BARRON'S
FINANCE AND
INVESTMENT
HANDBOOK

BARRON'S
FINANCE AND INVESTMENT
HANDBOOK

Second Edition

John Downes
Consultant
Office for Economic Development, City of New York
Former Vice President, AVCO Financial Services, Inc.

Jordan Elliot Goodman
Senior Finance and Investment Reporter
Money Magazine, Time Incorporated

BARRON'S

New York • London • Sydney • Toronto

Inquiries about purchasing parts of this book in electronic form should be directed to the publisher.

©Copyright 1987, 1986 by Barron's Educational Series, Inc.
Second Edition

All inquiries should be addressed to:
Barron's Educational Series, Inc.
250 Wireless Boulevard
Hauppauge, New York 11788

Library of Congress Catalog Card No. 86-10906

International Standard Book No. 0-8120-5729-5

Library of Congress Cataloging-in-Publication Data

Downes, John.
    Barron's finance and investment handbook.

    Bibliography: p. 967
    Includes index.
    1. Finance—Handbooks, manuals, etc. 2. Investments—Handbooks, manuals, etc. 3. Finance—Dictionaries. 4. Investments—Dictionaries. I. Goodman, Jordan Elliot. II. Barron's Educational Series, inc. III. Title. IV. Title: Finance and investment handbook.
HG173.D66   1986   332.6'78   86-10906
ISBN 0-8120-5729-5

PRINTED IN THE UNITED STATES OF AMERICA
4 5 6 7 8   9

CONTENTS

PART II   HOW TO READ AN ANNUAL REPORT

PART III   HOW TO READ THE FINANCIAL PAGES

PART IV   DICTIONARY OF FINANCE AND INVESTMENT

PART V   FINANCE AND INVESTMENT READY REFERENCE

APPENDIX

ACKNOWLEDGMENTS

A project as massive as this *Handbook* is clearly the work of more than two people, and to thank all adequately would add considerably to its bulk. There are several individuals and organizations, however, without whose help the project in its present form would not have been feasible at all.

Eric Berk, information systems coordinator of *Money* Magazine, provided invaluable assistance by doing the computer programming required to compile the lists of publicly traded companies and producing the charts that appear in the section of historical data. For the data itself, we are indebted to Interactive Data Corporation and its New York City consultant, Richard Bernstein.

A number of leading organizations provided information used in the *Handbook's* reference lists and we are grateful for their generosity and cooperation. These organizations include:

JD Resources
American Association of Individual Investors
The American Banker
A.M. Best and Company
The Securities Industry Association
Robert Stanger & Company
Public Accounting Report
The Investment Company Institute
The No-Load Mutual Fund Association
Thomas J. Herzfeld and Company
American Stock Exchange
Chicago Board of Trade
Chicago Board Options Exchange
Chicago Mercantile Exchange
Chicago Rice and Cotton Exchange
Coffee, Sugar and Cocoa Exchange
Commodity Exchange, Inc.
Kansas City Board of Trade
MidAmerica Commodity Exchange
Montréal Exchange
Minneapolis Grain Exchange
The National Association of Securities Dealers
New York Cotton Exchange
New York Futures Exchange
New York Mercantile Exchange
New York Stock Exchange
Pacific Stock Exchange
Philadelphia Stock Exchange
Toronto Stock Exchange

Vancouver Stock Exchange
Winnipeg Commodity Exchange
Interactive Data Corporation
Duane E. Frederic
Wilshire Associates
Buttonwood Press

Other people made contributions for which the word acknowledgment is inadequate. Barron's Project Editor Thomas F. Hirsch has been a daily source of perspective, judgment, and encouragement, and a partner in the fullest sense. We are grateful for his professional guidance and friendship. For help with our section on How to Read the Financial Pages we called on a veteran New York financial newspaperman, the late Charles Koshetz. The best parts of that chapter are Charlie's work and a memorial to the insights of a first-rate financial journalist. Finally, we are indebted to Katie and Annie Downes and Suzanne Koblentz Goodman for their personal support and countless sacrifices during the months the book has been in progress. An extra credit is due Suzanne, whose tireless and meticulous work on the listing of Publicly Traded Companies helped bring the project to an earlier conclusion.

John Downes
Jordan Elliot Goodman

INTRODUCTION

Not since the Great Depression spurred massive reforms in banking and the securities markets has the world of finance and investment seen changes as revolutionary as those of the 1970s and 80s. Deregulation, major tax-law revisions, globalization of markets, and widespread applications of advanced computer and communications technology have altered the world of finance and investment in ways that affect everybody.

As those developments were reshaping the finance and investment landscape in fundamental ways, other historic—sometimes traumatic—events were taking place on the economic and monetary fronts—record high interest rates, world-wide double-digit inflation followed by a major international recession and then disinflation, unprecedented swings in the value of the dollar relative to foreign currencies, and new highs in stock and bond prices.

The far-reaching results include a wider, more complex range of investment choices available to an investment public much more broadly based economically and conscious of such factors as volatility, interest-rate risk, inflation protection, and foreign exchange risk; financial news and corporate reports that are more complex and difficult to understand; an expanded and revised finance and investment vocabulary; a financial marketplace that has increased in size and diversity while spawning a burgeoning information industry using both print and electronic means of communication; and a regulatory establishment that has grown and adapted to a more consumer-oriented investment industry. This *Handbook* is designed as a self-contained reference covering each of these areas — for the individual investor, the student, and the professional.

Deregulation in the brokerage and banking industries, beginning with the "May Day" lifting of fixed commission rates on United States stock exchanges May 1, 1975, and gaining major international thrust with London's "Big Bang" of October 27, 1986, has transformed the financial marketplace. Traditional financial institutions have become diversified organizations mass-marketing a bewildering variety of investment products and services.

The Tax Reform Act of 1986, the most sweeping income tax overhaul in U.S. history, was the last of five major federal tax bills to influence financial and investment decision-making in a single ten-year period. With its enactment, a burdensome marginal tax system fraught with loopholes that had made "tax effects" a key basis of investment judgments has given way to a promising new era of lower tax rates, fewer tax brackets, and investment choices based primarily on economic values.

Internationally, the world has emerged much more interdependent, giving rise to a wide range of investment options denominated in both dollars and foreign currencies, created by firms competing for debt and equity in world-wide markets. Generally, international investment activity has increased as foreign markets have also become deregulated, as communications have improved, and as businesses and financial institutions have expanded beyond national boundaries.

Advances in computer and communications technology, by making possible the linking of markets and the instant processing of tremendous amounts of data, have at once brought greater simplicity and greater complexity to the world of finance and investment, inspiring new investment vehicles, transactions, and methods of limiting risk not previously imaginable.

The *Finance and Investment Handbook* begins with a discussion of 30 key investment alternatives—with their many variations—as they have emerged from this period of historic change. Some are new, others are modernized versions of traditional investment vehicles. Each is presented with an introductory overview followed by questions and answers offering concise information on such crucial matters as costs; minimum purchase amounts; risks; liquidity; tax implications; and suitability for tax-deferred retirement plans. The section's purpose is not to offer specific recommendations, but rather to set forth in an easy-to-read format the vital features distinguishing the various investments so you will be able to make better-informed investment decisions.

Corporate annual reports and other communications of publicly held corporations, as an ironic result of stricter disclosure requirements, have become increasingly elaborate and difficult to understand, leaving many investors more befuddled than enlightened. The second section of the *Handbook* explains what corporate reports contain, what to focus on, and how to analyze and interpret the data provided.

You must know how to read and understand financial information in newspapers in order to make intelligent investment choices and then to follow their progress. Not surprisingly, the proliferation of investment products and the broadening of public participation in the securities markets has fattened the financial sections of daily newspapers with information aimed at individual and institutional investors. Also, with the growth of cable television, many investors are getting their financial news from channels displaying a running ticker tape throughout the business day. The third part of the *Handbook* explains how to read the financial pages and the ticker tape.

Essential to decision-making in any field is understanding the language in which information is communicated. In a technical, dynamic field like finance and investment, keeping up with changing terminology would be a challenge in any event, but developments of the last decade have added a whole new lexicon of finance and investment terms and largely redefined the traditional vocabulary. The argot of the field has also been spiced by a wave of new Wall Street takeover buzzwords, like "greenmail," "poison pill," and "white knight." These and more than 2500 other key terms are defined clearly and comprehensively, with examples and illustrations, in the *Handbook's* fourth major section, the Dictionary of Finance and Investment.

The fifth section of the *Handbook* presents wide-ranging reference material. The information, arranged in an easily accessible manner, is designed to be *used* by investors—beginners and professionals alike—to locate specific data as well as to gain a broader understanding of finance and investment.

The finance and investment marketplace has not only grown in size but has changed character as a result of diversification, mergers, and the introduction of new firms that exist either to market new investment products or to provide information on them. The regulatory establishment, which consists of federal and state government agencies as well as self-regulatory organizations, and relevant trade association and consumer protection groups have expanded and adapted to an industry that has become more consumer-oriented. The most important of these government and nongovernment organizations—including those of Canada—are listed in the opening portions of the *Handbook's* reference listings.

The growing importance of the individual consumer in the investment community has been a catalyst for the burgeoning financial information industry. The *Handbook* lists the major finance and investment publications from national magazines to specialized newsletters, providing addresses and telephone numbers so they can be contacted easily. The industry also has an important electronic dimension in the form of computer databases and software, and the major sources of these products are presented.

"You can't tell the players without a scorecard" goes an old baseball adage, which certainly applies to today's major leagues of financial services. Despite diversification, financial institutions continue to be discussed mainly in terms of their principal and traditional activities—that is, as commercial banks, thrifts, brokerage firms, and life insurance companies. The *Handbook* lists the 100 largest in each of these categories. Also listed are the Federal Reserve and Federal Home Loan banks and branches, the primary government securities dealers, major limited partnership sponsors, the 25 largest accounting firms, and the world's major security and commodity exchanges.

Highly useful information, including name, address, phone number, and investment objective of both open-end and closed-end mutual funds and fund families is provided for those who would rather leave portfolio decisions to a professional manager.

Increasingly, U.S. and Canadian exchanges, in response to growing investor interest, are listing options and futures on financial instruments, stock indexes, and foreign currencies, as well as traditional stock options and futures on agricultural and other commodities. The *Handbook* provides a complete and detailed summary of contracts of all types on all U.S. and Canadian exchanges.

No handbook would be complete if it didn't supply the historical framework of the investment markets and the overall economy. This *Handbook* includes easy to understand but telling historical graphs together with background information and related statistical data on the principal stock and bond market indexes, as well as key economic indicators.

To facilitate ordering through brokers, particularly discount brokers, and to help you take advantage of an increasing willingness on the part of corporations to communicate directly with shareholders or potential shareholders, the *Handbook* provides a list—not readily available elsewhere—of the name, stock symbol, address, phone number, and line of business of approximately 4700 public companies in which you can buy shares or American Depositary Receipts on the New York Stock Exchange, the American Stock Exchange, the Toronto Stock Exchange, and over the counter on the NASDAQ National Market System. In addition, we indicate stocks on which listed options are traded and those offering dividend reinvestment plans. A limited number of companies offer free merchandise or other items or services of value as part of their shareholder relations efforts. You'll find a list of companies providing such "freebies."

The Appendix is an important part of the *Handbook*. In it you will find an annotated bibliography of selected key works on finance and investment. There is also a listing of the currencies of independent countries, which will be helpful in tracking international developments. At the conclusion of the *Handbook* is one of its most important assets — the index — which will make it easier to find all the information on a particular topic in the book.

HOW TO USE THIS *HANDBOOK* EFFECTIVELY

Each section of this *Handbook* is a self-contained entity. At the same time, however, the relevance of the various sections to each other is clear, since the objective of the *Handbook* is to join in one volume the different elements that together make up today's world of finance and investment. Tempting though it was from an editorial standpoint, cross-referencing has been kept to a minimum in the belief that readers would prefer not to be distracted by such editorial devices. At certain points, however, where reliance on the fuller explanation of a term in the *Handbook's* Dictionary of Finance and Investment seemed preferable to a discussion, cross-references to the dictionary are indicated by small capitals (for instance, ABC AGREEMENT). In any case, the dictionary is a source of comprehensive information on terms and concepts used throughout the *Handbook* and should be consulted whenever an aspect of finance and investment is not clear to you. The Table of Contents and especially the Index will also help you locate related information in different parts of the *Handbook* and should be consulted regularly.

* * *

Although the *Handbook* was a collaborative effort in every sense of the word, primary responsibility was divided as follows: The sections on investment alternatives and reading financial reports were written by John Downes. The section on reading the financial pages was written by Charles Koshetz and edited by John Downes and Jordan Elliot Goodman. The Dictionary of Finance and Investment was authored coequally by John Downes and Jordan Elliot Goodman. The reference lists and the accompanying explanatory material were compiled, edited, and written by Jordan Elliot Goodman.

PART I

How to Invest Your Money: 30 Key Personal Investment Opportunities

INTRODUCTION

Perhaps the most important benefit of deregulation and other recent landmark changes in the securities and banking industries has been the availability to the average individual of investment alternatives that were formerly reserved for the wealthy. But welcome though this development is, it has brought with it choices that are bewildering both in range and complexity. Traditional investment vehicles have been modernized, new ones have been introduced, and, as the marketing departments of financial services conglomerates have sought to give their products mass appeal, the distinctions between different investment alternatives have become blurred.

This section presents 30 basic investment alternatives as they have emerged from the revolutionary events of the 1970s and 80s. It is divided into 30 *basic* alternatives; each discussion, however, includes important variations, which, if counted separately, would more than double the number of alternatives.

The purpose of the section is not to provide advice. Investment decisions must always be made in subjective terms, taking into account one's financial position, risk comfort level, and goals. Rather, the section is designed to set forth in current terms the vital features distinguishing different investments, so you can talk knowledgeably with your investment counselor or, if you are a finance or investment professional, so you can be a better source of advice.

Preceding the discussions of investments is a table showing important characteristics of each investment. The chart is a quick way to learn pertinent facts, but should be used in conjunction with the discussions themselves to make sure you are aware of nuances and exceptions associated with a particular type of investment.

The discussions of investment alternatives begin with short overviews designed to describe the essential features of the investment and, where helpful, provide some historical perspective. These overviews are followed by sections in question-and-answer format designed to present concisely and informatively the basic data needed to evaluate investment alternatives. Let's look at the questions and what they mean. (Remember, if you don't understand a finance or investment term, consult the extensive dictionary in this *Handbook*.)

Buying, Selling, and Holding

How do I buy and sell it? A few years ago, things were simpler: you bought your stocks and bonds from a broker, your life insurance from an insurance agent, and went to a bank with your savings or your loan request. The trend today is toward FULL-SERVICE BROKERS and FINANCIAL SUPERMARKETS that offer all these services and more. We have tried to be as helpful as possible, but there is no universality as to what full-service means from one firm to the next. One thing can be said for certain, though: you won't sound foolish these days if you ask a bank or broker if a given investment—no matter how specialized—can be bought or sold through his or her firm. DISCOUNT BROKERS are a special breed. They handle a variety of securities, but as a rule function strictly as brokers; do not look to them for investment guidance.

Is there a minimum purchase amount, and what is the price range? This question is aimed at giving you an idea of what it costs to get in the game, which is often more than just the minimum DENOMINATION or UNIT in which an investment is issued. The question cannot always be answered in absolute terms, since broker policies vary in terms of minimum orders and there may be SUITABILITY RULES requiring that you prove a certain financial capacity to take the risks associated with a particular investment. Certain securities trade in ROUND LOTS (for instance, 100 shares of common stock), though it is usually possible to buy ODD LOT quantities (for instance, 35 shares) at a higher commission per unit. In any event, call the broker and ask; many large firms have special programs that combine small orders from different investors and thereby make it possible to buy and sell modest amounts at modest commissions.

What fees and charges are involved? Again, we have been specific wherever possible, but with some investments, notably common stocks, commissions are sometimes negotiated, based on the size and nature of the transaction. DISCOUNT BROKERS, which as a rule do not give investment advice but execute trades at rates that are roughly half those of most full-service brokers, also have different rates for different transactions. See the entries for SHARE BROKER and VALUE BROKER in this *Handbook*'s dictionary for discussions of different categories of discount broker. You will also frequently see references to DEALER spreads. This term refers to the MARKDOWNS and markups that are deducted from your selling price or added to your buying price when a broker-dealer is operating as a DEALER rather than simply as a BROKER.

Does it mature, expire, or otherwise terminate? Some investments are issued with a fixed MATURITY DATE, others are not. But even those with a fixed maturity date may be CALLABLE—that is, bought back at the pleasure of the issuer, or as part of a SINKING FUND provision. Others may have PUT OPTIONS, permitting REDEMPTION by the investor before maturity.

Can I sell it quickly? This question has to do with LIQUIDITY, the ability to convert an investment into cash without significant loss of value. Investments normally enjoying high liquidity are those with an active SECONDARY MARKET, in which they are actively traded among other investors subsequent to their original issue. Shares of LISTED SECURITIES have high liquidity. Liquidity can also be provided in other ways: for example, the SPONSOR of a unit investment trust might offer to MAKE A MARKET—to find a buyer to match you as a seller, should the need arise for you to sell.

How is market value determined and how do I keep track of it? MARKET VALUE is the price your investment would fetch in the open market, assuming that it is traded in a SECONDARY MARKET. In these discussions you will often encounter the word, VOLATILE, referring to the extent to which the market price of an investment fluctuates. Professionals use the term SYSTEMATIC RISK or its synonym market risk when discussing an investment's tendency to rise or fall in price as a result of market forces.

Investment Objectives

Should I buy this if my objective is capital appreciation? The purpose here is to identify investments likely to gain in value—to produce CAPITAL GAINS. Although APPRECIATION does not refer to capital growth due to factors such as reinvested dividends or compound interest, such factors are noted as a matter of relevance where they exist to a substantial degree. In the same category is appreciation due to ORIGINAL ISSUE DISCOUNT on fixed-income securities, which is considered interest. Other fixed-income investments bought in the market at a DISCOUNT from PAR because rising rates (or other factors) caused lower prices, create appreciation in the sense of capital gains either at REDEMPTION or when resold in the market at a higher price. Prices can also be at a PREMIUM, meaning higher than par value, when speaking of fixed-income investments.

Should I buy this if my objective is income? Here the purpose is to identify investments whose primary feature is providing regular income, as distinguished from alternatives primarily featuring capital gains or other potential values.

To what extent does it protect against inflation? If the value of an investment usually rises at the same rate or a higher rate than the rate of INFLATION erodes the value of the dollar, the investment is inflation-sensitive. Investments vary in the degree of protection they provide—some provide no protection.

Is it suitable for tax-deferred retirement accounts? Such accounts include INDI-VIDUAL RETIREMENT ACCOUNTS (IRAs), KEOGH PLANS, 401(K) PLANS, and other pension plans that are TAX-DEFERRED. The question addresses both the legality and, in some cases, the practicality of using a particular investment in such an account. Investments that might be ruled out for an IRA because of the $2000 annual maximum per person, might be appropriate for an IRA ROLLOVER.

Can I borrow against it? This question considers the general value of an investment as COLLATERAL at a bank or other lending institution, and also the eligibility of an investment for trading in MARGIN ACCOUNTS with brokers under Federal Reserve Board MARGIN REQUIREMENTS. A key consideration is the concept of LEVERAGE, the ability to control a given amount of value with a smaller amount of cash. Borrowing can also be a way of raising cash when an investment is ILLIQUID.

Risk Considerations

How assured can I be of getting my full investment back? Here the discussion concerns safety of PRINCIPAL, which has mainly to do with two types of risk: (1) market or SYSTEMATIC RISK and (2) financial or CREDIT RISK (risk that an issuer will DEFAULT on a contractual obligation or that an EQUITY investment will lose value because of financial difficulty or BANKRUPTCY of an issuer). Insurance considerations and HEDGING, protecting against loss of value through an offsetting position, are also discussed where appropriate.

How assured is my income? Assuming an investment produces income, this question deals with market risk as it may (or may not) affect income, with an issuer's legal obligation to pay income, and with priority of claim in LIQUIDATION.

Are there any other risks unique to this investment? This question intends only to highlight risks peculiar to a particular investment. It is not meant to imply that any risks not included do not exist.

Is it commercially rated? Commercial RATING agencies, such as MOODY'S INVESTORS SERVICE and STANDARD & POOR'S CORPORATION, analyze and rate certain securities and their issuers on a continuous basis. Most ratings are designed to indicate a company's financial strength and thus guide investors as to the degree of CREDIT RISK a security represents, though sometimes other factors are rated. Rating changes usually affect market values.

Tax Considerations

What tax advantages (or disadvantages) does it offer? This discussion is designed to present the tax considerations associated with an investment. Obviously, each individual's tax situation is unique and each investor should obtain professional advice to determine whether an investment with certain tax features represents an advantage or disadvantage in his or her particular case. The differential between ORDINARY INCOME and CAPITAL GAIN tax rates, formerly a key consideration, phases out by 1988 under the TAX REFORM ACT OF 1986.

Economic Considerations

What economic factors most affect buy, hold, and sell decisions? Here again, only the most general economic considerations are covered and what applies in general might not apply to you.

PERSONAL INVESTMENTS AT A GLANCE

The following chart applies nine key investment criteria to the 30 personal investment alternatives discussed in this section. It is designed simply to answer the question: Is this alternative one I might want to learn more about in view of my own investment objectives? A bullet (●) means that a given characteristic is usually associated, to one degree or another, with a particular alternative. A blank means it is not. A V means that variation within the investment category exists to such an extent that even broad classification would be misleading.

Exceptions abound, and in every case there is a question of degree. In the modern universe of investment alternatives, just about nothing is pure; that fact is indeed what this section of the *Handbook* is all about. So with cognizance of its limitations, use this chart for quick and handy reference and refer to the overviews and questionnaires for more complete understanding.

Investment	Regular Current Income	Capital Appreciation	Tax Benefits	Safety of Principal	Liquidity	Inflation Protection	Leverage*	Future Income or Security	Suitability for IRAs and other Tax-Deferred Accounts
Annuity		●	●	●		V		●	
Bond, Corporate	●	●		●	●				●
Closed-End Fund	●	●		V	●	V			●
Collectible		●				●			
Common Stock	●	●		V	●	●	●		●
Convertible Security	●	●		●	●	●	●		●
Foreign Stocks and Bonds	●	●		V	V	●			●
Futures Contract on a Commodity		●			●		●		
Futures Contract on an Interest Rate		●			●		●		
Futures Contract on a Stock Index		●			●		●		
Government Agency Security	●	●	●	●	●				●
Life Insurance (Cash Value)		●	●	●		V		●	
Limited Partnership	●	●	●	V		V			●

Investment							
Money Market Fund	●	●	●	●	●		●
Mortgage-Backed (Pass-Through) Security	●	●	●	●	●		●
Municipal Security	●●	●	●	●			
Mutual Fund (Open-End)	●●	●	v	●	v	●	●
Option Contract (Put or Call)	●	●				●	
Option Contract on a Futures Contract (Futures Option)		●				●	
Option Contract on an Interest Rate (Debt Option)		●				●	
Option Contract on a Stock Index		●				●	
Option Contract or Futures Contract on a Currency		●				●	
Precious Metals	●	●	v	●		●	
Preferred Stock (Nonconvertible)	●	●	●	●	●		●
Real Estate Investment Trust (REIT and FREIT)	●	●	v	●	●		●
Real Estate, Physical	v	●	●●	●		●	
Savings Alternatives	●	●	v	●			v
Treasury Securities	●	●	●●	●			●
Unit Investment Trust	●	v	v	v	v		●
Zero-Coupon Security	●	●	●	●	●	●	●

* Refers to margin securities and investments wherein large amounts of value can be controlled with small amounts of cash. The general value of investments as loan collateral is covered in the discussions of each of the investment alternatives.

HOW TO INVEST YOUR MONEY:
30 KEY PERSONAL INVESTMENT
OPPORTUNITIES

ANNUITY

After a period of modernization, tax rulings, and the shock of a big insurance company bankruptcy, the time-honored annuity is again gaining popularity as an investment alternative. It comes in several varieties, with two basic attractions: (1) tax-deferred capital growth and (2) the option of income for life or a guaranteed period. Among the drawbacks are high penalties (by insurers and the Internal Revenue Service) on premature withdrawal and lower investment returns than could usually be realized directly.

Traditionally, annuities provided fixed income payments for an individual's remaining lifetime in exchange for a lump-sum cash payment. But inflation's negative impact on fixed-income annuities combined with increased life expectancy gave rise, in the late 1950s, to the variable annuity, invested in assets, like stocks, that rise with inflation, thus preserving some purchasing power, although at the price of some market risk.

In the late 1960s and early 70s came the wraparound annuity, which enabled investors to wrap their own mutual funds, savings accounts, or other investments in the annuity vehicle, thus sheltering them from taxes. In the early 1980s, the IRS blew the whistle, ruling that to qualify for tax deferral, annuity investments had to be managed by insurance companies and be available only to annuity contract holders. The annuity has once again become a vehicle largely limited to retirement goals, but it has gained appeal with the modern features acquired along the way.

Annuities are available in two basic types:

Fixed annuities are "fixed" in two ways: (1) The amount you invest earns interest (tax-deferred) at a guaranteed rate (1% to 2% under long-term U.S. government bonds, typically) while your principal is guaranteed not to lose value. (2) When you withdraw or opt to "annuitize" (begin taking monthly income) you receive a guaranteed amount based on your age, sex, and selection of payment options. Inflation protection is, of course, minimal.

Variable annuities, in contrast, are "variable" in two ways: (1) The amount you put in is invested in your choice of a stock, fixed-income bond or money market account, the value and/or earnings of which vary with market conditions. (2) Market value determines the amount available for withdrawals, or (with actuarial factors) the amount the annuitant is paid from one month to the next. Variable annuities thus offer inflation protection in exchange for market risk (minimized somewhat when switching among funds is permitted).

The bankruptcy in the early 1980s of the Baldwin-United Corporation, the biggest name in deferred annuities, shook the confidence of an investor community that had learned to take the financial strength of insurance companies for granted. As it turned out, arrangements were made for investors to regain most of their money, and confidence in the industry, which is heavily regulated and high on any scale of safety, was restored.

In general, annuities, with a variety of optional features for both accumulation and payout, are for long-term investors willing to trade liquidity and some degree of return for safety and tax-deferred capital growth, and whose objective is to defer taxability until later (lower tax-rate) years and/or to guarantee retirement income.

*   *   *

What Is an Annuity?

An annuity is a contract between an insurance company and an annuitant whereby the company, in exchange for a single or flexible premium (i.e., paid in a lump sum or in installments) guarantees a fixed or variable payment to the annuitant at a future time.

Buying, Selling, and Holding

How do I buy and sell it? Insurance brokers, insurance company sales agents, savings institutions, full-service brokers, commercial banks, and other financial service organizations sell annuities.

Is there a minimum purchase amount, and what is the price range? It varies with the plan, but deferred annuities typically have minimums ranging from $1000 to $5000.

What fees and charges are involved? Fees and charges may include front-end load sales charges ranging from 1% to 10% (although there is a trend toward no initial commissions), premium taxes (imposed on the insurance company by some states and passed on to contract holders), annual fees (typically $15 to $30 per year up to a maximum of 1½% of account value), early withdrawal penalties (typically starting at 7% and decreasing to zero over a seven-year period), and other charges. (See Tax Considerations, below, for tax penalties).

Does it mature, expire, or otherwise terminate? Yes; both the accumulation period and the payout period are specified in the contract.

Can I sell it quickly? Accumulated cash value (principal payments plus investment earnings) can always be withdrawn, but there may be substantial withdrawal penalties as well as tax penalties.

How is market value determined and how do I keep track of it? Annuities do not have secondary market value, but information concerning account balances is supplied by the insurance company.

Investment Objectives

Should I buy an annuity if my objective is capital appreciation? Not in the sense that you would buy an investment at one price and hope to sell it at a higher price. But deferred annuities accumulate value through (tax-deferred) compounding, and variable annuities may be invested in stocks or other securities having capital gains potential.

Should I buy this if my objective is income? Annuities are designed to provide income for future guaranteed periods, so you would not buy a deferred annuity for current income needs.

To what extent does it protect against inflation? Fixed annuities provide no inflation protection. Variable annuities provide protection when their portfolios are invested in inflation-sensitive securities.

Is it suitable for tax-deferred retirement accounts? Yes, but since annuities have tax-deferred status themselves, it may be wiser to use them as supplements to IRAs, Keoghs, and other tax-deferred programs.

Can I borrow against it? Yes.

Risk Considerations

How assured can I be of getting back my full investment in an annuity? Insurance companies are heavily regulated and required to maintain reserves, so with established companies there is low risk of loss due to corporate failure. Most annuities permit early withdrawal of principal, but penalties may apply. Once annuitized (i.e., when payments by the insurance company begin) it becomes a question of how long you live. The insurance company (with the odds in its favor) bets you will die before the annuity is fully paid out.

How assured is my income? While variable annuity income can fluctuate, the risk of default is low. (See previous question.)

Are there any other risks unique to this investment? Although heavily regulated, insurance companies are potentially subject to mismanagement and fraud, and policyholders are not themselves covered by federal protection as bank depositors, for example, are covered by the Federal Deposit Insurance Corporation (FDIC).

Is it commercially rated? Yes. Insurance companies are rated by Best's Rating Service.

Tax Considerations

What tax advantages (or disadvantages) does an annuity offer? Earnings on money invested in deferred annuities, including all interest, dividends, and capital gains, accumulate and compound tax-deferred. Portions of payments to annuitants are returns of investor's principal and thus are not subject to income taxes. Withdrawals of accumulated earnings prior to age 59½ or within 5 years of the purchase date (whichever comes first) are subject to a 10% tax penalty. (An exception is made for life annuities, payable for the lifetimes, or life expectancies, of one or more annuitants.)

Economic Considerations

What economic factors most affect buy, hold, and sell decisions? Although factors such as inflationary expectations and anticipated interest rate movements may guide choices among types of annuities, the decision to buy and hold is based on insurance rather than economic considerations. Annuities are appropriate for people without dependents or heirs, who seek assured income for their remaining lives.

BOND, CORPORATE (INTEREST-BEARING)

The traditional attractions of a corporate bond have been (1) higher yield compared to government bonds and (2) relative safety. Whether secured (usually a mortgage bond) or unsecured (called a debenture), it has a higher claim on earnings than equity investments. If the firm goes out of business, bonds also have a higher claim on the assets of the issuer, whose financial well-being is safeguarded by provisions in bond indentures and is closely monitored by the major bond rating services. Interest on corporates is fully taxable.

Much publicized in the 1980s because of their widespread use in financing corporate takeovers, have been so-called junk bonds, corporate bonds with lower than investment-grade ratings that pay high yields to compensate for high risk. While there have been few defaults, junk bonds have not been tested in a prolonged period of business adversity.

Bonds are contracts between borrowers and lenders in which the issuer (borrower) promises the bondholder (lender) a specified rate of interest and repayment of principal at maturity.

The face, or par, value of a corporate bond is almost always $1000 (the exceptions being baby bonds with pars of $500 or less), but bonds do not necessarily sell at par value. Particularly in the secondary market, bonds are traded at discounts or premiums relative to par in order to bring their stated (coupon) rates in line with market rates. This inverse relationship between bond prices and interest rate movements causes market risk as the term applies to bonds; when interest rates rise, there is a decline in the price of a bond with a lower fixed interest rate.

Bond prices also vary with the time remaining to maturity. This is because of the time value of money and because time involves risk and risk means higher yield. Bond yields thus normally decrease (and prices increase) as the bond approaches maturity. The concept of yield-to-maturity is basic to bond pricing, and it takes into account the price paid for the bond and all cash inflows and their timing.

The safety and value of corporate bonds are also related to credit risk, quite simply the borrower's ability to pay interest and principal when due. The relative financial strength of the issuer, as reflected in the regularly updated rating assigned to its bonds by the major services, influences yield, which is adjusted by changes in the market price.

Other considerations influencing corporate bond prices include the existence of call features, which empower the issuer to redeem prior to maturity, often to the disadvantage of the bondholder; call protection periods, which benefit holders; sinking funds, which require the issuer to set aside funds for the retirement of the bonds at maturity; put options, which give the investor the right to redeem prior to maturity; subordinations, which give issues precedence over other issues in liquidation; and guarantees or insurance.

Variable-rate issues, usually called floating-rate notes even though some issues have terms of 30 years, adjust interest rates periodically in line with market rates. These issues generally have lower yields to compensate for the benefit to the holder, but they enjoy greater price stability to the extent the rate adjustments are responsive to market rate movements.

See also the discussions of Convertible Securities and Zero-Coupon Securities.

* * *

What Is a Corporate Bond?

A corporate bond is a debt security of a corporation requiring the issuer to pay the holder the par value at a specified maturity and to make agreed scheduled interest payments.

Buying, Selling, and Holding

How do I buy and sell a corporate bond? Through a securities broker-dealer.

Is there a minimum purchase amount, and what is the price range? Bonds are normally issued with $1000 par values, with baby bonds in smaller denominations. Issuers often have 5-bond minimums and broker-dealers trade in round lots of 10 or 100 units. Odd lots may be available at higher brokerage commissions or dealer spreads.

What fees and charges are involved? A per-bond commission of $2.50 to $20, depending on the broker and negotiations with the customer. However, a minimum charge of $30 is common. New issues involve no charges to the investor.

Does it mature, expire, or otherwise terminate? All bonds have maturity dates, but may be callable prior to maturity.

Can I sell it quickly? Usually yes. Most major issues are actively traded, but in large amounts. Small lots can be harder to trade and may involve some price sacrifice and higher transaction costs.

How is market value determined and how do I keep track of it? The market value of a fixed-income bond is a function of its yield to maturity and prevailing market interest rates. Prices thus decline when interest rates rise and rise when interest rates decline to result in an appropriate competitive yield. A change in the issuer's rating can also cause a change in yield, which is adjusted by a change in the market price of the bond. Bond prices are quoted in daily newspapers and electronic databases.

Investment Objectives

Should I buy a corporate bond if my objective is capital appreciation? Usually not, although capital appreciation is possible when bonds can be bought at a discount to their par value, bought prior to a drop in market interest rates, or bought at a favorable price because of a decline in the issuer's credit rating.

Should I buy this if my objective is income? Yes; bonds pay interest, usually semiannually. Yields on top-rated bonds are lower than on bonds of less than investment grade, called junk bonds, which pay more and have higher credit risk.

To what extent does it protect against inflation? Although normal inflationary expectations are built into interest rates, fixed-rate bonds offer no protection against high inflation. Variable-rate issues offer some protection.

Is it suitable for tax-deferred retirement accounts? Yes.

Can I borrow against it? Yes, subject to Federal Reserve margin rules (convertible bonds only) and brokerage-firm and lending-institution policies.

Risk Considerations

How assured can I be of getting my full investment back? If you hold to maturity, it will depend on the issuer's credit, which is evaluated regularly by the major investor's rating services and reflected in ratings from AAA down to D. If you plan to sell in the secondary market before maturity, you are subject also to market risk, the risk that bond prices will be down as a result of higher interest rates. Sophisticated investors sometimes protect against loss of value due to market risk by hedging, using options and futures available on long-term Treasury securities which are similarly affected by interest rate changes.

How assured is my income? Uninterrupted payment of interest depends on the issuer's financial strength and stability of earnings, factors reflected in its bond rating. Inflation can erode the dollar value of fixed-interest payments.

Are there any other risks unique to this investment? A callable bond can be redeemed by the issuer after a certain period has elapsed. Issuers normally force redemption when interest rates have declined and financing can be obtained more cheaply. Under just those circumstances, however, the investor finds the holding most attractive; the market price is up and the coupon interest rate is higher than the prevailing market interest rate. Look for bonds with call protection (typically 10 years).

Is it commercially rated? Yes. Fitch Investors Service, Moody's Investors Service, and Standard & Poor's Corporation are the major rating services.

Tax Considerations

What tax advantages (or disadvantages) does a corporate bond offer? None. Bond interest is taxed as ordinary income and appreciation is subject to capital gains tax, except that appreciation resulting from original issue discounts is taxed (as earned) at ordinary income rates.

Economic Considerations

What economic factors most affect buy, hold, or sell decisions? It is best to buy a corporate bond when interest rates are high and the best yields can be obtained. Holding is most attractive when rates are declining, causing an upward move in the market values of fixed-income securities. High inflation erodes the dollar value of fixed interest payments. Poor business conditions over a prolonged period can cause financial weakness and jeopardize a firm's ability to pay.

CLOSED-END FUND

Closed-end funds, so-called because, unlike open-end mutual funds, their sponsoring investment companies do not stand ready to issue and redeem shares on a continuous basis, have a fixed capitalization represented by publicly traded shares that are often listed on the major stock exchanges.

Closed-end funds tend to have specialized portfolios of stocks, bonds, convertibles, or combinations thereof, and may be oriented toward income, capital gains, or a combination of those objectives. Examples are the Japan Fund, which specializes in the stock of Japanese firms, and ASA Ltd., which invests in South African gold mining stocks. Both are traded on the New York Stock Exchange.

The attraction of a closed-end fund is twofold: (1) Because management is not concerned with continuous buying and selling to accommodate new investors and redemptions, a responsibility of open-end funds that frequently conflicts with ideal market timing, a well-managed closed-end fund can often buy and sell on more favorable terms. (2) Because the popular investor perception is just the opposite— that closed-end funds have less flexibility than open-end funds—shares of closed-end funds can usually be obtained at a discount from net asset value. As a result of these combined factors, annual earnings of closed-end funds sometimes exceed earnings of open-end funds with comparable portfolios.

A special form of closed-end fund is the *dual-purpose fund.* These hybrids have two classes of stock. Preferred shareholders receive all the income from the portfolio—dividends and interest—while common shareholders receive all capital gains realized on the sale of securities in the fund's portfolio. Dual-purpose funds are set up with a specific expiration date, when preferred shares are redeemed at a predetermined price and common shareholders claim the remaining assets, voting either to liquidate or continue the fund on an open-end basis.

Closed-end funds, of which about 70 are publicly traded, are regulated by the Securities and Exchange Commission.

See also the discussion of Mutual Funds.

*   *   *

What Is a Closed-End Fund?

A closed-end fund is a type of mutual fund that invests in diversified holdings and has a fixed number of shares that are publicly traded.

Buying, Selling, and Holding

How do I buy and sell a closed-end fund? Through a securities broker-dealer.

Is there a minimum purchase amount, and what is the price range? Round-lot 100 share purchases save commissions. Prices vary but many funds sell for $25 or less per share.

What fees and charges are involved? Standard brokerage commissions plus an annual management fee averaging ½% to 1% of the investment.

Does it mature, expire, or otherwise terminate? Funds can be liquidated or converted to open-end funds or operating companies if a majority of shareholders approve. Dual-purpose funds expire, typically in ten years.

Can I sell it quickly? Usually yes. Most funds offer good liquidity.

How is market value determined and how do I keep track of it? By supply and demand factors affecting shares in the market. Whether shares trade at a premium (rare) or at more or less of a discount (the rule) relative to the net asset value of the fund, can depend on the portfolio, yield, the general market, and factors like year-end tax selling. *The Wall Street Journal* on Monday reports the net asset value, price, and discount or premium for the previous week on actively traded funds.

Investment Objectives

Should I buy a closed-end fund if my objective is capital appreciation? Although fund shares rise and fall in the marketplace, influenced, among other factors, by the value of the fund's portfolio, investors seeking to participate in capital gains would select a fund having appreciation as its primary objective—an aggressive stock fund, for example, as opposed to a bond fund, though gains and losses are possible in both. Dual-purpose funds offer two classes of stock, common shareholders benefiting from all the capital gains, preferred shareholders getting all the interest and dividend income. Funds bought at a discount offer the prospect of additional appreciation through increases in fund share prices.

Should I buy this if my objective is income? Yes, especially funds whose objective is income. (See the preceding question.)

To what extent does it protect against inflation? Some portfolios are more sensitive (less vulnerable) to inflation than others, stocks being better than bonds, for example. Of course, increases in the portfolio benefit investors only when passed on in capital gains distributions or reflected in higher fund share values.

Is it suitable for tax-deferred retirement accounts? Yes.

Can I borrow against it? Yes, subject to Federal Reserve margin requirements and individual lender policies.

Risk Considerations

How assured can I be of getting my full investment back? Fund shares can be just as volatile as common stock. Professionals use various techniques to hedge funds selling at discounts or premiums or converting to open-end funds. These techniques include purchasing options and selling short other funds, treasury securities and futures, and stocks in the same fund's portfolio.

How assured is my income? It depends on the quality of the portfolio and the risk characteristics of the investments comprising it.

Are there any other risks unique to this investment? The risk unique to closed-end funds is that the value of fund shares can move independently of the value of the securities comprising the fund's portfolio. If this causes shares to trade at a discount to net asset values, it is bad for holders, although it can be viewed as a buying opportunity.

Is it commercially rated? Funds are not usually rated, but information helpful to investors is provided by Standard & Poor's Stock Record Sheets, Moody's Finance Manuals, and other sources.

Tax Considerations

What tax advantages (or disadvantages) does a closed-end fund offer? The tax treatment of closed-end fund shares is the same as for common stock except that until 1988 capital gains distributions enjoy preferential long-term capital gains treatment regardless of how long the fund has been held.

Economic Considerations

What economic factors most affect buy, hold or sell decisions? Most experts say to buy when shares can be obtained at a good discount and the stock market seems poised for a rise. Otherwise, decisions should consider the effects of different economic and market scenarios on various types of portfolios, such as bonds, stocks, or convertibles. It is probably wise to view closed-end funds as long-term investments and to sell when significant appreciation has occurred.

COLLECTIBLE

Collectibles, the name for a diverse range of physical possessions presumed to gain value with time, enjoyed a wave of popularity as a haven for investment money during the inflation-ravaged 1970s. Then the 1981–82 recession revealed how fickle the marketplace can be and how vulnerable collectibles are to adverse economic conditions. When that period was followed by one in which inflation was brought under control and financial investments became attractive again, enthusiasm for collectibles as an investment alternative, exclusive of their utility or personal enjoyment value, waned considerably. Some collectibles did, however, perform very well: One study listing investments that outperformed inflation between 1975 and 1980 included five categories of collectibles along with gold, silver, residential real estate, and money market funds.

There is no universal definition of a collectible. Some experts apply the criteria of rarity, quality, uniqueness, and age, while others put commodities with utilitarian value (like gemstones) or intrinsic value (like coins with gold or silver content) in addition to collector's value in separate categories.

In the broadest definition, however, collectibles are physical assets (not financial or real, in the sense of real estate), that have psychic or utilitarian value for their owners, are unique or in limited supply, and can be expected to increase in value with time and demand. The category thus includes stamps, coins, antiques, gemstones, fine art, photographs, and an almost endless list of other groups and subdivisions ranging from folk art and crafts to baseball cards, comic books, antique automobiles, and miscellaneous collectible junk.

While books have been written on the major categories of collectibles, certain common denominators exist to varying degrees from an investment perspective: often high costs to trade and own; high price volatility; no current income; and undependable or poor liquidity.

These factors plus the opportunity cost of an unproductive investment lead to one conclusion: Collectibles, especially when the relevant group of collectors is solidly in place and in good communication, will probably gain value and outstrip inflation over the long term, but the costs and risks of holding collectibles for investment purposes can be justified only when the assets also provide their owners pleasure or utility.

∗ ∗ ∗

What Is a Collectible?

A collectible is a physical asset of a non-real estate and nonfinancial nature that exists in limited supply, usually provides enjoyment or utility to its owner, and is expected to increase in value because of inflation or supply and demand factors such as popularity and rarity.

Buying, Selling, and Holding

How do I buy and sell a collectible? Through dealers, galleries, auctions, private owners, flea markets, and catalogs and other collector publications.

Is there a minimum purchase amount, and what is the price range? Minimums and price ranges vary with the collectible and run a gamut from a few pennies to millions of dollars.

What fees and charges are involved? This depends on the collectible, where it is traded, and many other factors, but fees are an important consideration. Costs may include dealer profits (markups), sales taxes, appraisal fees, storage and safekeeping, maintenance, insurance, as well as opportunity cost—the return you would get if your money were invested more productively.

Does it mature, expire, or otherwise terminate? No.

Can I sell it quickly? A collectible varies in liquidity, from one, like a painting or an antique, bought through established dealers standing ready to repurchase at an agreed-on price, to another salable only through consignment to dealers or auction houses.

How is market value determined and how do I keep track of it? Market value is determined by supply and demand. Some collectibles are more vulnerable to fads than others, and the marketplace can be more efficient in one type of collectible than another because it has more dealers and better communication among dealers and collectors. Some major newspapers, like *The New York Times,* carry advertisements for collectibles of various types; most of the main categories of collectibles are served by specialized periodicals or newsletters; and a number of national magazines contain classified sections and even articles aimed at collectors within their fields of interest. Dealers and appraisers are a source of information about market value, but it is important to satisy oneself as to their objectivity.

Investment Objectives

Should I buy a collectible if my objective is capital appreciation? Yes, but short-term profits depend on a combination of expertise and luck, and long-term appreciation can be affected by fads as well as economic developments.

Should I buy this if my objective is income? No.

To what extent does it protect against inflation? Although there are many risks that can undermine the value of a collectible, if the condition of the collectible remains good and supply and demand factors stay favorable, values will increase with inflation.

Is it suitable for tax-deferred retirement accounts? Collectibles are not legal investments in such accounts unless they are part of portfolios directed by trustees.

Can I borrow against it? Yes; many lenders will accept marketable collectibles as collateral.

Risk Considerations

How assured can I be of getting my full investment back? With most collectibles, this has mainly to do with your level of expertise and the amount of time you hold the asset. In the short term, it is likely that costs and commissions will offset whatever small gain might be realized. In the long run, collectibles become more limited in supply and (assuming good quality and condition) more valuable, but only if the demand has continued strong and economic conditions have not eroded purchasing power. Many collectibles are vulnerable to fads, though some bought from well-established and reputable dealers may be sold back at agreed upon prices.

How assured is my income? Collectibles normally provide no income, and are in fact a drain on cash that might otherwise be invested for income.

Are there any other risks unique to this investment? Collectibles are subject to a wide range of unique risks—forgery and other frauds; physical risk, such as deterioration, fire, and theft; "warehouse finds," where a large supply of a previously limited item is suddenly discovered and becomes a drug on the market; the reverse situation, where a large chunk of a given collectible's supply goes "in collection," leaving so little in circulation that diminished interest reduces demand. Each category has its own special risks and prospective collectors are advised to research them.

Is it commercially rated? No.

Tax Considerations

What tax advantages (or disadvantages) does it offer? Realized capital gains and capital losses are subject to standard rates for capital assets. Other tax advantages may pertain, depending on whether the collecting is done as a hobby or as a for-profit investment activity. Tax advice should be obtained.

Economic Considerations

What economic factors most affect buy, hold, and sell decisions? Collectibles have traditionally been favored by investors in times of inflation, though the value of this investment category as an inflation hedge is tempered by the many risks.

The marketability of collectibles is more dependent on good economic conditions than most other investments.

COMMON STOCK

For total return over the long term, no publicly traded investment alternative offers more potential under normal conditions than common stock.

A share of common stock is the basic unit of equity ownership in a corporation. The shareholder is usually entitled to vote in the election of directors and on other important matters and to share in the wealth created by corporate activities, both through the appreciation of share values and the payment of dividends out of the earnings remaining after debt obligations and holders of preferred stock are satisfied. In the event of liquidation of assets, common shareholders divide the assets remaining after creditors and preferred shareholders have been repaid.

In public corporations, shares have market values primarily based on investor expectations of future earnings and dividends. The relationship of this market price to the actual or expected earnings, called the price-earnings ratio or "multiple," is a measure of these expectations. Stock values are also affected by forecasts of business activity in general and by whatever "investor psychology" is produced by the immediate business and economic environment.

Stocks of young, fast-growing companies, particularly those in industries that are cyclical or high technology-oriented, tend to be volatile, to have high price-earnings ratios, and generally to carry a high degree of risk. Called *growth stocks,* they seldom pay dividends, since earnings are reinvested to finance growth. These stocks are often traded in the over-the-counter market or on the American Stock Exchange.

At the other end of the spectrum, stocks of old, established firms in mature industries and with histories of regular earnings and dividends tend to be characterized by relative price stability and low multiples. These stocks are usually found listed on the New York Stock Exchange (although there are exceptions) and the cream of the crop are known as blue chips. As a general category, these regular dividend payers are called *income stocks.*

Spanning the growth/income continuum is a wide range of common stock investment choices that can be made only in terms of one's personal objectives and risk comfort level. To help in the process is a professional establishment comprised of brokers, investment advisers, and financial planners supported by practitioners of various securities analysis approaches—those trained in fundamental analysis, technical analysis, chartists, and others.

Investors with limited means can gain the advantages of common stock ownership together with the benefits of professional management and portfolio diversification through mutual funds, which are discussed elsewhere in this section.

*   *   *

What Is Common Stock?

A common stock represents ownership in a corporation, usually carries voting rights, and often earns dividends (paid out at the discretion of the corporation's board of directors).

Buying, Selling, and Holding

How do I buy and sell common stock? Through a securities broker-dealer.

Is there a minimum purchase amount, and what is the price range? There is no minimum, but buying in round lots (usually 100 shares) saves extra odd-lot (under 100 shares) charges. Some brokers offer programs allowing odd-lot purchases at regular rates. Stock prices range widely, with the majority under $50.

What fees and charges are involved? The brokerage commission, the principal charge, varies by the value and/or size of transaction. Discount brokers charge less than full-service brokers. A nominal transfer tax is imposed on sellers by the federal government and several state governments. Interest and other charges may be incurred in margin accounts, in which qualifying stocks can be traded on credit within requirements of the Federal Reserve Board and individual brokerage firms.

Does it mature, expire, or otherwise terminate? No, although tender offers by issuing companies and outside acquirers often give shareholders the opportunity to sell within a set period at a premium over prevailing stock market prices.

Can I sell it quickly? Usually, yes. Shares of publicly held and actively traded companies are highly liquid.

How is market value determined and how do I keep track of it? Market value is basically determined by investor expectations of future earnings and dividend payments, although the value of assets is also important. Prices may also be affected temporarily by large transactions creating bid-offer imbalances, by rumors of various sorts, and by public tender offers. Newspapers and electronic databases show daily prices on stocks traded on exchanges and over the counter.

Investment Objectives

Should I buy common stock if my objective is capital appreciation? Yes, especially growth stocks of younger firms, which tend to reinvest earnings rather than pay dividends as older, established firms do.

Should I buy this if my objective is income? Yes, especially if your objectives also include some capital appreciation and inflation protection. Established companies are more likely to pay dividends regularly than are fast-growing firms that tend to reinvest earnings.

To what extent does it protect against inflation? Over the long run, stocks rise in value and increase dividends with inflation, though they do not protect against hyperinflation.

Is it suitable for tax-deferred retirement accounts? Yes. Stocks are suitable for IRAs, Keoghs, 401(K) plans, and other tax-deferred plans.

Can I borrow against it? Yes, subject to Federal Reserve margin rules and lender policies concerning marketable securities collateral.

Risk Considerations

How assured can I be of getting my full investment back? There is no concrete assurance. There is always the risk that market prices will decline in value, though some stocks are more volatile than others. When a company goes out of business and liquidates its assets, common shareholders are paid last—after preferred stockholders and creditors.

How assured is my income? Dividends come out of earnings and are declared at the discretion of the board of directors. They can be suspended if profits are off, or if the directors decide reinvestment is preferable. Older, established, blue chip companies are the most dependable dividend payers; young, growth-oriented firms tend to reinvest earnings and thus pay no (or low) dividends.

Are there any other risks unique to this investment? Anything that can affect the fortunes of a company can affect its stock value and dividend payments.

Is it commercially rated? Yes, Moody's, Standard & Poor's, Value Line Investment Survey, and others rate many publicly traded issues.

Tax Considerations

What tax advantages (or disadvantages) does common stock offer? Dividends to individuals, formerly subject to a $100 exclusion ($200 on joint returns), became fully taxable as of December 31, 1986. Gains on the sale of stock held more than six months received preferential long-term capital gains treatment prior to 1987 and were subject to a maximum rate of 28% in 1987. The tax rate differential between ordinary income and capital gains, regardless of the holding period, was scheduled to end effective with the 1988 tax year. After-tax corporate earnings not paid out as dividends accumulate without being taxed, if not deemed excessive. Corporations can exclude 80% of dividends received from other domestic corporations.

Economic Considerations

What economic factors most affect buy, hold, or sell decisions? Stocks are most attractive as holdings when inflation is moderate, interest rates are low, and business conditions are generally favorable to growth and bigger profits.

CONVERTIBLE SECURITY

Convertible securities—bonds (debentures) or preferred stock convertible into common stock (usually of the issuer but, in rare cases, of the issuer's subsidiary or affiliate)—offer both fixed income and appreciation potential but are not quite the best of both worlds. The yield on the convertible bond or preferred is normally less than that of a "straight" bond or preferred, and the potential for capital gain is less than with a common stock investment.

On the other hand, convertibles (sometimes called CVs and identified that way in the newspaper bond tables, but not the stock tables) do offer less credit risk and market risk than common shares while providing an opportunity to share in the future wealth of the corporation for whose shares the convertible can be exchanged.

In terms of priority of claim on earnings and assets, convertible bonds and convertible preferred stock have the same status as regular bonds and preferred. Bonds, whether convertible or straight, receive payments before preferred stock, whatever its type, and both bonds and preferred have precedence over common stock.

From the investor's standpoint, convertibles must be understood in terms of what is called their *investment value* and their *conversion value*. Investment value is the market value the convertible would have if it were not convertible—its value as a straight bond or straight preferred. Conversion value is the market price of the common stock times the number of shares into which the bond or preferred is convertible (called the conversion rate or ratio).

Since convertible owners hope to capitalize on rises in common shares through conversion and therefore value the conversion privilege, CVs begin trading at a premium over conversion value. As the common rises and the CV is viewed more and more as a common stock investment, the CV tends to sell for its common stock equivalent. Conversion is not advisable until the common dividend has more value than the income on the CV and it is normal for the common price to rise beyond the CV price until that equation is reached.

Of course, common-share prices cannot be guaranteed to rise, and in a down market convertible holders look at their investment in terms of its value as a bond or preferred stock. This investment value represents downside risk protection in the sense that the convertible will never be worth less than this value. Investment value is, however, subject to market risk; it can be pushed down by a general rise in interest rates. But should that happen, investors have downside protection in that the CV will never drop significantly below its conversion value.

Conventional wisdom holds that investors should not buy convertibles unless attracted by the soundness of the underlying common stock. They should be wary also of issues selling at high premiums over the value of the common stock or the prices at which they are callable.

See also the discussion of Zero-coupon Securities.

∗   ∗   ∗

What Is a Convertible Security?

A convertible security is a preferred stock or debenture (unsecured bond) paying a fixed dividend or rate of interest and convertible into common stock, usually of the issuer, at a specified price or conversion ratio.

Buying, Selling, and Holding

How do I buy and sell a convertible security? Through a securities broker-dealer.

Is there a minimum purchase amount and what is the price range? Convertible preferred stock typically trades in 10-share round lots and has par values ranging from $100 down to $10. Bonds sell in $1000 units but exceptions, called baby bonds, can have lower par values, usually $500 down to $25. Brokers often have minimum orders of 10 bonds or, frequently, 100 bonds. Odd lots involve higher commissions or dealer spreads.

What fees and charges are involved? Standard brokerage commissions or dealer spreads. Bonds usually involve a per-bond commission of $2.50 to $20, depending on the broker and the size of the order. However, a minimum of $30 is common.

Does it mature, expire, or otherwise terminate? Bonds mature; preferred stocks do not. Both may be callable, however, and the regular redemption and retirement of both shares and bonds may be provided for by sinking fund agreements. Of course, once converted to common stock, there are no maturities or calls.

Can I sell it quickly? Most can be readily sold, but trading volume is not ordinarily heavy and prices can fluctuate significantly.

How is market value determined and how do I keep track of it? Market value is influenced both by the market price of the underlying common stock and the investment value of the convertible security—that is, its value as a bond or preferred stock exclusive of the conversion feature. When the conversion premium—the amount by which the price of the convertible security exceeds the price of the underlying common stock—is high, the convertible trades like a bond or preferred stock. When trading like a fixed-income investment, its value fluctuates in inverse relation to interest rates, though it will not decline below its investment value. Once parity has been reached—that is, the price of the convertible and its value assuming conversion are the same—the convertible will rise along with the underlying common stock. Prices of convertibles are reported in the stock or bond tables of daily newspapers and in electronic databases.

Investment Objectives

Should I buy a convertible security if my objective is capital appreciation? Yes; convertibles offer the opportunity to capitalize on growth in common share values while enjoying the greater yield and safety of bonds or preferred.

Should I buy this if my objective is income? Yes; but since growth is a feature, the yield is less than on a straight bond or preferred.

To what extent does it protect against inflation? Convertible prices tend to rise with common share prices, which tend to rise with inflation.

Is it suitable for tax-deferred retirement accounts? Yes, CVs qualify for IRAs, Keoghs, 401(K) plans, and other tax-deferred plans.

Can I borrow against it? Yes, subject to margin rules. CVs are acceptable general collateral, with bonds having more loan value than stock.

Risk Considerations

How assured can I be of getting my full investment back? CVs have downside protection in that their value will not sink below the market value the same investment would have as a straight (nonconvertible) bond or preferred. That "investment value" varies inversely with rates, however, so when rates go up the "floor" goes down. The price of a CV is determined, on the other hand, by the value of its conversion feature, so as long as the common holds up, the CV should not decline to its investment value. Of course, once converted, your investment becomes subject to all the risks of common stock. In liquidation, convertible bonds are paid before convertible preferred stock, and both have precedence over the corporation's common stock.

How assured is my income? The interest on convertible bonds, as a legal obligation of the issuer, has a higher claim on earnings than dividends on convertible preferred stock, which can be omitted if the issuer gets tight for cash. Preferred dividends must be paid before common dividends, however. Assuming the issuer is strong financially and has dependable earnings, there is little to worry about.

Are there any other risks unique to this investment? Dilution—a decrease in the value of common shares into which the CV converts—can happen for many reasons. Provision for such obvious corporate actions as stock splits, new issues, or spin-offs of stock or other properties, is normally made in the bond indenture or preferred stock agreement, but subtle developments, such as small quarterly stock dividends or unplanned events, can be a risk.

Is it commercially rated? Yes, by Moody's, Standard & Poor's, Value Line, and other services.

Tax Considerations

What tax advantages (or disadvantages) does it offer? None, except that gains resulting from conversion to the issuer's common stock are not treated as gains for tax purposes, provided the stock you receive is that of the same corporation that issued the convertible. Corporations can exclude from taxes 80% of preferred dividends.

Economic Considerations

What economic factors most affect buy, hold, or sell decisions? Assuming economic conditions are not threatening the issuer's financial health, convertibles offer holders protection from adverse factors affecting both common stock and fixed-income securities. The CV is thus a security for all seasons, though the price of having it both ways is less appreciation potential than common stock and less yield than straight bonds or preferred stock. It follows that CVs are popular in times of economic and market uncertainty. The ideal time to buy is when rates are high and stocks are low and the best time to hold is in a rising stock market. Stagflation is the worst scenario because stocks are hurt by the stagnation and fixed-income securities are hurt by the inflation; both the conversion and investment values of CVs thus suffer.

FOREIGN STOCKS AND BONDS

Foreign stocks and bonds—those of foreign issuers denominated in foreign currencies—offer opportunities (1) to invest where economies or industry sectors may be faster growing than those at home and (2) to augment total returns through profits on currency movements.

Foreign securities have acquired luster in recent years, as ways to shift money from sluggish United States markets into more vibrant overseas economies (while gaining an edge on domestic inflation) and as "dollar plays," ways of capitalizing on expected declines in the value of the U.S. dollar vis-à-vis foreign currencies. Generally, foreign investment activity has picked up with deregulation of foreign markets, improved communications, and increased internationalization of businesses, banks, and broker-dealers.

Problems that remain, depending on the issue and the market, include inadequate financial information and regulation; high minimum purchase requirements; additional transaction costs and risks; taxes; possible illiquidity; political risk; and the possibility of currency losses. Unless you are wealthy, able to take big risks, and sophisticated in the ways of international interest rates and foreign exchange, you are better advised to achieve international diversification through open-end and closed-end funds or other investment pools specializing in foreign securities.

An exception for some investors might be American Depositary Receipts (ADRs). Many foreign stocks can be owned by way of these negotiable receipts, which are issued by United States banks and represent actual shares held in their foreign branches. ADRs are actively traded on the major stock exchanges and in the over-the-counter market. Although currency risks and foreign withholding taxes remain, the depositary pays dividends and capital gains in U.S. dollars and handles rights offerings, splits, stock dividends, and other corporate actions. ADRs eliminate trading inconveniences and custodial problems that otherwise exist with foreign stocks.

Eurobonds—bonds issued by governments and their agencies, banks, international institutions, and corporations (U.S. and foreign) and sold outside their countries through international syndicates for purchase by international investors—also warrant a special word. They may be denominated in foreign currencies, Eurodollars, or composite currency units, such as Special Drawing Rights (SDRs) or European Units of Account (EUAs) whose certificates representing the combined value of two or more currencies are designed to minimize the effects of currency fluctuations. Most are fixed-income obligations, but some Eurodollar issues have floating rates tied to the London Interbank Offered Rate (LIBOR). Eurobonds, which are issued in bearer form, attract upscale personal investors because they are available in a wide range of maturities, are not subject to a withholding tax, and offer good liquidity.

New issues of Eurobonds may not be sold legally to United States investors until a 90-day seasoning period has expired. Actually, most United States broker-dealers extend this rule to include all new issues in foreign currencies; foreign banks and broker-dealers are generally more solicitous of United States investors in selling new issues. Except for Yankee bonds, obligations of foreign borrowers issued in the United States and denominated in dollars, foreign bonds are not subject to Securities and Exchange Commission regulation.

*   *   *

What Are Foreign Stocks and Bonds?

Foreign stocks and bonds are stock of foreign companies listed on foreign exchanges; stock of foreign companies listed on United States exchanges or represented by listed American Depositary Receipts (ADRs); bonds of foreign government entities and corporations, including Eurobonds and nondollar-denominated bonds issued by local syndicates.

Buying, Selling, and Holding

How do I buy and sell foreign stocks and bonds? Through securities broker-dealers with foreign offices or with expertise in foreign markets, and through foreign banks and their American offices. (ADRs and shares traded on U.S. exchanges can be bought and sold through any broker.)

Is there a minimum purchase amount, and what is the price range? ADRs and U.S. exchange-listed foreign stocks trade just like domestic common stock. Minimums on other stocks and bonds vary widely by issue and dealer, but are often high. With the extra risks, diversification is important, which raises the cost even higher. Unless you are wealthy, you should probably opt for one of the mutual funds or other investment vehicles pooling foreign securities.

What fees and charges are involved? Transaction costs can be a significant consideration. They vary depending on many factors, but may include custodial fees, local turnover or transfer taxes, and currency conversion fees, in addition to broker commissions or dealer spreads. Transaction and custodial costs are minimized with ADRs.

Do foreign stocks and bonds mature, expire, or otherwise terminate? Bonds mature; stocks do not. However remote, the risk exists that a sovereign government will confiscate or devalue assets of foreign investors.

Can I sell them quickly? U.S. exchange-listed foreign stocks and ADRs normally enjoy high liquidity. With other foreign securities, illiquidity is often a problem. Even widely held issues are often kept as permanent investments by governments, banks, and other companies and may not trade actively. Canada, England, and Japan have high average turnover on their stock exchanges.

How is market value determined and how do I keep track of it? Economic, market, and monetary (interest-rate) factors affect foreign stock and bond values the same way they do domestic equity and debt securities, though conditions and growth rates differ among countries. Traditionally, foreign stocks, on average, have been less volatile than domestic issues, because issuers tended to be older firms whose stock was held largely by long-term investors. Today, foreign exchanges list a growing number of young, dynamic companies whose shares are actively traded and often quite volatile. *The Wall Street Journal,* the *Financial Times* (London), and other leading newspapers report on major foreign exchanges, as well as ADRs and foreign stocks and bonds traded in domestic markets.

Investment Objectives

Should I buy foreign stocks and bonds if my objective is capital appreciation? Especially in growing economies, stocks offer potential for both capital and currency appreciation. Unless bought at a discount or in a period of declining interest rates, bonds do not appreciate, although gains due to currency movements are possible.

Should I buy them if my objective is income? Yes, but most foreign stocks have lower dividend yields than domestic stocks, and exchange-rate fluctuations are a factor in the expected returns of both stocks and bonds.

To what extent do they protect against inflation? Foreign stocks can hedge inflation to the extent local economies and industry sectors offer better growth prospects than exist in the United States. But gains from dividends and appreciation can be eroded by foreign-exchange losses.

Are they suitable for tax-deferred retirement accounts? Yes.

Can I borrow against them? Yes; quality securities are acceptable collateral at most banks, and banks headquartered in the country of the issuer will often lend higher percentages of value. Foreign stocks listed on American exchanges are subject to Federal Reserve margin requirements.

Risk Considerations

How assured can I be of getting my full investment back? Although more young, growing firms appear every day on foreign exchanges, most shares represent solid issuers and volatility has traditionally been low, so foreign equities, on average, may actually be safer than many domestic issues, assuming no adverse currency fluctuations. Bondholders, who lack regulatory protection and full credit information, have more credit risk than owners of domestic issues, in addition to having political, interest rate, and currency risks. (Foreign exchange risk can be hedged using currency futures and options.)

How assured is my income? Since issuers tend to be established, reputable firms or governments, there have historically been few defaults on payments of interest or instances of omitted dividends. On the other hand, a lack of full financial disclosure and regulatory supervision makes it difficult to anticipate adverse financial developments. Also, many newer companies, whose securities are riskier than those of traditional foreign issuers, are likewise listed on foreign exchanges. Foreign-exchange risk can also affect income.

Are there any other risks unique to this investment? Political or sovereign risk— the risk, for example, that foreign assets might be expropriated or devalued or that local tax policies might adversely affect debt or equity holders; the risk of transactional losses caused by settlement delays or fraud; with stock not registered with the Securities and Exchange Commission, there are legal difficulties for Americans in subscribing to rights offerings, a fact which can also affect the salability of rights (rights problems do not exist with ADRs or U.S. exchange-listed foreign shares).

Are they commercially rated? Some foreign debt issues are rated. Information can be found in a publication called *Credit Week International,* available at some larger brokerage firms.

Tax Considerations

What tax advantages (or disadvantages) do they offer? Some countries impose a withholding tax, typically from 15% to 20%, on dividends and interest (except Eurobonds). U.S. tax treaties can result in partial reclamation of withholdings in some countries, and the tax can be offset to some extent against federal income taxes. There is usually no capital gains tax imposed by foreign governments, though such gains are taxed by the U.S. government. Special rules apply to 10% or more ownership of a foreign corporation.

Economic Considerations

What economic factors most affect buy, hold, or sell decisions? Foreign securities are best bought when the U.S. dollar is strong against the currency of denomination. To profit from currency movements (or, conversely, to avoid losses) it is best to hold when the dollar is declining against the local currency. Foreign equities are attractive relative to American investments when the foreign economy or industrial sector has a better outlook than its domestic counterpart. Foreign bonds rise and fall in inverse relation to market interest rates.

FUTURES CONTRACT ON A COMMODITY

A futures contract is a commitment to buy or sell a specified quantity of a commodity or financial instrument at a specified price during a particular delivery month. Once restricted largely to agricultural commodities and metals, futures contracts have in recent years been extended to include what are broadly termed financial futures—contracts on debt instruments, such as Treasury bonds and Government National Mortgage Association (''Ginnie Mae'') certificates and on foreign currencies—and, even more recently, contracts on stock indexes. Contract prices are determined through open outcry—a system of verbal communication between sellers and buyers on the floors of regulated commodities exchanges.

The futures markets are broadly divided into two categories of participants: (1) Hedgers have a position in (i.e., own) the underlying commodity or instrument (such as a farmer in the case of an agricultural commodity or an investor in the case of a financial or index future). Hedgers use futures to create countervailing positions, thus protecting against loss due to price (or rate) changes. (2) Speculators do not own the underlying asset for commercial or investment purposes, but instead aim to capitalize on the ups and downs (the volatility) of the contracts themselves. It is the speculators who provide the liquidity essential to the efficient operation of the futures markets.

As with option contracts, which are also discussed in this section, the great majority of futures contracts are closed out before their expiration—or delivery—date. This is done by buying or selling an offsetting contract. It is vital to note that with futures, in contrast to options (which simply expire), the alternative to an offset is a delivery, though this is done with title documentation or, in the case of index futures, cash, not by the legendary dumping of pork bellies on the front steps of absentminded contract holders. When the future is a contract to buy value, delivery of the future is avoided by buying an offsetting future to sell.

The attraction of futures for speculators, again like options, is the enormous leverage they provide. Although brokers normally require investors to meet substantial net worth and income requirements, it is possible to trade contracts with outlays of cash (or sometimes U.S. Treasury securities) equal to 5% to 10% of contract values. Such "margins" (actually good-faith deposits, more in the nature of performance bonds and required of both buyers and sellers) are set by the exchanges, although brokers normally have their own maintenance requirements. Margin calls are normally made when deposits drop to one half the original percentage value.

The commodity exchanges, with oversight by the Commodities Futures Trading Commission (CFTC), each day set limits, based on the previous day's closing price, to the extent a given contract's trading price may vary. While these trading limits help preclude exaggerated short-term volatility and thus make it possible for margin requirements to be kept low, they can also lock a trader into a losing position, where he must meet a margin call but is prevented from trading out of the position because the contract is either up limit or down limit (as high or as low as the daily limit permits it to be traded).

Speculators in futures contracts fall into three groups: (1) the exchange floor traders (scalpers), who make markets in contracts and turn small profits usually within the trading day; (2) spread traders, who hope to profit from offsetting positions in contracts having different maturities but the same underlying commodity or instrument, similar maturities but different (although usually closely related) underlying commodities, or similar contracts in different markets; and (3) position traders, who have the expertise and financial ability to analyze longer-term factors and ride out shorter term fluctuations in the expectation of ultimate gains.

While speculation in futures contracts is not recommended for the average investor, individuals with the money and risk tolerance may participate by choosing among the following alternatives: trading for one's own account, which involves time and expertise; trading through a managed account or a discretionary account with a commodities broker, which utilizes a professional's time and expertise for a fee or sometimes involves a participation in profits; or mutual funds, which offer both professional management and diversification and are regulated by both the CFTC and the Securities and Exchange Commission.

*   *   *

What Is a Commodity Futures Contract?

A commodity futures contract is an agreement to buy or sell a specific amount of a commodity at a particular price in a stipulated future month.

Buying, Selling, and Holding

How do I buy and sell it? Through a full-service broker or firm specializing in commodities transactions.

Is there a minimum purchase amount, and what is the price range? Contract sizes and unit prices vary widely from commodity to commodity, but the exchanges have liberal margin rules making it possible to trade with as little as 5% to 10% down. In some commodities, that can be $100, but brokers often have minimum deposits of $1000 to $2500. (They may also have strict personal income and net worth rules for investors.) One national exchange, the Mid-America Commodity Exchange, offers minicontracts in a number of commodities, currencies, and instruments; they range from one fifth to one half the size of regular contracts.

What fees and charges are involved? Broker commissions, which vary by contract but average $25 to $50 for a round-turn (buy and sell) trade with lower rates for intraday and spread (e.g., buy soybeans, sell soybean oil) transactions. Managed accounts involve management fees and, sometimes, participation in profits.

Does a commodity futures contract mature, expire, or otherwise terminate? Yes. All contracts have a stipulated expiration date.

Can I sell it quickly? Most established contracts are liquid, though daily price limits can create illiquidity when a commodity is down limit or up limit (as high or as low as the daily trading limit permits).

How is market value determined and how do I keep track of it? By supply and demand, which is affected by natural causes as well as general economic developments. Futures prices are quoted daily in the financial pages of newspapers and electronic databases.

Investment Objectives

Should I buy a commodity futures contract if my objective is capital appreciation? Only if you are expert, wealthy, and have a high tolerance for risk. Then, with the high leverage possible, capital gains (and losses) can be huge.

Should I buy this if my objective is income? No. Contracts pay no income.

To what extent does it protect against inflation? Forward commodity prices reflect inflation expectations, but since contracts are short-term oriented, inflation protection is a secondary consideraton.

Is it suitable for tax-deferred retirement accounts? Although not prohibited by the Internal Revenue Service, most brokerage firms rule out futures contracts as too risky for retirement accounts. They may have a limited role in managed accounts, primarily as a hedging tool. Certain pooled investment vehicles trading in futures may be appropriate in selected situations for people with high risk tolerance.

Can I borrow against it? Futures are not acceptable collateral with most lenders. Of course, they provide leverage inherently because of the relatively small deposits required to control contracts.

Risk Considerations

How assured can I be of getting my full investment back? Commodity futures are inherently speculative and it is actually possible to lose more than your investment (though margin calls would usually limit losses to the amount deposited if the account was sold out—that is, liquidated by the broker to meet the margin call).

How assured is my income? Futures provide no income.

Are there any other risks unique to this investment? The possibility of losses in excess of investment and the risk of illiquidity when a contract is down or up limit (thus making it impossible to trade out of a position) are risks unique to commodity futures trading. Of course, there is the risk (nightmare?) of actual delivery of a commodity if you fail to close out a position prior to expiration of a contract.

Is it commercially rated? No.

Tax Considerations

What tax advantages (or disadvantages) does a commodity futures contract offer? Speculators' open positions are marked to market at year end and paper profits and losses taxed as though realized. Prior to the Tax Reform Act of 1986, 60% of profits were taxed as long-term capital gains and 40% at short-term (ordinary income) rates, for a maximum rate of 32%. With the capital gains exclusion ended, net profits are taxable at ordinary rates, although net trading losses can be applied against capital gains on other investments and unused portions carried forward. Other tax treatments apply to nonspeculative and hedging uses and tax advice is recommended.

Economic Considerations

What economic factors most affect buy, hold, and sell decisions? Anything that affects supply and demand for a commodity makes contract values move up and down.

FUTURES CONTRACT ON AN INTEREST RATE

For a general discussion of a futures contract, see Futures Contract on a Commodity.

∗   ∗   ∗

What Is a Futures Contract on an Interest Rate?

A futures contract on an interest rate is an agreement to buy or sell a given amount of a fixed-income security, such as a Treasury bill, bond, or note or Government National Mortgage Association security at a particular price in a stipulated future month.

Buying, Selling, and Holding

How do I buy and sell it? Through a full-service broker or firm specializing in commodities transactions.

Is there a minimum purchase amount, and what is the price range? Contract sizes vary with the underlying security and the exchange, but range from $20,000 to $1 million; since exchange margin rules allow trading with as little as 5% deposited, the actual cost of investing can be relatively low.

What fees and charges are involved? Broker commissions averaging $25 to $50 per contract transaction.

Does it mature, expire, or otherwise terminate? Yes; futures contracts have specific expiration dates.

Can I sell it quickly? Yes, except that liquidity may become a problem if the contract reaches the maximum price movement allowable in one day, in effect locking you into a position.

How is market value determined and how do I keep track of it? By market interest rate movements, essentially. When rates go up, the prices of fixed-income securities (and futures related to them) go down, and vice versa. Prices are reported daily in newspapers and electronic databases.

Investment Objectives

Should I buy a futures contract on an interest rate if my objective is capital appreciation? Speculators use the leverage available with futures to capitalize on expected interest rate movements, standing to gain (or lose) substantially more than the amount invested.

Should I buy this if my objective is income? No, though you might use futures to hedge the value of securities bought for income or to lock in the yield on a security to be bought at a later date.

To what extent does it protect against inflation? To the extent inflation expectations are a factor in the volatility of fixed-income investments, futures can offer some protection against loss.

Is it suitable for tax-deferred retirement accounts? Although not prohibited by the Internal Revenue Service, most brokerage firms rule out futures contracts as too risky for retirement accounts. They may have a limited role in managed accounts, primarily as a hedging tool. Certain pooled investment vehicles trading in futures may be appropriate in selected situations for people with high risk tolerance.

Can I borrow against it? No; futures contracts are not acceptable collateral at most lenders. Of course, there is considerable leverage inherent in the small deposit required to control contracts.

Risk Considerations

How assured can I be of getting my full investment back? Just as interest rate movements cannot be predicted with certainty, interest rate futures can result in losses as well as gains; it is in fact possible to lose more than your investment (called open-ended risk) but margin calls would normally limit losses to the amount invested, assuming the account was sold out (liquidated) to meet the call.

How assured is my income? Futures do not provide income.

Are there any other risks unique to this investment? Open-ended risk and the risk of illiquidity when a contract is down limit or up limit, making it impossible to trade out of a position, are risks unique to futures contracts.

Is it commercially rated? No.

Tax Considerations

What tax advantages (or disadvantages) does it offer? Speculators' open positions are marked to market at year end and paper profits and losses taxed as though realized. Prior to the Tax Reform Act of 1986, 60% of profits were taxed as long-term capital gains and 40% at short-term (ordinary income) rates, for a maximum rate of 32%. With the capital gains exclusion ended, net profits are taxable at ordinary rates, although net trading losses can be applied against capital gains on other investments and unused portions carried forward. Other tax treatments apply to nonspeculative and hedging uses and tax advice is recommended.

Economic Considerations

What economic factors most affect buy, hold, and sell decisions? Economic and monetary factors affecting interest rates govern choices having to do with interest rate futures.

FUTURES CONTRACT ON A STOCK INDEX

For a general discussion of a futures contract, see Futures Contract on a Commodity.

*   *   *

What Is a Futures Contract on a Stock Index?

A futures contract on a stock index is an agreement to buy or sell a stock index at a price based on the index value in a stipulated future month with settlement in cash.

Buying, Selling, and Holding

How do I buy and sell it? Through a full-service broker or firm specializing in commodities transactions.

Is there a minimum purchase amount, and what is the price range? Contracts are priced according to formulas based on index values, and vary in terms both of formulas and index values. For example, the contracts on the New York Stock Exchange Composite Index, the Standard & Poor's 500 Stock Index, and The Value Line Stock Index are priced by multiplying $500 times the index value, which ranges roughly between 100 and 300; if one of those indexes had a value of 200, a contract would cost $100,000, which might require a deposit of 10% or $10,000. To play, though, you would probably have to meet an income and liquid net worth test requiring substantial means.

What fees and charges are involved? Broker commissions.

Does it mature, expire, or otherwise terminate? Yes, all contracts have specific expirations.

Can I sell it quickly? Yes, except that liquidity may become a problem if the contract reaches the maximum price movement allowable in one day (i.e., becomes down limit or up limit).

How is market value determined and how do I keep track of it? By the market performance of the stocks comprising the index as they affect the index value. Index futures are reported with other futures prices in the financial pages of daily newspapers and electronic databases.

Investment Objectives

Should I buy a futures contract on a stock index if my objective is capital appreciation? Speculators use the leverage available with futures to capitalize on expected market movements, standing to gain (or lose) substantially more than the amount invested.

Should I buy this if my objective is income? No, but they are used, mainly by professionals, to hedge the value of income-producing stocks.

To what extent does it protect against inflation? This is not an investment you would hold as an inflation hedge.

Is it suitable for tax-deferred retirement accounts? Although not prohibited by the Internal Revenue Service, most brokerage firms rule out futures contracts as too risky for retirement accounts. They may have a limited role in managed accounts, primarily as a hedging tool. Certain pooled investment vehicles trading in futures may be appropriate in selected situations for people with high risk tolerance.

Can I borrow against it? No; futures are not acceptable collateral at most lenders. Of course, there is considerable leverage inherent in the relatively small deposit required to control contracts.

Risk Considerations

How assured can I be of getting my full investment back? Just as market movements cannot be predicted with certainty, index futures can result in losses as well as gains; in fact, it is quite possible to lose more than your investment (called open-ended risk), although margin calls are a safeguard against losses in excess of investment if an account is sold out (liquidated) to meet the call.

How assured is my income? Index futures do not provide income.

Are there any other risks unique to this investment? Index futures and the individual stocks comprising the index may not move exactly together, so it is not a perfect hedging tool.

Is it commercially rated? No.

Tax Considerations

What tax advantages (or disadvantages) does it offer? Speculators' open positions are marked to market at year end and paper profits and losses taxed as though realized. Prior to the Tax Reform Act of 1986, 60% of profits were taxed as long-term capital gains and 40% at short-term (ordinary income) rates, for a maximum rate of 32%. With the capital gains exclusion ended, net profits are taxable at ordinary rates, although net trading losses can be applied against capital gains on other investments and unused portions carried forward. Other tax treatments apply to nonspeculative and hedging uses and tax advice is recommended.

Economic Considerations

What economic factors most affect buy, hold, and sell decisions? The myriad factors affecting the market outlook affect choices having to do with stock index futures, whether they are used to speculate or as a hedging tool.

GOVERNMENT AGENCY SECURITY

Government agency securities, popularly called agencies, are indirect obligations of the United States government, issued by federal agencies and government-sponsored corporations under authority from the United States Congress, but, with a few exceptions, not backed, as U.S. Treasury securities are, by the full faith and credit of the government.

While it is highly unlikely—even unthinkable—that they could ever be allowed to default on principal or interest, these agency securities cannot be considered absolutely risk-free, and therein lies their attraction—because of the slight difference in safety, they generally yield as much as a half percentage point more than direct obligations.

Agencies are also, like Treasuries, exempt from state and local taxes, although there are exceptions—for example, issues of the Government National Mortgage Association (GNMA), the Federal National Mortgage Association (FNMA) and the Federal Home Loan Mortgage Corporation (FHLMC), including both mortgage-backed pass-throughs and bonds and notes issued to finance their operations.

Unlike Treasuries, agencies are not sold by auction but rather are marketed at the best yield possible by the Federal Reserve Bank of New York, as fiscal agent, through its network of primary dealers. Information can be obtained from the Federal Reserve Bank of New York, Treasury and Agency Issues Division, from the issuing agencies, or from dealer commercial banks and securities brokers.

Issuers of government agency securities include:

Asian Development Bank

District of Columbia Armory Board (D.C. Stadium)

Export-Import Bank of the United States

Farmers Home Administration

Federal Farm Credit Consolidated System-Wide Securities

Federal Home Loan Banks

Federal Home Loan Mortgage Corporation

Federal Housing Administration (FHA)

Federal National Mortgage Association (FNMA)

Government National Mortgage Association (GNMA)

Interamerican Development Bank

International Bank for Reconstruction and Development (World Bank)

Maritime Administration

Small Business Administration (SBA)

Student Loan Marketing Association (SLMA)

Tennessee Valley Authority (TVA)

United States Postal Service

Washington Metropolitan Area Transit Authority

*   *   *

What Is a Government Agency Security?

A government agency security is a negotiable debt obligation of an agency of the United States government, which may be backed by the full faith and credit of the federal government but is more often guaranteed by the sponsoring agency with the implied backing of Congress.

Buying, Selling, and Holding

How do I buy and sell it? Through a securities broker-dealer or at many commercial banks.

Is there a minimum purchase amount, and what is the price range? Denominations and minimums vary widely from $1000 to $25,000 and up, depending on the issue, the issuing agency, and the dealer.

What fees and charges are involved? None in the case of new issues bought from a member of the underwriting group; otherwise a commission or dealer markup.

Does it mature, expire, or otherwise terminate? Yes, maturities range from 30 days to 25 years.

Can I sell it quickly? Yes, but bid and asked spreads tend to be wider than with direct Treasury obligations, which raises the cost of trading in the secondary market.

How is market value determined and how do I keep track of it? Market values vary inversely with market interest rate movements. Daily newspapers, brokers, and large banks provide price information.

Investment Objectives

Should I buy a government agency security if my objective is capital appreciation? No, though appreciation is possible when fixed-rate securities are bought prior to a drop in market interest rates.

Should I buy this if my objective is income? Yes. Yields are a bit higher than those of direct government obligations, but lower than those of corporate obligations.

To what extent does it protect against inflation? As fixed-income securities, agencies offer no protection, though shorter-term issues offer less exposure to inflation risk.

Is it suitable for tax-deferred retirement accounts? Yes.

Can I borrow against it? Yes; lenders will often lend 90% of value.

Risk Considerations

How assured can I be of getting my full investment back? Agencies are second only to Treasury securities as good credit risks. Market prices fall as interest rates rise, however, so you may not get a full return of principal if you sell in the secondary market prior to maturity. Some sophisticated investors hedge market risk using options, futures, and futures options that are available on certain Treasury securities and Government National Mortgage Association securities.

How assured is my income? Very assured. It is highly unlikely the U.S. Treasury, Congress, or a regulatory body like the Federal Reserve Board would allow a government agency to default on interest.

Are there any other risks unique to a government agency security? No, but mortgage-backed pass-through securities issued by government-sponsored entities have different characteristics and are covered separately in this section.

Is it commercially rated? Some issues are rated by major services.

Tax Considerations

What tax advantages (or disadvantages) does it offer? Agencies are fully taxable at the federal level but are exempt from state and local taxes with certain exceptions, such as issues of the Federal National Mortgage Association and the Government National Mortgage Association.

Economic Considerations

What economic factors most affect buy, hold, or sell decisions? It is best to buy when interest rates are high and the best yields can be obtained. Holding is most attractive when rates are declining, causing an upward move in the market values of fixed-income securities, and high inflation is not present to erode the value of fixed returns.

LIFE INSURANCE (CASH VALUE)

For young families as yet without sufficient financial security to provide for expenses in the event of the premature death of the breadwinner or homemaker, life insurance provides essential protection. By far the cheapest and simplest way to obtain that protection is *term life insurance,* a no-frills deal whereby premiums buy insurance but do not create cash value. The alternatives—variously called cash value, straight, whole, permanent, or ordinary life insurance—combine protection with an investment program.

The traditional cash value policy requires a fixed premium for the life of the insured and promises a fixed sum of money on the death of the insured. A portion of the premium covers expenses and actual insurance, the rest earns interest in a tax-deferred savings program, gradually building up a cash value. The latter can be cashed in by canceling the policy (hence the term "cash surrender value"), can be used to buy more protection, or can be borrowed at a below-market or even zero interest rate with the loan balance deducted from the death benefit. On the death of the insured, the beneficiary receives only the death benefit.

Variations called single-premium or limited-payment life policies, have higher up-front premiums so that a policy becomes paid-up—the cash value becomes sufficient to cover the death benefit without further premiums. Later, if the insured is still living, the policy begins paying benefits that can supplement retirement income or be converted to an annuity, thus guaranteeing income for life.

The one serious drawback of cash value policies has been that the interest rate is not competitive with other investments. With soaring interest rates and inflation in the 1970s and in the excitement of new investment products spawned by deregulation in the 1980s, upwardly mobile young investors began questioning the value of insurance policies providing neither competitive investment returns nor the flexibility their dynamic personal financial circumstances required. Faced with cancellations and poor sales, insurers came forth with the following:

> *Universal Life,* which clearly separates the cash value and protection elements of the policy and invests the cash value in a tax-deferred savings program tied to a money market rate. The cost of the insurance is fixed, based on the insured's age and sex, so depending on what the cash value portion earns (it is guaranteed to earn a minimum rate, but can earn more if market rates rise), the premium can vary. The insured may also change the amount of protection at any time. Flexibility is the main feature of this type of policy.

> *Variable Life,* which has a fixed premium like straight life, but the cash value goes into a choice of stock, bond, or money market portfolios, which the investor can alternate. The insurer guarantees a minimum death benefit regardless of portfolio performance, although excess gains buy additional coverage. The attraction here is capital growth opportunity.

> *Universal Variable Life,* a mid-1980s innovation that combines the flexibility of universal life with the growth potential of variable life.

Even with modern policies, however, the question persists: Why sacrifice a portion of income to an insurance company when pure protection can be more cheaply obtained through term insurance and returns as good or better can be obtained by investing directly? The answer depends on an individual's expertise, self-confidence, and willingness to spend time managing investments.

*   *   *

What Is Cash Value Life Insurance?

Cash value life insurance is a contract combining payment to beneficiaries, in the event of the insured's premature death, with investment programs.

Buying, Selling, and Holding

How do I buy and sell it? Through insurance brokers, insurance company sales agents, savings institutions, full-service brokers, commercial banks, financial planners, and other financial services organizations.

Is there a minimum purchase amount, and what is the price range? Annual premiums vary widely with the type of policy and such factors as the age and sex of the insured.

What fees and charges are involved? Cost of coverage, sales commissions, and insurance company operating costs are built into premiums. Some policies have penalties for cancellation before specified dates.

Does it mature, expire, or otherwise terminate? Policies mature in 10 years to life, depending on the program.

Can I sell it quickly? Yes. Policies can be canceled and cash values claimed anytime (although actual payment may require several weeks of processing time).

How is market value determined and how do I keep track of it? Policies are not traded in a secondary market. Cash values are determined by accumulated premiums plus investment income and performance.

Investment Objectives

Should I buy cash value life insurance if my objective is capital appreciation? Assuming death benefits are your primary objective, you might buy a variable life insurance policy or a universal variable life insurance policy with investments in a stock fund to gain capital appreciation.

Should I buy this if my objective is income? No, although policies combining annuities provide for income payments on annuitization.

To what extent does it protect against inflation? Universal, variable, and universal variable policies can offer some inflation protection through adjustable death benefits and the investment of cash values in inflation-sensitive securities.

Is it suitable for tax-deferred retirement accounts? No; life insurance is not an eligible investment.

Can I borrow against it? Yes. Insurance companies will normally loan cash value at lower-than-market rates and reduce the death benefit by the amount of the loan.

Risk Considerations

How assured can I be of getting my full investment back? Insurance companies are highly regulated and there is little risk they will not meet commitments. However, policies that provide for market returns on cash value investments also carry market risk: e.g., a variable life policy invested in a bond fund would lose cash value if interest rates rose, while one invested in stocks would lose in a down market.

How assured is my income? That depends on how cash values are invested. Policies that invest cash value in money market instruments, for example, are subject to fluctuating income.

Are there any other risks unique to cash value life insurance? Although heavily regulated, insurance companies are potentially subject to mismanagement and fraud and are not themselves covered by federal protection in the sense that banks, for example, are covered by the Federal Deposit Insurance Corporation.

Is it commercially rated? Yes. Insurance companies are rated by Best's Rating Service.

Tax Considerations

What tax advantages (or disadvantages) does it offer? Income earned on cash value accumulates and compounds tax-deferred. Though subject to federal estate taxes (after a $600,000 exclusion) and local inheritance taxes, life insurance proceeds paid to a named beneficiary avoid probate. Proceeds to beneficiaries are normally not subject to federal income taxes. Single-premium life insurance, which offers tax-free cash value accumulation and tax-free access to funds in the form of policy loans, is one of the few tax shelters to survive the Tax Reform Act of 1986.

Economic Considerations

What economic factors most affect buy, hold, and sell decisions? Inflation and volatility of interest rates gave rise to life insurance policies whose cash values vary with market conditions. Investors concerned about such factors can choose among such "new breed" alternatives, rather than buying traditional fixed-rate policies, and make their choices based on their expectations. Thus an investor anticipating high inflation and high interest rates would not choose a variable life policy invested in fixed-income bonds but might choose one with a stock fund or one that is money market-oriented. Variable and universal variable life insurance permit switching between bond, stock, and money market funds to afford maximum market flexibility.

LIMITED PARTNERSHIP (LP)

The unique feature of a limited partnership is that financial and tax events flow directly through to individual investors. Until recently this meant that limited partners in real estate ventures, oil and gas projects, and other activities (see page 630) could use liberal tax benefits such as depreciation, depletion, intangible drilling costs, and tax credits, as well as operating losses, as deductions against taxable income from wages and investment income.

The Tax Reform Act of 1986 severely curtailed the use of LPs as tax shelters by ruling that losses from "passive" sources, like LPs, could be used only against passive income. And while "economic programs"—those LPs emphasizing income, appreciation, and safety—may continue to provide attractive returns, their ability to shelter cash flow has been lessened by reduced benefits, notably the elimination of accelerated depreciation of real property and the repeal of the investment credit.

A limited partnership is an organization comprising a general partner with unlimited liability, who is both sponsor and manager, and limited partners, who provide most of the capital, have limited liability, and have no active management role. Most LPs aim to sell or refinance their assets within seven to ten years and distribute proceeds to shareholders.

Limited partnerships may be private, which are restricted to small numbers of wealthy investors and not required to register with the Securities and Exchange Commission, or public, which market shares in typical amounts of $1000 to $5000 to as many limited partners as the sponsor desires. Public LPs must register with the SEC and provide investors with a prospectus and other disclosures.

Limited partnerships are also distinguished in terms of their use of leverage to finance assets. *Leveraged programs,* whose assets are financed 50% or more with borrowed money, offer greater tax benefits because (1) with a larger asset base they generate more deductions, such as depreciation, and because (2) the interest is deductible. *Unleveraged programs* are favored by investors seeking maximum income and less risk.

From the investor's standpoint, one drawback of limited partnerships traditionally has been lack of liquidity. There is no active secondary market for shares, and although some sponsors offer market-making services to investors under some circumstances, the selling of shares during the life of the partnership is generally discouraged.

Inspired by investor reservations about the future of tax-advantaged partnerships after tax reform, some sponsors in the mid-1980s began marketing programs featuring depositary receipts, which represent unit interests and can be traded in the open marketplace. Liquidity provided this way is a feature of *master limited partnerships,* a mid-1980s innovation in which corporate assets or private partnerships are reorganized as public limited partnerships combining various objectives.

* * *

What Is a Limited Partnership?

A limited partnership is a form of business organization, having any of a variety of activities and investment objectives, which is made up of a general partner who organizes and manages the partnership and its operations, and limited partners who contribute capital, have limited liability, and assume no active role in day-to-day business affairs.

Buying, Selling, and Holding

How do I buy and sell it? Unit shares are bought through a securities broker-dealer or financial planner.

Is there a minimum purchase amount, and what is the price range? Public limited partnerships usually have a $1000 to $5000 minimum, with a $2000 minimum for IRAs. Private limited partnerships require at least $20,000. Offerings frequently involve suitability rules, requiring that individuals meet minimum net worth, income, and tax bracket criteria.

What fees and charges are involved? Brokerage commissions and other front-end costs, often totaling 20% or more of the amount invested. There may be additional management fees during the partnership's operating phase.

Does it mature, expire, or otherwise terminate? Most partnerships intend to dispose of their holdings within a specified period (7 to 10 years typically) and distribute the proceeds as capital gains to investors.

Can I sell it quickly? Usually not. There is no secondary market for partnership shares, although some sponsors offer to try to make a market to accommodate investors under certain circumstances. Certain private firms buy LP shares from holders, but the price for this kind of marketability can be high. Some partnerships offer liquidity through depositary receipts, which represent shares and are traded in secondary markets.

How is market value determined and how do I keep track of it? There is no active secondary market for limited partnerships shares. Share values to be ultimately realized as capital gains are affected by various factors, depending on the activities of the partnership and assets it holds.

Investment Objectives

Should I buy a share in a limited partnership if my objective is capital appreciation? Certain types of partnerships emphasize capital gains potential; others do not. Those offering the greatest potential are the riskiest.

Should I buy this if my objective is income? Yes, though not all partnerships have income as a primary objective and some emphasize the tax sheltering of income from other passive sources.

To what extent does it protect against inflation? Some, like all-cash equity programs with investments in inflation-sensitive real estate, offer high protection. Others, such as programs specializing in fixed-rate mortgages, suffer.

Is it suitable for tax-deferred retirement accounts? Yes.

Can I borrow against it? Because of their low liquidity, partnership shares may not be acceptable as marketable securities with many lenders.

Risk Considerations

How assured can I be of getting my full investment back? Safety of principal depends on the type of partnership and the quality of its holdings. Insured mortgage programs held for the life of the partnership offer high safety, but no appreciation, while leveraged programs aimed at high capital gains involve commensurate risk.

How assured is my income? Only insured mortgage programs offer any real assurance of income. Other income partnerships vary with the type and quality of their portfolios.

Are there any other risks unique to this investment? Yes, because limited partners have no active role in management, everything depends on the integrity and management ability of the general partner. In fact, some partnerships (such as those in real estate) are sold as blind pools—that is, the general partner has not even made property selections at the time that investment is made. Programs set up primarily as tax shelters run the risk of being declared abusive, subjecting the investor to heavy penalties and interest as well as back taxes.

Is it commercially rated? Several firms, such as Robert A. Stanger & Co., analyze limited partnerships and rate such factors as offering terms.

Tax Considerations

What tax advantages (or disadvantages) does it offer? Tax benefits flow through to limited partners. Losses thus generated through 1986 may be used to offset taxable income from any source. After 1986, however, such ''passive'' losses may be used only to offset income from other passive sources and not earned or investment income. The provision phases in over five years, so that 35% of passive losses will be disallowed in 1987, 60% in 1988, 80% in 1989, 90% in 1990, and 100% in 1991. Net losses are tax preference items (at 100% in 1987). Unused losses may be carried forward, and after offsetting any gain from the disposition of the passive investment, may be used against any other passive investment. Any excess losses then remaining can be generally applied. At risk rules now include real estate.

Economic Considerations

What economic factors most affect buy, hold, and sell decisions? Because limited partnership investments are generally held for the life of the partnership, hold and sell decisions have limited applicability. Buy decisions should be guided by the outlook for the type of activity in which the partnership specializes and such factors as the expected life of the program and whether it is leveraged or unleveraged.

MONEY MARKET FUND

This special breed of mutual fund gives personal investors the opportunity to own money market instruments that would otherwise be available only to large institutional investors. The attraction is higher yields than individuals could obtain on their own or from most bank money market deposit accounts, plus a high degree of safety and excellent liquidity, complete with checkwriting.

Money market funds are sponsored by mutual fund organizations (investment companies), brokerage firms, and institutions, like insurance companies, which sell and redeem shares without any sales charges or commissions. The company charges only an annual management fee, usually under 1%, although extra services may entail additional charges. Income earned from interest-bearing investments is credited and reinvested (in effect compounded) for shareholders on a daily basis.

The disadvantage of money market funds over other short-term investment alternatives is that income (although normally paid out monthly) fluctuates daily as investments in the fund's portfolio mature and are replaced with new investments bearing current interest rates. In a declining rate market, this can be a disadvantage as compared, say, to a certificate of deposit, which would continue to pay an above-market rate until maturity. As a general rule, fund dividend rates lag behind money market rate changes by a month or so, depending on the average length of their portfolios, which is controlled to an extent by the manager's expectations as to where rates will go. Major sponsors permit switching among different funds in their families.

The market value of a money market fund investment is normally maintained at a constant figure, usually $1 a share. This means capital gains (and the favorable tax treatment they receive) are not a feature of money market funds, though investors may achieve some growth through compounding by opting to reinvest monthly payments.

Funds may differ in terms of the type of securities comprising their portfolios, some specializing only in U.S. Treasury bills or in tax-exempt municipal securities. A general portfolio, however, would typically be comprised of bank and industrial commercial paper, certificates of deposit, acceptances, repurchase agreements, direct and indirect U.S. government obligations, Eurodollar CDs, and other safe and liquid investments. Bonds and foreign debt securities are sometimes included to lift yields.

Money market funds are not covered by federal insurance the way bank deposits are, although funds sponsored by brokerage firms are insured by the Securities Investor Protection Corporation (SIPC) against losses caused by a failure of the firm. Some funds may also be covered by private insurance.

For longer-term investment purposes, alternative investments offer better yield with comparable safety while also providing growth opportunity, tax advantages, and similar inflation protection. The convenience and income of money market funds, although increasingly challenged by bank deposit products, remain attractive for providing for emergencies and for parking temporarily idle cash.

*   *   *

What Is a Money Market Fund?

A money market fund is a type of mutual fund in which a pool of money is invested in various money market securities (short-term debt instruments) and which compounds interest daily and pays out (or reinvests) dividends to shareholders monthly.

Buying, Selling, and Holding

How do I buy and sell it? Through sponsoring brokerage firms and mutual fund organizations. Accounts are also offered by insurance companies and other financial institutions as a parking place for temporarily idle funds.

Is there a minimum purchase amount, and what is the price range? The minimum investment usually ranges from $500 to $5000. For funds offered through brokers, $1000 is typical; $2500 is a typical minimum investment for funds offered directly by fund sponsors. Additional investment is usually allowed in increments as small as $100.

What fees and charges are involved? Most are no-load (without sales fee), charging only an annual management fee, which is usually less than 1% of the investment. There may be extra fees for special services, such as money transfers.

Does it mature, expire, or otherwise terminate? No.

Can I sell it quickly? Yes. Shares are redeemable anytime and most funds offer checkwriting privileges, though $500 minimums for checks are common.

How is market value determined and how do I keep track of it? Market values of shares are kept constant. Yields change in response to money market conditions as investments turn over and are calculated on a daily basis. Seven and 30-day average yields are reported weekly in the financial pages of newspapers and current information can be obtained directly by calling the sponsoring organizations.

Investment Objectives

Should I buy this if my objective is capital appreciation? No.

Should I buy this if my objective is income? Yes. The attraction of money market funds is that the individuals can earn the same high yields that would otherwise be available only to institutional investors. Of course, income fluctuates and there is little protection against a decline in market rates.

To what extent does it protect against inflation? Because interest rates on newly offered debt instruments rise with inflation, money market funds, being composed of constantly rotating short-term investments, have performed well in inflation and paid dividends that kept pace with rising price levels.

Is it suitable for tax-deferred retirement accounts? Yes.

Can I borrow against it? Yes, banks and brokers will lend a high percentage (often 90%) of the value of your shares.

Risk Considerations

How assured can I be of getting my full investment back? Your investment in a money market fund is quite safe, since portfolios comprise securities of banks, governments, and top corporations. Investors seeking maximum safety can choose funds investing exclusively in U.S. government direct obligations, though at some sacrifice of yield; while this does not mean the fund is guaranteed by Uncle Sam, the fact that its investments are so guaranteed actually does provide a high degree of security. Some funds are privately insured against default.

How assured is my income? While the risk of default is very small, there is no way of preventing fluctuations in money market interest rates. Dividend rates could therefore decline, although the reaction to market rate changes may be more or less delayed, depending on the average maturity of a portfolio. Most fund sponsors permit shifting into other investment vehicles within their families when adverse developments can be foreseen or when better opportunities exist.

Are there any other risks unique to this investment? A fund that invested relatively long-term just prior to a drastic rise in rates could be forced to sell investments at a loss to meet redemptions. Well-managed and established funds are aware of this obvious risk and take measures to avoid it. Overall, the industry, which is regulated by the Securities and Exchange Commission, has enjoyed an excellent safety record.

Is it commercially rated? A number of organizations record past performance and a few predict future yields, but money market funds are not rated in the sense that bonds and stocks are.

Tax Considerations

What tax advantages (or disadvantages) does it offer? Where portfolios are comprised of tax-exempt securities, investors are exempt from federal taxes and, depending on state laws, possibly state and local taxes. (States may treat tax-exempt funds differently from tax-exempt direct investments.) Otherwise, dividends are fully taxable. Some states that do not tax interest earned on direct investments will tax dividends from funds, even though the fund's income is from interest earned.

Economic Considerations

What economic factors most affect buy, hold, and sell decisions? Money market funds are most attractive when short-term interest rates are high and alternative investments are beset with uncertainty. As a rule, investors use money market funds to park cash temporarily, choosing other investments for longer-term purposes.

MORTGAGE-BACKED (PASS-THROUGH) SECURITY

A mortgage-backed (pass-through) security offers one of the best risk/return deals available to investors, plus excellent liquidity. Two drawbacks, though, are that monthly income payments fluctuate and the term of the investment cannot be predicted with certainty.

Pass-through securities represent shares in pools of home mortgages having approximately the same terms and interest rates. They were introduced in the 1960s to make lenders liquid and stimulate home buying.

The process begins when prospective homeowners apply for mortgages to banks, savings and loan associations and mortgage bankers. The loan paper is sold to intermediaries, such as Freddie Mac or private organizations who repackage it in units represented by certificates, which are marketed to investors. Interest and principal, including prepayments, pass from the homeowner through the intermediary to the investor. When the mortgages mature or are prepaid, the investment expires.

Pass-throughs also enjoy an active secondary market, where securities trade either at discounts or premiums depending on prevailing interest rates. Interestingly, pass-throughs representing pools of low-rate mortgages, when they can be bought favorably to result in attractive yields, are the most desirable holdings because the prepayment risk is low.

The following are principal mortgage-backed securities:

Government National Mortgage Association (GNMA): Ginnie Maes are the most widely-held pass-throughs and are backed by Federal Housing Administration (FHA)-insured and Veterans Administration (VA)-guaranteed mortgages plus the general guarantee of GNMA, which (by virtue of rulings of the Treasury and Justice departments) brings the full faith and credit of the U.S. government behind these securities. They are as safe as Treasury bonds but typically yield 1% to 2% higher.

Federal Home Loan Mortgage Corporation (FHLMC): Freddie Mac PCs (Participation Certificates) are backed by both FHA and VA mortgages and privately insured conventional mortgages plus the general guarantee of FHLMC, a privately managed public institution owned by the Federal Home Loan Bank Board System members. With less safety, PCs yield 15-40 basis points more than GNMAs.

Federal National Mortgage Association (FNMA): Fannie Mae MBSs (Mortgage-Backed Securities) are issued and guaranteed by FNMA, a government-sponsored, publicly held (NYSE-traded) company, and backed by both conventional and FHA and VA mortgages. They are essentially similar to Freddie Macs and tend to have similar yields.

Private mortgage participation certificates issued by lending institutions or conduit firms have varying characteristics and different ratings, depending on such factors as private mortgage insurance, cash-fund backing, and over-collateralization (the extent to which the market values of underlying properties exceed the mortgages). These include jumbo pools of mortgages from different lenders.

Collateralized mortgage obligations (CMOs), a variation issued by Freddie Mac and private issuers, are paid off at different speeds. All CMOs receive monthly interest, but principal repayments flow first to fast-paying CMOs, then to intermediate CMOs, then long-term CMOs. For a slight sacrifice of yield, CMOs lessen the anxiety that pass-through holders might have about the uncertain life of their investments.

The Tax Reform Act of 1986 created a new tax entity, termed the *real estate mortgage investment conduit* (REMIC), a pass-through vehicle designed for multiclass mortgage pools. REMICs offer flexibility and protection from double taxation, a problem CMOs have avoided with legal technicalities, and are expected to breed a proliferation of mortgage-backed securities with widely varying risk/return characteristics.

$$* \quad * \quad *$$

What Is a Mortgage-Backed (Pass-Through) Security?

A mortgage-backed security is a share in an organized pool of residential mortgages, the principal and interest payments on which are passed through to shareholders, usually monthly. The category includes collateralized mortgage obligations (CMOs), technically mortgage-backed bonds, that provide for payout in short, intermediate, or longer time frames. It does not include mortgage-backed securities that are corporate bonds or government agency securities and are covered in those sections.

Buying, Selling, and Holding

Where do I buy and sell it? At a securities broker-dealer.

Is there a minimum purchase amount, and what is the price range? Most new pass-throughs are sold in minimum amounts of $25,000, although some older issues can be bought with less and some private issues and CMOs can be bought for as little as $1000. Shares of funds, limited partnerships, and unit investment trusts that buy such securities range from $1000–$5000.

What fees and charges are involved? This varies among vehicles and brokers, but can be either a flat fee or a dealer spread. Sponsors deduct modest fees from passed-through income.

Does it mature, expire, or otherwise terminate? Yes, the life of a pool, and its related securities, ends when the mortgages mature or are prepaid. CMOs offer investors a choice of earlier or later payouts.

Can I sell it quickly? Yes, liquidity is very good.

How is market value determined and how do I keep track of it? Market value, to the extent mortgage pools have fixed-rate obligations, goes up when market interest rates go down, and vice versa. On the other hand, prepayments rise when rates decline, shrinking the pool and lowering share values. Daily price and yield information is published in the financial pages of newspapers and in electronic databases.

Investment Objectives

Should I buy this if my objective is capital appreciation? Although most investors plan to hold for the life of the issue, capital appreciation is possible as the result of declining market interest rates.

Should I buy this if my objective is income? Yes; mortgage pass-throughs generally offer good yields. Ginnie Maes normally yield at least 1% more than U.S. Treasury bonds and have the same safety from default.

To what extent does it protect against inflation? Because they are based largely on fixed-income mortgages, pass-throughs suffer in high inflation.

Is it suitable for tax-deferred retirement accounts? Yes; except for rollovers, however, the minimum investments exceed IRA limits.

Can I borrow against it? Yes.

Risk Considerations

How assured can I be of getting my full investment back? Although some issues are safer than others (Ginnie Maes are U.S. government-guaranteed against default on underlying mortgages, for example) most pass-throughs are either government-sponsored or otherwise insured in addition to being over-collateralized (i.e., the market value of the real estate behind the mortgages exceeds the face value of the mortgages). They thus offer a high degree of credit safety, although loss of value due to rising interest rates is a risk if sold in the secondary market.

How assured is my income? Income is safe from the credit standpoint (see the previous question) but can vary from month to month as the result of prepayments and other factors.

Are there any other risks unique to this investment? Prepayments may shorten the life of the investment, although the cash they create is of course passed through to investors.

Is it commercially rated? Yes, Standard & Poor's and other services rate mortgage-backed securities.

Tax Considerations

What tax advantages (or disadvantages) does it offer? None. Interest is taxed as ordinary income and profits or losses from the sale of pass-through securities in the secondary market are taxed as capital gains or losses. But the monthly payment received by an investor in a pass-through is only partly interest. Because payments to the investor are simply pass-throughs of payments by homeowners on their mortgages, and those payments are part interest and part principal, the investor pays taxes only on the portion of his payment representing interest; the rest, as principal, is treated as a nontaxable return of capital. Since home mortgage payments have a higher ratio of interest to principal in the earlier years of the mortgage, it follows that income payments on pass-through securities normally have a higher proportion of taxable interest in the earlier years of the life of the pool.

Economic Considerations

What economic factors most affect buy, hold, and sell decisions? Mortgage-backed pass-throughs are most attractive to hold when general interest rates are low relative to the yield on the mortgage pool. However, this scenario can also cause a high rate of prepayments just when the investment is most attractive. The best holding is a pool of low-rate mortgages whose shares are bought at a good discount; that results in an attractive yield for investors, but since the homeowners are also happy with their low-rate mortgages, the risk of prepayment is much less. Of course, inflation erodes the value of fixed payments, which are the basis of income from pass-throughs.

MUNICIPAL SECURITY

A municipal security, or muni, is a debt obligation of a U.S. state or political subdivision, such as a county, city, town, village, or authority.

What has historically made munis special has been their exemption from federal income taxes and, frequently, from state and local income taxes as well. Because of this tax-exempt status, munis have traditionally paid lower rates of interest than taxable securities, making their after-tax return more attractive as an individual's income moved into higher brackets.

The Tax Reform Act of 1986 changed the municipal bond investment environment in fundamental ways primarily by dividing obligations into two basic groups:

> *Public purpose bonds,* also called traditional government purpose bonds or essential purpose bonds, continue to be tax-exempt and to be issued without limit.

> *Private purpose bonds,* vaguely defined as a bond involving more than a 10% benefit to private parties, are taxable unless specifically exempted. Such exempted *permitted private purpose bonds* are subject, with exceptions, to caps.

Whether tax-exempt or not, munis are either (1) *general obligations,* notes or bonds backed by the full faith and credit (including the taxing power) of the issuing entity and used to finance capital expenditures or improvements; or (2) *revenue obligations,* which are used to finance specific projects and are repaid from the revenues of the facilities they finance.

Although munis vary in the degree of credit strength backing them, and although there have been some famous defaults, such as the Washington Public Power Supply System (WHOOPS) in the 1980s, their safety record has generally been excellent, earning them a place between Treasuries and high-grade corporate bonds in terms of investor confidence.

In addition to taxable bonds, recent innovations in the municipal securities field have included *tax-exempt commercial paper,* short-term discounted notes usually backed by bank lines of credit; *bonds with put options* typically exercisable after one to five years, which carry a somewhat lower yield in exchange for the put privilege; *floating (or variable) rate* issues tied to the Treasury bill or another market rate; and *enhanced security* issues, in which the credit of the municipal entity is supplemented by bank lines of credit or other outside resources.

For smaller investors, open and closed-end funds, unit investment trusts, and other pooled vehicles with portfolios of municipal obligations offer diversification and professional management with lower minimums.

Munis are also available as zero-coupon securities and are covered in the section dealing with that investment alternative.

∗   ∗   ∗

What Is a Municipal Security?

A municipal security is a negotiable bond or note issued by a U.S. state or subdivision. A muni may be a general obligation backed by the full faith and credit (i.e., the borrowing and taxing power) of a government; a revenue obligation paid out of the cash flow from an income-producing project; or a special assessment obligation paid out of taxes specially levied to finance specific public works. Some municipal bonds, such as those to finance low-income housing, may be backed by a federal government agency.

Buying, Selling, and Holding

How do I buy and sell it? Most securities broker-dealers handle municipal securities.

Is there a minimum purchase amount, and what is the price range? Although munis are issued in units of $5000 or $1000 par value as a rule, with exceptions as low as $100, broker-dealers usually require minimum orders of at least $5000 and often want $10,000, $25,000, or up to $100,000. Odd lots are sometimes available from broker-dealers at extra commissions or spreads. Smaller investments can be made through mutual funds, closed-end funds, unit investment trusts and other pooled vehicles with tax-exempt portfolios.

What fees and charges are involved? Sometimes a commission, but usually a spread (rarely exceeding 5%) between the dealer's buying and selling prices.

Does it mature, expire, or otherwise terminate? Yes. Maturities range from one month (notes) to 30 years (bonds). Serial bonds mature in scheduled stages. Munis may also be callable or have put features.

Can I sell it quickly? Some munis have good liquidity, although issues of obscure municipalities and authorities can have inactive markets and be hard to sell.

How is market value determined and how do I keep track of it? Most munis are fixed-income securities and thus rise and fall in opposite relationship to market interest rates. Variable-rate issues, whose rates are periodically adjusted to reflect changes in U.S. Treasury bill yields or other money market rates, tend to sell at or close to their par values. Muni quotes are not normally published in daily newspapers, but prices published in *The Daily Bond Buyer* (mainly new muni issues) and the *Blue List of Current Municipal Offerings* (a Standard and Poor's publication reporting details of secondary market offerings and their size) are available through brokers or directly by subscription.

Investment Objectives

Should I buy a municipal security if my objective is capital appreciation? No, although appreciation is possible when munis sell at discounts because rates have risen or credit questions arise.

Should I buy this if my objective is income? Yes, but only if the after-tax yield in your tax bracket compares favorably to the yield on a taxable investment of comparable safety.

To what extent does it protect against inflation? Fixed-income munis offer no inflation protection. Variable-rate munis would offer some, if interest rates rose.

Is it suitable for tax-deferred accounts? Tax-exempt issues bearing a lower interest rate than a taxable security are not suitable. Taxable munis are suitable.

Can I borrow against it? You can, but the interest you pay is not tax-deductible if the proceeds are used to buy municipals. With the lower rate you earn on most munis, it would hardly pay. While munis are acceptable collateral for other loans, care must be taken to avoid the appearance of a violation of the rule against deducting interest.

Risk Considerations

How assured can I be of getting my full investment back? In most cases, you can be quite sure of getting your investment back at maturity. Munis generally rank between U.S. government securities and corporate bonds in credit safety. But the risk of default varies with the credit of the issuer and the type of obligation (mainly general obligation or revenue obligations). Some munis are covered for default by private insurers. Of course, prices of all fixed-income securities decline when interest rates go up.

How assured is my income? Munis are relatively safe (see the preceding question) but defaults are possible due to such factors as limited ability to impose taxes or disappointing revenues from the use of facilities. Issues may also be callable, enabling the issuer to force redemption after specified times.

Are there any other risks unique to this investment? Munis are not subject to Securities and Exchange Commission regulation, so the legality of the issue must be established. Make sure a legal opinion accompanies the issue.

Is it commercially rated? Moody's Investors Service, Standard & Poor's, and others rate credit. White's Tax-Exempt Bond Rating Service rates market risk.

Tax Considerations

What tax advantages (or disadvantages) does it offer? Interest may be exempt from federal income taxes and frequently from state and local income taxes (36 states tax exempt munis of other states but not their own; 5 states tax their own exempt munis and those of other states; 9 states plus the District of Columbia do not tax any exempt munis). Capital gains are taxable. Permitted private purpose bond interest may be a tax preference item in computing the Alternative Minimum Tax.

Economic Considerations

What economic factors most affect buy, hold, or sell decisions? Personal tax considerations, of course, then interest rate levels and the inflation rate. Buy when rates are high to get good yields; hold as rates decline to see market values rise. Because tax-exempt munis pay a relatively low interest rate, inflation is especially devastating if the rate is fixed. Prolonged economic downturns can increase the risk of municipal defaults. Special supply and demand factors owing to the uncertain status of tax-exempt issues under tax reform legislation then pending, caused abnormally high municipal yields in the mid-1980s.

MUTUAL FUNDS (OPEN END)

An open-end mutual fund is so named because its sponsoring organization, called an investment company or a management company, stands ready at any time to issue new shares or to redeem existing shares at their daily-computed net asset value. An open-end fund offers investors with moderate means the diversification, professional management (for a fee), economy of scale, and, where it might not otherwise exist, the liquidity available only to large investors.

Mutual funds are available with portfolio compositions designed for an almost infinite variety of investment objectives and risk levels. The following is a partial list of types of funds, with their basic portfolio or mode of operation:

Income Fund (stocks paying dividends, preferred stocks, corporate bonds)

Growth Fund (growth stocks)

Aggressive Growth Fund (smaller, riskier growth stocks)

Balanced Fund (growth and income securities)

Performance Fund (high-risk stocks, venture capital investments, etc.)

Conservative Balanced Fund (high-grade income and growth securities)

United States Government Bond Fund (U.S. Treasury or agency bonds)

International Fund (foreign stocks or bonds)

Global Fund (foreign and U.S. stocks or bonds)

Investment Grade Bond Fund (corporates with investment-grade ratings)

Junk Bond Fund (high-yielding corporates below investment grade)

Municipal Bond Fund (tax-exempt municipal securities)

Special Situations Fund (venture capital, debt/equity securities)

Stock Index Fund (replicating or representative of the major stock indexes)

Market Sector Fund or *Specialized Fund* (securities of high-growth industries or specialized industries like gold-mining)

Tax-managed Fund (utility stocks whose dividends are reinvested for long-term capital gains)

Speculative Fund (engages in selling short and leverage)

Commodities Fund (commodity futures contracts)

Option Fund (sells puts and calls for extra income, sometimes speculating by taking positions without owning underlying securities or instruments)

Socially-conscious Fund (excludes investments offensive on moral or ethical grounds)

Fund of Fund (invests in other funds with top performance)

Money Market Fund (short-term, interest-bearing debt instruments)

Tax-exempt Money Market Fund (trades long-term and short-term municipals for best yields and capital gains)

Ginnie-Mae Fund (mortgage-backed pass-through securities guaranteed by Government National Mortgage Association)

Major sponsors allow switching of investments from shares of one fund to another within their fund families. Other services commonly available to investors include term life insurance; automatic reinvestment plans; regular income checks; open account plans allowing fractional share purchases with Social Security or pension checks or other relatively small amounts of cash; loan programs; and toll-free information services.

∗   ∗   ∗

What Is an Open-End Mutual Fund?

An open-end mutual fund is an investment company that pools shareholder funds and invests in a diversified securities portfolio having a specified objective. It provides professional management and stands ready to sell new shares and redeem outstanding shares on a continuous (open-end) basis.

Buying, Selling, and Holding

Where do I buy and sell it? Load funds, in which a sales charge is deducted from the amount invested, are bought from securities brokers and financial planners. No-load funds are bought directly from the sponsor. Shares are not sold in the sense that shares of stock are transferred to other owners; rather they are redeemed (by phone, mail, or checkwriting privilege) by the fund at net asset value.

Is there a minimum purchase amount, and what is the price range? Some funds have a minimum deposit of $1000, others have no minimum. Share prices vary, but a majority are under $20. Many funds offer convenient share accumulation plans for investors of modest means.

What fees and charges are involved? Load funds charge a sales commission, typically 8½% of the amount invested, though with larger purchases the load can go as low as 1½%. No-load funds have no sales commissions. A hybrid, low-load funds, charge commissions of 3% or less. Both load and no-load funds charge annual management fees of from ½% to 1% of the value of the investment. There is usually no redemption charge (back-end load) with load funds; no-loads may or may not have a 1% to 2% redemption fee to discourage short-term trading. Various share accumulation plans may involve extra service charges. 12B-1 mutual funds, a type of load fund that builds assets through advertising and publicity, typically charge a promotion fee of 1% or less of the fund's value.

Does it mature, expire, or otherwise terminate? No.

Can I sell it quickly? Funds stand ready to redeem shares daily. Some managing companies allow switching among different funds they sponsor at either no charge (no-load fund families) or a small transaction fee.

How is market value determined and how do I keep track of it? Market value, called net asset value, depends on the way various economic and market forces affect the type of investments comprising a particular fund's portfolio; a given economic or interest-rate scenario will have a different effect on bond fund values than stock fund values. Mutual fund quotations are reported daily in newspapers and a fund management company reports, usually quarterly, on the composition of portfolios and transactions during the reporting period.

Investment Objectives

Should I buy an open-end mutual fund if my objective is capital appreciation? Yes, but you would buy a fund with capital gains as a primary objective, such as a growth stock or special situations fund.

Should I buy this if my objective is income? Yes, but you would buy a fund with income as its primary objective, such as a bond or money market fund or a stock fund investing in high-yield stocks.

To what extent does it protect against inflation? That depends on the type of fund. Equity-oriented funds or money market funds offer more protection than fixed-income bond portfolios, which provide little or no protection.

Is it suitable for tax-deferred retirement accounts? Yes, except when the fund is invested in tax-exempt securities, such as municipal bonds.

Can I borrow against it? Yes, subject to Federal Reserve margin rules. Collateral value varies with the type of fund. A lender that might loan 90% of the value of money market fund shares might find a high-risk fund unacceptable as collateral.

Risk Considerations

How assured can I be of getting my full investment back? It depends on the type of fund, the quality of the portfolio, and the adroitness of management in avoiding adverse developments. A money market fund has high safety of principal, whereas a bond fund is vulnerable to interest rate movements and a stock fund is subject to market risk, for example.

How assured is my income? Again, it depends on the type of portfolio, its quality, and the skill of the manager. A fund with AAA bonds will be a safer source of income than one comprised of higher-yielding but riskier junk bonds. Other funds stress capital growth at the expense of income. Money market funds offer assured income at a conservative rate, which goes up and down with market conditions.

Are there any other risks unique to this investment? Except for the fact that funds provide automatic diversification, the same risk considerations apply as affect individual investments.

Is it commercially rated? No, but some funds invest exclusively in securities with given commercial ratings, and a number of organizations rate mutual funds in terms of historical performance.

Tax Considerations

What tax advantages (or disadvantages) does it offer? Income is subject to the same federal income taxes as the investments from which it derives. Thus, a shareholder pays taxes just as if he owned the portfolio directly, except that all capital gains distributions are considered long-term, regardless of the time the fund has been held. Funds invested in tax-exempt municipal securities (some are triple— federal, state, and local—tax-exempt) provide tax-free income, at least at the federal level. States vary in their tax treatment of income from municipal securities (see the discussion of tax considerations in the section on Municipal Securities) and the same rules usually apply to fund income. Some states that would not tax interest will tax dividends from funds, however, even though the fund's income is from interest earned. In such states, dividends from a tax-exempt fund would be taxable.

Economic Considerations

What economic factors most affect buy, hold, or sell decisions? The same economic and market forces that affect individual investments affect funds made up of those investments, so choices should be made in the same terms.

OPTION CONTRACT (PUT or CALL)

Put and call options are contracts that give holders the right, for a price, called a premium, to sell or buy an underlying stock or financial instrument at a specified price, called the exercise or strike price, before a specified expiration date. Option sellers are called writers—covered writers if they own the underlying security or financial instrument, naked writers if they don't—and buyers of options are called option buyers. A put is an option to sell and a call is an option to buy.

Listed options are options traded (since 1973) on national stock and commodity exchanges and thus have both visibility and liquidity, as opposed to conventional over-the-counter options, which are individually negotiated, more expensive, and less liquid. Listed options are available on stocks, stock indexes, debt instruments, foreign currencies, and futures of different types. The issuance and settlement—all the mechanics of options clearing—are handled by the options clearing corporation (OCC), which is owned by the exchanges.

Options make it possible to control a large amount of value with a much smaller amount of money. Because a small percentage change in the value of a financial instrument can result in a much larger percentage change in the value of an option, large gains (and losses) are possible with the leverage that options provide. Although sometimes options are bought with the idea of holding the underlying security as an investment after the exercise of the option, options are usually bought and sold without ever being exercised and settled. They have a life of their own.

The value of options—that is, the amount of their premiums—is mainly determined by the relationship between the exercise price and the market price of the underlying instrument, by the volatility of the underlying instrument, and by the time remaining before expiration.

When the relationship between an option's strike price (exercise price) and the underlying market price is such that the holder would profit (transaction costs aside) by exercising it, an option has intrinsic value and is said to be in the money. In contrast, there is no intrinsic value in an out-of-the-money option—such as a put whose strike price is below the market price or a call whose strike price is above the market price. A premium will normally trade for at least its intrinsic value, if any. An out-of-the-money option, on the other hand, has obviously more risk and a lower premium than an option that is more likely to become profitable. Options on highly volatile securities and instruments command higher premiums because they are more likely to produce profits when and if they move.

Time value influences premiums because the longer the time remaining, the greater the chance of a favorable movement and the higher the present value of the underlying instrument if exercised. This time value, also called net premium, decreases as the option approaches its expiration. (For this reason, options are called wasting assets.) The value of an out-of-the-money option is all time value; that of an in-the-money option is a combination of time value and intrinsic value. In general, the greater the potential for gain, the greater the risk of not achieving it. The farther from expiration and the greater the volatility, the higher the premium an option will have.

Professional traders have multioption strategies, some quite complex, designed to limit risk while capitalizing on premium movements. Called straddles, combinations, and spreads (which have many varieties), they involve close monitoring, expertise, and sometimes onerous commissions. Options trading is not for the average investor.

Options do have a conservative role, however, for personal as well as institutional investors. Options can be used very much like term life insurance policies to protect investors against losses in investments already owned. Option selling (writing) can be a source of added returns.

The use of options as insurance involves the purchase of a put to limit losses or lock in the profit on a position already owned, or the purchase of a call to limit losses or lock in the profit on a short sale. For example, an individual with 100 shares of XYZ at a market value of $60 who expects the price to rise to $70 might buy, at a premium of $125, a put at $55 expiring in three months. If the stock rises, the insurance would have cost $125 and that amount would have to be subtracted from the capital gain. If the stock dropped, however, the put could be exercised and the stock sold for no lower than $55; that would limit the investor's loss to $625—$60 less $55 (times 100 shares) plus the premium of $125. The investor who thought the stock would drop could have sold it short and bought a call to assure the ability to buy the shares to cover at the call price.

Covered option writing—writing calls on stock or other instruments that are owned—is a safe way to increase the income return on an investment, provided the investor is prepared to sell the underlying holding at the exercise price if the price moves that way. Potential gains are limited to the amount of the premium (a significant drawback if the underlying holding rises in value and the option is exercised).

Calls can be written at, in, deep in, out of, or deep out of the money. The farther out of the money it is, the less the chance of exercise and the lower the premium it will command. The main problem with writing covered calls is that to warrant a premium high enough to offset the commissions, the underlying asset has to be volatile, and the option close to the money; the more volatile it is and the closer the option is to the money, the greater the chance it will be exercised. If it's exercised the writer's profit is limited to the premium, when a greater profit could have been made by holding the investment.

Mutual funds that make their income by writing and trading options are an alternative for small investors.

*   *   *

What Is an Option Contract (Put or Call)?

An option contract is a contract that grants the right, in exchange for a price or premium to buy (call) or sell (put) an underlying security at a specified price within a specified period of time.

Buying, Selling, and Holding

Where do I buy and sell it? At a full-service or discount broker.

Is there a minimum purchase amount, and what is the price range? The minimum is one option contract covering 100 shares. Contracts typically cost a few hundred dollars (usually less than $500).

What fees and charges are involved? In addition to the premium, brokerage commissions are charged for buying, selling, and exercising options. The maximum charge is $25 for a transaction covering one option; the average for multiple-contract transactions is about $14.

Does it mature, expire, or otherwise terminate? Yes; options have a specified expiration date, usually within nine months.

Can I sell it quickly? Yes; most options enjoy good liquidity.

How is market value determined and how do I keep track of it? The market value of an option is its premium value, which is determined by a combination of its intrinsic value (the difference between its exercise price and the market value of the underlying stock) and its time value (the value investors place on the amount of time until the expiration of the option). A small change in a stock price can cause a larger percentage change in an option premium; premium changes are reported daily in the financial sections of newspapers.

Investment Objectives

Should I buy an option contract if my objective is capital appreciation? Because a small change in a stock price causes a higher percentage change in a related option premium, speculators gain leverage using options. Of course, if the underlying stock fails to move in the right direction, the speculator is out the cost of the premium. Options are also used as hedging tools to protect the value of shares held for capital gains.

Should I buy this if my objective is income? Although sellers (writers) of options receive income from premiums and thereby augment the income return on the underlying holding, they may be forced to buy or sell the underlying holding if its price moves adversely. Options are not themselves income-producing investments, although speculators and some mutual funds create income through option writing and various spread strategies.

To what extent does it protect against inflation? Puts and calls, as short-term options, are not designed to capitalize on longer-term movements in common stock prices as might be caused by inflationary factors. Of course, subscription warrants and employee stock options, which are related to put and call options, could be viewed as inflation protection.

Is it suitable for tax-deferred retirement accounts? Although not prohibited by the Internal Revenue Service, most brokerage firms rule out options contracts as too risky for retirement accounts. They may have a limited role in managed accounts, primarily as a hedging tool. Mutual funds or other pooled investments that generate income by writing and speculating in options may be appropriate investments in selected situations for people with high risk tolerance.

Can I borrow against it? No. Although Federal Reserve margin rules allow options transactions in margin accounts, options cannot be used as part of the borrowing base. Of course, options are themselves a source of considerable leverage.

Risk Considerations

How assured can I be of getting my full investment back? Your investment is the premium plus commissions. It is recovered only if the underlying stock or instrument moves favorably to such an extent that the profit gained from selling or exercising the option exceeds the investment; whether it does or not is pure speculation.

How assured is my income? The only income that options provide is from premiums earned in selling them. That is assured income, but it can be more than offset if the underlying stock moves adversely and the option is exercised by its holder.

Are there any other risks unique to this investment? The risk in options ranges from the simple loss of a premium if the option proves valueless to the risk of a magnified loss in the case of uncovered or naked positions—that is, where a put or call is sold without owning the underlying security or instrument. Upon exercise, the security or instrument must be bought or sold at a market price that may be in wide variance from the exercise price.

Is it commercially rated? No.

Tax Considerations

What tax advantages (or disadvantages) does it offer? Options on stocks are subject to the same capital gains taxation as the stocks themselves. Some traditional uses of options to defer income from one year to another have been curtailed by recent tax legislation and advice should be sought. See also the entry for Tax Straddle in Part IV.

Economic Considerations

What economic factors most affect buy, hold, and sell decisions? The same economic factors that affect stock investments in the short term apply essentially to decisions involving put and call options used in speculation and hedging.

OPTION CONTRACT ON A FUTURES CONTRACT (FUTURES OPTION)

For a general discussion of an option, see Option Contract (Put or Call).

*   *   *

What Is an Option Contract on a Futures Contract?

A futures option is a contract that grants the right, in exchange for a price (premium) to buy (call) or sell (put) a specified futures contract within a specified period of time.

Buying, Selling, and Holding

How do I buy and sell it? At a full-service or discount broker.

Is there a minimum purchase amount, and what is the price range? The minimum purchase is one option on one futures contract. It can cost several hundred to several thousand dollars, depending on the underlying future.

What fees and charges are involved? In addition to the premium, brokerage commissions are charged for buying, selling, and exercising an option. Generally, the maximum charge is $25, and the average charge for multiple option transactions is around $14, with lower rates for high-volume transactions.

Does it mature, expire, or otherwise terminate? Yes; options have a specified expiration date, usually within one year.

Can I sell it quickly? Yes; most futures options have good liquidity and they are not subject to daily trading limits that can affect the liquidity of futures themselves.

How is market value determined and how do I keep track of it? The same factors that affect the market value of futures affect the premium values of futures options. (See the sections Futures Contract on a Commodity and Futures Contract on an Interest Rate.) Prices are reported daily in newspapers and electronic databases.

Investment Objectives

Should I buy a futures option if my objective is capital appreciation? Only if you are a speculator attracted to the high degree of leverage offered by options, although options on futures are used by investors to hedge the value of other investments held for capital gains.

Should I buy this if my objective is income? Although selling options is a source of income, options are not themselves an income-producing investment. Some mutual funds trade in options for the purpose of generating income, however.

To what extent does it protect against inflation? Only to the limited extent that futures offer the opportunity to capitalize on inflation expectations and their effects on interest rates and commodity prices.

Is it suitable for tax-deferred retirement accounts? Although not prohibited by the Internal Revenue Service, most brokerage firms rule out options contracts as too risky for retirement accounts. They may have a limited role in managed accounts, primarily as a hedging tool. Mutual funds or other pooled investments that generate income by writing and speculating in options may be appropriate investments in selected situations for people with high risk tolerance.

Can I borrow against it? No. Although Federal Reserve margin rules allow options transactions in margin accounts, options cannot be used as part of the borrowing base. Of course, options are themselves a source of significant leverage.

Risk Considerations

How assured can I be of getting my full investment back? Your investment is the premium plus commissions. It is recovered only if the underlying futures contract moves favorably to such an extent that the proceeds realized from selling or exercising the option exceed the amount expended; whether it does or not is pure speculation.

How assured is my income? The only income that options provide is from premiums earned in selling them. That is assured income, but it can be more than offset if the underlying future moves adversely and the option is exercised by the holder.

Are there any other risks unique to this investment? Essentially the same risks apply as are involved with regular options and futures on the same underlying assets. A special positive feature, however, is that futures options, particularly on debt instruments, have better liquidity than either straight options or straight futures; that is because of less restrictive trading limits on futures options than on futures, and because the open interest on futures options tends to be much higher than on regular interest-rate (debt) options.

Is it commercially rated? No.

Tax Considerations

What tax advantages (or disadvantges) does it offer? Options on futures are subject to the same tax treatment as futures are. See the section on a Futures Contract on a Commodity.

Economic Considerations

What economic factors most affect buy, hold, and sell decisions? The same economic forces that affect interest rate and commodity futures affect the options available on those contracts.

OPTION CONTRACT ON AN INTEREST RATE (DEBT OPTION)

For a general discussion of an option, see Option Contract (Put or Call).

*   *   *

What Is an Option Contract on an Interest Rate?

An interest-rate option is a contract that grants the right, in exchange for a price (premium), to buy (call option) or sell (put option) a certain debt security at a specified price within a specified period of time, thereby producing a particular yield.

Buying, Selling, and Holding

How do I buy and sell it? Through a full-service or discount broker.

Is there a minimum purchase amount, and what is the price range? The minimum purchase is one contract. Premiums, where the underlying security is interest-bearing, are determined as a percentage (in 32nds for Treasury bonds and notes) of par value. Thus a contract on a $100,000 par value U.S. Treasury bond with a premium of 2.50 (2 and $^{16}/_{32}$) would cost $2500, while a $20,000 minicontract with a premium of 1.24 (1 and $^{24}/_{32}$ or 1¾) would cost $350. Where the underlying security is discounted rather than interest-bearing, as with the 13-week Treasury bill, premiums are quoted with reference to basis point (100ths of one percent) differences between prices, expressed as complements of annualized discount rates. For example, with a 9% yield, a 13-week Treasury bill (par value $1 million) would have a price basis of 91 and might have an option trading at 92.20. With a premium thus quoted at 1.20 (120 basis points), it would cost $3000, calculated: .012 $\times$ $^{13}/_{52}$ $\times$ $1 million. (A quick way of approximating dollar premiums is to multiply basis points times $25.)

What fees and charges are involved? Brokerage commissions are charged for buying, selling, or exercising options. The maximum charge is $25 for a transaction covering one contract, with reduced rates for larger trades. Margin accounts may entail interest and other added charges. There may also be income and net worth rules to qualify investors.

Does it mature, expire, or otherwise terminate? Yes. All options have expiration dates, usually within nine months.

Can I sell it quickly? Interest rate options have generally good liquidity. Those with the most contracts outstanding (represented by open interest figures in newspapers) are usually easiest to trade.

How is market value determined and how do I keep track of it? Market value, which is premium value, is determined by a combination of intrinsic value (exercise value less market value of the underlying security) and time value (the diminishing value investors place on the time remaining to expiration). Intrinsic value changes with interest rate movements, which are influenced by Federal Reserve Board monetary policy and other economic factors. Option prices are reported daily in newspapers and electronic databases.

Investment Objectives

Should I buy an interest-rate option if my objective is capital appreciation? Speculators use the high leverage possible with options to capitalize on the price volatility resulting from interest rate movements.

Should I buy this if my objective is income? Option writers earn income in addition to the interest they receive on the underlying security, while taking the risk that the option will be exercised if rates move adversely. Investors also use interest rate options to hedge the value of other income-producing investments.

To what extent does it protect against inflation? As short-term instruments, interest-rate options are not designed for dealing with the longer-term effects of inflation on debt securities. However, inflation expectations are a factor in the term structure of interest rates, and it is possible, using options, to capitalize on short-term movements.

Is it suitable for tax-deferred retirement accounts? Although not prohibited by the Internal Revenue Service, most brokerage firms rule out options contracts as too risky for retirement accounts. They may have a limited role in managed accounts, primarily as a hedging tool. Mutual funds or other pooled investments that generate income by writing and speculating in options may be appropriate investments in selected situations for people with high risk tolerance.

Can I borrow against it? No. Although Federal Reserve margin rules allow options transactions in margin accounts, options cannot be used as part of the borrowing base. Of course, options are themselves a source of considerable leverage.

Risk Considerations

How assured can I be of getting my full investment back? Your investment is recovered only if interest rates move favorably to the extent that the proceeds of the sale of the option exceed the premium plus commissions already expended; that is a matter of pure speculation.

How assured is my income? The only income is from premiums earned in selling options and even that can be negated by losses resulting from exercise by the holder.

Are there any other risks unique to this investment? The marketplace of interest-rate options is dominated on one hand by large institutional investors and their portfolio managers and on the other by dealers who handle the large volumes of high-denomination securities that underlie the options. This puts the smaller investor at a disadvantage in terms both of information and transaction cost. Other special risks have to do with the Option Clearing Corporation's power to remedy shortages of underlying securities by permitting substitutions and adjusting strike prices, and with trading hour differences between options and underlying debt instruments. Sellers of options on discount instruments settled in current instruments take a risk to the extent that they cannot hedge perfectly against exercise.

Is it commercially rated? No.

Tax Considerations

What tax advantages (or disadvantages) does it offer? Unlike regular put and call options, traders in interest-rate options are subject to tax rules covering futures trading; this means open positions are marked to market at year-end with paper gains or losses treated as if realized and taxed as net capital gains (see page 31). Tax advice should be sought.

Economic Considerations

What economic factors most affect buy, hold, and sell decisions? Economic and monetary factors affecting interest rates govern choices having to do with interest-rate options.

OPTION CONTRACT ON A STOCK INDEX

For a general discussion of an option, see Option Contract (Put or Call).

*   *   *

What Is an Option Contract on a Stock Index?

A stock-index option is a contract that grants the right, in exchange for a price (premium), to buy (call option) or sell (put option) the value of an underlying stock index or subindex at a specified price within a specified period of time with settlement in cash.

Buying, Selling, and Holding

How do I buy and sell it? Through a full-service or discount broker.

Is there a minimum purchase amount, and what is the price range? The minimum purchase is one contract. The premium is the difference in index values times $100. A contract based on a 5-point difference between the current (base) value and the exercise value would thus cost $500. Because contracts are settled in cash, margin security in the form of cash or securities is required by brokers, who may also have suitability requirements calling for substantial net worth and income.

What fees and charges are involved? In addition to the premium, brokerage commissions are charged for buying, selling, and exercising options. The maximum charge is $25 for a transaction covering one contract, with reduced rates for large trades. Margin accounts may entail interest and other additional charges.

Does it mature, expire, or otherwise terminate? Yes; options have a specified expiration date.

Can I sell it quickly? Most stock-index options have good liquidity, though newly introduced contracts may have less active markets than contracts that are better established and more popular. Those with many contracts outstanding (represented by large open interest figures in the newspapers) are generally the easiest to trade.

How is market value determined and how do I keep track of it? Premium value is determined by a combination of intrinsic value (exercise price less the index value) and time value (the value investors place on the amount of time remaining to expiration). The intrinsic value is subject to all the forces that make the stock market go up and down; a small movement in the market, as represented by the index, will result in a much larger percentage change in premium value. Indexes are revalued constantly during the trading day and closing prices are published in daily newspapers and electronic databases along with the option values based on them.

Investment Objectives

Should I buy a stock-index option if my objective is capital appreciation? You might if you were a speculator expecting a move in the stock market and were attracted to the high leverage provided by options. You might also use index options to hedge against possible losses in other securities being held for capital gains.

Should I buy this if my objective is income? Although sellers of options receive premium income and thereby increase the income return on their portfolios, options are not themselves income securities.

To what extent does it protect against inflation? Index options are short-term investments and not designed to capitalize on longer-term market movements as might be caused by inflation.

Is it suitable for tax-deferred retirement accounts? Although not prohibited by the Internal Revenue Service, most brokerage firms rule out options contracts as too risky for retirement accounts. They may have a limited role in managed accounts, primarily as a hedging tool. Mutual funds or other pooled investments that generate income by writing and speculating in options may be appropriate investments in selected situations for people with high risk tolerance.

Can I borrow against it? No. Although Federal Reserve margin rules allow options transactions in margin accounts, options cannot be used as part of the borrowing base. Of course, options are themselves a source of significant leverage.

Risk Considerations

How assured can I be of getting my full investment back? Your investment is recovered only if the underlying index value moves favorably to such an extent that the proceeds gained from selling or exercising the option exceed the cost plus commissions; whether it does is pure speculation.

How assured is my income? The only income that options provide is from premiums earned in selling the options. Even that, however, can be negated if the underlying index moves adversely and the option is exercised by the holder.

Are there any other risks unique to this investment? Index options share the same risks as regular puts and calls, but have a few that are unique. These have basically to do with (1) the limitations of index options as a hedging tool (it is impractical to compose a portfolio that duplicates an index exactly and even then there is rarely dollar-for-dollar variation) and with (2) the fact that settlement is made in cash; the settlement figure is the difference between the strike price and the closing value of the index on the day of exercise, and since the seller is not informed of the assignment until the next business day or even later, his hedge position may have lost value. This timing risk must be considered in all multioption strategies using index options. Other risks have to do with trading halts affecting underlying shares (but not the indexes) and causing index values to be based on noncurrent prices, or trading halts in the index options themselves, with the risk that the index value will move adversely before a position can be closed out.

Is it commercially rated? No.

Tax Considerations

What tax advantages (or disadvantages) does it offer? Unlike regular put and call options, index options are subject to tax rules covering futures trading. This means open positions are marked to market at year-end; paper profits or losses are treated as if realized and taxed as net capital gains (see page 31). Tax advice should be sought.

Economic Considerations

What economic factors most affect buy, hold, and sell decisions? Index options are used to make market bets or to protect other holdings against market risk. Any and all economic factors affecting the market become relevant to decisions involving stock options.

OPTION CONTRACT OR FUTURES CONTRACT ON A CURRENCY

For a general discussion of an option, see Option Contract (Put or Call); for a general discussion of a futures contract, see Futures Contract on a Commodity.

*   *   *

What Is a Futures Contract or an Option Contract on a Currency?

They are contracts to buy or sell (futures) or that represent rights (options) to buy or sell a foreign currency at a particular price within a specified period of time.

Buying, Selling, and Holding

How do I buy and sell them? Through a full-service broker or commodities dealer.

Is there a minimum purchase amount, and what is the price range? Contract sizes vary with different currencies and different markets. The minimum purchase is one contract, which, for an option, typically costs a few hundred dollars. Futures contracts tend to be sizable (standard-size contracts are 12.5 million yen and 125,000 Swiss francs, for example, which on one day in the mid-1980s both equalled about $62,500) but they can be bought with small (1.5% to 4.2%) margins. Also, mini-contracts are traded in several currencies on the Mid-America Commodity Exchange—6.25 million yen and 62,500 Swiss francs, for example.

What fees and charges are involved? Broker's commissions, typically $25 or less per contract for options; $50 to $80 for a round-trip futures contract transaction (purchase and sale). In the event of actual delivery, other fees, charges, or taxes may be required.

Do they mature, expire, or otherwise terminate? Yes; all contracts have specified expiration dates.

Can I sell them quickly? Yes; option and futures contracts enjoy good liquidity, although daily price limits on futures can create illiquidity when contracts are down limit or up limit and it is impossible to trade out of a position, because maximum allowable price movement has occurred during the trading day.

How is market value determined and how do I keep track of it? Premiums and contract values change as the exchange rate between the dollar and the foreign currency changes. The exchange rate is determined by the relative value of two currencies, which can change as events affect either or both of the underlying currencies. Daily prices are published in newspapers and electronic databases.

Investment Objectives

Should I buy them if my objective is capital appreciation? Speculators use the high leverage afforded by options and futures contracts to seek gains on relative currency values.

Should I buy them if my objective is income? Except for premium income earned from selling (writing) options, contracts do not provide income. Contracts are frequently used in hedging strategies to protect other income-producing securities from losses due to currency values.

To what extent do they protect against inflation? Because they are short-term contracts, currency options and futures are not affected directly by inflation.

Are they suitable for tax-deferred retirement accounts? Although not prohibited by the Internal Revenue Service, most brokerage firms rule out options and futures contracts as too risky for retirement accounts. They may have a limited role in managed accounts, primarily as a hedging tool. Mutual funds or other pooled investments that generate income through options and futures may be appropriate investments in selected situations for people with high risk tolerance.

Can I borrow against them? Options can be traded in margin accounts but cannot be used as collateral. Moreover, since foreign currency does not have borrowing value either for margin purposes, purchases as the result of exercise may require extra cash or securities. Futures cannot be used as collateral, but provide leverage because they can be held with small margins, actually good faith deposits.

Risk Considerations

How assured can I be of getting my full investment back? With options, the only investment is the premium plus commissions and it is recovered only when the underlying rate of exchange moves favorably to such an extent that the proceeds gained from sale or exercise exceed the amount expended. Futures are inherently speculative and it is possible to lose more than your investment, although margin calls would normally limit losses to the amount invested, assuming the account was closed out (liquidated) to meet the call.

How assured is my income? Other than premium income from option writing (selling), options and futures provide no income.

Are there any other risks unique to these investments? Since two currencies are involved, developments in either country can affect the values of options and futures. Risks include general economic factors as well as government actions affecting currency valuation and the movements of currencies from one country to another. The quantities of currency underlying option contracts represent odd lots in a market dominated by transactions between banks; this can mean extra transaction costs upon exercise. The fact that options markets may be closed while round-the-clock interbank currency markets are open can create problems due to price and rate discrepancies. With futures, there is always the risk of actual delivery if a position is not closed out prior to expiration of the contract.

Are they commercially rated? No, neither options nor futures are rated.

Tax Considerations

What tax advantages (or disadvantages) do they offer? Options are subject to the same capital gains rules as the underlying assets. Futures are subject to special rules requiring that open positions be marked to market at year-end and be taxed as realized capital gains (see page 31). Net trading losses can be applied against capital gains on other investments and unused portions carried forward. Other tax treatments may apply where contracts are used for hedging purposes. Tax advice should be sought.

Economic Considerations

What economic factors most affect buy, hold, and sell decisions? All factors that affect either currency affect the values of options and futures contracts.

PRECIOUS METALS

Precious metals—gold, silver, platinum, and palladium—are bought by investors primarily to hedge against inflation, economic uncertainty, and foreign exchange risk, in the belief that these metals are repositories of absolute value, whereas paper currencies and securities denominated in such currencies have relative value and are vulnerable to loss.

The economics of precious metals have less to do with the production process, industrial demand, or their greatly diminished monetary role than with the psychology of the financial marketplace. There, precious metals—gold especially—are perceived to be the best store of value available when anxiety causes the value of other assets to go into a tailspin. Historically, in such scenarios gold and other precious metals have risen.

The most famous example was in January 1980 when high international inflation due to rising oil prices, the American-hostage crisis in Iran, and civil disorder in Saudi Arabia combined to cause abnormally heavy buying of precious metals, which drove gold to a record price of $887.50 per ounce and led silver and platinum to peak levels as well. When calmer times returned, however, prices soon fell and stabilized at lower levels. It was a memorable lesson in how volatile this store of value can be.

Physical ownership is one way of owning precious metals, available in bullion form in units ranging from 400-Troy-ounce gold bars to 1-ounce platinum ingots. These are sold by dealers at markups or premiums that fall as weights and dollar values rise. Gold can also be held in coins, such as the South African Krugerrand, the Canadian Maple Leaf, and the U.S. Eagle series, introduced in 1986. Generally, the more popular the coin, the greater its liquidity and the higher its premium. Silver can be bought in bags containing U.S. coins of $1000 total face value, priced at a discount to the silver value to cover melting and refining costs. The drawbacks of physical ownership are mainly the high premiums, safekeeping and insurance costs, and sales taxes.

Certificates—actually warehouse receipts issued by some banks, dealers, and full-service brokers—represent gold, silver, platinum, or palladium held in safe-keeping. Typically, for a fee of 3% or higher, the bank or dealer will buy metals in $1000 units and, for a small annual charge, provide insurance and storage. It will also, for 1% or so, sell the bullion or deliver it without a sales tax. The attraction is the convenience and lower transaction costs compared to physical ownership.

Other alternatives include *securities* of companies engaged in mining or processing, including some exchange-traded South African companies (many represented by American Depositary Receipts) as well as highly speculative penny stocks, traded over-the-counter or on regional or Canadian exchanges. There are also *mutual funds* and *closed-end funds* that specialize in both debt and equity issues of precious metals firms.

Finally, *commodity futures, options,* and *options on futures* are traded on precious metals. They provide leverage and hedging opportunities for well-capitalized investors with high expertise and risk tolerance. See separate discussions of these investment vehicles.

*   *   *

What Are Investments in Precious Metals?

Investments in precious metals involve gold, silver, platinum, and palladium as commodities (i.e., not as money), owned by investors, in physical form or through securities, because of their presumed value as stores of wealth and as hedges against inflation and economic uncertainty. Precious metals are traded by speculators who hope to profit from volatility in the financial marketplace.

Buying, Selling, and Holding

How do I buy and sell them? Through various dealers and brokers, depending on the form of ownership. Coins and certificates are bought and sold through major banks.

Is there a minimum purchase amount, and what is the price range? Precious metals can be bought with almost any amount of money, depending on the form of investment. Certificates generally have $1000 minimums.

What fees and charges are involved? Bullion involves a dealer markup, varying with quantity. Certificates cost 3% and up, with storage and insurance another 1% or more and sales fees of 1% or higher. Domestic and foreign securities and other forms of investment, like mutual funds, are subject to standard fees and commissions. Depending on the form of ownership, other costs may include sales or transfer taxes, shipping and handling, assay fees, insurance, storage, and safekeeping. Physical ownership involves an opportunity cost as well, since the money tied up could otherwise be invested in assets producing income.

Do they mature, expire, or otherwise terminate? Certain investment vehicles, such as options and futures, have specified expirations.

Can I sell them quickly? Usually yes, though platinum and palladium are less liquid than gold and silver. Larger ingots and less popular gold coins can have uncertain liquidity.

How is market value determined and how do I keep track of it? Market value is a complex affair. While investor demand is highest when inflation and economic uncertainty loom largest, industrial demand depends on economic health and certainty. Other factors, such as interest rates and foreign exchange rates, play a key role, and speculators are active. Different forms of investment may be affected in different ways at different times. Dealers are a source of information concerning physical assets; securities and commodities information is reported in the financial pages of daily newspapers.

Investment Objectives

Should I invest in precious metals if my objective is capital appreciation? Yes, but myriad forces affect market value, and a high degree of expertise is required to achieve short-term gains.

Should I buy them if my objective is income? Some forms of ownership, like stocks and mutual funds, may provide income, while others, like physical ownership, provide none and may involve negative returns. In general, precious metals are not purchased for income.

To what extent do they protect against inflation? Although used by investors primarily to hedge political and economic uncertainty, precious metals over the long term have risen in value with inflation. Investors buying precious metals for inflation protection should be mindful, however, that many factors can cause volatility in the shorter term.

Are they suitable for tax-deferred retirement accounts? Except for American Eagle coins, physical investment is not permitted. Common stocks and mutual fund shares involving precious metals may be suitable for some accounts.

Can I borrow against them? Yes; depending on the form of investment, there are various ways to leverage investments and use them as loan collateral.

Risk Considerations

How assured can I be of getting my full investment back? Precious metals tend to be volatile and offer no assurance that values will be retained.

How assured is my income? Where such investments provide income at all, such as mining stocks paying dividends, the risk is often great.

Are there any other risks unique to these investments? Many investors in precious metals have lost money doing business with unscrupulous dealer-brokers. Political risks in countries where mining is done and related developments, such as the sentiment in the mid-1980s for divestiture of shares of firms doing business in South

Africa, can jeopardize investment values. Inaccurate or misleading estimates of reserves of mining companies is another risk.

Are they commercially rated? Some common stocks are rated by Standard & Poor's and other major services.

Tax Considerations

What tax advantages (or disadvantages) do they offer? Assuming you are not engaged in mining or processing or using gold in a business or profession, dividend income and capital gains and losses are subject to the usual tax treatment. In addition, you may have to pay state sales taxes on physical purchases.

Economic Considerations

What economic factors most affect buy, hold, and sell decisions? Investors favor precious metals to hedge anticipated high inflation; however, many other economic factors can affect the value of precious metals and related investment alternatives, often in different ways.

PREFERRED STOCK (NONCONVERTIBLE)

Preferred stock is a hybrid security that combines features of both common stock and bonds. It is equity, not debt, however, and is thus riskier than bonds. It rarely carries voting rights.

Preferred dividends, like bond interest, are usually a fixed percentage of par value, so share prices, like bond prices, go up when interest rates move down and vice versa. But whereas bond interest is a contractual expense of the issuer, preferred dividends, although payable before common dividends, can be skipped if earnings are low. If the issuer goes out of business, preferred shareholders do not share in assets until bondholders are paid in full, though preferred shareholders rank ahead of common stockholders. Like bonds, preferreds may have sinking funds, be callable, or be redeemable by their holders.

Because preferred issues are designed for insurance companies and other institutional investors which, as corporations, enjoy an 80% tax exclusion on dividends earned, fully taxable yields for individuals are not much better than those on comparable bonds offering more safety. Moreover, trading is often inactive or in big blocks, meaning less liquidity and higher transaction costs for small investors.

Still, personal investors do hold preferred stock. A broker can usually find good buys as investor perceptions of risk in different industrial sectors create yield differences in stocks that are otherwise comparable. Capital appreciation can result from shares bought at a discount from the prices at which a sinking fund will purchase them, or from discounted shares of turnaround firms with dividend arrearages.

Different types of preferred stock include:

> *Convertible preferred,* convertible into common shares and thus offering growth potential plus fixed income; tends to behave differently in the marketplace than straight preferred (see Convertible Security).

Noncumulative preferred is a hangover from the heyday of the railroads and is rare today. Dividends, if unpaid, do not accumulate.

Cumulative preferred is the most common type. Dividends, if skipped, accrue, and common dividends cannot be paid while arrearages exist.

Participating preferred is unusual and typically issued by firms desperate for capital. Holders share in profits with common holders by way of extra dividends declared after regular dividends are paid. This type may have voting rights.

Adjustable (floating or *variable) rate preferred* adjusts the dividend rate quarterly (usually based on the 3-month U.S. Treasury bill) to reflect money market rates. It is aimed at corporate investors seeking after-tax yields combined with secondary market price stability. Individuals, looking at modest, fully taxable dividends that can go down as well as up, might prefer the safety of a money market fund.

Prior preferred stock (or preference shares) has priority of claim on assets and earnings over other preferred shares.

$$* \quad * \quad *$$

What Is Nonconvertible Preferred Stock?

Nonconvertible preferred is a form of owner's equity, usually nonvoting, paying dividends at a specified rate and having prior claim over common stock on earnings and assets in liquidation.

Buying, Selling, and Holding

How do I buy and sell it? Through a securities broker-dealer.

Is there a minimum purchase amount, and what is the price range? Buying round lots (usually 10 shares) saves commissions. Shares have par (face) values normally ranging from $100 down to $10, and market prices may be higher or lower than par values to bring yields in line with prevailing interest rate levels.

What fees and charges are involved? Standard commissions, with added transaction charges on inactively traded shares.

Does it mature, expire, or otherwise terminate? Preferred stock may be outstanding indefinitely, but many issues have call features or sinking fund provisions, whereby the issuer, usually for a small premium over par value, can require holders to redeem shares. Preferred issues may also have put features, which allow holders to redeem shares.

Can I sell it quickly? In most cases, yes. As a rule, preferreds are less liquid than common stocks and more liquid than bonds. Because large corporate investors dominate, smaller lots can sometimes be difficult for brokers to transact quickly.

How is market value determined and how do I keep track of it? Assuming good financial condition, fixed-income preferreds vary inversely with market interest rates. *Adjustable-rate preferreds* tend to be less volatile because dividends are adjusted quarterly to reflect money market conditions. Preferred prices are reported daily in the stock tables of newspapers and in databases, identified by the abbreviation ''PF'' in newspapers and ''PR'' in most electronic media.

Investment Objectives

Should I buy nonconvertible preferred stock if my objective is capital appreci-

ation? No, although appreciation is possible in shares bought at a discount from par or redemption value or bought prior to a decline in interest rates. Substantial appreciation is possible in turnaround situations where cumulative preferred issues of troubled companies are selling at big discounts and there is a sizable accumulated dividend obligation.

Should I buy this if my objective is income? Yes, but unless you're a corporation or you buy at a discount, your yield won't be much better than that on a comparable corporate bond, and bonds are less risky in terms of both income and principal.

To what extent does it protect against inflation? Fixed-rate preferred offers no protection against inflation. Adjustable-rate preferred offers some.

Is it suitable for tax-deferred retirement accounts? Yes.

Can I borrow against it? Yes, subject to lender policies and Federal Reserve margin requirements.

Risk Considerations

How assured can I be of getting my full investment back? The market value of fixed-rate preferred stock declines as interest rates rise. (Adjustable-rate preferred has greater price stability.) In liquidation, holders of preferred stock are paid after bondholders but before common stockholders.

How assured is my income? Dividends, unlike interest, are not legal obligations and are paid from earnings, so income is as reliable as the issuer's earnings are stable. Established companies, such as utilities, with predictable cash flows are better bets than young firms or firms in cyclical industries, such as housing. Preferred dividends must be paid before common distributions, however; that means common dividends wait until all unpaid preferred dividends of cumulative issues are satisfied.

Are there any other risks unique to this investment? Call features, when present, allow the issuer to force holders to redeem shares, usually at par value plus a small premium. Firms normally call issues when market rates have declined and they can obtain financing more cheaply. But it is exactly under such circumstances that shares are enjoying higher market values and paying higher than market yields to holders who bought before rates declined. So call features represent a risk to investors; indeed the very presence of a call feature can limit upside price potential. Another risk of preferred stock is that should a dividend be omitted, the market may perceive financial weakness and drive down the share values.

Is it commercially rated? Yes. Major issues are rated by Moody's, Standard & Poor's, Value Line Investment Survey, and other services.

Tax Considerations

What tax advantages (or disadvantages) does it offer? None for personal investors. Corporations enjoy an 80% exemption from federal income taxes on dividends from other domestic corporations, effectively raising returns.

Economic Considerations

What economic factors most affect buy, hold, or sell decisions? Since most preferred stock pays a fixed dividend, it is best to buy when market rates are high and the issuer is forced to offer a competitive yield. Prices vary inversely with interest rates, so values increase as interest rates decline. Fixed-rate preferred stock loses value in inflation. Poor business conditions may affect profits and threaten dividends.

REAL ESTATE INVESTMENT TRUST (REIT and FREIT)

Real Estate Investment Trusts, or REITs as they are commonly called, were authorized by Congress in the early 1960s to provide small investors with an opportunity to invest in large-scale real estate and to share in the tax benefits available. After a tumultuous period in the mid-1970s, when rising interest rates and tight money pressured builders, causing loan defaults and forcing many REITs into financial difficulty, the industry, wiser for the experience, enjoyed a resurgence.

Like shares of stock, REITs trade publicly, and like mutual funds their money is invested in a diverse array of assets, from shopping malls and office buildings to apartment complexes and hotels, usually with geographical diversification as well.

Some REITs, called *equity REITs*, take ownership positions in real estate; shareholders receive income from the rents received from the properties and receive capital gains as properties are sold at a profit. Because both rents and property values rise with inflation, inflation protection is an important benefit of equity-oriented real estate investments.

Other REITs specialize in lending money to real estate developers. Called *mortgage REITs*, they pass interest income on to shareholders.

Still other REITs feature a mix of equity and debt investments.

By law, REITs must derive 75% of income from rents, dividends, interest, and gains from the sale of real estate properties, and must pay out 95% to shareholders. Companies meeting those requirements are exempt from federal taxation at the corporate level, although dividends are taxable to shareholders.

REITs thus allow investors to share, with limited liability, the financial and tax benefits of real estate while avoiding the double taxation of corporate ownership. REITs also offer liquidity, since you can sell your shares on the market any time you wish.

On the negative side, REIT shares can be just as volatile as shares of stock. When conditions are unfavorable, such as when interest rates are high, materials are short, and the real-estate market is overbuilt, share values suffer. There is also a limit to the tax benefits REITs provide, in that losses cannot be passed through to investors, only tax-sheltered income. That is not the case with limited partnerships.

A variation of the REIT is the *finite life real estate investment trust,* or FREIT. FREITs, like limited partnerships, are self-liquidating—that is, they aim to sell or finance their holdings by a given date and distribute the proceeds to investors, thereby enabling them to realize capital gains.

Investors thus have the choice of (1) selling their FREIT shares in the market (share values tend to more closely reflect market values of property holdings than with REITs) or of (2) waiting to receive the full value of their shares when the portfolio is sold and the cash is distributed.

Of course, the disadvantages of REITs apply to FREITs as well—the risk of a drop in market prices of shares should you wish to sell, and the inability to share in tax-deductible losses.

* * *

What Is a Real Estate Investment Trust (REIT)?

A REIT is a trust that invests in real estate properties or mortgages with funds obtained by selling shares, usually publicly traded, to investors.

Buying, Selling, and Holding

How do I buy and sell it? Through a securities broker-dealer.

Is there a minimum purchase amount, and what is the price range? Like common stocks, shares trade in round lots of 100 shares, with odd-lot transactions involving higher commissions. Prices vary, but most shares trade under $50.

What fees and charges are involved? Standard brokerage commissions.

Does it mature, expire, or otherwise terminate? Not normally. A recent development, called the finite life real estate investment trust or FREIT, is self-liquidating—that is, the management has an expressed intention to sell all its properties and distribute the proceeds within a specified time frame.

Can I sell it quickly? Yes, good liquidity is a major attraction.

How is market value determined and how do I keep track of it? Shares of equity REITs reflect property values, rent trends, and market sentiment about real estate. Mortgage REITs fluctuate as market interest rates affect profits. Balanced REITs— part equity, part mortgage—tend to have greater price stability. FREITs, because shareholders will sooner or later realize capital gains income, tend to have share values somewhat more reflective of underlying property values. Share prices are reported in the stock tables of daily newspapers and in electronic databases.

Investment Objectives

Should I buy this if my objective is capital appreciation? Yes, but the potential for share value increases is greater with equity REITs than mortgage REITs. Also, automatic reinvestment of dividends increases capital gains potential. FREITs aim to pay out realized capital gains within a targeted period.

Should I buy this if my objective is income? Yes, especially since yields are not reduced by taxation at the corporate level. Mortgage REITs are more income-oriented than equity REITs.

To what extent does it protect against inflation? Since income from rents and capital gains increases with inflation, equity REITs provide excellent inflation protection. Mortgage REITs provide less.

Is it suitable for tax-deferred retirement accounts? Yes.

Can I borrow against it? Yes, subject to Federal Reserve margin rules and individual lender policies.

Risk Considerations

How assured can I be of getting my full investment back? REITs shares have the same market risks as common stocks plus the risk of a decline in property values. Mortgage REIT shares suffer when rising interest rates squeeze profits, and unless insured, can involve the risk of default on mortgages. You should not buy REITs if safety of principal is a paramount concern.

How assured is my income? Assuming REITs are well managed, income, which derives from rents or mortgage interest primarily, should be relatively secure. Still, real estate is sensitive to economic adversity, and there are many safer ways to invest for income.

Are there any other risks unique to this investment? Much depends on expert management in terms of selecting, diversifying, and managing portfolios. Valuation of real estate is anything but an exact science. Certain types of REIT portfolios are riskier than others, those whose portfolios comprise short-term construction loan paper being the riskiest.

Is it commercially rated? Yes, by Standard & Poor's, Moody's, and others.

Tax Considerations

What tax advantages (or disadvantages) does it offer? REITs are not taxed at the corporate level, so dividends are higher. But shareholders personally are taxed. Unlike real estate limited partnerships, REITs cannot offer flow-through tax benefits, but some trustees pass on tax-sheltered cash flow (in excess of income) as a non-taxable return of capital. When shares are sold, however, the cost basis must be adjusted by such returns of capital in calculating capital gains taxes. To meet Internal Revenue Service tax-exemption requirements, 75% of a REIT's income must be real-estate related and 95% of it must be paid out to shareholders.

Economic Considerations

What economic factors most affect buy, hold, or sell decisions? REITs are most attractive to buy and hold when interest rates are low and supply and demand factors in the real estate industry favor growth in property values. Shares tend to be inflation-sensitive as values increase and dividends rise with higher rentals. Real estate is a cyclical industry and the risk-return relationship is maximized when investments are made over the longer term.

REAL ESTATE, PHYSICAL

No investment alternative has been more ballyhooed as a way to get rich quick than real estate. With inflation a fact of life for half a century, this inflation-sensitive investment, with its high potential for leverage through mortgage financing and its abundant tax benefits, has indeed made many millionaires and provided millions of average home owners with nest eggs in the form of home equity.

Real estate has many drawbacks and risks, however, whether owned as an individual; in one of the several forms of joint ownership, which are distinguished mainly in terms of how an interest can be terminated and what happens to it in death or divorce; or through a corporation, which has the advantage of limited liability and the disadvantage of double taxation.

Among the problems of real estate ownership are high carrying costs in the form of property taxes, insurance, maintenance, and repairs; the risk of illiquidity; the risk of loss of value as the result of demographic factors, declining neighborhoods, local economic changes, or government policies (such as a rise in property taxes or the imposition of rent controls); competition from professional and institutional investors affecting local supply and demand factors; changes in federal tax provisions; high costs of selling; and a host of special risks associated with specific types of holdings.

Physical real estate can be categorized as (1) residential, where, because the owner lives there, the utility of shelter or recreational use is an important part of the value but depreciation and maintenance are not allowable tax deductions; (2) rental, where income and tax benefits are primary goals, and appreciation secondary; (3) speculative, where income and utilitarian values are traded off for capital gains potential and losses can result from carrying costs (an example is investment in raw land); and (4) multipurpose, such as a multifamily residence used partly to live in and partly to rent, or a vacation property combining recreational use and rental income (tax implications where the status is not clearly established can be serious).

Properties can also be held in forms of shared ownership, which bring tax advantages and other benefits of home ownership to apartments and town houses. Cooperatives, where owners hold shares in total projects, and condominiums, where apartment units are owned along with a share of commonly shared facilities and amenities, often require a tradeoff of certain lifestyle prerogatives (e.g., a ban on pets) and have eligibility criteria, advertising restrictions, or even prohibitions against renting that can severely limit liquidity. Condominium time-shares, where each of two or more owners has exclusive right of occupancy for a defined period, make condominium units much more affordable. The occupancy rights of some time-shared property even trade in a secondary market, not unlike securities.

The inflation protection, tax breaks, and total returns of real estate are also available through limited partnerships and real estate investment trusts (REITs). Such syndications offer diversification (by type of holding and geography), professional management, economies of scale, and limited liability for small investments, along with some risks and costs of their own.

*   *   *

What Is Physical Real Estate?

Physical real estate includes personal residences and investment properties in the form of developed and undeveloped land, established commercial or residential properties, condominiums, and cooperatives.

Buying, Selling, and Holding

How do I buy and sell it? Through a real estate broker or direct negotiation.

Is there a minimum purchase amount, and what is the price range? There is no minimum purchase amount; the price range is limitless. Properties can generally be financed with a down payment of 5% to 50% of value.

What fees and charges are involved? Real estate involves broker commissions and carrying costs in the form of debt interest, real estate taxes, and maintenance costs. Though there are many tax benefits associated with such costs, they can nonetheless be highly burdensome, especially if a property is not producing income.

Does it mature, expire, or otherwise terminate? Not in a financial sense, although related debt instruments have fixed maturities. Physical real estate is, of course, subject to destructive acts of nature, vandalism, and deterioration from use and time.

Can I sell it quickly? Liquidity varies with the type of property and market conditions; as a general rule, real estate is not a liquid investment.

How is market value determined and how do I keep track of it? Although general economic conditions and such factors as money supply and mortgage interest rates have an important effect, real estate is often characterized by independent markets. One segment of the industry (such as residential homes) can be booming, while another (such as office buildings) is depressed, and market conditions can vary widely from one community or geographical area to another. There is no formalized source of information about real estate prices. Trade associations can be a source of national and regional statistics and real estate brokers keep abreast of local values.

Investment Objectives

Should I buy this if my objective is capital appreciation? Yes.

Should I buy this if my objective is income? Yes, but only rental properties provide regular income.

To what extent does it protect against inflation? Real estate is inflation-sensitive, that is, both property values and rental income increase with inflation.

Is it suitable for tax-deferred retirement accounts? Personal residences are not legal investments. Real estate securities, such as real estate investment trusts (REITs) or income-oriented limited partnerships, can be appropriate investments, however.

Can I borrow against it? Yes; first, second, even third mortgages are common ways of borrowing against real estate. Home equity loans, a popular product of banks and other financial services institutions, are a convenient form of borrowing for home owners. On a professional scale, substantial fortunes have been made and lost using the financial leverage provided by real estate.

Risk Considerations

How assured can I be of getting my full investment back? Real estate offers no guarantees that values will not decline.

How assured is my income? A lease assures income for its term, to the extent the tenant is dependable and creditworthy.

Are there any other risks unique to this investment? Yes, many—including some not invented yet. Common risks include shifting population centers, changing local economies (including tax policies and rent control legislation), zoning changes, acts of nature, crimes like vandalism and arson, and physical deterioration.

Is it commercially rated? No.

Tax Considerations

What tax advantages (or disadvantages) does it offer? The main tax benefits are deductibility from federal income taxes of mortgage interest and property taxes, and on investment property, depreciation (which reduces taxable income without affecting cash flow) and deductible maintenance costs. All rental income is passive, but $25,000 of passive activity losses can be offset against nonpassive income (phased out for high-income taxpayers). Owners of personal residences can defer capital gains taxes by reinvesting the proceeds in another residence of equal or greater value within two years and are entitled to a one-time exemption from capital gains taxes up to certain limits after age 55. Unlike other consumer interest, which becomes nondeductible under the Tax Reform Act of 1986, interest on loans secured by home equity is deductible up to the original purchase price plus improvements plus amounts used for educational and medical expenses.

Economic Considerations

What economic factors most affect buy, hold, and sell decisions? Real estate values parallel general economic cycles but are also subject to supply and demand conditions in local markets and in segments of the industry (such as commercial, industrial, residential). The most successful real estate investors have diversified portfolios (in terms of geography and type of holding) and stay in an investment until it becomes profitable. These opportunities, together with professional management and economies of scale, are available to individuals through real estate investment trusts (REITs) and limited partnerships.

SAVINGS ALTERNATIVES

For emergencies and for the sake of prudence, every investor should keep a certain amount of money in cash and in risk-free financial assets. Depending on one's need for liquidity, this often means choosing among the deposit accounts and certificates of deposit offered by banks and thrift institutions and U.S. Savings Bonds.

The following are brief descriptions of major savings alternatives:

Deposit accounts Depositors are federally insured up to $100,000 in banks, savings and loans, and credit unions (belonging to the FDIC, FSLIC, or NCUA), but different accounts have different features.

Prior to changes in banking laws in the late 1970s and bank deregulation in the early 1980s, choices were relatively simple—a noninterest bearing checking account for day-to-day cash transactions and a passbook savings account paying a modest rate that was limited by law. Then came *Negotiated Order of Withdrawal (NOW) Accounts,* which allowed checkwriting in insured savings accounts but kept the low-interest ceilings. They were followed in 1982 by insured *Money Market Deposit Accounts (MMDAs)* requiring minimum balances but offering liquidity (with limited checkwriting), and paying money market-based rates only slightly lower, on average, than money market mutual funds. In 1983, insured *Super NOW Accounts* were introduced with a minimum balance of $2500, unlimited checking, and market-determined rates that tended to be just under those of MMDAs. Also available were products like *sweep accounts,* which combined insured low-interest savings accounts with MMDAs or money market funds, and *retail repos* (repurchase agreements), representing uninsured shares in an institution's government securities portfolio.

Much of that became history in 1986, when institutions became legally free to pay any rate of interest. It should be noted, however, that certain restrictions on checkwriting and penalties for early withdrawals of time deposits, which had been scheduled to end with full deregulation in March 1986, were extended. Because banks and thrift institutions must keep costly reserves, however, and because their federal insurance gives them a marketing advantage, their rates tend generally to be a hair below money market mutual funds. The exceptions are the more aggressive money center banks and institutions with riskier (thus higher-yielding) loan portfolios or skimpier services.

Certificates of Deposit CDs are issued by banks, savings and loan associations (S&Ls), and credit unions, in various denominations and maturities (some institutions offer designer CDs, with maturities to suit the customer) are also federally insured at member institutions. CDs, which can have similar maturities and vary a couple of points between issuers, are issued both in discount and interest-bearing form and sometimes with variable rates. Other variations include split-rate CDs, where a higher rate is paid early in the CD's term than in its later life; convertible-term CDs, which convert from fixed-rate to variable-rate instruments; and expandable CDs, which allow adding to the investment at the original rate. CDs can also be bought from some brokers, who make bulk purchases of high-yielding CDs from issuing institutions around the country and then resell them; since the brokers make markets in such CDs, buyers have liquidity they would not enjoy as direct investors.

Savings Bonds   Savings bonds, 1980s style, come with flexible yields (Series EEs, issued on a zero-coupon basis, pay 85% of the average U.S. Treasury note return with a minimum of 6% if held for 5 years), plus deferred federal taxability and exemption from state and local taxes. Previously issued Series E and H bonds can be rolled into EEs or HHs, which are interest-bearing and pay 6% over 10 years.

*   *   *

What Are Savings Alternatives?

Savings alternatives include interest-bearing deposit accounts at banks, savings and loans, and credit unions; bank certificates of deposit (CDs); and Series EE and HH U.S. Savings Bonds.

Buying, Selling, and Holding

How do I buy and sell them? Deposit accounts, CDs, and savings bonds may be transacted at banks or other savings and financial services institutions. Series EE bonds may also be available through employer-sponsored payroll savings programs. Series HH bonds can be acquired by exchanging Series E, EE, and freedom share bonds at Federal Reserve banks and branches or the Bureau of Public Debt (Washington, DC 20226). The Federal Reserve or BPD will also redeem HH bonds after six months from issue.

Is there a minimum purchase amount, and what is the price range? Deposit accounts are available with no minimum deposits, but interest may vary with balances and some banks impose charges (negative interest) when low balances become an administrative burden. CDs are usually issued for $500 and up, although some $100 CDs are available. Jumbo CDs are issued for $100,000 and up. Series EE bonds sell for $25 ($50 face value) to $5000 ($10,000 face value). Series HH bonds are issued in $500 to $10,000 denominations.

What fees and charges are involved? Fees and charges on deposit accounts vary with the institution and its product. As a general rule, the higher the balance, the longer the commitment, and the less service, the less the cost to the depositor. Such factors usually are reflected both in rates and in fees and charges. Although CDs involve no fees or charges to buy or to redeem at maturity, the Federal Reserve Board voted in March 1986 to impose a penalty of seven days' interest on amounts withdrawn within the first week from personal CDs. (Institutional CDs were made subject to other penalties for early withdrawal.) Savings bonds involve no fees or charges.

Do they mature, expire, or otherwise terminate? CDs have maturities ranging from 32 days to 10 years. Series EE bonds have adjustable maturities. Series HH bonds mature in 10 years.

Can I sell them quickly? Certain deposit accounts may require notice of withdrawal. CDs may be subject to early withdrawal penalties or the issuer may refuse withdrawal prior to maturity, except in cases of hardship. (Of course, it is usually possible to borrow against such collateral and interest is tax-deductible.) NOW accounts offer instant liquidity through checkwriting. CDs bought through brokers can be sold in the secondary market. Savings bonds may be redeemed after 6 months, but there may be interest penalties.

How is market value determined and how do I keep track of it? Large CDs traded by dealers and institutional investors and smaller CDs marketed by brokers have secondary market values that rise and fall in inverse relation to prevailing interest rates. There is no secondary market for consumer-size CDs bought directly from banks and other issuing institutions or for savings bonds and deposit accounts.

Investment Objectives

Should I buy these if my objective is capital appreciation? Other than interest compounding, there is no capital gains opportunity except in CDs traded in the secondary market.

Should I buy these if my objective is income? Deposit accounts provide income, although they vary in terms of how rates are determined, how interest is compounded and credited, and how effective annual yields compare competitively. CDs are used for income, but those due in less than one year and zero-coupon CDs are issued on a discount basis—that is, they are sold at less than face value and redeemed at face value. Series EE bonds do not pay interest until maturity and must be held 5 years to receive the full rate on redemption. Series HH bonds pay a fixed rate of 6%.

To what extent do they protect against inflation? To the extent rates move with inflation, deposit accounts offer some protection. Fixed-rate CDs provide none, but short maturities limit risk. Variable-rate CDs provide some protection. Series EE bonds offer some protection because the rate is adjustable. Series HH bonds have a fixed rate and offer none.

Are they suitable for tax-deferred retirement accounts? Deposit accounts are legally eligible, but CDs are a better choice due to their higher yields. Because savings bonds already offer tax deferral, there would be no advantage in putting them in such accounts.

Can I borrow against them? Yes.

Risk Considerations

How assured can I be of getting my full investment back? Most deposits and CDs are insured to $100,000 per depositor by the FDIC, FSLIC, or NCUA, which are federally-sponsored agencies. (Nonmembers are insured by state-backed or private insurers, but check the exact conditions.) Savings bonds are direct obligations of the federal government and are risk-free.

How assured is my income? Although rates may in some cases fluctuate, income is very safe because the agencies that insure principal oversee the financial affairs of the institutions.

Are there any other risks unique to these investments? No.

Are they commercially rated? Moody's and other services rate CDs.

Tax Considerations

What tax advantages (or disadvantages) do they offer? Savings bonds are exempt from state and local taxes. Interest on Series EE bonds is tax-deferred until cashed-in or redeemed at maturity; when exchanged for Series HH bonds, interest is tax-deferred until the HH bonds are redeemed. Interest on deposit accounts and CDs is fully taxable.

Economic Considerations

What economic factors most affect buy, hold, and sell decisions? Safety and growth of principal through interest compounding are the main objectives with savings vehicles, although expectations concerning interest rate movements and inflation may guide decisions.

TREASURY SECURITIES (BILLS, BONDS, and NOTES)

United States Treasury securities, called Treasuries for short, are backed by the full faith and credit of the U.S. government and are issued to finance activities ranging from daily cash management to the refinancing of long-term bonded debt.

Investors seeking income thus have a wide choice of maturities, yields, and denominations along with the utmost safety. The government would have to become insolvent before default could occur, and as long as it has the power to create money, that is not a real possibility.

Treasuries also offer excellent liquidity and exemption from taxation at the state and local (but not federal) levels, an advantage that can add significantly to yield in high-tax states and localities.

Being fixed-income securities, however, Treasuries are not immune to the ravages of high inflation, nor are they safe from market risk. When general interest rates move up, the prices of Treasuries, like all fixed-rate investments, move down—unluckily for investors forced to sell prior to maturity in the secondary market. On the other hand, Treasuries, unlike many other fixed-income investments, are not usually callable. Except for some long-term Treasury bonds that become callable five years before maturity, the government cannot force redemption when rates move down.

The major categories of Treasury securities are:

Treasury bills   Called T-bills for short, they are issued weekly with 13-week and 26-week maturities and monthly with a 52-week maturity, on a discount basis and in denominations beginning at $10,000 with multiples of $5000 thereafter. They are issued through the Federal Reserve System, and investors may submit tenders either on a competitive basis, specifying terms and risking rejection, or on a noncompetitive basis, in which case the average rate established in the regular auction applies and purchase is assured. T-bills can also be bought for a fee through banks and other dealers.

Treasury bonds and notes   These are interest-bearing, paying semi-annually in most cases, and, like T-bills, sold through Federal Reserve banks and branches on a competitive or noncompetitive basis. Maturities of bonds range from 10 to 30 years, those of notes from 2 to 10 years. Bonds and notes can be bought in denominations as low as $1000. Except for 2-year notes, which are usually sold monthly, bonds and notes are offered as the need arises. Of course, outstanding issues with almost any maturity can be bought in the secondary market.

Other Treasury securities, covered elsewhere, include Series EE and HH Savings Bonds and zero-coupon products created by separating the principal and interest coupons from Treasury bonds. A special class, known as flower bonds, is discussed under Tax Considerations below.

Investors may also buy shares of mutual funds or unit investment trusts that invest in portfolios of Treasury securities.

$$*\quad*\quad*$$

What Is a Treasury Security?

A Treasury security is a negotiable debt obligation of the United States government, backed by its full faith and credit, and issued with various maturities.

Buying, Selling, and Holding

How do I buy and sell it? New issues of bills, bonds, and notes may be purchased through competitive or noncompetitive auction at Federal Reserve banks and branches. They can also be bought and sold at commercial banks, securities broker-dealers, and other financial services companies.

Is there a minimum purchase amount, and what is the price range? Treasury bills are issued in minimum denominations of $10,000 and multiples of $5000 thereafter. Notes and bonds are issued in denominations of $1000, $5000, $10,000, $100,000, and $1 million. Notes due in less than 4 years are usually issued in $5000 denominations.

What fees and charges are involved? Treasury securities bought and redeemed through Federal Reserve banks and branches are without fees. Purchases and sales through banks or broker-dealers involve modest fees (about $25) and/or markups.

Does it mature, expire, or otherwise terminate? Yes. Maturities range from 23 days (cash management bills) to 30 years (bonds).

Can I sell it quickly? Yes; bills, bonds, and notes enjoy an active secondary market and are highly liquid.

How is market value determined and how do I keep track of it? As fixed-income securities, Treasuries rise and fall in price in inverse relation to market interest rates. Because they are risk-free investments, money flows into Treasuries when investors are worried about the credit safety of other debt securities, causing lower yields and higher prices. The financial sections of daily newspapers report new offerings and secondary market yields. The Bureau of Public Debt (Washington, DC 20226) or the Federal Reserve bank or branch in your district will respond to inquiries concerning upcoming offerings.

Investment Objectives

Should I buy this if my objective is capital appreciation? No, but appreciation is possible if market rates decline.

Should I buy this if my objective is income? Yes, particularly Treasuries with longer maturities, but you are sacrificing yield in return for safety. After-tax yields get a boost in high-tax states and localities because interest is not taxed at the state and local levels.

To what extent does it protect against inflation? There is no protection, though short maturities offer less exposure to the risk of inflation.

Is it suitable for tax-deferred retirement accounts? Yes.

Can I borrow against it? Yes, to 90% at most banks and brokers.

Risk Considerations

How assured can I be of getting my full investment back? From the credit standpoint, Treasuries offer the highest degree of safety available. You can be assured of getting your money back at maturity. Should you wish to sell earlier in the secondary market, you may find market prices have declined because of rising market interest rates. (Experts sometimes hedge this risk using interest-rate options, futures, and futures options.) Inflation, of course, erodes dollar values.

How assured is my income? There is virtually no risk the government will default on interest. Some long-term bonds may be callable in the final years, terminating interest prematurely. Inflation, of course, can erode the value of fixed-interest payments, and low-yielding securities, like Treasuries, are especially vulnerable in hyperinflation, where the inflation rate can exceed the interest rate.

Are there any other risks unique to this investment? No.

Is it commercially rated? No, since Treasuries are risk-free, there is no need for commercial credit ratings.

Tax Considerations

What tax advantages (or disadvantages) does it offer? Treasuries are fully taxable at the federal level but are exempt from state and local taxes. A special class, called estate tax anticipation bonds or flower bonds, can be used, regardless of cost, at par value in payment of estate taxes, if legally held by the decedent at time of death.

Economic Considerations

What economic factors most affect buy, hold, or sell decisions? As with any fixed-income investment, it is best to buy when market rates are high and issues carry a competitive yield. Since prices vary inversely with market interest rates, the holding becomes more attractive as market rates decline. As low-yielding, fixed-income securities, treasuries fare poorly in inflation. Because they are virtually default-proof, they are highly desirable holdings when poor business conditions make other investments vulnerable to default, though yields of Treasuries may decline as a result.

UNIT INVESTMENT TRUST

Like a mutual fund, a unit investment trust (UIT) offers to small investors the advantages of a large, professionally selected and diversified portfolio. Unlike a mutual fund, however, its portfolio is fixed; once structured, it is not actively managed, except for some limited surveillance. It is also self-liquidating, distributing principal as debt securities mature or are redeemed, and paying out the proceeds from equities as they are sold in accordance with predetermined timetables. A one-time sales charge of less than 5% is the only significant cost, and considering this buys you a share in a "millionaire's portfolio," it is one of the attractions.

While sponsors commonly offer instant liquidity as a feature of UITs, liquidity is provided specifically through agreements to make markets in shares or to redeem them; there is not an active secondary market in the public sense, and investors should read the prospectus to determine whether and by what means liquidity provisions exist.

The most common form of UIT is made up of tax-exempt bonds, put together by an investment firm with special expertise in the municipals field. The bonds are deposited with a trustee, usually a bank, which distributes interest and the proceeds from redemptions, calls, and maturities and provides unitholders with audited annual reports. Since unitholders pay taxes as though they were direct investors, portions of income payments representing interest are not taxable, nor are portions representing principal, which are tax-free returns of capital. Capital gains, however, are taxable, technically at the time the trust realizes them, although unitholders commonly recognize them only after their investment in the trust has been recovered from distributions of principal or at the time they sell their shares. It is important to get tax advice on this.

Unit investment trusts are also available with portfolios of money market securities; corporate bonds of different grades; mortgage-backed securities; U.S. government securities; adjustable and fixed-rate preferred stocks; utility common stocks; foreign bonds; replications of stock indexes; and other investments. New varieties of UITs are being created all the time.

Some sponsors offer additional conveniences to investors, including checkwriting, reinvestment options, and exchanging or swapping, for modest fees, among other unit investment trusts under their sponsorship.

* * *

What Is a Unit Investment Trust?

A unit investment trust (UIT) is a trust that invests in a fixed portfolio of income-producing securities and sells shares to investors.

Buying, Selling, and Holding

How do I buy and sell it? UITs are bought from sponsoring broker-dealers, who usually stand ready to redeem shares.

Is there a minimum purchase amount, and what is the price range? Shares (units) costing $1000 are typical.

What fees and charges are involved? A sales charge (load) ranging from less than 1% to 5% of your investment (4% is typical, with discounts for volume). An annual fee, usually 0.15%, is factored into the yield. Additional fees (0.30% typically) may apply when the portfolio is insured.

Does it mature, expire, or otherwise terminate? Trusts are self-liquidating. Proceeds are distributed as securities mature or are sold. The life of most UITs is 25 to 30 years, but 10-year trusts are common and some are as short as six months.

Can I sell it quickly? Liquidity is not guaranteed, but it usually exists to some extent because of most sponsors' intentions, once shares are sold, to make markets as an accommodation to holders wishing to sell. Trustees may also redeem shares, but such provisions should be investigated before buying shares. Sponsors may also allow switching into their other investment products at little or no cost.

How is market value determined and how do I keep track of it? Since shares represent units in an investment pool, values are determined by the forces affecting the securities in the pool. Thus trusts composed of fixed-income bonds will increase in value as interest rates decline and vice versa. A trust made up of stocks will be affected by market movements and earnings forecasts for individual stocks, among other factors. Details of a particular trust and its portfolio are set forth in the prospectus that, by law, is provided to investors.

Investment Objectives

Should I buy this if my objective is capital appreciation? UITs usually are set up to provide income (but even with a fixed portfolio, capital gains and losses can result from interest rate movements and other factors). Stock index trusts have capital gains as a primary goal.

Should I buy this if my objective is income? Yes.

To what extent does it protect against inflation? Bond trusts offer no protection; equity trusts and floating-rate trusts offer some.

Is it suitable for tax-deferred retirement accounts? Yes, except those with portfolios of securities that are already tax-exempt.

Can I borrow against it? Yes, subject to Federal Reserve margin rules. The lack of an active secondary market raises a question about ready marketability and the attractiveness of shares as collateral.

Risk Considerations

How assured can I be of getting my full investment back? This varies with the safety of the investments in the trust, government bonds and common equities being at opposite ends of the spectrum. Interest rates may decrease the value of bonds, and therefore of shares, unless held for the life of the trust; market risk is always a question with equities. A growing number of trusts purchase insurance against credit risk.

How assured is my income? Portfolios are well diversified, making income relatively secure.

Are there any other risks unique to this investment? The lack of active management, once the portfolio is established and the shares sold, limits responsive corrective action in the face of adverse portfolio developments. Diversification provides some protection, however.

Is it commercially rated? Yes.

Tax Considerations

What tax advantages (or disadvantages) does it offer? None. UITs are subject to the same taxes (or exemptions) as the investments comprising them. But trusts composed of municipal bonds, some specializing in triple-tax-exempt portfolios for qualified residents, are common, and many taxable UITs are designed for tax-deferred retirement programs.

Economic Considerations

What economic factors most affect buy, hold, or sell decisions? Unit investment trusts are bought with the intention of holding until they self-liquidate. The same considerations that would guide an investor in choosing debt, equity, or money market securities would guide the choice of a particular UIT.

ZERO-COUPON SECURITY

Zero-coupon securities don't pay out their fixed rate of interest like other debt securities; they are issued at deep discounts and accumulate and compound the interest, then pay the full face value at maturity. The attractions for the investor are mainly twofold: (1) They can be bought at very low prices because of the deep discount and (2) Their yield to maturity is locked in, which takes the guesswork out of interest reinvestment.

The mathematical effects of a zero-coupon security, unless one is used to thinking in terms of compound interest over long periods, can seem astonishing: $30.31 invested today in a 12%, 30-year zero-coupon bond will bring $1000 at maturity!

The disadvantages of zeros are that income taxes (unless they are tax-exempt) are payable as interest accrues (and out of cash raised from another source); they are highly volatile; and their value at maturity can erode with inflation. Credit risk, especially with corporate zeros, can be greater than with a regular bond; if the issuer defaults after a certain amount of time has passed, the investor has more to lose, since nothing has been received along the way.

Not surprisingly, a popular use of taxable zeros, with their low purchase prices and automatic compounding, is tax-deferred retirement accounts, where they are sheltered from taxability on imputed interest.

The following are principal types of zeros:

> *Corporate zero-coupon securities*   These are not usually recommended for individual investors because of credit risk and because the yield tends not to be competitive in relation to the risk. One explanation is that these issues are marketed to investors who do not have to pay taxes on imputed interest, such as foreign investors.
>
> *Strips and STRIPS*   Strips are U.S. Treasury or municipal securities that brokerage firms have separated into principal and interest which, represented by certificates (the actual securities are held in escrow), are marketed as zero-coupon securities under proprietary acronyms like Salomon Brothers' CATS (Certificates of Accrual on Treasury Securities) and M-CATS (Certificates of Accrual on Tax-exempt Securities). Although the obligor is actually the broker, the escrow arrangement assures a high degree of security. Free of risk altogether are STRIPS, Separate Trading of Registered Interest and Principal of Securities, the Treasury's acronym for its own issue of prestripped zero-coupon securities.
>
> *Municipal zero-coupon securities*   These securities are issued by state and local governments and are usually exempt from federal taxes and from state taxes in the state of issue. They provide a convenient way of providing for the future goals of high-bracket investors who get an after-tax benefit from their lower interest rates. One caveat, however: some are issued with call features, which can defeat the purpose of a zero from the investor's standpoint, so avoid those.
>
> *Zero-coupon convertibles*   Introduced in the mid-1980s, these convertibles come in two varieties: one, issued with a put option, converts into common stock, thus providing growth potential; the other, usually a municipal bond, converts into an interest-paying bond, thus enabling the investor to lock in a rate, then, 15 years later, to begin collecting interest.

*   *   *

What Is a Zero-Coupon Security?

A zero-coupon security is a debt security or instrument that does not pay periodic interest but is issued at a deep discount and redeemed at face value.

Buying, Selling, and Holding

How do I buy and sell it? Through a securities broker-dealer and many banks. Some products are proprietary, available only at the dealers marketing them.

Is there a minimum purchase amount, and what is the price range? Because of their deep discount, zero-coupon securities can be bought quite cheaply; a $1000 20-year bond yielding 12% would cost about $97, for example. Broker-dealer minimums of 10 bonds or more are common.

What fees and charges are involved? A broker commission or a dealer spread.

Does it mature, expire or otherwise terminate? Yes; zero-coupon securities have a specified maturity, although some may have put options or be convertible into common stock or interest-bearing bonds. Some zeros have been issued with call features.

Can I sell it quickly? Investors generally buy zeros intending to hold them until maturity. Should you need to sell, the broker-dealer you bought it from can probably make a market, although you would certainly pay a higher transaction cost. Zeros based on treasury securities are somewhat more liquid than corporate or municipal zeros.

How is market value determined and how do I keep track of it? Zeros, being essentially fixed-rate investments, rise and fall in inverse relation to interest rates and are especially volatile. Zeros are listed along with regular bonds in daily newspapers.

Investment Objectives

Should I buy zeros if my objective is capital appreciation? Investing one sum of money and getting back a larger sum is what zeros are all about, so the answer is really yes. Strictly speaking, however, the appreciation is not a capital gain, but is rather compounded interest. Capital gains are possible from secondary market sales after interest rates have declined, but zeros are not usually traded for capital gain.

Should I buy this if my objective is income? No. Zeros pay no periodic income.

To what extent does it protect against inflation? As fixed-rate investments, zeros generally offer no inflation protection. Zeros convertible into common stock offer some.

Is it suitable for tax-deferred retirement accounts? Because zeros are taxed as though annual interest were being paid, they are considered ideal candidates for tax-deferred plans. An exception, of course, would be municipal zeros, which are tax-exempt anyway.

Can I borrow against it? Yes, subject to Federal Reserve margin rules and lender policies.

Risk Considerations

How assured can I be of getting my full investment back? Corporate and municipal issues, unless insured, vary with the credit of the issuer, so credit ratings are important. Treasury issues that are stripped (split into two parts—principal and interest) by brokerage houses and marketed separately as zero-coupon securities represented by receipts or certificates, are highly safe as long as the broker holds the underlying Treasury security in escrow, as is the practice. Some municipal strips issued by brokers (e.g., M-CATS) have indirect U.S. government backing, since they represent prerefundings invested in Treasury securities. Direct Treasury zeros (STRIPS) are risk-free. Zeros sold in the secondary market are susceptible to interest rate risk and a wide dealer spread. Of course, full investment, when talking zeros, means face value, not the small amount originally invested, since money is assumed to have a time value.

How assured is my income? Zeros do not pay income; the income return is built into the redemption value.

Are there any other risks unique to this investment? Other than the small risk of an issuing firm going bankrupt in the case of receipts and certificates issued by brokerages, the unique risk of zeros has to do with the degree of exposure; should a zero default, there is more to lose compared with an interest-bearing security, where some portion of interest would have been paid out and presumably been reinvested. Some municipal issues may be callable, which largely defeats the purpose for which most investors hold zeros.

Is it commercially rated? Municipal and corporate issues are rated.

Tax Considerations

What tax advantages (or disadvantages) does it offer? Interest is taxable as it accrues each year, just as if it were paid out. An exception, of course, are tax-exempt municipal zeros, which may also be exempt from taxes in the state of issue. U.S. government zeros are taxable at the federal level but exempt from state and local taxes.

Economic Considerations

What economic factors most affect buy, hold, and sell decisions? Zeros are purchased based on competitive yield considerations and are normally held until maturity, their appeal being a locked-in interest rate as opposed to a yield that varies with the reinvestment value of periodic interest payments in changing markets. Should it be necessary to sell in the secondary market, lower rates mean higher prices. Considerations governing convertible zeros are complex and vary with the provisions of the issue.

PART II

How to Read an Annual Report

How to Read a Quarterly Report

HOW TO READ AN ANNUAL REPORT

Weekend sailors know an axiom that if you can understand a dinghy you can sail a yacht. It's all in grasping the fundamentals. Annual reports are the yachts of corporate communications, and in full regalia they can be as formidable as they are majestic. Fashioned by accountants and lawyers as well as marketers and executives, and costing major companies as much as $250,000 to $750,000 to publish, the reports are aimed at a variety of audiences—stockholders, potential stockholders, securities analysts, lenders, customers, and even employees. Essentially, however, they are financial statements, and if you can understand the basics, you will find that the rest is elaboration, much of which is legally required and very helpful. Of course, there are other parts that are simply embellishment, and those you take with a grain of salt. First, let's look at a "dinghy."

Basically, a financial statement comprises a *balance sheet* and an *income statement*. Exhibit 1 illustrates a statement reduced to "bare timbers."

EXHIBIT 1

BALANCE SHEET
December 31, 19XX

Cash/near cash	**5**	Accounts and notes payable	15
Accounts receivable	**20**	Accrued liabilities	5
Inventory	35	Current portion, long-term debt	5
CURRENT ASSETS	**60**	**CURRENT LIABILITIES**	**25**
		Long-term liabilities	25
		TOTAL LIABILITIES	**50**
Net fixed assets	35		
Other assets	5	Capital stock	10
		Retained earnings	40
		NET WORTH	**50**
TOTAL ASSETS	**$100**	**TOTAL LIABILITIES AND NET WORTH**	**$100**

THE BASIC BALANCE SHEET

A balance sheet (also called a statement of financial position or a statement of condition) is simply the status of a company's accounts at one moment in time, usually the last business day of a quarter or year. It is often compared to a snapshot, in contrast to a motion picture. On one side, it lists what the company owns—its assets. On the other side it lists what the company owes—its liabilities—and its net worth, or owners' equity, which is what investors have put into the firm plus earnings that have been retained in the business rather than paid out in dividends. The two sides are always equal. Even if a firm were insolvent—that is, owed more than it had in assets—the sides would be equalized by showing a negative (or deficit) net worth. (A minor technical point: Balance sheets can be presented with opposing sides, as just described, which is known as the account form, or with the assets above the liabilities and owners' equity, which is called the report form.)

EXHIBIT 1

INCOME STATEMENT
for the year ended December 31, 19XX

SALES		**$110**
Cost of goods sold	80	
Depreciation	5	
Selling, general, and administrative expenses	15	
	100	
NET OPERATING PROFIT		**10**
Other income or expense	1	
Interest expense	2	
Income taxes	2	
	5	
NET INCOME		**5**

THE BASIC INCOME STATEMENT

The income statement, which goes by such other names as statement of profit and loss, operating statement, and earnings statement, reports the results of operations over a specified period of time—12 months in the case of an annual report. As customers are billed, and as the costs and expenses of producing goods, running the business, and creating sales are incurred and recorded, the information summarized in the income statement is accumulated.

The income statement will be discussed below in more detail; it is enough for now to understand that its highlights are sales (or revenues), net operating profit (or operating income), and net income. It is this last amount—popularly called the bottom line because it comes after interest expense, unusual income and charges, and income taxes—that is available to pay dividends to shareholders or to be kept in the business as retained earnings.

A word about one expense item, called depreciation, which is important to understand because it is a major factor in cash flow, the net amount of cash taken into the business during a given period and the cash paid out during that period. Depreciation, which is sometimes combined in the figure for cost of goods sold, is merely a bookkeeping entry that reduces income without reducing cash. In other words, depreciation is a noncash expense, and it is added back to net income to determine a company's cash earnings. Net income plus depreciation equals cash flow from operations. More about depreciation and cash flow later.

BASIC RATIO TESTS

With the foregoing information on balance sheets and income statements, it is possible to look at a firm's year-to-year financial statements and make some tentative judgments about the firm's basic financial health and operating trends, particularly if you can compare the figures with those of other firms in a comparable industry. An in-depth look at important financial ratios is at the end of the discussion of the annual report, but much can be learned at a glance by applying the following basic ratio tests.

Current Ratio The current ratio is current assets divided by current liabilities. Current assets are assets expected to be converted to cash within a normal business cycle (usually one year), and current liabilities are obligations that must be paid during the same short-term period. For a manufacturing company (standards vary from industry to industry), a ratio of between 1.5 to 1 and 2 to 1—$1.50 to $2.00 of current assets for each $1.00 of current liabilities—is generally considered an indication that the firm is sufficiently liquid. In other words, there is enough net working capital (the difference between the two figures) to ensure that the firm can meet its current obligations and operate comfortably.

It is important that a company have this cushion because the liquidity of current assets, with the exception of cash and its equivalents, cannot be taken for granted; receivables can become slow or uncollectible (although a reserve for expected write-offs is normally provided) and inventory can lose value or become unsalable. Such things happen in recessions, and can result from poor credit, purchasing, or marketing decisions. Liabilities, unfortunately, remain constant. Of course, a company can have too much liquidity, suggesting inefficient use of cash resources, shrinking operations, or even vulnerability to a takeover attempt by an outside party. Well-run companies are lean, not fat.

Quick Ratio The quick ratio, which is also known as the acid-test ratio, is the current ratio, with inventory, its least liquid and riskiest component, excluded. It is calculated by adding cash, near-cash (for instance, marketable securities), and accounts receivable (sometimes collectively termed monetary assets), and dividing by current liabilities. Assuming no negative trends are revealed in year-to-year comparisons,a ratio of between .50 to 1 and 1 to 1 generally signifies good health, depending on the quality of the accounts receivable.

Average Collection Period A quick way of testing accounts receivable quality is to divide annual sales by 360 and divide the result into the accounts receivable. That tells you the average number of days it takes to collect an account. Since terms of sale in most industries are 30 days, a figure of 30 to 60 would indicate normal collections and basically sound receivables—at least up to the date of the statement. It may be helpful to compare a company's figure with that of other firms in the same industry.

Inventory Turnover Inventory turnover ratio tells the approximate number of times inventory is sold and replaced over a 12 month period and can be a tipoff, when compared with prior years' figures or comparative industry data, to unhealthy accumulations. Inventory should be kept adequate but trim, because it ties up costly working capital and carries market risks. To calculate turnover, divide the balance sheet inventory into sales. (*Note:* Industry comparative data published by Dun & Bradstreet and other firms providing financial data on companies compute this ratio using sales, not cost of goods sold. While cost of goods sold, because it does not include profit, produces a purer result, it is necessary to use sales for the sake of comparability.) As a general rule, high inventory turnover reflects efficient inventory management, but there are exceptions. A firm may be stockpiling raw materials in anticipation of shortages, for instance, or preparing to meet firm orders not yet reflected as sales. If inventory turnover is falling compared to prior years or is out of line with industry data, you should investigate the reasons. Year-to-year comparisons of inventory turnover are of particular significance in high volume–low profit margin industries such as garment manufacturing and retailing.

Debt-to-Equity Ratio   The debt-to-equity ratio can be figured in several ways, but for our purposes it is total liabilities divided by net worth. It measures reliance on creditors to finance operations and is one of several capitalization ratios summarized below. Although financial leverage—using other people's money to increase earnings per share—is desirable to a point, too much debt can be a danger sign. Debt involves contractual payments that must be made regardless of earnings levels; it must usually be refinanced when it matures at prevailing (perhaps much higher) money costs; and it has a prior claim on assets in the event of liquidation. Moreover, debt can limit a company's ability to finance additional growth and can adversely affect a firm's credit rating, with implications for the market value of shares. What is considered a proper debt-to-equity ratio varies with the type of company. Those with highly stable earnings, such as many utilities, are able to afford higher ratios than companies with volatile or cyclical earnings. For a typical industrial company, a debt-to-equity ratio significantly higher than 1 to 1 should be looked at carefully.

Operating Profit Margin   This figure, obtained by dividing a firm's net operating profit by sales, is a measure of operating efficiency. (Analysts sometimes add depreciation back into net operating profit since it is not a cash expense.) Year-to-year comparisons can be a reflection on cost control or on purchasing and pricing policies. Comparisons with other firms in the same industry provide insight into a company's ability to compete.

Return on Equity   This is the bottom line as a percentage of net worth (net worth is divided into net income), and it tells how much the company is earning on shareholder investment. Compared with the figures of prior years and similar companies, it is a measure of overall efficiency—a reflection on financial as well as operational management. But it can also be affected by factors beyond the control of management, such as general economic conditions or higher tax rates. And be suspicious of a firm with abnormally high returns; it could be in for competition from firms willing to sacrifice returns to gain a larger market share. As a rule of thumb, return on equity should be between 10% and 20%.

By applying the foregoing ratio tests to a company's basic balance sheet and income statement, particularly with the help of data on the company's prior years and on other companies in the same industry, you get a sense of whether the company's financial structure and operational trends are essentially sound. There is, however, a great deal you still don't know, such as:

- How reliable are the numbers?
- Are results affected by changes in accounting methods?
- Have there been changes in the company's top management?
- From what product lines did sales and profits largely derive?
- Did any special events affect last year's results?

- What new products are on the horizon?
- Are there any lawsuits or other contingent liabilities that could affect future results or asset values?
- To what extent are the company's operations multinational, and what is its exposure to foreign exchange fluctuations and/or political risk?
- If the company is labor-intensive, what is the status of its union contracts?
- What is the status of the company's debt? Is any financing or refinancing planned that could affect share values?
- How sensitive is the company to changes in interest rates?
- What were the sources and applications of cash?
- Are any major capital expenditures (for instance, real estate, machinery, equipment) being planned? How are existing fixed assets depreciated?
- How much is allocated to research and development?
- What other operational or financial changes has management planned?
- Does the company have a broad base of customers, or a few major customers?
- To what extent is the company dependent on government contracts?
- What is the company's pension liability, and what are its pension assets?

WHAT THE ANNUAL REPORT INCLUDES

The majority of annual reports of major public companies include a table of contents on the inside front cover. The following is typical:

Contents
Highlights
Letter to Shareholders
Review of Operations
Financial Statements
   Report of Independent Accountants
   Consolidated Financial Statements
   Statement of Changes in Financial Condition
   Notes to Financial Statements
   Supplementary Tables
   Management's Discussion and Analysis
Investor's Information
Directors and Officers

Highlights

The highlights greet you at the start of an annual report. Often including charts and other graphics, they present basic information in a clear, comparative way that requires little explanation. At the very least, you should expect to find the company's total sales for the past two years and its net income, expressed both as a total and on a per-share basis. Needless to say, upward trends (usually, but with exceptions) are positive and downward trends negative. But what is most important to understand is that the company and its public relations advisors can include here whatever other information they feel will create the desired impression on the shareholder. That usually means you can expect to find highlights that add up to a positive impression, although it has become lately a matter both of fashion and good business to include a downward trend or two for the sake of credibility. Basically, though, what you can expect to find highlighted, aside from the unavoidable, are the statistics of which the company is most proud. If dividends were up, they will probably be highlighted; if they were down, the same space might be devoted to an increase in research and development (R&D) expenditures, with the implicit promise of a future payoff for shareholders.

Occasionally, you will see information about common shares presented on a primary basis and on a basis assuming full dilution. Dilution occurs when an increased number of shares compete for the same amount of earnings, and it is a potential development when a company has convertible bonds, convertible preferred stock, warrants, or other securities outstanding that, if converted or exercised, would result in the issuance of additional shares. When dilution would significantly affect shareholders, companies are required to report earnings per share on both bases: before dilution (primary) and assuming conversion or exercise of all dilutive securities.

Should you encounter any other unfamiliar figures in the highlights, consult the Ratio Analysis Summary at the end of this discussion of an annual report.

Letter to Shareholders

In the many spoofs that have been written about corporate annual reports and their reputation for obfuscation, the least mercy has been reserved for the letter to shareholders. This review of the year just passed and look at the year ahead leads off the textual part of the report. It is usually signed by the chairperson and president and is often accompanied by a picture of the two together, suggesting amity not always characteristic of their day-to-day relationship.

While it is certainly true that the letter to shareholders is worded to put the best face on the past year's results and to soothe any anxieties that might be aroused by the financial figures to follow, it is nonetheless a statement of management's intentions and, when compared to prior years' messages, a test of management's credibility. Although it is not an audited, formal part of the report, it purports to be a serious comment on the year's results and their financial impact, a report that puts into perspective the major developments affecting shareholders, a statement of management's position on relevant social issues, and an expression of management's plans for the company's future. An impressive letter is one that compares past predictions with actual results and explains in a candid way the disappointments as well as the successes. Be wary of euphemisms (a ''challenging'' year was probably a bad one) and wording that is vague or qualified; a product area ''positioned for growth'' may sound promising, but it's not growing yet. If it were, the letter would say so. Much of the meaning of the letter to shareholders is between the lines.

Review of Operations

This review section consists of pictures and prose and often occupies the bulk of the pages of an annual report. Frequently slick, public relations-oriented, and designed to impress a corporation's various publics, the review can nonetheless be a valuable source of information about the company's products, services, facilities, and future direction. Unfortunately, it is also sometimes designed to divert the reader's attention from unpleasant realities. Be suspicious of reviews that stress the future and give the present short shrift or that are built around themes, such as the loyalty of employees or the company's role in building a stronger America. Also, what is not discussed can be more significant that what is discussed. Lack of reference to an aspect of operations described in the preceding year's annual report as an area of rapid growth and expansion may indicate that the company's expectations were not fulfilled and a write-off may be on the horizon. By and large, though, companies are responding to pressures for greater straightforwardness in the way they present themselves. In addition, companies these days are required to provide detailed financial information about the various segments contributing to their sales and profits. Although that information appears later in the supplementary financial data, it allows you to relate the activities being "promoted" to actual results and thus to evaluate the financial significance of different product areas. The Securities and Exchange Commission (SEC) has imposed stricter disclosure requirements in recent years, and these requirements have had a generally positive effect in terms of making annual reports more credible documents.

Financial Statements

Financial statements are, of course, the basic purpose of annual reports, and as the result both of expanded SEC disclosure regulation and companies' own interest in satisfying the information requirements of securities and credit analysts, financial statements have evolved over the years into presentations that elaborate substantially on the basic balance sheet and income statements. Reporting has also become more complex due to the complexity of the companies themselves, which have become diversified in terms both of product lines and geography, with a trend toward multinational operations involving political and currency risks.

Report of Independent Accountants: This report, also known as the auditor's opinion, is sometimes found at the beginning of the financial statement section and sometimes at the end, but it should be the first thing you read. Numbers are only numbers, and the opinion of an independent accounting firm, which is legally required of public companies, certifies that the financial statements were examined and validated. An unqualified opinion—we'll get to what a qualified opinion means in a minute—typically reads as shown in Exhibit 2, either in one paragraph of two.

EXHIBIT 2

Report of Independent Accountants

To the Shareholders of XYZ Corporation:

We have examined the statement of financial position of XYZ Corporation as of December 31,19X6 and 19X5, and the related statements of earnings and changes of financial position for each of the years in the three-year period ended December 31, 19X6. Our examinations were made in accordance with generally accepted auditing standards and accordingly included such tests of the accounting records and such other auditing procedures as we considered necessary in the circumstances.

In our opinion, the aforementioned financial statements present fairly the financial position of XYZ Corporation at December 31, 19X6 and 19X5, and the results of their operations for each of the years in the three-year period ended December 31, 19X6, in conformity with generally accepted accounting principles applied on a consistent basis.

[Signed and dated.]

What you should be on the lookout for is a qualified opinion. The tipoff is usually that the opinion section has more than two paragraphs and contains the words "except that" or "subject to." An opinion is qualified when the auditor (the accounting firm) has reservations about the report or sees the prospect of a significant modification to the figures as the result of some expected development. Examples might be a pending lawsuit that, if lost, would materially affect the firm's finances;

an indeterminable tax liability relating to an unusual transaction; or an inability to confirm a portion of inventory because of an inaccessible location.

It is important to understand that a qualified opinion does not question the accuracy of the report, nor is it necessarily negative. It should simply serve as a red flag and prompt investigation. The footnotes to the financial statements and/or the management's discussion and analysis section will usually provide details.

Rarely, but occasionally, seen are two other types of auditor's opinion, the disclaimer of opinion and the adverse opinion. A disclaimer of opinion states that an opinion is not possible because of a material restriction on the scope of the audit (for example, an inability to verify inventory quantities) or a material uncertainty about the accounts (for example, doubt about the company's continued existence as a going concern). An adverse opinion states that the company's financial statements do not present fairly the financial position or results of operations in accordance with generally accepted accounting principles. Either type of opinion is cause for concern, but you are unlikely to run into these types of opinions since the company will normally take the auditor's advice and make the necessary corrections.

You should be wary of a company's figures if the company regularly replaces the independent auditors. Such conduct could indicate that the company is opinion shopping—looking for auditors whose approach would produce the most favorable sales and earnings figures for the company and thereby perhaps hide problem areas or potential problem areas.

Report by Management: Usually accompanying the Report of Independent Accountants is a similar Report by Management certifying responsibility for the information examined by the accounting firm. This section attests to the objectivity and integrity of the data, estimates, and judgments on which the financial statements were based. It alludes to the company's internal controls and oversight responsibility of the board of directors for the financial statements as carried out through an audit committee composed of directors who are not employees. It is sometimes signed by the chief financial officer of the company and/or the chief executive officer.

Consolidated Financial Statements—Part 1: The Balance Sheet: In the following pages, we will discuss the financial statement of our hypothetical company, XYZ Corporation. As required, the statement presents comparative balance sheets as of the company's two most recent fiscal year ends and income statements for the past three years. Many variations exist on the accounts discussed below, and there are as many unique items as there are companies. But if you grasp the following, you will understand the basis of the vast majority of balance sheets and income statements.

First, an item-by-item explanation of XYZ's balance sheet (see Exhibit 3).

Current Assets

Cash and Short-term Securities

Cash requires little explanation; it is cash in the bank, on its way to the bank, or in the till. Short-term securities, sometimes listed separately under cash and called marketable securities, represent idle funds invested in highly safe, highly liquid securities, such as U.S. Treasury bills, certificates of deposit, and commercial paper. They are carried at the lower of their cost or market value. If they are shown at cost, their market value is indicated parenthetically or in a footnote.

EXHIBIT 3

XYZ CORPORATION
Balance Sheet
As of December 31
(Dollars in Millions)

	19X6	19X5
ASSETS		
Cash and short-term securities	**7.6**	7.0
Accounts and notes receivable	**10.2**	9.5
Inventories	**23.0**	20.9
Prepaid expenses	**.3**	.2
Total Current Assets	**41.1**	37.6
Property, plant and equipment	**83.3**	79.4
Less: Accumulated Depreciation	**23.5**	21.3
Net Fixed Assets	**59.8**	58.1
Other assets	**3.8**	3.0
Intangible assets	**.9**	.9
TOTAL ASSETS	**105.6**	99.6
LIABILITIES AND SHAREHOLDERS' EQUITY		
Accounts payable	**4.2**	4.3
Notes payable	**.8**	—
Accrued liabilities	**3.2**	2.7
Federal income taxes payable	**8.2**	7.1
Current portion (maturity) of long-term debt	**.7**	.8
Dividends payable	**1.4**	.9
Total Current Liabilities	**18.5**	15.8
Other liabilities	**2.0**	1.4
Long-term debt	**16.2**	17.0
Deferred federal income taxes	**.9**	.7
TOTAL LIABILITIES	**37.6**	34.9
6% cumulative preferred stock ($100 par value; authorized and outstanding: 50,000 shares)	**5.0**	5.0
Common stock ($10 par value; authorized 2,500,000 shares; outstanding 1,555,000 shares)	**15.6**	15.6
Capital surplus	**8.2**	8.2
Retained earnings	**39.2**	35.9
TOTAL STOCKHOLDERS' EQUITY	**68.0**	64.7
TOTAL LIABILITIES AND STOCKHOLDERS' EQUITY	**105.6**	99.6

Accounts and Notes Receivable

These are customer balances owing. When a company makes a sale, a customer is required either to pay in cash (cash sales) or, as in the majority of cases, within credit terms (credit sales), which tend to be standardized within industries but are typically 30 days and rarely more than 90 days. Accounts receivable—sometimes called just receivables—are credit accounts that are not yet received. Often there is a reference to a footnote containing an aging schedule, a breakdown of accounts in terms of where they stand in relation to their due dates. This reveals delinquency and trends and is a valuable tool for analysts. Of course, a company expects a certain percentage of uncollectible accounts and, based on its historical experience and current policies (it might, for example decide to liberalize credit policy to boost sales), it sets up a reserve (or allowance) for bad debts, which is deducted from gross receivables to arrive at the balance sheet value. This is either noted on the balance sheet or explained in a footnote. Special attention should be paid to accounts receivable if a company does a significant percentage of its business with a few key customers. If any of these key customers were to have financial problems, the worth of the receivables carried on the company's books would quickly be in jeopardy. Notes receivable normally account for a small portion of the total and usually represent cases in which special terms were granted and obligations were documented with promissory notes. If a short-term note receivable arose out of a loan or the sale of property or some other nontrade transaction, it would, if material, normally be shown separately or footnoted.

Inventories

This figure, when a company is engaged in manufacturing, is a combination of finished goods, work in process, and raw materials. Conservative accounting practice requires that inventories be carried at the lower of cost or market value, but there are different methods of inventory valuation, principally First In, First Out (FIFO) and Last In, First Out (LIFO).

Under the FIFO method, inventory is assumed to be sold in the chronological order in which it was purchased. Under the LIFO method, the reverse is true: The goods sold in a period are assumed to be those most recently bought. When prices are rising or falling, the difference is reflected in the balance sheet value of inventory. A company using the LIFO method during a period of inflation, because its cost of goods sold reflects the most recent—and higher—prices, will show lower profits on its income statement and a lower balance sheet inventory, since its ending inventory remains valued at older (lower) prices. Because LIFO produces lower taxable income in times of inflation, it is the method adopted by a majority of companies in recent years. Thus, the balance sheet inventories of these companies are undervalued—in other words, they have a "LIFO cushion." It is important to remember that *de*flation would produce the opposite result. An explanation of inventory valuation methods (or, significantly, any change in methods) is provided in the footnotes to the statements, which will also explain adjustments required by the 1986 tax act.

A company's inventory figure cannot be analyzed in a vacuum. To determine if a company is maintaining adequate inventory control, relate the inventory figure to the growth in sales. Inventory growth should keep pace with sales growth, not exceed it. A buildup of inventory relative to sales should be viewed with skepticism.

Prepaid Expenses

This account represents expenses paid in advance, such as rent, insurance, subscriptions, or utilities, that are capitalized—that is, recognized as asset values, and gradually written off as expenses, as their benefit is realized during the current accounting period. If the amount is important, this account is usually deducted from current assets in computing the current ratio. However, it usually represents an insignificant percentage of current assets and is thus ignored for analytical purposes.

Net Fixed Assets

Property, Plant and Equipment

This section of the balance sheet lists the company's fixed assets, sometimes called capital assets or long-term assets. These assets include land, buildings, machinery and equipment, furniture and fixtures, and leasehold improvements—relatively permanent assets that are used in the production of income. The word tangible is sometimes used in describing these assets, to distinguish them from intangible assets (described below), which similarly produce economic benefits for more than a year but which lack physical substance.

Fixed assets are carried—that is, recorded on the books of the company and therefore reported on its balance sheet—at original cost (the cost the company incurred to acquire them) less accumulated depreciation—the cumulative amount of that original cost that the company has written off through annual depreciation expenses charged to income. Land, however, because it is assumed to have unlimited useful life, is not depreciated. (Companies engaged in mining and other extractive industries, whose capital assets represent natural resources, enjoy depletion allowances, a concept similar to depreciation write-offs.) As a result of depreciation write-downs and inflation, it is not unusual for the book value of a company's fixed assets to be considerably lower than their market value. On the other hand, market value is an indication of what it will cost to keep fixed assets up to date and maintain sufficient capacity to support sales growth. The relationship between sales levels and capital expenditures is therefore an important factor in evaluating a firm's viability. However, businesses vary in terms of how capital-intensive they are; manufacturers rely more on fixed assets to produce sales than wholesalers, for example.

The existence of fully depreciated assets on a company's balance sheet may signal that the company is a likely candidate for a takeover attempt or a leveraged buyout. The company's plant, for instance, has most likely appreciated in market value over the years and the depreciated basis on which it is carried on the balance sheet may have no relationship to reality. Thus, new owners could in part finance the purchase of the company by selling some assets at their higher market value.

Other Assets

This category can include any number of items such as cash surrender value of life insurance policies taken out to insure the lives of key executives; notes receivable after one year; long-term advance payments; small properties not used in daily business operations; and minority stock ownership in other companies or in subsidiaries that for some reason are not consolidated. Additional types of assets, if significant, would be discussed in the footnotes.

Another category of other assets, which is sometimes broken out separately (as in our example), is generally called intangible assets. These are nonphysical rights or resources presumed to represent an advantage to the firm in the marketplace. The most common intangibles are (1) goodwill and (2) a grouping typically labeled patents, trademarks, and copyrights.

Goodwill refers to a company's worth as an operating entity, or going concern—the prestige and visibility of its name, the morale of its employees, the loyalty of its customers, and other going-concern values. These are values beyond the book value of the firm's assets. Thus, when a company is purchased at a price exceeding its book value, the difference—the value of its goodwill—represents a real cost to the acquiring company. Goodwill, though intangible and abstract, *can* be valued.

Because it has no liquidation value, however, it is classified as an intangible asset and must be amortized (written off) over time, in accordance with generally accepted accounting principles. As with fixed assets and depreciation, this is done by annual noncash charges to income. Unlike the case of depreciation deductions, however, there is no tax benefit to the company when intangibles are written off.

Patents, trademarks and copyrights, the other most common intangible assets, have economic value in the sense that they translate into profits, but their carrying value is based on their cost. Being intangibles, they are written off over what accounting practice deems to be their useful lives.

Other intangible assets might include capitalized advertising costs, organization costs, licenses, permits of various sorts, brand names, and franchises.

Because intangible assets are assumed not to have value in liquidation, they are excluded from most ratios used in analyzing values. The term tangible net worth is used to mean shareholder equity less intangible assets.

Current Liabilities

Accounts Payable

This account represents amounts owed to suppliers for raw materials and other goods, supplies, and services purchased on credit for use in the normal operating cycle of the business. In other words, one company's account payable is another company's account receivable. As with receivables, conventional credit terms vary from industry to industry, but 30 days is standard and anything over 90 days is the exception (except in highly seasonal industries, such as garment manufacturing, where longer-term dating is commonplace and liquidity is provided by cashing accounts receivable with finance companies known as factors). The level of accounts payable should vary with sales levels, or, more specifically, with the amount of annual purchases—a part of the cost of goods sold. Any bulging of accounts payable in relation to purchase could mean a firm is relying to an unhealthy extent on trade suppliers as a source of working capital.

Notes Payable

These are usually amounts due banks or financial institutions on short-term loans, often under lines of credit. A line of credit is an arrangement by which a company may borrow working capital up to a limit, and details are usually covered in the footnotes. Notes payable may also be due suppliers under special credit arrangements.

Accrued Liabilities

Accrued liabilities arise when an expense is recognized as an obligation but the cash has not yet actually been paid out. Expenses commonly reflected in this account include payroll, commissions, rent, interest, taxes, and other routine expenses.

Federal Income Taxes Payable

This account is similar to accrued liabilities, but is usually broken out in recognition of its importance. (It is to be distinguished from the account called deferred federal income taxes, a noncurrent liability discussed below.)

Current Portion (Maturity) of Long-Term Debt

When a company has a long-term debt obligation that requires regular payments, the amount due in the next 12 months is recorded here as a current liability.

Dividends Payable

These represent dividends that have been declared by the board of directors but have not been paid. Dividends become an obligation when they are declared, and are normally paid quarterly. They include both preferred and common dividends.

Long-term Liabilities

These are debt obligations due after one year. Included are term loans from financial institutions, mortgages, and debentures (unsecured bonds), as well as capital lease obligations, pension liabilities, and estimated liabilities under long-term warranties. Details are provided in footnotes.

Depending on a company's accounting practices, long-term liabilities may also include an item called deferred federal income taxes. This is often due to the fact that companies may use different rules for tax purposes and reporting purposes, and this creates timing differences. For example, a company using accelerated depreciation for tax purposes would get large depreciation write-offs in the early years of an asset's life, thus saving taxes, but would have higher taxable income in the later years. For reporting purposes, however, the company might wish to use the straight line method of depreciation, which each year produces equal (and lower) charges, thus resulting in higher reported earnings. The amount of taxes deferred are shown on the statement used for reporting purposes (the annual report) as deferred federal income taxes. Adjustments caused by the lower corporate tax rates provided in the Tax Reform Act of 1986 should be explained in footnotes.

Shareholders' Equity

This section of the balance sheet represents the owner's interest—the value of assets after creditors, who have a prior legal claim, have all been paid. It includes accounts for preferred stock, common stock, capital surplus, and retained earnings.

Preferred Stock

Not all companies issue preferred stock, and it exists in several varieties. Several general characteristics are particularly notable: It usually pays a fixed dividend that must be paid before common dividends can be paid; it has precedence over common stock in the distribution of assets in liquidation; and if it is cumulative, unpaid dividends accumulate and must be paid in full before common dividends can be declared.

In recent years companies have used preferred stock as part of antitakeover programs. Referred to as poison-pill preferreds, these shares are created when a hostile takeover attempt is imminent. The new class of preferred stock is designed to raise the cost of the acquisition to a point where it may be abandoned by the company attempting the takeover. You should check whether a company has issued preferred specifically to fend off a takeover attempt and, if so, try to determine the implications such preferred may have for common shareholders.

Common Stock

Shares of common stock are the basic units of ownership in a corporation. Common shareholders follow behind creditors and preferred shareholders in claims on assets and therefore take all the risks inherent in the business. But, with rare exceptions, they vote in elections of directors and on all important matters, and while they may or may not receive dividends, depending on earnings and whether the directors vote to declare dividends, the book value of their shares stands to grow as net worth (shareholders' equity) expands through earnings retained in the business. Common shareholders in publicly traded companies also stand to profit from increases in market prices of shares, which normally reflect expectations of future earnings. But on the balance sheet, common shares are listed either at a par or stated value, an accounting/legal value signifying nothing other than the lowest price at which shares can be initially sold. Sometimes different classes of stock exist and are listed separately, with the privileges or limitations of each indicated parenthetically or in referenced notes.

Capital Surplus

Sometimes seen as additional paid-in capital (as preferred stock and common stock are sometimes called paid-in capital), this account reflects proceeds from issuances of stock that were in excess of the par or stated value of shares. For example, XYZ common has a par value of $10 per share; when 100,000 shares were issued at $12 a share, $1,000,000 was added to common stock and $200,000 was added to capital surplus.

Retained Earnings

This account is made up of corporate earnings not paid out in dividends and instead retained in the business. Retained earnings are not put in a special bank account or stuffed into a figurative mattress—they are simply absorbed as working capital or to finance fixed assets in order to generate more earnings.

Consolidated Financial Statements—Part 2: The Income Statement: The income statement shows the results of operations over a period of 12 months. Results of the two years prior to the year reported on are included for comparative purposes (see Exhibit 4).

Net Sales

Most income statements (or, more formally, Statements of Income), lead off with Net Sales—the total of cash sales (negligible for most industrial companies) and credit sales for the accounting period (12 months for annual reports). Net simply means after returns of merchandise shipped; freight-out; and allowances for shortages, breakage, and other adjustments having to do with day-to-day commerce. (Note that some service companies, including utilities, and financial organizations use the term revenues instead of sales.) Needless to say, the trend of sales as revealed in the three years' worth of figures is a key indicator of how a company is faring in the marketplace. The figures should of course be adjusted for inflation to give an accurate reading of year-to-year changes.

Changes in the components of a company's sales can be more significant than changes in sales figures. If, for example, a chemical company can shift from marketing bulk chemicals (which have a relatively small profit margin) to marketing specialty chemicals (which have a relatively large profit margin) it will ultimately earn more even without an increase in sales. Changes in sales components can be determined by reviewing the business segment information in the annual report (discussed below.)

Cost of Goods Sold

This is the cost of producing inventory and includes raw materials, direct labor, and other overhead that can be directly related to production. It is directly affected by the company's choice of the FIFO or LIFO inventory valuation methods (see Inventories, above). The reason becomes clear when you look at the formula by which cost of goods sold is determined:

Beginning inventory + Purchases during the period – Ending inventory
$$= \text{Cost of goods sold}$$

When the ending inventory (the balance sheet inventory) is the oldest stock, which is the case when the LIFO method is used, the cost of goods sold, assuming prices are rising with inflation, becomes a higher number than would be the case using FIFO. Of course, the higher the cost of goods sold, the lower will be taxable income, as we will see.

EXHIBIT 4

XYZ CORPORATION
Income Statement
Fiscal Year Ended December 31
(Dollars in Millions)

	19X6	19X5	19X4
Net Sales	98.4	93.5	88.8
Cost of goods sold	64.9	62.2	59.7
Depreciation and amortization	2.2	3.0	2.0
Selling, general, and administrative expenses	12.1	11.1	10.3
	79.2	76.3	72.0
Net Operating Profit	19.2	17.2	16.8
Other Income or (Expenses)			
Income from dividends and interest	.2		
Interest expense	(1.0)	(.9)	(1.0)
Earnings before income taxes	18.4	16.3	15.8
Provision for income taxes	8.3	7.5	7.3
Net Income	10.1	8.8	8.5

Common shares outstanding: 1,555,000
Net earnings per share (after preferred dividend
requirements in 19X6 and 19X5: 19X6: $6.30; 19X5:
$5.47; 19X4: $5.47.

Statement of Retained Earnings

	19X6	19X5	19X4
Retained Earnings Beginning of Year	35.9	33.6	31.3
Net Income for Year	10.1	8.8	8.5
Less: Dividends Paid on:			
Preferred stock ($6 per share)	.3	.3	
Common stock (per share):19X6: $4.20; 19X5: $4.00; 19X4: $4.00).	6.5	6.2	6.2
Retained Earnings End of Year	39.2	35.9	33.6

Depreciation

This noncash expense was alluded to at the start of the discussion of an annual report and again under Deferred Federal Income Taxes Payable in the discussion of balance sheet liabilities. To encourage firms to keep facilities modern and thus spur the economy, the U.S. government provides businesses a way to pay less tax and thereby conserve cash. This is accomplished by allowing firms to take an annual percentage (called a depreciation write-off) of what they spent for certain types of fixed assets, such as buildings, machinery, and equipment, and to treat the amount as though it were an actual expense, thus reducing taxable income without requiring an outlay of cash.

Depreciation is a highly complex tax accounting concept, and for purposes of reading annual reports it is not necessary to understand it completely. It is enough to know that tax rules make it possible for companies to recover the cost of certain fixed asset investments on an accelerated basis and thus to get the benefit of tax savings sooner than they would using the straight-line method (now required for newly purchased real property). At the same time, companies are allowed, for purposes of annual reports, to reflect depreciation charges based on the straight line method, whereby the estimated useful life of the asset is divided into its cost to get a uniform annual depreciation charge, which is generally much lower than the figure used for tax purposes. Annual reports thus show higher earnings, while the stockholder has the satisfaction of knowing that the company's tax liability has been minimized. It is all spelled out in the footnotes.

What is more important to know is that depreciation charges have a relationship to the age of the assets and vary with the amount of investment in fixed assets. An increase in depreciation usually reflects increases in depreciable assets—fixed assets like plant and equipment. Decreases usually mean fixed assets have been disposed of or have become fully depreciated. Particularly since straight line depreciation is used by most companies for reporting purposes, lower depreciation charges can signal a need for fixed asset expenditures, meaning long-term financing, which has implications for shareholders in the form either of dilution of share values or higher interest costs. Of course, increased or modernized plant capacity should also translate eventually into higher sales, greater operating efficiency and higher earnings per share.

Selling, General, and Administrative (SG&A) Expenses

These are all the expenses associated with the normal operations of the business that were not included in cost of goods sold, which represented direct costs of production. Salaries, rent, utilities, advertising, travel and entertainment, commissions, office payroll, office expenses, and other such items are representative of this category, which varies from industry to industry in terms of its composition and the relative importance of selling expenses versus administrative expenses.

A good test of the quality of a company's management is its ability to control selling, general, and administrative expenses. Many companies have fallen into bankruptcy simply because management was unable or unwilling to control expenses and keep them in line with the growth of sales.

Net Operating Profit

The net operating profit is what is left over after costs of goods sold, depreciation, and SG&A expenses are deducted from sales, and it tells you the company's profit on a normal operating basis—that is, without taking into account unusual items of income or expense or nonoperating expenses such as interest and taxes. As stated above, it is a measure of operating efficiency, and significant variations from year to year or from industry standards should be investigated by looking more closely at the figures behind the totals, many of which are supplied in footnotes or published in the company's form 10-K (see Investor's Information, below). Lower than expected profit due to a rise in SG&A expenses as a percentage of sales might be traceable to a single factor, such as a rise in officers' salaries, for example.

Other Income or Expenses

This category picks up any unusual or nonoperating income or expense items. Examples might include income, gains, or losses from other investments; gains or losses on the sale of fixed assets; or special payments to employees. Nonrecurring items are usually explained in detail in footnotes. In this category is *interest expense,* which, unlike dividends, is a pretax expense. For companies with bonds or other debt outstanding, however, interest expense is a recurring item. Because interest on funded debt is a contractual, fixed expense that, if unpaid, becomes an event of default, analysts follow closely a company's fixed-charge coverage—how many times such fixed charges are covered by pretax annual earnings.

Earnings Before Income Taxes

This figure nets out all pretax income and expense items, but it would not be accurate to say it is the figure on which federal income taxes are based. That is because tax returns of corporations, as we have seen, use difficult methods of depreciation for tax purposes than they use for reporting to shareholders and because other factors, such as tax-loss carrybacks and carryforwards, which are not visible on the current year's statement, may affect the company's tax liability.

Provision for Income Taxes

After taking advantage of all available benefits, this is the company's tax liability for the year in question. Note that it is termed a *provision.* Payments based on estimated taxes have been made during the year, and net payments on this liability are payable according to a timetable determined by the Internal Revenue Service. A portion of the liability will be reflected as a accrued liability, as described above.

A company's effective tax rate should be compared with other companies in the same or similar industries. Although many tax loopholes have been ended by recent tax legislation, it may be a mark of smart and aggressive management if a company has a lower effective rate than other companies similarly engaged.

Net Income

This is the bottom line, the "after everything except dividends" figure. Dividends, by law, must be paid out of earnings, though not necessarily out of current earnings. Below the bottom line, figures for common shares outstanding and earnings per common share are given. Securities analysts usually focus on earnings per share in assessing a company's status. As a rule, earnings per share are expected to grow from year to year, and it may be a sign of trouble if they do not grow according to predictions or if they do not grow at all.

Consolidated Financial Statements—Part 3: The Statement of Retained Earnings:
What typically follows the Income Statement is an analysis showing retained earnings at the beginning of the period; how net income increased retained earnings;
dividends paid on preferred stock and common stock during the period; and the
retained earnings account at the end of the fiscal year being reported (see Exhibit
4). The last figure will, of course, be the same as the retained earnings figure in
the stockholders' equity section of the balance sheet.

A Statement of Retained Earnings may reflect stock dividends—new shares issued to existing shareholders. Stock dividends are accounted for by decreasing
retained earnings and increasing common stock in equal amounts (using par or stated
value if the stock dividend represents more than 20 to 25 percent of outstanding
shares, and market value if it represents less). Many investors are attracted to
companies that regularly declare stock dividends. It should be borne in mind, however, that stock dividends in no way enhance the actual assets of a company.

Statement of Changes in Financial Condition: The statement of changes in financial
condition (Exhibit 5) is really a reformulation of information already presented in
the balance sheet and income statement. Represented this way, however, it enables
you to see how working capital is derived and used. This statement, sometimes
called the Sources and Uses (or Application) of Funds Statement, focuses on changes
in net working capital—the difference between current assets and current liabilities—
but also includes significant changes not affecting working capital. An exchange of
bonds for stock, for example, would not affect working capital but would be shown
as a change in financial condition.

Working capital increases when long-term liabilities or shareholder equity increase or when noncurrent assets decrease. It decreases when long-term liabilities
or shareholder equity decrease or noncurrent assets increase. For example, the sale
of a fixed asset increases working capital by creating a current asset either in the
form of cash or a note receivable; a repayment of long-term debt, on the other hand,
uses cash and thus reduces working capital. (It should be noted that not all companies
focus on net working capital in their analysis of sources and uses of funds. A
minority of firms focus on the cash account itself, listing every change that increased
or decreased cash. Since most companies use the net working capital basis, the
discussion here assumes that basis. In any event, a breakdown of changes in the
components of working capital is provided, so if additions to working capital were
becoming stuck in slow-moving inventory and not being converted into cash, for
example, you could still detect such a development.)

To fully appreciate the importance of following funds flows—and thus the importance of this statement—you have to consider that a firm can be profitable, have
assets well in excess of liabilities, and still go bankrupt. Sound financial planning
is essentially a matter of assuring adequate liquidity—so that when obligations
payable in cash are due, adequate cash is at hand. Capital budgeting, which attempts
to arrive at the optimum mixture of short- and long-term debt and of debt and equity,
is a sophisticated subject beyond the scope of this discussion, but a basic rule of
thumb should be kept in mind as you evaluate the statement of changes in financial
position: In a conservatively operated company, *permanent* capital requirements—
fixed assets and the portion of working capital that is not seasonal—should be
financed through a combination of retained earnings and either long-term debt or
equity. *Short-term* requirements should be financed with short-term liabilities in a
cycle that begins when accounts payable are created to purchase inventory, which
in turn is sold to create accounts receivable, which are collected to produce cash,
and so on.

EXHIBIT 5

XYZ CORPORATION
Statement of Changes in Financial Condition
Fiscal Year Ended December 31
(Dollars in Millions)

	19X6	19X5	19X4
Sources of Funds (working capital)			
From operations:			
Net income	10.1	8.8	8.5
Items not requiring working capital:			
Depreciation and amortization	2.2	3.0	2.0
Increase in other liabilities	.6	1.4	1.0
Deferred income taxes	.2	.3	.2
Total funds provided by operations:	13.1	13.5	11.7
Proceeds from sales of preferred stock		5.0	
Total Sources of Funds	13.1	18.5	11.7
Uses of Funds (working capital)			
Additions to property, plant and equipment	3.9	4.2	2.8
Dividends paid on preferred stock	.3	.3	–
Dividends paid on common stock	6.5	6.2	6.2
Payments on long-term debt	.8	6.5	1.0
Increase in other assets	.8	.9	.5
Total Uses of Funds	12.3	18.1	10.5
NET INCREASE IN WORKING CAPITAL	.8	.4	1.2

Changes in Components of Working Capital

	19X6	19X5	19X4
Increase (decrease) in current assets			
Cash and short-term securities	.6	.5	.7
Accounts and notes receivable	.7	.6	.8
Inventories	2.1	1.9	1.2
Prepaid expenses	.1	-	.1
	3.5	3.0	2.8
Increase (decrease) in current liabilities			
Accounts payable	(.1)	1.2	.7
Notes payable	.8	–	–
Accrued liabilities	.5	.3	.3
Federal income taxes payable	1.1	.8	.6
Current portion of long-term debt	(.1)	–	–
Dividends payable	.5	.3	–
	2.7	2.6	1.6
NET INCREASE IN WORKING CAPITAL	.8	.4	1.2

XYZ Company has been showing increases in working capital which generally support its steadily increasing sales. Its funds-flow from operations has enabled it to make annual additions and improvements to its plant and machinery and still pay dividends without impairing its working capital. In 19X5, the statement reveals, the company, despite profitable operations, would have had a negative cash flow—more cash flowing out than in—as the result of meeting $6.5 million of long-term debt repayments—if management had not properly planned for the requirement by issuing $5 million of preferred stock.

Notes to Financial Statements: Footnotes to financial statements, sometimes just called notes, are unfortunately named if there's any implication that they represent superfluous detail. Indeed, both the balance sheet and the income statement contain the sentence: "The Notes to Financial Statements are an integral part of this statement." Footnotes set forth the accounting policies of the business—and provide additional disclosure. They contain information having profound significance for the financial values presented elsewhere in the financial statements. For example, the Tax Reform Act of 1986 introduced important changes in corporate accounting rules, which relevant footnotes can be expected to clarify.

It would be impossible to list here all the types of information one might find in the notes to financial statements. Here is a sampling, though, and if it succeeds in impressing you with the importance of reading this section of a financial report, it will have accomplished its purpose.

Accounting procedure changes   A change in the method of valuing inventory or a change in the company's method of depreciating fixed assets can have significant effects on reported earnings and asset values. You should investigate further if a company frequently changes accounting procedures. The company may, for instance, be trying to hide weak aspects of its operations.

Pension fund and profit-sharing plans   A number of companies recently have used overfunded pension plans to generate cash windfalls. In some instances, the existence of such excess funding can be detected by reading relevant notes about the actuarial assumptions on which the pension plan is based and relating them to the number of past and present employees covered by the pension plan. Management has discretion over the rate at which pension liabilities are funded, and in some cases officers of a company have used this power to smooth reported earnings by reducing charges in poor years and increasing charges in good years.

Long-term debt   Detail on debt maturities makes it possible to anticipate refinancing needs, which have implications for investors in terms of the effect of interest costs on profits or potential dilution of common share values. A company's ability to manage its debt structure so as to obtain money at the lowest rate for the longest maturity is viewed by analysts as demonstrating that the company has a capable management team.

Treasury stock   By buying their own shares in the market, companies decrease shares outstanding and thus increase earnings per share for existing stockholders. The existence of an active stock purchase program can be viewed as a two-edged sword. On the one hand, such a program provides in effect a support price for the company's shares as well as a buyer with deep pockets—the company itself. On the other hand, a stock purchase program is frequently used as a defense against a hostile takeover attempt and raises the question whether repurchase of stock is the best way to use assets of the company.

Taxes The prospect of an assessment for a prior year's taxes may be disclosed in the footnotes. Of particular significance is any footnote disclosing that a company's tax returns are being audited or that any of the assumptions utilized by the company in determining the taxable basis of its assets are being questioned by the Internal Revenue Service.

Leases One of the most significant of the off balance sheet liabilities is the long-term noncapital lease. A footnote dealing with a long-term lease should be reviewed carefully.

Supplementary Tables: The principal supplementary tables are the following.

Segment Reporting

The Financial Accounting Standards Board (FASB) requires companies meeting certain criteria having to do with product and geographical diversification to present certain information in segment form—that is, by product or industry category or markets serviced and by geographical territory. The information required, which covers the same three-year period as the income statement, includes sales or revenues; operating profit or loss; the book value of identifiable assets; aggregate depreciation, depletion, or amortization; and capital expenditures.

These breakdowns enable shareholders to evaluate a company's exposure to the vagaries of various geographical markets, including political and other risks to a company that has foreign operations. For industry or product-line segments, a stockholder is able to evaluate the company's activities in particular areas in terms of the amount of its investment and the return it is realizing on the investment, as well as the year-to-year trends.

Financial Reporting and Changing Prices

Another ruling of the FASB is aimed at accounting for the effect of inflation on the inventory, fixed assets, and the income statement values for cost of goods sold and depreciation as they are related to those assets. Thus, companies are required to present the last five years' figures showing the effects of declines in the purchasing power of the dollar in contrast to the primary values as shown in the financial statements, based on historical cost.

Five-Year Summary of Operations

This required schedule essentially extends the three-year income statement to five years, including preferred and common stock dividend history. It is a useful supplement in terms of permitting analysis of operating trends, and a number of corporations have taken it upon themselves to provide summaries of the last ten years of operations.

Two-Year Quarterly Data

This schedule provides a quarterly breakdown of sales, net income, the high and low stock price, and the common dividend. The operating data is most valuable when a company's operations are subject to seasonal factors, as, for example, a retailer is subject to heavy demand during the Christmas season. The market price and dividend data reveal stock price volatility and the regularity with which the company has made dividend payments.

Management's Discussion and Analysis: The general credibility and informational value of annual reports was significantly advanced in the mid-1980s when the Securities and Exchange Commission began requiring and monitoring the section Management's Discussion and Analysis of the Financial Condition and Results of Operations. This is a narrative presentation designed to present management's candid comments on three key areas of a company's business: results of operations, capital resources, and liquidity. Companies are required to address all material developments affecting these three key areas, favorable or unfavorable, including the effects of inflation. In discussing results of operations, companies are required not only to detail operating and unusual events that affected results for the period under discussion, but also any trends or uncertainties that might affect results in the future. The capital resources part involves questions of fixed asset expenditures and considerations of whether it benefits shareholders more to finance such outlays with stock, bonds, or through lease arrangements. Addressing liquidity means discussing anything that affects net working capital, such as the convertibility into cash of accounts receivable or inventory and the availability of bank lines of credit.

When it made this section a requirement, the SEC sought to elicit, in a company's own words, an interpretation of the significance of past and future financial developments. Its intentions were clearly revealed following enactment of the Tax Reform Act of 1986, when it voted to direct companies to use this section of their 1986 reports to shareholders to quantify certain effects of the new law, such as a reduction in current liabilities for future taxes. Whether it will prove to be a satisfactory substitute for one's own analysis remains to be seen.

Investor's Information

This section of the annual report lists the name of the transfer agent, registrar, and trustees; the exchanges on which the company's securities are traded; the date, time, and place of the annual meeting; and a notice as to when proxy materials will be made available to shareholders of record. If the company has an automatic dividend reinvestment plan, the terms and procedures for participating are stated here.

The number of common shareholders (and preferred, if any) as of the fiscal year-end is also usually indicated in this section.

This section may also invite requests for Form 10-K, the annual Securities and Exchange Commission filing corporations are required to make available to shareholders. The 10-K is filed within 90 days of a company's fiscal year-end. It is a thick, drab report containing a mass of detail. Much of what it contains is in the annual report to shareholders or is incorporated by reference to the public annual report, but other information is unique to the 10-K. Such unique information includes historical background; names of principal security holders; security holdings of management; more detailed financial schedules; information about products or services, properties, markets, distribution systems, backlogs, and competitive factors; detail about patents, licenses, or franchises; number of employees; environmental and other regulatory compliances; information concerning amounts paid directors and their share holdings; and background, including employment history, of executives and their relationships to the firm.

Form 10-Q is a shorter, unaudited, update of the 10-K. It must be filed within 45 days of the end of a company's first, second, and third fiscal quarters. It is mainly useful as a source of information about changes in the status of securities outstanding, compliance with debt agreements, and information on matters to be voted on by shareholders, such as the election of directors.

Directors and Officers

The names of members of the board of directors and their affiliations are listed here as are the names and titles of senior executives. Also usually indicated is the membership of board members on various committees, such as the executive committee, the finance committee, the compensation committee, the committee on corporate responsibility, the research and development committee, and the audit committee. Corporations vary in terms of the use to which they put the backgrounds of their directors—in some cases the role of directors is ceremonial, in others directors are used to advantage—and this section can sometimes provide meaningful insight. The absence of directors unaffiliated with management may indicate a company dominated by senior officers and not responsive to the concerns of outside shareholders. Senior management can also become more entrenched in companies that stagger the terms of directors to help prevent a hostile takeover.

*   *   *

RATIO ANALYSIS SUMMARY

Ratios are the principal tools of financial statement analysis. By definition, however, ratios indicate relationships, and by excluding considerations such as dollar amounts and the overall size of a company, their meaning in and of themselves can be limited if not misleading. Ratios have their greatest significance when used to make year-to-year comparisons for the purpose of determining trends or when used in comparison with industry data. Composite ratios for different industries are published by Standard & Poor's Corporation, Dun & Bradstreet, Robert Morris Associates, and the Federal Trade Commission. The following is a summary of key ratios and what they signify. Each ratio is computed for XYZ Corporation, whose hypothetical financial statements are shown in the discussion above of the annual report.

Ratios That Measure Liquidity

Ratio	Calculation	XYZ Computation
Current ratio	$\dfrac{\text{Current assets}}{\text{Current liabilities}}$	$\dfrac{41.1}{18.5} = 2.22$

The current ratio measures the extent to which the claims of a firm's short-term creditors are covered by assets expected to be converted to cash within the same short-term period. In XYZ's industry, the standard is 1.9, so its 2.2 ratio indicates comfortable liquidity, although down slightly from last year's ratio of 2.4. In a recession, extra liquidity protection could make a vital difference; slack consumer demand would mean that XYZ's wholesale customers would have lower sales. That would mean less sales and lower inventory turnover for XYZ. As XYZ's customers became tighter for cash and slower paying, or went out of business, XYZ's accounts receivable would become less collectible. Ultimately that could mean insolvency. Hence the importance of this key measure of short-term solvency. Of course, in other types of companies, the current ratio would have less significance. A company whose sales were largely under United States government contracts would have less receivables and inventory risk, for example, and could thus afford a lower current ratio.

Quick ratio	$\dfrac{\text{Current assets-inventory}}{\text{Current liabilities}}$	$\dfrac{41.1 - 23.0}{18.5} = .97$

A refinement of the current ratio, the quick or acid-test ratio answers the question: If sales stopped, could the company meet its current obligations with the readily convertible assets on hand? XYZ has a quick ratio of .97, almost a dollar of quick assets for each dollar of current liabilities, and virtually in line with the industry standard of 1.0. Last year it was slightly better, 1.04 times, but that small a year-to-year difference is probably not enough to signify a negative trend.

Ratios That Measure Activity

Ratio	Calculation	XYZ Computation
Inventory turnover	$\dfrac{\text{Cost of goods sold}}{\text{Inventory}}$	$\dfrac{64.9}{23.0} = 2.8$ times

This tells us the number of times inventory is sold in the course of the year. As a general rule, high turnover means efficient inventory management and more marketable inventory with a lower risk of illiquidity. But it could also be a reflection on pricing policies or could reflect shortages and an inability to meet new orders. XYZ's turnover ratio is 4.3 times, down slightly from the prior year's 4.5 times, and the industry standard is 6.7 times. This should be looked into.

Average collection period	$\dfrac{\text{Accounts receivable}}{\text{Annual credit sales/360 days}}$	$\dfrac{10.2}{.270} = 37$ days

Assuming a company's terms of sale are standard for its industry, the average collection period—which tells if customers are paying bills on time—can be a reflection on credit policy (a liberal policy, involving relaxed credit standards to generate higher sales volume, will usually result in a longer average collection period); on the diligence of a firm's collection effort; on the attractiveness of discounts offered for prompt payment; or on general economic conditions as they affect the finances of the firm's customers. XYZ's collection period was 38 days this year and 37 days last year compared with an industry average of 37 days. It thus enjoys typical collections, apparently reflecting a sound and competitive credit policy. Of course, there could be potential problems not revealed by this test; for example, a concentration of accounts receivable in one industry or with a few customers, which, if affected by adversity, would have a disproportionate effect on the total receivables portfolio. Footnotes to the financial statements will often contain information concerning the composition of accounts receivable and their age relative to the invoice date.

Fixed assets turnover	$\dfrac{\text{Net sales}}{\text{Net fixed assets}}$	$\dfrac{98.4}{59.8} = 1.6$ times

Measured over time and against competitors, this ratio indicates how efficiently a firm is using its property, plant and equipment—its "plant capacity." Increases in fixed assets should produce increases in sales, although the investment will normally lag the sales effect. If, given time, sales fail to increase in relation to plant capacity, it usually reflects poor marketing strategy. XYZ's ratio is low by industry standards. It has recently added to its capacity and has plans to pursue a more aggressive policy aimed at higher sales and increased market share.

Total assets turnover	$\dfrac{\text{Net sales}}{\text{Total assets}}$	$\dfrac{98.4}{105.6} = .93$ times

This ratio measures the amount of sales volume the company is generating on its investment in assets and is thus an indication of the efficiency with which assets are utilized. The relationship between sales and assets is sometimes called operating leverage, since any sales increases that can be generated from the same amount of assets increase profits and return on equity and vice versa. XYZ's turnover of .93, virtually unchanged from the prior year, is considerably under the industry standard of 2.1 meaning XYZ had better increase sales or dispose of some assets. As we observed above, however, it has plans to increase sales and recently added fixed assets in preparation.

Ratios That Measure Profitability

Ratio	Calculation	XYZ Computation
Operating profit margin	$\dfrac{\text{Net operating profit}}{\text{Net sales}}$	$\dfrac{19.2}{98.4} = 19.5\%$

This ratio is the key to measuring a firm's operating efficiency. It is a reflection on management's purchasing and pricing policies and its success in controlling costs and expenses directly associated with the running of the business and the creation of sales, excluding other income and expenses, interest, and taxes. (Some analysts exclude depreciation from this ratio, but we include it here for the sake of comparability.) XYZ's operating profit margin has been quite consistent over the past three years and is somewhat higher than industry averages. That could mean it is in for some competition or that it is exceptionally good at controlling costs. To zero in on the reasons for XYZ's better-than-average performance, relate cost of goods sold to sales and selling, general, and administrative expenses to sales. The explanation may lie in pricing policy or somewhere in the area of selling, general, and administrative expenses.

Net profit margin	$\dfrac{\text{Net income}}{\text{Net sales}}$	$\dfrac{10.1}{98.4} = 10.3\%$

This measures management's overall efficiency—its success not only in managing operations but in terms of borrowing money at a favorable rate, investing idle cash to produce extra income, and taking advantage of tax benefits. XYZ's ratio of 10.3% compares favorably with industry standards. A company in a field where the emphasis was on high volume—a supermarket, for instance—might show a net profit margin of much less—2% for example.

Return on equity	$\dfrac{\text{Net income}}{\text{Total stockholders' equity}}$	$\dfrac{10.1}{68.0} = 15\%$

This ratio measures the overall return on stockholders' equity. It is the bottom line measured against the money shareholders have invested. XYZ's 15% return is above average for the industry, which is good for shareholders as long as it doesn't invite competition.

Ratios That Measure Capitalization (Leverage)

Ratio	Calculation	XYZ Computation
Debt to total assets	$\dfrac{\text{Total liabilities}}{\text{Total assets}}$	$\dfrac{37.6}{105.6} = 36\%$

This measures the proportion of assets financed with debt as opposed to equity. Creditors, such as bankers, prefer that this ratio be low, since it means a greater cushion in the event of liquidation. Owners, on the other hand, may seek higher leverage in order to magnify earnings or may prefer to finance the company's activities through debt rather than yield control. XYZ's ratio is about average for its industry.

Ratio	Calculation	XYZ Computation
Long-term debt to total capitalization	$\dfrac{\text{Long-term debt}}{\text{Long-term debt + stockholders' equity}}$	$\dfrac{16.2}{68.0} = 24\%$

This ratio tells us the proportion of permanent financing that is represented by long-term debt versus equity. XYZ's ratio of 24% (24% of its permanent capital is debt) is low by industry standards, suggesting it might consider increasing its leverage—that is, financing its future growth through bonds rather than stock.

Ratio	Calculation	XYZ Computation
Debt to equity (debt ratio)	$\dfrac{\text{Total liabilities}}{\text{Total stockholders' equity}}$	$\dfrac{37.6}{68.0} = 55\%$

This is the basic ratio. It measures the reliance on creditors—short and long term—to finance total assets and becomes critical in the event of liquidation, when the proceeds from the sale of assets go to creditors before owners. Since assets tend to shrink in liquidation, the lower this ratio the more secure owners can feel. Also, a high debt ratio makes it more difficult to borrow should the need arise. XYZ's debt ratio of 55% is very conservative, and is another indication that its shareholders could safely benefit from greater leverage.

Ratio	Calculation	XYZ Computation
Times interest earned	$\dfrac{\text{Earnings before taxes and interest charges}}{\text{Interest charges}}$	$\dfrac{19.4}{1.0} = 19 \text{ times}$

This ratio measures the number of times fixed interest charges are covered by earnings. Since failure to meet interest payments would be an event of default under the terms of most debenture agreements, this coverage ratio indicates a margin of safety. Put another way, it indicates the extent to which earnings could shrink—in a recession, for example—before the firm became unable to meet its contractual interest charges. XYZ earns 19 times its annual interest payments, which is substantially more than is normally considered conservative. It is another indication that XYZ should consider increasing its leverage.

Ratio	Calculation	XYZ Computation
Fixed charge coverage	$\dfrac{\text{Earnings before taxes and interest charges}}{\text{Interest charges + lease payments}}$	$\dfrac{19.4}{1.0} = 19 \text{ times}$

This is the times interest earned ratio expanded to include other fixed charges, notably annual lease payments. XYZ has no lease obligations, so the ratio is the same. It is important to note, however, that the extent of this coverage should be sufficient to ensure that a company can meet its fixed contractual obligations in bad times as well as good times.

Ratios That Measure Stock Values

Ratio	Calculation	XYZ Computation
Price-earnings ratio	$\dfrac{\text{Market price of common share}}{\text{Earnings per common share}}$	$\dfrac{63.00}{6.30} = 10 \text{ times}$

This ratio reflects the value the marketplace puts on a company's earnings and the prospect of future earnings. It is important to shareholders because it represents the value of their holdings, and it is also important from the corporate standpoint in that it is an indication of the firm's cost of capital—the price it could expect to receive if it were to issue new shares. XYZs multiple of ten times earnings is about average for an established company.

Ratio	Calculation	XYZ Computation
Market-to-book ratio	$\dfrac{\text{Market price of common share}}{\text{Book value per share (total assets } - \text{ intangible assets } - \text{ total liabilities and preferred stock/common shares outstanding)}}$	$\dfrac{63.00}{40.00} = 1.58$ times

This indicates the value the market places on a firm's expected earnings—its value as a going concern—in relation to the value of its shares if the company were to be liquidated and the proceeds from the sale of assets, after creditor claims were satisfied, were paid to shareholders. XYZ's common shares have a market value that is half again as much as their value in liquidation, assuming its assets could be liquidated at book value.

Dividend payout ratio	$\dfrac{\text{Dividends per common share}}{\text{Earnings per common share}}$	$\dfrac{4.20}{6.30} = 67\%$

This ratio indicates the percentage of common share earnings that are paid out in dividends. As a general rule, young, growing companies tend to reinvest their earnings to finance expansion and thus have low dividend payout ratios or ratios of zero. XYZ's ratio of 67% is higher than most established companies show.

HOW TO READ A QUARTERLY REPORT

In addition to annual reports, publicly held companies issue interim reports usually on a quarterly basis, which update shareholders about sales and earnings and report any material changes in the company's affairs. Companies are also required to file quarterly information with the Securities and Exchange Commission on Form 10-Q within 45 days of the end of the first, second, and third fiscal quarters. These reports, which contain unaudited financial information and news of changes in securities outstanding, compliance with debt agreements, and matters to be voted on by shareholders, may be available from companies directly; at SEC libraries in Atlanta, Boston, Chicago, Denver, Fort Worth, Los Angeles, New York, Seattle, and the District of Columbia; or through firms that provide all SEC filings (and which advertise in the financial sections of newspapers).

Quarterly shareholder reports vary in comprehensiveness. Some reports provide complete, though usually unaudited, financial statements, but most simply contain summarized updates of the operating highlights of the annual report. Accounting regulations require that companies give at least the following information.

- Sales (or revenues)
- Net income (before and after potential dilution, if pertinent)
- Provision for federal income taxes
- Nonrecurring items of income or expense, with tax implications
- Significant acquisitions or disposals of business segments
- Material contingencies, such as pending lawsuits
- Accounting changes
- Significant changes in financial position, including working capital and capital structure

Accounting regulations require that figures be presented either for the quarter in question or cumulatively for the year-to-date, but prior year data must be included on a comparative basis. That requirement is designed to deal with seasonal factors. For example, the quarterly results of a department store, to cite an industry with marked seasonality (sales bulge at Christmastime), would be meaningless unless compared with the same quarter of the prior year.

The main thing to remember about quarterly reports is that they are designed to update existing shareholders, not to provide prospective shareholders with an overall perspective on the company. They should be read in conjunction with the annual report.

PART III

How to Read the
Financial Pages

How to Read Ticker Tapes

HOW TO READ THE FINANCIAL PAGES

Financial news is a swift-running stream that can be harnessed to power your investment decision-making—or drown you in a flood of statistics. Its volume has expanded greatly since the 1970s, following deregulation of the financial markets and other developments that increased public participation in a growing investment marketplace, prompting many of us to become our own money managers.

As a result, the financial press has staffed up and daily financial sections have been expanded and redesigned, often along the lines of *The New York Times* free-standing section. *The Wall Street Journal* added a second section. A relative newcomer, *Investor's Daily,* creates graphs from its computerized data base to show price movements of individual securities. *USA Today* uses innovative graphics to include as much financial information as possible in its pages.

The Financial Times of London responded to the growing appetite for foreign financial news by increasing its international distribution. *Barron's National Business and Financial Weekly,* long an important weekly source of information for professionals, became more consumer-oriented and added many useful tables and features not found elsewhere.

These and other financial publications have three major goals: (1) To pack as much news as possible into a given space; (2) to attract as many readers as possible; and (3) to allow busy readers to obtain a quick overview and/or easily find whatever specific information they are seeking. These aims are accomplished through packaging the news, and as readers, we must understand how this is done so we can unpackage it to suit ourselves.

THE FIRST PAGE

The outside of the news package—the first page of the financial section of a major daily general-interest newspaper or daily financial newspaper—is aimed at the broadest audience: the consumer, the investor, the civic minded, the curious—all of us, in one way or another. As you move to the inside pages, the information becomes more specific: reports on individual people, companies, markets. The tabular material is the most specific of all, and is included for readers who seek detail—a stock price, currency exchange rates, bond yield, corporate earnings report, or information on a new securities offering, for example. The outside of the package may contain, depending on news developments, one or more of the following elements.

The Digest

The digest presents major stories of the preceding day in summary form, along with summaries of the more important analytical feature stories from that day's newspaper. A good digest also gives you an idea of why an event was important, and what it could lead to. It will also tell you what page to turn to for the full story.

The Economics Story

The fact that a general economics story often appears on the front page of the package is a tribute to the sophistication and interest of the readership. It also reflects the fact that government economic data is scheduled for release well in advance, giving editors and reporters time to reserve space, pull out charts for updating, and line up experts to offer commentary. A monthly cycle of major statistics often starts with the release of data on construction spending and the employment situation (the latter generally is released on the first Friday of the month) and continues with statistics on chain-store sales, crop production, consumer installment credit, industrial production, capacity utilization, housing starts and building permits, producer (wholesale) prices, personal income and outlays, consumer prices, average hourly wages, savings flows, and other matters. The month often ends with a report on the indexes of leading, coincident, and lagging economic indicators. Most of the statistics refer to the previous month, some to two months before. Motor-vehicle manufacturers report on sales every ten days.

Important statistics are also released on a quarterly basis. These statistics include information on U.S. import and export prices, corporate profits, and—of particular significance—the gross national product (GNP). The GNP (especially its inflation-adjusted version, constant dollar or real GNP) is a measure of the total value of goods and services produced by the United States economy. Of key interest is how the seasonally adjusted annual growth rate of the GNP in a particular quarter compares to the previous quarter and to the same quarter in the previous year. Trends in the GNP are our primary measures of whether the U.S. economy is strong or weak, growing or in recession.

For investment purposes, watch for basic themes in overall stories on the economy. Favorable economic signals bode well for corporate profits, and therefore usually for stock prices, and unfavorable signals can have the opposite effect. A weakening economy can lift bond prices, however, because economic slackness means weaker demand for credit and thus lower rates for new loans, which translates into higher prices for existing bonds and notes. But one monthly figure doesn't make a trend, and other factors, including speculation about Federal Reserve Board monetary policy, also affect securities prices. In any event, between the time economic data is released and its appearance in newspapers, there has been ample opportunity for financial markets to react—to "discount the news," as they say on Wall Street. Most stock markets remained open until 4 P.M. EST the day before (the Pacific Stock Exchange closes 30 minutes later) while the bond market, which is mainly located in brokerage house trading rooms, has no official closing. Thus, the opportunity to react effectively to an economic event may have passed by the time you read of it in the newspaper.

The Interest Rate/Bond Market Story

As market interest rates move up or down, the prices of fixed income securities move in the opposite direction to adjust yields to market levels. Yield determines price, and vice versa. Thus, the daily bond market story is essentially an interest rate story. Major daily newspapers always reserve inside space for this story and move it to the outside of the financial package when warranted by major developments. The event could be a big move in bond values, a new prediction by a widely followed interest-rate forecaster, Congressional testimony or other action by the Federal Reserve Board (especially its chairman), or policy changes by foreign central banks. The bigger the development, the more attention will be focused on its significance to consumers—the prospect of higher or lower mortgage and personal borrowing costs, for instance. A complete story will also explain the significance of such news to investors and include comments by analysts and economists. The Federal Reserve's weekly report on the money supply (usually released on Thursday) provides much of the grist for late-week interest rate stories. If the money supply grows faster than the Federal Reserve had planned, the Fed may be tempted to adopt a restrictive monetary policy. That is, the Federal Reserve may reduce the amount of money in the economy to prevent a rise in inflation. Tighter money means higher interest rates, at least on short-term loans and securities, which usually exerts downward pressure on stock and bond prices. If the Fed thinks the money supply is growing too slowly, especially during an economic slowdown, the Fed could be expected to try to ease monetary policy and stimulate money growth. This often leads to lower interest rates and higher prices for fixed income securities, as well as to optimism and higher prices in the stock markets.

The Commodities Story

The roller coaster action in the prices of oil, gold, and silver in recent years helped make activity in the commodities markets a more frequent front-of-the-package story. When the commodities story gets front-page treatment, the consumer implications—for example, the effects on retail prices of gasoline or orange juice—will usually receive most attention. But there will also be economic and market forecasts and comments by professional analysts and traders, designed to inform investors about commodities futures or futures options contracts. Typical questions answered include: How fast has the price of the commodity futures contract reversed direction in the past? Are there new sources of supply that could affect prices—for example, soybeans from Brazil to replace those from Kansas, or beef from Argentina to replace meat from Texas? Is anything happening that could limit supply? What is the outlook for a political development causing activity in precious metals contracts?

The Takeover or Merger Story

Major takeover bids (called public tender offers) or merger announcements make big news partly because they have important implications for the securities prices of the companies involved. In a takeover or merger story look for (1) the price, total and per share, that's being offered for the target company. Also look at the form of payment—cash, securities, or a combination—and how it's being raised. A leveraged buyout, for instance, can sometimes leave the acquired company laden with debt. (2) The reasons for the merger—to combine businesses for greater financial or marketing strength; to avoid an unfriendly takeover; to bail out a troubled corporation, for example. An unfriendly or hostile tender offer could trigger a bidding war which would drive up the price of the target company's stock or legal action. Also, a large-scale takeover or merger runs the risk of antitrust action by the federal government in addition to other impediments. When takeover plans are set back or collapse, the price of the target's stock will most likely drop. (3) Comments by analysts on the acquirer's motives and management skills. A bid substantially above market could mean shares are undervalued or that the acquirer has exciting plans; particularly with reduced float, it might be wiser to hold than tender.

A complete takeover or merger story will also uncover what the risk arbitragers—professional traders who speculate in merger situations—are doing. Heavy buying of the stock of the takeover target combined with short selling of the shares of the acquirer, usually means the professionals think the takeover will succeed.

The Stock Market Story

This daily feature shifts to the front of the financial package when stock indexes undergo an especially big move. Although broader-based and more scientifically weighted indexes exist, the Dow Jones Industrial Average, which tracks 30 blue chip stocks, continues to be the most widely watched barometer and almost invariably is featured in the stock market story. A good roundup should give you the widest possible exploration of factors—the effect of other markets (bonds, commodities, currencies, and to an increased extent, stock options and financial futures), corporate earnings, takeover bids and merger rumors, economic developments, and changing market forecasts. The article should differentiate between different groups of stocks and different markets. The New York Stock Exchange activity often reflects buying and selling by institutional investors while the American Stock Exchange and over the counter (NASDAQ) markets reflect a higher proportion of activity by individual investors interested in less well-known growth stocks. Increasingly, market volatility is caused by program trades, the massive buying and selling by institutions and traders of all stocks in a program or index on which options or futures are traded. This phenomenon can create such drama on the third Friday of March, June, September, and December (when index options, index futures, and stock options expire together) that the closing that day has become known as the triple witching hour. A complete stock market story will usually include predictions by analysts who engage either in fundamental analysis, which focuses on business conditions and the financial strength of companies, or technical analysis, which concentrates on the conditions of the stock market, such as the supply and demand for shares and the emotional cycles of investors. Technical analysts, including those called chartists, are usually more willing than fundamentalists to predict near-term market movements for newspaper stories.

The Company Story

Sometimes company stories are the result of breaking news—a profit report, a takeover attempt, a new product—and sometimes they are features that have been planned, and even written, well in advance of publication. Newspapers often carry a company stock story as part of their regular stock market coverage or because it is an important company to the newpaper's readership (it has a plant in town, for instance). Because stories on publicly owned companies can influence market values, there are laws to prevent capitalizing on advance knowledge of their content.

Among the things that you, as an investor or potential investor in a company, want to learn are: (1) The nature of the company's business, and whether or not it's diversified or a one-product operation; the size of its customer base; whether it does business mainly with the government or with private firms; whether it relies heavily on exports and is therefore sensitive to fluctuations in the dollar's value; whether its sources of supply are secure; and whether it can easily pass costs on to consumers. (2) The amount of debt of the company relative to its overall capital and whether it plans to borrow funds, issue more shares, or pay back loans. Among other things, this financial information will tell you whether the value of shares you may already own will undergo dilution, which could reduce earnings per share and thus reduce the market value of shares. (3) The nature of the company's ownership. Is a substantial proportion of stock held by the company's founders or by its current management? Closely held companies cannot be taken over by unwelcome acquirers as easily as widely held companies, but that can also deprive shareholders of profits they might otherwise gain through public tender offers at premiums to market value. You should also be told if financial institutions own large blocks of shares; big institutional positions are an indication of how professional investors regard the company. In the case of companies with relatively few shares, however, that can also cause substantial price swings should institutions gobble up or dump large amounts of shares. Trends in insider or institutional ownership can be solid signals as to the prospects of a company—if top management is accumulating shares, they may know before the public about events that might cause the stock to rise. (4) Trends in the company's earnings history. How steady have profits been? Have they been increasing on a per-share basis? Is the company emerging from a period of weakness? Are earnings mainly the result of ongoing operations or of one-time extraordinary items, such as the sale of company property? (5) Trends in dividend payments.

The Industry Story

You'll find many of the same elements of a company story in an industry story, and you will in addition have the opportunity to look at one company in relation to others. These stories are often accompanied by charts comparing companies in an industrial sector (computer chip makers, retailers, or utilities, for instance) according to sales, per-share earnings, stock price range, recent stock price, price-earnings ratio, and other important data.

Advertisements

Throughout the financial pages of most newspapers—even on the front page— you will find advertisements for bank deposit instruments, mutual funds, and other investments. Early in the year many advertisements for individual retirement accounts appear. Some ads include order forms and encourage you to send a check— sometimes for a hefty amount—right away. Mutual funds and sponsors of other publicly offered securities, however, can't accept an investment from you without first sending you a prospectus. A mutual fund sometimes will print the prospectus as part of the advertisement. Never react impulsively to an attractive rate or yield or special deal. It is difficult to compare rates, yields, and terms because each situation is unique and different institutions use various methods to compute yields. Some have withdrawal penalties and other restrictions that might not be obvious in the ad.

You will also find advertisements for financial publications, advisory newsletters, and computer databases and software, among other products. Often these products can be very helpful, but it is usually best to request a sample or a demonstration to make sure the product suits your needs.

SCANNING THE INSIDE FINANCIAL PAGES

You can get a quick picture of current financial events and trends by scanning the financial pages. The news digest, already discussed, is a good starting point. The inside pages are peppered with daily, weekly, or monthly charts and graphs to give you a snapshot of aspects of business and economics. Among the items that appear in many newspapers are the following:

Stock Market Arrow Box

This simple but telling illustration shows you the general direction of the New York Stock Exchange on the previous day. The illustration will vary somewhat from newspaper to newspaper, but in our illustration the number next to the upward-pointing arrow indicates the number of issues that rose on the NYSE, the downward-pointing arrow indicates the number of issues that fell, and the number in the middle shows the number of issues that remained unchanged. When more stocks advance than decline, it is considered a favorable or bullish sign. When declines outnumber advances, it is considered an unfavorable or bearish indication. Below the arrow box are major indexes measuring stock prices—the NYSE composite index, Standard & Poor's composite index (the S&P 500), and the Dow Jones Industrial Average, along with their closing level and change from the previous trading day. The three indexes are based on different groups of stocks, and analysts may draw significance if the percentage change varies considerably between two indexes or among all three. If the indexes move in tandem, on the other hand, they are usually said to reveal or underscore a trend. Below the indexes the trading volume of NYSE-listed shares is broken down by the number of shares exchanged on the NYSE and on regional stock exchanges and the NASDAQ system.

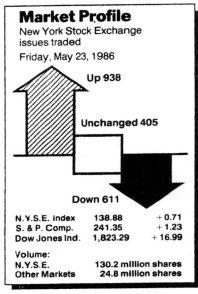

Market Profile
New York Stock Exchange issues traded

Friday, May 23, 1986

Up 938

Unchanged 405

Down 611

N.Y.S.E. Index	138.88	+ 0.71
S. & P. Comp.	241.35	+ 1.23
Dow Jones Ind.	1,823.29	+ 16.99

Volume:
N.Y.S.E.	130.2 million shares
Other Markets	24.8 million shares

An advantage of the arrow box is that you see at a glance how the NYSE, which has a broad impact on finance, performed the day before. A disadvantage is that you don't see what happened on other important stock markets, notably the American Stock Exchange and NASDAQ, which may not have moved in the same direction as the NYSE. And, of course how the NYSE performed doesn't tell you how particular stocks fared.

Earnings Reports

Quarterly profit reports for corporations are carried in major newspapers like *The New York Times* or *Wall Street Journal* as well as in many other newspapers. In most cases, the abbreviated reports appear in one place, and include the latest sales, net income, net income per share, and shares outstanding, compared with the year-earlier figures. Using year-earlier comparisons rather than comparisons with the previous quarter excludes purely seasonal fluctuations. Department stores, for example, as a rule report the most sales in the fourth quarter, owing to the Christmas season. Comparing the fourth and third quarters, therefore, might give an inaccurate impression of the health of a department-store chain. It is very important also to look at earnings on a per-share basis. Per-share earnings, more than total earnings, are a major determinant of stock prices.

By the time you read the brief earnings reports, the stock market usually has had time to react, since the reports are usually released during trading hours. Occasionally, a company releases earnings after the close of trading, and you may see the price of the stock market react to the news when trading resumes. (Some companies release disappointing earnings late Friday in the hope they will be overlooked or their impact lessened because of the two-day break in trading.)

XYZ PRODUCTS (N)

Qtr to March 31	1986	1985
Revenue	$5,600,000	$4,980,000
Net income	463,000	452,000
Share earns	.22	.22
Shares outstanding	2,100,000	2,050,000

Dividend Reports

Lists of quarterly dividends, organized alphabetically by corporation, appear in greater number during the third through fifth weeks of each calendar quarter when earnings reports are most numerous. The dividend reports are generally divided into categories: Irregular, Increased, Reduced, and Regular. The organization of columns looks like this:

DIVIDEND REPORTS

		Regular		
	Period	Rate	Stk of Record	Pay able
XYZ Corp.	Q	.30	4-10	4-30

The table tells you that the regular dividend for the hypothetical XYZ Corporation is paid quarterly, that the dividend is 30 cents per share (which would result in $1.20 per share annually if the rate held steady), that the dividend will be paid to shareowners of record April 10, and that the actual payment will be made on April 30. It's important to remember that stocks go ex-dividend during the interval between the dividend announcement and the actual payment. This means that the dividend isn't payable to investors who buy the stock during that interval. (On the other hand, if you sell the stock during the ex-dividend period, you still collect the dividend.) Shares listed on the NYSE generally go ex-dividend four days before the stockholder of record date. Stocks normally decline by the amount of the dividend when they enter an ex-dividend trading period.

Securities Offerings

Announcements of newly issued or about-to-be issued stocks and bonds come in two forms. Large newspapers include calendars and digests of expected and newly announced securities issues to be distributed by underwriting groups or syndicates. These groups of investment banking houses also place paid advertisements, known as tombstones in the language of Wall Street, which give a very basic summary of the offerings. (Tombstone ads are also used for other purposes, such as announcing major personnel changes or a firm's important role in an acquisition or merger.)

The newspaper listings come under such headings as Finance Briefs (*The New York Times*) or Financing Business (*The Wall Street Journal*). Because a high proportion of the offerings are bonds, these listings can usually be found near the bond tables and the interest rate/bond market news story.

One advantage of buying new issues (which are often reserved for favored customers) over buying existing securities, is that the buyer pays no commission. The broker-dealer is paid out of the underwriting spread, the difference between the price at which the securities are sold to the public and the lower price paid to the issuer by the underwriters. Even if you're not interested in purchasing securities, these notices give you an idea of the prevailing interest rates (in the case of bonds) and the types of companies that are able to attract capital by issuing shares.

New Issue   October 2, 19--

750,000 Shares

ABXY Corporation

**Common Stock
($.10 par value)**

Price $30 per Share

First XYZ Inc.

MNO Inc.

TUV Securities

ABC Inc.   CDE & Co.   Monopoly Inc.

Ajax Inc.   Dustby Inc.   ZXZ Inc.

HIJ Securities

In the accompanying illustration of a typical tombstone ad, the boilerplate (standard legal language) advises you to read the the prospectus before you buy. Many investors, of course, simply rely on the word of their brokers anyway, but the prospectus is a legally required summary of the facts and risks concerning the issue, and investors are well-advised to read it. The tombstone lists the names of the firms comprising the underwriting group and, by alphabetically organized groups, the relative importance of their participation. The par value of the stock, if any, is usually listed, but has no meaning in terms of market value. The offering price, of course, is included; however, this announcement doesn't tell you anything more, for example, how the proceeds of the sale are to be used.

Tender Offer Announcements

In both friendly and unfriendly takeover situations, the advertisements placed by corporations soliciting your shares may offer the greatest source of practical information regarding what you should or could do with your shares. Among other things, these comprehensive tombstone type notices identify the company seeking to acquire another company; state the price being offered for your shares and whether payment will be in cash or securities or a combination of the two; inform you of various deadlines to send in your shares or to withdraw your offer; and announce various other conditions, such as the minimum number of shares the acquiring company requires for the deal to be completed. These notices also include the names of companies that act as soliciting and information agents, such as D.F. King & Co., Georgeson & Co., or the Carter Organization, along with their addresses and phone numbers. Such companies have been paid to provide you with information and prospectuses. Of course, these ads can also be biased and are often followed in a few days with ads placed by the target company, citing reasons to reject the bid.

Redemption Notices

Callable bonds and preferred stock can be redeemed by the issuer prior to maturity, and the likelihood of this happening is greatest when the issuer can replace them with new securities providing lower interest rate or dividends. When redemption takes place, issuers often place paid notices in a local newspaper and/or a major publication, such as *The Wall Street Journal*. These notices provide the serial numbers and demoninations of the securities being redeemed and the call price of the securities.

Short Interest

Around the twentieth of each month, the New York and American stock exchanges release data on short interest—shares sold when they are not actually owned by the seller (usually they are borrowed). The exchanges break down the statistics by individual stocks and also give a total number of shorted shares of their listed companies compared to the total the month before.

Short interest figures generally signify that professional investors anticipate a decline in share prices. However, the figures are somewhat inflated by the inclusion of the short positions of exchange floor specialists; they sell short as part of their stabilizing function as well as for investment purposes. Market analysts also view large short interest positions as potential buying pressure since short positions must ultimately be covered by purchasing shares.

Interest Rate Charts

These charts give you a general idea of borrowing costs and the value of fixed-income securities. Rising rates depress prices of fixed-income investments, and falling rates boost their value. A typical daily chart looks like this:

INTEREST RATES

	In Percent		
	Yesterday	Previous Day	Year Ago
Prime Rate	9.50	9.50	10.50
Discount Rate	7.50	7.50	8.00
Federal Funds	7.88	7.95	8.73
3-Mo. Treasury Bills	6.96	7.09	8.73
6-Mo. Treasury Bills	7.01	7.05	8.80
7-Yr. Treasury Notes	7.88	8.03	11.75
30-Yr. Treasury Bonds	8.10	8.30	11.90
Telephone Bonds	9.34	9.43	12.89
Municipal Bonds	7.92	8.03	10.39

The prime rate, which is the rate banks charge their most creditworthy customers for short-term loans, and the discount rate, which is the rate the Federal Reserve Bank charges member banks for short-term loans, don't fluctuate daily. The other rates and yields (most of these numbers are yields—the percentage return based on the price of a fixed-income security, combined with its annual interest rate) do change daily, making a comparison of the yesterday and previous day columns worthwhile. The year ago column gives you an idea of the longer-term trend in both rates and fixed-income security values.

Prime Rate   This gives businesspeople an idea of basic borrowing costs. Most bank customers pay more than the prime rate for short-term loans, although the rate charged is based on the prime and often floats with it. Because the prime rate is adjusted only when money market conditions have changed significantly, a change in the prime rate is usually considered a major event and is interpreted as a harbinger of rising or falling loan demand and economic activity. Securities prices are thus affected by changes or expected changes in this bellwether rate.

Discount Rate   Like the prime rate, the discount rate doesn't change often. It is one of the means the Federal Reserve Board has of tightening or easing the growth of the money supply, and it is used judiciously. Therefore, when the Federal Reserve Board makes a change, it's considered a major event and can be expected to have an impact on securities prices, especially bonds. While cuts in the discount rate are usually aimed at stimulating the economy—a positive development for stocks—they could also reflect a degree of concern on the part of the Fed about weakness in the economy. This could, depending on circumstances, undermine the securities markets. The value of stocks and bonds often depends on how far into the future investors are willing to look when they interpret the meaning of rate changes.

Federal Funds   This rate on short-term loans of funds between banks fluctuates, especially every other Wednesday when banks must have their books in order to meet proper reserve levels (some banks borrow to comply with reserve requirements). The Fed influences this rate by setting bank reserves levels and by open market operations. Federal funds rates are thus considered a reflection of Federal Reserve policy and accordingly can have an impact on stock and bond prices.

3-month Treasury Bills   This yield is a closely watched indicator of the direction of short-term rates. The 3-month T-bill rate also gives you an idea of the anticipated changes in rates paid by banks on deposits and in charges for adjustable rate credit.

6-month Treasury Bills   The significance of this yield is very similar to that of 3-month T-bills. Ordinarily, yields on 6-month T-bills should be a little higher than those on 3-month bills, issued at the same time since investors' money is tied up for a longer term.

7-year Treasury Notes   This yield gives you an idea of the prevailing rates for intermediate term fixed-income securities. Yields on corporate and other non-Treasury securities, which aren't as safe, will be appropriately higher than those of this risk-free benchmark.

30-year Treasury bonds   This is probably the most widely watched bond yield. It is also referred to as the long bond yield. The entire bond market, and sometimes the stock market as well, often moves in step with changes in the price of 30-year Treasuries, which move in the opposite direction of their yield.

Telephone Bonds   Newspaper rate charts typically use a top-rated telephone company or utility bond yield as a benchmark for corporate bond yields in general. Yields on most other corporate bonds will be higher because they are not considered as safe.

Municipal Bonds   This yield is often taken from an index of municipal bonds produced by a major brokerage like Merrill Lynch or Salomon Brothers or by the *Bond Buyer,* a trade paper for municipal bond issuers, underwriters, and dealers. If the yields rise, your municipal bond portfolio has probably dropped in value. If yields drop, the opposite is most likely the case. Since the interest paid on municipals has traditionally been partly or wholly tax free, municipal-bond investors have been willing to accept lower yields than they would on fully taxable long-term securities.

Major newspapers usually carry additional lists of rates mainly of interest to professional traders. These include rates for Eurodollar time deposits, bankers acceptances, and commercial paper, as well as the London Interbank Offered Rate (LIBOR). Another listing, the broker loan rate (or call loan rate), the rate brokers pay banks for overnight loans to cover securities positions of customers, has considerable importance to individual investors, too, because it determines what brokerages charge customers for margin loans.

Some major newspapers, such as *The Wall Street Journal* and *Barron's,* carry weekly listings of the banks currently offering the highest interest rates on deposit accounts and certificates of deposit.

Other Economic and Financial Indicators

Among the more common weekly graphic features relating to business activity, securities prices, and returns on your savings are the following:

Treasury Bill Bar Chart: This appears in many newspapers, usually on Tuesday, following the Treasury bill auction of the preceding day. This table of 3-month Treasury bill yields shows how discount rates have changed on a weekly basis over the past three months, and gives the year-earlier yield as well. This chart gives you an idea of the direction in which rates on adjustable rate mortgages are heading, and whether you'll earn more or less income from a money market fund or an adjustable rate CD.

Money Supply Chart: This type of chart appears on Friday, following the weekly report on the nation's money supply released by the Federal Reserve Board at 4:30 P.M. EST on Thursday. The chart contains a "cone," made up of diverging lines that indicate the upper and lower targets of money supply growth laid down by the Federal Reserve Board. If the line representing M–1 money supply growth moves above the cone, watch out for jittery speculation about tighter monetary policy— speculation that could hurt bond prices. If the M–1 line is below the cone, be prepared for speculation that the Federal Reserve Board intends to loosen monetary policy and push rates lower—speculation that often supports bond prices. M–1, however, fluctuates week to week because it's narrowly based. Broader measures of the money supply, M–2 and M–3, are reported monthly, and articles often include similar charts for these figures.

Gold Prices: Gold receives more daily attention in the press than most other commodities because many experts consider it to be:

1. A measure of inflationary expectations. Gold is often used by investors as a hedge against inflation, because, in the past at least, it has often increased in value in times of severe inflation.

2. A measure of international tension. International financial crises, wars, and the threat of war often cause investors and speculators to bid up the price of bullion and bullion futures contracts.

3. A measure of confidence in the dollar. Gold is now considered an alternative investment to the dollar. If the dollar weakens, the chances of gold prices rising, or at least holding steady, often improve.

Gold prices may be given as follows:

GOLD PRICES

Comex Thurs.	(In U.S. dollars per troy ounce) London PM Thurs.	London AM Thurs.	Comex Wed.
337.30	336.90	337.85	336.40

The two largest gold markets are the Commodity Exchange (Comex) in New York and the London network of gold dealers, which is considered a single market. This type of chart gives you a 24-hour view, starting with the most recent Comex close on the left and proceeding to earlier price quotations in London and the previous day's Comex close. The Comex close is actually a settlement price determined shortly after trading ends, and represents the futures contract set to expire soonest, the so-called nearest month contract. The London prices represent the morning and afternoon gold fixings.

Commodity Index: The Commodity Reserach Bureau Index that tracks 27 commodity prices is often placed at the head of the commodities tables. The index may look like this:

COMMODITY INDEX

Today	Previous Day	Year Ago
211.9	209.04	238.6

This table gives you a one-year perspective on prices—everything from grain to gold—and perhaps an idea about inflationary trends. Lower commodity prices, for example, can signal lower inflation, which in turn can lead to lower interest rates and yields and higher bond prices. The disadvantage of this table is that it doesn't provide insights into the daily fluctuations of specific commodities.

Dollar Indexes: The Federal Reserve Board and Morgan Guaranty Trust Co. compile indexes of the value of the dollar. The Federal Reserve's index, for example, is included at the bottom of the currency table in *The New York Times,* and includes the previous two days' indexes along with the year-earlier number. The average of 10 other major currencies' dollar value, weighted according to the various countries' trade activity with the U.S., is an important resource for those who want to try to discern the trend of the dollar for business purposes or for overseas investments.

Currency Exchange Rates: We've come to appreciate much more keenly the effect of varying currency exchange rates. When the dollar becomes stronger, that is, when it buys more British pounds, West German marks, Japanese yen, and so on, it becomes cheaper in terms of dollars to travel and shop abroad, to import foreign goods, and to buy foreign stocks and bonds. On the other hand, companies (and their shares) based in the United States may suffer under such conditions because cheaper imported goods can hurt the sale of those produced in the United States. When the dollar becomes weaker, that is, when it buys fewer units of foreign currencies and foreign currencies buy more dollars, the cost of foreign travel and imports rise while U.S. exports become more competitive in world markets. The prices of foreign securities, in terms of dollars, rise. Investing in foreign stock markets often means tracking the value of the dollar.
    A quick view of major currency fluctuations may be provided as follows:

CURRENCY RATES

	New York Thurs.	Home Mkt. Thurs. (In U.S. dollars)	New York Wed.
British pound	1.4700	1.4795	1.4840
Canadian dollar	0.7066	0.7062	0.7161
(In foreign units to U.S. dollar)			
French franc	6.8105	6.7920	6.7343
Japanese yen	180.60	178.60	181.10
Swiss franc	1.8725	1.8665	1.8805
West German mark	2.2153	2.2085	2.2285

The dollar loses value when a unit of foreign currency buys more dollars or a dollar buys fewer units of foreign currency. The dollar rises in value when a unit of foreign currency buys fewer dollars or a dollar buys more units of foreign currency.

The British pound and Canadian dollar are often quoted in U. S. dollars. For this reason, the currency rate table is set up as it is. (Currency tables vary somewhat from newspaper to newspaper.) The accompanying table shows a rising dollar as you move from the most recent New York late price (actually, there's never an official close to this market, only late-day prices) the previous day to the earlier price (except for Canada, which operates in the same timeframe as the United States) in the home market and the previous day's price in New York.

For most other foreign currencies, prices are expressed in terms of the amount of foreign currency that can be bought with a dollar. In this table, the dollar buys more French francs in New York as time progresses (the dollar is "up" against the French franc) while it buys fewer Japanese yen, Swiss francs, and West German marks.

Major publications usually carry full exchange tables, listed alphabetically by country, which provide the previous two days' exchange rates in four columns—two in terms of dollars per unit of foreign currency, and two in terms of units of foreign currency per dollar.

THE STOCK MARKETS: DAILY SUMMARIES

Key Stock Market Indexes and Charts

It's possible for all but the busiest person to get a quick overview of stock market activity—and even some sense of future market movement—by reviewing the key market indexes and charts clustered at the beginning of the daily stock tables. At first, the mass of figures may overwhelm you. But you can train your eyes and brain to march through such displays, dividing them into mentally digestible components. The principal displays of *The Wall Street Journal* appears on the inside back page. The Market Indicators package of *The New York Times,* shown here, appears at the beginning of its New York Stock Exchange listings. It can be broken down as follows:

> *Charts 1 to 4* These sets of market indexes for the NYSE (1), Amex (2), and NASDAQ (3) and Value Line and Wilshire Associates indexes (4—they include stocks listed on all three markets) are price averages. They simply tell you in which direction the overall group of stocks each covers moved during the most recent trading session. The NYSE receives the most attention, with its list tracked by three families of indexes: the Dow Jones, Standard & Poor's, and the exchange's own NYSE composite. A composite index includes all the stocks traded on a particular market. A narrower index, such as those that appear here for utilities or transportation shares, tracks relatively few stocks. Utility and financial stocks are sensitive to interest rate changes—and by extension—to the bond market because these industries depend on huge amounts of credit. Therefore, pluses for these indexes immediately indicate the likelihood that the rate situation is stable or improving. Scanning the pluses and minuses in the various markets tells you if the previous day's movements were broadly based or varied from one market to another. Declines for the Amex and NASDAQ next to rising indexes for the NYSE may indicate that institutional investors are more optimistic than individual investors.

Charts 5 and 6   Volume can help you determine in which direction the stock market will continue to move. If stock prices rise amid heavy volume, the indication is that many investors chose to invest heavily in stocks, and they intend to hold out for further price rises. Similarly, a market drop on heavy volume is considered a more serious setback than a drop on light volume. A market rise on light volume will cause the market rise to be questioned. The trick, of course, is to have an idea of what normal volume is for any given exchange during any particular season. Both *The New York Times* and *The Wall Street Journal* carry bar charts that indicate daily volume for the NYSE for the past three months and six months, respectively.

Charts 7 to 9   Called Market Diary here, these figures, like the volume numbers, help you confirm or doubt the validity of changes in the price index. If, for example, the indexes have risen sharply in one of the markets, but the number of issues that advanced are fairly evenly matched with the number of issues that declined, it's possible that the movement of a few stocks was responsible for the rising indexes. Thus, the market isn't as strong as it first appeared. Similarly, the number of stocks that hit 52-week highs during the session indicates how strong the market really was. Major financial sections and publications carry lists of stocks that hit 52-week highs and lows. Obviously, you want to know if any of your stocks are included on these lists.

Charts 10 to 12   The most active issues—stocks with the heaviest trading volume—are given in the descending order of shares traded for each issue—15 for the NYSE and 10 each for the Amex and NASDAQ markets. Sometimes stocks appear on the most active list because of a news items or a rumor regarding profits, mergers, or new products. Some stocks, however, constantly appear because they are actively traded by financial institutions, which often are restricted to buying stocks with large market capitalizations (the number of outstanding shares times the market price).

Charts 13 to 15   Because up and down price changes are expressed in percentage terms, you can get a quick idea of the importance of your gain or loss if one of your stocks appears on this list. Cheaper stocks are more apt to be included on this list, since small point changes translate into bigger percentage changes for cheaper stocks than for expensive ones. The list may also help you find (or avoid) volatile stocks.

Chart 16   The up and down share volume helps you gauge the daily strength and weakness of the NYSE and Amex. The Advanced column presents the number of shares in each market that were rising when they changed hands, while the Declined column indicates the number of shares sold below the price of the previous sale. Shares sold at the same price are not included. These figures can signal an underlying weakness or strength often masked by the indexes. If stocks rose according to the indexes, but were sold on "weakness" (that is, when the shares were dropping) rather than on "strength" (that is, on rising prices), this could mean that investors were using an overall price rise to take their profits and get out.

Chart 17   Odd-lots, usually stock transactions of fewer than 100 shares, indicate what small investors are doing. Although unflattering to small

MARKET INDICATORS

N.Y.S.E. Issues

Consolidated Trading

(1)

Dow Jones Stock Averages

	Open	High	Low	Close	Chg.
30 Industrials	1812.25	1842.14	1804.69	1823.29	+16.99
20 Transports	796.25	803.97	790.73	797.96	+ 2.94
15 Utilities	183.78	185.54	182.65	184.35	+ 0.67
65 Stocks	703.46	713.10	699.81	706.71	+ 4.96

S.&P. Index

	High	Low	Close	Chg.
400 Indust	270.52	268.21	269.49	+ 1.28
20 Transpt	204.21	202.83	203.85	+ 0.93
40 Utilities	103.78	103.04	103.44	+ 0.34
40 Financl	29.60	29.18	29.54	+ 0.36
500 Stocks	242.16	240.12	241.35	+ 1.23

N.Y.S.E. Index

	High	Low	Last	Chg.
Composite	139.23	138.69	138.88	+0.71
Industrial	160.82	160.31	160.37	+0.76
Transport	123.68	123.31	123.51	+0.39
Utility	69.20	69.05	69.05	+0.21
Finance	154.04	152.89	153.84	+1.65

(10)

Most Active

	Vol.	Last	Chg.
Noeast Util	8,217,800	19¾	+ ⅛
DartKrft	1,929,300	59	+1½
IBM	1,667,200	143⅞	+ ½
Interfst	1,641,500	7⅜	....
Amer T&T	1,632,200	24⅝	− ⅛
EstKodak	1,335,200	58⅞	+ ⅞
IrvngBk	1,300,800	54⅞	+1¼
DominResc	1,247,600	39	+ ¼
Phila Elec	1,091,100	17⅝	....
Safeway	1,076,200	44¾	+2½
MorganJP	1,057,400	88½	+1½
Chrysler s	991,300	37¾	−1⅛
McDermInt	976,700	19⅞	+ ⅞
Comw Edis	973,200	30	− ⅜
GenElec	919,700	79⅞	+1⅞

(13)

Changes—Up

	Last	Chg.	Pct.
Tricentrl	2⅛	+ ¼	13.3
HarprRow s	22½	+ 2⅛	10.4
GalvstHou	2¾	+ ¼	10.0
Pier 1 Inc	24	+ 2⅛	9.7
McDrmInt wt	3	+ ¼	9.1
SwstForest	14⅛	+ 1⅛	8.7
Kollmor	18⅝	+ 1⅜	8.0
TitanCp	10⅝	+ ¾	7.6
StPacCp s	32¼	+ 2⅛	7.1
WinterJack	9½	+ ⅝	7.0

Changes—Down

	Last	Chg.	Pct.
viAmfesco	4	− ½	11.1
WyleLabs	14	− 1⅝	10.4
LLCCorp	2⅜	− ¼	9.5
RiverOak	2⅜	− ¼	9.5
IntegRsc	24	− 2⅜	9.0
SuaveShoe	9½	− ⅞	8.4
StgdBusin	14¼	− 1¼	8.1
Ensource s	8⅜	− ⅝	6.9
StorageEqt	14⅛	− ⅞	5.8
HowellCp	10⅞	− ⅝	5.4

(5)

Volume by Exchanges

Markets	Shares
NYSE	130,160,000
Pacific	4,196,800
Midwest	8,848,200
NASD	5,731,940
Boston	2,611,300
Cinci	272,800
Phila	3,091,350
Instinet	49,300
Total	154,961,690

Volume Comparisons

Day's Sales	130,160,000
Thursday's Sales	144,920,000
Year Ago	85,970,000
1986 to Date	14,345,842,116
1985 to Date	10,925,327,587

(7)

Market Diary

	Today	Prev.
Advanced	938	1218
Declined	611	452
Unchanged	405	360
Total issues	1954	2030
New highs	118	101
New lows	7	11

(16)

Up-Down Share Volume

	Advanced	Declined
N.Y.S.E.	79,588,960	33,487,900
Amex	5,593,630	5,985,415

(17)

Odd-Lot Trading

Previous Day's Trading

purchases of 317,956 shares; sales of 443,910 shares including 13,203 sales sold short.

FRIDAY, May 23, 1986

Amex Issues
Consolidated Trading

(2) **Market Value Index**

High	Low	Close	Chg.
278.15	275.99	277.98	+1.76

(6) **Volume Comparisons**

Day's Sales	13,705,055
Thursday's Sales	12,624,355
Year Ago	5,393,165
1986 to Date	1,327,554,684
1985 to Date	871,375,140

(8) **Market Diary**

	Today	Prev
Advanced	339	324
Declined	241	241
Unchanged	214	259
Total issues	794	824
New highs	44	31
New lows	6	5

(11) **Most Active**

	Vol.	Last	Chg.
DomePtrl	2,331,800	1	–3-16
Wickes	1,198,900	6¼	....
AmExpFFd wt	600,700	4⅝	+ ⅛
Hasbro	438,700	49	– ⅜
FtAustPr n	400,900	10⅜	– ⅛
TexasAirCp	394,400	33⅝	+1¼
ICH Cp s	381,000	25	+ ⅞
LorimarTel n	368,500	30⅛	–1⅝
WangLabB	306,100	16⅞	– ⅛
BAT Ind	275,900	5⅞	+3-16

(14) **Changes—Up**

	Last	Chg.	Pct.
Kidde wt	4⅛	+ ⅝	17.9
UnivPat	17⅜	+ 2⅜	15.8
RBW Cp	9⅜	+ 1¼	15.4
Foote Minl	9¼	+ 1⅛	13.8
Pier 1 Inc wt	18½	+ 2¼	13.8
DWG Corp	2¼	+ ¼	12.5
UnFoodsA	2½	+ ¼	11.1
UnFoodsB	2½	+ ¼	11.1
ConStor s	35¼	+ 3½	11.0
Vintage Ent	3⅞	+ ⅜	10.7

Changes—Down

	Last	Chg.	Pct
Shopwell s	30½	– 4⅛	11.9
ActonCp	2	– ¼	11.1
Hinderliter	4⅝	– ½	9.8
WinnEntB	4	– ⅜	8.6
TriangCp	14¾	– 1¼	7.8
LSB Ind	3	– ¼	7.7
GrandAuto	19⅝	– 1½	7.1
MatecCp	5	– ⅜	7.0
MountMed	6⅞	– ½	6.8
VircoMf	21	– 1½	6.7

Over-the-Counter
Nasdaq Quotes

Index (3)

Index	Close.	Chg.	Week Ago.	Month Ago.
Composite	391.91	+2.29	384.67	392.34
Indust	399.56	+2.12	391.92	399.93
NMS Comp	166.60	+0.97	163.49	166.98
NMS Inds	150.06	+0.78	147.15	150.42

Market Diary (9)

Advanced	1,242
Declined	771
Unchanged	2,219
Total issues	4,232
New highs	203
New lows	29
Total sales	115,107,000

Most Active (12)

Name	Volume	Last or Bid	Asked	Chg.
Quotrn	1,897,800	18⅞		– ⅛
Intecm	1,261,900	5 9-16		....
Intel	1,002,900	25⅝		– ¾
Seagate	886,000	12⅝		– ½
MCI	878,300	10		....
Tandem	822,100	31¼		–1⅝
Beechm	813,500	6	6 1-16	....
GlaxH s..	728,500	14¾	14⅞	....
BearAu	719,500	13⅝	13⅞	+ ⅛
DSC	712,800	11⅛		+ ⅛

Changes—Up (15)

	Last	Chg.	Pct.
ClinicalDta	2½	+ ⅝	33.3
Sequel	3¼	+ ¾	30.0
Neurotech	2⅜	+ ½	26.7
Supradur	9½	+ 2	26.7
EnvirnPrc	2½	+ ½	25.0
BrilundLtd	3	+ 9/16	23.1
InfoSolu	4	+ ¾	23.1
WespacInv 2	2¾	+ ½	22.2
AveryInc	6¼	+ 1⅛	22.0
AdvanTob	4½	+ ¾	20.0

Changes—Down

	Last	Chg	Pct.
MktSyst un	7⅛	– 1⅞	20.8
ChemLawn	21¾	– 5	18.7
AmRestaur	3⅜	– ½	12.9
ECI Telcm	5¼	– ¾	12.5
PionrCm un	3¾	– ½	11.8
Kaypro	2	– ¼	11.1
VanzettiSy	3½	– ⅜	9.7
Finalco	3	– 5/16	9.4
VuittonL	38	– 3⅞	9.3
CueInd	2½	– ¼	9.1

Other Indexes (4)

NEW YORK (AP) — The Value Line Index of 1,685 NYSE, American and OTC stocks was 242.31 Friday, up 1.02 or 0.42 percent from Thursday. A year ago the index was 198.29.

SANTA MONICA, Calif. (AP) — The Wilshire Associates' 5,000 Equity Index, the market value of 5,000 NYSE, American and OTC issues, was $2,491.752 billion Friday up $12.805 billion or 0.52 percent from Thursday. A year ago the index was $1,931.417 billion.

investors, odd-lot buying or selling is used by contrarian analysts as an example of what *not* to do. In other words, odd-lotters are widely believed to be wrong more often than right. When the proportion of odd-lot short sales rises above normal levels, many analysts predict an imminent market rally. Note that this data, which encompasses NYSE trading, appears two days after the session to which the statistics refer, rather than on the day following the session.

New York Stock Exchange and American Stock Exchange Consolidated Tables

You have to reach into stock tables to find specific information. Stock tables remain the heart of daily financial publications and sections, although the commodity, options, and bond tables are becoming increasingly more important as readers become more familiar with other types of investments. The tables for the two major New York City stock exchanges, the New York and American stock exchanges, follow the same format. The information in each encompasses consolidated trading, which also includes trading on regional exchanges and on the over-the-counter market. Starting with the name of each stock, which we'll call Column 1, the tables offer:

1. Name It's not always easy to locate a particular stock, because the names are usually radically abbreviated. The abbreviation systems used by the Associated Press and United Press International, which supply most of the tables you see, are different (and not to be confused with stock ticker symbols used on the exchanges); thus, the alphabetical order will differ from one system to the other. Stocks like IBM and AT&T are easy to find; few investors, however, would know immediately that WTPTP is West Point Pepperell. Unless otherwise identified, these are names of common stock. A ''pf'' identifies preferred stock. Preferred stocks that are convertible to common shares are identified as preferred stock, but the convertability feature is not indicated in the stock tables as it is in the corporate bond tables. A ''v'' indicates that trading was suspended in the primary market. Stock tables are usually accompanied by explanatory notes defining any letters that may appear. An ''A,'' ''B,'' or other capital letter differentiates between one class of stock and another. A ''wt'' identifies the security as a warrant. A ''vj'' indicates that the company is in bankruptcy proceedings, and ''wi'' means when issued, signifying that the shares have not yet been issued. If the issuance is canceled, the trades will also be canceled. Also included but not identified are exchange-listed American Depositary Receipts (ADRs), which are negotiable receipts representing shares of foreign issuers.

NEW YORK STOCK EXCHANGE

⑨		①	②	③	④	⑤	⑥		⑦	⑧
52-Week				**Yid**	**PE**	**Sales**				
High	**Low**	**Stock**	**Div**	**%**	**Ratio**	**100s**	**High**	**Low**	**Last**	**Chg.**
25	18	XYZ Corp.	.92	2.0	7	623	17⅜	17⅛	17⅜	+ ⅛

2. Annual dividend Dividends are listed by dollars and cents per share. Don't confuse this figure with the amount you'll receive in the mail each quarter. The annual dividend is an estimate, based on the most recent quarterly dividend multiplied by four. If a company has a history of steadily rising dividends, consider this a conservative estimate. An "e" in this column indicates that dividends have been irregular, and that the figure represents the amount paid over the past year, rather than an estimate of future dividends. A "g" means dividends are paid in Canadian currency, although the other stock market data is given in terms of U.S. dollars.

3. Yield This is the current dividend divided by the lastest closing price, rounded off to the nearest tenth of a percent. A low- or no-yield stock may be a growth stock, which means that profits are reinvested rather than paid out in dividends. Investors purchase growth stocks for capital gains, not for dividends; they hope that stock prices will increase as profits do. Some investors, however, purchase stocks for dividends, or income. This yield figure allows you to compare the dividend income with the income from other types of investments. Remember, however, that while the yield on a stock represents the potential income, the yield on bonds is a combination of both the annual interest income and the lump-sum capital gain or loss that occurs when the bond is redeemed. In a way, therefore, comparing stock and bond yields is similar to comparing apples and oranges.

4. PE ratio The price earnings ratio is the latest price divided by the last 12 months' earnings per share, rounded to the nearest whole number. Be sure not to confuse PEs with dividends. PEs are used to compare the perceived value of stocks in the marketplace. PEs indicate how investors view the value of a company's profits. Stocks representing solid, uninflated profits that are expected to grow usually have higher PEs than stocks with questionable profits and profit-growth potential. Growth companies may have PEs of 20 or more. On the other hand, a high PE could be the result of a recent drop in earnings, and the prelude to a drop in the stock's price that will drop the PE to its former, lower level. A start-up or turnaround company could be attractive, but could have no earnings—and therefore no PE. PEs give you a way to calculate per share earnings roughly: divide the stock price by the PE.

5. Sales This column gives you the trading volume, in hundreds of shares. A "5," in most cases, means 500 shares changed hands; a "1067" means 106,700 shares were traded. A "z," however, indicates that the full figure is being given. Volume measures how liquid a stock is. Stocks that consistently show large volume and small price changes are liquid; it takes a large imbalance between buy and sell orders to move the price much. Stocks with consistently low trading volume may be subject to wide price swings when large orders are finally placed. Sudden surges in volume, accompanied by rising prices, may indicate that an individual or an organization is building up a stake. (If five percent or more of a company's stock is acquired, however, SEC rule 13(d) requires that information, including a statement of intentions, be filed with its offices, with the company, and with the relevant stock exchange.) Volume surges often trigger takeover rumors, which in turn result in even greater volume and price movements.

Financial analysts and journalists often ask company executives about the reasons for unusually heavy volume. A response of "no known reason" may cool speculation, while a "no comment" may fuel the guessing game.

An "x" in the volume column means the stock is ex-dividend. During this time buyers do not receive the most recently declared dividend. Stock prices decline by the amount of the dividend when the shares go ex-dividend, and then usually recover gradually.

6. *High/Low* These twin columns give the highest and lowest prices during the trading session. A "u" indicates a 52-week high; a "d" indicates a 52-week low.

7. *Last sale* The last sale is the closing price. Prices are usually expressed in "eighths"; an eighth equals 12.5 cents. Increments of sixteenths (6.25 cents) and thirty-seconds (3.125 cents) are used for cheaper stocks. You'll see these increments most often with over-the-counter stocks. Tables provided by Associated Press don't indicate the location of the last sale. United Press International does include the location, using "p" for Pacific Stock Exchange, "x" for Philadelphia Stock Exchange, "u" for Midwest Stock Exchange, and "g" for over-the-counter.

8. *Change* This figure represents the change in closing price from the previous day.

9. *52-week High-Low* The high-low column gives you the annual trading range, the highest and lowest prices of the previous 52 weeks plus the current trading week, up to, but not through, the last session. A broad range indicates that a stock has demonstrated the potential to make—and lose—money for shareholders. Sometimes, a stock that has traded up and down within a range will meet resistance when it approaches its previous high point, because some investors will use this high point as a benchmark to sell. Similarly, the low point could serve as a buffer against further price drops. At the low point, buyers, hoping history will repeat itself and the stock rise, may purchase shares and thus provide support for the stock's price.

Over-the-Counter Stock Tables

The quantity of information available for over-the-counter stocks has grown dramatically over the years. It's still often necessary, however, to call your broker for a price because many of the lesser-known, less expensive stocks aren't included in the daily tables. Your broker will use the pink sheets published by the National Quotations Bureau, which list bid and asked prices, to give you a price. *Barron's* provides extensive over-the-counter tables on a weekly basis. The *National OTC Stock Journal,* another weekly, carries information about penny stocks, which usually sell for less than $1.00. The daily tables included in large newspapers have expanded, in part because of the efforts of the National Association of Securities Dealers, the umbrella group for over-the-counter dealers. Since the early 1970s, the NASD Automated Quotations, or NASDAQ system, has allowed dealers using desktop terminals to view each other's bid quotations (the highest prices they're willing to pay), and asked quotations (the lowest prices they'd accept). NASDAQ also passes this information on to wire services for use in daily stock tables. Since the early 1980s, the system has been upgraded to allow dealers to enter transaction prices and sizes of trades. As a result, the tables for the more expensive or more heavily traded NASDAQ stocks look much like the NYSE and Amex tables, replete with price and volume information. Stocks that are subject to this full-line reporting system are included in tables carrying such headings as NASDAQ National Market or NASDAQ National Market Issues.

NASDAQ National Market

NASDAQ NATIONAL MARKET

⑦		①	②	③	④		⑤	⑥
52-week				**Sales**				**Net**
High	**Low**	**Stock**	**Div**	**100s**	**High**	**Low**	**Last**	**Chg.**
12¼	7¾	XYZ		149	9¼	8⅞	9¼	+ ½
23½	6½	AVc s		26	21¼	22	21¼	− ⅜

The NASDAQ National Market table includes the following major elements:

1. The name of the stock, as abbreviated and alphabetized by Associated Press or United Press International.

2. The dividend, in cents (or dollars and cents) per share on an annual basis. These stocks are generally no- or low-dividend payers. As with the NYSE and Amex listings, an ''s'' in the name column indicates a dividend was paid with stock, not cash.

3. Sales, or volume, in hundreds of shares. Because there are many dealers in the over-the-counter market, the volume figure may reflect mainly transactions between dealers, rather than sales and purchases by investors.

4. High and low prices for the trading day.

5. Last refers to the last sale of the day, which ends at 4 P.M. EST. This is the asked, not the bid, price; the spread between bid and asked prices generally is greater on a percentage basis than for NYSE or Amex listed stocks.

6. Change, the difference between the price at the close of the day and the price at the previous close.

7. The 52-week high and low prices, just as on the NYSE and Amex.

Two categories found in the NYSE and Amex tables are missing here—yield and price-earnings (PE) ratio. You can calculate the yield by dividing the estimated annual dividend by the price. To determine the PE, you can look up earnings in the Standard & Poor's Stock Guide or ask your broker for them, and divide the annual earnings by the price. Or, use the weekly National Market System table in *Barron's,* which includes PEs.

Other Over-the-Counter Tables   Not all the companies meeting NASD criteria to have their shares listed as part of the National Market System are included there. Instead, more limited market information for the shares of these and other NAS-DAQ-listed companies is included under the headings of NASDAQ National List or NASDAQ Bid and Asked Quotations. In these tables, you'll mainly find volume figures and closing bid and asked quotations along with the daily change in the bid price from the previous day's closing bid.

NASDAQ NATIONAL LIST

① Stock & Div	② Sales 100s	③ Bid	④ Asked	⑤ Net Chg.
ABZ Sys	90	$\frac{3}{8}$	$\frac{7}{8}$	$-\frac{1}{4}$
Quiljax	2	6	$6\frac{3}{4}$	. . .
Zextap Inc .08	14	$15\frac{1}{2}$	16	$-\frac{1}{2}$

The NASDAQ Bid and Asked Quotations table presents the following elements:

1. Name of the stock and its annual dividend, if any.

2. Sales, in hundreds of shares.

3. Last bid of the session, that is, the most a dealer will pay you for a share. You'll note that the spread between bid and asked prices often is considerable.

4. Last asked quotation of the day, that is, the lowest a dealer will accept for a share.

5. Change in the bid from the end of the previous trading day.

Many over-the-counter stocks appear on neither the National Market nor the National List. Some of the larger financial publications and sections include as many of these stocks as they see fit, usually in an abbreviated form that includes only the name, bid, and asked, but no volume or daily change. These stocks are listed under various headings, including Additional OTC Quotes and NASDAQ Supplemental OTC.

Regional and Foreign Stock Market Tables

A relatively small number of stocks are listed only on regional exchanges, such as the Midwest, Pacific, Philadelphia, and Boston stock exchanges. These shares usually aren't very actively traded and attract mainly a regional following. Regional stock trading information in newspapers usually provides daily data on volume; high, low, and closing prices; and change in price. Readers must calculate dividends, yield, the PE ratio, and seek out 52-week high and low prices.

Of increasing importance are stocks traded on foreign markets. Information about the more important stocks are carried in such major newspapers as *The New York Times* and *The Wall Street Journal.* The stocks are organized by the exchange on which they're traded. The information carried for the Toronto and Montréal markets in Canada is the same as the information carried for the U.S. regional exchange-listed stocks. The data carried for other foreign stocks is more limited: often only the name and the closing price, given in local currency, such as Japanese yen, British pence, French francs, Swiss francs, West German marks, and so on. It's up to the reader to track the daily change, and, if necessary, make use of the foreign exchange tables to translate the price into U.S. dollars and cents. Other tables show foreign securities traded over the counter. The majority of these issues are American Depositary Receipts, representing ownership of securities physically deposited abroad. Where they are not ADRs, the indication "n" is used. Quotes are in U.S. dollars and these tables typically have four columns: sales, bid price, asked price, and net change.

STOCK OPTIONS TABLES

Stock options give you both a conservative way to increase the income on your holdings or insure your portfolio against losses, as well as relatively inexpensive and highly speculative ways to invest in stocks. In any case, don't assume you understand these investment vehicles until you at least understand the stock option tables. Although unheard of a generation ago, these tables now comprise a major portion of the inside of financial news packages. The longest tables are generated by the principal options exchanges, the Chicago Board Options Exchange, the American Stock Exchange, and the Philadelphia Stock Exchange. Shorter tables are included for small options trading operations found on other exchanges.

Daily Stock Options Tables

Options tables give you the prices of wasting assets. These contracts, which as a rule last no longer than nine months, give the holder the right, but not the obligation, to buy (call) or sell (put) shares of stock at a specified strike price by a specified expiration date. The daily table format, and what it includes, by columns, is as follows.

STOCK OPTIONS

	①	②	③ Calls—Last			④ Puts—Last		
	Option & NY Close	Strike Price	May	Aug	Nov	May	Aug	Nov
Ⓐ	XYZ	35	7	6½	6¾	¾	¼	r
Ⓑ	40	40	2	1½	r	1	1½	r
Ⓒ	40	45	¾	¼	r	7	6½	r

1. Name of the underlying stock and under it, the closing price of the underlying stock, repeated for each row of strike prices. (Since New York Stock Exchange tables now generally include sales of NYSE stocks on other exchanges, the NY Close may differ from the NYSE table, which reports later sales on the Pacific Stock Exchange and elsewhere.) In this example, XYZ Corporation stock closed at 40 on the principal stock exchange on which it's traded, most likely the New York Stock Exchange. Because the stock is worth $40 per share, each 100-share options contract has an exercise value of $4000.

2. The strike price is given in this column. This is the price per share at which the option holder is entitled to buy or sell the stock. The accompanying table includes options series for three strike prices— $35, $40, and $45 per share. Therefore, the values of the 100-share contracts are $3500, $4000, and $4500, respectively.

3. and 4. These figures represent the closing prices, or premiums, that were paid for the various puts and calls. The prices are expressed on a per share basis, meaning that you must multiply by 100 shares to determine the cost of the contract. These prices are given for the different months of expiration, usually spaced three months apart. Each contract has a specific month of expiration, with expiration set at 11:59 A.M. EST on the third Saturday of that month. Whether you gain or lose in options trading usually depends on movements in the premium price. That is because options positions are generally closed out with an offsetting purchase or sale or are allowed to expire. Having to exercise the option, that is, actually buying the stock in the case of calls or coming up with the shares to sell in the case of puts, involves more cash than many options holders want to commit.

Notice how the strike prices of the options series straddle the current market value of the stock. This gives investors a choice of intrinsically worthless—but cheap—options as well as options that have considerable value, but which are expensive to buy. Options exchanges constantly create series with new strike prices to maintain this situation as the price of the underlying stock changes. For stocks selling at $25 to $50 per share, the strike prices are usually set in increments of $5; the increments are $10 on contracts for stocks priced $50 to $200 per share. For options on stocks worth $200 or more per share, strike prices are set $20 apart, and for options on stocks worth less than $25 per share, the increments are $2.50.

Using the Associated Press system of symbols, "r" in the premium column means options for that particular strike price and month of expiration did not trade. An "s" indicates that the Options Clearing Corporation, which guarantees your cash or shares when options are exercised or traded, isn't offering that particular contract. United Press International uses "nt" if an option did not trade, and "no" if the OCC isn't offering an option. Associated Press expresses sixteenths as "¹⁄₁₆" while United Press uses "1s" to represent that fraction.

The cheapest options are those on which you would lose money (even before considering commission costs) if you exercised them. These are referred to as out-of-the-money options. For example, an XYZ May45 call, giving you the right to pay $45 per share or $4500 per contract for 100 shares of XYZ, costs only ³⁄₄—75 cents per share or $75 per contract. (See Line C, Column 3.) In other words, someone is willing to pay these prices for the right to later pay out $4500 for a stock currently worth $4000. Of course, the hope is that XYZ stock will rise. For example, if the stock rises to $43 per share (which would still mean that the option is intrinsically worthless and out of the money) another investor may be willing to pay more for that option—perhaps 1½ or $1.50 a share. The second investor hopes that the stock will rise to the point at which the option would produce a profit if exercised. In any case, the first buyer, who paid $75 for the contract, could get $150 for the contract—doubling his or her money before subtracting commission costs.

Options with intrinsic value, such as the XYZ May35 calls (which give you the right to pay $3500 for something already worth $4000) are naturally more expensive than those with no intrinsic value. In this table, these options finished the previous section at $7 per share (Line C, Column 4), or $700 per contract. The percentage gains or losses on such options are less than the volatile out-of-the-money options, but there is also less chance that these options will have to be allowed to expire worthless.

These tables also indicate how much money you can make by selling options and thus increase the income from your stock portfolio. For example, if you own

100 shares of XYZ, you may decide to sell calls; that is, you may give another person the right to buy your shares. In return, you receive the premium. Assuming the price of options held steady from the previous day's closing levels, you could expect to receive $150 for selling an XYZ Aug40 call (Line B, Column 3). Of course, if the stock price should rise, the call holder could exercise the option, and you would lose the capital gain. Ideally, you would hope that XYZ stock would hold at around 40 until the option you sold expired. In that case, after brokerage commissions were factored into the equation, it would not be worthwhile for another investor to exercise the option you sold.

If you are worried that your XYZ stock might drop, you can lock in a value of $35 a share through most of August by buying an Aug 35 put (which gives you the right to get $35 a share) for $25 a contract (Line A, Column 4).

In addition to options on individual stocks, options are traded on debt instruments (interest rate options), foreign currencies, stock indexes, and certain futures contracts. What applies to puts and calls on stocks also applies to options on other instruments, with one major exception—index options. Because they are settled in cash and have other distinct features, they deserve special attention.

Daily Index Options Tables

Index options, which give you the right to buy and sell the dollar value of an index (rather than 100 shares of stock, as with stock options) are relatively few; sometimes, however, they are extremely popular. They often dominate the most-active lists that appear at the head of daily option tables. Index options tables run under their exchange headings: Chicago Board Options Exchange (often referred to in the tables as Chicago Board or just Chicago), the American, Philadelphia, Pacific, and New York stock exchanges, and NASD.

Index options are popular because they allow investors to play the whole market, in the case of broad-based indexes, or segments of the market, in the case of indexes that track technology stocks or gold stocks, among others. An index is assigned a value of a certain number of dollars per point—$100, for example. Standard & Poor's has allowed its indexes to be used for such purposes, as have the New York Stock Exchange and Value Line. Sometimes indexes are created specifically for trading options on them. Using the usual format, a hypothetical XYZ index option, which for example, tracks hundreds of stocks, would appear like the accompanying example.

INDEX OPTIONS

	①		②			③	
XYZ Index							
Strike Price	**Calls—Last**			**Puts—Last**			
	Feb	**Mar**	**Apr**	**Feb**	**Mar**	**Apr**	
Ⓐ 290	12⅞	14¼	14⅛	³⁄₁₆	2	4¼	
Ⓑ 295	7⅝	10¼	11⅜	¹¹⁄₁₆	3¼	6¾	
Ⓒ 300	3¾	7¾	8⅛	1⅞	5⅜	9⅛	
Ⓓ 305	1³⁄₁₆	4⅞	6½	4⅜	10½	12	
Ⓔ 310	⅜	2⅞	4½	...	14	...	

Ⓕ Total call volume 27,435 Total call open int. 78,121
Ⓖ Total put volume 17,477 Total call open int. 75, 940
Ⓗ The index: High 302.55; Low 296.90;
Close 302.51. + 4.32

Index option tables have the following components:

1. The strike price is the price you would pay (if you owned a call) or would receive (if you owned a put) if the option were exercised. To compute the dollar value, multiple by $100 per point, because the XYZ Index has an assigned value of $100 per point. The 290 strike price, for example, would require the payment of $29,000.

2. Calls-last are the closing prices, or premiums, for calls. Unlike the much longer time periods available for stock options, index options expire in about three months at most. As you can see, investors were paying 12⁷/₈, or $1287.50 per contract, for the expensive, deep-in-the-money Feb290 calls (Line A, Column 2). That's because the index closed at 302.51—the index's closing level is given on Line H—making its monetary value $30,251. The holder of a call with a strike price of 290, or $29,000, has an option with an intrinsic value of $1251 and hopes the value will rise even higher so the option can be sold or exercised at a profit after commissions.

Meanwhile, the 310 strike price call options have no intrinsic value; they are out of the money and thus, cheap. A Feb310 cost only ³/₈, or $37.50 per contract (Line E, Column 2), because it gives the buyer the right to pay $31,000 for an investment that's currently worth only $30,251.

3. Premiums on puts move in the opposite direction of calls. The March puts with a 310 strike price (Line E, Column 3) are expensive, ($1400 per contract) because they are deep in the money; they give the holder the right to demand $31,000 for an index that's worth only $30,152.

F. This line indicates the number of call contracts that were traded during the session and the number of contracts still open (open interest). To some extent, these figures measure investor optimism, because calls are bets that the market index will rise.

G. This line presents the same type of information given in line F, except that line G deals with puts. These figures reflect investor pessimism, because puts are bets that the market will drop, at least insofar as the group of stocks being tracked by the index is concerned.

H. This line indicates how the index performed during the session, in terms of its highest, lowest, and closing values, and change from its previous close. The gain shown in this example, 4.32 points, signifies that the value of the XYZ index rose $432.

Weekly Options Tables

Weekly options tables, such as those found in *Barron's* or the Sunday *New York Times,* follow a format different from the daily tables. Calls and puts are stacked rather than placed next to each other. More information is included in these tables. Index options are still run separately.

In the accompanying example of a typical stock-option table, the columns include the following information:

WEEKLY OPTIONS TABLE

①	②	③	④		⑤	⑥	⑦
Option	Sales	Open Int.	High	Low	Last	Net Chg.	Stock close
ABZ Mar35	1437	10921	6⅛	3¾	4	−1⅛	39
ABZ Mar35 p	99	5089	¹⁄₁₆	¹⁄₁₆	¹⁄₁₆	−¹⁄₁₆	39
ABZ Mar40	5981	7332	1¹⁵⁄₁₆	½	⁹⁄₁₆	−¹⁄₁₆	39
ABZ Mar40 p	237	402	2	1	1¾	+⅜	39

1. Name of the option, as identified by the underlying stock, the expiration month, and the strike price. The closest expiration months and lowest strike prices appear first. A "p" identifies puts; the other options are calls.

2. Sales for the week, in terms of the number of contracts that changed hands.

3. Open interest—the number of contracts in investor and dealer hands that haven't been exercised or closed out yet. Comparing the number of outstanding calls to puts helps you assess the direction speculators expect the price of the stock to take.

4. The highest and lowest premiums, per share, paid for a particular contract during the past week.

5. The closing premium, or price, per share, at the end of the week.

6. Net Change—how much premiums per share rose or fell from the previous weekly close. The 1⅛ ($1.125 per share) loss for ABZ Mar35 calls indicates that the contracts lost $112.50 each.

7. The closing price of the underlying shares, which, when multiplied by 100, equals the exercise value of the contracts, $3900.

FUTURES TABLES

Futures tables are grouped by broad categories—agricultural (grains, edible oils, livestock, coffee, sugar, cocoa, orange juice), metals (gold, silver, platinum, palladium, copper), industrials (lumber, cotton, crude oil, heating oil, gasoline), and financial (U.S. Treasury bonds, notes, and bills, foreign currencies, certificates of deposit, stock index futures). About 50 contracts are listed in various futures markets and included in newspaper tables. Commodity contracts are agreements to deliver or take delivery of a commodity in the future. Hence, the "Futures Prices" label for these tables. Most investors in commodities futures contracts are speculators who hope to make big profits by predicting correctly the change in commodity prices. The contracts are identified by their delivery months. A typical table, in this case for cattle, is presented here. The type of contract and the exchange (CME, or Chicago Mercantile Exchange) as well as the size (44,000 pounds) and the units of trade (pennies per pound) are shown in lines B and C.

CATTLE FUTURES

	① ... Season ...		②		③	④	⑤	⑥
Ⓐ	High	Low	High	Low	Close	Chg.	Open Int.

Ⓑ CATTLE, LIVE BEEF (CME)
Ⓒ 44,000 lb.; ¢ per lb.

	High	Low	High	Low	Close	Chg.	Open Int.
Ⓓ	67.07	55.30 Apr	61.75	60.32	60.40	−.30	29,042
Ⓔ	66.60	56.25 Jun	60.52	59.35	59.47	−.28	17.547
Ⓕ	61.75	55.20 Aug	58.40	57.45	57.47	−.25	5,939
Ⓖ	60.60	55.70 Oct	57.20	56.37	56.50	−.15	2,705
Ⓗ	61.75	57.55 Dec	58.80	58.10	58.35	−.02	612
Ⓘ	60.20	58.00 Feb	58.90	58.77	58.77	+.07	56

Ⓙ Est. sales 21,859. Wed's sales 21.607.
Ⓚ Wed.'s open Int 55,901, up 63.

Other information is presented as follows:

1. The highest and lowest prices paid for a particular delivery month contract since the contract was listed. This indicates the price swings of the contract. The April futures (*Line D*) ranged between 67.07 cents and 55.30 cents per pound, or $29,510 and $24,332 per 44,000-pound contract—a difference of $5178. An investor smart enough or lucky enough to invest $2433 (10% margin when the contract reached its $24,332 low point) and sell when prices peaked would have more than doubled his or her money. On the other hand, someone who invested at the high point could easily have lost all of his or her money. When the loss of a contract's value equals the amount of money that's been invested, brokers will usually demand more margin. If they don't get it, they will sell the contract.

2. The delivery months differentiate one contract from another. The spacing between delivery months and the length of the longest contract varies from one commodity to the next. Most contracts last no longer than one year.

3. The daily high and low prices.

4. The closing price. At 60.40 cents, the close in the April future made that contract worth $26,576.

5. The change in price—the difference from one close to the next. The .3 cent loss for April cattle signifies a $132 loss for the contract.

6. The open interest—the number of contracts that have not been closed through delivery or offsetting transactions. This indicates which contracts will experience the heaviest trading in the future, as most contracts will be closed out through either a sale or a purchase of an offsetting contract, rather than by the delivery of the commodity.

J. This line estimates the number of contracts that changed hands during the last session, as well as the volume of the previous session.

K. This line presents the total open interest of the two previous days, and the change in the number of open contracts.

A great deal of information is omitted from these tables, including delivery days, delivery specifications (the locations to which the commodities would be sent and how they would arrive), and the daily limits in price changes that exchanges impose on most futures contracts. The contract specifications are available from the exchange on which the commodity is traded. Commodities don't possess the uniform qualities of options contracts; the sequence of delivery months and the maximum length of contracts varies from one commodity to another.

Comprehensive commodities tables also include a listing of cash prices, gathered from various sources each day—exchanges, warehouses, fabricators—which give you the immediate value of many of the commodities for which futures contracts are traded as well as other materials, such as wool and cloth and mercury, which have no formal futures market. In the case of futures-related commodities, remember that the current cash price, while often determining the direction of futures contract prices, is usually different. A glut in grain during the harvest could cause an immediate plunge in prices, while prices in the futures market, which anticipate conditions further down the road, could rise.

CORPORATE BOND TABLES

Although corporate bond tables give you valuable insight into a key financial market, they present only part of the picture. While several thousand corporate bonds are traded on the New York and American stock exchanges, many more that are traded through broker/dealers do not appear in the tables of exchange-listed bonds. In addition, exchange-listed bonds traded in lots of 10 or more are also handled off the exchange. According to the Nine Bond Rule, only lots of nine or fewer must be sent to the exchange floor.

Nevertheless, these tables are important because they (1) give you specific information about bonds you may own or are considering buying and (2) indicate the prevailing yields, which can help you estimate the value of similar bonds that you may have in your portfolio or are considering buying.

The table listings look like this:

CORPORATE BONDS

	①	②	③	④		⑤	⑥
Bonds		**Current Yield**	**Sales in $1,000**	**High**	**Low**	**Last**	**Net Chg.**
ABZ	9⅜s01	11.6	42	81¼	81	81¼	+¼
MXY	8.15x00	9.5	285	85½	84½	85½	−1
KLO	10s09f	18	113	55½	55	55½	+⅛
STU	zr88	...	17	69⅜	68⅞	69	+½
WVX	9½ 05	cv	101	141½	139	141	−1

The accompanying typical bond table presents information as follows:

1. The company abbreviations may vary from the abbreviations used in the stock tables. Also included in this column is the annual interest each bond pays, expressed as a percentage of the par or face value.

Most corporate bonds are available in $1000 denominations (though prices are quoted in $100 units), which would mean that ABZ's 9⅜ payout would total $93.75 annually. Where a rate cannot be expressed as a fraction, decimals are used, for example, 8.15 for MXY. The annual interest rate is also referred to as the coupon. Noninterest-paying zero coupon securities are identified by a "zr," as with STU here. The last two numbers in the name cluster represent the year in which the bonds will mature—01 for 2001, 88 for 1988. Among the qualifiers that may also appear after the name is "f," meaning that the bond is trading flat or without accrued interest, and that an interest payment has been missed. The "s" often seen after the bond name is a stylistic embellishment that reflects the verbal description of bonds; for example. "ABZ nine and three eighths of 2001."

2. The current yield represents the annual interest payment as a percentage of the last closing price. It provides a comparison with yields for other types of investments. In the case of convertible bonds, or convertibles, where prices, and therefore yields, are governed by movements in the underlying shares, no yield is given. Instead, "cv" is inserted in the yield column to indicate that this is a convertible issue. Of course, no yield is given with zero coupon bonds either.

3. This is volume on the exchange, expressed in sales of $1000 bonds, which is the normal corporate bond denomination. Events—mergers, earnings news, and so on—can cause volume surges, especially in the case of the convertibles. The amount of volume will tell you how liquid the bonds are.

4. These figures represent the highest and lowest prices during the session. Weekly bond tables also include 52-week highs and lows. Prices are quoted as a percentage of par value, as though the face value was $100, not $1000. For example, a $1000 face value bond sold at 81¼ actually sold at $812.50.

5. The last sale, in terms of $100 units. Multiply by 10 to get the price per $1000 bond.

6. The net change indicates the gain or loss since the previous close, expressed as a percentage of par. Therefore, the +¼ gain for ABZ translates into 25 cents per $100 face value, or $2.50 per $1000 bond. The −1 for WVX indicates a $10 loss for $1000 bond. Price changes reflect changes in interest rates. If bond prices have dropped it means interest rates probably rose, and vice versa.

You should also be familiar with the following information, which is not included in the corporate bond tables:

Ratings These indicate the risk of default by the issuer on payments of interest or principal. The major bond rating agencies are Fitch Investors Service, Moody's Investors Service and Standard and Poor's Corporation.

Denominations Not all bonds are available in denominations of $1000. Some, called baby bonds, are denominated in amounts of $500 or less.

Yield to maturity This represents the return, including both the annual interest payments and the gain or loss realized when the bonds are redeemed, taking into account the timing of payments and the time value of money. Yield to maturity will vary depending on whether you bought the bonds at a discount or a premium in relation to their face value, and with the time remaining to maturity. This type of yield calculation allows you to more easily compare bonds with other types of fixed income investments.

Payment dates Interest payments on corporate bonds are usually, but not always, made semiannually. In any case, the payment cycles vary.

Callability If a bond can be redeemed prior to maturity by the issuer, it will most likely be called when rates decline and conditions are favorable to the issuer. For this reason, another yield calculation, yield to call, can have more significance than yield to maturity.

GOVERNMENT SECURITIES TABLES

There's no uniform method of quoting the prices of government securities. In addition, the methods of presenting the values of these bills, notes, and bonds are sometimes as obscure as these markets once were to general investors. Because of the numbers of investors who are now familiar with these markets, however, it's worthwhile for you to know how to extract information from these tables.

Treasury Bills

These obligations—or IOUs—of the U.S. Treasury, are backed by the full faith and credit of the U.S. government. They always mature within one year (3 months, 6 months, 9 months and one year), and are included in many major daily newspapers in the form used in the accompanying table. Information is provided as follows.

TREASURY BILLS

① Date	② Bid	③ Asked	④ Chg	⑤ Yield
Mar 13	5.61	5.55	+0.09	5.63

1. This is the date on which the bills mature. The maturity date distinguishes one bill from another.

2. The bid is the price dealers were willing to pay late (there is never an official end) in the last trading session. A bid is presented in a way you may find confusing. It's the discount from the face value demanded by dealers, expressed as an annual percentage. The reason for this is that Treasury bills do not pay interest in the usual sense. Instead, you pay less than the face value of the bills, but you receive the full value when the bills mature. The difference equals the interest you would receive. Thus, if you pay $9000 for a one-year $10,000 bill ($10,000 is the minimum size for a Treasury bill), you're paying 10% less than par, or buying the bill at a 10% discount. A bid of 10 would appear in the table. The higher the discount, the lower the price.

3. The asked price is the price the dealer is willing to accept, again expressed as an annualized percentage discount rate. In these tables, the percentages are carried out to the nearest hundredth, or basis point. Note that the dealer demands a smaller discount—a higher price—when he resells the bonds.

4. The change indicates how much the bid discount rate rose or fell during the session. A plus change actually represents a drop in prices, because it indicates an increased discount from par. Just as a larger discount on merchandise in a store window signifies lower prices, so the .09%, or 9 basis point, indicates an increase in the discount. A minus change means that Treasury bill prices have risen and that the discount rate—and often other types of yields and rates—has dropped.

5. The yield represents a yield to maturity, based on the price you would actually pay for the Treasury bill, rather than its face value. The 10% discount rate tells you that you would pay 10% less than $10,000— or $9000—for a one year Treasury bill, for a difference—representing interest—of $1000. The actual yield, however, is better expressed in terms of the amount you would really pay for this investment—$9000. In addition, a return of $1000 on a $9000 investment is greater than the 10% discount rate; it's an 11.11% yield. Note that the yield shown in the sample table, 5.63, is higher than the 5.61 discount rate bid shown in column 2.

Treasury Notes and Bonds

Treasury note and bond prices are included in the same tables. The only difference is that the notes, designated by an ''n'' or a ''p,'' mature in from one to ten years after they are issued, while bonds mature in ten years or longer. These tables present the securities in the order of their maturity dates, with the closest maturity date at the top and the furthest (always the much-quoted government long bond) at the bottom. Notice the increase in yields as the period of maturity increases; this reflects the fact that lenders demand a greater return for locking up their money for longer time periods. As with other government bonds, prices are given as dealer bid and asked quotes, not in terms of last sales. The reason for this is that there is no way for the extensive network of government bond dealers to report transaction prices and amounts in order to register them onto a last-sale ''tape.'' Extra care must be taken in reading the bid and asked quotes because the two digits following the decimal points are 32nds rather than hundredths, reflecting the traditional language of the government bond market.

The information on a typical daily table is as follows:

TREASURY BONDS

① Date	② Rate	③ Bid	④ Asked	⑤ Chg.	⑥ Yield
Apr 86 n	11¾	100.19	100.23	+ .4	6.13
Feb 93	6¾	95.18	96.18	+ 1.2	7.39
Nov 02-07	7⅞	97.19	98.3	+ 1.2	8.06
Nov 15 k	9⅜	118.1	118.5	+ 2.2	8.23

1. The date identifies the note or bond by its month and year of maturity; thus an "89" means 1989, a "16" means 2016. In addition, an "n" signifies a note (a "p" signifies notes not subject to withholding tax for foreign owners) while no notation (or a "k" if no withholding tax for foreigner owners is required) appears for bonds. When the maturity figure consists of two years, such as the 02–07 in this table, the second year (2007 here) represents the maturity, while the first year (2002 here) indicates that the bonds could be repaid early, beginning in 2002. Such callability is rare with Treasury securities; it is found only in the final five years of certain 30-year bond issues.

2. The rate is the coupon rate, or the annual interest rate, expressed as a percentage of the face value ($1000 minimum denominations for bonds and $1000 or $5000 for notes).

3. The bid is the price dealers were offering to pay late in the session. It's presented as a percentage of face value. Note, however, that the two digits following the decimal point are 32nds, not tenths or hundredths. The 113.13 bid for the Oct 89 notes equals 113 13/32%. Because 1/32% of $1000 is 31¼ cents, 13/32 equals $4.06¼; the total bid, per $1000 of notes, equals $1134.06¼.

4. The asked, the price at which dealers are offering to sell the securities, is calculated similarly to the bid.

5. The daily change from two previous sessions to yesterday's session is based on the rise or fall of the bid price.

6. This figure represents yield to maturity, which combines your current yield (the percentage return in interest based on the price you actually pay) and the difference between the price you paid and the face value at redemption.

Government Agency Bonds

Securities of U.S. agencies such as the Federal Home Loan Bank and Government National Mortgage Association that appear in *The Wall Street Journal* and *The New York Times* use the same type of bid and asked quotes, expressed in 32nds of a percent, as appear in the Treasury note and bond tables.

Municipal Bonds

You probably won't find municipal bond prices in the financial pages. Even major financial publications include only a sampling of revenue bonds—those repaid from the income of a particular project rather than from general tax dollars. Such tables, typically headed Tax-exempt Authority Bonds, include the issuer's name, maturity date, the bid, the asked, and the daily change in the bid. Information on general obligation bonds is even harder to find. One way of approximating the value of your holdings, though, is to look at yields on newly issued bonds as revealed in tombstone ads placed by underwriters or in the short lists of new issues some papers provide. If the yields on new issues are lower than those your municipals are earning, your bonds are probably selling above face value and vice-versa, assuming the bonds are comparable in terms of quality and type of issuer.

The Tax Reform Act of 1986 profoundly altered the municipal bond landscape, and there are now taxable as well as tax-exempt general obligation and revenue issues. There will undoubtedly be a period of sorting out before reporting practices become conventionally adopted.

MUTUAL FUNDS TABLES

Mutual fund prices are listed several ways in newspapers. Prices of a fund offered by an open-end management company that invests in long-term securities—either stocks or bonds—change with changes in market segments or the market as a whole. These funds sell and redeem their own shares. Large newspapers generally list these prices under the heading Mutual Funds.

MUTUAL FUNDS

①	② NAV	③ Buy	④ Chg.
ABZ Grp:			
Genrl Fd	14.38	NL	+ .03
AB Growth	10.50	11.03	+ .01
ABZ Incm	5.22	NL	+ .02
Tax Ex	8.21	NL	− .01

These tables contain the following information, by column:

1. The names of mutual funds are clustered by family of funds—funds sponsored by a particular management company. The names often reflect the type of investments that comprise each fund; for example, a general stock fund, growth stock fund, income fund, or tax-exempt bond fund.

Some fund names are followed by lowercase letters such as a (meaning a stock dividend was paid in the past 12 months), d (new 52-week low), f (quotation refers to previous day), r (redemption charge may apply), u (new 52-week high), and x (fund is trading ex-dividend).

2. NAV stands for net asset value, the per-share value of the fund's assets, minus management costs. This is the amount you would receive, per share, if you redeemed your shares. The numbers indicate dollars and cents per share. Sometimes the column carries the heading Sell, meaning that you would receive this amount per share if you were the seller.

3. The Buy column may also be headed Offer Price. It tells you, in dollars and cents per share, the price per share, the price you would pay to buy the shares. Funds that carry a sales charge, or front end load, cost more per share than their net asset value. Funds with back end loads discourage withdrawals by charging a fee to redeem your shares. Many funds, however, carry no sales charge; these are no-load funds whose buy-in costs are the same as their net asset values. These funds carry an "NL" or just "n" in the Buy column.

4. Change refers to the daily change in net asset value, determined at the close of each trading day.

Share prices of a fund offered by a closed-end management company, which issues a fixed number of shares that are then traded among investors, are often included in the daily stock tables. Some newspapers also provide weekly tables listing the prices and values of the shares as of the previous day's close-of-the-market.

CLOSED-END FUNDS

①	② N.A. Value	③ Stk Price	④ % Diff
Diversified funds			
ABZ Fund	17.55	21½	+3.1
WXY Fund	10.81	11⅜	−1.8
ZBF Fund	24.74	20½	−5.0
Specialized Equity and Convertible Funds			
ABZ Gold	33.10	33½	+2.2
XYZ Conv	15.77	16	+1.6
XYZ Tech	9.97	10⅛	−4.4

1. Fund names are grouped alphabetically by fund type.

2. Net Asset Values, as of the last close (unless otherwise indicated) are listed in terms of dollars and cents per share.

3. Stock prices are the last close.

4. Percent difference represents the weekly rise or fall of the net asset value of the shares.

Listings of shares of dual purpose funds can be found in stock exchange tables. These closed-end funds have two classes of shares. One class entitles shareholders to capital gains based on the market value of the assets. The other class entitles holders to dividend and interest income from the fund. Some major newspapers also carry weekly tables of the per-share prices of the capital shares, the net asset value of the capital shares, and the weekly percentage or loss of price of those shares. These tables are useful because the daily stock tables don't include net asset values.

Tables for money market funds appear weekly, usually Thursday, after the release of data by Donoghue's money fund average or the National Association of Securities Dealers. Some newspapers print the tables again on Sunday. If you need information on a money market fund before Thursday, you can call the fund organizations. Many fund groups have toll-free 800 phone numbers for shareholders. Most investors need no more than weekly updates because per share values should remain constant at $1.00. These funds, which invest in short-term debt instruments, often are bought because they are liquid (most allow checkwriting) and the yield fluctuates with short-term interest rates. Market movements and the accompanying capital gains and losses don't play a major role in the decision to buy or sell shares. The yield is the main information included in such tables.

MONEY MARKET FUNDS

① Fund	② Assets ($ million)	③ Average maturity (days)	④ 7-day average yield (%)	⑤ 30-day average yield (%)
ABzz Safety Fst	344.7	20	10.3	9.7
Blxx Liquid Secs	1,343.9	26	10.1	9.6
Xymo Govt. Fund	299.0	22	9.9	9.5

The accompanying table includes the following information, by column:

1. Name of the money-market fund.

2. Assets are stated in millions of dollars, to the nearest $100,000. These figures indicate the size of the fund. Investors constantly debate the advantages and disadvantages of size.

3. The average maturity figure represents how long, on average, it takes for the securities in a money fund's portfolio to mature. Shorter average maturities mean that the fund's yield will react more quickly to general interest-rate changes in the fixed-income securities market. This is beneficial when rates are rising, but disadvantageous when rates are dropping. In the latter case, you would want your fund to hold onto higher-yielding securities as long as possible. The move in the average maturity figure is considered by some to be a good predictor of short-term interest rate direction. If a fund's average maturity increases by several days for several weeks, this is an indication that portfolio managers expect short-term rates to drop. If the average maturity decreases, the managers probably expect short-term rates to rise.

4. The 7-day average yield indicates the average daily total return for that period, and is determined largely by subtracting the fund's costs from the investment income. The result is expressed as a percentage of the average share price:

5. The 30-day average yield allows you to compare the performance of one fund with another over a longer and more meaningful period of time.

HOW TO READ TICKER TAPES

With the growth of cable television, an increasing number of investors pick up financial news from cablecasters that cover the securities and commodities markets continuously throughout the business day. Like daily newspapers, the purveyors of electronic financial news aim for a broad audience. Through the creative use of graphics and commentary, they manage generally to communicate complex information in a way nonprofessionals can understand.

But unless you work for an investment firm or spend your leisure time sitting around a board room of a brokerage, the figures and symbols that pass constantly—sometimes with maddening rapidity—across the lower portion of the TV screen may require explanation. What you see there is the stock ticker tape, the same report of trading activity displayed on the floors of the major stock exchanges. The only difference is that to give stock exchange members an advantage, it is transmitted with a 15-minute delay.

The most frequently seen display is the consolidated tape, a combination of two networks (not to be confused with television networks): Network A reports all New York Stock Exchange issues traded on the NYSE or other identified markets, which include five regional exchanges, the over-the-counter market, and other markets, such as Instinet, a computerized market in which large institutional blocks are traded. Network B reports all American Stock Exchange issues traded on the Amex or other identified markets. National Association of Securities Dealers (NASDAQ) over-the-counter quotes are presented separately in the lower band.

Elements of the consolidated tape; which reports actual transactions (the term quotes is loosely used to mean trades in ticker tape jargon, although its proper financial meaning refers to bid and asked quotations) are explained as follows:

Stock Symbol   The first letters are the stock ticker symbol—XON for Exxon, CCI for Citicorp. IBM for IBM, for example. (There is one exception to this, which is that the prefix Q is used when a company is in receivership or bankruptcy.) The ticker symbol may be followed by an abbreviation designating a type of issue, such as Pr to signify preferred stock, which may, in turn, be followed by a letter indicating a class of preferred. Thus XYZPrE means XYZ Corporation's preferred stock series E. If XYZ's preferred stock series E was convertible, the abbreviation .CV would be added to read XYZPrE.CV. Common stock classes, if any, are indicated by a period plus a letter following the ticker symbol. Thus XYZ's class B common would be designated XYZ.B.

Other abbreviations placed after the ticker symbol as necessary are rt for rights; wi for when issued; .WD for when distributed; .WS for warrants (the abbreviation may be preceded by another period and letter to identify the particular issue of warrant); and .XD for ex-dividend.

Market Identifiers   When the information about the stock is followed by an ampersand (&) and a letter, the transaction took place in a market other than the New York Stock Exchange, if you are looking at Network A, or the American Stock Exchange, if you are looking at Network B. The letter identifies the market as follows:

A	American Stock Exchange
B	Boston Stock Exchange
C	Cincinnati Stock Exchange
M	Midwest Stock Exchange
N	New York Stock Exchange
O	Other Markets (mainly Instinet)
P	Pacific Stock Exchange
T	Third market (mainly NASDAQ)
X	Philadelphia Stock Exchange

Volume   The next portion of the transaction information provided on a ticker tape may appear below or to the right of the above stock symbol and market designation. It reports the number of shares traded. However, if the trade is in a round lot of 100 shares, which it usually is, no volume is indicated and the tape simply shows the issue and the price. Thus XYZ 26½ simply means that 100 shares of XYZ were traded at 26.50 a share. Where larger round lot transactions take place, the number of round lots is indicated followed by the letter "s" followed by the price. Thus, XYZ 4 s 26½ means 400 shares were traded at $26.50 a share. Similarly, 1700 shares would be XYZ 17 s 26½ and so on, except that when the volume is 10,000 shares or more the full number is given—XYZ 16,400 s 26½, for example.

Odd lots—quantities other than multiples of 100 or whatever other unit represents the round lot—are not printed on the ticker tape unless approved by an exchange official. If approval is given, odd lots of 50 shares and 150 shares of XYZ would be displayed respectively: XYZ 50 SHRS 26½ and XYZ 150 SHRS 26½.

A limited number of issues—mainly inactive stocks or higher priced preferred issues—trade in round lots of less than 100 shares. On the New York Stock Exchange such round lots are always 10 shares, but on the Amex these round lots can be 10, 25, or 50 shares. Transactions in these special round lots are designated by a number indicating how many lots were traded followed by the symbols $_s^s$. Thus, on the New York Stock Exchange, XYZ Pr 3 $_s^s$ 55 means 3 10-share lots (30 shares) of XYZ preferred stock were traded at $55 a share. If XYZ were listed on the Amex, you would not know by looking at the tape whether the lot involved was 10, 25, or 50 shares. For that information, you would have to consult a stock guide.

Active Market Procedures   When trading becomes sufficiently heavy to cause the tape to run more than a minute behind, shortcuts are implemented. The most frequently taken measure to keep up with heavy trading is signified by the tape printout DIGITS AND VOLUME DELETED. This means only the unit price digit and fraction will be printed (for example, 9½ instead of 19½) except when the price ends in zero or is an opening transaction. In addition, volume information will be deleted except when trades are 5000 shares or more (the threshold can be raised if required). Another common procedure is to announce REPEAT PRICES OMITTED, meaning that successive transactions at the same price will not be repeated. A third measure is MINIMUM PRICE CHANGES OMITTED, meaning trades will not be displayed unless the price difference exceeds ⅛ of a point. The second and third measures do not apply to opening transactions or to trades of 5000 shares or more. When activity slackens to a more normal level, the tape will read DIGITS AND VOLUME RESUMED with similar indications for the other measures.

Other Abbreviations   When a transaction is being reported out of its proper order, the letters .SLD will follow the symbol as in XYZ .SLD 3s 26½. SLR followed by a number signifies seller's option and number of days until settlement. This indication is found after the price. CORR indicates that a correction of information follows. ERR or CXL indicates a print is to be ignored. OPD signifies an opening transaction that was delayed or one whose price is significantly changed from the previous day's close.

HOW TO USE THIS DICTIONARY EFFECTIVELY

Alphabetization: All entries are alphabetized by letter rather than by word so that multiple-word terms are treated as single words. For example, **NET ASSET VALUE** follows **NET ASSETS** as though it were spelled **NETASSETVALUE,** without spacing. Similarly, **ACCOUNT EXECUTIVE** follows **ACCOUNTANT'S OPINION.** In unusual cases, abbreviations or acronyms appear as entries in the main text, in addition to appearing in the back of the book in the separate listing of Abbreviations and Acronyms. This is when the short form, rather than the formal name, predominates in common business usage. For example, NASDAQ is more commonly used in speaking of the National Association of Securities Dealers Automated Quotations system than the name itself, so the entry is at **NASDAQ.** Numbers in entry titles are alphabetized as if they were spelled out.

Where a term has several meanings, alphabetical sequence is used for subheads, except in special instances where clarity dictates a different order (for example, under **LEVERAGE** the subhead **Operating leverage** precedes **Financial leverage**). In some entries, the various meanings of the term are presented with simple numerical headings. Securities and Exchange Commission rules are presented in the official numerical order.

Cross references: In order to gain a fuller understanding of a term, it will sometimes help to refer to the definition of another term. In these cases the additional term is printed in SMALL CAPITALS. Such cross references appear in the body of the definition or at the end of the entry (or subentry). Cross references at the end of an entry (or subentry) may refer to related or contrasting concepts rather than give more information about the concept under discussion. As a rule, a term is printed in small capitals only the first time it appears in an entry. Where an entry is fully defined at another entry, a reference rather than a definition is provided; for example, **EITHER-OR ORDER** *see* ALTERNATIVE ORDER.

Italics: Italic type is generally used to indicate that another term has a meaning identical or very closely related to that of the entry. Occasionally, italic type is also used to highlight the fact that a word used is a business term and not just a descriptive phrase. Italics are also used for the titles of publications.

Parentheses: Parentheses are used in entry titles for two reasons. The first is to indicate that an entry's opposite is such an integral part of the concept that only one discussion is necessary; for example, **REALIZED PROFIT (OR LOSS).** The second and more common reason is to indicate that an abbreviation is used with about the same frequency as the term itself; for example, **OVER THE COUNTER (OTC).**

Examples, Illustrations, and Tables: The numerous examples in this Dictionary are designed to help readers gain understanding and to help them relate abstract concepts to the real world of finance and investment. Line drawings are provided in addition to text to clarify concepts best understood visually; for example, technical chart patterns used by securities analysts and graphic concepts used in financial analysis. Tables supplement definitions where essential detail is more effectively condensed and expressed in tabular form; for example, components of the U.S. money supply.

Special Definitions: Some entries are given expanded treatment to enhance their reference value. Examples are **ECONOMIC RECOVERY TAX ACT OF 1981, SECURITIES AND COMMODITIES EXCHANGES, SECURITIES AND EXCHANGE COMMISSION RULES, STOCK INDEXES AND AVERAGES,** and **TAX REFORM ACT OF 1986.**

DICTIONARY OF FINANCE
AND INVESTMENT

a

ABC AGREEMENT agreement between a brokerage firm and one of its employees spelling out the firm's rights when it purchases a New York Stock Exchange membership for the employee. Only individuals can be members of the NYSE, and it is common practice for a firm to finance the purchase of a membership, or seat, by one of its employees. (A membership in the mid-1980s cost in excess of $300,000.) The NYSE-approved ABC Agreement contains the following provisions regarding the future disposition of the seat: (1) The employee may retain the membership and buy another seat for an individual designated by the firm. (2) The employee may sell the seat and give the proceeds to the firm. (3) The employee may transfer the seat to another employee of the firm.

ABILITY TO PAY

Finance: borrower's ability to meet principal and interest payments on long-term obligations out of earnings. Also called *ability to service. See also* FIXED CHARGE COVERAGE.

Industrial relations: ability of an employer, especially a financial organization, to meet a union's financial demands from operating income.

Municipal bonds: issuer's present and future ability to generate enough tax revenue to meet its contractual obligations, taking into account all factors concerned with municipal income and property values.

Taxation: the concept that tax rates should vary with levels of wealth or income; for example, the progressive income tax.

ABOVE PAR *see* PAR VALUE.

ABSOLUTE PRIORITY RULE *see* BANKRUPTCY.

ABSORBED

Business: a cost that is treated as an expense rather than passed on to a customer. Also, a firm merged into an acquiring company.

Cost accounting: indirect manufacturing costs (such as property taxes and insurance) are called *absorbed costs.* They are differentiated from variable costs (such as direct labor and materials). *See also* DIRECTOVERHEAD.

Finance: an account that has been combined with related accounts in preparing a financial statement and has lost its separate identity. Also called *absorption account* or *adjunct account.*

Securities: issue that an underwriter has completely sold to the public.

Also, in market trading, securities are absorbed as long as there are corresponding orders to buy and sell. The market has reached the *absorption point* when further assimilation is impossible without an adjustment in price. *See also* UNDIGESTED SECURITIES.

ABUSIVE TAX SHELTER LIMITED PARTNERSHIP the Internal Revenue Service deems to be claiming illegal tax deductions—typically, one that inflates the value of acquired property beyond its fair market value. If these writeoffs are denied by the IRS, investors must pay severe penalties and interest charges, on top of back taxes.

ACCELERATED COST RECOVERY SYSTEM (ACRS) provision instituted by the ECONOMIC RECOVERY TAX ACT OF 1981 (ERTA) and modified by the TAX REFORM ACT OF 1986, which establishes rules for the DEPRECIATION (the recovery of cost through tax deductions) of qualifying assets within a shorter period than the asset's expected useful (economic) life. With certain exceptions, the 1986 Act modifications, which generally provide for greater acceleration over longer periods of time than ERTA rules, are effective for property placed in service after 1986. (There are special transition rules applicable to property under contract or construction prior to March 1, 1986, and to specific kinds of property).

The modified rules specify seven ACRS classes determined with reference to their ASSET DEPRECIATION RANGE (ADR). The ADR system, in effect prior to 1981 and now revived, provides upper and lower limits for the designated lifetimes of different types of assets. Thus, the ACRS *three-year* class includes property with an ADR midpoint of four years or less, the *five-year* class includes assets with an ADR midpoint of more than four but less than 10 years, and so on.

ACRS three-year, five-year, seven-year, and ten-year classes are subject to the DOUBLE DECLINING BALANCE DEPRECIATION METHOD (DDB); the fifteen and twenty-year classes use a variation, *the 150% declining balance method*. The real property class, which comprises residential and nonresidential subclasses depreciable over 27½ and 31½ years, respectively (real property was unfavorably affected by the 1986 tax act), uses STRAIGHT-LINE DEPRECIATION.

ACCELERATED DEPRECIATION Internal Revenue Service-approved methods used in the DEPRECIATION of fixed assets placed in service prior to 1980 when the ACCELERATED COST RECOVERY SYSTEM (ACRS) became mandatory. Such methods provided for faster recovery of cost and earlier tax advantages than traditional STRAIGHT LINE DEPRECIATION and included such methods as DOUBLE-DECLINING BALANCE METHOD (now used in some ACRS classes) and SUM-OF-THE-YEARS' DIGITS METHOD.

ACCELERATION CLAUSE provision, normally present in an INDENTURE agreement, mortgage, or other contract, that the unpaid balance is to become due and payable if specified events of default should occur. Such events include failure to meet interest, principal, or sinking fund payments; insolvency; and nonpayment of taxes on mortgaged property.

ACCEPTANCE

In general: agreement created when the drawee of a TIME DRAFT (bill of exchange) writes the word "accepted" above the signature and designates a date of payment. The drawee becomes the acceptor, responsible for payment at maturity.

Also, paper issued and sold by sales finance companies, such as General Motors Acceptance Corporation.

Banker's acceptance: time draft drawn on and accepted by a bank, the customary means of effecting payment for merchandise sold in import-export transactions and a source of financing used extensivelyin international trade. With the credit strength of a bank behind it, the banker's acceptance usually qualifies as a MONEY MARKET instrument. The liability assumed by the bank is called its acceptance liability. *See also* LETTER OF CREDIT.

Trade acceptance: time draft drawn by the seller of goods on the buyer, who becomes the acceptor, and which is therefore only as good as the buyer's credit.

ACCOUNT

In general: contractual relationship between a buyer and seller under which payment is made at a later time. The term *open account* or *charge account* is used, depending on whether the relationship is commercial or personal.

Also, the historical record of transactions under the contract, as periodically shown on the *statement of account*.

Banking: relationship under a particular name, usually evidenced by a deposit against which withdrawals can be made. Among them are demand, time, custodial, joint, trustee, corporate, special, and regular accounts. Administrative responsibility is handled by an *account officer*.

Bookkeeping: assets, liabilities, income, and expenses as represented by individual ledger pages to which debit and credit entries are chronologically posted to record changes in value. Examples are cash, accounts receivable, accrued interest, sales, and officers' salaries. The system of recording, verifying, and reporting such information is called accounting. Practitioners of accounting are called *accountants*.

Investment banking: financial and contractual relationship between parties to an underwriting syndicate, or the status of securities owned and sold.

Securities: relationship between a broker-dealer firm and its client wherein the firm, through its registered representatives, acts as agent in buying and selling securities and sees to related administrative matters. *See also* ACCOUNT EXECUTIVE; ACCOUNT STATEMENT.

ACCOUNTANT'S OPINION statement signed by an independent public accountant describing the scope of the examination of an organization's books and records. Because financial reporting involves considerable discretion, the accountant's opinion is an important assurance to a lender or investor. Depending on the scope of an audit and the auditor's confidence in the veracity of the information, the opinion can be unqualified or, to some degree, qualified. Qualified opinions, though not necessarily negative, warrant investigation. Also called *auditor's certificate*.

ACCOUNT EXECUTIVE brokerage firm employee who advises and handles orders for clients and has the legal powers of an AGENT. Every account executive must pass certain tests and be registered with the NATIONAL ASSOCIATION OF SECURITIES DEALERS (NASD) before soliciting orders from customers. Also called *registered representative*. *See also* BROKER.

ACCOUNTING PRINCIPLES BOARD (APB) board of the American Institute of Certified Public Accountants (AICPA) that issued (1959–73) a series of ACCOUNTANT'S OPINIONS constituting much of what is known as GENERALLY ACCEPTED ACCOUNTING PRINCIPLES. *See also* FINANCIAL ACCOUNTING STANDARDS BOARD (FASB).

ACCOUNTS PAYABLE amounts owing on open account to creditors for goods and services. Analysts look at the relationship of accounts payable to purchases for indications of sound day-to-day financial management. *See also* TRADE CREDIT.

ACCOUNTS RECEIVABLE money owed to a business for merchandise or services sold on open account, a key factor in analyzing a company's LIQUIDITY—its ability to meet current obligations without additional revenues. *See also* ACCOUNTS RECEIVABLE TURNOVER; AGING SCHEDULE; COLLECTION RATIO.

ACCOUNTS RECEIVABLE FINANCING short-term financing whereby accounts receivable serve as collateral for working capital advances. *See also* FACTORING.

ACCOUNTS RECEIVABLE TURNOVER ratio obtained by dividing total credit sales by accounts receivable. The ratio indicates how many times the receivables portfolio has been collected during the accounting period. *See also* ACCOUNTS RECEIVABLE; AGING SCHEDULE; COLLECTIONRATIO.

ACCOUNT STATEMENT

In general: any record of transactions and their effect on charge or open-account balances during a specified period.

Banking: summary of all checks paid, deposits recorded, and resulting balances during a defined period. Also called a *bank statement*.

Securities: statement summarizing all transactions and showing the status of an account with a broker-dealer firm, including long and short positions. Such statements must be issued quarterly, but are generally provided monthly when accounts are active. Also, the OPTION AGREEMENT required when an option account is opened.

ACCREDITED INVESTOR under Securities and Exchange Commission Regulation D, a wealthy investor who does not count as one of the maximum of 35 people allowed to put money into a PRIVATE LIMITED PARTNERSHIP. To be accredited, such an investor must have a net worth of at least $1 million or an annual income of at least $200,000, or must put at least $150,000 into the deal, and the investment must not account for more than 20% of the investor's worth. Private limited partnerships use accredited investors to raise a larger amount of capital than would be possible if only 35 less-wealthy people could contribute.

ACCRETION
1. asset growth through internal expansion, acquisition, or such causes as aging of whisky or growth of timber.
2. adjustment of the difference between the price of a bond bought at an original discount and the par value of the bond.

ACCRUAL BASIS accounting method whereby income and expense items are recognized as they are earned or incurred, even though they may not have been received or actually paid in cash. The alternative is CASH BASIS accounting.

ACCRUED INTEREST interest that has accumulated between the most recent payment and the sale of a bond or other fixed-income security. At the time of sale, the buyer pays the seller the bond's price plus accrued interest, calculated by multiplying the coupon rate by the number of days that have elapsed since the last payment.

Accrued interest is also used in a real estate LIMITED PARTNERSHIP when the seller of a building takes a lump sum in cash at the time of sale and gives a second mortgage for the remainder. If the rental income from the building does not cover the mortgage payments, the seller agrees to let the interest accrue until the building is sold to someone else. Accrued interest deals were curtailed by the 1984 tax act.

ACCUMULATED DIVIDEND dividend due, usually to holders of cumulative preferred stock, but not paid. It is carried on the books as a liability until paid. *See also* CUMULATIVE PREFERRED.

ACCUMULATED PROFITS TAX surtax on earnings retained in a business to avoid the higher personal income taxes they would be subject to if paid out as dividends to the owners.

Accumulations above the specified limit, which is set fairly high to benefit small firms, must be justified by the reasonable needs of the business or be subject to the surtax. Because determining the reasonable needs of a business involves considerable judgment, companies have been known to pay excessive dividends or even to make merger decisions out of fear of the accumulated profits tax. Also called *accumulated earnings tax.*

ACCUMULATION

Corporate finance: profits that are not paid out as dividends but are instead added to the company's capital base. *See also* ACCUMULATED PROFITS TAX.

Investments: purchase of a large number of shares in a controlled way so as to avoid driving the price up. An institution's accumulation program, for instance, may take weeks or months to complete.

Mutual funds: investment of a fixed dollar amount regularly and reinvestment of dividends and capital gains.

ACCUMULATION AREA price range within which buyers accumulate shares of a stock. Technical analysts spot accumulation areas when a stock does not drop below a particular price. Technicians who use the ON-BALANCE VOLUME method of analysis advise buying stocks that have hit their accumulation area, because the stocks can be expected to attract more buying interest. *See also* DISTRIBUTION AREA.

ACCUMULATION AREA

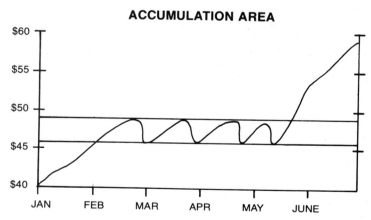

ACID-TEST RATIO *See* QUICK RATIO.

ACKNOWLEDGMENT verification that a signature on a banking or brokerage document is legitimate and has been certified by an authorized person. Acknowledgment is needed when transferring an account from one broker to another, for instance. In banking, an acknowledgment verifies that an item has been received by the paying bank and is or is not available for immediate payment.

ACQUIRED SURPLUS uncapitalized portion of the net worth of a successor company in a POOLING OF INTERESTS combination. In other words, the part of the combined net worth not classified as CAPITAL STOCK.

    In a more general sense, the surplus acquired when a company is purchased.

ACQUISITION one company taking over controlling interest in another company. Investors are always looking out for companies that are likely to be acquired, because those who want to acquire such companies are often willing to pay more than the market price for the shares they need to complete the acquisition. *See also* MERGER; POOLING OF INTERESTS; TAKEOVER.

ACROSS THE BOARD movement in the stock market that affects almost all stocks in the same direction. When the market moves up across the board, almost every stock gains in price.

    An across-the-board pay increase in a company is a raise of a fixed percent or amount for all employees.

ACTING IN CONCERT two or more investors working together to achieve the same investment goal—for example, all buying stock in a company they want to take over. Such investors must inform the Securities and Exchange Commission if they intend to oust the company's top management or acquire control. It is illegal for those acting in concert to manipulate a stock's price for their own gain.

ACTIVE BOND CROWD members of the bond department of the New York Stock Exchange responsible for the heaviest volume of bond trading. The opposite of the active crowd is the CABINET CROWD, which deals in bonds that are infrequently traded. Investors who buy and sell bonds in the active crowd will tend to get better prices for their securities than in the inactive market, where spreads between bid and asked prices are wider.

ACTIVE BOX collateral available for securing brokers' loans or customers' margin positions in the place—or *box*—where securities are held in safekeeping for clients of a broker-dealer or for the broker-dealer itself. Securities used as collateral must be owned by the firm or hypothecated—that is, pledged or assigned—by the customer to the firm, then by the broker to the lending bank. For margin loans, securities must be hypothecated by the customer to the broker.

ACTIVE MARKET heavy volume of trading in a particular stock, bond, or commodity. The spread between bid and asked prices is usually narrower in an active market than when trading is quiet.

    Also, a heavy volume of trading on the exchange as a whole. Institutional money managers prefer such a market because their trades of large blocks of stock tend to have less impact on the movement of prices when trading is generally active.

ACTUALS any physical commodity, such as gold, soybeans, or pork bellies. Trading in actuals ultimately results in delivery of the commodity to the buyer when the contract expires. This contrasts with trading in commodities of, for example, index options, where the contract is settled in cash, and no physical commodity is delivered upon expiration. However, even when trading is in actuals most futures and options contracts are closed out before the contract expires, and so these transactions do not end in delivery.

ACTUARY mathematician employed by an insurance company to calculate premiums, reserves, dividends, and insurance, pension, and annuity rates, using risk factors obtained from experience tables. These tables are based on both the company's history of insurance claims and other industry and general statistical data.

ADDITIONAL PAID-IN CAPITAL *see* PAID-IN CAPITAL.

ADJUSTABLE RATE MORTGAGE (ARM) mortgage agreement between a financial institution and a real estate buyer stipulating predetermined adjustments of the interest rate at specified intervals. Mortgage payments are tied to some index outside the control of the bank or savings and loan institution, such as the interest rates on U.S. Treasury bills or the average national mortgage rate. Adjustments are made regularly, usually at intervals of one, three, or five years. In return for taking some of the risk of a rise in interest rates, borrowers get lower rates at the beginning of the ARM than they would if they took out a fixed rate mortgage covering the same term. A homeowner who is worried about sharply rising interest rates should probably choose a fixed rate mortgage, whereas one who thinks rates will rise modestly, stay stable, or fall should choose an adjustable rate mortgage. Critics of ARMs charge that these mortgages entice young homeowners to undertake potentially onerous commitments.

ADJUSTED BASIS base price from which to judge capital gains or losses upon sale of an asset like a stock or bond. The cost of commissions in effect is deducted at the time of sale when net proceeds are used for tax purposes. The price must be adjusted to account for any stock splits that have occurred since the initial purchase before arriving at the adjusted basis.

ADJUSTED DEBIT BALANCE (ADB) formula for determining the position of a margin account, as required under Regulation T of the Federal Reserve Board. The ADB is calculated by netting the balance owing the broker with any balance in the SPECIAL MISCELLANEOUS ACCOUNT (SMA), and any paper profits on short accounts. Although changes made in Regulation T in 1982 diminished the significance of ADBs, the formula is still useful in determining whether withdrawals of cash or securities are permissible based on SMA entries.

ADJUSTED EXERCISE PRICE term used in put and call options on Government National Mortgage Association (Ginnie Mae) contracts. To make sure that all contracts trade fairly, the final exercise price of the option is adjusted to take into account the coupon rates carried on all GNMA mortgages. If the standard GNMA mortgage carries an 8% yield, for instance, the price of GNMA pools with 12% mortgages in them are adjusted so that both instruments have the same yield to the investor.

ADJUSTED GROSS INCOME income on which an individual computes federal income tax. Adjusted gross income is determined by subtracting from gross income any unreimbursed business expenses and other deductions—for example Individual Retirement Account (with exceptions outlined in the TAX REFORM ACT OF 1986) and Keogh payments, alimony payments, and disability income. Adjusted gross income is the individual's or couple's income before itemized deductions for such items as medical expenses, state and local income taxes, and real estate taxes.

ADJUSTMENT BOND bond issued in exchange for outstanding bonds when recapitalizing a corporation that faces bankruptcy. Authorization for the exchange comes from the bondholders, who consider adjustment bonds a lesser evil. These bonds promise to pay interest only to the extent earned by the corporation. This gives them one of the characteristics of income bonds, which trade flat—that is, without accrued interest.

ADMINISTRATOR court-appointed individual or bank charged with carrying out the court's decisions with respect to a decedent's estate until it is fully distributed to all claimants. Administrators are appointed when a person dies without having made a will or without having named an executor, or when the named executor cannot or will not serve. The term *administratrix* is sometimes used if the individual appointed is a woman.

In a general sense, an administrator is a person who carries out an organization's policies.

AD VALOREM Latin term meaning "according to value" and referring to a way of assessing duties or taxes on goods or property. As one example, ad valorem DUTY assessment is based on value of the imported item rather than on its weight or quantity. As another example, the city of Englewood, New Jersey, levies an ad valorem tax based on the assessed value of property rather than its size.

ADVANCE-DECLINE (A-D) measurement of the number of stocks that have advanced and the number that have declined over a particular period. It is the ratio of one to the other and shows the general direction of the market. It is considered bullish if more stocks advance than decline on any trading day. It is bearish if declines outnumber advances. The steepness of the A-D line graphically shows whether a strong bull or bear market is underway.

ADVANCE-DECLINE LINE

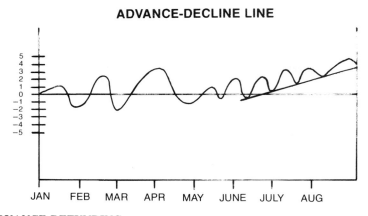

ADVANCE REFUNDING

Government securities: exchange of maturing government securities prior to their due date for issues with a later maturity. It is through advance refunding that the national debt is extended as an alternative to the economic disruptions that would result from eliminating the debt all at once.

Municipal bonds: sale of new bonds (a *refunding issue*) in advance, usually by some years, of the first call date of the old bonds (*issue to be refunded*). The refunding issue would normally have a lower rate than the issue to be refunded, and the proceeds would be invested, usually in government securities, until the higher-rate bonds become callable. This practice was curtailed by the 1986 federal Tax Act.

AFFILIATE

In general: two companies are affiliated when one owns less than a majority of the voting stock of the other, or when both are subsidiaries of a third company.

A SUBSIDIARY is a company of which more than 50% of the voting shares are owned by another corporation, termed the PARENT COMPANY. A subsidiary is always, by definition, an affiliate, but subsidiary is the preferred term when majority control exists. In everyday use, affiliate is the correct word for intercompany relationships, however indirect, where the parent-subsidiary relationship does not apply.

Banking Act of 1933: any organization that a bank owns or controls by stock holdings, or which the bank's shareholders own, or whose officers are also directors of the bank.

Internal Revenue Service: for purposes of consolidated tax returns an affiliated group is composed of companies whose parent or other inclusive corporation owns at least 80% of voting stock.

Interstate Commerce Commission, Account 706: 1. Controlled by the accounting company alone or with others under a joint agreement. **2.** Controlling the accounting company alone or with others under a joint agreement.

Investment Company Act: company in which there is any direct or indirect ownership of 5% or more of the outstanding voting securities.

AFFILIATED PERSON individual in a position to exert direct influence on the actions of a corporation. Among such persons are owners of 10% or more of the voting shares, directors, and senior elected officers and any persons in a position to exert influence through them—such as members of their immediate family and other close associates. Sometimes called a *control person.*

AFTER ACQUIRED CLAUSE clause in a mortgage agreement providing that any additional mortgageable property acquired by the borrower after the mortgage is signed will be additional security for the obligation.

While such provisions can help give mortgage bonds a good rating and enable issuing corporations to borrow at favorable rates, by precluding additional first mortgages, they make it difficult to finance growth through new borrowings. This gives rise to various maneuvers to remove after acquired clauses, such as redemption or exchange of bonds or changes in indenture agreements.

AFTERMARKET *see* SECONDARY MARKET.

AFTERTAX BASIS basis for comparing the returns on a corporate taxable bond and a municipal tax-free bond. For example, a corporate bond paying 10% would have an aftertax return of 7.2% for someone in the 28% tax bracket. So any municipal bond paying higher than 7.2% would yield a higher aftertax return.

AFTERTAX REAL RATE OF RETURN amount of money, adjusted for inflation, that an investor can keep, out of the income and capital gains earned from investments. Every dollar loses value to inflation, so investors have to keep an eye on the aftertax real rate of return whenever they commit their capital. By and large, investors seek a rate of return that will match if not exceed the rate of inflation.

AGAINST THE BOX SHORT SALE by the holder of a LONG POSITION in the same stock. *Box* refers to the physical location of securities held in safekeeping. When a stock is sold against the box, it is sold short, but only in effect. A short sale is usually defined as one where the seller does not own the shares. Here the seller *does* own the shares (holds a long position) but does not wish to disclose ownership; or perhaps the long shares are too inaccessible to deliver in the time required; or he may be holding his existing position to get the benefit of long-term capital gains tax treatment. In any event, when the sale is made against the box, the shares needed to cover are borrowed, probably from a broker.

AGED FAIL contract between two broker-dealers that is still not settled 30 days after the settlement date. At that point the open balance no longer counts as an asset, and the receiving firm must adjust its capital accordingly.

AGENCY

In general: relationship between two parties, one a principal and the other an AGENT who represents the principal in transactions with a third party.

Finance: certain types of accounts in trust institutions where individuals, usually trust officers, act on behalf of customers. Agency services to corporations are related to stock purchases and sales. Banks also act as agents for individuals.

Government: securities issued by government-sponsored corporations such as Federal Home Loan Banks or Federal Land Banks. Agency securities are exempt from Securities and Exchange Commission (SEC) registration requirements.

Investment: act of buying or selling for the account and risk of a client. Generally, an agent, or broker, acts as intermediary between buyer and seller, taking no financial risk personally or as a firm, and charging a commission for the service.

AGENT individual authorized by another person, called the principal, to act in the latter's behalf in transactions involving a third party. Banks are frequently appointed by individuals to be their agents, and so authorize their employees to act on behalf of principals. Agents have three basic characteristics:
1. They act on behalf of and are subject to the control of the principal.
2. They do not have title to the principal's property.
3. They owe the duty of obedience to the principal's orders.
See also ACCOUNT EXECUTIVE; BROKER; TRANSFER AGENT.

AGGREGATE EXERCISE PRICE in stock options trading, the number of shares in a put or call CONTRACT (normally 100) multiplied by the EXERCISE PRICE. The price of the option, called the PREMIUM, is a separate figure not included in the aggregate exercise price. A July call option on 100 XYZ at 70 would, for example, have an aggregate exercise price of 100 (number of shares) times $70 (price per share), or $7,000, if exercised on or before the July expiration date.

In options traded on debt instruments, which include GOVERNMENT NATIONAL MORTGAGE ASSOCIATION (GNMA) pass-throughs, Treasury bills, Treasury notes, Treasury bonds, and certain municipal bonds, the aggregate exercise price is determined by multiplying the FACE VALUE of the underlying security by the exercise price. For example, the aggregate exercise price of put option Treasury bond December 90 would be $90,000 if exercised on or before its December expiration date, the calculation being 90% times the $100,000 face value of the underlying bond.

AGGREGATE SUPPLY in MACROECONOMICS, the total amount of goods and services supplied to the market at alternative price levels in a given period of time; also called *total output*. The central concept in SUPPLY-SIDE ECONOMICS, it corresponds with aggregate demand, defined as the total amount of goods and services demanded in the economy at alternative income levels in a given period, including both consumer and producers' goods; aggregate demand is also called *total spending*. The aggregate supply curve describes the relationship between price levels and the quantity of output that firms are willing to provide.

AGING SCHEDULE classification of trade ACCOUNTS RECEIVABLE by date of sale. Usually prepared by a company's auditor, the *aging,* as the schedule is called, is a vital tool in analyzing the quality of a company's receivables investment. It is frequently required by grantors of credit.

The schedule is most often seen as: (1) a list of the amount of receivables by the month in which they were created; (2) a list of receivables by maturity, classified as current or as being in various stages of delinquency. The following is a typical aging schedule:

	dollars (in thousands)	
Current (under 30 days)	$14,065	61%
1–30 days past due	3,725	16
31–60 days past due	2,900	12
61–90 days past due	1,800	8
Over 90 days past due	750	3
	$23,240	100%

The aging schedule reveals patterns of delinquency and shows where collection efforts should be concentrated. It helps in evaluating the adequacy of the reserve for BAD DEBTS, because the longer accounts stretch out the more likely they are to become uncollectible. Using the schedule can help prevent the loss of future sales, since old customers who fall too far behind tend to seek out new sources of supply.

AGREEMENT AMONG UNDERWRITERS contract between participating members of an investment banking SYNDICATE; sometimes called *syndicate contract* or *purchase group agreement.* It is distinguished from the *underwriting agreement,* which is signed by the company issuing the securities and the SYNDICATE MANAGER, acting as agent for the underwriting group.

The agreement among underwriters: (1) appoints the originating investment banker as syndicate manager and agent; (2) appoints additional managers, if considered advisable; (3) defines the members' proportionate liability (usually limited to the amount of their participation) and agrees to pay each member's share on settlement date; (4) authorizes the manager to form and allocate units to a SELLING GROUP, and agrees to abide by the rules of the selling group agreement; (5) states the life of the syndicate, usually running until 30 days after termination of the selling group, or ending earlier by mutual consent.

AIR POCKET STOCK stock that falls sharply, usually in the wake of such negative news as unexpected poor earnings. As shareholders rush to sell, and few buyers can be found, the price plunges dramatically, like an airplane hitting an air pocket.

ALIEN CORPORATION company incorporated under the laws of a foreign country regardless of where it operates. ''Alien corporation'' can be used as a synonym for the term *foreign corporation.* However, ''foreign corporation'' also is used in U.S. state law to mean a corporation formed in a state other than that in which it does business.

ALLIED MEMBER general partner or voting stockholder of a member firm of the New York Stock Exchange who is not personally a member. Allied members cannot do business on the trading floor. A member firm need have no more than one partner or voting stockholder who owns a membership. So even the chairman of the board of a member firm may be no more than an allied member.

ALLIGATOR SPREAD spread in the options market that "eats the investor alive" with high commission costs. The term is used when a broker arranges a combination of puts and calls that generates so much commission the client is unlikely to turn a profit even if the markets move as anticipated.

ALL OR NONE (AON)

Investment banking: an offering giving the issuer the right to cancel the whole issue if the underwriting is not fully subscribed.

Securities: buy or sell order marked to signify that no partial transaction is to be executed. The order will not automatically be canceled, however, if a complete transaction is not executed; to accomplish that, the order entry must be marked FOK, meaning FILL (for the full number of units) OR KILL.

ALLOTMENT amount of securities assigned to each of the participants in an investment banking SYNDICATE formed to underwrite and distribute a new issue, called *subscribers* or *allottees*. The financial responsibilities of the subscribers are set forth in an allotment notice, which is prepared by the SYNDICATE MANAGER.

ALLOWANCE deduction from the value of an invoice, permitted by a seller of goods to cover damages or shortages. *See also* RESERVE.

ALL-SAVERS CERTIFICATE *see* ECONOMIC RECOVERY TAX ACT OF 1981 (ERTA).

ALPHA *see* VOLATILE.

ALTERNATIVE MINIMUM TAX (AMT) federal tax, revamped by the TAX REFORM ACT OF 1986, aimed at ensuring that wealthy individuals and corporations pay at least some income tax. For individuals, the AMT is computed by adding TAX PREFERENCE ITEMS such as PASSIVE losses from tax shelters, tax-exempt interest on PRIVATE-PURPOSE BONDS issued after August 8, 1986, and deductions claimed for charitable contributions of stock, real estate, art work, and other appreciated property to adjusted gross income, then subtracting $40,000 for a married couple filing jointly or $30,000 if filing singly; 21% of the remainder is the payable tax. The exemption amounts are phased out by 25 cents for each $1 that AMT income exceeds $150,000 for joint filers ($112,500 for individuals). The corporate AMT has the same exemptions but a rate of 20%. Preferences include 50% of the excess of "book" (financial statement) income over total taxable income plus other preferences such as untaxed appreciation of charitable contributions, certain "excess" accelerated depreciation on assets put in service after 1986, tax-exempt interest on private-purpose bonds issued after August 8, 1986, and other industry-specific preferences. After 1989, the corporate AMT is set to be based on the tax definition of earnings and profits, not book income.

ALTERNATIVE ORDER order giving a broker a choice between two courses of action; also called an *either-or order* or a *one cancels the other order*. Such orders are either to buy or to sell, never both. Execution of one course automatically makes the other course inoperative. An example is a combination buy limit/buy stop order, wherein the buy limit is below the current market and the buy stop is above.

AMBAC Indemnity Corporation *see* MUNICIPAL BOND INSURANCE.

AMENDMENT addition to, or change, in a legal document. When properly signed, it has the full legal effect of the original document.

AMERICAN DEPOSITARY RECEIPT (ADR) receipt for the shares of a foreign-based corporation held in the vault of a U.S. bank and entitling the shareholder to all dividends and capital gains. Instead of buying shares of foreign-based companies in overseas markets, Americans can buy shares in the U.S. in the form of an ADR. ADR's are available for hundreds of stocks from numerous countries. Also called *American Depositary Share.*

AMERICAN STOCK EXCHANGE (AMEX) stock exchange located at 86 Trinity Place in downtown Manhattan. The Amex was known until 1921 as the *Curb Exchange,* and it is still referred to as the *Curb* today. For the most part, the stocks and bonds traded on the Amex are those of small to medium-size companies, as contrasted with the huge companies whose shares are traded on the New York Stock Exchange. A large number of oil and gas companies, in particular, are traded on the Amex. The Amex also houses the trading of options on many New York Stock Exchange stocks and some OVER THE COUNTER stocks. More foreign shares are traded on the Amex than on any other U.S. exchange.

AMORTIZATION accounting procedure that gradually reduces the cost value of a limited life or intangible asset through periodic charges to income. For fixed assets the term used is DEPRECIATION, and for wasting assets (natural resources) it is depletion, both terms meaning essentially the same thing as amortization. Most companies follow the conservative practice of writing off, through amortization, INTANGIBLE ASSETS such as goodwill. It is also common practice to amortize any premium over par value paid in the purchase of preferred stock or bond investments. The purpose of amortization is to reflect resale or redemption value.

Amortization also refers to the reduction of debt by regular payments of interest and principal sufficient to pay off a loan by maturity.

Discount and expense on funded debt are amortized by making applicable charges to income in accordance with a predetermined schedule. While this is normally done systematically, charges to profit and loss are permissible at any time in any amount of the remaining discount and expense. Such accounting is detailed in a company's annual report.

ANALYST person in a brokerage house, bank trust department, or mutual fund group who studies a number of companies and makes buy or sell recommendations on the securities of particular companies and industry groups. Most analysts specialize in a particular industry, but some investigate any company that interests them, regardless of its line of business. Some analysts have considerable influence, and can therefore affect the price of a company's stock when they issue a buy or sell recommendation. *See also* CREDIT ANALYST.

AND INTEREST phrase used in quoting bond prices to indicate that, in addition to the price quoted, the buyer will receive ACCRUED INTEREST.

ANNUAL BASIS statistical technique whereby figures covering a period of less than a year are extended to cover a 12-month period. The procedure, called *annualizing,* must take seasonal variations (if any) into account to be accurate.

ANNUAL MEETING once-a-year meeting when the managers of a company report to stockholders on the year's results, and the board of directors stands for election for the next year. The chief executive officer usually comments on the outlook for the coming year and, with other senior officers, answers questions from shareholders. Stockholders can also request that resolutions on corporate policy be voted on by all those owning stock in the company. Stockholders unable to attend the annual meeting may vote for directors and pass on resolutions through the use of PROXY material, which must legally be mailed to all shareholders of record.

ANNUAL PERCENTAGE RATE (APR) cost of credit that consumers pay, expressed as a simple annual percentage. According to the federal Truth in Lending Act, every consumer loan agreement must disclose the APR in large bold type. *See also* CONSUMER CREDIT PROTECTION ACT OF 1968.

ANNUAL RENEWABLE TERM INSURANCE *See* TERM INSURANCE.

ANNUAL REPORT yearly record of a corporation's financial condition that must be distributed to shareholders under SECURITIES AND EXCHANGE COMMISSION regulations. Included in the report is a description of the company's operations as well as its balance sheet and income statement. The long version of the annual report with more detailed financial information—called the 10-K—is available upon request from the corporate secretary.

ANNUITIZE to begin a series of payments from the capital that has built up in an ANNUITY. The payments may be a fixed amount, or for a fixed period of time, or for the lifetimes of one or two *annuitants,* thus guaranteeing income payments that cannot be outlived. *See also* DEFERRED PAYMENT ANNUITY; FIXED ANNUITY; IMMEDIATE PAYMENT ANNUITY; VARIABLE ANNUITY.

ANNUITY form of contract sold by life insurance companies that guarantees a fixed or variable payment to the annuitant at some future time, usually retirement. In a FIXED ANNUITY the amount will ultimately be paid out in regular installments varying only with the payout method elected. In a VARIABLE ANNUITY, the amount of the payout will vary with the value of the account. All capital and investment proceeds that remain inside the annuity accumulate tax-deferred. Key considerations when buying an annuity are the financial soundness of the insurance company (*see* BEST'S RATING), the returns it has paid on annuities in the past, and the level of fees and commissions paid to annuity salesmen.

ANTICIPATED HOLDING PERIOD time during which a limited partnership expects to hold onto an asset. In the prospectus for a real estate limited partnership, for instance, a sponsor will typically say that the anticipated holding period for a particular property is five to seven years. At the end of that time the property is sold, and, usually, the capital received is returned to the limited partners in one distribution.

ANTICIPATION

In general: paying an obligation before it falls due.

Finance: repayment of debt obligations before maturity, usually to save interest. If a formalized discount or rebate is involved, the term used is *anticipation rate.*

Mortgage instrument: when a provision allows prepayment without penalty, the mortgagee is said to have the *right of anticipation.*

Trade payments: bill that is paid before it is due, not discounted.

ANTITRUST LAWS federal legislation designed to prevent monopolies and restraint of trade. Landmark statutes include:
1. the Sherman Anti-Trust Act of 1890, which prohibited acts or contracts tending to create monopoly and initiated an era of trustbusting.
2. the Clayton Anti-Trust Act of 1914, which was passed as an amendment to the Sherman Act and dealt with local price discrimination as well as with the INTERLOCKING DIRECTORATES. It went further in the areas of the HOLDING COMPANY and restraint of trade.
3. the Federal Trade Commission Act of 1914, which created the Federal Trade

Commission or FTC, with power to conduct investigations and issue orders preventing unfair practices in interstate commerce.

ANY-AND-ALL-BID offer to pay an equal price for all shares tendered by a deadline; contrasts with TWO-TIER BID. *See also* TAKEOVER.

APPRECIATION increase in the value of an asset such as a stock, bond, commodity, or real estate.

APPROVED LIST *see* LEGAL LIST.

ARBITRAGE profiting from differences in price when the same security, currency, or commodity is traded on two or more markets. For example, an *arbitrageur* simultaneously buys one contract of gold in the New York market and sells one contract of gold in the Chicago market, locking in a profit because at that moment the price on the two markets is different. (The arbitrageur's selling price is higher than the buying price.) *Index arbitrage* exploits price differences between STOCK INDEX FUTURES and underlying stocks. By taking advantage of momentary disparities in prices between markets, arbitrageurs perform the economic function of making those markets trade more efficiently. *See also* RISK ARBITRAGE.

ARBITRAGE BONDS bonds issued by a municipality in order to gain an interest rate advantage by refunding higher-rate bonds in advance of their call date. Proceeds from the lower-rate refunding issue are invested in treasuries until the first call date of the higher-rate issue being refunded. Arbitrage bonds, which always raised a question of tax exemption, were further curtailed by the TAX REFORM ACT OF 1986.

ARBITRATION *see* BOARD OF ARBITRATION.

ARITHMETIC MEAN simple average obtained by dividing the sum of two or more items by the number of items.

ARM'S LENGTH TRANSACTION transaction that is conducted as though the parties were unrelated, thus avoiding any semblance of conflict of interest. For example, under current law parents may rent real estate to their children and still claim business deductions such as depreciation as long as the parents charge their children what they would charge if someone who is not a relative were to rent the same property.

ARREARAGE

In general: amount of any past-due obligation.

Investments: amount by which interest on bonds or dividends on CUMULATIVE PREFERRED stock is due and unpaid. In the case of cumulative preferred stock, common dividends cannot be paid by a company as long as preferred dividends are in arrears.

ARTICLES OF INCORPORATION document filed with a U.S. state by the founders of a corporation. After approving the articles, the state issues a certificate of incorporation; the two documents together become the CHARTER that gives the corporation its legal existence. The charter embodies such information as the corporation's name, purpose, amount of authorized shares, and number and identity of directors. The corporation's powers thus derive from the laws of the state and from the provisions of the charter. Rules governing its internal management are set forth in the corporation's BYLAWS, which are drawn up by the founders.

ASCENDING TOPS chart pattern tracing a security's price over a period of time and showing that each peak in a security's price is higher than the preceding peak. This upward movement is considered bullish, meaning that the upward trend is likely to continue. *See also* DESCENDING TOPS.

ASCENDING TOPS

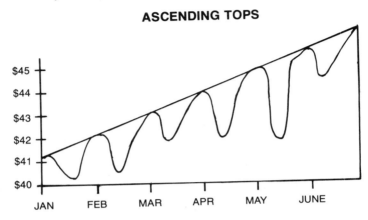

ASE INDEX *see* STOCK INDEXES AND AVERAGES.

ASKED PRICE
1. price at which a security or commodity is offered for sale on an exchange or in the over-the-counter market. Generally, it is the lowest round lot price at which a dealer will sell. Also called the *ask price, asking price, ask,* or OFFERING PRICE.
2. per-share price at which mutual fund shares are offered to the public, usually the NET ASSET VALUE per share plus a sales charge, if any.

ASSAY test of a metal's purity to verify that it meets the standards for trading on a commodities exchange. For instance, a 100 troy-ounce bar of refined gold must be assayed at a fineness of not less than 995 before the Comex will allow it to be used in settlement of a gold contract.

ASSESSED VALUATION dollar value assigned to property by a municipality for purposes of assessing taxes, which are based on the number of mills per dollar of assessed valuation. If a house is assessed at $100,000 and the tax rate is 50 mills, the tax is $5000. Assessed valuation is important not only to homeowners but also to investors in municipal bonds that are backed by property taxes.

ASSET anything having commercial or exchange value that is owned by a business, institution, or individual. *See also* CAPITAL ASSET; CURRENT ASSETS; DEFERRED CHARGE; FIXED ASSET; INTANGIBLE ASSET; NONCURRENT ASSET.

ASSET COVERAGE extent to which a company's net assets cover a particular debt obligation, class of preferred stock, or equity position.
Asset coverage is calculated as follows: from assets at their total book value or liquidation value, subtract intangible assets, current liabilities, and all obligations prior in claim to the issue in question. Divide the result by the dollar amount of the subject issue (or loan) to arrive at the asset coverage ratio. The same information can be expressed as a percentage or, by using units as the divisor, as a dollar figure of coverage per unit. The variation to determine pre-

ferred stock coverage treats all liabilities as paid; the variation to arrive at common stock coverage considers both preferred stock and liabilities paid. The term most often used for the common stock calculation is *net book value per share of common stock.*

These calculations reveal *direct* asset coverage. *Overall* asset coverage is obtained by including the subject issue with the total of prior obligations and dividing the aggregate into total tangible assets at liquidating value.

Asset coverage is important as a cushion against losses in the event of liquidation.

ASSET DEPRECIATION RANGE SYSTEM (ADR) range of depreciable lives allowed by the Internal Revenue Service for particular classes of depreciable assets. The ADR system was replaced when the ECONOMIC RECOVERY TAX ACT OF 1981 (ERTA) introduced the ACCELERATED COST RECOVERY SYSTEM (ACRS) but was revived with modifications of ACRS under the TAX REFORM ACT OF 1986. The ADR system assigns an upper and lower limit to the estimated useful lives of asset classes. ACRS classes are based on the mid-points of these ranges. Under the alternative depreciation system, taxpayers may elect STRAIGHT LINE DEPRECIATION over the applicable ADR-class life.

ASSET FINANCING financing that seeks to convert particular assets into working cash in exchange for a security interest in those assets. The term is replacing *commercial financing* as major banks join commercial finance companies in addressing the financing needs of companies that do not fit the traditional seasonal borrower profile. Although the prevalent form of asset financing continues to be loans against accounts receivable, *inventory loans* are common and *second mortgage loans,* predicated as they usually are on market values containing a high inflation factor, seem to gain popularity by the day. *See also* ACCOUNTS RECEIVABLE FINANCING.

ASSET-LIABILITY MANAGEMENT matching an individual's level of debt and amount of assets. Someone who is planning to buy a new car, for instance, would have to decide whether to pay cash, thus lowering assets, or to take out a loan, thereby increasing debts (or liabilities). Such decisions should be based on interest rates, on earning power, and on the comfort level with debt. Financial institutions carry out asset-liability management when they match the maturity of their deposits with the length of their loan commitments to keep from being adversely affected by rapid changes in interest rates.

ASSET MANAGEMENT ACCOUNT account at a brokerage house, bank, or savings institution that combines banking services like checkwriting, credit cards, and debit cards; brokerage features like buying securities and making loans on margin; and the convenience of having all financial transactions listed on one monthly statement.

ASSET PLAY stock market term for a stock that is attractive because the current price does not reflect the value of the company's assets. For example, an analyst could recommend a hotel chain, not because its hotels are run well but because its real estate is worth far more than is recognized in the stock's current price. Asset play stocks are tempting targets for takeovers because they provide an inexpensive way to buy assets.

ASSIGN sign a document transferring ownership from one party to another. Ownership can be in a number of forms, including tangible property, rights (usually arising out of contracts), or the right to transfer ownership at some later time.

The party who assigns is called the *assignor* and the party who receives the transfer of title—the assignment—is the *assignee*.

Stocks and registered bonds can be assigned by completing and signing a form printed on the back of the certificate—or, as is sometimes preferred for safety reasons, by executing a separate form, called an *assignment separate from certificate* or *stock/bond power*.

When the OPTIONS CLEARING CORPORATION learns of the exercise of an option, it prepares an assignment form notifying a broker-dealer that an option written by one of its clients has been exercised. The firm in turn assigns the exercise in accordance with its internal procedures.

An assignment for the benefit of creditors, sometimes called simply an *assignment*, is an alternative to bankruptcy, whereby the assets of a company are assigned to the creditors and liquidated for their benefit by a trustee.

ASSIMILATION absorption of a new issue of stock by the investing public after all shares have been sold by the issue's underwriters. *See also* ABSORBED.

ASSUMPTION act of taking on responsibility for the liabilities of another party, usually documented by an *assumption agreement*. In the case of a MORTGAGE assumption, the seller remains secondarily liable unless released from the obligation by the lender.

AT PAR at a price equal to the face, or nominal, value of a security. *See also* PAR VALUE.

AT RISK exposed to the danger of loss. Investors in a limited partnership can claim tax deductions only if they can prove that there's a chance of never realizing any profit and of losing their investment as well. Deductions will be disallowed if the limited partners are not exposed to economic risk—if, for example, the general partner guarantees to return all capital to limited partners even if the business venture should lose money.

AT THE CLOSE order to buy or sell a security within the final 30 seconds of trading. Brokers never guarantee that such orders will be executed.

AT THE MARKET *see* MARKET ORDER.

AT THE MONEY at the current price, as an option with an exercise price equal to or near the current price of the stock or underlying futures contract. *See also* DEEP IN/OUT OF THE MONEY; IN THE MONEY; OUT OF THE MONEY.

AT THE OPENING customer's order to a broker to buy or sell a security at the price that applies when an exchange opens. If the order is not executed at that time, it is automatically canceled.

AUCTION MARKET system by which securities are bought and sold through brokers on the securities exchanges, as distinguished from the over-the-counter market, where trades are negotiated. Best exemplified by the NEW YORK STOCK EXCHANGE, it is a double auction system or TWO-SIDED MARKET. That is because, unlike the conventional auction with one auctioneer and many buyers, here we have many sellers and many buyers. As in any auction, a price is established by competitive bidding between brokers acting as agents for buyers and sellers. That the system functions in an orderly way is the result of several trading rules: (1) The first bid or offer at a given price has priority over any other bid or offer at the same price. (2) The high bid and low offer "have the floor." (3) A new auction begins whenever all the offers or bids at a given price are exhausted. (4) Secret transactions are prohibited. (5) Bids and offers must be made in an audible voice.

Also, the competitive bidding by which Treasury bills are sold. *See also* BILL; DUTCH AUCTION.

AUDIT professional examination and verification of a company's accounting documents and supporting data for the purpose of rendering an opinion as to their fairness, consistency, and conformity with GENERALLY ACCEPTED ACCOUNTING PRINCIPLES. *See also* ACCOUNTANT'S OPINION.

AUDITOR'S CERTIFICATE *see* ACCOUNTANT'S OPINION.

AUDIT TRAIL step-by-step record by which accounting data can be traced to their source. Questions as to the validity or accuracy of an accounting figure can be resolved by reviewing the sequence of events from which the figure resulted.

AUTEX SYSTEM electronic system for alerting brokers that other brokers want to buy or sell large blocks of stock. Once a match is made, the actual transaction takes place over the counter or on the floor of an exchange.

AUTHENTICATION identification of a bond certificate as having been issued under a specific indenture, thus validating the bond. Also, legal verification of the genuineness of a document, as by the certification and seal of an authorized public official.

AUTHORITY BOND bond issued by and payable from the revenue of a government agency or a corporation formed to administer a revenue-producing public enterprise. One such corporation is the Port Authority of New York and New Jersey, which operates bridges and tunnels in the New York City area. Because an authority usually has no source of revenue other than charges for the facilities it operates, its bonds have the characteristics of revenue bonds. The difference is that bondholder protections may be incorporated in the authority bond contract as well as in the legislation that created the authority.

AUTHORIZED SHARES maximum number of shares of any class a company may legally create under the terms of its ARTICLES OF INCORPORATION. Normally, a corporation provides for future increases in authorized stock by vote of the stockholders. The corporation is not required to issue all the shares authorized and may initially keep issued shares at a minimum to hold down taxes and expenses. Also called *authorized stock*.

AUTOMATIC REINVESTMENT *see* CONSTANT DOLLAR PLAN; DIVIDEND REINVESTMENT PLAN.

AUTOMATIC WITHDRAWAL mutual fund program that entitles shareholders to a fixed payment each month or each quarter. The payment comes from dividends, including realized capital gains and income on securities held by the fund.

AVERAGE appropriately weighted and adjusted ARITHMETIC MEAN of selected securities designed to represent market behavior generally or important segments of the market. Among the most familiar averages are the Dow Jones industrial and transportation averages.

Because the evaluation of individual securities involves measuring price trends of securities in general or within an industry group, the various averages are important analytical tools.

AVERAGE DOWN strategy to lower the average price paid for a company's shares. An investor who wants to buy 1000 shares, for example, could buy 400 at the current market price and three blocks of 200 each as the price fell. The average cost would then be lower than it would have been if all 1000 shares had been bought at once. Investors also average down in order to realize tax losses. Say someone buys shares at $20, then watches them fall to $10. Instead of doing nothing, the investor can buy at $10, then sell the $20 shares at a capital loss, which can be used at tax time to offset other gains. However, the WASH SALE rule says that in order to claim the capital loss, the investor must not sell the $20 stock until at least 30 days after buying the stock at $10. *See also* CONSTANT DOLLAR PLAN.

AVERAGE EQUITY average daily balance in a trading account. Brokerage firms calculate customer equity daily as part of their procedure for keeping track of gains and losses on uncompleted transactions, called MARK TO THE MARKET. When transactions are completed, profits and losses are booked to each customer's account together with brokerage commissions. Even though daily fluctuations in equity are routine, average equity is a useful guide in making trading decisions and ensuring sufficient equity to meet MARGIN REQUIREMENTS.

AVERAGE UP buy on a rising market so as to lower the overall cost. Buying an equal number of shares at $50, $52, $54, and $58, for instance, will make the average cost $53.50. This is a mathematical reality, but it does not determine whether the stock is worth buying at any or all of these prices.

AVERAGING *see* CONSTANT DOLLAR PLAN.

AWAY FROM THE MARKET expression used when the bid on a LIMIT ORDER is lower or the offer price is higher than the current market price for the security. Away from the market limit orders are held by the specialist for later execution unless FILL OR KILL (FOK) is stipulated on the order entry.

b

BABY BOND convertible or straight debt bond having a par value of less than $1000, usually $500 to $25. Baby bonds bring the bond market within reach of small investors and, by the same token, open a source of funds to corporations that lack entree to the large institutional market. On the negative side, they entail higher administrative costs (relative to the total money raised) for distribution and processing and lack the large and active market that ensures the liquidity of conventional bonds.

BACKDATING

In general: dating any statement, document, check or other instrument earlier than the date drawn.

Mutual funds: feature permitting fundholders to use an earlier date on a promise to invest a specified sum over a specified period in exchange for a reduced sales charge. Backdating, which usually accompanies a large transaction, gives retroactive value to purchases from the earlier date in order to meet the requirements of the promise, or LETTER OF INTENT.

BACK-END LOAD redemption charge an investor pays when withdrawing money from an investment. Most common in mutual funds and annuities, the back-end load is designed to discourage withdrawals.

BACKING AWAY broker-dealer's failure, as market maker in a given security, to make good on a bid for the minimum quantity. This practice is considered unethical under the RULES OF FAIR PRACTICE of the NATIONAL ASSOCIATION OF SECURITIES DEALERS.

BACKLOG value of unfilled orders placed with a manufacturing company. Whether the firm's backlog is rising or falling is a clue to its future sales and earnings.

BACK OFFICE bank or brokerage house departments not directly involved in selling or trading. The back office sees to accounting records, compliance with government regulations, and communication between branches. When stock-market trading is particularly heavy, order processing can be slowed by massive volume; this is called a back office crunch.

BACK UP turn around; reverse a stock market trend. When prices are moving in one direction, traders would say of a sudden reversal that the market backed up.

BACK UP

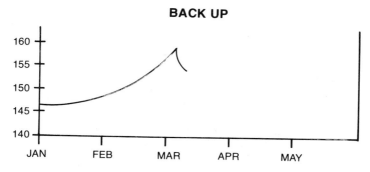

BACKUP LINE BANK LINE of credit in the name of an issuer of commercial paper, covering maturing notes in the event that new notes cannot be marketed to replace them. Ideally, the unused line should always equal the commercial paper outstanding. In practice, something less than total coverage is commonplace, particularly because the compensating balances normally required in support of the line are also available to meet maturing paper.

BACKWARDATION
1. pricing structure in commodities or foreign-exchange trading in which deliveries in the near future have a higher price than those made later on. Backwardation occurs when demand is greater in the near future. *See also* CONTANGO.
2. London Stock Exchange term for the fees and interest due on short sales of stock with delayed delivery.

BAD DEBT open account balance or loan receivable that has proven uncollectible and is written off. Traditionally, companies and financial institutions have maintained a RESERVE for uncollectible accounts, charging the reserve for actual bad debts and making annual tax deductible charges to income to replenish or increase the reserve. The TAX REFORM ACT OF 1986 required companies and large banks ($500 million or more in assets) to convert from the reserve method to a direct charge-off method for tax purposes beginning in 1987, although bad debt reserves will continue to appear on balance sheets for reporting purposes. Small banks and thrift institutions were allowed to continue using the reserve method for tax purposes, although with stricter limitations. The relationship of bad debt write-offs and recoveries to accounts receivable can reveal how liberal or conservative a firm's credit and charge-off policies are.

BAD DELIVERY opposite of GOOD DELIVERY.

BALANCED BUDGET *see* BUDGET.

BALANCED MUTUAL FUND fund that buys common stock, preferred stock, and bonds in an effort to obtain the highest return consistent with a low-risk strategy. A balanced fund typically offers a higher yield than a pure stock fund and performs better than such a fund when stocks are falling. In a rising market, however, a balanced mutual fund usually will not keep pace with all-equity funds.

BALANCE OF PAYMENTS system of recording all of a country's economic transactions with the rest of the world during a particular time period. Double-entry bookkeeping is used, and there can be no surplus or deficit on the overall balance of payments. The balance of payments is typically divided into three accounts—current, capital, and gold—and these can show a surplus or deficit. The current account covers imports and exports of goods and services; the capital account covers movements of investments; and the gold account covers gold movements. The balance of payments helps a country evaluate its competitive strengths and weaknesses and forecast the strength of its currency. From the standpoint of a national economy, a surplus on a part of the balance of payments is not necessarily good, nor is a deficit necessarily bad; the state of the national economy and the manner of financing the deficit are important considerations. *See also* BALANCE OF TRADE.

BALANCE OF TRADE net difference over a period of time between the value of a country's imports and exports of merchandise. Movable goods such as automobiles, foodstuffs, and apparel are included in the balance of trade; payments abroad for services and for tourism are not. When a country exports more than it imports, it is said to have a favorable balance of trade; when imports predominate the balance is called unfavorable. The balance of trade should be viewed in the context of the country's entire international economic position, however. For example, a country may consistently have an unfavorable balance of trade that is offset by considerable exports of services; this country would be judged to have a good international economic position. *See also* BALANCE OF PAYMENTS.

BALANCE SHEET financial report, also called *statement of condition* or *statement of financial position,* showing the status of a company's assets, liabilities, and owners' equity on a given date, usually the close of a month. One way of looking at a business enterprise is as a mass of capital (ASSETS) arrayed against the sources of that capital (LIABILITIES and EQUITY). Assets are equal to liabilities and equity, and the balance sheet is a listing of the items making up the two sides of the equation. Unlike a PROFIT AND LOSS STATEMENT, which shows the results of operations over a period of time, a balance sheet shows the state of affairs at one point in time. It is a snapshot, not a motion picture, and must be analyzed with reference to comparative prior balance sheets and other operating statements.

BALLOON final payment on a debt that is substantially larger than the preceding payments. Loans or mortgages are structured with balloon payments when some projected event is expected to provide extra cash flow or when refinancing is anticipated. Balloon loans are sometimes called *partially amortized loans.*

BALLOON INTEREST in serial bond issues, the higher COUPON rate on bonds with later maturities.

BALLOON MATURITY bond issue or long-term loan with larger dollar amounts of bonds or payments falling due in the later years of the obligation.

BANKER'S ACCEPTANCE *see* ACCEPTANCE.

BANK HOLDING COMPANY company that owns or controls two or more banks or other bank holding companies. As defined in the Bank Holding Company Act of 1956, such companies must register with the BOARD OF GOVERNORS of the FEDERAL RESERVE SYSTEM and hence are called registered bank holding companies. Amendments to the 1956 act set standards for acquisitions (1966) and ended the exemption enjoyed by one-bank holding companies (1970), thus restricting bank holding companies to activities related to banking.

BANK LINE bank's moral commitment, as opposed to its contractual commitment, to make loans to a particular borrower up to a specified maximum during a specified period, usually one year. Because a bank line—also called a *line of credit*—is not a legal commitment, it is not customary to charge a commitment fee. It *is* common, however, to require that compensating balances be kept on deposit—typically 10% of the line, with an additional 10% of any borrowings under the line. A line about which a customer is officially notified is called an *advised line* or *confirmed line.* A line that is an internal policy guide about which the customer is not informed is termed a *guidance line.*

BANK QUALITY *see* INVESTMENT GRADE.

BANKRUPTCY state of insolvency of an individual or an organization—in other words, an inability to pay debts. There are two kinds of legal bankruptcy under U.S. law: involuntary, when one or more creditors petition to have a debtor judged insolvent by a court; and voluntary, when the debtor brings the petition. In both cases, the objective is an orderly and equitable settlement of obligations.

The 1978 Bankruptcy Reform Act removed some of the rigidities of the old law and permitted more flexibility in procedures. The Bankruptcy Reform Act of 1984 curtailed some of the more liberal provisions (mainly affecting consumer bankruptcy) of the 1978 act.

Chapter 7 of the 1978 act, dealing with LIQUIDATION, provides for a court-appointed interim trustee with broad powers and discretion to make management changes, arrange unsecured financing, and generally operate the debtor business in such a way as to prevent loss. Only by filing an appropriate bond is the debtor able to regain possession from the trustee.

Chapter 11, which deals with REORGANIZATION, provides that, unless the court rules otherwise, the debtor remains in possession of the business and in control of its operation. Debtor and creditors are allowed considerable flexibility in working together. The 1978 law relaxes the old *absolute priority rule,* which gave creditor claims categorical precedence over ownership claims. It also makes possible the negotiation of payment schedules, the restructuring of debt, and even the granting of loans by the creditors to the debtor.

BANK TRUST DEPARTMENT part of a bank engaged in settling estates, administering trusts and guardianships, and performing AGENCY services. As part of its personal trust and ESTATE PLANNING services, it manages investments for large accounts—typically those with at least $50,000 in assets. People who cannot or do not want to make investment decisions are commonly bank trust department clients. Known for their conservative investment philosophy, such departments have custody over billions of dollars, making them a major factor in the movement of stock and bond prices.

Among other things, the departments also act as trustee for corporate bonds, administer pension and profit-sharing plans, and function as TRANSFER AGENTS.

BANK WIRE computerized message system owned and administered by about 250 participating banks in about 75 U.S. cities. Like the FED WIRE, the bank wire transmits large dollar credit transfer information. It also provides information about loan participations, securities transactions, Federal Reserve System funds borrowings, credit history, the payment or nonpayment of ''wire fate'' items, and other essential matters requiring prompt communication.

BAROMETER selective compilation of economic and market data designed to represent larger trends. Consumer spending, housing starts, and interest rates are barometers used in economic forecasting. The Dow Jones Industrial Average and the Standard & Poor's 500 Stock Index are prominent stock market barometers. The Dow Jones Utility Average is a barometer of market trends in the utility industry.

A *barometer stock* has a price movement pattern that reflects the market as a whole, thus serving as a market indicator. General Motors, for example, is considered a barometer stock.

BARRON'S CONFIDENCE INDEX weekly index of corporate bond yields published by *Barron's*, a Dow Jones financial newspaper. The index shows the ratio of Barron's average yield on 10 top-grade bonds to the Dow Jones average yield on 40 bonds. People who are worried about the economic outlook tend to seek high quality, whereas investors who feel secure about the economy are more likely to buy lower-rated bonds. The spread between high- and low-grade bonds thus reflects investor opinion about the economy.

BARTER trade of goods or services without use of money. When money is involved, whether in such forms as wampum, checks, or bills or coins, a transaction is called a SALE. Although barter is usually associated with undeveloped economies, it occurs in modern complex societies. In conditions of extreme inflation, it can be a preferred mode of commerce. Where a population lacks confidence in its currency or banking system, barter becomes commonplace. In international trade, barter can provide a way of doing business with countries whose soft currencies would otherwise make them unattractive trading partners.

BASE MARKET VALUE average market price of a group of securities at a given time. It is used as a basis of comparison in plotting dollar or percentage changes for purposes of market INDEXING.

BASE PERIOD particular time in the past used as the yardstick when measuring economic data. A base period is usually a year or an average of years; it can also be a month or other time period. The U.S. rate of inflation is determined by measuring current prices against those of a base year; for instance, the consumer price index for May 1983 was determined by comparing prices in that month with prices in the base year of 1967.

BASIS

In general: original cost plus out-of-pocket expenses that must be reported to the Internal Revenue Service when an investment is sold and must be used in calculating capital gains or losses. If a stock was bought for $1000 two years ago and is sold today for $2000, the basis is $1000 and the profit is a capital gain.

Bonds: an investor's YIELD TO MATURITY at a given bond price. A 10% bond selling at 100 has a 10% basis.

Commodities: the difference between the cash price of a hedged money market instrument and a FUTURES CONTRACT.

BASIS POINT smallest measure used in quoting yields on bonds and notes. One basis point is 0.01% of yield. Thus a bond's yield that changed from 10.67% to 11.57% would be said to have moved 90 basis points.

BASIS PRICE

In general: price an investor uses to calculate capital gains when selling a stock or bond. *See also* BASIS.

Odd-lot trading: the price arbitrarily established by an exchange floor official at the end of a trading session for a buyer or seller of an odd lot when the market bid and asked prices are more than $2 apart, or if no round-lot transactions have occurred that day. The customer gets the basis price plus or minus the odd-lot differential, if any. This procedure for determining prices is rare, since most odd lots are transacted at the market bid (if a sale) or asked (if a buy) or at prices based on the next round-lot trade.

BD FORM document that every brokerage house must file with the Securities and Exchange Commission, detailing the firm's financial position and naming its officers. The form must constantly be brought up to date.

BEAR person who thinks a market will fall. Bears may sell a stock short or buy a PUT OPTION to take advantage of the anticipated drop.

BEARER BOND *see* COUPON BOND.

BEARER FORM security not registered on the books of the issuing corporation and thus payable to the one possessing it. A bearer bond has coupons attached, which the bondholder sends in or presents on the interest date for payment, hence the alternative name COUPON BONDS. Bearer stock certificates are negotiable without endorsement and are transferred by delivery. Dividends are payable by presentation of dividend coupons, which are dated or numbered. Most securities issued today are in registered form, though municipal bonds and many foreign equity securities continue to be issued in bearer form.

In effect, REGISTERED SECURITIES become bearer certificates when properly endorsed, since they can theoretically be negotiated by their holder.

BEAR MARKET prolonged period of falling prices. A bear market in stocks is usually brought on by the anticipation of declining economic activity, and a bear market in bonds is caused by rising interest rates.

BEAR RAID attempt by investors to manipulate the price of a stock by selling large numbers of shares short. The manipulators pocket the difference between the initial price and the new, lower price after this maneuver. Bear raids are illegal under Securities and Exchange Commission rules, which stipulate that every SHORT SALE be executed on an UPTICK (the last price was higher than the price before it) or a ZERO PLUS TICK (the last price was unchanged but higher than the last preceding different price).

BEAR SPREAD strategy in the options market designed to take advantage of a fall in the price of a security or commodity. Someone executing a bear spread could buy a combination of calls and puts on the same security at different *strike prices* in order to profit as the security's price fell. Or the investor could buy a put of short maturity and a put of long maturity in order to profit from the difference between the two puts as prices fell. *See also* BULL SPREAD.

BELL signal that opens and closes trading on major exchanges—sometimes actually a bell but sometimes a buzzer sound.

BELLWETHER security seen as an indicator of a market's direction. In stocks, International Business Machines (IBM) has long been considered a bellwether because so much of its stock is owned by institutional investors who have much control over supply and demand on the stock market. Institutional trading actions tend to influence smaller investors and therefore the market generally. In bonds, the 20-year U.S. Treasury bond is considered the bellwether, denoting the direction in which all other bonds are likely to move.

BELOW PAR *see* PAR VALUE.

BENEFICIAL OWNER person who enjoys the benefits of ownership even though title is in another name. When shares of a mutual fund are held by a custodian bank or when securities are held by a broker in STREET NAME, the real owner is the beneficial owner, even though, for safety or convenience, the bank or broker holds title.

BENEFICIARY
1. person to whom an inheritance passes as the result of being named in a will.
2. recipient of the proceeds of a life insurance policy.
3. party in whose favor a LETTER OF CREDIT is issued.
4. one to whom the amount of an ANNUITY is payable.
5. party for whose benefit a TRUST exists.

BEST EFFORT arrangement whereby investment bankers, acting as agents, agree to do their best to sell an issue to the public. Instead of buying the securities outright, these agents have an option to buy and an authority to sell the securities. Depending on the contract, the agents exercise their option and buy enough shares to cover their sales to clients, or they cancel the incompletely sold issue altogether and forgo the fee. Best efforts deals, which were common prior to 1900, entailed risks and delays from the issuer's standpoint. What is more, the broadening of the securities markets has made marketing new issues easier, and the practice of outright purchase by investment bankers, called FIRM COMMITMENT underwriting, has become commonplace. For the most part, the best efforts deals we occasionally see today are handled by firms specializing in the more speculative securities of new and unseasoned companies. *See also* BOUGHT DEAL.

BEST'S RATING rating of financial soundness given to insurance companies by Best's Rating Service. The top rating is A+. A Best's rating is important to buyers of insurance or annuities because it informs them whether a company is financially sound. Best's Ratings are also important to investors in insurance stocks.

BETA COEFFICIENT measure of a stock's relative volatility. The beta is the covariance of a stock in relation to the rest of the stock market. The Standard & Poor's 500 Stock Index has a beta coefficient of 1. Any stock with a higher beta is more volatile than the market, and any with a lower beta can be expected to rise and fall more slowly than the market. A conservative investor whose main concern is preservation of capital should focus on stocks with low betas, whereas one willing to take high risks in an effort to earn high rewards should look for high-beta stocks.

BID AND ASKED bid is the highest price a prospective buyer is prepared to pay at a particular time for a trading unit of a given security; asked is the lowest price acceptable to a prospective seller of the same security. Together, the two prices constitute a QUOTATION; the difference between the two prices is the SPREAD. Although the bid and asked dynamic is common to all securities trading, "bid and asked" usually refers to UNLISTED SECURITIES traded OVER THE COUNTER.

BIDDING UP practice whereby the price bid for a security is successively moved higher lest an upswing in prices leaves orders unexecuted. An example would be an investor wanting to purchase a sizable quantity of shares in a rising market, using buy limit orders (orders to buy at a specified price or lower) to ensure the most favorable price. Since offer prices are moving up with the market, the investor must move his limit buy price upward to continue accumulating shares. To some extent the buyer is contributing to the upward price pressure on the stock, but most of the price rise is out of his control.

BID WANTED (BW) announcement that a holder of securities wants to sell and will entertain bids. Because the final price is subject to negotiation, the bid submitted in response to a BW need not be specific. A BW is frequently seen on published market quotation sheets.

BIG BANG deregulation on October 27, 1986, of London-based securities markets, an event comparable to MAY DAY in the United States and marking a major step toward a single world financial market.

BIG BOARD popular term for the NEW YORK STOCK EXCHANGE.

BIG EIGHT largest U.S. accounting firms as measured by revenue. They do the accounting and auditing for most major corporations, signing the auditor's certificate that appears in every annual report. The eight, in alphabetical order, in the mid-1980s were Arthur Andersen & Co.; Coopers and Lybrand; Ernst & Whinney; Deloitte Haskins & Sells; Peat, Marwick Mitchell & Co.; Price Waterhouse & Co.; Touche Ross & Co.; and Arthur Young & Co. A worldwide list would include a ninth firm, Klynveld Main Goerdeler, based in Amsterdam, which outranks several of the U.S. Big Eight. Merger discussions are often underway among accounting firms, and mergers could lead to a change in the composition of the Big Eight.

BILL

In general: (1) short for *bill of exchange,* an order by one person directing a second to pay a third. (2) document evidencing a debtor's obligation to a creditor, the kind of bill we are all familiar with. (3) paper currency, like the $5 bill. (4) *bill of sale,* a document used to transfer the title to certain goods from seller to buyer in the same way a deed to real property passes.

Investments: short for *due bill,* a statement of money owed. Commonly used to adjust a securities transaction when dividends, interest, and other distributions are reflected in a price but have not yet been disbursed. For example, when a stock is sold ex-dividend, but the dividend has not yet been paid, the buyer would sign a due bill stating that the amount of the dividend is payable to the seller.

A due bill may accompany delivered securities to give title to the buyer's broker in exchange for shares or money.

U.S. Treasury bill: commonly called bill or T-bill by money market people, a Treasury bill is a short-term (maturities up to a year), discounted government security sold through competitive bidding at weekly and monthly auctions in denominations from $10,000 to $1 million.

The auction at which bills are sold differs from the two-sided auction used by exchanges. Here, in what is sometimes termed a *Dutch auction,* the Treasury invites anyone interested to submit a bid, called a TENDER, then awards units to the highest bidders going down a list. Three- and six-month bills are auctioned weekly, nine-month and one-year bills monthly. Although the yield on bills may barely top the inflation rate, the high degree of safety together with the liquidity provided by an active SECONDARY MARKET make bills popular with corporate money managers as well as with banks and other government entities.

Individuals may also purchase bills directly, in amounts under $500,000, at no transaction charge, from a Federal Reserve bank, the Bureau of Federal Debt, or certain commercial banks. Bills bought on this basis are priced by noncompetitive bidding, with subscribers paying an average of the accepted bids.

Treasury bills are the most widely used of all government debt securities and are a primary instrument of Federal Reserve monetary policy.

See also TAX ANTICIPATION BILL.

BILLING CYCLE interval between periodic billings for goods sold or services rendered, normally one month, or a system whereby bills or statements are mailed at periodic intervals in order to distribute the clerical workload.

BILL OF EXCHANGE *see* DRAFT.

BLACK FRIDAY sharp drop in a financial market. The original Black Friday was September 24, 1869, when a group of financiers tried to corner the gold market and precipitated a business panic followed by a depression. The panic of 1873 also began on Friday.

BLACK MONDAY October 19, 1987, when the Dow Jones Industrial Average plunged a record 508 points following sharp drops the previous week, reflecting investor anxiety about inflated stock price levels, federal budget and trade deficits, and foreign market activity. Many blamed PROGRAM TRADING for the extreme VOLATILITY.

BLACK-SCHOLES OPTION PRICING MODEL model developed by Fischer Black and Myron Scholes to gauge whether options contracts are fairly valued. The model incorporates such factors as the volatility of a security's return, the level of interest rates, the relationship of the underlying stock's price to the *strike price* of the option, and the time remaining until the option expires. Current valuations using this model are developed by the Options Monitor Service and are available from Monchik-Weber Associates.

BLANKET CERTIFICATION FORM *see* NASD FORM FR-1.

BLANKET FIDELITY BOND insurance coverage against losses due to employee dishonesty. Brokerage firms are required to carry such protection in proportion to their net capital as defined by the Securities and Exchange Commission. Contingencies covered include securities loss, forgery, and fraudulent trading. Also called *blanket bond*.

BLANKET RECOMMENDATION communication sent to all customers of a brokerage firm recommending that they buy or sell a particular stock or stocks in a particular industry regardless of investment objectives or portfolio size.

BLIND POOL limited partnership that does not specify the properties the general partner plans to acquire. If, for example, a real estate partnership is offered in the form of a blind pool, investors can evaluate the project only by looking at the general partner's track record. In a *specified pool*, on the other hand, investors can look at the prices paid for property and the amount of rental income the buildings generate, then evaluate the partnership's potential. In general, blind pool partnerships do not perform better or worse than specified pool partnerships.

BLOCK large quantity of stock or large dollar amount of bonds held or traded. As a general guide, 10,000 shares or more of stock and $200,000 or more worth of bonds would be described as a block.

BLOCK POSITIONER dealer who, to accommodate the seller of a block of securities, will take a position in the securities, hoping to gain from a rise in the market price. Block positioners must register with the Securities and Exchange Commission and the New York Stock Exchange (if member firms). Typically they engage in ARBITRAGE, HEDGING, and SELLING SHORT in order to protect their risk and liquidate their position.

BLOWOUT quick sale of all shares in a new offering of securities. Corporations like to sell securities in such environments, because they get a high price for their stock. Investors are likely to have a hard time getting the number of shares they want during a blowout. Also called *going away* or *hot issue*.

BLUE CHIP common stock of a nationally known company that has a long record of profit growth and dividend payment and a reputation for quality management, products, and services. Some examples of blue chip stocks: International Business Machines, General Electric, and Du Pont. Blue chip stocks typically are relatively high priced and low yielding.

BLUE LIST daily financial publication listing bonds offered for sale by some 700 dealers and banks and representing more than $3 billion in par value. The Blue List mainly contains data on municipal bonds. With its pertinent price, yield, and other data, the Blue List is the most comprehensive source of information on activity and volume in the SECONDARY MARKET for TAX-EXEMPT SECURITIES. Some corporate bonds offered by the same dealers are also included. Full name, Blue List of Current Municipal Offerings.

BLUE-SKY LAW law of a kind passed by various states to protect investors against securities fraud. These laws require sellers of new stock issues or mutual funds to register their offerings and provide financial details on each issue so that investors can base their judgments on relevant data. The term is said to have originated with a judge who asserted that a particular stock offering had as much value as a patch of blue sky.

BOARD BROKER employee of the CHICAGO BOARD OPTIONS EXCHANGE who handles AWAY FROM THE MARKET orders, which cannot immediately be executed. If board brokers act as agents in executing such orders, they notify the exchange members who entered the orders.

BOARD OF ARBITRATION group of three to five individuals selected to adjudicate cases between securities firms. Arbitration is the method approved by the NATIONAL ASSOCIATION OF SECURITIES DEALERS, the MUNICIPAL SECURITIES RULE-MAKING BOARD, and the exchanges for resolving disputes, and it applies to both member and nonmember firms. Once the parties to a dispute agree to bring the matter before an arbitration board, the board's ruling is final and binding.

BOARD OF DIRECTORS group of individuals elected, usually at an annual meeting, by the shareholders of a corporation and empowered to carry out certain tasks as spelled out in the corporation's charter. Among such powers are appointing senior management, naming members of executive and finance committees (if any), issuing additional shares, and declaring dividends. Boards normally include the top corporate executives, termed *inside directors,* as well as OUTSIDE DIRECTORS chosen from business and from the community at large to advise on matters of broad policy. Directors meet several times a year and are paid for their services. They are considered control persons under the securities laws, meaning that their shares are restricted. As insiders, they cannot (1) buy and sell the company's stock within a 6-month period; (2) sell short in the company's stock, and if they sell owned shares must deliver in 20 days and/or place certificates in mail within 5 days; (3) effect any foreign or arbitrage transaction in the company's stock; (4) trade on material information not available to the public.

BOARD OF GOVERNORS OF THE FEDERAL RESERVE SYSTEM seven-member managing body of the FEDERAL RESERVE SYSTEM, commonly called the Federal Reserve Board. The board sets policy on issues relating to banking regulations as well as to the MONEY SUPPLY.

BOARD ROOM
Brokerage house: room where customers can watch an electronic board that displays stock prices and transactions.
Corporation: room where the board of directors holds its meetings.

BOILERPLATE standard legal language, often in fine print, used in most contracts, wills, indentures, prospectuses, and other legal documents. Although what the boilerplate says is important, it rarely is subject to change by the parties to the agreement, since it is the product of years of legal experience.

BOILER ROOM place where high-pressure salespeople use banks of telephones to call lists of potential investors (known in the trade as sucker lists) in order to peddle speculative, even fraudulent, securities. They are called boiler rooms because of the high-pressure selling. Boiler room methods, if not illegal, clearly violate the National Association of Securities Dealers' RULES OF FAIR PRACTICE, particularly those requiring that recommendations be suitable to a customer's account. *See also* BUCKET SHOP.

BOND any interest-bearing or discounted government or corporate security that obligates the issuer to pay the bondholder a specified sum of money, usually at specific intervals, and to repay the principal amount of the loan at maturity. Bondholders have an IOU from the issuer, but no corporate ownership privileges, as stockholders do.

An owner of *bearer bonds* presents the bond coupons and is paid interest, whereas the owner of *registered bonds* appears on the records of the bond issuer.

A SECURED BOND is backed by collateral which may be sold by the bondholder to satisfy a claim if the bond's issuer fails to pay interest and principal when they are due. An *unsecured bond* or DEBENTURE is backed by the full faith and credit of the issuer, but not by any specific collateral.

A CONVERTIBLE bond gives its owner the privilege of exchange for other securities of the issuing company at some future date and under prescribed conditions.

Also, a bond, in finance, is the obligation of one person to repay a debt taken on by someone else, should that other person default. A bond can also be money or securities deposited as a pledge of good faith.

A surety or PERFORMANCE BOND is an agreement whereby an insurance company becomes liable for the performance of work or services provided by a contractor by an agreed-upon date. If the contractor does not do what was promised, the surety company is financially responsible. *See also* INDENTURE.

BOND ANTICIPATION NOTE (BAN) short-term debt instrument issued by a state or municipality that will be paid off with the proceeds of an upcoming bond issue. To the investor, BANs offer a safe, tax-free yield that may be higher than other tax-exempt debt instruments of the same maturity.

BOND BROKER broker who executes bond trades on the floor of an exchange. Also, one who trades corporate, U.S. government, or municipal debt issues over the counter, mostly for large institutional accounts.

***BOND BUYER*, THE** daily publication containing most of the key statistics and indexes used in the fixed-income markets. *See also* BOND BUYER'S INDEX; THIRTY-DAY VISIBLE SUPPLY.

BOND BUYER'S INDEX index published daily by the *BOND BUYER,* a newspaper covering the municipal bond market. The index provides the yardsticks against which municipal bond yields are measured. One index is composed of 20 long-term bonds rated A or better, and another is made up of 11 AA-rated bonds. Both use newly issued municipals selling at par. The *Bond Buyer* also lists long-term government bonds and compares their aftertax yield with the yield from tax-free municipals. Investors use the publication's Bond Buyer Indexes to plot interest rate patterns.

BOND CROWD exchange members who transact bond orders on the floor of the exchange. The work area in which they congregate is separate from the stock traders, hence the term bond crowd.

BOND POWER form used in the transfer of registered bonds from one owner to another. Sometimes called *assignment separate from certificate,* it accomplishes the same thing as the assignment form on the back of the bond certificate, but has a safety advantage in being separate. Technically, the bond power appoints an attorney-in-fact with the power to make a transfer of ownership on the corporation's books.

BOND RATING method of evaluating the possibility of default by a bond issuer. Standard & Poor's, Moody's Investors Service, and Fitch's Investors Service analyze the financial strength of each bond's issuer, whether a corporation or a government body. Their ratings range from AAA (highly unlikely to default) to D (in default). Bonds rated B or below are not INVESTMENT GRADE—in other words, institutions that invest other people's money may not under most state laws buy them. *See also* RATING.

BOND RATIO *leverage* ratio measuring the percentage of a company's capitalization represented by bonds. It is calculated by dividing the total bonds due after one year by the same figure plus all equity. A bond ratio over 33% indicates high leverage—except in utilities, where higher bond ratios are normal. *See also* DEBT-TO-EQUITY RATIO.

BOND SWAP simultaneous sale of one bond issue and purchase of another. The motives for bond swaps vary: *maturity swaps* aim to stretch out maturities but can also produce a profit because of the lower prices on longer bonds; *yield swaps* seek to improve return and *quality swaps* seek to upgrade safety; *tax swaps* create tax-deductible losses through the sale, while the purchase of a substitute bond effectively preserves the investment. *See also* SWAP, SWAP ORDER.

BOOK
1. in an underwriting of securities, (1) preliminary indications of interest rate on the part of prospective buyers of the issue ("What is the book on XYZ Company?") or (2) record of activity in the syndicate account ("Who is managing the book on XYZ?").
2. record maintained by a specialist of buy and sell orders in a given security. The term derives from the notebook that specialists traditionally used for this purpose. Also, the aggregate of sell orders left with the specialist, as in BUY THE BOOK.
3. as a verb, to book is to give accounting recognition to something. ("They booked a profit on the transaction.")
4. collectively, books are the journals, ledgers, and other accounting records of a business.
   See also BOOK VALUE.

BOOK-ENTRY SECURITIES securities that are not represented by a certificate. Purchases and sales of some municipal bonds, for instance, are merely recorded on customers' accounts; no certificates change hands. This is increasingly popular because it cuts down on paperwork for brokers and leaves investors free from worry about their certificates. *See also* CERTIFICATELESS MUNICIPALS.

BOOK PROFIT OR LOSS *see* UNREALIZED PROFIT OR LOSS.

BOOK VALUE
1. value at which an asset is carried on a balance sheet. For example, a piece of manufacturing equipment is put on the books at its cost when purchased. Its value is then reduced each year as depreciation is charged to income. Thus, its book value at any time is its cost minus accumulated depreciation. However, the primary purpose of accounting for depreciation is to enable a company to recover its cost, not replace the asset or reflect its declining usefulness. Book value may therefore vary significantly from other objectively determined values, most notably MARKET VALUE.
2. net asset value of a company's securities, calculated by using the following formula:
   Total assets *minus* intangible assets (goodwill, patents, etc.) *minus* current liabilities *minus* any long-term liabilities and equity issues that have a prior claim (subtracting them here has the effect of treating them as paid) *equals* total net assets available for payment of the issue under consideration.

The total net asset figure, divided by the number of bonds, shares of preferred stock, or shares of common stock, gives the *net asset value*—or book value—per bond or per share of preferred or common stock.

Book value can be a guide in selecting underpriced stocks and is an indication of the ultimate value of securities in liquidation. *See also* ASSET COVERAGE.

BORROWED RESERVES funds borrowed by member banks from a FEDERAL RESERVE BANK for the purpose of maintaining the required reserve ratios. Actually, the proper term is *net borrowed reserves,* since it refers to the difference between borrowed reserves and excess or free reserves. Such borrowings, usually in the form of advances secured by government securities or eligible paper, are kept on deposit at the Federal Reserve bank in the borrower's region. Net borrowed reserves are an indicator of heavy loan demand and potentially TIGHT MONEY.

BORROWING POWER OF SECURITIES amount of money that customers can invest in securities on MARGIN, as listed every month on their brokerage account statements. This margin limit usually equals 50% of the value of their stocks, 30% of the value of their bonds, and the full value of their CASH EQUIVALENT assets, such as MONEY MARKET account funds. The term also refers to securities pledged (hypothecated) to a bank or other lender as loan COLLATERAL. The loan value in this case depends on lender policy and type of security.

BOSTON STOCK EXCHANGE *see* REGIONAL STOCK EXCHANGES.

BOT
1. stockbroker shorthand for bought, the opposite of SL for sold.
2. in finance, abbreviation for balance of trade.
3. in the mutual savings bank industry, abbreviation for board of trustees.

BOTTOM

In general: support level for market prices of any type. When prices fall below that level and appear to be continuing downward without check, we say that the *bottom dropped out.* When prices begin to trend upward again, we say they have *bottomed out.*

Economics: lowest point in an economic cycle.

Securities: lowest market price of a security or commodity during a day, a season, a year, a cycle. Also, lowest level of prices for the market as a whole, as measured by any of the several indexes.

BOTTOM FISHER investor who is on the lookout for stocks that have fallen to their bottom prices before turning up. In extreme cases, bottom fishers buy stocks and bonds of bankrupt or near-bankrupt firms.

BOTTOM-UP APPROACH TO INVESTING search for outstanding performance of individual stocks before considering the impact of economic trends. The companies may be identified from research reports, stock screens, or personal knowledge of the products and services. This approach assumes that individual companies can do well, even in an industry that is not performing well. *See also* TOP-DOWN APPROACH TO INVESTING.

BOUGHT DEAL in securities underwriting, a FIRM COMMITMENT to purchase an entire issue outright from the issuing company. Differs from a STAND-BY COMMITMENT, wherein, with conditions, a SYNDICATE of investment bankers agrees to purchase part of an issue if it is not fully subscribed. Also differs from a BEST

EFFORTS commitment, wherein the syndicate agrees to use its best efforts to sell the issue. Most issues in recent years have been bought deals. Typically, the syndicate puts up a portion of its own capital and borrows the rest from commercial banks. Then, perhaps through a selling group, the syndicate resells the issue to the public at slightly more than the purchase price.

BOUTIQUE small, specialized brokerage firm that deals with a limited clientele and offers a limited product line. A highly regarded securities analyst may form a research boutique, which clients use as a resource for buying and selling certain stocks. A boutique is the opposite of a FINANCIAL SUPERMARKET, which offers a wide variety of services to a wide variety of clients.

BOX physical location of securities or other documents held in safekeeping. The term derives from the large metal tin, or tray, in which brokerage firms and banks actually place such valuables. Depending on rules and regulations concerned with the safety and segregation of clients' securities, certificates held in safekeeping may qualify for stock loans or as bank loan collateral.

BRACKET CREEP edging into higher tax brackets as income rises to compensate for inflation. The TAX REFORM ACT OF 1986 collapsed the marginal rate system into two broad brackets, effective in 1988, virtually eliminating bracket creep as a potential problem.

BRANCH OFFICE MANAGER person in charge of a branch of a securities brokerage firm or bank. Branch office managers who oversee the activities of three or more brokers must pass tests administered by various stock exchanges. A customer who is not able to resolve a conflict with a REGISTERED REPRESENTATIVE should bring it to the attention of the branch office manager, who is responsible for resolving such differences.

BREADTH OF THE MARKET percentage of stocks participating in a particular market move. Analysts say there was good breadth if two thirds of the stocks listed on an exchange rose during a trading session. A market trend with good breadth is more significant and probably more long-lasting than one with limited breadth, since more investors are participating. Breadth-of-the-market indexes are alternatively called ADVANCE/DECLINE indexes.

BREAK

Finance: in a pricing structure providing purchasing discounts at different levels of volume, a point at which the price changes—for example, a 10% discount for ten cases.

Investments: (1) sudden, marked drop in the price of a security or in market prices generally; (2) discrepancy in the accounts of brokerage firms; (3) stroke of good luck.

BREAKEVEN POINT

Finance: the point at which sales equal costs. The point is located by breakeven analysis, which determines the volume of sales at which fixed and variable costs will be covered. All sales over the breakeven point produce profits; any drop in sales below that point will produce losses.

Because costs and sales are so complex, breakeven analysis has limitations as a planning tool and is being supplanted by computer-based financial planning systems. *See also* LEVERAGE (operating).

Securities: dollar price at which a transaction produces neither a gain nor a loss.

In options strategy the term has the following definitions:
1. long calls and short uncovered calls: strike price plus premium.
2. long puts and short uncovered puts: strike price minus premium.
3. short covered call: purchase price minus premium.
4. short put covered by short stock: short sale price of underlying stock plus premium.

BREAKING THE SYNDICATE terminating the investment banking group formed to underwrite a securities issue. More specifically, terminating the AGREEMENT AMONG UNDERWRITERS, thus leaving the members free to sell remaining holdings without price restrictions. The agreement among underwriters usually terminates the syndicate 30 days after the selling group, but the syndicate can be broken earlier by agreement of the participants.

BREAKOUT rise in a security's price above a resistance level (commonly its previous high price) or drop below a level of support (commonly the former lowest price). A breakout is taken to signify a continuing move in the same direction.

BREAKOUT

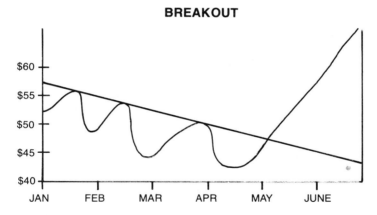

BREAKPOINT SALE in mutual funds, the dollar investment required to make the fundholder eligible for a lower sales charge. *See also* LETTER OF INTENT; RIGHT OF ACCUMULATION.

BRETTON WOODS AGREEMENT OF 1944 *see* FIXED EXCHANGE RATE.

BRIDGE LOAN short-term loan, also called a *swing loan,* made in anticipation of intermediate-term or long-term financing.

BROAD TAPE enlargement of the Dow Jones news ticker tape, projected on a screen in the board room of a brokerage firm. It continually reports major news developments and financial information. The term can also refer to similar information provided by Associated Press, United Press International, Reuters, or Munifacts. The broad tape is not allowed on the exchange floor because it would give floor traders an unfair edge.

BROKER

Insurance: person who finds the best insurance deal for a client and then sells the policy to the client.

Real estate: person who represents the seller and gets a commission when the property is sold.

Securities: person who acts as an intermediary between a buyer and seller, usually charging a commission. A broker who specializes in stocks, bonds, commodities, or options acts as AGENT and must be registered with the exchange where the securities are traded. Hence the term *registered representative. See also* ACCOUNT EXECUTIVE; DEALER; DISCOUNT BROKER.

BROKER-DEALER *see* DEALER.

BROKER LOAN RATE interest rate at which brokers borrow from banks to cover the securities positions of their clients. The broker loan rate usually hovers a percentage point or so above such short-term interest rates as the federal funds rate and the Treasury bill rate. Since brokers' loans and their customers' margin accounts are usually covered by the same collateral, the term REHYPOTHECATION is used synonymously with *broker loan borrowing*. Because broker loans are callable on 24-hour notice, the term *call loan rate* is also used, particularly in money rate tables published in newspapers.

BUCKET SHOP illegal brokerage firm, of a kind now almost extinct, which accepts customer orders but does not execute them right away as Securities and Exchange Commission regulations require. Bucket-shop brokers confirm the price the customer asked for, but in fact make the trade at a time advantageous to the broker, whose profit is the difference between the two prices. Sometimes bucket shops neglect to fill the customer's order and just pocket the money. *See also* BOILER ROOM.

BUDGET estimate of revenue and expenditure for a specified period. Of the many kinds of budgets, a CASH BUDGET shows cash flow, an expense budget shows projected expenditures, and a CAPITAL BUDGET shows anticipated capital outlays. The term refers to a preliminary financial plan. In a *balanced budget* revenues cover expenditures.

BULGE quick, temporary price rise that applies to an entire commodities or stock market, or to an individual commodity or stock.

BULL person who thinks prices will rise. One can be bullish on the prospects for an individual stock, bond, or commodity, an industry segment, or the market as a whole. In a more general sense, bullish means optimistic, so a person can be bullish on the economy as a whole.

BULL MARKET prolonged rise in the prices of stocks, bonds, or commodities. Bull markets usually last at least a few months and are characterized by high trading volume.

BULL SPREAD option strategy, executed with puts or calls, that will be profitable if the underlying stock rises in value. The following are three varieties of bull spread:

Vertical spread: simultaneous purchase and sale of options of the same class at different strike prices, but with the same expiration date.

Calendar spread: simultaneous purchase and sale of options of the same class and the same price but at different expiration dates.

Diagonal spread: combination of vertical and calendar spreads wherein the investor buys and sells options of the same class at different strike prices and different expiration dates.

An investor who believes, for example, that XYZ stock will rise, perhaps only moderately, buys an XYZ 30 call for 1½ and sells an XYZ 35 call for ½; both options are OUT OF THE MONEY. The 30 and 35 are strike prices and the 1½ and ½ are premiums. The net cost of this spread, or the difference between the premiums, is $1. If the stock rises to 35 just prior to expiration, the 35 call becomes worthless and the 30 call is worth $5. Thus the spread provides a profit of $4 on an investment of $1. If on the other hand the price of the stock goes down, both options expire worthless and the investor loses the entire premium.

BUNCHING

1. combining many round-lot orders for execution at the same time on the floor of an exchange. This technique can also be used with odd-lot orders, when combining many small orders can save the odd-lot differential for each customer.
2. pattern on the ticker tape when a series of trades in the same security appear consecutively.

BURNOUT exhaustion of a tax shelter's benefits, when an investor starts to receive income from the investment. This income must be reported to the Internal Revenue Service, and taxes must be paid on it.

BUSINESS CYCLE recurrence of periods of expansion (RECOVERY) and contraction (RECESSION) in economic activity with effects on inflation, growth, and employment. One cycle extends from a GNP base line through one rise and one decline and back to the base line, a period averaging about 2½ years. A business cycle affects profitability and CASH FLOW, making it a key consideration in corporate dividend policy, and is a factor in the rise and fall of the inflation rate, which in turn affects return on investments.

BUSINESS DAY

In general: hours when most businesses are in operation. Although individual working hours may differ, and particular firms may choose staggered schedules, the conventional business day is 9 A.M. to 5 P.M.

Finance and investments: day when financial marketplaces are open for trading. In figuring the settlement date on a *regular way* securities transaction—which is the fifth business day after the trade date—Saturday, Sunday, and a legal holiday would not be counted, for example.

BUSINESS SEGMENT REPORTING reporting the results of the divisions, subsidiaries, or other segments of a business separately so that income, sales, and assets can be compared. Allocation of central corporate expenses is not required by the Financial Accounting Standards Board. Also called line of business reporting.

BUTTERFLY SPREAD complex option strategy that involves selling two calls and buying two calls on the same or different markets, with several maturity dates. One of the options has a higher exercise price and the other has a lower exercise price than the other two options. An investor in a butterfly spread will profit if the underlying security makes no dramatic movements because the premium income will be collected when the options are sold.

BUY acquire property in return for money. Buy can be used as a synonym for bargain.

BUY AND HOLD STRATEGY strategy that calls for accumulating shares in a company over the years. This allows the investor to pay favorable long-term capital gains tax on profits and requires far less attention than a more active trading strategy.

BUY AND WRITE STRATEGY conservative options strategy that entails buying stocks and then writing covered call options on them. Investors receive both the dividends from the stock and the premium income from the call options. However, the investor may have to sell the stock below the current market price if the call is exercised.

BUYBACK purchase of a long contract to cover a short position, usually arising out of the short sale of a commodity. Also, purchase of identical securities to cover a short sale. Synonym: *short covering*.

Bond buyback: corporation's purchase of its own bonds at a discount in the open market. This is done in markets characterized by rapidly rising interest rates and commensurately declining bond prices.

BUYER'S MARKET market situation that is the opposite of a SELLER'S MARKET.

BUY HEDGE *see* LONG HEDGE.

BUY IN

Options trading: procedure whereby the responsibility to deliver or accept stock can be terminated. In a transaction called *buying-in* or CLOSING PURCHASE, the writer buys an identical option (only the premium or price is different). The second of these options offsets the first, and the profit or loss is the difference in premiums.

Securities: transaction between brokers wherein securities are not delivered on time by the broker on the sell side, forcing the buy side broker to obtain shares from other sources.

BUYING CLIMAX rapid rise in the price of a stock or commodity, setting the stage for a quick fall. Such a surge attracts most of the potential buyers of the stock, leaving them with no one to sell their stock to at higher prices. This is what causes the ensuing fall. Technical chartists see a buying climax as a dramatic runup, accompanied by increased trading volume in the stock.

BUYING ON MARGIN buying securities with credit available through a relationship with a broker, called a MARGIN ACCOUNT. Arrangements of this kind are closely regulated by the Federal Reserve Board. *See also* MARGIN.

BUYING POWER amount of money available to buy securities, determined by tabulating the cash held in brokerage accounts, and adding the amount that could be spent if securities were margined to the limit. The market cannot rise beyond the available buying power. *See also* PURCHASING POWER.

BUY MINUS order to buy a stock at a price lower than the current market price. Traders try to execute a buy minus order on a temporary dip in the stock's price.

BUY ON THE BAD NEWS strategy based on the belief that, soon after a company announces bad news, the price of its stock will plummet. Those who buy at this stage assume that the price is about as low as it can go, leaving plenty of room for a rise when the news improves. If the adverse development is indeed temporary, this technique can be quite profitable. *See also* BOTTOM FISHER.

BUY ORDER in securities trading, an order to a broker to purchase a specified quantity of a security at the MARKET PRICE or at another stipulated price.

BUYOUT purchase of at least a controlling percentage of a company's stock to take over its assets and operations. A buyout can be accomplished through negotiation or through a tender offer. A LEVERAGED BUYOUT occurs when a small group borrows the money to finance the purchase of the shares. The loan is ultimately repaid out of cash generated from the acquired company's operations or from the sale of its assets. *See also* GOLDEN PARACHUTE.

BUY STOP ORDER BUY ORDER marked to be held until the market price rises to the STOP PRICE, then to be entered as a MARKET ORDER to buy at the best available price. Sometimes called a *suspended market order,* because it remains suspended until a market transaction elects, activates, or triggers the stop. Such an order is not permitted in the over-the-counter market. *See also* STOP ORDER.

BUY THE BOOK order to a broker to buy all the shares available from the specialist in a security and from other brokers and dealers at the current offer price. The book is the notebook in which specialists keep track of buy and sell orders. The most likely source of such an order is a professional trader or a large institutional buyer.

BYLAWS rules governing the internal management of an organization which, in the case of business corporations, are drawn up at the time of incorporation. The charter is concerned with such broad matters as the number of directors and the number of authorized shares; the bylaws, which can usually be amended by the directors themselves, cover such points as the election of directors, the appointment of executive and finance committees, the duties of officers, and how share transfers may be made. Bylaws, which are also prevalent in not-for-profit organizations, cannot countermand laws of the government.

BYPASS TRUST agreement allowing parents to pass assets on to their children to reduce estate taxes. The trust must be made irrevocable, meaning that the terms can never be changed. Assets put in such a trust usually exceed the amount that children and other heirs can receive tax-free at a parent's death. Under the 1981 Tax Act, this amount reaches $600,000 in 1987. Parents can arrange to receive income from the assets during their lifetimes and may even be able to touch the principal in case of dire need. One variation of a bypass trust is the qualified terminable interest property trust, or Q-TIP TRUST.

C

CABINET CROWD members of the New York Stock Exchange who trade in infrequently traded bonds. Also called *inactive bond crowd* or *book crowd.* Buy and sell LIMIT ORDERS for these bonds are kept in steel racks, called cabinets, at the side of the bond trading floor; hence the name cabinet crowd.

CABINET SECURITY stock or bond listed on a major exchange but not actively traded. There are a considerable number of such bonds and a limited number of such stocks, mainly those trading in ten-share units. Cabinets are the metal storage racks that LIMIT ORDERS for such securities are filed in pending execution or cancellation. *See also* CABINET CROWD.

CAGE section of a brokerage firm's back office where funds are received and disbursed.

Also, the installation where a bank teller works.

CALENDAR list of securities about to be offered for sale. Separate calendars are kept for municipal bonds, corporate bonds, government bonds, and new stock offerings.

CALENDAR SPREAD options strategy that entails buying two options on the same security with different maturities. If the EXERCISE PRICE is the same (a June 50 call and a September 50 call) it is a HORIZONTAL SPREAD. If the exercise prices are different (a June 50 call and a September 45 call), it is a DIAGONAL SPREAD. Investors gain or lose as the difference in price narrows or widens.

CALL

Banking: demand to repay a secured loan usually made when the borrower has failed to meet such contractual obligations as timely payment of interest. When a banker calls a loan, the entire principal amount is due immediately. *See also* BROKER LOAN RATE.

Securities: issuer's right to redeem bonds or preferred stock before maturity (if any). The first dates when an issuer may call securities is specified in the prospectus and in the INDENTURE or preferred stock agreement.
See also CALLABLE; CALL PRICE.

CALLABLE redeemable by the issuer before the scheduled maturity. The issuer must pay the holders a premium price if such a security is retired early. Bonds are usually called when interest rates fall so significantly that the issuer can save money by floating new bonds at lower rates. *See also* CALL PRICE; DEMAND LOAN.

CALLED AWAY term for a bond redeemed before maturity, or a call or put option exercised against the stockholder, or a delivery required on a short sale.

CALL FEATURE part of the agreement a bond issuer makes with a buyer, called the indenture, describing the schedule and price of redemptions before maturity. Most corporate and municipal bonds have 10-year call features (termed CALL PROTECTION by holders); government securities usually have none. *See also* CALL PRICE.

CALL LOAN RATE *see* BROKER LOAN RATE.

CALL OPTION right to buy 100 shares of a particular stock or stock index at a predetermined price before a preset deadline, in exchange for a premium. For buyers who think a stock will go up dramatically, call options permit a profit from a smaller investment than it would take to buy the stock. These options can also produce extra income for the seller, who gives up ownership of the stock if the option is exercised.

CALL PREMIUM amount that the buyer of a call option has to pay to the seller for the right to purchase a stock or stock index at a specified price by a specified date.

In bonds, preferreds, and convertibles, the amount over par that an issuer has to pay to an investor for redeeming the security early.

CALL PRICE price at which a bond or preferred stock with a *call provision* or

CALL FEATURE can be redeemed by the issuer; also known as *redemption price*. To compensate the holder for loss of income and ownership, the call price is usually higher than the par value of the security, the difference being the CALL PREMIUM. *See also* CALL PROTECTION.

CALL PROTECTION length of time during which a security cannot be redeemed by the issuer. U.S. government securities are generally not callable, although there is an exception in certain 30-year Treasury bonds, which become callable after 25 years. Corporate and municipal issuers generally provide 10 years of call protection. Investors who plan to live off the income from a bond should be sure they have call protection, because without it the bond could be CALLED AWAY at any time specified in the indenture.

CANCEL

In general: void a negotiable instrument by annulling or paying it; also, prematurely terminate a bond or other contract.

Securities trading: void an order to buy or sell. *See also* GOOD TILL CANCELED ORDER.

CAPITAL ASSET long-term asset that is not bought or sold in the normal course of business. Generally speaking, the term includes FIXED ASSETS—land, buildings, equipment, furniture and fixtures, and so on. The Internal Revenue Service definition of capital assets includes security investments.

CAPITAL ASSET PRICING MODEL (CAPM) sophisticated model of the relationship between *expected risk* and *expected return*. The model is grounded in the theory that investors demand higher returns for higher risks. It says that the return on an asset or a security is equal to the risk-free return—such as the return on a short-term Treasury security—plus a risk premium.

CAPITAL BUDGET program for financing long-term outlays such as plant expansion, research and development, and advertising. Among the methods used in arriving at a capital budget are NET PRESENT VALUE (NPV), INTERNAL RATE OF RETURN (IRR), and PAYBACK PERIOD.

CAPITAL CONSUMPTION ALLOWANCE amount of depreciation included in the GROSS NATIONAL PRODUCT (GNP), normally around 11%. This amount is subtracted from GNP, on the theory that it is needed to maintain the productive capacity of the economy, to get *net national product (NNP)*. Adjusted further for indirect taxes, NNP equals *national income*. Economists use GNP rather than NNP in the analyses we read every day largely because capital consumption allowance figures are not always available or reliable. *See also* DEPRECIATION.

CAPITAL EXPENDITURE outlay of money to acquire or improve CAPITAL ASSETS such as buildings and machinery.

CAPITAL FLIGHT movement of large sums of money from one country to another to escape political or economic turmoil or to seek higher rates of return. For example, periods of high inflation or political revolution have brought about an exodus of capital from many Latin American countries to the United States, which is perceived as a safe haven for capital.

CAPITAL FORMATION creation or expansion, through savings, of capital or of *producer's goods*—buildings, machinery, equipment—that produce other goods and services, the result being economic expansion.

CAPITAL GAIN difference between an asset's purchase price and selling price, when the difference is positive. When the TAX REFORM ACT OF 1986 was passed, the profit on a CAPITAL ASSET held six months was considered a long-term gain taxable at a lower rate. The 1986 law provided that the differential between long-term capital gain and ordinary income rates be phased out.

CAPITAL GAINS DISTRIBUTION mutual fund's distribution to shareholders of the profits derived from the sale of stocks or bonds. Traditionally, mutual fund shareholders have benefited from a lower long-term capital gains tax rate regardless of how long they held fund shares. The TAX REFORM ACT OF 1986 provides for the elimination by 1988 of the rate differential favoring long-term capital gains.

CAPITAL GAINS TAX tax on profits from the sale of CAPITAL ASSETS. The tax law has traditionally specified a minimum HOLDING PERIOD after which a CAPITAL GAIN was taxed at a more favorable rate (recently a maximum of 20% for individuals) than ordinary income. The TAX REFORM ACT OF 1986 provided that all capital gains be taxed at a maximum of 28% in 1987 and at ordinary income rates starting in 1988.

CAPITAL GOODS goods used in the production of other goods—industrial buildings, machinery, equipment—as well as highways, office buildings, government installations. In the aggregate such goods form a country's productive capacity.

CAPITAL-INTENSIVE requiring large investments in CAPITAL ASSETS. Motor-vehicle and steel production are capital-intensive industries. To provide an acceptable return on investment, such industries must have a high margin of profit or a low cost of borrowing. The term capital-intensive is sometimes used to mean a high proportion of fixed assets to labor.

CAPITALISM economic system in which (1) private ownership of property exists; (2) aggregates of property or capital provide income for the individuals or firms that accumulated it and own it; (3) individuals and firms are relatively free to compete with others for their own economic gain; (4) the profit motive is basic to economic life.

Among the synonyms for capitalism are LAISSEZ-FAIRE economy, private enterprise system, and free-price system. In this context *economy* is interchangeable with *system*.

CAPITALIZATION see CAPITALIZE; CAPITAL STRUCTURE; MARKET CAPITALIZATION.

CAPITALIZATION RATE rate of interest used to convert a series of future payments into a single PRESENT VALUE.

CAPITALIZATION RATIO analysis of a company's capital structure showing what percentage of the total is debt, preferred stock, common stock, and other equity. The ratio is useful in evaluating the relative RISK and leverage that holders of the respective levels of security have. *See also* BOND RATIO.

CAPITALIZE
1. convert a schedule of income into a principal amount, called *capitalized value*, by dividing by a rate of interest.
2. issue securities to finance *capital outlays* (rare).
3. record capital outlays as additions to asset accounts, not as expenses. *See also* CAPITAL EXPENDITURE.

4. convert a lease obligation to an asset/liability form of expression called a *capital lease,* that is, to record a leased asset as an owned asset and the lease obligation as borrowed funds.
5. turn something to one's advantage economically—for example, sell umbrellas on a rainy day.

CAPITAL LEASE lease that under Statement 13 of the Financial Accounting Standards Board must be reflected on a company's balance sheet as an asset and corresponding liability. Generally, this applies to leases where the lessee acquires essentially all of the economic benefits and risks of the leased property.

CAPITAL LOSS amount by which the proceeds from the sale of a CAPITAL ASSET are less than the cost of acquiring it. Until the TAX REFORM ACT OF 1986, $2 of LONG-TERM LOSS could be used to offset $1 of LONG-TERM GAIN and (for non-corporate taxpayers) up to $3000 of ORDINARY INCOME, while short-term losses could be applied dollar-for-dollar against short-term gains and $3000 of ordinary income. Starting in 1987, capital losses are offsetable dollar-for-dollar against capital gains and $3000 of ordinary income. The short-term/long-term distinction ends starting 1988. *See also* TAX LOSS CARRYBACK, CARRYFORWARD.

CAPITAL MARKETS markets where capital funds—debt and equity—are traded. Included are private placement sources of debt and equity as well as organized markets and exchanges.

CAPITAL OUTLAY *see* CAPITAL EXPENDITURE.

CAPITAL REQUIREMENTS
1. permanent financing needed for the normal operation of a business; that is, the long-term and working capital.
2. appraised investment in fixed assets and normal working capital. Whether patents, rights, and contracts should be included is moot.

CAPITAL STOCK stock authorized by a company's charter and having PAR VALUE, STATED VALUE, or NO PAR VALUE. The number and value of issued shares are normally shown, together with the number of shares authorized, in the capital accounts section of the balance sheet.

Informally, a synonym for COMMON STOCK, though capital stock technically also encompasses PREFERRED STOCK.

CAPITAL STRUCTURE corporation's financial framework, including LONG-TERM DEBT, PREFERRED STOCK, and NET WORTH. It is distinguished from FINANCIAL STRUCTURE, which includes additional sources of capital such as short-term debt, accounts payable, and other liabilities. It is synonymous with *capitalization,* although there is some disagreement as to whether capitalization should include long-term loans and mortgages. Analysts look at capital structure in terms of its overall adequacy and its composition as well as in terms of the DEBT-TO-EQUITY RATIO, called *leverage. See also* CAPITALIZATION RATIO; PAR VALUE.

CAPITAL SURPLUS
1. EQUITY—or NET WORTH—not otherwise classifiable as CAPITAL STOCK or RETAINED EARNINGS. Here are five ways of creating surplus:
   a. from stock issued at a premium over par or stated value.
   b. from the proceeds of stock bought back and then sold again.
   c. from a reduction of par or stated value or a reclassification of capital stock.
   d. from donated stock.

    e. from the acquisition of companies that have capital surplus.
    2. common umbrella term for more specific classifications such as ACQUIRED
    SURPLUS, ADDITIONAL PAID-IN CAPITAL, DONATED SURPLUS, and REEVALUA-
    TION SURPLUS (arising from appraisals). Most common synonyms: *paid-in
    surplus; surplus*.

CAPITAL TURNOVER annual sales divided by average stockholder equity (net
worth). When compared over a period, it reveals the extent to which a company
is able to grow without additional capital investment. Generally, companies with
high profit margins have a low capital turnover and vice versa. Also called *equity
turnover*.

CAPTIVE FINANCE COMPANY company, usually a wholly owned subsidiary,
that exists primarily to finance consumer purchases from the parent company.
Prominent examples are General Motors Acceptance Corporation and Ford Motor
Credit Corporation. Although these subsidiaries stand on their own financially,
parent companies frequently make SUBORDINATED LOANS to add to their equity
positions. This supports the high leverage on which the subsidiaries operate and
assures their active participation in the COMMERCIAL PAPER and bond markets.

CARRYBACK, CARRYFORWARD *see* TAX LOSS CARRYBACK, CARRYFORWARD.

CARRYING CHARGE
    Commodities: charge for carrying the actual commodity, including interest, stor-
    age, and insurance costs.
    Margin accounts: fee that a broker charges for carrying securities on credit.
    Real estate: carrying cost, primarily interest and taxes, of owning land prior to
    its development and resale.
    Retailing: seller's charge for installment credit, which is either added to the
    purchase price or to unpaid installments.

CARRYOVER *see* TAX LOSS CARRYBACK, CARRYFORWARD.

CARTEL group of businesses or nations that agree to influence prices by regulating
production and marketing of a product. The most famous contemporary cartel is
the Organization of Petroleum Exporting Countries (OPEC), which, notably in
the 1970s, restricted oil production and sales and raised prices. A cartel has less
control over an industry than a MONOPOLY. A number of nations, including the
United States, have laws prohibiting cartels. TRUST is sometimes used as a synonym for cartel.

CASH asset account on a balance sheet representing paper currency and coins,
negotiable money orders and checks, and bank balances. Also, transactions handled in cash.
    To cash is to convert a negotiable instrument, usually into paper currency
and coins.

CASH ACCOUNT brokerage firm account whose transactions are settled on a cash
basis. It is distinguished from a MARGIN ACCOUNT, for which the broker extends
credit. Some brokerage customers have both cash and margin accounts. By law,
a CUSTODIAL ACCOUNT for a minor must be a cash account.

CASH BASIS

Accounting: method that recognizes revenues when cash is received and recognizes expenses when cash is paid out. In contrast, the *accrual method* recognizes revenues when goods or services are sold and recognizes expenses when obligations are incurred. A third method, called *modified cash basis,* uses accrual accounting for long-term assets and is the basis usually referred to when the term cash basis is used.

Series EE Savings Bonds: paying the entire tax on these bonds when they mature. The alternative is to prorate the tax each year until the bonds mature.

CASHBOOK accounting book that combines cash receipts and disbursements. Its balance ties to the cash account in the general ledger on which the balance sheet is based.

CASH BUDGET estimated cash receipts and disbursements for a future period. A comprehensive cash budget schedules daily, weekly, or monthly expenditures together with the anticipated CASH FLOW from collections and other operating sources. Cash flow budgets are essential in establishing credit and purchasing policies, as well as in planning credit line usage and short-term investments in COMMERCIAL PAPER and othersecurities.

CASH COMMODITY commodity that is owned as the result of a completed contract and must be accepted upon delivery. Contrasts with futures contracts, which are not completed until a specified future date. The cash commodity contract specifications are set by the commodity exchanges.

CASH CONVERSION CYCLE elapsed time, usually expressed in days, from the outlay of cash for raw materials to the receipt of cash after the finished goods have been sold. Because a profit is built into the sales, the term *earnings cycle* is also used. The shorter the cycle, the more WORKING CAPITAL a business generates and the less it has to borrow. This cycle is directly affected by production efficiency, credit policy, and other controllable factors.

CASH COW business that generates a continuing flow of cash. Such a business usually has well-established brand names whose familiarity stimulates repeated buying of the products. For example, a magazine company that has a high rate of subscription renewals would be considered a cash cow. Stocks that are cash cows have dependable dividends.

CASH DIVIDEND cash payment to a corporation's shareholders, distributed from current earnings or accumulated profits and taxable as income. Cash dividends are distinguished from STOCK DIVIDENDS, which are payments in the form of stock. *See also* YIELD.

INVESTMENT COMPANY cash dividends are usually made up of dividends, interest income, and capital gains received on its investment portfolio.

CASH EARNINGS cash revenues less cash expenses—specifically excluding non-cash expenses such as DEPRECIATION.

CASH EQUIVALENTS instruments or investments of such high liquidity and safety that they are virtually as good as cash. Examples are a MONEY MARKET FUND and a TREASURY BILL.

CASH FLOW

1. in a larger financial sense, an analysis of all the changes that affect the cash account during an accounting period. Cash flow from OPERATIONS is one factor in a breakdown usually shown as *sources of cash* and *uses of cash*. The cash sale of a fixed asset is a source, for example, whereas the cash purchase of an asset is a use. When more cash comes in than goes out, we speak of a *positive cash flow;* the opposite is a *negative cash flow*. Companies with assets well in excess of liabilities may nevertheless go bankrupt because they cannot generate enough cash to meet current obligations.

2. in investments, NET INCOME plus DEPRECIATION and other noncash charges. In this sense, it is synonymous with CASH EARNINGS. Investors focus on cash flow from operations because of their concern with a firm's ability to pay dividends. *See also* CASH BUDGET.

CASHIERING DEPARTMENT *see* CAGE.

CASH MARKET transactions in the cash or spot markets that are completed; that is, ownership of the commodity is transferred from seller to buyer and payment is given on delivery of the commodity. The cash market contrasts with the futures market, in which contracts are completed at a specified time in the future.

CASH ON DELIVERY (COD)

Commerce: transaction requiring that goods be paid for in full by cash or certified check or the equivalent at the point of delivery. The term *collect on delivery* has the same abbreviation and same meaning. If the customer refuses delivery, the seller has round-trip shipping costs to absorb or other, perhaps riskier, arrangements to make.

Securities: a requirement that delivery of securities to institutional investors be in exchange for assets of equal value—which, as a practical matter, means cash. Alternatively called *delivery against cost* (DAC) or *delivery versus payment* (DVP). On the other side of the trade, the term is *receive versus payment*.

CASH OR DEFERRED ARRANGEMENT (CODA) *see* 401(K) PLAN.

CASH RATIO ratio of cash and marketable securities to current liabilities; a refinement of the QUICK RATIO. The cash ratio tells the extent to which liabilities could be liquidated immediately. Sometimes called *liquidity ratio*.

CASH SURRENDER VALUE in insurance, the amount the insurer will return to a policyholder on cancellation of the policy. Sometimes abbreviated *CSVLI* (cash surrender value of life insurance), it shows up as an asset on the balance sheet of a company that has life insurance on its principals, called *key man insurance*. Insurance companies make loans against the cash value of policies, often at a better-than-market rate.

CASUALTY LOSS financial loss caused by damage, destruction, or loss of property as the result of an identifiable event that is sudden, unexpected, or unusual. Casualty and theft losses are considered together for tax purposes; are covered by most *casualty insurance* policies; and are tax deductible provided the loss is (1) not covered by insurance or (2) if covered, a claim has been made and denied.

CATS *see* CERTIFICATE OF ACCRUAL ON TREASURY SECURITIES.

CATS AND DOGS speculative stocks that have short histories of sales, earnings, and dividend payments. In bull markets, analysts say disparagingly that even the cats and dogs are going up.

CAVEAT EMPTOR, CAVEAT SUBSCRIPTOR *buyer beware, seller beware.* A variation on the latter is *caveat venditor.* Good advice when markets are not adequately protected, which was true of the stock market before the watchdog SECURITIES AND EXCHANGE COMMISSION was established in the 1930s.

CENTRAL BANK country's bank that (1) issues currency; (2) administers monetary policy, including OPEN MARKET OPERATIONS; (3) holds deposits representing the reserves of other banks; and (4) engages in transactions designed to facilitate the conduct of business and protect the public interest. In the United States, central banking is a function of the FEDERAL RESERVE SYSTEM.

CERTIFICATE formal declaration that can be used to document a fact, such as a birth certificate.

The following are certificates with particular relevance to finance and investments.

1. auditor's certificate, sometimes called certificate of accounts, or ACCOUNTANT'S OPINION.
2. bond certificate, certificate of indebtedness issued by a corporation containing the terms of the issuer's promise to repay principal and pay interest, and describing collateral, if any. Traditionally, bond certificates had coupons attached, which were exchanged for payment of interest. Now that most bonds are issued in registered form, coupons are less common. The amount of a certificate is the par value of the bond.
3. CERTIFICATE OF DEPOSIT.
4. certificate of INCORPORATION.
5. certificate of indebtedness, government debt obligation having a maturity shorter than a bond and longer than a treasury bill (such as a Treasury Note).
6. PARTNERSHIP certificate, showing the interest of all participants in a business partnership.
7. PROPRIETORSHIP certificate, showing who is legally responsible in an individually owned business.
8. STOCK CERTIFICATE, evidence of ownership of a corporation showing number of shares, name of issuer, amount of par or stated value represented or a declaration of no-par value, and rights of the shareholder. Preferred stock certificates also list the issuer's responsibilities with respect to dividends and voting rights, if any.

CERTIFICATELESS MUNICIPALS MUNICIPAL BONDS that have no certificate of ownership for each bondholder. Instead, one certificate is valid for the entire issue. Certificateless municipals save paperwork for brokers and municipalities and allow investors to trade their bonds without having to transfer certificates. *See also* BOOK ENTRY SECURITIES.

CERTIFICATE OF ACCRUAL ON TREASURY SECURITIES (CATS) U.S. Treasury issues, sold at a deep discount from face value. A ZERO-COUPON security, they pay no interest during their lifetime, but return the full face value at maturity. They are appropriate for retirement or education planning. As TREASURY SECURITIES, CATS cannot be CALLED AWAY.

CERTIFICATE OF DEPOSIT (CD) debt instrument issued by a bank that usually pays interest. Institutional CDs are issued in denominations of $100,000 or more, and individual CDs start as low as $100. Maturities range from a few weeks to several years. Interest rates are set by competitive forces in the marketplace.

CERTIFICATE OF DEPOSIT ROLLOVER sophisticated investment strategy that defers taxes from one year to the next. An investor buys a certificate of deposit on margin that will mature in the following year, deducts the interest cost on the loan this year, and moves the income from the certificate into the next year. Internal Revenue Service rules say the interest deduction can be applied against any net investment income, which includes dividends, interest, royalties, and capital gains. Prior to the TAX REFORM ACT OF 1986, $10,000 of investment related interest over and above investment income was deductible. Under the 1986 law, the excess over income will be brought to zero by 1991.

CERTIFIED CHECK check for which a bank guarantees payment. When the check is certified, it legally becomes an obligation of the bank, and the funds to cover it are immediately withdrawn from the depositor's account.

CERTIFIED FINANCIAL PLANNER (CFP) person who has passed examinations administered by the Denver-based College for Financial Planning, testing the ability to coordinate a client's banking, estate, insurance, investment, and tax affairs. Financial planners usually specialize in one or more of these areas and consult outside experts as needed. Some planners charge only fees and make no money on the implementation of their plans. Others charge a smaller fee but collect a commission on each product or service they sell.

CERTIFIED PUBLIC ACCOUNTANT (CPA) accountant who has passed certain exams, achieved a certain amount of experience, reached a certain age, and met all other statutory and licensing requirements of the U.S. state where he or she works. In addition to accounting and auditing, CPAs prepare tax returns for corporations and individuals.

CHAIRMAN OF THE BOARD member of a corporation's board of directors who presides over its meetings and who is the highest ranking officer in the corporation. The chairman of the board may or may not have the most actual executive authority in a firm. The additional title of CHIEF EXECUTIVE OFFICER (CEO) is reserved for the principal executive, and depending on the particular firm, that title may be held by the chairman, the president, or even an executive vice president. In some corporations, the position of chairman is either a prestigious reward for a past president or an honorary position for a prominent person, a large stockholder, or a family member; it may carry little or no real power in terms of policy or operating decision making.

CHAPTER 7 *see* BANKRUPTCY.

CHAPTER 11 *see* BANKRUPTCY.

CHARGE OFF *see* BAD DEBT.

CHARTER *see* ARTICLES OF INCORPORATION.

CHARTIST technical analyst who charts the patterns of stocks, bonds, and commodities to make buy and sell recommendations to clients. Chartists believe recurring patterns of trading can help them forecast future price movements. *See also* TECHNICAL ANALYSIS.

CHECK bill of exchange, or draft on a bank drawn against deposited funds to pay a specified sum of money to a specified person on demand. A check is considered as cash and is NEGOTIABLE when endorsed.

CHECKING THE MARKET canvassing securities market-makers by telephone or other means in search of the best bid or offer price.

CHICAGO BOARD OF TRADE *see* SECURITIES AND COMMODITIES EXCHANGES.

CHICAGO BOARD OPTIONS EXCHANGE *see* SECURITIES AND COMMODITIES EXCHANGES.

CHICAGO MERCANTILE EXCHANGE *see* SECURITIES AND COMMODITIES EXCHANGES.

CHIEF EXECUTIVE OFFICER (CEO) officer of a firm principally responsible for the activities of a company. CEO is usually an additional title held by the CHAIRMAN OF THE BOARD, the president, or another senior officer such as a vice chairman or an executive vice president.

CHIEF FINANCIAL OFFICER (CFO) executive officer who is responsible for handling funds, signing checks, keeping financial records, and financial planning for a corporation. He or she typically has the title of vice president-finance or financial vice president in large corporations, that of treasurer or controller (also spelled comptroller) in smaller companies. Since many state laws require that a corporation have a treasurer, that title is often combined with one or more of the other financial titles.

The controllership function requires an experienced accountant to direct internal accounting programs, including cost accounting, systems and procedures, data processing, acquisitions analysis, and financial planning. The controller may also have internal audit responsibilities.

The treasury function is concerned with the receipt, custody, investment, and disbursement of corporate funds and for borrowings and the maintenance of a market for the company's securities.

CHIEF OPERATING OFFICER officer of a firm, usually the president or an executive vice president, responsible for day-to-day management. The chief operating officer reports to the CHIEF EXECUTIVE OFFICER and may or may not be on the board of directors (presidents typically serve as board members). *See also* CHAIRMAN OF THE BOARD.

CHURNING excessive trading of a client's account. Churning increases the broker's commissions, but usually leaves the client worse off or no better off than before. Churning is illegal under SEC and exchange rules, but is difficult to prove.

CINCINNATI STOCK EXCHANGE (CSE) stock exchange established in 1887. The CSE became the first completely automated stock exchange, handling members' transactions without the benefit of a physical trading floor by using computers. The CSE has nominal jurisdiction over the National Securities Trading System (NSTS), known popularly as the ''Cincinnati experiment.'' Participating brokerage firms enter orders into the NSTS computer, which then matches orders and clears the orders back to the brokers. The NSTS contains some of the features envisioned for a national exchange market system.

CIRCLE underwriter's way of designating potential purchasers and amounts of a securities issue during the REGISTRATION period, before selling is permitted. Registered representatives canvass prospective buyers and report any interest to the underwriters, who then circle the names on their list.

CITIZEN BONDS form of CERTIFICATELESS MUNICIPALS. Citizen bonds may be registered on stock exchanges, in which case their prices are listed in daily newspapers, unlike other municipal bonds. *See also* BOOK-ENTRY SECURITIES.

CLASS
1. securities having similar features. Stocks and bonds are the two main classes; they are subdivided into various classes—for example, mortgage bonds and debentures, issues with different rates of interest, common and preferred stock, or Class A and Class B common. The different classes in a company's capitalization are itemized on its balance sheet.
2. options of the same type—put or call—with the same underlying security. A class of option having the same expiration date and EXERCISE PRICE is termed a SERIES.

CLASS A/CLASS B SHARES *see* CLASSIFIED STOCK.

CLASSIFIED STOCK separation of equity into more than one CLASS of common, usually designated Class A and Class B. The distinguishing features, set forth in the corporation charter and bylaws, usually give an advantage to the Class A shares in terms of voting power, though dividend and liquidation privileges can also be involved. Classified stock is less prevalent today than in the 1920s, when it was used as a means of preserving minority control.

CLAYTON ANTI-TRUST ACT *see* ANTITRUST LAWS.

CLEAN
Finance: free of debt, as in a clean balance sheet. In banking, corporate borrowers have traditionally been required to *clean up* for at least 30 days each year to prove their borrowings were seasonal and not required as permanent working capital.
International trade: without documents, as in clean vs. documentary drafts.
Securities: block trade that matches corresponding buy or sell orders, thus sparing the block positioner any inventory risk. If the transaction appears on the exchange tape, it is said to be *clean on the tape*. Sometimes such a trade is called a *natural:* "We did a natural for 80,000 XYZ common."

CLEAR
Banking: COLLECTION of funds on which a check is drawn, and payment of those funds to the holder of the check. *See also* CLEARING HOUSE FUNDS.
Finance: asset not securing a loan and not otherwise encumbered. As a verb, to clear means to make a profit: "After all expenses, we *cleared* $1 million."
Securities: COMPARISON of the details of a transaction between brokers prior to settlement; final exchange of securities for cash on delivery.

CLEARING HOUSE FUNDS funds represented by checks or drafts that are transferred between banks through the FEDERAL RESERVE SYSTEM. Unlike FEDERAL FUNDS, which are drawn on reserve balances and are good the same day, clearing house funds require three days to clear. Also, funds used to settle transactions on which there is one day's FLOAT.

CLIFFORD TRUST trust set up for at least ten years and a day which makes it possible to turn over title to income-producing assets, then to reclaim the assets when the trust expires. Prior to the TAX REFORM ACT OF 1986, such trusts were popular ways of shifting income-producing assets from parents to children, whose income was taxed at lower rates. The 1986 Tax Act makes monies put in Clifford

Trusts after March 1, 1986, subject to taxation at the grantor's tax rate, thus defeating their purpose. For trusts established before that date, taxes on earnings over $1000 will be paid at the grantor's rate, but only if the child is under the age of 14. *See also* INTER VIVOS TRUST.

CLONE FUND in a FAMILY OF FUNDS, new fund set up to emulate a successful existing fund.

CLOSE
1. the price of the final trade of a security at the end of a trading day.
2. the last half hour of a trading session on the exchanges.
3. in commodities trading, the period just before the end of the session when trades marked for execution AT THE CLOSE are completed.
4. to consummate a sale or agreement. In a REAL ESTATE closing, for example, rights of ownership are transferred in exchange for monetary and other considerations. At a *loan* closing, notes are signed and checks are exchanged. At the close of an *underwriting* deal, checks and securities are exchanged.
5. in accounting, the transfer of revenue and expense accounts at the end of the period—called *closing the books*.

CLOSE A POSITION to eliminate an investment from one's portfolio. The simplest example is the outright sale of a security and its delivery to the purchaser in exchange for payment. In commodities futures and options trading, traders commonly close out positions through offsetting transactions. Closing a position terminates involvement with the investment; hedging, though similar, requires further actions at some point in the future.

CLOSED CORPORATION corporation whose shares are owned by a few people, usually members of management or a family. Shares are not for sale and there is no public market. Also known as *close corporation* or *private corporation*.

CLOSED-END MANAGEMENT COMPANY INVESTMENT COMPANY that operates a mutual fund with a limited number of shares outstanding. Unlike an OPEN-END MANAGEMENT COMPANY, which creates new shares to meet investor demand, a closed-end fund starts with a set number of shares. These are often listed on an exchange.

CLOSED-END MORTGAGE mortgage-bond issue with an indenture that prohibits repayment before maturity and the repledging of the same collateral without the permission of the bondholders; also called closed mortgage. It is distinguished from an OPEN-END MORTGAGE.

CLOSED OUT liquidated the position of a client unable to meet a margin call or cover a short sale. *See also* CLOSE A POSITION.

CLOSELY HELD corporation most of whose voting stock is held by a few shareholders; differs from a CLOSED CORPORATION because enough stock is publicly held to provide a basis for trading. Also, the shares held by the controlling group and not considered likely to be available for purchase.

CLOSING COSTS expenses involved in transferring real estate from a seller to a buyer, among them lawyer's fees, survey charges, title searches and insurance, and fees to file deeds and mortgages.

CLOSING PRICE price of the last transaction completed during a day's trading session on an organized securities exchange. *See also* CLOSING RANGE.

CLOSING PURCHASE option seller's purchase of another option having the same features as an earlier one. The two options cancel each other out and thus liquidate the seller's position.

CLOSING QUOTE last bid and offer prices recorded by a specialist or market maker at the close of a trading day.

CLOSING RANGE range of prices (in commodities trading) within which an order to buy or sell a commodity can be executed during one trading day.

CLOSING SALE sale of an option having the same features (i.e., of the same series) as an option previously purchased. The two have the effect of canceling each other out. Such a transaction demonstrates the intention to liquidate the holder's position in the underlying securities upon exercise of the buy.

CODE OF ARBITRATION *see* BOARD OF ARBITRATION.

CODE OF PROCEDURE NATIONAL ASSOCIATION OF SECURITIES DEALERS (NASD) guide for its District Business Conduct Committees in hearing and adjudicating complaints filed between or against NASD members under its Rules of Fair Practice.

COINSURANCE sharing of an insurance risk, common when claims could be of such size that it would not be prudent for one company to underwrite the whole risk. Typically, the underwriter is liable up to a stated limit, and the coinsurer's liability is for amounts above that limit.

Policies on hazards such as fire or water damage often require coverage of at least a specified coinsurance percentage of the replacement cost. Such clauses induce the owners of property to carry full coverage or close to it.

COLLATERAL ASSET pledged to a lender until a loan is repaid. If the borrower defaults, the lender has the legal right to seize the collateral and sell it to pay off the loan.

COLLATERALIZE *see* ASSIGN; COLLATERAL; HYPOTHECATION.

COLLATERALIZED MORTGAGE OBLIGATION (CMO) mortgage-backed bond that separates mortgage pools into short-, medium-, and long-term portions. Investors who want a fast return of capital can buy 5-year CMOs; those who want a long-term investment can buy a share in a 20-year pool. Each class is paid a fixed rate of interest at regular intervals. The fact that investors in Ginnie Maes and other mortgage-backed securities could never predict the pace at which their capital would be repaid gave rise to CMOs, which split the pools into different time frames, called *tranches*.

COLLATERAL TRUST BOND corporate debt security backed by other securities, usually held by a bank or other trustee. Such bonds are backed by collateral trust certificates and are usually issued by parent corporations that are borrowing against the securities of wholly owned subsidiaries.

COLLECTIBLE rare object collected by investors. Examples: stamps, coins, oriental rugs, antiques, baseball cards, photographs. Collectibles typically rise sharply in value during inflationary periods, when people are trying to move their assets from paper currency as an inflation hedge, then drop in value during low inflation. Collectible trading for profit can be quite difficult, because of the limited number of buyers and sellers.

COLLECTION
1. presentation of a negotiable instrument such as a draft or check to the place at which it is payable. The term refers not only to check clearing and payment, but to such special banking services as foreign collections, coupon collection, and collection of returned items (bad checks).
2. referral of a past due account to specialists in collecting loans or accounts receivable, either an internal department or a private collection agency.
3. in a general financial sense, conversion of accounts receivable into cash.

COLLECTION PERIOD *see* COLLECTION RATIO.

COLLECTION RATIO ratio of a company's accounts receivable to its average daily sales. Average daily sales are obtained by dividing sales for an accounting period by the number of days in the accounting period—annual sales divided by 365, if the accounting period is a year. That result, divided into accounts receivable (an average of beginning and ending accounts receivable is more accurate), is the collection ratio—the average number of days it takes the company to convert receivables into cash. It is also called *average collection period. See* ACCOUNTS RECEIVABLE TURNOVER for a discussion of its significance.

COLLECTIVE BARGAINING process by which members of the labor force, operating through authorized union representatives, negotiate with their employers concerning wages, hours, working conditions, and benefits.

COMBINATION
1. arrangement of options involving two long or two short positions with different expiration dates or strike (exercise) prices. A trader could order a combination with a long call and a long put or a short call and a short put.
2. joining of competing companies in an industry to alter the competitive balance in their favor is called a combination in restraint of trade.
3. joining two or more separate businesses into a single accounting entity; also called *business combination. See also* MERGER.

COMBINATION BOND bond backed by the full faith and credit of the governmental unit issuing it as well as by revenue from the toll road, bridge, or other project financed by the bond.

COMBINATION ORDER *see* ALTERNATIVE ORDER.

COMBINED FINANCIAL STATEMENT financial statement that brings together the assets, liabilities, net worth, and operating figures of two or more affiliated companies. In its most comprehensive form, called a combining statement, it includes columns showing each affiliate on an "alone" basis; a column "eliminating" offsetting intercompany transactions; and the resultant combined financial statement. A combined statement is distinguished from a CONSOLIDATED FINANCIAL STATEMENT of a company and subsidiaries, which must reconcile investment and capital accounts. Combined financial statements do not necessarily represent combined credit responsibility or investment strength.

COMEX *see* SECURITIES AND COMMODITIES EXCHANGES.

COMFORT LETTER
1. independent auditor's letter, required in securities underwriting agreements, to assure that information in the registration statement and prospectus is correctly prepared and that no material changes have occurred since its prepara-

tion. It is sometimes called *cold comfort letter*—cold because the accountants do not state positively that the information is correct, only that nothing has come to their attention to indicate it is not correct.

2. letter from one to another of the parties to a legal agreement stating that certain actions not clearly covered in the agreement will—or will not—be taken. Such declarations of intent usually deal with matters that are of importance only to the two parties and do not concern other signers of the agreement.

COMMERCIAL HEDGERS companies that take positions in commodities markets in order to lock in prices at which they buy raw materials or sell their products. For instance, Alcoa might hedge its holdings of aluminum with contracts in aluminum futures, or Eastman Kodak, which must buy great quantities of silver for making film, might hedge its holdings in the silver futures market.

COMMERCIAL LOAN short-term (typically 90-day) renewable loan to finance the seasonal WORKING CAPITAL needs of a business, such as purchase of inventory or production and distribution of goods. Commercial loans—shown on the balance sheet as notes payable—rank second only to TRADE CREDIT in importance as a source of short-term financing. Interest is based on the prime rate. *See also* CLEAN.

COMMERCIAL PAPER short-term obligations with maturities ranging from 2 to 270 days issued by banks, corporations, and other borrowers to investors with temporarily idle cash. Such instruments are unsecured and usually discounted, although some are interest-bearing. They can be issued directly—*direct issuers* do it that way—or through brokers equipped to handle the enormous clerical volume involved. Issuers like commercial paper because the maturities are flexible and because the rates are usually marginally lower than bank rates. Investors— actually lenders, since commercial paper is a form of debt—like the flexibility and safety of an instrument that is issued only by top-rated concerns and is nearly always backed by bank lines of credit. Both Moody's and Standard & Poor's assign ratings to commercial paper.

COMMERCIAL WELLS oil and gas drilling sites that are productive enough to be commercially viable. A limited partnership usually syndicates a share in a commercial well.

COMMINGLING

Securities: mixing customer-owned securities with those owned by a firm in its proprietary accounts. REHYPOTHECATION—the use of customers' collateral to secure brokers' loans—is permissible with customer consent, but certain securities and collateral must by law be kept separate.

Trust banking: pooling the investment funds of individual accounts, with each customer owning a share of the total fund. Similar to a MUTUAL FUND.

COMMISSION

Real estate: percentage of the selling price of the property, paid by the seller.

Securities: fee paid to a broker for executing a trade based on the number of shares traded or the dollar amount of the trade. Since 1975, when regulation ended, brokers have been free to charge whatever they like.

COMMISSION BROKER broker, usually a floor broker, who executes trades of stocks, bonds, or commodities for a commission.

COMMITMENT FEE lender's charge for contracting to hold credit available. Fee may be replaced by interest when money is borrowed or both fees and interest may be charged, as with a REVOLVING CREDIT.

COMMITTEE ON UNIFORM SECURITIES IDENTIFICATION PROCE-DURES (CUSIP) committee that assigns identifying numbers and codes for all securities. These CUSIP numbers and symbols are used when recording all buy or sell orders. For International Business Machines the CUSIP symbol is IBM and the CUSIP number is 45920010.

COMMODITIES bulk goods such as grains, metals, and foods traded on a commodities exchange or on the SPOT MARKET. *See also* SECURITIES AND COMMODITIES EXCHANGES.

COMMODITIES EXCHANGE CENTER *see* SECURITIES AND COMMODITIES EXCHANGES.

COMMODITIES FUTURES TRADING COMMISSION *see* REGULATED COMMODITIES.

COMMODITY-BACKED BOND bond tied to the price of an underlying commodity. An investor whose bond is tied to the price of silver or gold receives interest pegged to the metal's current price, rather than a fixed dollar amount. Such a bond is meant to be a hedge against inflation, which drives up the prices of most commodities.

COMMODITY PAPER inventory loans or advances secured by commodities. If the commodities are in transit, a bill of lading is executed by a common carrier. If they are in storage, a trust receipt acknowledges that they are held and that proceeds from their sale will be transmitted to the lender; a warehouse receipt lists the goods.

COMMON MARKET *see* EUROPEAN ECONOMIC COMMUNITY.

COMMON STOCK units of ownership of a public corporation. Owners typically are entitled to vote on the selection of directors and other important matters as well as to receive dividends on their holdings. In the event that a corporation is liquidated, the claims of secured and unsecured creditors and owners of bonds and preferred stock take precedence over the claims of those who own common stock. For the most part, however, common stock has more potential for appreciation. *See also* CAPITAL STOCK.

COMMON STOCK EQUIVALENT preferred stock or bond convertible into common stock, or warrant to purchase common stock at a specified price or discount from market price. Common stock equivalents represent potential dilution of existing common shareholder's equity, and their conversion or exercise is assumed in calculating fully diluted earnings per share. *See also* FULLY DILUTED EARNINGS PER SHARE.

COMMON STOCK FUND MUTUAL FUND that invests only in common stocks.

COMMON STOCK RATIO percentage of total capitalization represented by common stock. From a creditor's standpoint a high ratio represents a margin of safety in the event of LIQUIDATION. From an investor's standpoint, however, a high ratio can mean a lack of *leverage*. What the ratio should be depends largely on the stability of earnings. Electric utilities can operate with low ratios because their earnings are stable. As a general rule, when an industrial company's stock ratio is below 30%, analysts check on earnings stability and fixed charge coverage in bad times as well as good.

COMMUNITY PROPERTY property and income accumulated by a married couple and belonging to them jointly. The two have equal rights to the income from stocks, bonds, and real estate, as well as to the appreciated value of those assets.

COMPANY organization engaged in business as a proprietorship, partnership, corporation, or other form of enterprise. Originally, a firm made up of a group of people as distinguished from a sole proprietorship. However, since few proprietorships owe their existence exclusively to one person, the term now applies to proprietorships as well.

COMPARATIVE STATEMENTS financial statements covering different dates but prepared consistently and therefore lending themselves to comparative analysis, as accounting convention requires. Comparative figures reveal trends in a company's financial development and permit insight into the dynamics behind static balance sheet figures.

COMPARISON
1. short for *comparison ticket,* a memorandum exchanged prior to settlement by two brokers in order to confirm the details of a transaction to which they were parties. Also called comparison sheet.
2. verification of collateral held against a loan, by exchange of information between two brokers or between a broker and a bank.

COMPENSATING BALANCE *or* **COMPENSATORY BALANCE** average balance required by a bank for holding credit available. The more or less standard requirement for a bank line of credit, for example, is 10% of the line plus an additional 10% of the borrowings. Compensating balances increase the effective rate of interest on borrowings.

COMPETITIVE BID sealed bid, containing price and terms, submitted by a prospective underwriter to an issuer, who awards the contract to the bidder with the best price and terms. Many municipalities and virtually all railroads and public utilities use this bid system. Industrial corporations generally prefer to negotiate with their investment bankers on stock issues but sometimes use competitive bidding to select underwriters for bond issues. *See also* NEGOTIATED UNDERWRITING.

COMPLETE AUDIT usually the same as an unqualified audit, because it is so thoroughly executed that the auditor's only reservations have to do with unobtainable facts. A complete audit examines the system of internal control and the details of the books of account, including subsidiary records and supporting documents. This is done with an eye to legality, mathematical accuracy, accountability, and the application of accepted accounting principles.

COMPLETED CONTRACT METHOD accounting method whereby revenues and expenses (and therefore taxes) on long-term contracts, such as government defense contracts, are recognized in the year the contract is concluded, except that losses are recognized in the year they are forecast. This method differs from the *percentage-of-completion method,* where sales and costs are recognized each year based on the value of the work performed. Under the TAX REFORM ACT OF 1986, manufacturers with long-term contracts must elect either the latter method or the *percentage-of-completion capitalized cost method,* requiring that 40% of the contract be included under the percentage-of-completion method and 60% under the taxpayer's normal accounting method.

COMPLETION PROGRAM oil and gas limited partnership that takes over drilling when oil is known to exist in commercial quantities. A completion program is a conservative way to profit from oil and gas drilling, but without the capital gains potential of exploratory wildcat drilling programs.

COMPLIANCE DEPARTMENT department set up in all organized stock exchanges to oversee market activity and make sure that trading complies with Securities and Exchange Commission and exchange regulations. A company that does not adhere to the rules can be delisted, and a trader or brokerage firm that violates the rules can be barred from trading.

COMPOUND GROWTH RATE rate of growth of a number, compounded over several years. Securities analysts check a company's compound growth rate of profits for five years to see the long-term trend in profitability.

COMPOUND INTEREST interest earned on principal plus interest that was earned earlier. If $100 is deposited in a bank account at 10%, the depositor will be credited with $110 at the end of the first year and $121 at the end of the second year. That extra $1, which was earned on the $10 interest from the first year, is the compound interest. This example involves interest compounded annually; interest can also be compounded on a daily, quarterly, half-yearly, or other basis.

COMPTROLLER OF THE CURRENCY federal official, appointed by the President and confirmed by the Senate, who is responsible for chartering, examining, supervising, and liquidating all national banks. In response to the *comptroller's call,* national banks are required to submit *call reports* of their financial activities at least four times a year and to publish them in local newspapers. National banks can be declared insolvent only by the Comptroller of the Currency.

COMPUTERIZED MARKET TIMING SYSTEM system of picking buy and sell signals that puts together voluminous trading data in search of patterns and trends. Often, changes in the direction of moving average lines form the basis for buy and sell recommendations. These systems, commonly used by commodity funds and by services that switch between mutual funds, tend to work well when markets are moving steadily up or down, but not in trendless markets.

CONCESSION
1. selling group's per-share or per-bond compensation in a corporate underwriting.
2. right, usually granted by a government entity, to use property for a specified purpose, such as a service station on a highway.

CONDOMINIUM form of real estate ownership in which individual residents hold a deed and title to their houses or apartments and pay a maintenance fee to a management company for the upkeep of common property such as grounds, lobbies, and elevators as well as for other amenities. Condominium owners pay real estate taxes on their units and can sublet or sell as they wish. Some real estate limited partnerships specialize in converting rental property into condominiums. *See also* COOPERATIVE.

CONFIRMATION
1. formal memorandum from a broker to a client giving details of a securities transaction. When a broker acts as a dealer, the confirmation must disclose that fact to the customer.
2. document sent by a company's auditor to its customers and suppliers requesting verification of the book amounts of receivables and payables. *Positive confirmations* request that every balance be confirmed, whereas *negative confirmations* request a reply only if an error exists.

CONFORMED COPY copy of an original document with the essential legal features, such as the signature and seal, being typed or indicated in writing.

CONGLOMERATE corporation composed of companies in a variety of businesses. Conglomerates were popular in the 1960s, when they were thought to provide better management and sounder financial backing, and therefore generate more profit, than small independent companies. Some conglomerates became so complex that they were difficult to manage. In the 1980s, some conglomerates sold off divisions and concentrated on a few core businesses. Analysts generally consider stocks of conglomerates difficult to evaluate.

CONSIDERATION something of value that one party gives to another in exchange for a promise or act. In law, a requirement of valid contracts. A consideration can be in the form of money, commodities, or personal services; in many industries the forms have become standardized.

CONSOLIDATED FINANCIAL STATEMENT financial statement that brings together all assets, liabilities, and operating accounts of a parent company and its subsidiaries. *See also* COMBINED FINANCIAL STATEMENT.

CONSOLIDATED MORTGAGE BOND bond issue that covers several units of property and may refinance separate mortgages on these properties. The consolidated mortgage with a single coupon rate is a traditional form of financing for railroads because it is economical to combine many properties in one agreement.

CONSOLIDATED TAPE combined tapes of the New York Stock Exchange and the American Stock Exchange. It became operative in June 1975. Network A covers NYSE-listed securities and identifies the originating market. Network B does the same for Amex-listed securities and securities listed on regional exchanges. *See also* TICKER TAPE.

CONSOLIDATED TAX RETURN return combining reports of companies in what the tax law defines as an affiliated group. A firm is part of an affiliated group if at least 80% owned by another corporation. "Owned" refers to voting stock. (Before the TAX REFORM ACT OF 1986 it also included nonvoting stock.)

CONSOLIDATION LOAN loan that combines and refinances other loans or debt. It is normally an installment loan designed to reduce the dollar amount of an individual's monthly payments.

CONSORTIUM group of companies formed to promote a common objective or engage in a project of benefit to all the members. The relationship normally entails cooperation and a sharing of resources, sometimes even common ownership.

CONSTANT DOLLAR PLAN method of accumulating assets by investing a fixed amount of dollars in securities at set intervals. The investor buys more shares when the price is low and fewer shares when the price is high; the overall cost is lower than it would be if a constant number of shares were bought at set intervals. *See also* DOLLAR COST AVERAGING.

CONSTANT DOLLARS dollars of a base year, used as a gauge in adjusting the dollars of other years in order to ascertain actual purchasing power. Denoted as C$ by the FINANCIAL ACCOUNTING STANDARDS BOARD (FASB), which defines constant dollars as hypothetical units of general purchasing power.

CONSTRUCTION LOAN short-term real estate loan to finance building costs. The funds are disbursed as needed or in accordance with a prearranged plan, and the money is repaid on completion of the project, usually from the proceeds of a mortgage loan. The rate is normally higher than prime, and there is usually an origination fee. The effective yield on these loans tends to be high, and the lender has a security interest in the real property.

CONSTRUCTIVE RECEIPT term used by Internal Revenue Service for the date when a taxpayer received dividends or other income. IRS rules say that constructive receipt of income is established if the taxpayer has the right to claim it, whether or not the choice is exercised. For instance, if a bond pays interest on December 29, the taxpayer must report the income in that tax year and not in the following year.

CONSUMER CREDIT PROTECTION ACT OF 1968 landmark federal legislation establishing rules of disclosure that lenders must observe in dealings with borrowers. The act stipulates that consumers be told annual percentage rates, potential total cost, and any special loan terms. The act, enforced by the Federal Reserve Bank, is also known as the *Truth in Lending Act.*

CONSUMER DEBENTURE investment note issued by a financial institution and marketed directly to the public. Consumer debentures were a popular means of raising lendable funds for banks during tight money periods prior to deregulation, since these instruments, unlike certificates of deposit, could compete freely with other money-market investments in a high-rate market.

CONSUMER FINANCE COMPANY *see* FINANCE COMPANY.

CONSUMER GOODS goods bought for personal or household use, as distinguished from CAPITAL GOODS or *producer's goods,* which are used to produce other goods. The general economic meaning of consumer goods encompasses consumer services. Thus the *market basket* on which the CONSUMER PRICE INDEX is based includes clothing, food, and other goods as well as utilities, entertainment, and other services.

CONSUMER PRICE INDEX (CPI) measure of change in consumer prices, as determined by a monthly survey of the U.S. Bureau of Labor Statistics. Many pension and employment contracts are tied to changes in consumer prices, as protection against inflation and reduced purchasing power. Among the CPI components are the costs of housing, food, transportation, and electricity. Also known as the *cost-of-living index.*

CONSUMPTION TAX *see* VALUE-ADDED TAX (VAT).

CONTANGO

1. pricing situation in which futures prices get progressively higher as maturities get progressively longer, creating negative spreads as contracts go farther out. The increases reflect carrying costs, including storage, financing, and insurance. The reverse condition, an inverted market, is termed BACKWARDATION.
2. in finance, the costs that must be taken into account in analyses involving forecasts.

CONTINGENT LIABILITY

Banking: potential obligation of a guarantor or accommodation endorser; or the position of a customer who opens a letter of credit and whose account will be charged if a draft is presented. The bank's own responsibility for letters of credit and other commitments, individually and collectively, is its contingent liability.

Corporate reports: pending lawsuits, judgments under appeal, disputed claims, and the like, representing financial liability in the event of an adverse outcome.

CONTINGENT ORDER securities order whose execution depends on the execution of another order; for example, a sell order and a buy order with prices stipulated. Where the purpose is to effect a swap, a price difference might be stipulated as a condition of the order's execution. Generally, brokers discourage these orders, preferring to deal with firm instructions.

CONTINUOUS NET SETTLEMENT (CNS) method of securities clearing and settlement that eliminates multiple fails in the same securities. This is accomplished by using a clearing house, such as the National Securities Clearing Corporation, and a depository, such as DEPOSITORY TRUST COMPANY, to match transactions to securities available in the firm's position, resulting in one net receive or deliver position at the end of the day. By including the previous day's fail position in the next day's selling trades, the firm's position is always up to date and money settlement or withdrawals can be made at any time with the clearing house. The alternative to CNS is window settlement, where the seller delivers securities to the buyer's cashier and receives payment.

CONTRA BROKER broker on the opposite side—the buy side of a sell order or the sell side of a buy order.

CONTRACT in general, agreement by which rights or acts are exchanged for lawful consideration. To be valid, it must be entered into by competent parties, must cover a legal and moral transaction, must possess mutuality, and must represent a meeting of minds.

CONTRACTUAL PLAN plan by which fixed dollar amounts of mutual fund shares are accumulated through periodic investments for 10 or 15 years. The legal vehicle for such investments is the *plan company* or *participating unit investment trust*, a selling organization operating on behalf of the fund's underwriter. The plan company must be registered with the Securities and Exchange Commission, as the underlying fund must be, so the investor receives two prospectuses. Investors in these plans commonly receive other benefits in exchange for their fixed periodic payments, such as decreasing term life insurance. *See also* FRONT END LOAD.

CONTRARIAN investor who does the opposite of what most investors are doing at any particular time. According to contrarian opinion, if everyone is certain that something is about to happen, it won't. This is because most people who say the market is going up are fully invested and have no additional purchasing power, which means the market is at its peak. When people predict decline they have already sold out, so the market can only go up. Some mutual funds follow a contrarian investment strategy, and some investment advisers suggest only out-of-favor securities, whose price/earnings ratio is lower than the rest of the market or industry.

CONTROLLED COMMODITIES commodities regulated by the Commodities Exchange Act of 1936, which set up trading rules for futures in commodities markets in order to prevent fraud and manipulation.

CONTROLLED WILDCAT DRILLING drilling for oil and gas in an area adjacent to but outside the limits of a proven field. Also known as a *field extension*. Limited partnerships drilling in this area take greater risks than those drilling in areas of proven energy reserves, but the rewards can be considerable if oil is found.

CONTROLLER *or* COMPTROLLER chief accountant of a company. In small companies the controller may also serve as treasurer. In a brokerage firm, the controller prepares financial reports, supervises internal audits, and is responsible for compliance with Securities and Exchange Commission regulations.

CONTROLLING INTEREST ownership of more than 50% of a corporation's voting shares. A much smaller interest, owned individually or by a group in combination, can be controlling if the other shares are widely dispersed and not actively voted.

CONTROL PERSON *see* AFFILIATED PERSON.

CONTROL STOCK shares owned by holders who have a CONTROLLING INTEREST.

CONVENTIONAL MORTGAGE residential mortgage loan, usually from a bank or savings and loan association, with a fixed rate and term. It is repayable in fixed monthly payments over a period usually 30 years or less, secured by real property, and not insured by the FEDERAL HOUSING ADMINISTRATION or guaranteed by the Veterans Administration.

CONVENTIONAL OPTION put or call contract arranged off the trading floor of a listed exchange and not traded regularly. It was commonplace when options were banned on certain exchanges, but is now rare.

CONVERGENCE movement of the price of a futures contract toward the price of the underlying CASH COMMODITY. At the start of the contract price is higher because of the time value. But as the contract nears expiration the futures price and the cash price converge.

CONVERSION
1. exchange of a convertible security such as a bond into a fixed number of shares of the issuing corporation's common stock.
2. transfer of mutual-fund shares without charge from one fund to another fund in a single family; also known as fund switching.
3. in insurance, switch from short-term to permanent life insurance.

CONVERSION PARITY common-stock price at which a convertible security can become exchangeable for common shares of equal value.

CONVERSION PREMIUM amount by which the price of a convertible tops the market price of the underlying stock. If a stock is trading at $50 and the bond convertible at $45 is trading at $50, the premium is $5. If the premium is high the bond trades like any fixed income bond. If the premium is low the bond trades like a stock.

CONVERSION PRICE the dollar value at which convertible bonds, debentures, or preferred stock can be converted into common stock, as announced when the convertible is issued.

CONVERSION RATIO relationship that determines how many shares of common stock will be received in exchange for each convertible bond or preferred share when the conversion takes place. It is determined at the time of issue and is expressed either as a ratio or as a conversion price from which the ratio can be figured by dividing the par value of the convertible by the conversion price. The indentures of most convertible securities contain an antidilution clause whereby the conversion ratio may be raised (or the conversion price lowered) by the percentage amount of any stock dividend or split, to protect the convertible holder against dilution.

CONVERSION VALUE

In general: value created by changing from one form to another. For example, converting rental property to condominiums adds to the value of the property.

Convertibles: the price at which the exchange can be made for common stock.

CONVERTIBLES corporate securities (usually preferred shares or bonds) that are exchangeable for a set number of another form (usually common shares) at a prestated price. Convertibles are appropriate for investors who want higher income than is available from common stock, together with greater appreciation potential than regular bonds offer. From the issuer's standpoint, the convertible feature is usually designed as a sweetener, to enhance the marketability of the stock or preferred.

COOLING-OFF PERIOD
1. interval (usually 20 days) between the filing of a preliminary prospectus with the Securities and Exchange Commission and the offer of the securities to the public. *See also* REGISTRATION.
2. period during which a union is prohibited from striking, or an employer from locking out employees. The period, typically 30 to 90 days, may be required by law or provided for in a labor agreement.

COOPERATIVE organization owned by its members.

In real estate, a property whose residents own shares in a cooperative giving them exclusive use of their apartments. Decisions about common areas—hallways, elevators, grounds—are made by a vote of members' shares. Members also approve sales of apartments.

Agriculture cooperatives help farmers sell their products more efficiently. Food cooperatives buy food for their members at wholesale prices, but usually require members to help run the organization.

CORNERING THE MARKET purchasing a security or commodity in such volume that control over its price is achieved. A cornered market in a security would be unhappy news for a short seller, who would have to pay an inflated price to cover. Cornering has been illegal for some years.

CORPORATE BOND debt instrument issued by a private corporation, as distinct from one issued by a government agency or a municipality. Corporates typically have four distinguishing features: (1) they are taxable; (2) they have a par value of $1000; (3) they have a term maturity—which means they come due all at once—and are paid for out of a sinking fund accumulated for that purpose; (4) they are traded on major exchanges, with prices published in newspapers. *See also* BOND; MUNICIPAL BOND.

CORPORATE EQUIVALENT YIELD comparison that dealers in government bonds include in their offering sheets to show the after-tax yield of government bonds selling at a discount and corporate bonds selling at par.

CORPORATE FINANCING COMMITTEE NATIONAL ASSOCIATION OF SECURITIES DEALERS standing committee that reviews documentation submitted by underwriters in compliance with Securities and Exchange Commission requirements to ensure that proposed markups are fair and in the public interest.

CORPORATE INCOME FUND (CIF) UNIT INVESTMENT TRUST with a fixed portfolio made up of high-grade securities and instruments, similar to a MONEY MARKET FUND. Most CIFs pay out investment income monthly.

CORPORATE INSIDER *see* INSIDER.

CORPORATION legal entity, chartered by a U.S. state or by the federal government, and separate and distinct from the persons who own it, giving rise to a jurist's remark that it has "neither a soul to damn nor a body to kick." Nonetheless, it is regarded by the courts as an artificial person; it may own property, incur debts, sue, or be sued. It has three chief distinguishing features:
1. limited liability; owners can lose only what they invest.
2. easy transfer of ownership through the sale of shares of stock.
3. continuity of existence.

Other factors helping to explain the popularity of the corporate form of organization are its ability to obtain capital through expanded ownership, and the shareholders' ability to profit from the growth of the business.

CORPUS Latin for *body*.
1. in trust banking, the property in a trust—real estate, securities and other personal property, cash in bank accounts, and any other items included by the donor.
2. body of an investment or note, representing the principal or capital as distinct from the interest or income.

CORRECTION reverse movement, usually downward, in the price of an individual stock, bond, commodity, or index. If prices have been rising on the market as a whole, then fall dramatically, this is known as a *correction within an upward trend*. Technical analysts note that markets do not move straight up or down and that corrections are to be expected during any long-term move. *See* illustration, page 222.

CORRELATION COEFFICIENT statistical measure of the degree to which the movements of two variables are related.

CORRESPONDENT financial organization that regularly performs services for another in a market inaccessible to the other. In banking there is usually a depository relationship that compensates for expenses and facilitates transactions.

CORRECTION

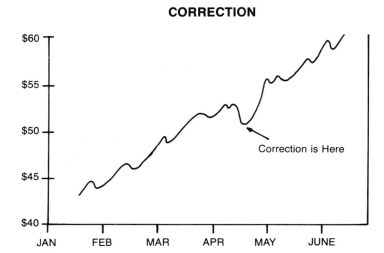

COST ACCOUNTING branch of accounting concerned with providing the information that enables the management of a firm to evaluate production costs.

COST BASIS original price of an asset, used in determining capital gains. It usually is the purchase price, but in the case of an inheritance it is the appraised value of the asset at the time of the donor's death.

COST-BENEFIT ANALYSIS method of measuring the benefits expected from a decision, calculating the cost of the decision, then determining whether the benefits outweigh the costs. Corporations use this method in deciding whether to buy a piece of equipment, and the government uses it in determining whether federal programs are achieving their goals.

COST OF CAPITAL rate of return that a business could earn if itchose another investment with equivalent risk—in other words, the OPPORTUNITY COST of the funds employed as the result of an investment decision. Cost of capital is also calculated using a weighted average of a firm's costs of debt and classes of equity. This is also called the *composite cost of capital.*

COST OF CARRY out-of-pocket costs incurred while an investor has an investment position, among them interest on long positions in margin accounts, dividends lost on short margin positions, and incidentalexpenses.

COST OF GOODS SOLD figure representing the cost of buying raw materials and producing finished goods. Depreciation is considered a part of this cost but is usually listed separately. Included in the direct costs are clear-cut factors such as direct factory labor as well as others that are less clear-cut, such as overhead. *Cost of sales* may be used as a synonym or may mean selling expenses. See also DIRECT OVERHEAD; FIRST IN, FIRST OUT; LAST IN, FIRST OUT.

COST-OF-LIVING ADJUSTMENT (COLA) adjustment of wages designed to offset changes in the cost of living, usually as measured by the CONSUMER PRICE INDEX. COLAs are key bargaining issues in labor contracts and are politically sensitive elements of social security payments and federal pensions because they affect millions of people.

COST-OF-LIVING INDEX *see* CONSUMER PRICE INDEX.

COST OF SALES *see* COST OF GOODS SOLD.

COST-PLUS CONTRACT contract basing the selling price of a product on the total cost incurred in making it plus a stated percentage or a fixed fee—called a *cost-plus-fixed-fee contract.* Cost-plus contracts are common when there is no historical basis for estimating costs and the producer would run a risk of loss— defense contracts involving sophisticated technology, for example. The alternative is a FIXED PRICE contract.

COST-PUSH INFLATION inflation caused by rising prices, which follow on the heels of rising costs. This is the sequence: When the demand for raw materials exceeds the supply, prices go up. As manufacturers pay more for these raw materials they raise the prices they charge merchants for the finished products, and the merchants in turn raisethe prices they charge consumers. *See also* DEMAND-PULL INFLATION;INFLATION.

COST RECORDS
1. investor records of the prices at which securities were purchased, which provide the basis for computing capital gains.
2. in finance, anything that can substantiate the costs incurred in producing goods, providing services, or supporting an activity designed to be productive. Ledgers, schedules, vouchers, and invoices are cost records.

COUNCIL OF ECONOMIC ADVISERS group of economists appointed by the President of the United States to provide counsel on economic policy. The council helps to prepare the President's budget message to Congress, and its chairman frequently speaks for the administration's economic policy.

COUPON interest rate on a debt security the issuer promises to pay to the holder until maturity, expressed as an annual percentage of face value. For example, a bond with a 10% coupon will pay $10 per $100 of the face amount per year, usually in installments paid every six months. The term derives from the small detachable segment of a bond certificate which, when presented to the bond's issuer, entitles the holder to the interest due on that date. As the REGISTERED BOND becomes more widespread, coupons are gradually disappearing.

COUPON BOND bond issued with detachable coupons that must be presented to a paying agent or the issuer for semiannual interest payment. These are bearer bonds, so whoever presents the coupon is entitled to the interest. Once universal, the coupon bond has been gradually giving way to the REGISTERED BOND, some of which pay interest through electronic transfers. *See also* BOOK-ENTRY SECURITIES; CERTIFICATELESS MUNICIPALS; COUPON.

COUPON COLLECTION *see* COLLECTION.

COVARIANCE statistical term for the correlation between two variables multiplied by the standard deviation for each of the variables.

COVENANT promise in a trust indenture or other formal debt agreement that certain acts will be performed and others refrained from. Designed to protect the lender's interest, covenants cover such matters as working capital, debt-equity ratios, and dividend payments. Also called *restrictive covenant* or *protective covenant.*

COVER
1. to buy back contracts previously sold; said of an investor who has sold stock or commodities short.
2. in corporate finance, to meet fixed annual charges on bonds, leases, and other obligations, out of earnings.
3. amount of net-asset value underlying a bond or equity security. Coverage is an important aspect of a bond's safety rating.

COVERED OPTION option contract backed by the shares underlying the option. For instance, someone who owns 300 shares of XYZ and sells three XYZ call options is in a covered option position. If the XYZ stock price goes up and the option is exercised, the investor has the stock to deliver to the buyer. Selling a call brings a premium from the buyer. *See also* NAKED OPTION.

COVERED WRITER seller of covered options—in other words, an owner of stock who sells options against it to collect premium income. For example, when writing a CALL OPTION, if a stock price stays stable or drops, the seller will be able to hold onto the stock. If the price rises sharply enough, it will have to be given up to the option buyer.

COVERING SHORT *see* COVER.

CRASH precipitate drop in stock prices and economic activity, as in the crash of 1929, which initiated the Great Depression. Crashes are usually brought on by a loss in investor confidence following periods of high inflation.

CREDIT
In general: loans, bonds, charge-account obligations, and openaccount balances with commercial firms. Also, available but unused bank letters of credit and other standby commitments as well as a variety of consumer credit facilities.

On another level, discipline in which lending officers and industrial credit people are professionals. At its loftiest it is defined in Dun & Bradstreet's motto: "Credit—Man's Confidence in Man."

Accounting: entry—or the act of making an entry—that increases liabilities, owners' equity, revenue, and gains, and decreases assets and expenses. *See also* CREDIT BALANCE.

Customer's statement of account: adjustment in the customer's favor, or increase in equity.

CREDIT ANALYST person who (1) analyzes the record and financial affairs of an individual or a corporation to ascertain creditworthiness or (2) determines the credit ratings of corporate and municipal bonds by studying the financial condition and trends of the issuers.

CREDIT BALANCE
In general: account balance in the customer's favor. *See also* CREDIT.

Securities: in cash accounts with brokers, money deposited and remaining after purchases have been paid for, plus the uninvested proceeds from securities sold. In margin accounts, (1) proceeds from short sales, held in escrow for the securities borrowed for these sales; (2) free credit balances, or net balances, which can be withdrawn at will. SPECIAL MISCELLANEOUS ACCOUNT balances are not counted as free credit balances.

CREDIT INSURANCE protection against *abnormal* losses from unpaid accounts receivable, often a requirement of banks lending against accounts receivable.

In consumer credit, life or accident coverage protecting the creditor against loss in the event of death or disability, usually stated as a percentage of the loan balance.

CREDITOR'S COMMITTEE group representing firms that have claims on a company in financial difficulty or bankruptcy; sometimes used as an alternative to legal bankruptcy, especially by smaller firms.

CREDIT RATING formal evaluation of an individual's or company's credit history and capability of repaying obligations. Any number of firms investigate, analyze, and maintain records on the credit responsibility of individuals and businesses— TRW (individuals) and Dun & Bradstreet (commercial firms), for example. The bond ratings assigned by Standard & Poor's and Moody's are also a form of credit RATING. Most large companies and lending institutions assign credit ratings to existing and potential customers.

CREDIT RISK financial and moral risk that an obligation will not be paid and a loss will result.

CREDIT SPREAD difference in the value of two options, when the value of the one sold exceeds the value of the one bought. The opposite of a DEBIT SPREAD.

CREDIT UNION not-for-profit financial institution typically formed by employees of a company, a labor union, or a religious group and operated as a cooperative. Credit unions may offer a full range of financial services and pay higher rates on deposits and charge lower rates on loans than commercial banks. Federally chartered credit unions are regulated and insured by the National Credit Union Administration.

CROSS securities transaction in which the same broker acts as agent in both sides of the trade. The practice—called crossing—is legal only if the broker first offers the securities publicly at a price higher than the bid.

CROSSED TRADE manipulative practice prohibited on major exchanges whereby buy and sell orders are offset without recording the trade on the exchange, thus perhaps depriving the investor of the chance to trade at a more favorable price. Also called *crossed sale*.

CROWD group of exchange members with a defined area of function tending to congregate around a trading post pending execution of orders. These are specialists, floor traders, odd-lot dealers, and other brokers as well as smaller groups with specialized functions—the INACTIVE BOND CROWD, for example.

CROWDING OUT heavy federal borrowing at a time when businesses and consumers also want to borrow money. Because the government can pay any interest rate it has to and individuals and businesses can't, the latter are crowded out of credit markets by high interest rates. Crowding out can thus cause economic activity to slow.

CROWN JEWELS the most desirable entities within a diversified corporation as measured by asset value, earning power and business prospects. The crown jewels usually figure prominently in takeover attempts; they typically are the main objective of the acquirer and may be sold by a takeover target to make the rest of the company less attractive to the acquirer.

CROWN LOAN demand loan by a high-income individual to a low-income relative, usually a child or elderly parent. This device was named for Chicago industrialist Harry Crown, who first used it. The money would be invested and the income would be taxable at the borrower's lower rates. For years, the crown loan provided a substantial tax benefit for all parties involved, since such loans could be made interest-free. In 1984 the U.S. Supreme Court ruled that such loans had to be made at the market rate of interest or be subject to gift taxes.

CUM DIVIDEND with dividend; said of a stock whose buyer is eligible to receive a declared dividend. Stocks are usually cum dividend for trades made on or before the fifth day preceding the RECORD DATE, when the register of eligible holders is closed for that dividend period. Trades after the fifth day go EX-DIVIDEND.

CUM RIGHTS with rights; said of stocks that entitle the purchaser to buy a specified amount of stock that is yet to be issued. The cut-off date when the stocks go from cum rights to EX-RIGHTS (without rights) is stipulated in the prospectus accompanying the rights distribution.

CUMULATIVE PREFERRED preferred stock whose dividends if omitted because of insufficient earnings or any other reason accumulate until paid out. They have precedence over common dividends, which cannot be paid if a cumulative preferred obligation exists. Most preferred stock issued today is cumulative.

CUMULATIVE VOTING voting method that improves minority shareholders' chances of naming representatives on the board of directors. In regular or statutory voting, stockholders must apportion their votes equally among candidates for director. Cumulative voting allows shareholders to cast all their votes for one candidate. Assuming one vote per share, 100 shares owned, and six directors to be elected, the regular method lets the shareholder cast 100 votes for each of six candidates for director, a total of 600 votes. The cumulative method lets the same 600 votes be cast for one candidate or split as the shareholder wishes. Cumulative voting is a popular cause among advocates of corporate democracy, but it remains the exception rather than the rule.

CURB *see* AMERICAN STOCK EXCHANGE.

CURRENCY FUTURES contracts in the futures markets that are for delivery in a major currency such as U.S. dollars, British pounds, French francs, German marks, Swiss francs, or Japanese yen. Corporations that sell products around the world can hedge their currency risk with these futures.

CURRENCY IN CIRCULATION paper money and coins circulating in the economy, counted as part of the total money in circulation, which includes DEMAND DEPOSITS in banks.

CURRENT ASSETS cash, accounts receivable, inventory, and other assets such as inventory that are likely to be converted into cash, sold, exchanged, or expensed in the normal course of business, usually within a year.

CURRENT COUPON BOND corporate, federal, or municipal bond with a coupon within half a percentage point of current market rates. These bonds are less volatile than similarly rated bonds with lower coupons because the interest they pay is competitive with current market instruments.

CURRENT LIABILITY debt or other obligation coming due within a year.

CURRENT MARKET VALUE present worth of a client's portfolio at today's market price, as listed in a brokerage statement every month—or more often if stocks are bought on margin or sold short. For listed stocks and bonds the current market value is determined by closing prices; for over-the-counter securities the bid price is used.

CURRENT MATURITY interval between the present time and the maturity date of a bond issue, as distinguished from original maturity, which is the time difference between the issue date and the maturity date. For example, in 1987 a bond issued in 1985 to mature in 2005 would have an original maturity of 20 years and a current maturity of 18 years.

CURRENT PRODUCTION RATE top interest rate allowed on current GOVERNMENT NATIONAL MORTGAGE ASSOCIATION mortgage-backed securities, usually half a percentage point below the current mortgage rate to defray administrative costs of the mortgage servicing company. For instance, when homeowners are paying 13½% on mortgages, an investor in a GNMA pool including those mortgages will get a current production rate of 13%.

CURRENT RATIO current assets divided by current liabilities. The ratio shows a company's ability to pay its current obligations from current assets. For the most part, a company that has a small inventory and readily collectible accounts receivable can operate safely with a lower current ratio than a company whose cash flow is less dependable. *See also* QUICK RATIO.

CURRENT YIELD annual interest on a bond divided by the market price. It is the actual income rate of return as opposed to the coupon rate (the two would be equal if the bond were bought at par) or the yield to maturity. For example, a 10% (coupon rate) bond with a face (or par) value of $1000 is bought at a market price of $800. The annual income from the bond is $100. But since only $800 was paid for the bond, the current yield is $100 divided by $800, or 12½%.

CUSHION
1. interval between the time a bond is issued and the time it can be called. Also termed CALL PROTECTION.
2. margin of safety for a corporation's financial ratios. For instance, if its DEBT-TO-EQUITY RATIO has a cushion of up to 40% debt, anything over that level might be cause for concern.
3. *see* LAST IN, FIRST OUT.

CUSHION BOND callable bond with a coupon above current market interest rates that is selling for a premium. Cushion bonds lose less of their value as rates rise and gain less in value as rates fall, making them suitable for conservative investors interested in high income.

CUSHION THEORY theory that a stock's price must rise if many investors are taking short positions in it, because those positions must be covered by purchases of the stock. Technical analysts consider it particularly bullish if the short positions in a stock are twice as high as the number of shares traded daily. This is because price rises force short sellers to cover their positions, making the stock rise even more.

CUSTODIAL ACCOUNT account that parents create for a minor, usually at a bank or brokerage firm. Minors cannot make securities transactions without the approval of the account trustee. The TAX REFORM ACT OF 1986 taxes earnings over $1000 in a custodial account at the parent's tax rate, but only if the child is younger than 14 years old. For a child 14 years or older, earnings are taxed at the child's rate. *See also* CLIFFORD TRUST; CROWN LOAN; UNIFORM GIFTS TO MINORS ACT.

CUSTODIAN bank or other financial institution that keeps custody of stock certificates and other assets of a mutual fund, individual, or corporate client. *See also* CUSTODIAL ACCOUNT.

CUSTOMER'S LOAN CONSENT agreement signed by a margin customer permitting a broker to borrow margined securities to the limit of the customer's debit balance for the purpose of covering other customers' short positions and certain failures to complete delivery.

CUSTOMER'S MAN traditionally a synonym for *registered representative, account executive,* or *account representative.* Now used rarely, as more women work in brokerages.

CUSTOMERS' NET DEBIT BALANCE total credit extended by New York Stock Exchange member firms to finance customer purchases of securities.

CUTOFF POINT in capital budgeting, the minimum rate of return acceptable on investments.

CYCLE *see* BUSINESS CYCLE.

CYCLICAL STOCK stock that tends to rise quickly when the economy turns up and to fall quickly when the economy turns down. Examples are housing, automobiles, and paper. Stocks of noncyclical industries—such as foods, insurance, drugs—are not as directly affected by economic changes.

d

DAILY TRADING LIMIT maximum that many commodities and options markets are allowed to rise or fall in one day. When a market reaches its limit early and stays there all day, it is said to be having an up-limit or down-limit day. Exchanges usually impose a daily trading limit on each contract. For example, the Chicago Board of Trade limit is two points ($2000 per contract) up or down on its treasury bond futures options contract.

DAISY CHAIN trading between market manipulators to create the appearance of active volume as a lure for legitimate investors. When these traders drive the price up, the manipulators unload their holdings, leaving the unwary investors without buyers to trade with in turn.

DATED DATE date from which accrued interest is calculated on new bonds and other debt instruments. The buyer pays the issuer an amount equal to the interest accrued from the dated date to the issue's settlement date. With the first interest payment on the bond, the buyer is reimbursed.

DATE OF RECORD date on which a shareholder must officially own shares in order to be entitled to a dividend. For example, the board of directors of a corporation might declare a dividend on November 1 payable on December 1 to stockholders of record on November 15. After the date of record the stock is said to be EX-DIVIDEND. Also called *record date.*

DATING in commercial transactions, extension of credit beyond the supplier's customary terms—for example, 90 days instead of 30 days. In industries marked by high seasonality and long lead time, dating, combined with ACCOUNTS RECEIVABLE FINANCING, makes it possible for manufacturers with lean capital to continue producing goods. Also called *seasonal dating, special dating.*

DAY LOAN loan from a bank to a broker for the purchase of securities pending delivery through the afternoon clearing. Once delivered the securities are pledged as collateral and the loan becomes a regular broker's call loan. Also called *morning loan.*

DAY ORDER order to buy or sell securities that expires unless executed or canceled the day it is placed. All orders are day orders unless otherwise specified. The main exception is a GOOD-TILL-CANCELED ORDER, though even it can be executed the same day if conditions are right.

DAY TRADE purchase and sale of a position during the same day.

DEALER
1. individual or firm acting as a PRINCIPAL in a securities transaction. Principals trade for their own account and risk. When buying from a broker acting as a dealer, a customer receives securities from the firm's inventory; the confirmation must disclose this. When specialists trade for their own account, as they must as part of their responsibility for maintaining an orderly market, they act as dealers. Since most brokerage firms operate both as brokers and as principals, the term *broker-dealer* is commonly used.
2. one who purchases goods or services for resale to consumers. The element of inventory risk is what distinguishes a dealer from an agent or sales representative.

DEBENTURE general debt obligation backed only by the integrity of the borrower and documented by an agreement called an INDENTURE. An *unsecured bond* is a debenture.

DEBENTURE STOCK stock issued under a contract providing for fixed payments at scheduled intervals and more like preferred stock than a DEBENTURE, since their status in liquidation is equity and not debt.
    Also, a type of bond issued by Canadian and British corporations, which refer to debt issues as stock.

DEBIT BALANCE
1. account balance representing money owed to the lender or seller.
2. money a margin customer owes a broker for loans to purchase securities.

DEBIT SPREAD difference in the value of two options, when the value of the one bought exceeds the value of the one sold. The opposite of a CREDIT SPREAD.

DEBT
1. money, goods, or services that one party is obligated to pay to another in accordance with an expressed or implied agreement. Debt may or may not be secured.
2. general name for bonds, notes, mortgages, and other forms of paper evidencing amounts owed and payable on specified dates or ondemand.

DEBT INSTRUMENT written promise to repay a debt; for instance, a BILL, NOTE, BOND, banker's ACCEPTANCE, CERTIFICATE OF DEPOSIT, or COMMERCIAL PAPER.

DEBTOR person or business that owes money. The person or business on the other side of the transaction is the *creditor*.

DEBT RETIREMENT repayment of debt. The most common method of retiring corporate debt is to set aside money each year in a SINKING FUND.

Most municipal bonds and some corporates are issued in serial form, meaning different portions of an issue—called series—are retired at different times, usually on an annual or semiannual schedule.

Sinking fund bonds and serial bonds are not classes of bonds, just methods of retiring them that are adaptable to debentures, convertibles, and so on. *See also* REFUNDING.

DEBT SECURITY security representing money borrowed that must be repaid and having a fixed amount, a specific maturity or maturities, and usually a specific rate of interest or an original purchase discount. For instance, a BILL, BOND, COMMERCIAL PAPER, or a NOTE.

DEBT SERVICE cash required in a given period, usually one year, for payments of interest and current maturities of principal on outstanding debt. In corporate bond issues, the annual interest plus annual sinking fund payments; in government bonds, the annual payments into the debt service fund. *See also* ABILITY TO PAY.

DEBT-TO-EQUITY RATIO
1. total liabilities divided by total shareholders' equity. This shows to what extent owner's equity can cushion creditors' claims in the event of liquidation.
2. total long-term debt divided by total shareholders' equity. This is a measure of LEVERAGE—the use of borrowed money to enhance the return on owners' equity.
3. long-term debt and preferred stock divided by common stock equity. This relates securities with fixed charges to those without fixed charges.

DECLARE authorize the payment of a dividend on a specified date, an act of the board of directors of a corporation. Once declared, a dividend becomes an obligation of the issuing corporation.

DEDUCTION
1. expense allowed by the Internal Revenue Service as a subtraction from adjusted gross income in arriving at a person's taxable income. Such deductions include interest paid, state and local taxes, charitable contributions.
2. adjustment to an invoice allowed by a seller for a discrepancy, shortage, and so on.

DEED written instrument containing some transfer, bargain, or contract relating to property—most commonly, conveying the legal title to real estate from one party to another.

DEEP DISCOUNT BOND bond selling for a discount of more than about 20% from its face value. Unlike a CURRENT COUPON BOND, which has a higher interest rate, a deep discount bond will appreciate faster as interest rates fall and drop faster as rates rise. Unlike ORIGINAL ISSUE DISCOUNT bonds, deep discounts were issued at a par value of $1000.

DEEP IN/OUT OF THE MONEY CALL OPTION whose exercise price is well below the market price of the underlying stock (deep *in* the money) or well above the market price (deep *out of* the money). The situation would be exactly the opposite for a PUT OPTION. The premium for buying a deep-in-the-money option is high, since the holder has the right to purchase the stock at a striking price considerably below the current price of the stock. The premium for buying a deep-out-of-the-money option is very small, on the other hand, since the option may never be profitable.

DEFAULT failure of a debtor to make timely payments of interest and principal as they come due or to meet some other provision of a bond indenture. In the event of default, bondholders may make claims against the assets of the issuer in order to recoup their principal.

DEFEASANCE

In general: provision found in some debt agreements whereby the contract is nullified if specified acts are performed.

Corporate finance: short for in-substance defeasance, a technique whereby a corporation discharges old, low-rate debt without repaying it prior to maturity. The corporation uses newly purchased securities with a lower face value but paying higher interest or having a higher market value. The objective is a cleaner (more debt free) balance sheet and increased earnings in the amount by which the face amount of the old debt exceeds the cost of the new securities. The use of defeasance in modern corporate finance began in 1982 when Exxon bought and put in an irrevocable trust $312 million of U.S. government securities yielding 14% to provide for the repayment of principal and interest on $515 million of old debt paying 5.8% to 6.7% and maturing in 2009. Exxon removed the defeased debt from its balance sheet and added $132 million—the after-tax difference between $515 million and $312 million—to its earnings that quarter.

In another type of defeasance, a company instructs a broker to buy, for a fee, the outstanding portion of an old bond issue of the company. The broker then exchanges the bond issue for a new issue of the company's stock with an equal market value. The broker subsequently sells the stock at a profit.

DEFENSIVE SECURITIES stocks and bonds that are more stable than average and provide a safe return on an investor's money. When the stock market is weak, defensive securities tend to decline less than the overall market.

DEFERRAL OF TAXES postponement of tax payments from this year to a later year. For instance, an INDIVIDUAL RETIREMENT ACCOUNT (IRA) defers taxes until the money is withdrawn.

DEFERRED ACCOUNT account that postpones taxes until a later date. Some examples: INDIVIDUAL RETIREMENT ACCOUNT, KEOGH PLAN accounts, ANNUITY, PROFIT-SHARING PLAN, SALARY REDUCTION PLAN.

DEFERRED CHARGE expenditure carried forward as an asset until it becomes relevant, such as an advance rent payment or insurance premium. The opposite is *deferred income,* such as advance rent received.

DEFERRED INTEREST BOND bond that pays interest at a later date. A ZERO COUPON BOND, which pays interest and repays principal in one lump sum at maturity, is in this category. In effect, such bonds automatically reinvest the interest at a fixed rate. Prices are more volatile for a deferred interest bond than for a CURRENT COUPON BOND.

DEFERRED PAYMENT ANNUITY annuity whose contract provides that payments to the annuitant be postponed until a number of periods have elapsed—for example, when the annuitant attains a certain age. Also called a *deferred annuity*.

DEFICIENCY LETTER written notice from the Securities and Exchange Commission to a prospective issuer of securities that the preliminary prospectus needs revision or expansion. Deficiency letters require prompt action; otherwise, the registration period may be prolonged.

DEFICIT
1. excess of liabilities and debts over income and assets. Deficits usually are corrected by borrowing or by selling assets.
2. in finance, an excess of expenditures over budget.

DEFICIT FINANCING borrowing by a government agency to make up for a revenue shortfall. Deficit financing stimulates the economy for a time but eventually can become a drag on the economy by pushing up interest rates. *See also* CROWDING OUT; KEYNESIAN ECONOMICS.

DEFICIT NET WORTH excess of liabilities over assets and capital stock, perhaps as a result of operating losses. Also called *negative net worth*.

DEFICIT SPENDING excess of government expenditures over government revenue, creating a shortfall that must be financed through borrowing. *See also* DEFICIT FINANCING.

DEFINED BENEFIT PENSION PLAN plan that promises to pay a specified amount to each person who retires after a set number of years of service. Such plans pay no taxes on their investments. Employees contribute to them in some cases; in others, all contributions are made by the employer.

DEFLATION decline in the prices of goods and services. Deflation is the reverse of INFLATION; it should not be confused with DISINFLATION, which is a slowing down in the rate of price increases. Generally, the economic effects of deflation are the opposite of those produced by inflation, with two notable exceptions: (1) prices that increase with inflation do not necessarily decrease with deflation— union wage rates, for example; (2) while inflation may or may not stimulate output and employment, marked deflation has always affected both negatively.

DEFLATOR statistical factor or device designed to adjust the difference between real or constant value and value affected by inflation—the *GNP deflator*, for example. *See also* CONSTANT DOLLARS.

DEFLECTION OF TAX LIABILITY legal shift of one person's tax burden to someone else through such methods as the CLIFFORD TRUST, CUSTODIAL ACCOUNTS, and SPOUSAL REMAINDER TRUSTS. Such devices were curtailed but not eliminated by the TAX REFORM ACT OF 1986.

DELAYED DELIVERY delivery of securities later than the scheduled date, which is ordinarily five business days after the trade date. A contract calling for delayed delivery, known as a SELLER'S OPTION, is usually agreed to by both parties to a trade. *See also* DELIVERY DATE.

DELAYED OPENING postponement of the start of trading in a stock until a gross imbalance in buy and sell orders is overcome. Such an imbalance is likely to follow on the heels of a significant event such as a takeover offer.

DELINQUENCY failure to make a payment on an obligation when due. In finance company parlance, the amount of past due balances, determined either on a contractual or recency-of-payment basis.

DELISTING removal of a company's security from an exchange because the firm did not abide by some regulation or the stock does not meet certain financial ratios or sales levels.

DELIVERABLE BILLS financial futures and options trading term meaning Treasury bills that meet all the criteria of the exchange on which they are traded. One such criterion is that the deliverable T-bill is the current bill for the week in which settlement takes place.

DELIVERY DATE
1. first day of the month in which delivery is to be made under a futures contract. Since sales are on a SELLER'S OPTION basis, delivery can be on any day of the month, as long as proper notice is given.
2. fifth business day following a REGULAR WAY transaction on the New York Stock Exchange. Seller's option delivery can be anywhere from 5 to 60 days, though there may be a purchase-price adjustment to compensate for DELAYED DELIVERY. In the case of bonds, regular way delivery means the next business day following a bond sale.

DELIVERY NOTICE
1. notification from the seller to the buyer of a futures contract indicating the date when the actual commodity is to be delivered.
2. in general business transactions, a formal notice documenting that goods have been delivered or will be delivered on a certain date.

DELIVERY VERSUS PAYMENT securities industry procedure, common with institutional accounts, whereby delivery of securities sold is made to the buying customer's bank in exchange for payment, usually in the form of cash. (Institutions are required by law to require "assets of equal value" in exchange for delivery.) Also called CASH ON DELIVERY, delivery against payment, delivery against cash, or, from the sell side, RECEIVE VERSUS PAYMENT.

DELTA measure of the relationship between an option price and the underlying futures contract or stock price. For a call option, a delta of 0.50 means a half-point rise in premium for every dollar that the stock goes up. For a put option contract, the premium rises as stock prices fall. As options near expiration, IN-THE-MONEY contracts approach a delta of 1.

DEMAND DEPOSIT account balance which, without prior notice to the bank, can be drawn on by check, cash withdrawal from an automatic teller machine, or by transfer to other accounts using the telephone or home computers. Demand deposits are the largest component of the U.S. MONEY SUPPLY, and the principal medium through which the Federal Reserve implements monetary policy. *See also* COMPENSATING BALANCE.

DEMAND LOAN loan with no set maturity date that can be called for repayment when the lender chooses. Banks usually bill interest on these loans at fixed intervals.

DEMAND-PULL INFLATION price increases occurring when supply is not adequate to meet demand. *See also* COST-PUSH INFLATION.

DEMONETIZATION withdrawal from circulation of a specified form of currency. For example, the Jamaica Agreement between major INTERNATIONAL MONETARY FUND countries officially demonetized gold starting in 1978, ending its role as the major medium of international settlement.

DENOMINATION face value of currency units, coins, and securities. *See also* PAR VALUE.

DEPLETION accounting treatment available to companies that extract oil and gas, coal, or other minerals, usually in the form of an allowance that reduces taxable income. Oil and gas limited partnerships pass the allowance on to their limited partners, who can use it to reduce other tax liabilities.

DEPOSIT
1. cash, checks, or drafts placed with a financial institution for credit to a customer's account. Banks broadly differentiate between demand deposits (checking accounts on which the customer may draw at any time) and time deposits, which usually pay interest and have a specified maturity or require 30 days' notice before withdrawal.
2. securities placed with a bank or other institution or with a person for a particular purpose.
3. sums lodged with utilities, landlords, and service companies as security.
4. money put down as evidence of an intention to complete a contract and to protect the other party in the event that the contract is not completed.

DEPOSITARY RECEIPT *see* AMERICAN DEPOSITARY RECEIPT.

DEPOSITORY INSTITUTIONS DEREGULATION AND MONETARY CON-TROL ACT federal legislation of 1980 providing for deregulation of the banking system. The act established the Depository Institutions Deregulation Committee, composed of five voting members, the Secretary of the Treasury and the chair of the Federal Reserve Board, the Federal Home Loan Bank Board, the Federal Deposit Insurance Corporation, and the National Credit Union Administration, and one nonvoting member, the Comptroller of the Currency. The committee is charged with phasing out regulation of interest rates of banks and savings institutions over a six-year period (passbook accounts were deregulated effective April, 1986, under a different federal law). The act authorized interest-bearing NEGOTIABLE ORDER OF WITHDRAWAL (NOW) accounts to be offered anywhere in the country. The act also overruled state usury laws on home mortgages over $25,000 and otherwise modernized mortgages by eliminating dollar limits, permitting second mortgages, and ending territorial restrictions in mortgage lending. Another part of the law permitted stock brokerages to offer checking accounts. *See also* DEREGULATION.

DEPOSITORY TRUST COMPANY central securities repository where stock and bond certificates are exchanged. Most of these exchanges now take place electronically, and few paper certificates actually change hands. The DTC is a member of the Federal Reserve System and is owned by most of the brokerage houses on Wall Street and the New York Stock Exchange.

DEPRECIATED COST original cost of a fixed asset less accumulated DEPRECIATION; this is the *net book value* of the asset.

DEPRECIATION
Economics: consumption of capital during production—in other words, wearing

out of plant and capital goods, such as machines and equipment.

Finance: amortization of fixed assets, such as plant and equipment, so as to allocate the cost over their depreciable life. Depreciation reduces taxable income but does not reduce cash.

Among the most commonly used methods are STRAIGHT-LINE DEPRECIATION; ACCELERATED DEPRECIATION; and the ACCELERATED COST RECOVERY SYSTEM. Others include the annuity, appraisal, compound interest, production, replacement, retirement, and sinking fund methods.

Foreign Exchange: decline in the price of one currency relative to another.

DEPRESSION economic condition characterized by falling prices, reduced purchasing power, an excess of supply over demand, rising unemployment, accumulating inventories, deflation, plant contraction, public fear and caution, and a general decrease in business activity. The Great Depression of the 1930s, centered in the United States and Europe, had worldwide repercussions.

DEREGULATION greatly reducing government regulation in order to allow freer markets to create a more efficient marketplace. After the stock-brokerage industry was deregulated in the mid-1970s, commissions were no longer fixed. After the banking industry was deregulated in the early 1980s, banks were given greater freedom in setting interest rates on deposits and loans. Industries such as communications and transportation have also been deregulated, with similar results: increased competition, heightened innovation, and mergers among weaker competitors. Some government oversight usually remains after deregulation.

DESCENDING TOPS chart pattern wherein each new high price for a security is lower than the preceding high. The trend is considered bearish.

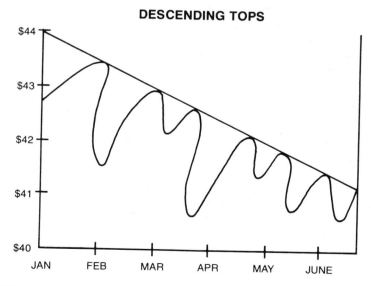

DESCENDING TOPS

DESK trading desk, or Securities Department, at the New York FEDERAL RESERVE BANK, which is the operating arm of the FEDERAL OPEN MARKET COMMITTEE. The Desk executes all transactions undertaken by the FEDERAL RESERVE SYSTEM in the money market or the government securities market, serves as the Treasury Department's eyes and ears in these and related markets, and encompasses a foreign desk which conducts transactions in the FOREIGN EXCHANGE market.

DEVALUATION lowering of the value of a country's currency relative to gold and/or the currencies of other nations. Devaluation can also result from a rise in value of other currencies relative to the currency of a particular country.

DEVELOPMENTAL DRILLING PROGRAM drilling for oil and gas in an area with proven reserves to a depth known to have been productive in the past. Limited partners in such a program, which is considerably less risky than an EXPLORATORY DRILLING PROGRAM or WILDCAT DRILLING, have a good chance of steady income, but little chance of enormous profits.

DIAGONAL SPREAD strategy based on a long and short position in the same class of option (two puts or two calls in the same stock) at different striking prices and different expiration dates. Example: a six-month call sold with a striking price of 40 and a three-month call sold with a striking price of 35. *See also* CALENDAR SPREAD; VERTICAL SPREAD.

DIAMOND INVESTMENT TRUST unit trust that invests in high-quality diamonds. Begun in the early 1980s by Thomson McKinnon, these trusts let shareholders invest in diamonds without buying and holding a particular stone. Shares in these trusts do not trade actively and are therefore difficult to sell if diamond prices fall, as they did soon after the first trust was set up.

DIFFERENTIAL small extra charge sometimes called the *odd-lot-differential*— usually ⅛ of a point—that dealers add to purchases and subtract from sales in quantities less than the standard trading unit or ROUND LOT.

Also, the extent to which a dealer widens his quote to compensate for lack of volume, even though the transaction involves normal trading units.

DIGITS DELETED designation on securities exchange tape meaning that because the tape has been delayed, some digits have been dropped. For example, 26½ . . . 26⅝ . . . 26⅛ becomes 6½ . . . 6⅝ . . . 6⅛.

DILUTION effect on earnings per share and book value per share if all convertible securities were converted or all warrants or stock options were exercised. *See* FULLY DILUTED EARNINGS PER (COMMON) SHARE.

DIP slight drop in securities prices after a sustained uptrend. Analysts often advise investors to buy on dips, meaning buy when a price is momentarily weak.

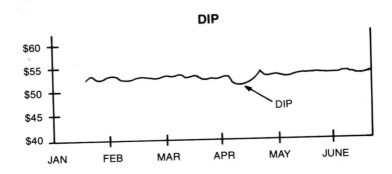

DIP

DIRECTOR *see* BOARD OF DIRECTORS.

DIRECT OVERHEAD portion of overhead costs—rent, lights, insurance—allocated to manufacturing, by the application of a standard factor termed a *burden rate*. This amount is absorbed as an INVENTORY cost and ultimately reflected as a COST OF GOODS SOLD.

DIRECT PARTICIPATION PROGRAM program letting investors participate directly in the cash flow and tax benefits of the underlying investments. Such programs are usually organized as LIMITED PARTNERSHIPS, although their uses as tax shelters have been severely curtailed by tax legislation affecting PASSIVE investments.

DIRECT PLACEMENT direct sale of securities to one or more professional investors, typically life-insurance companies. About one third of the new securities offerings in the early 1980s were direct placements, almost all of them bond issues. Also called PRIVATE PLACEMENT.

DISBURSEMENT paying out of money in the discharge of a debt or an expense, as distinguished from a distribution.

DISCHARGE OF BANKRUPTCY order terminating bankruptcy proceedings, ordinarily freeing the debtor of all legal responsibility for specified obligations.

DISCHARGE OF LIEN order removing a lien on property after the originating legal claim has been paid or otherwise satisfied.

DISCLOSURE release by companies of all information, positive or negative, that might bear on an investment decision, as required by the Securities and Exchange Commission and the stock exchanges. *See also* FINANCIAL PUBLIC RELATIONS; INSIDE INFORMATION; INSIDER.

DISCOUNT
1. difference between a bond's current market price and its face or redemption value.
2. manner of selling securities such as treasury bills, which are issued at less than face value and are redeemed at face value.
3. relationship between two currencies. The French franc may sell at a discount to the English pound, for example.
4. to apply all available news about a company in evaluating its current stock price. For instance, taking into account the introduction of an exciting new product.
5. method whereby interest on a bank loan or note is deducted inadvance.
6. reduction in the selling price of merchandise or a percentage off the invoice price in exchange for quick payment.

DISCOUNT BOND bond selling below its redemption value. *See also* DEEP DISCOUNT BOND.

DISCOUNT BROKER brokerage house that executes orders to buy and sell securities at commission rates lower than those charged by a FULL SERVICE BROKER.

DISCOUNT DIVIDEND REINVESTMENT PLAN *see* DIVIDEND REINVESTMENT PLAN.

DISCOUNTED CASH FLOW value of future expected cash receipts and expenditures at a common date, which is calculated using NET PRESENT VALUE or INTERNAL RATE OF RETURN and is a factor in analyses of both capital investments and securities investments. The net present value (NPV) method applies a rate of discount (interest rate) based on the marginal cost of capital to future cash flows to bring them back to the present. The internal rate of return (IRR) method finds the average return on investment earned through the life of the investment. It determines the discount rate that equates the present value of future cash flows to the cost of the investment.

DISCOUNTING THE NEWS bidding a firm's stock price up or down in anticipation of good or bad news about the company's prospects.

DISCOUNT RATE
1. interest rate that the Federal Reserve charges member banks for loans, using government securities or ELIGIBLE PAPER as collateral. This provides a floor on interest rates, since banks set their loan rates a notch above the discount rate.
2. interest rate used in determining the PRESENT VALUE of future CASH FLOWS. *See also* CAPITALIZATION RATE.

DISCOUNT WINDOW place in the Federal Reserve where banks go to borrow money at the DISCOUNT RATE. Borrowing from the Fed is a privilege, not a right, and banks are discouraged from using the privilege except when they are short of reserves.

DISCOUNT YIELD yield on a security sold at a discount—U.S. treasury bills sold at \$9750 and maturing at \$10,000 in 90 days, for instance. To figure the annual yield, divide the discount (\$250) by the face amount (\$10,000) and multiply that number by the approximate number of days in the year (360) divided by the number of days to maturity (90). The calculation looks like this:

$$\frac{\$250}{\$10,000} \times \frac{360}{90} = .025 \times 4 = .10 = 10\%.$$

DISCRETIONARY ACCOUNT account giving a broker the power to buy and sell securities, without the client's prior knowledge or consent. Some clients set broad guidelines, such as limiting investments to blue chip stocks.

DISCRETIONARY INCOME amount of a consumer's income spent after essentials like food, housing, and utilities and prior commitments have been covered. The total amount of discretionary income can bea key economic indicator because spending this money can spur theeconomy.

DISCRETIONARY ORDER order to buy a particular stock, bond, or commodity that lets the broker decide when to execute the trade and at what price.

DISCRETIONARY TRUST
1. mutual fund or unit trust whose investments are not limited to a certain kind of security. The management decides on the best way to use the assets.
2. personal trust that lets the trustee decide how much income or principal to provide to the beneficiary. This can be used to prevent the beneficiary from dissipating funds.

DISINFLATION slowing down of the rate at which prices increase—usually during a recession, when sales drop and retailers are not always able to pass on higher prices to consumers. Not to be confused with DEFLATION, when prices actually drop.

DISINTERMEDIATION movement of funds from low-yielding accounts at traditional banking institutions to higher-yielding investments in the general market—for example, withdrawal of funds from a passbook savings account paying 5½% to buy a Treasury bill paying 10%. As a counter move, banks may pay higher rates to depositors, then charge higher rates to borrowers, which leads to tight money and reduced economic activity. Since banking DEREGULATION, disintermediation is not the economic problem it once was.

DISINVESTMENT reduction in capital investment either by disposing of capital goods (such as plant and equipment) or by failing to maintain or replace capital assets that are being used up.

DISPOSABLE INCOME personal income remaining after personal taxes and noncommercial government fees have been paid. This money can be spent on essentials or nonessentials or it can be saved. *See also* DISCRETIONARY INCOME.

DISTRIBUTING SYNDICATE group of brokerage firms or investment bankers that join forces in order to facilitate the DISTRIBUTION of a large block of securities. A distribution is usually handled over a period of time to avoid upsetting the market price. The term distributing syndicate can refer to a primary distribution or a secondary distribution, but the former is more commonly called simply a syndicate or an underwriting syndicate.

DISTRIBUTION
Corporate finance: allocation of income and expenses to the appropriate subsidiary accounts.
Economics: (1) movement of goods from manufacturers; (2) way in which wealth is shared in any particular economic system.
Estate law: parceling out of assets to the beneficiaries named in a will, as carried out by the executor under the guidance of a court.
Mutual funds and closed-end investment companies: payout of realized capital gains on securities in the portfolio of the fund or closed-end investment company.
Securities: sale of a large block of stock in such manner that the price is not adversely affected. Technical analysts look on a pattern of distribution as a tipoff that the stock will soon fall in price. The opposite of distribution, known as ACCUMULATION, may signal a rise in price.

DISTRIBUTION AREA price range in which a stock trades for a long time. Sellers who want to avoid pushing the price down will be careful not to sell below this range. ACCUMULATION of shares in the same range helps to account for the stock's price stability. Technical analysts consider distribution areas in predicting when stocks may break up or down from that price range. *See also* ACCUMULATION AREA.

DISTRIBUTION STOCK stock part of a block sold over a period of time in order to avoid upsetting the market price. May be part of a primary (underwriting) distribution or a secondary distribution following SHELF REGISTRATION.

DISTRIBUTOR wholesaler of goods to dealers that sell to the consumer market.

DIVERSIFICATION
1. spreading of risk by putting assets in several categories of investments—stocks, bonds, money market instruments, and precious metals, for instance, or several industries, or a mutual fund, with its broad range of stocks in one portfolio.

2. at the corporate level, entering different business areas, as a CONGLOMERATE does.

DIVERSIFIED INVESTMENT COMPANY mutual fund or unit trust that invests in a wide range of securities. Under the Investment Company Act of 1940, such a company may not have more than 5% of its assets in any one stock, bond, or commodity and may not own more than 10% of the voting shares of any one company.

DIVESTITURE disposition of an asset or investment by outright sale, employee purchase, liquidation, and so on.

Also, one corporation's orderly distribution of large blocks of another corporation's stock, which were held as an investment. Du Pont was ordered by the courts to divest itself of General Motors stock, for example.

DIVIDEND distribution of earnings to shareholders, prorated by class of security and paid in the form of money, stock, scrip, or, rarely, company products or property. The amount is decided by the board of directors and is usually paid quarterly. Dividends must be declared as income in the year they are received.

Mutual fund dividends are paid out of income, usually on a quarterly basis from the fund's investments. The tax on such dividends depends on whether the distributions resulted from capital gains, interest income, or dividends received by the fund, although these distinctions will largely disappear in 1988 under the 1986 Tax Act.

DIVIDEND EXCLUSION pre-TAX REFORM ACT OF 1986 provision allowing for subtraction from dividends qualifying as taxable income under Internal Revenue Service rules—$100 for individuals and $200 for married couples filing jointly. The 1986 Tax Act eliminated this exclusion effective for the 1987 tax year.

Domestic corporations may exclude from taxable income 80% of dividends received from other domestic corporations. The exclusion was 85% prior to the 1986 Act.

DIVIDEND PAYOUT RATIO percentage of earnings paid to shareholders in cash. In general, the higher the payout ratio, the more mature the company. Electric and telephone utilities tend to have the highest payout ratios, whereas fast-growing companies usually reinvest all earnings and pay no dividends.

DIVIDEND RECORD publication of Standard & Poor's Corporation that provides information on corporate dividend policies and payment histories.

DIVIDEND REINVESTMENT PLAN automatic reinvestment of shareholder dividends in more shares of the company's stock. Some companies absorb most or all of the applicable brokerage fees, and some also discount the stock price. Dividend reinvestment plans allow shareholders to accumulate capital over the long term using DOLLAR COST AVERAGING. For corporations, dividend reinvestment plans are a means of raising capital funds without the FLOTATION COSTS of a NEW ISSUE.

DIVIDEND REQUIREMENT amount of annual earnings necessary to pay contracted dividends on preferred stock.

DIVIDEND ROLLOVER PLAN method of buying and selling stocks around their EX-DIVIDEND dates so as to collect the dividend and make a small profit on the trade. This entails buying shares about two weeks before a stock goes ex-dividend. After the ex-dividend date the price will drop by the amount of the dividend, then work its way back up to the earlier price. By selling slightly above the purchase price, the investor can cover brokerage costs, collect the dividend, and realize a small capital gain in three or four weeks. This is a short-term gain and is taxed at regular rates.

DIVIDENDS PAYABLE dollar amount of dividends that are to be paid, as reported in financial statements. These dividends become an obligation once declared by the board of directors and are listed as liabilities in annual and quarterly reports.

DOCUMENTARY DRAFT *see* DRAFT.

DOLLAR BOND
1. municipal revenue bond quoted and traded on a dollar price basis instead of yield to maturity.
2. bond denominated in U.S. dollars but issued outside the United States, principally in Europe.
3. bond denominated in U.S. dollars and issued in the United States by foreign companies.
See also EUROBOND; EURODOLLAR BOND.

DOLLAR COST AVERAGING *see* CONSTANT DOLLAR PLAN.

DOLLAR DRAIN amount by which a foreign country's imports from the United States exceed its exports to the United States. As the country spends more dollars to finance the imports than it receives in payment for the exports, its dollar reserves drain away.

DOLLAR SHORTAGE situation in which a country that imports from the United States can no longer pay for its purchases without U.S. gifts or loans to provide the necessary dollars. After World War II a worldwide dollar shortage was alleviated by massive infusions of American money through the European Recovery Program (Marshall Plan) and other grant and loan programs.

DOMESTIC ACCEPTANCE *see* ACCEPTANCE.

DOMESTIC CORPORATION corporation doing business in the U.S. state in which it was incorporated. In all other U.S. states its legal status is that of a FOREIGN CORPORATION.

DONATED STOCK fully paid capital stock of a corporation contributed without CONSIDERATION to the same issuing corporation. The gift is credited to the DONATED SURPLUS account at PAR VALUE.

DONATED SURPLUS shareholder's equity account that is credited when contributions of cash, property, or the firm's own stock are freely given to the company. Also termed *donated capital*. Not to be confused with contributed surplus or contributed capital, which is the balances in CAPITAL STOCK accounts plus capital contributed in excess of par or STATED VALUE accounts.

DONOGHUE'S MONEY FUND AVERAGE average of all major money-market fund yields, published weekly for 7- and 30-day yields. Donoghue also tracks the maturity of securities in money-fund portfolios—a short maturity reflecting the conviction of fund managers that interest rates are going to rise. The Donoghue Average is published in many newspapers.

DO NOT REDUCE (DNR) instruction on a LIMIT ORDER to buy, or on a STOP ORDER to sell, or on a STOP-LIMIT ORDER to sell, not to reduce the order when the stock goes EX-DIVIDEND and its price is reduced by the amount of the dividend as usually happens. DNRs do not apply to rights or stock dividends.

DON'T FIGHT THE TAPE don't trade against the market trend. If stocks are falling, as reported on the BROAD TAPE, some analysts say it would be foolish to buy aggressively. Similarly, it would be fighting the tape to sell short during a market rally.

DON'T KNOW Wall Street slang for a *questioned trade*. Brokers exchange comparison sheets to verify the details of transactions between them. Any discrepancy that turns up is called a don't know or a *QT*.

DOUBLE AUCTION SYSTEM *see* AUCTION MARKET.

DOUBLE-BARRELED municipal revenue bond whose principal and interest are guaranteed by a larger municipal entity. For example, a bridge authority might issue revenue bonds payable out of revenue from bridge tolls. If the city or state were to guarantee the bonds, they would be double-barreled, and the investor would be protected against default in the event that bridge usage is disappointing and revenue proves inadequate.

DOUBLE-DECLINING-BALANCE DEPRECIATION METHOD (DDB) method of accelerated depreciation, approved by the Internal Revenue Service, permitting twice the rate of annual depreciation as the straight-line method. It is also called the 200 percent declining-balance method. The two methods are compared below, assuming an asset with a total cost of $1000, a useful life of four years, and no SALVAGE VALUE.

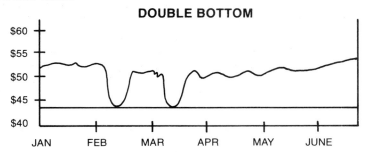

DOUBLE BOTTOM

DOUBLE-DECLINING-BALANCE DEPRECIATION METHOD (DDB) method of accelerated depreciation, approved by the Internal Revenue Service, permitting twice the rate of annual depreciation as the straight-line method. The two methods are compared below, assuming an asset with a total cost of $1000, a useful life of four years, and no SALVAGE VALUE.

YEAR	STRAIGHT LINE		DOUBLE DECLINING BALANCE	
	Expense	Cumulative	Expense	Cumulative
1	$250	$250	$500	$500
2	250	500	250	750
3	250	750	125	875
4	250	1000	63	938
	$1000		$938	

With STRAIGHT-LINE DEPRECIATION the useful life of the asset is divided into the total cost to arrive at the uniform annual charge of $250, or 25% a year. DDB permits twice the straight-line annual percentage rate—50% in this case—to be applied each year to the undepreciated value of the asset. Hence: 50% × $1000 = $500 the first year, 50% × $500 = $250 the second year, and so on.

A variation of DDB, called *150 percent declining balance method,* uses 150% of the straight-line annual percentage rate.

A switch to straight-line from declining balance depreciation is permitted once in the asset's life—logically, at the third year in our example. When the switch is made, however, salvage value must be considered. *See also* ACCELERATED COST RECOVERY SYSTEM; DEPRECIATION.

DOUBLE TAXATION taxation of earnings at the corporate level, then again as stockholder dividends.

DOUBLE TOP technical chart pattern showing a rise to a high price, then a drop, then another rise to the same high price. This means the security is encountering resistance to a move higher. However, if the price does move through that level, the security is expected to go on to a new high. *See also* DOUBLE BOTTOM.

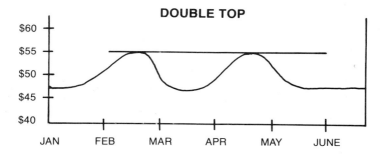

DOW JONES AVERAGES *see* STOCK INDEXES AND AVERAGES.

DOW JONES INDUSTRIAL AVERAGE *see* STOCK INDEXES AND AVERAGES.

DOWNSIDE RISK estimate that a security will decline in value and the extent of the decline, taking into account the total range of factors affecting market price.

DOWNSTREAM flow of corporate activity from parent to subsidiary. Financially, it usually refers to loans, since dividends and interest generally flow upstream.

DOWNTICK sale of a security at a price below that of the preceding sale. If a stock has been trading at $15 a share, for instance, the next trade is a downtick if it is at 14⅞. Also known as MINUS TICK.

DOWNTURN shift of an economic or stock market cycle from rising to falling. The economy is in a downturn when it moves from expansion to recession, and the stock market is in a downturn when it changes from a bull to a bear market.

DOW THEORY theory that a major trend in the stock market must be confirmed by a similar movement in the Dow Jones Industrial Average and the Dow Jones Transportation Average. According to Dow Theory, a significant trend is not confirmed until both Dow Jones indexes reach the new highs or lows; if they don't, the market will fall back to its former trading range. Dow Theory proponents often disagree on when a true breakout has occurred and, in any case, miss a major portion of the up or down move while waiting for their signals.

DRAFT signed, written order by which one party (drawer) instructs another party (drawee) to pay a specified sum to a third party (payee). Payee and drawer are usually the same person. In foreign transactions, a draft is usually called a *bill of exchange*. When prepared without supporting papers, it is a *clean draft*. With papers or documents attached, it is a *documentary draft*. A *sight draft* is payable on demand. A *time draft* is payable either on a definite date or at a fixed time after sight or demand.

DRAINING RESERVES actions by the Federal Reserve System to decrease the money supply by curtailing the funds banks have available to lend. The Fed does this in three ways: (1) by raising reserve requirements, forcing banks to keep more funds on deposit with Federal Reserve banks; (2) by increasing the rate at which banks borrow to maintain reserves, thereby making it unattractive to deplete reserves by making loans; and (3) by selling bonds in the open market at such attractive rates that dealers reduce their bank balances to buy them. *See also* MULTIPLIER.

DRAWBACK rebate of taxes or duties paid on imported goods that have been reexported. It is in effect a government subsidy designed to encourage domestic manufacturers to compete overseas.

DRAWER *see* DRAFT.

DRILLING PROGRAM *see* BALANCED DRILLING PROGRAM; COMPLETION PROGRAM; DEVELOPMENTAL DRILLING PROGRAM; EXPLORATORY DRILLING PROGRAM; OIL AND GAS LIMITED PARTNERSHIP.

DUAL BANKING U.S. system whereby banks are chartered by the state or federal government. This makes for differences in banking regulations, in lending limits, and in services available to customers.

DUAL CURRENCY SECURITY stock or bond denominated in more than one currency.

DUAL LISTING listing of a security on more than one exchange to increase liquidity and extend the number of hours when the stock can be traded. Securities may not be listed on both the New York and American stock exchanges.

DUAL PURPOSE FUND exchange-listed closed-end mutual fund that has two classes of shares. One class entitles shareholders to all dividends and interest income received by the fund. The other class gives shareholders the benefit of capital gains realized on the sale of securities held by the fund. Dual purpose funds are not closely followed on Wall Street, and there is little trading in them.

DUE BILL *see* BILL.

DUE DILIGENCE MEETING meeting conducted by the underwriter of a new offering at which brokers can ask representatives of the issuer questions about the issuer's background and financial reliability and the intended use of the proceeds. Brokers who recommend investment in new offerings without very careful due diligence work may face lawsuits if the investment should go sour later. Although, in itself, the legally required due diligence meeting typically is a perfunctory affair, most companies, recognizing the importance of due diligence, hold informational meetings, often in different regions of the country, at which top management representatives are available to answer questions of securities analysts and institutional investors.

DUMPING

International finance: selling goods abroad below cost in order to eliminate a surplus or to gain an edge on foreign competition. The U.S. Antidumping Act of 1974 was designed to prevent the sale of imported goods below cost in the United States.

Securities: offering large amounts of stock with little or no concern for price or market effect.

DUN & BRADSTREET (D & B) company that combines credit information obtained directly from commercial firms with data solicited from their creditors, then makes this available to subscribers in reports and a ratings directory. D & B also offers an accounts receivable collection service and publishes financial composite ratios and other financial information. A subsidiary, MOODY'S INVESTORS SERVICE, rates bonds and commercial paper.

DUN'S NUMBER short for Dun's Market Identifier. It is published as part of a list of firms giving information such as an identification number, address code, number of employees, corporate affiliations, and trade styles. Full name: Data Universal Numbering System.

DUTCH AUCTION auction system in which the price of an item is gradually lowered until it meets a responsive bid and is sold. U.S. Treasury bills are sold under this system. Contrasting is the two-sided or DOUBLE AUCTION SYSTEM exemplified by the major stock exchanges. *See also* BILL.

DUTCH AUCTION PREFERRED STOCK type of adjustable-rate PREFERRED STOCK whose dividend is determined every seven weeks in a DUTCH AUCTION process by corporate bidders. Shares are bought and sold at FACE VALUES ranging from $100,000 to $500,000 per share. Also known as *Money Market Preferred Stock* (Shearson Lehman Brothers Inc.) and by such proprietary acronyms as DARTS (Salomon Brothers Inc.).

DUTY tax imposed on the importation, exportation, or consumption of goods. *See also* TARIFF.

e_____

EACH WAY commission made by a broker involved on both the purchase and the sale side of a trade. *See also* CROSSED TRADE.

EARLY WITHDRAWAL PENALTY charge assessed against holders of fixed-term investments if they withdraw their money before maturity. Such a penalty would be assessed, for instance, if someone who has a six-month certificate of deposit were to withdraw the money after four months.

EARNED INCOME income (especially wages and salaries) generated by providing goods or services. Also, pension or annuity income.

EARNED SURPLUS *see* RETAINED EARNINGS.

EARNINGS BEFORE TAXES corporate profits after interest has been paid to bondholders, but before taxes have been paid.

EARNINGS PER SHARE portion of a company's profit allocated to each outstanding share of common stock. For instance, a corporation that earned $10 million last year and has 10 million shares outstanding would report earnings of $1 per share. The figure is calculated after paying taxes and after paying preferred shareholders and bondholders. Earnings per share are a key statistic in evaluating a stock's outlook.

EARNINGS-PRICE RATIO relationship of earnings per share to current stock price. Also known as *earnings yield,* it is used in comparing the relative attractiveness of stocks, bonds, and money market instruments. Inverse of PRICE-EARNINGS RATIO.

EASY MONEY *see* TIGHT MONEY.

ECONOMETRICS use of computer analysis and modeling techniques to describe in mathematical terms the relationship between key economic forces such as labor, capital, interest rates, and government policies, then test the effects of changes in economic scenarios. For instance, an econometric model might show the relationship of housing starts and interest rates.

ECONOMIC GROWTH RATE rate of change in the GROSS NATIONAL PRODUCT, as expressed in an annual percentage. If adjusted for inflation, it is called the *real economic growth rate.* Two consecutive quarterly drops in the growth rate mean recession, and two consecutive advances in the growth rate reflect an expanding economy.

ECONOMIC INDICATORS key statistics showing the direction of the economy. Among them are the unemployment rate, inflation rate, factory utilization rate, and balance of trade. *See also* LEADING INDICATORS.

ECONOMIC RECOVERY TAX ACT OF 1981 (ERTA) tax-cutting legislation. Among the key provisions:
1. across-the-board tax cut, which took effect in three stages ending in 1983.
2. indexing of tax brackets to the inflation rate.
3. lowering of top tax rates on long-term capital gains from 28% to 20%. The top rate on dividends, interest, rents, and royalties income dropped from 70% to 50%.
4. lowering of MARRIAGE PENALTY tax, as families with two working spouses could deduct 10% from the salary of the lower-paid spouse, up to $3000.
5. expansion of INDIVIDUAL RETIREMENT ACCOUNTS to all working people, who can contribute up to $2000 a year, and $250 annually for nonworking spouses. Also, expansion of the amount self-employed people can contribute to KEOGH PLAN account contributions.
6. creation of the *all-savers certificate,* which allowed investors to exempt up to $1000 a year in earned interest. The authority to issue these certificates expired at the end of 1982.
7. deductions for reinvesting public utility dividends.
8. reductions in estate and gift taxes, phased in so that the first $600,000 of property can be given free of estate tax starting in 1987. Annual gifts that can be given free of gift tax were raised from $3000 to $10,000. Unlimited deduction for transfer of property to a spouse at death.
9. lowering of rates on the exercise of stock options.
10. change in rules on DEPRECIATION and INVESTMENT CREDIT.
    See also TAX REFORM ACT OF 1986.

EDGE ACT banking legislation, passed in 1919, which allows national banks to conduct foreign lending operations through federal or state chartered subsidiaries, called Edge Act corporations. Such corporations can be chartered by other states and are allowed, unlike domestic banks, to own banks in foreign countries and to invest in foreign commercial and industrial firms. The act also permitted the FEDERAL RESERVE SYSTEM to set reserve requirements on foreign banks that do business in America. Edge Act corporations benefited further from the 1978 International Banking Act, which instructs the Fed to strike any regulations putting American banks at a disadvantage compared with U.S. operations of foreign banks.

EEC *see* EUROPEAN ECONOMIC COMMUNITY.

EFFECTIVE DATE

In general: date on which an agreement takes effect.

Securities: date when an offering registered with the Securities and Exchange Commission may commence, usually 20 days after filing the registration statement. *See also* SHELF REGISTRATION.

Banking and insurance: time when an insurance policy goes into effect. From that day forward, the insured party is covered by the contract.

EFFECTIVE DEBT total debt owed by a firm, including the capitalized value of lease payments.

EFFECTIVE NET WORTH net worth plus subordinated debt, as viewed by senior creditors. In small business banking, loans payable to principals are commonly subordinated to bank loans. The loans for principals thus can be regarded as effective net worth as long as a bank loan is outstanding and the subordination agreement is in effect.

EFFECTIVE RATE yield on a debt instrument as calculated from the purchase price. The effective rate on a bond is determined by the price, the coupon rate, the time between interest payments, and the time until maturity. Every bond's effective rate thus depends on when it was bought. The effective rate is a more meaningful yield figure than the coupon rate. *See also* RATE OF RETURN.

EFFECTIVE SALE price of a ROUND LOT that determines the price at which the next ODD LOT will be sold. If the last round-lot price was 15, for instance, the odd-lot price might be 15⅛. The added fraction is the *odd-lot differential*.

EFFICIENT MARKET theory that market prices reflect the knowledge and expectations of all investors. Those who adhere to this theory consider it futile to seek undervalued stocks or to forecast market movements. Any new development is reflected in a firm's stock price, they say, making it impossible to beat the market. This vociferously disputed hypothesis also holds that an investor who throws darts at a newspaper's stock listings has as good a chance to outperform the market as any professional investor.

EFFICIENT PORTFOLIO portfolio that has a maximum expected return for any level of risk or a minimum level of risk for any expected return. It is arrived at mathematically, taking into account the expected return and standard deviation of returns for each security, as well as the covariance of returns between different securities in the portfolio.

EITHER-OR ORDER *see* ALTERNATIVE ORDER.

ELASTICITY OF DEMAND AND SUPPLY

Elasticity of demand: responsiveness of buyers to changes in price. Demand for luxury items may slow dramatically if prices are raised, because these purchases are not essential, and can be postponed. On the other hand, demand for necessities such as food, telephone service, and emergency surgery is said to be inelastic. It remains about the same despite price changes because buyers cannot postpone their purchases without severe adverse consequences.

Elasticity of supply: responsiveness of output to changes in price. As prices move up, the supply normally increases. If it does not, it is said to be inelastic. Supply is said to be elastic if the rise in price means a rise in production.

ELECT

In general: choose a course of action. Someone who decides to incorporate a certain provision in a will elects to do so.

Securities trading: make a conditional order into a market order. If a customer has received a guaranteed buy or sell price from a specialist on the floor of an exchange, the transaction is considered elected when that price is reached. If the guarantee is that a stock will be sold when it reaches 20, and a stop order is put at that price, the sale will be elected at 20.

ELIGIBLE PAPER commercial and agricultural paper, drafts, bills of exchange, banker's acceptances, and other negotiable instruments that were acquired by a bank at a discount and that the Federal Reserve Bank will accept for rediscount.

EMANCIPATION freedom to assume certain legal responsibilities normally associated only with adults, said of a minor who is granted this freedom by a court. If both parents die in an accident, for instance, the 16-year-old eldest son may be emancipated by a judge to act as guardian for his younger brothers and sisters.

EMBARGO government prohibition against the shipment of certain goods to another country. An embargo is most common during wartime, but is sometimes applied for economic reasons as well. For instance, the Organization of Petroleum Exporting Countries placed an embargo on the shipment of oil to the West in the early 1970s to protest Israeli policies and to raise the price of petroleum.

EMERGENCY HOME FINANCE ACT OF 1970 act creating the quasigovernmental Federal Home Loan Mortgage Corporation, also known as Freddie Mac, to stimulate the development of a secondary mortgage market. The act authorized Freddie Mac to package and sell Federal Housing Administration and Veterans Administration-guaranteed mortgage loans. More than half the home mortgages were subsequently packaged and sold to investors in the secondary market in the form of pass-through securities.

EMPLOYEE RETIREMENT INCOME SECURITY ACT (ERISA) 1974 law governing the operation of most private pension and benefit plans. The law eased pension eligibility rules, set up the PENSION BENEFIT GUARANTY CORPORATION, and established guidelines for the management of pension funds.

EMPLOYEE STOCK OWNERSHIP PLAN (ESOP) program encouraging employees to purchase stock in their company. Employees may participate in the management of the company and even take control to rescue the company or a particular plant that would otherwise go out of business. Employees may offer wage and work-rule concessions in return for ownership privileges in an attempt to keep a marginal facility operating.

ENCUMBERED owned by one party but subject to another party's valid claim. A homeowner owns his mortgaged property, for example, but the bank has a security interest in it as long as the mortgage loan is outstanding.

ENDORSE transfer ownership of an asset by signing the back of a negotiable instrument. One can endorse a check to receive payment or endorse a stock or bond certificate to transfer ownership.
See also QUALIFIED ENDORSEMENT.

ENERGY MUTUAL FUND mutual fund that invests solely in energy stocks such as oil, oil service, gas, solar energy, and coal companies and makers of energy-saving devices.

ENTERPRISE a business firm. The term often is applied to a newly formed venture.

ENTREPRENEUR person who takes on the risks of starting a new business. Many entrepreneurs have technical knowledge with which to produce a saleable product or to design a needed new service. Often, VENTURE CAPITAL is used to finance the startup in return for a piece of the equity. Once an entrepreneur's business is established, shares may be sold to the public as an INITIAL PUBLIC OFFERING, assuming favorable market conditions.

EOM DATING arrangement—common in the wholesale drug industry, for example—whereby all purchases made through the 25th of one month are payable within 30 days of the end of the following month; EOM means *end of month*. Assuming no prompt payment discount, purchases through the 25th of April, for example, will be payable by the end of June. If a discount exists for payment in ten days, payment would have to be made by June 10th to take advantage of it. End of month dating with a 2% discount for prompt payment (10 days) would be expressed in the trade either as: *2%-10 days, EOM, 30,* or *2/10 prox. net 30,* where prox., or proximo, means "the next."

EQUAL CREDIT OPPORTUNITY ACT federal legislation passed in the mid-1970s prohibiting discrimination in granting credit, based on race, religion, sex, ethnic background, or whether a person is receiving public assistance or alimony. The Federal Trade Commission enforces the act.

EQUILIBRIUM PRICE
1. price when the supply of goods in a particular market matches demand.
2. for a manufacturer, the price that maximizes a product's profitability.
See illustration, page 250.

EQUIPMENT LEASING PARTNERSHIP limited partnership that buys equipment such as computers, railroad cars, and airplanes, then leases it to businesses. Limited partners receive income from the lease payments as well as tax benefits such as depreciation. Whether a partnership of this kind works out well depends on the GENERAL PARTNER's expertise. Failure to lease the equipment can be disastrous, as happened with railroad hopper cars in the mid-1970s.

EQUIPMENT TRUST CERTIFICATE bond, usually issued by a transportation company such as a railroad or shipping line, used to pay for new equipment. The

EQUILIBRIUM PRICE

certificate gives the bondholder the first right to the equipment in the event that interest and principal are not paid when due. Title to the equipment is held in the name of the trustee, usually a bank, until the bond is paid off.

EQUITY

In general: fairness. Law courts, for example, try to be equitable in their judgments when splitting up estates or settling divorce cases.

Banking: difference between the amount a property could be sold for and the claims held against it.

Brokerage account: excess of securities over debit balance in a margin account. For instance, equity would be $28,000 in a margin account with stocks and bonds worth $50,000 and a debit balance of $22,000.

Investments: ownership interest possessed by shareholders in a corporation— stock as opposed to bonds.

EQUITY FINANCING raising money by issuing shares of common or preferred stock. Usually done when prices are high and the most capital can be raised for the smallest number of shares.

EQUITY FUNDING type of investment combining a life insurance policy and a mutual fund. The fund shares are used as collateral for a loan to pay the insurance premiums, giving the investor the advantages of insurance protection and investment appreciation potential.

EQUITY KICKER offer of an ownership position in a deal that involves loans. For instance, a mortgage real estate limited partnership that lends to real estate developers might receive as an equity kicker a small ownership position in a building that can appreciate over time. When the building is sold, limited partners receive the appreciation payout. In return for that equity kicker, the lender is likely to charge a lower interest rate on the loan. Convertible features and warrants are offered as equity kickers to make securities attractive to investors.

EQUITY REIT REAL ESTATE INVESTMENT TRUST that takes an ownership position in the real estate it invests in. Stockholders in equity REITs earn dividends on rental income from the buildings and earn appreciation if properties are sold for a profit. The opposite is a MORTGAGE REIT.

EQUIVALENT BOND YIELD comparison of discount yields and yields on bonds with coupons. For instance, if a 10%, 90-day Treasury bill with a face value of $10,000 cost $9,750, the equivalent bond yield would be:

$$\frac{\$250}{\$9,750} \times \frac{365}{90} = 10.40\%$$

EQUIVALENT TAXABLE YIELD comparison of the taxable yield on a corporate bond and the tax-free yield on a municipal bond. Depending on the tax bracket, an investor's aftertax return may be greater with a municipal bond than with a corporate bond offering a higher interest rate. For someone in a 28% tax bracket, for instance, a 10% municipal bond would have an equivalent taxable yield of 13.9%. See YIELD EQUIVALENCE for method of calculation.

ERISA see EMPLOYEE RETIREMENT INCOME SECURITY ACT.

ERTA see ECONOMIC RECOVERY TAX ACT OF 1981.

ESCALATOR CLAUSE provision in a contract allowing cost increases to be passed on. In an employment contract, an escalator clause might call for wage increases to keep employee earnings in line with inflation. In a lease, an escalator clause could obligate the tenant to pay for increases in fuel or other costs.

ESCHEAT return of property (for example, land, bank balances, insurance policies) to the state if abandoned or left by a person who died without making a will. If rightful owners or heirs later appear, they can claim the property.

ESCROW money, securities, or other property or instruments held by a third party until the conditions of a contract are met.

ESTATE all the assets a person possesses at the time of death—such as securities, real estate, interests in business, physical possessions, and cash. The estate is distributed to heirs according to the dictates of the person's will or, if there is no will, a court ruling.

ESTATE PLANNING planning for the orderly handling, disposition, and administration of an estate when the owner dies. Estate planning includes drawing up a will, setting up trusts, and minimizing estate taxes, perhaps by passing property to heirs before death or by setting up a BYPASS TRUST or a TESTAMENTARY TRUST.

ESTATE TAX tax imposed by a state or the federal government on assets left to heirs in a will. Under the Economic Recovery Tax Act of 1981, there is no estate tax on transfers of property between spouses. An exclusion that began at $250,000 in 1982 rose to $600,000 in 1987.

ESTIMATED TAX amount of anticipated tax for the coming tax year, minus tax credits, based on the higher of regular or ALTERNATIVE MINIMUM TAX (AMT). Corporations, estates and trusts, self-employed persons, and persons for whom less than a fixed percentage of income is withheld by employers compute estimated tax and make quarterly payments. The total of withholdings and estimated taxes paid must equal 100% of the prior year's actual tax or (after 1986) 90% of the estimated year's tax.

EUROBOND bond denominated in U.S. dollars or other currencies and sold to investors outside the country whose currency is used. The bonds are usually issued by large underwriting groups composed of banks and issuing houses from many countries. An example of a Eurobond transaction might be a dollar-denominated debenture issued by a Belgian corporation through an underwriting group comprised of the overseas affiliate of a New York investment banking house, a bank in Holland, and a consortium of British merchant banks; a portion of the issue is sold to French investors through Swiss investment accounts. The Eurobond market is an important source of capital for multinational companies and foreign governments, including Third World governments.

EUROCURRENCY Money deposited by corporations and national governments in banks away from their home countries, called *Eurobanks*. The terms Eurocurrency and Eurobanks do not necessarily mean the currencies or the banks are European, though more often than not, that is the case. For instance, dollars deposited in a British bank or Italian lire deposited in a Japanese bank are considered to be Eurocurrency. The Eurodollar is only one of the Eurocurrencies, though it is the most prevalent. Also known as *Euromoney*.

EURODOLLAR U.S. currency held in banks outside the United States, mainly in Europe, and commonly used for settling international transactions. Some securities are issued in Eurodollars—that is, with a promise to pay interest in dollars deposited in foreign bank accounts.

EURODOLLAR BOND bond that pays interest and principal in Eurodollars, U.S. dollars held in banks outside the United States, primarily in Europe. Such a bond is not registered with the Securities and Exchange Commission, and because there are fewer regulatory delays and costs in the Euromarket, Eurodollar bonds generally can be sold at lower than U.S. interest rates. *See also* EUROBOND.

EURODOLLAR CERTIFICATE OF DEPOSIT CDs issued by banks outside the United States, primarily in Europe, with interest and principal paid in dollars. Such CDs usually have minimum denominations of $100,000 and short-term maturities of less than two years. The interest rate on these CDs is usually pegged to the LONDON INTERBANK OFFERED RATE (LIBOR).

EUROPEAN ECONOMIC COMMUNITY (EEC) economic alliance formed in 1957 by Belgium, France, Italy, Luxembourg, The Netherlands, and West Germany to foster trade and cooperation among its members. Membership was subsequently extended to Great Britain, Ireland, and Denmark (1973); Greece (1984); and Spain and Portugal (1986). Trade barriers were gradually abolished and import duties were standardized with non-EEC countries. Many former European dependencies in Africa and the Caribbean, now independent countries, have preferential trade agreements with the EEC. Central staff headquarters are in Brussels, Belgium. Also known as the *European Community* and the *Common Market*.

EUROPEAN OPTION PUT OPTION or CALL OPTION exercisable for a limited time just before expiration. In contrast, an *American option* is exercisable at any time before expiration.

EVALUATOR independent expert who appraises the value of property for which there is limited trading—antiques in an estate, perhaps, or rarely traded stocks or bonds. The fee for this service is sometimes a flat amount, sometimes a percentage of the appraised value.

EXACT INTEREST *see* ORDINARY INTEREST.

EX-ALL sale of a security without dividends, rights, warrants, or any other privileges associated with that security.

EXCESS MARGIN equity in a brokerage firm's customer account, expressed in dollars, above the legal minimum for a margin account or the maintenance requirement. For instance, with a margin requirement of $25,000, as set by REGULATION T and a maintenance requirement of $12,500 set by the stock exchange, the client whose equity is $100,000 would have excess margin of $75,000 and $87,500 in terms of the initial and maintenance requirements, respectively.

EXCESS PROFITS TAX extra federal taxes placed on the earnings of a business. Such taxes may be levied during a time of national emergency, such as in wartime, and are designed to increase national revenue. The excess profits tax is to be distinguished from the WINDFALL PROFITS TAX, designed to prevent excessive corporate profits in special circumstances.

EXCESS RESERVES money a bank holds over and above the RESERVE REQUIREMENT. The money may be on deposit with the Federal Reserve System or with an approved depository bank, or it may be in the bank's possession. Excess reserves are available for loans to other banks or customers or for other corporate uses.

EXCHANGE DISTRIBUTION block trade carried out on the floor of an exchange between customers of a member firm. Someone who wants to sell a large block of stock in a single transaction can get a broker to solicit and bunch a large number of orders. The seller transmits the securities to the buyers all at once, and the trade is announced on the BROAD TAPE as an exchange distribution. The seller, not the buyers, pays a special commission to the broker who executes the trade.

EXCHANGE PRIVILEGE right of a shareholder to switch from one mutual fund to another within one fund family—often, at no additional charge. This enables investors to put their money in an aggressive growth-stock fund when they expect the market to turn up strongly, then switch to a money-market fund when they anticipate a downturn. Some discount brokers allow shareholders to switch between fund families in pursuit of the best performance.

EXCHANGE RATE price at which one country's currency can be converted into another's. The exchange rate between the U.S. dollar and the British pound is different from the rate between the dollar and the West German mark, for example. A wide range of factors influences exchange rates, which generally change slightly each trading day. Some rates are fixed by agreement; *see* FIXED EXCHANGE RATE.

EXCISE TAX federal or state tax on the sale or manufacture of a commodity, usually a luxury item. Examples: federal and state taxes on alcohol and tobacco.

EXCLUSION
1. item not covered by a contract. For instance, an insurance policy may list certain hazards that are excluded from coverage.
2. on a tax return, items that must be reported, but are not taxed. For example, corporations are allowed to exclude 80% of dividends received from other domestic corporations.

EX-DIVIDEND interval between the announcement and the payment of the next dividend. An investor who buys shares during that interval is not entitled to the dividend. Typically, a stock's price moves up by the dollar amount of the dividend as the ex-dividend date approaches, then falls by the amount of the dividend after that date. A stock that has gone ex-dividend is marked with an x in newspaper listings.

EX-DIVIDEND DATE date on which a stock goes EX-DIVIDEND, typically about three weeks before the dividend is paid to shareholders of record. Shares listed on the New York Stock Exchange go ex-dividend four business days before the RECORD DATE. This NYSE rule is generally followed by the other exchanges.

EXECUTION
Securities: carrying out a trade. A broker who buys or sells shares is said to have executed an order.
Law: the signing, sealing, and delivering of a contract or agreement making it valid.

EXECUTOR person designated to carry out the wishes expressed in a will as to the administration of the estate and the distribution of the assets in it. An executor may be a bank trust officer or a family member or trusted friend.

EXEMPT SECURITIES stocks and bonds exempt from certain Securities and Exchange Commission and Federal Reserve Board rules. For instance, government and municipal bonds are exempt from SEC registration requirements and from Federal Reserve Board margin rules.

EXERCISE make use of a right available in a contract. In options trading a buyer of a call contract may exercise the right to buy underlying shares at a particular price by informing the option seller. A put buyer's right is exercised when the underlying shares are sold at the agreed-upon price.

EXERCISE LIMIT limit on the number of option contracts of any one class that can be exercised in a span of five business days. For options on stocks, the exercise limit is usually 2000 contracts.

EXERCISE NOTICE notification by a broker that a client wants to exercise a right to buy the underlying stock in an option contract. Such notice is transmitted to the option seller through the Options Clearing Corporation, which ensures that stock is delivered as agreed upon.

EXERCISE PRICE price at which the stock or commodity underlying a call or put option can be purchased (call) or sold (put) over the specified period. For instance, a call contract may allow the buyer to purchase 100 shares of XYZ at any time in the next three months at an exercise or STRIKE PRICE of $63.

EXHAUST PRICE price at which broker must liquidate a client's holding in a stock that was bought on margin and has declined, but has not had additional funds put up to meet the MARGIN CALL.

EXIMBANK *see* EXPORT-IMPORT BANK.

EX-LEGAL municipal bond that does not have the legal opinion of a bond law firm printed on it, as most municipal bonds do. When such bonds are traded, buyers must be warned that legal opinion is lacking.

EXPECTED RETURN *see* MEAN RETURN.

EXPENSE RATIO amount, expressed as a percentage of total investment, that shareholders pay for mutual fund operating expenses and management fees. This money, which may be as high as 1% of shareholder assets, is taken out of the fund's current income and is disclosed in the annual report to shareholders.

EXPIRATION

Banking: date on which a contract or agreement ceases to be effective.

Options trading: last day on which an option can be exercised. If it is not, traders say that the option *expired worthless*.

EXPIRATION CYCLE cycle of expiration dates used in options trading. For example, contracts may be written for one of three cycles: January, April, July, October; February, May, August, November; March, June, September, December. Since options are traded in three-, six-, and nine-month contracts, only three of the four months in the set are traded at once. In our example, when the January contract expires, trading begins on the October contract. Commodities futures expiration cycles follow other schedules.

EX-PIT TRANSACTION purchase of commodities off the floor of the exchange where they are regularly traded and at specified terms.

EXPLORATORY DRILLING PROGRAM search for an undiscovered reservoir of oil or gas—a very risky undertaking. Exploratory wells are called *wildcat* (in an unproven area); *controlled wildcat* (in an area outside the proven limits of an existing field); or *deep test* (within a proven field but to unproven depths). Exploratory drilling programs are usually syndicated, and units are sold to limited partners.

EXPORT-IMPORT BANK (EXIMBANK) bank set up by Congress in 1934 to encourage U.S. trade with foreign countries. Eximbank is an independent entity that borrows from the U.S. Treasury to (1) finance exports and imports; (2) grant direct credit to non-U.S. borrowers;(3) provide export guarantees, insurance against commercial and political risk, and discount loans.

EX-RIGHTS without the RIGHT to buy a company's stock at a discount from the prevailing market price, which was distributed until a particular date. Typically, after that date the rights trade separately from the stock itself. *See also* EX-WARRANTS.

EX-STOCK DIVIDENDS interval between the announcement and payment of a stock dividend. An investor who buys shares during that interval is not entitled to the announced stock dividend; instead, it goes to the seller of the shares, who was the owner on the last recorded date before the books were closed and the stock went EX-DIVIDEND. Stocks cease to be ex-dividend after the payment date.

EXTERNAL FUNDS funds brought in from outside the corporation, perhaps in the form of a bank loan, or the proceeds from a bond offering, or an infusion of cash from venture capitalists. External funds supplement internally generated CASH FLOW and are used for expansion, as well as for seasonal WORKING CAPITAL needs.

EXTRA DIVIDEND dividend paid to shareholders in addition to the regular dividend. Such a payment is made after a particularly profitable year in order to reward shareholders and engender loyalty.

EXTRAORDINARY ITEM nonrecurring occurrence that must be explained to shareholders in an annual or quarterly report. Some examples: writeoff of a division, acquisition of another company, sale of a large amount of real estate, or uncovering of employee fraud that negatively affects the company's financial condition. Earnings are usually reported before and after taking into account the effects of extraordinary items.

EX-WARRANTS stock sold with the buyer no longer entitled to the WARRANT attached to the stock. Warrants allow the holder to buy stock at some future date at a specified price. Someone buying a stock on June 3 that had gone ex-warrants on June 1 would not receive those warrants. They would be the property of the stockholder of record on June 1.

f

FACE-AMOUNT CERTIFICATE debt security issued by face-amount certificate companies, one of three categories of mutual funds defined by the INVESTMENT COMPANY ACT OF 1940. The holder makes periodic payments to the issuer, and the issuer promises to pay the purchaser the face value at maturity or a surrender value if the certificate is presented prior to maturity.

FACE VALUE value of a bond, note, mortgage, or other security as given on the certificate or instrument. Corporate bonds are usually issued with $1000 face values, municipal bonds with $5000 face values, and federal government bonds with $10,000 face values. Although the bonds fluctuate in price from the time they are issued until redemption, they are redeemed at maturity at their face value, unless the issuer defaults. If the bonds are retired before maturity, bondholders normally receive a slight premium over face value. The face value is the amount on which interest payments are calculated. Thus, a 10% bond with a face value of $1000 pays bondholders $100 per year. Face value is also referred to as PAR VALUE or *nominal value*.

FACTORING type of financial service whereby a firm sells or transfers title to its accounts receivable to a factoring company, which then acts as principal, not as agent. The receivables are sold without recourse, meaning that the factor cannot turn to the seller in the event accounts prove uncollectible. Factoring can be done either on a *notification basis,* where the seller's customers remit directly to the factor, or on a *nonnotification basis,* where the seller handles the collections and remits to the factor. There are two basic types of factoring:
1. **Discount factoring** arrangement whereby seller receives funds from the factor prior to the average maturity date, based on the invoice amount of the receivable, less cash discounts, less an allowance for estimated claims, returns, etc. Here the factor is compensated by an interest rate based on daily balances and typically 2% to 3% above the bank prime rate.
2. **Maturity factoring** arrangement whereby the factor, who performs the entire credit and collection function, remits to the seller for the receivables sold each month on the average due date of the factored receivables. The factor's commission on this kind of arrangement ranges from 0.75% to 2%, depending on the bad debt risk and the handling costs.
   Factors also accommodate clients with "overadvances," loans in anticipation of sales, which permit inventory building prior to peak selling periods. Factoring has traditionally been most closely associated with the garment industry, but is used by companies in other industries as well.

FAIL POSITION securities undelivered due to the failure of selling clients to deliver the securities to their brokers so the latter can deliver them to the buying brokers. Since brokers are constantly buying and selling, receiving and delivering, the term usually refers to a net delivery position—that is, a given broker owes more securities to other brokers on sell transactions than other brokers owe to it on buy transactions. *See also* FAIL TO DELIVER; FAIL TO RECEIVE.

FAIL TO DELIVER situation where the broker-dealer on the sell side of a contract has not delivered securities to the broker-dealer on the buy side. A fail to deliver is usually the result of a broker not receiving delivery from its selling customer. As long as a fail to deliver exists, the seller will not receive payment. *See also* FAIL TO RECEIVE.

FAIL TO RECEIVE situation where the broker-dealer on the buy side of a contract has not received delivery of securities from the broker-dealer on the sell side. As long as a fail to receive exists, the buyer will not make payment for the securities. *See also* FAIL TO DELIVER.

FAIR CREDIT REPORTING ACT federal law enacted in 1971 giving the right to see and challenge credit records at credit bureaus. *See also* CREDIT RATING.

FAIR MARKET VALUE price at which an asset or service passes from a willing seller to a willing buyer. It is assumed that both buyer and seller are rational and have a reasonable knowledge of relevant facts. *See also* MARKET.

FAIR-PRICE AMENDMENT AMENDMENT, aimed at hostile TWO-TIER BIDS, providing that a SUPERMAJORITY AMENDMENT will be waived if a fair price is offered for all shares of a TAKEOVER target.

FAIR RATE OF RETURN level of profit that a utility is allowed to earn as determined by federal and/or state regulators. Public utility commissions set the fair rate of return based on the utility's needs to maintain service to its customers, pay adequate dividends to shareholders and interest to bondholders, and maintain and expand plant and equipment.

FAIR TRADE ACTS state laws protecting manufacturers from price-cutting by permitting them to establish minimum retail prices for their goods. Fair trade pricing was effectively eliminated in 1975 when Congress repealed the federal laws upholding resale price maintenance.

FAMILY OF FUNDS group of mutual funds managed by the same investment management company. Each fund typically has a different objective; one may be a growth-oriented stock fund, whereas another may be a bond fund or a money market fund. Shareholders in one of the funds can usually switch their money into any of the family's other funds, sometimes at no charge. This system makes it convenient for shareholders to move their assets as different investments become more or less appropriate at different points in the economic cycle, or as their investment needs change. There may be tax consequences when money is transferred from one fund to another. Families of funds with no sales charges are called *no-load families* and are sold directly to investors. Those with sales fees are called *load families* and are typically sold by a broker. *See also* INVESTMENT COMPANY.

FANNIE MAE nickname for the FEDERAL NATIONAL MORTGAGE ASSOCIATION.

FARTHER OUT; FARTHER IN relative length of option-contract maturities with reference to the present. For example, an options investor in January would call an option expiring in October farther out than an option expiring in July. The July option is farther in than the October option. *See also* DIAGONAL SPREAD.

FAVORABLE TRADE BALANCE situation that exists when the value of a nation's exports is in excess of the value of its imports. *See* BALANCE OF PAYMENTS; BALANCE OF TRADE.

FAVORITE FIFTY *See* NIFTY FIFTY.

FEDERAL AGENCY SECURITY debt instrument issued by an agency of the federal government such as the Federal National Mortgage Association, Federal Farm Credit Bank, and the Tennessee Valley Authority (TVA). Though not general obligations of the U.S. Treasury, such securities are sponsored by the government and therefore have high safety ratings.

FEDERAL DEFICIT federal shortfall that results when the government spends more in a fiscal year than it receives in revenue. To cover the shortfall, the government usually borrows from the public by floating long- and short-term debt. Federal deficits, which started to rise in the 1970s and exploded to enormous proportions in the early 1980s, are said by economists to be a cause of high interest rates and inflation, since they compete with private borrowing by businesses and consumers for funds, and add to monetary demand. *See also* CROWDING OUTNATIONAL DEBT.

FEDERAL DEPOSIT INSURANCE CORPORATION (FDIC) federal agency established in 1933 that guarantees (within limits) funds on deposit in member banks and performs other functions such as making loans to or buying assets from member banks to facilitate mergers or prevent failures.

FEDERAL FARM CREDIT BANK government-sponsored institution that consolidates the financing activities of the Federal Land Banks, the Federal Intermediate Credit Banks, and the Banks for Cooperatives. *See* FEDERAL FARM CREDIT SYSTEM.

FEDERAL FARM CREDIT SYSTEM system established by the Farm Credit Act of 1971 to provide credit services to farmers and farm-related enterprises through a network of 12 Farm Credit districts. Each district has a Federal Land Bank, a Federal Intermediate Credit Bank, and a Bank for Cooperatives to carry out policies of the system. The system sells short-term (5- to 270-day) notes in increments of $50,000 on a discounted basis through a national syndicate of securities dealers. Rates are set by the FEDERAL FARM CREDIT BANK, a unit established to consolidate the financing activities of the various banks. An active secondary market is maintained by several dealers. The system also issues Federal Farm Credit System Consolidated Systemwide Bonds on a monthly basis with 6- and 9-month maturities. The bonds are sold in increments of $5000 with rates set by the system. The bonds enjoy a secondary market even more active than that for the discounted notes. *See also* SECONDARY MARKET.

FEDERAL FUNDS
  1. funds deposited by commercial banks at Federal Reserve Banks, including funds in excess of bank reserve requirements. Banks may lend federal funds to each other on an overnight basis at the federal funds rate. Member banks may also transfer funds among themselves or on behalf of customers on a same-day basis by debiting and crediting balances in the various reserve banks. *See* FED WIRE.

2. money used by the Federal Reserve to pay for its purchases of government securities.

3. funds used to settle transactions where there is no FLOAT.

FEDERAL FUNDS RATE interest rate charged by banks with excess reserves at a Federal Reserve district bank to banks needing overnight loans to meet reserve requirements. The federal funds rate is the most sensitive indicator of the direction of interest rates, since it is set daily by the market, unlike the PRIME RATE and the DISCOUNT RATE, which are periodically changed by banks and by the Federal Reserve Board, respectively.

FEDERAL HOME LOAN BANK SYSTEM system supplying credit reserves for SAVINGS AND LOANS, cooperative banks, and other mortgage lenders in a manner similar to the Federal Reserve's role with commerical banks. The Federal Home Loan Bank System is made up of 12 regional Federal Home Loan Banks. It raises money by issuing notes and bonds and lends money to savings and loans and other mortgage lenders based on the amount of collateral the institution can provide. The system was established in 1932 after a massive wave of bank failures.

FEDERAL HOME LOAN MORTGAGE CORPORATION (FHLMC) publicly chartered agency that buys qualifying residential mortgages from lenders, packages them into new securities backed by those pooled mortgages, provides certain guarantees, and then resells the securities on the open market. The corporation's stock is owned by savings institutions across the U.S. and is held in trust by the Federal Home Loan Bank System. The corporation, nicknamed Freddie Mac, has created an enormous secondary market, which provides more funds for mortgage lending and allows investors to buy high-yielding securities backed by federal guarantees. Freddie Mac formerly packaged only mortgages backed by the Veteran's Administration or the Federal Housing Administration, but now it also resells nongovernmentally backed mortgages. The corporation was established in 1970. *See also* MORTGAGE BACKED CERTIFICATES.

FEDERAL HOUSING ADMINISTRATION (FHA) federally sponsored agency that insures lenders against loss on residential mortgages. It was founded in 1934 in response to the Great Depression to execute the provisions of the National Housing Act. The FHA was the forerunner of a group of government agencies responsible for the growing secondary market for mortgages, such as the Government National Mortgage Association (Ginnie Mae) and the Federal National Mortgage Association (Fannie Mae).

FEDERAL INTERMEDIATE CREDIT BANK one of 12 banks that make funds available to production credit associations, commercial banks, agricultural credit corporations, livestock loan companies, and other institutions extending credit to crop farmers and cattle raisers. Their stock is owned by farmers and ranchers, and the banks raise funds largely from the public sale of short-term debentures. *See also* FEDERAL FARM CREDIT BANK; FEDERAL FARM CREDIT SYSTEM.

FEDERAL LAND BANK one of 12 banks under the U.S. Farm Credit Administration that extend long-term mortgage credit to crop farmers and cattle raisers for buying land, refinancing debts, or other agricultural purposes. To obtain a loan, a farmer or rancher must purchase stock equal to 5% of the loan in any one of approximately 500 local land bank associations; these, in turn, purchase an equal amount of stock in the Federal Land bank. The stock is retired when the loan is repaid. The banks raise funds by issuing Consolidated Systemwide Bonds to the public. *See also* FEDERAL FARM CREDIT BANK; FEDERAL FARM CREDIT SYSTEM.

FEDERAL NATIONAL MORTGAGE ASSOCIATION (FNMA)publicly owned, government-sponsored corporation chartered in 1938 to purchase mortgages from lenders and resell them to investors. The agency, known by the nickname Fannie Mae, mostly packages mortgages backed by the Federal Housing Administration, but also sells some nongovernmentally backed mortgages. Shares of FNMA itself, known as Fannie Maes, are traded on the New York Stock Exchange. The price usually soars when interest rates fall and plummets when interest rates rise, since the mortgage business is so dependent on the direction of interest rates.

FEDERAL OPEN MARKET COMMITTEE (FOMC) key committee in the FEDERAL RESERVE SYSTEM, which sets short-term monetary policy for the Federal Reserve (the Fed). The committee comprises the seven Federal Reserve governors and the presidents of six Federal Reserve Banks. To tighten the money supply, which decreases the amount of money available in the banking system, the Fed sells government securities. The meetings of the committee, which are secret, are the subject of much speculation on Wall Street, as analysts try to guess whether the Fed will tighten or loosen the money supply, thereby causing interest rates to rise or fall. *See also* DESK.

FEDERAL RESERVE BANK one of the 12 banks that, with their branches, make up the FEDERAL RESERVE SYSTEM. These banks are located in Boston, New York, Philadelphia, Cleveland, Richmond, Atlanta, Chicago, St. Louis, Minneapolis, Kansas City, Dallas, and San Francisco. The role of each Federal Reserve Bank is to monitor the commercial and savings banks in its region to ensure that they follow Federal Reserve Board regulations and to provide those banks with access to emergency funds from the DISCOUNT WINDOW. The reserve banks act as depositories for member banks in their regions, providing money transfer and other services. Each of the banks is owned by the member banks in its district.

FEDERAL RESERVE BOARD (FRB) governing board of the FEDERAL RESERVE SYSTEM. Its seven members are appointed by the President of the United States, subject to Senate confirmation, and serve 14-year terms. The Board establishes Federal Reserve System policies on such key matters as reserve requirements and other bank regulations, sets the discount rate, tightens or loosens the availability of credit in the economy, and regulates the purchase of securities on margin.

FEDERAL RESERVE OPEN MARKET COMMITTEE *see* FEDERAL OPEN MARKET COMMITTEE.

FEDERAL RESERVE SYSTEM system established by the Federal Reserve Act of 1913 to regulate the U.S. monetary and banking system. The Federal Reserve System (the Fed) is comprised of 12 regional Federal Reserve Banks, their 25 branches, and all national and state banks that are part of the system. National banks are stockholders of the FEDERAL RESERVE BANK in their region.

The Federal Reserve System's main functions are to regulate the national money supply, set reserve requirements for member banks, supervise the printing of currency at the mint, act as clearinghouse for the transfer of funds throughout the banking system, and examine member banks to make sure they meet various Federal Reserve regulations. Although the members of the system's governing board are appointed by the President of the United States and confirmed by the Senate, the Federal Reserve System is considered an independent entity, which is supposed to make its decisions free of political influence. Governors are appointed for terms of 14 years, which further assures their independence. *See also* FEDERAL OPEN MARKET COMMITTEE; FEDERAL RESERVE BOARD; OPEN MARKET OPERATIONS.

FEDERAL SAVINGS AND LOAN ASSOCIATION federally chartered institution with a primary responsibility to collect people's savings deposits and to provide mortgage loans for residential housing. Federal Savings and Loans may be owned either by stockholders, who can trade their shares on stock exchanges, or by depositors, in which case the associations are considered mutual organizations. Federal Savings and Loans are members of the Federal Home Loan Bank System. In the 1970s and early 80s S&Ls expanded into nonhousing-related financial services such as discount stock brokerage, financial planning, credit cards, and consumer loans. *See also* FINANCIAL SUPERMARKET; MUTUAL ASSOCIATION; SAVINGS AND LOAN ASSOCIATION.

FEDERAL SAVINGS AND LOAN INSURANCE CORPORATION (FSLIC) federal agency established in 1934 that insures deposits in member savings institutions.

FEDERAL TRADE COMMISSION (FTC) federal agency established in 1914 to foster free and fair business competition and prevent monopolies and activities in restraint of trade. It administers both antitrust and consumer protection legislation.

FED WIRE high-speed, computerized communications network that connects all 12 Federal Reserve Banks, their 24 branches, the Federal Reserve Board office in Washington, D.C., U.S. Treasury offices in Washington, D.C., and Chicago, and the Washington, D.C. office of the Commodity Credit Corporation; also spelled FedWire and Fedwire. The Fed wire has been called the central nervous system of money transfer in the United States. It enables banks to transfer reserve balances from one to another for immediate available credit and to transfer balances for business customers. Using the Fed wire, Federal Reserve Banks can settle interdistrict transfers resulting from check collections, and the Treasury can shift balances from its accounts in different reserve banks quickly and without cost. It is also possible to transfer bearer short-term Government securities within an hour at no cost. This is done through a procedure called CPD (Commissioner of Public Debt of the Treasury) transfers, whereby one Federal Reserve Bank ''retires'' a seller's security, while another reserve bank makes delivery of a like amount of the same security from its unissued stock to the buyer.

FICTITIOUS CREDIT the credit balance in a securities MARGIN ACCOUNT representing the proceeds from a short sale and the margin requirement under Federal Reserve Board REGULATION T (which regulates margin credit). Because the proceeds, which are held as security for the loan of securities made by the broker to effect the short sale, and the margin requirement are both there to protect the broker's position, the money is not available for withdrawal by the customer; hence the term ''fictitious'' credit. It is in contrast to a free credit balance, which can be withdrawn anytime.

FIDELITY BOND *see* BLANKET FIDELITY BOND.

FIDUCIARY person, company, or association holding assets in trust for a beneficiary. The fiduciary is charged with the responsibility of investing the money wisely for the beneficiary's benefit. Some examples of fiduciaries are executors of wills and estates, receivers in bankruptcy, trustees, and those who administer the assets of underage or incompetent beneficiaries. Most U.S. states have laws about what a fiduciary may or may not do with a beneficiary's assets. For instance, it is illegal for fiduciaries to invest or misappropriate the money for their personal gain. *See also* LEGAL LIST; PRUDENT MAN RULE.

FIFO *see* FIRST IN, FIRST OUT.

FILL execute a customer's order to buy or sell a stock, bond, or commodity. An order is filled when the amount of the security requested is supplied. When less than the full amount of the order is supplied, it is known as a *partial fill*.

FILL OR KILL (FOK) order to buy or sell a particular security which, if not executed immediately, is canceled. Often, fill or kill orders are placed when a client wants to buy a large quantity of shares of a particular stock at a particular price. If the order is not executed because it will significantly upset the market price for that stock, the order is withdrawn.

FINANCE CHARGE cost of credit, including interest, paid by a customer for a consumer loan. Under the Truth in Lending Act, the finance charge must be disclosed to the customer in advance. *See also* CONSUMER CREDIT PROTECTION ACT OF 1968; REGULATION Z.

FINANCE COMPANY company engaged in making loans to individuals or businesses. Unlike a bank, it does not receive deposits but rather obtains its financing from banks, institutions, and other money market sources. Generally, finance companies fall into three categories:(1) consumer finance companies, also known as *small loan* or *direct loan companies,* lend money to individuals under the small loan laws of the individual U.S. states; (2) sales finance companies, also called *acceptance companies,* purchase retail and wholesale paper from automobile and other consumer and capital goods dealers; (3) commercial finance companies, also called *commercial credit companies,* make loans to manufacturers and wholesalers; these loans are secured by accounts receivable, inventories, and equipment. Finance companies typically enjoy high credit ratings and are thus able to borrow at the lowest market rates, enabling them to make loans at rates not much higher than banks. Even though their customers usually do not qualify for bank credit, these companies have experienced a low rate of default. Finance companies in general tend to be interest rate-sensitive—increases and decreases in market interest rates affect their profits directly. For this reason, publicly held finance companies are sometimes referred to as "money stocks." *See also* CAPTIVE FINANCE COMPANY.

FINANCIAL ACCOUNTING STANDARDS BOARD (FASB) independent board responsible for establishing and interpreting generally accepted accounting principles. It was formed in 1973 to succeed and continue the activities of the Accounting Principles Board (APB). *See* GENERALLY ACCEPTED ACCOUNTING PRINCIPLES.

FINANCIAL FUTURE FUTURES CONTRACT based on a financial instrument. Such contracts usually move under the influence of interest rates. As rates rise, contracts fall in value; as rates fall, contracts gain in value. Examples of instruments underlying financial futures contracts: Treasury bills, Treasury notes, Government National Mortgage Association (Ginnie Mae) pass-throughs, foreign currencies, and certificates of deposit. Trading in these contracts is governed by the federal Commodities Futures Trading Commission. Traders use these futures to speculate on the direction of interest rates. Financial institutions (banks, insurance companies, brokerage firms) use them to hedge financial portfolios against adverse fluctuations in interest rates.

FINANCIAL INSTITUTION institution that collects funds from the public to place in financial assets such as stocks, bonds, money market instruments, bank deposits, or loans. Depository institutions (banks, savings and loans, savings banks, credit unions) pay interest on deposits and invest the deposit money mostly in loans. Nondepository institutions (insurance companies, pension plans) collect money by selling insurance policies or receiving employer contributions and pay it out for legitimate claims or for retirement benefits. Increasingly, many institutions are performing both depository and nondepository functions. For instance, brokerage firms now place customers' money in certificates of deposit and money market funds and sell insurance. *See* FINANCIAL SUPERMARKET.

FINANCIAL INTERMEDIARY commercial bank, savings and loan, mutual savings bank, credit union, or other "middleman" that smooths the flow of funds between "savings surplus units" and "savings deficit units." In an economy viewed as three sectors—households, businesses, and government—a *savings surplus unit* is one where income exceeds consumption; a *savings deficit unit* is one where current expenditures exceed current income and external sources must be called upon to make up the difference. As a whole, households are savings surplus units, whereas businesses and governments are savings deficit units. Financial intermediaries redistribute savings into productive uses and, in the process, serve two other important functions: By making savers infinitesimally small "shareholders" in huge pools of capital, which in turn are loaned out to a wide number and variety of borrowers, the intermediaries provide both diversification of risk and liquidity to the individual saver. *See also* DISINTERMEDIATION; FINDER'S FEE.

FINANCIAL LEASE lease in which the service provided by the lessor to the lessee is limited to financing equipment. All other responsibilities related to the possession of equipment, such as maintenance, insurance, and taxes, are borne by the lessee. A financial lease is usually noncancellable and is fully paid out *(amortized)* over its term.

FINANCIAL LEVERAGE *see* LEVERAGE.

FINANCIAL MARKET market for the exchange of capital and credit in the economy. Money markets concentrate on short-term debt instruments; capital markets trade in long-term debt and equity instruments. Examples of financial markets: stock market, bond market, commodities market, and foreign exchange market.

FINANCIAL POSITION status of a firm's assets, liabilities, and equity accounts as of a certain time, as shown on its FINANCIAL STATEMENT. Also called *financial condition*.

FINANCIAL PUBLIC RELATIONS branch of public relations specializing in corporate disclosure responsibilities, stockholder relations, and relations with the professional investor community. Financial public relations is concerned not only with matters of corporate image and the cultivation of a favorable financial and investment environment but also with legal interpretation and adherence to Securities and Exchange Commission and other government regulations, as well as with the DISCLOSURE requirements of the securities exchanges. Its practitioners, therefore, include lawyers with expertise in such areas as tender offers and takeovers, public offerings, proxy solicitation, and insider trading.

FINANCIAL PYRAMID
1. risk structure many investors aim for in spreading their investments between low-, medium-, and high-risk vehicles. In a financial pyramid, the largest part

of the investor's assets is in safe, liquid investments that provide a decent return. Next, some money is invested in stocks and bonds that provide good income and the possibility for long-term growth of capital. Third, a smaller portion of one's capital is committed to speculative investments which may offer higher returns if they work out well. At the top of the financial pyramid, where only a small amount of money is committed, are high-risk ventures that have a slight chance of success, but which will provide substantial rewards if they succeed.

2. acquisition of holding company assets through financial leverage. *See* PYRAMIDING.

Financial pyramid is not to be confused with fraudulent selling schemes, also sometimes called *pyramiding*.

FINANCIAL PYRAMID

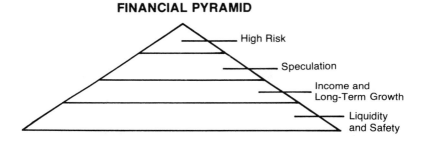

FINANCIAL STATEMENT written record of the financial status of an individual, association, or business organization. The financial statement includes a BALANCE SHEET and an INCOME STATEMENT (or operating statement or profit and loss statement) and may also include a statement of changes in working capital and net worth.

FINANCIAL STRUCTURE makeup of the right-hand side of a company's BALANCE SHEET, which includes all the ways its assets are financed, such as trade accounts payable and short-term borrowings as well as long-term debt and ownership equity. Financial structure is distinguished from CAPITAL STRUCTURE, which includes only long-term debt and equity. A company's financial structure is influenced by a number of factors, including the growth rate and stability of its sales, its competitive situation (i.e., the stability of its profits), its asset structure, and the attitudes of its management and its lenders. It is the basic frame of reference for analyses concerned with financial leveraging decisions.

FINANCIAL SUPERMARKET company that offers a wide range of financial services under one roof. For example, some large retail organizations offer stock, insurance, and real estate brokerage, as well as banking services. For customers, having all their assets with one institution can make financial transactions and planning more convenient and efficient, since money does not constantly have to be shifted from one institution to another. For institutions, such all-inclusive relationships are more profitable than dealing with just one aspect of a customer's financial needs. Institutions often become financial supermarkets in order to capture all the business of their customers.

FINDER'S FEE fee charged by a person or company acting as a finder (intermediary) in a transaction.

FINITE LIFE REAL ESTATE INVESTMENT TRUST (FREIT) REAL ESTATE INVESTMENT TRUST (REIT) that promises to try to sell its holdings within a specified period to realize CAPITAL GAINS.

FIRM

1. general term for a business, corporation, partnership, or proprietorship. Legally, a firm is not considered a corporation since it may not be incorporated and since the firm's principals are not recognized as separate from the identity of the firm itself. This might be true of a law or accounting firm, for instance.
2. solidity with which an agreement is made. For example, a firm order with a manufacturer or a firm bid for a stock at a particular price means that the order or bid is assured.

FIRM COMMITMENT

Securities Underwriting: arrangement whereby investment bankers make outright purchases from the issuer of securities to be offered to the public; also called *firm commitment underwriting.* The underwriters, as the investment bankers are called in such an arrangement, make their profit on the difference between the purchase price—determined through either competitive bidding or negotiation—and the public offering price. Firm commitment underwriting is to be distinguished from conditional arrangements for distributing new securities, such as standby commitments and best efforts commitments. The word *underwriting* is frequently misused with respect to such conditional arrangements. It is used correctly only with respect to firm commitment underwritings or, as they are sometimes called, BOUGHT DEALS. *See also* BEST EFFORT; STANDBY COMMITMENT.

Lending: term used by lenders to refer to an agreement to make a loan to a specific borrower within a specific period of time and, if applicable, on a specific property. *See also* COMMITMENT FEE.

FIRM ORDER

Commercial transaction: written or verbal order that has been confirmed and is not subject to cancellation.

Securities: (1) order to buy or sell for the proprietary account of the broker-dealer firm; (2) buy or sell order not conditional upon the customer's confirmation.

FIRM QUOTE securities industry term referring to any round lot bid or offer price of a security stated by a market maker and not identified as a nominal (or subject) quote. Under National Association of Securities Dealers' (NASD) rules and practice, quotes requiring further negotiation or review must be identified as nominal quotes. *See also* NOMINAL QUOTATION.

FIRST BOARD delivery dates for futures as established by the Chicago Board of Trade and other exchanges trading in futures.

FIRST CALL DATE first date specified in the indenture of a corporate or municipal bond contract on which part or all of the bond may be redeemed at a set price. An XYZ bond due in 2010, for instance, may have a first call date of May 1, 1993. This means that, if XYZ wishes, bondholders may be paid off starting on that date in 1993. Bond brokers typically quote yields on such bonds with both yield to maturity (in this case, 2010) and yield to call (in this case, 1993). *See also* YIELD TO CALL; YIELD TO MATURITY.

FIRST IN, FIRST OUT (FIFO) method of accounting for inventory whereby, quite literally, the inventory is assumed to be sold in the chronological order in which it was purchased. For example, the following formula is used in computing the cost of goods sold:

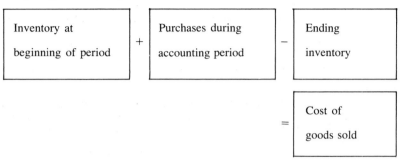

Under the FIFO method, inventory costs flow from the oldest purchases forward, with beginning inventory as the starting point and ending inventory representing the most recent purchases. The FIFO method contrasts with the LIFO or LAST IN, FIRST OUT method, which is FIFO in reverse. The significance of the difference becomes apparent when inflation or deflation affects inventory prices. In an inflationary period, the FIFO method produces a higher ending inventory, a lower cost of goods sold figure, and a higher gross profit. LIFO, on the other hand, produces a lower ending inventory, a higher cost of goods sold figure, and a lower reported profit.

In accounting for the purchase and sale of securities for tax purposes, FIFO is assumed by the IRS unless it is advised of the use of an alternative method.

FIRST MORTGAGE real estate loan that gives the mortgagee (lender) a primary lien against a specified piece of property. A primary lien has precedence over all other mortgages in case of default. *See also* JUNIOR MORTGAGE; SECOND MORTGAGE.

FIRST PREFERRED STOCK preferred stock that has preferential claim on dividends and assets over other preferred issues and common stock.

FISCAL AGENT
1. usually a bank or a trust company acting for a corporation under a corporate trust agreement. The fiscal agent handles such matters as disbursing funds for dividend payments, redeeming bonds and coupons, handling taxes related to the issue of bonds, and paying rents.
2. agent of the national government or its agencies or of a state or municipal government that performs functions relating to the issue and payment of bonds. For example, the Federal Reserve is the U.S. government's fiscal agent.

FISCAL POLICY federal taxation and spending policies designed to level out the business cycle and achieve full employment, price stability, and sustained growth in the economy. Fiscal policy basically follows the economic theory of the 20th-century English economist John Maynard Keynes that insufficient demand causes unemployment and excessive demand leads to inflation. It aims to stimulate demand and output in periods of business decline by increasing government purchases and cutting taxes, thereby releasing more disposable income into the spending stream, and to correct overexpansion by reversing the process. Working to balance these deliberate fiscal measures are the so-called built-in stabilizers, such as the progressive income tax and unemployment benefits, which automatically respond countercyclically. Fiscal policy is administered independently of MONETARY POLICY, by which the Federal Reserve Board attempts to regulate economic activity by controlling the money supply. The goals of fiscal and monetary policy are the same, but Keynesians and Monetarists disagree as to which of the two approaches works best. At the basis of their differences are questions dealing with the velocity (turnover) of money and the effect of changes in the money supply on the equilibrium rate of interest (the rate at which money demand equals money supply). *See also* KEYNESIAN ECONOMICS.

FISCAL YEAR (FY) accounting period covering 12 consecutive months, 52 consecutive weeks, 13 four-week periods, or 365 consecutive days, at the end of which the books are closed and profit or loss is determined. A company's fiscal year is often, but not necessarily, the same as the calendar year. A seasonal business will frequently select a fiscal rather than a calendar year, so that its year-end figures will show it in its most liquid condition, a choice which also has the advantage of having less inventory to verify physically. The fiscal year of the U.S. government runs from October 1 to September 30.

FIT securities industry jargon describing a situation where the features of a particular investment perfectly match the portfolio requirements of an investor.

FITCH INVESTORS SERVICE, INC. New York and Denver-based RATING firm, which rates corporate and municipal bonds, preferred stock, commercial paper, and obligations of health-care and not-for-profit institutions.

FITCH SHEETS sheets indicating the successive trade prices of securities listed on the major exchanges. They are published by Francis Emory Fitch, Inc. in New York City.

FIVE HUNDRED DOLLAR RULE REGULATION T provision of the Federal Reserve that exempts deficiencies in MARGIN requirements amounting to $500 or less from mandatory remedial action. Brokers are thus not forced to resort to the liquidation of an account to correct a trivial deficiency in a situation where, for example, a customer is temporarily out of town and cannot be reached.

FIVE PERCENT RULE one of the Rules of Fair Practice of the National Association of Securities Dealers (NASD). It proposes an ethical guideline for spreads in dealer transactions and commissions in brokerage transactions, including PROCEEDS SALES and RISKLESS TRANSACTIONS.

FIXATION setting of a present or future price of a commodity, such as the twice-daily London GOLD FIXING. In other commodities, prices are fixed further into the future for the benefit of both buyers and sellers of that commodity.

FIXED ANNUITY investment contract sold by an insurance company that guarantees fixed payments, either for life or for a specified period, to an annuitant. In fixed annuities, the insurer takes both the investment and the mortality risks. A fixed annuity contrasts with a VARIABLE ANNUITY, where payments depend on an uncertain outcome, such as prices in the securities markets. *See also* ANNUITY.

FIXED ASSET tangible property used in the operations of a business, but not expected to be consumed or converted into cash in the ordinary course of events.

Plant, machinery and equipment, furniture and fixtures, and leasehold improvements comprise the fixed assets of most companies. They are normally represented on the balance sheet at their net depreciated value.

FIXED-CHARGE COVERAGE ratio of profits before payment of interest and income taxes to interest on bonds and other contractual long-term debt. It indicates how many times interest charges have been earned by the corporation on a pretax basis. Since failure to meet interest payments would be a default under the terms of indenture agreements, the coverage ratio measures a margin of safety. The amount of safety desirable depends on the stability of a company's earnings. (Too much safety can be an indication of an undesirable lack of leverage.) In cyclical companies, the fixed-charge coverage in periods of recession is a telling ratio. Analysts also find it useful to calculate the number of times that a company's *cash flow*—i.e., *after*-tax earnings plus noncash expenses (for example, depreciation)—covers fixed charges. Also known as *times fixed charges*.

FIXED COST cost that remains constant regardless of sales volume. Fixed costs include salaries of executives, interest expense, rent, depreciation, and insurance expenses. They contrast with *variable costs* (direct labor, materials costs), which are distinguished from *semivariable costs*. Semivariable costs vary, but not necessarily in direct relation to sales. They may also remain fixed up to a level of sales, then increase when sales enter a higher range. For example, expenses associated with a delivery truck would be fixed up to the level of sales where a second truck was required. Obviously, no costs are purely fixed; the assumption, however, serves the purposes of cost accounting for limited planning periods. Cost accounting is also concerned with the allocation of portions of fixed costs to inventory costs, also called indirect costs, overhead, factory overhead, and supplemental overhead. *See also* DIRECT OVERHEAD; VARIABLE COST.

FIXED EXCHANGE RATE set rate of exchange between the currencies of countries. At the Bretton Woods international monetary conference in 1944, a system of fixed exchange rates was set up, which existed until the early 1970s, when a FLOATING EXCHANGE RATE system was adopted.

FIXED INCOME INVESTMENT security that pays a fixed rate of return. This usually refers to government, corporate, or municipal bonds, which pay a fixed rate of interest until the bonds mature, and to preferred stock, which pays a fixed dividend. Such investments are advantageous in a time of low inflation, but do not protect holders against erosion of buying power in a time of rising inflation, since the bondholder or preferred shareholder gets the same amount of interest or dividends, even though consumer goods cost more.

FIXED PRICE

Investment: in a public offering of new securities, price at which investment bankers in the underwriting SYNDICATE agree to sell the issue to the public. The price remains fixed as long as the syndicate remains in effect. The proper term for this kind of system is *fixed price offering system*. In contrast, Eurobonds, which are also sold through underwriting syndicates, are offered on a basis that permits discrimination among customers; i.e., the underwriting spread may be adjusted to suit the particular buyer. *See also* EUROBOND.

Contracts: type of contract where the price is preset and invariable, regardless of the actual costs of production. *See also* COST-PLUS CONTRACT.

FIXED RATE (LOAN) type of loan in which the interest rate does not fluctuate with general market conditions. There are fixed rate mortgage (also known as conventional mortgage) and consumer installment loans, as well as fixed rate business loans. Fixed rate loans tend to have higher original interest rates than flexible rate loans such as an ADJUSTABLE RATE MORTGAGE (ARM), because lenders are not protected against a rise in the cost of money when they make a fixed rate loan.

The term fixed rate may also refer to fixed currency exchange rates. *See* FIXED EXCHANGE RATE.

FIXED TRUST UNIT INVESTMENT TRUST that has a fixed portfolio of previously agreed upon securities; also called *fixed investment trust*. The securities are usually of one type, such as corporate, government, or municipal bonds, in order to afford a regular income to holders of units. A fixed trust is distinguished from a PARTICIPATING TRUST.

FIXTURE attachment to real property that is not intended to be moved and would create damage to the property if it were moved—for example, a plumbing fixture. Fixtures are classified as part of real estate when they share the same useful life. Otherwise, they are considered equipment.

FLAG technical chart pattern resembling a flag shaped like a parallelogram with masts on either side, showing a consolidation within a trend. It results from price fluctuations within a narrow range, both preceded and followed by sharp rises or declines. If the flag—the consolidation period—is preceded by a rise, it will usually be followed by a rise; a fall will follow a fall.

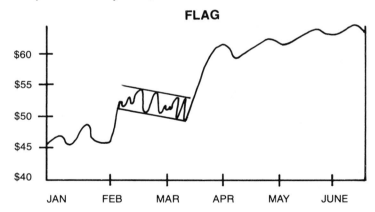

FLASH tape display designation used when volume on an exchange is so heavy that the tape runs more than five minutes behind. The flash interrupts the display to report the current price—called the *flash price*—of a heavily traded security. Current prices of two groups of 50 stocks are flashed at five-minute intervals as long as the tape is seriously behind.

FLAT
  1. in bond trading, without accrued interest. This means that accrued interest will be received by the buyer if and when paid but that no accrued interest is payable to the seller. Issues in default and INCOME BONDS are normally quoted and traded flat. The opposite of a flat bond is an AND INTEREST bond. *See also* LOANED FLAT.

2. inventory of a market maker with a net zero position—i.e., neither long nor short.

3. position of an underwriter whose account is completely sold.

FLAT MARKET market characterized by HORIZONTAL PRICE MOVEMENT. It is usually the result of low activity. However, STABILIZATION, consolidation, and DISTRIBUTION are situations marked by both horizontal price movement and active trading.

FLAT SCALE

Industry: labor term denoting a uniform rate of pay that makes no allowance for volume, frequency, or other factors.

Municipal bonds: bond trader's term describing a situation where shorter and longer term yields show little difference over the maturity range of a new serial bond issue.

FLAT TAX tax applied at the same rate to all levels of income. It is often discussed as an alternative to the PROGRESSIVE TAX. Proponents of a flat tax argue that people able to retain larger portions of higher income would have added incentive to earn, thus stimulating the economy. Advocates also note its simplicity. Opponents argue it is a REGRESSIVE TAX in effect, comparing it to the sales tax, a uniform tax that puts a greater burden on households with lower incomes. The TAX REFORM ACT OF 1986 instituted a *modified flat tax system*—a progressive tax with fewer tax brackets and lower rates.

FLEXIBLE BUDGET statement of projected revenue and expenditure based on various levels of production. It shows how costs vary with different rates of output or at different levels of sales volume.

FLEXIBLE EXCHANGE RATE *see* FLOATING EXCHANGE RATE.

FLIGHT OF CAPITAL *see* CAPITAL FLIGHT.

FLIGHT TO QUALITY moving capital to the safest possible investment to protect oneself from loss during an unsettling period in the market. For example, when a major bank fails, cautious money market investors may buy only government-backed money market securities instead of those issued by major banks. A flight to quality can be measured by the differing yields resulting from such a movement of capital. In the example just given, the yields on bank-issued money market paper will rise since there will be less demand for it, and the rates on government securities will fall, because there will be more demand for them.

FLOAT

Banking: time between the deposit of a check in a bank and payment. Long floats are to the advantage of checkwriters, whose money may earn interest until a check clears. They are to the disadvantage of depositors, who must wait for a check to clear before they have access to the funds. As a rule, the further away the paying bank is from the deposit bank, the longer it will take for a check to clear. Some U.S. states limit the amount of float a bank can impose on the checks of its depositors. *See also* UNCOLLECTED FUNDS.

Investments: number of shares of a corporation that are outstanding and available for trading by the public. A small float means the stock will be more volatile, since a large order to buy or sell shares can influence the stock's price dramatically. A larger float means the stock will be less volatile.

FLOATER debt instrument with a variable interest rate tied to another interest rate—for example, the rate paid by Treasury bills. A FLOATING RATE NOTE, for instance, provides a holder with additional interest if the applicable interest rate rises and less interest if the rate falls. It is generally best to buy floaters if it appears that interest rates will rise. If the outlook is for falling rates, investors typically concentrate on fixed-rate instruments. Floaters spread risk between issuers and debtholders.

FLOATING AN ISSUE *see* NEW ISSUE; UNDERWRITE.

FLOATING DEBT continuously renewed or refinanced short-term debt of companies or governments used to finance ongoing operating needs.

FLOATING EXCHANGE RATE movement of a foreign currency exchange rate in response to changes in the market forces of supply and demand; also known as *flexible exchange rate*. Currencies strengthen or weaken based on a nation's reserves of hard currency and gold, its international trade balance, its rate of inflation and interest rates, and the general strength of its economy. Nations generally do not want their currency to be too strong, because this makes the country's goods too expensive for foreigners to buy. A weak currency, on the other hand, may signify economic instability if it has been caused by high inflation or a weak economy. The opposite of the floating exchange rate is the FIXED EXCHANGE RATE system. *See also* PAR VALUE OF CURRENCY.

FLOATING RATE NOTE debt instrument with a variable interest rate. Interest adjustments are made periodically, often every six months, and are tied to a money-market index such as Treasury bill rates. Floating rate notes usually have a maturity of about five years. They provide holders with protection against rises in interest rates, but pay lower yields than fixed rate notes of the same maturity. Also known as a FLOATER.

FLOATING SECURITIES
1. securities bought for the purpose of making a quick profit on resale and held in a broker's name.
2. outstanding stock of a corporation that is traded on an exchange.
3. unsold units of a newly issued security.

FLOATING SUPPLY

Bonds: total dollar amount of municipal bonds in the hands of speculators and dealers that is for sale at any particular time as offered in the BLUE LIST. Someone might say, for instance, "There is $10 billion in floating supply available now in the municipal bond market."

Stocks: number of shares of a stock available for purchase. A dealer might say, "The floating supply in this stock is about 200,000 shares." Sometimes called simply the *float*.

FLOOR BROKER member of an exchange who is an employee of a member firm and executes orders, as agent, on the floor of the exchange for clients. The floor broker receives an order via teletype machine from his firm's trading department, then proceeds to the appropriate trading post on the exchange floor. There he joins other brokers and the specialist in the security being bought or sold, and executes the trade at the best competitive price available. On completion of the transaction, the customer is notified through his registered representative back at the firm, and the trade is printed on the consolidated ticker tape, which is displayed electronically around the country. A floor broker should not be confused with a FLOOR TRADER, who trades as a principal for his or her own account, rather than as a broker.

FLOOR OFFICIAL securities exchange employee, who is present on the floor of the exchange to settle disputes in the auction procedure, such as questions about priority or precedence in the settling of an auction. The floor official makes rulings on the spot and his or her judgment is usually accepted.

FLOOR TICKET summary of the information entered on the ORDER TICKET by the registered representative on receipt of a buy or sell order from a client. The floor ticket gives the floor broker the information needed to execute a securities transaction. The information required on floor tickets is specified by securities industry rules.

FLOOR TRADER member of a stock or commodities exchange who trades on the floor of that exchange for his or her own account. The floor trader must abide by trading rules similar to those of the exchange specialists who trade on behalf of others. The term should not be confused with FLOOR BROKER. *See also* REGISTERED COMPETITIVE TRADER.

FLOTATION (FLOATATION) COST cost of issuing new stocks or bonds. It varies with the amount of underwriting risk and the job of physical distribution. It comprises two elements: (1) the compensation earned by the investment bankers (the underwriters) in the form of the spread between the price paid to the issuer (the corporation or government agency) and the offering price to the public, and (2) the expenses of the issuer (legal, accounting, printing, and other out-of-pocket expenses). Securities and Exchange Commission studies reveal that flotation costs are higher for stocks than for bonds, reflecting the generally wider distribution and greater volatility of common stock as opposed to bonds, which are usually sold in large blocks to relatively few investors. The SEC also found that flotation costs as a percentage of gross proceeds are greater for smaller issues than for larger ones. This occurs because the issuer's legal and other expenses tend to be relatively large and fixed; also, smaller issues tend to originate with less estab-lished issuers, requiring more information development and marketing expense. An issue involving a RIGHTS OFFERING can involve negligible underwriting risk and selling effort and therefore minimal flotation cost, especially if the under-pricing is substantial.

The UNDERWRITING SPREAD is the key variable in flotation cost, historically ranging from 23.7% of the size of a small issue of common stock to as low as 1.25% of the par value of high-grade bonds. Spreads are determined by both negotiation and competitive bidding.

FLOWER BOND type of U.S. government bond that, regardless of its cost price, is acceptable at par value in payment of estate taxes if the decedent was the legal holder at the time of death; also called *estate tax anticipation bond*. Flower bonds were issued as recently as 1971, and the last of them, with a 3½% coupon, will mature in 1998.

FLOW OF FUNDS

Economics: in referring to the national economy, the way funds are transferred from savings surplus units to savings deficit units through financial intermediaries. *See also* FINANCIAL INTERMEDIARY.

Municipal bonds: statement found in the bond resolutions of municipal revenue issues showing the priorities by which municipal revenue will be applied. Typically, the flow of funds in decreasing order of priority is operation and maintenance, bond debt service, expansion of the facility, and sinking fund for retirement of debt prior to maturity. The flow of funds statement varies in detail from issue to issue.

FLUCTUATION

1. change in prices or interest rates, either up or down. Fluctuation may refer to either slight or dramatic changes in the prices of stocks, bonds, or commodities. *See also* FLUCTUATION LIMIT.
2. the ups and downs in the economy.

FLUCTUATION LIMIT limits placed on the daily ups and downs of futures prices by the commodity exchanges. The limit protects traders from losing too much on a particular contract in one day. If a commodity reaches its limit, it may not trade any further that day. *See also* LIMIT UP, LIMIT DOWN.

FNMA *see* FEDERAL NATIONAL MORTGAGE ASSOCIATION.

FOB *see* FREE ON BOARD.

FOCUS REPORT FOCUS is an acronym for the Financial and Operational Combined Uniform Single report, which broker-dealers are required to file monthly and quarterly with self-regulatory organizations (SROs). The SROs include exchanges, securities associations, and clearing organizations registered with the Securities and Exchange Commission and required by federal securities laws to be self-policing. The FOCUS report contains figures on capital, earnings, trade flow, and other required details.

FORBES 500 annual listing by *Forbes* magazine of the largest U.S. publicly owned corporations ranked four ways: by sales, assets, profits, and market value. *See also* FORTUNE 500.

FORCED CONVERSION when a CONVERTIBLE security is called in by its issuer. Convertible owners may find it to their financial advantage either to sell or to convert their holdings into common shares of the underlying company or to accept the call price. Such a conversion usually takes place when the convertible is selling above its CALL PRICE because the market value of the shares of the underlying stock has risen sharply. *See also* CONVERTIBLE.

FORECASTING projecting current trends using existing data.

Stock market forecasters predict the direction of the stock market by relying on technical data of trading activity and fundamental statistics on the direction of the economy.

Economic forecasters foretell the strength of the economy, often by utilizing complex econometric models as a tool to make specific predictions of future levels of inflation, interest rates, and employment. *See also* ECONOMETRICS.

Forecasting can also refer to various PROJECTIONS used in business and financial planning.

FORECLOSURE process by which a homeowner who has not made timely payments of principal and interest on a mortgage loses title to the home. The holder of the mortgage, whether it be a bank, a savings and loan, or an individual, must go to court to seize the property, which may then be sold to satisfy the claims of the mortgage.

FOREIGN CORPORATION
1. corporation chartered under the laws of a state other than the one in which it conducts business. Because of inevitable confusion with the term ALIEN CORPORATION, *out-of-state corporation* is preferred.
2. corporation organized under the laws of a foreign country; the term ALIEN CORPORATION is usually preferred.

FOREIGN CROWD New York Stock Exchange members who trade on the floor in foreign bonds.

FOREIGN DIRECT INVESTMENT
1. investment in U.S. businesses by foreign citizens; usually involves majority stock ownership of the enterprise.
2. joint ventures between foreign and U.S. companies.

FOREIGN EXCHANGE instruments employed in making payments between countries—paper currency, notes, checks, bills of exchange, and electronic notifications of international debits and credits.

FORM 3 form filed with the Securities and Exchange Commission and the pertinent stock exchange by all holders of 10% or more of the stock of a company registered with the SEC and by all directors and officers, even if no shares are owned. Form 3 details the number of shares owned as well as the number of warrants, rights, convertible bonds, and options to purchase common stock. Individuals required to file Form 3 are considered insiders, and they are required to update their information whenever changes occur. Such changes are reported on FORM 4.

FORM 4 document, filed with the Securities and Exchange Commission and the pertinent stock exchange, which is used to report changes in the holdings of (1) those who own at least 10% of a corporation's outstanding stock and (2) directors and officers, even if they own no stock. When there has been a major change in ownership, Form 4 must be filed within ten days of the end of the month in which the change took place. Form 4 filings must be constantly updated during a takeover attempt of a company when the acquirer buys more than 10% of the outstanding shares.

FORM 8-K Securities and Exchange Commission required form that a publicly held company must file, reporting on any material event that might affect its financial situation or the value of its shares, ranging from merger activity to amendment of the corporate charter or bylaws. The SEC considers as material all matters about which an average, prudent investor ought reasonably to be informed before deciding whether to buy, sell, or hold a registered security. Form 8-K must be filed within a month of the occurrence of the material event. Timely disclosure rules may require a corporation to issue a press release immediately concerning an event subsequently reported on Form 8-K.

FORM 10-K annual report required by the Securities and Exchange Commission of every issuer of a registered security, every exchange-listed company, and any company with 500 or more shareholders or $1 million or more in gross assets. The form provides for disclosure of total sales, revenue, and pretax operating income, as well as sales by separate classes of products for each of a company's separate lines of business for each of the past five years. A source and application of funds statement presented on a comparative basis for the last two fiscal years is also required. Form 10-K becomes public information when filed with the SEC.

FORM 10-Q quarterly report required by the Securities and Exchange Commission of companies with listed securities. Form 10-Q is less comprehensive than the FORM 10-K annual report and does not require that figures be audited. It may cover the specific quarter or it may be cumulative. It should include comparative figures for the same period of the previous year.

FORMULA INVESTING investment technique based on a predetermined timing or asset allocation model that eliminates emotional decisions. One type of formula investing, called dollar cost averaging, involves putting the same amount of money into a stock or mutual fund at regular intervals, so that more shares will be bought when the price is low and less when the price is high. Another formula investing method calls for shifting funds from stocks to bonds or vice versa as the stock market reaches particular price levels. If stocks rise to a particular point, a certain amount of the stock portfolio is sold and put in bonds. On the other hand, if stocks fall to a particular low price, money is brought out of bonds into stocks. *See also* CONSTANT DOLLAR PLAN.

FORTUNE 500 annual listing by *Fortune* magazine of the 500 largest U.S. industrial (manufacturing) corporations, ranked by sales. The magazine also ranks the assets, net income, stockholders' equity, number of employees, net income as a percent of sales or of stockholders' equity, earnings per share, and total return to investors.

Fortune publishes another annual directory—the Fortune Service 500—which ranks the 500 largest nonmanufacturing U.S. companies by sales or revenue and by the other criteria used in the Fortune 500 directory. These nonindustrial companies are divided into seven categories: diversified service (housing, health care, etc.), commercial banking, diversified financial (S&Ls, Student Loan Marketing Association, etc.), life insurance, retailing, transportation, and utilities. *See also* FORBES 500.

FORWARD CONTRACT purchase or sale of a specific quantity of a commodity, government security, foreign currency, or other financial instrument at the current or SPOT PRICE, with delivery and settlement at a specified future date. Because it is a completed contract—as opposed to an options contract, where the owner has the choice of completing or not completing—a forward contract can be a COVER for the sale of a FUTURES CONTRACT. *See* HEDGE.

FORWARD EXCHANGE TRANSACTION purchase or sale of foreign currency at an exchange rate established now but with payment and delivery at a specified future time. Most forward exchange contracts have one-, three-, or six-month maturities, though contracts in major currencies can normally be arranged for delivery at any specified date up to a year, and sometimes up to three years.

FORWARD PRICING Securities and Exchange Commission requirement that open-end investment companies, whose share price is always determined by the NET ASSET VALUE of the outstanding shares, base all incoming buy and sell orders on the next net asset valuation of fund shares. *See also* INVESTMENT COMPANY.

FOR YOUR INFORMATION (FYI) prefix to a security price quote by a market maker that indicates the quote is ''for your information'' and is not a firm offer to trade at that price. FYI quotes are given as a courtesy for purposes of valuation. FVO (for valuation only) is sometimes used instead.

401(K) PLAN also called *cash or deferred arrangement* (CODA) or SALARY REDUCTION PLAN, plan whereby an employee may elect, as an alternative to receiving taxable cash in the form of compensation or a bonus, to contribute pre-tax dollars to a qualified tax-deferred retirement plan. Effective in 1987, elective deferrals are limited to $7000 (previously $30,000), although employers may continue to contribute the smaller of 25% of compensation or $30,000, less the amount of salary deferral. Withdrawals from 401(K) plans prior to age 59½ are subject to a 10% penalty tax except for death, disability, termination of employment, or qualifying hardship. "Highly compensated" employees are subject to special limitations.

FOURTH MARKET direct trading of large blocks of securities between institutional investors to save brokerage commissions. The fourth market is aided by computers, notably by a computerized subscriber service called *INSTINET,* an acronym for Institutional Networks Corporation. INSTINET is registered with the Securities and Exchange Commission as a stock exchange and numbers among its subscribers a large number of mutual funds and other institutional investors linked to each other by computer terminals. The system permits subscribers to display tentative volume interest and bid-ask quotes to others in the system.

FRACTIONAL DISCRETION ORDER buy or sell order for securities that allows the broker discretion within a specified fraction of a point. For example, "Buy 1000 XYZ at 28, discretion ½ point" means that the broker may execute the trade at a maximum price of 28½.

FRACTIONAL SHARE unit of stock less than one full share. For instance, if a shareholder is in a dividend reinvestment program, and the dividends being reinvested are not adequate to buy a full share at the stock's current price, the shareholder will be credited with a fractional share until enough dividends have been accumulated to purchase a full share.

FRANCHISE

In general: (1) privilege given a dealer by a manufacturer or franchise service organization to sell the franchisor's products or services in a given area, with or without exclusivity. Such arrangements are sometimes formalized in a *franchise agreement,* which is a contract between the franchisor and franchisee wherein the former may offer consultation, promotional assistance, financing, and other benefits in exchange for a percentage of sales or profits. (2) The business owned by the franchisee, who usually must meet an initial cash investment requirement.

Government: legal right given to a company or individual by a government authority permitting the performance of some economic function. For example, an electrical utility might have the right, under the terms of a franchise, to use city property to provide electrical service to city residents.

FRANCHISE TAX state tax, usually regressive (that is, the rate decreases as the tax base increases), imposed on a state-chartered corporation for the right to do business under its corporate name. Franchise taxes are usually levied on a number of value bases, such as capital stock, capital stock plus surplus, or profits.

FRAUD intentional misrepresentation, concealment, or omission of the truth for the purpose of deception or manipulation to the detriment of a person or an organization. Fraud is a legal concept and the application of the term in a specific instance should be determined by a legal expert.

FREDDIE MAC
   1. nickname for FEDERAL HOME LOAN MORTGAGE CORPORATION (FHLMC).

2. mortgage-backed securities, issued in minimum denominations of $25,000, that are packaged, guaranteed, and sold by the FHLMC. Mortgage-backed securities are issues in which residential mortgages are packaged and sold to investors.

FREE AND OPEN MARKET market in which price is determined by the free, unregulated interchange of supply and demand. The opposite is a *controlled market,* where supply, demand, and price are artificially set, resulting in an *inefficient market.*

FREE BOX securities industry jargon for a secure storage place (''box'') for fully paid (''free'') customers' securities, such as a bank vault or the DEPOSITORY TRUST COMPANY.

FREED UP securities industry jargon meaning that the members of an underwriting syndicate are no longer bound by the price agreed upon and fixed in the AGREEMENT AMONG UNDERWRITERS. They are thus free to trade in the security on a market basis.

FREE ON BOARD (FOB) transportation term meaning that the invoice price includes delivery at the seller's expense to a specified point and no further. For example, ''FOB our Newark warehouse'' means that the buyer must pay all shipping and other charges associated with transporting the merchandise from the seller's warehouse in Newark to the buyer's receiving point. Title normally passes from seller to buyer at the FOB point by way of a bill of lading.

FREERIDING
1. practice, prohibited by the Securities and Exchange Commission and the National Association of Securities Dealers, whereby an underwriting SYNDICATE member withholds a portion of a new securities issue and later resells it at a price higher than the initial offering price.
2. practice whereby a brokerage client buys and sells a security in rapid order without putting up money for the purchase. The practice violates REGULATION T of the Federal Reserve Board concerning broker-dealer credit to customers. The penalty requires that the customer's account be frozen for 90 days. *See also* FROZEN ACCOUNT.

FREE RIGHT OF EXCHANGE ability to transfer securities from one name to another without paying the charge associated with a sales transaction. The free right applies, for example, where stock in STREET NAME (that is, registered in the name of a broker-dealer) is transferred to the customer's name in order to be eligible for a dividend reinvestment plan. *See also* REGISTERED SECURITY.

FRONT-END LOAD sales charge applied to an investment at the time of initial purchase. There may be a front-end load on a mutual fund, for instance, which is sold by a broker. Annuities, life insurance policies, and limited partnerships can also have front-end loads. From the investor's point of view, the earnings from the investment should make up for this up-front fee within a relatively short period of time. *See also* INVESTMENT COMPANY.

FRONT RUNNING securities industry jargon referring to a practice whereby a trader with advance knowledge of a BLOCK transaction that will influence the price of a security enters into OPTION transactions to capitalize on the trade.

FROZEN ACCOUNT

Banking: bank account from which funds may not be withdrawn until a lien is satisfied and a court order is received freeing the balance.

A bank account may also be frozen by court order in a dispute over the ownership of property.

Investments: brokerage account under disciplinary action by the Federal Reserve Board for violation of REGULATION T. During the period an account is frozen (90 days), the customer may not sell securities until their purchase price has been fully paid and the certificates have been delivered. The penalty is invoked commonly in cases of FREERIDING.

FULL COUPON BOND bond with a coupon rate that is near or above current market interest rates. If interest rates are generally about 10%, for instance, a 9½% or 11% bond is considered a full coupon bond.

FULL DISCLOSURE

In general: requirement to disclose all material facts relevant to a transaction.

Securities industry: public information requirements established by the Securities Act of 1933, the Securities Exchange Act of 1934, and the major stock exchanges.

See also DISCLOSURE.

FULL FAITH AND CREDIT phrase meaning that the full taxing and borrowing power, *plus* revenue other than taxes, is pledged in payment of interest and repayment of principal of a bond issued by a government entity. U.S. government securities and general obligation bonds of states and local governments are backed by this pledge.

FULL-SERVICE BROKER broker who provides a wide range of services to clients. Unlike a DISCOUNT BROKER, who just executes trades, a full-service broker offers advice on which stocks, bonds, commodities, and mutual funds to buy or sell. A full-service broker may also offer an ASSET MANAGEMENT ACCOUNT; advice on financial planning, tax shelters, and INCOME LIMITED PARTNERSHIPS; and new issues of stock. A full-service broker's commissions will be higher than those of a discount broker. The term *brokerage* is gradually being replaced by variations of the term *financial services* as the range of services offered by brokers expands.

FULLY DILUTED EARNINGS PER (COMMON) SHARE figure showing earnings per common share after assuming the exercise of warrants and stock options, and the conversion of convertible bonds and preferred stock (all potentially *dilutive* securities). Actually, it is more analytically correct to define the term as the smallest earnings per common share figure that can be obtained by computing earnings per share (EPS) for all possible combinations of assumed exercise or conversion (because antidilutive securities—securities whose conversion would add to EPS—may not be assumed to be exercised or converted). Fully diluted EPS must be reported on the profit and loss statement when the figure is 97% or less of earnings available to common shareholders divided by the average number of common shares outstanding during the period. *See also* DILUTION; PRIMARY EARNINGS PER (COMMON) SHARE.

FULLY DISTRIBUTED term describing a new securities issue that has been completely resold to the investing public (that is, to institutions and individuals and other investors rather than to dealers).

FULLY VALUED said of a stock that has reached a price at which analysts think the underlying company's fundamental earnings power has been recognized by the market. If the stock goes up from that price, it is called OVERVALUED. If the stock goes down, it is termed UNDERVALUED.

FUNDAMENTAL ANALYSIS

Economics: research of such factors as interest rates, gross national product, inflation, unemployment, and inventories as tools to predict the direction of the economy.

Investment: analysis of the balance sheet and income statements of companies in order to forecast their future stock price movements. Fundamental analysts consider past records of assets, earnings, sales, products, management, and markets in predicting future trends in these indicators of a company's success or failure. By appraising a firm's prospects, these analysts assess whether a particular stock or group of stocks is UNDERVALUED or OVERVALUED at the current market price. The other major school of stock market analysis is TECHNICAL ANALYSIS, which relies on price and volume movements of stocks and does not concern itself with financial statistics.

FUNDED DEBT

1. debt that is due after one year and is formalized by the issuing of bonds or long-term notes.
2. bond issue whose retirement is provided for by a SINKING FUND.
   See also FLOATING DEBT.

FUNDING

1. refinancing a debt on or before its maturity; also called REFUNDING and, in certain instances, PREREFUNDING.
2. putting money into investments or another type of reserve fund, to provide for future pension or welfare plans.
3. in corporate finance, the word *funding* is preferred to *financing* when referring to bonds in contrast to stock. A company is said to be funding its operations if it floats bonds.
4. to provide funds to finance a project, such as a research study.
   See also SINKING FUND.

FUNGIBLES bearer instruments, securities, or goods that are equivalent, substitutable, and interchangeable. Commodities such as soybeans or wheat, common shares of the same company, and dollar bills are all familiar examples of fungibles.

Fungibility (interchangeability) of listed options, by virtue of their common expiration dates and strike prices, makes it possible for buyers and sellers to close out their positions by putting offsetting transactions through the OPTIONS CLEARING CORPORATION. *See also* OFFSET; STRIKE PRICE.

FURTHEST MONTH in commodities or options trading, the month that is furthest away from settlement of the contract. For example, Treasury bill futures may have outstanding contracts for three, six, or nine months. The six- and nine-month contracts would be the furthest months, and the three-month contract would be the NEAREST MONTH.

FUTURES CONTRACT agreement to buy or sell a specific amount of a commodity or financial instrument at a particular price in a stipulated future month. The price is established between buyer and seller on the floor of a commodity exchange, using the OPEN OUTCRY system. A futures contract obligates the buyer to purchase the underlying commodity and the seller to sell it, unless the contract is sold to another before settlement date, which may happen if a trader waits to take a profit or cut a loss. This contrasts with options trading, in which the option buyer may choose whether or not to exercise the option by the exercise date. *See also* FORWARD CONTRACT; FUTURES MARKET.

FUTURES MARKET commodity exchange where FUTURES CONTRACTS are traded. Different exchanges specialize in particular kinds of contracts. The major exchanges are Amex Commodity Exchange, the Commodity Exchange Inc. (Comex), the New York Coffee, Sugar and Cocoa Exchange, the New York Cotton Exchange, the New York Mercantile Exchange, and the New York Futures Exchange, all in New York; the Chicago Board of Trade, the International Monetary Market, the Chicago Mercantile Exchange, the Chicago Rice and Cotton Exchange, and the MidAmerica Commodity Exchange, all in Chicago; the Kansas City Board of Trade, in Kansas City, MO; and the Minneapolis Grain Exchange, in Minneapolis. *See also* SPOT MARKET.

FUTURES OPTION OPTION on a FUTURES CONTRACT.

FVO (FOR VALUATION ONLY) *see* FOR YOUR INFORMATION.

g

GAP

Finance: amount of a financing need for which provision has yet to be made. For example, ABC company might need $1.5 million to purchase and equip a new plant facility. It arranges a mortgage loan of $700,000, secures equipment financing of $400,000, and obtains new equity of $150,000. That leaves a gap of $250,000 for which it seeks gap financing. Such financing may be available from state and local governments concerned with promoting economic development.

Securities: securities industry term used to describe the price movement of a stock or commodity when one day's trading range for the stock or commodity

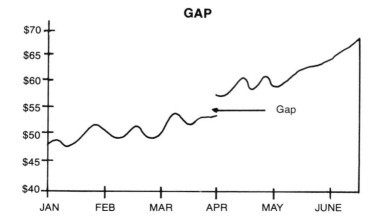

GAP

does not overlap the next day's, causing a range, or gap, in which no trade has occurred. This usually takes place because of some extraordinary positive or negative news about the company or commodity. *See also* PRICE GAP.

GARAGE annex floor on the north side of the main trading floor of the New York Stock Exchange.

GARNISHMENT court order to an employer to withhold all or part of an employee's wages and send the money to the court or to a person who has won a lawsuit against the employee. An employee's wages will be *garnished* until the court-ordered debt is paid. Garnishing may be used in a divorce settlement or for repayment of creditors.

GATHER IN THE STOPS stock-trading tactic that involves selling a sufficient amount of stock to drive down the price to a point where stop orders (orders to buy or sell at a given price) are known to exist. The stop orders are then activated to become market orders (orders to buy or sell at the best available price), in turn creating movement which touches off other stop orders in a process called SNOWBALLING. Because this can cause sharp trading swings, floor officials on the exchanges have the authority to suspend stop orders in individual securities if that seems advisable. *See also* STOP ORDER.

GENERAL ACCOUNT Federal Reserve Board term for brokerage customer margin accounts subject to REGULATION T, which covers extensions of credit by brokers for the purchase and short sale of securities. The Fed requires that all transactions in which the broker advances credit to the customer be made in this account. *See also* MARGIN ACCOUNT.

GENERAL LEDGER formal ledger containing all the financial statement accounts of a business. It contains offsetting debit and credit accounts, the totals of which are proved by a trial balance. Certain accounts in the general ledger, termed *control accounts,* summarize the detail booked on separate subsidiary ledgers.

GENERAL LIEN LIEN against an individual that excludes real property. The lien carries the right to seize personal property to satisfy a debt. The property seized need not be the property that gave rise to the debt.

GENERAL LOAN AND COLLATERAL AGREEMENT continuous agreement under which a securities broker-dealer borrows from a bank against listed securities to buy or carry inventory, finance the underwriting of new issues, or carry the margin accounts of clients. Synonymous with *broker's loan. See also* BROKER LOAN RATE; MARGIN ACCOUNT; UNDERWRITE.

GENERALLY ACCEPTED ACCOUNTING PRINCIPLES (GAAP) conventions, rules, and procedures that define accepted accounting practice, including broad guidelines as well as detailed procedures. The basic doctrine was set forth by the Accounting Principles Board of the American Institute of Certified Public Accountants, which was superseded in 1973 by the FINANCIAL ACCOUNTING STANDARDS BOARD (FASB), an independent self-regulatory organization.

GENERAL MORTGAGE mortgage covering all the mortgageable properties of a borrower and not restricted to any particular piece of property. Such a blanket mortgage can be lower in priority of claim in liquidation than one or more other mortgages on specific parcels.

GENERAL OBLIGATION BOND municipal bond backed by the FULL FAITH AND

CREDIT (which includes the taxing and further borrowing power) of a municipality. A *GO bond,* as it is known, is repaid with general revenue and borrowings, in contrast to the revenue from a specific facility built with the borrowed funds, such as a tunnel or a sewer system. *See also* REVENUE BOND.

GENERAL PARTNER
1. one of two or more partners who are jointly and severally responsible for the debts of a partnership.
2. managing partner of a LIMITED PARTNERSHIP, who is responsible for the operations of the partnership and, ultimately, any debts taken on by the partnership. The general partner's liability is unlimited. In a real estate partnership, the general partner will pick the properties to be bought and will manage them. In an oil and gas partnership, the general partner will select drilling sites and oversee drilling activity. In return for these services, the general partner collects certain fees and often retains a percentage of ownership in the partnership.

GENERAL REVENUE when used in reference to state and local governments taken separately, the term refers to total revenue less revenue from utilities, sales of alcoholic beverages, and insurance trusts. When speaking of combined state and local total revenue, the term refers only to taxes, charges, and miscellaneous revenue, which avoids the distortion of overlapping intergovernmental revenue.

GENERAL REVENUE SHARING unrestricted funds (usable for any purpose) provided by the federal government to the 50 states and to more than 38,000 cities, towns, counties, townships, Indian tribes, and Alaskan native villages under the State and Local Fiscal Assistance Act of 1972. It is set to expire in 1987.

GIFT TAX graduated tax, levied on the donor of a gift by the federal government and most state governments when assets are passed from one person to another. The more money that is given as a gift, the higher the tax rate. The Economic Recovery Tax Act of 1981 allowed a $10,000 federal gift tax exemption per recipient. This means that $10,000 a year can be given free of gift tax to one person ($20,000 to a married couple). The gift tax is computed on the dollar value of the asset being transferred above the $10,000 exemption level. Gifts between spouses are not subject to gift tax. Many states match the $10,000 gift tax exemption, but some allow a smaller amount to be gifted free of tax.

GILT-EDGED SECURITY stock or bond of a company that has demonstrated over a number of years that it is capable of earning sufficient profits to cover dividends on stocks and interest on bonds with great dependability. The term is used with corporate bonds more often than with stocks, where the term BLUE CHIP is more common.

GINNIE MAE nickname for the GOVERNMENT NATIONAL MORTGAGE ASSOCIATION and the certificate issued by that agency. *See also* GINNIE MAE PASS-THROUGH.

GINNIE MAE PASS-THROUGH security backed by a pool of mortgages and guaranteed by the GOVERNMENT NATIONAL MORTGAGE ASSOCIATION (Ginnie Mae), which passes through to investors the interest and principal payments of homeowners. Homeowners make their mortgage payments to the bank or savings and loan that originated their mortgage. After a service charge, usually ½%, the bank forwards the mortgage payments to the pass-through buyers, who may be institutional investors or individuals. Ginnie Mae guarantees that investors will receive timely principal and interest payments even if homeowners do not make mortgage payments on time.

The introduction of Ginnie Mae pass-throughs has benefited the home mortgage market, since more capital has become available for lending. Investors, who are able to receive high, government-guaranteed interest payments, have also benefited. For investors, however, the rate of principal repayment on a Ginnie Mae pass-through is uncertain. If interest rates fall, principal will be repaid faster, since homeowners will refinance their mortgages. If rates rise, principal will be repaid more slowly, since homeowners will hold onto the underlying mortgages. *See also* HALF-LIFE.

GIVE UP
1. term used in a securities transaction involving three brokers, as illustrated by the following scenario: Broker A, a FLOOR BROKER, executes a buy order for Broker B, another member firm broker who has too much business at the time to execute the order. The broker with whom Broker A completes the transaction (the sell side broker) is Broker C. Broker A "gives up" the name of Broker B, so that the record shows a transaction between Broker B and Broker Ceven though the trade was actually executed between Broker A and Broker C.
2. another application of the term: A customer of brokerage firm ABC Co. travels out of town and, finding no branch office of ABC, places an order with DEF Co., saying he is an account of ABC. After confirming the account relationship, DEF completes a trade with GHI Co., advising GHI that DEF is acting for ABC ("giving up" ABC's name). ABC will then handle the clearing details of the transaction with GHI. Alternatively, DEF may simply send the customer's order directly to ABC for execution. Whichever method is used, the customer pays only one commission.

GLAMOR STOCK stock with a wide public and institutional following. Glamor stocks achieve this following by producing steadily rising sales and earnings over a long period of time. In bull (rising) markets, glamor stocks tend to rise faster than market averages. Although a glamor stock is often in the category of a BLUE CHIP stock, the glamor is characterized by a higher earnings growth rate.

GLASS-STEAGALL ACT OF 1933 legislation passed by Congress authorizing deposit insurance and prohibiting commercial banks from owning brokerage firms. Under Glass-Steagall, these banks may not engage in investment banking activities, such as underwriting corporate securities or municipal revenue bonds. The law was designed to insulate bank depositors from the risk involved when a bank dealt in securities and to prevent a banking collapse like the one that occurred in the Great Depression. In the mid-1980s banks challenged the Glass-Steagall Act by offering money market funds, discount brokerage services, commercial paper, and other investment services.

GNOMES OF ZÜRICH term coined by Labour ministers of Great Britain, during the sterling crisis of 1964, to describe the financiers and bankers in Zürich, Switzerland, who were engaged in foreign exchange speculation.

GNP *see* GROSS NATIONAL PRODUCT.

GO AROUND term used to describe the process whereby the trading desk at the New York Federal Reserve Bank ("the DESK"), acting on behalf of the FEDERAL OPEN MARKET COMMITTEE, contacts primary dealers for bid and offer prices. Primary dealers are those banks and investment houses approved for direct purchase and sale transactions with the Federal Reserve System in its OPEN MARKET OPERATIONS.

GO-GO FUND MUTUAL FUND that invests in highly risky but potentially rewarding stocks. During the 1960s many go-go funds shot up in value, only to fall dramatically later and, in some cases, to go out of business as their speculative investments fizzled.

GOING AHEAD unethical securities brokerage act whereby the broker trades first for his own account before filling his customers' orders. Brokers who go ahead violate the RULES OF FAIR PRACTICE of the National Association of Securities Dealers.

GOING AWAY bonds purchased by dealers for immediate resale to investors, as opposed to bonds purchased *for stock*—that is, to be held in inventory for resale at some future time. The significance of the difference is that bonds bought going away will not overhang the market and cause adverse pressure on prices.

The term is also used in new offerings of serial bonds to describe large purchases, usually by institutional investors, of the bonds in a particular maturity grouping (or series).

GOING-CONCERN VALUE value of a company as an operating business to another company or individual. The excess of going-concern value over asset value, or LIQUIDATING VALUE, is the value of the operating organization as distinct from the value of its assets. In acquisition accounting, going-concern value in excess of asset value is treated as an intangible asset, termed *goodwill*. Goodwill is generally understood to represent the value of a well-respected business name, good customer relations, high employee morale, and other such factors expected to translate into greater than normal earning power. However, because this intangible asset has no independent market or liquidation value, accepted accounting principles require that goodwill be written off over a period of time.

GOING LONG purchasing a stock, bond, or commodity for investment or speculation. Such a security purchase is known as a LONG POSITION. The opposite of going long is GOING SHORT, when an investor sells a security he does not own and thereby creates a SHORT POSITION.

GOING PRIVATE movement from public ownership to private ownership of a company's shares either by the company's repurchase of shares or through purchases by an outside private investor. A company usually goes private when the market price of its shares is substantially below their BOOK VALUE and the opportunity thus exists to buy the assets cheaply. Another motive for going private is to ensure the tenure of existing management by removing the company as a takeover prospect.

GOING PUBLIC securities industry phrase used when a private company first offers its shares to the public. The firm's ownership thus shifts from the hands of a few private stockowners to a base that includes public shareholders. At the moment of going public, the stock is called an INITIAL PUBLIC OFFERING. From that point on, or until the company goes private again, its shares have a MARKET VALUE. *See also* NEW ISSUE; GOING PRIVATE.

GOING SHORT selling a stock or commodity that the seller does not have. An investor who goes short borrows stock from his or her broker, hoping to purchase other shares of it at a lower price. The investor will then replace the borrowed stock with the lower priced stock and keep the difference as profit. *See also* SELLING SHORT; GOING LONG.

GOLD BOND bond backed by gold. Such debt obligations are issued by gold-mining companies, who peg interest payments to the level of gold prices. Investors who buy these bonds therefore anticipate a rising gold price. Silver mining companies also issue silver-backed bonds that tie interest payments to silver prices.

GOLDBUG analyst enamored of gold as an investment. Goldbugs usually are worried about possible disasters in the world economy, such as a depression or hyperinflation, and therefore recommend gold as a HEDGE.

GOLDEN HANDCUFFS contract that ties a broker to a brokerage firm. If the broker stays at the firm, he or she will earn lucrative commissions, bonuses, and other compensation. But if the broker leaves and tries to lure clients to another firm, the broker must promise to give back to the firm much of the compensation received while working there. Golden handcuffs are a response by the brokerage industry to the frequent movement of brokers from one firm to another.

GOLDEN PARACHUTE lucrative contract given to a top executive to provide lavish benefits in case the company is taken over by another firm, resulting in the loss of the job. A golden parachute might include generous severance pay, stock options, or a bonus. The TAX REFORM ACT OF 1984 eliminated the deductability of ''excess compensation'' and imposed an excise tax. The TAX REFORM ACT OF 1986 covered matters of clarification.

GOLD FIXING daily determination of the price of gold by selected gold specialists and bank officials in London, Paris, and Zürich. The price is fixed at 10:30 A.M. and 3:30 P.M. London time every business day, according to the prevailing market forces of supply and demand.

GOLD MUTUAL FUND mutual fund that invests in the shares of gold mining concerns. Some gold mutual funds invest in only U.S. and Canadian stocks; others invest in North American and South African shares. These funds offer investors diversification among many gold mining shares and, frequently, high dividend income, since South African mines typically pay out almost all their earnings as dividends. Such funds have usually performed best during periods of rising inflation. They offer a way of participating in gold as an inflation HEDGE, without the risks incurred by an unsophisticated investor dealing in gold commodities futures trading, bullion, or individual gold stocks.

GOLD STANDARD monetary system under which units of currency are convertible into fixed amounts of gold. Such a system is said to be anti-inflationary. The United States has been on the gold standard in the past. *See also* HARD MONEY.

GOOD DELIVERY securities industry designation meaning that a certificate has the necessary endorsements and meets all other requirements (signature guarantee, proper denomination, and other qualifications), so that title can be transferred by delivery to the buying broker, who is then obligated to accept it. Exceptions constitute *bad delivery*.

GOOD FAITH DEPOSIT

In general: token amount of money advanced to indicate intent to pursue a contract to completion.

Commodities: initial margin deposit required when buying or selling a futures contract. Such deposits generally range from 2% to 10% of the contract value.

Securities:
1. deposit, usually 25% of a transaction, required by securities firms of individuals who are not known to them but wish to enter orders with them.
2. deposit left with a municipal bond issuer by a firm competing for the underwriting business. The deposit typically equals 1% to 5% of the principal amount of the issue and is refundable to the unsuccessful bidders.

GOOD MONEY

Banking: federal funds, which are good the same day, in contrast to CLEARING HOUSE FUNDS. Clearing house funds are understood in two ways: (1) funds requiring three days to clear and (2) funds used to settle transactions on which there is a one-day FLOAT.

Gresham's Law: theory that money of superior intrinsic value, "good money," will eventually be driven out of circulation by money of lesser intrinsic value. *See also* GRESHAM'S LAW.

GOOD-THIS-MONTH ORDER (GTM) order to buy or sell securities (usually at a LIMIT PRICE or STOP PRICE set by the customer) that remains in effect until the end of the month. In the case of a limit price, the customer instructs the broker either to buy at the stipulated limit price or anything lower, or to sell at the limit price or anything higher. In the case of a stop price, the customer instructs the broker to enter a market order once a transaction in the security occurs at the stop price specified.

A variation on the GTM order is the *good-this-week-order* (GTW), which expires at the end of the week if it is not executed.

See also DAY ORDER; GOOD-TILL-CANCELED ORDER; LIMIT ORDER; OPEN ORDER; STOP ORDER.

GOOD THROUGH order to buy or sell securities or commodities at a stated price for a stated period of time, unless canceled, executed, or changed. It is a type of LIMIT ORDER and may be specified GTW (good this week), GTM (GOOD this MONTH ORDER), or for shorter or longer periods.

GOOD-TILL-CANCELED ORDER (GTC) brokerage customer's order to buy or sell a security, usually at a particular price, that remains in effect until executed or canceled. If the GTC order remains unfilled after a long period of time, a broker will usually periodically confirm that the customer still wants the transaction to occur if the stock reaches the target price. *See also* DAY ORDER; GOOD-THIS-MONTH ORDER; OPEN ORDER; TARGET PRICE.

GOODWILL *see* GOING-CONCERN VALUE.

GOVERNMENT NATIONAL MORTGAGE ASSOCIATION (GNMA) government-owned corporation, nicknamed Ginnie Mae, which is an agency of the U.S. Department of Housing and Urban Development. GNMA guarantees, with the full faith and credit of the United States Government, full and timely payment of all monthly principal and interest payments on the mortgage-backed PASS-THROUGH SECURITIES of registered holders. The securities, which are issued by private firms, such as MORTGAGE BANKERS and savings institutions, and typically marketed through security broker-dealers, represent pools of residential mortgages insured or guaranteed by the Federal Housing Administration (FHA), the Farmer's Home Administration (FmHA), or the Veterans Administration (VA). *See also* FEDERAL HOME LOAN MORTGAGE CORPORATION; FEDERAL NATIONAL MORTGAGE ASSOCIATION; GINNIE MAE PASS-THROUGH.

GOVERNMENT OBLIGATIONS U.S. government debt instruments (Treasury bonds, bills, notes, savings bonds) the government has pledged to repay. *See* GOVERNMENTS.

GOVERNMENTS

1. securities issued by the U.S. government, such as Treasury bills, bonds, notes, and savings bonds. Governments are the most creditworthy of all debt instruments since they are backed by the FULL FAITH AND CREDIT of the U.S. government, which if necessary can print money to make payments. Also called TREASURIES.
2. debt issues of federal agencies, which are not directly backed by the U.S. government. *See also* GOVERNMENT SECURITIES.

GOVERNMENT SECURITIES securities issued by U.S. government agencies, such as the Federal Home Loan Bank or the Federal Land Bank; also called *agency securities*. Although these securities have high credit ratings, they are not considered to be GOVERNMENT OBLIGATIONS and therefore are not directly backed by the FULL FAITH AND CREDIT of the government as TREASURIES are.

GRACE PERIOD

In general: period of time provided in most loan contracts and insurance policies during which default or cancellation will not occur even though payment is past due.

Banking: a provision in some long-term loans, notably EUROCURRENCY syndication loans to foreign governments and multinational firms by groups of banks, whereby repayment of principal does not begin until some point well into the life of the loan. The grace period, which can be as long as five years, is an important point of negotiation between a borrower and a lender; borrowers will sometimes accept a higher interest rate to obtain a longer grace period.

GRADUATED-PAYMENT MORTGAGE (GPM) mortgage featuring lower monthly payments at first, which steadily rise until they level off after a few years. GPMs, also known as ''jeeps,'' are designed for young couples whose income is expected to grow as their careers advance. A graduated-payment mortgage allows such a family to buy a house that would be unaffordable if mortgage payments started out at a high level. Persons planning to take on such a mortgage must be confident that their income will be able to keep pace with the rising payments. *See also* ADJUSTABLE-RATE MORTGAGE; CONVENTIONAL MORTGAGE; REVERSE-ANNUITY MORTGAGE; VARIABLE-RATE MORTGAGE.

GRADUATED SECURITY security whose listing has been upgraded by moving from one exchange to another—for example, from the American Stock Exchange to the more prestigious New York Stock Exchange, or from a regional exchange to a national exchange. An advantage of such a transfer is to widen trading in the security.

GRAHAM AND DODD METHOD OF INVESTING investment approach outlined in Benjamin Graham and David Dodd's landmark book *Security Analysis,* published in the 1930s. Graham and Dodd founded the modern discipline of security analysis with their work. They believed that investors should buy stocks with undervalued assets and that eventually those assets would appreciate to their true value in the marketplace. Graham and Dodd advocated buying stocks in companies where current assets exceed current liabilities and all long-term debt, and where the stock is selling at a low PRICE/EARNINGS RATIO. They suggested that the stocks be sold after a profit objective of between 50% and 100% was reached, which they assumed would be three years or less from the time of purchase. Analysts today who call themselves Graham and Dodd investors hunt for stocks selling below their LIQUIDATING VALUE and do not necessarily concern themselves with the potential for earnings growth.

GRANDFATHER CLAUSE provision included in a new rule that exempts from the rule a person or business already engaged in the activity coming under regulation. For example, an opinion of the Accounting Principles Board (now the Financial Accounting Standards Board) adopted in 1970 requires that businesses amortize (write off) goodwill. The opinion contains a grandfather clause, however, which exempts goodwill acquired before 1970 from the required amortization.

GRANTOR

Investments: options trader who sells a CALL OPTION or a PUT OPTION and collects PREMIUM INCOME for doing so. The grantor sells the right to buy a security at a certain price in the case of a call, and the right to sell at a certain price in the case of a put.

Law: one who executes a deed conveying title to property or who creates a trust. Also called a *settlor*.

GRAVEYARD MARKET bear market wherein investors who sell are faced with substantial losses, while potential investors prefer to stay liquid, that is, to keep their money in cash or cash equivalents until market conditions improve. Like a graveyard, those who are in can't get out and those who are out have no desire to get in.

GREENMAIL payment by a TAKEOVER target to a potential acquirer, usually to buy back shares at a premium. In exchange, the acquirer agrees not to pursue the takeover bid further. *See also* STANDSTILL AGREEMENT.

GREEN SHOE clause in an underwriting agreement saying that, in the event of exceptional public demand, the issuer will authorize additional shares for distribution by the syndicate.

GRESHAM'S LAW theory in economics that bad money drives out good money. Specifically, people faced with a choice of two currencies of the same nominal value, one of which is preferable to the other because of metal content or because it resists mutilation, will hoard the good money and spend the bad money, thereby driving the good money out of circulation. The observation is named for Sir Thomas Gresham, master of the mint in the reign of Queen Elizabeth I.

GROSS ESTATE total value of a person's assets before liabilities such as debts and taxes are deducted. After someone dies, the executor of the will makes an assessment of the stocks, bonds, real estate, and personal possessions that comprise the gross estate. Debts and taxes are paid, as are funeral expenses and estate administration costs. Beneficiaries of the will then receive their portion of the remainder, which is called the *net estate*.

GROSS LEASE property lease under which the lessor (landlord) agrees to pay all the expenses normally associated with ownership (insurance, taxes, utilities, repairs). An exception might be that the lessee (tenant) would be required to pay real estate taxes above a stipulated amount or to pay for certain special operating expenses (snow removal, grounds care in the case of a shopping center, or institutional advertising, for example). Gross leases are the most common type of lease contract and are typical arrangements for short-term tenancy. They normally contain no provision for periodic rent adjustments, nor are there preestablished renewal arrangements. *See also* NET LEASE.

GROSS NATIONAL PRODUCT (GNP) total value of goods and services produced in the U.S. economy over a particular period of time, usually one year. The GNP growth rate is the primary indicator of the status of the economy. GNP is made up of consumer and government purchases, private domestic and foreign investments in the U.S., and the total value of exports. Figures for GNP on an annual basis are released every quarter, as is an inflation-adjusted version, called *real GNP*.

GROSS PROFIT net sales less the COST OF GOODS SOLD. Also called *gross margin*. *See also* NET PROFIT.

GROSS SALES total sales at invoice values, not reduced by customer discounts, returns or allowances, or other adjustments. *See also* NET SALES.

GROSS SPREAD difference (spread) between the public offering price of a security and the price paid by an underwriter to the issuer. The spread breaks down into the manager's fee, the dealer's (or underwriter's) discount, and the selling concession (i.e., the discount offered to a selling group). *See also* CONCESSION; FLOTATION (FLOATATION) COST.

GROUP OF TEN ten major industrialized countries that try to coordinate monetary and fiscal policies to create a more stable world economic system. The ten are Belgium, Canada, France, Italy, Japan, The Netherlands, Sweden, the United Kingdom, the United States, and West Germany. Also known as the *Paris Club*.

GROUP SALES term used in securities underwriting that refers to block sales made to institutional investors. The securities come out of a syndicate "pot" with credit for the sale prorated among the syndicate members in proportion to their original allotments.

GROWTH FUND mutual fund that invests in growth stocks. The goal is to provide capital appreciation for the fund's shareholders over the long term. Growth funds are more volatile than more conservative income or money market funds. They tend to rise faster than conservative funds in bull (advancing) markets and to drop more sharply in bear (falling) markets. *See also* GROWTH STOCK.

GROWTH STOCK stock of a corporation that has exhibited faster-than-average gains in earnings over the last few years and is expected to continue to show high levels of profit growth. Over the long run, growth stocks tend to outperform slower-growing or stagnant stocks. Growth stocks are riskier investments than average stocks, however, since they usually sport higher price/earnings ratios and make little or no dividend payments to shareholders. *See also* PRICE/EARNINGS RATIO.

GUARANTEE to take responsibility for payment of a debt or performance of some obligation if the person primarily liable fails to perform. A guarantee is a CONTINGENT LIABILITY of the guarantor—that is, it is a potential liability not recognized in accounts until the outcome becomes probable in the opinion of the company's accountant.

GUARANTEED BOND bond on which the principal and interest are guaranteed by a firm other than the issuer. Such bonds are nearly always railroad bonds, arising out of situations where one road has leased the road of another and the security holders of the leased road require assurance of income in exchange for giving up control of the property. Guaranteed securities involved in such situations may also include preferred or common stocks when dividends are guaranteed. Both guaranteed stock and guaranteed bonds become, in effect, DEBENTURE (unsecured) bonds of the guarantor, although the status of the stock may be questionable in the event of LIQUIDATION. In any event, if the guarantor enjoys stronger credit than the railroad whose securities are being guaranteed, the securities have greater value.

Guaranteed bonds may also arise out of parent-subsidiary relationships where bonds are issued by the subsidiary with the parent's guarantee.

GUARANTEED INCOME CONTRACT contract between an insurance company and a corporate profit-sharing or pension plan that guarantees a specific rate of return on the invested capital over the life of the contract. Although the insurance company takes all market, credit, and interest rate risks on the investment portfolio, it can profit if its returns exceed the guaranteed amount. For pension and profit-sharing plans, guaranteed income contracts are a conservative way of assuring beneficiaries that their money will achieve a certain rate of return.

GUARANTEED STOCK *see* GUARANTEED BOND.

GUARANTEE LETTER letter by a commercial bank that guarantees payment of the EXERCISE PRICE of a client's PUT OPTION (the right to sell a given security at a particular price within a specified period) if or when a notice indicating its exercise, called an assignment notice, is presented to the option seller (writer).

GUARANTEE OF SIGNATURE certificate issued by a bank or brokerage firm vouching for the authenticity of a person's signature. Such a document may be necessary when stocks, bonds, or other registered securities are transferred from a seller to a buyer. Banks also require guarantees of signature before they will process certain transactions.

GUN JUMPING
1. trading securities on information before it becomes publicly disclosed.
2. illegally soliciting buy orders in an underwriting, before a Securities and Exchange Commission REGISTRATION is complete.

h

HAIRCUT securities industry term referring to the formulas used in the valuation of securities for the purpose of calculating a broker-dealer's net capital. The haircut varies according to the class of a security, its market risk, and the time to maturity. For example, cash equivalent GOVERNMENTS could have a 0% haircut, equities could have an average 30% haircut, and fail positions (securities with past due delivery) with little prospect of settlement could have a 100% haircut. *See also* CASH EQUIVALENTS; FAIL POSITION.

HALF-LIFE point in time in which half the principal has been repaid in a mortgage-backed security guaranteed or issued by the GOVERNMENT NATIONAL MORTGAGE ASSOCIATION, the FEDERAL NATIONAL MORTGAGE ASSOCIATION, or the FEDERAL HOME LOAN MORTGAGE CORPORATION. Such a security normally has a half-life of

12 years. But specific mortgage pools can have vastly longer or shorter half-lives, depending on interest rate trends. If interest rates fall, more homeowners will refinance their mortgages, meaning that principal will be paid off more quickly, and half-lives will drop. If interest rates rise, homeowners will hold onto their mortgages longer than anticipated, and half-lives will rise.

HALF-STOCK common or preferred stock with a $50 par value instead of the more conventional $100 par value.

HAMMERING THE MARKET intense selling of stocks by those who think prices are inflated. Speculators who think the market is about to drop, and therefore sell short, are said to be hammering the market. *See also* SELLING SHORT.

HARD DOLLARS actual payments made by a customer for services, including research, provided by a brokerage firm. For instance, if a broker puts together a financial plan for a client, the fee might be $1000 in hard dollars. This contrasts with SOFT DOLLARS, which refers to compensation by way of the commissions a broker would receive if he were to carry out any trades called for in that financial plan. Brokerage house research is sold for either hard or soft dollars.

HARD MONEY (HARD CURRENCY)
1. currency in which there is widespread confidence. It is the currency of an economically and politically stable country, such as the U.S. or Switzerland. Countries that have taken out loans in hard money generally must repay them in hard money.
2. gold or coins, as contrasted with paper currency, which is considered *soft money*. Some hard-money enthusiasts advocate a return to the GOLD STANDARD as a method of reducing inflation and promoting economic growth.

HEAD AND SHOULDERS patterns resembling the head and shoulders outline of a person, which is used to chart stock price trends. The pattern signals the reversal of a trend. As prices move down to the right shoulder, a head and shoulders top is formed, meaning that prices should be falling. A reverse head and shoulders pattern has the head at the bottom of the chart, meaning that prices should be rising.

HEAD AND SHOULDERS

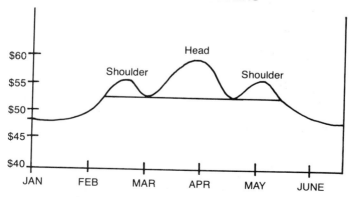

HEAVY MARKET stock, bond, or commodity market with falling prices resulting from a larger supply of offers to sell than bids to buy.

HEDGE/HEDGING strategy used to offset investment risk. A perfect hedge is one eliminating the possibility of future gain or loss.

A stockholder worried about declining stock prices, for instance, can hedge his or her holdings by buying a PUT OPTION on the stock or selling a CALL OPTION. Someone owning 100 shares of XYZ stock, selling at $70 per share, can hedge his position by buying a put option giving him the right to sell 100 shares at $70 at any time over the next few months. This investor must pay a certain amount of money, called a PREMIUM, for these rights. If XYZ stock falls during that time, the investor can exercise his option—that is, sell the stock at $70—thereby preserving the $70 value of the XYZ holdings. The same XYZ stockholder can also hedge his position by selling a call option. In such a transaction, he sells the right to buy XYZ at $70 per share for the next few months. In return, he receives a premium. If XYZ stock falls in price, that premium income will offset to some extent the drop in value of the stock.

SELLING SHORT is another widely used hedging technique.

Investors often try to hedge against inflation by purchasing assets that will rise in value faster than inflation.

Large commercial firms that want to be assured of the price they will receive or pay for a commodity will hedge their position by buying and selling simultaneously in the FUTURES MARKET. For example, Hershey's, the chocolate company, will hedge its supplies of cocoa in the futures market to limit the risk of a rise in cocoa prices.

HEDGE CLAUSE disclaimer seen in market letters, security research reports, or other printed matter having to do with evaluating investments, which purports to absolve the writer from responsibility for the accuracy of information obtained from usually reliable sources. Despite such clauses, which may mitigate liability, writers may still be charged with negligence in their use of information. Typical language of a hedge clause: "The information furnished herein has been obtained from sources believed to be reliable, but its accuracy is not guaranteed."

HEDGED TENDER SELLING SHORT a portion of the shares being tendered to protect against a price drop in the event all shares tendered are not accepted. For example, ABC Company or another company wishing to acquire ABC Company announces a TENDER OFFER at $52 a share when ABC shares are selling at a market price of $40. The market price of ABC will now rise to near the tender price of $52. An investor wishing to sell all his or her 2000 shares at $52 will tender 2000 shares, but cannot be assured all shares will be accepted. To lock in the $52 price on the tendered shares the investor thinks might not be accepted—say half of them or 1000 shares—he or she will sell short that many shares. Assuming the investor has guessed correctly and only 1000 shares are accepted, when the tender offer expires and the market price of ABC begins to drop, the investor will still have sold all 2000 shares for $52 or close to it—half to the tenderer and the other half when the short sale is consummated.

HEDGE FUND securities industry term used to describe certain mutual funds that use hedging techniques. For example, the Prudential-Bache Option Growth Fund has used futures contracts on stock market indexes and short sales with stock options to limit risks (i.e., "to make money in any market environment"). *See* HEDGE/HEDGING.

HEMLINE THEORY whimsical idea that stock prices move in the same general direction as the hemlines of women's dresses. Short skirts in the 1920s and 1960s were considered bullish signs that stock prices would rise, whereas longer dresses in the 1930s and 1940s were considered bearish (falling) indicators. Despite its sometimes uncanny way of being prophetic, the hemline theory has remained more in the area of wishful thinking than serious market analysis.

HIGH CREDIT

Banking: maximum amount of loans outstanding recorded for a particular customer.

Finance: the highest amount of TRADE CREDIT a particular company has received from a supplier at one time.

HIGH FLYER high-priced and highly speculative stock that moves up and down sharply over a short period. The stock of unproven high-technology companies might be high flyers, for instance.

HIGH-GRADE BOND bond rated triple-A or double-A by Standard & Poor's or Moody's rating services. *See also* RATING.

HIGH-PREMIUM CONVERTIBLE DEBENTURE bond with a long-term, high-premium, common stock conversion feature and also offering a fairly competitive interest rate. Premium refers in this case to the difference between the market value of the CONVERTIBLE security and the value at which it is convertible into common stock. Such bonds are designed for bond-oriented portfolios, with the "KICKER," the added feature of convertibility to stock, intended as an inflation hedge.

HIGHS stocks that have hit new high prices in daily trading for the current 52-week period. (They are listed as "highs" in daily newspapers.) Technical analysts consider the ratio between new highs and new LOWS in the stock market to be significant for pointing out stock market trends.

HIGH-TECH STOCK stock of companies involved in high-technology fields (computers, semiconductors, biotechnology, robotics, electronics). Successful high-tech stocks have above-average earnings growth and therefore typically very volatile stock prices.

HISTORICAL COST accounting principle requiring that all financial statement items be based on original cost or acquisition cost. The dollar is assumed to be stable for the period involved.

HISTORICAL TRADING RANGE price range within which a stock, bond, or commodity has traded since going public. A VOLATILE stock will have a wider trading range than a more conservative stock. Technical analysts see the top of a historical range as the RESISTANCE LEVEL and the bottom as the SUPPORT LEVEL. They consider it highly significant if a security breaks above the resistance level or below the support level. Usually such a move is interpreted to mean that the security will go onto new highs or new lows, thus expanding its historical trading range.

HISTORICAL YIELD yield provided by a mutual fund, typically a money market fund, over a particular period of time. For instance, a money market fund may advertise that its historical yield averaged 10% over the last year.

HIT THE BID to accept the highest price offered for a stock. For instance, if a stock's ask price is $50¼ and the current bid price is $50, a seller will hit the bid if he or she accepts $50 a share.

HOLDER OF RECORD owner of a company's securities as recorded on the books of the issuing company or its TRANSFER AGENT as of a particular date. Dividend declarations always specify payability to holders of record as of a specific date.

HOLDING COMPANY corporation that owns enough voting stock in another corporation to influence its board of directors and therefore to control its policies and management. A holding company need not own a majority of the shares of its subsidiaries or be engaged in similar activities. However, to gain the benefits of tax consolidation, which include tax-free dividends to the parent and the ability to share operating losses, the holding company must own 80% or more of the subsidiary's voting stock.

Among the advantages of a holding company over a MERGER as an approach to expansion are the ability to control sizeable operations with fractional owner-ship and commensurately small investment; the somewhat theoretical ability to take risks through subsidiaries with liability limited to the subsidiary corporation; and the ability to expand through unobtrusive purchases of stock, in contrast to having to obtain the approval of another company's shareholders.

Among the disadvantages of a holding company are partial multiple taxation when less than 80% of a subsidiary is owned, plus other special state and local taxes; the risk of forced DIVESTITURE (it is easier to force dissolution of a holding company than to separate merged operations); and the risks of negative leverage effects in excessive PYRAMIDING.

The following types of holding companies are defined in special ways and are subject to particular legislation: public utility holding company (*see* PUBLIC UTILITY HOLDING COMPANY ACT), BANK HOLDING COMPANY, railroad holding com-pany, and air transport holding company.

HOLDING PERIOD length of time an asset is held by its owner. Through 1987, capital assets held for six months or more qualify for special CAPITAL GAINS TAX treatment. *See also* ANTICIPATED HOLDING PERIOD; INVESTMENT LETTER.

HOLDING THE MARKET entering the market with sufficient buy orders to create price support for a security or commodity, for the purpose of stabilizing a down-ward trend. The Securities and Exchange Commission views ''holding'' as a form of illegal manipulation except in the case of stabilization of a new issue cleared with the SEC beforehand.

HOMEOWNER'S EQUITY ACCOUNT credit line offered by banks and bro-kerage firms allowing a homeowner to tap the built-up equity in his or her home. Such an account is, in effect, a REVOLVING-CREDIT second mortgage, which can be accessed with the convenience of a check. When a homeowner writes a check (takes a loan), a LIEN is automatically placed against the house; the lien is removed after the loan is repaid. A homeowner's equity account often carries a lower interest rate than a second mortgage; typically, the rate is tied to the PRIME RATE. Most such programs require an initial signup fee and payment of additional fees called *points* when the credit line is tapped. Interest on such loans is tax deductible up to the amount of the original purchase price of the home plus improvements plus borrowings for educational and medical expenses. *See also* SECOND MORTGAGE LENDING.

HOME RUN large gain by an investor in a short period of time. Someone who aims to hit an investment home run may be looking for a potential TAKEOVER target, for example, since takeover bids result in sudden price spurts. Such in-vesting is inherently more risky than the strategy of holding for the long term.

HORIZON ANALYSIS method of measuring the discounted cash flow (time-adjusted return) from an investment, using time periods or series *(horizons)* that differ from the investment's contractual maturity. The horizon date might be the end of a BUSINESS CYCLE or some other date determined in the perspective of the investor's overall portfolio requirements. Horizon analysis calculations, which include reinvestment assumptions, permit comparison with alternative investments that is more realistic in terms of individual portfolio requirements than traditional YIELD-TO-MATURITY calculations.

HORIZONTAL PRICE MOVEMENT movement within a narrow price range over an extended period of time. A stock would have a horizontal price movement if it traded between $35 and $37 for over six months, for instance. Also known as *sideways price movement. See also* FLAT MARKET.

HORIZONTAL PRICE MOVEMENT

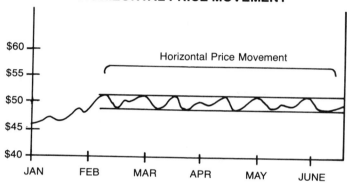

HORIZONTAL SPREAD options strategy that involves buying and selling the same number of options contracts with the same exercise price, but with different maturity dates; also called a CALENDAR SPREAD. For instance, an investor might buy ten XYZ call options with a striking price of $70 and a maturity date of October. At the same time, he would sell ten XYZ call options with the same striking price of $70 but a maturity date of July. The investor hopes to profit by moves in XYZ stock by this means.

HOSPITAL REVENUE BOND bond issued by a municipal or state agency to finance construction of a hospital or nursing home. The latter is then operated under lease by a not-for-profit organization or a for-profit corporation such as Hospital Corporation of America. A hospital revenue bond, which is a variation on the INDUSTRIAL DEVELOPMENT BOND, is tax exempt, but there may be limits to the exemption. *See also* REVENUE BOND.

HOT ISSUE newly issued stock that is in great public demand. Hot issue stocks usually shoot up in price at their initial offering, since there is more demand than there are shares available. Special National Association of Securities Dealers rules apply to the distribution of hot issues by the selling investment banking syndicate. *See also* UNDERWRITE.

HOT STOCK
1. stock that has been stolen.
2. newly issued stock that rises quickly in price. *See* HOT ISSUE.

HOUSE
1. firm or individual engaged in business as a broker-dealer in securities and/or investment banking and related services.
2. nickname for the London Stock Exchange.

HOUSE ACCOUNT account handled at the main office of a brokerage firm or managed by an executive of the firm; in other words, an account distinguished from one that is normally handled by a salesperson in the territory. Ordinarily, a salesperson does not receive a commission on a house account, even though the account may actually be in his or her territory.

HOUSE CALL brokerage house notification that the customer's EQUITY in a MARGIN ACCOUNT is below the maintenance level. If the equity declines below that point, a broker must call the client, asking for more cash or securities. If the client fails to deliver the required margin, his or her position will be liquidated. House call limits are usually higher than limits mandated by the National Association of Securities Dealers (NASD), a self-regulatory group, and the major exchanges with jurisdiction over these rules. Such a margin MAINTENANCE REQUIREMENT is in addition to the initial margin requirements set by REGULATION T of the Federal Reserve Board. *See also* HOUSE MAINTENANCE REQUIREMENT; MARGIN CALL.

HOUSE MAINTENANCE REQUIREMENT internally set and enforced rules of individual broker-dealers in securities with respect to a customer's MARGIN ACCOUNT. House maintenance requirements set levels of EQUITY that must be maintained to avoid putting up additional equity or having collateral sold out. These levels are normally higher than maintenance levels required by the NATIONAL ASSOCIATION OF SECURITIES DEALERS (NASD) and the stock exchange. *See also* HOUSE CALL; MINIMUM MAINTENANCE.

HOUSE OF ISSUE investment banking firm that underwrites a stock or bond issue and offers the securities to the public. *See also* UNDERWRITE.

HOUSE RULES securities industry term for internal rules and policies of individual broker-dealer firms concerning the opening and handling of customers' accounts and the activities of the customers in such accounts. House rules are designed to assure that firms are in comfortable compliance with the requirements of outside regulatory authorities and in most cases are more stringent than the outside regulations. *See also* HOUSE CALL; HOUSE MAINTENANCE REQUIREMENT.

HOUSING AND URBAN DEVELOPMENT, DEPARTMENT OF (HUD) cabinet-level federal agency, founded in 1965, which is responsible for stimulating housing development in the United States. HUD has several programs to subsidize low- and moderate-income housing and urban renewal projects, often through loan guarantees. The GOVERNMENT NATIONAL MORTGAGE ASSOCIATION (Ginnie Mae), which fosters the growth of the secondary mortgage market, is within HUD.

HOUSING BOND short- or long-term bond issued by a local housing authority to finance short-term construction of (typically) low- or middle-income housing or long-term commitments for housing, plants, pollution control facilities, or similar projects. Such bonds are free from federal income taxes and from state and local taxes where applicable.

Shorter-term bonds sell in $5000 denominations and have maturities from 18 months to 4 years. They cannot be called (redeemed prior to maturity) and are paid at maturity with the proceeds from Federal Housing Administration-insured loans. Longer-term bonds are typically issued by local authorities under federal agency contracts, thus providing complete safety. Yields are competitive.

HULBERT RATING rating by *Hulbert Financial Digest* of how well the recommendations of various investment advisory newsletters have performed over the past few years. The *Digest* ranks several dozen investment advisory newsletters by tabulating the profits and losses of newsletter readers had they followed the advice.

HUNG UP term used to describe the position of an investor whose stocks or bonds have dropped in value below their purchase price, presenting the problem of a substantial loss if the securities were sold.

HURDLE RATE term used in the budgeting of capital expenditures, meaning the REQUIRED RATE OF RETURN in a DISCOUNTED CASH FLOW analysis. If the *expected rate of return* on an investment is below the hurdle rate, the project is not undertaken. The hurdle rate should be equal to the INCREMENTAL COST OF CAPITAL.

HYBRID ANNUITY contract offered by an insurance company that allows an investor to mix the benefits of both fixed and variable annuities. For instance, an annuity buyer may put a portion of his assets in a FIXED ANNUITY, which promises a certain rate of return, and the remainder in a stock or bond fund VARIABLE ANNUITY, which offers a chance for higher return but takes more risk.

HYPOTHECATION

Banking: pledging property to secure a loan. Hypothecation does not transfer title, but it does transfer the right to sell the hypothecated property in the event of default.

Securities: pledging of securities to brokers as collateral for loans made to purchase securities or to cover short sales, called margin loans. When the same collateral is pledged by the broker to a bank to collateralize a broker's loan, the process is called *rehypothecation*.

i

ILLEGAL DIVIDEND dividend declared by a corporation's board of directors in violation of its charter or of state laws. Most states, for example, stipulate that dividends be paid out of current income or RETAINED EARNINGS; they prohibit dividend payments that come out of CAPITAL SURPLUS or that would make the corporation insolvent. Directors who authorize illegal dividends may be sued by stockholders and creditors and may also face civil and criminal penalties. Stockholders who receive such dividends may be required to return them in order to meet the claims of creditors.

ILLIQUID

Finance: firm that lacks sufficient CASH FLOW to meet current and maturing obligations.

Investments: not readily convertible into cash, such as a stock, bond, or commodity that is not traded actively and would be difficult to sell at once without taking a large loss. Other assets for which there is not a ready market, and which therefore may take some time to sell, include real estate and collectibles such as rare stamps, coins, or antiquefurniture.

IMBALANCE OF ORDERS too many orders of one kind—to buy or to sell—without matching orders of the opposite kind. An imbalance usually follows a dramatic event such as a takeover, the death of a key executive, or a government ruling that will significantly affect the company's business. If it occurs before the stock exchange opens, trading in the stock is delayed. If it occurs during the trading day, the specialist suspends trading until enough matching orders can be found to make for an orderly market.

IMF *see* INTERNATIONAL MONETARY FUND.

IMMEDIATE FAMILY parents, brothers, sisters, children, relatives supported financially, father-in-law, mother-in-law, sister-in-law, and brother-in-law. This definition is incorporated in the NATIONAL ASSOCIATION OF SECURITIES DEALERS RULES OF FAIR PRACTICE on abuses of *hot issues* through such practices as FREE-RIDING and WITHHOLDING. The ruling prohibits the sale of such securities to members of a broker-dealer's own family or to persons buying and selling for institutional accounts and their families.

IMMEDIATE OR CANCEL ORDER buy or sell order requiring that all or part of the order be executed as soon as the broker enters a bid or offer; the portion not executed is automatically canceled. Such stipulations usually accompany large orders.

IMMEDIATE PAYMENT ANNUITY annuity contract bought with a single payment and with a specified payout plan. Payments may be for a specified period or for the life of the annuitant and are usually on a monthly basis.

IMPAIRED CAPITAL total capital that is less than the stated or par value of the company's CAPITAL STOCK. *See also* DEFICIT NET WORTH.

IMPORT DUTY *see* TARIFF.

IMPUTED VALUE logical or implicit value that is not recorded in any accounts. Examples: in projecting annual figures, values are imputed for months about which actual figures are not yet available; cash invested unproductively has an imputed value consisting of what it would have earned in a productive investment (OPPORTUNITY COST); in calculating national income, the U.S. Department of Commerce imputes a dollar value for wages and salaries paid in kind, such as food and lodging provided on ships at sea.

INACTIVE ASSET asset not continually used in a productive way, such as an auxiliary generator.

INACTIVE BOND CROWD *see* CABINET CROWD.

INACTIVE POST trading post on the New York Stock Exchange at which inactive stocks are traded in 10-share units rather than the regular 100-share lots. Known to traders as *Post 30. See also* ROUND LOT.

INACTIVE STOCK/BOND security traded relatively infrequently, either on an exchange or over the counter. The low volume makes the security ILLIQUID, and small investors tend to shy away from it.

IN-AND-OUT TRADER someone who buys and sells the same security in one day, endeavoring to profit from sharp price moves. *See also* DAY TRADE.

INCENTIVE FEE compensation for producing above-average results. Incentive fees are common for commodities trading advisers who achieve or top a preset return, as well as for a GENERAL PARTNER in a real estate or oil and gas LIMITED PARTNERSHIP.

INCENTIVE STOCK OPTION plan created by the ECONOMIC RECOVERY TAX ACT OF 1981 (ERTA) under which qualifying options are free of tax at the date of grant and the date of exercise. Profits on shares sold after being held one year after exercise are subject to favorable CAPITAL GAINS TAX rates until 1987, when such capital gains become taxable at ordinary rates.

INCESTUOUS SHARE DEALING buying and selling of shares in each other's companies to create a tax or other financial advantage.

INCOME AVAILABLE FOR FIXED CHARGES *see* FIXED-CHARGE COVERAGE.

INCOME AVERAGING method of computing personal income tax whereby tax is figured on the average of the total of current year's income and that of the three preceding years. According to 1984 U.S. tax legislation, income averaging was used when a person's income for the current year exceeded 140% of the average taxable income in the preceding three years. The TAX REFORM ACT OF 1986 repealed income averaging.

INCOME BOND obligation on which the payment of interest is contingent on sufficient earnings from year to year. Such bonds are traded FLAT—that is, with no accrued interest—and are often an alternative to bankruptcy. *See* ADJUSTMENT BOND.

INCOME INVESTMENT COMPANY management company that operates an income-oriented MUTUAL FUND for investors who value income over growth. These funds may invest in bonds or high-dividend stocks or may write covered call options on stocks. *See also* INVESTMENT COMPANY.

INCOME LIMITED PARTNERSHIP real estate, oil and gas, or equipment leasing LIMITED PARTNERSHIP whose aim is high income, much of which may be taxable. Such a partnership may be designed for tax-sheltered accounts like Individual Retirement Accounts, Keogh plan accounts, or pension plans.

INCOME PROPERTY real estate bought for the income it produces. The property may be placed in an INCOME LIMITED PARTNERSHIP, or it may be owned by one individual or company. Buyers also hope to achieve capital gains when they sell the property.

INCOME SHARES one of two kinds or classes of capital stock issued by a DUAL-PURPOSE FUND or split investment company, the other kind being *capital shares*. Holders of income shares receive dividends from both classes of shares, generated from income (dividends and interest) produced by the portfolio, whereas holders of capital shares receive capital gains payouts on both classes. Income shares normally have a minimum income guarantee, which is cumulative.

INCOME STATEMENT *see* PROFIT AND LOSS STATEMENT.

INCOME TAX annual tax on income levied by the federal government and by certain state and local governments. There are two basic types: the personal income tax, levied on incomes of households and unincorporated businesses, and the corporate (or corporation) income tax, levied on net earnings of corporations.

The U.S. income tax was instituted in 1913 by the Sixteenth Amendment to the Constitution. It has typically accounted for more than half the federal government's total annual revenue. Nearly all states tax individual and corporate incomes, as do many cities, though sales and property taxes are the main sources of state and local revenue. The personal income tax, and to a lesser extent the corporate income tax, were designed to be progressive—that is, to take a larger percentage of higher incomes than lower incomes. The ranges of incomes to which progressively higher rates apply are called TAX BRACKETS, which also determine the value of DEDUCTIONS, such as business costs and expenses, state and local income taxes, or charitable contributions.

In 1986, the individual income tax comprised 15 marginal tax brackets (including the ZERO BRACKET AMOUNT) ranging to a high of 50%. Corporations paid a base rate on the first $25,000 of income, a higher rate on the second $25,000, and a still higher rate on anything over $50,000. LONG-TERM CAPITAL GAINS received preferential tax treatment both for individuals and corporations. Because capital gains rates rewarded taxpayers in a position to take risks, and because LOOPHOLES and TAX SHELTERS enabled the wealthiest corporations and individuals to escape the higher tax brackets, the progressiveness of the tax system was often more theoretical than real.

Spurred by SUPPLY SIDE ECONOMICS, the TAX REFORM ACT OF 1986 introduced a modified FLAT TAX system and contained the most sweeping changes in tax laws since 1913. Signed into law in the Fall of 1986, it drastically reduced tax rates for both individuals and corporations, collapsed the marginal rate structure for individuals into two basic brackets, ended preferential capital gains tax treatment, curtailed loopholes and shelters, and imposed a much stricter ALTERNATIVE MINIMUM TAX applicable to corporations as well as individuals.

INCORPORATION process by which a company receives a state charter allowing it to operate as a corporation. The fact of incorporation must be acknowledged in the company's legal name, using the word *incorporated*, the abbreviation *inc.*, or other acceptable variations. *See also* ARTICLES OF INCORPORATION.

INCREMENTAL CASH FLOW net of cash outflows and inflows attributable to a corporate investment project.

INCREMENTAL COST OF CAPITAL weighted cost of the additional capital raised in a given period. Weighted cost of capital, also called *composite cost of capital*, is the weighted average of costs applicable to the issues of debt and classes of equity that compose the firm's capital structure. Also called *marginal cost of capital*.

INDEMNIFY agree to compensate for damage or loss. The word is used in insurance policies promising that, in the event of a loss, the insured will be restored to the financial position that existed prior to the loss.

INDENTURE formal agreement, also called a deed of trust, between an issuer of bonds and the bondholder covering such considerations as:(1) form of the bond; (2) amount of the issue; (3) property pledged (if not a debenture issue); (4) protective COVENANTS including any provision for a sinking fund; (5) WORKING CAPITAL and CURRENT RATIO; and(6) redemption rights or call privileges. The indenture also provides for the appointment of a trustee to act on behalf of the bondholders, in accordance with the TRUST INDENTURE ACT OF 1939.

INDEPENDENT BROKER New York Stock Exchange member who executes orders for other floor brokers who have more volume than they can handle, or for firms whose exchange members are not on the floor. Formerly called $2 brokers because of their commission for a round lot trade, independent brokers are compensated by commission brokers with fees that once were fixed but are now negotiable. *See also* GIVE UP.

INDEX statistical composite that measures changes in the economy or in financial markets, often expressed in percentage changes from a base year or from the previous month. For instance, the CONSUMER PRICE INDEX uses 1967 as the base year. That index, made up of key consumer goods and services, moves up and down as the rate of inflation changes. By the early 1980s the index had climbed from 100 in 1967 into the low 300s, meaning that the basket of goods the index is based on had risen in price by more than 200%.

Indexes also measure the ups and downs of stock, bond, and commodities markets, reflecting market prices and the number of shares outstanding for the companies in the index. Some well-known indexes are the New York Stock Exchange Index, the American Stock Exchange Index, Standard & Poor's Index, and the Value Line Index. Subindexes for industry groups such as beverages, railroads, or computers are also tracked. Stock market indexes form the basis for trading in INDEX OPTIONS.

INDEX FUND MUTUAL FUND whose portfolio matches that of a broad-based index such as Standard & Poor's Index and whose performance therefore mirrors the market as a whole. Many institutional investors, especially believers in the EFFICIENT MARKET theory, put money in index funds on the assumption that trying to beat the market averages over the long run is futile, and their investments in these funds will at least keep up with the market.

INDEXING
1. weighting one's portfolio to match a broad-based index such as Standard & Poor's so as to match its performance—or buying shares in an INDEX FUND.
2. tying wages, taxes, or other rates to an index. For example, a labor contract may call for indexing wages to the consumer price index to protect against loss of purchasing power in a time of rising inflation.

INDEX OF LEADING INDICATORS *see* LEADING INDICATORS.

INDEX OPTIONS calls and puts on indexes of stocks. These options are traded on the New York, American, and Chicago Board Options Exchanges, among others. Broad-based indexes cover a wide range of companies and industries, whereas narrow-based indexes consist of stocks in one industry or sector of the economy. Index options allow investors to trade in a particular market or industry group without having to buy all the stocks individually. For instance, someone who thought oil stocks were about to fall could buy a put on the oil index instead of selling short shares in half a dozen oil companies.

INDICATED YIELD coupon or dividend rate as a percentage of the current market price. For fixed rate bonds it is the same as CURRENT YIELD. For common stocks, it is the market price divided into the annual dividend. For preferred stocks, it is the market price divided into the contractual dividend.

INDICATION approximation of what a security's TRADING RANGE (bid and offer prices) will be when trading resumes after a delayed opening or after being halted because of an IMBALANCE OF ORDERS or another reason. Also called *indicated market*.

INDICATION OF INTEREST securities underwriting term meaning a dealer's or investor's interest in purchasing securities that are still *in registration* (awaiting clearance by) the Securities and Exchange Commission. A broker who receives an indication of interest should send the client a preliminary prospectus on the securities. An indication of interest is not a commitment to buy, an important point because selling a security while it is in registration is illegal. *See* CIRCLE.

INDICATOR technical measurement securities market analysts use to forecast the market's direction, such as investment advisory sentiment, volume of stock trading, direction of interest rates, and buying or selling by corporate insiders.

INDIRECT COST AND EXPENSE *see* DIRECT OVERHEAD; FIXED COST.

INDIRECT LABOR COSTS wages and related costs of factory employees, such as inspectors and maintenance crews, whose time is not charged to specific finished products.

INDIVIDUAL RETIREMENT ACCOUNT (IRA) personal, TAX DEFERRED, retirement account that an employed person can set up with a deposit limited to $2000 per year ($4000 for a couple when both work, or $2250 for a couple when one works and the other's income is $250 or less). Under the TAX REFORM ACT OF 1986, rules effective in the tax year 1987 include: deductibility of IRA contributions regardless of income if neither the taxpayer nor the taxpayer's spouse is covered by a QUALIFIED PLAN OR TRUST; even if covered by a qualified plan, taxpayers may deduct IRA contributions if ADJUSTED GROSS INCOME is below $40,000 on a joint return or $25,000 on a single return; couples with incomes of $40,000 to $50,000 and single taxpayers with incomes of $25,000 to $35,000 are allowed partial deductions in amounts reduced proportionately over the $10,000 range with a minimum deduction of $200; taxpayers with incomes over $50,000 (joint) and $35,000 (single) are not allowed deductions, but may make the same contributions (treated as a nontaxable RETURN OF CAPITAL upon withdrawal) and thus gain the benefit of tax-deferral; taxpayers who cannot make deductible contributions because of participation in qualified retirement plans may make nondeductible contributions. Withdrawals from IRAs prior to age 59½ are generally subject to a 10% (of principal) penalty tax.

INDIVIDUAL RETIREMENT ACCOUNT (IRA) ROLLOVER provision of the IRA law that enables persons receiving lump-sum payments from their company's pension or profit-sharing plan because of retirement or other termination of employment to ROLL OVER the amount into an IRA investment plan within 60 days. Also, current IRAs may themselves be transferred to other investment options within the 60-day period. Through an IRA rollover, the capital continues to accumulate tax-deferred until time of withdrawal.

INDUSTRIAL in stock market vernacular, general, catch-all category including firms producing or distributing goods and services that are not classified as utility, transportation, or financial companies.

INDUSTRIAL DEVELOPMENT BOND (IDB) type of MUNICIPAL REVENUE BOND issued to finance FIXED ASSETS that are then leased to private firms, whose payments AMORTIZE the debt. IDBs were traditionally tax-exempt to buyers, but under the TAX REFORM ACT OF 1986, large IDB issues ($1 million plus) are taxable effective August 15, 1986 while tax-exempt small issues for commercial and manufacturing purposes are prohibited after 1986 and 1989 respectively. Also, effective August 8, 1986, banks lost their 80% interest deductibility on borrowings to buy IDBs.

INDUSTRIAL PRODUCTION monthly statistic released by the FEDERAL RESERVE BOARD on the total output of all U.S. factories and mines. These numbers are a key ECONOMIC INDICATOR.

INDUSTRIAL REVENUE BOND *see* INDUSTRIAL DEVELOPMENT BOND.

INEFFICIENCY IN THE MARKET failure of investors to recognize that a particular stock or bond has good prospects or may be headed for trouble. According to the EFFICIENT MARKET theory, current prices reflect all knowledge about securities. But some say that those who find out about securities first can profit by exploiting that information; stocks of small, little-known firms with a large growth potential most clearly reflect the market's inefficiency, they say.

INELASTIC DEMAND OR SUPPLY *see* ELASTICITY OF DEMAND OR SUPPLY.

INFANT INDUSTRY ARGUMENT case made by developing sectors of the economy that their industries need protection against international competition while they establish themselves. In response to such pleas, the government may enact a TARIFF or import duty to stifle foreign competition. The infant industry argument is frequently made in developing nations that are trying to lessen their dependence on the industrialized world. In Brazil, for example, such infant industries as automobile production argue that they need protection until their technological capability and marketing prowess are sufficient to enable competition with well-established foreigners.

INFLATION rise in the prices of goods and services, as happens when spending increases relative to the supply of goods on the market—in other words, too much money chasing too few goods. Moderate inflation is a common result of economic growth. Hyperinflation, with prices rising at 100% a year or more, causes people to lose confidence in the currency and put their assets in hard assets like real estate or gold, which usually retain their value in inflationary times. *See also* COST-PUSH INFLATION; DEMAND-PULL INFLATION.

INFLATION ACCOUNTING showing the effects of inflation in financial statements. The Financial Accounting Standards Board (FASB) requires major companies to supplement their traditional financial reporting with information showing the effects of inflation. The ruling applies to public companies having inventories and fixed assets of more than $125 million or total assets of more than $1 billion.

INFLATION RATE rate of change in prices. Two primary U.S. indicators of the inflation rate are the CONSUMER PRICE INDEX and the PRODUCER PRICE INDEX, which track changes in prices paid by consumers and by producers. The rate can be calculated on an annual, monthly, or other basis.

INFRASTRUCTURE a nation's basic system of transportation, communication, and other aspects of its physical plant. Building and maintaining road, bridge, sewage, and electrical systems provides millions of jobs nationwide. For developing countries, building an infrastructure is a first step in economic development.

INGOT bar of metal. The Federal Reserve System's gold reserves are stored in ingot form. Individual investors may take delivery of an ingot of a precious metal such as gold or silver or may buy a certificate entitling them to a share in an ingot.

INHERITANCE TAX RETURN state counterpart to the federal ESTATE TAX return, required of the executor or administrator to determine the amount of state tax due on the inheritance.

INITIAL MARGIN amount of cash or eligible securities required to be deposited with a broker before engaging in MARGIN transactions. A margin transaction is one in which the broker extends credit to the customer in a MARGIN ACCOUNT. Under REGULATION T of the Federal Reserve Board, the initial margin is $2000 plus 50% of the purchase price when buying eligible stock or convertible bonds or 50% of the proceeds of a short sale. *See also* MINIMUM MAINTENANCE.

INITIAL PUBLIC OFFERING (IPO) corporation's first offering of stock to the public. IPO's are almost invariably an opportunity for the existing investors and participating venture capitalists to make big profits, since for the first time their shares will be given a market value reflecting expectations for future growth. *See also* HOT ISSUE.

INJUNCTION court order instructing a defendant to refrain from doing something that would be injurious to the plaintiff, or face a penalty. The usual procedure is to issue a temporary restraining order, then hold hearings to determine whether a permanent injunction is warranted.

IN PLAY stock affected by TAKEOVER rumors or activities.

INSIDE INFORMATION corporate affairs that have not yet been made public. The officers of a firm would know in advance, for instance, if the company was about to be taken over, or if the latest earnings report was going to differ significantly from information released earlier. Under Securities and Exchange Commission rules, an INSIDER is not allowed to trade on the basis of such information.

INSIDE MARKET bid or asked quotes between dealers trading for their own inventories. Distinguished from the retail market, where quotes reflect the prices that customers pay to dealers. Also known as *interdealer market; wholesale market.*

INSIDER person with access to key information before it is announced to the public. Usually the term refers to directors, officers, and key employees, but the definition has been extended legally to include relatives and others in a position to capitalize on INSIDE INFORMATION. Insiders are prohibited from trading on their knowledge.

INSOLVENCY inability to pay debts when due. *See also* BANKRUPTCY; CASH FLOW; SOLVENCY.

INSTALLMENT SALE
In general: sale made with the agreement that the purchased goods or services will be paid for in fractional amounts over a specified period of time.
Securities: transaction with a set contract price, paid in installments over a period of time. Gains or losses are generally taxable on a prorated basis.

INSTINET *see* FOURTH MARKET.

INSTITUTIONAL BROKER broker who buys and sells securities for banks, mutual funds, insurance companies, pension funds, or other institutional clients. Institutional brokers deal in large volumes of securities and generally charge their customers lower per-unit commission rates than individuals pay.

INSTITUTIONAL BROKER'S ESTIMATE SYSTEM (IBES) service run by the New York City brokerage firm of Lynch Jones and Ryan, which assembles analysts' estimates of future earnings for thousands of publicly traded companies. These estimates are tabulated, and companies are pinpointed whose estimates have shifted significantly. Reports also detail how many estimates are available on each company and the high, low, and average estimates for each.

INSTITUTIONAL INVESTOR organization that trades large volumes of securities. Some examples are mutual funds, banks, insurance companies, pension funds, labor union funds, corporate profit-sharing plans, and college endowment funds. Typically, more than 50% and sometimes upwards of 70% of the daily trading on the New York Stock Exchange is on behalf of institutional investors.

INSTRUMENT legal document in which some contractual relationship is given formal expression or by which some right is granted—for example, notes, contracts, agreements. *See also* NEGOTIABLE INSTRUMENT.

INSTRUMENTALITY federal agency whose obligations, while not direct obligations of the U.S. Government, are sponsored or guaranteed by the government and backed by the FULL FAITH AND CREDIT of the government. Well over 100 series of notes, certificates, and bonds have been issued by such instrumentalities as Federal Intermediate Credit Banks, Federal Land Banks, Federal Home Loan Bank Board, and Student Loan Marketing Association.

INSURANCE system whereby individuals and companies that are concerned about potential hazards pay premiums to an insurance company, which reimburses them in the event of loss. The insurer profits by investing the premiums it receives. Some common forms of insurance cover business risks, automobiles, homes, boats, worker's compensation, and health. Life insurance guarantees payment to the beneficiaries when the insured person dies. In a broad economic sense, insurance transfers risk from individuals to a larger group, which is better able to pay for losses.

INSURED ACCOUNT account at a bank, savings and loan association, credit union, or brokerage firm that belongs to a federal or private insurance organization. Bank accounts are insured by the FEDERAL DEPOSIT INSURANCE CORPORATION; savings and loan accounts are insured by the FEDERAL SAVINGS AND LOAN INSURANCE CORPORATION. Credit union accounts are insured by the *National Credit Union Administration*. Brokerage accounts are insured by the SECURITIES INVESTOR PROTECTION CORPORATION. Such insurance protects depositors against loss in the event that the institution becomes insolvent. Federal insurance systems were set up in the 1930s, after bank failures threatened the banking system with collapse. Some money market funds are covered by private insurance companies.

INTANGIBLE ASSET right or nonphysical resource that is presumed to represent an advantage to the firm's position in the marketplace. Such assets include copyrights, patents, TRADEMARKS, goodwill, computer programs, capitalized advertising costs, organization costs, licenses, LEASES, FRANCHISES, exploration permits, and import and exportpermits.

INTANGIBLE COST tax-deductible cost. Such costs are incurred in drilling, testing, completing, and reworking oil and gas wells—labor, core analysis, fracturing, drill stem testing, engineering, fuel, geologists' expenses; also abandonment losses, management fees, delay rentals, and similar expenses.

INTERBANK RATE *see* LONDON INTERBANK OFFERED RATE (LIBOR).

INTERCOMMODITY SPREAD spread consisting of a long position and a short position in different but related commodities—for example, a long position in gold futures and a short position in silver futures. The investor hopes to profit from the changing price relationship between the commodities.

INTERDELIVERY SPREAD futures or options trading technique that entails buying one month of a contract and selling another month in the same contract—for instance, buying a June wheat contract and simultaneously selling a September wheat contract. The investor hopes to profit as the price difference between the two contracts widens or narrows.

INTEREST
1. cost of using money, expressed as a rate per period of time, usually one year, in which case it is called an annual rate of interest.
2. share, right, or title in property.

INTEREST COVERAGE *see* FIXED-CHARGE COVERAGE.

INTEREST EQUALIZATION TAX (IET) tax of 15% on interest received by foreign borrowers in U.S. capital markets, imposed in 1963 and removed in 1974.

INTEREST-SENSITIVE STOCK stock of a firm whose earnings change when interest rates change, such as a bank or utility, and which therefore tends to go up or down on news of rate movements.

INTERIM DIVIDEND DIVIDEND declared and paid before annual earnings have been determined, generally quarterly. Most companies strive for consistency and plan quarterly dividends they are sure they can afford, reserving changes until fiscal year results are known.

INTERIM LOAN *see* CONSTRUCTION LOAN.

INTERIM STATEMENT financial report covering only a portion of a fiscal year. Public corporations supplement the annual report with quarterly statements informing shareholders of changes in the balance sheet and income statement, as well as other newsworthy developments.

INTERLOCKING DIRECTORATE membership on more than one company's board of directors. This is legal so long as the companies are not competitors. Consumer activists often point to interlocking directorates as an element in corporate conspiracies. The most flagrant abuses were outlawed by the Clayton Anti-Trust Act of 1914.

INTERMARKET SPREAD *see* INTERDELIVERY SPREAD.

INTERMARKET TRADING SYSTEM (ITS) video-computer display system that links the posts of specialists at the New York, American, Boston, Midwest, Philadelphia, and Pacific Stock Exchanges who are trading the same securities. The quotes are displayed and are firm (good) for at least 100 shares. A broker at one exchange may direct an order to another exchange where the quote is better by marking a card and sending the order electronically. A transaction that is accepted by the broker at the other exchange is termed an electronic handshake; the actual contract is made by telex or telephone.

INTERMEDIARY person or institution empowered to make investment decisions for others. Some examples are banks, savings and loan institutions, insurance companies, brokerage firms, mutual funds, and credit unions. These specialists are knowledgeable about investment alternatives and can achieve a higher return than the average investor can. Furthermore, they deal in large dollar volumes, have lower transaction costs, and can diversify their assets easily. Also called *financial intermediary*.

INTERMEDIATE TERM period between the short and long term, the length of time depending on the context. Stock analysts, for instance, mean 6 to 12 months, whereas bond analysts most often mean 3 to 10 years.

INTERMEDIATION placement of money with a financial INTERMEDIARY like a broker or bank, which invests it in bonds, stocks, mortgages, or other loans, money-market securities, or government obligations so as to achieve a targeted return. More formally called *financial intermediation*. The opposite is DISINTER-MEDIATION, the withdrawal of money from an intermediary.

INTERNAL CONTROL method, procedure, or system designed to promote efficiency, assure the implementation of policy, and safeguard assets.

INTERNAL EXPANSION asset growth financed out of internally generated cash— usually termed INTERNAL FINANCING—or through ACCRETION or APPRECIATION. *See also* CASH EARNINGS.

INTERNAL FINANCING funds produced by the normal operations of a firm, as distinguished from external financing, which includes borrowings and new equity. *See also* INTERNAL EXPANSION.

INTERNAL RATE OF RETURN (IRR) discount rate at which the present values of the future cash flows of an investment equal the cost of the investment. It is found by a process of trial and error; when the net present values of cash outflows (the cost of the investment) and cash inflows (returns on the investment) equal zero, the rate of discount being used is the IRR. When IRR is greater than the required return—called the hurdle rate in capital budgeting—the investment is acceptable.

INTERNAL REVENUE SERVICE (IRS) U.S. agency charged with collecting nearly all federal taxes, including personal and corporate income taxes, social security taxes, and excise and gift taxes. Major exceptions include taxes having to do with alcohol, tobacco, firearms, and explosives, and customs duties and tariffs. The IRS administers the rules and regulations that are the responsibility of the U.S. Department of the Treasury and investigates and prosecutes (through the U.S. Tax Court) tax illegalities.

INTERNATIONAL BANK FOR RECONSTRUCTION AND DEVELOP-MENT (IBRD) organization set up by the Bretton Woods Agreement of 1944 to help finance the reconstruction of Europe and Asia after World War II. That task accomplished, the *World Bank,* as IBRD is known, turned to financing commercial and infrastructure projects, mostly in developing nations. It does not compete with commercial banks, but it may participate in a loan set up by a commercial bank. World Bank loans must be backed by the government in the borrowing country.

INTERNATIONAL MONETARY FUND (IMF) organization set up by the Bretton Woods Agreement in 1944. Unlike the World Bank, whose focus is on foreign exchange reserves and the balance of trade, the IMF focus is on lowering trade barriers and stabilizing currencies. While helping developing nations pay their debts, the IMF usually imposes tough guidelines aimed at lowering inflation, cutting imports, and raising exports. IMF funds come mostly from the treasuries of industrialized nations. *See also* INTERNATIONAL BANK FOR RECONSTRUCTION AND DEVELOPMENT.

INTERNATIONAL MONETARY MARKET (IMM) division of the Chicago Mercantile Exchange that trades futures in U.S. Treasury bills, foreign currency, certificates of deposit, and Eurodollar deposits.

INTERNATIONAL MUTUAL FUND MUTUAL FUND that invests in securities markets throughout the world so that if one market is in a slump, money can still be made in others. Fund managers must be alert to trends in foreign currencies as well as in world markets. Otherwise, seemingly profitable investments in a rising market could lose money if the national currency is rising against the dollar.

INTERPOLATION estimation of an unknown number intermediate between known numbers. Interpolation is a way of approximating price or yield using bond tables that do not give the net yield on every amount invested at every rate of interest and for every maturity. Interpolation is based on the assumption that a certain percentage change in yield will result in the same percentage change in price. The assumption is not altogether correct, but the variance is small enough to ignore.

INTERPOSITIONING placement of a second broker in a securities transaction between two principals or between a customer and a marketmaker. The practice is regulated by the Securities and Exchange Commission, and abuses such as interpositioning to create additional commission income are illegal.

INTERSTATE COMMERCE COMMISSION (ICC) federal agency created by the Interstate Commerce Act of 1887 to insure that the public receives fair and reasonable rates and services from carriers and transportation service firms involved in interstate commerce. Legislation enacted in the 1970s and 80s substantially curtailed the regulatory activities of the ICC, particularly in the rail, truck, and bus industries.

INTER VIVOS TRUST trust established between living persons—for instance, between father and child. In contrast, a TESTAMENTARY TRUST goes into effect when the person who establishes the trust dies. Also called *living trust*.

IN THE MONEY option contract on a stock whose current market price is above the striking price of a call option or below the striking price of a put option. A call option on XYZ at a striking price of 100 would be in the money if XYZ were selling for 102, for instance, and a put option with the same striking price would be in the money if XYZ were selling for 98. *See also* AT THE MONEY; OUT OF THE MONEY.

IN THE TANK slang expression meaning market prices are dropping rapidly. Stock market observers may say, "The market is in the tank" after a day in which stock prices fell.

INTRACOMMODITY SPREAD futures position in which a trader buys and sells contracts in the same commodity on the same exchange, but for different months. For instance, a trader would place an intracommodity spread if he bought a pork bellies contract expiring in December and at the same time sold a pork bellies contract expiring in April. His profit or loss would be determined by the price difference between the December and April contracts.

INTRADAY within the day; often used in connection with high and low prices of a stock, bond, or commodity. For instance, ''The stock hit a new intraday high today'' means that the stock reached an all-time high price during the day but fell back to a lower price by the end of the day. The listing of the high and low prices at which a stock is traded during a day is called the *intraday price range.*

INTRINSIC VALUE

Financial analysis: valuation determined by applying data inputs to a valuation theory or model. The resulting value is comparable to the prevailing market price.

Options trading: difference between the EXERCISE PRICE or strike price of an option and the market value of the underlying security. For example, if the strike price is $53 on a call option to purchase a stock with a market price of $55, the option has an intrinsic value of $2. Or, in the case of a put option, if the strike price was $55 and the market price of the underlying stock was $53, the intrinsic value of the option would also be $2. Options AT THE MONEY or OUT OF THE MONEY have no intrinsic value.

INVENTORY

Corporate finance: value of a firm's raw materials, work in process, supplies used in operations, and finished goods. Since inventory value changes with price fluctuations, it is important to know the method of valuation. There are a number of inventory valuation methods; the most widely used are FIRST IN, FIRST OUT (FIFO) and LAST IN, FIRST OUT (LIFO). Financial statements normally indicate the basis of inventory valuation, generally the lower figure of either cost price or current market price, which precludes potentially overstated earnings and assets as the result of sharp increases in the price of raw materials.

Personal finance: list of all assets owned by an individual and the value of each, based on cost, market value, or both. Such inventories are usually required for property insurance purposes and are sometimes required with applications for credit.

Securities: net long or short position of a dealer or specialist. Also, securities bought and held by a dealer for later resale.

INVENTORY FINANCING

Factoring: sometimes used as a synonym for overadvances in FACTORING, where loans in excess of accounts receivable are made against inventory in anticipation of future sales.

Finance companies: financing by a bank or sales finance company of the inventory of a dealer in consumer or capital goods. Such loans, also called wholesale financing or *floorplanning,* are secured by the inventory and are usually made as part of a relationship in which retail installment paper generated by sales to the public is also financed by the lender. *See also* FINANCE COMPANY.

INVENTORY TURNOVER ratio of annual sales to inventory, which shows how many times the inventory of a firm is sold and replaced during an accounting period; sometimes called *inventory utilization ratio.* Compared with industry averages, a low turnover might indicate a company is carrying excess stocks of inventory, an unhealthy sign because excess inventory represents an investment with a low or zero rate of return and because it makes the company more vulnerable to falling prices. A steady drop in inventory turnover, in comparison with prior periods, can reveal lack of a sufficiently aggressive sales policy or ineffective buying.

Two points about the way inventory turnover may be calculated: (1) Because sales are recorded at market value and inventories are normally carried at cost, it is more realistic to obtain the turnover ratio by dividing inventory into cost of goods sold rather than into sales. However, it is conventional to use sales as the numerator because that is the practice of Dun & Bradstreet and other compilers of published financial ratios, and comparability is of overriding importance. (2) To minimize the seasonal factor affecting inventory levels, it is better to use an average inventory figure, obtained by adding yearly beginning and ending inventory figures and dividing by 2.

INVERTED SCALE serial bond offering where earlier maturities have higher yields than later maturities. *See also* SERIAL BOND.

INVERTED YIELD CURVE unusual situation where short-term interest rates are higher than long-term rates. Normally, lenders receive a higher yield when committing their money for a longer period of time; this situation is called a POSITIVE YIELD CURVE. An inverted YIELD CURVE occurs when a surge in demand for short-term credit drives up short-term rates on instruments like Treasury bills and money-market funds, while long-term rates move up more slowly, since borrowers are not willing to commit themselves to paying high interest rates for many years. This situation happened in the early 1980s, when short-term interest rates were around 20%, while long-term rates went up to only 16% or 17%. The existence of an inverted yield curve can be a sign of an unhealthy economy, marked by high inflation and low levels of confidence. Also called *negative yield curve*.

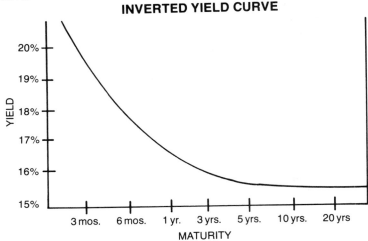

INVESTMENT use of capital to create more money, either through income-producing vehicles or through more risk-oriented ventures designed to result in capital gains. *Investment* can refer to a financial investment (where an investor puts money into a vehicle) or to an investment of effort and time on the part of an individual who wants to reap profits from the success of his labor. Investment connotes the idea that safety of principal is important. SPECULATION, on the other hand, is far riskier.

INVESTMENT ADVISERS ACT legislation passed by Congress in 1940 that requires all investment advisers to register with the Securities and Exchange Commission. The Act is designed to protect the public from fraud or misrepresentation by investment advisers. One requirement, for example, is that advisers must disclose all potential *conflicts of interest* with any recommendations they make to those they advise. A potential conflict of interest might exist where the adviser had a position in a security he was recommending. *See also* INVESTMENT ADVISORY SERVICE.

INVESTMENT ADVISORY SERVICE service providing investment advice for a fee. Investment advisers must register with the Securities and Exchange Commission and abide by the rules of the INVESTMENT ADVISERS ACT. Investment advisory services usually specialize in a particular kind of investment—for example, emerging growth stocks, international stocks, mutual funds, or commodities. Some services only offer advice through a newsletter; others will manage a client's money. The performance of many investment advisory services is ranked by the *Hulbert Financial Digest. See* HULBERT RATING.

INVESTMENT BANKER firm, acting as underwriter or agent, that serves as intermediary between an issuer of securities and the investing public. In what is termed FIRM COMMITMENT underwriting, the investment banker, either as manager or participating member of an investment banking syndicate, makes outright purchases of new securities from the issuer and distributes them to dealers and investors, profiting on the spread between the purchase price and the selling (public offering) price. Under a conditional arrangement called BEST EFFORT, the investment banker markets a new issue without underwriting it, acting as agent rather than principal and taking a commission for whatever amount of securities the banker succeeds in marketing. Under another conditional arrangement, called STANDBY COMMITMENT, the investment banker serves clients issuing new securities by agreeing to purchase for resale any securities not taken by existing holders of RIGHTS.

Where a client relationship exists, the investment banker's role begins with preunderwriting counseling and continues after the distribution of securities is completed, in the form of ongoing expert advice and guidance, often including a seat on the board of directors. The direct underwriting responsibilities include preparing the Securities and Exchange Commission registration statement; consulting on pricing of the securities; forming and managing the syndicate; establishing a selling group if desired; and PEGGING (stabilizing) the price of the issue during the offering and distribution period.

In addition to new securities offerings, investment bankers handle the distribution of blocks of previously issued securities, either through secondary offerings or through negotiations; maintain markets for securities already distributed; and act as finders in the private placement of securities.

Along with their investment banking functions, the majority of investment bankers also maintain broker-dealer operations, serving both wholesale and retail clients in brokerage and advisory capacities and offering a growing number of related financial services. *See also* FLOTATION COST; SECONDARY DISTRIBUTION; UNDERWRITE.

INVESTMENT CERTIFICATE certificate evidencing investment in a savings and loan association and showing the amount of money invested. Investment certificates do not have voting rights and do not involve stockholder responsibility. Also called *mutual capital certificate. See also* MUTUAL ASSOCIATION.

INVESTMENT CLUB group of people who pool their assets in order to make joint investment decisions. Each member of the club contributes a certain amount of capital, with additional money to be invested every month or quarter. Decisions on which stocks or bonds to buy are made by a vote of members. Besides helping each member become more knowledgeable about investing, these clubs allow people with small amounts of money to participate in larger investments and therefore pay lower commissions. There is a National Association of Investment Clubs, based in Royal Oak, Michigan.

INVESTMENT COMPANY firm that, for a management fee, invests the pooled funds of small investors in securities appropriate for its stated investment objectives. It offers participants more diversification, liquidity, and professional management service than would normally be available to them as individuals.

There are two basic types of investment companies: (1) *open-end*, better known as a MUTUAL FUND, which has a floating number of outstanding shares (hence the name *open-end*) and stands prepared to sell or redeem shares at their current NET ASSET VALUE; and (2) *closed-end*, also known as an *investment trust*, which, like a corporation, has a fixed number of outstanding shares that are traded like stock, often on the major exchanges.

Open-end management companies are divided into two categories, based on their acquisition cost policies: (1) *load funds,* which are sold in the over-the-counter market by broker-dealers, who do not receive a sales commission; instead, a "loading charge" is added to the net asset value at time of purchase. The charge typically runs 8½%, with a reduction for quantity that ranges as low as 4%. There is no redemption charge when load fund shares are sold. (2) *no-load funds,* which are bought directly from sponsoring companies. Such companies do not charge a loading fee, although small redemption charges are not uncommon.

Dealers in closed-end investment companies obtain their sales revenue from regular brokerage commissions.

Both open-end and closed-end investment companies charge annual management fees, typically ranging from ½% to 1% of the value of the investment.

Under the INVESTMENT COMPANY ACT OF 1940, the registration statement and prospectus of every investment company must state its specific investment objectives. Basically, the companies fall into the following categories: diversified common stock funds; balanced funds (mixing bonds and preferred and common stocks); bond and preferred stock funds (featuring fixed income); specialized funds (by industry, groups of industries, geography, size of company); income funds (high-yield securities); performance funds (growth stocks); dual-purpose funds (a form of closed-end investment company offering a choice of dividend shares or capital gain shares); and money market funds (money market instruments).

INVESTMENT COMPANY ACT OF 1940 legislation passed by Congress requiring registration and regulation of investment companies by the Securities and Exchange Commission. The Act sets the standards by which mutual funds and other investment vehicles of investment companies operate, in such areas as promotion, reporting requirements, pricing of securities for sale to the public, and allocation of investments within a fund portfolio. *See also* INVESTMENT COMPANY.

INVESTMENT COUNSEL person with the responsibility for providing investment advice to clients and executing investment decisions.

INVESTMENT CREDIT reduction in income tax liability granted by the federal government over the years to firms making new investments in certain asset categories, primarily equipment; also called *investment tax credit.* The investment credit, designed to stimulate the economy by encouraging capital expenditure, has been a feature of tax legislation on and off, and in varying percentage amounts, since 1962; in 1985 it was 6% or 10% of the purchase price, depending on the life of the asset. As a credit, it has been deducted from the tax bill, not from pretax income, and it has been independent of DEPRECIATION. The TAX REFORM ACT OF 1986 generally repealed the investment credit retroactively for any property placed in service after January 1, 1986. The 1986 Act also provided for a 35% reduction of the value of credits carried over from previous years.

INVESTMENT GRADE term used to describe bonds suitable for purchase by prudent investors. Standard & Poor's rating service designates the bonds in its four top categories (AAA down to BBB) as investment grade. In their FIDUCIARY roles, institutional investors, such as pension funds, insurance companies, and banks, must maintain a certain level of credit quality in the bond portfolios they purchase, so they tend to buy mostly investment grade bonds. Any debt issue below investment grade is considered speculative and is often referred to as a JUNK BOND.

INVESTMENT HISTORY body of prior experience establishing "normal investment practice" with respect to the account relationship between a member firm and its customer. For example, the Rules of Fair Practice of the National Association of Securities Dealers (NASD) prohibit the sale of a new issue to members of a distributing dealer's immediate family unless it can be demonstrated that the number of securities ordered conformed to normal investment practice. In other words, if there was sufficient precedent in the investment history of this particular dealer-customer relationship, the sale would not be a violation of NASD rules.

INVESTMENT LETTER in the private placement of new securities, a letter of intent between the issuer of securities and the buyer establishing that the securities are being bought as an investment and are not for resale. This is necessary to avoid having to register the securities with the Securities and Exchange Commission. (Under provisions of SEC Rule 144, a purchaser of such securities may eventually resell them to the public if certain specific conditions are met, including a mimimum holding period of at least two years.) Use of the investment letter gave rise to the terms *letter stock* and *letter bond* in referring to unregistered issues. *See also* LETTER SECURITY.

INVESTMENT STRATEGY plan to allocate assets among such choices as stocks, bonds, CASH EQUIVALENTS, commodities, and real estate. An investment strategy should be formulated based on an investor's outlook on interest rates, inflation, and economic growth, among other factors, and also taking into account the investor's age, tolerance for risk, amount of capital available to invest, and future needs for capital, such as for financing childrens' college educations or buying a house. An investment adviser will help to devise such a strategy. *See also* INVESTMENT ADVISORY SERVICE.

INVESTMENT STRATEGY COMMITTEE committee in the research department of a brokerage firm that sets the overall investment strategy the firm recommends to clients. The director of research, the chief economist, and several top analysts typically sit on this committee. The group advises clients on the amount of money that should be placed into stocks, bonds, or CASH EQUIVALENTS, as well as the industry groups or individual stocks or bonds that look particularly attractive.

INVESTMENT TAX CREDIT *see* INVESTMENT CREDIT.

INVESTMENT TRUST *see* INVESTMENT COMPANY.

INVESTMENT VALUE OF A CONVERTIBLE SECURITY estimated price at which a CONVERTIBLE security (CV) would be valued by the marketplace if it had no stock conversion feature. The investment value for CVs of major companies is determined by investment advisory services and, theoretically, should never fall lower than the price of the related stock. It is arrived at by estimating the price at which a nonconvertible ("straight") bond or preferred share of the same issuing company would sell. The investment value reflects the interest rate; therefore, the market price of the security will go up when rates are down and vice versa. *See also* PREMIUM OVER BOND VALUE.

INVESTOR RELATIONS DEPARTMENT in major listed companies, a staff position responsible for investor relations, reporting either to the chief financial officer or to the director of public relations. The actual duties will vary, depending on whether the company retains an outside financial public relations firm, but the general responsibilities are as follows:
- to see that the company is understood, in terms of its activities and objectives, and is favorably regarded in the financial and capital markets and the investment community; this means having input into the annual report and other published materials, coordinating senior management speeches and public statements with the FINANCIAL PUBLIC RELATIONS effort, and generally fostering a consistent and positive corporate image.
- to ensure full and timely public DISCLOSURE of material information, and to work with the legal staff in complying with the rules of the SEC, the securities exchanges, and other regulatory authorities.
- to respond to requests for reports and information from shareholders, professional investors, brokers, and the financial media.
- to maintain productive relations with the firm's investment bankers, the specialists in its stock, major broker-dealers, and institutional investors who follow the company or hold sizeable positions in its securities.
- to take direct measures, where necessary, to see that the company's shares are properly valued. This involves identifying the firm's particular investment audience and the professionals controlling its stock float, arranging analysts' meetings and other presentations, and generating appropriate publicity.

The most successful investor relations professionals have been those who follow a policy of full and open dissemination of relevant information, favorable and unfavorable, on a consistent basis. The least successful, over the long run, have been the "touts"—those who emphasize promotion at the expense of credibility.

INVESTORS SERVICE BUREAU New York Stock Exchange public service that responds to written inquiries of all types concerning securities investments.

INVOICE bill prepared by a seller of goods or services and submitted to the purchaser. The invoice lists all the items bought, together with amounts.

INVOLUNTARY BANKRUPTCY *see* BANKRUPTCY.

IRA *see* INDIVIDUAL RETIREMENT ACCOUNT.

IRA ROLLOVER *see* INDIVIDUAL RETIREMENT ACCOUNT ROLLOVER.

IRREDEEMABLE BOND

1. bond without a CALL FEATURE (issuer's right to redeem the bond before maturity) or a REDEMPTION privilege (holder's right to sell the bond back to the issuer before maturity).
2. PERPETUAL BOND.

IRREVOCABLE TRUST trust that cannot be changed or terminated by the one who created it without the agreement of the BENEFICIARY.

IRS *see* INTERNAL REVENUE SERVICE.

ISSUE

1. stock or bonds sold by a corporation or a government entity at a particular time.
2. selling new securities by a corporation or government entity, either through an underwriter or by a private placement.
3. descendants, such as children and grandchildren. For instance, "This man's estate will be passed, at his death, to his issue."

ISSUED AND OUTSTANDING shares of a corporation, authorized in the corporate charter, which have been issued and are outstanding. These shares represent capital invested by the firm's shareholders and owners, and may be all or only a portion of the number of shares authorized. Shares that have been issued and subsequently repurchased by the company are called *treasury stock,* because they are held in the corporate treasury pending reissue or retirement. Treasury shares are legally issued but are not considered outstanding for purposes of voting, dividends, or earnings per share calculations. Shares authorized but not yet issued are called *unissued shares.* Most companies show the amount of authorized, issued and outstanding, and treasury shares in the capital section of their annual reports. *See also* TREASURY STOCK.

ISSUER legal entity that has the power to issue and distribute a security. Issuers include corporations, municipalities, foreign and domestic governments and their agencies, and investment trusts. Issuers of stock are responsible for reporting on corporate developments to shareholders and paying dividends once declared. Issuers of bonds are committed to making timely payments of interest and principal to bondholders.

j

JEEP *see* GRADUATED PAYMENT MORTGAGE.

JOBBER

1. wholesaler, especially one who buys in small lots from manufacturers, importers, and/or other wholesalers and sells to retailers.
2. London Stock Exchange term for MARKET MAKER.

JOINT ACCOUNT bank or brokerage account owned jointly by two or more people. Joint accounts may be set up in two ways: (1) either all parties to the account must sign checks and approve all withdrawals or brokerage transactions or (2) any one party can take such actions on his or her own. *See also* JOINT TENANTS WITH RIGHT OF SURVIVORSHIP.

JOINT ACCOUNT AGREEMENT form needed to open a JOINT ACCOUNT at a bank or brokerage. It must be signed by all parties to the account regardless of the provisions it may contain concerning signatures required to authorize transactions.

JOINT AND SURVIVOR ANNUITY annuity that makes payments for the lifetime of two or more beneficiaries, often a husband and wife. When one of the annuitants dies, payments continue to the survivor annuitant in the same amount or in a reduced amount as specified in the contract.

JOINT BOND bond that has more than one obligator or that is guaranteed by a party other than the issuer; also called *joint and several bond*. Joint bonds are common where a parent corporation wishes to guarantee the bonds of a subsidiary. *See* GUARANTEED BOND.

JOINTLY AND SEVERALLY

In general: legal phrase used in definitions of liability meaning that an obligation may be enforced against all obligators jointly or against any one of them separately.

Securities: term used to refer to municipal bond underwritings where the account is undivided and syndicate members are responsible for unsold bonds in proportion to their participations. In other words, a participant with 5% of the account would still be responsible for 5% of the unsold bonds, even though that member might already have sold 10%. *See also* SEVERALLY BUT NOT JOINTLY.

JOINT STOCK COMPANY form of business organization that combines features of a corporation and a partnership. Under U.S. law, joint stock companies are recognized as corporations with unlimited liability for their stockholders. As in a conventional corporation, investors in joint stock companies receive shares of stock they are free to sell at will without ending the corporation; they also elect directors. Unlike in a limited liability corporation, however, each shareholder in a joint stock company is legally liable for all debts of the company.

There are some advantages to this form of organization compared with limited-liability corporations: fewer taxes, greater ease of formation under the common law, more security for creditors, mobility, and freedom from regulation, for example. However, the disadvantages—such as the fact that the joint stock company usually cannot hold title to real estate and, particularly, the company's unlimited liability—tend to outweigh the advantages, with the result that it is not a popular form of organization.

JOINT TENANTS WITH RIGHT OF SURVIVORSHIP when two or more people maintain a JOINT ACCOUNT with a brokerage firm or a bank, it is normally agreed that, upon the death of one account holder, ownership of the account assets passes to the remaining account holders. This transfer of assets escapes probate, but estate taxes may be due, depending on the amount of assets transferred.

JOINT VENTURE agreement by two or more parties to work on a project together. Frequently, a joint venture will be formed when companies with complementary technology wish to create a product or service that takes advantage of the strengths of the participants. A joint venture, which is usually limited to one project, differs from a partnership, which forms the basis for cooperation on many projects.

JUDGMENT decision by a court of law ordering someone to pay a certain amount of money. For instance, a court may order someone who illegally profited by trading on INSIDE INFORMATION to pay a judgment amounting to all the profits from the trade, plus damages. The term also refers to condemnation awards by government entities in payment for private property taken for public use.

JUMBO CERTIFICATE OF DEPOSIT certificate with a minimum denomination of $100,000. Jumbo CDs are usually bought and sold by large institutions such as banks, pension funds, money market funds, and insurance companies.

JUNIOR ISSUE issue of debt or equity that is subordinate in claim to another issue in terms of dividends, interest, principal, or security in the event of liquidation. *See also* JUNIOR SECURITY; PREFERRED STOCK; PRIORITY; PRIOR LIEN BOND; PRIOR PREFERRED STOCK.

JUNIOR MORTGAGE mortgage that is subordinate to other mortgages—for example, a second or a third mortgage. If a debtor defaults, the first mortgage will have to be satisfied before the junior mortgage.

JUNIOR REFUNDING refinancing government debt that matures in one to five years by issuing new securities that mature in five years or more.

JUNIOR SECURITY security with lower priority claim on assets and income than a SENIOR SECURITY. For example, a PREFERRED STOCK is junior to a DEBENTURE, but a debenture, being an unsecured bond, is junior to a MORTGAGE BOND. COMMON STOCK is junior to all corporate securities. Some companies—finance companies, for example—have senior SUBORDINATED and junior subordinated issues, the former having priority over the latter, but both ranking lower than senior (unsubordinated) debt.

JUNK BOND bond with a credit rating of BB or lower by RATING agencies. Junk bonds are issued by companies without long track records of sales and earnings, or by those with questionable credit strength. They are a popular means of financing TAKEOVERS. Since they are more volatile and pay higher yields than INVESTMENT GRADE bonds, many risk-oriented investors specialize in trading them. Institutions with FIDUCIARY responsibilities are regulated. *See* LEGAL LIST.

JURISDICTION defined by the American Bankers Association as "the legal right, power or authority to hear and determine a cause; as in the jurisdiction of a court." The term frequently comes up in finance and investment discussions in connection with the jurisdictions of the various regulatory authorities bearing on the field. For example, the Federal Reserve Board, not the Securities and Exchange Commission (as might be supposed), has jurisdiction in a case involving a brokerage MARGIN ACCOUNT (*see also* REGULATION T).

The term also is important with respect to EUROCURRENCY loan agreements, where it is possible for a loan to be funded in one country but made in another by a group of international banks each from different countries, to a borrower in still another country. The determination of jurisdiction, not to mention the willingness of courts in different countries to accept that jurisdiction, is a matter of obvious urgency in such cases.

JURY OF EXECUTIVE OPINION forecasting method whereby a panel of experts—perhaps senior corporate financial executives—prepare individual forecasts based on information made available to all of them. Each expert then reviews the others' work and modifies his or her own forecasts accordingly. The resulting composite forecast is supposed to be more realistic than any individual effort could be. Also known as *Delphi forecast.*

JUSTIFIED PRICE fair market price an informed buyer will pay for an asset, whether it be a stock, a bond, a commodity, or real estate. *See also* FAIR MARKET VALUE.

JUST TITLE title to property that is supportable against all legal claims. Also called *clear title, good title, proper title*.

k
_____

KAFFIRS term used in Great Britain that refers to South African gold mining shares. These shares are traded over the counter in the U.S. in the form of American Depositary Receipts, which are claims to share certificates deposited in a foreign bank. Under South African law, Kaffirs must pay out almost all their earnings to shareholders as dividends. These shares thus not only provide stockholders with a gold investment to hedge against inflation, but also afford substantial income in the form of high dividend payments. However, investors in Kaffirs must also consider the political risks of investing in South Africa, as well as the risk of fluctuations in the price of gold. *See also* AMERICAN DEPOSITARY RECEIPT.

KANSAS CITY BOARD OF TRADE (KCBT) futures exchange on which contracts for wheat and the Value Line Stock Index are traded.

KEOGH PLAN tax-deferred pension account designated for employees of unincorporated businesses or for persons who are self-employed (either full-time or part-time). As of 1984, eligible people could contribute up to 25% of earned income, up to a maximum of $30,000. Like the INDIVIDUAL RETIREMENT ACCOUNT (IRA), the Keogh plan allows all investment earnings to grow tax deferred until capital is withdrawn, as early as age 59½ and starting no later than age 70½. Almost any investment except precious metals or collectibles can be used for a Keogh account. Typically, people place Keogh assets in stocks, bonds, money-market funds, certificates of deposit, mutual funds, or limited partnerships. The Keogh plan was established by Congress in 1962 and was expanded in 1976 and again in 1981 as part of the Economic Recovery Tax Act.

KEY INDUSTRY industry of primary importance to a nation's economy. For instance, the defense industry is called a key industry since it is crucial to maintaining a country's safety. The automobile industry is also considered key since so many jobs are directly or indirectly dependent on it.

KEYNESIAN ECONOMICS body of economic thought originated by the British economist and government adviser, John Maynard Keynes (1883–1946), whose landmark work, *The General Theory of Employment, Interest and Money,* was published in 1935. Writing during the Great Depression, Keynes took issue with the classical economists, like Adam Smith, who believed that the economy worked best when left alone. Keynes believed that active government intervention in the marketplace was the only method of ensuring economic growth and stability. He held essentially that insufficient demand causes unemployment and that excessive demand results in inflation; government should therefore manipulate the level of aggregate demand by adjusting levels of government expenditure and taxation. For example, to avoid depression Keynes advocated increased government spending and EASY MONEY, resulting in more investment, higher employment, and increased consumer spending.

Keynesian economics has had great influence on the public economic policies of industrial nations, including the United States. In the 1980s, however, after repeated recessions, slow growth, and high rates of inflation in the U.S., a contrasting outlook, uniting monetarists and "supply siders," blamed excessive government intervention for troubles in the economy.

See also AGGREGATE SUPPLY; LAISSEZ-FAIRE; MACROECONOMICS; MONETARIST; SUPPLY-SIDE ECONOMICS.

KICKBACK

Finance: practice whereby sales finance companies reward dealers who discount installment purchase paper through them with cash payments.

Government and private contracts: payment made secretly by a seller to someone instrumental in awarding a contract or making a sale—an illegal payoff.

Labor relations: illegal practice whereby employers require the return of a portion of wages established by law or union contract, in exchange for employment.

KICKER added feature of a debt obligation, usually designed to enhance marketability by offering the prospect of equity participation. For instance, a bond may be convertible to stock if the shares reach a certain price. This makes the bond more attractive to investors, since the bondholder potentially gets the benefit of an equity security in addition to interest payments. Other examples of equity kickers are RIGHTS and WARRANTS. Some mortgage loans also include kickers in the form of ownership participation or in the form of a percentage of gross rental receipts. Kickers are also called *sweeteners*.

KILLER BEES those who aid a company in fending off a takeover bid. "Killer bees" are usually investment bankers who devise strategies to make the target less attractive or more difficult to acquire.

KITING

Commercial banking: (1) depositing and drawing checks between accounts at two or more banks and thereby taking advantage of the FLOAT—that is, the time it takes the bank of deposit to collect from the paying bank. (2) fraudently altering the figures on a check to increase its face value.

Securities: driving stock prices to high levels through manipulative trading methods, such as the creation of artificial trading activity by the buyer and the seller working together and using the same funds.

KNOW YOUR CUSTOMER ethical concept in the securities industry either stated or implied by the rules of the exchanges and the other authorities regulating broker-dealer practices. Its meaning is expressed in the following paragraph from Article 3 of the NASD Rules of Fair Practice: "In recommending to a customer the purchase, sale or exchange of any security, a member shall have reasonable grounds for believing that the recommendation is suitable for such customer upon the basis of the facts, if any, disclosed by such customer as to his other security holdings and as to his financial situation and needs." Customers opening accounts at brokerage firms must supply financial information that satisfies the know your customer requirement for routine purposes.

KONDRATIEFF WAVE theory of the Soviet economist Nikolai Kondratieff in the 1920s that the economies of the Western capitalist world were prone to major up-and-down "supercycles" lasting 50 to 60 years. He claimed to have predicted the economic crash of 1929–30 based on the crash of 1870, 60 years earlier. The

Kondratieff wave theory has adherents, but is controversial among economists. Also called *Kondratieff cycle*.

KRUGERRAND gold bullion coin minted by the Republic of South Africa and containing one troy ounce of gold. Krugerrands usually sell for slightly more than the current value of their gold content. Krugerrands were banned for further import into the United States in 1985, although existing coins could still be traded. Other gold coins traded include the Mexican 50-peso, Austrian 100-corona, and Canadian Maple Leaf pieces and the United States Eagle series.

L

LABOR-INTENSIVE requiring large pools of workers. Said of an industry in which labor costs are more important than capital costs. Deep-shaft coal mining, for instance, is labor-intensive.

LAFFER CURVE curve named for U.S. economics professor Arthur Laffer, postulating that economic output will grow if marginal tax rates are cut. The curve is used in explaining SUPPLY-SIDE ECONOMICS, a theory that noninflationary growth is spurred when tax policies encourage productivity and investment.

LAISSEZ-FAIRE doctrine that interference of government in business and economic affairs should be minimal. Adam Smith's *The Wealth Of Nations* (1776) described laissez-faire economics in terms of an "invisible hand" that would provide for the maximum good for all, if businessmen were free to pursue profitable opportunities as they saw them. The growth of industry in England in the early 19th century and American industrial growth in the late 19th century both occurred in a laissez-faire capitalist environment. The laissez-faire period ended by the beginning of the 20th century, when large monopolies were broken up and government regulation of business became the norm. The Great Depression of the 1930s saw the birth of KEYNESIAN ECONOMICS, an influential approach advocating government intervention in economic affairs. The movement toward deregulation of business in the U.S. in the 1970s and 80s is to some extent a return to the laissez-faire philosphy. Laissez-faire is French for "allow to do."

LAPSED OPTION OPTION that reached its expiration date without being exercised and is thus without value.

LAST IN FIRST OUT (LIFO) method of accounting for INVENTORY that ties the cost of goods sold to the cost of the most recent purchases. The formula for cost of goods sold is:

beginning inventory + purchases − ending inventory = cost of goods sold

In contrast to the FIRST IN, FIRST OUT (FIFO) method, in a period of rising prices LIFO produces a higher cost of goods sold and a lower gross profit and taxable income. The artificially low balance sheet inventories resulting from the use of LIFO in periods of inflation give rise to the term *LIFO cushion*.

LAST SALE most recent trade in a particular security. Not to be confused with the final transaction in a trading session, called the CLOSING SALE. The last sale is the point of reference for two Securites and Exchange Commission rules: (1) On a national exchange, no SHORT SALE may be made below the price of the last regular sale. (2) No short sale may be made at the same price as the last sale unless the last sale was at a price higher than the preceding different price. PLUS

TICK, MINUS TICK, ZERO MINUS TICK, and ZERO PLUS TICK, used in this connection, refer to the last sale.

LAST TRADING DAY final day during which a futures contract may be settled. If the contract is not OFFSET, either an agreement between the buying and selling parties must be arranged or the physical commodity must be delivered from the seller to the buyer.

LATE TAPE delay in displaying price changes because trading on a stock exchange is particularly heavy. If the tape is more than five minutes late, the first digit of a price is deleted. For instance, a trade at 62¾ is reported as 2¾. *See also* DIGITS DELETED.

LAY OFF

Investment banking: reduce the risk in a standby commitment, under which the bankers agree to purchase and resell to the public any portion of a stock issue not subscribed to by shareowners who hold rights. The risk is that the market value will fall during the two to four weeks when shareholders are deciding whether to exercise or sell their rights. To minimize the risk, investment bankers (1) buy up the rights as they are offered and, at the same time, sell the shares represented by these rights; and (2) sell short an amount of shares proportionate to the rights that can be expected to go unexercised—to ½% of the issue, typically. Also called *laying off.*

Labor: temporarily or permanently remove an employee from a payroll because of an economic slowdown or a production cutback, not because of poor performance or an infraction of company rules.

LEADER
1. stock or group of stocks at the forefront of an upsurge or a downturn in a market. Typically, leaders are heavily bought and sold by institutions that want to demonstrate their own market leadership.
2. product that has a large market share.

LEADING INDICATORS components of an index released monthly by the U.S. Commerce Department's Bureau of Economic Analysis. The components in 1985 were average workweek of production workers; average weekly claims for state unemployment insurance; new orders for consumer goods and materials; vendor performance (companies receiving slower deliveries from suppliers); net business formation; contracts for plant and equipment; new building permits; inventory changes; sensitive materials prices; stock prices; MONEY SUPPLY (M-2); and business and consumer borrowing. The index of leading indicators, the components of which are adjusted for inflation, has accurately forecast ups and downs in the business cycle. Official full name: *Composite Index of 12 Leading Indicators.*

LEASE contract granting use of real estate, equipment, or other fixed assets for a specified time in exchange for payment, usually in the form of rent. The owner of the leased property is called the lessor, the user the lessee. *See also* CAPITAL LEASE; FINANCIAL LEASE; OPERATING LEASE; SALE AND LEASEBACK.

LEASE ACQUISITION COST price paid by a real estate LIMITED PARTNERSHIP, when acquiring a lease, including legal fees and related expenses. The charges are prorated to the limited partners.

LEASEHOLD asset representing the right to use property under a LEASE.

LEASEHOLD IMPROVEMENT modification of leased property. The cost is added to fixed assets and then amortized.

LEASE-PURCHASE AGREEMENT agreement providing that portions of LEASE payments may be applied toward the purchase of the property under lease.

LEG
1. sustained trend in stock market prices. A prolonged bull or bear market may have first, second, and third legs.
2. one side of a spread transaction. For instance, a trader might buy a CALL OPTION that has a particular STRIKE PRICE and expiration date, then combine it with a PUT OPTION that has the same striking price and a different expiration date. The two options are called legs of the spread.
   Selling one of the options is termed LIFTING A LEG.

LEGAL computerized data base maintained by the New York Stock Exchange to track enforcement actions against member firms, audits of member firms, and customer complaints. LEGAL is not an acronym, but is written in all capitals.

LEGAL ENTITY person or organization that has the legal standing to enter into a contract and may be sued for failure to perform as agreed in the contract. A child under legal age is not a legal entity; a corporation is a legal entity since it is a person in the eyes of the law.

LEGAL INVESTMENT investment permissible for investors with FIDUCIARY responsibilities. INVESTMENT GRADE bonds, as rated by Standard & Poor's or Moody's, usually qualify as legal investments. Guidelines designed to protect investors are set by the state in which the fiduciary operates. *See also* LEGAL LIST.

LEGAL LIST securities selected by a state agency, usually a banking department, as permissible holdings of mutual savings banks, pension funds, insurance companies, and other FIDUCIARY institutions. To protect the money that individuals place in such institutions, only high quality debt and equity securities are generally included. As an alternative to the list, some states apply the PRUDENT MAN RULE.

LEGAL MONOPOLY exclusive right to offer a particular service within a particular territory. In exchange, the company agrees to have its policies and rates regulated. Electric and water utilities are legal monopolies.

LEGAL OPINION
1. statement as to legality, written by an authorized official such as a city attorney or an attorney general.
2. statement as to the legality of a MUNICIPAL BOND issue, usually written by a law firm specializing in public borrowings. It is part of the *official statement*, the municipal equivalent of a PROSPECTUS. Unless the legality of an issue is established, an investor's contract is invalid at the time of issue and he cannot sue under it. The legal opinion is therefore required by a SYNDICATE MANAGER and customarily accompanies the transfer of municipal securities as long as they are outstanding.

LEGAL TRANSFER transaction that requires documentation other than the standard stock or bond power to validate the transfer of a stock certificate from a seller to a buyer—for example, securities registered to a corporation or to a deceased person. It is the selling broker's responsibility to supply proper documentation to the buying broker in a legal transfer.

LENDER individual or firm that extends money to a borrower with the expectation of being repaid, usually with interest. Lenders create debt in the form of loans, and in the event of LIQUIDATION they are paid off before stockholders receive distributions. But the investor deals in both debt (bonds) and equity (stocks). It is useful to remember that investors in commercial paper, bonds, and other debt instruments are in fact lenders with the same rights and powers enjoyed by banks.

LENDER OF LAST RESORT
1. characterization of a central bank's role in bolstering a bank that faces large withdrawals of funds. The U.S. lender of last resort is the FEDERAL RESERVE BANK. Member banks may borrow from the DISCOUNT WINDOW to maintain reserve requirements or to meet large withdrawals. The Fed thereby maintains the stability of the banking system, which would be threatened if major banks were to fail.
2. government small business financing programs and municipal economic development organizations whose precondition to making loans to private enterprises is an inability to obtain financing from other lending sources.

LENDING AT A PREMIUM term used when one broker lends securities to another broker to cover customer's short position and imposes a charge for the loan. Such charges, which are passed on to the customer, are the exception rather than the rule, since securities are normally LOANED FLAT between brokers, that is, without interest. Lending at a premium might occur when the securities needed are in very heavy demand and are therefore difficult to borrow. The premium is in addition to any payments the customer might have to make to the lending broker to MARK TO THE MARKET or to cover dividends or interest payable on the borrowed securities.

LENDING AT A RATE paying interest to a customer on the credit balance created from the proceeds of a SHORT SALE. Such proceeds are held in ESCROW to secure the loan of securities, usually made by another broker, to cover the customer's short position. Lending at a rate is the exception rather than the rule.

LENDING SECURITIES securities borrowed from a broker's inventory, other MARGIN ACCOUNTS, or from other brokers, when a customer makes a SHORT SALE and the securities must be delivered to the buying customer's broker. As collateral, the borrowing broker deposits with the lending broker an amount of money equal to the market value of the securities. No interest or premium is ordinarily involved in the transaction. The Securities and Exchange Commission requires that brokerage customers give permission to have their securities used in loan transactions, and the point is routinely covered in the standard agreement signed by customers when they open general accounts.

LETTER BOND *see* LETTER SECURITY.

LETTER OF CREDIT (L/C) instrument or document issued by a bank guaranteeing the payment of a customer's drafts up to a stated amount for a specified period. It substitutes the bank's credit for the buyer's and eliminates the seller's risk. It is used extensively in international trade. A *commercial letter of credit* is normally drawn in favor of a third party, called the beneficiary. A *confirmed letter of credit* is provided by a correspondent bank and guaranteed by the issuing bank. A *revolving letter of credit* is issued for a specified amount and automatically renewed for the same amount for a specified period, permitting any number of drafts to be drawn so long as they do not exceed its overall limit. A *traveler's* *letter of credit* is issued for the convenience of a traveling customer and typically lists correspondent banks at which drafts will be honored. A *performance letter of credit* is issued to guarantee performance under a contract.

LETTER OF INTENT

1. any letter expressing an intention to take (or not take) an action, sometimes subject to other action being taken. For example, a bank might issue a letter of intent stating it will make a loan to a customer, subject to another lender's agreement to participate. The letter of intent, in this case, makes it possible for the customer to negotiate the participation loan.
2. preliminary agreement between two companies that intend to merge. Such a letter is issued after negotiations have been satisfactorily completed.
3. promise by a MUTUAL FUND shareholder to invest a specified sum of money monthly for about a year. In return, the shareholder is entitled to lower sales charges.
4. INVESTMENT LETTER for a LETTER SECURITY.

LETTER SECURITY stock or bond that is not registered with the Securities and Exchange Commission and therefore cannot be sold in the public market. When an issue is sold directly by the issuer to the investor, registration with the SEC can be avoided if a LETTER OF INTENT, called an INVESTMENT LETTER, is signed by the purchaser establishing that the securities are being bought for investment and not for resale. The letter's integral association with the security gives rise to the terms *letter security, letter stock,* and *letter bond.*

LETTER STOCK *see* LETTER SECURITY.

LEVEL DEBT SERVICE provision in a municipal charter stipulating that payments on municipal debt be approximately equal every year. This makes it easier to project the amount of tax revenue needed to meet obligations.

LEVERAGE

Operating leverage: extent to which a company's costs of operating are fixed (rent, insurance, executive salaries) as opposed to variable (materials, direct labor). In a totally automated company, whose costs are virtually all fixed, every dollar of increase in sales is a dollar of increase in operating income once the BREAKEVEN POINT has been reached, because costs remain the same at every level of production. In contrast, a company whose costs are largely variable would show relatively little increase in operating income when production and sales increased because costs and production would rise together. The leverage comes in because a small change in sales has a magnified percentage effect on operating income and losses. The *degree of operating leverage*—the ratio of the percentage change in operating income to the percentage change in sales or units sold—measures the sensitivity of a firm's profits to changes in sales volume. A firm using a high degree of operating leverage has a breakeven point at a relatively high sales level.

Financial leverage: debt in relation to equity in a firm's capital structure—its LONG-TERM DEBT (usually bonds), PREFERRED STOCK, and SHAREHOLDERS' EQUITY— measured by the DEBT-TO-EQUITY RATIO. The more long-term debt there is, the greater the financial leverage. Shareholders benefit from financial leverage to the extent that return on the borrowed money exceeds the interest costs and the market value of their shares rises. For this reason, financial leverage is popularly called *trading on the equity.* Because leverage also means required interest and principal payments and thus ultimately the risk of default, how much leverage is desirable is largely a question of stability of earnings. As a rule of thumb, an industrial company with a debt to equity ratio of more than 30% is highly leveraged, exceptions being firms with dependable earnings and cash flow, such as electric utilities.

Since long-term debt interest is a fixed cost, financial leverage tends to take over where operating leverage leaves off, further magnifying the effects on earnings per share of changes in sales levels. In general, high operating leverage should accompany low financial leverage, and vice versa.

Investments: means of enhancing return or value without increasing investment. Buying securities on margin is an example of leverage with borrowed money, and extra leverage may be possible if the leveraged security is convertible into common stock. RIGHTS, WARRANTS, and OPTION contracts provide leverage, not involving borrowings but offering the prospect of high return for little or no investment.

LEVERAGED BUYOUT TAKEOVER of a company, using borrowed funds. Most often, the target company's assets serve as security for the loans taken out by the acquiring firm, which repays the loans out of cash flow of the acquired company. Management may use this technique to retain control by converting a company from public to private. A group of investors may also borrow from banks, using their own assets as collateral, to take over another firm. In almost all leveraged buyouts, public shareholders receive a premium over the current market value for their shares.

LEVERAGED COMPANY company with debt in addition to equity in its capital structure. In its popular connotation, the term is applied to companies that are highly leveraged. Although the judgment is relative, industrial companies with more than one third of their capitalization in the form of debt are considered highly leveraged. *See also* LEVERAGE.

LEVERAGED INVESTMENT COMPANY

1. open-end INVESTMENT COMPANY, or MUTUAL FUND, that is permitted by its charter to borrow capital from a bank or other lender.
2. dual-purpose INVESTMENT COMPANY, which issues both income and capital shares. Holders of income shares receive dividends and interest on investments, whereas holders of capital shares receive all capital gains on investments. In effect each class of shareholder leverages the other.

LEVERAGED LEASE LEASE that involves a lender in addition to the lessor and lessee. The lender, usually a bank or insurance company, puts up a percentage of the cash required to purchase the asset, usually more than half. The balance is put up by the lessor, who is both the equity participant and the borrower. With the cash the lessor acquires the asset, giving the lender (1) a mortgage on the asset and (2) an assignment of the lease and lease payments. The lessee then makes periodic payments to the lessor, who in turn pays the lender. As owner of the asset, the lessor is entitled to tax deductions for DEPRECIATION on the asset and INTEREST on the loan.

LEVERAGED STOCK stock financed with credit, as in a MARGIN ACCOUNT. Although not, strictly speaking, leveraged stock, securities that are convertible into common stock provide an extra degree of leverage when bought on margin. Assuming the purchase price is reasonably close to the INVESTMENT VALUE and CONVERSION VALUE, the downside risk is no greater than it would be with the same company's common stock, whereas the appreciation value is much greater.

LIABILITY claim on the assets of a company or individual—excluding ownership EQUITY. Characteristics: (1) It represents a transfer of assets or services at a specified or determinable date. (2) The firm or individual has little or no discretion to avoid the transfer. (3) The event causing the obligation has already occurred. *See also* BALANCE SHEET.

LIBOR *see* LONDON INTERBANK OFFERED RATE.

LIEN creditor's claim against property. For example, a mortgage is a lien against a house; if the mortgage is not paid on time, the house can be seized to satisfy the lien. Similarly, a bond is a lien against a company's assets; if interest and principal are not paid when due, the assets may be seized to pay the bondholders. As soon as a debt is paid, the lien is removed. Liens may be granted by courts to satisfy judgments. *See also* MECHANIC'S LIEN.

LIFE EXPECTANCY age to which an average person can be expected to live, as calculated by an ACTUARY. Insurance companies base their projections of benefit payouts on actuarial studies of such factors as sex, heredity, and health habits and base their rates on actuarial analysis. Life expectancy can be calculated at birth or at some other age and generally varies according to age. Thus, all persons at birth might have an average life expectancy of 70 years and all persons aged 40 years might have an average life expectancy of 75 years.

Life expectancy projections determine such matters as the ages when an INDIVIDUAL RETIREMENT ACCOUNT may start and finish paying out funds. Annuities payable for lifetimes are usually based on separate male or female tables, except that a QUALIFIED PLAN OR TRUST must use unisex tables.

LIFE INSURANCE IN FORCE amount of life insurance that a company has issued, including the face amount of all outstanding policies together with all dividends that have been paid to policyholders. Thus a life insurance policy for $500,000 on which dividends of $10,000 have been paid would count as life insurance in force of $510,000.

LIFO *see* LAST IN, FIRST OUT.

LIFT rise in securities prices as measured by the Dow Jones Industrial Average or other market averages, usually caused by good business or economic news.

LIFTING A LEG closing one side of a HEDGE, leaving the other side as a long or short position. A leg, in Wall Street parlance, is one side of a hedged transaction. A trader might have a STRADDLE—that is, a call and a put on the same stock, at the same price, with the same expiration date. Making a closing sale of the put, thereby lifting a leg—or *taking off a leg,* as it is sometimes called—would leave the trader with the call, or the LONG LEG.

LIMITED COMPANY form of business most common in Britain, where registration under the Companies Act is comparable to incorporation under state law in the United States. It is abbreviated Ltd. or PLC.

LIMITED DISCRETION agreement between broker and client allowing the broker to make certain trades without consulting the client—for instance, sell an option position that is near expiration or sell a stock on which there has just been adverse news.

LIMITED PARTNERSHIP organization made up of a GENERAL PARTNER, who manages a project, and limited partners, who invest money but have limited liability, are not involved in day-to-day management, and usually cannot lose more than their capital contribution. Usually limited partners receive income, capital gains, and tax benefits; the general partner collects fees and a percentage of capital gains and income. Typical limited partnerships are in real estate, oil and gas, and equipment leasing, but they also finance movies, research and development, and other projects. Typically, public limited partnerships are sold through brokerage firms, for minimum investments of $5000, whereas private limited partnerships are put together with fewer than 35 limited partners who invest more than $20,000 each. *See also* INCOME LIMITED PARTNERSHIP; MASTER LIMITED PARTNERSHIP; OIL AND GAS LIMITED PARTNERSHIP; RESEARCH AND DEVELOPMENT LIMITED PARTNERSHIP; UNLEVERAGED PROGRAM.

LIMITED RISK risk in buying an options contract. For example, someone who pays a PREMIUM to buy a CALL OPTION on a stock will lose nothing more than the premium if the underlying stock does not rise during the life of the option. In contrast, a FUTURES CONTRACT entails *unlimited risk,* since the buyer may have to put up more money in the event of an adverse move. Thus options trading offers limited risk unavailable in futures trading.

Also, stock analysts may say of a stock that has recently fallen in price, that it now has limited risk, reasoning that the stock is unlikely to fall much further.

LIMITED TAX BOND MUNICIPAL BOND backed by the full faith of the issuing government but not by its full taxing power; rather it is secured by the pledge of a special tax or group of taxes, or a limited portion of the real estate tax.

LIMITED TRADING AUTHORIZATION *see* LIMITED DISCRETION.

LIMIT ORDER order to buy or sell a security at a specific price or better. The broker will execute the trade only within the price restriction. For example, a customer puts in a limit order to buy XYZ Corp. at 30 when the stock is selling for 32. Even if the stock reached 30⅛ the broker will not execute the trade. Similarly, if the client put in a limit order to sell XYZ Corp. at 33 when the price is 31, the trade will not be executed until the stock price hits 33.

LIMIT ORDER INFORMATION SYSTEM electronic system that informs subscribers about securities traded on participating exchanges, showing the specialist, the exchange, the order quantities, and the bid and offer prices. This allows subscribers to shop for the most favorable prices.

LIMIT PRICE price set in a LIMIT ORDER. For example, a customer might put in a limit order to sell shares at 45 or to buy at 40. The broker executes the order at the limit price or better.

LIMIT UP, LIMIT DOWN maximum price movement allowed for a commodity FUTURES CONTRACT during one trading day. In the face of a particularly dramatic development, a future's price may move limit up or limit down for several consecutive days.

LINE OF CREDIT *see* BANK LINE.

LIPPER MUTUAL FUND INDUSTRY AVERAGE average performance level of all mutual funds, as reported by Lipper Analytical Services of New York. The performance of all mutual funds is ranked quarterly and annually, by type of fund—such as aggressive growth fund or income fund. Mutual fund managers try to beat the industry average as well as the other funds in their category. *See also* MUTUAL FUND.

LIQUID ASSET cash or easily convertible into cash. Some examples: money-market fund shares, U.S. Treasury bills, bank deposits. An investor in an ILLIQUID investment such as a real estate or oil and gas LIMITED PARTNERSHIP is required to have substantial liquid assets, which would serve as a cushion if the illiquid deal did not work out favorably.

In a corporation's financial statements, liquid assets are cash, marketable securities, and accounts receivable.

LIQUIDATING DIVIDEND distribution of assets in the form of a DIVIDEND from a corporation that is going out of business. Such a payment may come when a firm goes bankrupt or when management decides to sell off a company's assets and pass the proceeds on to shareholders.

LIQUIDATING VALUE projected price for an asset of a company that is going out of business—for instance, a real estate holding or office equipment. Liquidating value, also called *auction value,* assumes that assets are sold separately from the rest of the organization; it is distinguished from GOING CONCERN VALUE, which may be higher because of what accountants term *organization value* or *goodwill.*

LIQUIDATION
1. dismantling of a business, paying off debts in order of priority, and distributing the remaining assets in cash to the owners. Involuntary liquidation is covered under Chapter 7 of the federal BANKRUPTCY law. *See also* JUNIOR SECURITY; PREFERRED STOCK.
2. forced sale of a brokerage client's securities or commodities after failure to meet a MARGIN CALL. *See also* SELL OUT.

LIQUIDITY
1. characteristic of a security or commodity with enough units outstanding to allow large transactions without a substantial drop in price. A stock, bond, or commodity that has a great many shares outstanding therefore has liquidity. Institutional investors are inclined to seek out liquid investments so that their trading activity will not influence the market price.
2. ability of an individual or company to convert assets into cash or cash equivalents without significant loss. Investments in money-market funds and listed stocks are much more liquid than investments in real estate, for instance. Having a good amount of liquidity means being able to meet maturing obligations promptly, earn trade discounts, benefit from a good credit rating, and take advantage of market opportunities.

LIQUIDITY DIVERSIFICATION purchase of bonds whose maturities range from short to medium to long term, thus helping to protect against sharp fluctuations in interest rates.

LIQUIDITY FUND Emeryville, California, company that will buy a limited partner's interest in a real estate LIMITED PARTNERSHIP for cash at 25% to 30% below the appraised value.

LIQUIDITY RATIO measure of a firm's ability to meet maturing short-term obligations. *See also* CURRENT RATIO; NET QUICK ASSETS; QUICK RATIO.

LISTED OPTION put or call OPTION that an exchange has authorized for trading, properly called an *exchange-traded option*.

LISTED SECURITY stock or bond that has been accepted for trading by one of the organized and registered securities exchanges in the United States, which list more than 6000 issues of securities of some 3500 corporations. Generally, the advantages of being listed are that the exchanges provide (1) an orderly market-place; (2) liquidity; (3) fair price determination; (4) accurate and continuous reporting on sales and quotations; (5) information on listed companies; and (6) strict regulations for the protection of security holders. Each exchange has its own listing requirements, those of the New York Stock Exchange being most stringent. Listed securities include stocks, bonds, convertible bonds, preferred stocks, warrants, rights, and options, although not all forms of securities are accepted on all exchanges. Unlisted securites are traded in the OVER-THE-COUNTER market. *See also* LISTING REQUIREMENTS; STOCK EXCHANGE.

LISTING REQUIREMENTS rules that must be met before a stock is listed for trading on an exchange. Among the requirements of the New York Stock Exchange: a corporation must have a minimum of one million publicly held shares with a minimum aggregate market value of $16 million as well as an annual net income topping $2.5 million before federal income tax.

LIVING TRUST *see* INTER VIVOS TRUST.

LOAD sales charge paid by an investor who buys shares in a load MUTUAL FUND or ANNUITY. Loads are usually charged when shares or units are purchased; a charge for withdrawing is called a BACK-END LOAD (or *rear-end load*). A fund that does not charge this fee is called a NO-LOAD FUND. *See also* INVESTMENT COMPANY.

LOAD FUND MUTUAL FUND that is sold for a sales charge by a brokerage firm or other sales representative. Such funds may be stock, bond, or commodity funds, with conservative or aggressive objectives. The stated advantage of a load fund is that the salesperson will explain the fund to the customer, and advise him or her when it is appropriate to sell the fund, as well as when to buy more shares. A NO-LOAD FUND, which is sold without a sales charge directly to investors by a fund company, does not give advice on when to buy or sell. *See also* INVESTMENT COMPANY.

LOAD SPREAD OPTION method of allocating the annual sales charge on some contractual mutual funds. In a CONTRACTUAL PLAN, the investor accumulates shares in the fund through periodic fixed payments. During the first four years of the contract, up to 20% of any single year's contributions to the fund may be credited against the sales charge, provided that the total charges for these four years do not exceed 64% of one year's contributions. The sales charge is limited to 9% of the entire contract.

LOAN transaction wherein an owner of property, called the LENDER, allows another party, the *borrower*, to use the property. The borrower customarily promises to return the property after a specified period with payment for its use, called INTEREST. The documentation of the promise is called a PROMISSORY NOTE when the property is cash.

LOAN CROWD stock exchange members who lend or borrow securities required to cover the positions of brokerage customers who sell short—called a crowd because they congregate at a designated place on the floor of the exchange. *See also* LENDING SECURITIES.

LOANED FLAT loaned without interest, said of the arrangement whereby brokers lend securities to one another to cover customer SHORT SALE positions. *See also* LENDING AT A PREMIUM; LENDING AT A RATE; LENDING SECURITIES.

LOAN STOCK *see* LENDING SECURITIES.

LOAN VALUE
1. amount a lender is willing to loan against collateral. For example, at 50% of appraised value, a piece of property worth $800,000 has a loan value of $400,000.
2. with respect to REGULATION T of the FEDERAL RESERVE BOARD, the maximum percentage of the current market value of eligible securities that a broker can lend a margin account customer. Regulation T applies only to securities formally registered or having an unlisted trading privilege on a national securities exchange. For securities exempt from Regulation T, which comprise U.S. government securities, municipal bonds, and bonds of the International Bank for Reconstruction and Development, loan value is a matter of the individual firm's policy.

LOCK BOX
1. cash management system whereby a company's customers mail payments to a post office box near the company's bank. The bank collects checks from the lock box—sometimes several times a day—deposits them to the account of the firm, and informs the company's cash manager by telephone of the deposit. This reduces processing FLOAT and puts cash to work more quickly. The bank's fee for its services must be weighed against the savings from reduced float to determine whether this arrangement is cost-effective.
2. bank service that entails holding a customer's securities and, as agent, receiving and depositing income such as dividends on stock and interest on bonds.
3. box rented in a post office where mail is stored until collected.

LOCKED IN
1. unable to take advantage of preferential tax treatment on the sale of an asset because the required HOLDING PERIOD has not elapsed. *See also* CAPITAL GAIN.
2. commodities position in which the market has an up or down limit day, and investors cannot get in or out of the market.
3. said of a rate of return that has been assured for a length of time through an investment such as a certificate of deposit or a fixed rate bond; also said of profits or yields on securities or commodities that have been protected through HEDGING techniques.

LOCKED MARKET highly competitive market environment with identical bid and ask prices for a stock. The appearance of more buyers and sellers unlocks the market.

LOCK-UP OPTION privilege offered a WHITE KNIGHT (friendly acquirer) by a TARGET COMPANY of buying CROWN JEWELS or additional equity. The aim is to discourage a hostile TAKEOVER.

LONDON INTERBANK OFFERED RATE (LIBOR) rate that the most creditworthy international banks dealing in EURODOLLARS charge each other for large loans. The LIBOR rate is usually the base for other large Eurodollar loans to less creditworthy corporate and government borrowers. For instance, a Third World country may have to pay one point over LIBOR when it borrows money.

LONG BOND 30-year TREASURIES or any bond that matures in more than 10 years. Since these bonds commit investors' money for a long time, they are riskier than shorter-term bonds of the same quality and thus normally pay a higher yield.

LONG COUPON

1. bond issue's first interest payment covering a longer period than the remaining payments, or the bond issue itself. Conventional schedules call for interest payments at six-month intervals. A long COUPON results when a bond is issued more than six months before the date of the first scheduled payment. *See also* SHORT COUPON.
2. interest-bearing bond maturing in more than 10 years.

LONG HEDGE

1. FUTURES CONTRACT bought to protect against a rise in the cost of honoring a future commitment. Also called a *buy hedge*. The hedger benefits from a narrowing of the BASIS (difference between cash price and future price) if the future is bought below the cash price, and from a widening of the basis if the future is bought above the cash price.
2. FUTURES CONTRACT or CALL OPTION bought in anticipation of a drop in interest rates, so as to lock in the present yield on a fixed-income security.

LONG LEG part of an OPTION SPREAD representing a commitment to buy the underlying security. For instance, if a spread consists of a long CALL OPTION and a short PUT OPTION, the long call is the long LEG.

LONG POSITION

1. ownership of a security, giving the investor the right to transfer ownership to someone else by sale or by gift; the right to receive any income paid by the security; and the right to any profits or losses as the security's value changes.
2. investor's ownership of securities held by a brokerage firm.

LONG TERM

1. HOLDING PERIOD of six months or longer, according to the TAX REFORM ACT OF 1984 and applicable in calculating the CAPITAL GAINS TAX until 1988.
2. investment approach to the stock market in which an investor seeks appreciation by holding a stock for a year or more.
3. bond with a maturity of ten years or longer.
   See also LONG BOND; LONG-TERM DEBT; LONG-TERM FINANCING; LONG-TERM GAIN; LONG-TERM LOSS.

LONG-TERM DEBT liability due in a year or more. Normally, interest is paid periodically over the term of the loan, and the principal amount is payable as notes or bonds mature. Also, a LONG BOND with a maturity of 10 years or more.

LONG-TERM FINANCING liabilities not repayable in one year and all equity. *See also* LONG-TERM DEBT.

LONG-TERM GAIN subsequent to the TAX REFORM ACT OF 1984 and prior to provisions of the TAX REFORM ACT OF 1986 effective in 1988, a gain on the sale of a CAPITAL ASSET where the HOLDING PERIOD was six months or more and the profit was subject to the long-term CAPITAL GAINS TAX.

LONG-TERM LOSS negative counterpart to LONG-TERM GAIN as defined by the same legislation. A CAPITAL LOSS can be used to offset a CAPITAL GAIN plus $3000 of ORDINARY INCOME (but the gain and loss must both be either long-term or short-term until the distinction ends in 1988).

LOOPHOLE technicality making it possible to circumvent a law's intent without violating its letter. For instance, a TAX SHELTER may exploit a loophole in the tax law, or a bank may take advantage of a loophole in the GLASS STEAGALL ACT to acquire a DISCOUNT BROKER.

LOSS RATIO ratio of losses paid or accrued by an insurer to premiums earned, usually for a one-year period. *See also* BAD DEBT.

LOSS RESERVE *see* BAD DEBT.

LOT in a general business sense, a lot is any group of goods or services making up a transaction. *See also* ODD LOT; ROUND LOT.

LOW bottom price paid for a security over the past year or since trading in the security began; in the latter sense also called *historic low*.

LUMP-SUM DISTRIBUTION single payment to a beneficiary covering the entire amount of an agreement. Participants in Individual Retirement Accounts, pension plans, profit-sharing, and executive stock option plans generally can opt for a lump-sum distribution if the taxes are not too burdensome when they become eligible.

LUXURY TAX tax on goods considered nonessential.

m

MACROECONOMICS analysis of a nation's economy as a whole, using such aggregate data as price levels, unemployment, inflation, and industrial production. *See also* MICROECONOMICS.

MAINTENANCE BOND bond that guarantees against defects in workmanship or materials for a specified period following completion of a contract.

MAINTENANCE CALL call for additional money or securities when a brokerage customer's margin account equity falls below the requirements of the National Association of Securities Dealers (NASD), of the exchanges, or of the brokerage firm. Unless the account is brought up to the levels complying with equity maintenance rules, some of the client's securities may be sold to remedy the deficiency. *See also* MAINTENANCE REQUIREMENT; MINIMUM MAINTENANCE; SELL OUT.

MAINTENANCE FEE annual charge to maintain certain types of brokerage accounts. Such a fee may be attached to an ASSET MANAGEMENT ACCOUNT, which combines securities and money market accounts. Banks and brokers may also charge a maintenance fee for an INDIVIDUAL RETIREMENT ACCOUNT (IRA).

MAINTENANCE REQUIREMENT *see* MINIMUM MAINTENANCE.

MAJORITY SHAREHOLDER one of the shareholders who together control more than half the outstanding shares of a corporation. If the ownership is widely scattered and there are no majority shareholders, effective control may be gained with far less than 51% of the outstanding shares. *See also* WORKING CONTROL.

MAKE A MARKET maintain firm bid and offer prices in a given security by standing ready to buy or sell ROUND LOTS at publicly quoted prices. The dealer is called a *market maker* in the over-the-counter market and a SPECIALIST on the exchanges. A dealer who makes a market over a long period is said to *maintain* a market. *See also* REGISTERED COMPETITIVE MARKET MAKER.

MAKE A PRICE *see* MAKE A MARKET.

MALONEY ACT legislation, also called the Maloney Amendment, enacted in 1938 to amend the SECURITIES EXCHANGE ACT OF 1934 by adding Section 15A, which provides for the regulation of the OVER-THE-COUNTER market (OTC) through national securities associations registered with the Securities and Exchange Commission. *See also* NATIONAL ASSOCIATION OF SECURITIES DEALERS (NASD).

MANAGED ACCOUNT investment account consisting of money that one or more clients entrust to a manager, who decides when and where to invest it. Such an account may be handled by a bank trust department or by an investment advisory firm. Clients are charged a MANAGEMENT FEE and share in proportion to their participation in any losses and gains.

MANAGEMENT combined fields of policy and administration and the people who provide the decisions and supervision necessary to implement the owners' business objectives and achieve stability and growth. The formulation of policy requires analysis of all factors having an effect on short- and long-term profits. The administration of policies is carried out by the CHIEF EXECUTIVE OFFICER, his or her immediate staff, and everybody else who possesses authority delegated by people with supervisory responsibility. Thus the size of management can range from one person in a small organization to multilayered management hierarchies in large, complex organizations. The top members of management, called senior management, report to the owners of a firm; in large corporations, the CHAIRMAN OF THE BOARD, the PRESIDENT, and sometimes other key senior officers report to the BOARD OF DIRECTORS, comprising elected representatives of the owning stockholders. The application of scientific principles to decision-making is called management science. *See also* ORGANIZATION CHART.

MANAGEMENT COMPANY same as INVESTMENT COMPANY.

MANAGEMENT FEE charge against investor assets for managing the portfolio of an open- or closed-end MUTUAL FUND as well as for such services as shareholder relations or administration. The fee, as disclosed in the PROSPECTUS, is a fixed percentage of the fund's asset value, typically 1% or less per year. The fee also applies to a MANAGED ACCOUNT.

MANAGING UNDERWRITER leading—and originating—investment banking firm of an UNDERWRITING GROUP organized for the purchase and distribution of a new issue of securities. The AGREEMENT AMONG UNDERWRITERS authorizes the managing underwriter, or syndicate manager, to act as agent for the group in purchasing, carrying, and distributing the issue as well as complying with all federal and state requirements; to form the selling group; to determine the allocation of securities to each member; to make sales to the selling group at a specified discount—or CONCESSION—from the public offering price; to engage in open market transactions during the underwriting period to stabilize the market price of the security; and to borrow for the syndicate account to cover costs. *See also* FLOTATION COST; INVESTMENT BANKER; UNDERWRITE.

MANIPULATION buying or selling a security to create a false appearance of active trading and thus influence other investors to buy or sell shares. This may be done by one person or by a group acting in concert. Those found guilty of manipulation are subject to criminal and civil penalties. *See also* MINI-MANIPULATION.

MARGIN

In general: amount a customer deposits with a broker when borrowing from the broker to buy securities. Under Federal Reserve Board regulation, the initial margin required since 1945 has ranged from 50 to 100 percent of the security's purchase price. In the mid-1980s the minimum was 50% of the purchase or short sale price, in cash or eligible securities, with a minimum of $2000. Thereafter, MINIMUM MAINTENANCE requirements are imposed by the National Association of Securities Dealers (NASD) and the New York Stock Exchange, in the mid-1980s 25% of the market value of margined securities, and by the individual brokerage firm, whose requirement is typically higher.

Banking: difference between the current market value of collateral backing a loan and the face value of the loan. For instance, if a $100,000 loan is backed by $50,000 in collateral, the margin is $50,000.

Corporate finance: difference between the price received by a company for its products and services and the cost of producing them. Also known as *gross profit margin*.

Futures trading: good-faith deposit an investor must put up when buying or selling a contract. If the futures price moves adversely, the investor must put up more money to meet margin requirements.

MARGIN ACCOUNT brokerage account allowing customers to buy securities with money borrowed from the broker. Margin accounts are governed by REGULATION T, by the National Association of Securities Dealers (NASD), by the New York Stock Exchange, and by individual brokerage house rules. Margin requirements can be met with cash or with eligible securities. In the case of securities sold short, an equal amount of the same securities is normally borrowed without interest from another broker to cover the sale, while the proceeds are keptin escrow as collateral for the lending broker. *See also* MINIMUMMAINTENANCE.

MARGIN AGREEMENT document that spells out the rules governing a MARGIN ACCOUNT, including the HYPOTHECATION of securities, how much equity the customer must keep in the account, and the interest rate on margin loans. Also known as a *hypothecation agreement*.

MARGINAL COST increase or decrease in the total costs of a business firm as the result of one more or one less unit of output. Also called *incremental cost* or *differential cost*. Determining marginal cost is important in deciding whether or not to vary a rate of production. In most manufacturing firms, marginal costs decrease as the volume of output increases due to economies of scale, which include factors such as bulk discounts on raw materials, specialization of labor, and more efficient use of machinery. At some point, however, diseconomies of scale enter in and marginal costs begin to rise; diseconomies include factors like more intense managerial supervision to control a larger work force, higher raw materials costs because local supplies have been exhausted, and generally less efficient input. The marginal cost curve is typically U-shaped on a graph.

A firm is operating at optimum output when marginal cost coincides with average total unit cost. Thus, at less than optimum output, an increase in the rate of production will result in a marginal unit cost lower than average total unit cost; production in excess of the optimum point will result in marginal cost higher than average total unit cost. In other words, a sale at a price higher than marginal unit cost will increase the net profit of the manufacturer even though the sales price does not cover average total unit cost; marginal cost is thus the lowest amount at which a sale can be made without adding to the producer's loss or subtracting from his profits.

MARGINAL COST

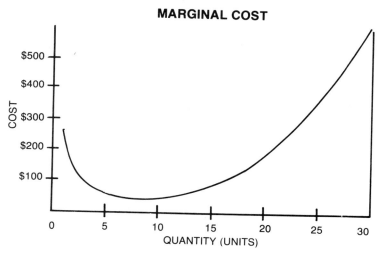

MARGINAL EFFICIENCY OF CAPITAL annual percentage yield earned by the last additional unit of capital. It is also known as *marginal productivity of capital, natural interest rate, net capital productivity,* and *rate of return over cost.* The significance of the concept to a business firm is that it represents the market rate of interest at which it begins to pay to undertake a capital investment. If the market rate is 10%, for example, it would not pay to undertake a project that has a return of 9½%, but any return over 10% would be acceptable. In a larger economic sense, marginal efficiency of capital influences long-term interest rates. This occurs because of the law of diminishing returns as it applies to the yield on capital. As the highest yielding projects are exhausted, available capital moves into lower yielding projects and interest rates decline. As market rates fall, investors are able to justify projects that were previously uneconomical. This process is called *diminishing marginal productivity* or *declining marginal effi-ciency of capital.*

MARGINAL REVENUE change in total revenue caused by one additional unit of output. It is calculated by determining the difference between the total revenues produced before and after a one-unit increase in the rate of production. As long as the price of a product is constant, price and marginal revenue are the same; for example, if baseball bats are being sold at a constant price of $10 apiece, a one-unit increase in sales (one baseball bat) translates into an increase in total revenue of $10. But it is often the case that additional output can be sold only if the price is reduced, and that leads to a consideration of MARGINAL COST—the added cost of producing one more unit. Further production is not advisable when marginal cost exceeds marginal revenue since to do so would result in a loss. Conversely, whenever marginal revenue exceeds marginal cost, it is advisable to produce an additional unit. Profits are maximized at the rate of output where marginal revenue equals marginal cost.

MARGINAL TAX RATE amount of tax imposed on an additional dollar of income. In the U.S. progressive income tax system, the marginal tax rate increases as income rises. Economists believing in SUPPLY-SIDE ECONOMICS hold that this reduces the incentive to be productive and discourages business investment. In urging that marginal tax rates be cut for individuals and businesses, they argue that the resulting increased work effort and business investment would reduce STAGFLATION. *See also* FLAT TAX.

MARGIN CALL demand that a customer deposit enough money or securities to bring a margin account up to the INITIAL MARGIN or MINIMUM MAINTENANCE requirements. If a customer fails to respond, securities in the account may be liquidated. *See also* FIVE HUNDRED DOLLAR RULE; SELL OUT.

MARGIN DEPARTMENT section within a brokerage firm that monitors customer compliance with margin regulations, keeping track of debits and credits, short sales, and purchases of stock on margin, and all other extensions of credit by the broker. Also known as the *credit department*. *See also* MARK TO THE MARKET.

MARGIN OF PROFIT relationship of gross profits to net sales. Returns and allowances are subtracted from gross sales to arrive at net sales. Cost of goods sold (sometimes including depreciation) is subtracted from net sales to arrive at gross profit. Gross profit is divided by net sales to get the profit margin, which is sometimes called the *gross margin*. The result is a ratio, and the term is also written as *margin of profit ratio*.

The term profit margin is less frequently used to mean the *net margin,* obtained by deducting operating expenses in addition to cost of goods sold and dividing the result by net sales. Operating expenses are usually shown on profit and loss statements as "selling, general and administrative (SG&A) expenses."

Both gross and net profit margins, when compared with prior periods and with industry statistics, can be revealing in terms of a firm's operating efficiency and pricing policies and its ability to compete successfully with other companies in its field.

MARGIN REQUIREMENT minimum amount that a client must deposit in the form of cash or eligible securities in a margin account as spelled out in REGULATION T of the Federal Reserve Board. Reg T requires a minimum of $2000 or 50% of the purchase price of eligible securities bought on margin or 50% of the proceeds of short sales. Also called INITIAL MARGIN. *See also* MARGIN; MARGIN SECURITY; MINIMUM MAINTENANCE; SELLING SHORT.

MARGIN SECURITY security that may be purchased or sold in a MARGIN ACCOUNT with a broker. REGULATION T, which controls margin buying, divides securities into three categories: (1) Registered securities are listed and registered or have an unlisted trading privilege on a national securities exchange. These may be purchased or sold short in a margin account. (2) U.S. government securities, municipal bonds, and bonds of the International Bank for Reconstruction and Development are exempt from Regulation T control, but they qualify as margin securities and their loan value is determined by the policy of the brokerage firm. (3) Securities that are not registered on a national securities exchange and are not in the exempt category do not qualify as margin securities. All transactions in them must be in cash.

MARITAL DEDUCTION provision in the Economic Recovery Tax Act of 1981 allowing all the assets of a marriage partner to pass to the surviving spouse free of estate taxes. Previously, a portion of the estate was taxed. The change eliminated double taxation of the surviving spouse's estate.

MARKDOWN

1. amount subtracted from the selling price, when a customer sells securities to a dealer in the OVER THE COUNTER market. Had the securities been purchased from the dealer, the customer would have paid a *markup,* or an amount added to the purchase price. The National Association of Securities Dealers (NASD) RULES OF FAIR PRACTICE established 5% as a reasonable guideline in markups and markdowns, though many factors enter into the question of fairness, and exceptions are common.
2. reduction in the price at which the underwriters offer municipal bonds after the market has shown a lack of interest at the original price.
3. downward adjustment of the value of securities by banks and investment firms, based on a decline in market quotations.
4. reduction in the original retail selling price, which was determined by adding a percentage factor, called a markon, to the cost of the merchandise. Anything added to the markon is called a markup, and the term markdown does not apply unless the price is dropped below the original selling price.

MARKET

1. public place where products or services are bought and sold, directly or through intermediaries. Also called *marketplace.*
2. aggregate of people with the present or potential ability and desire to purchase a product or service; equivalent to demand.
3. securities markets in the aggregate, or the New York Stock Exchange in particular.
4. short for *market value,* the value of an asset based on the price it would command on the open market, usually as determined by the MARKET PRICE at which similar assets have recently been bought and sold.
5. as a verb, to sell. *See also* MARKETING.

MARKETABILITY speed and ease with which a particular security may be bought and sold. A stock that has a large amount of shares outstanding and is actively traded is highly marketable and also liquid. In common use, marketability is interchangeable with LIQUIDITY, but liquidity implies the preservation of value when a security is bought or sold.

MARKETABLE SECURITIES securities that are easily sold. On a corporation's balance sheet, they are assets that can be readily converted into cash—for example, government securities, banker's acceptances, and commercial paper. In keeping with conservative accounting practice, these are carried at cost or market value, whichever is lower.

MARKET ANALYSIS

1. research aimed at predicting or anticipating the direction of stock, bond, or commodity markets, based on technical data about the movement of market prices or on fundamental data such as corporate earnings prospects or supply and demand.

2. study designed to define a company's markets, forecast their directions, and decide how to expand the company's share and exploit any new trends.

MARKET CAPITALIZATION value of a corporation as determined by the market price of its issued and outstanding common stock. It is calculated by multiplying the number of outstanding shares by the current market price of a share. Institutional investors often use market capitalization as one investment criterion, requiring, for example, that a company have a market capitalization of $100 million or more to qualify as an investment. Analysts look at market capitalization in relation to book, or accounting, value for an indication of how investors value a company's future prospects.

MARKET IF TOUCHED ORDER (MIT) order to buy or sell a security or commodity as soon as a preset market price is reached, at which point it becomes a MARKET ORDER. When corn is selling for $4.75 a bushel, someone might enter a market if touched order to buy at $4.50. As soon as the price is dropped to $4.50, the contract would be bought on the customer's behalf at whatever market price prevails when the order is executed.

MARKET INDEX numbers representing weighted values of the components that make up the index. A stock market index, for example, is weighted according to the prices and number of outstanding shares of the various stocks. The Standard and Poor's 500 Stock Index is one of the most widely followed, but myriad other indexes track stocks in various industry groups.

MARKETING moving goods and services from the provider to consumer. This involves product origination and design, development, distribution, advertising, promotion, and publicity as well as market analysis to define the appropriate market.

MARKET LETTER newsletter provided to brokerage firm customers or written by an independent market analyst, registered as an investment adviser with the Securities and Exchange Commission, who sells the letter to subscribers. These letters assess the trends in interest rates, the economy, and the market in general. Brokerage letters typically reiterate the recommendations of their own research departments. Independent letters take on the personality of their writers—concentrating on growth stocks, for example, or basing their recommendations on technical analysis. A HULBERT RATING is an evaluation of such a letter's performance.

MARKET MAKER see MAKE A MARKET.

MARKET ORDER order to buy or sell a security at the best available price. Most orders executed on the exchanges are market orders.

MARKET OUT CLAUSE escape clause sometimes written into FIRM COMMITMENT underwriting agreements which essentially allows the underwriters to be released from their purchase commitment if material adverse developments affect the securities markets generally. It is not common practice for the larger investment banking houses to write "outs" into their agreements, since the value of their commitment is a matter of paramount concern. See also UNDERWRITE.

MARKETPLACE see MARKET.

MARKET PRICE last reported price at which a security was sold on an exchange. For stocks or bonds sold OVER THE COUNTER, the combined bid and offer prices available at any particular time from those making a market in the stock. For an inactively traded security, evaluators or other analysts may determine a market price if needed—to settle an estate, for example.

In the general business world, market price refers to the price agreed upon by buyers and sellers of a product or service, as determined by supply and demand.

MARKET RESEARCH exploration of the size, characteristics, and potential of a market to find out, before developing any new product or service, what people want and need. Market research is an early step in marketing—which stretches from the original conception of a product to its ultimate delivery to the consumer.

In the stock market, market research refers to TECHNICAL ANALYSIS of factors such as volume, price advances and declines, and market breadth, which analysts use to predict the direction of prices.

MARKET RISK *see* SYSTEMATIC RISK.

MARKET SHARE percentage of industry sales of a particular company or product.

MARKET TIMING decisions on when to buy or sell securities, in light of economic factors such as the strength of the economy and the direction of interest rates, or technical indications such as the direction of stock prices and the volume of trading. Investors in mutual funds may implement their market timing decisions by switching from a stock fund to a bond fund to a money market fund and back again, as the market outlook changes.

MARKET TONE general health and vigor of a securities market. The market tone is good when dealers and market makers are trading actively on narrow bid and offer spreads; it is bad when trading is inactive and bid and offer spreads are wide.

MARKET VALUE

In general: market price—the price at which buyers and sellers trade similar items in an open marketplace. In the absence of a market price, it is the estimated highest price a buyer would be warranted in paying and a seller justified in accepting, provided both parties were fully informed and acted intelligently and voluntarily.

Investments: current market price of a security—as indicated by the latest trade recorded.

Accounting: technical definition used in valuing inventory or marketable securities in accordance with the conservative accounting principle of ''lower of cost or market.'' While cost is simply acquisition cost, market value is estimated net selling price less estimated costs of carrying, selling, and delivery, and, in the case of an unfinished product, the costs to complete production. The market value arrived at this way cannot, however, be lower than the cost at which a normal profit can be made.

MARKET VALUE-WEIGHTED INDEX index whose components are weighted according to the total market value of their outstanding shares. The impact of a component's price change is proportional to the issue's overall market value, which is the share price times the number of shares outstanding. For example, the Computer Technology Index, traded on the American Stock Exchange, has 30 component stocks. The weighting of each stock constantly shifts with changes in the stock's price and the number of shares outstanding. The index fluctuates in line with the price moves of the stocks.

MARK TO THE MARKET

1. adjust the valuation of a security or portfolio to reflect current market values. For example, MARGIN ACCOUNTS are marked to the market to ensure compliance with maintenance requirements. OPTION and FUTURES CONTRACTS are marked to the market at year end with PAPER PROFIT OR LOSS recognized for tax purposes.
2. in a MUTUAL FUND, the daily net asset value reported to shareholders is the result of marking the fund's current portfolio to current market prices.

MARKUP *see* MARKDOWN.

MARRIAGE PENALTY effect of a tax code that makes a married couple pay more than the same two people would pay if unmarried and filing singly. The $3000 (maximum) two-earner deduction instituted by the ECONOMIC RECOVERY TAX ACT OF 1981 (ERTA) to counter the marriage penalty was repealed, effective for the tax year 1987, by the TAX REFORM ACT OF 1986, which substituted lower tax rates, wider TAX BRACKETS, and an increased STANDARD DEDUCTION.

MARRIED PUT option to sell a certain number of securities at a particular price by a specified time, bought simultaneously with securities of the underlying company so as to hedge the price paid for the securities. *See also* OPTION; PUT OPTION.

MASTER LIMITED PARTNERSHIP public LIMITED PARTNERSHIP composed of corporate assets spun off (*roll out*) or private limited partnerships (*roll up*) with income, capital gains, and/or TAX SHELTER orientations. Interests are represented by depositary receipts traded in the SECONDARY MARKET. Investors thus enjoy LIQUIDITY in addition to flow-through benefits.

MATCHED AND LOST report of the results of flipping a coin by two securities brokers locked in competition to execute equal trades.

MATCHED BOOK term used for the accounts of securities dealers when their borrowing costs are equal to the interest earned on loans to customers and other brokers.

MATCHED MATURITIES coordination of the maturities of a financial institution's loans and certificates of deposit. For instance, a savings and loan might make 10-year mortgages at 14%, using the money received for 10-year certificates of deposit with 11% yields. The bank is thus positioned to make a three-point profit for 10 years. If a bank granted 20-year mortgages at a fixed 12%, on the other hand, using short-term funds from money market accounts paying 9%, the bank would lose dramatically if the money market accounts began paying 14%. Such a situation, called a *maturity mismatch,* can cause tremendous problems for the financial institution if it persists.

MATCHED ORDERS

1. illegal manipulative technique of offsetting buy and sell orders to create the impression of activity in a security, thereby causing upward price movement that benefits the participants in the scheme.
2. action by a SPECIALIST to create an opening price reasonably close to the previous close. When an accumulation of one kind of order—either buy or sell—causes a delay in the opening of trading on an exchange, the specialist tries to find counterbalancing orders or trades long or short from his own inventory in order to narrow the spread.

MATCHED SALE PURCHASE TRANSACTION FEDERAL OPEN MARKET COMMITTEE procedure whereby the Federal Reserve Bank of New York sells government securities to a nonbank dealer against payment in FEDERAL FUNDS. The agreement requires the dealer to sell the securities back by a specified date, which ranges from one to 15 days. The Fed pays the dealer a rate of interest equal to the discount rate. These transactions, also called reverse repurchase agreements, decrease the money supply for temporary periods by reducing dealer's bank balances and thus excess reserves. The Fed is thus able to adjust an abnormal monetary expansion due to seasonal or other factors. *See also* REPURCHASE AGREEMENT.

MATRIX TRADING bond swapping whereby traders seek to take advantage of temporary aberrations in YIELD SPREAD differentials between bonds of the same class but with different ratings or between bonds of different classes.

MATURE ECONOMY economy of a nation whose population has stabilized or is declining, and whose economic growth is no longer robust. Such an economy is characterized by a decrease in spending on roads or factories and a relative increase in consumer spending. Many of Western Europe's economies are considerably more mature than that of the United States and in marked contrast to the faster-growing economies of the Far East.

MATURITY DATE
1. date on which the principal amount of a note, draft, acceptance, bond, or other debt instrument becomes due and payable. Also, termination or due date on which an installment loan must be paid in full.
2. in FACTORING, average due date of factored receivables, when the factor remits to the seller for receivables sold each month.

MAXIMUM CAPITAL GAINS MUTUAL FUND fund whose objective is to produce large capital gains for its shareholders. During a bull market it is likely to rise much faster than the general market or conservative mutual funds. But in a falling market, it is likely to drop much farther than the market averages. This increased volatility results from a policy of investing in small, fast-growing companies whose stocks characteristically are more volatile than those of large, well-established companies.

MAY DAY May 1, 1975, when fixed minimum brokerage commissions ended in the United States. Instead of a mandated rate to execute exchange trades, brokers were allowed to charge whatever they chose. The May Day changes ushered in the era of discount brokerage firms that execute buy and sell orders for low commissions, but give no investment advice. The end of fixed commissions also marked the beginning of diversification by the brokerage industry into a wide range of financial services utilizing computer technology and advanced communications systems.

MEAN RETURN in security analysis, expected value, or mean, of all the likely returns of investments comprising a portfolio; in capital budgeting, mean value of the probability distribution of possible returns. The portfolio approach to the analysis of investments aims at quantifying the relationship between risk and return. It assumes that while investors have different risk-value preferences, rational investors will always seek the maximum rate of return for every level of acceptable risk. It is the mean, or expected, return that an investor attempts to maximize at each level of risk. Also called *expected return. See also* CAPITAL ASSET PRICING MODEL, EFFICIENT PORTFOLIO, PORTFOLIO THEORY.

MECHANIC'S LIEN LIEN against buildings or other structures, allowed by some states to contractors, laborers, and suppliers of materials used in their construction or repair. The lien remains in effect until these people have been paid in full and may, in the event of a liquidation before they have been paid, give them priority over other creditors.

MEDIUM-TERM BOND bond with a maturity of 2 to 10 years. *See also* INTERMEDIATE TERM; LONG TERM; SHORT TERM.

MEMBER BANK bank that is a member of the FEDERAL RESERVE SYSTEM, including all nationally chartered banks and any state-chartered banks that apply for membership and are accepted. Member banks are required to purchase stock in the FEDERAL RESERVE BANK in their districts equal to 6% of their own PAID-IN CAPITAL and paid-in surplus. Half of that investment is carried as an asset of the member bank. The other half is callable by the Fed at any time. Member banks are also required to maintain a percentage of their deposits as reserves in the form of currency in their vaults and balances on deposit at their Fed district banks. These reserve balances make possible a range of money transfer and other services using the FED WIRE system to connect banks in different parts of the country.

MEMBER FIRM brokerage firm that has at least one membership on a major stock exchange, even though, by exchange rules, the membership is in the name of an employee and not of the firm itself. Such a firm enjoys the rights and privileges of membership, such as voting on exchange policy, together with the obligations of membership, such as the commitment to settle disputes with customers through exchange arbitration procedures.

MEMBER SHORT SALE RATIO ratio of the total shares sold short for the accounts of New York Stock Exchange members in one week divided by the total short sales for the same week. Because the specialists, floor traders, and off-the-floor traders who trade for members' accounts are generally considered the best minds in the business, the ratio is a valuable indicator of market trends. A ratio of 82% or higher is considered bearish; a ratio of 68% or lower is positive and bullish. The member short sale ratio appears with other NYSE round lot statistics in the Monday edition of *The Wall Street Journal* and in *Barron's,* a weekly financial newspaper.

MERCANTILE AGENCY organization that supplies businesses with credit ratings and reports on other firms that are or might become customers. Such agencies may also collect past due accounts or trade collection statistics, and they tend to industry and geographical specialization. The largest of the agencies, DUN & BRADSTREET, was founded in 1841 under the name Mercantile Agency. It provides credit information on companies of all descriptions along with a wide range of other credit and financial reporting services.

MERCHANT BANK
  1. European financial institution that engages in investment banking, counseling, and negotiating in mergers and acquisitions, and a variety of other services including securities portfolio management for customers, insurance, the acceptance of foreign bills of exchange, dealing in bullion, and participating in commercial ventures. Deposits in merchant banks are negligible, and the prominence of such names as Rothschild, Baring, Lazard, and Hambro attests to their role as counselors and negotiators in large-scale acquisitions, mergers, and the like.

2. American bank that has entered into an agreement with a merchant to accept deposits generated by bank credit/charge card transactions.

MERGER combination of two or more companies, either through a POOLING OF INTERESTS, where the accounts are combined; a purchase, where the amount paid over and above the acquired company's book value is carried on the books of the purchaser as goodwill; or a consolidation, where a new company is formed to acquire the net assets of the combining companies. Strictly speaking, only combinations in which one of the companies survives as a legal entity are called mergers or, more formally, statutory mergers; thus consolidations, or statutory consolidations, are technically not mergers, though the term merger is commonly applied to them. Mergers meeting the legal criteria for pooling of interests, where common stock is exchanged for common stock, are nontaxable and are called tax-free mergers. Where an acquisition takes place by the purchase of assets or stock using cash or a debt instrument for payment, the merger is a taxable capital gain to the selling company or its stockholders. There is a potential benefit to such taxable purchase acquisitions, however, in that the acquiring company can write up the acquired company's assets by the amount by which the market value exceeds the book value; that difference can then be charged off to depreciation with resultant tax savings.

Mergers can also be classified in terms of their economic function. Thus a *horizontal merger* is one combining direct competitors in the same product lines and markets; a *vertical merger* combines customer and company or supplier and company; a *market extension merger* combines companies selling the same products in different markets; a *product extension merger* combines companies selling different but related products in the same market; a *conglomerate merger* combines companies with none of the above relationships or similarities. *See also* ACQUISITION.

MEZZANINE BRACKET members of a securities underwriting group whose participations are of such a size as to place them in the tier second to the largest participants. In the newspaper TOMBSTONE advertisements that announce new securities offerings, the underwriters are listed in alphabetical groups, first the lead underwriters, then the mezzanine bracket, then the remaining participants.

MEZZANINE LEVEL stage of a company's development just prior to its going public, in VENTURE CAPITAL language. Venture capitalists entering at that point have a lower risk of loss than at previous stages and can look forward to early capital appreciation as a result of the MARKET VALUE gained by an INITIAL PUBLIC OFFERING.

MICROECONOMICS study of the behavior of basic economic units such as companies, industries, or households. Research on the companies in the airline industry would be a microeconomic concern, for instance. *See also* MACROECONOMICS.

MIDWEST STOCK EXCHANGE *see* REGIONAL STOCK EXCHANGES.

MIG-1 *see* MOODY'S INVESTMENT GRADE.

MILL one-tenth of a cent, the unit most often used in expressing property tax rates. For example, if a town's tax rate is 5 mills per dollar of assessed valuation, and the assessed valuation of a piece of property is \$100,000, the tax is \$500, or 0.005 times \$100,000.

MINI-MANIPULATION trading in a security underlying an option contract so as to manipulate the stock's price, thus causing an increase in the value of the options. In this way the manipulator's profit can be multiplied many times, since a large position in options can be purchased with a relatively small amount of money.

MINIMUM MAINTENANCE equity level that must be maintained in brokerage customers' margin accounts, as required by the New York Stock Exchange (NYSE), the National Association of Securities Dealers (NASD), and individual brokerage firms. Under REGULATION T, $2000 in cash or securities must be deposited with a broker before *any* credit can be extended; then an INITIAL MARGIN requirement must be met, currently 50% of the market value of eligible securities long or short in customers' accounts. The NYSE and NASD, going a step further, both require that a margin be *maintained* equal to 25% of the market value of securities in margin accounts. Brokerage firm requirements are typically a more conservative 30%. When the market value of margined securities falls below these minimums a MARGIN CALL goes out requesting additional equity. If the customer fails to comply, the broker may sell the margined stock and close the customer out. *See also* MARGIN REQUIREMENT; MARGIN SECURITY; MARK TO THE MARKET; SELL OUT.

MINI-WAREHOUSE LIMITED PARTNERSHIP partnership that invests in small warehouses where people can rent space to store belongings. Such partnerships offer tax benefits such as depreciation allowances, but mostly they provide income derived from rents. When the partnership is liquidated, the general partner may sell the warehouse for a profit, providing capital gains to limited partners.

MINORITY INTEREST interest of shareholders who, in the aggregate, own less than half the shares in a corporation. On the consolidated balance sheets of companies whose subsidiaries are not wholly owned, the minority interest is shown as a separate equity account or as a liability of indefinite term. On the income statement, the minority's share of income is subtracted to arrive at consolidated net income.

MINUS symbol (−) preceding a fraction or number in the change column at the far right of newspaper stock tables designating a closing sale lower than that of the previous day.

MINUS TICK *see* DOWNTICK.

MISSING THE MARKET failing to execute a transaction on terms favorable to a customer and thus being negligent as a broker. If the order is subsequently executed at a price demonstrably less favorable, the broker, as the customer's agent, may be required to make good on the amount lost.

MIXED ACCOUNT brokerage account in which some securities are owned (in long positions) and some borrowed (in short positions).

MOBILE HOME CERTIFICATE mortgage-backed security guaranteed by the GOVERNMENT NATIONAL MORTGAGE ASSOCIATION consisting of mortgages on mobile homes. Although the maturity tends to be shorter on these securities than on single-family homes, they have all the other characteristics of regular Ginnie Maes, and the timely payment of interest and the repayment of principal are backed by the FULL FAITH AND CREDIT of the U.S. government.

MODELING designing and manipulating a mathematical representation of an economic system or corporate financial application so that the effect of changes can be studied and forecast. For example, in ECONOMETRICS, a complex economic model can be drawn up, entered into a computer, and used to predict the effect of a rise in inflation or a cut in taxes on economic output.

MODERN PORTFOLIO THEORY *see* PORTFOLIO THEORY.

MOMENTUM rate of acceleration of an economic, price, or volume movement. An economy with strong growth that is likely to continue is said to have a lot of momentum. In the stock market, technical analysts study stock momentum by charting price and volume trends.

MONETARIST economist who believes that the MONEY SUPPLY is the key to the ups and downs in the economy. Monetarists such as Milton Friedman think that the money supply has far more impact on the economy's future course than, say, the level of federal spending—a factor on which KEYNESIAN ECONOMICS puts great stress. Monetarists advocate slow but steady growth in the money supply.

MONETARY POLICY FEDERAL RESERVE BOARD decisions on the MONEY SUPPLY. To make the economy grow faster, the Fed can supply more credit to the banking system through its OPEN MARKET OPERATIONS, or it can lower the member bank reserve requirement or lower the DISCOUNT RATE—which is what banks pay to borrow additional reserves from the Fed. If, on the other hand, the economy is growing too fast and inflation is an increasing problem, the Fed might withdraw money from the banking system, raise the reserve requirement, or raise the discount rate, thereby putting a brake on economic growth. Other instruments of monetary policy range from selective credit controls to simple but often highly effective MORAL SUASION. Monetary policy differs from FISCAL POLICY, which is carried out through government spending and taxation. Both seek to control the level of economic activity as measured by such factors as industrial production, employment, and prices.

MONEY CENTER BANK bank in one of the major financial centers of the world, among them New York, Chicago, San Francisco, Los Angeles, London, Paris, and Tokyo. These banks play a major national and international economic role because they are large lenders, depositories, and buyers of money market instruments and securities as well as large lenders to governments and international corporations. In the stock market, bank analysts usually categorize the money center banks as separate from regional banks—those that focus on one area of the country. Also known as *money market bank.*

MONEY MARKET market for SHORT-TERM DEBT INSTRUMENTS—negotiable certificates of deposit, Eurodollar certificates of deposit, commercial paper, banker's acceptances, Treasury bills, and discount notes of the Federal Home Loan Bank, Federal National Mortgage Association, and Federal Farm Credit System, among others. Federal funds borrowings between banks, bank borrowings from the Federal Reserve Bank WINDOW, and various forms of repurchase agreements are also elements of the money market. What these instruments have in common are safety and LIQUIDITY. The money market operates through dealers, MONEY CENTER BANKS, and the Open Market Trading DESK at the New York Federal Reserve Bank. New York City is the leading money market, followed by London and Tokyo. The dealers in the important money markets are in constant communication with each other and with major borrowers and investors to take advantage of ARBITRAGE opportunities, a practice which helps keep prices uniform worldwide. *See also* MONEY MARKET FUND.

MONEY MARKET DEPOSIT ACCOUNT market-sensitive bank account that has been offered since December 1982. Under Depository Institutions Deregulatory Committee rules, such accounts must have a minimum of $1000 (scheduled to be eliminated in 1986) and only three checks may be drawn per month, although unlimited transfers may be carried out at an automatic teller machine. The funds are therefore liquid—that is, they are available to depositors at any time without penalty. The interest rate is generally comparable to rates on money market mutual funds, though any individual bank's rate may be higher or lower. These accounts are insured by the FEDERAL DEPOSIT INSURANCE CORPORATION or the FEDERAL SAVINGS AND LOAN INSURANCE CORPORATION.

MONEY MARKET FUND open-ended MUTUAL FUND that invests in commercial paper, banker's acceptances, repurchase agreements, government securities, certificates of deposit, and other highly liquid and safe securities, and pays money market rates of interest. Launched in the middle 1970s, these funds were especially popular in the early 1980s when interest rates and inflation soared. Management's fee is less than 1% of an investor's assets; interest over and above that amount is credited to shareholders monthly. The fund's net asset value remains a constant $1 a share—only the interest rate goes up or down. Such funds usually offer the convenience of checkwriting privileges.

Most funds are not federally insured, but some are covered by private insurance. Some funds invest only in government-backed securities, which give shareholders an extra degree of safety.

Many money market funds are part of fund families. This means that investors can switch their money from one fund to another and back again without charge. Money in an ASSET MANAGEMENT ACCOUNT usually is automatically swept into a money market fund until the accountholder decides where to invest it next. *See also* DONOGHUE'S MONEY FUND AVERAGE; FAMILY OF FUNDS; MONEY MARKET DEPOSIT ACCOUNT.

MONEY SPREAD *see* VERTICAL SPREAD.

MONEY SUPPLY total stock of money in the economy, consisting primarily of (1) currency in circulation and (2) deposits in savings and checking accounts. Too much money in relation to the output of goods tends to push interest rates down and push prices and inflation up; too little money tends to push interest rates up, lower prices and output, and cause unemployment and idle plant capacity. The bulk of money is in demand deposits with commercial banks, which are regulated by the Federal Reserve Board. It manages the money supply by raising or lowering the reserves that banks are required to maintain and the DISCOUNT RATE at which they can borrow from the Fed, as well as by its OPEN MARKET OPERATIONS—trading government securities to take money out of the system or put it in.

Changes in the financial system, particularly since banking deregulation in the 1980s, have caused controversy among economists as to what really constitutes the money supply at a given time. In response to this, a more comprehensive analysis and breakdown of money was developed. Essentially, the various forms of money are now grouped into two broad divisions: M-1, M-2, and M-3, representing money and NEAR MONEY; and L, representing longer-term liquid funds. The accompanying table shows a detailed breakdown of all four categories. *See also* MONETARY POLICY.

MONEY SUPPLY

Classification	Components
M-1	currency in circulation commercial bank demand deposits NOW and ATS (automatic transfer from savings) accounts credit union share drafts mutual savings bank demand deposits nonbank travelers checks
M-2	M-1 overnight repurchase agreements issued by commercial banks overnight Eurodollars savings accounts time deposits under $100,000 money market mutual fund shares
M-3	M-2 time deposits over $100,000. term repurchase agreements
L	M-3 and other liquid assets such as: Treasury bills savings bonds commercial paper bankers' acceptances Eurodollar holdings of United States residents (nonbank)

MONOPOLY control of the production and distribution of a product or service by one firm or a group of firms acting in concert. In its pure form, monopoly, which is characterized by an absence of competition, leads to high prices and a general lack of responsiveness to the needs and desires of consumers. Although the most flagrant monopolistic practices in the United States were outlawed by ANTITRUST LAWS enacted in the late 19th century and early 20th century, monopolies persist in some degree as the result of such factors as patents, scarce essential materials, and high startup and production costs that discourage competition in certain industries. *Public monopolies*—those operated by the government, such as the post office, or closely regulated by the government, such as utilities—ensure the delivery of essential products and services at acceptable prices and generally avoid the disadvantages produced by private monopolies. *Monopsony,* the dominance of a market by one buyer or group of buyers acting together, is less prevalent than monopoly. *See also* CARTEL; OLIGOPOLY; PERFECT COMPETITION.

MONTHLY COMPOUNDING OF INTEREST *see* COMPOUND INTEREST.

MONTHLY INVESTMENT PLAN plan whereby an investor puts a fixed dollar amount into a particular investment every month, thus building a position at advantageous prices by means of *dollar cost averaging* (*see* CONSTANT DOLLAR PLAN).

MOODY'S INVESTMENT GRADE rating assigned by MOODY'S INVESTORS SER-

VICE to certain municipal short-term debt securities, classified as MIG-1, 2, 3, and 4 to signify best, high, favorable, and adequate quality, respectively. All four are investment grade or bank quality.

MOODY'S INVESTORS SERVICE headquartered with its parent company, Dun & Bradstreet, in downtown Manhattan, Moody's is one of the two best known bond rating agencies in the country, the other being Standard & Poor's. Moody's also rates commercial paper, preferred and common stocks, and municipal short-term issues. The six bound manuals it publishes annually, supplemented weekly or semiweekly, provide great detail on issuers and securities. The company also publishes the quarterly *Moody's Handbook of Common Stocks,* which charts more than 500 companies, showing industry group trends and company stock price performance. Also included are essential statistics for the past decade, an analysis of the company's financial background, recentfinancial developments, and the outlook. Moody's rates most of the publicly held corporate and municipal bonds and many Treasury and government agency issues, but does not usually rate privately placed bonds.

MORAL OBLIGATION BOND tax-exempt bond issued by a municipality or a state financial intermediary and backed by the moral obligation pledge of a state government. (State financial intermediaries are organized by states to pool local debt issues into single bond issues, which can be used to tap larger investment markets.) Under a moral obligation pledge, a state government indicates its intent to appropriate funds in the future if the primary OBLIGOR, the municipality or intermediary, defaults. The state's obligation to honor the pledge is moral rather than legal because future legislatures cannot be legally obligated to appropriate the funds required.

MORAL SUASION persuasion through influence rather than coercion, said of the efforts of the FEDERAL RESERVE BOARD to achieve member bank compliance with its general policy. From time to time, the Fed uses moral suasion to restrain credit or to expand it.

MORTGAGE debt instrument by which the borrower (mortgagor) gives the lender (mortgagee) a lien on property as security for the repayment of a loan. The borrower has use of the property, and the lien is removed when the obligation is fully paid. A mortgage normally involves real estate. For personal property, such as machines, equipment, or tools, the lien is called a *chattel mortgage. See also* ADJUSTABLE RATE MORTGAGE; CLOSED-END MORTGAGE; CONSOLIDATED MORTGAGE BOND; MORTGAGE BOND; OPEN-END MORTGAGE; VARIABLE RATE MORTGAGE.

MORTGAGE-BACKED CERTIFICATE security backed by mortgages. Such certificates are issued by the FEDERAL HOME LOAN MORTGAGE CORPORATION and the FEDERAL NATIONAL MORTGAGE ASSOCIATION. Others are guaranteed by the GOVERNMENT NATIONAL MORTGAGE ASSOCIATION. Investors receive payments out of the interest and principal on the underlying mortgages. Sometimes banks issue certificates backed by CONVENTIONAL MORTGAGES, selling them to large institutional investors. The growth of mortgage-backed certificates and the secondary mortgage market in which they are traded has helped keep mortgage money available for home financing. *See also* PASS-THROUGH SECURITY.

MORTGAGE-BACKED SECURITY *see* MORTGAGE-BACKED CERTIFICATE.

MORTGAGE BANKER company, or individual, that originates mortgage loans, sells them to other investors, services the monthly payments, keeps related records, and acts as escrow agent to disperse funds for taxes and insurance. A mortgage banker's income derives from origination and servicing fees, profits on the resale of loans, and the spread between mortgage yields and the interest paid on borrowings while a particular mortgage is held before resale. To protect against negative spreads or mortgages that can't be resold, such companies seek commitments from institutional lenders or buy them from the FEDERAL NATIONAL MORTGAGE ASSOCIATION or the GOVERNMENT NATIONAL MORTGAGE ASSOCIATION. Mortgage bankers thus play an important role in the flow of mortgage funds even though they are not significant mortgage holders.

MORTGAGE BOND bond issue secured by a mortgage on the issuer's property, the lien on which is conveyed to the bondholders by a deed of trust. A mortgage bond may be designated senior, underlying, first, prior, overlying, junior, second, third, and so forth, depending on the priority of the lien. Most of those issued by corporations are first mortgage bonds secured by specific real property and also representing unsecured claims on the general assets of the firm. As such, these bonds enjoy a preferred position relative to unsecured bonds of the issuing corporation. *See also* CONSOLIDATED MORTGAGE BOND; MORTGAGE.

MORTGAGE POOL group of mortgages sharing similar characteristics in terms of class of property, interest rate, and maturity. Investors buy participations and receive income derived from payments on the underlying mortgages. The principal attractions to the investor are DIVERSIFICATION and LIQUIDITY, along with a relatively attractive yield. Those backed by government-sponsored agencies such as the FEDERAL HOME LOAN MORTGAGE CORPORATION, FEDERAL NATIONAL MORTGAGE ASSOCIATION, and GOVERNMENT NATIONAL MORTGAGE ASSOCIATION have become popular not only with individual investors but with life insurance companies, pension funds, and even foreign investors.

MORTGAGE REIT REAL ESTATE INVESTMENT TRUST that lends stockholder capital to real estate builders and buyers. Mortgage REITs also borrow from banks and relend that money at higher interest rates. This kind of REIT is highly sensitive to interest rates; as rates rise, its profits are squeezed, because the cost of funds rises faster than income. Profits expand when rates fall, however, as loan income stays the same but the cost of funds drops. The other kind of real estate investment trust—called an EQUITY REIT—takes an ownership position in real estate, as opposed to acting as a lender. Some REITs do both.

MORTGAGE SERVICING administration of a mortgage loan, including collecting monthly payments and penalties on late payments, keeping track of the amount of principal and interest that has been paid at any particular time, acting as escrow agent for funds to cover taxes and insurance, and, if necessary, curing defaults and foreclosing when a homeowner is seriously delinquent. For mortgage loans that are sold in the secondary market and packaged into a MORTGAGE-BACKED CERTIFICATE the local bank or savings and loan that originated the mortgage typically continues servicing the mortgages and collects a fee for doing so.

MOST ACTIVE LIST stocks with the most shares traded on a given day. Unusual VOLUME can be caused by TAKEOVER activity, earnings releases, institutional trading in a widely-held issue, and other factors.

MOVING AVERAGE average of security or commodity prices constructed on a period as short as a few days or as long as several years and showing trends for the latest interval. For example, a thirty-day moving average includes yesterday's figures; tomorrow the same average will include today's figures and will no longer show those for the earliest date included in yesterday's average. Thus every day it picks up figures for the latest day and drops those for the earliest day.

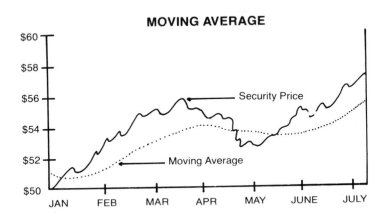

MOVING AVERAGE

MULTINATIONAL CORPORATION corporation that has production facilities or other fixed assets in at least one foreign country and makes its major management decisions in a global context. In marketing, production, research and development, and labor relations, its decisions must be made in terms of host-country customs and traditions. In finance, many of its problems have no domestic counterpart—the payment of dividends in another currency, for example, or the need to shelter working capital from the risk of devaluation, or the choices between owning and licensing. Economic and legal questions must be dealt with in drastically different ways. In addition to foreign exchange risks and the special business risks of operating in unfamiliar environments, there is the specter of political risk—the risk that sovereign governments may interfere with operations or terminate them altogether.

MULTIPLE see PRICE-EARNINGS RATIO.

MULTIPLIER the multiplier—also called the *multiplier effect* or the *multiplier principal*—has two major applications in finance and investments.
1. *investment multiplier* or *Keynesian multiplier:* multiplies the effects of investment spending in terms of total income. An investment in a small plant facility, for example, increases the incomes of the workers who built it, the merchants who provide supplies, the distributors who supply the merchants, the manufacturers who supply the distributors, and so on. Each recipient spends a portion of the income and saves the rest. By making an assumption as to the percentage each recipient saves, it is possible to calculate the total income produced by the investment.
2. *deposit multiplier* or *credit multiplier:* magnifies small changes in bank deposits into changes in the amount of outstanding credit and the money supply. For example, a bank receives a deposit of $100,000, and the RESERVE REQUIREMENT is 20%. The bank is thus required to keep $20,000 in the form of reserves. The remaining $80,000 becomes a loan, which is deposited in the

$100,000 could expand into a total of $500,000 in deposits and $400,000 in credit.

MUNICIPAL BOND debt obligation of a state or local government entity. The funds may support general governmental needs or special projects. Issuance must be approved by referendum or by an electoral body. Prior to the TAX REFORM ACT OF 1986, the terms municipal and tax-exempt were synonymous, since virtually all municipal obligations were exempt from federal income taxes and most from state and local income taxes, at least in the state of issue. The 1986 Act, however, divided municipals into two broad groups: (1) PUBLIC PURPOSE BONDS, which remain tax-exempt and can be issued without limitation, and (2) PRIVATE PURPOSE BONDS, which are taxable unless specifically exempted. The tax distinction between public and private purpose is based on the percentage extent to which the bonds benefit private parties: if a tax-exempt public purpose bond involves more than a 10% benefit to private parties, it is taxable. *Permitted private purpose bonds* (those specified as tax-exempt) are generally TAX PREFERENCE ITEMS in computing the ALTERNATIVE MINIMUM TAX and, effective August 15, 1986, are subject to volume caps. *See also* ADVANCE REFUNDING; GENERAL OBLIGATION BOND; HOSPITAL REVENUE BOND; INDUSTRIAL DEVELOPMENT BOND; LIMITED TAX BOND; MUNICIPAL INVESTMENT TRUST; MUNICIPAL REVENUE BOND; SINGLE STATE MUNICIPAL BOND FUND; SPECIAL ASSESSMENT BOND; TAXABLE MUNICIPAL BOND; TAX EXEMPT SECURITY; UNDERLYING DEBT.

MUNICIPAL BOND INSURANCE policies underwritten by private insurers guaranteeing municipal bonds in the event of default. The insurance can be purchased either by the issuing government entity or the investor; it provides that bonds will be purchased from investors at par should default occur. Such insurance is available from a number of large insurance companies, but a major portion is written by two organizations: AMBAC (formerly called American Municipal Bond Assurance Corporation), a private corporation, and Municipal Bond Insurance Association (MBIA), a pool of private insurers. Insured municipal bonds generally enjoy the highest rating resulting in greater marketability and lower cost to their issuers. From the investor's standpoint, however, their yield is typically lower than similarly rated uninsured bonds because the cost of the insurance is passed on by the issuer to the investor. Some unit investment trusts and mutual funds feature insured municipal bonds for investors willing to trade marginally lower yield for the extra degree of safety.

MUNICIPAL BOND INSURANCE ASSOCIATION *see* MUNICIPAL BOND INSURANCE.

MUNICIPAL IMPROVEMENT CERTIFICATE Certificate issued by a local government in lieu of bonds to finance improvements or services, such as widening a sidewalk, or installing a sewer, or repairing a street. Such an obligation is payable from a special tax assessment against those who benefit from the improvement, and the payments may be collected by the contractor performing the work. Interest on the certificate is usually free of federal, state, and local taxes. *See also* GENERAL OBLIGATION BOND.

MUNICIPAL INVESTMENT TRUST (MIT) UNIT INVESTMENT TRUST that buys municipal bonds and passes the tax-free income on to shareholders. Bonds in the trust's portfolio are normally held until maturity, unlike the constant trading of bonds in an open-ended municipal bond fund's portfolio. MITs are sold through brokers, typically for a sales charge of about 3% of the principal paid, with a minimum investment of $1000. The trust offers diversification, professional management of the portfolio, and monthly interest, compared with the semiannual payments made by individual municipal bonds.

Many MITs invest in the securities of just one state. For California residents who buy a California-only MIT, for example, all the interest is free of federal, state, and local taxes. In contrast, a Californian who buys a national MIT might have to pay state and local taxes on interest derived from out-of-state bonds in the trust's portfolio.

MUNICIPAL NOTE in common usage, a municipal debt obligation with an original maturity of two years or less.

MUNICIPAL REVENUE BOND bond issued to finance public works such as bridges or tunnels or sewer systems and supported directly by the revenues of the project. For instance, if a municipal revenue bond is issued to build a bridge, the tolls collected from motorists using the bridge are committed for paying off the bond. Unless otherwise specified in the indenture, holders of these bonds have no claims on the issuer's other resources.

MUNICIPAL SECURITIES RULEMAKING BOARD *see* SELF-REGULATORY ORGANIZATION.

MUTILATED SECURITY certificate that cannot be read for the name of the issue or the issuer, or for the detail necessary for identification and transfer, or for the exercise of the holder's rights. It is then the seller's obligation to take corrective action, which usually means having the transfer agent guarantee the rights of ownership to the buyer.

MUTUAL ASSOCIATION SAVINGS AND LOAN ASSOCIATION organized as a co-operative owned by its members. Members' deposits represent shares; shareholders vote on association affairs and receive income in the form of dividends. Unlike state-chartered corporate S&Ls, which account for a minority of the industry, mutual associations are not permitted to issue stock, and they are usually chartered by the Federal Home Loan Bank Board and belong to the Federal Savings and Loan Insurance Corporation. Deposits are technically subject to a waiting period before withdrawal, although in practice withdrawals are usually allowed on demand, the association's liquidity being assured by its ability to borrow from the Federal Home Loan Bank using home mortgages as collateral.

MUTUAL COMPANY corporation whose ownership and profits are distributed among members in proportion to the amount of business they do with the company. The most familiar examples are (1) mutual insurance companies, whose members are policy holders entitled to name the directors or trustees and to receive dividends or rebates on future premiums; (2) state-chartered MUTUAL SAVINGS BANKS, whose members are depositors sharing in net earnings but having nothing to do with management; and (3) federal savings and loan associations, MUTUAL ASSOCIATIONS whose members are depositors entitled to vote and receive dividends.

MUTUAL FUND fund operated by an INVESTMENT COMPANY that raises money from shareholders and invests it in stocks, bonds, options, commodities, or money market securities. These funds offer investors the advantages of diversification and professional management. For these services they charge a management fee, typically 1% or less of assets per year.

Mutual funds may invest aggressively or conservatively. Investors should assess their own tolerance for risk before they decide which fund would be appropriate for them. In addition, the timing of buying or selling depends on the outlook for the economy, the state of the stock and bond markets, interest rates, and other factors.

MUTUAL FUND CUSTODIAN commercial bank or trust company that provides safekeeping for the securities owned by a mutual fund and may also act as TRANSFER AGENT, making payments to and collecting investments from shareholders. Mutual fund custodians must comply with the rules set forth in the INVESTMENT COMPANY ACT OF 1940.

MUTUAL IMPROVEMENT CERTIFICATE certificate issued by a local government in lieu of bonds to finance improvements or services, such as widening a sidewalk, or installing a sewer, or repairing a street. Such an obligation is payable from a special tax assessment against those who benefit from the improvement, and the payments may be collected by the contractor performing the work. Interest on the certificate is free of federal, state, and local taxes. *See also* GENERAL OBLIGATION BOND.

MUTUAL SAVINGS BANK SAVINGS BANK organized under state charter for the ownership and benefit of its depositors. A local board of trustees makes major decisions as fiduciaries, independently of the legal owners. Traditionally, income is distributed to depositors after expenses are deducted and reserve funds are set aside as required. In recent times, many mutual savings banks have begun to issue stock and offer consumer services such as credit cards and checking accounts, as well as commercial services such as corporate checking accounts and commercial real estate loans.

n

NAKED OPTION OPTION for which the buyer or seller has no underlying security position. A writer of a naked CALL OPTION, therefore, does not own a LONG POSITION in the stock on which the call has been written. Similarly, the writer of a naked PUT OPTION does not have a SHORT POSITION in the stock on which the put has been written. Naked options are very risky—although potentially very rewarding. If the underlying stock or stock index moves in the direction sought by the investor, profits can be enormous, because the investor would only have had to put down a small amount of money to reap a large return. On the other hand, if the stock moved in the opposite direction, the writer of the naked option could be subject to huge losses.

For instance, if someone wrote a naked call option at $60 a share on XYZ stock without owning the shares, and if the stock rose to $70 a share, the writer of the option would have to deliver XYZ shares to the call buyer at $60 a share. In order to acquire those shares, he or she would have to go into the market and buy them for $70 a share, sustaining a $10-a-share loss on his or her position. If, on the other hand, the option writer already owned XYZ shares when writing the option, he or she could just turn those shares over to the option buyer. This latter strategy is known as writing a COVERED CALL.

NAKED POSITION securities position that is not hedged from market risk—for example, the position of someone who writes a CALL or PUT option without having the corresponding LONG POSITION or SHORT POSITION on the underlying security. The potential risk or reward of naked positions is greater than that of covered positions. *See* COVERED CALL; HEDGE; NAKED OPTION.

NARROWING THE SPREAD closing the SPREAD between the bid and asked prices of a security as a result of bidding and offering by market makers and specialists in a security. For example, a stock's bid price—the most anyone is willing to pay—may be $10 a share, and the asked price—the lowest price at which anyone will sell—may be $10¾. If a broker or market maker offers to buy shares at $10¼, while the asked price remains at $10¾, the spread has effectively been narrowed.

NARROW MARKET securities or commodities market characterized by light trading and greater fluctuations in prices relative to volume than would be the case if trading were active. The market in a particular stock is said to be narrow if the price falls more than a point between ROUND LOT trades without any apparent explanation, suggesting lack of interest and too few orders. The terms THIN MARKET and *inactive market* are used as synonyms for narrow market.

NASDAQ National Association of Securities Dealers Automated Quotations system, which is owned and operated by the NATIONAL ASSOCIATION OF SECURITIES DEALERS. NASDAQ is a computerized system that provides brokers and dealers with price quotations for securities traded OVER THE COUNTER as well as for many New York Stock Exchange listed securities. NASDAQ quotes are published in the financial pages of most newspapers.

NASD FORM FR-1 form required of foreign dealers in securities subscribing to new securities issues in the process of distribution, whereby they agree to abide by NATIONAL ASSOCIATION OF SECURITIES DEALERS rules concerning a HOT ISSUE. Under NASD Rules of Fair Practice, firms participating in the distribution must make a bona fide public offering at the public offering price. Any sale designed to capitalize on a hot issue—one that on the first day of trading sells at a substantial premium over the public offering price—would be in violation of NASD rules. Violations include a sale to a member of the dealer's family or to an employee, assuming such sales could not be defended as "normal investment practice." Also called *blanket certification form*.

NATIONAL ASSOCIATION OF INVESTMENT CLUBS association that helps investment clubs get established. Investment clubs are formed by people who pool their money and make common decisions about how to invest those assets. *See also* INVESTMENT CLUB.

NATIONAL ASSOCIATION OF SECURITIES DEALERS (NASD) nonprofit organization formed under the joint sponsorship of the Investment Bankers' Conference and the Securities and Exchange Commission to comply with the MALONEY ACT. NASD members include virtually all investment banking houses and firms dealing in the OVER THE COUNTER market. Operating under the supervision of the SEC,the NASD's basic purposes are to (1) standardize practices in the field, (2) establish high moral and ethical standards in securities trading,(3) provide a representative body to consult with the government and investors on matters of common interest, (4) establish and enforce fair and equitable rules of securities trading, and (5) establish a disciplinary body capable of enforcing the above provisions. The NASD also requires members to maintain quick assets in excess of current liabilities at all times. Periodic examinations and audits are conducted to ensure a high level of solvency and financial integrity among members. A special Investment Companies Department is concerned with the problems of investment companies and has the responsibility of reviewing companies' sales literature in that segment of the securities industry.

NATIONAL BANK commercial bank whose charter is approved by the U.S. Comptroller of the Currency rather than by a state banking department. National banks are required to be members of the FEDERAL RESERVE SYSTEM and to purchase stock in the FEDERAL RESERVE BANK in their district (*see* MEMBER BANK). They must also belong to the FEDERAL DEPOSIT INSURANCE CORPORATION.

NATIONAL DEBT debt owed by the Federal government. The national debt is made up of such debt obligations as Treasury bills, Treasury notes, and Treasury bonds. Congress imposes a ceiling on the national debt, which has been increased on occasions when federal spending has risen to the level of the ceiling. In the mid-1980s, the national debt stood at about $1.5 trillion. The interest due on the national debt is one of the major annual expenses of the federal government.

NATIONALIZATION takeover of a private company's assets or operations by a government. The company may or may not be compensated for the loss of assets. In developing nations, an operation is typically nationalized if the government feels the company is exploiting the host country and exporting too high a proportion of the profits. By nationalizing the firm, the government hopes to keep profits at home. In developed countries, industries are often nationalized when they need government subsidies to survive. For instance, the French government nationalized steel and chemical companies in the mid-1980s in order to preserve jobs that would have disappeared if free market forces had prevailed. In some developed countries, however, nationalization is carried out as a form of national policy, often by Socialist governments, and is not designed to rescue ailing industries.

NATIONAL MARKET ADVISORY BOARD board appointed by the Securities and Exchange Commission under provisions of the 1975 Securities Act to study and advise the commission on a national exchange market system (NEMS). NEMS is envisioned as a highly automated, national exchange with continuous auction markets and competing specialists or market makers, but one that would preserve the existing regional exchanges.

NATIONAL MARKET SYSTEM
1. system of trading OVER THE COUNTER stocks under the sponsorship of the NATIONAL ASSOCIATION OF SECURITIES DEALERS (NASD) and NASDAQ. Stocks trading in the National Market System must meet certain criteria for size, profitability, and trading activity. More comprehensive information is available for National Market System stocks than for other stocks traded over the counter. For most over-the-counter stocks, newspapers list the stock name, dividend, trading volume, bid and ask prices, and the change in those prices during a trading day. For National Market System stocks, the listing includes the stock name, dividend, high and low price for the past 52 weeks, trading volume, high and low price during the trading day, closing price on that day, and price change for that day.
2. national system of trading whereby the prices for stocks and bonds are listed simultaneously on the New York Stock Exchange and all regional exchanges. Buyers and sellers therefore are able to get the best prices by executing their trades on the exchange with the most favorable price at the time. This system is not to be confused with the national exchange market system (NEMS) being studied by the Securities and Exchange Commission and other planning groups. *See also* NATIONAL MARKET ADVISORY BOARD.

NATIONAL QUOTATION BUREAU daily service to subscribers that collects bid and offer quotes from MARKET MAKERS in stocks and bonds traded OVER THE COUNTER. Quotes are distributed on PINK SHEETS (for stocks) and YELLOW SHEETS (for corporate bonds). The Bureau is a subsidiary of the Commerce Clearing House, a company engaged in financial publishing.

NATIONAL SECURITIES CLEARING CORPORATION (NSCC) securities clearing organization formed in 1977 by merging subsidiaries of the New York and American Stock Exchanges with the National Clearing Corporation. It functions essentially as a medium through which brokerage firms, exchanges, and other clearing corporations reconcile accounts with each other. *See also* CONTINUOUS NET SETTLEMENT.

NEAREST MONTH in commodity futures or OPTION trading, the expiration dates, expressed as months, closest to the present. For a commodity or an option that had delivery or expiration dates available in September, December, March, and June, for instance, the nearest month would be September if a trade were being made in August. Nearest month contracts are always more heavily traded than FURTHEST MONTH contracts.

NEAR MONEY assets that are easily convertible into cash. Some examples are government securities, bank TIME DEPOSITS, and MONEY MARKET FUND shares. Bonds close to REDEMPTION date are also called near money.

NEGATIVE CARRY situation when the cost of money borrowed to finance securities is higher than the yield on the securities. If an investor borrowed at 12% to finance, or ''carry,'' a bond yielding 10%, the bond would have a negative carry, for example. Negative carry does not necessarily mean a loss to the investor, however, and a positive yield can result on an after-tax basis. In this case, the income from the 10% bond may be tax exempt, whereas the interest on the 12% loan is tax deductible.

NEGATIVE CASH FLOW situation in which a business spends more cash than it receives through earnings or other transactions in an accounting period. *See also* CASH FLOW.

NEGATIVE INCOME TAX proposed system of providing financial aid to poverty-level individuals and families, using the mechanisms already in place to collect income taxes. After filing a tax return showing income below subsistence levels, instead of paying an income tax, low-income people would receive a direct subsidy, called a negative income tax, sufficient to bring them up to the subsistence level.

NEGATIVE PLEDGE CLAUSE negative covenant or promise in an INDENTURE agreement that states the corporation will not pledge any of its assets if doing so would result in less security to the debtholders covered under the indenture agreement. Also called *covenant of equal coverage*.

NEGATIVE WORKING CAPITAL situation in which the current liabilities of a firm exceed its current assets. For example, if the total of cash, MARKETABLE SECURITIES, ACCOUNTS RECEIVABLE and notes receivable, inventory, and other current assets is less than the total of ACCOUNTS PAYABLE, short-term notes payable, long-term debt due in one year, and other current liabilities, the firm has a negative working capital. Unless the condition is corrected, the firm will not be able to pay debts when due, threatening its ability to keep operating and possibly resulting in bankruptcy.

To remedy a negative working capital position, a firm has these alternatives: (1) it can convert a long-term asset into a current asset—for example, by selling a piece of equipment or a building, by liquidating a long-term investment, or by renegotiating a long-term loan receivable; (2) it can convert short-term liabilities into long-term liabilities—for example, by negotiating the substitution of a current account payable with a long-term note payable; (3) it can borrow long term; (4) it can obtain additional equity through a stock issue or other sources of paid-in capital; (5) it can retain or "plow back" profits. *See also* WORKING CAPITAL.

NEGATIVE YIELD CURVE situation in which yields on short-term securities are higher than those on long-term securities of the same quality. Normally, short-term rates are lower than long-term rates because those who commit their money for longer periods are taking more risk. But if interest rates climb high enough, borrowers become unwilling to lock themselves into high rates for long periods and borrow short-term instead. Therefore, yields rise on short-term funds and fall or remain stable on long-term funds. Also called an INVERTED YIELD CURVE. *See also* YIELD CURVE.

NEGOTIABLE

In general:
1. something that can be sold or transferred to another party in exchange for money or as settlement of an obligation.
2. matter of mutual concern to one or more parties that involves conditions to be worked out to the satisfaction of the parties. As examples: In a lender-borrower arrangement, the interest rate may be negotiable; in securities sales, brokerage commissions are now negotiable, having historically been fixed; and in divorce cases involving children, the terms of visiting rights are usually negotiable.

Finance: instrument meeting the qualifications of the Uniform Commercial Code dealing with negotiable instruments. *See* NEGOTIABLE INSTRUMENT.

Investments: type of security the title to which is transferable by delivery. A stock certificate with the stock power properly signed is negotiable, for example.

NEGOTIABLE CERTIFICATE OF DEPOSIT large-dollar-amount, short-term certificate of deposit. Such certificates are issued by large banks and bought mainly by corporations and institutional investors. They are payable either to the bearer or to the order of the depositor, and, being NEGOTIABLE, they enjoy an active SECONDARY MARKET, where they trade in round lots of $5 million. Although they can be issued in any denomination from $100,000 up, the typical amount is $1 million. They have a minimum original maturity of 14 days; most original maturities are under six months. Also called a JUMBO CERTIFICATE OF DEPOSIT.

NEGOTIABLE INSTRUMENT unconditional order or promise to pay an amount of money, easily transferable from one person to another. Examples: check, promissory note, draft (bill of exchange). The Uniform Commercial Code requires that for an instrument to be negotiable it must be signed by the maker or drawer, must contain an unconditional promise or order to pay a specific amount of money, must be payable on demand or at a specified future time, and must be payable to order or to the bearer.

NEGOTIABLE ORDER OF WITHDRAWAL a bank or savings and loan withdrawal ticket that is a NEGOTIABLE INSTRUMENT. The accounts from which such withdrawals can be made, called NOW accounts, are thus, in effect, interest-bearing checking accounts. They were first introduced in the late 1970s and became available nationally in January 1980. In the early and mid-1980s the interest rate on NOW accounts was capped at 5½%; the cap was phased out in the late 1980s. *See also* SUPER NEGOTIABLE ORDER OF WITHDRAWAL (NOW) ACCOUNT.

NEGOTIATED UNDERWRITING underwriting of new securities issue in which the SPREAD between the purchase price paid to the issuer and the public offering price is determined through negotiation rather than multiple competitive bidding. The spread, which represents the compensation to the investment bankers participating in the underwriting (collectively called the *syndicate*), is negotiated between the issuing company and the MANAGING UNDERWRITER, with the consent of the group. Most corporate stock and bond issues and municipal revenue bond issues are priced through negotiation, whereas municipal general obligation bonds and new issues of public utilities are generally priced through competitive bidding. Competitive bidding is mandatory for new issues of public utilities holding companies. *See also* COMPETITIVE BID.

NEST EGG assets put aside for a person's retirement. Such assets are usually invested conservatively to provide the retiree with a secure standard of living for the rest of his or her life. Investment in an INDIVIDUAL RETIREMENT ACCOUNT would be considered part of a nest egg.

NET

In general: figure remaining after all relevant deductions have been made from the gross amount. For example: net sales are equal to gross sales minus discounts, returns, and allowances; net profit is gross profit less operating (sales, general, and administrative) expenses; net worth is assets (worth) less liabilities.

Investments: dollar difference between the proceeds from the sale of a security and the seller's adjusted cost of acquisition—that is, the gain or loss.

As a verb:
1. to arrive at the difference between additions and subtractions or plus amounts and minus amounts. For example, in filing tax returns, capital losses are netted against capital gains.
2. to realize a net profit, as in "last year we netted a million dollars after taxes."

NET ASSETS difference between a company's total assets and liabilities; another way of saying *owner's equity* or NET WORTH. *See* ASSET COVERAGE for a discussion of net asset value per unit of bonds, preferred stock, or common stock.

NET ASSET VALUE (NAV)
1. in mutual funds, the market value of a fund share, synonymous with *bid price*. In the case of no-load funds, the NAV, market price, and offering price are all the same figure, which the public pays to buy shares; load fund market or offer prices are quoted after adding the sales charge to the net asset value. NAV is calculated by most funds after the close of the exchanges each day by taking the closing market value of all securities owned plus all other assets such as cash, subtracting all liabilities, then dividing the result (total net assets) by the total number of shares outstanding. The number of shares outstanding can vary each day depending on the number of purchases and redemptions.
2. book value of a company's different classes of securities, usually stated as net asset value per bond, net asset value per share of preferred stock, and net book value per common share of common stock. The formula for computing net asset value is total assets less any INTANGIBLE ASSET less all liabilities and securities having a prior claim, divided by the number of units outstanding

(i.e., bonds, preferred shares, or common shares). *See* BOOK VALUE for a discussion of how these values are calculated and what they mean.

NET CAPITAL REQUIREMENT Securities and Exchange Commission requirement that member firms as well as nonmember broker-dealers in securities maintain a maximum ratio of indebtedness to liquid capital of 15 to 1; also called *net capital rule* and *net capital ratio*. Indebtedness covers all money owed to a firm, including MARGIN loans and commitments to purchase securities, one reason new public issues are spread among members of underwriting syndicates. Liquid capital includes cash and assets easily converted into cash.

NET CHANGE difference between the last trading price on a stock, bond, commodity, or mutual fund from one day to the next. The net change in individual stock prices is listed in newspaper financial pages. The designation $+2\frac{1}{2}$, for example, means that a stock's final price on that day was $2.50 higher than the final price on the previous trading day. The net change in prices of OVER THE COUNTER stocks is usually the difference between bid prices from one day to the next.

NET CURRENT ASSETS difference between current assets and current liabilities; another name for WORKING CAPITAL. Some security analysts divide this figure (after subtracting preferred stock, if any) by the number of common shares outstanding to arrive at working capital per share. Believing working capital per share to be a conservative measure of LIQUIDATING VALUE (on the theory that fixed and other noncurrent assets would more than compensate for any shrinkage in current assets if assets were to be sold), they compare it with the MARKET VALUE of the company's shares. If the net current assets per share figure, or "minimum liquidating value," is higher than the market price, these analysts view the common shares as a bargain (assuming, of course, that the company is not losing money and that its assets are conservatively valued). Other analysts believe this theory ignores the efficiency of capital markets generally and, specifically, obligations such as pension plans, which are not reported as balance sheet liabilities under present accounting rules.

NET EARNINGS *see* NET INCOME.

NET ESTATE *see* GROSS ESTATE.

NET INCOME

In general: sum remaining after all expenses have been met or deducted; synonymous with *net earnings* and with *net profit* or *net loss* (depending on whether the figure is positive or negative).

For a business: difference between total sales and total costs and expenses. Total costs comprise cost of goods sold including depreciation; total expenses comprise selling, general, and administrative expenses, plus INCOME DEDUCTIONS. Net income is usually specified as to whether it is before income taxes or after income taxes. Net income after taxes is the *bottom line* referred to in popular vernacular. It is out of this figure that dividends are normally paid. *See also* OPERATING PROFIT (OR LOSS).

For an individual: gross income less expenses incurred to produce gross income. Those expenses are mostly deductible for tax purposes.

NET INCOME PER SHARE OF COMMON STOCK amount of profit or earnings allocated to each share of common stock after all costs, taxes, allowances for depreciation, and possible losses have been deducted. Net income per share is stated in dollars and cents and is usually compared with the corresponding period a year earlier. For example, XYZ might report that second-quarter net income per share was $1.20, up from 90 cents in the previous year's second quarter. Also known as *earnings per common share* (EPS).

NET INCOME TO NET WORTH RATIO *see* RETURN ON EQUITY.

NET INVESTMENT INCOME PER SHARE income received by an investment company from dividends and interest on securities investments during an accounting period, less management fees and administrative expenses and divided by the number of outstanding shares. Short-term trading profits (net profits from securities held for less than six months) are considered dividend income. The dividend and interest income is received by the investment company, which in turn pays shareholders the net investment income in the form of dividends prorated according to each holder's share in the total PORTFOLIO.

NET LEASE financial lease stipulating that the user (rather than the owner) of the leased property shall pay all maintenance costs, taxes, insurance, and other expenses. Many real estate and oil and gas limited partnerships are structured as net leases with ESCALATOR CLAUSES, to provide limited partners with both depreciation tax benefits and appreciation of investment, minus cash expenses. *See also* GROSS LEASE.

NET OPERATING LOSS (NOL) tax term for the excess of business expenses over income in a tax year. Under TAX LOSS CARRYBACK, CARRYFORWARD provisions, NOLs can (if desired) be carried back three years and forward 15 years. The TAX REFORM ACT OF 1986 limits the use of NOLs, in cases where an acquired loss corporation has had a 50% or more change in ownership, to the loss corporation's FAIR MARKET VALUE multiplied by the long-term tax-exempt bond rate.

NET PRESENT VALUE (NPV) method used in evaluating investments whereby the net present value of all cash outflows (such as the cost of the investment) and cash inflows (returns) is calculated using a given discount rate, usually a REQUIRED RATE OF RETURN. An investment is acceptable if the NPV is positive. In capital budgeting, the discount rate used is called the HURDLE RATE and is usually equal to the INCREMENTAL COST OF CAPITAL.

NET PROCEEDS amount (usually cash) received from the sale or disposition of property, from a loan, or from the sale or issuance of securities after deduction of all costs incurred in the transaction. In computing the gain or loss on a securities transaction for tax purposes, the amount of the sale is the amount of the net proceeds.

NET PROFIT *see* NET INCOME.

NET QUICK ASSETS cash, MARKETABLE SECURITIES, and ACCOUNTS RECEIVABLE, minus current liabilities. *See also* QUICK RATIO.

NET REALIZED CAPITAL GAINS PER SHARE amount of CAPITAL GAINS that an investment company realized on the sale of securities, NET of CAPITAL LOSSES and divided by the number of outstanding shares. Such net gains are distributed at least annually to shareholders in proportion to their shares in the total portfolio. Such distributions have traditionally been treated as tax-favored long-term capital gains to the shareholders, regardless of the length of time they have held shares in the investment company. Capital gains are to be taxed at ORDINARY income rates starting in 1988. *See also* REGULATED INVESTMENT COMPANY.

NET SALES gross sales less returns and allowances, freight out, and cash discounts allowed. Cash discounts allowed is seen less frequently than in past years, since it has become conventional to report as net sales the amount finally received from the customer. Returns are merchandise returned for credit; allowances are deductions allowed by the seller for merchandise not received or received in damaged condition; freight out is shipping expense passed on to the customer.

NET TANGIBLE ASSETS PER SHARE total assets of a company, less any INTANGIBLE ASSET such as goodwill, patents, and trademarks, less all liabilities and the par value of preferred stock, divided by the number of common shares outstanding. *See* BOOK VALUE for a discussion of what this calculation means and how it can be varied to apply to bonds or preferred stock shares. *See also* NET ASSET VALUE.

NET TRANSACTION securities transaction in which the buyer and seller do not pay fees or commissions. For instance, when an investor buys a new issue, no commission is due. If the stock is initially offered at $15 a share, the buyer's total cost is $15 per share.

NET WORTH amount by which assets exceed liabilities. For a corporation, net worth is also known as *stockholders' equity* or NET ASSETS. For an individual, net worth is the total value of all possessions, such as a house, stocks, bonds, and other securities, minus all outstanding debts, such as mortgage and revolving-credit loans. In order to qualify for certain high-risk investments, brokerage houses require that an individual's net worth must be at or above a certain dollar level.

NET YIELD RATE OF RETURN on a security net of out-of-pocket costs associated with its purchase, such as commissions or markups. *See also* MARKDOWN.

NEW ACCOUNT REPORT document filled out by a broker that details vital facts about a new client's financial circumstances and investment objectives. The report may be updated if there are material changes in a client's financial position. Based on the report, a client may or may not be deemed eligible for certain types of risky investments, such as commodity trading or highly leveraged LIMITED PARTNERSHIP deals. *See also* KNOW YOUR CUSTOMER.

NEW ISSUE stock or bond being offered to the public for the first time, the distribution of which is covered by Securities and Exchange Commission (SEC) rules. New issues may be initial public offerings by previously private companies or additional stock or bond issues by companies already public and often listed on the exchanges. New PUBLIC OFFERINGS must be registered with the SEC. PRIVATE PLACEMENTS can avoid SEC registration if a LETTER OF INTENT establishes that the securities are purchased for investment and not for resale to the public. *See also* HOT ISSUE; LETTER SECURITY; PUBLIC OFFERING; UNDERWRITE.

NEW MONEY amount of additional long-term financing provided by a new issue or issues in excess of the amount of a maturing issue or by issues that are being refunded.

NEW MONEY PREFERRED PREFERRED STOCK issued after October 1, 1942, when the tax exclusion for corporate investors receiving preferred stock dividends was raised from 60% to 85%, to equal the exclusion on common stock dividends.

The change benefited financial institutions, such as insurance companies, which are limited in the amount of common stocks they can hold, typically 5% of assets. New money preferreds offer an opportunity to gain tax advantages over bond investments, which have fully taxable interest. The corporate tax exclusion on dividends was lowered to 80% starting in 1987.

NEW YORK COFFEE, SUGAR AND COCOA EXCHANGE *see* SECURITIES AND COMMODITIES EXCHANGES.

NEW YORK COTTON EXCHANGE *see* SECURITIES AND COMMODITIES EXCHANGES.

NEW YORK CURB EXCHANGE *see* AMERICAN STOCK EXCHANGE.

NEW YORK FUTURES EXCHANGE *see* SECURITIES AND COMMODITIES EXCHANGES.

NEW YORK MERCANTILE EXCHANGE *see* SECURITIES AND COMMODITIES EXCHANGES.

NEW YORK STOCK EXCHANGE (NYSE) oldest (1792) and largest stock exchange in the United States, located at 11 Wall Street in New York City; also known as the *Big Board* and *The Exchange*. The NYSE is an unincorporated association governed by a board of directors headed by a full-time paid chairman and comprised of individuals representing the public and the exchange membership in about equal proportion. Operating divisions of the NYSE are market operations, member firm regulation and surveillance, finance and office services, product development and planning, and market services and customer relations. Staff groups handle other specialized functions, such as legal problems, government relations, and economic research; certain operational functions are handled by affiliated corporations, such as DEPOSITORY TRUST COMPANY, NATIONAL SECURITIES CLEARING CORPORATION (NSCC), and SECURITIES INDUSTRY AUTOMATION CORPORATION (SIAC). Total voting membership is currently fixed at 1366 "seats," which are owned by individuals, usually partners or officers of securities firms. The number of firms represented is about 550, some of which are specialists responsible for the maintenance of an orderly market in the securities they handle. Most members execute orders for the public, although a small number—about 30, who are called FLOOR TRADERS—deal exclusively for their own accounts. More than 1500 companies are listed on the NYSE, representing large firms meeting the exchange's uniquely stringent LISTING REQUIREMENTS. STOCKS, BONDS, WARRANTS, OPTIONS, and RIGHTS are traded at 14 electronically equipped installations, called TRADING POSTS, on the FLOOR of the exchange. In the mid-1980s'NYSE-listed shares made up approximately 60% of the total shares traded on organized national exchanges in the United States.

NEW YORK STOCK EXCHANGE INDEX *see* STOCK INDEXES AND AVERAGES.

NICHE particular specialty in which a firm has garnered a large market share. Often, the market will be small enough so that the firm will not attract very much competition. For example, a company that makes a line of specialty chemicals for use by only the petroleum industry is said to have a niche in the chemical industry. Stock analysts frequently favor such companies, since their profit margins can often be wider than those of firms facing more competition.

NIFTY FIFTY 50 stocks most favored by institutions. The membership of this group is constantly changing, although companies that continue to produce consistent earnings growth over a long time tend to remain institutional favorites. Nifty Fifty stocks also tend to have higher than market average price/earnings ratios, since their growth prospects are well recognized by institutional investors. The Nifty Fifty stocks were particularly famous in the bull markets of the 1960s and early 1970s, when many of the price/earnings ratios soared to 50 or more. *See also* PRICE/EARNINGS RATIO.

NINE-BOND RULE New York Stock Exchange (NYSE) requirement that orders for nine bonds or less be sent to the floor for one hour to seek a market. Since bond trading tends to be inactive on the NYSE (because of large institutional holdings and because many of the listed bond trades are handled OVER THE COUNTER), Rule 396 is designed to obtain the most favorable price for small investors. Customers may request that the rule be waived, but the broker-dealer in such cases must then act only as a BROKER and not as a PRINCIPAL (dealer for his own account).

NO-ACTION LETTER letter requested from the Securities and Exchange Commission wherein the Commission agrees to take neither civil nor criminal action with respect to a specific activity and circumstances. LIMITED PARTNERSHIPS designed as TAX SHELTERS, which are frequently venturing in uncharted legal territory, often seek no-action letters to clear novel marketing or financing techniques.

NO-BRAINER term used to describe a market the direction of which has become obvious, and therefore requires little or no analysis. This means that most of the stocks will go up in a strong bull market and fall in a bear market, so that it does not matter very much which stock investors buy or sell.

NOISE stock-market activity caused by PROGRAM TRADES and other phenomena not reflective of general sentiment.

NO-LOAD FUND MUTUAL FUND offered by an open-end investment company that imposes no sales charge (load) on its shareholders. Investors buy shares in no-load funds directly from the fund companies, rather than through a BROKER, as is done in load funds. Many no-load fund families (*see* FAMILY OF FUNDS) allow switching of assets between stock, bond, and money market funds. The listing of the price of a no-load fund in a newspaper is accompanied with the designation NL. The net asset value, market price, and offer prices of this type of fund are exactly the same, since there is no sales charge. *See also* LOAD FUND.

NOMINAL EXERCISE PRICE EXERCISE PRICE (strike price) of a GOVERNMENT NATIONAL MORTGAGE ASSOCIATION (GNMA or Ginnie Mae) option contract, obtained by multiplying the unpaid principal balance on a Ginnie Mae certificate by the ADJUSTED EXERCISE PRICE. For example, if the unpaid principal balance is $96,000 and the adjusted exercise price is 58, the nominal exercise price is $55,680.

NOMINAL INTEREST RATE *see* NOMINAL YIELD.

NOMINAL QUOTATION bid and offer prices given by a market maker for the purpose of valuation, not as an invitation to trade. Securities industry rules require that nominal quotations be specifically identified as such; usually this is done by prefixing the quote with the letters FYI (FOR YOUR INFORMATION) or FVO (for valuation only).

NOMINAL YIELD annual dollar amount of income received from a fixed-income security divided by the PAR VALUE of the security and stated as a percentage. Thus a bond that pays $90 a year and has a par value of $1000 has a nominal yield of 9%, called its *coupon rate*. Similarly, a preferred stock that pays a $9 annual dividend and has a par value of $100 has a nominal yield of 9%. Only when a stock or bond is bought exactly at par value is the nominal yield equal to the actual yield. Since market prices of fixed-income securities go down when market interest rates go up and vice versa, the actual yield, which is determined by the market price and coupon rate (nominal yield), will be higher when the purchase price is below par value and lower when the purchase price is above par value. *See also* RATE OF RETURN.

NOMINEE person or firm, such as a bank official or brokerage house, into whose name securities or other properties are transferred by agreement. Securities held in STREET NAME, for example, are registered in the name of a BROKER (nominee) to facilitate transactions, although the customer remains the true owner.

NONCALLABLE preferred stock or bond that cannot be redeemed at the option of the issuer. A bond may offer CALL PROTECTION for a particular length of time, such as ten years. After that, the issuer may redeem the bond if it chooses and can justify doing so. U.S. government bond obligations are not callable until close to maturity. Provisions for noncallability are spelled out in detail in a bond's INDENTURE agreement or in the prospectus issued at the time a new preferred stock is floated. Bond yields are often quoted to the first date at which the bonds could be called. *See also* YIELD TO CALL.

NONCLEARING MEMBER member firm of the New York Stock Exchange or another organized exchange that does not have the operational facilities for clearing transactions and thus pays a fee to have the services performed by another member firm, called a *clearing member*. The clearing process involves comparison and verification of information between the buying and selling brokers and then the physical delivery of certificates in exchange for payment, called the *settlement*.

NONCOMPETITIVE BID method of buying Treasury bills without having to meet the high minimum purchase requirements of the regular DUTCH AUCTION; also called *noncompetitive tender*. The process of bidding for Treasury bills is split into two parts: competitive and noncompetitive bids.

COMPETITIVE BIDS are entered by large government securities dealers and brokers, who buy millions of dollars worth of bills. They offer the best price they can for the securities, and the highest bids are accepted by the Treasury in what is called the Dutch auction.

Noncompetitive bids are submitted by smaller investors through a Federal Reserve Bank, the Bureau of Federal Debt, or certain commercial banks. These bids will be executed at the average of the prices paid in all the competitive bids accepted by the Treasury. The minimum noncompetitive bid for a Treasury bill is $10,000.

NONCUMULATIVE term describing a preferred stock issue in which unpaid dividends do not accrue. Such issues contrast with CUMULATIVE PREFERRED issues, where unpaid dividends accumulate and must be paid before dividends on common shares. Most preferred issues are cumulative. On a noncumulative preferred, omitted dividends will, as a rule, never be paid. Some older railroad preferred stocks are of this type.

NONCURRENT ASSET asset not expected to be converted into cash, sold, or exchanged within the normal operating cycle of the firm, usually one year. Examples of noncurrent assets include FIXED ASSETS, such as real estate, machinery, and other equipment; LEASEHOLD IMPROVEMENTS; INTANGIBLE ASSETS, such as goodwill, patents, and trademarks; notes receivable after one year; other investments; miscellaneous assets not meeting the definition of a CURRENT ASSET. Prepaid expenses (also called DEFERRED CHARGES or *deferred expenses*), which include such items as rent paid in advance, prepaid insurance premiums, and subscriptions, are usually considered current assets by accountants. Credit analysts, however, prefer to classify these expenses as noncurrent assets, since prepayments do not represent asset strength and protection in the way that other current assets do, with their convertibility into cash during the normal operating cycle and their liquidation value should operations be terminated.

NONMEMBER FIRM brokerage firm that is not a member of an organized exchange. Such firms execute their trades either through member firms, on regional exchanges, or in the THIRD MARKET. *See* MEMBER FIRM; REGIONAL STOCK EXCHANGES.

NONPARTICIPATING PREFERRED STOCK *see* PARTICIPATING PREFERRED STOCK.

NONPRODUCTIVE LOAN type of commercial bank loan that increases the amount of spending power in the economy but does not lead directly to increased output; for example, a loan to finance a LEVERAGED BUYOUT. The Federal Reserve has on occasion acted to curtail such lending as one of its early steps in implementing monetary restraint.

NONPUBLIC INFORMATION information about a company, either positive or negative, that will have a material effect on the stock price when it is released to the public. Insiders, such as corporate officers and members of the board of directors, are not allowed to trade on material nonpublic information until it has been released to the public, since they would have an unfair advantage over unsuspecting investors. Some examples of important nonpublic information are an imminent takeover announcement, a soon-to-be-released earnings report that is more favorable than most analysts expect, or the sudden resignation of a key corporate official. *See also* DISCLOSURE; INSIDER.

NONPURPOSE LOAN loan for which securities are pledged as collateral but which is not used to purchase or carry securities. Under Federal Reserve Board REGULATION U, a borrower using securities as collateral must sign an affidavit called a PURPOSE STATEMENT, indicating the use to which the loan is to be put. Regulation U limits the amount of credit a bank may extend for purchasing and carrying margin securities, where the credit is secured directly or indirectly by stock.

NONQUALIFYING ANNUITY annuity purchased outside of an IRS-approved pension plan. The contributions to such an annuity are made with after-tax dollars. Just as with a QUALIFYING ANNUITY, however, the earnings from the nonqualifying annuity can accumulate tax deferred until withdrawn. Assets may be placed in either a FIXED ANNUITY, a VARIABLE ANNUITY, or a HYBRID ANNUITY.

NONQUALIFYING STOCK OPTION employee stock option not meeting the Internal Revenue Service criteria for QUALIFYING STOCK OPTIONS (INCENTIVE STOCK

OPTIONS) and therefore triggering a tax upon EXERCISE. (The issuing employer, however, can deduct the nonqualifying option during the period when it is exercised, whereas it would not have a deduction when a qualifying option is exercised.) A STOCK OPTION is a right issued by a corporation to an individual, normally an executive employee, to buy a given amount of shares at a stated price within a specified period of time. Gains realized on the exercise of nonqualifying options are treated as ordinary income in the tax year in which the options are exercised. Qualifying stock options, in contrast, are taxed neither at the time of granting nor the time of exercise; only when the underlying stock is sold and a CAPITAL GAIN realized, does a tax event occur.

NONRECOURSE LOAN type of financial arrangement used by limited partners in a DIRECT PARTICIPATION PROGRAM, whereby the limited partners finance a portion of their participation with a loan secured by their ownership in the underlying venture. They benefit from the LEVERAGE provided by the loan. In case of default, the lender has no recourse to the assets of the partnership beyond those held by the limited partners who borrowed the money.

NONRECURRING CHARGE one-time expense or WRITE-OFF appearing in a company's financial statement; also called *extraordinary charge*. Nonrecurring charges would include, for example, a major fire or theft, the write-off of a division, and the effect of a change in accounting procedure.

NONREFUNDABLE provision in a bond INDENTURE that either prohibits or sets limits on the issuer's retiring the bonds with the proceeds of a subsequent issue, called REFUNDING. Such a provision often does not rule out refunding altogether but protects bondholders from REDEMPTION until a specified date. Other such provisions may preclude refunding unless new bonds can be issued at a specified lower rate. *See also* CALL PROTECTION.

NONVOTING STOCK corporate securities that do not empower a holder to vote on corporate resolutions or the election of directors. Such stock is sometimes issued in connection with a takeover attempt, when management creates nonvoting shares to dilute the target firm's equity and thereby discourage the merger attempt. Except in very special circumstances, the New York Stock Exchange does not list nonvoting stock. Preferred stock is normally nonvoting stock. *See also* VOTING STOCK; VOTING TRUST CERTIFICATE.

NO-PAR-VALUE STOCK stock with no set (par) value specified in the corporate charter or on the stock certificate; also called *no-par stock*. Companies issuing no-par value shares may carry whatever they receive for them either as part of the CAPITAL STOCK account or as part of the CAPITAL SURPLUS (paid-in capital) account, or both. Whatever amount is carried as capital stock has an implicit value, represented by the number of outstanding shares divided into the dollar amount of capital stock.

The main attraction of no-par stock to issuing corporations, historically, had to do with the fact that many states imposed taxes based on PAR VALUE, while other states, like Delaware, encouraged incorporations with no-par-value stock.

For the investor, there are two reservations: (1) that unwise or inept directors may reduce the value of outstanding shares by accepting bargain basement prices on new issues (shareholders are protected, to some extent, from this by PRE-EMPTIVE RIGHT—the right to purchase enough of a new issue to protect their power and equity) and (2) that too great an amount of net worth may be channeled into the capital surplus account, which is restricted by the law of many states from being a source of dividend payments. *See* ILLEGAL DIVIDEND.

Still, no-par stock, along with low-par stock, remains an appealing alternative, from the issuer's standpoint, to par-value shares because of investor confusion of par value and real value.

Most stock issued today is either no-par or low-par value.

NORMAL INVESTMENT PRACTICE history of investment in a customer account with a member of the National Association of Securities Dealers as defined in their rules of fair practice. It is used to test the bona fide PUBLIC OFFERINGS requirement that applies to the allocation of a HOT ISSUE. If the buying customer has a history of purchasing similar amounts in normal circumstances, the sale qualifies as a bona fide public offering and is not in violation of the Rules of Fair Practice. A record of buying only hot issues is not acceptable as normal investment practice. *See also* NASD FORM FR-1.

NORMAL TRADING UNIT standard minimum size of a trading unit for a particular security; also called a ROUND LOT. For instance, stocks have a normal trading unit of 100 shares, although inactive stocks trade in 10-share round lots. Any securities trade for less than a round lot is called an ODD LOT trade.

NOTE written promise to pay a specified amount to a certain entity on demand or on a specified date. *See also* MUNICIPAL NOTE; PROMISSORY NOTE; TREASURIES.

NOT-FOR-PROFIT type of incorporated organization in which no stockholder or trustee shares in profits or losses and which usually exists to accomplish some charitable, humanitarian, or educational purpose; also called *nonprofit*. Such groups are exempt from corporate income taxes but are subject to other taxes on income-producing property or enterprises. Donations to these groups are usually tax deductible for the donor. Some examples are hospitals, colleges and universities, foundations, and such familiar groups as the Red Cross and Girl Scouts.

NOT HELD instruction (abbreviated NH) on a market order to buy or sell securities, indicating that the customer has given the FLOOR BROKER time and price discretion in executing the best possible trade but will not hold the broker responsible if the best deal is not obtained. Such orders, which are usually for large blocks of securities, were originally designed for placement with specialists, who could hold an order back if they felt prices were going to rise. The Securities and Exchange Commission no longer allows specialists to handle NH orders, leaving floor brokers without any clear alternative except to persuade the customer to change the order to a LIMIT ORDER. The broker can then turn the order over to a SPECIALIST, who could sell pieces of the block to floor traders or buy it for his own account. *See* SPECIALIST BLOCK PURCHASE AND SALE. An older variation of NH is DRT, meaning disregard tape.

NOT RATED indication used by securities rating services (such as Standard & Poor's or Moody's) and mercantile agencies (such as Dun & Bradstreet) to show that a security or a company has not been rated. It has neither negative nor positive implications. The abbreviation NR is used.

NOVATION

1. agreement to replace one party to a contract with a new party. The novation transfers both rights and duties and requires the consent of both the original and the new party.
2. replacement of an older debt or obligation with a newer one.

NOW ACCOUNT *see* NEGOTIABLE ORDER OF WITHDRAWAL.

O

OBLIGATION BOND type of mortgage bond in which the face value is greater than the value of the underlying property. The difference compensates the lender for costs exceeding the mortgage value.

OBLIGOR one who has an obligation, such as an issuer of bonds, a borrower of money from a bank or another source, or a credit customer of a business supplier or retailer. The obligor (*obligator, debtor*) is legally bound to pay a debt, including interest, when due.

ODD LOT securities trade made for less than the NORMAL TRADING UNIT (termed a ROUND LOT). In stock trading, any purchase or sale of less than 100 shares is considered an odd lot, although inactive stocks generally trade in round lots of 10 shares. An investor buying or selling an odd lot pays a higher commission rate than someone making a round-lot trade. This odd-lot differential varies among brokers but for stocks is often ⅛ of a point (12½¢) per share. For instance, someone buying 100 shares of XYZ at $70 would pay $70 a share plus commission. At the same time, someone buying only 50 shares of XYZ would pay $70⅛ a share plus commission. *See also* ODD-LOT DEALER; ODD-LOT SHORT-SALE RATIO; ODD-LOT THEORY.

ODD-LOT DEALER originally a dealer who bought round lots of stock and resold it in odd lots to retail brokers who, in turn, accommodated their smaller customers at the regular commission rate plus an extra charge, called the odd-lot differential. The assembling of round lots from odd lots is now a service provided free by New York Stock Exchange specialists to member brokers, and odd-lot transactions can be executed through most brokers serving the retail public. Brokers handling odd lots do, however, receive extra compensation; it varies with the broker, but ⅛ of a point (12½¢) per share in addition to a regular commission is typical. *See also* ODD-LOT.

ODD-LOT SHORT-SALE RATIO ratio obtained by dividing ODD LOT short sales by total odd-lot sales, using New York Stock Exchange (NYSE) statistics; also called the *odd-lot selling indicator*. Historically, odd-lot investors—those who buy and sell in less than 100-share round lots—react to market highs and lows; when the market reaches a low point, odd-lot short sales reach a high point, and vice versa. The odd-lot ratio has followed the opposite pattern of the NYSE MEMBER SHORT SALE RATIO. *See also* ODD-LOT THEORY.

ODD-LOT THEORY historical theory that the ODD LOT investor—the small personal investor who trades in less than 100-share quantities—is usually guilty of bad timing and that profits can be made by acting contrary to odd-lot trading patterns. Heavy odd-lot buying in a rising market is interpreted by proponents of this theory as a sign of technical weakness and the signal of a market reversal. Conversely, an increase of odd-lot selling in a declining market is seen as a sign of technical strength and a signal to buy. In fact, analyses of odd-lot trading over the years fail to bear out the theory with any real degree of consistency, and it has fallen into disfavor in recent years. It is also a fact that odd-lot customers generally, who tend to buy market leaders, have fared rather well in the upward market that has prevailed over the last fifty years or so. *See also* ODD-LOT SHORT-SALE RATIO.

OFF-BOARD off the exchange (the New York Stock Exchange is known as the Big Board, hence the term). The term is used either for a trade that is executed OVER THE COUNTER or for a transaction entailing listed securities that is not completed on a national exchange. Over-the-counter trading is handled by telephone, with competitive bidding carried on constantly by market makers in a particular stock. The other kind of off-board trade occurs when a block of stock is exchanged between customers of a brokerage firm, or between a customer and the firm itself if the brokerage house wants to buy or sell securities from its own inventory. *See also* THIRD MARKET.

OFFER price at which someone who owns a security offers to sell it; also known as the ASKED PRICE. This price is listed in newspapers for stocks traded OVER THE COUNTER. The bid price—the price at which someone is prepared to buy—is also shown. The bid price is always lower than the offer price. *See also* OFFERING PRICE.

OFFERING *see* PUBLIC OFFERING.

OFFERING CIRCULAR *see* PROSPECTUS.

OFFERING DATE date on which a distribution of stocks or bonds will first be available for sale to the public. *See also* DATED DATE; PUBLIC OFFERING.

OFFERING PRICE price per share at which a new or secondary distribution of securities is offered for sale to the public; also called PUBLIC OFFERING PRICE. For instance, if a new issue of XYZ stock is priced at $40 a share, the offering price is $40.

When mutual fund shares are made available to the public, they are sold at NET ASSET VALUE, also called the *offering price* or the ASKED PRICE, plus a sales charge, if any. In a NO-LOAD FUND, the offering price is the same as the net asset value. In a LOAD FUND, the sales charge is added to the net asset value, to arrive at the offering price. *See also* OFFER.

OFFERING SCALE prices at which different maturities of a SERIAL BOND issue are offered to the public by an underwriter. The offering scale may also be expressed as yields to maturity. *See also* YIELD TO MATURITY.

OFFER WANTED (OW) notice by a potential buyer of a security that he or she is looking for an offer by a potential seller of the security. The abbreviation OW is frequently seen in the PINK SHEETS (listing of stocks) and YELLOW SHEETS (listing of corporate bonds) published by the NATIONAL QUOTATION BUREAU for securities traded by OVER THE COUNTER dealers. *See also* BID WANTED.

OFF-FLOOR ORDER order to buy or sell a security that originates off the floor of an exchange. These are customer orders originating with brokers, as distinguished from orders of floor members trading for their own accounts (ON-FLOOR ORDERS). Exchange rules require that off-floor orders be executed before orders initiated on the floor.

OFFICE OF MANAGEMENT AND BUDGET (OMB) at the federal level, an agency within the Office of the President responsible for (1) preparing and presenting to Congress the president's budget; (2) working with the Council of

Economic Advisers and the Treasury Department in developing a fiscal program; (3) reviewing the administrative policies and performance of government agencies; and (4) advising the president on legislative matters.

OFFICIAL NOTICE OF SALE notice published by a municipality inviting investment bankers to submit competitive bids for an upcoming bond issue. The notice provides the name of a municipal official from whom further detail can be obtained and states certain basic information about the issue, such as its par value and important conditions. The *Bond Buyer* regularly carries such notices.

OFFICIAL STATEMENT *see* LEGAL OPINION.

OFFSET

Accounting: (1) amount equaling or counterbalancing another amount on the opposite side of the same ledger or the ledger of another account. *See also* ABSORBED. (2) amount that cancels or reduces a claim of any sort.

Banking: (1) bank's legal right to seize deposit funds to cover a loan in default—called *right of offset*. (2) number stored on a bank card that, when related to the code number remembered by the cardholder, represents the depositor's identification number, called *PAN-PIN pair*.

Securities, commodities, options: (1) closing transaction involving the purchase or sale of an OPTION having the same features as one already held. (2) HEDGE, such as the SHORT SALE of a stock to protect a capital gain or the purchase of a future to protect a commodity price, or a STRADDLE representing the purchase of offsetting put and call options on a security.

OFFSHORE term used in the United States for any financial organization with a headquarters outside the country. A MUTUAL FUND with a legal domicile in the Bahamas or the Cayman Islands, for instance, is called an *offshore fund*. To be sold in the United States, such funds must adhere to all pertinent federal and state regulations. Many banks have offshore subsidiaries that engage in activities that are either heavily regulated or taxed or not allowed under U.S. law.

OIL AND GAS LIMITED PARTNERSHIP partnership consisting of one or more limited partners and one or more general partners that is structured to find, extract, and market commercial quantities of oil and natural gas. The limited partners, who assume no liability beyond the funds they contribute, buy units in the partnership, typically for at least $5000 a unit, from a broker registered to sell that partnership. All the limited partners' money then goes to the GENERAL PARTNER, the partner with unlimited liability, who either searches for oil and gas (an exploratory or wildcat well), drills for oil and gas in a proven oil field (a DEVELOPMENTAL DRILLING PROGRAM), or pumps petroleum and gas from an existing well (a COMPLETION PROGRAM). The riskier the chance of finding oil and gas, the higher the potential reward or loss to the limited partner. Conservative investors who mainly want to collect income from the sale of proven oil and gas reserves are safest with a developmental or completion program.

In addition to the potential income from such a program, limited partners also receive tax breaks, such as depreciation deductions for equipment used for drilling and oil depletion allowances for the value of oil extracted from the fields. If the partnership borrows money for increased drilling, limited partners also can get deductions for the interest cost of the loans. *See also* EXPLORATORY DRILLING PROGRAM; INCOME LIMITED PARTNERSHIP; INTANGIBLE COSTS; LIMITED PARTNERSHIP.

OIL AND GAS LOTTERY program run by the Bureau of Land Management at the U.S. Department of the Interior that permits anyone filing an application to be selected for the right to drill for oil and gas on selected parcels of federal land. Both large oil companies and small speculators enter this lottery. An individual winning the drawing for a particularly desirable plot of land may sublet the property to an oil company, which will pay him or her royalties if the land yields commercial quantities of oil and gas.

OLIGOPOLY market situation in which a small number of selling firms control the market supply of a particular good or service and are therefore able to control the market price. An oligopoly can be *perfect*—where all firms produce an identical good or service (cement)—or *imperfect*—where each firm's product has a different identity but is essentially similar to the others (cigarettes). Because each firm in an oligopoly knows its share of the total market for the product or service it produces, and because any change in price or change in market share by one firm is reflected in the sales of the others, there tends to be a high degree of interdependence among firms; each firm must make its price and output decisions with regard to the responses of the other firms in the oligopoly, so that oligopoly prices, once established, are rigid. This encourages nonprice competition, through advertising, packaging, and service—a generally nonproductive form of resource allocation. Two examples of oligopoly in the United States are airlines serving the same routes and tobacco companies. *See also* OLIGOPSONY.

OLIGOPSONY market situation in which a few large buyers control the purchasing power and therefore the output and market price of a good or service; the buy-side counterpart of OLIGOPOLY. Oligopsony prices tend to be lower than the prices in a freely competitive market, just as oligopoly prices tend to be higher. For example, the large tobacco companies purchase all the output of a large number of small tobacco growers and therefore are able to control tobacco prices.

OMITTED DIVIDEND dividend that was scheduled to be declared by a corporation, but instead was not voted for the time being by the board of directors. Dividends are sometimes omitted when a company has run into financial difficulty and its board decides it is more important to conserve cash than to pay a dividend to shareholders. The announcement of an omitted dividend will typically cause the company's stock price to drop, particularly if the announcement is a surprise.

ON ACCOUNT

In general: in partial payment of an obligation.

Finance: on credit terms. The term applies to a relationship between a seller and a buyer wherein payment is expected sometime after delivery and the obligation is not documented by a NOTE. Synonymous with *open account*.

ON A SCALE *see* SCALE ORDER.

ON-BALANCE VOLUME TECHNICAL ANALYSIS method that attempts to pinpoint when a stock, bond, or commodity is being accumulated by many buyers or is being distributed by many sellers. The on-balance volume line is superimposed on the stock price line on a chart, and it is considered significant when the two lines cross. The chart indicates a buy signal when accumulation is detected and a sell signal when distribution is spotted. The on-balance method can be used to diagnose an entire market or an individual stock, bond, or commodity.

ONE-CANCELS-THE-OTHER ORDER *see* ALTERNATIVE ORDER.

ON-FLOOR ORDER security order originating with a member on the floor of an exchange when dealing for his or her own account. The designation separates such orders from those for customers' accounts (OFF-FLOOR ORDERS), which are generally given precedence by exchange rules.

ON MARGIN *see* MARGIN.

OPD ticker tape symbol designating (1) the first transaction of the day in a security after a DELAYED OPENING or (2) the opening transaction in a security whose price has changed significantly from the previous day's close—usually 2 or more points on stocks selling at $20 or higher, 1 or more points on stocks selling at less than $20.

OPEN

Securities:
1. status of an order to buy or sell securities that has still not been executed. A GOOD-TILL-CANCELED ORDER that remains pending is an example of an open order.
2. to establish an account with a broker.

Banking: to establish an account or a LETTER OF CREDIT.

Finance: unpaid balance.

See also OPEN-END LEASE; OPEN-END MANAGEMENT COMPANY; OPEN-END MORTGAGE; OPEN INTEREST; OPEN ORDER; OPEN REPO.

OPEN-END LEASE lease agreement providing for an additional payment after the property is returned to the lessor, to adjust for any change in the value of the property.

OPEN-END MANAGEMENT COMPANY INVESTMENT COMPANY that sells MUTUAL FUNDS to the public. The terms arises from the fact that the firm continually creates new shares on demand. Mutual fund shareholders buy the shares at NET ASSET VALUE and can redeem them at any time at the prevailing market price, which may be higher or lower than the price at which the investor bought. The shareholder's funds are invested in stocks, bonds, or money market instruments, depending on the type of mutual fund company. The opposite of an open-end management company is a CLOSED-END MANAGEMENT COMPANY, which issues a limited number of shares, which are then traded on a stock exchange.

OPEN-END MORTGAGE

Real estate finance: MORTGAGE that allows the issuance of additional bonds having equal status with the original issue, but that protects the original bondholders with specific restrictions governing subsequent borrowing under the original mortgage. For example, the terms of the original INDENTURE might permit additional mortgage-bond financing up to 75% of the value of the property acquired, but only if total fixed charges on all debt, including the proposed new bonds, have been earned a stated number of times over the previous 5 years. The open-end mortgage is a more practical and acceptable (to the mortgage holder) version of the *open mortgage,* which allows a corporation to issue unlimited amounts of bonds under the original first mortgage, with no protection to the original bondholders. An even more conservative version is the *limited open-end mortgage,* which usually contains the same restrictions as the open-end, but places a limit on the amount of first mortgage bonds that can be issued, and typically provides that proceeds from new bond issues be used to retire outstanding bonds with the same or prior security.

Trust banking: corporate trust indenture that permits the trustee to authenticate and deliver bonds from time to time in addition to the original issue. *See also* AUTHENTICATION.

OPENING

1. price at which a security or commodity starts a trading day. Investors who want to buy or sell as soon as the market opens will put in an order at the opening price.

2. short time frame of market opportunity. For instance, if interest rates have been rising for months, and for a few days or weeks they fall, a corporation that has wanted to FLOAT bonds at lower interest rates might seize the moment to issue the bonds. This short time frame would be called an *opening in the market* or a *window of opportunity. See also* WINDOW.

OPEN INTEREST total number of contracts in a commodity or options market that are still open; that is, they have not been exercised, closed out, or allowed to expire. The term also applies to a particular commodity or, in the case of options, to the number of contracts outstanding on a particular underlying security. The level of open interest is reported daily in newspaper commodity and options pages.

OPEN-MARKET OPERATIONS activities by which the Securities Department of the Federal Reserve Bank of New York—popularly called the DESK—carries out instructions of the FEDERAL OPEN MARKET COMMITTEE designed to regulate the money supply. Such operations involve the purchase and sale of government securities, which effectively expands or contracts funds in the banking system. This, in turn, alters bank reserves, causing a MULTIPLIER effect on the supply of credit and, therefore, on economic activity generally. Open-market operations represent one of three basic ways the Federal Reserve implements MONETARY POLICY, the others being changes in the member bank RESERVE REQUIREMENTS and raising or lowering the DISCOUNT RATE charged to banks borrowing from the Fed to maintain reserves.

OPEN-MARKET RATES interest rates on various debt instruments bought and sold in the open market that are directly responsive to supply and demand. Such open-market rates are distinguished from the DISCOUNT RATE, set by the FEDERAL RESERVE BOARD as a deliberate measure to influence other rates, and from bank commercial loan rates, which are directly influenced by Federal Reserve policy. The rates on short-term instruments like COMMERCIAL PAPER and banker's ACCEPTANCES are examples of open-market rates, as are yields on interest-bearing securities of all types traded in the SECONDARY MARKET.

OPEN ON THE PRINT BLOCK POSITIONER's term for a BLOCK trade that has been completed with an institutional client and "printed" on the consolidated tape, but that leaves the block positioner open—that is, with a risk position to be covered. This usually happens when the block positioner is on the sell side of the transaction and sells SHORT what he lacks in inventory to complete the order.

OPEN ORDER buy or sell order for securities that has not yet been executed or canceled; a GOOD-TILL-CANCELED ORDER.

OPEN OUTCRY method of trading on a commodity exchange. The term derives from the fact that traders must shout out their buy or sell offers. When a trader shouts he wants to sell at a particular price and someone else shouts he wants to buy at that price, the two traders have made a contract that will be recorded.

OPEN REPO REPURCHASE AGREEMENT in which the repurchase date is unspecified and the agreement can be terminated by either party at any time. The agreement continues on a day-to-day basis with interest rate adjustments as the market changes.

OPERATING LEASE type of LEASE, normally involving equipment, whereby the contract is written for considerably less than the life of the equipment and the lessor handles all maintenance and servicing; also called *service lease*. Operating leases are the opposite of capital leases, where the lessee acquires essentially all the economic benefits and risks of ownership. Common examples of equipment financed with operating leases are office copiers, computers, automobiles, and trucks. Most operating leases are cancellable, meaning the lessee can return the equipment if it becomes obsolete or is no longer needed.

OPERATING LEVERAGE *see* LEVERAGE.

OPERATING PROFIT (OR LOSS) the difference between the revenues of a business and the related costs and expenses, excluding income derived from sources other than its regular activities and before income deductions; synonymous with *net operating profit (or loss), operating income (or loss),* and *net operating income (or loss).* Income deductions are a class of items comprising the final section of a company's income statement, which, although necessarily incurred in the course of business and customarily charged before arriving at net income, are more in the nature of costs imposed from without than costs subject to the control of everyday operations. They include interest; amortized discount and expense on bonds; income taxes; losses from sales of plants, divisions, major items of property; prior-year adjustments; charges to contingency reserves; bonuses and other periodic profit distributions to officers and employees; write-offs of intangibles; adjustments arising from major changes in accounting methods, such as inventory valuation base; fire, flood, and other extraordinary losses; losses on foreign exchange; and other material and nonrecurrent items.

OPERATING RATIO any of a group of ratios that measure a firm's operating efficiency and effectiveness by relating various income and expense figures from the profit and loss statement to each other and to balance sheet figures. Among the ratios used are sales to cost of goods sold, operating expenses to operating income, net profits to gross income, net income to net worth. Such ratios are most revealing when compared with those of prior periods and with industry averages.

OPERATIONS DEPARTMENT BACK OFFICE of a brokerage firm where all clerical functions having to do with clearance, settlement, and execution of trades are handled. This department keeps customer records and handles the day-to-day monitoring of margin positions.

OPM
 1. other people's money; Wall Street slang for the use of borrowed funds by individuals or companies to increase the return on invested capital. *See also* FINANCIAL LEVERAGE.
 2. options pricing model. *See* BLACK-SCHOLES OPTION PRICING MODEL.

OPPORTUNITY COST

In general: highest price or rate of return an alternative course of action would provide.

Corporate finance: concept widely used in business planning; for example, in evaluating a CAPITAL INVESTMENT project, a company must measure the projected return against the return it would earn on the highest yielding alternative investment involving similar risk. *See also* COST OF CAPITAL.

Securities investments: cost of forgoing a safe return on an investment in hopes of making a larger profit. For instance, an investor might buy a stock that shows great promise but yields only 4%, even though a higher safe return is available in a money market fund yielding 10%. The 6% yield difference is called the opportunity cost.

OPTIMUM CAPACITY level of output of manufacturing operations that produces the lowest cost per unit. For example, a tire factory may produce tires at $30 apiece if it turns out 10,000 tires a month, but the tires can be made for $20 apiece if the plant operates at its optimum capacity of 100,000 tires a month. *See also* MARGINAL COST.

OPTION

In general: right to buy or sell property that is granted in exchange for an agreed-upon sum. If the right is not exercised after a specified period, the option expires and the option buyer forfeits the money. *See also* EXERCISE.

Securities: securities transaction agreement tied to stocks, commodities, or stock indexes. Options are traded on many exchanges.

1. a CALL OPTION gives its buyer the right to buy 100 shares of the underlying security at a fixed price before a specified date in the future—usually three, six, or nine months. For this right, the call option buyer pays the call option seller, called the writer, a fee called a PREMIUM, which is forfeited if the buyer does not exercise the option before the agreed-upon date. A call buyer therefore speculates that the price of the underlying shares will rise within the specified time period. For example, a call option on 100 shares of XYZ stock may grant its buyer the right to buy those shares at $100 apiece anytime in the next three months. To buy that option, the buyer may have to pay a premium of $2 a share, or $200. If at the time of the option contract XYZ is selling for $95 a share, the option buyer will profit if XYZ's stock price rises. If XYZ shoots up to $120 a share in two months, for example, the option buyer can EXERCISE his or her option to buy 100 shares of the stock at $100 and then sell the shares for $120 each, keeping the difference as profit (minus the $2 premium per share). On the other hand, if XYZ drops below $95 and stays there for three months, at the end of that time the call option will expire and the call buyer will receive no return on the $2 a share investment premium of $200.

2. the opposite of a call option is a PUT OPTION, which gives its buyer the right to sell a specified number of shares of a stock at a particular price within a specified time period. Put buyers expect the price of the underlying stock to fall. Someone who thinks XYZ's stock price will fall might buy a three-month XYZ put for 100 shares at $100 apiece and pay a premium of $2. If XYZ falls to $80 a share, the put buyer can then exercise his or her right to sell 100 XYZ shares at $100. The buyer will first purchase 100 shares at $80 each and then sell them to the put option seller (writer) at $100 each, thereby making a profit of $18 a share (the $20 a share profit minus the $2 a share cost of the option premium).

In practice, most call and put options are rarely exercised. Instead, investors buy and sell options before expiration, trading on the rise and fall of premium prices. Because an option buyer must put up only a small amount of money (the premium) to control a large amount of stock, options trading provides a great deal of LEVERAGE and can prove immensely profitable. Options traders can write either covered options, in which they own the underlying security, or far riskier naked options, for which they do not own the underlying security. Often, options traders lose many premiums on unsuccessful trades before they make a very profitable trade. More sophisticated traders combine various call and put options in SPREAD and STRADDLE positions. Their profits or losses result from the narrowing or widening of spreads between option prices.

An *incentive stock option* is granted to corporate executives if the company achieves certain financial goals, such as a level of sales or profits. The executive is granted the option of buying company stock at a below-market price and selling the stock in the market for a profit.

See also CALL; COVERED OPTION; DEEP IN (OUT OF) THE MONEY; IN THE MONEY; NAKED OPTION; OPTION WRITER; OUT OF THE MONEY.

OPTION AGREEMENT form filled out by a brokerage firm's customer when opening an option account. It details financial information about the customer, who agrees to follow the rules and regulations of options trading. This agreement, also called the *option information form,* assures the broker that the customer's financial resources are adequate to withstand any losses that may occur from options trading. The customer must receive a prospectus from the OPTIONS CLEARING CORPORATION before he or she can begin trading.

OPTIONAL DIVIDEND dividend that can be paid either in cash or in stock. The shareholder entitled to the dividend makes the choice.

OPTIONAL PAYMENT BOND bond whose principal and/or interest are payable, at the option of the holder, in one or more foreign currencies as well as in domestic currency.

OPTION HOLDER someone who has bought a call or put OPTION but has not yet exercised or sold it. A call option holder wants the price of the underlying security to rise; a put option holder wants the price of the underlying security to fall.

OPTION MUTUAL FUND MUTUAL FUND that either buys or sells options in order to increase the value of fund shares. OPTION mutual funds may be either conservative or aggressive. For instance, a conservative fund may buy stocks and increase shareholders' income through the PREMIUM earned by selling put and call options on the stocks in the fund's portfolio. This kind of fund would be called an *option income fund.* At the opposite extreme, an aggressive *option growth fund* may buy puts and calls in stocks that the fund manager thinks are about to fall or rise sharply; if the fund manager is right, large profits can be earned through EXERCISE of the options. The LEVERAGE that options provide makes it possible to multiply the return on invested funds many times over.

OPTION PREMIUM amount per share paid by an OPTION buyer to an option seller for the right to buy (call) or sell (put) the underlying security at a particular price within a specified period. Option premium prices are quoted in increments of eighths or sixteenths of 1% and are printed in the options tables of daily newspapers. A PREMIUM of $5 per share means an option buyer would pay $500 for an option on 100 shares. *See also* CALL OPTION; PUT OPTION.

OPTIONS CLEARING CORPORATION (OCC) corporation that handles options transactions on the stock exchanges and is owned by the exchanges. It issues all options contracts and guarantees that the obligations of both parties to a trade are fulfilled. The OCC also processes the exchange of money on all options trades and maintains records of those trades. Its prospectus is given to all investors to read before they can trade in options. This prospectus outlines the rules and risks of trading and sets the standards for ethical conduct on the part of options traders. *See also* OPTION.

OPTION SERIES options of the same class (puts or calls with the same underlying security) that also have the same EXERCISE PRICE and maturity month. For instance, all XYZ October 80 calls are a series, as are all ABC July 100 puts. *See also* OPTION.

OPTION SPREAD buying and selling of options within the same CLASS at the same time. The investor who uses the OPTION spread strategy hopes to profit from the widening or narrowing of the SPREAD between the various options. Option spreads can be designed to be profitable in either up or down markets.

Some examples:

(1) entering into two options at the same EXERCISE PRICE, but with different maturity dates. For instance, an investor could buy an XYZ April 60 call and sell an XYZ July 60 call.

(2) entering into two options at different STRIKE PRICES with the same expiration month. For example, an investor could buy an XYZ April 60 call and sell an XYZ April 70 call.

(3) entering into two options at different strike prices with different expiration months. For instance, an investor could buy an XYZ April 60 call and sell an XYZ July 70 call.

OPTION WRITER person or financial institution that sells put and call options. A writer of a PUT OPTION contracts to buy 100 shares of stock from the put option buyer by a certain date for a fixed price. For example, an option writer who sells XYZ April 50 put agrees to buy XYZ stock from the put buyer at $50 a share any time until the contract expires in April.

A writer of a CALL OPTION, on the other hand, guarantees to sell the call option buyer the underlying stock at a particular price before a certain date. For instance, a writer of an XYZ April 50 call agrees to sell stock at $50 a share to the call buyer any time before April.

In exchange for granting this right, the option writer receives a payment called an OPTION PREMIUM. For holders of large portfolios of the premiums from stocks, option writing therefore is a source of additional income.

OR BETTER Indication, abbreviated OB on the ORDER TICKET of a LIMIT ORDER to buy or sell securities, that the broker should transact the order at a price better than the specified LIMIT PRICE if a better price can be obtained.

ORDER

Investments: instruction to a broker or dealer to buy or sell securities or commodities. Securities orders fall into four basic categories: MARKET ORDER, LIMIT ORDER, time order, and STOP ORDER.

Law: direction from a court of jurisdiction, or a regulation.

Negotiable instruments: payee's request to the maker, as on a check stating, "Pay to the order of (when presented by) John Doe."

Trade: request to buy, sell, deliver, or receive goods or services which commits the issuer of the order to the terms specified.

ORDER TICKET form completed by a registered representative (ACCOUNT EXECUTIVE) of a brokerage firm, upon receiving order instructions from a customer. It shows whether the order is to buy or to sell, the number of units, the name of the security, the kind of order (ORDER MARKET, LIMIT ORDER or STOP ORDER) and the customer's name or code number. After execution of the order on the exchange floor or in the firm's trading department (if over the counter), the price is written and circled on the order ticket, and the completing broker is indicated by number. The order ticket must be retained for a certain period in compliance with federal law.

ORDINARY INCOME income from the normal activities of an individual or business, as distinguished from CAPITAL GAINS from the sale of assets. Prior to the TAX REFORM ACT OF 1986, the long-term CAPITAL GAINS TAX was lower than that on ordinary income. The 1986 Act eliminated the preferential capital gains rate, but it kept the separate statutory language to allow for future increases in ordinary income rates.

ORDINARY INTEREST simple interest based on a 360-day year rather than on a 365-day year (the latter is called *exact interest*). The difference between the two bases when calculating daily interest on large sums of money can be substantial. The ratio of ordinary interest to exact interest is 1.0139.

ORGANIZATION CHART chart showing the interrelationships of positions within an organization in terms of authority and responsibility. There are basically three patterns of organization: *line organization,* in which a single manager has final authority over a group of foremen or middle management supervisors; *functional organization,* in which a general manager supervises a number of managers identified by function; and *line and staff organization,* which is a combination of line and functional organization, with specialists in particular functions holding staff positions where they advise line officers concerned with actual production.

ORIGINAL COST
1. in accounting, all costs associated with the acquisition of an asset.
2. in public utilities accounting, the acquisition cost incurred by the entity that first devotes a property to public use; normally, the utility company's cost for the property. It is used to establish the rate to be charged customers in order to provide the utility company with a FAIR RATE OF RETURN on capital.

ORIGINAL ISSUE DISCOUNT discount from PAR VALUE at the time a bond is issued. (Although the par value of bonds is normally $1000, $100 is used when traders quote prices.) A bond may be issued at $50 ($500) per bond instead of $100 ($1000), for example. The bond will mature at $100 ($1000), however, so that an investor has a built-in gain if the bond is held until maturity. The most extreme version of an original issue discount is a ZERO-COUPON BOND, which is originally sold at far below par value and pays no interest until it matures.

    The tax treatment of original issue discount bonds is complex. The Internal Revenue Service assumes a certain rate of appreciation of the bond every year until maturity. No capital gain or loss will be incurred if the bond is sold for that estimated amount. But if the bond is sold for more than the assumed amount, a CAPITAL GAINS TAX or a tax at the ORDINARY INCOME rate is due.

ORIGINAL MATURITY interval between the issue date and the maturity date of a bond, as distinguished from current maturity, which is the time difference between the present time and the maturity date. For example, in 1987 a bond issued in 1985 to mature in 2005 would have an original maturity of 20 years and a current maturity of 18 years.

ORIGINATOR
1. bank, savings and loan, or mortgage banker that initially made the mortgage loan comprising part of a pool of mortgages.
2. investment banking firm that worked with the issuer of a new securities offering from the early planning stages and that usually is appointed manager of the underwriting SYNDICATE; more formally called the *originating investment banker*.
3. in banking terminology, the initiator of money transfer instructions.

OTC *see* OVER THE COUNTER.

OTC MARGIN STOCK shares of certain large firms traded OVER THE COUNTER that qualify as margin securities under REGULATION T of the Federal Reserve Board. Such stock must meet rigid criteria, and the list of eligible OTC shares is under constant review by the Fed. *See also* MARGIN SECURITY.

OTHER INCOME heading on a profit and loss statement for income from activities not in the normal course of business; sometimes called *other revenue*. Examples: interest on customers' notes, dividends and interest from investments, profit from the disposal of assets other than inventory, gain on foreign exchange, miscellaneous rent income. *See also* EXTRAORDINARY ITEM.

OTHER PEOPLE'S MONEY *see* OPM.

OUT-OF-FAVOR INDUSTRY OR STOCK industry or stock that is currently unpopular with investors. For example, the investing public may be disenchanted with an industry's poor earnings outlook. If interest rates were rising, interest-sensitive stocks such as banks and savings and loans would be out of favor because rising rates might harm these firms' profits. CONTRARIAN investors—those who consciously do the opposite of most other investors—tend to buy out-of-favor stocks because they can be bought cheaply. When the earnings of these stocks pick up, contrarians typically sell the stocks. Out-of-favor stocks tend to have a low PRICE/EARNINGS RATIO.

OUT OF LINE term describing a stock that is too high or too low in price in comparison with similar-quality stocks. A comparison of this sort is usually based on the PRICE/EARNINGS RATIO (PE), which measures how much investors are willing to pay for a firm's earnings prospects. If most computer industry stocks had PEs of 15, for instance, and XYZ Computers had a PE of only 10, analysts would say that XYZ's price is out of line with the rest of the industry.

OUT OF THE MONEY term used to describe an OPTION whose STRIKE PRICE for a stock is either higher than the current market value, in the case of a CALL, or lower, in the case of a PUT. For example, an XYZ December 60 CALL option would be out of the money when XYZ stock was selling for $55 a share. Similarly, an XYZ December 60 PUT OPTION would be out of the money when XYZ stock was selling for $65 a share.

    Someone buying an out-of-the-money option hopes that the option will move IN THE MONEY, or at least in that direction. The buyer of the above XYZ call would want the stock to climb above $60 a share, whereas the put buyer would like the stock to drop below $60 a share.

OUTSIDE DIRECTOR member of a company's BOARD OF DIRECTORS who is not an employee of the company. Such directors are considered important because they are presumed to bring unbiased opinions to major corporate decisions and also can contribute diverse experience to the decision-making process. A retailing company may have outside directors with experience in finance and manufacturing, for instance. To avoid conflict of interest, outside directors never serve on the boards of two directly competing corporations. Directors receive fees from the company in return for their service, usually a set amount for each board meeting they attend.

OUTSTANDING
1. unpaid; used of ACCOUNTS RECEIVABLE and debt obligations of all types.
2. not yet presented for payment, as a check or draft.
3. stock held by shareholders, shown on corporate balance sheets under the heading of CAPITAL STOCK issued and outstanding.

OUT THE WINDOW term describing the rapid way a very successful NEW ISSUE of securities is marketed to investors. An issue that goes out the window is also called a BLOWOUT. *See also* HOT ISSUE.

OVERALL MARKET PRICE COVERAGE total assets less intangibles divided by the total of (1) the MARKET VALUE of the security issue in question and (2) the BOOK VALUE of liabilities and issues having a prior claim. The answer indicates the extent to which the market value of a particular CLASS of securities is covered in the event of a company's liquidation.

OVERBOOKED *see* OVERSUBSCRIBED.

OVERBOUGHT description of a security or a market that has recently experienced an unexpectedly sharp price rise and is therefore vulnerable to a price drop (called a CORRECTION by technical analysts). When a stock has been overbought, there are fewer buyers left to drive the price up further. *See also* OVERSOLD.

OVERHANG sizable block of securities or commodities contracts that, if released on the market, would put downward pressure on prices. Examples of overhang include shares held in a dealer's inventory, a large institutional holding, a secondary distribution still in registration, and a large commodity position about to be liquidated. Overhang inhibits buying activity that would otherwise translate into upward price movement.

OVERHEAD
1. costs of a business that are not directly associated with the production or sale of goods or services. Also called INDIRECT COSTS AND EXPENSES, *burden* and, in Great Britain, *oncosts*.
2. sometimes used in a more limited sense, as in manufacturing or factory overhead.
  See also DIRECT OVERHEAD.

OVERHEATING term describing an economy that is expanding so rapidly that economists fear a rise in INFLATION. In an overheated economy, too much money is chasing too few goods, leading to price rises, and the productive capacity of a nation is usually nearing its limit. The remedies in the United States are usually a tightening of the money supply by the Federal Reserve and curbs in federal government spending. *See also* MONETARY POLICY; OPTIMUM CAPACITY.

OVERISSUE shares of CAPITAL STOCK issued in excess of those authorized. Preventing overissue is the function of a corporation's REGISTRAR (usually a bank acting as agent), which works closely with the TRANSFER AGENT in canceling and reissuing certificates presented for transfer and in issuing new shares.

OVERLAPPING DEBT municipal accounting term referring to a municipality's share of the debt of its political subdivisions or the special districts sharing its geographical area. It is usually determined by the ratio of ASSESSED VALUATION of taxable property lying within the corporate limits of the municipality to the assessed valuation of each overlapping district. Overlapping debt is often greater than the direct debt of a municipality, and both must be taken into account in determining the debt burden carried by taxable real estate within a municipality when evaluating MUNICIPAL BOND investments.

OVERNIGHT POSITION broker-dealer's LONG POSITION or SHORT POSITION in a security at the end of a trading day.

OVERNIGHT REPO overnight REPURCHASE AGREEMENT; an arrangement whereby securities dealers and banks finance their inventories of Treasury bills, notes, and bonds. The dealer or bank sells securities to an investor with a temporary surplus of cash, agreeing to buy them back the next day. Such transactions are settled in immediately available FEDERAL FUNDS, usually at a rate below the federal funds rate (the rate charged by banks lending funds to each other).

OVERSOLD description of a stock or market that has experienced an unexpectedly sharp price decline and is therefore due, according to some proponents of TECHNICAL ANALYSIS, for an imminent price rise. If all those who wanted to sell a stock have done so, there are no sellers left, and so the price will rise. *See also* OVERBOUGHT.

OVERSUBSCRIBED underwriting term describing a new stock issue for which there are more buyers than available shares. An oversubscribed, or *overbooked*, issue often will jump in price as soon as its shares go on the market, since the buyers who could not get shares will want to buy once the stock starts trading. In some cases, an issuer will increase the number of shares available if the issue is oversubscribed. *See also* GREEN SHOE; HOT ISSUE.

OVER THE COUNTER (OTC)

1. security that is not listed and traded on an organized exchange.
2. market in which securities transactions are conducted through a telephone and computer network connecting dealers in stocks and bonds, rather than on the floor of an exchange.

Over-the-counter stocks are traditionally those of smaller companies that do not meet the LISTING REQUIREMENTS of the New York Stock Exchange or the American Stock Exchange. In recent years, however, many companies that qualify for listing have chosen to remain with over-the-counter trading, because they feel that the system of multiple trading by many dealers is preferable to the centralized trading approach of the New York Stock Exchange, where all trading in a stock has to go through the exchange SPECIALIST in that stock. The rules of over-the-counter stock trading are written and enforced largely by the NATIONAL ASSOCIATION OF SECURITIES DEALERS (NASD), a self-regulatory group. Prices of over-the-counter stocks are published in daily newspapers, with the NATIONAL MARKET SYSTEM stocks listed separately from the rest of the over-the-counter market. Other over-the-counter markets include those for government and municipal bonds. *See also* NASDAQ.

OVERTRADING

Finance: practice of a firm that expands sales beyond levels that can be financed with normal WORKING CAPITAL. Continued overtrading leads to delinquent ACCOUNTS PAYABLE and ultimately to default on borrowings.

New issue underwriting: practice whereby a member of an underwriting group induces a brokerage client to buy a portion of a new issue by purchasing other securities from the client at a premium. The underwriter breaks even on the deal because the premium is offset by the UNDERWRITING SPREAD.

Securities: excessive buying and selling by a broker in a DISCRETIONARY ACCOUNT. *See also* CHURNING.

OVERVALUED description of a stock whose current price is not justified by the earnings outlook or the PRICE/EARNINGS RATIO. It is therefore expected that the stock will drop in price. Overvaluation may result from an emotional buying spurt, which inflates the market price of the stock, or from a deterioration of the company's financial strength. The opposite of overvalued is UNDERVALUED. *See also* FULLY VALUED.

OVERWRITING speculative practice by an OPTION WRITER who believes a security to be overpriced or underpriced and sells CALL OPTIONS or PUT OPTIONS on the security in quantity, assuming they will not be exercised. *See also* OPTION.

P

PACIFIC STOCK EXCHANGE *See* REGIONAL STOCK EXCHANGES.

PAC-MAN STRATEGY technique used by a corporation that is the target of a takeover bid to defeat the acquirer's wishes. The TARGET COMPANY defends itself by threatening to take over the acquirer and begins buying its common shares. For instance, if company A moves to take over company B against the wishes of the management of company B, company B will begin buying shares in company A in order to thwart A's takeover attempt. The Pac-Man strategy is named after a popular video game of the early 1980s, in which each character that does not swallow its opponents is itself consumed. *See also* TAKEOVER; TENDER OFFER.

PAID-IN CAPITAL capital received from investors in exchange for stock, as distinguished from capital generated from earnings or donated. The paid-in capital account includes CAPITAL STOCK and contributions of stockholders credited to accounts other than capital stock, such as an excess over PAR value received from the sale or exchange of capital stock. It would also include surplus resulting from RECAPITALIZATION. Paid-in capital is sometimes classified more specifically as *additional paid-in capital, paid-in surplus,* or *capital surplus.* Such accounts are distinguished from RETAINED EARNINGS or its older variation, EARNED SURPLUS. *See also* DONATED STOCK.

PAID-IN SURPLUS see PAID-IN CAPITAL.

PAINTING THE TAPE
1. illegal practice by manipulators who buy and sell a particular security among themselves to create artificial trading activity, causing a succession of trades to be reported on the CONSOLIDATED TAPE and luring unwary investors to the "action." After causing movement in the market price of the security, the manipulators hope to sell at a profit.
2. consecutive or frequent trading in a particular security, resulting in its repeated appearances on the ticker tape. Such activity is usually attributable to special investor interest in the security.

PAIRED SHARES common stocks of two companies under the same management that are sold as a unit, usually appearing as a single certificate printed front and back. Also called *Siamese shares* or *stapled stock.*

P & L *see* PROFIT AND LOSS STATEMENT.

PAPER PROFIT OR LOSS unrealized CAPITAL GAIN or CAPITAL LOSS in an investment or PORTFOLIO. Paper profits and losses are calculated by comparing the current market prices of all stocks, bonds, mutual funds, and commodities in a portfolio to the prices at which those assets were originally bought. These profits or losses become realized only when the securities are sold.

PAR equal to the nominal or FACE VALUE of a security. A bond selling at par, for instance, is worth the same dollar amount it was issued for or at which it will be redeemed at maturity—typically, $1000 per bond.

With COMMON STOCK, par value is set by the company issuing the stock. At one time, par value represented the original investment behind each share of stock in goods, cash, and services, but today this is rarely the case. Instead, it is an assigned amount (such as $1 a share) used to compute the dollar accounting value of the common shares on a company's balance sheet. Par value has no relation to MARKET VALUE, which is determined by such considerations as NET ASSET VALUE, YIELD, and investors' expectations of future earnings. Some companies issueNO-PAR VALUE STOCK. *See also* STATED VALUE.

Par value has more importance for bonds and PREFERRED STOCK. The interest paid on bonds is based on a percentage of a bond's par value—a 10% bond pays 10% of the bond's par value annually. Preferred dividends are normally stated as a percentage of the par value of the preferred stock issue.

PAR BOND bond that is selling at PAR, the amount equal to its nominal value or FACE VALUE. A corporate bond redeemable at maturity for $1000 is a par bond when it trades on the market for $1000.

PARENT COMPANY company that owns or controls subsidiaries through the ownership of voting stock. A parent company is usually an operating company in its own right; where it has no business of its own, the term HOLDING COMPANY is often preferred.

PARETO'S LAW theory that the pattern of income distribution is constant, historically and geographically, regardless of taxation or welfare policies; also called *law of the trivial many and the critical few* or *80-20 law.* Thus, if 80% of a nation's income will benefit only 20% of the population, the only way to improve the economic lot of the poor is to increase overall output and income levels.

Other applications of the law include the idea that in most business activities a small percentage of the work force produces the major portion of output or that 20% of the customers account for 80% of the dollar volume of sales. The law is attributed to Vilfredo Pareto, an Italian-Swiss engineer and economist (1848–1923).

Pareto is also credited with the concept called *Paretian optimum* (or *optimality*) that resources are optimally distributed when an individual cannot move into a better position without putting someone else into a worse position.

PARITY PRICE price for a commodity or service that is pegged to another price or to a composite average of prices based on a selected prior period. As the two sets of prices vary, they are reflected in an index number on a scale of 100. For example, U.S. farm prices are pegged to prices based on the purchasing power of farmers in the period from 1910 to 1914. If the parity ratio is below 100, reflecting a reduction in purchasing power to the extent indicated, the government compensates the farmer by paying a certain percentage of parity, either in the form of a direct cash payment, in the purchase of surplus crops, or in a NONRE-COURSE LOAN.

The concept of parity is also widely applied in industrial wage contracts as a means of preserving the real value of wages.

PARKING placing assets in a safe investment while other investment alternatives are under consideration. For instance, an investor will park the proceeds of a stock or bond sale in an interest-bearing money market fund while considering what other stocks or bonds to purchase.

PARTIAL DELIVERY term used when a broker does not deliver the full amount of a security or commodity called for by a contract. If 10,000 shares were to be delivered, for example, and only 7000 shares are transferred, it is called a partial delivery.

PARTICIPATING PREFERRED STOCK PREFERRED STOCK that, in addition to paying a stipulated dividend, gives the holder the right to participate with the common stockholder in additional distributions of earnings under specified conditions. One example would be an arrangement whereby preferred shareholders are paid $5 per share, then common shareholders are paid $5 per share, and then preferred and common shareholders share equally in further dividends up to $1 per share in any one year.

Participating preferred issues are rare. They are used when special measures are necessary to attract investors. Most preferred stock is *nonparticipating preferred stock,* paying only the stipulated dividends.

PARTICIPATION CERTIFICATE certificate representing an interest in a POOL of funds or in other instruments, such as a MORTGAGE POOL. The following quasi-governmental agencies issue and/or guarantee such certificates (also called PASS-THROUGH SECURITIES): FEDERAL HOME LOAN MORTGAGE CORPORATION, FEDERAL NATIONAL MORTGAGE ASSOCIATION, GOVERNMENT NATIONAL MORTGAGE ASSOCIATION.

PARTICIPATION LOAN

Commercial lending: loan made by more than one lender and serviced (administered) by one of the participants, called the *lead bank* or *lead lender.* Participation loans make it possible for large borrowers to obtain bank financing when the amount involved exceeds the legal lending limit of an individual bank (approximately 10% of a bank's capital).

Real estate: mortgage loan, made by a lead lender, in which other lenders own an interest.

PARTNERSHIP contract between two or more people in a joint business who agree to pool their funds and talent and share in the profits and losses of the enterprise. Those who are responsible for the day-to-day management of the partnership's activities, whose individual acts are binding on the other partners, and who are personally liable for the partnership's total liabilities are called *general partners.* Those who contribute only money and are not involved in management decisions are called *limited partners;* their liability is limited to their investment.

Partnerships are a common form of organization for service professions such as accounting and law. Each accountant or lawyer made a partner earns a percentage of the firm's profits.

Limited partnerships are also sold to investors by brokerage firms, financial planners, and other registered representatives. These partnerships may be either public (meaning that a large number of investors will participate and the partnership's plans must be filed with the Securities and Exchange Commission) or private (meaning that only a limited number of investors may participate and the plan‚need not be filed with the SEC). Both public and private limited partnerships invest in real estate, oil and gas, research and development, and equipment leasing. Some of these partnerships are oriented towards offering tax advantages and capital gains to limited partners, while others are designed to provide mostly income and some capital gains.

See also GENERAL PARTNER; LIMITED PARTNERSHIP; OIL AND GAS LIMITED PARTNERSHIP; PRIVATE LIMITED PARTNERSHIP; PUBLIC LIMITED PARTNERSHIP.

PAR VALUE *see* PAR.

PAR VALUE OF CURRENCY ratio of one nation's currency unit to that of another country, as defined by the official exchange rates between the two countries; also called *par of exchange* or *par exchange rate*. Since 1971, exchange rates have been allowed to float; that is, instead of official rates of exchange, currency values are being determined by the forces of supply and demand in combination with the buying and selling by countries of their own currencies in order to stabilize the market value, a form of PEGGING.

PASSED DIVIDEND *see* OMITTED DIVIDEND; CUMULATIVE PREFERRED.

PASSIVE income or loss from activities in which a taxpayer does not materially participate, such as LIMITED PARTNERSHIPS, as distinguished from (1) income from wages and active trade or business or (2) INVESTMENT INCOME, such as dividends and interest. Under the TAX REFORM ACT OF 1986, losses and credits from passive activities are deductible only against income and tax from passive activities, although one passive activity can offset another and unused passive losses can be carried forward. For preenactment passive interests, 65% of net passive losses can be applied against nonpassive income in 1987, 40% in 1988, 20% in 1989, and 10% in 1990. Real estate rental activities are considered passive regardless of material participation, but $25,000 can be deducted against nonpassive activities (phasing out for incomes over $100,000 with special provisions for low-income and rehabilitation housing).

PASSIVE BOND BOND that yields no interest. Such bonds sometimes arise out of reorganizations or are used in NOT-FOR-PROFIT fund raising.

PASS-THROUGH SECURITY security, representing pooled debt obligations repackaged as shares, that passes income from debtors through the intermediary to investors. The most common type of pass-through is a MORTGAGE-BACKED CERTIFICATE, usually government-guaranteed, where homeowners' principal and interest payments pass from the originating bank or savings and loan through a governmental agency or investment bank to investors, net of service charges. Pass-throughs representing other types of assets, such as auto loan paper or student loans, are also widely marketed. *See also* COLLATERALIZED MORTGAGE OBLIGATION; REMIC.

PAYBACK PERIOD in capital budgeting; the length of time needed to recoup the cost of a CAPITAL INVESTMENT. The payback period is the ratio of the initial investment (cash outlay) to the annual cash inflows for the recovery period. The major shortcoming of the payback period method is that it does not take into account cash flows after the payback period and is therefore not a measure of the profitability of an investment project. For this reason, analysts generally prefer the DISCOUNTED CASH FLOW methods of capital budgeting—namely, the INTERNAL RATE OF RETURN and the NET PRESENT VALUE methods.

PAYDOWN

Bonds: refunding by a company of an outstanding bond issue through a smaller new bond issue, usually to cut interest costs. For instance, a company that issued $100 million of 12% bonds a few years ago will pay down (refund) that debt with a new $80 million issue with an 8% yield. The amount of the net deduction is called the paydown.

Lending: repayment of principal short of full payment. *See also* ON ACCOUNT.

PAYING AGENT agent, usually a bank, that receives funds from an issuer of bonds or stock and in turn pays principal and interest to bondholders and dividends to stockholders, usually charging a fee for the service. Sometimes called *disbursing agent*.

PAYMENT DATE date on which a declared stock dividend or a bond interest payment is scheduled to be paid.

PAYOUT RATIO percentage of a firm's profits that is paid out to shareholders in the form of dividends. Young, fast-growing companies reinvest most of their earnings in their business and usually do not pay dividends. Regulated electric, gas, and telephone utility companies have historically paid out larger proportions of their highly dependable earnings in dividends than have other industrial corporations. Since these utilities are limited to a specified return on assets and are thus not able to generate from internal operations the cash flow needed for expansion, they pay large dividends to keep their stock attractive to investors desiring yield and are able to finance growth through new securities offerings. *See also* RETENTION RATE.

PAY UP

1. situation when an investor who wants to buy a stock at a particular price hesitates and the stock begins to rise. Instead of letting the stock go, he "pays up" to buy the shares at the higher prevailing price.
2. when an investor buys shares in a high quality company at what is felt to be a high price. Such an investor will say "I realize that I am paying up for this stock, but it is worth it because it is such a fine company."

PEGGING stabilizing the price of a security, commodity, or currency by intervening in a market. For example, until 1971 governments pegged the price of gold at certain levels to stabilize their currencies and would therefore buy it when the price dropped and sell when the price rose. Since 1971, a FLOATING EXCHANGE RATE system has prevailed, in which countries use pegging—the buying or selling of their own currencies—simply to offset fluctuations in the exchange rate. The U.S. government uses pegging in another way to support the prices of agricultural commodities; *see* PARITY PRICE.

In floating new stock issues, the managing underwriter is authorized to try to peg the market price and stabilize the market in the issuer's stock by buying shares in the open market. With this one exception, securities price pegging is illegal and is regulated by the Securities and Exchange Commission. *See also* STABILIZATION.

PENALTY CLAUSE clause found in contracts, borrowing agreements, and savings instruments providing for penalties in the event a contract is not kept, a loan payment is late, or a withdrawal is made prematurely. *See also* PREPAYMENT PENALTY.

PENNANT technical chart pattern resembling a pointed flag, with the point facing to the right. Unlike a FLAG pattern, in which rallies and peaks occur in a uniform range, it is formed as the rallies and peaks that give it its shape become less pronounced. A pennant is also characterized by diminishing trade volume. With these differences, this pattern has essentially the same significance as a flag; that is, prices will rise or fall sharply once the pattern is complete.

PENNANT

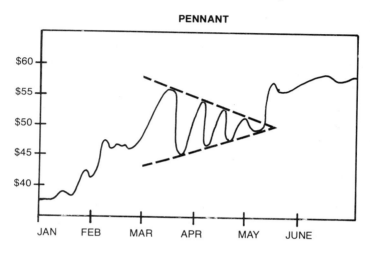

PENNY STOCK stock that typically sells for less than $1 a share, although it may rise to as much as $10 a share after the initial PUBLIC OFFERING, usually because of heavy promotion. Penny stocks are issued by companies with a short or erratic history of revenues and earnings, and therefore such stocks are more VOLATILE than those of large, well-established firms traded on the New York or American stock exchanges. Many brokerage houses therefore have special precautionary rules about trading in these stocks.

All penny stocks are traded OVER-THE-COUNTER, many of them in the local markets of Denver, Vancouver, or Salt Lake City. These markets have had a history of boom and bust, with a speculative fervor for oil, gas, and gold-mining stocks in the Denver penny stock market in the late 1970s turning to bust by the early 1980s.

PENSION BENEFIT GUARANTY CORPORATION (PBGC) federal corporation established under the EMPLOYEE RETIREMENT INCOME SECURITY ACT of 1974 (ERISA) to guarantee basic pension benefits in covered plans by administering terminated plans and placing liens on corporate assets for certain pension liabilities that were not funded. To be covered, a plan must promise clearly defined benefits to more than 25 employees. *See also* PENSION FUND.

PENSION FUND fund set up by a corporation, labor union, governmental entity, or other organization to pay the pension benefits of retired workers. Pension funds invest billions of dollars annually in the stock and bond markets, and are therefore a major factor in the supply-demand balance of the markets. Earnings on the investment portfolios of pension funds are TAX DEFERRED. Fund managers make actuarial assumptions about how much they will be required to pay out to pensioners and then try to ensure that the RATE OF RETURN on their portfolios equals or exceeds that anticipated payout need. *See also* APPROVED LIST; EMPLOYEE RETIREMENT INCOME SECURITY ACT; PRUDENT-MAN RULE; VESTING.

PER CAPITA DEBT total bonded debt of a municipality, divided by its population. A more refined version, called *net per capita debt,* divides the total bonded debt less applicable sinking funds by the total population. The result of either ratio, compared with ratios of prior periods, reveals trends in a municipality's debt burden, which bond analysts evaluate, bearing in mind that, historically, defaults in times of recession have generally followed overexpansion of debts in previous boom periods.

PERCENTAGE-OF-COMPLETION CAPITALIZED COST METHOD *See* COMPLETED CONTRACT METHOD.

PERCENTAGE ORDER order to a securities broker to buy or sell a specified number of shares of a stock after a fixed number of these shares have been traded. It can be a LIMIT ORDER or a MARKET ORDER and usually applies to one day.

PERFECT COMPETITION market condition wherein no buyer or seller has the power to alter the market price of a good or service. Characteristics of a perfectly competitive market are a large number of buyers and sellers, a homogeneous (similar) good or service, an equal awareness of prices and volume, an absence of discrimination in buying and selling, total mobility of productive resources, and complete freedom of entry. Perfect competition exists only as a theoretical ideal. Also called *pure competition.*

PERFORMANCE BOND surety bond given by one party to another, protecting the second party against loss in the event the terms of a contract are not fulfilled. The surety company is primarily liable with the principal (the contractor) for nonperformance. For example, a homeowner having a new kitchen put in may request a performance bond from the home improvement contractor so that the homeowner would receive cash compensation if the kitchen was not done satisfactorily within the agreed upon time.

PERFORMANCE FEE *see* INCENTIVE FEE.

PERFORMANCE FUND MUTUAL FUND designed for growth of capital. A performance fund invests in high-growth companies that do not pay dividends or that pay small dividends. Investors in such funds are willing to take higher-than-average risks in order to earn higher-than-average returns on their invested capital. *See also* GROWTH STOCK; PERFORMANCE STOCK.

PERFORMANCE STOCK high-growth stock that an investor feels will significantly rise in value. Also known as GROWTH STOCK, such a security tends to pay either a small dividend or no dividend at all. Companies whose stocks are in this category tend to retain earnings rather than pay dividends in order to finance their rapid growth. *See also* PERFORMANCE FUND.

PERIODIC PAYMENT PLAN plan to accumulate capital in a mutual fund by making regular investments on a monthly or quarterly basis. The plan has a set pay-in period, which may be 10 or 20 years, and a mechanism to withdraw funds from the plan after that time. Participants in periodic payment plans enjoy the advantages of DOLLAR COST AVERAGING and the diversification among stocks or bonds that is available through a mutual fund. Some plans also include completion insurance, which assures that all scheduled contributions to the plan will continue so that full benefits can be passed on to beneficiaries in the event the participant dies or is incapacitated.

PERIODIC PURCHASE DEFERRED CONTRACT ANNUITY contract for which fixed-amount payments, called *premiums,* are paid either monthly or quarterly and that does not begin paying out until a time elected by the holder (the *annuitant*). In some cases, premium payments may continue after payments from the annuity have begun. A periodic purchase deferred contract can be either fixed or variable. *See also* FIXED ANNUITY; VARIABLE ANNUITY.

PERIOD OF DIGESTION time period after the release of a NEW ISSUE of stocks or bonds during which the trading price of the security is established in the marketplace. Particularly when an INITIAL PUBLIC OFFERING is released, the period of digestion may entail considerable VOLATILITY, as investors try to ascertain an appropriate price level for it.

PERMANENT FINANCING

Corporate finance: long-term financing by means of either debt (bonds or long-term notes) or equity (common or preferred stock).

Real estate: long-term mortgage loan or bond issue, usually with a15-, 20-, or 30-year term, the proceeds of which are used to repay a CONSTRUCTION LOAN.

PERPENDICULAR SPREAD option strategy using options with similar expiration dates and different strike prices (the prices at which the options can be exercised). A perpendicular spread can be designed for either a bullish or a bearish outlook.

PERPETUAL BOND bond that has no maturity date, is not redeemable, and pays a steady stream of interest indefinitely; also called *annuity bond.* The only notable perpetual bonds in existence are the consols first issued by the British Treasury to pay off smaller issues used to finance the Napoleonic Wars (1814). Some persons in the United States believe it would be more realistic to issue perpetual government bonds than constantly to refund portions of the national debt, as is the practice.

PERPETUAL INVENTORY inventory accounting system whereby book inventory is kept in continuous agreement with stock on hand; also called *continuous inventory.* A daily record is maintained of both the dollar amount and the physical quantity of inventory, and this is reconciled to actual physical counts at short intervals. Perpetual inventory contrasts with *periodic inventory.*

PERPETUAL WARRANT investment certificate giving the holder the right to buy a specified number of common shares of stock at a stipulated price with no expiration date. *See also* SUBSCRIPTION WARRANT.

PETRODOLLARS dollars paid to oil-producing countries and deposited in Western banks. In the 1970s, Middle Eastern oil producers built up huge surpluses of petrodollars, which the banks lent to oil-importing countries around the world. By the mid-1980s, these surpluses had shrunk, and many of the borrowing countries were having trouble repaying their huge debts. The flow of petrodollars, therefore, is very important in understanding the current world economic situation. Also called *petrocurrency* or *oil money*.

PHANTOM STOCK PLAN executive incentive concept whereby an executive receives a bonus based on the market appreciation of the company's stock over a fixed period of time. The hypothetical (hence phantom) amount of shares involved in the case of a particular executive is proportionate to his or her salary level. The plan works on the same principle as a CALL OPTION (a right to purchase a fixed amount of stock at a set price by a particular date). Unlike a call option, however, the executive pays nothing for the option and therefore has nothing to lose.

PHILADELPHIA STOCK EXCHANGE *see* REGIONAL STOCK EXCHANGES.

PHYSICAL COMMODITY actual commodity that is delivered to the contract buyer at the completion of a commodity contract in either the SPOT MARKET or the FUTURES MARKET. Some examples of physical commodities are corn, cotton, gold, oil, soybeans, and wheat. The quality specifications and quantity of the commodity to be delivered are specified by the exchange on which it is traded.

PHYSICAL VERIFICATION procedure by which an auditor actually inspects the assets of a firm, particularly inventory, to confirm their existence and value, rather than relying on written records. The auditor may use statistical sampling in the verification process.

PICKUP value gained in a bond swap. For example, bonds with identical coupon rates and maturities may have different market values, mainly because of a difference in quality, and thus in yields. The higher yield of the lower-quality bond received in such a swap compared with the yield of the higher-quality bond that was exchanged for it results in a net gain for the trader, called his or her pickup on the transaction.

PICKUP BOND bond that has a relatively high coupon (interest) rate and is close to the date at which it is callable—that is, can be paid off prior to maturity—by the issuer. If interest rates fall, the investor can look forward to picking up a redemption PREMIUM, since the bond will in all likelihood be called.

PICTURE Wall Street jargon used to request bid and asked prices and quantity information from a specialist or from a dealer regarding a particular security. For example, the question "What's the picture on XYZ?" might be answered, "58⅜ [best bid] to ¾ [best offer is 58¾], 1000 either way [there are both a buyer and a seller for 1000 shares]."

PIGGYBACK REGISTRATION situation when a securities UNDERWRITER allows existing holdings of shares in a corporation to be sold in combination with an offering of new public shares. The PROSPECTUS in a piggyback registration will reveal the nature of such a public/private share offering and name the sellers of the private shares. *See also* PUBLIC OFFERING.

PINK SHEETS daily publication of the NATIONAL QUOTATION BUREAU that details the BID AND ASKED prices of thousands of OVER THE COUNTER (OTC) stocks. Many of these stocks are not carried in daily OTC newspaper listings. Brokerage firms subscribe to the pink sheets—named for their color—because the sheets not only give current prices but list market makers who trade each stock. Debt securities are listed separately on YELLOW SHEETS.

PIPELINE term referring to the underwriting process that involves securities being proposed for public distribution. The phrase used is "in the pipeline." The entire underwriting process, including registration with the Securities and Exchange Commission, must be completed before a security can be offered for public sale. Underwriters attempt to have several securities issues waiting in the pipeline so that the issues can be sold as soon as market conditions become favorable. In the municipal bond market, the pipeline is called the "Thirty Day Visible Supply" in the *Daily Bond Buyer* newspaper.

PLACE to market new securities. The term applies to both public and private sales but is more often used with reference to direct sales to institutional investors, as in PRIVATE PLACEMENT. The terms FLOAT and *distribute* are preferred in the case of a PUBLIC OFFERING.

PLACEMENT RATIO ratio, compiled by the *Daily Bond Buyer* as of the close of business every Thursday, indicating the percentage of the past week's new MUNICIPAL BOND offerings that have been bought from the underwriters. Only issues of $1 million or more are included.

PLANT assets comprising land, buildings, machinery, natural resources, furniture and fixtures, and all other equipment permanently employed. Synonymous with FIXED ASSET.

In a limited sense, the term is used to mean only buildings or only land and buildings: "property, plant, and equipment" and "plant and equipment."

PLEDGING transferring property, such as securities or the CASH SURRENDER VALUE of life insurance, to a lender or creditor as COLLATERAL for an obligation. *Pledge* and *hypothecate* are synonymous, as they do not involve transfer of title. ASSIGN, although commonly used interchangeably with *pledge* and *hypothecate,* implies transfer of ownership or of the right to transfer ownership at a later date. *See also* HYPOTHECATION.

PLOW BACK to reinvest a company's earnings in the business rather than pay out those profits as dividends. Smaller, fast-growing companies usually plow back most or all earnings in their businesses, whereas more established firms pay out more of their profits as dividends.

PLUS
1. plus sign (+) that follows a price quotation on a Treasury note or bond, indicating that the price (normally quoted as a percentage of PAR value refined to 32ds) is refined to 64ths. Thus 95.16 + (95^{16}/$_{32}$ + or 95^{32}/$_{64}$ +) means 95^{33}/$_{64}$.
2. plus sign after a transaction price in a listed security (for example, 39½ +), indicating that the trade was at a higher price than the previous REGULAR WAY transaction. *See also* PLUS TICK.
3. plus sign before the figure in the column labeled "Change" in the newspaper stock tables, meaning that the closing price of the stock was higher than the previous day's close by the amount stated in the "Change" column.

PLUS TICK expression used when a security has been traded at a higher price than the previous transaction in that security. A stock price listed as 28 + on the CONSOLIDATED TAPE has had a plus tick from 27⅞ or below on previous trades. It is a Securities and Exchange Commission rule that short sales can be executed only on plus ticks or ZERO PLUS TICKS. Also called *uptick. See also* MINUS TICK; TICK; ZERO-MINUS TICK.

POINT

Bonds: percentage change of the face value of a bond expressed as a point. For example, a change of 1% is a move of one point. For a bond with a $1000 face value, each point is worth $10, and for a bond with a $5000 face value, each point is $50.

Bond yields are quoted in basis points: 100 basis points make up 1% of yield. *See* BASIS POINT.

Real estate and other commercial lending: upfront fee charged by the lender, separate from interest but designed to increase the overall yield to the lender. A point is 1% of the total principal amount of the loan. For example, on a $100,000 mortgage loan, a charge of 3 points would equal $3000.

Stocks: change of $1 in the market price of a stock. If a stock has risen 5 points, it has risen by $5 a share.

The movements of stock market averages, such as the Dow Jones Industrial Average, are also quoted in points. However, those points refer not to dollar amounts but to units of movement in the average, which is a composite of weighted dollar values. For example, a 10-point move in the Dow Jones Average from 1200 to 1210 does *not* mean the Dow now stands at $1210.

POINT AND FIGURE CHART graphic technique used in TECHNICAL ANALYSIS to follow the up or down momentum in the price moves of a security. Point and figure charting disregards the element of time and is solely used to record changes in price. Every time a price move is upward, an X is put on the graph above the previous point. Every time the price moves down, an O is placed one square down. When direction changes, the next column is used. The resulting lines of

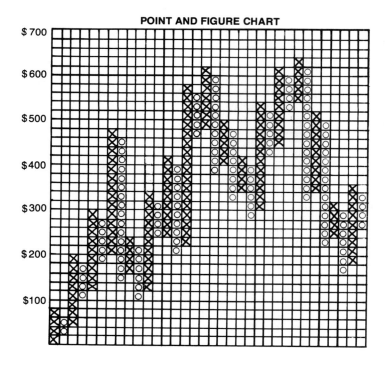

POINT AND FIGURE CHART

Xs and Os will indicate whether the security being charted has been maintaining an up or a down momentum over a particular time period.

POISON PILL strategic move by a takeover-target company to make its stock less attractive to an acquirer. For instance, a firm may issue a new series of PREFERRED STOCK that gives shareholders the right to redeem it at a premium price after a TAKEOVER. Such a poison pill will raise the cost of an ACQUISITION, hopefully deterring a takeover bid.

POLICY LOAN loan from an insurance company secured by the CASH SURRENDER VALUE of a life insurance policy. The amount available for such a loan depends on the number of years the policy has been in effect, the insured's age when the policy was issued, and the size of the death benefit. Such loans are often made at below-market interest rates to policyholders, although more recent policies usually only allow borrowing at rates that fluctuate in line with money market rates. If the loan is not repaid by the insured, the death benefit of the life insurance policy will be reduced by the amount of the loan plus accrued interest.

POOL

Capital Budgeting: as used in the phrase "pool of financing," the concept that investment projects are financed out of a pool of funds rather than out of bonds, preferred stock, and common stock individually. A weighted average cost of capital is thus used in analyses evaluating the return on investment projects. *See also* COST OF CAPITAL.

Industry: joining of companies to improve profits by reducing competition. Such poolings are generally outlawed in the United States by various ANTITRUST LAWS.

Insurance: association of insurers who share premiums and losses in order to spread risk and give small insurers an opportunity to compete with larger ones.

Investments:

1. combination of resources for a common purpose or benefit. For example, an INVESTMENT CLUB pools the funds of its members, giving them the opportunity to share in a PORTFOLIO offering greater diversification and the hope of a better return on their money than they could get individually. A *commodities pool* entrusts the funds of many investors to a trading professional and distributes profits and losses among participants in proportion to their interests.

2. group of investors joined together to use their combined power to manipulate security or commodity prices or to obtain control of a corporation. Such pools are outlawed by regulations governing securities and commodities trading. *See also* MORTGAGE POOL.

POOLING OF INTERESTS accounting method used in the combining or merging of companies following an acquisition, whereby the balance sheets (assets and liabilities) of the two companies are simply added together, item by item. This tax-free method contrasts with the PURCHASE ACQUISITION method, in which the buying company treats the acquired company as an investment and any PREMIUM paid over the FAIR MARKET VALUE of the assets is reflected on the buyer's balance sheet as GOODWILL. Because reported earnings are higher under the pooling of interests method, most companies prefer it to the purchase acquisition method, particularly when the amount of goodwill is sizable.

The pooling of interests method can be elected only when the following conditions are met:

1. The two companies must have been autonomous for at least two years prior

to the pooling and one must not have owned more than 10% of the stock of the other.

2. The combination must be consummated either in a single transaction or in accordance with a specific plan within one year after the plan is initiated; no contingent payments are permitted.

3. The acquiring company must issue its regular common stock in exchange for 90% or more of the common stock of the other company.

4. The surviving corporation must not later retire or reacquire common stock issued in the combination, must not enter into an arrangement for the benefit of former stockholders, and must not dispose of a significant portion of the assets of the combining companies for at least 2 years.

See also MERGER.

PORTFOLIO combined holding of more than one stock, bond, commodity, real estate investment, CASH EQUIVALENT, or other asset by an individual or institutional investor. The purpose of a portfolio is to reduce risk by diversification. See also PORTFOLIO BETA SCORE; PORTFOLIO THEORY.

PORTFOLIO BETA SCORE relative VOLATILITY of an individual securites portfolio, taken as a whole, as measured by the BETA COEFFICIENTS of the securities making it up.

PORTFOLIO INSURANCE the use, by a PORTFOLIO MANAGER, of STOCK INDEX FUTURES to protect stock portfolios against market declines. Instead of selling actual stocks as they lose value, managers sell the index futures; if the drop continues, they repurchase the futures at a lower price, using the profit to offset losses in the stock portfolio. See also PROGRAM TRADING.

PORTFOLIO MANAGER professional responsible for the securities PORTFOLIO of an individual or INSTITUTIONAL INVESTOR. A portfolio manager may work for a mutual fund, pension fund, profit-sharing plan, bank trust department, or insurance company, as well as private investors. In return for a fee, the manager has the fiduciary responsibility to manage the assets prudently and make them grow as much as possible. In making such decisions, a portfolio manager must choose whether stocks, bonds, CASH EQUIVALENTS, real estate, or some other assets present the best opportunities for profit at any particular time. See also PORTFOLIO THEORY; PRUDENT-MAN RULE.

PORTFOLIO THEORY sophisticated investment decision approach that permits an investor to classify, estimate, and control both the kind and the amount of expected risk and return; also called *portfolio management theory* or *modern portfolio theory*. Essential to portfolio theory are its quantification of the relationship between risk and return and the assumption that investors must be compensated for assuming risk. Portfolio theory departs from traditional security analysis in shifting emphasis from analyzing the characteristics of individual investments to determining the statistical relationships among the individual securities that comprise the overall portfolio. The portfolio theory approach has four basic steps: *security valuation*—describing a universe of assets in terms of expected return and expected risk; *asset allocation decision*—determining how assets are to be distributed among classes of investment, such as stocks or bonds; *portfolio optimization*—reconciling risk and return in selecting the securities to be included, such as determining which portfolio of stocks offers the best return for a given level of expected risk; and *performance measurement*—dividing each stock's performance (risk) into market-related (systematic) and industry/security-related (residual) classifications.

POSITION

Banking: bank's net balance in a foreign currency.

Finance: firm's financial condition.

Investments:

1. investor's stake in a particular security or market. A LONG POSITION equals the number of shares *owned;* a SHORT POSITION equals the number of shares *owed* by a dealer or an individual. The dealer's long positions are called his *inventory of securities.*

2. Used as a verb, to take on a long or a short position in a stock.

POSITION BUILDING process of buying shares to accumulate a LONG POSITION or of selling shares to accumulate a SHORT POSITION. Large institutional investors who want to build a large position in a particular security do so over time to avoid pushing up the price of the security.

POSITION LIMIT

Commodities trading: number of contracts that can be acquired in a specific commodity before a speculator is classified as a "large trader." Large traders are subject to special oversight by the COMMODITIES FUTURES TRADING COMMISSION (CFTC) and the exchanges and are limited as to the number of contracts they can add to their positions. The position limit varies with the type of commodity.

Options trading: maximum number of exchange-listed OPTION contracts that can be owned or controlled by an individual holder, or by a group of holders acting jointly, in the same underlying security. The current limit is 2000 contracts on the same side of the market (for example, long calls and short puts are one side of the market); the limit applies to all expiration dates.

POSITION TRADER commodities trader who takes a long-term approach—six months to a year or more—to the market. Usually possessing more than average experience, information, and capital, these traders ride through the ups and downs of price fluctuations until close to the delivery date, unless drastic adverse developments threaten. More like insurance underwriters than gamblers, they hope to achievelong-term profits from calculated risks as distinguished from pure speculation.

POSITIVE CARRY situation in which the cost of money borrowed to finance securities is lower than the yield on the securities. For example, if a fixed-income bond yielding 13% is purchased with a loan bearing 11% interest, the bond has positive carry. The opposite situation is called NEGATIVE CARRY.

POSITIVE YIELD CURVE situation in which interest rates are higher on long-term debt securities than on short-term debt securities of the same quality. For example, a positive yield curve exists when 20-year Treasury bonds yield 14% and 3-month Treasury bills yield 10%. Such a situation is common, since an investor who ties up his money for a longer time is taking more risk and is usually compensated by a higher yield. When short-term interest rates rise above long-term rates, there is a NEGATIVE YIELD CURVE. *See* illustration, page 396. .

POST

Accounting: to transfer from a journal of original entry detailed financial data,

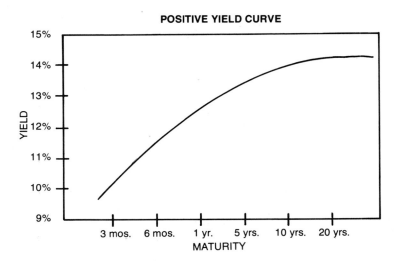

POSITIVE YIELD CURVE

in the chronological order in which it was generated, into a ledger book. Banks post checking account deposits and withdrawalsin a ledger, then summarize these transactions on the monthly bankstatement.

Investments: horseshoe-shaped structure on the floor of the New York Stock Exchange where specialists trade specific securities. Video screens surround the post, displaying the bid and offer prices available for stocks traded at that location. Also called *trading post.*

POT securities underwriting term meaning the portion of a stock or bond issue returned to the MANAGING UNDERWRITER by the participating investment bankers to facilitate sales to INSTITUTIONAL INVESTORS. Institutions buying from the pot designate the firms to be credited with pot sales. *See also* RETENTION.

POT IS CLEAN MANAGING UNDERWRITER'S announcement to members of the underwriting group that the POT—the portion of the stock or bond issue withheld to facilitate institutional sales—has been sold.

POWER OF ATTORNEY

In general: written document that authorizes a particular person to perform certain acts on behalf of the one signing the document. The document, which must be witnessed by a notary public or some other public officer, may bestow either *full power of attorney* or *limited power of attorney.* It becomes void upon the death of the signer.

Investments: *full power of attorney* might, for instance, allow assets to be moved from one brokerage or bank account to another. A *limited power of attorney,* on the other hand, would only permit transactions within an existing account. A broker given a limited power of attorney, for instance, may buy and sell securities in an account but may not remove them. Such an account is called a DISCRETIONARY ACCOUNT. *See also* DISCRETIONARY ORDER; PROXY; STOCK POWER.

PRECEDENCE priority of one order over another on the floor of the exchanges, according to rules designed to protect the DOUBLE-AUCTION SYSTEM. The rules basically are that the highest bid and lowest offer have precedence over other bids and offers, that the first bid or first offer at a price has priority over other bids or offers at that price, and that the size of the order determines precedence thereafter, large orders having priority over smaller orders. Where two orders of equal size must compete for the same limited quantity after the first bid is filled, the impasse is resolved by a flip of the coin. *See also* MATCHED AND LOST. Exchange rules also require that public orders have precedence over trades for floor members' own accounts. *See also* OFF-FLOOR ORDER; ON-FLOOR ORDER.

PRECOMPUTE in installment lending, methods of charging interest whereby the total amount of annual interest either is deducted from the face amount of the loan at the time the loan proceeds are disbursed or is added to the total amount to be repaid in equal installments. In both cases, the EFFECTIVE RATE to the borrower is higher than the stated annual rate used in the computation. "Truth in lending" laws require that the effective annual rate be expressed in SIMPLE INTEREST terms.

PREEMPTIVE RIGHT right giving existing stockholders the opportunity to purchase shares of a NEW ISSUE before it is offered to others. Its purpose is to protect shareholders from dilution of value and control when new shares are issued. Although 48 U.S. states have preemptive right statutes, most states also either permit corporations to pay stockholders their preemptive rights or state in their statutes that the preemptive right is valid only if set forth in the corporate charter. As a result, preemptive rights are the exception rather than the rule. Where they do exist, the usual procedure is for each existing stockholder to receive, prior to a new issue, a SUBSCRIPTION WARRANT indicating how many new shares the holder is entitled to buy—normally, a proportion of the shares he or she already holds. Since the new shares would typically be priced below the market, a financial incentive exists to exercise the preemptive right. *See also* SUBSCRIPTION RIGHT.

PREFERENCE ITEM *see* TAX PREFERENCE ITEM.

PREFERENCE SHARES *see* PRIOR-PREFERRED STOCK.

PREFERRED DIVIDEND COVERAGE net income after interest and taxes (but before common stock dividends) divided by the dollar amount of preferred stock dividends. The result tells how many times over the preferred dividend requirement is covered by current earnings.

PREFERRED STOCK class of CAPITAL STOCK that pays dividends at a specified rate and that has preference over common stock in the payment of dividends and the liquidation of assets. Preferred stock does not ordinarily carry voting rights.

Most preferred stock is *cumulative;* if dividends are passed (not paid for any reason), they accumulate and must be paid before common dividends. A PASSED DIVIDEND on *noncumulative preferred* stock is generally gone forever. *Participating preferred* stock entitles its holders to share in profits above and beyond the declared dividend, along with common shareholders, as distinguished from *nonparticipating preferred,* which is limited to the stipulated dividend. *Adjustable-rate preferred* stock pays a dividend that is adjustable, usually quarterly, based on changes in the Treasury bill rate or other money market rates. *Convertible preferred stock* is exchangeable for a given number of common shares and thus tends to be more VOLATILE than *nonconvertible preferred,* which behaves more like a fixed-income bond. *See also* CONVERTIBLE; CUMULATIVE PREFERRED; PARTICIPATING PREFERRED; PRIOR-PREFERRED STOCK.

PREFERRED STOCK RATIO PREFERRED STOCK at PAR value divided by total CAPITALIZATION; the result is the percentage of capitalization—bonds and net worth—represented by preferred stock.

PRELIMINARY PROSPECTUS first document released by an underwriter of a NEW ISSUE to prospective investors. The document offers financial details about the issue but does not contain all the information that will appear in the final or statutory prospectus, and parts of the document may be changed before the final prospectus is issued. Because portions of the cover page of the preliminary prospectus are printed in red ink, it is popularly called the *red herring*.

PREMIUM

In general: extra payment usually made as an incentive.

Bonds:

1. amount by which a bond sells above its face (PAR) value. For instance, a bond with a face value of $1000 would sell for a $100 premium when it cost $1100. The same meaning also applies to preferred stock. *See also* PREMIUM BOND; PREMIUM OVER BOND VALUE; PREMIUM OVER CONVERSION VALUE.
2. amount by which the REDEMPTION PRICE to the issuer exceeds the face value when a bond is called. *See also* CALL PREMIUM.

Insurance: fee paid to an insurance company for insurance protection. Also, the single or multiple payments made to build an ANNUITY fund.

Options: price a put or call buyer must pay to a put or call seller (writer) for an option contract. The premium is determined by market supply and demand forces. *See also* OPTION; PREMIUM INCOME.

Stocks:

1. charge occasionally paid by a short seller when stock is borrowed to make delivery on a SHORT SALE.
2. amount by which a stock's price exceeds that of other stocks to which it is comparable. For instance, securities analysts might say that XYZ Foods is selling at a 15% premium to other food company stocks—an indication that the stock is more highly valued by investors than its industry peers. It does not necessarily mean that the stock is overpriced, however. Indeed, it may indicate that the investment public has only begun to recognize the stock's market potential and that the price will continue to rise. Similarly, analysts might say that the food industry is selling for a 20% premium to Standard & Poor's 500 index, indicating the relative price strength of the industry group to the stock market as a whole.
3. in new issues, amount by which the trading price of the shares exceeds the OFFERING PRICE.
4. amount over market value paid in a *tender offer*. *See also* PREMIUM RAID.

PREMIUM BOND bond with a selling price above face or redemption value. A bond with a face value of $1000, for instance, would be called a premium bond if it sold for $1050. This price does not include any ACCRUED INTEREST due when the bond is bought. When a premium bond is called before scheduled maturity, bondholders are usually paid more than face value, though the amount may be less than the bond is selling for at the time of the CALL.

PREMIUM INCOME income received by an investor who sells a PUT OPTION or a CALL OPTION. An investor collects premium income by writing a COVERED OPTION, if he or she owns the underlying stock, or a NAKED OPTION, if he or she does not own the stock. An investor who sells options to collect premium income hopes that the underlying stock will not rise very much (in the case of a call) or fall very much (in the case of a put).

PREMIUM OVER BOND VALUE upward difference between the market value of a CONVERTIBLE bond and the price at which a straight bond of the same company would sell in the same open market. A convertible bond, eventually convertible to common stock, will normally sell at a PREMIUM over its bond value because investors place a value on the conversion feature. The higher the market price of the issuer's stock is relative to the price at which the bond is convertible, the greater the premium will be, reflecting the investor's tendency to view it more as a stock than as a bond. When the stock price falls near or below the conversion price, investors then tend to view the convertible as a bond and the premium narrows or even disappears. Other factors affecting the prices of convertible bonds generally include lower transaction costs on the convertibles than would be incurred in buying the stock outright, an attraction that exerts some upward pressure on the premium; the demand from life insurance companies and other institutional investors that are limited by law as to the common stock investments they can have and that gain their equity participation through convertibles; the duration period of the option to convert—the longer it is, the more valuable the future and the higher the premium; high dividends on the issuer's common stock, a factor increasing demand for the common versus the convertible, and therefore a downward pressure. *See also* PREMIUM OVER CONVERSION VALUE.

PREMIUM OVER CONVERSION VALUE amount by which the MARKET PRICE of a CONVERTIBLE preferred stock or convertible bond exceeds the price at which it is convertible. Convertibles (CVs) usually sell at a PREMIUM for two basic reasons: (1) if the convertible is a bond, the bond value—defined as the price at which a straight bond of the same company would sell in the same open market— is the lowest value the CV will reach; it thus represents DOWNSIDE RISK protection, which is given a value in the marketplace, generally varying with the VOLATILITY of the common stock; (2) the conversion privilege is given a value by investors because they might find it profitable eventually to convert the securities.

At relatively high common-stock price levels, a convertible tends to sell for its common stock equivalent and the conversion value becomes negligible. This occurs because investors are viewing the security as a common stock, not as a bond, and because conversion would be preferable to redemption if the bond were called. On the other hand, when the market value of the convertible is close to its bond value, the conversion feature has little value and the security is valued more as a bond. It is here that the CONVERSION PREMIUM is highest. The conversion premium is also influenced to some extent by transaction costs, insurance company investment restrictions, the duration of the conversion OPTION, and the size of common dividends. *See also* PREMIUM OVER BOND VALUE.

PREMIUM RAID surprise attempt to acquire a position in a company's stock by offering holders an amount—or premium—over the market value of their shares. The term *raid* assumes that the motive is control and not simply investment. Attempts to acquire control are regulated by federal laws that require disclosure of the intentions of those seeking shares. *See also* TENDER OFFER; WILLIAMS ACT.

PRENUPTIAL CONTRACT agreement between a future husband and wife that details how the couple's financial affairs are to be handled both during the marriage and in the event of divorce. The agreement may cover insurance protection, ownership of housing and securities, and inheritance rights. Such contracts may not be accepted in a court of law.

PREPAYMENT

In general: paying a debt obligation before it comes due.

Accounting: expenditure for a future benefit, which is recorded in a BALANCE SHEET asset account called a DEFERRED CHARGE, then written off in the period when the benefit is enjoyed. For example, prepaid rent is first recorded as an asset, then charged to expense as the rent becomes due on a monthly basis.

Banking: paying a loan before maturity. Some loans (particularly mortgages) have a prepayment clause that allows prepayment at any time without penalty, while others charge a fee if a loan is paid off before due.

Installment credit: making payments before they are due. *See also* RULE OF THE 78s.

Securities: paying a seller for a security before the settlement date.

Taxes: prepaying taxes, for example, to have the benefit of deducting state and local taxes from one's federal income tax return in the current calendar year rather than in the next year.

PREPAYMENT PENALTY fee paid by a borrower to a bank when a loan or mortgage that does not have a prepayment clause is repaid before its scheduled maturity.

PREREFUNDING procedure in which a bond issuer floats a second bond in order to pay off the first bond at the first CALL date. The proceeds from the sale of the second bond are safely invested, usually in Treasury securities, that will mature at the first call date of the first bond issue. Those first bonds are said to be prerefunded after this operation has taken place. Bond issuers prerefund bonds during periods of lower interest rates in order to lower their interest costs. *See also* ADVANCE REFUNDING; REFUNDING.

PRESALE ORDER order to purchase part of a new MUNICIPAL BOND issue that is accepted by an underwriting SYNDICATE MANAGER before an announcement of the price or COUPON rate and before the official PUBLIC OFFERING. Municipals are exempt from registration requirements and other rules of the Securities and Exchange Commission, which forbids preoffering sales of corporate bond issues. *See also* PRESOLD ISSUE.

PRESENT VALUE value today of a future payment, or stream of payments, discounted at some appropriate compound interest—or discount—rate. For example, the present value of $100 to be received 10 years from now is about $38.55, using a discount rate equal to 10% interest compounded annually.

The present value method, also called the DISCOUNTED CASH FLOW method, is widely used in corporate finance to measure the return on a CAPITAL INVESTMENT project. In security investments, the method is used to determine how much money should be invested today to result in a certain sum at a future time. Present value calculations are facilitated by present value tables, which are compound interest tables in reverse. Also called *time value of money*.

PRESIDENT highest-ranking officer in a corporation after the CHAIRMAN OF THE BOARD, unless the title CHIEF EXECUTIVE OFFICER (CEO) is used, in which case the president can outrank the chairman. The president is appointed by the BOARD OF DIRECTORS and usually reports directly to the board. In smaller companies the president is usually the CEO, having authority over all other officers in matters of day-to-day management and policy decision-making. In large corporations the CEO title is frequently held by the chairman of the board, leaving the president as CHIEF OPERATING OFFICER, responsible for personnel and administration on a daily basis.

PRESIDENTIAL ELECTION CYCLE THEORY hypothesis of investment advisers that major stock market moves can be predicted based on the four-year presidential election cycle. According to this theory, stocks decline soon after a president is elected, as the chief executive takes the harsh and unpopular steps necessary to bring inflation, government spending, and deficits under control. During the next two years or so, taxes may be raised and the economy will slip into a recession. About midway into the four-year cycle, stocks should start to rise in anticipation of the economic recovery that the incumbent president wants to be roaring at full steam by election day. The cycle then repeats itself with the election of a new president or the reelection of an incumbent. This theory worked remarkably well from the late 1960s to the mid-1980s.

PRESOLD ISSUE issue of MUNICIPAL BONDS or government bonds that is completely sold out before the price or yield is publicly announced. Corporate bond issues, which must be offered to the public with a Securities and Exchange Commission registration statement, cannot legally be presold. *See also* PRESALE ORDER.

PRETAX EARNINGS OR PROFITS NET INCOME (earnings or profits) before federal income taxes.

PRETAX RATE OF RETURN yield or capital gain on a particular security before taking into account an individual's tax situation. *See also* RATE OF RETURN.

PRICE CHANGE net rise or fall of the price of a security at the close of a trading session, compared to the previous session's CLOSING PRICE. A stock that rose $2 in a day would have a +2 after its final price in the newspaper stock listings. A stock that fell $2 would have a −2. The average of the price changes for groups of securities, in indicators such as the Dow Jones Industrial Average and Standard & Poor's 500 Stock Index, is calculated by taking into account all the price changes in the components of the average or index.

PRICE/EARNINGS RATIO (P/E) price of a stock divided by its earnings per share. The P/E ratio may either use the reported earnings from the latest year (called a *trailing P/E*) or employ an analyst's forecast of next year's earnings (called a *forward P/E*). The trailing P/E is listed along with a stock's price and trading activity in the daily newspapers. For instance, a stock selling for $20 a share that earned $1 last year has a trailing P/E of 20. If the same stock has projected earnings of $2 next year, it will have a forward P/E of 10.

The price/earnings ratio, also known as the *multiple,* gives investors an idea of how much they are paying for a company's earning power. The higher the P/E, the more investors are paying, and therefore the more earnings growth they are expecting. High P/E stocks—those with multiples over 20—are typically young, fast-growing companies. They are far riskier to trade than low P/E stocks, since it is easier to miss high-growth expectations than low-growth predictions. Low P/E stocks tend to be in low-growth or mature industries, in stock groups that have fallen out of favor, or in old, established, BLUE-CHIP companies with long records of earnings stability and regular dividends. In general, low P/E stocks have higher yields than high P/E stocks, which often pay no dividends at all.

PRICE GAP term used when a stock's price either jumps or plummets from its last trading range without overlapping that trading range. For instance, a stock might shoot up from a closing price of $20 a share, marking the high point of an $18–$20 trading range for that day, and begin trading in a $22–$24 range the next day on the news of a takeover bid. Or a company that reports lower than expected earnings might drop from the $18–$20 range to the $13–$15 range without ever trading at intervening prices. Price gaps are considered significant movements by technical analysts, who note them on charts, because such gaps are often indications of an OVERBOUGHT or OVERSOLD position.

PRICE LIMIT *see* LIMIT PRICE.

PRICE RANGE high/low range in which a stock has traded over a particular period of time. In the daily newspaper, a stock's 52-week price range is given. In most companies' annual reports, a stock's price range is shown for the FISCAL YEAR.

PRICE SPREAD OPTIONS strategy in which an investor simultaneously buys and sells two options covering the same security, with the same expiration months, but with different exercise prices. For example, an investor might buy an XYZ May 100 call and sell an XYZ May 90 call.

PRICE SUPPORT government-set price floor designed to aid farmers or other producers of goods. For instance, the government sets a minimum price for sugar that it guarantees to sugar growers. If the market price drops below that level, the government makes up the difference. *See also* PARITY PRICE.

PRICE-WEIGHTED INDEX index in which component stocks are weighted by their price. Higher-priced stocks therefore have a greater percentage impact on the index than lower-priced stocks. In recent years, the trend of using price-weighted indexes has given way to the use of MARKET-VALUE WEIGHTED INDEXES.

PRICEY term used of an unrealistically low bid price or unrealistically high offer price. If a stock is trading at $15, a pricey bid might be $10 a share, and a pricey offer $20 a share.

PRIMARY DEALER one of the three dozen or so banks and investment dealers authorized to buy and sell government securities in direct dealings with the FEDERAL RESERVE BANK of New York in its execution of Fed OPEN MARKET OPERATIONS. Such dealers must be qualified in terms of reputation, capacity, and adequacy of staff and facilities.

PRIMARY DISTRIBUTION sale of a new issue of stocks or bonds, as distinguished from a SECONDARY DISTRIBUTION, which involves previously issued stock. All issuances of bonds are primary distributions. Also called *primary offering,* but not to be confused with *initial public offering,* which refers to a corporation's *first* distribution of stock to the public.

PRIMARY EARNINGS PER (COMMON) SHARE earnings available to common stock (which is usually net earnings after taxes and preferred dividends) divided by the number of common shares outstanding. This figure contrasts with earnings per share after DILUTION, which assumes warrants, rights, and options have been exercised and convertibles have been converted. *See also* CONVERTIBLE; FULLY DILUTED EARNINGS PER (COMMON) SHARE; SUBSCRIPTION WARRANT.

PRIMARY MARKET market for new issues of securities, as distinguished from the SECONDARY MARKET, where previously issued securities are bought and sold. A market is primary if the proceeds of sales go to the issuer of the securities sold.

The term also applies to government securities auctions and to opening option and futures contract sales.

PRIME

Banking: PRIME RATE.

Investments: acronym for Prescribed Right to Income and Maximum Equity. PRIME is a UNIT INVESTMENT TRUST, sponsored by the Americus Shareowner Service Corporation, which separates the income portion of a stock from its appreciation potential. The income-producing portion is called PRIME, and the appreciation potential is called SCORE (an acronym for Special Claim on Residual Equity). PRIME and SCORE together make up a unit share investment trust, known by the acronym USIT. Both PRIME and SCORE trade on the New York Stock Exchange.

The first version of this unit came into existence with American Telephone and Telegraph stock in late 1983, as AT&T was undergoing divestiture. PRIME units entitled their holders to the dividend income that a holder of one common share of the old AT&T would have gotten plus a proportionate share of the dividends of the seven regional operating companies split off from AT&T. PRIME holders also received all price APPRECIATION in the stock up to the equivalent of $75 a share. SCORE holders received all appreciation over $75, but no dividend income.

This form of unit trust allows investors who want income from a stock to maximize that income, and investors who want capital gains to have increased leverage in achieving those gains. *See also* CAPITAL GAIN.

PRIME PAPER highest quality COMMERCIAL PAPER, as rated by Moody's Investor's Service and other rating agencies. Prime paper is considered INVESTMENT GRADE, and therefore institutions with FIDUCIARY responsibility can invest in it. Moody's has three ratings of prime paper:

    P-1: Highest quality
    P-2: Higher quality
    P-3: High quality

Commercial paper below P-3 is not considered prime paper.

PRIME RATE interest rate banks charge to their most creditworthy customers. The rate is determined by the market forces affecting a bank's cost of funds and the rates that borrowers will accept. The prime rate tends to become standard across the banking industry when a major bank moves its prime rate up or down. The rate is a key interest rate, since loans to less-creditworthy customers are often tied to the prime rate. For example, a BLUE CHIP company may borrow at a prime rate of 10%, but a less-well-established small business may borrow from the same bank at prime plus 2, or 12%. Although the major bank prime rate is the definitive "best rate" reference point, many banks, particularly those in outlying regions, have a two-tier system, whereby smaller companies of top credit standing may borrow at an even lower rate.

PRINCIPAL

In General:
1. major party to a transaction, acting as either a buyer or a seller. A principal buys and sells for his or her own account and at his or her own risk.
2. owner of a privately held business.

Banking and Finance:
1. face amount of a debt instrument or deposit on which interest is either owed or earned.

2. balance of an obligation, separate from interest. *See also* PRINCIPAL AMOUNT.

Investments: basic amount invested, exclusive of earnings.

PRINCIPAL AMOUNT FACE VALUE of an obligation (such as a bond or a loan) that must be repaid at maturity, as separate from the INTEREST.

PRINCIPAL STOCKHOLDER stockholder who owns a significant number of shares in a corporation. Under Securities and Exchange Commission (SEC) rules, a principal stockholder owns 10% or more of the voting stock of a REGISTERED COMPANY. These stockholders are often on the board of directors and are considered insiders by SEC rules, so that they must report buying and selling in the company's stock. *See also* AFFILIATED PERSON; CONTROL STOCK; INSIDER.

PRINCIPAL SUM

Finance: also used as a synonym for PRINCIPAL, in the sense of the obligation due under a debt instrument exclusive of interest. Synonymous with CORPUS. *See also* TRUST.

Insurance: amount specified as payable to the beneficiary under a policy, such as the death benefit.

PRIORITY system used in an AUCTION MARKET, in which the first bid or offer price is executed before other bid and offer prices, even if subsequent orders are larger. Orders originating off the floor (*see* OFF-FLOOR ORDER) of an exchange also have priority over ON-FLOOR ORDERS. *See also* MATCHED AND LOST; PRECEDENCE.

PRIOR-LIEN BOND bond that has precedence over another bond of the same issuing company even though both classes of bonds are equally secured. Such bonds usually arise from REORGANIZATION. *See also* JUNIOR ISSUE.

PRIOR-PREFERRED STOCK PREFERRED STOCK that has a higher claim than other issues of preferred stock on dividends and assets in the event of LIQUIDATION; also known as *preference shares.*

PRIVATE LIMITED PARTNERSHIP LIMITED PARTNERSHIP not registered with the Securities and Exchange Commission (SEC) and having a maximum of 35 limited partners. *See also* ACCREDITED INVESTOR.

PRIVATE PLACEMENT sale of stocks, bonds, or other investments directly to an institutional investor like an insurance company. A PRIVATE LIMITED PARTNERSHIP is also considered a private placement. A private placement does not have to be registered with the Securities and Exchange Commission, as a PUBLIC OFFERING does, if the securities are purchased for investment as opposed to resale. *See also* LETTER SECURITY.

PRIVATE PURPOSE BOND category of MUNICIPAL BOND distinguished from PUBLIC PURPOSE BOND in the TAX REFORM ACT OF 1986 because 10% or more of the bond's benefit goes to private activities. Private purpose obligations, which are also called *private activity bonds* or *nonessential function bonds,* are taxable unless their use is specifically exempted. Even tax-exempt *permitted private activity bonds,* if issued after August 8, 1986, are TAX PREFERENCE ITEMS, except those issued for 501(c)(3) organizations (hospitals, colleges, universities). Private purpose bonds specifically *prohibited* from tax-exemption effective August 15, 1986, include those for sports, trade, and convention facilities and large-issue (over $1 million) INDUSTRIAL DEVELOPMENT BONDS. Permitted issues, except those for 501(c)(3) organizations, airports, docks, wharves, and government-owned solid-waste disposal facilities, are subject to volume caps, effective August 15, 1986, of $75 per capita or $250 million per state (whichever is larger), dropping to $50 per capita or $150 million per state in 1988. *See also* TAXABLE MUNICIPAL BOND.

PROBATE judicial process whereby the will of a deceased person is presented to a court and an EXECUTOR or ADMINISTRATOR is appointed to carry out the will.

PROCEEDS
1. funds given to a borrower after all interest costs and fees are deducted.
2. money received by the seller of an asset after commissions are deducted—for example, the amount a stockholder receives from the sale of shares, less broker's commission. *See also* PROCEEDS SALE.

PROCEEDS SALE OVER THE COUNTER securities sale where the PROCEEDS are used to purchase another security. Under the FIVE PERCENT RULE of the NATIONAL ASSOCIATION OF SECURITIES DEALERS (NASD), such a trade is considered one transaction and the NASD member's total markup or commission is subject to the 5% guideline.

PRODUCER PRICE INDEX measure of change in wholesale prices (formerly called the *wholesale price index*), as released monthly by the U.S. Bureau of Labor Statistics. The index is broken down into components by commodity, industry sector, and stage of processing. *See also* CONSUMER PRICE INDEX.

PRODUCTION RATE coupon (interest) rate at which a PASS-THROUGH SECURITY of the GOVERNMENT NATIONAL MORTGAGE ASSOCIATION (GNMA) is issued. The rate is set a half percentage point under the prevailing Federal Housing Administration (FHA) rate, the maximum rate allowed on residential mortgages insured and guaranteed by the FHA and the Veterans Administration.

PROFIT
Finance: positive difference that results from selling products and services for more than the cost of producing these goods. *See also* NET PROFIT.
Investments: difference between the selling price and the purchase price of commodities or securities when the selling price is higher.

PROFIT AND LOSS STATEMENT (P & L) summary of the revenues, costs, and expenses of a company during an accounting period; also called INCOME STATEMENT, *operating statement, statement of profit and loss, income and expense statement.* Together with the BALANCE SHEET as of the end of the accounting period, it constitutes a company's financial statement. *See also* COST OF GOODS SOLD; NET INCOME; NET SALES.

PROFIT CENTER segment of a business organization that is responsible for producing profits on its own.

PROFIT MARGIN *see* MARGIN OF PROFIT.

PROFIT-SHARING PLAN agreement between a corporation and its employees that allows the employees to share in company profits. Annual contributions are made by the company, when it has profits, to a profit-sharing account for each employee, either in cash or in a deferred plan, which may be invested in stocks, bonds, or cash equivalents. The funds in a profit-sharing account generally accumulate tax deferred until the employee retires or leaves the company. Many plans allow employees to borrow against profit-sharing accounts for major expenditures such as purchasing a home or financing children's education. Because corporate profit-sharing plans have custody over billions of dollars, they are major institutional investors in the stock and bond markets.

PROFIT TAKING action by short-term securities or commodities traders to cash in on gains earned on a sharp market rise. Profit taking pushes down prices, but only temporarily; the term implies an upward market trend.

PRO FORMA Latin for "as a matter of form"; refers to a presentation of data, such as a BALANCE SHEET or INCOME STATEMENT, where certain amounts are hypothetical. For example, a pro forma balance sheet might show a debt issue that has been proposed but has not yet been consummated.

PROGRAM TRADING computerized buying (*buy program*) or selling (*sell program*), by institutions or index ARBITRAGE specialists, of all stocks in a program or index. PORTFOLIO INSURANCE is a variation of program trading.

PROGRESSIVE TAX INCOME TAX system in which those with higher incomes pay taxes at higher rates than those with lower incomes; also called *graduated tax*. *See also* FLAT TAX; REGRESSIVE TAX.

PROGRESS PAYMENTS
1. periodic payments to a supplier, contractor, or subcontractor for work satisfactorily performed to date. Such schedules are provided in contracts and can significantly reduce the amount of WORKING CAPITAL required by the performing party.
2. disbursements by lenders to contractors under construction loan arrangements. As construction progresses, bills and LIEN waivers are presented to the bank or savings and loan, which advances additional funds.

PROJECTION estimate of future performance made by economists, corporate planners, and credit and securities analysts. Economists use econometric models to project GROSS NATIONAL PRODUCT (GNP), inflation, unemployment, and many other economic factors. Corporate financial planners project a company's operating results and CASH FLOW, using historical trends and making assumptions where necessary, in order to make budget decisions and to plan financing. Credit analysts use projections to forecast DEBT SERVICE ability. Securities analysts tend to focus their projections on earnings trends and cash flow per share in order to predict market values and dividend coverage. *See also* ECONOMETRICS.

PROJECT LINK econometric model linking all the economies in the world and forcasting the effects of changes in different economies on other economies. The project is identified with 1980 Nobel Memorial Prize in Economics winner Lawrence R. Klein. *See also* ECONOMETRICS.

PROJECT NOTE short-term debt issue of a municipal agency, usually a housing authority, to finance the construction of public housing. When the housing is finished, the notes are redeemed and the project is financed with long-term bonds. Both project notes and bonds usually pay tax-exempt interest to note- and bondholders, and both are also guaranteed by the U.S. Department of Housing and Urban Development.

PROMISSORY NOTE written promise committing the maker to pay the payee a specified sum of money either on demand or at a fixed or determinable future date, with or without interest. Instruments meeting these criteria are NEGOTIABLE. Often called, simply, a NOTE.

PROPORTIONAL REPRESENTATION method of stockholder voting, giving individual shareholders more power over the election of directors than they have under STATUTORY VOTING, which, by allowing one vote per share per director, makes it possible for a majority shareholder to elect all the directors. The most familiar example of proportional representation is CUMULATIVE VOTING, under which a shareholder has as many votes as he has shares of stock, multiplied by the number of vacancies on the board, all of which can be cast for one director. This makes it possible for a minority shareholder or a group of small shareholders to gain at least some representation on the board. Another variety provides for the holders of specified classes of stock to elect a number of directors in certain circumstances. For example, if the corporation failed to pay preferred dividends, the preferred holders might then be given the power to elect a certain proportion of the board. Despite the advocacy of stockholders' rights activists, proportional representation has made little headway in American corporations.

PROPRIETORSHIP unincorporated business owned by a single person. The individual proprietor has the right to all the profits from the business and also has responsibility for all the firm's liabilities. Since proprietors are considered self-employed, they are eligible for Keogh accounts for their retirement funds. *See also* KEOGH PLAN.

PRO RATA Latin for "according to the rate"; a method of proportionate allocation. For example, a pro rata property tax rebate might be divided proportionately (prorated) among taxpayers based on their original assessments, so that each gets the same percentage.

PROSPECTUS formal written offer to sell securities that sets forth the plan for a proposed business enterprise or the facts concerning an existing one that an investor needs to make an informed decision. Prospectuses are also issued by MUTUAL FUNDS, describing the history, background of managers, fund objectives, a financial statement, and other essential data. A prospectus for a PUBLIC OFFERING must be filed with the Securities and Exchange Commission and given to prospective buyers of the offering. The prospectus contains financial information and a description of a company's business history, officers, operations, pending litigation (if any), and plans (including the use of the proceeds from the issue).

Before investors receive the final copy of the prospectus, called the *statutory prospectus,* they may receive a PRELIMINARY PROSPECTUS, commonly called a *red herring.* This document is not complete in all details, though most of the major facts of the offering are usually included. The final prospectus is also called the *offering circular.*

Offerings of limited partnerships are also accompanied by prospectuses. Real estate, oil and gas, equipment leasing, and other types of limited partnerships are described in detail, and pertinent financial information, the background of the general partners, and supporting legal opinions are also given.

PROTECTIVE COVENANT *see* COVENANT.

PROVISION *see* ALLOWANCE.

PROXY

In general: person authorized to act or speak for another.

Business:

1. written POWER OF ATTORNEY given by shareholders of a corporation, authorizing a specific vote on their behalf at corporate meetings. Such proxies normally pertain to election of the BOARD OF DIRECTORS or to various resolutions
submitted for shareholders' approval.

2. person authorized to vote on behalf of a stockholder of a corporation.

PROXY FIGHT technique used by an acquiring company to attempt to gain control
of a TAKEOVER target. The acquirer tries to persuade the shareholders of the
TARGET COMPANY that the present management of the firm should be ousted in
favor of a slate of directors favorable to the acquirer. If the shareholders, through
their PROXY votes, agree, the acquiring company can gain control of the company
without paying a PREMIUM price for the firm.

PROXY STATEMENT information that the Securities and Exchange Commission
requires must be provided to shareholders before they vote by proxy on company
matters. The statement contains proposed members of the BOARD OF DIRECTORS,
inside directors' salaries, and pertinent information regarding their bonus and
option plans, as well as any resolutions of minority stockholders and of management.

PRUDENT-MAN RULE standard adopted by some U.S. states to guide those with
responsibility for investing the money of others. Such fiduciaries (executors of
wills, trustees, bank trust departments, and administrators of estates) must act as
a prudent man or woman would be expected to act, with discretion and intelligence, to seek reasonable income, preserve capital, and, in general, avoid speculative investments. States not using the prudent-man system use the LEGAL LIST
system, allowing fiduciaries to invest only in a restricted list of securities, called
the *legal list.*

PUBLIC HOUSING AUTHORITY BOND obligation of local public housing
agencies, which is centrally marketed through competitive sealed-bid auctions
conducted by the U.S. Department of Housing and Urban Development (HUD).
These obligations are secured by an agreement between HUD and the local housing agency that provides that the federal government will loan the local authority
a sufficient amount of money to pay PRINCIPAL and INTEREST to maturity.

The proceeds of such bonds provide low-rent housing through new construction, rehabilitation of existing buildings, purchases from private builders or developers, and leasing from private owners. Under special provisions, low-income
families may also purchase such housing.

The interest on such bonds is exempt from federal income taxes and may
also be exempt from state and local income taxes.

PUBLIC LIMITED PARTNERSHIP real estate, oil and gas, equipment leasing,
or other PARTNERSHIP that is registered with the Securities and Exchange Commission and offered to the public through registered broker/dealers. Such partnerships may be oriented to producing income or capital gains, or to generating
tax advantages for limited partners. The number of investors in such a partnership
is limited only by the sponsor's desire to cap the funds raised. On the other hand,
a PRIVATE LIMITED PARTNERSHIP is limited to 35 accredited investors. *See also*
LIMITED PARTNERSHIP.

PUBLICLY HELD corporation that has shares available to the public at large. Such companies are regulated by the Securities and Exchange Commission.

PUBLIC OFFERING

1. offering to the investment public, after registration requirements of the Securities and Exchange Commission (SEC) have been complied with, of new securities, usually by an investment banker or a syndicate made up of several investment bankers, at a public offering price agreed upon between the issuer and the investment bankers. Public offering is distinguished from PRIVATE PLACEMENT of new securities, which is subject to different SEC regulations. *See also* REGISTERED NEW ISSUE; UNDERWRITE.

2. SECONDARY DISTRIBUTION of previously issued stock. *See also* REGISTERED SECONDARY OFFERING.

PUBLIC OFFERING PRICE price at which a NEW ISSUE of securities is offered to the public by underwriters. *See also* OFFERING PRICE; UNDERWRITE.

PUBLIC OWNERSHIP

Government: government ownership and operation of a productive facility for the purpose of providing some good or service to citizens. The government supplies the capital, controls management, sets prices, and generally absorbs all risks and reaps all profits—similar to a private enterprise. When public ownership displaces private ownership in a particular instance, it is called NATIONALIZATION.

Investments: portion of a corporation's stock that is publicly traded.

PUBLIC PURPOSE BOND category of MUNICIPAL BOND, as defined in the TAX REFORM ACT OF 1986, which is exempt from federal income taxes provided it provides no more than 10% benefit to private parties; also called *public activity, traditional government purpose,* and *essential purpose* bond. Although not defined in specific terms, public purpose bonds are presumed to include purposes such as roads, libraries, and government buildings.

PUBLIC SECURITIES ASSOCIATION association representing dealers, banks, and brokers underwriting municipal, U.S. government, and federal agency debt securities, as well as dealers in mortgage-backed securities.

PUBLIC UTILITY HOLDING COMPANY ACT OF 1935 major landmark in legislation regulating the securities industry, which reorganized the financial structures of HOLDING COMPANIES in the gas and electric utility industries and regulated their debt and dividend policies. Prior to the Act, abuses by holding companies were rampant, including WATERED STOCK, top-heavy capital structures with excessive fixed-debt burdens, and manipulation of the securities markets.

To summarize the four basic provisions of the Act:

1. It requires holding companies operating interstate and persons exercising a controlling influence on utilities and holding companies to register with the Securities and Exchange Commission (SEC) and to provide information on the organizational structure, finances, and means of control.

2. It provides for SEC control of the operation and performance of registered holding companies and SEC approval of all new securities offerings, resulting in such reforms as the elimination of NONVOTING STOCK, the prevention of the milking of subsidiaries, and the outlawing of the upstreaming of dividends (payment of dividends by operating companies to holding companies).

3. It provides for uniform accounting standards, periodic administrative and financial reports, and reports on holdings by officers and directors, and for the end of interlocking directorates with banks or investment bankers.

4. It began the elimination of complex organizational structures by allowing only one intermediate company between the top holding company and its operating companies (the GRANDFATHER CLAUSE).

PURCHASE ACQUISITION accounting method used in a business MERGER whereby the purchasing company treats the acquired company as an investment and adds the acquired company's assets to its own at their fair market value. Any premium paid over and above the FAIR MARKET VALUE of the acquired assets is reflected as GOODWILL on the buyer's BALANCE SHEET and must be written off against future earnings. Goodwill amortization is not deductible for tax purposes, so the reduction of reported future earnings can be a disadvantage of this method of merger accounting as compared with the alternative POOLING OF INTERESTS method. The purchase acquisition method is mandatory unless all the criteria for a pooling of interests combination are met.

PURCHASE FUND provision in some PREFERRED STOCK contracts and BOND indentures requiring the issuer to use its best efforts to purchase a specified number of shares or bonds annually at a price not to exceed par value. Unlike SINKING FUND provisions, which require that a certain number of bonds be retired annually, purchase funds require only that a tender offer be made; if no securities are tendered, none are retired. Purchase fund issues benefit the investor in a period of rising rates when the redemption price is higher than the market price and the proceeds can be put to work at a higher return.

PURCHASE GROUP group of investment bankers that, operating under the AGREEMENT AMONG UNDERWRITERS, agrees to purchase a NEW ISSUE of securities from the issuer for resale to the investment public; also called the UNDERWRITING GROUP or *syndicate*. The purchase group is distinguished from the SELLING GROUP, which is organized by the purchase group and includes the members of the purchase group along with other investment bankers. The selling group's function is DISTRIBUTION.

The agreement among underwriters, also called the *purchase group agreement,* is distinguished from the underwriting or purchase agreement, which is between the underwriting group and the issuer. *See also* UNDERWRITE.

PURCHASE GROUP AGREEMENT *see* PURCHASE GROUP.

PURCHASE-MONEY MORTGAGE MORTGAGE given by a buyer in lieu of cash for the purchase of property. Such mortgages make it possible to sell property when mortgage money is unavailable or when the only buyers are unqualified to borrow from commercial sources.

PURCHASE ORDER written authorization to a vendor to deliver specified goods or services at a stipulated price. Once accepted by the supplier, the purchase order becomes a legally binding purchase CONTRACT.

PURCHASING POWER

Economics: value of money as measured by the goods and services it can buy. For example, the PURCHASING POWER OF THE DOLLAR can be determined by comparing an index of consumer prices for a given base year to the present.

Investment: amount of credit available to a client in a brokerage account for the purchase of additional securities. Purchasing power is determined by the dollar amount of securities that can be margined. For instance, a client with purchasing power of $20,000 in his or her account could buy securities worth $40,000 under the Federal Reserve's currently effective 50% MARGIN REQUIREMENT. *See also* MARGIN SECURITY.

PURCHASING POWER OF THE DOLLAR measure of the amount of goods and services that a dollar can buy in a particular market, as compared with prior periods, assuming always an INFLATION or a DEFLATION factor and using an index of consumer prices. It might be reported, for instance, that one dollar in 1970 has 59 cents of purchasing power in 1985 because of the erosion caused by inflation. Deflation would increase the dollar's purchasing power.

PURE PLAY stock market jargon for a company that is virtually all devoted to one line of business. An investor who wants to invest in that line of business looks for such a pure play. For instance, General Dynamics may be considered a pure play in the defense business. The opposite of a pure play is a widely diversified company, such as a CONGLOMERATE.

PURPOSE LOAN loan backed by securities and used to buy other securities under Federal Reserve Board MARGIN and credit regulations.

PURPOSE STATEMENT form filed by a borrower that details the purpose of a loan backed by securities. The borrower agrees not to use the loan proceeds to buy securities in violation of any Federal Reserve regulations. *See also* NONPURPOSE LOAN; REGULATION U.

PUT BOND bond that allows its holder to redeem the issue on specified dates before maturity and receive full FACE VALUE. In return for this privilege, a bond buyer sacrifices some yield when choosing a put bond over a fixed-rate bond, that cannot be redeemed before maturity.

PUT-CALL RATIO total puts divided by total calls outstanding on a security or index. The ratio is one of the SENTIMENT INDICATORS.

PUT OPTION

Bonds: bondholder's right to redeem a bond before maturity. *See also* PUT BOND.

Options: contract that grants the right to sell at a specified price a specific number of shares by a certain date. The put option buyer gains this right in return for payment of an OPTION PREMIUM. The put option seller grants this right in return for receiving this premium. For instance, a buyer of an XYZ May 70 put has the right to sell 100 shares of XYZ at $70 to the put seller at any time until the contract expires in May. A put option buyer hopes the stock will drop in price, while the put option seller (called a *writer*) hopes the stock will remain stable, rise, or drop by an amount less than his or her profit on the premium.

PUT TO SELLER phrase used when a PUT OPTION is exercised. The OPTION WRITER is obligated to buy the underlying shares at the agreed-upon price. If an XYZ June 40 put were ''put to seller,'' for instance, the writer would have to buy 100 shares of XYZ at $40 a share from the put holder even though the current market price of XYZ may be far less than $40 a share.

PYRAMIDING

In general: form of business expansion that makes extensive use of financial LEVERAGE to build complex corporate structures.

Fraud: scheme that builds on nonexistent values, often in geometric progression, such as a chain letter, now outlawed by mail fraud legislation. A famous example was the Ponzi scheme, perpetrated by Charles Ponzi in the late 1920s. Investors were paid "earnings" out of money received from new investors until the scheme collapsed.

Investments: using unrealized profits from one securities or commodities POSITION as COLLATERAL to buy further positions with funds borrowed from a broker. This use of leverage creates increased profits in a BULL MARKET, and causes MARGIN CALLS and large losses in a BEAR MARKET.

Marketing: legal marketing strategy whereby additional distributorships are sold side-by-side with consumer products in order to multiply market reach and maximize profits to the sales organization.

q

Q-TIP TRUST *q*ualified *t*erminable *i*nterest *p*roperty *trust,* which allows assets to be transferred between spouses. The grantor of a Q-tip trust directs income from the assets to his or her spouse for life but has the power to distribute the assets upon the death of the spouse. Such trusts qualify the grantor for the unlimited marital deduction if the spouse should die first.

A Q-tip trust is often used to provide for the welfare of a spouse while keeping the assets out of the estate of another (such as a future marriage partner) if the grantor dies first.

QUALIFIED ENDORSEMENT endorsement (signature on the back of a check or other NEGOTIABLE INSTRUMENT transferring the amount to someone other than the one to whom it is payable) that contains wording designed to limit the endorser's liability. "Without recourse," the most frequently seen example, means that if the instrument is not honored, the endorser is not responsible. Where qualified endorsements are restrictive (such as "for deposit only") the term *restricted endorsement* is preferable.

QUALIFIED OPINION language in the auditor's opinion accompanying financial statements that calls attention to limitations of the audit or exceptions the auditor takes to items in the statements. Typical reasons for qualified opinions: a pending lawsuit that, if lost, would materially affect the financial condition of the company; an indeterminable tax liability relating to an unusual transaction; inability to confirm a portion of the inventory because of inaccessible location. *See also* ACCOUNTANT'S OPINION.

QUALIFIED PLAN OR TRUST plan set up by an employer for the benefit of employees that adheres to the rules set forth by the Internal Revenue Service (IRS) in 1954. Such a plan—for example, a profit-sharing or a pension plan—allows employees to build up savings, which are paid out at retirement or upon termination of employment. The employees pay taxes on this money only when they draw it out, usually at retirement; until such time, the funds accumulate tax deferred. The employer makes the payments to the plan, and is therefore entitled to certain deductions and other tax benefits as stated in the IRS Code.

QUALIFYING ANNUITY ANNUITY approved by the Internal Revenue Service (IRS) for inclusion as an investment in Keogh plans, IRAs, and other IRS-approved pension and profit-sharing plans. *See also* KEOGH PLAN; INDIVIDUAL RETIREMENT ACCOUNT (IRA).

QUALIFYING SHARE share of COMMON STOCK owned in order to qualify as a director of the issuing corporation.

QUALIFYING STOCK OPTION privilege granted to an employee of a corporation that permits the purchase, for a special price, of shares of its CAPITAL STOCK, under conditions sustained in the Internal Revenue Service Code. The law states (1) that the OPTION plan must be approved by the stockholders, (2) that the option is not transferable, (3) that the EXERCISE PRICE must not be less than the MARKET PRICE of the shares at the time the option is issued, and (4) that the grantee may not own more than 5% of the company's voting power or 5% of the value of all classes of its outstanding stock (10% if equity capital is under $1 million). No income tax is payable by the employee either at the time of the grant or at the time the option is exercised. If the stock is sold, the holding period required for long-term capital gains treatment is one year through 1987. Beginning in 1988, capital gains and ordinary income are taxable at the same rates under the TAX REFORM ACT OF 1986, which provides that (1) the FIRST IN, FIRST OUT (FIFO) method is no longer required for options exercised after 1986, meaning that if the market price falls below the option price, another option with a lower exercise price can be issued, and (2) starting in 1987, there is a $100,000 per employee limit on the value of stock covered by options that are exercisable in any one calendar year. Also called INCENTIVE STOCK OPTION.

QUALIFYING UTILITY utility in which shareholders were able (until the end of 1985) to defer taxes by reinvesting up to $750 in dividends ($1500 for a couple filing jointly) in the company's stock. Taxes were due when the stock was sold. This plan was enacted by the Economic Recovery Tax Act of 1981 as a means of helping utilities raise investment capital cheaply. Most of the utilities qualifying for the plan were electric utilities.

QUALITATIVE ANALYSIS

In general: analysis that evaluates factors that cannot be precisely measured.

Securities and credit analysis: analysis that is concerned with such questions as the experience, character, and general caliber of management; employee morale; and the status of labor relations rather than with the actual financial data about a company. *See also* QUANTITATIVE ANALYSIS.

QUALITY CONTROL process of assuring that products are made to consistently high standards of quality. Inspection of goods at various points in their manufacture is usually an important part of the quality control process.

QUALITY OF EARNINGS phrase describing a corporation's earnings that are attributable to increased sales and cost controls, as distinguished from artificial profits created by inflationary values in inventories or other assets. In a period of high inflation, the quality of earnings tends to suffer, since a large portion of a firm's profits is generated by the rising value of inventories. In a lower inflation period, a company that achieves higher sales and maintains lower costs produces a higher quality of earnings—a factor often appreciated by investors, who are frequently willing to pay more for a higher quality of earnings.

QUANTITATIVE ANALYSIS analysis dealing with measurable factors as distinguished from such qualitative considerations as the character of management or the state of employee morale. In credit and securities analysis, examples of quantitative considerations are the value of assets; the cost of capital; the historical and projected patterns of sales, costs, and profitability and a wide range of considerations in the areas of economics; the money market; and the securities markets. Although quantitative and qualitative factors are distinguishable, they must be combined to arrive at sound business and financial judgments. *See also* QUALITATIVE ANALYSIS.

QUARTERLY
In general: every three months (one quarter of a year).

Securities: basis on which earnings reports to shareholders are made; also, usual time frame of dividend payments.

QUARTER STOCK stock with a par value of $25 per share.

QUASI-PUBLIC CORPORATION corporation that is operated privately and often has its stock traded publicly, but that also has some sort of public mandate and often has the government's backing behind its direct debt obligations; for instance, the FEDERAL NATIONAL MORTGAGE ASSOCIATION (Fannie Mae), and the STUDENT LOAN MARKETING ASSOCIATION (Sallie Mae).

QUICK RATIO cash, MARKETABLE SECURITIES, and ACCOUNTS RECEIVABLE divided by current liabilities. By excluding inventory, this key LIQUIDITY ratio focuses on the firm's more LIQUID ASSETS, and helps answer the question "If sales stopped, could this firm meet its current obligations with the readily convertible assets on hand?" Assuming there is nothing happening to slow or prevent collections, a quick ratio of 1 to 1 or better is usually satisfactory. Also called *acid-test ratio, quick asset ratio*.

QUID PRO QUO
In general: from the Latin, meaning "something for something." By mutual agreement, one party provides a good or service for which he or she gets another good or service in return.

Securities industry: arrangement by a firm using institutional research that it will execute all trades based on that research with the firm providing it, instead of directly paying for the research. This is known as paying in SOFT DOLLARS.

QUIET PERIOD period an ISSUER is "in registration" and subject to an SEC embargo on promotional publicity. It dates from the preunderwriting decision to 40 or 90 days after the EFFECTIVE DATE.

QUOTATION
Business: price estimate on a commercial project or transaction.

Investments: highest bid and lowest offer (asked) price currently available on a security or a commodity. An investor who asks for a quotation ("quote") on XYZ might be told "60 to 60½," meaning that the best bid price (the highest price any buyer wants to pay) is currently $60 a share and that the best offer (the lowest price any seller is willing to accept) is $60½ at that time. Such quotes assume ROUND-LOT transactions—for example, 100 shares for stocks.

QUOTATION BOARD electronically controlled board at a brokerage firm that displays current price quotations and other financial data such as dividends, price ranges of stocks, and current volume of trading.

QUOTED PRICE price at which the last sale and purchase of a particular security or commodity took place.

r

RADAR ALERT close monitoring of trading patterns in a company's stock by senior managers to uncover unusual buying activity that might signal a TAKEOVER attempt. *See also* SHARK WATCHER.

RAIDER individual or corporate investor who intends to take control of a company by buying a controlling interest in its stock and installing new management. Raiders who accumulate 5% or more of the outstanding shares in the TARGET COMPANY must report their purchases to the Securities and Exchange Commission, the exchange of listing, and the target itself. *See also* BEAR RAID; WILLIAMS ACT.

RALLY marked rise in the price of a security, commodity future, or market after a period of decline or sideways movement.

R & D *see* RESEARCH AND DEVELOPMENT.

RANDOM WALK theory about the movement of stock and commodity futures prices hypothesizing that past prices are of no use in forecasting future price movements. According to the theory, stock prices reflect reactions to information coming to the market in random fashion, so they are no more predictable than the walking pattern of a drunken person. The random walk theory was first espoused in 1900 by the French mathematician Louis Bachelier and revived in the 1960s. It is hotly disputed by advocates of TECHNICAL ANALYSIS, who say that charts of past price movements enable them to predict future price movements.

RANGE high and low end of a security, commodity future, or market's price fluctuations over a period of time. Daily newspapers publish the 52-week high and low price range of stocks traded on the New York Stock Exchange, American Stock Exchange, and over-the-counter markets. Advocates of TECHNICAL ANALYSIS attach great importance to trading ranges because they consider it of great significance if a security breaks out of its trading range by going higher or lower. *See also* BREAKOUT.

RATE BASE value established for a utility by a regulatory body such as a Public Utility Commission on which the company is allowed to earn a particular rate of return. Generally the rate base includes the utility's operating costs but not the cost of constructing new facilities. Whether modernization costs should be included in the rate base, and thus passed on to customers, is a subject of continuing controversy. *See also* FAIR RATE OF RETURN.

RATE COVENANT provision in MUNICIPAL REVENUE BOND agreements or resolutions covering the rates, or methods of establishing rates, to be charged users of the facility being financed. The rate covenant usually promises that rates will be adjusted when necessary to cover the cost of repairs and maintenance while continuing to provide for the payment of bond interest and principal.

RATE OF EXCHANGE *see* EXCHANGE RATE; PAR VALUE OF CURRENCY.

RATE OF INFLATION *see* CONSUMER PRICE INDEX; INFLATION RATE; PRODUCER PRICE INDEX.

RATE OF RETURN

Fixed-income securities (bonds and preferred stock): CURRENT YIELD, that is, the coupon or contractual dividend rate divided by the purchase price. *See also*

YIELD TO AVERAGE LIFE; YIELD TO CALL; YIELD TO MATURITY.

Common stock: (1) dividend yield, which is the annual dividend divided by the purchase price. (2) TOTAL RETURN rate, which is the dividend plus capital appreciation.

Corporate finance: RETURN ON EQUITY or RETURN ON INVESTED CAPITAL.

Capital budgeting: INTERNAL RATE OF RETURN.

See also FAIR RATE OF RETURN; HORIZON ANALYSIS; MEAN RETURN; REAL INTEREST RATE; REQUIRED RATE OF RETURN; TOTAL RETURN; YIELD.

RATING

Credit and investments: evaluation of securities investment and credit risk by rating services such as Fitch Investors Service, MOODY'S INVESTORS SERVICE, STANDARD & POOR'S CORPORATION, and VALUE LINE INVESTMENT SURVEY. See also CREDIT RATING; NOT RATED.

Insurance: using statistics, mortality tables, probability theory, experience, judgment, and mathematical analysis to establish the rates on which insurance premiums are based. There are three basic rating systems: class rate, applying to a homogeneous grouping of clients; schedule system, relating positive and negative factors in the case of a particular insured (for example, a smoker or nonsmoker in the case of a life policy) to a base figure; and experience rating, reflecting the historical loss experience of the particular insured. Also called rate-making.

Insurance companies are also rated; see BEST'S RATING.

LEADING BOND RATING SERVICES Explanation of corporate/municipal bond ratings	RATING SERVICE		
	Fitch	Moody's	Standard & Poor's
Highest quality, "gilt edged"	AAA	Aaa	AAA
High quality	AA	Aa	AA
Upper medium grade	A	A	A
Medium grade	BBB	Baa	BBB
Predominantly speculative	BB	Ba	BB
Speculative, low grade	B	B	B
Poor to default	CCC	Caa	CCC
Highest speculation	CC	Ca	CC
Lowest quality, no interest	C	C	C
In default, in arrears, questionable value	{ DDD DD D		DDD DD D

Fitch and Standard & Poor's may use + or − to modify some ratings. Moody's uses the numerical modifiers 1 (highest), 2, and 3 in the range from Aa1 through Ca3.

RATIO ANALYSIS method of analysis, used in making credit and investment judgments, which utilizes the relationship of figures found in financial statements to determine values and evaluate risks and compares such ratios to those of prior periods and other companies to reveal trends and identify eccentricities. Ratio analysis is only one tool among many used by analysts. See also ACCOUNTS RECEIVABLE TURNOVER; ACID TEST RATIO; BOND RATIO; CAPITALIZATION RATIO; CAPITAL TURNOVER; CASH RATIO; COLLECTION PERIOD; COMMON STOCK RATIO; CURRENT RATIO; DEBT-TO-EQUITY RATIO; DIVIDEND PAYOUT RATIO; EARNINGS-PRICE RATIO; FIXED CHARGE COVERAGE; LEVERAGE; NET TANGIBLE ASSETS PER SHARE; OPERATING RATIO; PREFERRED STOCK RATIO; PRICE-EARNINGS RATIO; PROFIT MARGIN; QUICK RATIO; RETURN ON EQUITY; RETURN ON INVESTED CAPITAL; RETURN ON SALES.

RATIO WRITER OPTIONS writer who sells more CALL contracts than he has underlying shares. For example, an investor who writes (sells) 10 calls, 5 of them covered by the 500 owned shares of the underlying stock and the other 5 of them uncovered (or "naked"), has a 2 for 1 ratio write.

REACHBACK ability of a LIMITED PARTNERSHIP or other tax shelter to offer deductions at the end of the year that reach back for the entire year. For instance, the investor who buys an OIL AND GAS LIMITED PARTNERSHIP in late December might be able to claim deductions for the entire year's drilling costs, depletion allowance, and interest expenses. Reachback on tax shelters was considered to be abusive by the Internal Revenue Service, and it was substantially eliminated in 1983 and 1984.

REACTION drop in securities prices after a sustained period of advancing prices, perhaps as the result of PROFIT TAKING or adverse developments. *See also* CORRECTION.

READING THE TAPE judging the performance of stocks by monitoring changes in price as they are displayed on the TICKER tape. An analyst reads the tape to determine whether a stock is acting strongly or weakly, and therefore is likely to go up or down. An investor reads the tape to determine whether a stock trade is going with or against the flow of market action. *See also* DON'T FIGHT THE TAPE.

REAL ESTATE piece of land and all physical property related to it, including houses, fences, landscaping, and all rights to the air above and earth below the property. Assets not directly associated with the land are considered *personal property*.

REAL ESTATE INVESTMENT TRUST (REIT) company, usually traded publicly, that manages a portfolio of real estate in order to earn profits for shareholders. Patterned after INVESTMENT COMPANIES, REITs make investments in a diverse array of real estate from shopping centers and office buildings to apartment complexes and hotels. Some REITs, called EQUITY REITS, take equity positions in real estate; shareholders receive income from the rents received from the properties and receive capital gains as buildings are sold at a profit. Other REITs specialize in lending money to building developers; such MORTGAGE REITS pass interest income on to shareholders. Some REITs have a mix of equity and debt investments. To avoid taxation at the corporate level, 75% or more of the REIT's income must be from real property and 95% of its taxable income must be distributed to shareholders. The TAX REFORM ACT OF 1986 generally gave REITs more flexibility.

REAL INCOME income of an individual, group, or country adjusted for changes in PURCHASING POWER caused by inflation. A price index is used to determine the difference between the purchasing power of a dollar in a base year and the purchasing power now. The resulting percentage factor, applied to total income, yields the value of that income in constant dollars, termed real income. For instance, if the cost of a market basket increases from $100 to $120 in ten years, reflecting a 20% decline in purchasing power, salaries must rise by 20% if real income is to be maintained.

REAL INTEREST RATE current interest rate minus inflation rate. The real interest rate may be calculated by comparing interest rates with present or, more frequently, with predicted inflation rates. The real interest rate gives investors in bonds and other fixed-rate instruments a way to see whether their interest will allow them to keep up with or beat the erosion in dollar values caused by inflation.

With a bond yielding 10% and inflation of 3%, for instance, the real interest rate of 7% would bring a return high enough to beat inflation. If inflation were at 15%, however, the investor would fall behind as prices rise.

REALIZED PROFIT (OR LOSS) profit or loss resulting from the sale or other disposal of a security. Capital gains taxes may be due when profits are realized; realized losses can be used to offset realized gains for tax purposes. Such profits and losses differ from a PAPER PROFIT OR LOSS, which (except for OPTION and FUTURES CONTRACTS) has no tax consequences.

REAL RATE OF RETURN RETURN on an investment adjusted for inflation.

REBATE
1. in lending, unearned interest refunded to a borrower if the loan is paid off before maturity.
2. in consumer marketing, payment made to a consumer after a purchase is completed, to induce purchase of a product. For instance, a customer who buys a television set for $500 may be entitled to a rebate of $50, which is received after sending a proof of purchase and a rebate form to the television manufacturer. *See also* RULE OF THE 78S.

RECAPITALIZATION alteration of a corporation's CAPITAL STRUCTURE, such as an exchange of bonds for stock. BANKRUPTCY is a common reason for recapitalization; debentures might be exchanged for REORGANIZATION BONDS that pay interest only when earned A healthy company might seek to improve its tax situation by replacing preferred stock with bonds to take advantage of the tax deductibility of interest. *See also* DEFEASANCE.

RECAPTURE
1. contract clause allowing one party to recover some degree of possession of an asset. In leases calling for a percentage of revenues, such as those for shopping centers, the recapture clause provides that the developer get a percentage of profits in addition to a fixed rent.
2. in the tax code, the reclamation by the government of tax benefits previously taken. For example, where a portion of the profit on the sale of a depreciable asset represented ACCELERATED DEPRECIATION or the INVESTMENT CREDIT, all or part of that gain would be "recaptured" and taxed as ORDINARY INCOME, with the balance subject to the favorable CAPITAL GAINS TAX. Effective with the TAX REFORM ACT OF 1986, dispositions of property are taxed at ordinary rates uniformly. Recapture also has specialized applications in oil and other industries. Recapture assumed a new meaning under the 1986 Act whereby banks with assets of $500 million or more were required to take into income the balance of their RESERVE for BAD DEBTS. The Act called for recapture of income at the rate of 10%, 20%, 30%, and 40% for the years 1987 through 1990, respectively.

RECEIVER court-appointed person who takes possession of, but not title to, the assets and affairs of a business or estate that is in a form of BANKRUPTCY called *receivership* or is enmeshed in a legal dispute. The receiver collects rents and other income and generally manages the affairs of the entity for the benefit of its owners and creditors until a disposition is made by the court.

RECEIVER'S CERTIFICATE debt instrument issued by a RECEIVER, who uses the proceeds to finance continued operations or otherwise to protect assets in receivership. The certificates constitute a LIEN on the property, ranking ahead of all other secured or unsecured liabilities in LIQUIDATION.

RECEIVE VERSUS PAYMENT instruction accompanying sell orders by institutions that only cash will be accepted in exchange for delivery of the securities at the time of settlement. Institutions are generally required by law to accept only cash. Also called *receive againstpayment*.

RECESSION downturn in economic activity, defined by many economists as at least two consecutive quarters of decline in a country's GROSS NATIONAL PRODUCT.

RECLAMATION

Banking: restoration or correction of a NEGOTIABLE INSTRUMENT—or the amount thereof—that has been incorrectly recorded by the *clearing house*.

Finance: restoration of an unproductive asset to productivity, such as by using landfill to make a swamp developable.

Securities: right of either party to a securities transaction to recover losses caused by *bad delivery* or other irregularities in the settlement process.

RECORD DATE *see* DATE OF RECORD; EX-DIVIDEND DATE; PAYMENT DATE.

RECOURSE LOAN

1. loan for which an endorser or guarantor is liable for payment in the event the borrower defaults.
2. loan made to a DIRECT PARTICIPATION PROGRAM or LIMITED PARTNERSHIP whereby the lender, in addition to being secured by specific assets, has recourse against the general assets of the partnership. *See also* NONRECOURSE LOAN.

RECOVERY

Economics: period in a business cycle when economic activity picks up and the GROSS NATIONAL PRODUCT grows, leading into the expansion phase of the cycle.

Finance: (1) absorption of cost through the allocation of DEPRECIATION; (2) collection of an ACCOUNT RECEIVABLE that had been written off as a bad debt; (3) residual cost, or salvage value, of a fixed asset after all allowable depreciation.

Investment: period of rising prices in a securities or commodities market after a period of falling prices.

REDEEMABLE BOND *see* CALLABLE.

REDEMPTION repayment of a debt security or preferred stock issue, at or before maturity, at PAR or at a premium price.

Mutual fund shares are redeemed at NET ASSET VALUE when a shareholder's holdings are liquidated.

REDEMPTION PRICE *see* CALL PRICE.

RED HERRING *see* PRELIMINARY PROSPECTUS.

REDISCOUNT DISCOUNT short-term negotiable debt instruments, such as banker's ACCEPTANCES and COMMERCIAL PAPER, that have been *discounted* with a bank—in other words, exchanged for an amount of cash adjusted to reflect the current interest rate. The bank then discounts the paper a second time for its own benefit with another bank or with a Federal Reserve bank. Rediscounting was once the primary means by which banks borrowed additional reserves from the Fed. Today most banks do this by discounting their own notes secured by GOVERNMENT SECURITIES or other ELIGIBLE PAPER. But *rediscount rate* is still used as a synonym for DISCOUNT RATE, the rate charged by the Fed for all bank borrowings.

REFINANCING

Banking: extending the maturity date, or increasing the amount of existing debt, or both.

Bonds: REFUNDING; retiring existing bonded debt by issuing new securities to reduce the interest rate, or to extend the maturity date, or both.

Personal finance: revising a payment schedule, usually to reduce the monthly payments and often to modify interest charges.

REFUNDING

1. replacing an old debt with a new one, often in order to lower the interest costs of the issuer. For instance, a corporation or municipality that has issued 14% bonds may want to refund them by issuing 10% bonds if interest rates have dropped. *See also* PREREFUNDING; REFINANCING.
2. in merchandising, returning money to the purchaser—for example, a consumer who has paid for an appliance and is not happy with it.

REGIONAL BANK bank that specializes in collecting deposits and making loans in one region of the country, as distinguished from a MONEY CENTER BANK, which operates nationally and internationally.

REGIONAL STOCK EXCHANGES organized national securities exchanges located outside of New York City and registered with the Securities and Exchange Commission. They include: the Boston, Cincinnati, Intermountain (Salt Lake City), Midwest (Chicago), Pacific (Los Angeles and San Francisco), Philadelphia (Philadelphia and Miami), and Spokane stock exchanges. These exchanges list not only regional issues, but many of the securities that are listed on the New York exchanges. Companies listed on the NEW YORK STOCK EXCHANGE and the AMERICAN STOCK EXCHANGE will often be listed on regional exchanges as well to broaden the market for their securities. Using the INTERMARKET TRADING SYSTEM (ITS), a SPECIALIST on the floor of one of the New York or regional exchanges can see competing prices for the securities he trades on video screens. Regional exchanges handle only a small percentage of the total volume of the New York exchanges, though more than 50% of companies listed in New York are also listed regionally. *See also* DUAL LISTING; GRADUATED SECURITY; SECURITIES AND COMMODITIES EXCHANGES.

REGISTERED BOND bond that is recorded in the name of the holder on the books of the issuer or the issuer's REGISTRAR and can be transferred to another owner only when ENDORSED by the registered owner. A bond registered for principal only, and not for interest, is called a *registered coupon bond*. One that is not registered is called a *bearer bond;* one issued with detachable coupons for presentation to the issuer or a paying agent when interest or principal payments are due is termed a COUPON BOND. Bearer bonds are NEGOTIABLE INSTRUMENTS payable to the holder and therefore do not legally require endorsement. Bearer bonds that may be changed to registered bonds are called *interchangeable bonds.*

REGISTERED CHECK check issued by a bank for a customer who places funds aside in a special register. The customer writes in his name and the name of the payee and the amount of money to be transferred. The bank, which collects a fee for the service, then puts on the bank's name and the amount of the check and gives the check a special number. The check has two stubs, one for the customer and one for the bank. The registered check is similar to a money order for someone who does not have a checking account at the bank.

REGISTERED COMPANY company that has filed a REGISTRATION STATEMENT with the Securities and Exchange Commission in connection with a PUBLIC OFFERING of securities and must therefore comply with SEC DISCLOSURE requirements.

REGISTERED COMPETITIVE MARKET MAKER

1. securities dealer registered with the NATIONAL ASSOCIATION OF SECURITIES DEALERS (NASD) as a market maker in a particular OVER-THE-COUNTER stock—that is, one who maintains firm bid and offer prices in the stock by standing ready to buy or sell round lots. Such dealers must announce their quotes through NASDAQ, which requires that there be at least two market makers in each stock listed in the system; the bid and asked quotes are compared to ensure that the quote is a *representative spread*. *See also* MAKE A MARKET.
2. REGISTERED COMPETITIVE TRADER on the New York Stock Exchange. Such traders are sometimes called market makers because, in addition to trading for their own accounts, they are expected to help correct an IMBALANCE OF ORDERS. *See also* REGISTERED EQUITY MARKET MAKER.

REGISTERED COMPETITIVE TRADER one of a group of New York Stock Exchange members who buy and sell for their own accounts. Because these members pay no commissions, they are able to profit on small changes in market prices and thus tend to trade actively in stocks doing a high volume. Like SPECIALISTS, registered competitive traders must abide by exchange rules, including a requirement that 75% of their trades be *stabilizing*. This means they cannot sell unless the last trading price on a stock was up, or buy unless the last trading price was down. Orders from the general public take precedence over those of registered competitive traders, which account for less than 1% of volume. Also called *floor trader* or *competitive trader*.

REGISTERED COUPON BOND *see* REGISTERED BOND.

REGISTERED EQUITY MARKET MAKER AMERICAN STOCK EXCHANGE member firm registered as a trader for its own account. Such firms are expected to make stabilizing purchases and sales when necessary to correct imbalances in particular securities. *See also* REGISTERED COMPETITIVE MARKET MAKER.

REGISTERED INVESTMENT COMPANY investment company, such as an open-end or closed-end MUTUAL FUND, which files a registration statement with the Securities and Exchange Commission and meets all the other requirements of the INVESTMENT COMPANY ACT OF 1940.

REGISTERED OPTIONS TRADER specialist on the floor of the AMERICAN STOCK EXCHANGE who is responsible for maintaining a fair and orderly market in an assigned group of options.

REGISTERED REPRESENTATIVE employee of a stock exchange member broker/dealer who acts as an ACCOUNT EXECUTIVE for clients. As such, the registered representative gives advice on which securities to buy and sell, and he collects a percentage of the commission income he generates as compensation. To qualify as a registered representative, a person must acquire a background in the securities business and pass a series of tests, including the General Securities Examination and state securities tests. ''Registered'' means licensed by the Securities and Exchange Commission and by the New York Stock Exchange.

REGISTERED SECONDARY OFFERING offering, usually through investment bankers, of a large block of securities that were previously issued to the public, using the abbreviated Form S-16 of the Securities and Exchange Commission. Such offerings are usually made by major stockholders of mature companies who may be *control persons* or institutions who originally acquired the securities in a private placement. Form S-16 relies heavily on previously filed SEC documents such as the S-1, the 10-K, and quarterly filings. Where listed securities are concerned, permission to sell large blocks off the exchange must be obtained from the appropriate exchange. *See also* LETTER SECURITY; SECONDARY DISTRIBUTION; SECONDARY OFFERING; SHELF REGISTRATION.

REGISTERED SECURITY
1. security whose owner's name is recorded on the books of the issuer or the issuer's agent, called a *registrar*—for example, a REGISTERED BOND as opposed to a *bearer bond,* the former being transferable only by endorsement, the latter payable to the holder.
2. securities issue registered with the Securities and Exchange Commission as a new issue or as a SECONDARY OFFERING. *See also* REGISTERED SECONDARY OFFERING; REGISTRATION.

REGISTRAR agency responsible for keeping track of the owners of bonds and the issuance of stock. The registrar, working with the TRANSFER AGENT, keeps current files of the owners of a bond issue and the stockholders in a corporation. The registrar also makes sure that no more than the authorized amount of stock is in circulation. For bonds, the registrar certifies that a bond is a corporation's genuine debt obligation.

REGISTRATION process set up by the Securities Exchange Acts of 1933 and 1934 whereby securities that are to be sold to the public are reviewed by the Securities and Exchange Commission. The REGISTRATION STATEMENT details pertinent financial and operational information about the company, its management, and the purpose of the offering. Incorrect or incomplete information will delay the offering.

REGISTRATION FEE charge made by the Securities and Exchange Commission and paid by the issuer of a security when a public offering is recorded with the SEC.

REGISTRATION STATEMENT document detailing the purpose of a proposed public offering of securities. The statement outlines financial details, a history of the company's operations and management, and other facts of importance to potential buyers. *See also* REGISTRATION.

REGRESSION ANALYSIS statistical technique used to establish the relationship of a dependent variable, such as the sales of a company, and one or more independent variables, such as family formations, GROSS NATIONAL PRODUCT, per capita income, and other ECONOMIC INDICATORS. By measuring exactly how large and significant each independent variable has historically been in its relation to the dependent variable, the future value of the dependent variable can be predicted. Essentially, regression analysis attempts to measure the degree of correlation between the dependent and independent variables, thereby establishing the latter's predictive value. For example, a manufacturer of baby food might want to determine the relationship between sales and housing starts as part of a sales forecast. Using a technique called a scatter graph, it might plot on the X and Y axes the historical sales for ten years and the historical annual housing starts foɪ the same period. A line connecting the average dots, called the regression line, would reveal the degree of correlation between the two factors by showing the amount of unexplained variation—represented by the dots falling outside the line. Thus, if the regression line connected all the dots, it would demonstrate a direct relationship between baby food sales and housing starts, meaning that one could be predicted on the basis of the other. The proportion of dots scattered outside the regression line would indicate, on the other hand, the degree to which the relationship was less direct, a high enough degree of unexplained variation meaning there was no meaningful relationship and that housing starts have no predictive value in terms of baby food sales. This proportion of unexplained variations is termed the *coefficient of determination,* and its square root the CORRELATION COEFFICIENT. The correlation coefficient is the ultimate yardstick of regression analysis: a correlation coefficient of 1 means the relationship is direct—baby food and housing starts move together; − 1 means there is a negative relationship— the more housing starts there are, the less baby food is sold; a coefficient of zero means there is no relationship between the two factors.

Regression analysis is also used in securities' markets analysis and in the risk-return analyses basic to PORTFOLIO THEORY.

REGRESSION ANALYSIS SCATTER GRAPH

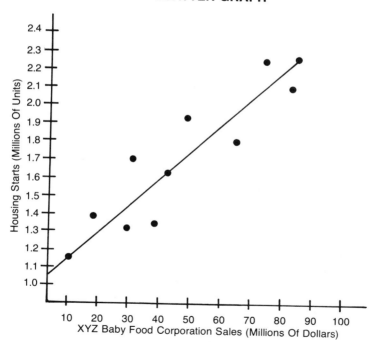

REGRESSIVE TAX

1. system of taxation in which tax rates decline as the tax base rises. For example, a system that taxed values of $1000 to $5000 at 5%, $5000 to $10,000 at 4% and so on would be regressive. A regressive tax is the opposite of a PRO-

GRESSIVE TAX.

2. tax system that results in a higher tax for the poor than for the rich, in terms of percentage of income. In this sense, a sales tax is regressive even though the same rate is applied to all sales, because people with lower incomes tend to spend most of their incomes on goods and services. Similarly, payroll taxes are regressive because they are borne largely by wage earners and not by higher income groups. Local property taxes also tend to be regressive because poorer people spend more of their incomes on housing costs, which are directly affected by property taxes. *See also* FLAT TAX.

REGULAR WAY DELIVERY (AND SETTLEMENT) completion of securities transaction at the office of the purchasing broker on (but not before) the fifth full business day following the date of the transaction, as required by the NEW YORK STOCK EXCHANGE. Government transactions are an exception; for them, regular way means delivery and settlement the next business day following a transaction.

REGULATED COMMODITIES commodities under the jurisdiction of the COMMODITIES FUTURES TRADING COMMISSION, which include all commodities traded in organized contract markets. The CFTC was established in 1974 by the U.S. Congress, succeeding the Commodities Exchange Act of 1936. It polices matters of information and disclosure, fair trading practices, registration of firms and individuals, and the protection of customer funds, record keeping, and the maintenance of orderly futures and options markets.

REGULATED INVESTMENT COMPANY MUTUAL FUND or UNIT INVESTMENT TRUST eligible under *Regulation M* of the Internal Revenue Service to pass capital gains, dividends, and interest earned on fund investments directly to its shareholders to be taxed at the personal level. The process, designed to avoid double taxation, is called the *conduit theory*. To qualify as a regulated investment company, the fund must meet such requirements as 97% minimum distribution of interest and dividends received on investments and 90% distribution of capital gain net income. Shareholders must pay taxes even if they reinvest their distributions.

REGULATION A

1. Securities and Exchange Commission provision for simplified REGISTRATION of small issues of securities. A Regulation A issue requires a shorter form of PROSPECTUS and carries lesser liability for officers and directors for false or misleading statements.
2. Federal Reserve Board statement of the means and conditions under which Federal Reserve banks make loans to member and other banks at what is called the DISCOUNT WINDOW. *See also* REDISCOUNT.

REGULATION G Federal Reserve Board rule regulating lenders other than commercial banks, brokers or dealers who, in the ordinary course of business, extend credit to individuals to purchase or carry securities. Special provision is made for loans by corporations and credit unions to finance purchases under employee stock option and stock purchase plans.

REGULATION Q Federal Reserve Board ceiling on the rates that banks and other savings institutions can pay on savings and other time deposits. THE DEPOSITORY INSTITUTIONS DEREGULATION AND MONETARY CONTROL ACT OF 1980 provided for phasing out Regulation Q by 1986.

REGULATION T Federal Reserve Board regulation covering the extension of credit to customers by securities brokers, dealers, and members of the national securities exchanges. It establishes INITIAL MARGIN requirements and defines registered (eligible), unregistered (ineligible), and exempt securities. *See also* MARGIN REQUIREMENT; MARGIN SECURITIES.

REGULATION U Federal Reserve Board limit on the amount of credit a bank may extend a customer for purchasing and carrying MARGIN SECURITIES. *See also* NONPURPOSE LOAN.

REGULATION Z Federal Reserve Board regulation covering provisions of the CONSUMER CREDIT PROTECTION ACT OF 1968, known as the Truth in Lending Act.

REHYPOTHECATION pledging by brokers of securities in customers' MARGIN ACCOUNTS to banks as collateral for broker loans under a GENERAL LOAN AND COLLATERAL AGREEMENT. Broker loans cover the positions of brokers who have made margin loans to customers for margin purchases and SELLING SHORT. Margin loans are collateralized by the HYPOTHECATION of customers' securities to the broker. Their rehypothecation is authorized when the customer originally signs a GENERAL ACCOUNT agreement.

REINSURANCE sharing of RISK among insurance companies. Part of the insurer's risk is assumed by other companies in return for a part of the premium fee paid by the insured. By spreading the risk, reinsurance allows an individual company to take on clients whose coverage would be too great a burden for one insurer to carry alone.

REINVESTMENT PRIVILEGE right of a shareholder to reinvest dividends in order to buy more shares in the company or MUTUAL FUND, usually at no additional sales charge.

REINVESTMENT RATE rate of return resulting from the reinvestment of the interest from a bond or other fixed-income security. The reinvestment rate on a ZERO-COUPON BOND is predictable and locked in, since no interest payments are ever made, and therefore all imputed interest is reinvested at the same rate. The reinvestment rate on coupon bonds is less predictable because it rises and falls with market interest rates.

REIT *see* REAL ESTATE INVESTMENT TRUST.

REJECTION

Banking: refusal to grant credit to an applicant because of inadequate financial strength, a poor credit history, or some other reason.

Insurance: refusal to underwrite a risk, that is, to issue a policy.

Securities: refusal of a broker or a broker's customer to accept the security presented to complete a trade. This usually occurs because the security lacks the necessary endorsements, or because of other exceptions to the rules for GOOD DELIVERY.

RELEASE CLAUSE provision in a MORTGAGE agreement allowing the freeing of pledged property after a proportionate amount of payment has been made.

REMARGINING putting up additional cash or eligible securities to correct a deficiency in EQUITY deposited in a brokerage MARGIN ACCOUNT to meet MINIMUM MAINTENANCE REQUIREMENTS. Remargining usually is prompted by a MARGIN CALL.

REMIC acronym for *real estate mortgage investment conduit,* a pass-through vehicle created under the TAX REFORM ACT OF 1986 to issue multiclass mortgage-backed securities. REMICs may be organized as corporations, partnerships, or trusts, and those meeting qualifications are not subject to DOUBLE TAXATION. Interests in REMICs may be *regular* (debt instruments) or *residual* (equity interests).

REMIT pay for purchased goods or services by cash, check, or electronic payment.

REORGANIZATION financial restructuring of a firm in BANKRUPTCY. *See also* TRUSTEE IN BANKRUPTCY; VOTING TRUST CERTIFICATE.

REORGANIZATION BOND debt security issued by a company in REORGANIZATION proceedings. The bonds are generally issued to the company's creditors on a basis whereby interest is paid only if and when it is earned. *See also* ADJUSTMENT BOND; INCOME BOND.

REPATRIATION return of the financial assets of an organization or individual from a foreign country to the home country.

REPLACEMENT COST ACCOUNTING accounting method allowing additional DEPRECIATION on part of the difference between the original cost and current replacement cost of a depreciable asset.

REPURCHASE AGREEMENT (REPO; RP) agreement between a seller and a buyer, usually of U.S. Government securities, whereby the seller agrees to repurchase the securities at an agreed upon price and, usually, at a stated time. Repos, also called RPs or buybacks, are widely used both as a money market investment vehicle and as an instrument of Federal Reserve MONETARY POLICY. Where a repurchase agreement is used as a short-term investment, a government securities dealer, usually a bank, borrows from an investor, typically a corporation with excess cash, to finance its inventory, using the securities as collateral. Such RPs may have a fixed maturity date or be OPEN REPOS, callable at any time. Rates are negotiated directly by the parties involved, but are generally lower than rates on collateralized loans made by New York banks. The attraction of repos to corporations, which also have the alternatives of COMMERCIAL PAPER, CERTIFICATES OF DEPOSIT, TREASURY BILLS and other short-term instruments, is the flexibility of maturities that makes them an ideal place to "park" funds on a very temporary basis. Dealers also arrange *reverse repurchase agreements*, whereby they agree to buy the securities and the investor agrees to repurchase them at a later date.

The FEDERAL RESERVE BANK also makes extensive use of repurchase agreements in its OPEN MARKET OPERATIONS as a method of fine tuning the MONEY SUPPLY. To temporarily expand the supply, the Fed arranges to buy securities from nonbank dealers who in turn deposit the proceeds in their commercial bank accounts thereby adding to reserves. Timed to coincide with whatever length of time the Fed needs to make the desired adjustment, usually 1 to 15 days, the dealer repurchases the securities. Such transactions are made at the Federal Reserve DISCOUNT RATE and accounts are credited in FEDERAL FUNDS. When it wishes to reduce the money supply temporarily, the Fed reverses the process. Using a procedure called the MATCHED SALE PURCHASE TRANSACTION, it sells securities to a nonbank dealer who either draws down bank balances directly or takes out a bank loan to make payment, thereby draining reserves.

In a third variation of the repurchase agreement, banks and thrift institutions can raise temporary capital funds with a device called the *retail repurchase agreement*. Using pooled government securities to secure loans from individuals, they agree to repurchase the securities at a specified time at a price including interest. Despite its appearance of being a deposit secured by government securities, the investor has neither a special claim on the securities nor protection by the FEDERAL DEPOSIT INSURANCE CORPORATION in the event the bank liquidates.

See also OVERNIGHT REPO.

REQUIRED RATE OF RETURN return required by investors before they will commit money to an investment at a given level of risk. Unless the expected return exceeds the required return, an investment is unacceptable. *See also* HURDLE RATE; INTERNAL RATE OF RETURN; MEAN RETURN.

RESCIND cancel a contract agreement. The Truth in Lending Act confers the RIGHT OF RESCISSION, which allows the signer of a contract to nullify it within three business days without penalty and have any deposits refunded. Contracts may also be rescinded in cases of fraud, failure to comply with legal procedures, or misrepresentation. For example, a contract signed by a child under legal age may be rescinded, since children do not have the right to take on contractual obligations.

RESEARCH AND DEVELOPMENT (R&D) scientific and marketing evolution of a new product or service. Once such a product has been created in a laboratory or other research setting, marketing specialists attempt to define the market for the product. Then, steps are taken to manufacture the product to meet the needs of the market. Research and development spending is often listed as a separate item in a company's financial statements. In industries such as high-technology and pharmaceuticals, R&D spending is quite high, since products are outdated or attract competition quickly. Investors looking for companies in such fast-changing fields check on R&D spending as a percentage of sales because they consider this an important indicator of the company's prospects. *See also* RESEARCH AND DEVELOPMENT LIMITED PARTNERSHIP.

RESEARCH AND DEVELOPMENT LIMITED PARTNERSHIP plan whose investors put up money to finance new product RESEARCH AND DEVELOPMENT. In return, the investors get a percentage of the product's profits, if any, together with such benefits as DEPRECIATION of equipment. R&D partnerships may be offered publicly or privately, usually through brokerage firms. Those that are offered to the public must be registered with the Securities and Exchange Commission. *See also* LIMITED PARTNERSHIP.

RESEARCH DEPARTMENT division within a brokerage firm, investment company, bank trust department, insurance company, or other institutional investing organization that analyzes markets and securities. Research departments include analysts who focus on particular securities, commodities, and whole industries as well as generalists who forecast movements of the markets as a whole, using both FUNDAMENTAL ANALYSIS and TECHNICAL ANALYSIS. An analyst whose advice is followed by many investors can have a major impact on the prices of individual securities.

RESERVE
1. segregation of RETAINED EARNINGS to provide for such payouts as dividends, contingencies, improvements, or retirement of preferred stock.
2. VALUATION RESERVE, also called ALLOWANCE, for DEPRECIATION, BAD DEBT

losses, shrinkage of receivables because of discounts taken, and other provisions created by charges to the PROFIT AND LOSS STATEMENT.

3. hidden reserves, represented by understatements of BALANCE SHEET values.

4. deposit maintained by a commercial bank in a FEDERAL RESERVE BANK to meet the Fed's RESERVE REQUIREMENT.

RESERVE REQUIREMENT FEDERAL RESERVE SYSTEM rule mandating the financial assets that member banks must keep in the form of cash and other liquid assets as a percentage of DEMAND DEPOSITS and TIME DEPOSITS. This money must be in the bank's own vaults or on deposit with the nearest regional FEDERAL RESERVE BANK. Reserve requirements, set by the Fed's Board of Governors, are one of the key tools in deciding how much money banks can lend, thus setting the pace at which the nation's money supply and economy grow. The higher the reserve requirement, the tighter the money—and therefore the slower the economic growth. *See also* MONETARY POLICY; MONEY SUPPLY; MULTIPLIER.

RESIDENTIAL ENERGY CREDIT tax credit granted to homeowners prior to 1986 by the federal government for improving the energy efficiency of their homes. Installation of storm windows and doors, insulation, or new fuel-saving heating systems before the end of 1985 meant a maximum federal credit on expenditures of $300. Equipping a home with renewable energy devices such as solar panels or windmills meant a maximum federal credit of $4000. Many states offer incentives for installing such devices.

RESIDUAL SECURITY SECURITY that has a potentially dilutive effect on earnings per common share. Warrants, rights, convertible bonds, and preferred stock are potentially dilutive because exercising or converting them into common stock would increase the number of common shares competing for the same earnings, and earnings per share would be reduced. *See also* DILUTION: FULLY DILUTED EARNINGS PER (COMMON) SHARE.

RESIDUAL VALUE
1. realizable value of a FIXED ASSET after costs associated with the sale.
2. amount remaining after all allowable DEPRECIATION charges have been subtracted from the original cost of a depreciable asset.
3. scrap value, which is the value to a junk dealer.
   Also called *salvage value*.

RESISTANCE LEVEL price ceiling at which technical analysts note persistent selling of a commodity or security. If XYZ's stock generally trades between a low of $50 and a high of $60 a share, $50 is called the SUPPORT LEVEL and $60 is called the resistance level. Technical analysts think it significant when the stock breaks through the resistance level because that means it usually will go on to new high prices. *See also* BREAKOUT; TECHNICAL ANALYSIS. *See* illustration, page 429.

RESOLUTION
1. in general, expression of desire or intent.
2. formal document representing an action of a corporation's BOARD OF DIRECTORS—perhaps a directive to management, such as in the declaration of a dividend, or a corporate expression of sentiment, such as acknowledging the services of a retiring officer. A *corporate resolution*, which defines the authority and powers of individual officers, is a document given to a bank.
3. legal order or contract by a government entity—called a *bond resolution*—

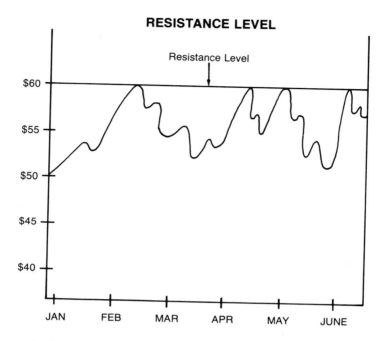

RESISTANCE LEVEL

Resistance Level

authorizing a bond issue and spelling out the rights of bondholders and the obligations of the issuer.

RESTRICTED ACCOUNT MARGIN ACCOUNT with a securities broker in which the EQUITY is less than the INITIAL MARGIN requirement set by the Federal Reserve Board's REGULATION T. A customer whose account is restricted may not make further purchases and must, in accordance with Regulation T's *retention requirement*, retain in the account a percentage of the proceeds of any sales so as to reduce the deficiency (debit balance). This retention requirement is currently set at 50%. *See also* MARGIN CALL.

RESTRICTED SURPLUS portion of RETAINED EARNINGS not legally available for the payment of dividends. Among the circumstances giving rise to such restriction: dividend arrearages in CUMULATIVE PREFERRED stock, a shortfall in the minimum WORKING CAPITAL ratio specified in an INDENTURE, or simply a vote by the BOARD OF DIRECTORS. Also called *restricted retained earnings*.

RESTRICTIVE COVENANT *see* COVENANT.

RESYNDICATION LIMITED PARTNERSHIP partnership in which existing properties are sold to new limited partners, who can gain tax advantages that had been exhausted by the old partnership. For instance, a partnership with government-subsidized housing may have given partners substantial tax benefits five years ago. Now the same housing development may be sold to a resyndication partnership, which will start the process of DEPRECIATION over again and claim additional tax benefits for its new limited partners. Resyndication partnerships are usually offered as PRIVATE PLACEMENTS through brokerage houses, although a few have been offered to the public.

RETAIL HOUSE brokerage firm that caters to retail investors instead of institutions. Such a firm may be a large national broker called a WIRE HOUSE, with a large RESEARCH DEPARTMENT and a wide variety of products and services for individuals, or it may be a small BOUTIQUE serving an exclusive clientele with specialized research or investment services.

RETAIL INVESTOR investor who buys securities and commodities futures on his own behalf, not for an organization. Retail investors typically buy shares of stock or commodity positions in much smaller quantities than institutions such as mutual funds, bank trust departments, and pension funds and therefore are usually charged commissions higher than those paid by the institutions. In recent years, market activity has increasingly been dominated by INSTITUTIONAL INVESTORS.

RETAINED EARNINGS net profits kept to accumulate in a business after dividends are paid. Also called *undistributed profits* or *earned surplus*. Retained earnings are distinguished from *contributed capital*—capital received in exchange for stock, which is reflected in CAPITAL STOCK or CAPITAL SURPLUS and DONATED STOCK or DONATED SURPLUS. STOCK DIVIDENDS—the distribution of additional shares of capital stock with no cash payment—reduce retained earnings and increase capital stock. Retained earnings plus the total of all the capital accounts represent the NET WORTH of a firm. *See also* ACCUMULATED PROFITS TAX; PAID-IN CAPITAL.

RETAINED EARNINGS STATEMENT reconciliation of the beginning and ending balances in the RETAINED EARNINGS account on a company's BALANCE SHEET. It breaks down changes affecting the account, such as profits or losses from operations, dividends declared, and any other items charged or credited to retained earnings. A retained earnings statement is required by GENERALLY ACCEPTED ACCOUNTING PRINCIPLES whenever comparative balance sheets and income statements are presented. It may appear in the balance sheet, in a combined PROFIT AND LOSS STATEMENT and retained earnings statement, or as a separate schedule. It may also be called *statement of changes in earned surplus* (or *retained income*).

RETENTION in securities underwriting, the number of units allocated to a participating investment banker (SYNDICATE member) minus the units held back by the syndicate manager for facilitating institutional sales and for allocation to firms in the selling group that are not also members of the syndicate. *See also* UNDERWRITE.

RETENTION RATE percentage of aftertax profits credited to RETAINED EARNINGS. It is the opposite of the DIVIDEND PAYOUT RATIO.

RETENTION REQUIREMENT *see* RESTRICTED ACCOUNT.

RETIREMENT
1. cancellation of stock or bonds that have been reacquired or redeemed. *See also* CALLABLE; REDEMPTION.
2. removal from service after a fixed asset has reached the end of its useful life or has been sold and appropriate adjustments have been made to the asset and depreciation accounts.
3. repayment of a debt obligation.
4. permanent withdrawal of an employee from gainful employment in accordance with an employer's policies concerning length of service, age, or disability. A retired employee may have rights to a pension or other retirement provisions

offered by the employer. Employer retirement benefits may supplement payments from an INDIVIDUAL RETIREMENT ACCOUNT (IRA) or KEOGH PLAN.

RETURN

Finance and investment: profit on a securities or capital investment, usually expressed as an annual percentage rate. *See also* RATE OF RETURN; RETURN ON EQUITY; RETURN ON INVESTED CAPITAL; RETURN ON SALES; TOTAL RETURN.

Retailing: exchange of previously sold merchandise for REFUND or CREDIT against future sales.

Taxes: form on which taxpayers submit information required by the government when they file with the INTERNAL REVENUE SERVICE. For example, form 1040 is the tax return used by individual tax payers.

Trade: physical return of merchandise for credit against an invoice.

RETURN OF CAPITAL distribution of cash resulting from DEPRECIATION tax savings, the sale of a CAPITAL ASSET or of securities in a portfolio, or any other transaction unrelated to RETAINED EARNINGS. Returns of capital are not directly taxable but may result in higher CAPITAL GAINS taxes later on if they reduce the acquisition cost base of the property involved. Also called *return of basis.*

RETURN ON EQUITY amount, expressed as a percentage, earned on a company's common stock investment for a given period. It is calculated by dividing common stock equity (NET WORTH) at the beginning of the accounting period into NET INCOME for the period after preferred stock dividends but before common stock dividends. Return on equity tells common shareholders how effectually their money is being employed. Comparing percentages for current and prior periods reveals trends, and comparison with industry composites reveals how well a company is holding its own against its competitors.

RETURN ON INVESTED CAPITAL amount, expressed as a percentage, earned on a company's total capital—its common and preferred stock EQUITY plus its long-term FUNDED DEBT—calculated by dividing total capital into earnings before interest, taxes, and dividends. Return on invested capital, usually termed *return on investment,* or *ROI,* is a useful means of comparing companies, or corporate divisions, in terms of efficiency of management and viability of product lines.

RETURN ON SALES net pretax profits as a percentage of NET SALES—a useful measure of overall operational efficiency when compared with prior periods or with other companies in the same line of business. It is important to recognize, however, that return on sales varies widely from industry to industry. A supermarket chain with a 2% return on sales might be operating efficiently, for example, because it depends on high volume to generate an acceptable RETURN ON INVESTED CAPITAL. In contrast, a manufacturing enterprise is expected to average 4% to 5%, so a return on sales of 2% is likely to be considered highly inefficient.

REVALUATION change in the value of a country's currency relative to others that is based on the decision of authorities rather than on fluctuations in the market. Revaluation generally refers to an increase in the currency's value; DEVALUATION refers to a decrease. *See also* FLOATING EXCHANGE RATE; PAR VALUE OF CURRENCY.

REVENUE ANTICIPATION NOTE (RAN) short-term debt issue of a municipal entity that is to be repaid out of anticipated revenues such as sales taxes. When the taxes are collected, the RAN is paid off. Interest from the note is usually tax-free to RAN holders.

REVENUE BOND *See* MUNICIPAL REVENUE BOND.

REVENUE NEUTRAL guiding criterion in drafting the TAX REFORM ACT OF 1986 whereby provisions estimated to add revenue were offset by others estimated to reduce revenue, so that on paper the new bill would generate the same amount of revenue as the old tax laws. The concept was theoretical rather than real, since estimates are subject to variation.

REVENUE SHARING

Limited partnerships: percentage split between the general partner and limited partners of profits, losses, cash distributions, and other income or losses which result from the operation of a real estate, oil and gas, equipment leasing, or other partnership. *See also* LIMITED PARTNERSHIP.

Taxes: return of tax revenue to a unit of government by a larger unit, such as from a state to one of its municipalities. GENERAL REVENUE SHARING between the federal government and states, localities, and other subunits existed between 1972 and 1987.

REVERSAL change in direction in the stock or commodity futures markets, as charted by technical analysts. If the Dow Jones Industrial Average has been climbing steadily from 1100 to 1200, for instance, chartists would speak of a reversal if the average started a sustained fall back toward 1100.

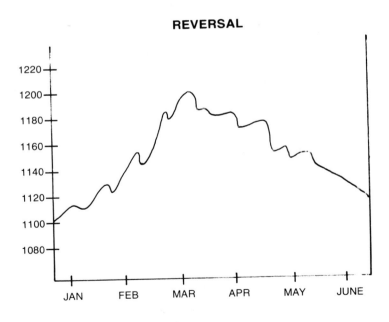

REVERSE ANNUITY MORTGAGE MORTGAGE instrument that allows an elderly person to live off the equity in a fully paid-for house. Such a homeowner would enter into a reverse annuity mortgage agreement with a financial institution such as a bank, which would guarantee a lifelong fixed monthly income in return for gradually giving up ownership of the house. The longer the payments continue, the less equity the elderly owner would retain. At the owner's death the bank gains title to the real estate, which it can sell at a profit. The law also permits such arrangements between relatives, so that, for instance, a son or daughter might enter into a reverse annuity mortgage transaction with his or her retiring parents, thus providing the parents with cash to invest in income-yielding securities and the son or daughter with the depreciation and other tax benefits of real estate ownership. *See also* ARM'S LENGTH TRANSACTION.

REVERSE A SWAP restore a bond portfolio to its former position following a swap of one bond for another to gain the advantage of a YIELD SPREAD or a tax loss. The reversal may mean that the yield differential has disappeared or that the investor, content with a short-term profit, wishes to stay with the original bond for the advantages that may be gained in the future. *See also* BOND SWAP.

REVERSE CONVERSION technique whereby brokerage firms earn interest on their customers' stock holdings. A typical reverse conversion would work like this: A brokerage firm sells short the stocks it holds in customers' margin accounts, then invests this money in short-term money market instruments. To protect against a sharp rise in the markets, the firm hedges its short position by buying CALL options and selling PUT options. To unwind the reverse conversion, the firm buys back the stocks, sells the call, and buys the put. *See also* MARGIN ACCOUNT; OPTION.

REVERSE REPURCHASE AGREEMENT *see* REPURCHASE AGREEMENT.

REVERSE SPLIT procedure whereby a corporation reduces the number of shares outstanding. The total number of shares will have the same market value immediately after the reverse split as before it, but each share will be worth more. For example, if a firm with 10 million outstanding shares selling at $10 a share executes a reverse 1 for 10 split, the firm will end up with 1 million shares selling for $100 each. Such splits are usually initiated by companies wanting to raise the price of their outstanding shares because they think the price is too low to attract investors. Also called *split down*. *See also* SPLIT.

REVOCABLE TRUST agreement whereby income-producing property is deeded to heirs. The provisions of such a TRUST may be altered as many times as the GRANTOR pleases, or the entire trust agreement can be canceled, unlike irrevocable trusts. The grantor receives income from the assets, but the property passes directly to the beneficiaries at the grantor's death, without having to go through PROBATE court proceedings. Since the assets are still part of the grantor's estate, however, estate taxes must be paid on this transfer. This kind of trust differs from an IRREVOCABLE TRUST, which permanently transfers assets from the estate during the grantor's lifetime and therefore escapes estate taxes.

REVOLVING CREDIT

Commercial banking: contractual agreement between a bank and its customer, usually a company, whereby the bank agrees to make loans up to a specified maximum for a specified period, usually a year or more. As the borrower repays a portion of the loan, an amount equal to the repayment can be borrowed again under the terms of the agreement. In addition to interest borne by notes, the bank charges a fee for the commitment to hold the funds available. A COMPENSATING BALANCE may be required in addition.

Consumer banking: loan account requiring monthly payments of less than the full amount due, and the balance carried forward is subject to a financial charge.

Also, an arrangement whereby borrowings are permitted up to a specified limit and for a specified period, usually a year, with a fee charged for the commitment. Also called *open-end credit* or *revolving line of credit*.

REVOLVING LINE OF CREDIT *see* REVOLVING CREDIT.

RICH
1. term for a security whose price seems too high in light of its price history. For bonds, the term may also imply that the yield is too low.
2. term for rate of interest that seems too high in relation to the borrower's risk.
3. synonym for *wealthy*.

RIGGED MARKET situation in which the prices for a security are manipulated so as to lure unsuspecting buyers or sellers. *See also* MANIPULATION.

RIGHT *see* SUBSCRIPTION RIGHT.

RIGHT OF REDEMPTION right to recover property transferred by a MORTGAGE or other LIEN by paying off the debt either before or after foreclosure. Also called *equity of redemption*.

RIGHT OF RESCISSION right granted by the federal CONSUMER CREDIT PROTECTION ACT OF 1968 to void a contract within three business days with full refund of any down payment and without penalty. The right is designed to protect consumers from high-pressure door-to-door sales tactics and hastily made credit commitments which involve their homes as COLLATERAL, such as loans secured by second mortgages.

RIGHT OF SURVIVORSHIP right entitling one owner of property held jointly to take title to it when the other owner dies. *See also* JOINT TENANTS WITH RIGHT OF SURVIVORSHIP; TENANTS IN COMMON.

RIGHTS OFFERING offering of COMMON STOCK to existing shareholders who hold rights that entitle them to buy newly issued shares at a discount from the price at which shares will later be offered to the public. Rights offerings are usually handled by INVESTMENT BANKERS under what is called a STANDBY COMMITMENT, whereby the investment bankers agree to purchase any shares not subscribed to by the holders of rights. *See also* PREEMPTIVE RIGHT; SUBSCRIPTION RIGHT.

RING location on the floor of an exchange where trades are executed. The circular arrangement where traders can make bid and offer prices is also called a *pit*, particularly when commodities are traded.

RISING BOTTOMS technical chart pattern showing a rising trend in the low prices of a security or commodity. As the range of prices is charted daily, the lows reveal an upward trend. Rising bottoms signify higher and higher basic SUPPORT LEVELS for a security or commodity. When combined with a series of ASCENDING TOPS, the pattern is one a follower of TECHNICAL ANALYSIS would call bullish.

RISK measurable possibility of losing or not gaining value. Risk is differentiated from uncertainty, which is not measurable. Among the commonly encountered types of risk are these:
Actuarial risk: risk an insurance underwriter covers in exchange for premiums, such as the risk of premature death.

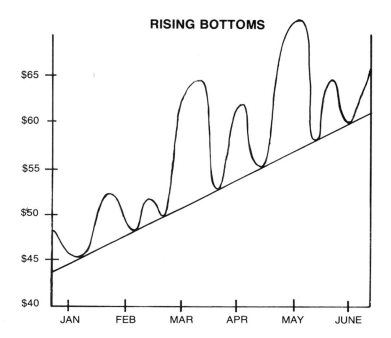

RISING BOTTOMS

Exchange risk: chance of loss on foreign currency exchange.

Inflation risk: chance that the value of assets or of income will be eroded as inflation shrinks the value of a country's currency.

Interest rate risk: possibility that a fixed-rate debt instrument will decline in value as a result of a rise in interest rates.

Inventory risk: possibility that price changes, obsolescence, or other factors will shrink the value of INVENTORY.

Liquidity risk: possibility that an investor will not be able to buy or sell a commodity or security quickly enough or in sufficient quantities because buying or selling opportunities are limited.

Political risk: possibility of NATIONALIZATION or other unfavorable government action.

Repayment (credit) risk: chance that a borrower or trade debtor will not repay an obligation as promised.

Risk of principal: chance that invested capital will drop in value.

Underwriting risk: risk taken by an INVESTMENT BANKER that a new issue of securities purchased outright will not be bought by the public and/or that the market price will drop during the offering period.

RISK-ADJUSTED DISCOUNT RATE in PORTFOLIO THEORY and CAPITAL BUDGET analysis, the rate necessary to determine the PRESENT VALUE of an uncertain or risky stream of income; it is the risk-free rate (generally the return on short-term U.S. Treasury securities) plus a risk premium that is based on an analysis of the risk characteristics of the particular investment or project.

RISK ARBITRAGE ARBITRAGE involving risk, as in the simultaneous purchase of stock in a company being acquired and sale of stock in its proposed acquirer. Also called *takeover arbitrage*. Traders called *arbitrageurs* attempt to profit from TAKEOVERS by cashing in on the expected rise in the price of the target company's shares and drop in the price of the acquirer's shares. If the takeover plans fall through, the traders may be left with enormous losses. Risk arbitrage differs from riskless arbitrage, which entails locking in or profiting from the differences in the prices of two securities or commodities trading on different exchanges. *See also* RISKLESS TRANSACTION.

RISK AVERSE term referring to the assumption that, given the same return and different risk alternatives, a rational investor will seek the security offering the least risk—or, put another way, the higher the degree of risk, the greater the return that a rational investor will demand. *See also* CAPITAL ASSET PRICING MODEL; EFFICIENT PORTFOLIO; MEAN RETURN; PORTFOLIO THEORY.

RISK CAPITAL *see* VENTURE CAPITAL.

RISK CATEGORY classification of risk elements used in analyzing MORTGAGES.

RISKLESS TRANSACTION
1. trade guaranteeing a profit to the trader that initiates it. An *arbitrageur* may lock in a profit by trading on the difference in prices for the same security or commodity in different markets. For instance, if gold were selling for $400 an ounce in New York and $398 in London, a trader who acts quickly could buy a contract in London and sell it in New York for a riskless profit.
2. concept used in evaluating whether dealer MARKUPS and MARKDOWNS in OVER THE COUNTER transactions with customers are reasonable or excessive. In what is known as the FIVE PERCENT RULE, the NATIONAL ASSOCIATION OF SECURITIES DEALERS (NASD) takes the position that markups (when the customer buys) and markdowns (when the customer sells) should not exceed 5%, the proper charge depending on the effort and risk of the dealer in completing a trade. The maximum would be considered excessive for a riskless transaction, in which a security has high marketability and the dealer does not simply act as a broker and take a commission but trades from or for inventory and charges a markup or markdown. Where a dealer satisfies a buy order by making a purchase in the open market for inventory, then sells the security to the customer, the trade is called a *simultaneous transaction*. To avoid NASD criticism, broker-dealers commonly disclose the markups and markdowns to customers in transactions where they act as dealers.

ROCKET SCIENTIST investment firm creator of innovative securities.

ROLL DOWN move from one OPTION position to another one having a lower EXERCISE PRICE. The term assumes that the position with the higher exercise price is closed out.

ROLL FORWARD move from one OPTION position to another with a later expiration date. The term assumes that the earlier position is closed out before the later one is established. If the new position involves a higher EXERCISE PRICE, it is called a *roll-up and forward*; if a lower exercise price, it is called a *roll-down and forward*. Also called *rolling over*.

ROLLING STOCK equipment that moves on wheels, used in the transportation industry. Examples include railroad cars and locomotives, tractor-trailers, and trucks.

ROLLOVER

1. movement of funds from one investment to another. For instance, an INDI-VIDUAL RETIREMENT ACCOUNT may be rolled over when a person retires into an ANNUITY or other form of pension plan payout system. When a BOND or CERTIFICATE OF DEPOSIT matures, the funds may be rolled over into another bond or certificate of deposit. The proceeds from the sale of a house may be rolled over into the purchase of another house within two years without tax penalty. A stock may be sold and the proceeds rolled over into the same stock, establishing a different cost basis for the shareholder. *See also* THIRTY DAY WASH RULE.

2. term often used by banks when they allow a borrower to delay making a PRINCIPAL payment on a loan. Also, a country that has difficulty in meeting its debt payments may be granted a rollover by its creditors. With governments themselves, rollovers in the form of REFUNDINGS or REFINANCINGS are routine. *See also* CERTIFICATE OF DEPOSIT ROLLOVER.

ROLL UP move from one OPTION position to another one having a higher EXERCISE PRICE. The term assumes that the earlier position is closed out before the new position is established. *See also* MASTER LIMITED PARTNERSHIP.

ROUND LOT generally accepted unit of trading on a securities exchange. On the New York Stock Exchange, for example, a round lot is 100 shares for stock and $1000 or $5000 par value for bonds. In inactive stocks, the round lot is 10 shares. Increasingly, there seems to be recognition of a 500-share round lot for trading by institutions. Large-denomination CERTIFICATES OF DEPOSIT trade on the OVER THE COUNTER market in units of $1 million. Investors who trade in round lots do not have to pay the DIFFERENTIAL charged on ODD LOT trades.

ROUND TRIP TRADE purchase and sale of a security or commodity within a short time. For example, a trader who continually is making short-term trades in a particular commodity is making round trip or *round turn* trades. Commissions for such a trader are likely to be quoted in terms of the total for a purchase and sale—$100 for the round trip, for instance. Excessive round trip trading is called CHURNING.

ROYALTY payment to the holder for the right to use property such as a patent, copyrighted material, or natural resources. For instance, inventors may be paid royalties when their inventions are produced and marketed. Authors may get royalties when books they have written are sold. Land owners leasing their property to an oil or mining company may receive royalties based on the amount of oil or minerals extracted from their land. Royalties are set in advance as a percentage of income arising from the commercialization of the owner's rights or property.

ROYALTY TRUST oil or gas company *spin-off* of oil reserves to a trust, which avoids DOUBLE TAXATION, eliminates the expense and risk of new drilling, and provides DEPLETION tax benefits to shareholders. In the mid-1980s Mesa Royalty Trust, which pioneered the idea, led other trusts in converting to a MASTER LIMITED PARTNERSHIP form of organization, offering tax advantages along with greater flexibility and liquidity.

RULE 405 New York Stock Exchange codification of an ethical concept recognized industrywide by those dealing with the investment public. These so-called KNOW YOUR CUSTOMER rules recognize that what is suitable for one investor may be less appropriate for another and require investment people to obtain pertinent facts about a customer's other security holdings, financial condition, and objectives. *See also* SUITABILITY RULES.

RULE OF 72 formula for approximating the time it will take for a given amount of money to double at a given COMPOUND INTEREST rate. The formula is simply 72 divided by the interest rate. In six years $100will double at a compound annual rate of 12%, thus: 72 divided by 12equals 6.

RULE OF THE 78s method of computing REBATES of interest on installment loans. It uses the SUM-OF-THE-YEAR'S-DIGITS basis in determining the interest earned by the FINANCE COMPANY for each month of a year, assuming equal monthly payments, and gets its name from the fact that the sum of the digits 1 through 12 is 78. Thus interest is equal to12/78ths of the total annual interest in the first month, 11/78ths in the second month, and so on.

RULES OF FAIR PRACTICE set of rules established by the Board of Governors of the NATIONAL ASSOCIATION OF SECURITIES DEALERS (NASD), a self-regulatory organization comprising investment banking houses and firms dealing in the OVER THE COUNTER securities market. As summarized in the NASD bylaws, the rules are designed to foster just and equitable principles of trade and business; high standards of commercial honor and integrity among members; the prevention of fraud and manipulative practices; safeguards against unreasonable profits, commissions, and other charges; and collaboration with governmental and other agencies to protect investors and the public interest in accordance with Section 15A of the MALONEY ACT. *See also* FIVE PERCENT RULE; IMMEDIATE FAMILY; KNOW YOUR CUSTOMER; MARKDOWN; RISKLESS TRANSACTION.

RUN

Banking: demand for their money by many depositors all at once. If large enough, a run on a bank can cause it to fail, as hundreds of banks did in the Great Depression of the 1930s. Such a run is caused by a breach of confidence in the bank, perhaps as a result of large loan losses or fraud.

Securities:
1. list of available securities, along with current bid and asked prices, which a market maker is currently trading. For bonds the run may include the par value as well as current quotes.
2. when a security's price rises quickly, analysts say it had a quick run up, possibly because of a positive earnings report.

RUNDOWN

In general: status report or summary.

Municipal bonds: summary of the amounts available and the prices on units in a SERIAL BOND that has not yet been completely sold to the public.

RUNNING AHEAD illegal practice of buying or selling a security for a broker's personal account before placing a similar order for a customer. For example, when a firm's analyst issues a positive report on a company, the firm's brokers may not buy the stock for their own accounts before they have told their clients the news. Some firms prohibit brokers from making such trades for a specific period, such as two full days from the time of the recommendation.

RUNOFF printing of an exchange's closing prices on a TICKER tape after the market has closed. The runoff may take a long time when trading has been very heavy and the tape has fallen far behind the action.

S

SAFE HARBOR

1. financial or accounting step that avoids legal or tax consequences. Commonly used in reference to *safe harbor leasing*, as permitted by the ECONOMIC RECOVERY TAX ACT OF 1981 (ERTA). An unprofitable company unable to use the INVESTMENT CREDIT and ACCELERATED COST RECOVERY SYSTEM (ACRS) liberalized depreciation rules, could transfer those benefits to a profitable firm seeking to reduce its tax burden. Under such an arrangement, the profitable company would own an asset the unprofitable company would otherwise have purchased itself; the profitable company would then lease the asset to the unprofitable company, presumably passing on a portion of the tax benefits in the form of lower lease rental charges. Safe harbor leases were curtailed by provisions in the TAX EQUITY AND FISCAL RESPONSIBILITY ACT OF 1982 (TEFRA).
2. provision in a law that excuses liability if the attempt to comply in good faith can be demonstrated. For example, safe harbor provisions would protect management from liability under Securities and Exchange Commission rules for financial PROJECTIONS made in good faith.
3. form of SHARK REPELLENT whereby a TARGET COMPANY acquires a business so onerously regulated it makes the target less attractive, giving it, in effect, a safe harbor.

SAFEKEEPING
storage and protection of a customer's financial assets, valuables, or documents, provided as a service by an institution serving as AGENT and, where control is delegated by the customer, also as custodian. An individual, corporate, or institutional investor might rely on a bank or a brokerage firm to hold stock certificates or bonds, keep track of trades, and provide periodic statements of changes in position. Investors who provide for their own safekeeping usually use a *safe deposit box*, provided by financial institutions for a fee. *See also* STREET NAME.

SALARY REDUCTION PLAN
plan allowing employees to contribute pretax compensation to a qualified TAX-DEFERRED retirement plan. Until the TAX REFORM ACT OF 1986, the term was synonymous with 401(K) PLAN, but the 1986 Act prohibited employees of state and local governments and tax-exempt organizations from establishing new 401(K) plans and added restrictions to existing government and tax-exempt unfunded deferred compensation arrangements and tax-sheltered annuity arrangements creating, in effect, a broadened definition of salary reduction plan. The 1986 law limits annual maximum deferral amounts for unfunded deferred compensation arrangements to the lesser of $7500 or ⅓ of an individual's compensation and imposes a $9500 annual limit on elective deferrals under 403(B) Plans (annuity programs for municipalities and not-for-profits).

SALE

In general: any exchange of goods or services for money. *Contrast with* BARTER.

Finance: income received in exchange for goods and services recorded for a given accounting period, either on a cash basis (as received) or on an accrual basis (as earned). *See also* GROSS SALES.

Securities: in securities trading, a sale is executed when a buyer and a seller have agreed on a price for the security.

SALE AND LEASEBACK form of LEASE arrangement in which a company sells an asset to another party—usually an insurance or finance company, a leasing company, a limited partnership, or an institutional investor—in exchange for cash, then contracts to lease the asset for a specified term. Typically, the asset is sold for its MARKET VALUE, so the lessee has really acquired capital that would otherwise have been tied up in a long-term asset. Such arrangements frequently have tax benefits for the lessee, although there is normally little difference in the effect on income between the lease payments and the interest payments that would have existed had the asset been purchased with borrowed money. A company generally opts for the sale and leaseback arrangement as an alternative to straight financing when the rate it would have to pay a lender is higher than the cost of rental or when it wishes to show less debt on its BALANCE SHEET (called *off-balance-sheet financing*). *See also* CAPITAL LEASE.

SALES CHARGE fee paid to a brokerage house by a buyer of shares in a load MUTUAL FUND or a LIMITED PARTNERSHIP. Normally, the sales charge for a mutual fund starts at 8½% of the capital invested and decreases as the size of the investment increases. The sales charge for a limited partnership is often even higher—typically 10%. In return for the sales charge, investors are entitled to investment advice from the broker on which fund or partnership is best for them. A fund that carries no sales charge is called a NO-LOAD FUND. *See also* FRONT-END LOAD; LETTER OF INTENT; LOAD FUND.

SALES LITERATURE

In general: written material designed to help sell a product or a service.
Investments: written material issued by a securities brokerage firm, mutual fund, underwriter, or other institution selling a product that explains the advantages of the investment product. Such literature must be truthful and must comply with disclosure regulations issued by the Securities and Exchange Commission and state securities agencies.

SALES LOAD *see* SALES CHARGE.

SALLIE MAE *see* STUDENT LOAN MARKETING ASSOCIATION.

SALVAGE VALUE *see* RESIDUAL VALUE.

SAME-DAY SUBSTITUTION offsetting changes in a MARGIN ACCOUNT in the course of one day, resulting in neither a MARGIN CALL nor a credit to the SPECIAL MISCELLANEOUS ACCOUNT. Examples: a purchase and a sale of equal value; a decline in the MARKET VALUE of some margin securities offset by an equal rise in the market value of others.

SATURDAY NIGHT SPECIAL sudden attempt by one company to take over another by making a public TENDER OFFER. The term was coined in the 1960s after a rash of such surprise maneuvers, which were often announced over weekends. The WILLIAMS ACT of 1968 placed severe restrictions on tender offers and required disclosure of direct or indirect ownership of 5% or more of any class of EQUITY. It thus marked the end of what, in its traditional form, was known as the "creeping tender."

SAUCER technical chart pattern signaling that the price of a security or a commodity has formed a bottom and is moving up. An inverse saucer shows a top in the security's price and signals a downturn. *See also* TECHNICAL ANALYSIS.

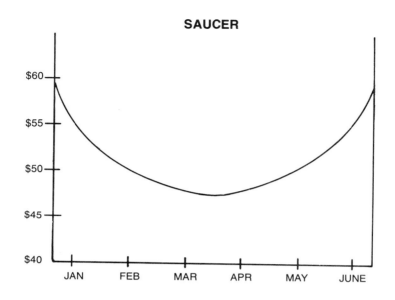

SAUCER

SAVINGS AND LOAN ASSOCIATION depository financial institution, federally or state chartered, that obtains the bulk of its deposits from consumers and holds the majority of its assets as home mortgage loans. A few such specialized institutions were organized in the 19th century under state charters but with minimal regulation. Reacting to the crisis in the banking and home building industries precipitated by the Great Depression, Congress in 1932 passed the Federal Home Loan Bank Act, establishing the FEDERAL HOME LOAN BANK SYSTEM to supplement the lending resources of state-chartered savings and loans (S&Ls). The Home Owners' Loan Act of 1933 created a system for the federal chartering of S&Ls under the supervision of the Federal Home Loan Bank Board. Deposits in federal S&Ls were insured with the formation of the Federal Savings and Loan Insurance Corporation in 1934.

A second wave of restructuring occurred in the 1980s. The DEPOSITORY INSTITUTIONS DEREGULATION AND MONETARY CONTROL ACT of 1980 set a six-year timetable for the removal of interest rate ceilings, including the S&Ls' quarter-point rate advantage over the commercial bank limit on personal savings accounts. The act also allowed S&Ls limited entry into some markets previously open only to commercial banks (commercial lending, nonmortgage consumer lending, trust services) and, in addition, permitted MUTUAL ASSOCIATIONS to issue INVESTMENT CERTIFICATES. In actual effect, interest rate parity was achieved by the end of 1982.

The Garn-St Germain Depository Institutions Act of 1982 accelerated the pace of deregulation and gave the Federal Home Loan Bank Board wide latitude in shoring up the capital positions of S&Ls weakened by the impact of record-high interest rates on portfolios of old, fixed-rate mortgage loans. The 1982 act also encouraged the formation of stock savings and loans or the conversion of existing mutual (depositor-owned) associations to the stock form, which gave the associations another way to tap the capital markets and thereby to bolster their net worth. *See also* SAVINGS BANK.

SAVINGS BANK depository financial institution that primarily accepts consumer deposits and makes home mortgage loans. Historically, savings banks were of the mutual (depositor-owned) form and chartered in only 16 states; the majority of savings banks were located in the New England states, New York, and New Jersey. Prior to the passage of the Garn-St Germain Depository Institutions Act of 1982, state-chartered savings bank deposits were insured along with commercial bank deposits by the FEDERAL DEPOSIT INSURANCE CORPORATION. The GarnSt Germain Act gave savings banks the options of a federal charter, mutual-to-stock conversion, supervision by the Federal Home Loan Bank Board, and insurance from the FEDERAL SAVINGS AND LOAN INSURANCE CORPORATION. *See also* MUTUAL SAVINGS BANK; SAVINGS AND LOAN ASSOCIATION.

SAVINGS BOND U.S. government bond issued in FACE VALUE denominations ranging from $50 to $10,000. Issued at a discount, these bonds are redeemed at face value at maturity. From 1941 to 1979, the government issued SERIES E BONDS. Starting in 1980, Series EE and HH bonds were issued. Series EE bonds range from $50 to $10,000; Series HH bonds, from $500 to $10,000. Both earn interest for ten years, though the U.S. Congress often extends that date. As of November 1, 1986, Series EE bonds, if held for five years, pay 85% of the average yields on five-year Treasury securities or 6%, whichever is more. Series HH bonds, available only through an exchange of at least $500 in Series E or EE bonds, pay a fixed annual 6% rate in two semiannual payments.

The interest from savings bonds is exempt from state and local taxes, and no federal tax is due until the bonds are redeemed. Bondholders wanting to defer the tax liability on their maturing Series EE bonds can exchange them for Series HH.

SCALE

Labor: wage rate for specific types of employees. For example: ''Union scale for carpenters is $15.60 per hour.''

Production economics: amount of production, as in ''economy or diseconomy of scale.'' *See also* MARGINAL COST.

Serial bonds: vital data for each of the scheduled maturities in a new SERIAL BOND issue, including the number of bonds, the date they mature, the COUPON rate, and the offering price.

See also SCALE ORDER.

SCALE ORDER order for a specified number of shares that is to be executed in stages in order to average the price. Such an order might provide for the purchase of a total of 5000 shares to be executed in lots of 500 shares at each quarter-point interval as the market declines. Since scale orders are clerically cumbersome, not all brokers will accept them.

SCALPER

In general: speculator who enters into quasi-legal or illegal transactions to turn a quick and sometimes unreasonable profit. For example, a scalper buys tickets at regular prices for a major event and when the event becomes a sellout, resells the tickets at the highest price possible.

Securities:

1. investment adviser who takes a position in a security before recommending it, then sells out after the price has risen as a result of the recommendation. *See also* INVESTMENT ADVISERS ACT.

2. market maker who, in violation of the RULES OF FAIR PRACTICE of the NAT-

IONAL ASSOCIATION OF SECURITIES DEALERS, adds an excessive markup or takes an excessive MARKDOWN on a transaction. *See also* FIVE PERCENT RULE.

3. commodity trader who trades for small gains, usually establishing and liquidating a position within one day.

SCHEDULE 13D form required under Section 13d of the SECURITIES ACT OF 1934 within ten business days of acquiring direct or BENEFICIAL OWNERSHIP of 5% or more of any class of equity securities in a PUBLICLY HELD corporation. In addition to filing with the Securities and Exchange Commission, the purchaser of such stock must also file the 13d with the stock exchange on which the shares are listed (if any) and with the company itself. Required information includes the way the shares were acquired, the purchaser's background, and future plans regarding the target company. The law is designed to protect against insidious TAKEOVER attempts and to keep the investing public aware of information that could affect the price of their stock. *See also* WILLIAMS ACT.

SCORCHED-EARTH POLICY technique used by a company that has become the target of a TAKEOVER attempt to make itself unattractive to the acquirer. For example, it may agree to sell off the most attractive parts of its business, called the CROWN JEWELS, or it may schedule all debt to become due immediately after a MERGER. *See also* POISON PILL; SHARK REPELLENT.

SCORE acronym for "Special Claim on Residual Equity," a certificate issued by the Americus Shareowner Service Corporation, a privately held company formed to market the product. A SCORE gives its holder the right to all the appreciation on an underlying security above a specified price, but none of the dividend income from the security. Its counterpart, called PRIME, passes all dividend income to its holders, who get the benefit of price appreciation up to the limit where SCORE begins. PRIME and SCORE together form a unit share investment trust (USIT), and both are listed on the New York Stock Exchange. A buyer of a SCORE unit is hoping that the underlying stock will rise steeply in value.

The first USIT was formed with the shares of American Telephone and Telegraph. PRIME holders got all dividends and price appreciation in AT&T up to $75 a share; SCORE holders received all appreciation above $75.

SCREEN (STOCKS) to look for stocks that meet certain predetermined investment and financial criteria. Often, stocks are screened using a computer and a data base containing financial statistics on thousands of companies. For instance, an investor may want to screen for all those companies that have a PRICE/EARNINGS RATIO of less than 10, an earnings growth rate of more than 15%, and a dividend yield of more than 4%.

SCRIP

In general: receipt, certificate, or other representation of value recognized by both payer and payee. Scrip is not currency, but may be convertible into currency.

Securities: temporary document that is issued by a corporation and that represents a fractional share of stock resulting from a SPLIT, exchange of stock, or SPIN-OFF. Scrip certificates may be aggregated or applied toward the purchase of full shares. Scrip dividends have historically been paid in lieu of cash dividends by companies short of cash.

SCRIPOPHILY practice of collecting stock and bond certificates for their scarcity value, rather than for their worth as securities. The certificate's price rises with the beauty of the illustration on it and the importance of the issuer in world finance and economic development. Many old certificates, such as those issued by railroads in the 19th century or by Standard Oil before it was broken up in the early 20th century, have risen greatly in value since their issue, even though the issuing companies no longer exist.

SDR *see* SPECIAL DRAWING RIGHTS.

SEASONALITY variations in business or economic activity that recur with regularity as the result of changes in climate, holidays, and vacations. The retail toy business, with its steep sales buildup between Thanksgiving and Christmas and pronounced dropoff thereafter, is an example of seasonality in a dramatic form, though nearly all businesses have some degree of seasonal variation. It is often necessary to make allowances for seasonality when interpreting or projecting financial or economic data, a process economists call *seasonal adjustment*.

SEASONED ISSUE securities (usually from established companies) that have gained a reputation for quality with the investing public and enjoy LIQUIDITY in the SECONDARY MARKET.

SEAT figurative term for a membership on a securities or commodities exchange. Seats are bought and sold at prices set by supply and demand. A seat on the New York Stock Exchange, for example, traded for more than $300,000 in the mid-1980s. *See also* ABC AGREEMENT; MEMBER FIRM.

SEC *see* SECURITIES AND EXCHANGE COMMISSION.

SECONDARY DISTRIBUTION public sale of previously issued securities held by large investors, usually corporations, institutions, or other AFFILIATED PERSONS, as distinguished from a NEW ISSUE or PRIMARY DISTRIBUTION, where the seller is the issuing corporation. As with a primary offering, secondaries are usually handled by INVESTMENT BANKERS, acting alone or as a syndicate, who purchase the shares from the seller at an agreed price, then resell them, sometimes with the help of a SELLING GROUP, at a higher PUBLIC OFFERING PRICE, making their profit on the difference, called the SPREAD. Since the offering is registered with the Securities and Exchange Commission, the syndicate manager can legally stabilize—or peg—the market price by bidding for shares in the open market. Buyers of securities offered this way pay no commissions, since all costs are borne by the selling investor. If the securities involved are listed, the CONSOLIDATED TAPE will announce the offering during the trading day, although the offering is not made until after the market's close. Among the historically large secondary distributions were the Ford Foundation's offering of Ford Motor Company stock in 1956 (approximately $658 million) handled by 7 firms under a joint management agreement and the sale of Howard Hughes' TWA shares ($566 million) through Merrill Lynch, Pierce, Fenner & Smith in 1966.

A similar form of secondary distribution, called the SPECIAL OFFERING, is limited to members of the New York Stock Exchange and is completed in the course of the trading day.

See also EXCHANGE DISTRIBUTION; REGISTERED SECONDARY OFFERING; SECURITIES AND EXCHANGE COMMISSION RULES 144 and 237.

SECONDARY MARKET

1. exchanges and over-the-counter markets where securities are bought and sold subsequent to original issuance, which took place in the PRIMARY MARKET. Proceeds of secondary market sales accrue to the selling dealers and investors, not to the companies that originally issued the securities.

2. market in which money-market instruments are traded among investors.

SECONDARY MORTGAGE MARKET buying, selling, and trading of existing mortgage loans and mortgage-backed securities. Original lenders are thus able to sell loans in their portfolios in order to build LIQUIDITY to support additional lending. Mortgages originated by lenders are purchased by government agencies (such as the FEDERAL HOME LOAN MORTGAGE CORPORATION, and the FEDERAL NATIONAL MORTGAGE ASSOCIATION) and by investment bankers. These agencies and bankers, in turn, create pools of mortgages, which they repackage as mortgage-backed securities, called PASS-THROUGH SECURITIES or PARTICIPATION CERTIFICATES, which are then sold to investors. The secondary mortgage market thus encompasses all activity beyond the PRIMARY MARKET, which is between the homebuyers and the originating mortgage lender.

SECONDARY OFFERING *see* SECONDARY DISTRIBUTION.

SECOND MORTGAGE LENDING advancing funds to a borrower that are secured by real estate previously pledged in a FIRST MORTGAGE loan. In the case of DEFAULT, the first mortgage has priority of claim over the second.

A variation on the second mortgage is the *home equity loan*, in which the loan is secured by independent appraisal of the property value. A home equity loan may also be in the form of a line of credit, which may be drawn down on by using a check or even a credit card. *See also* HOMEOWNER'S EQUITY ACCOUNT; RIGHT OF RESCISSION.

SECOND-PREFERRED STOCK preferred stock issue that ranks below another preferred issue in terms of priority of claim on dividends and on assets in liquidation. Second-preferred shares are often issued with a CONVERTIBLE feature or with a warrant to make them more attractive to investors. *See also* JUNIOR SECURITY; PREFERRED STOCK; PRIOR-PREFERRED STOCK; SUBSCRIPTION WARRANT.

SECOND ROUND intermediate stage of VENTURE CAPITAL financing, coming after the SEED MONEY (for START-UP) and *first round* stages and before the MEZZANINE LEVEL, when the company has matured to the point where it might consider a LEVERAGED BUYOUT by management or an INITIAL PUBLIC OFFERING (IPO).

SECTOR particular group of stocks, usually found in one industry. SECURITIES ANALYSTS often follow a particular sector of the stock market, such as airline or chemical stocks.

SECTOR FUND SPECIALIZED MUTUAL FUND that invests in one industry.

SECULAR long-term (10–50 years or more) as distinguished from seasonal or cyclical time frames.

SECURED BOND bond backed by the pledge of COLLATERAL, a MORTGAGE, or other LIEN. The exact nature of the security is spelled out in the INDENTURE. Secured bonds are distinguished from unsecured bonds, called DEBENTURES.

SECURED DEBT debt guaranteed by the pledge of assets or other COLLATERAL. *See also* ASSIGN; HYPOTHECATION.

SECURITIES ACT OF 1933 first law enacted by Congress to regulate the securities markets, approved May 26, 1933, as the Truth in Securities Act. It requires REGISTRATION of securities prior to public sale and adequate DISCLOSURE of pertinent financial and other data in a PROSPECTUS to permit informed analysis by potential investors. It also contains antifraud provisions prohibiting false representations and disclosures. Enforcement responsibilities were assigned to the SECURITIES AND EXCHANGE COMMISSION by the SECURITIES EXCHANGE ACT OF 1934. The 1933 act did not supplant BLUE SKY LAWS of the various states.

SECURITIES ACTS AMENDMENTS OF 1975 federal legislation enacted on June 4, 1975, to amend the SECURITIES EXCHANGE ACT OF 1934. The 1975 amendments directed the SECURITIES AND EXCHANGE COMMISSION to work with the industry toward establishing a NATIONAL MARKET SYSTEM together with a system for the nationwide clearance and settlement of securities transactions. Because of these provisions, the 1975 laws are sometimes called the *National Exchange Market System Act*. New regulations were also introduced to promote prompt and accurate securities handling, and clearing agencies were required to register with and report to the SEC. The 1975 amendments required TRANSFER AGENTS other than banks to register with the SEC and provided that authority with respect to bank transfer agents would be shared by the SEC and bank regulatory agencies. The Municipal Securities Rulemaking Board was created to regulate brokers, dealers, and banks dealing in municipal securities, with rules subject to SEC approval and enforcement shared by the NATIONAL ASSOCIATION OF SECURITIES DEALERS and bank regulatory agencies. The law also required the registration of broker-dealers in municipals, but preserved the exemption of issuers from REGISTRATION requirements. The amendments contained the prohibition of fixed commission rates, adopted earlier by the SEC in its Rule 19b-3.

SECURITIES ANALYST individual, usually employed by a stock brokerage house, bank, or investment institution, who performs investment research and examines the financial condition of a company or group of companies in an industry and in the context of the securities markets. Many analysts specialize in a single industry or SECTOR and make investment recommendations to buy, sell, or hold in that area. Among a corporation's financial indicators most closely followed by ANALYSTS are sales and earnings growth, CAPITAL STRUCTURE, stock price trend and PRICE/EARNINGS RATIO, DIVIDEND PAYOUTS, and RETURN ON INVESTED CAPITAL. Securities analysts promote corporate financial disclosure by sponsoring forums through local associations, the largest of which is the New York Society of Security Analysts, and through its national body, the Financial Analysts Federation. *See also* FORECASTING; FUNDAMENTAL ANALYSIS; QUALITATIVE ANALYSIS; QUANTITATIVE ANALYSIS; TECHNICAL ANALYSIS.

SECURITIES AND COMMODITIES EXCHANGES organized, national exchanges where securities, options, and futures contracts are traded by members for their own accounts and for the accounts of customers. The stock exchanges are registered with and regulated by the SECURITIES AND EXCHANGE COMMISSION (SEC); the commodities exchanges are registered with and regulated by the Commodity Futures Trading Commission (*see* REGULATED COMMODITIES); where options are also traded on an exchange, such activity is regulated by the SEC.

STOCKS, BONDS, SUBSCRIPTION RIGHTS, SUBSCRIPTION WARRANTS and in some cases OPTIONS are traded on nine STOCK EXCHANGES in the United States. The FUTURES MARKET is represented by 13 leading commodities exchanges.

Exchanges listing basic securities—stocks, bonds, rights, warrants and options on individual stocks—are described under the entries for New York Stock Exchange, American Stock Exchange, and regional stock exchanges. The exchanges listing commodity and other futures contracts and options in addition to those on individual stocks are:

American Stock Exchange (New York) *index options:* Computer Technology Index, Institutional Index, Major Market Index, Oil Index. *interest rate options:* U.S. Treasury bills, U.S. Treasury notes.

Amex Commodities Corporation (New York) *options:* gold bullion.

Chicago Board of Trade (Chicago) *futures:* corn, gold, Government National Mortgage Association mortgages, Major Market Index, Major Market Index "MAXI", Municipal Bond Index, NASDAQ-100 Index, oats, silver, soybeans, soybean meal, soybean oil, Treasury bonds, Treasury notes, wheat. *futures options:* corn, silver, soybeans, Treasury bonds, Treasury notes.

Chicago Board Options Exchange (Chicago) *foreign currency options:* British pound, Canadian dollar, Deutsche Mark, French franc, Japanese yen, Swiss franc. *index options:* Standard and Poor's 100 Index, Standard and Poor's 500 Index, Standard and Poor's Over The Counter 250 Index. *interest rate options:* U.S. Treasury bonds, U.S. Treasury notes.

Chicago Mercantile Exchange (Chicago) *futures:* feeder cattle, live cattle, live hogs, lumber, Over The Counter 250 Industrial Stock Price Index, pork bellies, Standard and Poor's 100 Index, Standard and Poor's 500 Index. *futures options:* British pound, Deutsche Mark, Eurodollars, live cattle, live hogs, Standard and Poor's 500 stock Index, Swiss franc.

Chicago Rice and Cotton Exchange (Chicago) *futures:* rough rice, short staple cotton.

Coffee, Sugar & Cocoa Exchange, Inc.* (New York) *futures:* cocoa, coffee, consumer price index-wages, sugar number 11, sugar number 14. *futures options:* cocoa, coffee, sugar.

Commodity Exchange, Inc. (COMEX)* (New York) *futures:* aluminum, copper, gold, silver. *futures options:* copper, gold, silver.

International Monetary Market at Chicago Mercantile Exchange (Chicago) *futures:* bank certificates of deposit, British pound, Canadian dollar, Deutsche Mark, Eurodollars, European Currency Units (ECUs), French franc, gold, Japanese yen, Swiss franc, U.S. Treasury bills.

Kansas City Board of Trade (Kansas City) *futures:* Value Line Maxi Index, Value Line Mini Index, wheat. *futures options:* wheat.

MidAmerica Commodity Exchange (Chicago) *futures:* British pound, Canadian dollar, copper, corn, Deutsche Mark, gold, Japanese yen, live cattle, live hogs, oats, platinum, silver, soybeans, soybean meal, Swiss franc, U.S. Treasury bills, U.S. Treasury bonds, wheat. *futures options:* gold, soybeans, wheat.

Minneapolis Grain Exchange (Minneapolis) *futures:* high fructose corn syrup, spring wheat, winter wheat. *futures options:* spring wheat.

National Association of Securities Dealers Quotation System (NASDAQ) *index option:* NASDAQ 100 index.

New York Cotton Exchange* (New York) *futures:* cotton, orange juice, propane. *futures options:* cotton, orange juice. **Finex** (a division of the Cotton Exchange): European Currency Unit futures, U.S. dollar futures, U.S. dollar futures options.

New York Futures Exchange (division of the New York Stock Exchange) (New York) *futures:* Commodity Research Bureau Futures Price Index, NYSE Composite Index. *futures options:* NYSE Composite Index.

New York Mercantile Exchange* (New York) *futures:* crude oil, gasoline (leaded and unleaded), no. 2 heating oil, palladium, platinum, potatoes. *futures options:* crude oil.

New York Stock Exchange (New York) *index options:* New York Stock Exchange Beta Index, New York Stock Exchange Options Index.

Pacific Stock Exchange (San Francisco) *index options:* Technology Index.

Philadelphia Stock Exchange (Philadelphia) *foreign currency futures:* Australian dollar, British pound, Canadian dollar, Deutsche Mark, European Currency Unit,

*These exchanges, though independent, share space and other facilities at 4 World Trade Center, in New York City, and are collectively called the Commodity Exchange Center.

French franc, Japanese yen, Swiss franc. *foreign currency options:* British pound, Canadian dollar, Deutsche Mark, European Currency Unit, French franc, Japanese yen, Swiss franc. *futures:* National Over-The-Counter Index Futures (Philadelphia Board of Trade). *index options:* Gold/Silver Index, National OTC Index, Value Line Composite Index. *interest rate options:* Eurodollar deposits, European Currency Units.

SECURITIES AND EXCHANGE COMMISSION (SEC) federal agency created by the SECURITIES EXCHANGE ACT OF 1934 to administer that act and the SECURITIES ACT OF 1933, formerly carried out by the FEDERAL TRADE COMMISSION. The SEC is made up of five commissioners, appointed by the President of the United States on a rotating basis for five-year terms. The chairman is designated by the President and, to insure its independence, no more than three members of the commission may be of the same political party. The statutes administered by the SEC are designed to promote full public DISCLOSURE and protect the investing public against malpractice in the securities markets. All issues of securities offered in interstate commerce or through the mails must be registered with the SEC; all national securities exchanges and associations are under its supervision, as are INVESTMENT COMPANIES, investment counselors and advisers, OVER THE COUNTER brokers and dealers, and virtually all other individuals and firms operating in the investment field. In addition to the 1933 and 1934 securities acts, responsibilities of the SEC include the PUBLIC UTILITY HOLDING COMPANY ACT of 1935, the TRUST INDENTURE ACT of 1939, the INVESTMENT COMPANY ACT of 1940 and the INVESTMENT ADVISERS ACT of 1940. It also administers the SECURITIES ACTS AMENDMENTS OF 1975, which directed the SEC to facilitate the establishment of a NATIONAL MARKET SYSTEM and a nationwide system for clearance and settlement of transactions and established the Municipal Securities Rulemaking Board, a self-regulatory organization whose rules are subject to SEC approval. *See also* SECURITIES AND EXCHANGE COMMISSION RULES.

SECURITIES AND EXCHANGE COMMISSION RULES The following are some of the more commonly encountered rules of the SEC. The list highlights the most prominent features of the rules and is not intended as a legal interpretation. The rules are listed in numerical order.

Rule 3b-3: Definition of Short Sale defines short sale as one in which the seller does not own the SECURITY sold or which is consummated by delivery of a borrowed security; ownership is defined in terms of securities, CONVERTIBLES, OPTIONS, and SUBSCRIPTION WARRANTS.

Rule 10a-1: Short sales known as the SHORT SALE RULE, prohibits a short sale of securities below the price of the last regular trade and at that price unless it was higher than the last different price preceding it. In determining the price at which a short sale can be made after a security goes EX-DIVIDEND, EX-RIGHTS, or ex- any other distribution, all sales prices prior to the ex- date may be reduced by the amount of the distribution.

Rule 10b-2: Solicitation of purchases on an exchange to facilitate distribution of securities prohibits parties concerned with a PRIMARY DISTRIBUTION or a SECONDARY DISTRIBUTION of a security from soliciting orders for the issue other than through the offering circular or formal PROSPECTUS.

Rule 10b-4: Short tendering of securities prohibits a SHORT TENDER—the sale of borrowed securities (as in SELLING SHORT) to a person making a TENDER OFFER.

Rule 10b-6: Prohibitions against trading by persons interested in a distribution rule that prohibits issuers, underwriters, broker-dealers, or others involved in a DISTRIBUTION of securities from buying the issue, or rights to it, during the distribution. The section permits transactions between the issuer and the underwriters and among the participating underwriters as required to carry out a distribution. The law extends to a repurchase by the issuer or to a purchase by participants in a new issue of CONVERTIBLE securities already on the market and convertible into the securities being offered.

Rule 10b-7: Stabilizing to effect a distribution provisions governing market STABILIZATION activities by issuers or underwriters in securities offerings.

Rule 10b-8: Distributions through rights prohibits market price MANIPULATION by interested parties in a RIGHTS OFFERING.

Rule 10b-10: Confirmation of transactions sets minimum information and disclosure requirements for the written confirmations of sales or purchases that broker-dealers send to clients, including disclosure of whether a firm is acting as AGENT (broker) or as PRINCIPAL (dealer).

Rule 10b-13: Other purchases during tender offer or exchange offer prohibits a person making a cash TENDER OFFER or an offer to exchange one EQUITY security for another from taking a position in the security being tendered or in a security CONVERTIBLE into the security being tendered until the tender offer or exchange offer expires.

Rule 10b-16: Credit terms in margin transactions terms and conditions concerning the interest charges on MARGIN loans to brokerage customers and the broker's disclosure responsibilities to borrowers.

Rule 11A: Floor trading regulations rules governing floor trading by exchange members, including those concerning PRIORITY and PRECEDENCE of transactions, transactions for the accounts of persons associated with members, HEDGE transactions, exchange bond trading, transactions by REGISTERED COMPETITIVE MARKET MAKERS and REGISTERED EQUITY MARKET MAKERS, and member transactions.

Rule 12b–1: *See* 12b-1 MUTUAL FUND.

Rule 13d: Acquisition of beneficial interest disclosures required by any person who directly or indirectly acquires a beneficial interest of 5% or more of any class of a registered equity security. *See also* WILLIAMS ACT.

Rule 13e: Repurchase of shares by issuers prohibits purchase by an issuer of its own shares during a TENDER OFFER for its shares and regulates GOING PRIVATE transactions by issuers or their affiliates.

Rule 14a: Solicitation of proxies sets forth the information and documentation required with PROXY materials distributed to shareholders of a public corporation.

Rule 14d: Tender offers regulations and restrictions covering public TENDER OFFERS and related disclosure requirements. *See also* WILLIAMS ACT.

Rule 15c2-1: Hypothecation of customers' securities regulates a broker-dealer's SAFEKEEPING of customers' securities in a MARGIN ACCOUNT, prohibiting the COMMINGLING of customers' accounts without the consent of the respective customers and the commingling of customers' accounts with the securities of non-customers, and limiting broker borrowings secured by customers' collateral to the aggregate amount of customers' indebtedness. *See also* HYPOTHECATION.

Rule 15c3-1: Net capital requirements for brokers or dealers covers NET CAPITAL REQUIREMENTS relative to the aggregate indebtedness of brokers and dealers of different types.

Rule 15c3-2: Customers' free credit balances requires a broker-dealer to notify customers with credit balances in their accounts that such balances may be withdrawn on demand.

Rule 15c3-3: Customer-protection reserves and custody of securities regulates the handling of customers' fully paid securities and excess MARGIN securities (security value in excess of MARGIN REQUIREMENTS) with broker-dealers. Fully paid securities must be segregated, and the broker must make weekly deposits to a Special Reserve Bank Account for the Exclusive Benefit of Customers.

Rule 17f-1: Missing, lost, counterfeit, or stolen securities requires exchanges, broker-dealers, clearing agencies, banks and transfer agents to report promptly to both the SEC and the appropriate law enforcement agency any knowledge of missing, lost, counterfeit, or stolen securities and to check with the SEC whenever a security comes into their possession to make sure it has not been reported at large.

Rule 19b-3: Prohibiting fixing of rates of commission by exchanges prohibits fixed commissions on stock exchange transactions pursuant to the SECURITIES ACT AMENDMENTS OF 1975.

Rule 19c-3: Off-board trading by exchange members permits securities listed on an exchange after April 26, 1979, to be traded off the exchange by member firms, a step toward an experimental NATIONAL MARKET SYSTEM in compliance with the SECURITIES ACT AMENDMENTS OF 1975.

Rule 144: Public sale of unregistered securities sets forth the conditions under which a holder of unregistered securities may make a public sale without filing a formal REGISTRATION STATEMENT. No LETTER SECURITY purchased through a PRIVATE PLACEMENT may be sold for at least two years after the date of purchase. Thereafter, during any three-month period, the following amounts may be sold: if listed securities, the greater of 1 % of the amount outstanding or the average trading volume within the preceding weeks; if unlisted, 1 % of outstandings. Securities may be sold only in broker's transactions.

Rule 145: Securities acquired in recapitalization persons who acquire securities as a result of reclassification, MERGER, consolidation, or transfer of corporate assets may sell such securities without REGISTRATION under stipulated conditions.

Rule 156: Mutual fund sales literature forbids false and misleading sales materials promoting INVESTMENT COMPANY securities.

Rule 237: Public sale of unregistered securities expanding on Rule 144, provides that five years after full payment for the purchase of privately placed securities, the lesser of $50,000 of such securities or 1% of the securities outstanding in a particular CLASS may be sold within a one year period.

Rule 254: Registration of small issues provides for simplified registration of small issues ($1.5 million or less in the mid-1980s) including a short-form REGISTRATION STATEMENT and PROSPECTUS. *See also* REGULATION A.

Rule 415: Shelf registration permits corporations to file a REGISTRATION for securities they intend to issue in the future when market conditions are favorable. *See also* SHELF REGISTRATION.

SECURITIES EXCHANGE ACT OF 1934 law governing the securities markets, enacted June 6, 1934. The act outlaws misrepresentation, MANIPULATION, and other abusive practices in the issuance of securities. It created the SECURITIES AND EXCHANGE COMMISSION (SEC) to enforce both the SECURITIES ACT OF 1933 and the Securities Exchange Act of 1934.

Principal requirements of the 1934 act are as follows:

1. REGISTRATION of all securities listed on stock exchanges, and periodic DISCLOSURES by issuers of financial status and changes in condition.
2. regular disclosures of holdings and transactions of "INSIDERS"—the officers and directors of a corporation and those who control at least 10% of equity securities.
3. solicitation of PROXIES enabling shareholders to vote for or against policy proposals.
4. registration with the SEC of stock exchanges and brokers and dealers to ensure their adherence to SEC rules through self-regulation.
5. surveillance by the SEC of trading practices on stock exchanges and over-the-

counter markets to minimize the possibility of insolvency among brokers and dealers.

6. regulation of MARGIN REQUIREMENTS for securities purchased on credit; the FEDERAL RESERVE BOARD sets those requirements.
7. SEC subpoena power in investigations of possible violations and in enforcement actions.

The SECURITIES ACT AMENDMENTS OF 1975 ratified the system of free-market determination of brokers' commissions and gave the SEC authority to oversee development of a NATIONAL MARKET SYSTEM.

SECURITIES INDUSTRY ASSOCIATION (SIA) trade group that represents
broker-dealers. The SIA lobbies for legislation affecting the brokerage industry. It also educates its members and the public about industry trends and keeps statistics on revenues and profits of brokers. The SIA represents only the segment of broker-dealers that sells taxable securities. Tax-exempt bond, government bond, and mortgage-backed security dealers are represented by the PUBLIC SECURITIES ASSOCIATION.

SECURITIES INDUSTRY AUTOMATION CORPORATION (SIAC) organization established in 1972 to provide communications and computer systems and services for the New York Stock Exchange (NYSE) and the American Stock Exchange (AMEX). It is two-thirds owned by NYSE and one-third owned by AMEX.

SECURITIES INVESTOR PROTECTION CORPORATION (SIPC) nonprofit corporation, established by Congress under the Securities Investors Protection Act of 1970, that insures the securities and cash in the customer accounts of member brokerage firms against the failure of those firms. All brokers and dealers registered with the Securities and Exchange Commission and with national stock exchanges are required to be members of SIPC. The Corporation acts similarly to the FEDERAL DEPOSIT INSURANCE CORPORATION (FDIC), which insures banks, and the FEDERAL SAVINGS AND LOAN INSURANCE CORPORATION (FSLIC), which insures savings and loans. When a brokerage firm fails, SIPC will first try to merge it into another brokerage firm. If this fails, SIPC will liquidate the firm's assets and pay off account holders up to an overall maximum of $500,000 per customer, with a limit of $100,000 on cash or cash equivalents. SIPC does not protect investors against market risk. See also SEPARATE CUSTOMER.

SECURITIES LOAN
1. loan of securities by one broker to another, usually to cover a customer's short sale. The lending broker is secured by the cash proceeds of the sale.
2. in a more general sense, loan collateralized by MARKETABLE SECURITIES. These would include all customer loans made to purchase or carry securities by broker-dealers under Federal Reserve Board REGULATION T margin rules, as well as by banks under REGULATION U and other lenders under REGULATION G. Loans made by banks to brokers to cover customers' positions are also collateralized by securities, but such loans are called *broker's loans* or *call loans. See also* HYPOTHECATION; LENDING AT A PREMIUM; LENDING AT A RATE; LENDING SECURITIES; REHYPOTHECATION; SELLING SHORT.

SECURITY
Finance: collateral offered by a debtor to a lender to secure a loan called *collateral security.* For instance, the security behind a mortgage loan is the real

estate being purchased with the proceeds of the loan. If the debt is not repaid, the lender may seize the security and resell it.

Personal security refers to one person or firm's GUARANTEE of another's primary obligation.

Investment: instrument that signifies an ownership position in a corporation (a stock), a creditor relationship with a corporation or governmental body (a bond), or rights to ownership such as those represented by an OPTION, SUBSCRIPTION RIGHT, and SUBSCRIPTION WARRANT.

SECURITY MARKET LINE relationship between the REQUIRED RATE OF RETURN on an investment and its SYSTEMATIC RISK.

SECURITY RATINGS evaluations of the credit and investment risk of securities issues by commercial RATING agencies.

SEED MONEY venture capitalist's first contribution toward the financing or capital requirements of a START-UP business. It frequently takes the form of a loan, often SUBORDINATED, or an investment in convertible bonds or preferred stock. Seed money provides the basis for additional capitalization to accommodate growth. *See also* MEZZANINE LEVEL; SECOND ROUND; VENTURE CAPITAL.

SEEK A MARKET to look for a buyer (if a seller) or a seller (if a buyer) of securities.

SEGREGATION OF SECURITIES Securities and Exchange Commission rules (8c and 15c2-1) designed to protect customers' securities used by broker-dealers to secure broker loans. Specifically, broker-dealers may not (1) commingle the securities of different customers without the written consent of each customer, (2) commingle a customer's securities with those of any person other than a bonafide customer, or (3) borrow more against customers' securities than the customers, in the aggregate, owe the broker-dealer against the same securities. *See also* COMMINGLING; HYPOTHECATION; REHYPOTHECATION; SECURITIES AND EXCHANGE COMMISSION RULE 15c2-1.

SELECTED DEALER AGREEMENT agreement governing the SELLING GROUP in a securities underwriting and distribution. *See also* UNDERWRITE.

SELF-DIRECTED IRA INDIVIDUAL RETIREMENT ACCOUNT (IRA) that can be actively managed by the account holder, who designates a CUSTODIAN to carry out investment instructions. The account is subject to the same conditions and early withdrawal limitations as a regular IRA. Investors who withdraw money from a qualified IRA plan have 60 days in which to roll over the funds to another plan before they become liable for tax penalties. Most corporate and U.S. government securities are eligible to be held by a self-directed IRA, as are limited partnerships, but collectibles and precious metals (art, gems, gold coins) are not.

SELF-REGULATORY ORGANIZATION (SRO) principal means contemplated by the federal securities laws for the enforcement of fair, ethical, and efficient practices in the securities and commodities futures industries. It is these organizations that are being referred to when "industry rules" are mentioned, as distinguished from the regulatory agencies such as the Securities and Exchange Commission or the Federal Reserve Board. The SROs include all the national SECURITIES AND COMMODITIES EXCHANGES as well as the NATIONAL ASSOCIATION OF SECURITIES DEALERS (NASD), which represents all the firms operating in the over-the-counter market, and the *Municipal Securities Rulemaking Board,* created under the Securities Acts Amendments of 1975 to regulate brokers, dealers and banks dealing in municipal securities. Rules made by the MSRB are subject to approval by the SEC and are enforced by the NASD and bank regulatory agencies.

SELF-SUPPORTING DEBT bonds sold for a project that will produce sufficient revenues to retire the debt. Such debt is usually issued by municipalities building a public structure (for example, a bridge or tunnel) that will be producing revenue through tolls or other charges. The bonds are not supported by the taxing power of the municipality issuing them. *See also* REVENUE BOND.

SELLER'S MARKET situation in which there is more demand for a security or product than there is available supply. As a result, the prices tend to be rising, and the sellers can set both the prices and the terms of sale. It contrasts with a buyer's market, characterized by excess supply, low prices, and terms suited to the buyer's desires.

SELLER'S OPTION securities transaction in which the seller, instead of making REGULAR WAY DELIVERY, is given the right to deliver the security to the purchaser on the date the seller's option expires or before, provided written notification of the seller's intention to deliver is given to the buyer one full business day prior to delivery. Seller's option deliveries are normally not made before 6 business days following the transaction or after 60 days.

SELLING CLIMAX sudden plunge in security prices as those who hold stocks or bonds panic and decide to dump their holdings all at once. Technical analysts see a climax as both a dramatic increase in volume and a sharp drop in prices on a chart. To these analysts, such a pattern usually means that a short-term rally will soon follow, since there are few sellers left after the climax. Sometimes, a selling climax can signal the bottom of a BEAR MARKET, meaning that after the climax the market will start to rise.

SELLING CLIMAX

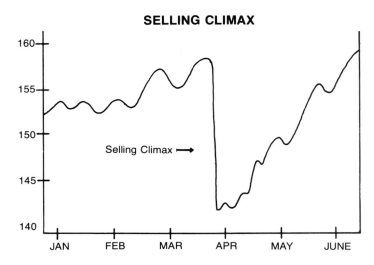

SELLING CONCESSION discount at which securities in a NEW ISSUE offering (or a SECONDARY DISTRIBUTION) are allocated to the members of a SELLING GROUP by the underwriters. Since the selling group cannot sell to the public at a price higher than the PUBLIC OFFERING PRICE, its compensation comes out of the difference between the price paid to the issuer by the underwriters and the public offering price, called the SPREAD. The selling group's portion, called the CONCESSION, is normally one half or more of the gross spread, expressed as a discount off the public offering price. *See also* FLOTATION COST; UNDERWRITE; UNDERWRITING SPREAD.

SELLING DIVIDENDS questionable practice by sales personnel dealing in MUTUAL FUNDS whereby a customer is induced to buy shares in a fund in order to get the benefit of a dividend scheduled in the near future. Since the dividend is already part of the NET ASSET VALUE of the fund and therefore part of the share price, the customer derives no real benefit.

SELLING, GENERAL, AND ADMINISTRATIVE (SG&A) EXPENSES grouping of expenses reported on a company's PROFIT AND LOSS STATEMENT between COST OF GOODS SOLD and INCOME DEDUCTIONS. Included are such items as salespersons' salaries and commissions, advertising and promotion, travel and entertainment, office payroll and expenses, and executives' salaries. SG&A expenses do not include such items as interest or amortization of INTANGIBLE ASSETS, which would be listed as income deductions. *See also* OPERATING PROFIT (OR LOSS).

SELLING GROUP group of dealers appointed by the syndicate manager of an UNDERWRITING GROUP, as AGENT for the other underwriters, to market a new or secondary issue to the public; also called *selling syndicate*. The selling group typically includes members of the underwriting group but varies in size with the size of the issue, sometimes running into several hundred dealers. The selling group is governed by the selling group agreement, also called the SELECTED DEALER AGREEMENT. It sets forth the terms of the relationship, establishes the commission (or SELLING CONCESSION, as it is called), and provides for the termination of the group, usually in 30 days. The selling group may or may not be obligated to purchase unsold shares. *See also* UNDERWRITE.

SELLING OFF selling securities or commodities under pressure to avoid further declines in prices. Technical analysts call such action a *sell-off*. *See also* DUMPING.

SELLING ON THE GOOD NEWS practice of selling a stock soon after a positive news development is announced. Most investors, cheered by the news of a successful new product or higher earnings, buy a stock because they think it will go higher; this pushes up the price. Someone selling on this good news believes that the stock will have reached its top price once all those encouraged by the development have bought the stock. Therefore, it is better to sell at this point than to wait for more good news or to be holding the stock if the next announcement is disappointing. *Compare with* BUYING ON THE BAD NEWS.

SELLING SHORT sale of a security or commodity futures contract not owned by the seller; a technique used (1) to take advantage of an anticipated decline in the price or (2) to protect a profit in a LONG POSITION (*see* SELLING SHORT AGAINST THE BOX).

An investor borrows stock certificates for delivery at the time of short sale. If the seller can buy that stock later at a lower price, a profit results; if the price rises, however, a loss results.

A commodity sold short represents a promise to deliver the commodity at a set price on a future date. Most commodity short sales are COVERED before the DELIVERY DATE.

Example of a short sale involving stock: An investor, anticipating a decline in the price of XYZ shares, instructs his or her broker to sell short 100 XYZ when XYZ is trading at $50. The broker then loans the investor 100 shares of XYZ, using either its own inventory, shares in the MARGIN ACCOUNT of another customer, or shares borrowed from another broker. These shares are used to make settlement with the buying broker within five days of the short sale transaction, and the proceeds are used to secure the loan. The investor now has what is known as a SHORT POSITION—that is, he or she still does not own the 100 XYZ and, at some point, must buy the shares to repay the lending broker. If the market price of XYZ drops to $40, the investor can buy the shares for $4000, repay the lending broker, thus covering the short sale, and claim a profit of $1000, or $10 a share.

Short selling is regulated by REGULATION T of the Federal Reserve Board. *See also* LENDING AT A RATE; LENDING AT A PREMIUM; LOANED FLAT; MARGIN REQUIREMENT; SHORT SALE RULE.

SELLING SHORT AGAINST THE BOX SELLING SHORT stock actually owned by the seller but held in SAFEKEEPING, called the BOX in Wall Street jargon. The motive for the practice, which assumes that the securities needed to COVER are borrowed as with any short sale, may be simply inaccessibility of the box or that the seller does not wish to disclose ownership. The main motive traditionally, however, has been to protect a CAPITAL GAIN in the shares that are owned, while deferring a LONG-TERM GAIN into another tax year. This practice had particular benefit when the tax rate on long-term gains was significantly lower than that on ORDINARY INCOME and a six-month HOLDING PERIOD was required to qualify. Under the TAX REFORM ACT of 1986, long-term capital gains rates for individuals rose to 28% in 1987 compared with a maximum ordinary income rate of 38.5% in that year. Beginning in 1988, capital gains and ordinary income become taxable at the same rates, eliminating the tax deferral motive for selling short against the box, except in extreme cases where taxpayers are moving from the 28% to the 15% bracket.

SELL OUT
1. liquidation of a MARGIN ACCOUNT by a broker after a MARGIN CALL has failed to produce additional equity to bring the margin to the required level. *See also* CLOSE A POSITION; MARGIN REQUIREMENT; MINIMUM MAINTENANCE.
2. action by a broker when a customer fails to pay for securities purchased and the securities received from the selling broker are sold to cover the transaction. Term also applies to commodities futures transactions.
3. expression used when all the securities in a NEW ISSUE underwriting have been distributed.

SELL PLUS sell order with instructions to execute only if the trading price in a security is higher than the last different preceding price. *See also* SHORT-SALE RULE.

SELL-STOP ORDER *see* STOP ORDER.

SELL THE BOOK order to a broker by the holder of a large quantity of shares of a security to sell all that can be ABSORBED at the current bid price. The term derives from the SPECIALIST'S BOOK—the record of all the buy and sell orders members have placed in the stock he or she handles. In this scenario, the buyers potentially include those in the specialist's book, the specialist for his or her own account, and the broker-dealer CROWD.

SENIOR DEBT loans or DEBT SECURITIES that have claim prior to junior obligations and EQUITY on a corporation's assets in the event of LIQUIDATION. Senior debt commonly includes funds borrowed from banks, insurance companies, or other financial institutions, as well as notes, bonds, or debentures not expressly defined as junior or subordinated.

SENIOR REFUNDING replacement of securities maturing in 5 to 12 years with issues having original maturities of 15 years or longer. The objectives may be to reduce the bond issuer's interest costs, to consolidate several issues into one, or to extend the maturity date.

SENIOR SECURITY security that has claim prior to a junior obligation and EQUITY on a corporation's assets and earnings. Senior securities are repaid before JUNIOR SECURITIES in the event of LIQUIDATION. Debt, including notes, bonds, and debentures, is senior to stock; first mortgage bonds are senior to second mortgage bonds; and all mortgage bonds are senior to debentures, which are unsecured.

SENSITIVE MARKET market easily swayed by good or bad news.

SENSITIVITY ANALYSIS study measuring the effect of a change in a variable (such as sales) on the risk or profitability of an investment.

SENTIMENT INDICATORS measures of the bullish or bearish mood of investors. Many technical analysts look at these indicators as contrary indicators—that is, when most investors are bullish, the market is about to drop, and when most are bearish, the market is about to rise. Some financial newsletters measure swings in investor sentiment by tabulating the number of INVESTMENT ADVISORY SERVICES that are bullish or bearish.

SEPARATE CUSTOMER concept used by the SECURITIES INVESTOR PROTECTION CORPORATION (SIPC) in allocating insurance coverage. If there is a difference in the way investment accounts are owned, each account is viewed as a separate customer entitled to the maximum protection; thus two accounts, one in the name of John Jones and the other in the name of John Jones and his wife Mary Jones, would be treated as separate accounts and separate persons. On the other hand, a CASH ACCOUNT, a MARGIN ACCOUNT, and a special convertible bond account all owned by John Jones are not treated as separate customer accounts but as one.

SERIAL BOND bond issue, usually of a municipality, with various MATURITY DATES scheduled at regular intervals until the entire issue is retired. Each bond certificate in the series has an indicated REDEMPTION DATE.

SERIES E BOND savings bond issued by the U.S. government from 1941 to 1979. The bonds were then replaced by Series EE and Series HH bonds. Outstanding Series E bonds, which may be exchanged for the newer varieties, will continue to pay interest for between 25 and 40 years from their issue date. Those issued from 1941 to 1952 accrue interest for 40 years; those issued in 1979, for 25 years. There is a sliding scale for Series E bonds issued between 1952 and 1979. Their interest is exempt from state and local taxes. *See also* SAVINGS BOND.

SERIES EE BOND *see* SAVINGS BOND.

SERIES HH BOND *see* SAVINGS BOND.

SERIES OF OPTION class of OPTION, either all CALL OPTIONS or all PUT OPTIONS, on the same underlying security, all of which have the same EXERCISE PRICE (strike price) and maturity date. For example, all XYZ May 50 calls would form a series of options.

SETTLE

In general: to pay an obligation.

Estates: distribution of an estate's assets by an executor to beneficiaries after all legal procedures have been completed.

Law: (1) to resolve a legal dispute short of adjudication; (2) to arrange for disposition of property, such as between spouses or between parents and children, if there has been a dispute such as a divorce.

Securities: to complete a securities trade between brokers acting as AGENTS or between a broker and his customer. A trade is settled when the customer has paid the broker for securities bought or when the customer delivers securities that have been sold and the customer receives the proceeds from the sale. *See also* CONTINUOUS NET SETTLEMENT.

SETTLEMENT DATE date by which an executed order must be settled, either by a buyer paying for the securities with cash or by a seller delivering the securities and receiving the proceeds of the sale for them. In a REGULAR-WAY DELIVERY of stocks and bonds, the settlement date is five business days after the trade was executed. For listed options and government securities, settlement is required by the next business day. *See also* SELLER'S OPTION.

SETTLOR person who creates an INTER VIVOS TRUST as distinguished from a TESTAMENTARY TRUST. Also called *donor, grantor*, or *trustor*.

SEVERALLY BUT NOT JOINTLY form of agreement used to establish the responsibility for selling a portion of the securities in an underwriting. UNDERWRITING GROUP members agree to buy a certain portion of an issue (severally) but do not agree to joint liability for shares not sold by other members of the syndicate. In a less common form of underwriting arrangement, called a *several and joint agreement*, syndicate members agree to sell not only the shares allocated to them, but also any shares not sold by the rest of the group. *See also* UNDERWRITE.

SG&A EXPENSES *see* SELLING, GENERAL, AND ADMINISTRATIVE EXPENSES.

SHADOW CALENDAR backlog of securities issues in REGISTRATION with the Securities and Exchange Commission for which no OFFERING DATE has been set pending clearance.

SHAKEOUT change in market conditions that results in the elimination of marginally financed participants in an industry. For example, if the market for microcomputers suddenly becomes glutted because there is more supply than demand, a shakeout will result, meaning that companies will fall by the wayside. In the securities markets, a shakeout occurs when speculators are forced by market events to sell their positions, usually at a loss.

SHARE

1. unit of equity ownership in a corporation. This ownership is represented by a stock certificate, which names the company and the shareowner. The number of shares a corporation is authorized to issue is detailed in its corporate charter. Corporations usually do not issue the full number of AUTHORIZED SHARES.
2. unit of ownership in a mutual fund. *See also* INVESTMENT COMPANY.

3. interest, normally represented by a certificate, in a general or LIMITED PARTNERSHIP.

SHARE BROKER DISCOUNT BROKER whose charges are based on the number of shares traded. The more shares in a trade, the lower the per-share cost will be. Trading with a share broker is usually advantageous for those trading at least 500 shares, or for those trading in high-priced shares, who would otherwise pay a percentage of the dollar amount. Those trading in small numbers of shares, or lower-priced ones, may pay lower commissions with a VALUE BROKER, the other kind of discount brokerage firm.

SHAREHOLDER
1. owner of one or more shares of STOCK in a corporation. A common shareholder is normally entitled to four basic rights of ownership: (1) claim on a share of the company's undivided assets in proportion to number of shares held; (2) proportionate voting power in the election of DIRECTORS and other business conducted at shareholder meetings or by PROXY; (3) DIVIDENDS when earned and declared by the BOARD OF DIRECTORS; and (4) PREEMPTIVE RIGHT to subscribe to additional stock offerings before they are available to the general public except when overruled by the ARTICLES OF INCORPORATION or in special circumstances, such as where stock is issued to effect a merger.
2. owner of one or more shares or units in a MUTUAL FUND. Mutual fund investors have voting rights similar to those of stock owners.

Shareholders' rights can vary according to the articles of incorporation or BYLAWS of the particular company.

See also PREFERRED STOCK.

SHAREHOLDER'S EQUITY total ASSETS minus total LIABILITIES of a corporation. Also called *stockholder's equity*, EQUITY, and NET WORTH.

SHARE REPURCHASE PLAN program by which a corporation buys back its own shares in the open market. It is usually done when shares are UNDERVALUED. Since it reduces the number of shares outstanding and thus increases EARNINGS PER SHARE, it tends to elevate the market value of the remaining shares held by stockholders. *See also* GOING PRIVATE; TREASURY STOCK.

SHARES AUTHORIZED number of shares of stock provided for in the ARTICLES OF INCORPORATION of a company. This figure is ordinarily indicated in the capital accounts section of a company's BALANCE SHEET and is usually well in excess of the shares ISSUED AND OUTSTANDING. A corporation cannot legally issue more shares than authorized. The number of authorized shares can be changed only by amendment to the corporate charter, with the approval of the shareholders. The most common reason for increasing authorized shares in a public company is to accommodate a stock SPLIT.

SHARES OUTSTANDING *see* ISSUED AND OUTSTANDING.

SHARK REPELLENT measure undertaken by a corporation to discourage unwanted TAKEOVER attempts. Also called *porcupine provision*. For example:
(1) fair price provision requiring a bidder to pay the same price to all shareholders. This raises the stakes and discourages TENDER OFFERS designed to attract only those shareholders most eager to replace management.
(2) GOLDEN PARACHUTE contract with top executives that makes it prohibitively expensive to get rid of existing management.
(3) defensive merger, in which a TARGET COMPANY combines with another or-

ganization that would create antitrust or other regulatory problems if the original, unwanted takeover proposal was consummated. *See also* SAFE HARBOR.

(4) STAGGERED BOARD OF DIRECTORS, a way to make it more difficult for a corporate RAIDER to install a majority of directors sympathetic to his or her views.

(5) supermajority provision, which might increase from a simple majority to two-thirds or three-fourths the shareholder vote required to ratify a takeover by an outsider.

See also POISON PILL; SCORCHED-EARTH POLICY.

SHARK WATCHER firm specializing in the early detection of TAKEOVER activity. Such a firm, whose primary business is usually the solicitation of proxies for client corporations, monitors trading patterns in a client's stock and attempts to determine the identity of parties accumulating shares.

SHELF REGISTRATION term used for SECURITIES AND EXCHANGE COMMISSION RULE 415 adopted in the 1980s, which allows a corporation to comply with REGISTRATION requirements up to two years prior to a PUBLIC OFFERING of securities. With the registration "on the shelf," the corporation, by simply updating regularly filed annual, quarterly, and related reports to the SEC, can go to the market as conditions become favorable with a minimum of administrative preparation. The flexibility corporate issuers enjoy as the result of shelf registration translates into substantial savings of time and expense.

SHELL CORPORATION company that is incorporated but has no significant assets or operations. Such corporations may be formed to obtain financing prior to starting operations, in which case an investment in them is highly risky. The term is also used of corporations set up by fraudulent operators as fronts to conceal tax evasion schemes.

SHERMAN ANTI-TRUST ACT OF 1890 *see* ANTITRUST LAWS.

SHOP
1. area of a business location where production takes place, as distinguished from the office or warehouse areas.
2. factory work force of an employer, as in a "union shop."
3. office of a broker-dealer in securities.
4. the act of canvassing dealers for the most favorable price, as in shopping securities dealers for the best bid or offer.
5. a small retail establishment.

SHORT AGAINST THE BOX *see* SELLING SHORT AGAINST THE BOX.

SHORT BOND
1. bond with a short maturity; a somewhat subjective concept, but generally meaning two years or less. *See also* SHORT TERM.
2. bond repayable in one year or less and thus classified as a CURRENT LIABILITY in accordance with the accounting definition of SHORT-TERM DEBT.
3. SHORT COUPON bond.

SHORT COUPON
1. bond interest payment covering less than the conventional six-month period. A short coupon payment occurs when the original issue date is less than a half year from the first scheduled interest payment date. Depending on how short the coupon is, the ACCRUED INTEREST makes a difference in the value of the

bond at the time of issue, which is reflected in the offering price.
2. bond with a relatively short maturity, usually two years or less.
    See also LONG COUPON.

SHORT COVERING actual purchase of securities by a short seller to replace those borrowed at the time of a short sale. *See also* LENDING SECURITIES; SELLING SHORT.

SHORT HEDGE transaction that limits or eliminates the risk of declining value in a security or commodity without entailing ownership. Examples:
(1) SELLING SHORT AGAINST THE BOX leaves the owned securities untouched, possibly to gain in value, while protecting against a decline in value, since that would be offset by a profit on the short sale.
(2) purchasing a PUT OPTION to protect the value of a security that is owned limits loss to the cost of the option.
(3) buying a futures contract on raw materials at a specific price protects a manufacturer committed to sell a product at a certain price at a specified future time but who cannot buy the raw materials at the time of the commitment. Thus, if the price of the materials goes up, the manufacturer makes a profit on the contract; if the price goes down, he or she makes a profit on the product.
    Compare with LONG HEDGE.

SHORT INTEREST total amount of shares of stock that have been sold short and have not yet been repurchased to close out SHORT POSITIONS. The short interest figure for the New York Stock Exchange, which is published monthly in newspapers, indicates how many investors think stock prices are about to fall. The Exchange reports all issues in which there are at least 5000 shares sold short, and in which the short interest position had changed by at least 2000 shares in the preceding month. The higher the short interest, the more people are expecting a downturn. Such short interest also represents potential buying pressure, however, since all short sales must eventually be covered by the purchase of shares. For this reason, a high short interest position is viewed as a bullish sign by many sophisticated market watchers. *See also* SELLING SHORT; SHORT INTEREST THEORY.

SHORT INTEREST THEORY theory that a large SHORT INTEREST in a stock presages a rise in the market price. It is based on the reasoning that even though short selling reflects a belief that prices will decline, the fact that short positions must eventually be covered is a source of upward price pressure. It is also called the CUSHION THEORY, since short sales can be viewed as a cushion of imminent buy orders. *See also* MEMBERS' SHORT-SALE RATIO; ODD-LOT SHORT-SALE RATIO; SELLING SHORT; SPECIALIST'S SHORT-SALE RATIO.

SHORT POSITION
Commodities: contract in which a trader has agreed to sell a commodity at a future date for a specific price.
Stocks: stock shares that an individual has sold short (by delivery of borrowed certificates) and has not covered as of a particular date.
    See also COVER; SELLING SHORT.

SHORT SALE *see* SELLING SHORT.

SHORT-SALE RULE Securities and Exchange Commission rule requiring that short sales be made only in a rising market; also called PLUS TICK rule. A short sale can be transacted only under these conditions: (1) if the last sale was at a higher price than the sale preceding it (called an UPTICK OR PLUS TICK); (2) if the last sale price is unchanged but higher than the last preceding different sale (called a ZERO-PLUS TICK). The short sale rule was designed to prevent abuses perpetuated by so-called pool operators, who would drive down the price of a stock by heavy short selling, then pick up the shares for a large profit.

SHORT SQUEEZE situation when prices of a stock or commodity futures contract start to move up sharply and many traders with short positions are forced to buy stocks or commodities in order to COVER their positions and prevent losses. This sudden surge of buying leads to even higher prices, further aggravating the losses of short sellers who have not covered their positions. *See also* SELLING SHORT.

SHORT TENDER using borrowed stock to respond to a TENDER OFFER. The practice is prohibited by SECURITIES AND EXCHANGE COMMISSION RULE 10b-4.

SHORT TERM

Accounting: assets expected to be converted into cash within the normal operating cycle (usually one year), or liabilities coming due in one year or less. *See also* CURRENT ASSETS; CURRENT LIABILITY.

Investment: investment with a maturity of one year or less. This includes bonds, although in differentiating between short-, medium-, and long-term bonds short term often is stretched to mean two years or less. *See also* SHORT BOND; SHORT-TERM DEBT; SHORT-TERM GAIN OR LOSS.

Taxes: HOLDING PERIOD of six months or less, used to differentiate SHORT-TERM GAIN OR LOSS from LONG TERM GAIN and LONG TERM LOSS until the TAX REFORM ACT OF 1986 eliminated the short/long distinction in 1988.

SHORT-TERM DEBT all debt obligations coming due within one year; shown on a balance sheet as current liabilities. *See also* CURRENT LIABILITY.

SHORT-TERM GAIN OR LOSS for tax purposes, the profit or loss realized from the sale of securities or other capital assets held six months or less. Short term gains are taxable at ordinary income rates to the extent they are not reduced by offsetting short term losses. *See also* CAPITAL GAIN; CAPITAL LOSS.

SIDE-BY-SIDE TRADING trading of a security and an OPTION on that security on the same exchange.

SIDEWAYS MARKET period in which prices trade within a narrow range, showing only small changes up or down. Also called HORIZONTAL PRICE MOVEMENT. *See also* FLAT MARKET.

SILENT PARTNER
1. limited partner in a DIRECT PARTICIPATION PROGRAM, such as real estate and oil and gas limited partnerships, in which CASH FLOW and tax benefits are passed directly through to shareholders. Such partners are called silent because, unlike general partners, they have no direct role in management and no liability beyond their individual investment.
2. general partner in a business who has no role in management but represents a sharing of the investment and liability. Silent partners of this type are often found in family businesses, where the intent is to distribute tax liability. *See also* LIMITED PARTNERSHIP.

SILVER THURSDAY the day—March 27, 1980—when the extremely wealthy Hunt brothers of Texas failed to meet a MARGIN CALL by the brokerage firm of Bache Halsey Stuart Shields (which later became Prudential-Bache Securities) for $100 million in silver futures contracts. Their position was later covered and Bache survived, but the effects on the commodities markets and the financial markets in general were traumatic.

SIMPLE INTEREST interest calculation based only on the original principal amount. Simple interest contrasts with COMPOUND INTEREST, which is applied to principal plus accumulated interest. For example, $100 on deposit at 12% simple interest would yield $12 per year (12% of $100). For computing interest on loans, simple interest is distinguished from various methods of calculating interest on a pre-computed basis. *See also* PRECOMPUTE; CONSUMER CREDIT PROTECTION ACT OF 1968.

SIMPLIFIED EMPLOYEE PENSION (SEP) PLAN pension plan in which both the employee and the employer contribute to an INDIVIDUAL RETIREMENT ACCOUNT (IRA). Under the TAX REFORM ACT OF 1986, employees (except those participating in SEPs of state or local governments) may elect to have employer contributions made to the SEP or paid to the employee in cash as with cash or deferred arrangements [401(K) PLANS]. Elective contributions, which are excludable from earnings for income tax purposes but includable for employment tax (FICA and FUTA) purposes, are limited to $7000, while employer contributions may not exceed $30,000. SEPs are limited to small employers (25 or fewer employees) and at least 50% of employees must participate. Special provisions concern the integration of SEP contributions and Social Security benefits and limit tax deferrals for highly compensated individuals.

SINGLE OPTION term used to distinguish a PUT OPTION or a CALL OPTION from a SPREAD or a STRADDLE, each of which involves two or more put or call options. *See also* OPTION.

SINGLE-PREMIUM DEFERRED ANNUITY (SPDA) tax-deferred investment similar to an INDIVIDUAL RETIREMENT ACCOUNT, without many of the IRA restrictions. An investor makes a lump-sum payment to an insurance company selling the annuity. That lump sum can be invested in either a fixed-return instrument like a CD or a variable-return portfolio that can be switched among stocks, bonds, and money-market accounts. Proceeds are taxed only when distributions are taken. In contrast to an IRA, there is no limit to the amount that may be invested in an SPDA. Like the IRA, the tax penalty for withdrawals before age 59½ is 10%.

SINGLE-PREMIUM LIFE INSURANCE WHOLE LIFE INSURANCE policy requiring one premium payment. Since this large, up-front payment begins accumulating cash value immediately, the policy holder will earn more than holders of policies paid up in installments. With its tax-free appreciation (assuming it remains in force); low or no net-cost; tax-free access to funds through POLICY LOANS; and tax-free proceeds to beneficiaries, this type of policy emerged as a popular TAX SHELTER under the TAX REFORM ACT OF 1986.

SINGLE-STATE MUNICIPAL BOND FUND MUTUAL FUND that invests entirely in tax-exempt obligations of governments and government agencies within a single state. Therefore, dividends paid on fund shares are not taxable to residents of that state when they file state tax returns, although capital gains, if any, are taxable (at ORDINARY INCOME rates starting in 1988).

SINKER industry term for a bond with a SINKING FUND.

SINKING FUND money accumulated on a regular basis in a separate custodial account that is used to redeem debt securities or preferred stock issues. A bond indenture or preferred stock charter may specify that payments be made to a sinking fund, thus assuring investors that the issues are safer than bonds (or preferred stocks) for which the issuer must make payment all at once, without the benefit of a sinking fund. *See also* PURCHASE FUND.

SIZE

1. number of shares or bonds available for sale. A market maker will say, when asked for a quote, that a particular number of shares (the size) is available at a particular price.
2. term used when a large number of shares are for sale—a trader will say that "shares are available in size," for instance.

SKIP-PAYMENT PRIVILEGE

1. clause in some MORTGAGE contracts and installment loan agreements that allows the borrower to miss a payment if payments are ahead of schedule.
2. option offered to bank credit-card holders meeting certain requirements whereby they may defer the December payment on balances due.

SLD LAST SALE indication, meaning "sold last sale," that appears on the CONSOLIDATED TAPE when a greater than normal change occurs between transactions in a security. The designation, which appears after the STOCK SYMBOL, is normally used when the change is a point or more on lower-priced issues (below $20) or two points or more on higher-priced issues.

SLEEPER stock in which there is little investor interest but which has significant potential to gain in price once its attractions are recognized. Sleepers are most easily recognized in retrospect, after they have already moved up in price.

SLEEPING BEAUTY potential TAKEOVER target that has not yet been approached by an acquirer. Such a company usually has particularly attractive features, such as a large amount of cash, or undervalued real estate or other assets.

SMALL BUSINESS ADMINISTRATION (SBA) federal agency created in 1953 to provide financial assistance (through direct loans and loan guarantees) as well as management assistance to businesses that lack the access to CAPITAL MARKETS enjoyed by larger more creditworthy corporations. Further legislation authorized the SBA to contribute to the VENTURE CAPITAL requirements of START-UP companies by licensing and funding small business investment companies (SBICs), to maintain a loan fund for rehabilitation of property damaged by natural disasters, and to provide loans, counseling and training for small businesses owned by minorities, the economically disadvantaged, and the disabled. The SBA finances its activities through direct grants approved by Congress.

SMALL INVESTOR individual investor who buys small amounts of stock or bonds, often in ODD LOT quantities; also called the RETAIL INVESTOR. Although there are millions of small investors, their total holdings are dwarfed by the share ownership of large institutions such as mutual funds and insurance companies. Together with the proliferation of mutual funds, recent developments in the brokerage industry and its diversification along full-service lines have brought new programs specifically designed to make investing more convenient for small investors. Thus, much cash traditionally kept in savings banks has found its way into the stock and bond markets. *See also* ODD-LOT SHORT-SALE RATIO; ODD-LOT THEORY.

SNOWBALLING process by which the activation of STOP ORDERS in a declining or advancing market causes further downward or upward pressure on prices, thus triggering more stop orders and more price pressure, and so on.

SOCIAL CONSCIOUSNESS MUTUAL FUND mutual fund that is managed for capital appreciation while at the same time investing in securities of companies that do not conflict with certain social priorities. As a product of the social consciousness movements of the 1960s and 1970s, this type of mutual fund might not invest in companies that derive significant profits from defense contracts or whose activities cause environmental pollution, nor in companies with significant interests in countries with repressive or racist governments.

SOFT CURRENCY funds of a country that are not acceptable in exchange for the hard currencies of other countries. Soft currencies, such as the Soviet Union's ruble, are fixed at unrealistic exchange rates and are not backed by gold, so that countries with hard currencies, like U.S. dollars or British pounds, are reluctant to convert assets into them. *See also* HARD MONEY (HARD CURRENCY).

SOFT DOLLARS means of paying brokerage firms for their services through commission revenue, rather than through direct payments, known as *hard-dollar fees*. For example, a mutual fund may offer to pay for the research of a brokerage firm by executing trades generated by that research through that brokerage firm. The broker might agree to this arrangement if the fund manager promises to spend at least $100,000 in commissions with the broker that year. Otherwise, the fund would have to pay a hard-dollar fee of $50,000 for the research. *Compare with* HARD DOLLARS.

SOFT MARKET market characterized by an excess of supply over demand. A soft market in securities is marked by inactive trading, wide bid-offer spreads, and pronounced price drops in response to minimal selling pressure. Also called *buyer's market*.

SOFT SPOT weakness in selected stocks or stock groups in the face of a generally strong and advancing market.

SOLD-OUT MARKET commodities market term meaning that futures contracts in a particular commodity or maturity range are largely unavailable because of contract liquidations and limited offerings.

SOLVENCY state of being able to meet maturing obligations as they come due. *See also* INSOLVENCY.

SOURCE AND APPLICATIONS OF FUNDS STATEMENT analysis of changes in the FINANCIAL POSITION of a firm from one accounting period to another; also called *sources and uses of funds statement*. It is usually presented as part of a complete FINANCIAL STATEMENT and appears in the ANNUAL REPORTS of publicly held companies. It consists of two parts: (1) *sources of funds* summarizes the transactions that increased WORKING CAPITAL, such as NET INCOME, DEPRECIATION, the issue of bonds, the sale of stock, or an increase in deferred taxes; (2) *applications of funds* summarizes the way funds were used, such as the purchase or improvement of plant and equipment, the payment of dividends, the repayment of long-term debt, or the redemption or repurchase of shares.

SOVEREIGN RISK risk that a foreign government will default on its loan or fail to honor other business commitments because of a change in national policy. A country asserting its prerogatives as an independent nation might prevent the REPATRIATION of a company or country's funds through limits on the flow of capital, tax impediments, or the nationalization of property. Sovereign risk became a factor in the growth of international debt that followed the oil price increases of the 1970s. Several developing countries that borrowed heavily from Western banks to finance trade deficits had difficulty later keeping to repayment schedules. Banks had to reschedule loans to such countries as Mexico and Argentina to keep them from defaulting. These loans ran the further risk of renunciation by political leaders, which also would have affected loans to private companies that had been guaranteed by previous governments. Beginning in the 1970s, banks and other multinational corporations developed sophisticated analytical tools to measure sovereign risk before committing to lend, invest, or begin operations in a given foreign country. Throughout periods of worldwide economic volatility, the United States has been able to attract foreign investment because of its perceived lack of sovereign risk. Also called *country risk* or *political risk.*

SPECIAL ARBITRAGE ACCOUNT special MARGIN ACCOUNT with a broker reserved for transactions in which the customer's risk is hedged by an offsetting security transaction or position. The MARGIN REQUIREMENT on such a transaction is substantially less than in the case of stocks bought on credit and subject to price declines. *See also* HEDGE/HEDGING.

SPECIAL ASSESSMENT BOND municipal bond that is repaid from taxes imposed on those who benefit directly from the neighborhood-oriented public works project funded by the bond; also called *special assessment limited liability bond, special district bond, special purpose bond,* SPECIAL TAX BOND. For example, if a bond finances the construction of a sewer system, the homeowners and businesses hooked up to the sewer system pay a special levy that goes to repay the bonds. The interest from special assessment bonds is tax free to resident bondholders. These are not normally GENERAL OBLIGATION BONDS, and the FULL FAITH AND CREDIT of the municipality is not usually behind them. Where the full faith and credit does back such bonds, they are called general obligation special assessment bonds.

SPECIAL BID infrequently used method of purchasing a large block of stock on the New York Stock Exchange whereby a MEMBER FIRM, acting as a broker, matches the buy order of one client, usually an institution, with sell orders solicited from a number of other customers. It is the reverse of an EXCHANGE DISTRIBUTION. The member broker makes a fixed price offer, which is announced in advance on the CONSOLIDATED TAPE. The bid cannot be lower than the last sale or the current regular market bid. Sellers of the stock pay no commissions; the buying customer pays both the selling and buying commissions. The transaction is completed during regular trading hours.

SPECIAL BOND ACCOUNT special MARGIN ACCOUNT with a broker that is reserved for transactions in U.S. government bonds, municipals, and eligible listed and unlisted nonconvertible corporate bonds. The restrictions under which brokers may extend credit with margin securities of these types are generally more liberal than in the case of stocks.

SPECIAL CASH ACCOUNT same as CASH ACCOUNT.

SPECIAL DISTRICT BOND *see* SPECIAL ASSESSMENT BOND.

SPECIAL DRAWING RIGHTS (SDR) measure of a nation's reserve assets in the international monetary system; known informally as "paper gold." First issued by the INTERNATIONAL MONETARY FUND (IMF) in 1970, SDRs are designed to supplement the reserves of gold and convertible currencies (or hard currencies) used to maintain stability in the foreign exchange market. For example, if the U.S. Treasury sees that the British pound's value has fallen precipitously in relation to the dollar, it can use its store of SDRs to buy excess pounds on the foreign exchange market, thereby raising the value of the remaining supply of pounds.

This neutral unit of account was made necessary by the rapid growth in world trade during the 1960s. International monetary officials feared that the supply of the two principal reserve assets—gold and U.S. dollars—would fall short of demand, causing the value of the U.S. currency to rise disproportionately in relation to other reserve assets. (At the time SDRs were introduced, the price of gold was fixed at about $35 per ounce.)

The IMF allocates to each of its more than 140 member countries an amount of SDRs proportional to its predetermined quota in the fund, which in turn is based on its GROSS NATIONAL PRODUCT (GNP). Each member agrees to back its SDRs with the full faith and credit of its government, and to accept them in exchange for gold or convertible currencies.

Originally, the value of one SDR was fixed at one dollar and at the dollar equivalent of other key currencies on January 1, 1970. As world governments adopted the current system of FLOATING EXCHANGE RATES, the SDR's value fluctuated relative to the "basket" of major currencies. Increasing reliance on SDRs in settling international accounts coincided with a decline in the importance of gold as a reserve asset.

Because of its inherent equilibrium relative to any one currency, the SDR has been used to denominate or calculate the value of private contracts, international treaties, and securities on the EUROBOND market.

SPECIALIST member of a stock exchange who maintains a fair and orderly market in one or more securities. A specialist or SPECIALIST UNIT performs two main functions: executing LIMIT ORDERS on behalf of other exchange members for a portion of the FLOOR BROKER's commission, and buying or selling—sometimes SELLING SHORT—for the specialist's own account to counteract temporary imbalances in supply and demand and thus prevent wide swings in stock prices. The specialist is prohibited by exchange rules from buying for his own account when there is an unexecuted order for the same security at the same price in the SPECIALIST'S BOOK, the record kept of limit orders in each price category in the sequence in which they are received. Specialists must meet strict minimum capital requirements before receiving formal approval by the New York Stock Exchange. *See also* SPECIALIST BLOCK PURCHASE AND SALE; SPECIALIST'S SHORT SALE RATIO.

SPECIALIST BLOCK PURCHASE AND SALE transaction whereby a SPECIALIST on a stock exchange buys a large block of securities either to sell for his own account or to try and place with another block buyer and seller, such as a FLOOR TRADER. Exchange rules require that such transactions be executed only when the securities cannot be ABSORBED in the regular market. *See also* NOT HELD.

SPECIALIST'S BOOK record maintained by a SPECIALIST that includes the specialist's own inventory of securities, market orders to sell short, and LIMIT ORDERS and STOP ORDERS that other stock exchange members have placed with the specialist. The orders are listed in chronological sequence. For example, for a stock trading at 57 a broker might ask for 500 shares when the price falls to 55. If successful at placing this limit order, the specialist notifies the member broker who entered the request, and collects a commission. The specialist is prohibited from buying the stock for his own account at a price for which he has previously agreed to execute a limit order.

SPECIALIST'S SHORT-SALE RATIO ratio of the amount of stock sold short by specialists on the floor of the New York Stock Exchange to total short sales. The ratio signals whether specialists are more or less bearish (expecting prices to decline) on the outlook for stock prices than other NYSE members and the public. Since specialists must constantly be selling stock short in order to provide for an orderly market in the stocks they trade, their short sales cannot be entirely regarded as an indication of how they perceive trends. Still, their overall short sales activity reflects knowledge, and technical analysts watch the specialist's short-sale ratio carefully for a clue to imminent upturns or downturns in stock prices. Traditionally, when the ratio rises above 60%, it is considered a bearish signal. A drop below 45% is seen as bullish and below 35% is considered extremely bullish. *See also* ODD-LOT SHORT-SALE RATIO; SELLING SHORT; SPECIALIST.

SPECIALIST UNIT stock exchange SPECIALIST (individual, partnership, corporation, or group of two or three firms) authorized by an exchange to deal as PRINCIPAL and AGENT for other brokers in maintaining a stable market in one or more particular stocks. A specialist unit on the New York Stock Exchange is required to have enough capital to buy at least 5000 shares of the common stock of a company it handles and 1000 shares of the company's CONVERTIBLE preferred stock.

SPECIALIZED MUTUAL FUND fund that limits its investments to a particular sector of the marketplace—for example, the energy industry or the health care-related field. In some mutual fund groups, there is a PORTFOLIO of specialized funds for shareholders to choose from, so that when one area no longer looks promising, they can shift assets into another area. For example, investors may want to sell their shares in an interest-sensitive financial services fund and reinvest the proceeds in a defense-stock fund if they think interest rates are about to rise and defense spending is about to increase dramatically.

SPECIAL MISCELLANEOUS ACCOUNT (SMA) memorandum account of the funds in excess of the MARGIN REQUIREMENT. Such excess funds may arise from the proceeds of sales, appreciation of market values, dividends, or cash or securities put up in response to a MARGIN CALL. An SMA is not under the jurisdiction of REGULATION T of the Federal Reserve Board, as is the INITIAL MARGIN requirement, but this does not mean the customer is free to withdraw balances from it. The account is maintained essentially so that the broker can gauge how far the customer might be from a margin call. Any withdrawals require the broker's permission.

SPECIAL OFFERING method of selling a large block of stock that is similar to a SECONDARY DISTRIBUTION but is limited to New York Stock Exchange members and takes place during normal trading hours. The selling member announces the impending sale on the CONSOLIDATED TAPE, indicating a fixed price, which is usually based on the last transaction price in the regular market. All costs and commissions are borne by the seller. The buyers are member firms that may be buying for customer accounts or for their own inventory. Such offerings must have approval from the Securities and Exchange Commission.

SPECIAL SITUATION

1. undervalued stock that should soon rise in value because of an imminent favorable turn of events. A special situation stock may be about to introduce a revolutionary new product or be undergoing a needed management change. Many securities analysts concentrate on looking for and analyzing special situation stocks.
2. stock that fluctuates widely in daily trading, often influencing market averages, because of a particular news development, such as the announcement of a TAKEOVER bid.

SPECIAL TAX BOND

1. MUNICIPAL REVENUE BOND that will be repaid through excise taxes on such purchases as gasoline, tobacco, and liquor. The bond is not backed by the ordinary taxing power of the municipality issuing it. The interest from these bonds is tax free to resident bondholders.
2. SPECIAL ASSESSMENT BOND.

SPECTAIL term for broker-dealer who is part retail broker but preponderantly dealer/speculator.

SPECULATION assumption of risk in anticipation of gain but recognizing a higher than average possibility of loss. Speculation is a necessary and productive activity. It can be profitable over the long term when engaged in by professionals, who often limit their losses through the use of various HEDGING techniques and devices, including OPTIONS trading, SELLING SHORT, STOP LOSS ORDERS, and transactions in FUTURES CONTRACTS. The term speculation implies that a business or investment risk can be analyzed and measured, and its distinction from the term INVESTMENT is one of degree of risk. It differs from gambling, which is based on random outcomes.

See also VENTURE CAPITAL.

SPIN-OFF form of corporate DIVESTITURE that results in a subsidiary or division becoming an independent company. In a traditional spin-off, shares in the new entity are distributed to the parent corporation's shareholders of record on a PRO RATA basis. Spin-offs can also be accomplished through a LEVERAGED BUYOUT by the subsidiary or division's management, or through an EMPLOYEE STOCK OWNERSHIP PLAN (ESOP).

SPLIT increase in a corporation's number of outstanding shares of stock without any change in the shareholders' EQUITY or the aggregate MARKET VALUE at the time of the split. In a split, also called a *split up*, the share price declines. If a stock at $100 par value splits 2-for-1, the number of authorized shares doubles (for example, from 10 million to 20 million) and the price per share drops by half, to $50. A holder of 50 shares before the split now has 100 shares at the lower price. If the same stock splits 4-for-1, the number of shares quadruples to 40 million and the share price falls to $25. Dividends per share also fall proportionately. Directors of a corporation will authorize a split to make ownership more affordable to a broader base of investors. Where stock splits require an increase in AUTHORIZED SHARES and/or a change in PAR VALUE of the stock, shareholders must approve an amendment of the corporate charter.

See also REVERSE SPLIT.

SPLIT COMMISSION commission divided between the securities broker who executes a trade and another person who brought the trade to the broker, such as an investment counselor or financial planner. Split commissions between brokers are also common in real estate transactions.

SPLIT DOWN *see* REVERSE SPLIT.

SPLIT OFFERING new municipal bond issue, part of which is represented by SERIAL BONDS and part by term maturity bonds.

SPLIT ORDER large transaction in securities that, to avoid unsettling the market and causing fluctuations in the market price, is broken down into smaller portions to be executed over a period of time.

SPLIT RATING situation in which two major rating agencies, such as Standard & Poor's and Moody's Investors Service, assign a different rating to the same security.

SPLIT UP *see* SPLIT.

SPONSOR

Limited partnerships: GENERAL PARTNER who organizes and sells a LIMITED PARTNERSHIP. Sponsors (also called *promoters*) rely on their reputation in past real estate, oil and gas, or other deals to attract limited partners to their new deals.

Mutual funds: investment company that offers shares in its funds. Also called the *underwriter*.

Stocks: important investor—typically, an institution, mutual fund, or other big trader—whose favorable opinion of a particular security influences other investors and creates additional demand for the security. Institutional investors often want to make sure a stock has wide sponsorship before they invest in it, since this should ensure that the stock will not fall dramatically.

SPOT COMMODITY COMMODITY traded with the expectation that it will actually be delivered to the buyer, as contrasted to a FUTURES CONTRACT that will usually expire without any physical delivery taking place. Spot commodities are traded in the SPOT MARKET.

SPOT DELIVERY MONTH nearest month of those currently being traded in which a commodity could be delivered. In late January, therefore, the spot delivery month would be February for commodities with a February contract trade.

SPOT MARKET commodities market in which goods are sold for cash and delivered immediately. Trades that take place in FUTURES CONTRACTS expiring in the current month are also called *spot market trades*. The spot market tends to be conducted OVER-THE-COUNTER—that is, through telephone trading—rather than on the floor of an organized commodity exchange. Also called *actual market, cash market* or *physical market*. *See also* FUTURES MARKET.

SPOT PRICE current delivery price of a commodity traded in the SPOT MARKET. Also called *cash price*.

SPOUSAL IRA INDIVIDUAL RETIREMENT ACCOUNT that may be opened in the name of a nonworking spouse. In the mid-1980s, the maximum annual IRA contribution for a married couple, only one of whom was employed, was $2250. The couple could allocate the $2250 any way they wished between two accounts, as long as either account did not exceed the $2000 limit imposed on all IRAs. If both spouses worked, they could each contribute up to $2000 to their respective IRAs, or a combined maximum of $4000.

SPOUSAL REMAINDER TRUST means used prior to the TAX REFORM ACT OF 1986 to shift income to a person taxable at a lower rate. Income-producing property, such as securities, is transferred by the grantor to the trust for a specific time, typically five years. Trust income is distributed to the beneficiary (or to a minor's CUSTODIAL ACCOUNT) to be used for expenses such as a child's college education. The income is therefore taxed at the beneficiary's lower tax rate. When the trust term expires, the property passes irrevocably to the grantor's spouse. The TAX REFORM ACT OF 1986 provided that effective for trusts established or contributions to trusts made after March 1, 1986, income must be taxed at the grantor's tax rate if the beneficiary is under age 14 and the property can revert to the grantor or the grantor's spouse.

SPREAD

Commodities: in futures trading, the difference between delivery months in the same or different markets.

Fixed-income securities:
1. difference between yields on securities of the same quality but different maturities. For example, the spread between 10% short-term Treasury bills and 14% long-term Treasury bonds is 4 percentage points.
2. difference between yields on securities of the same maturity but different quality. For instance, the spread between a 14% long-term Treasury bond and a 17% long-term bond of a B-rated corporation is 3 percentage points, since an investor's risk is so much less with the Treasury bond. *See also* YIELD SPREAD.

Foreign exchange: in ARBITRAGE terminology, a larger-than-normal difference in currency exchange rates between two markets.

Options: difference in premiums (prices) resulting from a combination of put and call OPTIONS within the same CLASS on the same underlying security. STRIKE PRICE and expiration month may be the same or different. For example, an investor could create a spread by buying an XYZ November 40 call and selling an XYZ November 30 call. *See also* BEAR SPREAD; BULL SPREAD; BUTTERFLY SPREAD; CALENDAR SPREAD; CREDIT SPREAD; DEBIT SPREAD; DIAGONAL SPREAD; OPTION; PRICE SPREAD; VERTICAL SPREAD.

Stocks and bonds:
1. difference between the bid and offer price. If a stock is bid at $45 and offered at $46, the spread is one dollar. This spread narrows or widens according to the supply and demand for the security being traded.
2. difference between the high and low price of a particular security over a given period.

Underwriting: difference between the proceeds an issuer of a new security receives and the price paid by the public for the issue. This spread is taken by the underwriting syndicate as payment for its services. A security issued at $100 may entail a spread of $2 for the underwriter, so the issuer receives $98 from the offering. *See also* UNDERWRITING SPREAD.

SPREADING practice of buying and selling OPTION contracts of the same CLASS on the same underlying security in order to profit from moves in the price of that security. *See also* SPREAD.

SPREAD OPTION SPREAD position involving the purchase of an OPTION at one EXERCISE PRICE and the simultaneous sale of another option on the same underlying security at a different exercise price and/or expiration date. *See also* DIAGONAL SPREAD; HORIZONTAL SPREAD; VERTICAL SPREAD.

SPREAD ORDER OPTIONS market term for an order designating the SERIES of LISTED OPTIONS the customer wishes to buy and sell, together with the desired SPREAD—or difference in option premiums (prices)—shown as a net debit or net credit. The transaction is completed if the FLOOR BROKER can execute the order at the requested spread.

SPREAD POSITION status of an account in which a SPREAD has been executed.

SPREADSHEET ledger sheet on which a company's financial statements, such as BALANCE SHEETS, INCOME STATEMENTS, and sales reports, are laid out in columns and rows. Spreadsheets are used by securities and credit analysts in researching companies and industries. Since the advent of personal computers, spreadsheets have come into wide use, because software makes them easy to use. In an electronic spreadsheet on a computer, any time one number is changed, all the other numbers are automatically adjusted according to the relationships the computer operator sets up. For instance, in a spreadsheet of a sales report of a company's many divisions, the updating of a single division's sales figure will automatically change the total sales for the company, as well as the percentage of total sales that division produced.

SQUEEZE

Finance: (1) tight money period, when loan money is scarce and interest rates are high, making borrowing difficult and expensive—also called a *credit crunch*; (2) any situation where increased costs cannot be passed on to customers in the form of higher prices.

Investments: situation when stocks or commodities futures start to move up in price, and investors who have sold short are forced to COVER their short positions in order to avoid large losses. When done by many short sellers, this action is called a SHORT SQUEEZE. *See also* SELLING SHORT; SHORT POSITION.

SRO *see* SELF-REGULATORY ORGANIZATION.

STABILIZATION

Currency: buying and selling of a country's own currency to protect its exchange value, also called PEGGING.

Economics: leveling out of the business cycle, unemployment, and prices through fiscal and monetary policies.

Market trading: action taken by REGISTERED COMPETITIVE TRADERS on the New York Stock Exchange in accordance with an exchange requirement that 75% of their trades be stabilizing—in other words, that their sell orders follow a PLUS TICK and their buy orders a MINUS TICK.

New issues underwriting: intervention in the market by a managing underwriter in order to keep the market price from falling below the PUBLIC OFFERING PRICE during the offering period. The underwriter places orders to buy at a specific price, an action called PEGGING that, in any other circumstance, is a violation of laws prohibiting MANIPULATION in the securities and commodities markets.

STAG speculator who makes it a practice to get in and out of stocks for a fast profit, rather than to hold securities for investment.

STAGFLATION term coined by economists in the 1970s to describe the previously unprecedented combination of slow economic growth and high unemployment (stagnation) with rising prices (inflation). The principal factor was the fourfold increase in oil prices imposed by the Organization of Petroleum Exporting Countries (OPEC) cartel in 1973-74, which raised price levels throughout the economy while further slowing economic growth. As is characteristic of stagflation, fiscal and monetary policies aimed at stimulating the economy and reducing unemployment only exacerbated the inflationary effects.

STAGGERED BOARD OF DIRECTORS board of directors of a company in which a portion of the directors are elected each year, instead of all at once. A board is often staggered in order to thwart unfriendly TAKEOVER attempts, since potential acquirers would have to wait longer than one ANNUAL MEETING before they could take control of a company's board through the normal voting procedure.

STAGGERING MATURITIES technique used to lower risk by a bond investor. Since long-term bonds are more volatile than short-term ones, an investor can HEDGE against interest rate movements by buyingshort-, medium- and long-term bonds. If interest rates decline, the long-term bonds will rise faster in value than the shorter-term bonds. If rates rise, however, the shorter-term bonds will hold their value better than ong-term debt obligations, which could fall precipitously.

STAGNATION

Economics: period of no or slow (3% or less) economic growth or of economic decline, in real (inflation-adjusted) terms.

Securities: period of low volume and inactive trading.

STAGS acronym for *S*terling *T*ransferable *A*ccruing *G*overnment *S*ecurities, ZERO-COUPON SECURITIES denominated in pounds sterling and created by separating interest payments from the principal of British Treasury bonds (gilts). *See also* STRIP.

STANDARD & POOR'S CORPORATION subsidiary of McGraw-Hill, Inc. that provides a broad range of investment services, including RATING corporate and municipal bonds, common stocks, preferred stocks, and COMMERCIAL PAPER; compiling the Standard & Poor's Composite Index of 500 Stocks, the Standard & Poor's 400 Industrial Index, and the Standard & Poor's 100 Index among other indexes; publishing a wide variety of statistical materials, investment advisory reports, and other financial information, including: *Bond Guide*, a summary of data on corporate and municipal bonds; *Earnings Forecaster*, earnings-per-share estimates on more than 1600 companies; *New Issue Investor*, information and analysis on the new issue market; *Stock Guide*, investment data on listed and unlisted common and preferred stocks and mutual funds; *Analyst's Handbook*, per-share data on the stocks and industry groups making up the 400 index, plus 15 transportation, financial and utility groups; *Corporation Records*, six volumes of information on more than 10,000 publicly held companies; *Stock Reports*, 2-page analytical reports on listed and unlisted companies. A subsidiary publishes the daily BLUE LIST of municipal and corporate bonds. Standard & Poor's also publishes *Poor's Register*, a national directory of companies and their officers; *Securities Dealers of North America*, a directory of investment banking and brokerage firms in North America; and provides a range of back office and electronic services. See also BOND RATING; STANDARD & POOR'S RATING; STOCK INDEXES AND AVERAGES.

STANDARD & POOR'S INDEX broad-based measurement of changes in stock-market conditions based on the average performance of 500 widely held common stocks; commonly known as the *Standard & Poor's 500* (or *S&P 500*). The selection of stocks, their relative weightings to reflect differences in the number of outstanding shares, and publication of the index itself are services of STANDARD & POOR'S CORPORATION, a financial advisory, securities rating, and publishing firm. The index tracks 400 industrial company stocks (also called the Standard & Poor's 400), 20 transportation stocks, 40 financial company stocks, and 40 public utilities. *See also* STOCK INDEXES AND AVERAGES.

STANDARD & POOR'S RATING classification of stocks and bonds according to risk issued by STANDARD AND POOR'S CORPORATION. S&P's top four grades—called INVESTMENT GRADE AAA, AA, A, and BBB—indicate a minimal risk that a corporate or municipal bond issue will default in its timely payment of interest and principal. These four RATINGS also apply to stocks in sound financial shape—those with healthy balance sheets and good prospects for earnings growth. Bonds or stocks rated BB or below by Standard & Poor's are considered speculative. *See also* LEGAL LIST.

STANDARD COST estimate, based on engineering and accounting studies, of what the costs of production should be, assuming normal operating conditions. Standard costs differ from budgeted costs, which are forecasts based on expectations. Variances between standard costs and actual costs measure productive efficiency and are a basis of cost control.

STANDARD DEDUCTION individual taxpayer alternative to itemizing deductions. Under the TAX REFORM ACT OF 1986, which indexes them to inflation in 1989, they are:

	1987	1988
Single Taxpayer	$2540	$3000
Head of Household	$2540	$4400
Married Filing Jointly	$3760	$5000
Married Filing Separately	$1880	$2500

STANDARD DEVIATION statistical measure of the degree to which an individual value in a probability distribution tends to vary from the mean of the distribution. It is widely applied in modern PORTFOLIO THEORY, for example, where the past performance of securities is used to determine the range of possible future performances and a probability is attached to each performance. The standard deviation of performance can then be calculated for each security and for the portfolio as a whole. The greater the degree of dispersion, the greater the risk. *See also* PORTFOLIO THEORY; REGRESSION ANALYSIS..

STANDARD INDUSTRIAL CLASSIFICATION (SIC) SYSTEM federally designed standard numbering system identifying companies by industry and providing other information. It is widely used by market researchers, securities analysts, and others. Computerized data bases frequently make use of the system.

STANDBY COMMITMENT

Securities: agreement between a corporation and an investment banking firm or group (the *standby underwriter*) whereby the latter contracts to purchase for resale, for a fee, any portion of a stock issue offered to current shareholders in a RIGHTS OFFERING that is not subscribed to during the two- to four-week standby period. A right, often issued to comply with laws guaranteeing the shareholder's PREEMPTIVE RIGHT, entitles its holder, either an existing shareholder or a person who has bought the right from a shareholder, to purchase a specified amount of shares before a PUBLIC OFFERING and usually at a price lower than the PUBLIC OFFERING PRICE.

The risk to the investment banker in a standby commitment is that the market price of shares will fall during the standby period. *See also* LAY OFF for a discussion of how standby underwriters protect themselves. *See also* FLOTATION COST; SUBSCRIPTION RIGHT; UNDERWRITE.

Lending: a bank commitment to loan money up to a specified amount for a specific period, to be used only in a certain contingency. The most common example would be a commitment to repay a construction lender in the event a permanent mortgage lender cannot be found. A COMMITMENT FEE is normally charged.

STANDBY UNDERWRITER *see* STANDBY COMMITMENT.

STANDSTILL AGREEMENT accord by a RAIDER to abstain from buying shares of a company for a specified period. *See also* GREENMAIL.

START-UP new business venture. In VENTURE CAPITAL parlance, start-up is the earliest stage at which a venture capital investor or investment pool will provide funds to an enterprise, usually on the basis of a business plan detailing the background of the management group along with market and financial PROJECTIONS. Investments or loans made at this stage are also called SEED MONEY.

STATE BANK bank organized under a charter granted by a regulatory authority in one of the 50 U.S. states, as distinguished from a NATIONAL BANK, which is federally chartered. The powers of a state-chartered commercial bank are generally consistent with those of national banks, since state laws tend to conform to federal initiatives and vice versa. State banks' deposits are insured by the FEDERAL DEPOSIT INSURANCE CORPORATION. State banks have the option of joining the FEDERAL RESERVE SYSTEM, and even if they reject membership, they may purchase support services from the Fed, including check-processing and coin and currency services.

STATED VALUE assigned value given to a corporation's stock for accounting purposes in lieu of par value. For example, the stated value may be set at $1 a share, so that if a company issued 10 million shares, the stated value of its stock would be $10 million. The stated value of the stock has no relation to its market price. It is, however, the amount per share that is credited to the CAPITAL STOCK account for each share outstanding and is therefore the legal capital of the corporation. Since state law generally prohibits a corporation from paying dividends or repurchasing shares when doing so would impair its legal capital, stated value does offer stockholders a measure of protection against loss of value.

STATEMENT
1. summary for customers of the transactions that occurred over the preceding month. A bank statement lists all deposits and withdrawals, as well as the running account balances. A brokerage statement shows all stock, bond, commodity futures, or options trades, interest and dividends received, margin debt outstanding, and other transactions, as well as a summary of the worth of the accounts at month end. A trade supplier provides a summary of open account transactions. *See also* ASSET MANAGEMENT ACCOUNT.
2. statement drawn up by businesses to show the status of their ASSETS and LIABILITIES and the results of their operations as of a certain date. *See also* FINANCIAL STATEMENT.

STATEMENT OF CONDITION

Banking: sworn accounting of a bank's resources, liabilities, and capital accounts as of a certain date, submitted in response to periodic "calls" by bank regulatory authorities.

Finance: summary of the status of assets, liabilities, and equity of a person or a business organization as of a certain date. *See also* BALANCE SHEET.

STATEMENT OF INCOME *see* PROFIT AND LOSS STATEMENT.

STATEMENT OF OPERATIONS *see* PROFIT AND LOSS STATEMENT.

STATUTORY INVESTMENT investment specifically authorized by state law for use by a trustee administering a trust under that state's jurisdiction.

STATUTORY MERGER legal combination of two or more corporations in which only one survives as a LEGAL ENTITY. It differs from *statutory consolidation*, in which all the companies in a combination cease to exist as legal entities and a new corporate entity is created. *See also* MERGER.

STATUTORY PROSPECTUS *see* PROSPECTUS.

STATUTORY VOTING one-share, one-vote rule that governs voting procedures in most corporations. Shareholders may cast one vote per share either for or against each nominee for the board of directors, but may not give more than one vote to one nominee. The result of statutory voting is that, in effect, those who control over 50% of the shares control the company by ensuring that the majority of the board will represent their interests. *Compare with* CUMULATIVE VOTING. *See also* PROPORTIONAL REPRESENTATION.

STAYING POWER ability of an investor to stay with (not sell) an investment that has fallen in value. For example, a commodity trader with staying power is able to meet margin calls as the commodities FUTURES CONTRACTS he has bought fall in price. He can afford to wait until the trade ultimately becomes profitable. In real estate, an investor with staying power is able to meet mortgage and maintenance payments on his or her properties and is therefore not harmed as interest rates rise or fall, or as the properties become temporarily difficult to sell.

STICKY DEAL new securities issue that the underwriter fears will be difficult to sell. Adverse market conditions, bad news about the issuing entity, or other factors may lead underwriters to say, "This will be a sticky deal at the price we have set." As a result, the price may be lowered or the offering withdrawn from the market.

STOCK

1. ownership of a CORPORATION represented by shares that are a claim on the corporation's earnings and assets. COMMON STOCK usually entitles the shareholder to vote in the election of directors and other matters taken up at shareholder meetings or by proxy. PREFERRED STOCK generally does not confer voting rights but it has a prior claim on assets and earnings—dividends must be paid on preferred stock before any can be paid on common stock. A corporation can authorize additional classes of stock, each with its own set of contractual rights. *See also* ARTICLES OF INCORPORATION; AUTHORIZED SHARES; BLUE CHIP; BOOK VALUE; CAPITAL STOCK; CERTIFICATE; CLASS; CLASSIFIED STOCK; CLOSELY HELD; COMMON STOCK; COMMON STOCK EQUIVALENT; CONVERTIBLES;

CONTROL STOCK; CORPORATION; CUMULATIVE PREFERRED; DIVIDEND; EARNINGS PER SHARE; EQUITY; FLOAT; FRACTIONAL SHARES; GOING PUBLIC; GROWTH STOCK; INACTIVE STOCK; INITIAL PUBLIC OFFERING; ISSUED AND OUTSTANDING; JOINT STOCK COMPANY; LETTER SECURITY; LISTED SECURITY; MARKET VALUE; NONVO-TING STOCK; NO-PAR VALUE STOCK; OVER THE COUNTER; PAR VALUE; PAR-TICIPATING PREFERRED; PENNY STOCK; PREEMPTIVE RIGHT; PREFERENCE SHARES; PREFERRED STOCK; PRIOR PREFERRED STOCK; QUARTER STOCK; REGISTERED SECURITY; REGISTRAR; REVERSE SPLIT; SCRIP; SECURITY; SHARE; SHAREHOLDER; SPLIT; STATED VALUE; STOCK CERTIFICATE; STOCK DIVIDEND; STOCK EXCHANGE; STOCKHOLDER; STOCKHOLDER OF RECORD; STOCK MARKET; STOCK POWER; STOCK PURCHASE PLAN; STOCK SYMBOL; STOCK WATCHER; TRANSFER AGENT; TREASURY STOCK; VOTING STOCK; VOTING TRUST CERTIFICATE; WATERED STOCK.

2. inventories of accumulated goods in manufacturing and retailing businesses.

3. *see* ROLLING STOCK.

STOCK AHEAD situation in which two or more orders for a stock at a certain price arrive about the same time, and the exchange's PRIORITY rules take effect. New York Stock Exchange rules stipulate that the bid made first should be exe-cuted first or, if two bids came in at once, the bid for the larger number of shares receives priority. The bid that was not executed is then reported back to the broker, who informs the customer that the trade was not completed because there was stock ahead. *See also* MATCHED AND LOST.

STOCK CERTIFICATE documentation of a shareholder's ownership in a cor-poration. Stock certificates are engraved intricately on heavy paper to deter for-gery. They indicate the number of shares owned by an individual, their PAR VALUE (if any), the CLASS of stock (for example, common or preferred), and attendant voting rights. To prevent theft, shareholders often store certificates in safe deposit boxes or take advantage of a broker's SAFEKEEPING service. Stock certificates become negotiable when endorsed.

STOCK DIVIDEND payment of a corporate dividend in the form of stock rather than cash. The stock dividend may be additional shares in the company, or it may be shares in a SUBSIDIARY being spun off to shareholders. The dividend is usually expressed as a percentage of the shares held by a shareholder. For in-stance, a shareholder with 100 shares would receive 5 shares as the result of a 5% stock dividend. From the corporate point of view, stock dividends conserve cash needed to operate the business. From the stockholder point of view, the advantage is that additional stock is not taxed until sold, unlike a cash dividend, which is declarable as income in the year it is received.

STOCK EXCHANGE organized marketplace in which stocks, COMMON STOCK EQUIVALENTS, and bonds are traded by members of the exchange, acting both as agents (brokers) and as principals (dealers or traders). Such exchanges have a physical location where brokers and dealers meet to execute orders from insti-tutional and individual investors to buy and sell securities. Each exchange sets its own requirements for membership; the New York Stock Exchange has the most stringent requirements. *See also* AMERICAN STOCK EXCHANGE; LISTING REQUIREMENTS; NEW YORK STOCK EXCHANGE; REGIONAL STOCK EXCHANGES; SECURITIES AND COMMODITIES EXCHANGES.

STOCKHOLDER individual or organization with an ownership position in a cor-poration; also called a SHAREHOLDER or *shareowner*. Stockholders must own at least one share, and their ownership is confirmed by either a stock certificate or a record by their broker, if shares are in the broker's custody.

STOCKHOLDER OF RECORD common or preferred stockholder whose name is registered on the books of a corporation as owning shares as of a particular date. Dividends and other distributions are made only to shareholders of record. Common stockholders are usually the only ones entitled to vote for candidates for the board of directors or on other matters requiring shareholder approval.

STOCK INDEXES AND AVERAGES indicators used to measure and report value changes in representative stock groupings. Strictly speaking, an AVERAGE is simply the ARITHMETIC MEAN of a group of prices whereas an INDEX is an average expressed in relation to an earlier established BASE MARKET VALUE. (In practice, the distinction between indexes and averages is not always clear; the AMEX Major Market Index is an average, for example.) Indexes and averages may be broad based—that is, comprised of many stocks and designed to be representative of the overall market—or narrow based—meaning made up of a smaller number of stocks and designed to reflect a particular industry or market SECTOR. Selected indexes and averages are also used as the underlying value of STOCK INDEX FUTURES, INDEX OPTIONS, or options on index futures, which enable investors to make a ''market bet'' or to HEDGE a POSITION against general market movement at relatively little cost. An extensive number and variety of indexes and averages exist. Among the best known and most widely used are:

AMEX Major Market Index price-weighted (high-priced issues have more influence than low-priced issues) average of 20 BLUE CHIP industrial stocks. It is designed to replicate the Dow Jones Industrial Average (DJIA) in measuring representative performance in the stocks of major industrial corporations. It is produced by the American Stock Exchange (AMEX) but is composed of stocks listed on the New York Stock Exchange (NYSE), 15 of which are also components of the DJIA. Futures on the Major Market Index are traded on the Chicago Board of Trade.

AMEX Market Value Index (AMVI) formerly known as the ASE Index and prepared on a different basis, AMVI is a capitalization or MARKET VALUE-WEIGHTED INDEX (i.e., the impact of a component's price change is proportionate to the overall market value of the issue) introduced at a base level of 100.00 in September 1973 and adjusted to half that level in July 1983. It measures the collective performance of more than 800 issues, representing all major industry groups, traded on the AMEX, including AMERICAN DEPOSITARY RECEIPTS and warrants as well as common stocks. Uniquely, cash dividends paid by component stocks are assumed to be reinvested and are thus reflected in the index. Options on the AMVI are listed on the American Stock Exchange.

Dow Jones Industrial Average (DJIA) price-weighted average of 30 actively traded blue chip stocks, primarily industrials but including American Express Company and American Telephone and Telegraph Company. Prepared and published by Dow Jones & Company, it is the oldest and most widely quoted of all the market indicators. The components, which change from time to time, represent between 15% and 20% of the market value of NYSE stocks. The DJIA is calculated by adding the closing prices of the component stocks and using a divisor that is adjusted for SPLITS and STOCK DIVIDENDS equal to 10% or more of the market value of an issue as well as for substitutions and mergers. The average is quoted in points, not in dollars. Dow Jones & Company has refused to allow the DJIA to be used as a basis for speculation with futures or options. Subindexes similarly prepared are the *Dow Jones Transportation Average (DJTA)*—20 railroad, airline and trucking stocks (*see also* DOW THEORY); and the *Dow Jones Utility Average (DJUA)*—15 geographically representative gas and electric utility companies.

The Dow Jones Composite, also called the *65 Stock Average,* combines the

DJIA, DJTA, and DJUA. Dow Jones also puts out two prominent bond averages—the *Dow Jones 40 Bond Average*, representative of six different bond groups, and the *Dow Jones Municipal Bond Yield Average*, a weekly average of leading state and major city tax-exempt yields.

New York Stock Exchange Composite Index market value-weighted index which relates all NYSE stocks to an aggregate market value as of December 31, 1965, adjusted for capitalization changes. The base value of the index is $50 and point changes are expressed in dollars and cents. Futures and futures options are traded on the New York Futures Exchange (NYFE), a division of the NYSE. Index options are traded on the NYSE itself. The *New York Stock Exchange Telephone Index*, similarly prepared, is comprised of the eight common stocks of companies that made up predivestiture AT&T. Index options in the Telephone Index are listed on the NYSE, but no futures are traded. NYSE subindexes include the *NYSE Industrial, NYSE Transportation, NYSE Utility,* and *NYSE Financial* Indexes.

Standard & Poor's Composite Index of 500 Stocks market value-weighted index showing the change in the aggregate market value of 500 stocks relative to the base period 1941-43. It is composed mostly of NYSE-listed companies with some AMEX and over-the-counter stocks, in the following proportions: 400 industrials, 60 transportation and utility companies, and 40 financial issues. The index represents about 80% of the market value of all issues traded on the NYSE. Index options are traded on the Chicago Board Options Exchange and futures and futures options are traded on the Chicago Mercantile Exchange. *The Standard & Poor's 100 Stock Index*, calculated on the same basis as the 500 stock index, is made up of stocks for which options are listed on the Chicago Board Options Exchange. Its components are mainly NYSE industrials, but some transportation, utility and financial stocks are also included. Options on the 100 Index are listed on the Chicago Board Options Exchange and futures are traded on the Chicago Mercantile Exchange. Futures options are not traded.

NASDAQ-OTC Price Index this index is based on the National Association of Securities Dealers Automated Quotations (NASDAQ) and represents all domestic OVER-THE-COUNTER stocks except those traded on exchanges and those having only one MARKET MAKER, a total of some 3500 stocks. It is market value-weighted and was introduced with a base value of 100.00 on February 5, 1971. Options and futures are not traded on this index.

Value Line Composite Index equally-weighted geometric average of approximately 1700 NYSE, AMEX, and over the counter stocks tracked by the VALUE LINE INVESTMENT SURVEY. The index uses a base value of 100.00 established June 30, 1961, and changes are expressed in index numbers rather than dollars and cents. This index is designed to reflect price changes of typical industrial stocks and being neither price nor market value-weighted, it largely succeeds. Options are traded on the Philadelphia Exchange, and futures are available on the Kansas City Board of Trade.

Wilshire 5000 Equity Index broadest of all the averages and indexes, the Wilshire Index is market value-weighted and represents the value, in billions of dollars, of all NYSE, AMEX, and over the counter issues for which quotes are available, some 5000 stocks in all. Changes are measured against a base value established December 31, 1980. Options and futures are not traded on the Wilshire Index, which is prepared by the Wilshire Associates of Santa Monica, California.

Barron's Group Stock Averages simple, arithmetic averages of stocks in more than 30 different industrial groupings, adjusted for splits and large stock dividends since 1937. Options and futures are not traded.

See also BARRON'S CONFIDENCE INDEX; BOND BUYER'S INDEX; LIPPER MUTUAL FUND INDUSTRY AVERAGE; SECURITIES AND COMMODITIES EXCHANGES.

STOCK INDEX FUTURE security that combines features of traditional commodity futures trading with securities trading using composite stock indexes. Investors can speculate on general market performance or can buy an index future contract to hedge a LONG POSITION or SHORT POSITION against a decline in value. Settlement is in cash, since it is obviously impossible to deliver an index of stocks to a futures buyer. Among the most popular stock index futures traded are the New York Stock Exchange Composite Index on the New York Futures Exchange (NYFE), the Standard & Poor's 500 Index on the Chicago Mercantile Exchange (CME), and the Value Line Composite Index on the Kansas City Board of Trade (KCBT).

It is also possible to buy options on stock index futures; the Standard & Poor's 500 Stock Index futures options are traded on the Chicago Mercantile Exchange and the New York Stock Exchange Composite Index futures options are traded on the New York Futures Exchange, for example. Unlike stock index futures or INDEX OPTIONS, however, futures options are not settled in cash; they are settled by delivery of the underlying stock index futures contracts.

See also FUTURES CONTRACT; HEDGE/HEDGING; SECURITIES AND COMMODITIES EXCHANGES.

STOCK LIST function of the organized stock exchanges that is concerned with LISTING REQUIREMENTS and related investigations, the eligibility of unlisted companies for trading privileges, and the delisting of companies that have not complied with exchange regulations and listing requirements. The New York Stock Exchange department dealing with listing of securities is called the Department of Stock List.

STOCK MARKET general term referring to the organized trading of securities through the various exchanges and the OVER THE COUNTER market. The securities involved include COMMON STOCK, PREFERRED STOCK, BONDS, CONVERTIBLES, OPTIONS, rights, and warrants. The term may also encompass commodities when used in its most general sense, but more often than not the stock market and the commodities (or futures) market are distinguished. The query "How did the market do today?" is usually answered by a reference to the Dow Jones Industrial Average, comprised of stocks listed on the New York Stock Exchange. *See also* SECURITIES AND COMMODITIES EXCHANGES.

STOCK OPTION
1. right to purchase or sell a stock at a specified price within a stated period. OPTIONS are a popular investment medium, offering an opportunity to hedge positions in other securities, to speculate in stocks with relatively little investment, and to capitalize on changes in the MARKET VALUE of options contracts themselves through a variety of options strategies.
   See also CALL OPTION; PUT OPTION.
2. widely used form of employee incentive and compensation, usually for the executives of a corporation. The employee is given an OPTION to purchase its shares at a certain price (at or below the market price at the time the option is granted) for a specified period of years.
   See also INCENTIVE STOCK OPTION; QUALIFYING STOCK OPTION.

STOCK POWER power of attorney form transferring ownership of a REGISTERED SECURITY from the owner to another party. A separate piece of paper from the

CERTIFICATE, it is attached to the latter when the security is sold or pledged to a brokerage firm, bank, or other lender as loan COLLATERAL. Technically, the stock power gives the owner's permission to another party (the TRANSFER AGENT) to transfer ownership of the certificate to a third party. Also called *stock/bond power*.

STOCK PURCHASE PLAN organized program for employees of a company to buy shares of its stock. The plan could take the form of compensation if the employer matches employee stock purchases. Also, a corporation can offer to reinvest dividends in additional shares as a service to shareholders, or it can set up a program of regular additional share purchases for participating shareholders who authorize periodic, automatic payments from their wages for this purpose.

Another form of stock purchase plan is the EMPLOYEE STOCK OWNERSHIP PLAN (ESOP), whereby employees regularly accumulate shares and may ultimately assume control of the company.

STOCK RECORD control, usually in the form of a ledger card or computer report, used by brokerage firms to keep track of securities held in inventory and their precise location within the firm. Securities are recorded by name and owner.

STOCK SPLIT *see* SPLIT.

STOCK SYMBOL letters used to identify listed companies on the securities exchanges on which they trade. These symbols, also called *trading symbols,* identify trades on the CONSOLIDATED TAPE and are used in other reports and documents whenever such shorthand is convenient. Some examples: ABT (Abbott Laboratories), AA (Aluminum Company of America), XON (Exxon), KO (Coca Cola). Stock symbols are not necessarily the same as abbreviations used to identify the same companies in the stock tables of newspapers. *See also* COMMITTEE ON UNIFORM SECURITIES IDENTIFICATION PROCEDURES (CUSIP).

STOCK-TRANSFER AGENT *see* TRANSFER AGENT.

STOCK WATCHER (NYSE) computerized service that monitors all trading activity and movement in stocks listed on the New York Stock Exchange. The system is set up to identify any unusual activity due to rumors or MANIPULATION or other illegal practices. The stock watch department of the NYSE is prepared to conduct investigations and to take appropriate action, such as issuing clarifying information or turning questions of legality over to the Securities and Exchange Commission. *See also* SURVEILLANCE DEPARTMENT OF EXCHANGES.

STOP-LIMIT ORDER order to a securities broker with instructions to buy or sell at a specified price or better (called the *stop-limit price*) but only after a given *stop price* has been reached or passed. It is a combination of a STOP ORDER and a LIMIT ORDER. For example, the instruction to the broker might be "buy 100 XYZ 55 STOP 56 LIMIT" meaning that if the MARKET PRICE reaches $55, the broker enters a limit order to be executed at $56 or a better (lower) price. A stop-limit order avoids some of the risks of a stop order, which becomes a MARKET ORDER when the stop price is reached; like all price-limit orders, however, it carries the risk of missing the market altogether, since the specified limit price or better may never occur. The American Stock Exchange prohibits stop-limit orders unless the stop and limit prices are equal.

STOP LOSS

Insurance: promise by a reinsurance company that it will cover losses incurred by the company it reinsures over and above an agreed-upon amount.

Stocks: customer order to a broker that sets the sell price of a stock below the current MARKET PRICE. A stop-loss order therefore will protect profits that have already been made or prevent further losses if the stock drops.

STOP ORDER order to a securities broker to buy or sell at the MARKET PRICE once the security has traded at a specified price called the *stop price*. A stop order may be a DAY ORDER, a GOOD-TILL-CANCELED ORDER, or any other form of time-limit order. A stop order to buy, always at a stop price above the current market price, is usually designed to protect a profit or to limit a loss on a short sale (*see* SELLING SHORT). A stop order to sell, always at a price below the current market price, is usually designed to protect a profit or to limit a loss on a security already purchased at a higher price. The risk of stop orders is that they may be triggered by temporary market movements or that they may be executed at prices several points higher or lower than the stop price because of market orders placed ahead of them. Also called *stop-loss order*. *See also* GATHER IN THE STOPS; STOP LIMIT ORDER; STOP LOSS (stocks).

STOP-OUT PRICE lowest dollar price at which Treasury bills are sold at a particular auction. This price and the beginning auction price are averaged to establish the price at which smaller purchasers may purchase bills under the NONCOMPETITIVE BID system. *See also* BILL; DUTCH AUCTION.

STOP PAYMENT revocation of payment on a check after the check has been sent or delivered to the payee. So long as the check has not been cashed, the writer has up to six months in which to request a stop payment. The stop payment right does not carry over to electronic funds transfers.

STOPPED OUT term used when a customer's order is executed under a STOP ORDER at the price predetermined by the customer, called the *stop price*. For instance, if a customer has entered a stop-loss order to sell XYZ at $30 when the stock is selling at $33, and the stock then falls to $30, his or her position will be stopped out. A customer may also be stopped out if the order is executed at a guaranteed price offered by a SPECIALIST. *See also* GATHER IN THE STOPS; STOPPED STOCK.

STOPPED STOCK guarantee by a SPECIALIST that an order placed by a FLOOR BROKER will be executed at the best bid or offer price then in the SPECIALIST'S BOOK unless it can be executed at a better price within a specified period of time.

STOP PRICE *see* STOP ORDER.

STORY compelling scenario for buying a particular stock. A securities analyst who favors a stock sells the stock to clients by means of a story—for instance, that new management has come in and is turning a losing company into a winning one. Story stocks are frequently from companies with some unique product or service that is difficult for competitors to copy.

STRADDLE strategy consisting of an equal number of PUT OPTIONS and CALL OPTIONS on the same underlying stock, stock index, or commodity future at the same STRIKE PRICE and maturity date. Each OPTION may be exercised separately, although the combination of options is usually bought and sold as a unit.

STRAIGHT-LINE DEPRECIATION method of depreciating a fixed asset whereby the asset's useful life is divided into the total cost less the estimated salvage value. The procedure is used to arrive at a uniform annual DEPRECIATION expense to be charged against income before figuring income taxes. Thus, if a new machine purchased for $1200 was estimated to have a useful life of ten years and a salvage value of $200, annual depreciation under the straight-line method would be $100, charged at $100 a year. This is the oldest and simplest method of depreciation and is used by many companies for financial reporting purposes, although faster depreciation of some assets with greater tax benefits in the early years is allowed under the ACCELERATED COST RECOVERY SYSTEM (ACRS).

STRAP OPTION contract combining one PUT OPTION and two CALL OPTIONS of the same SERIES, which can be bought at a lower total premium than that of the three options bought individually. The put has the same features as the calls—same underlying security, exercise price, and maturity. Also called *triple option*. *Compare with* STRIP.

STREET short for Wall Street, referring to the financial community in New York City and elsewhere. It is common to hear "The Street likes XYZ." This means there is a national consensus among securities analysts following XYZ that its prospects are favorable. *See also* STREET NAME.

STREET NAME phrase describing securities held in the name of a broker or another nominee instead of a customer. Since the securities are in the broker's custody, transfer of the shares at the time of sale is easier than if the stock were registered in the customer's name and physical certificates had to be transferred.

STRIKE PRICE *see* EXERCISE PRICE.

STRIP

Bonds: brokerage-house practice of separating a bond into its CORPUS and COUPONS, which are then sold separately as ZERO-COUPON SECURITIES. The 1986 Tax Act permitted MUNICIPAL BOND strips. Some, such as Salomon Brothers' tax-exempt M-CATS, represent PREREFUNDINGS backed by U.S. Treasury securities held in escrow. Other strips include Treasuries stripped by brokers, such as TIGERS, and stripped mortgage-backed securities of government-sponsored issuers like Fannie Mae. A variation known by the acronym STRIPS (Separate Trading of Registered Interest and Principal of Securities) is a prestripped zero-coupon bond that is a direct obligation of the U. S. Treasury.

Options: OPTION contract consisting of two PUT OPTIONS and one CALL OPTION on the same underlying stock or stock index with the same strike and expiration date. *Compare with* STRAP.

Stocks: to buy stocks with the intention of collecting their dividends. Also called *dividend stripping*. *See also* DIVIDEND ROLLOVER PLAN.

STUDENT LOAN MARKETING ASSOCIATION (SLMA) publicly traded stock corporation that guarantees student loans traded on the SECONDARY MARKET. It was established by federal decree in 1972 to increase the availability of education loans to college and university students made under the federally sponsored Guaranteed Student Loan Program and the Health, Education Assistance Loan Program. Known as *Sallie Mae*, it purchases student loans from originating financial institutions and provides financing to state student loan agencies. It also sells short- and medium-term notes, some FLOATING RATE NOTES.

SUBCHAPTER M Internal Revenue Service regulation dealing with what is commonly called the *conduit theory*, in which qualifying investment companies and real estate investment trusts avoid double taxation by passing interest and dividend income and capital gains directly through, without taxation, to shareholders, who are taxed as individuals. *See also* REAL ESTATE INVESTMENT TRUST; REGULATED INVESTMENT COMPANY.

SUBCHAPTER S section of the Internal Revenue Code giving a corporation that has 35 or fewer shareholders and meets certain other requirements the option of being taxed as if it were a PARTNERSHIP. Thus a small corporation can distribute its income directly to shareholders and avoid the corporate income tax while enjoying the other advantages of the corporate form. These companies are known as *S corporations, tax-option corporations,* or *small business corporations.*

SUBJECT Wall Street term referring to a bid and/or offer that is negotiable—that is, a QUOTATION that is not firm. For example, a broker looking to place a sizable order might call several dealers with the question, "Can you give me a *subject quote* on 20,000 shares of XYZ?"

SUBJECT QUOTE *see* SUBJECT.

SUBORDINATED junior in claim on assets to other debt, that is, repayable only after other debts with a higher claim have been satisfied. Some subordinated debt may have less claim on assets than other subordinated debt; a *junior subordinated debenture* ranks below a subordinated DEBENTURE, for example.
  It is also possible for unsubordinated (senior) debt to become subordinated at the request of a lender by means of a subordination agreement. For example, if an officer of a small company has made loans to the company instead of making a permanent investment in it, a bank might request the officer's loan be subordinated to its own loan as long as the latter is outstanding. This is accomplished by the company officer's signing a subordination agreement. *See also* EFFECTIVE NET WORTH; JUNIOR SECURITY.

SUBSCRIPTION agreement of intent to buy newly issued securities. *See also* NEW ISSUE; SUBSCRIPTION RIGHT; SUBSCRIPTION WARRANT.

SUBSCRIPTION PRICE price at which existing shareholders of a corporation are entitled to purchase common shares in a RIGHTS OFFERING or at which subscription warrants are exercisable. *See also* SUBSCRIPTION RIGHT; SUBSCRIPTION WARRANT.

SUBSCRIPTION PRIVILEGE right of existing shareholders of a corporation, or their transferees, to buy shares of a new issue of common stock before it is offered to the public. *See also* PREEMPTIVE RIGHT; SUBSCRIPTION RIGHT.

SUBSCRIPTION RATIO *see* SUBSCRIPTION RIGHT.

SUBSCRIPTION RIGHT privilege granted to existing shareholders of a corporation to subscribe to shares of a new issue of common stock before it is offered to the public; better known simply as a *right*. Such a right, which normally has a life of two to four weeks, is freely transferable and entitles the holder to buy the new common stock below the PUBLIC OFFERING PRICE. While in most cases one existing share entitles the stockholder to one right, the number of rights needed to buy a share of a new issue (called the *subscription ratio*) varies and is determined by a company in advance of an offering. To subscribe, the holder sends or delivers to the company or its agent the required number of rights plus the dollar price of the new shares.
  Rights are sometimes granted to comply with state laws that guarantee the

shareholders' PREEMPTIVE RIGHT—their right to maintain a proportionate share of ownership. It is common practice, however, for corporations to grant rights even when not required by law; protecting shareholders from the effects of DILUTION is seen simply as good business.

The actual certificate representing the subscription is technically called a SUBSCRIPTION WARRANT, giving rise to some confusion. The term *subscription warrant,* or simply *warrant,* is commonly understood in a related but different sense—as a separate entity with a longer life than a right—maybe 5, 10, or 20 years or even perpetual—and with a SUBSCRIPTION PRICE higher at the time of issue than the MARKET VALUE of the common stock.

Subscription rights are offered to shareholders in what is called a RIGHTS OFFERING, usually handled by underwriters under a STANDBY COMMITMENT.

SUBSCRIPTION WARRANT type of security, usually issued together with a BOND or PREFERRED STOCK, that entitles the holder to buy a proportionate amount of common stock at a specified price, usually higher than the market price at the time of issuance, for a period of years or to perpetuity; better known simply as a *warrant.* In contrast, rights, which also represent the right to buy common shares, normally have a subscription price lower than the current market value of the common stock and a life of two to four weeks. A warrant is usually issued as a SWEETENER, to enhance the marketability of the accompanying fixed income securities. Warrants are freely transferable and are traded on the major exchanges. They are also called *stock-purchase warrants. See also* PERPETUAL WARRANT; SUBSCRIPTION RIGHT.

SUBSIDIARY company of which more than 50% of the voting shares are owned by another corporation, called the PARENT COMPANY. *See also* AFFILIATE.

SUBSTITUTION

Banking: replacement of COLLATERAL by other collateral.

Contracts: replacement of one party to a contract by another. *See also* NOVATION.

Economics: concept that, if one product or service can be replaced by another, their prices should be similar.

Law: replacement of one attorney by another in the exercise of stock powers relating to the purchase and sale of securities. *See also* STOCK POWER.

Securities:
1. exchange or SWAP of one security for another in a client's PORTFOLIO. Securities analysts often advise substituting a stock they currently favor for a stock in the same industry that they believe has less favorable prospects.
2. substitution of another security of equal value for a security acting as COLLATERAL for a MARGIN ACCOUNT. *See also* SAME-DAY-SUBSTITUTION.

SUITABILITY RULES guidelines that those selling sophisticated and potentially risky financial products, such as limited partnerships or commodities futures contracts, must follow to ensure that investors have the financial means to assume the risks involved. Such rules are enforced through self-regulation administered by such organizations as the NATIONAL ASSOCIATION OF SECURITIES DEALERS, the SECURITIES AND COMMODITIES EXCHANGES, and other groups operating in the securities industry. Individual brokerage firms selling the products have their own guidelines and policies. They typically require the investor to have a certain level of NET WORTH and LIQUID ASSETS, so that he or she will not be irreparably harmed if the investment sours. A brokerage firm may be sued if it has allowed an unsuitable investor to buy an investment that goes sour. *See also* KNOW YOUR CUSTOMER.

SUM-OF-THE-YEARS'-DIGITS METHOD (SOYD) method of ACCELERATED DEPRECIATION that results in higher DEPRECIATION charges and greater tax savings in the earlier years of a FIXED ASSET's useful life than the STRAIGHT-LINE DEPRECIATION method, where charges are uniform throughout. Sometimes called just *sum-of-digits method*, it allows depreciation based on an inverted scale of the total of digits for the years of useful life. Thus, for four years of life, the digits 4, 3, 2, and 1 are added to produce 10. The first year's rate becomes 4/10ths of the depreciable cost of the asset (cost less salvage value), the second year's rate 3/10ths, and so on. The effects of this method of accelerated depreciation are compared with the straight-line method in the following illustration, which assumes an asset with a total cost of $1000, a useful life of four years, and no salvage value:

YEAR	STRAIGHT LINE		SUM-OF-YEARS' DIGITS	
	Expense	Cumulative	Expense	Cumulative
1	$250	$250	$400	$400
2	$250	$500	$300	$700
3	$250	$750	$200	$900
4	$250	$1000	$100	$1000
	$1000		$1000	

See also ACCELERATED COST RECOVERY SYSTEM (ACRS).

SUNRISE INDUSTRIES figurative term for the emerging growth sectors that some believe will be the mainstays of the future economy, taking the place of declining *sunset industries*. Although the latter, including such mature industries as the automobile, steel, and other heavy manufacturing industries, will continue to be important, their lead role as employers of massive numbers of workers is expected to be superseded by the electronics and other computer-related high-technology, biotechnology, and genetic engineering sectors and by service industries.

SUNSET PROVISION condition in a law or regulation that specifies an expiration date unless reinstated by legislation. For example, a sunset provision in the TAX REFORM ACT OF 1986 prohibits tax-exempt single-family mortgage bonds after 1988.

SUNSHINE LAWS state or federal laws (also called *government in the sunshine laws*) that require most meetings of regulatory bodies to be held in public and most of their decisions and records to be disclosed. Many of these statutes were enacted in the 1970s because of concern about government abuses during the Watergate period. Most prominent is the federal Freedom of Information (FOI) Act, which makes it possible to obtain federal documents.

SUPERMAJORITY AMENDMENT corporate AMENDMENT requiring that a substantial majority (usually 67% to 90%) of stockholders approve important transactions, such as mergers.

SUPER NOW ACCOUNT deregulated transaction account authorized for depository institutions in 1982. It paid interest higher than on a conventional NOW (NEGOTIABLE ORDER OF WITHDRAWAL) account but slightly lower than that on the MONEY MARKET DEPOSIT ACCOUNT (MMDA). With the deregulation of banking deposit accounts in 1986, however, banks are free to pay whatever rates they feel cost considerations and competitive conditions warrant. Although some banks continue to offer MMDA accounts which pay a slightly higher rate to compensate for the fact that checkwriting is limited to three checks a month, most banks now offer one transaction account with unlimited checkwriting.

SUPER SINKER BOND bond with long-term COUPONS (which might equal a 20-year-bond's yield) but with short maturity. Typically, super sinkers are HOUSING BONDS, which provide home financing. If homeowners move from their homes and prepay their mortgages, bondholders receive their principal back right away. Super sinkers may therefore have an actual life of as little as three to five years, even though their yield is about the same as bonds of much longer maturities.

SUPERVISORY ANALYST member firm research analyst who has passed a special New York Stock Exchange examination and is deemed qualified to approve publicly distributed research reports.

SUPPLEMENTAL AGREEMENT agreement that amends a previous agreement and contains additional conditions.

SUPPLY-SIDE ECONOMICS theory of economics contending that drastic reductions in tax rates will stimulate productive investment by corporations and wealthy individuals to the benefit of the entire society. Championed in the late 1970s by Professor Arthur Laffer (*see* LAFFER CURVE) and others, the theory held that MARGINAL TAX RATES had become so high (primarily as a result of big government) that major new private spending on plant, equipment, and other "engines of growth" was discouraged. Therefore, reducing the size of government, and hence its claim on earned income, would fuel economic expansion.

Supporters of the supply-side theory claimed they were vindicated in the first years of the administration of President Ronald W. Reagan, when marginal tax rates were cut just prior to a sustained economic recovery. However, members of the opposing KEYNESIAN ECONOMICS school maintained that the recovery was a classic example of "demand-side" economics—growth was stimulated not by increasing the supply of goods, but by increasing consumer demand as disposable incomes rose. Also clashing with the supply-side theory were MONETARIST economists, who contended that the most effective way of regulating aggregate demand is for the Federal Reserve to control growth in the money supply. *See also* AGGREGATE SUPPLY.

SUPPORT LEVEL price level at which a security tends to stop falling because there is more demand than supply. Technical analysts identify support levels as prices at which a particular security or market has bottomed in the past. When a stock is falling towards its support level, these analysts say it is "testing its support," meaning that the stock should rebound as soon as it hits the support price. If the stock continues to drop through the support level, its outlook is considered very bearish. The opposite of a support level is a RESISTANCE LEVEL. *See* illustration, page 487.

SURCHARGE charge added to a charge, cost added to a cost, or tax added to a tax. *See also* SURTAX.

SURPLUS connotes either CAPITAL SURPLUS or EARNED SURPLUS. *See also* PAID-IN CAPITAL; RETAINED EARNINGS.

SURTAX tax applied to corporations or individuals who have earned a certain level of income. For instance, a government might impose a surtax of 10% on all those with an ADJUSTED GROSS INCOME of $50,000 or more.

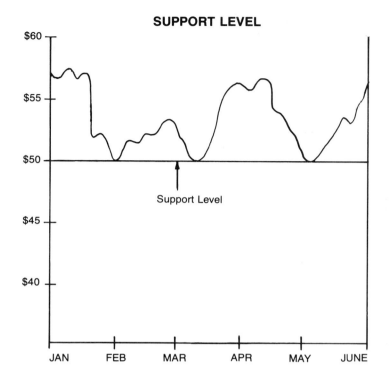

SUPPORT LEVEL

Support Level

JAN FEB MAR APR MAY JUNE

SURVEILLANCE DEPARTMENT OF EXCHANGES division of a stock exchange that is constantly watching to detect unusual trading activity in stocks, which may be a tipoff to an illegal practice. These departments cooperate with the Securities and Exchange Commission in investigating misconduct. *See also* STOCK WATCHER.

SUSPENDED TRADING temporary halt in trading in a particular security, in advance of a major news announcement or to correct an imbalance of orders to buy and sell. Using telephone alert procedures, listed companies with material developments to announce can give advance notice to the New York Stock Exchange Department of Stock List or the American Stock Exchange Securities Division. The exchanges can then determine if trading in the securities affected should be suspended temporarily to allow for orderly dissemination of the news to the public. Where advance notice is not possible, a SPECIALIST may halt trading to stabilize the price of a security affected by a rumor or news development. Destabilizing developments might include a MERGER announcement, an unfavorable earnings report, or a major resource discovery. *See also* DISCLOSURE; FORM 8-K; INVESTOR RELATIONS DEPARTMENT.

SUSPENSE ACCOUNT in accounting, an account used temporarily to carry receipts, disbursements, or discrepancies, pending their analysis and permanent classification.

SWAP exchange one security for another. A swap may be executed to change the maturities of a bond PORTFOLIO or the quality of the issues in a stock or bond portfolio, or because investment objectives have shifted. Investors with bond portfolio losses often swap for other higher-yielding bonds to be able to increase the return on their portfolio and realize tax losses. *See also* BOND SWAP; SUBSTITUTION.

SWAP ORDER *see* CONTINGENT ORDER.

SWEETENER feature added to a securities offering to make it more attractive to purchasers. A bond may have the sweetener of convertibility into common stock added, for instance. *See also* KICKER.

SWITCHING

Mutual Funds: moving assets from one mutual fund to another, either within a FAMILY OF FUNDS or between different fund families. There is no charge for switching within a no-load family of mutual funds, which offers a variety of stock, bond, and money market funds. A sales charge would have to be paid when switching from one LOAD FUND to another. Switching usually occurs at the shareholder's initiative, as a resultof changes in market conditions or investment objectives. *See also* NO-LOAD FUND.

Securities: selling stocks or bonds to replace them with other stocks and bonds with better prospects for gain. *See also* SWAP.

SWITCH ORDER *see* CONTINGENT ORDER.

SYNDICATE *see* PURCHASE GROUP; UNDERWRITING GROUP.

SYNDICATE MANAGER *see* MANAGING UNDERWRITER.

SYNERGY ideal sought in corporate mergers and acquisitions that the performance of a combined enterprise will exceed that of its previously separate parts. For example, a MERGER of two oil companies, one with a superior distribution network and the other with more reserves, would have synergy and would be expected to result in higher earnings per share than if the companies remained separate.

SYSTEMATIC RISK that part of a security's risk that is common to all securities of the same general class (stocks and bonds) and thus cannot be eliminated by DIVERSIFICATION; also known as *market risk*. The measure of systematic risk in stocks is the BETA COEFFICIENT. *See also* PORTFOLIO BETA SCORE, PORTFOLIO THEORY.

t

TAFT-HARTLEY ACT federal law (in full, Labor Management Relations Act) enacted in 1947, which restored to management in unionized industries some of the bargaining power it had lost in prounion legislation prior to World War II. Taft-Hartley prohibited a union from
- refusing to bargain in good faith
- coercing employees to join a union
- imposing excessive or discriminatory dues and initiation fees
- forcing employers to hire union workers to perform unneeded or nonexistent tasks (a practice known as *featherbedding*)
- striking to influence a bargaining unit's choice between two contesting unions (called a *jurisdictional strike*)

- engaging in secondary boycotts against businesses selling or handling nonunion goods
- engaging in sympathy strikes in support of other unions

Taft-Hartley also

- imposed disclosure requirements to regulate union business dealings and uncover fraud and racketeering
- prohibited unions from directly making contributions to candidates running for federal offices
- authorized the President of the United States to postpone strikes in industries deemed essential to national economic health or national security by declaring an 80-day "cooling-off period"
- permitted states to enact right-to-work laws, which outlaw compulsory unionization.

TAIL

Insurance: interval between receipt of premium income and payment of claims. For example, REINSURANCE companies have a long tail as compared to CASUALTY INSURANCE companies.

Treasury auctions: spread in price between the lowest COMPETITIVE BID accepted by the U.S. Treasury for bills, bonds, and notes and the average bid by all those offering to buy such Treasury securities. *See also* TREASURIES.

Underwriting: decimal places following the round-dollar amount of a bid by a potential UNDERWRITER in a COMPETITIVE BID underwriting. For instance, in a bid of $97.3347 for a particular bond issue, the tail is .3347.

TAILGATING unethical practice of a broker who, after a customer has placed an order to buy or sell a certain security, places an order for the same security for his or her own account. The broker hopes to profit either because of information the customer is known or presumed to have or because the customer's purchase is of sufficient size to put pressure on the security price.

TAKE

In general:
1. profit realized from a transaction.
2. gross receipts of a lottery or gambling enterprise.
3. open to bribery, as in *being on the take.*

Law: to seize possession of property. When a debtor defaults on a debt backed by COLLATERAL, that property is taken back by the creditor.

Securities: act of accepting an OFFER price in a transaction between brokers or dealers.

TAKE A BATH to suffer a large loss on a SPECULATION or investment, as in "I took a bath on my XYZ stock when the market dropped last week."

TAKE A FLIER to speculate, that is, to buy securities with the knowledge that the investment is highly risky.

TAKE A POSITION
1. to buy stock in a company with the intent of holding for the long term or, possibly, of taking control of the company. An acquirer who takes a position of 5% or more of a company's outstanding stock must file information with the Securities and Exchange Commission, the exchange the TARGET COMPANY is listed on, and the target company itself.

2. phrase used when a broker/dealer holds stocks or bonds in inventory. A position may be either long or short. *See also* LONG POSITION; SHORT POSITION.

TAKEDOWN
1. each participating INVESTMENT BANKER'S proportionate share of the securities to be distributed in a new or a secondary offering.
2. price at which the securities are allocated to members of the UNDERWRITING GROUP, particularly in municipal offerings.
    See also UNDERWRITE.

TAKE-OR-PAY CONTRACT agreement between a buyer and a seller that obligates the buyer to pay a minimum amount of money for a product or a service, even if the product or service is not delivered. These contracts are most often used in the utility industry to back bonds to finance new power plants. A take-or-pay contract stipulates that the prospective purchaser of the power will take the power from the bond issuer or, if construction is not completed, will repay bondholders the amount of their investment. Take-or-pay contracts are a common way to protect bondholders. In a precedent-setting case in 1983, however, the Washington State Supreme Court voided take-or-pay contracts that many utilities had signed to support the building of the Washington Public Power Supply System (known as WHOOPS) nuclear plants. This action caused WHOOPS to default on some of its bonds, putting a cloud over the validity of the take-or-pay concept.

TAKEOUT
Real estate finance: long-term mortgage loan made to refinance a short-term construction loan (INTERIM LOAN). *See also* STANDBY COMMITMENT.
Securities: withdrawal of cash from a brokerage account, usually after a sale and purchase has resulted in a net CREDIT BALANCE.

TAKEOVER change in the controlling interest of a corporation. A takeover may be a friendly acquisition or an unfriendly bid the TARGET COMPANY might fight with SHARK REPELLENT techniques. A hostile takeover (aiming to replace existing management) is usually attempted through a public TENDER OFFER. Other approaches might be unsolicited merger proposals to directors, accumulations of shares in the open market, or PROXY FIGHTS that seek to install new directors. *See also* ANY-AND-ALL BID; CROWN JEWELS; FAIR-PRICE AMENDMENT; GOLDEN PARACHUTE; GREENMAIL; IN PLAY; KILLER BEES; LEVERAGED BUYOUT; LOCK-UP OPTION; MERGER; PAC-MAN STRATEGY; POISON PILL; RADAR ALERT; RAIDER; RISK ARBITRAGE; SAFE HARBOR; SATURDAY NIGHT SPECIAL; SCHEDULE 13D; SCORCHED EARTH POLICY; SHARK WATCHER; SLEEPING BEAUTY; STAGGERED BOARD OF DIRECTORS; STANDSTILL AGREEMENT; SUPERMAJORITY AMENDMENT; TWO-TIER BID; WHITE KNIGHT; WHITE SQUIRE; WILLIAMS ACT.

TAKEOVER ARBITRAGE *see* RISK ARBITRAGE.

TAKING DELIVERY
In general: accepting receipt of goods from a common carrier or other shipper, usually documented by signing a bill of lading or other form of receipt.
Commodities: accepting physical delivery of a commodity under a FUTURES CONTRACT or SPOT MARKET contract. Delivery requirements, such as the size of the contract and the necessary quality of the commodity, are established by the exchange on which the commodity is traded.
Securities: accepting receipt of stock or bond certificates that have recently been purchased or transferred from another account.

TANGIBLE ASSET any asset not meeting the definition of an INTANGIBLE ASSET, which is a nonphysical right to something presumed to represent an advantage in the marketplace, such as a trademark or patent. Thus tangible assets are clearly those having physical existence, like cash, real estate, or machinery. Yet in accounting, assets such as ACCOUNTS RECEIVABLE are considered tangible, even though they are no more physical than a license or a lease, both of which are considered intangible. In summary: if an asset has physical form it is tangible; if it doesn't, consult a list of what accountants have decided are intangible assets.

TANGIBLE COST oil and gas drilling term meaning the cost of items that can be used over a period of time, such as casings, well fittings, land, and tankage, as distinguished from intangible costs such as drilling, testing, and geologist's expenses. In the most widely used LIMITED PARTNERSHIP sharing arrangements, tangible costs are borne by the GENERAL PARTNER (manager) while intangible costs are borne by the limited partners (investors), usually to be taken as tax deductions. In the event of a dry hole, however, all costs become intangibles. *See also* INTANGIBLE COST.

TANGIBLE NET WORTH total ASSETS less INTANGIBLE ASSETS and total LIABILITIES; also called *net tangible assets*. Intangible assets include nonmaterial benefits such as goodwill, patents, copyrights, and trademarks.

TAPE
1. service that reports prices and size of transactions on major exchanges. Also called *ticker tape,* because of the sound made by the machine that printed the tape before the process was computerized.
2. tape of Dow Jones and other news wires, usually called the BROAD TAPE. *See also* CONSOLIDATED TAPE.

TARGET COMPANY firm that has been chosen as attractive for TAKEOVER by a potential acquirer. The acquirer may buy up to 5% of the target's stock without public disclosure, but it must report all transactions and supply other information to the Securities and Exchange Commission, the exchange the target company is listed on, and the target company itself once 5% or more of the stock is acquired. *See also* TOEHOLD PURCHASE; SCHEDULE 13D; SLEEPING BEAUTY; TENDER OFFER; WILLIAMS ACT.

TARGET PRICE

Finance: price at which an acquirer aims to buy a company in a TAKEOVER.

Options: price of the underlying security after which a certain OPTION will become profitable to its buyer. For example, someone buying an XYZ 50 call for a PREMIUM of $200 could have a target price of 52, after which point the premium will be recouped and the CALL OPTION will result in a profit when exercised.

Stocks: price that an investor is hoping a stock he or she has just bought will rise to within a specified period of time. An investor may buy XYZ at $20, with a target price of $40 in one year's time, for instance.

TARIFF
1. federal tax on imports or exports usually imposed either to raise revenue (called a *revenue tariff*) or to protect domestic firms from import competition (called a *protective tariff*). A tariff may also be designed to correct an imbalance of payments. The money collected under tariffs is called DUTY or *customs duty*.
2. schedule of rates or charges, usually for freight.

TAXABLE INCOME amount of income (after all allowable deductions and adjustments to income) subject to tax. On an individual's federal income tax return, taxable income is ADJUSTED GROSS INCOME (the sum of wages, salaries, dividends, interest, capital gains, business income, etc., less adjustments for INDIVIDUAL RETIREMENT ACCOUNT contributions, moving expenses, unreimbursed business expenses) less itemized or standard deductions and the total of personal exemptions. Once taxable income is known, the individual taxpayer finds the total income tax obligation by checking the Internal Revenue Service tax tables or by calculating the tax according to a rate schedule. TAX CREDITS reduce the tax liability dollar-for-dollar.

NET INCOME of a self-employed person (self-proprietorship) and distributions to members of a partnership are included in adjusted gross income, and hence taxable income, on an individual tax return.

Taxable income of an incorporated business, also called *net income before taxes,* consists of total revenues less cost of goods sold, selling and administrative expenses, interest, and extraordinary items.

TAXABLE MUNICIPAL BOND taxable debt obligation of a state or local government entity, an outgrowth of the TAX REFORM ACT OF 1986 (which restricted the issuance of traditional TAX-EXEMPT SECURITIES). Taxable MUNICIPAL BONDS are issued as PRIVATE PURPOSE BONDS to finance such prohibited projects as a sports stadium; as MUNICIPAL REVENUE BONDS where caps apply; or as PUBLIC PURPOSE BONDS where the 10% private use limitation has been exceeded.

TAX AND LOAN ACCOUNT account in a private-sector depository institution, held in the name of the district Federal Reserve Bank as fiscal agent of the United States, that serves as a repository for operating cash available to the U.S. Treasury. Withheld income taxes, employers' contributions to the Social Security fund, and payments for U.S. government securities routinely go into a tax and loan account.

TAX ANTICIPATION BILL (TAB) short-term obligation issued by the U.S. Treasury in competitive bidding at maturities ranging from 23 to 273 days. TABs typically come due within 5 to 7 days after the quarterly due dates for corporate tax payments, but corporations can tender them at PAR value on those tax deadlines in payment of taxes without forfeiting interest income. Since 1975, TABs have been supplemented by cash management bills, due in 30 days or less, and issued in minimum $10 million blocks. These instruments, which are timed to coincide with the maturity of existing issues, provide the Treasury with additional cash management flexibility while giving large investors a safe place to park temporary funds.

TAX ANTICIPATION NOTE (TAN) short-term obligation of a state or municipal government to finance current expenditures pending receipt of expected tax payments. TAN debt evens out the cash flow and is retired once corporate and individual tax revenues are received.

TAX BASIS

Finance: original cost of an ASSET, less accumulated DEPRECIATION, that goes into the calculation of a gain or loss for tax purposes. Thus, a property acquired for $100,000 that has been depreciated by $40,000 has a tax basis of $60,000 assuming no other adjustments; sale of that property for $120,000 results in a taxable CAPITAL GAIN of $60,000.

Investments: price at which a stock or bond was purchased, plus brokerage commission. The law requires that a PREMIUM paid on the purchase of an investment be amortized.

TAX BRACKET point on the income-tax rate schedules where TAXABLE INCOME falls; also called *marginal tax bracket*. It is expressed as a percentage to be applied to each additional dollar earned over the base amount for that bracket. Under a PROGRESSIVE TAX system, increases in taxable income lead to higher marginal rates in the form of higher brackets. The TAX REFORM ACT OF 1986, introducing a modified flat tax system, reduced the number of tax brackets for individuals from 15 to 2, starting with the 1988 tax year. (A five-bracket structure, with rates ranging from 11% to 38.5%, was provided for the 1987 transition year.) The two brackets set by the law were 15% and 28%, but a 5% surtax effectively put high-income taxpayers in a marginal tax bracket of 33%. For example, a single taxpayer in the 15% bracket paid $15 on each taxable $100 up to $17,850, and 28%, or $28, of each taxable dollar over that level. The 5% surtax applied to single incomes between $43,150 and $89,560; different income figures were involved for heads of household and married couples filing jointly. A DEDUCTION came off the last marginal dollar earned; thus the 28% taxpayer in the above example would save $28 in taxes with each additional $100 of deductions until he worked his way back into the 15% bracket where each $100 deduction would save $15. (A deduction should not be confused with a TAX CREDIT.)

For corporations the 1986 law reduced the number of brackets from five to three. Effective July 1, 1987 (with blended rates applicable to any fiscal year that included that date), firms with taxable income of $50,000 or less were subject to a 15% rate; incomes from $50,000 to $75,000 were taxed at 25%; and incomes from $75,000 and up were taxed at 34%. An additional 5% tax was imposed on income between $100,000 and $335,000, which in effect created a flat tax rate of 34% for corporations with taxable income of $335,000 or more and a 39% effective rate on taxable income in the $100,000 to $335,000 phaseout range.

TAX CREDIT direct, dollar-for-dollar reduction in tax liability, as distinguished from a tax deduction, which reduces taxes only by the percentage of a taxpayer's TAX BRACKET. (A taxpayer in the 28% tax bracket would get a 28 cent benefit from each $1.00 deduction, for example.) In the case of a tax credit, a taxpayer owing $10,000 in tax would owe $9000 if he took advantage of a $1000 tax credit. Under certain conditions, tax credits are allowed for a pensioner above age 65, income tax paid to a foreign country, child care expenses, rehabilitation of historic properties, conducting research and development, building low-income housing, and providing jobs for economically disadvantaged people. The TAX REFORM ACT OF 1986 repealed many tax credits, such as the INVESTMENT CREDIT.

TAX DEFERRED term describing an investment whose accumulated earnings are free from taxation until the investor takes possession of them. For example, the holder of an INDIVIDUAL RETIREMENT ACCOUNT postpones paying taxes on interest, dividends, or capital appreciation if he or she waits until after age 59½ to cash in those gains. Other examples of tax-deferred investment vehicles include KEOGH PLANS; ANNUITIES; VARIABLE LIFE INSURANCE, WHOLE LIFE INSURANCE, and UNIVERSAL LIFE INSURANCE policies; STOCK PURCHASE or DIVIDEND REINVESTMENT PLANS; and Series EE and Series HH U.S. SAVINGS BONDS.

TAX EQUITY AND FISCAL RESPONSIBILITY ACT OF 1982 (TEFRA) federal legislation to raise tax revenue, mainly through closing various loopholes and instituting tougher enforcement procedures. Among its major components:

1. penalties for noncompliance with tax laws were increased, and various steps were taken to facilitate tax collection by the Internal Revenue Service (IRS).
2. ten percent of interest and dividends earned was required to be withheld from all bank and brokerage accounts and forwarded directly to the IRS. (This provision was later canceled by Congress after a major lobbying campaign to overturn it.)

3. TAX PREFERENCE ITEMS were added to the old add-on minimum tax to strengthen the ALTERNATIVE MINIMUM TAX.
4. the floor for medical expense deductions was raised from 3% to 5% of ADJUSTED GROSS INCOME.
5. casualty and theft losses were made deductible only if each loss exceeds $100 and the total excess losses exceed 10% of adjusted gross income.
6. deductions for original issue discount bonds were limited to the amount the issuer would deduct as interest if it issued bonds with a face amount equivalent to the actual proceeds and paying the market rate of interest. This amount must be reduced by the amount of deductions for actual interest.
7. more rapid rates for recovering costs under the ACCELERATED COST RECOVERY SYSTEM (ACRS), which had been scheduled to go into effect in 1985 and 1986, were repealed.
8. most of the rules providing for SAFE HARBOR leasing transactions authorized under the ECONOMIC RECOVERY TAX ACT OF 1981 were repealed. Formerly, companies were allowed to trade unusable tax benefits for cash, but Congress considered the practice abusive.
9. excise taxes were raised to 3% on telephone use, to 16 cents a pack on cigarettes, and to 8% on airline tickets.
10. the Federal Unemployment Tax Act wage base and tax rate were increased.
11. numerous tax incentives for corporate mergers and takeovers were reduced.
12. net extraction losses in foreign oil and gas operations in one country were allowed to offset net extraction income from such operations in other countries in the computation of oil and gas extraction taxes.
13. most bonds were required to be registered so that the government could ensure that bondholders are reporting interest.
14. As long as they are not prohibited by a Foreign Corrupt Practices Act, payments to foreign officials were authorized to be deducted as legitimate business expenses.
15. the basis of assets that generate tax INVESTMENT CREDITS was reduced by one-half the amount of the credit.
16. pension and profit-sharing qualified plans were curtailed with a series of new rules that restricted plan loans, required withholding on plan distributions, limited estate-tax exclusions on certain plan distributions, and restricted ''top-heavy'' plans, those tilted to benefit mostly the top-earning employees of a company.
17. changes were made in the way life insurance companies were taxed.

TAX-EXEMPT SECURITY obligation whose interest is exempt from taxation by federal, state, and/or local authorities. It is frequently called a MUNICIPAL BOND (or simply a *municipal*), even though it may have been issued by a state government or agency or by a county, town, or other political district or subdivision. The security is backed by the FULL FAITH AND CREDIT or by anticipated revenues of the issuing authority. Interest income from tax-exempt municipals is free from federal income taxation as well as from taxation in the jurisdiction where the securities have been issued. Thus, New York City obligations are TRIPLE TAX-EXEMPT to city residents whose income is taxed on the federal, state, and local levels. (A very few municipalities tax residents for their own otherwise tax-exempt issues.)

MUTUAL FUNDS that invest exclusively in tax-exempt securities confer the same tax advantages on their shareholders. However, while a fund's dividends would be entirely tax-exempt on a shareholder's federal tax return, they would be free from state income tax only in proportion to the amount of interest income derived from the taxpayer's home state, assuming no interstate reciprocity arrangements pertain.

The return to investors from a tax-exempt bond is less than that from a corporate bond, because the tax exemption provides extra compensation; the higher the TAX BRACKET of the investor, the more attractive the tax-free alternative becomes. Municipal bond yields vary according to local economic factors, the issuer's perceived ability to repay, and the security's quality RATING assigned by one of the bond-rating agencies. *See also* MORAL OBLIGATION BOND.

TAX LOSS CARRYBACK, CARRYFORWARD tax benefit that allows a company or individual to apply losses to reduce tax liability. A company may OFFSET the current year's capital or net operating losses against profits in the three immediately preceding years, with the earliest year first. After the carryback, it may carry forward (also called a *carryover*) capital losses five years and net operating losses up to 15 years. By then it will presumably have regained financial health.

Individuals may carry over capital losses until they are used up for an unlimited number of years to offset capital gains. Unlike corporations, however, individuals generally cannot carry back losses to apply to prior years' tax returns. The 1986 tax act curbed tax-motivated BUYOUTS by limiting the use of NOLs where a loss corporation has had a 50% or more ownership change in a three-year period. A special set of complex rules pertains to carryback of losses for trading in commodity futures contracts.

TAX PREFERENCE ITEM item specified by the tax law that a taxpayer must include when calculating ALTERNATIVE MINIMUM TAX (AMT). Under the TAX REFORM ACT OF 1986, preference items include: net PASSIVE losses at 100% of value (that is, without the transition benefits the regular tax allows for interests purchased before enactment); benefits from ACCELERATED DEPRECIATION (calculated in different ways for personal property and real property); certain INTANGIBLE COSTS; the excess of fair market value at exercise date over option cost for INCENTIVE STOCK OPTIONS; tax-exempt interest on PRIVATE PURPOSE BONDS of municipalities issued after August 8, 1986; and the untaxed appreciation of property contributed to charity. Corporate preferences are generally the same as for individuals, but in addition include: charges to increase BAD DEBT reserves when they exceed levels reflecting actual experience (applicable to small banks and other financial institutions); earnings based on percentage-of-completion accounting for long-term contracts entered into after February 1, 1986; gains on dispositions of dealer property in the year of disposition (as opposed to the installment method of accounting) effective March 1, 1986; and an amount equal to 50% of the difference between a corporation's book income and its AMT liability. The last-mentioned preference, which is aimed at profits reported to shareholders but not regularly taxed, is scheduled to expire in 1989. *See also* TAX REFORM ACT OF 1976; TAX EQUITY AND FISCAL RESPONSIBILITY ACT OF 1982.

TAX REFORM ACT OF 1976 federal legislation that tightened several provisions and benefits relating to taxation, beginning in the 1976 tax year. Among its major provisions:

1. extended the long-term CAPITAL GAINS holding period from six months to nine months in 1977 and to 12 months beginning in 1978.
2. instituted new rules on determining the TAX BASIS of inherited property.
3. set a new minimum capital gains tax on the sale of a house.
4. established, for homeowners over age 65, a once-in-a-lifetime exclusion of up to $35,000 in capital gains tax on the sale of a principal residence. (This amount was later raised by other tax bills, until it stood at $125,000 in the mid-1980s.)
5. increased the maximum net CAPITAL LOSS deduction from ordinary income on a personal income tax return to $3000 beginning in 1978.

6. extended the period of tax loss carryforward from five years to seven; gave companies the option of carrying losses forward without having first to carry them back; and prohibited acquiring corporations from taking advantage of an acquired firm's loss carryovers unless it gave the acquired firm's stockholders continuing ownership in the combined company.

7. limited deductions for home-office expenses to cases where homes are used as principal business locations, or for meeting with clients.

8. disallowed owners who rent their vacation homes from reporting losses, deducting maintenance costs or taking depreciation on those rentals unless the owners themselves used the homes less than two weeks per year, or less than 10% of total rental time.

9. instituted a deduction up to $3000 for "indirect" moving costs if a new job is more than 35 miles from a previous job.

10. established a child-care tax credit of up to $400 for one child and up to $800 for more than one child.

11. allowed a divorced parent, if contributing at least $1200 in child support, to claim a child as a dependent deduction.

12. instituted a spousal INDIVIDUAL RETIREMENT ACCOUNT, which allowed non-working spouses to contribute up to $250.

13. disallowed losses on tax shelters financed through loans made without any obligation to pay, or where taxpayer's risk is limited by a form of guarantee or REPURCHASE AGREEMENT, except for real estate investments.

14. treated the exercise of a STOCK OPTION as ordinary income rather than as a CAPITAL GAIN.

TAX REFORM ACT OF 1984 legislation enacted by Congress as part of the Deficit Reduction Act of 1984 to reduce the federal budget deficit. The following are highlights from the more than 100 provisions in the Act:

1. shortened the minimum holding period for assets to qualify for long-term capital gains treatment from one year to six months.

2. allowed contributions to be made to an INDIVIDUAL RETIREMENT ACCOUNT no later than April 15 after the tax year for which an IRA benefit is sought; previously the cut-off was the following October 15.

3. allowed the Internal Revenue Service to tax the benefits of loans made on below-market, interest-free, or "gift" terms.

4. tightened INCOME AVERAGING requirements.

5. set a $150 per capita limit on the amount of INDUSTRIAL DEVELOPMENT BONDS that a state could issue in a year, and permitted interest to be tax-exempt only for certain "small issues."

6. retained the 15% minimum tax on corporate TAX PREFERENCE ITEMS as in the TAX REFORM ACT OF 1976, but increased from 15% to 20% the deduction allowed for a tax preference item.

7. restricted GOLDEN PARACHUTE payments to executives by eliminating the corporate tax deductibility of these payments and subjecting them to a non-deductible 20% excise tax.

8. required registration of TAX SHELTERS with the Internal Revenue Service and set penalties for failure to comply. Also set penalties for overvaluing assets used for depreciation in a tax shelter.

9. expanded rules in ERTA to cover additional types of stock and options transactions that make up TAX STRADDLES.

10. repealed the 30% withholding tax on interest, dividends, rents, and royalties paid to foreign investors by U.S. corporations and government agencies.

11. raised the liquor tax, reduced the cigarette tax, and extended the 3% telephone excise tax.

12. delayed to 1987 the scheduled decline in estate and gift taxes.

13. granted a specific tax exemption for many fringe benefits.
14. extended mortgage subsidy bonds through 1988.
15. required ALTERNATIVE MINIMUM TAX quarterly estimated payments.
16. changed the rules affecting taxation of life insurance companies.
17. disqualified from eligibility for long-term capital gains tax the appreciation of market discounts on newly issued ORIGINAL ISSUE DISCOUNT bonds.
18. real estate depreciation was lengthened from 15 to 18 years.
19. delayed implementation of new finance leasing rules until 1988.
20. restricted the sale of unused depreciation tax deductions by tax-exempt entities to companies that can use the deductions.
21. phased out the graduated corporate income tax on the first $100,000 of income for corporations with income over $1 million.
22. created Foreign Sales Corporations (FSCs) to provide American companies with tax deferral advantages to encourage exports.
23. limited tax breaks for luxury automobiles to a maximum writeoff of $16,000 in the first three years of ownership.
24. increased the earned income tax credit for lower-income taxpayers from 10% to a maximum of 11% of the first $5000 of income.
25. eliminated the tax on property transfers in a divorce.
26. increased the standard automobile mileage rate from 9 cents a mile to 12 cents a mile for expenses incurred in volunteer charity work.
27. tightened rules and increased penalties for those who try to inflate deductions by overvaluing property donated to charity.

TAX REFORM ACT OF 1986 landmark federal legislation that made comprehensive changes in the system of U.S. taxation. Among the law's major provisions:

Provisions Affecting Individuals

1. lowered maximum marginal tax rates from 50% to 28%, beginning in 1988 and reduced the number of basic TAX BRACKETS from 14 to 2—28% and 15%. Also instituted a 5% rate surcharge for high-income taxpayers.
2. eliminated the preferential tax treatment of CAPITAL GAINS. Starting in 1988, all gains realized on asset sales are taxed at ordinary income rates, no matter how long the asset was held.
3. increased the personal exemption to $1900 in 1987, $1950 in 1988, and $2000 in 1989. Phased out exemption for high-income taxpayers.
4. increased the STANDARD DEDUCTION, and indexed it to inflation starting in 1989.
5. repealed the deduction for two-earner married couples.
6. repealed income averaging for all taxpayers.
7. repealed the $100 ($200 for couples) dividend exclusion.
8. restricted the deductibility of IRA contributions.
9. mandated the phaseout of consumer interest deductibility by 1991.
10. allowed investment interest expense to be offset against investment income, dollar-for-dollar, without limitation.
11. limited unreimbursed medical expenses that can be deducted to amounts in excess of 7.5% of adjusted gross income.
12. limited the tax deductibility of interest on a first or second home mortgage to the purchase price of the house plus the cost of improvements and amounts used for medical or educational purposes.
13. repealed the deductibility of state and local sales taxes.
14. limited miscellaneous deductions to expenses exceeding 2% of adjusted gross income.
15. limited the deductibility of itemized charitable contributions.
16. strengthened the ALTERNATIVE MINIMUM TAX, and raised the rate to 21%.

17. tightened home office deductions.
18. lowered the deductibility of business entertainment and meal expenses from 100% to 80%.
19. eliminated the benefits of CLIFFORD TRUSTS and other income-shifting devices by taxing unearned income over $1000 on gifts to children under 14 years old at the grantor's tax rate.
20. repealed the tax credit for political contributions.
21. limited the use of losses from PASSIVE activity to offsetting income from passive activity.
22. lowered the top rehabilitation tax credit from 25% to 20%.
23. made all unemployment compensation benefits taxable.
24. repealed the deduction for attending investment seminars.
25. eased the rules for exercise of INCENTIVE STOCK OPTIONS.
26. imposed new limitations on SALARY REDUCTION PLANS and SIMPLIFIED EMPLOYEE PENSION (SEP) PLANS.

Provisions Affecting Business
27. lowered the top corporate tax rate to 34% from 46%, and lowered the number of corporate tax brackets from five to three.
28. applied the ALTERNATIVE MINIMUM TAX (AMT) to corporations, and set a 20% rate.
29. repealed the investment tax credit for property placed in service after 1985.
30. altered the method of calculating DEPRECIATION.
31. limited the deductibility of charges to BAD DEBT reserves to financial institutions with less than $500 million in assets.
32. extended the research and development tax credit, but lowered the rate from 25% to 20%.
33. eliminated the deductibility of interest that banks pay to finance tax-exempt securities holdings.
34. eliminated the deductibility of GREENMAIL payments by companies warding off hostile takeover attempts.
35. restricted COMPLETED CONTRACT METHOD accounting for tax purposes.
36. limited the ability of a company that acquires more than 50% of another firm to use NET OPERATING LOSSES to offset taxes.
37. reduced the corporate DIVIDEND EXCLUSION from 85% to 80%.
38. limited cash and installment method accounting for tax purposes.
39. restricted tax-exemption on MUNICIPAL BONDS to PUBLIC PURPOSE BONDS and specified PRIVATE PURPOSE BONDS. Imposed caps on the dollar amount of permitted private purpose bonds. Limited PREREFUNDING. Made interest on certain private purpose bonds subject to the AMT.
40. amended the rules for qualifying as a REAL ESTATE INVESTMENT TRUST and the taxation of REITs.
41. set up tax rules for real estate mortgage investment conduits (REMICs).
42. changed many rules relating to taxation of foreign operations of U.S. multinational companies.
43. liberalized the requirements for employee VESTING rules in a company's qualified pension plan, and changed other rules affecting employee benefit plans.
44. enhanced benefit of SUBCHAPTER S corporation status.

TAX SELLING selling of securities, usually at year end, to realize losses in a PORTFOLIO, which can be used to OFFSET capital gains and thereby lower an investor's tax liability. *See also* LONG TERM GAIN; LONG TERM LOSS; SELLING SHORT AGAINST THE BOX; SHORT TERM GAIN OR LOSS; SWAP; THIRTY-DAY WASH RULE.

TAX SHELTER method used by investors to legally avoid or reduce tax liabilities. Legal shelters include those using DEPRECIATION of assets like real estate or equipment or DEPLETION allowances for oil and gas exploration. LIMITED PARTNERSHIPS have traditionally offered investors limited liability and tax benefits including "flow through" operating losses usable to offset income from other sources. The TAX REFORM ACT OF 1986 dealt a severe blow to such tax shelters by ruling that PASSIVE losses could be used only to offset passive income, by lengthening depreciation schedules, and by extending AT RISK rules to include real estate investments. Vehicles that allow tax-deferred capital growth, such as INDIVIDUAL RETIREMENT ACCOUNTS (IRAs) and KEOGH PLANS (which also provide current tax deductions for qualified taxpayers), SALARY REDUCTION PLANS, and SINGLE PREMIUM LIFE INSURANCE, are also popular tax shelters as are tax-exempt MUNICIPAL BONDS.

TAX STRADDLE technique whereby OPTION or FUTURES CONTRACTS are used to eliminate economic risk while creating an advantageous tax position. In its most common use, an investor with a CAPITAL GAIN would take a position creating an offsetting "artificial" loss in the current tax year and postponing the gain until the next tax year. The ECONOMIC RECOVERY TAX ACT OF 1981 curtailed this practice by requiring traders to MARK TO THE MARKET at year-end and include unrealized gains in taxable income. The TAX REFORM ACT OF 1986 introduced a change whereby an exception for COVERED WRITERS of calls is denied if the taxpayer fails to hold the covered CALL OPTION for 30 days after the related stock is disposed of at a loss, if gain on the termination or disposition of the option is included in the next year.

TAX UMBRELLA tax loss carryforwards stemming from losses of a company in past years, which act to shield profits earned in the current and future tax years from taxes. *See also* TAX LOSS CARRYBACK, CARRYFORWARD.

TEAR SHEET sheet from one of the six loose-leaf books comprising Standard & Poor's Corporation Records, which provide essential background and financial data on more than 7500 companies. Brokers often tear and mail these sheets to satisfy customer inquiries on specific companies (hence the name).

TECHNICAL ANALYSIS research into the demand and supply for securities and commodities based on trading volume and price studies. Technical analysts use charts or computer programs to identify price trends in a market, security, or commodity future, which they think will foretell price movements. Most analysis is done for the short- or intermediate-term outlook for the security or commodity in question, but some technicians also predict long-term cycles based on charts and other data. Unlike fundamental analysts, technical analysts generally do not concern themselves with the financial position of a company, such as its earnings, or the strength of its balance sheet. *See also* ADVANCE/DECLINE (A-D); ASCENDING TOPS; BREAKOUT; CORRECTION; DESCENDING TOPS; DIP; DOUBLE BOTTOM; DOUBLE TOP; FLAG; FUNDAMENTAL ANALYSIS; GAP; HEAD AND SHOULDERS; HORIZONTAL PRICE MOVEMENT; MOVING AVERAGE; PENNANT; POINT AND FIGURE CHART; RESISTANCE LEVEL; REVERSAL; RISING BOTTOMS; SAUCER; SELLING CLIMAX; SUPPORT LEVEL; TRIANGLE; V FORMATION; VERTICAL LINE CHARTING; W FORMATION.

TECHNICAL RALLY short rise in securities or commodities futures prices within a general declining trend. Such a rally may result because investors are bargain-hunting or because analysts have noticed a particular SUPPORT LEVEL at which securities usually bounce up.

TECHNICAL SIGN short-term trend that TECHNICAL ANALYSIS can identify as significant in the price movement of a security or a commodity.

TEFRA *see* TAX EQUITY AND FISCAL RESPONSIBILITY ACT OF 1982.

TELEPHONE SWITCHING process of shifting assets from one MUTUAL FUND or VARIABLE ANNUITY portfolio to another by telephone. Such a switch may be among the stock, bond, or money-market funds of a single FAMILY OF FUNDS, or it may be from a fund in one family to a fund in another. Transfers involving portfolios in annuity contracts do not trigger taxation of gains as do mutual fund switches.

TENANCY IN COMMON ownership of property by two or more persons in such a way that when one of them dies, the deceased's undivided interest passes to his or her heirs and not to the surviving tenant(s). This arrangement is distinguished from joint tenancy (*see* JOINT TENANTS WITH THE RIGHT OF SURVIVORSHIP) and tenancy by the entirety (a similar arrangement pertaining to a married couple where the husband or wife automatically acquires the other's share upon death).

TENANT

Real Estate: (1) holder or possessor of real property; (2) lessee.

Securities: part owner of a security.
   See also JOINT TENANTS WITH RIGHT OF SURVIVORSHIP; TENANCY IN COMMON.

TENDER
1. act of surrendering one's shares in a corporation in response to an offer to buy them at a set price. *See also* TENDER OFFER.
2. to submit a formal bid to buy a security, as in a U.S. Treasury bill auction. *See also* DUTCH AUCTION.
3. offer of money or goods in settlement of a prior debt or claim, as in the delivery of goods on the due date of a FUTURES CONTRACT.
4. agreed-upon medium for the settlement of financial transactions, such as U.S. currency, which is labeled ''legal tender for all debts, public and private.''

TENDER OFFER offer to buy shares of a corporation, usually at a PREMIUM above the shares' market price, for cash, securities, or both, often with the objective of taking control of the TARGET COMPANY. A tender offer may arise from friendly negotiations between the company and a corporate suitor or may be unsolicited and possibly unfriendly, resulting in countermeasures being taken by the target firm. The Securities and Exchange Commission requires any corporate suitor accumulating 5% or more of a target company to make disclosures to the SEC, the target company, and the relevant exchange. *See also* SCHEDULE 13D; TAKEOVER; TREASURY STOCK.

10-K REPORT *see* FORM 10-K.

TEN PERCENT GUIDELINE MUNICIPAL BOND analysts' guideline that funded debt over 10% of the ASSESSED VALUATION of taxable property in a municipality is excessive.

TERM
1. period of time during which the conditions of a contract will be carried out. This may refer to the time in which loan payments must be made, or the time when interest payments will be made on a certificate of deposit or a bond. It also may refer to the length of time a life insurance policy is in force. *See also* TERM LIFE INSURANCE.
2. provision specifying the nature of an agreement or contract, as in *terms and conditions*.

3. period of time an official or board member is elected or appointed to serve. For example, Federal Reserve governors are appointed for 14-year terms.

TERM CERTIFICATE CERTIFICATE OF DEPOSIT with a longer-term maturity date. Such CDs can range in length from one year to ten years, though the most popular term certificates are those for one or two years. Certificate holders usually receive a fixed rate of interest, payable semiannually during the term, and are subject to costly EARLY WITHDRAWAL PENALTIES if the certificate is cashed in before the scheduled maturity.

TERM LIFE INSURANCE form of life insurance, written for a specified period, that requires the policyholder to pay only for the cost of protection against death; that is, no cash value is built up as in WHOLE LIFE INSURANCE. Every time the policy is renewed, the premium is higher, since the insured is older and therefore statistically more likely to die. Term insurance is far cheaper than whole life, giving policyholders the alternative of using the savings to invest on their own.

TERM LOAN intermediate- to long-term (typically, two to ten years) secured credit granted to a company by a commercial bank, insurance company, or commercial finance company usually to finance capital equipment or provide working capital. The loan is amortized over a fixed period, sometimes ending with a BALLOON payment. Borrowers under term loan agreements are normally required to meet minimum WORKING CAPITAL and debt to net worth tests, to limit dividends, and to maintain continuity of management.

TEST

In general: examination to determine knowledge, competence, or qualifications.

Finance: criterion used to measure compliance with financial ratio requirements of indentures and other loan agreements (for example, a current asset to current liability test, or a debt to net worth test).

Securities: term used in reference to a price movement that approaches a SUPPORT LEVEL or a RESISTANCE LEVEL established earlier by a commodity future, security, or market. A test is passed if the levels are not penetrated and is failed if prices go on to new lows or highs. Technical analysts say, for instance, that if the Dow Jones Industrials last formed a solid base at 1000, and prices have been falling from 1100, a period of testing is approaching. If prices rebound once the Dow hits 1000 and go up further, the test is passed. If prices continue to drop below 1000, however, the test is failed. *See also* TECHNICAL ANALYSIS.

TESTAMENTARY TRUST trust created by a will, as distinguished from an INTER VIVOS TRUST created during the lifetime of the GRANTOR.

THEORETICAL VALUE (OF A RIGHT) mathematically determined MARKET VALUE of a SUBSCRIPTION RIGHT after the offering is announced but before the stock goes EX-RIGHTS. The formula includes the current market value of the common stock, the subscription price, and the number of rights required to purchase a share of stock:

theoretical value of a right

$$= \frac{\text{market value of common stock} - \text{subscription price per share}}{\text{number of rights needed to buy 1 share} + 1}$$

Thus, if the common stock market price is $50 per share, the subscription price is $45 per share, and the subscription ratio is 4 to 1, the value of one right would be $1:

$$\frac{50 - 45}{4 + 1} = \frac{5}{5} = 1$$

THIN MARKET market in which there are few bids to buy and few offers to sell. A thin market may apply to an entire class of securities or commodities futures— such as small OVER THE COUNTER stocks or the platinum market—or it may refer to a particular stock, whether exchange-listed or over-the-counter. Prices in thin markets are more volatile than in markets with great LIQUIDITY, since the few trades that take place can affect prices significantly. Institutional investors who buy and sell large blocks of stock tend to avoid thin markets, because it is difficult for them to get in or out of a POSITION without materially affecting the stock's price.

THIRD MARKET nonexchange-member broker/dealers and institutional investors trading OVER THE COUNTER in exchange-listed securities. The third market rose to importance in the 1950s when institutional investors began buying common stocks as an inflation hedge and fixed commission rates still prevailed on the exchanges. By trading large blocks with nonmember firms, they both saved commissions and avoided the unsettling effects on prices that large trades on the exchanges produced. After commission rates were deregulated in May 1975, a number of the firms active in the third market became member firms so they could deal with members as well as nonmembers. At the same time, member firms began increasingly to move large blocks of stock off the floor of the exchanges, in effect becoming participants in the third market. Before selling securities off the exchange to a nonmember, however, a member firm must satisfy all LIMIT ORDERS on the SPECIALIST'S BOOK at the same price or higher. *See also* OFF-FLOOR ORDER.

THIRD-PARTY CHECK

1. check negotiated through a bank, except one payable to the writer of the check (that is, a check written for cash). The *primary party* to a transaction is the bank on which a check is drawn. The *secondary party* is the drawer of the check against funds on deposit in the bank. The *third party* is the payee who endorses the check.
2. double-endorsed check. In this instance, the payee endorses the check by signing the back, then passes the check to a subsequent holder, who endorses it prior to cashing it. Recipients of checks with multiple endorsers are reluctant to accept them unless they can verify each endorser's signature.
3. payable-through drafts and other negotiable orders not directly serviced by the providing company. For example, a check written against a money market mutual fund is processed not by the mutual fund company but typically by a commercial bank that provides a ''third-party'' or ''payable-through'' service. Money orders, credit union share drafts, and checks drawn against a brokerage account are other examples of payable-through or third-party items.

THIRTY-DAY VISIBLE SUPPLY total dollar volume of new MUNICIPAL BONDS carrying maturities of 13 months or more that are scheduled to reach the market within 30 days. The figure is supplied on Thursdays in the *BOND BUYER*.

THIRTY-DAY WASH RULE Internal Revenue Service rule stating that losses on a sale of stock may not be used as losses for tax purposes (that is, used to OFFSET gains) if equivalent stock is purchased within 30 days before or 30 after the date of sale.

THRIFT INSTITUTION organization formed primarily as a depository for consumer savings, the most common varieties of which are the SAVINGS AND LOAN ASSOCIATION and the SAVINGS BANK. Traditionally, savings institutions have loaned most of their deposit funds in the residential mortgage market and continued to do so after legislation in the early 1980s expanded their range of depository services and allowed them to make commercial and consumer loans. CREDIT UNIONS are sometimes included in the thrift institution category, since their principal source of deposits is also personal savings, though they have traditionally made small consumer loans, not mortgage loans. *See also* DEPOSITORY INSTITUTIONS DEREGULATION AND MONETARY CONTROL ACT; MUTUAL ASSOCIATION; MUTUAL SAVINGS BANK.

TICK upward or downward price movement in a security's trades. Technical analysts watch the tick of a stock's successive up or down moves to get a feel of the stock's trend. *See also* DOWNTICK; MINUS TICK; PLUS TICK; SHORT SALE RULE; TECHNICAL ANALYSIS; UPTICK; ZERO-MINUS TICK; ZERO-PLUS TICK.

TICKER system that produces a running report of trading activity on the stock exchanges, called the TICKER TAPE. The name derives from machines that, in times past, printed information by punching holes in a paper tape, making an audible ticking sound as the tape was fed forth. Today's ticker tape is a computer screen and the term is used to refer both to the CONSOLIDATED TAPE, which shows the STOCK SYMBOL, latest price, and volume of trades on the exchanges, and to news ticker services. *See also* QUOTATION BOARD.

TICKER SYMBOL letters that identify a security for trading purposes on the CONSOLIDATED TAPE, such as XON for Exxon Corporation. *See also* STOCK SYMBOL; TICKER TAPE.

TICKER TAPE device that relays the STOCK SYMBOL and the latest price and volume on securities as they are traded to investors around the world. Prior to the advent of computers, this machine had a loud printing device that made a ticking sound. Since 1975, the New York Stock Exchange and the American Stock Exchange have used a CONSOLIDATED TAPE that indicates the New York or REGIONAL STOCK EXCHANGE on which a trade originated. Other systems, known as news tickers, pass along the latest economic, financial and market news developments. See also TAPE.

TL	MMM&P	IBM&T	XON&M	
3S41⅝	83½	4S124¼		2S41

Sample section of the consolidated tape.
Trades in Time, Inc., Minnesota Mining and Manufacturing, IBM, and Exxon are shown. Letters following the ampersands in the upper line indicate the marketplace in which the trade took place: P signifies the Pacific Stock Exchange, T the THIRD MARKET, M the Midwest Exchange; no indication means the New York Stock Exchange. Other codes not illustrated are X for Philadelphia Stock Exchange, B for Boston Stock Exchange, O for other markets, including INSTINET. In the lower line, where a number precedes the letter S, a multiple of 100 shares is indicated. Thus, 300 shares of Time, Inc. were transacted at a price of 41⅝ on the New York Stock Exchange; 100 shares of Minnesota Mining were traded on the Pacific Exchange at 83½, and so on.

TIGER acronym for Treasury Investors Growth Receipt, a form of ZERO-COUPON SECURITY first created by the brokerage firm of Merrill Lynch, Pierce, Fenner & Smith. TIGERS are U.S. government-backed bonds that have been stripped of their COUPONS. Both the CORPUS (principal) of the bonds and the individual coupons are sold separately at a deep discount from their face value. Investors receive FACE VALUE for the TIGERS when the bonds mature but do not receive periodic interest payments. Under Internal Revenue Service rules, however, TIGER holders owe income taxes on the imputed interest they would have earned had the bond been a FULL COUPON BOND. To avoid having to pay taxes without having the benefit of the income to pay them from, most investors put TIGERS in Individual Retirement or Keogh accounts or in other TAX DEFERRED plans. Also called *TIGR*.

TIGHT MARKET market in general or market for a particular security marked by active trading and narrow bid-offer price spreads. In contrast, inactive trading and wide spreads characterize a *slack market*. *See also* SPREAD.

TIGHT MONEY economic condition in which credit is difficult to secure, usually as the result of Federal Reserve action to restrict the MONEY SUPPLY. The opposite is *easy money*. *See also* MONETARY POLICY.

TIME DEPOSIT savings account or CERTIFICATE OF DEPOSIT held in a financial institution for a fixed term or with the understanding that the depositor can withdraw only by giving notice. While a bank is authorized to require 30 days' notice of withdrawal from savings accounts, passbook accounts are generally regarded as readily available funds. Certificates of deposit, on the other hand, are issued for a specified term of 30 days or more, and provide penalties for early withdrawal. Financial institutions are free to negotiate any maturity term a customer might desire on a time deposit or certificate, as long as the term is at least 30 days, and to pay interest rates as high or low as the market will bear. *See also* DEPOSITORY INSTITUTIONS DEREGULATION AND MONETARY CONTROL ACT; REGULATION Q.

TIME DRAFT DRAFT payable at a specified or determinable time in the future, as distinguished from a *sight draft*, which is payable on presentation and delivery.

TIMES FIXED CHARGES *see* FIXED-CHARGE COVERAGE.

TIME SPREAD OPTION strategy in which an investor buys and sells PUT OPTION and CALL OPTION contracts with the same EXERCISE PRICE but with different expiration dates. The purpose of this and other option strategies is to profit from the difference in OPTION PREMIUMS—the prices paid to buy the options. *See also* CALENDAR SPREAD; HORIZONTAL SPREAD; SPREAD.

TIME VALUE

In general: price put on the time an investor has to wait until an investment matures, as determined by calculating the PRESENT VALUE of the investment at maturity. *See also* YIELD TO MATURITY.

Options: that part of a stock option PREMIUM that reflects the time remaining on an option contract before expiration. The premium is composed of this time value and the INTRINSIC VALUE of the option.

Stocks: difference between the price at which a company is taken over and the price before the TAKEOVER occurs. For example, if XYZ Company is to be taken over at $30 a share in two months, XYZ shares might presently sell for $28.50.

The $1.50 per share difference is the cost of the time value those owning XYZ must bear if they want to wait two months to get $30 a share. As the two months pass, the time value will shrink, until it disappears on the day of the takeover. The time that investors hold XYZ has a price because it could be used to invest in something else providing a higher return. *See also* OPPORTUNITY COST.

TIP

In general: payment over and above a formal cost or charge, ostensibly given in appreciation for extra service, to a waiter, bellhop, cabdriver, or other person engaged in service. Also called a *gratuity*.

Investments: information passed by one person to another as a basis for buy or sell action in a security. Such information is presumed to be of material value and not available to the general public. The Securities and Exchange Commission regulates the use of such information by so-called insiders, and court cases have established the liability of persons receiving and using or passing on such information (called tippees) in certain circumstances. *See also* INSIDER; INSIDE INFORMATION.

TOEHOLD PURCHASE accumulation by an acquirer of less than 5% of the shares of a TARGET COMPANY. Once 5% is acquired, the acquirer is required to file with the Securities and Exchange Commission, the appropriate stock exchange, and the target company, explaining what is happening and what can be expected. *See also* SCHEDULE 13D; WILLIAMS ACT.

TOLL REVENUE BOND MUNICIPAL BOND supported by revenues from tolls paid by users of the public project built with the bond proceeds. Toll revenue bonds frequently are floated to build bridges, tunnels, and roads. *See also* REVENUE BOND.

TOMBSTONE advertisement placed in newspapers by investment bankers in a PUBLIC OFFERING of securities. It gives basic details about the issue and lists the UNDERWRITING GROUP members involved in the offering in alphabetically organized groupings according to the size of their participations. It is not ''an offer to sell or a solicitation of an offer to buy,'' but rather it calls attention to the PROSPECTUS, sometimes called the *offering circular*. A tombstone may also be placed by an investment banking firm to announce its role in a PRIVATE PLACEMENT, corporate MERGER, or ACQUISITION; by a corporation to announce a major business or real estate deal; or by a firm in the financial community to announce a personnel development or a principal's death. *See also* MEZZANINE BRACKET.

TON bond traders' jargon for $100 million.

TOP-DOWN APPROACH TO INVESTING method in which an investor first looks at trends in the general economy, and next selects industries and then companies that should benefit from those trends. For example, an investor who thinks inflation will stay low might be attracted to the retailing industry, since consumers' spending power will be enhanced by low inflation. The investor then might look at Macy's, Federated Department Stores, and other major retailers to see which company has the best earnings prospects in the near term. The opposite method is called the BOTTOM-UP APPROACH TO INVESTING.

TOPPING OUT term denoting a market or a security that is at the end of a period of rising prices and can now be expected to stay on a plateau or even to decline.

TOTAL CAPITALIZATION CAPITAL STRUCTURE of a company, including LONG-TERM DEBT and all forms of EQUITY.

TOTAL COST

Accounting: (usually pl.) sum of FIXED COSTS, semivariable costs, and VARIABLE COSTS.

Investments: contract price paid for a security plus the brokerage commission plus any ACCRUED INTEREST due the seller (if the security is a bond). The figure is not to be confused with the COST BASIS for the purpose of figuring the CAPITAL GAINS TAX, which may involve other factors such as amortization of bond premiums.

TOTAL RETURN annual return on an investment including appreciation and dividends or interest; a complete definition would also include personal tax considerations and present value adjustments. For bonds, total return is YIELD TO MATURITY. For stocks, future appreciation is projected using the current PRICE/EARNINGS RATIO. In options trading, total return means dividends plus capital gains plus premium income.

TOTAL VOLUME total number of shares or contracts traded in a stock, bond, commodity future, or option on a particular day. For stocks and bonds, this is the aggregate of trades on national exchanges like the New York and American stock exchanges and on regional exchanges. For commodities futures and options, it represents the volume of trades executed around the world in one day. For over-the-counter securities, total volume is measured by the NASDAQ index.

TOUT to promote a particular security aggressively, usually done by a corporate spokesman, public relations firm, broker, or analyst with a vested interest in promoting the stock. Touting a stock is unethical if it misleads investors. *See also* INVESTMENT ADVISERS ACT; INVESTOR RELATIONS DEPARTMENT.

TRADE

In general:
1. buying or selling of goods and services among companies, states, or countries, called *commerce*. The amount of goods and services imported minus the amount exported makes up a country's BALANCE OF TRADE. *See also* TARIFF; TRADE DEFICIT.
2. those in the business of selling products are called *members of the trade*. As such, they receive DISCOUNTS from the price the public has to pay.
3. group of manufacturers who compete in the same market. These companies form trade associations and publish trade journals.
4. commercial companies that do business with each other. For example, ACCOUNTS PAYABLE to suppliers are called *trade accounts payable*; the term TRADE CREDIT is used to describe accounts payable as a source of WORKING CAPITAL financing. Companies paying their bills promptly receive *trade discounts* when available.
5. synonymous with BARTER, the exchange of goods and services without the use of money.

Securities: to carry out a transaction of buying or selling a stock, a bond, or a commodity future contract. A trade is consummated when a buyer and seller agree on a price at which the trade will be executed. A TRADER frequently buys and sells for his or her own account securities for short-term profits, as contrasted with an investor who holds his positions in hopes of long-term gains.

TRADE BALANCE *see* BALANCE OF TRADE.

TRADE CREDIT open account arrangements with suppliers of goods and services, and a firm's record of payment with the suppliers. Trade liabilities comprise a company's ACCOUNTS PAYABLE. DUN & BRADSTREET is the largest compiler of trade credit information, rating commercial firms and supplying published reports. Trade credit data is also processed by MERCANTILE AGENCIES specializing in different industries.

Trade credit is an important external source of WORKING CAPITAL for a company, although such credit can be highly expensive. Terms of 2% 10 days, net 30 days (2% discount if paid in 10 days, the net [full] amount due in 30 days) translate into a 36% annual interest rate if not taken advantage of. On the other hand, the same terms translate into a borrowing rate of slightly over 15% if payment is made in 60 days instead of 30.

TRADE DATE day on which a security or a commodity future trade actually takes place. The SETTLEMENT DATE usually follows the trade date by five business days, but varies depending on the transaction and method of delivery used. *See also* DELAYED DELIVERY; DELIVERY DATE; REGULAR-WAY DELIVERY (AND SETTLEMENT); SELLER'S OPTION.

TRADE DEFICIT OR SURPLUS excess of imports over exports (*trade deficit*) or of exports over imports (*trade surplus*), resulting in a negative or positive BALANCE OF TRADE. The balance of trade is made up of transactions in merchandise and other movable goods and is only one factor comprising the larger *current account* (which includes services and tourism, transportation, and other *invisible items*, such as interest and profits earned abroad) in the overall BALANCE OF PAYMENTS. Factors influencing a country's balance of trade include the strength or weakness of its currency in relation to those of the countries with which it trades (a strong U.S. dollar, for example, makes goods produced in other countries relatively cheap for Americans), production advantages in key manufacturing areas (Japanese automobiles, for instance), or the domestic economy of a trading country where production may or may not be meeting demand.

TRADEMARK distinctive name, symbol, motto, or emblem that identifies a product, service, or firm. In the United States, trademark rights—the right to prevent competitors from using similar marks in selling or advertising—arise out of use; that is, registration is not essential to establish the legal existence of a mark. A trademark registered with the U.S. Patent and Trademark Office is good for 20 years, renewable as long as used. Products may be both patented and protected by trademark, the advantage being that when the patent runs out, exclusivity can be continued indefinitely with the trademark. A trademark is classified on a BALANCE SHEET as an INTANGIBLE ASSET.

Although, like land, trademarks have an indefinite life and cannot technically be amortized, in practice accountants do amortize trademarks over their estimated life, not to exceed 40 years.

TRADER

In general: anyone who buys and sells goods or services for profit; a DEALER or *merchant*. *See also* BARTER; TRADE.

Investments:
1. individual who buys and sells securities, such as STOCKS, BONDS, OPTIONS, or commodities, such as wheat, gold, or FOREIGN EXCHANGE, for his or her own account—that is, as a dealer or PRINCIPAL—rather than as a BROKER or AGENT.
2. individual who buys and sells securities or commodities for his or her own account on a short-term basis in anticipation of quick profits; a *speculator*.

See also DAY TRADE; COMPETITIVE TRADER; FLOOR TRADER; REGISTERED COMPETITIVE MARKET MAKER; REGISTERED COMPETITIVE TRADER; SPECULATION.

TRADING AUTHORIZATION document giving a brokerage firm employee acting as AGENT (BROKER) the POWER OF ATTORNEY in buy-sell transactions for a customer.

TRADING DIVIDENDS technique of buying and selling stocks in other firms by a corporation in order to maximize the number of DIVIDENDS it can collect. This action is advantageous, because 80% of the dividend income it receives from the stocks of other companies is not taxed, according to Internal Revenue Service regulations. *See also* DIVIDEND EXCLUSION.

TRADING HALT *see* SUSPENDED TRADING.

TRADING LIMIT *see* DAILY TRADING LIMIT; LIMIT UP, LIMIT DOWN.

TRADING PATTERN long-range direction of a security or commodity future price. This pattern is charted by drawing a line connecting the highest prices the security has reached and another line connecting the lowest prices the security has traded at over the same time frame. These two lines will be pointing either up or down, indicating the security's long-term trading pattern.

See also TRENDLINE.

TRADING PATTERN

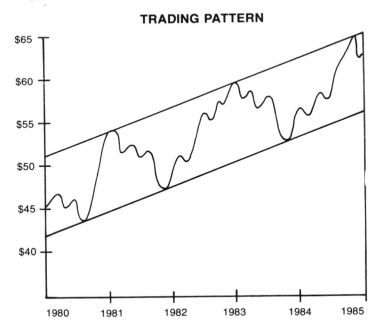

TRADING POST physical location on a stock exchange floor where particular securities are bought and sold. It is here that the SPECIALIST in a particular security performs his market-making functions and that the CROWD (floor brokers with orders in that security) congregates. The New York Stock Exchange, for example, has 22 trading posts, most handling around 100 stocks. *See also* FLOOR BROKER; FLOOR TRADER; MAKE A MARKET.

TRADING RANGE

Commodities: trading limit set by a COMMODITIES futures exchange for a particular commodity. The price of a commodity future contract may not go higher or lower than that limit during one day's trading. *See also* LIMIT UP, LIMIT DOWN.

Securities: range between the highest and lowest prices at which a security or a market has traded. The trading range for XYZ Corporation might be $40 to $60 over the last two years, for example. If a security or a market seems to be stuck in a narrow price range, analysts say that it is a trading range market, which will eventually be followed by a significant up or down move. *See also* FLAG; PENNANT; TRIANGLE; WEDGE.

TRADING UNIT number of SHARES, BONDS, or other securities that is generally accepted for ordinary trading purposes on the exchanges. *See also* ODD LOT; ROUND LOT; UNIT OF TRADING.

TRADING VARIATION fractions to which securities transaction prices are rounded. For example, stocks are rounded up or down to the nearest eighth of a point. Options over $3 are also rounded to an eighth, but options under $3 are rounded to $\frac{1}{16}$. Corporate and municipal bonds are rounded to $\frac{1}{8}$, medium- and long-term government notes and bonds to $\frac{1}{32}$, and shorter-term government bonds to $\frac{1}{64}$. *See also* PLUS.

TRANCH *see* COLLATERALIZED MORTGAGE OBLIGATION (CMO).

TRANSACTION

Accounting: event or condition recognized by an entry in the books of account.

Securities: execution of an order to buy or sell a security or commodity futures contract. After the buyer and seller have agreed on a price, the seller is obligated to deliver the security or commodity involved, and the buyer is obligated to accept it. *See also* TRADE.

TRANSFER AGENT agent, usually a commercial bank, appointed by a corporation, to maintain records of stock and bond owners, to cancel and issue certificates, and to resolve problems arising from lost, destroyed, or stolen certificates. (Preventing OVERISSUE of shares is the function of the REGISTRAR.) A corporation may also serve as its own transfer agent.

TRANSFER PRICE price charged by individual entities in a multi-entity corporation on transactions among themselves; also termed *transfer cost*. This concept is used where each entity is managed as a PROFIT CENTER—that is, held responsible for its own RETURN ON INVESTED CAPITAL—and must therefore deal with the other internal parts of the corporation on an arm's-length (or market) basis. *See also* ARM'S LENGTH TRANSACTION.

TRANSFER TAX

1. combined federal tax on gifts and estates. *See* ESTATE TAX; GIFT TAX.
2. federal tax on the sale of all bonds (except obligations of the United States, foreign governments, states, and municipalities) and all stocks. The tax is paid by the seller at the time ownership is transferred and involves a few pennies per $100 of value.
3. tax levied by some state and local governments on the transfer of such docu-

ments as deeds to property, securities, or licenses. Such taxes are paid, usually with stamps, by the seller or donor and are determined by the location of the transfer agent. States with transfer taxes on stock transactions are New York, Florida, South Carolina, and Texas. New York bases its tax on selling price; the other states apply the tax to PAR value (giving NO-PAR-VALUE STOCK a value of $100). Bonds are not taxed at the state level.

TRANSMITTAL LETTER letter sent with a document, security, or shipment describing the contents and the purpose of the transaction.

TREASURER company officer responsible for the receipt, custody, investment, and disbursement of funds, for borrowings, and, if it is a public company, for the maintenance of a market for its securities. Depending on the size of the organization, the treasurer may also function as the CONTROLLER, with accounting and audit responsibilities. The laws of many states require that a corporation have a treasurer. *See also* CHIEF FINANCIAL OFFICER (CFO).

TREASURIES NEGOTIABLE debt obligations of the U.S. government, secured by its FULL FAITH AND CREDIT and issued at various schedules and maturities. The income from Treasury securities is exempt from state and local, but not federal, taxes.
1. *Treasury bills*—short-term securities with maturities of one year or less issued at a discount from FACE VALUE. Auctions of 91-day and 182-day BILLS take place weekly, and the yields are watched closely in the money markets for signs of interest rate trends. Many floating-rate loans and variable-rate mortgages have interest rates tied to these bills. The Treasury also auctions 52-week bills once every four weeks. At times it also issues very short-term cash management bills, TAX ANTICIPATION BILLS, and treasury certificates of indebtedness. Treasury bills are issued in minimum denominations of $10,000, with $5000 increments above $10,000 (except for cash management bills, which are sold in minimum $10 million blocks). Individual investors who do not submit a COMPETITIVE BID are sold bills at the average price of the winning competitive bids. Treasury bills are the primary instrument used by the Federal Reserve in its regulation of MONEY SUPPLY through OPEN MARKET OPERATIONS. *See also* DUTCH AUCTION; REPURCHASE AGREEMENT.
2. *Treasury bonds*—long-term debt instruments with maturities of 10 years or longer issued in minimum denominations of $1000.
3. *Treasury notes*—intermediate securities with maturities of 1 to 10 years. Denominations range from $1000 to $1 million or more. The notes are sold by cash subscription, in exchange for outstanding or maturing government issues, or at auction.

TREASURY BILL *See* BILL; TREASURIES.

TREASURY BOND *see* TREASURIES.

TREASURY STOCK stock reacquired by the issuing company and available for RETIREMENT or resale. It is issued but not outstanding. It cannot be voted and it pays or accrues no dividends. It is not included in any of the ratios measuring values per common share. Among the reasons treasury stock is created are (1) to provide an alternative to paying taxable dividends, since the decreased amount of outstanding shares increases the per share value and often the market price; (2) to provide for the exercise of stock options and warrants and the conversion of convertible securities; (3) in countering a TENDER OFFER by a potential acquirer; (4) to alter the DEBT-TO-EQUITY RATIO by issuing bonds to finance the reacquisition of shares; (5) as a result of the STABILIZATION of the market price during a NEW ISSUE. Also called *reacquired stock* and *treasury shares*. *See also* ISSUED AND OUTSTANDING; UNISSUED STOCK.

TREND

In general: any general direction of movement. For example: "There is an upward (downward, level) trend in XYZ sales," or "There is a trend toward increased computerization of trading on Wall Street."

Securities: long-term price or trading volume movements either up, down, or sideways, which characterize a particular market, commodity or security. Also applies to interest rates and yields.

TRENDLINE line used by technical analysts to chart the past direction of a security or commodity future in order to help predict future price movements. The trendline is made by connecting the highest or lowest prices to which a security or commodity has risen or fallen within a particular time period. The angle of the resulting line will indicate if the security or commodity is in a downtrend or uptrend. If the price rises above a downward sloping trendline or drops below a rising uptrend line, technical analysts say that a new direction may be emerging. *See also* TECHNICAL ANALYSIS; TRADING PATTERN.

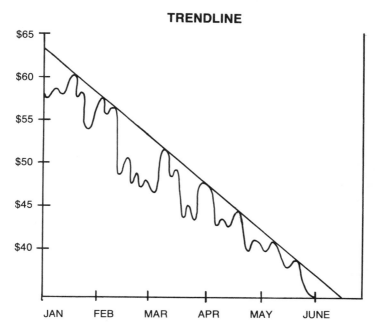

TRIANGLE technical chart pattern that has two base points and a top point, formed by connecting a stock's price movements with a line. In a typical triangle pattern, the apex points to the right, although in reverse triangles the apex points to the left. In a typical triangle, there are a series of two or more rallies and price drops where each succeeding peak is lower than the preceding peak, and each bottom is higher than the preceding bottom. In a right-angled triangle, the sloping part of the formation often points in the direction of the breakout. Technical analysts find it significant when a security's price breaks out of the triangle formation, either up or down, because that usually means the security's price will continue in that direction. *See also* PENNANT; TECHNICAL ANALYSIS; WEDGE.

TRIANGLE

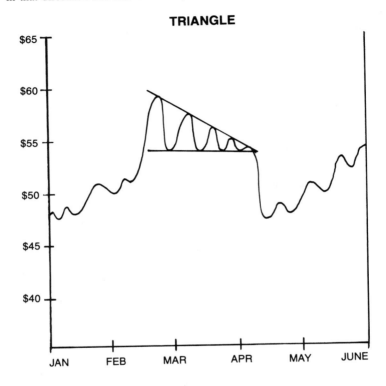

TRICKLE DOWN theory that economic growth can best be achieved by letting businesses flourish, since their prosperity will ultimately trickle down to middle- and lower-income people, who will benefit by increased economic activity. Economists who argue for this method say that it produces more long-term growth than if government made direct welfare grants to the middle- and lower-income sectors. *See also* SUPPLY-SIDE ECONOMICS.

TRIPLE TAX EXEMPT feature of MUNICIPAL BONDS in which interest is exempt from federal, state, and local taxation for residents of the states and localities that issue them. Such bonds are particularly attractive in states with high income tax rates. Many municipal bond funds buy only triple tax exempt bonds and market them to residents of the state and city of the issuer. *See also* SINGLE-STATE MUNIC-IPAL BOND FUND.

TRIPLE WITCHING HOUR last trading hour on the third Friday of March, June, September, and December, when OPTIONS and futures on stock indexes expire concurrently. Massive trades in index futures, options, and underlying stocks by hedge strategists and arbitrageurs cause abnormal activity (NOISE) and VOLATILITY. Smaller-scale *witching hours* occur in the other eight months, usually on the third Friday, when index futures or options expire.

TRUNCATION shortening of processing steps, in an effort to reduce paperwork and operating costs. For example, check truncation, or check SAFEKEEPING, where the bank holds the checks or microfilm records of them in a central file.

TRUST

Business: type of corporate combination that engaged in monopolies and restraint of trade and that operated freely until the ANTITRUST LAWS of the late 19th century and early 20th century. The name derived from the use of the voting trust, in which a small number of trustees vote a majority of the shares of a corporation. The voting trust survives as a means of facilitating the reorganization of firms in difficulty. *See also* INVESTMENT COMPANY; VOTING TRUST CERTIFICATE.

Law: FIDUCIARY relationship in which a person, called a *trustee,* holds title to property for the benefit of another person, called a BENEFICIARY. The person creating the trust is the *creator, settlor,* GRANTOR, or *donor;* the property itself is called the CORPUS, *trust res, trust fund,* or *trust estate,* which is distinguished from any income earned by it. If the trust is created while the donor is living, it is called a *living trust* or INTER VIVOS TRUST. A trust created by a will is called a TESTAMENTARY TRUST. The trustee is usually charged with investing trust property productively and, unless specifically limited, can sell, mortgage, or lease the property as he or she deems warranted. *See also* CLIFFORD TRUST; INVESTMENT TRUST; TRUST COMPANY; TRUSTEE IN BANKRUPTCY; TRUST INDENTURE ACT OF 1939.

TRUST COMPANY organization, usually combined with a commercial bank, which is engaged as a trustee, FIDUCIARY, or AGENT for individuals or businesses in the administration of TRUST funds, estates, custodial arrangements, stock transfer and registration, and other related services. Trust companies also engage in fiduciary investment management functions and estate planning. They are regulated by state law.

TRUSTEE *see* TRUST.

TRUSTEE IN BANKRUPTCY trustee appointed by a U.S. district court or by creditors to administer the affairs of a bankrupt company or individual. Under Chapter 7 of the U.S. BANKRUPTCY Code, the trustee has the responsibility for liquidating the property of the company and making distributions of liquidating dividends to creditors. Under the Chapter 11 provision, which provides for REORGANIZATION, a trustee may or may not be appointed. If one is, the trustee is responsible for seeing that a reorganization plan is filed and often assumes responsibility for the company.

TRUST INDENTURE ACT OF 1939 federal law requiring all corporate bonds and other debt securities to be issued under an INDENTURE agreement approved by the SECURITIES AND EXCHANGE COMMISSION (SEC) and providing for the appointment of a qualified trustee free of conflict of interest with the issuer. The Act provides that indentures contain protective clauses for bondholders, that bondholders receive semiannual financial reports, that periodic filings be made with the SEC showing compliance with indenture provisions, and that the issuer be liable for misleading statements. Securities exempted from regulation under the SECURITIES ACT OF 1933 are also exempted from the Trust Indenture Act, but some securities not requiring registration under the 1933 Act do fall under the provisions of the Trust Indenture Act, such as bonds issued in REORGANIZATION or RECAPITALIZATION.

TRUTH IN LENDING LAW legislation stipulating that lenders must disclose to borrowers the true cost of loans and make the interest rate and terms of the loan simple to understand. *See also* CONSUMER CREDIT PROTECTION ACT OF 1968; RIGHT OF RESCISSION.

TURKEY disappointing investment. The term may be used with reference to a business deal that went awry, or to the purchase of a stock or bond that dropped in value sharply, or to a new securities issue that did not sell well or had to be sold at a loss.

TURNAROUND favorable reversal in the fortunes of a company, a market, or the economy at large. Stock market investors speculating that a poorly performing company is about to show a marked improvement in earnings might profit handsomely from its turnaround.

TURNKEY any project constructed or manufactured by a company that ultimately turns it over in finished form to the company that will use it, so that all the user has to do is turn the key, so to speak, and the project is underway. The term is used of housing projects that, after construction, are turned over to property managers. There are also turnkey computer systems, for which the user needs no special computer knowledge and which can therefore be put right to work once they are installed.

TURNOVER

Finance:
1. number of times a given asset is replaced during an accounting period, usually a year. *See also* ACCOUNTS RECEIVABLE TURNOVER; INVENTORY TAKEOVER.
2. ratio of annual sales of a company to its NET WORTH, measuring the extent to which a company can grow without additional capital investment when compared over a period. *See also* CAPITAL TURNOVER.

Great Britain: annual sales volume.

Industrial relations: total employment divided by the number of employees replaced during a given period.

Securities: volume of shares traded as a percentage of total shares listed on an exchange during a period, usually either a day or a year. The same ratio is applied to individual securities and the portfolios of individual or institutional investors.

12b-1 MUTUAL FUND MUTUAL FUND that assesses shareholders for some of its promotion expenses. These funds are usually no-load, so no brokers are involved in the sale to the public. Instead, the funds normally rely on advertising and public relations to build their assets. The charge usually amounts to about 1% or less of a fund's assets. A 12b-1 fund must be specifically registered as such with the Securities and Exchange Commission, and the fact that such charges are levied must be disclosed. *See also* NO-LOAD FUND.

TWENTY-DAY PERIOD period required by the Securities and Exchange Commission (SEC) after filing of the REGISTRATION STATEMENT and PRELIMINARY PROSPECTUS in a NEW ISSUE or SECONDARY DISTRIBUTION during which they are reviewed and, if necessary, modified. The end of the twenty-day period—also called the COOLING-OFF PERIOD—marks the EFFECTIVE DATE when the issue may be offered to the public. The period may be extended by the SEC if more time is needed to respond to a DEFICIENCY LETTER.

TWENTY-FIVE PERCENT RULE MUNICIPAL BOND analyst's guideline that bonded debt over 25% of a municipality's annual budget is excessive.

TWENTY-PERCENT CUSHION RULE guideline used by analysts of MUNICIPAL REVENUE BONDS that estimated revenues from the financed facility should exceed the operating budget plus maintenance costs and DEBT SERVICE by a 20% margin or "cushion" to allow for unanticipated expenses or error in estimating revenues.

TWISTING unethical practice of convincing a customer to trade unnecessarily, thereby generating a commission for the broker or salesperson. For example, a broker may induce a customer to sell one mutual fund with a sales charge in order to buy another fund, also with a sales charge, thereby generating a commission. Also called CHURNING.

TWO-DOLLAR BROKER see INDEPENDENT BROKER.

200 PERCENT DECLINING BALANCE METHOD see DOUBLE DECLINING-BALANCE DEPRECIATION METHOD (DDB).

TWO-SIDED MARKET market in which both the BID AND ASKED sides are firm, such as that which a SPECIALIST and others who MAKE A MARKET are required to maintain. In a two-sided market, both buyers and sellers are assured of their ability to complete transactions. Also called *two-way market*.

TWO-TIER BID TAKEOVER bid where the acquirer offers to pay more for the shares needed to gain control than for the remaining shares; contrasts with ANY-AND-ALL BID.

U

ULTRA VIRES ACTIVITIES actions of a corporation that are not authorized by its charter and that may therefore lead to shareholder or third-party suits. *See also* ARTICLES OF INCORPORATION.

UNAMORTIZED BOND DISCOUNT difference between the FACE VALUE (par value) of a bond and the proceeds received from the sale of the bond by the issuing company, less whatever portion has been amortized, that is, written off to expense as recorded periodically on the PROFIT AND LOSS STATEMENT. At the time of issue, a company has two alternatives: (1) it can immediately absorb as an expense the amount of discount plus costs related to the issue, such as legal, printing, REGISTRATION, and other similar expenses, or (2) it can decide to treat the total discount and expenses as a DEFERRED CHARGE, recorded as an ASSET to be written off over the life of the bonds or by any other schedule the company finds desirable. The amount still to be expensed at any point is the unamortized bond discount.

UNAMORTIZED PREMIUMS ON INVESTMENTS unexpensed portion of the amount by which the price paid for a security exceeded its PAR value (if a BOND or PREFERRED STOCK) or MARKET VALUE (if common stock). A PREMIUM paid in acquiring an investment is in the nature of an INTANGIBLE ASSET, and conservative accounting practice dictates it be written off to expense over an appropriate period. *See also* GOING-CONCERN VALUE.

UNCOLLECTED FUNDS portion of bank deposit made up of checks that have not yet been collected by the depository bank—that is, payment has not yet been acknowledged by the bank on which a check was drawn. A bank will usually not let a depositor draw on uncollected funds. *See also* FLOAT.

UNCOVERED OPTION OPTION contract for which the owner does not hold the underlying investment (should delivery on the option be required). *See also* NAKED OPTION; UNDERLYING FUTURES CONTRACT; UNDERLYING SECURITY; WRITING NAKED.

UNDERBANKED said of a NEW ISSUE underwriting when the originating INVESTMENT BANKER is having difficulty getting other firms to become members of the UNDER-WRITING GROUP, or syndicate. *See also* UNDERWRITE.

UNDERBOOKED said of a NEW ISSUE of securities during the preoffering REGISTRATION period when brokers canvassing lists of prospective buyers report limited INDICATIONS OF INTEREST. The opposite of underbooked would be *fully circled. See also* CIRCLE.

UNDERCAPITALIZATION situation in which a business does not have enough capital to carry out its normal business functions. *See also* CAPITALIZATION; WORKING CAPITAL.

UNDERLYING DEBT MUNICIPAL BOND term referring to the debt of government entities within the jurisdiction of larger government entities and for which the larger entity has partial credit responsibility. For example, a township might share responsibility for the general obligations of a village within the township, the debt of the village being underlying debt from the township's standpoint. The term OVERLAPPING DEBT is also used to describe underlying debt, but overlapping debt can also exist with entities of equal rank where, for example, a school district crosses boundaries of two or more townships.

UNDERLYING FUTURES CONTRACT FUTURES CONTRACT that underlies an OPTION on that future. For example, the Chicago Board of Trade offers a U.S. Treasury bond futures option. The underlying future is the Treasury bond futures contract traded on the Board of Trade. If the option contract were exercised, delivery would be made in the underlying futures contract.

UNDERLYING SECURITY
Options: security that must be delivered if a PUT OPTION or CALL OPTION contract is exercised. Stock INDEX OPTIONS and STOCK INDEX FUTURES, however, are settled in cash, since it is not possible to deliver an index of stocks.
Securities: common stock that underlies certain types of securities issued by corporations. This stock must be delivered if a SUBSCRIPTION WARRANT or SUBSCRIPTION RIGHT is exercised, if a CONVERTIBLE bond or PREFERRED STOCK is converted into common shares, or if an INCENTIVE STOCK OPTION is exercised.

UNDERMARGINED ACCOUNT MARGIN ACCOUNT that has fallen below MARGIN REQUIREMENTS or MINIMUM MAINTENANCE requirements. As a result, the broker must make a MARGIN CALL to the customer.

UNDERVALUED security selling below its LIQUIDATION value or the MARKET VALUE analysts believe it deserves. A company's stock may be undervalued because the industry is out of favor, because the company is not well known or has an erratic history of earnings, or for many other reasons. Fundamental analysts try to spot companies that are undervalued so their clients can buy before the stocks become FULLY VALUED. Undervalued companies are also frequently targets of TAKEOVER attempts, since acquirers can buy assets cheaply this way. *See also* FUNDAMENTAL ANALYSIS.

UNDERWRITE

Insurance: to assume risk in exchange for a PREMIUM.

Investments: to assume the risk of buying a NEW ISSUE of securities from the issuing corporation or government entity and reselling them to the public, either directly or through dealers. The UNDERWRITER makes a profit on the difference between the price paid to the issuer and the PUBLIC OFFERING PRICE, called the UNDERWRITING SPREAD.

Underwriting is the business of investment bankers, who usually form an UNDERWRITING GROUP (also called a PURCHASE GROUP or syndicate) to pool the risk and assure successful distribution of the issue. The syndicate operates under an AGREEMENT AMONG UNDERWRITERS, also termed a *syndicate contract* or PURCHASE GROUP contract.

The underwriting group appoints a MANAGING UNDERWRITER, also known as *lead underwriter, syndicate manager,* or simply *manager,* that is usually the *originating investment banker*—the firm that began working with the issuer months before to plan details of the issue and prepare the REGISTRATION materials to be filed with the SECURITIES AND EXCHANGE COMMISSION. The manager, acting as agent for the group, signs the UNDERWRITING AGREEMENT (or *purchase contract*) with the issuer. This agreement sets forth the terms and conditions of the arrangement and the responsibilities of both issuer and underwriter. During the offering period, it is the manager's responsibility to stabilize the MARKET PRICE of the issuer's shares by bidding in the open market, a process called PEGGING. The manager may also appoint a SELLING GROUP, comprised of dealers and the underwriters themselves, to assist in DISTRIBUTION of the issue.

Strictly speaking, *underwrite* is properly used only in a FIRM COMMITMENT underwriting, also known as a BOUGHT DEAL, where the securities are purchased outright from the issuer.

Other investment banking arrangements to which the term is sometimes loosely applied are BEST EFFORT, ALL OR NONE, and STANDBY COMMITMENTS; in each of these, the risk is shared between the issuer and the INVESTMENT BANKER.

The term is also sometimes used in connection with a REGISTERED SECONDARY OFFERING, which involves essentially the same process as a new issue, except that the proceeds go to the selling investor, not to the issuer. For these arrangements, the term *secondary offering* or SECONDARY DISTRIBUTION is preferable to *underwriting,* which is usually reserved for new, or primary, distributions.

There are two basic methods by which underwriters are chosen by issuers and underwriting spreads are determined: NEGOTIATED UNDERWRITINGS and COMPETITIVE BID underwritings. Generally, the negotiated method is used in corporate equity (stock) issues and most corporate debt (bond) issues, whereas the competitive bidding method is used by municipalities and public utilities.

See also ALLOTMENT; BLOWOUT; FLOATING AN ISSUE; FLOTATION COST; HOT ISSUE; INITIAL PUBLIC OFFERING; PRESOLD ISSUE; PRIMARY MARKET; PUBLIC OFFERING; STANDBY UNDERWRITER.

UNDERWRITER

Insurance: company that assumes the cost risk of death, fire, theft, illness, etc., in exchange for payments, called *premiums.*

Securities: INVESTMENT BANKER who, singly or as a member of an UNDERWRITING GROUP or syndicate, agrees to purchase a NEW ISSUE of securities from an issuer and distribute it to investors, making a profit on the UNDERWRITING SPREAD. *See also* UNDERWRITE.

UNDERWRITING AGREEMENT agreement between a corporation issuing new securities to be offered to the public and the MANAGING UNDERWRITER as agent for the UNDERWRITING GROUP. Also termed the *purchase agreement* or *purchase contract*, it represents the underwriters' commitment to purchase the securities, and it details the PUBLIC OFFERING PRICE, the UNDERWRITING SPREAD (including all discounts and commissions), the net proceeds to the issuer, and the SETTLE- MENT DATE.

The issuer agrees to pay all expenses incurred in preparing the issue for resale, including the costs of REGISTRATION with the SECURITIES AND EXCHANGE COMMISSION (SEC) and of the PROSPECTUS, and agrees to supply the managing underwriter with sufficient copies of both the PRELIMINARY PROSPECTUS (red her- ring) and the final, statutory prospectus. The issuer guarantees (1) to make all required SEC filings and to comply fully with the provisions of the SECURITIES ACT OF 1933; (2) to assume responsibility for the completeness, accuracy, and proper certification of all information in the registration statement and prospectus; (3) to disclose all pending litigation; (4) to use the proceeds for the purposes stated; (5) to comply with state securities laws; (6) to work to get listed on the exchange agreed upon; and (7) to indemnify the underwriters for liability arising out of omissions or misrepresentations for which the issuer had responsibility.

The underwriters agree to proceed with the offering as soon as the registration is cleared by the SEC or at a specified date thereafter. The underwriters are authorized to make sales to members of a SELLING GROUP.

The underwriting agreement is not to be confused with the AGREEMENT AMONG UNDERWRITERS. *See also* BEST EFFORT; FIRM COMMITMENT; STANDBY COMMITMENT; UNDERWRITE.

UNDERWRITING GROUP temporary association of investment bankers, orga- nized by the originating INVESTMENT BANKER in a NEW ISSUE of securities. Op- erating under an AGREEMENT AMONG UNDERWRITERS, it agrees to purchase se- curities from the issuing corporation at an agreed-upon price and to resell them at a PUBLIC OFFERING PRICE, the difference representing the UNDERWRITING SPREAD. The purpose of the underwriting group is to spread the risk and assure successful distribution of the offering. Most underwriting groups operate under a *divided syndicate contract*, meaning that the liability of members is limited to their in- dividual participations. Also called DISTRIBUTING SYNDICATE, PURCHASE GROUP, *investment banking group*, or *syndicate. See also* FIRM COMMITMENT; UNDER- WRITE; UNDERWRITING AGREEMENT.

UNDERWRITING SPREAD difference between the amount paid to an issuer of securities in a PRIMARY DISTRIBUTION and the PUBLIC OFFERING PRICE. The amount of SPREAD varies widely, depending on the size of the issue, the financial strength of the issuer, the type of security involved (stock, bonds, rights), the status of the security (senior, junior, secured, unsecured), and the type of commitment made by the investment bankers. The range may be from a fraction of 1% for a bond issue of a big utility company to 25% for the INITIAL PUBLIC OFFERING of a small company. The division of the spread between the MANAGING UNDERWRITER, the SELLING GROUP, and the participating underwriters also varies, but in a two- point spread the manager might typically get 0.25%, the selling group 1%, and the underwriters 0.75%. It is usual, though, for the underwriters also to be mem- bers of the selling group, thus picking up 1.75% of the spread, and for the manager to be in all three categories, thus picking up the full 2%. *See also* COMPETITIVE BID; FLOTATION COST; GROSS SPREAD; NEGOTIATED UNDERWRITING; SELLING CONCESSION; UNDERWRITE.

UNDIGESTED SECURITIES newly issued stocks and bonds that remain undistributed because there is insufficient public demand at the OFFERING PRICE. *See also* UNDERWRITE.

UNDISTRIBUTED PROFITS (EARNINGS, NET INCOME) *see* RETAINED EARNINGS.

UNDIVIDED PROFITS account shown on a bank's BALANCE SHEET representing profits that have neither been paid out as DIVIDENDS nor transferred to the bank's SURPLUS account. Current earnings are credited to the undivided profits account and are then either paid out in dividends or retained to build up total EQUITY. As the account grows, round amounts may be periodically transferred to the surplus account.

UNEARNED DISCOUNT account on the books of a lending institution recognizing interest deducted in advance and which will be taken into income as earned over the life of the loan. In accordance with accounting principles, such interest is initially recorded as a LIABILITY. Then, as months pass and it is gradually "earned," it is recognized as income, thus increasing the lender's profit and decreasing the corresponding liability. *See also* UNEARNED INCOME.

UNEARNED INCOME (REVENUE)
Accounting: income received but not yet earned, such as rent received in advance or other advances from customers. Unearned income is usually classified as a CURRENT LIABILITY on a company's BALANCE SHEET, assuming that it will be credited to income within the normal accounting cycle. *See also* DEFERRED CHARGE.
Income taxes: income from sources other than wages, salaries, tips, and other employee compensation—for example, DIVIDENDS, INTEREST, rent.

UNEARNED INTEREST interest that has already been collected on a loan by a financial institution, but that cannot yet be counted as part of earnings because the principal of the loan has not been outstanding long enough. Also called DISCOUNT and UNEARNED DISCOUNT.

UNENCUMBERED property free and clear of all liens (creditors' claims). When a homeowner pays off his mortgage, for example, the house becomes unencumbered property. Securities bought with cash instead of on MARGIN are unencumbered.

UNIFIED CREDIT federal TAX CREDIT that may be applied against the gift tax, the estate tax, and, under specified conditions, the generation-skipping transfer tax.

UNIFORM GIFTS TO MINORS ACT (UGMA) law adopted by most U.S. states that sets up rules for the distribution and administration of assets in the name of a child. The Act provides for a CUSTODIAN of the assets, often the parents, but sometimes an independent TRUSTEE. When minors reach majority, custodial accounts become the child's property unless other arrangements have been specified. The practice of shifting income to a minor's account to gain lower income-tax rates was curtailed by the TAX REFORM ACT OF 1986, which made unearned income over $1000 to a child under 14 years old subject to taxation at the grantor's rate.

UNIFORM PRACTICE CODE rules of the NATIONAL ASSOCIATION OF SECURITIES DEALERS (NASD) concerned with standards and procedures for the operational handling of OVER THE COUNTER securities transactions, such as delivery, SETTLE-

MENT DATE, EX-DIVIDEND DATE, and other ex-dates (such as EX-RIGHTS and EX-WARRANTS), and providing for the arbitration of disputes through Uniform Practice committees.

UNIFORM SECURITIES AGENT STATE LAW EXAMINATION test required of prospective REGISTERED REPRESENTATIVES in many U.S. states. In addition to the examination requirements of states, all registered representatives, whether employees of member firms or OVER THE COUNTER brokers, must pass the General Securities Representative Examination (also known as the Series 7 Examination), administered by the National Association of Securities Dealers (NASD).

UNISSUED STOCK shares of a corporation's stock authorized in its charter but not issued. They are shown on the BALANCE SHEET along with shares ISSUED AND OUTSTANDING. Unissued stock may be issued by action of the board of directors, although shares needed for unexercised employee STOCK OPTIONS, rights, warrants, or convertible securities must not be issued while such obligations are outstanding. Unissued shares cannot pay dividends and cannot be voted. They are not to be confused with TREASURY STOCK, which is issued but not outstanding.

UNIT

In general: any division of quantity accepted as a standard of measurement or of exchange. For example, in the commodities markets, a unit of wheat is a bushel, a unit of coffee a pound, and a unit of shell eggs a dozen. The unit of U.S. currency is the dollar.

Banking: bank operating out of only one office, and with no branches, as required by states having unit banking laws.

Finance:
1. segment or subdivision (division or subsidiary, product line, or plant) of a company.
2. in sales or production, quantity rather than dollars. One might say, for example, "Unit volume declined but dollar volume increased after prices were raised."

Securities:
1. minimum amount of stocks, bonds, commodities, or other securities accepted for trading on an exchange. *See also* ODD LOT; ROUND LOT; UNIT OF TRADING.
2. group of specialists on a stock exchange, who maintain fair and orderly markets in particular securities. *See also* SPECIALIST; SPECIALIST UNIT.
3. more than one class of securities traded together; one common share and one SUBSCRIPTION WARRANT might sell as a unit, for example.
4. in primary and secondary distributions of securities, one share of stock or one bond.

UNITED STATES GOVERNMENT SECURITIES direct GOVERNMENT OBLIGATIONS—that is, debt issues of the U.S. government, such as Treasury bills, notes, and bonds and Series EE and Series HH SAVINGS BONDS as distinguished from government-sponsored AGENCY issues. *See also* GOVERNMENT SECURITIES; TREASURIES.

UNIT INVESTMENT TRUST investment vehicle, registered with the SECURITIES AND EXCHANGE COMMISSION under the INVESTMENT COMPANY ACT OF 1940, that purchases a fixed PORTFOLIO of income-producing securities, such as corporate, municipal, or government bonds, mortgage-backed securities, or PREFERRED STOCK.

Units in the trust, which usually cost at least $1000, are sold to investors by brokers, for a LOAD charge of about 4%. Unit holders receive an undivided interest in both the principal and the income portion of the portfolio in proportion to the amount of capital they invest. The portfolio of securities remains fixed until all the securities mature and unit holders have recovered their principal. Most brokerage firms maintain a SECONDARY MARKET in the trusts they sell, so that units can be resold if necessary.

In Britain, open-end mutual funds are called *unit trusts.*

See also INVESTMENT COMPANY; MORTGAGE-BACKED CERTIFICATE; UNIT SHARE INVESTMENT TRUST.

UNIT OF TRADING normal number of shares, bonds, or commodities comprising the minimum unit of trading on an exchange. For stocks, this is usually 100 shares, although inactive shares trade in 10-share units. For corporate bonds on the NYSE, the unit for exchange trading is $1000 or $5000 par value. Commodities futures units vary widely, according to the COMMODITY involved. *See also* FUTURES CONTRACT; ODD LOT; ROUND LOT.

UNIT SHARE INVESTMENT TRUST (USIT) specialized form of UNIT INVESTMENT TRUST comprising one unit of PRIME and one unit of SCORE.

UNIVERSAL LIFE INSURANCE form of life insurance, first marketed in the early 1980s, that combines the low-cost protection of TERM LIFE INSURANCE with a savings portion, which is invested in a tax-deferred account earning money-market rates of interest. The policy is flexible; that is, as age and income change, a policyholder can increase or decrease premium payments and coverage, or shift a certain portion of premiums into the savings account, without additional sales charges or complications. A new form of the policy; called *universal variable life insurance,* combines the flexibility of universal life with the growth potential of variable life. *See also* VARIABLE LIFE INSURANCE; WHOLE LIFE INSURANCE.

UNLEVERAGED PROGRAM LIMITED PARTNERSHIP whose use of borrowed funds to finance the acquisition of properties is 50% or less of the purchase price. In contrast, a *leveraged program* borrows 50% or more. Investors seeking to maximize income tend to favor unleveraged partnerships, where interest expense and other deductions from income are at a minimum. Investors looking for TAX SHELTERS favor leveraged programs despite the higher risk because of the larger DEPRECIATION writeoffs on the greater amount of property acquired with the borrowed money and the greater amount of tax deductible interest.

UNLIMITED TAX BOND MUNICIPAL BOND secured by the pledge to levy taxes at an unlimited rate until the bond is repaid.

UNLISTED SECURITY security that is not listed on an organized exchange, such as the NEW YORK STOCK EXCHANGE, the AMERICAN STOCK EXCHANGE, or the REGIONAL STOCK EXCHANGES, and is traded in the OVER THE COUNTER market.

UNLISTED TRADING trading of securities not listed on an organized exchange but traded on that exchange as an accommodation to its members. An exchange wishing to trade unlisted securities must file an application with the SECURITIES AND EXCHANGE COMMISSION and make the necessary information available to the investing public. The New York Stock Exchange does not allow unlisted trading privileges, and the practice has declined at the American Stock Exchange and other organized exchanges.

UNLOADING
Finance: selling off large quantities of merchandise inventory at below-market prices either to raise cash quickly or to depress the market in a particular product.
Investments: selling securities or commodities when prices are declining to preclude further loss.
See also DUMP; PROFIT TAKING; SELLING OFF.

UNPAID DIVIDEND dividend that has been declared by the board of directors of a corporation but has not reached its PAYMENT DATE. Once a board acts to DECLARE a dividend, it is then recognized as a corporate LIABILITY until paid.

UNREALIZED PROFIT (OR LOSS) profit or loss that has not become actual. It becomes a REALIZED PROFIT (OR LOSS) when the security or commodity future contract in which there is a gain or loss is actually sold. Also called a *paper profit or loss.*

UNREGISTERED STOCK *see* LETTER SECURITY.

UNSECURED DEBT obligation not backed by the pledge of specific COLLATERAL.

UNWIND A TRADE to reverse a securities transaction through an offsetting transaction. *See also* OFFSET.

UPSET PRICE term used in auctions that represents the minimum price at which a seller of property will entertain bids.

UPSIDE POTENTIAL amount of upward price movement an investor or an analyst expects of a particular stock, bond, or commodity. This opinion may result from either FUNDAMENTAL ANALYSIS or TECHNICAL ANALYSIS.

UPSTAIRS MARKET transaction completed within the broker-dealer's firm and without using the stock exchange. Securities and Exchange Commission and stock exchange rules exist to ensure that such trades do not occur at prices less favorable to the customer than those prevailing in the general market. *See also* OFF BOARD.

UPTICK transaction executed at a price higher than the preceding transaction in that security; also called PLUS TICK. A plus sign is displayed throughout the day next to the last price of each stock that showed a higher price than the preceding transaction in that stock at the TRADING POST of the SPECIALIST on the floor of the New York Stock Exchange. Short sales may only be executed on upticks or ZERO-PLUS TICKS. *See also* MINUS TICK; SELLING SHORT; TICK.

UPTREND upward direction in the price of a stock, bond, or commodity future contract or overall market. *See also* TRENDLINE.

UTILITY REVENUE BOND MUNICIPAL BOND issued to finance the construction of electric generating plants, gas, water and sewer systems, among other types of public utility services. These bonds are repaid from the revenues the project produces once it is operating. Such bonds usually have a reserve fund that contains an amount equal to one year's DEBT SERVICE, which protects bondholders in case there is a temporary cash shortage or revenues are less than anticipated. *See also* REVENUE BOND.

V

VALUATION RESERVE reserve or allowance, created by a charge to expenses (and therefore, in effect, taken out of profits) in order to provide for changes in the value of a company's assets. Accumulated DEPRECIATION, allowance for BAD DEBTS, and UNAMORTIZED BOND DISCOUNT are three familiar examples of valuation reserves. Also called *valuation account*.

VALUE-ADDED TAX (VAT) consumption tax levied on the value added to a product at each stage of its manufacturing cycle as well as at the time of purchase by the ultimate consumer. The value-added tax is a fixture in European countries and a major source of revenue for the European Common Market. Advocates of a value-added tax for the U.S. contend that it would be the most efficient method of raising revenue and that the size of its receipts would permit a reduction in income tax rates. Opponents argue that in its pure form it would be the equivalent of a national sales tax and therefore unfair and regressive, putting the greatest burden on those who can least afford it. As an example, for each part that goes into the assembling of an automobile, the auto manufacturer would pay a value-added tax to the supplier, probably a percentage of the purchase price, as is the case with a sales tax. When the finished car is sold, the consumer pays a value-added tax on the cost of the finished product less the material and supply costs that were taxed at earlier stages. This avoids double taxation and thus differs from a flat sales tax based on the total cost of purchase.

VALUE BROKER DISCOUNT BROKER whose rates are based on a percentage of the dollar value of each transaction. It is usually advantageous to place orders through a value broker for trades of low-priced shares or small numbers of shares, since commissions will be relatively smaller than if a shareholder used a SHARE BROKER, another type of discount broker, who charges according to the number and the price of the shares traded.

VALUE CHANGE change in a stock price adjusted for the number of outstanding shares of that stock, so that a group of stocks adjusted this way are equally weighted. A unit of movement of the group—called an INDEX—is thus representative of the average performance.

VALUE DATE

Banking: official date when money is transferred, that is, becomes good funds to the depositor. The value date differs from the *entry date* when items are received from the depositor, since the items must then be forwarded to the paying bank or otherwise collected. The term is used mainly with reference to foreign accounts, either maintained in a domestic bank or maintained by a domestic bank in foreign banks. *See also* FLOAT.

Eurodollar and foreign currency transactions: synonymous with SETTLEMENT DATE or DELIVERY DATE, which on spot transactions involving North American currencies (U.S. dollar, Canadian dollar, and Mexican peso) is one business day and on spot transactions involving other currencies, two business days. In the forward exchange market, value date is the maturity date of the contract plus one business day for North American currencies, two business days for other currencies. *See also* FORWARD EXCHANGE TRANSACTION; SPOT MARKET.

VALUE LINE INVESTMENT SURVEY investment advisory service that ranks hundreds of stocks for ''timeliness'' and safety. Using a computerized model based on a company's earnings momentum, Value Line projects which stocks will have the best or worst relative price performance over the next 12 months. In addition, each stock is assigned a risk rating, which identifies the VOLATILITY of a stock's price behavior relative to the market average. The service also ranks all major industry groups for timeliness. Value Line's ranking system for both timeliness and safety of individual stock is as follows:

1—highest rank
2—above average rank
3—average rank
4—below average rank
5—lowest rank

The weekly writeups of companies that Value Line subscribers receive include detailed financial information about a company, as well as such data as corporate INSIDER buying and selling decisions and the percentage of a company's shares held by institutions.

VA MORTGAGE *see* VETERANS ADMINISTRATION (VA) MORTGAGE.

VARIABLE ANNUITY life insurance ANNUITY contract whose value fluctuates with that of an underlying securities PORTFOLIO or other INDEX of performance. The variable annuity contrasts with a conventional or FIXED ANNUITY, whose rate of return is constant and therefore vulnerable to the effects of inflation. Income on a variable annuity may be taken periodically, beginning immediately or at any future time. The annuity may be a single-premium or multiple-premium contract. The return to investors may be in the form of a periodic payment that varies with the MARKET VALUE of the portfolio or a fixed minimum payment with add-ons based on the rate of portfolio appreciation. *See also* SINGLE PREMIUM DEFERRED ANNUITY.

VARIABLE COST cost that changes directly with the amount of production—for example, direct material or direct labor needed to complete a product. *See also* FIXED COST.

VARIABLE LIFE INSURANCE innovation in WHOLE LIFE INSURANCE that gives policyholders the opportunity to earn substantial CAPITAL GAINS on their insurance investment. As the inflation and high interest rates of the 1970s and early 80s made the rates of return on whole life policies uncompetitive, insurance companies began to underwrite a variable life policy that allows the cash value of the policy to be invested in stock, bond, or money market portfolios. Investors can elect to move from one portfolio to another or can rely on the company's professional money managers to make such decisions for them. As in whole life insurance, the annual premium is fixed, but part of it is earmarked for the investment PORTFOLIO. The policyholder bears the risk of securities investments, while the insurance company guarantees a minimum death benefit unaffected by any portfolio losses. When portfolio investments rise substantially, a portion of the increased cash value is put into additional insurance coverage. As in usual whole life policies, borrowings can be made against the accumulated cash value, or the policy can be cashed in. As in an INDIVIDUAL RETIREMENT ACCOUNT, earnings from variable life policies are tax deferred until distributed. Income is then taxed only to the extent that it exceeds the total premiums paid into the policy. Death benefits are taxed not as individual income but as taxable estate income, which has an exclusion rising to $600,000 in 1987.

Variable life insurance is different from UNIVERSAL LIFE INSURANCE. Universal life allows policyholders to increase or decrease premiums and change the death benefit. It also accrues interest at market-related rates on premiums over and above insurance charges and expenses.

VARIABLE-RATE DEMAND NOTE note representing borrowings (usually from a commercial bank) that is payable on demand and that bears interest tied to a money market rate, usually the bank PRIME RATE. The rate on the note is adjusted upward or downward each time the base rate changes.

VARIABLE RATE MORTGAGE (VRM) home mortgage loan with an interest rate that varies with money market rates or the lending institution's cost of funds. The VRM—also called ADJUSTABLE RATE MORTGAGE—grew out of a depressed mortgage market caused by record high interest rates in the late 1970s and reached a peak of popularity from 1980 to 1984 with lenders offering initial below-market rates. As rates began to fall in 1984, the popularity of the VRM began to wane and the fixed-rate mortgage, now affordable, again became attractive to home-buyers who placed a value on its predictability.

The VRM is not to be confused with a GRADUATED PAYMENT MORTGAGE, which is issued at a fixed rate with monthly payments designed to increase as the borrower's income grows.

VARIANCE

Accounting: difference between actual cost and STANDARD COST in the categories of direct material, direct labor, and DIRECT OVERHEAD. A positive variation (when the actual cost is lower than the standard or anticipated cost) would translate into a higher profit unless offset by negative variances elsewhere.

Finance:
1. difference between corresponding items on a comparative BALANCE SHEET and PROFIT AND LOSS STATEMENT.
2. difference between actual experience and budgeted or projected experience in any financial category. For example, if sales were projected to be $2 million for a period and were actually $2.5 million, there would be a positive variance of $500,000, or 25%.

Statistics: measure of the dispersion of a distribution. It is the sumof the squares of the deviations from the mean. *See also* STANDARDDEVIATION.

VELOCITY rate of spending, or turnover of money—in other words, how many times a dollar is spent in a given period of time. The concept of "income velocity of money" was first explained by the economist Irving Fisher in the 1920s as bearing a direct relationship to GROSS NATIONAL PRODUCT (GNP). GNP is the product of total MONEY SUPPLY and its velocity measure. Velocity affects the amount of economic activity generated by a given money supply, which includes bank deposits and cash in circulation. Velocity is a factor in the Federal Reserve Board's management of MONETARY POLICY, because an increase in velocity may obviate the need for a stimulative increase in the money supply. Conversely, a decline in velocity might dampen economic growth, even if the money supply holds steady. An increase in income velocity since World War II has been partly attributed to active cash management by corporations using electronic technology to move funds rapidly in and out of various bank accounts and investment ve-hicles. *See also* FISCAL POLICY.

VENDOR

1. supplier of goods or services of a commercial nature; may be a manufacturer, importer, or wholesale distributor. For example, one component of the Index of LEADING INDICATORS is vendor performance, meaning the rate at which

suppliers of goods are making delivery to their commercial customers.

2. retailer of merchandise, especially one without an established place of business, as in *sidewalk vendor*.

VENTURE CAPITAL important source of financing for START-UP companies or others embarking on new or TURNAROUND ventures that entail some investment risk but offer the potential for above average future profits; also called *risk capital*. Prominent among firms seeking venture capital in the 1980s are those classified as emerging-growth or high-technology companies. Sources of venture capital include wealthy individual investors; subsidiaries of banks and other corporations organized as small business investment companies (SBICs); groups of investment banks and other financing sources who pool investments in venture capital funds or VENTURE CAPITAL LIMITED PARTNERSHIPS. The SMALL BUSINESS ADMINISTRATION (SBA) promotes venture capital programs through the licensing and financing of SBICs. Venture capital financing supplements other personal or external funds that an ENTREPRENEUR is able to tap, or takes the place of loans of other funds that conventional financial institutions are unable or unwilling to risk. Some venture capital sources invest only at a certain stage of entrepreneurship, such as the start-up or SEED MONEY stage, the *first round* or SECOND ROUND phases that follow, or at the MEZZANINE LEVEL immediately preceding an INITIAL PUBLIC OFFERING. In return for taking an investment risk, venture capitalists are usually rewarded with some combination of PROFITS, PREFERRED STOCK, ROYALTIES on sales, and capital appreciation of common shares.

VENTURE CAPITAL LIMITED PARTNERSHIP investment vehicle organized by a brokerage firm or entrepreneurial company to raise capital for START-UP companies or those in the early processes of developing products and services. The partnership will usually take shares of stock in the company in return for capital supplied. Limited partners receive income from profits the company may earn. If the company is successful and goes public, limited partners' profits could be realized from the sale of formerly private stock to the public. This type of partnership differs from a RESEARCH AND DEVELOPMENT LIMITED PARTNERSHIP in that R&D deals receive revenue only from the particular products they UNDERWRITE, whereas a venture capital partnership participates in the profits of the company, no matter what product or service is sold. *See also* ENTREPRENEUR; LIMITED PARTNERSHIP.

VERTICAL LINE CHARTING form of technical charting on which the high, low, and closing prices of a stock or a market are shown on one vertical line with the closing price indicated by a short horizontal mark. Each vertical line represents another day, and the chart shows the trend of a stock or a market over a period of days, weeks, months, or years. Technical analysts discern from these charts whether a stock or a market is continually closing at the high or low end of its trading range during a day. This is useful in understanding whether the market's action is strong or weak, and therefore whether prices will advance or decline in the near future. *See also* TECHNICAL ANALYSIS. *See* illustration, page 527.

VERTICAL SPREAD OPTION strategy that involves purchasing an option at one STRIKE PRICE while simultaneously selling another option of the same class at the next higher or lower strike price. Both options have the same expiration date. For example, a vertical spread is created by buying an XYZ May 30 call and selling an XYZ May 40 call. The investor who buys a vertical spread hopes to profit as the difference between the option premium on the two option positions widens or narrows. Also called a PRICE SPREAD. *See also* OPTION PREMIUM.

VERTICAL LINE CHARTING

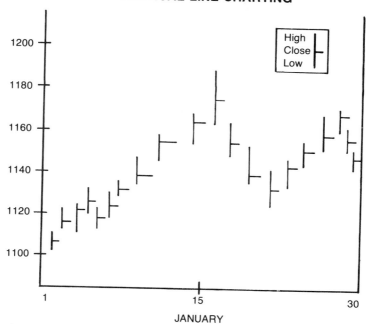

VESTING right an employee gradually acquires by length of service at a company to receive employer-contributed benefits, such as payments from a PENSION FUND, PROFIT-SHARING PLAN, or other QUALIFIED PLAN OR TRUST. Under the TAX REFORM ACT OF 1986, employees must be vested 100% after five years of service or at 20% a year starting in the third year and becoming 100% vested after seven years.

VETERANS ADMINISTRATION (VA) MORTGAGE home mortgage loan granted by a lending institution to qualified veterans of the U.S. armed forces or to their surviving spouses and guaranteed by the VA. The guarantee reduces risk to the lender for all or part of the purchase price on conventional homes, mobile homes, and condominiums. Because of this federal guarantee, banks and thrift institutions can afford to provide 30-year VA mortgages on favorable terms with a relatively low down payment even during periods of TIGHT MONEY. Interest rates on VA mortgages, formerly fixed by the Department of Housing and Urban Development together with those on Federal Housing Administration (FHA) mortgages, are now set by the VA.

VA mortgages comprise an important part of the mortgage pools packaged and sold as securities by such quasi-governmental organizations as the FEDERAL HOME MORTGAGE CORPORATION (Freddie Mac) and the GOVERNMENT NATIONAL MORTGAGE ASSOCIATION (Ginnie Mae).

V FORMATION technical chart pattern that forms a V. The V pattern indicates that the stock, bond, or commodity being charted has bottomed out and is now in a bullish (rising) trend. An upside-down (inverse) V is considered bearish (indicative of a falling market). *See also* BOTTOM; TECHNICAL ANALYSIS. *See* illustration, page 528.

V FORMATION

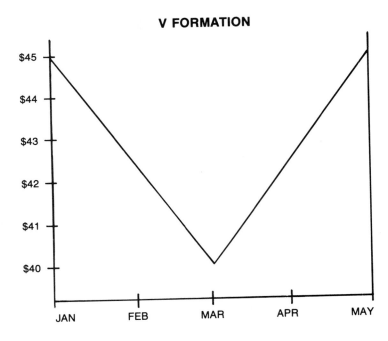

VOIDABLE contract that can be annulled by either party after it is signed because fraud, incompetence, or another illegality exists or because a RIGHT OF RESCISSION applies.

VOLATILE tending to rapid and extreme fluctuations. The term is used to describe the size and frequency of the fluctuations in the price of a particular stock, bond, or commodity. A stock may be volatile because the outlook for the company is particularly uncertain, because there are only a few shares outstanding (*see also* THIN MARKET), or because of various other reasons. Where the reasons for the volatility have to do with the particular security as distinguished from market conditions, volatility is measured by a concept called the alpha factor. A stock with an alpha factor of 1.25 is projected to rise in price by 25% in a year on the strength of its inherent values such as growth in earnings per share and regardless of the performance of the market as a whole. Market-related volatility, also called SYSTEMATIC RISK, is measured by the BETA COEFFICIENT.

VOLATILITY characteristic of a security, commodity, or market to rise or fall sharply in price within a short-term period. A measure of the relative volatility of a stock to the overall market is its BETA COEFFICIENT. *See also* VOLATILE.

VOLUME total number of stock shares, bonds, or commodities futures contracts traded in a particular period. Volume figures are reported daily by exchanges, both for individual issues trading and for the total amount of trading executed on the exchange. Technical analysts place great emphasis on the amount of volume that occurs in the trading of a security or a commodity futures contract. A sharp rise in volume is believed to signify future sharp rises or falls in price, because it reflects increased investor interest in a security, commodity, or market. *See also* TECHNICAL ANALYSIS; TURNOVER.

VOLUME DELETED note appearing on the CONSOLIDATED TAPE, usually when the tape is running behind by two minutes or more because of heavy trading, that only the STOCK SYMBOL and the trading price will be displayed for transactions of less than 5000 shares.

VOLUNTARY ACCUMULATION PLAN plan subscribed to by a MUTUAL FUND shareholder to accumulate shares in that fund on a regular basis over time. The amount of money to be put into the fund and the intervals at which it is to be invested are at the discretion of the shareholder. A plan that invests a set amount on a regular schedule is a dollar cost averaging plan or CONSTANT DOLLAR PLAN.

VOLUNTARY BANKRUPTCY legal proceeding that follows a petition of BANKRUPTCY filed by a debtor in the appropriate U.S. district court under the Bankruptcy Act. Petitions for voluntary bankruptcy can be filed by any insolvent business or individual except a building and loan association or a municipal, railroad, insurance, or banking corporation.

VOTING STOCK shares in a corporation that entitle the shareholder to voting and PROXY rights. When a shareholder deposits such stock with a CUSTODIAN that acts as a voting TRUST, the shareholder retains rights to earnings and dividends but delegates voting rights to the trustee. *See also* COMMON STOCK; PROPORTIONAL REPRESENTATION; VOTING TRUST CERTIFICATE.

VOTING TRUST CERTIFICATE transferable certificate of beneficial interest in a *voting trust,* a limited-life trust set up to center control of a corporation in the hands of a few individuals, called *voting trustees.* The certificates, which are issued by the voting trust to stockholders in exchange for their common stock, represent all the rights of common stock except voting rights. The common stock is then registered on the books of the corporation in the names of the trustees. The usual purpose for such an arrangement is to facilitate REORGANIZATION of a corporation in financial difficulty by preventing interference with management. Voting trust certificates are limited to the five-year life of a TRUST but can be extended with the mutual consent of the holders and trustees.

VULTURE FUND type of LIMITED PARTNERSHIP that invests in depressed property, usually real estate, aiming to profit when prices rebound.

W

WAITING PERIOD TWENTY-DAY period required by the SECURITIES AND EXCHANGE COMMISSION between the filing of a REGISTRATION in a securities offering and the time the securities can legally be offered to the investing public. This COOLING-OFF PERIOD may be extended if more time is needed to make corrections or add information to the REGISTRATION STATEMENT and PROSPECTUS.

WALLFLOWER stock that has fallen out of favor with investors. Such stocks tend to have a low PRICE/EARNINGS RATIO.

WALL STREET

1. common name for the financial district at the lower end of Manhattan in New York City, where the New York and American Stock Exchanges and numerous brokerage firms are headquartered. The New York Stock Exchange is actually located at the corner of Wall and Broad Streets.

2. investment community, such as in "Wall Street really likes the prospects for that company" or "Wall Street law firm," meaning a firm specializing in securities law and mergers. Also referred to as "the Street."

WANTED FOR CASH TICKER tape announcement that a bidder will pay cash the same day for a specified block of securities. Cash trades are executed for delivery and settlement at the time the transaction is made.

WAR BABIES jargon for the stocks and bonds of corporations engaged primarily as defense contractors. Also called *war brides*.

WAREHOUSE RECEIPT document listing goods or commodities kept for SA-FEKEEPING in a warehouse. The receipt can be used to transfer ownership of that commodity, instead of having to deliver the physical commodity. Warehouse receipts are used with many commodities, particularly precious metals like gold, silver, and platinum, which must be safeguarded against theft.

WARRANT *see* SUBSCRIPTION WARRANT.

WASH SALE purchase and sale of a security either simultaneously or within a short period of time. It may be done by a single investor or (where MANIPULATION is involved) by two or more parties conspiring to create artificial market activity in order to profit from a rise in the security's price. Wash sales taking place within 30 days of the underlying purchase do not qualify as tax losses under Internal Revenue Service rules.

Under the TAX REFORM ACT OF 1984, wash sale rules were extended to all taxpayers except those trading in securities in the normal course of business, such as securities dealers. Prior to the 1984 Act, noncorporate taxpayers engaged in a trade or business were exempt from wash sale rules. The Act also extended the wash sale prohibition to closing short sales of substantially identical securities, or to instances where short sales are made within 30 days of closing.

See also THIRTY-DAY WASH RULE.

WASTING ASSET
1. fixed asset, other than land, that has a limited useful life and is therefore subject to DEPRECIATION.
2. natural resource that diminishes in value because of extractions of oil, ores, or gas, or the removal of timber, or similar depletion and that is therefore subject to AMORTIZATION.
3. security with a value that expires at a particular time in the future. An OPTION contract, for instance, is a wasting asset, because the chances of a favorable move in the underlying stock diminish as the contract approaches expiration, thus reducing the value of the option.

WATCH LIST list of securities singled out for special surveillance by a brokerage firm or an exchange or other self-regulatory organization to spot irregularities. Firms on the watch list may be TAKEOVER candidates, companies about to issue new securities, or others that seem to have attracted an unusually heavy volume of trading activity. *See also* STOCK WATCHER; SURVEILLANCE DEPARTMENT OF EXCHANGES.

WATERED STOCK stock representing ownership of OVERVALUED assets, a condition of overcapitalized corporations, whose total worth is less than their invested capital. The condition may result from inflated accounting values, gifts of stock, operating losses, or excessive stock dividends. Among the negative features of watered stock from the shareholder's standpoint are inability to recoup full investment in LIQUIDATION, inadequate return on investment, possible liability exceeding the PAR value of shares, low MARKET VALUE because of poor dividends and possible adverse publicity, reduced ability of the firm to issue new stock or debt securities to capitalize on growth opportunity, and loss of competitive position because of the need to raise prices to provide a return acceptable to investors. To remedy the situation, a company must either increase its assets without increasing its OUTSTANDING shares or reduce outstanding shares without reducing assets. The alternatives are to increase RETAINED EARNINGS or to adjust the accounting values of assets or of stock.

WEAK MARKET market characterized by a preponderance of sellers over buyers and a general declining trend in prices.

WEDGE technical chart pattern similar to but varying slightly from a TRIANGLE. Two converging lines connect a series of peaks and troughs to form a wedge. These converging lines move in the same direction, unlike a triangle, in which one rises while the other falls or one rises or falls while the other line stays horizontal. Falling wedges usually occur as temporary interruptions of upward price rallies, rising wedges as interruptions of a falling price trend. *See also* TECHNICAL ANALYSIS.

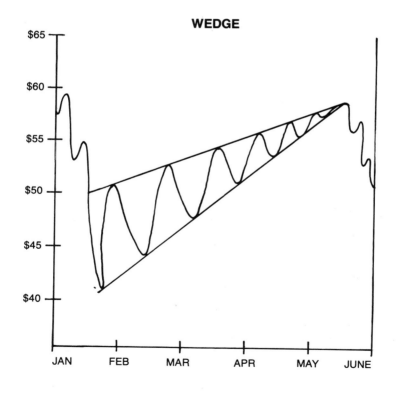

W FORMATION technical chart pattern of the price of a stock, bond, or commodity that shows the price has hit a SUPPORT LEVEL two times and is moving up; also called a *double bottom*.

A reverse W is just the opposite; the price has hit a resistance level and is headed down. This is called a DOUBLE TOP.

W FORMATION

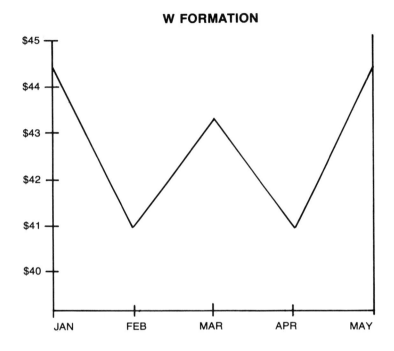

WHEN DISTRIBUTED transactions conditional on the SECONDARY DISTRIBUTION of shares ISSUED AND OUTSTANDING but CLOSELY HELD, as those of a wholly owned subsidiary, for example. *See also* WHEN ISSUED.

WHEN ISSUED short form of "when, as, and if issued." Term refers to a transaction made conditionally because a security, although authorized, has not yet been issued. NEW ISSUES of stocks and bonds, stocks that have SPLIT, and Treasury securities are all traded on a when issued basis. In a newspaper listing, a "WI" is placed next to the price of such a security. *See also* WHEN DISTRIBUTED.

WHIPSAWED to be caught in VOLATILE price movements and make losing trades as prices rise and fall. A trader is whipsawed if he or she buys just before prices fall and sells just before prices rise.

Term is also used in TECHNICAL ANALYSIS referring to misleading signals in the chart trends of markets or particular securities.

WHITE KNIGHT friendly acquirer sought by the target of an unfriendly TAKEOVER.

WHITE SQUIRE WHITE KNIGHT who buys less than a majority interest.

WHITE'S RATING White's Tax-Exempt Bond Rating Service's classification of municipal securities, which is based on market factors rather than credit considerations and which attempts to determine appropriate yields. *See also* MUNICIPAL BOND.

WHOLE LIFE INSURANCE form of life insurance policy that offers protection in case the insured dies and also builds up cash value. The policy stays in force for the lifetime of the insured, unless the policy is canceled or lapses. The policyholder usually pays a set annual PREMIUM for whole life, which does not rise as the person grows older (as in the case with TERM INSURANCE). The earnings on the cash value in the policy accumulate tax-deferred, and can be borrowed against in the form of a POLICY LOAN. The death benefit is reduced by the amount of the loan, if the loan is not repaid. Because whole life insurance traditionally offered a low return on the policyholder's investment, many policyholders beginning in the 1970s switched to new, higher-earning forms of whole life, such as UNIVERSAL LIFE INSURANCE and VARIABLE LIFE INSURANCE. Whole life insurance is also known as *ordinary* life, *permanent* life, or *straight* life insurance. *See also* SINGLE-PREMIUM LIFE INSURANCE.

WHOLE LOAN SECONDARY MORTGAGE MARKET term that distinguishes an investment representing an original residential mortgage loan (whole loan) from a loan representing a participation with one or more lenders or a PASS-THROUGH SECURITY representing a pool of mortgages.

WHOLESALE PRICE INDEX *see* PRODUCER PRICE INDEX.

WHOLESALER

In general: middleman or DISTRIBUTOR who sells mainly to retailers, JOBBERS, other merchants, and industrial, commercial, and institutional users as distinguished from consumers. *See also* VENDOR.
Securities:
1. INVESTMENT BANKER acting as an UNDERWRITER in a NEW ISSUE or as a distributor in a secondary offering of securities. *See also* SECONDARY DISTRIBUTION.
2. broker-dealer who trades with other broker-dealers, rather than with the retail investor, and receives discounts and selling commissions.
3. SPONSOR of a MUTUAL FUND.

WHOOPS nickname for the Washington Public Power Supply System. In the late 1970s and early 80s, WHOOPS raised billions of dollars through MUNICIPAL BOND offerings to finance construction of five nuclear plants in the state of Washington. Because of cost overruns, bad management, and numerous delays, two of the plants were canceled, and it was doubtful that two others would ever be completed. WHOOPS defaulted on the payments to bondholders on the two canceled plants after the Washington Supreme Court ruled that the TAKE-OR-PAY CONTRACTS with the many utilities in the Northwest that had backed the bonds were invalid. This was the largest municipal bond default in history.

WIDE OPENING abnormally large SPREAD between the BID AND ASKED prices of a security at the OPENING of a trading session.

WIDGET symbolic American gadget, used wherever a hypothetical product is needed to illustrate a manufacturing or selling concept.

WIDOW-AND-ORPHAN STOCK stock that pays high dividends and is very safe. It usually has a low BETA COEFFICIENT and is involved in a noncyclical business. For years American Telephone and Telegraph was considered the premier widow-and-orphan stock, but its status was being reevaluated following the court ordered-divestiture of local operating companies in the mid-1980s.

WILDCAT DRILLING exploring for oil or gas in an unproven area. A wildcat

OIL AND GAS LIMITED PARTNERSHIP is structured so that investors take high risks but can reap substantial rewards if oil or gas is found in commercial quantities.

WILLIAMS ACT federal legislation enacted in 1968 that imposes requirements with respect to public TENDER OFFERS. It was inspired by a wave of unannounced TAKEOVERS in the 1960s, which caught managers unawares and confronted stockholders with decisions they were ill prepared to make. The Williams Act and amendments now comprise Sections 13(d) and 14(d) of the SECURITIES EXCHANGE ACT OF 1934. The law requires the bidder opening a tender to file with both the SECURITIES AND EXCHANGE COMMISSION and the TARGET COMPANY a statement detailing the terms of the offer, the bidder's background, the cash source, and his or her plans for the company if there is a takeover. The same information is required within 10 days from any person or company acquiring 5% or more of another company. The law mandates a minimum offering period of 20 days and gives tendering shareholders 15 days to change their minds. If only a limited number of shares are accepted, they must be prorated among the tendering stockholders. *See also* SATURDAY NIGHT SPECIAL.

WINDFALL PROFIT profit that occurs suddenly as a result of an event not controlled by the person or company profiting from the event. For example, oil companies profited in the 1970s from an explosion in the price of oil brought about by the Arab oil embargo and the price increases demanded by the Organization of Petroleum Exporting Countries. *See also* WINDFALL PROFITS TAX.

WINDFALL PROFITS TAX tax on profits that result from a sudden windfall to a particular company or industry. In 1980, federal legislation was passed that levied such a tax on oil companies because of the profits they earned as a result of the sharp increase in oil prices in the 1970s.

WINDOW
1. limited time during which an opportunity should be seized, or it will be lost. For example, a period when new stock issues are welcomed by the public only lasts for a few months, or maybe as long as a year—that time is called the *window of opportunity*.
2. DISCOUNT WINDOW of a Federal Reserve bank.
3. cashier department of a brokerage firm, where delivery and settlement of securities transactions takes place.

WINDOW DRESSING
1. trading activity near the end of a quarter or fiscal year that is designed to dress up a PORTFOLIO to be presented to clients or shareholders. For example, a fund manager may sell losing positions in his portfolio so he can display only positions that have gained in value.
2. accounting gimmickry designed to make a FINANCIAL STATEMENT show a more favorable condition than actually exists—for example by omitting certain expenses, by concealing liabilities, by delaying WRITE-OFFS, by anticipating sales, or by other such actions, which may or may not be fraudulent.

WIRE HOUSE national or international brokerage firm whose branch offices are linked by a communications system that permits the rapid dissemination of prices, information, and research relating to financial markets and individual securities. Although smaller retail and regional brokers currently have access to similar data, the designation of a firm as a wire house dates back to the time when only the largest organizations had access to high-speed communications. Therefore, *wire house* still is used to refer to the biggest brokerage houses.

WIRE ROOM operating department of a brokerage firm that receives customers' orders from the REGISTERED REPRESENTATIVE and transmits the vital data to the exchange floor, where a FLOOR TICKET is prepared, or to the firm's trading department for execution. The wire room also receives notices of executed trades and relays them to the appropriate registered representatives. Also called *order department, order room,* or *wire and order.*

WITCHING HOUR *see* TRIPLE WITCHING HOUR.

WITHDRAWAL PLAN program available through most open-end MUTUAL FUND companies in which shareholders can receive fixed payments of income or CAPITAL GAINS (or both) on a regular basis, usually monthly or quarterly.

WITHHOLDING

Securities: violation of the RULES OF FAIR PRACTICE of the NATIONAL ASSOCIATION OF SECURITIES DEALERS whereby a participant in a PUBLIC OFFERING fails to make a bona fide public offering at the PUBLIC OFFERING PRICE—for example, by withholding shares for his or her own account or selling shares to a family member, an employee of the dealer firm, or another broker-dealer—in order to profit from the higher market price of a HOT ISSUE. *See also* IMMEDIATE FAMILY; INVESTMENT HISTORY.

Taxes:

1. deduction from salary payments and other compensation to provide for an individual's tax liability. Federal income taxes and Social Security contributions are withheld from paychecks and are deposited in a Treasury TAX AND LOAN ACCOUNT with a bank. The yearly amount of withholding is reported on an income statement (formW-2), which must be submitted with the federal, state, and local tax returns. Liability not provided for by withholding must be paid in four ESTIMATED TAX payments.
2. withholding by corporations and financial institutions of a flat 10% of interest and dividend payments due securities holders, as required under the TAX EQUITY AND FISCAL RESPONSIBILITY ACT OF 1982. The purpose was to levy a tax on people whose earnings escaped tracking by the Internal Revenue Service. The 10% withholding requirement was repealed in 1983. As a compromise, "backup withholding" was instituted, whereby, using Social Security numbers, payments can be reported to the IRS and matched against the actual income reported.
3. withholdings from pension and annuity distributions, sick pay, tips, and sizeable gambling winnings, as stipulated by law.
4. 30% withholding requirement on income from U.S. securities owned by foreigners—repealed by the TAX REFORM ACT OF 1984.

WORKING CAPITAL funds invested in a company's cash, ACCOUNTS RECEIVABLE, INVENTORY, and other CURRENT ASSETS (*gross working capital*); usually refers to *net working capital*—that is, current assets minus current liabilities (*see* CURRENT LIABILITY). Working capital finances the CASH CONVERSION CYCLE of a business—the length of time required to convert raw materials into finished goods, finished goods into sales, and accounts receivable into cash. These factors vary with the type of industry and the scale of production, which varies in turn with seasonality and with sales expansion and contraction.

Internal sources of working capital include RETAINED EARNINGS, operating efficiencies and the allocation of CASH FLOW from sources like DEPRECIATION or deferred taxes to working capital. External sources include bank and other short-term borrowings, TRADE CREDIT, and term debt and EQUITY FINANCING not channeled into long-term assets. *See also* CURRENT RATIO; NET CURRENT ASSETS.

WORKING CONTROL effective control of a corporation by a shareholder or shareholders with less than 51% voting interest. Working control by a minority holder, or by two or more minority holders working in concert, is possible when share ownership of a firm is otherwise widely dispersed.

WORKING INTEREST direct participation with unlimited liability, as distinguished from passive LIMITED PARTNERSHIP shares. The TAX REFORM ACT OF 1986 let investors with working interests in drilling ventures, such as GENERAL PARTNERS, offset losses against all types of income.

WORKOUT situation, such as a bad loan or troubled firm, where remedial measures are being taken.

WORLD BANK *see* INTERNATIONAL BANK FOR RECONSTRUCTION AND DEVELOPMENT.

WRAPAROUND ANNUITY ANNUITY contract allowing an annuitant discretion in the choice of underlying investments. Wraparound refers to the protection the annuity vehicle provides through its TAX-DEFERRED status, which becomes precarious when the annuity vehicle is being used as a technical way to avoid tax payment. The tax courts have ruled against tax deferment where money can be allocated by an annuity owner to a portfolio managed by an annuitant and where the annuitant can switch among funds of the sponsoring insurance company that are also marketed independently of annuities. On the other hand, the IRS has upheld tax deferral where an individual could not buy such funds without also buying the annuity. In any event, the insurer must legally own the annuity money.

WRAPAROUND MORTGAGE second mortgage that increases a borrower's indebtedness while leaving the original mortgage contract in force. The wraparound mortgage becomes the JUNIOR MORTGAGE and is held by the lending institution as security for the total mortgage debt. The borrower makes payments on both loans to the wraparound lender, who in turn makes scheduled installment payments on the original *senior mortgage*. It is a convenient way for a property owner to obtain additional credit without having to pay off an existing mortgage.

WRINKLE novel feature that may attract a buyer for a new product or a security. For example, ZERO COUPON SECURITIES were a new wrinkle when they were introduced in the early 1980s, but soon thereafter became quite commonplace.

WRITE-OFF charging an ASSET amount to expense or loss. The effect of a write-off is to reduce or eliminate the value of the asset and reduce profits. Write-offs are systematically taken in accordance with allowable tax DEPRECIATION of a FIXED ASSET, and with the AMORTIZATION of certain other assets, such as an INTANGIBLE ASSET and a capitalized cost (like premiums paid on investments). Write-offs are also taken when assets are, for whatever reason, deemed worthless, the most common example being uncollectible ACCOUNTS RECEIVABLE. Where such write-offs can be anticipated and therefore estimated, the usual practice has been to charge income regularly in amounts needed to maintain a RESERVE, the actual losses then being charged to the reserve. The TAX REFORM ACT OF 1986 required that BAD DEBT write-offs be charged directly to income by taxpayers other than small banks and thrift institutions. *See also* EXTRAORDINARY ITEM; NONRECURRING CHARGE.

WRITE OUT procedure followed when a SPECIALIST on an exchange makes a trade involving his own inventory, on one hand, and an order he is holding for a FLOOR

BROKER, on the other. Exchange rules require a two-part transaction: the broker first completes a trade with the specialist, who then completes the transaction by a separate trade with the customer. The write out involves no charge other than the normal broker's commission.

WRITER

1. person who sells PUT OPTION and CALL OPTION contracts, and therefore collects PREMIUM INCOME. The writer of a put option is obligated to buy (and the writer of a call option is obligated to sell) the UNDERLYING SECURITY at a predetermined price by a particular date if the OPTION is exercised. *See also* COVERED CALL; NAKED OPTION; WRITING NAKED.

2. insurance UNDERWRITER.

WRITING CASH-SECURED PUTS OPTION strategy that a trader who wants to sell PUT OPTIONS uses to avoid having to use a MARGIN ACCOUNT. Rather than depositing MARGIN with a broker, a put WRITER can deposit cash equal to the option EXERCISE PRICE. With this strategy, the put option writer is not subject to additional margin requirements in the event of changes in the underlying stock's price. The put writer can also be earning money by investing the PREMIUM he or she receives in MONEY MARKET instruments.

WRITING NAKED strategy used by an OPTION seller in which the trader does not own the UNDERLYING SECURITY. This strategy can lead to large profits if the stock moves in the hoped-for direction, but it can lead to large losses if the stock moves in the other direction, since the trader will have to go into the marketplace to buy the stock in order to deliver it to the option buyer. *See also* NAKED OPTION.

WRITING PUTS TO ACQUIRE STOCK strategy used by an OPTION writer (seller) who believes a stock is going to decline and that its purchase at a given price would represent a good investment. By writing a PUT OPTION exercisable at that price, the writer cannot lose. If the stock, contrary to his expectation, goes up, the option will not be exercised and he is at least ahead the amount of the PREMIUM he received. If, as expected, the stock goes down and the option is exercised, he has bought the stock at what he had earlier decided was a good buy, and he has the premium income in addition.

WRITTEN-DOWN VALUE BOOK VALUE of an asset after DEPRECIATION or other AMORTIZATION; also called *net book value*. For example, if the original cost of a piece of equipment was $1000 and accumulated depreciation charges totaled $400, the written-down value would be $600. *See also* INTANGIBLE ASSET.

WT abbreviation for *warrant*. *See also* SUBSCRIPTION WARRANT.

X

X or XD symbol used in newspapers to signify that a stock is trading EX-DIVIDEND, that is, without dividend. The symbol X is also used in bond tables to signify without interest.

XR symbol used in newspapers to signify that a stock is trading EX-RIGHTS, that is, without rights attached. *See also* SUBSCRIPTION RIGHT.

XW symbol used in newspapers to signify that a stock is trading EX-WARRANTS, that is, without warrants attached. *See also* SUBSCRIPTION WARRANT.

Y

YANKEE BOND MARKET dollar-denominated bonds issued in the U.S. by foreign banks and corporations. The bonds are issued in the U.S. when market conditions there are more favorable than on the EUROBOND market or in domestic markets overseas. Similarly, Yankee CERTIFICATES OF DEPOSIT are negotiable CDs issued in the U.S. by branches and agencies of foreign banks.

YELLOW SHEETS daily publication of the NATIONAL QUOTATION BUREAU that details the BID AND ASKED prices and firms that MAKE A MARKET in CORPORATE BONDS traded in the OVER THE COUNTER (OTC) market. Much of this information is not available in the daily OTC newspaper listings. The sheets are named for their color. OTC equity issues are covered separately on PINK SHEETS and regional OTC issues of both classes are listed on white sheets.

YEN BOND in general terms, any bond issue denominated in Japanese yen. International bankers using the term are usually referring to yen-denominated bonds issued or held outside Japan. Yen bonds have historically been an unimportant factor in international credit because of strict exchange controls and financial industry regulation by the Japanese government. An accord announced in May 1984 by the U.S. Treasury Department and Japanese Ministry of Finance was designed to open Japan to international money, capital, and securities markets and increase the importance of the yen in world trade and government reserve holdings. As a result, yen bonds are expected to increase their share of international debt offerings currently dominated by U.S. dollars. *See also* EUROBOND.

YIELD

In general: RETURN on an investor's CAPITAL INVESTMENT. A piece of real estate may yield a certain return, or a business deal may offer a particular yield. *See also* RETURN ON INVESTED CAPITAL.

Agriculture: agricultural output in terms of quantity of a crop.

Bonds:

1. COUPON rate of interest divided by the purchase price, called CURRENT YIELD. For example, a bond selling for $1000 with a 10% coupon offers a 10% current yield. If that same bond were selling for $500, however, it would offer a 20% yield to an investor who bought it for $500. (As a bond's price falls, its yield rises and vice versa.)

2. rate of return on a bond, taking into account the total of annual interest payments, the purchase price, the redemption value, and the amount of time remaining until maturity; called *maturity yield* or YIELD TO MATURITY. *See also* YIELD TO AVERAGE LIFE; YIELD TO CALL.

Lending: total money earned on a loan—that is, the ANNUAL PERCENTAGE RATE of interest multiplied by the term of the loan.

Stocks: percentage rate of return paid on a common or preferred stock in dividends. For example, a stock that sells for $20 and pays an annual dividend of $2 per share has a yield, also called a *dividend yield*, of 10%.

Taxes: amount of revenue received by a governmental entity as a result of a tax.

YIELD ADVANTAGE extra amount of return an investor will earn if he or she purchases a CONVERTIBLE security instead of the common stock of the same issuing corporation. If an XYZ Corporation convertible yields 10% and an XYZ common share yields 5%, the yield advantage is 5%. *See also* YIELD SPREAD.

YIELD CURVE graph showing the term structure of interest rates by plotting the yields of all bonds of the same quality with maturities ranging from the shortest to the longest available. The resulting curve shows if short-term interest rates are higher or lower than long-term rates. If short-term rates are lower, it is called a POSITIVE YIELD CURVE. If short-term rates are higher, it is called a NEGATIVE (or INVERTED) YIELD CURVE. If there is little difference between short-term and long-term rates, it is called a *flat yield curve*. For the most part, the yield curve is positive, since investors who are willing to tie up their money for a longer period of time usually are compensated for the extra risk they are taking by receiving a higher yield. The most common version of the yield curve graph plots Treasury securities, showing the range of yields from a three-month TREASURY BILL to a 20- or 30-year TREASURY BOND.

Fixed-income analysts study the yield curve carefully in order to make judgments about the direction of interest rates.

YIELD EQUIVALENCE the rate of interest at which a tax-exempt bond and a taxable security of similar quality provide the same return. In the day of the 50% TAX BRACKET, for example, a tax-exempt bond paying 10% was the equivalent of a taxable corporate bond of 20%. To calculate the yield that must be provided by a taxable security to equal that of a tax-exempt bond for investors in different tax brackets, the tax exempt yield is divided by the reciprocal of the tax bracket (100 less 28%, for example) to arrive at the taxable yield. Thus, a person in the 28% tax bracket, for example, who wished to figure the taxable equivalent of a 10% tax free municipal bond would divide 10% by 72% (100 minus 28%) to get 13.9%—the yield a corporate taxable bond would have to provide to be equivalent, after taxes, to the 10% municipal bond. To convert a taxable yield to a tax-exempt yield, the formula is reversed—that is, the tax exempt yield is equal to the taxable yield multiplied by the reciprocal of the tax bracket.

YIELD SPREAD difference in YIELD between various issues of securities. In comparing bonds, it usually refers to issues of different credit quality since issues of the same maturity and quality would normally have the same yields, as with Treasury securities, for example. Yield spread also refers to the differential between dividend yield on stocks and the CURRENT YIELD on bonds. The comparison might be made, for example, between the STANDARD & POOR'S INDEX (of 500 stocks) dividend yield and the current yield of an index of corporate bonds. A significant difference in bond and stock yields, assuming similar quality, is known as a *yield gap*.

YIELD TO AVERAGE LIFE yield calculation used, in lieu of YIELD TO MATURITY or YIELD TO CALL, where bonds are retired systematically during the life of the issue, as in the case of a SINKING FUND with contractual requirements. Because the issuer will buy its own bonds on the open market to satisfy its sinking fund requirements if the bonds are trading below PAR, there is to that extent automatic price support for such bonds; they therefore tend to trade on a yield-to-average-life basis.

YIELD TO CALL yield on a bond assuming the bond will be redeemed by the issuer at the first CALL date specified in the INDENTURE agreement. The same calculations are used to calculate yield to call as YIELD TO MATURITY except that the principal value at maturity is replaced by the first CALL PRICE and the maturity date is replaced by the first call date. Assuming the issuer will put the interest of the company before the interest of the investor and will call the bonds if it is favorable to do so, the lower of the yield to call and the yield to maturity can be viewed as the more realistic rate of return to the investor.

YIELD TO MATURITY (YTM) concept used to determine the rate of return an investor will receive if a long-term, interest-bearing investment, such as a bond, is held to its MATURITY DATE. It takes into account purchase price, REDEMPTION value, time to maturity, COUPON yield, and the time between interest payments. Recognizing time value of money, it is the DISCOUNT RATE at which the PRESENT VALUE of all future payments would equal the present price of the bond, also known as INTERNAL RATE OF RETURN. It is implicitly assumed that coupons are reinvested at the YTM rate. YTM can be approximated using a bond value table (also called a bond yield table) or can be determined using a programmable calculator equipped for bond mathematics calculations. *See also* HORIZON ANALYSIS; YIELD TO AVERAGE LIFE; YIELD TO CALL.

YO-YO STOCK stock that fluctuates in a VOLATILE manner, rising and falling quickly like a yo-yo.

Z

ZERO-BASE BUDGETING (ZBB) method of setting budgets for corporations and government agencies that requires a justification of all expenditures, not only those that exceed the prior year's allocations. Thus all budget lines are said to begin at a zero base and are funded according to merit rather than according to the level approved for the preceding year, when circumstances probably differed.

ZERO-BRACKET AMOUNT until the TAX REFORM ACT OF 1986, the STANDARD DEDUCTION, that is, the income automatically not subject to federal income tax for taxpayers choosing not to itemize deductions. The zero-bracket amount was built into the tax tables and schedules used to compute tax. The 1986 Act replaced the zero-bracket amount with an increased standard deduction, which was subtracted from income before computing taxes rather than being part of the rate tables. The new standard deduction, indexed to inflation and containing special provisions for the blind and elderly, was set to become fully effective in 1988.

ZERO-COUPON CONVERTIBLE SECURITY
1. Zero-coupon BOND convertible into the common stock of the issuing company when the stock reaches a predetermined price. Introduced as Liquid Yield Option Notes (LYONS), these securities have a PUT OPTION that permits holders to redeem the bonds within three years after the initial offering. They tend to trade at a small PREMIUM OVER CONVERSION VALUE and provide a lower YIELD TO MATURITY than their nonconvertible counterparts.
2. Zero-coupon bond, usually a MUNICIPAL BOND, convertible into an interest bearing bond at some time before maturity. For example, a zero-coupon (tax-free) municipal bond would automatically accumulate and compound interest for its first 15 years at which time it would convert to a regular income-paying bond. Thus, an investor is able to lock in a current interest rate with a small initial investment. Varieties are marketed under the acronyms GAINS (Growth And Income Securities) and FIGS (Future Income and Growth Securities).

ZERO-COUPON SECURITY security that makes no periodic interest payments but instead is sold at a deep discount from its face value. The buyer of such a bond receives the rate of return by the gradual APPRECIATION of the security, which is redeemed at FACE VALUE on a specified maturity date. For tax purposes, the Internal Revenue Service maintains that the holder of a zero-coupon bond owes income tax on the interest that has accrued each year, even though the bondholder does not actually receive the cash until maturity. Because of this interpretation, many financial advisors recommend that zero-coupon securities be used for INDIVIDUAL RETIREMENT ACCOUNTS or KEOGH ACCOUNTS, where they remain tax-sheltered.

There are many kinds of zero-coupon securities. The most commonly known is the zero-coupon bond, which either may be issued at a deep discount by a corporation or may be created by a brokerage firm when it strips the coupons off a bond and sells the CORPUS and the coupons separately. This technique is used frequently with Treasury bonds, and the zero-coupon issue is marketed under such names as Cat or Tiger. Zero-coupon bonds are also issued by municipalities. Buying a municipal zero frees its purchaser of the worry about paying taxes on imputed interest, since the interest is tax-exempt. Zero-coupon certificates of deposit and zero mortgages also exist; they work on the same principal as zero-coupon bonds—the CD or mortgage holder receives face value at maturity, and no payments until then.

Zero-coupon securities are frequently used to plan for a specific investment goal. For example, a parent knowing his child will enter college in 10 years can buy a zero that will mature in 10 years, and thus be assured of having money available for tuition. Similarly, a worker wanting to provide for retirement in 25 years can buy a 25-year zero.

Because zero-coupon securities bear no interest, they are the most VOLATILE of all fixed-income securities. Since zero-coupon bondholders do not receive interest payments, zeros fall more dramatically than bonds paying out interest on a current basis when interest rates rise. However, when interest rates fall, zero-coupon securities rise more rapidly in value, because the bonds have locked in a particular rate of reinvestment that becomes more attractive the further rates fall. The greater the number of years that a zero-coupon security has until maturity, the less an investor has to pay for it, and the more LEVERAGE is at work for him. For instance, a bond that will mature in 5 years may double, but one that matures in 25 years may increase in value 10 times, depending on the interest rate of the bond.

See also CERTIFICATE OF ACCRUAL ON TREASURY SECURITIES (CATS); COUPON BOND; DEEP DISCOUNT BOND; TIGER.

ZERO-MINUS TICK sale that takes place at the same price as the previous sale, but at a lower price than the last different price; also called a *zero downtick*. For instance, stock trades may be executed consecutively at prices of $52, $51, and $51. The final trade at $51 was made at a zero-minus tick, because it was made at the same price as the previous trade, but at a lower price than the last different price.

ZERO-PLUS TICK securities trade that takes place at the same price as the previous transaction but at a higher price than the last different price; also called *zero uptick*. For instance, with trades executed consecutively at $51, $52, and $52, the last trade at $52 was made at a zero-plus tick—the same price as the previous trade but a higher price than the last different price. Short sales must be executed only on zero-plus ticks or on PLUS TICKS. *See also* SHORT SALE RULE.

PART V

Finance and Investment
Ready Reference

INTRODUCTION

In today's complex world of finance and investment, it's crucial not only to know *how* different investments work, but also *where* to find the information essential to making wise decisions about those investments.

In the following pages you will find an enormous wealth of information concerning finance and investment. In some cases, the data presented is designed mainly to help you tap the many sophisticated sources available to investors. In other cases, we present well-organized data that can offer important insight into the workings of finance and investment. *In all cases, you are given information you can use.* The address and telephone number is given for just about every institution, organization, and firm listed, and you are encouraged to make direct contact in order to obtain the data required to make a well-informed investment decision.

The section is divided into the following principal parts:

Sources of Information and Assistance   Here you will find principal agencies and associations, both public and private, designed to help investors and consumers. Also listed are major financial publications and computer software and electronic databases useful in finance and investment.

Major Financial Institutions   In this part you will find some of the most influential players in the financial arena today. Among them are Federal Reserve System banks, primary government dealers. Federal Home Loan banks, the 100 largest commercial banks, the 100 largest thrift institutions, the 100 largest life insurance companies, the 100 largest brokerage firms, the largest sponsors of publicly available limited partnerships, the 25 largest accounting firms, and major stock and commodity exchanges around the world.

Mutual Funds   The burgeoning number of mutual funds, which allow individuals to invest with all the advantages of professional management, are listed in this part. The more widely known open-end mutual funds are given first, then the closed-end funds are presented.

Futures and Options Contracts   The increasingly important and complex world of futures and options is presented in this part. A list of contracts is given first, with a reference to the exchange on which the contracts are traded. Then detailed specifications of each contract are presented in tabular form, arranged by exchange.

Historical Data   To give you historical perspective on financial markets and the economy, this section provides graphs illustrating important longer-term financial and economic trends. In addition, important data is provided in tabular form so you can look up, say, the highest level the Dow Jones Industrial Average reached in 1979, as well as what the rate of inflation was that year.

Publicly Traded Companies Here can be found the most important companies in which you can buy shares. About 4700 companies are listed, broken down by the place where shares are traded. This section is led off by New York Stock Exchange companies and continues with American Stock Exchange companies, firms listed on the NASDAQ National Market System of the over-the-counter market, and selected major companies listed on the Toronto Stock Exchange. These listings provide you with each company's name, stock symbol, address, telephone number, and line of business. In addition, you can quickly determine whether a company offers a dividend reinvestment plan to shareholders or whether options are traded on the stock.

These listings are followed by a compilation of the most important American Depositary Receipts. ADRs allow Americans to buy conveniently the shares of major companies headquartered outside the United States. ADRs have become more important in recent years as American investors have increasingly looked to diversify investments beyond the borders of the United States.

The section on publicly traded companies concludes with a listing of benefits some firms offer to their shareholders in the form of free or reduced-price merchandise and/or services.

1. SOURCES OF INFORMATION AND ASSISTANCE

When trying to make decisions and keep up-to-date in the increasingly complex world of finance and investment, it is often necessary to turn to others. This section of the *Handbook* is designed to guide you to organizations that can help you.

Since financial markets are heavily regulated by the government today, it is important to know which federal and state regulators can be of assistance. The first part of this section gives a brief description of major federal, state, and provincial regulatory organizations in both the United States and Canada, and how to contact them.

A government agency sometimes is not the best place to turn. Private associations, trade groups, and self-regulatory organizations are often well equipped to deal with problems or questions related to finance and investment. The second part of this section lists many of these private groups.

For advice on where to invest and how to manage your financial affairs, there is an enormous pool of advice available in finance and investment publications. The third part of this section gives you the information you need to contact a great number of worthy publications that contain such advice.

To tap information about financial markets in an even speedier fashion, you can use computer databases, which are listed in the fourth part of this section. In addition, we have selected some of the best software that can make sense of the massive amounts of information these databases contain.

FEDERAL REGULATORY ORGANIZATIONS IN THE UNITED STATES AND CANADA

This is a list of the major governmental agencies that regulate the finance and investment markets in the United States and Canada. Each agency's address and telephone number is accompanied by a brief description of its major responsibilities. These agencies primarily oversee the fairness and efficiency of finance and investment markets. In that role, consumers and investors can complain to them about perceived abuses or illegality in the marketplace. Many of the agencies are discussed in more detail in the Dictionary section of the *Handbook,* along with the legislation that created the agency. The regulatory aspect of some of the agencies is less important than other functions.

Agencies of the United States Government

Commerce Department
14th Street & E Streets S.W.
Washington, D.C. 20230
(202) 377-4901

Regulates international trade and helps American businesses expand in a variety of ways. Publishes a large amount of data about the American economy.

Commodity Futures Trading Commission
2033 K Street N.W.
Washington, D.C. 20581
(202) 254-8630

Regulates the trading of commodity futures and options contracts. Investigates charges of fraud against commodity dealers. The CFTC also approves all new contracts that exchanges want to trade.

Comptroller of the Currency
490 L'Enfant Plaza S.W.
Washington, D.C. 20220
(202) 447-1600

Regulates all national banks in the United States. Handles consumer complaints against those banks.

Department of the Treasury
15th Street & Pennsylvania Avenue N.W.
Washington, D.C. 20220
(202) 566-2041

Regulates the issuance of government debt (Treasury bills, bonds, and notes) in coordination with the Federal Reserve and issues savings bonds. Plays a large role in coordinating economic and financial matters with foreign governments.

Federal Deposit Insurance Corporation
550 17th Street N.W.
Washington, D.C. 20429
(202) 393-8400

Insures deposits in member institutions up to $100,000 per depositor. Also regularly examines banks and replies to consumer complaints about federally insured state banks. Helps arrange the merger of weak banks into stronger ones.

Federal Home Loan Bank Board
1700 G Street N.W.
Washington, D.C. 20552
(202) 377-6000

Regulates and supplies credit to savings and loans. Responds to consumer complaints about federally chartered savings and loans.

Federal Home Loan Mortgage Corporation
1776 G Street N.W.
Washington, D.C. 20552
(202) 789-4448

Freddie Mac, as it is known, encourages the growth of the secondary mortgage market by buying mortgages from lenders, packaging and guaranteeing them, and reselling them as mortgage-backed securities.

Federal Reserve System
20th and Constitution St. N.W.
Washington, D.C. 20551
(202) 452-3000

Regulates national money supply, oversees activities of and supplies credit to member banks, and supervises the printing of money at the mint. Investors can also buy Treasury securities directly from the Fed or any of its district banks or branches.

Federal Savings and Loan Insurance Corporation
1700 G Street N.W.
Washington, D.C. 20552
(202) 377-6600

Insures deposits in member savings and loans up to $100,000 per depositor. Also regularly examines savings and loans and responds to consumer complaints about federally insured S&Ls. Helps arrange the merger of weak S&Ls into stronger ones.

Federal Trade Commission
Pennsylvania Avenue at Sixth Street N.W.
Washington, D.C. 20580
(202) 523-3598

Enforces antitrust laws and consumer protection legislation. For instance, the FTC oversees the Truth-in-Lending laws, and seeks to curtail unfair sales practices and deceptive advertising.

Internal Revenue Service
1111 Constitution Avenue N.W.
Washington, D.C. 20224
(202) 566-4743

Collects personal and corporate taxes for the federal government and administers rules and regulations of the Treasury Department.

National Credit Union Administration
1776 G Street N.W.
Washington, D.C. 20456
(202) 357-1050

Regulates federally chartered credit unions and offers assistance in setting up credit unions.

Securities and Exchange Commission
450 Fifth Street, N.W.
Washington, D.C. 20549
(202) 272-2650

Regulates the securities industry. Registers issues of securities, investigates fraud and insider trading, supervises investment companies, investment advisers, accounting firms, and self-regulatory organizations like the stock exchanges and the National Association of Securities Dealers.

Securities Investor Protection Corporation
900 17th Street N.W.
Washington, D.C. 20006
(202) 223-8400

Insures brokerage customers' holdings up to $500,000 per customer, with a limit of $100,000 in cash or cash equivalents against losses due to financial failure of a brokerage firm. SIPC does not cover losses due to market fluctuations or default by the issuers of securities. Helps arrange mergers of failing brokerage firms into stronger firms.

Small Business Administration
1441 L Street N.W.
Washington, D.C. 20416
(202) 653-7561

Offers advice and below-market rate loans and loan guarantees to qualifying small businesses, with special programs for veterans and women, among other groups. Also licenses and funds Small Business Investment Companies (SBICs).

United States Tax Court
400 Second Street N.W.
Washington, D.C. 20217
(202) 376-2754

Hears cases involving disputes between the IRS and taxpayers.

Agencies of the Canadian Government

Bank of Canada
Ottawa, Ontario K1A 0G9
(613) 782-8111

Regulates the money supply of Canada. It also acts as fiscal agent for the government of Canada in managing the public debt. The Bank of Canada also has the sole right to issue Canadian paper money.

Business Centre
Department of Regional Industrial Expansion
235 Queen Street
Ottawa, Ontario K1A 0H5
(613) 995-5771

The center helps business people get useful information about federal programs and services, industrial and trade topics, and in general improves the relationship of government with the business community.

Canada Deposit Insurance Corporation
P.O. Box 2340, Station D
Ottawa, Ontario K1P 5W5
(613) 996-2081

Insures deposits up to $60,000 per depositor in member institutions. Membership in the Corporation is restricted to banks, trust companies, and mortgage loan companies.

Canada Mortgage and Housing Corporation
682 Montreal Road
Ottawa, Ontario K1A 0P7
(613) 748-2000

The corporation administers the National Housing Act and is responsible for delivering housing assistance to increase the supply of housing. The corporation also insures mortgage loans made by approved lenders on the open market, and makes direct loans to areas not served by approved lenders.

Consumer and Corporate Affairs Canada
Place du Portage, Tower 1
Ottawa/Hull, Ontario K1A OC9
(819) 997-1670

Regulates many business activities and oversees consumer protection. Among its many responsibilities, the agency regulates product safety, consumer complaints, misleading advertising, federal corporation law, patents, copyrights and trademark law, and inspection of meat, fish, and other foods.

Export Development Corporation
151 O'Connor Street
Ottawa, Ontario K1P 5T9
(613) 598-2500

Assists Canadian companies to export their products and services.

External Affairs Department, International
  Trade Development
125 Sussex Drive
Ottawa, Ontario K1A OG2
(800) 267-8376

Coordinates international trade policy, and helps Canadian companies export their products and services.

Federal Business Development Bank
800 Place Victoria
Montréal, Québec H42 1L4
(514) 283-5904

Provides capital and equity financing and management services to Canadian businesses.

Finance Department
Ottawa, Ontario K1A OG5
(613) 992-1573

Conducts the financial affairs and economic planning for the Canadian government.

Inspector-General of Banks
Department of Finance
Ottawa, Ontario K1A OG5
(613) 992-0377

Division of the Finance Department that inspects banks for soundness of their financial condition.

Insurance Department Canada
Jackson Building
Ottawa, Ontario K1A OH2
(613) 996-8587

Regulates all insurance companies in Canada, including life insurance, health insurance, and property and casualty insurance.

Revenue Canada, Taxation
Communications Directorate
875 Heron Road
Ottawa, Ontario K1A OL8
(613) 957-3503

Collects corporate and individual taxes from Canadians.

Statistics Canada
Ottawa, Ontario K1A OT6
(613) 990-9851

Compiles many of the economic and financial statistics for the government of Canada.

Treasury Board
140 O'Connor Street
Ottawa, Ontario K1A OR5
(613) 957-2422

A Cabinet committee, brought into existence by the Financial Administration Act, which advises the rest of the Cabinet on the optimum allocation of public funds among government programs to permit the most efficient use of the government's manpower and financial and material resources.

U.S. STATE ATTORNEY GENERALS' OFFICES

The attorney general's office in a state is the place to go for a wide variety of consumer complaints. The attorney general is particularly concerned with stopping fraud, and frequently several attorneys general will coordinate their efforts to stop a multistate fraudulent business. Those who suspect a solicitation to be fraudulent should contact the relevant attorney general on this list before handing over any money.

Besides taking consumer complaints, the attorney general's office promulgates rules and regulations to promote fair business practices. Areas in their jurisdiction include deceptive advertising and contract law, for example. When appropriate, attorneys general also appeal to legislative bodies to pass new consumer protection laws. To enforce these laws, attorneys general pursue both civil and criminal prosecution of violators.

Attorney generals' offices may also be a source of help when considering a purchase decision. These offices usually publish helpful publications giving tips on what to avoid in entering certain kinds of sales contracts, for instance. Even if one is not sure where to turn for help for a particular consumer problem, the attorney general is often a good place to start.

ALABAMA
Attorney General
Alabama State House
Montgomery, Alabama 36130
(205) 261-7300 (800) 392-5658

ALASKA
Attorney General
Suite 110, 1031 West Fourth Avenue
Anchorage, Alaska 99501
(907) 279-0429

ARIZONA
Attorney General
1275 West Washington Street
Phoenix, Arizona 85007
(602) 255-5763 (800) 352-8431

ARKANSAS
Attorney General
Justice Building
Little Rock, Arkansas 72201
(501) 371-2341 (800) 482-8982

CALIFORNIA
Attorney General
Suite 511, 1515 K Street
Sacramento, California 95814
(916) 455-9555 (800) 952-5548

COLORADO
Attorney General
1525 Sherman Street
Denver, Colorado 80203
(303) 866-3611

CONNECTICUT
Attorney General
30 Trinity Street
Hartford, Connecticut 06106
(203) 566-5374 (800) 842-2649

DELAWARE
Attorney General
820 North French Street
Wilmington, Delaware 19801
(302) 571-3250

DISTRICT OF COLUMBIA
Department of Consumer and Regulatory
 Affairs
614 H Street, N.W.
Washington, D.C. 20001
(202) 727-7000

FLORIDA
Attorney General
State Capitol
Tallahassee, Florida 32399
(904) 488-9105 (800) 342-2176

GEORGIA
Attorney General
132 State Judicial Building
Atlanta, Georgia 30334
(404) 656-3345 (800) 282-5808

HAWAII
Office of Consumer Protection
250 South King Street
Honolulu, Hawaii 96812
(808) 548-2540

IDAHO
Attorney General
Room 210
State House
Boise, Idaho 83720
(208) 334-2400

ILLINOIS
Attorney General
500 South Second Street
Springfield, Illinois 62706
(217) 782-9011

INDIANA
Attorney General
219 State House
Indianapolis, Indiana 46204
(317) 232-6330 (800) 382-5516

IOWA
Attorney General
1300 East Walnut Street
Des Moines, Iowa 50319
(515) 281-5926

KANSAS
Attorney General
Kansas Judicial Center
Topeka, Kansas 66612
(913) 296-3751 (800) 432-2310

KENTUCKY
Attorney General
209 Saint Clair Street
Frankfort, Kentucky 40601
(502) 564-2200 (800) 432-9257

LOUISIANA
Attorney General
1885 Woodale Boulevard
Baton Rouge, Louisiana 70806
(504) 925-4181

MAINE
Attorney General
State House Station Number 6
Augusta, Maine 04333
(207) 289-3716

MARYLAND
Attorney General
7 North Calvert Street
Baltimore, Maryland 21202
(301) 528-8662

MASSACHUSETTS
Attorney General
One Ashburton Place
Boston, Massachusetts 02108
(617) 727-8400

MICHIGAN
Attorney General
670 Law Building
Lansing, Michigan 48913
(517) 373-1140

MINNESOTA
Attorney General
124 Ford Building
117 University Avenue
St. Paul, Minnesota 55155
(612) 296-2331

MISSISSIPPI
Attorney General
P.O. Box 220
Jackson, Mississippi 39215
(601) 359-3095 (800) 222-7622

MISSOURI
Attorney General
P.O. Box 899
Jefferson City, Missouri 65102
(314) 751-2616 (800) 392-8222

MONTANA
Consumer Affairs Unit
Commerce Department
1424 Ninth Avenue
Helena, Montana 59620
(406) 444-4312

NEBRASKA
Attorney General
State Capitol Building
Lincoln, Nebraska 68509
(402) 471-2682

NEVADA
Commissioner of Consumer Affairs
Department of Commerce
State Mail Room Complex
Las Vegas, Nevada 89158
(702) 386-5293 (800) 992-0900

NEW HAMPSHIRE
Attorney General
State House Annex
Concord, New Hampshire 03301
(603) 271-3641

NEW JERSEY
Attorney General
1100 Raymond Boulevard
Newark, New Jersey 07102
(201) 648-3510

NEW MEXICO
Attorney General
P.O. Drawer 1508
Santa Fe, New Mexico 87504
(505) 827-6910

NEW YORK
Attorney General
State Capitol
Albany, New York 12224
(518) 474-5481

NORTH CAROLINA
Attorney General
Department of Justice Building
P.O. Box 629
Raleigh, North Carolina 27602
(919) 733-7741

NORTH DAKOTA
Attorney General
State Capitol Building
Bismarck, North Dakota 58505
(701) 224-2210 (800) 472-2600

OHIO
Attorney General
30 East Broad Street
Columbus, Ohio 43215
(614) 466-8831 (800) 282-0515

OKLAHOMA
Attorney General
112 State Capitol Building
Oklahoma City, Oklahoma 73105
(405) 521-3921

OREGON
Department of Justice
Justice Building
Salem, Oregon 97310
(503) 378-4732

PENNSYLVANIA
Attorney General
Strawberry Square
Harrisburg, Pennsylvania 17120
(717) 787-9707

PUERTO RICO
Department of Justice
P.O. Box 192
Old San Juan, Puerto Rico 00902
(809) 721-2900

RHODE ISLAND
Attorney General
72 Pine Street
Providence, Rhode Island 02903
(401) 274-4400

SOUTH CAROLINA
Attorney General
P.O. Box 11549
Columbia, South Carolina 29211
(803) 758-3040 (800) 922-1594

SOUTH DAKOTA
Attorney General
Anderson Building
Pierre, South Dakota 57501
(605) 773-4400 (800) 592-1865

TENNESSEE
Attorney General
450 James Robertson Parkway
Nashville, Tennessee 37219
(615) 741-2672 (800) 342-8385

TEXAS
Attorney General
P.O. Box 12548, Capitol Station
Austin, Texas 78711
(512) 463-2100

UTAH
Attorney General
130 State Capitol
Salt Lake City, Utah 84114
(801) 533-5319

VERMONT
Attorney General
109 State Street
Montpelier, Vermont 05602
(802) 828-3186 (800) 642-5149

VIRGINIA
Attorney General
Supreme Court Building
101 North Eighth Street
Richmond, Virginia 23219
(804) 786-3433 (800) 552-9963

VIRGIN ISLANDS OF THE UNITED STATES
Consumer Services Administration
P.O. Box 5468
Charlotte Amalie, St. Thomas
U.S. Virgin Islands 00801
(809) 774-3130

WASHINGTON
Attorney General
1300 Dexter Horton Building
Seattle, Washington 98104
(206) 464-7744 (800) 551-4636

WEST VIRGINIA
Attorney General
1204 Kanawha Boulevard East
Charleston, West Virginia 25301
(304) 348-8986

WISCONSIN
Department of Justice
P.O. Box 7856
Madison, Wisconsin 53707
(608) 266-1852 (800) 362-8189

WYOMING
Attorney General
123 State Capitol Building
Cheyenne, Wyoming 82002
(307) 777-7841

U.S. STATE BANKING REGULATORS

The regulators listed here are charged with supervising the activities of state-chartered banks. These are banks not regulated at the national level, where the Comptroller of the Currency and Federal Reserve Board do the supervision. Depending on the state, state-chartered banks may have more or fewer powers than federally regulated banks. For example, the amount of money state banks can lend to customers as a percent of deposits varies widely from state to state. State banking regulators also oversee the financial soundness of banks in their jurisdictions, and help to merge failing banks into healthy ones. These regulators do not insure state bank deposits, however; that is usually done by the Federal Deposit Insurance Corporation.

State bank regulators also pursue consumer complaints against banks in their state. For example, it would be appropriate to contact a regulator if a state bank was preventing checks from clearing within a reasonable time or if fees were excessive. Complaints about deceptive advertising or promotional materials by banks can also be addressed to these agencies. Questions about credit, and the denial of credit privileges, are also handled by the agencies in this list.

State banking agencies are also helpful when shopping for a bank. They will usually publish helpful literature about banks and bank services. Do not expect these agencies to do comparisons of yields paid on bank accounts or interest rates charged on loans—these numbers change too frequently for the agencies to track them.

ALABAMA
Superintendent of Banks
166 Commerce Street, 3rd Floor
Montgomery, Alabama 36130
(205) 261-3452

ALASKA
Director of Banking and Securities
Post Office Box D
Juneau, Alaska 99811
(907) 465-2521

ARIZONA
Superintendent of Banks
Suite 815, Century Plaza
3225 North Central
Phoenix, Arizona 85012
(602) 255-4421

ARKANSAS
State Bank Commissioner
Suite 500, 323 Center, Tower Building
Little Rock, Arkansas 72201
(501) 371-1117

CALIFORNIA
Superintendent of Banks
Suite 750, 235 Montgomery Street
San Francisco, California 94104
(415) 557-3535

COLORADO
State Bank Commissioner
Room 700
303 West Colfax
Denver, Colorado 80204
(303) 866-3131

CONNECTICUT
Banking Commissioner
44 Capitol Avenue
Hartford, Connecticut 06106
(203) 566-4560

DELAWARE
State Bank Commissioner
P.O. Box 1401
Dover, Delaware 19903
(302) 736-4235

DISTRICT OF COLUMBIA
Comptroller of the Currency
490 L'Enfant Plaza, S.W.
Washington, D.C. 20219
(202) 447-1750

FLORIDA
State Comptroller
State Capitol Building
Tallahassee, Florida 32399
(904) 488-0370

GEORGIA
Commissioner of Banking and Finance
Suite 200, 2990 Brandywine Road
Atlanta, Georgia 30341
(404) 393-7330

HAWAII
Division of Financial Institutions
P.O. Box 2054
Honolulu, Hawaii 96805
(808) 548-5855

IDAHO
Department of Finance
Statehouse Mail
Boise, Idaho 83720
(208) 334-3313

ILLINOIS
Commissioner of Banks and Trust Companies
Room 400, Reisch Building
119 South 5th Street
Springfield, Illinois 62701
(217) 782-7966

INDIANA
Department of Financial Institutions
Room 1024, Indiana State Office Building
Indianapolis, Indiana 46204
(317) 232-3955

IOWA
Superintendent of Banking
Room 530, 418 Sixth Avenue
Des Moines, Iowa 50309
(515) 281-4014

KANSAS
State Bank Commissioner
Suite 300, 700 Jackson Street
Topeka, Kansas 66603
(913) 296-2266

KENTUCKY
Office of Financial Institutions
911 Leawood Drive
Frankfort, Kentucky 40601
(502) 564-3390

LOUISIANA
Commissioner of Financial Institutions
P.O. Box 94095, Capitol Station
Baton Rouge, Louisiana 70804
(504) 925-4661

MAINE
Superintendent of Banking
State House Station—36
Augusta, Maine 04333
(207) 289-3231

MARYLAND
Bank Commissioner
Suite 800, The Brokerage
34 Market Place
Baltimore, Maryland 21202
(301) 659-6262

MASSACHUSETTS
Commissioner of Banks
100 Cambridge Street
Boston, Massachusetts 02202
(617) 727-3120

MICHIGAN
Financial Institutions Bureau
P.O. Box 30224
Lansing, Michigan 48909
(517) 373-3460

MINNESOTA
Deputy Commissioner of Commerce
5th floor, 500 Metro Square Building
St. Paul, Minnesota 55101
(612) 296-2715

MISSISSIPPI
Department of Banking and Consumer Finance
P.O. Box 731
Jackson, Mississippi 39205
(601) 359-1031

MISSOURI
Commissioner of Finance
P.O. Box 716
Jefferson City, Missouri 65102
(314) 751-3397

MONTANA
Commissioner of Financial Institutions
1424 9th Avenue
Helena, Montana 59620
(406) 444-2091

NEBRASKA
Director of Banking and Finance
301 Centennial Mall South
Lincoln, Nebraska 68509
(402) 471-2171

NEVADA
Administrator of Financial Institutions
406 East Second Street
Carson City, Nevada 89710
(702) 885-4260

NEW HAMPSHIRE
Bank Commissioner
45 South Main Street
Concord, New Hampshire 03301
(603) 271-3561

NEW JERSEY
Commissioner of Banking
36 West State Street
Trenton, New Jersey 08625
(609) 292-3420

NEW MEXICO
Financial Institutions Division
Regulations and Licensing Department
Bataan Memorial Building
Santa Fe, New Mexico 87503
(505) 827-7740

NEW YORK
Superintendent of Banks
2 Rector Street
New York, New York 10006
(212) 618-6553

NORTH CAROLINA
Commissioner of Banks
P.O. Box 29512
Raleigh, North Carolina 27626
(919) 733-3016

NORTH DAKOTA
Commissioner of Banking and Financial
  Institutions
Room 1301, State Capitol
Bismarck, North Dakota 58505
(701) 224-2253

OHIO
Superintendent of Banks
2 Nationwide Plaza
Columbus, Ohio 43266
(614) 466-2932

OKLAHOMA
Bank Commissioner
Malco Building
4100 North Lincoln Boulevard
Oklahoma City, Oklahoma 73105
(405) 521-2783

OREGON
Administrator of the Financial Institutions
  Division
280 Court Street, N.E.
Salem, Oregon 97310
(503) 378-4140

PENNSYLVANIA
Secretary of Banking
16th Floor, 333 Market Street
Harrisburg, Pennsylvania 17101-2290
(717) 787-6991

PUERTO RICO
Bureau of Banks and Financial Institutions
P.O. Box 5-4515
San Juan, Puerto Rico 00905
(809) 721-5242

RHODE ISLAND
Banking and Securities
100 North Main Street
Providence, Rhode Island 02903
(401) 277-2405

SOUTH CAROLINA
Director of Banking
Room 217, 1026 Sumter Street
Columbia, South Carolina 29201
(803) 758-2116

SOUTH DAKOTA
Director of Banking and Finance
500 East Capitol Avenue
Pierre, South Dakota 57501
(605) 773-3421

TENNESSEE
Commissioner of Financial Institutions
James K. Polk State Office Building
505 Deaderick Street
Nashville, Tennessee 37219
(615) 741-2236

TEXAS
Banking Commissioner
2601 North Lamar
Austin, Texas 78705
(512) 479-1200

UTAH
Commissioner of Financial Institutions
P.O. Box 89
Salt Lake City, Utah 84110
(801) 530-6502

VERMONT
Commissioner of Banking and Insurance
State Office Building
Montpelier, Vermont 05602
(802) 828-3301

VIRGINIA
Commissioner of Financial Institutions
Suite 1600, 701 East Byrd Street
Richmond, Virginia 23205
(804) 786-3657

VIRGIN ISLANDS OF THE UNITED STATES
Chairman of the Banking Board
P.O. Box 450
St. Thomas, Virgin Islands 00801
(809) 774-2991

WASHINGTON
Supervisor of Banking
Room 219, General Administration Building
Olympia, Washington 98504
(206) 753-6520

WEST VIRGINIA
Commissioner of Banking
Room 311, State Office Building 3
Charleston, West Virginia 25305
(304) 348-2294

WISCONSIN
Commissioner of Banking
P.O. Box 7876
Madison, Wisconsin 53707
(608) 266-1621

WYOMING
State Examiner
4th Floor West, Herschler Building
Cheyenne, Wyoming 82002
(307) 777-6600

U.S. STATE INSURANCE REGULATORS

Every U.S. state has its own laws and regulations governing all types of insurance. Unlike most other areas in the financial services field, there is very little regulation of the insurance industry at the federal level. The state agencies listed here enforce all state insurance laws. Insurance commissioners must approve of the sale of all life, health, automobile, and homeowners insurance products in their states. Some states, such as New York and California, are particularly rigorous in approving new products for sale to state residents. If a product has been approved for sale in one of those states, it is often approved elsewhere as well.

When there are problems with an insurance company, these regulators step in. For example, they oversee the process of merging failing insurance companies into strong ones. They also protect policyholders by assuring that insurance companies keep adequate reserves. In the case of an insurance company failure, they see to it that policyholders' interests are protected as much as possible. State insurance offices also respond to consumer complaints against insurance companies on such issues as unfair pricing, denial of insurance claims, and deceptive advertising practices. Before bringing a complaint to one of these agencies, however, it is important to complain to the insurance company first. If the problem has not been resolved at that level, then these agencies should be consulted.

These insurance regulators also offer assistance to those looking to purchase insurance coverage. They may provide helpful literature about the kinds of insurance policies being offered, and also be able to inform buyers about patterns of complaints against particular companies.

ALABAMA
Commissioner of Insurance
135 South Union Street
Montgomery, Alabama 36130
(205) 269-3550

ALASKA
Director of Insurance
P.O. Box D
Juneau, Alaska 99811
(907) 465-2515

ARIZONA
Director of Insurance
801 East Jefferson
Phoenix, Arizona 85007
(602) 255-5400

ARKANSAS
Insurance Commissioner
400 University Tower Building
Little Rock, Arkansas 72204
(501) 371-1325

CALIFORNIA
Insurance Commissioner
600 South Commonwealth, 14th Floor
Los Angeles, California 90005
(213) 736-2551

COLORADO
Commissioner of Insurance
303 West Colfax, 5th Floor
Denver, Colorado 80204
(303) 866-3201

CONNECTICUT
Insurance Commissioner
Room 425, 165 Capitol Avenue
State Office Building
Hartford, Connecticut 06106
(203) 566-2810

DELAWARE
Insurance Commissioner
841 Silver Lake Plaza
Dover, Delaware 19901
(302) 736-4251

DISTRICT OF COLUMBIA
Superintendent of Insurance
Suite 516, 614 H Street, N.W.
Washington, D.C. 20001
(202) 727-7419

FLORIDA
Insurance Commissioner
Plaza Level 11, State Capitol Building
Tallahassee, Florida 32399
(904) 488-3440

GEORGIA
Insurance Commissioner
Suite 716, West Tower Floyd Building
#2 Martin Luther King Jr. Drive
Atlanta, Georgia 30334
(404) 656-2056

HAWAII
Insurance Commissioner
1010 Richards Street
Honolulu, Hawaii 96813
(808) 548-5450

IDAHO
Director of Insurance
700 West State Street
Boise, Idaho 83720
(208) 334-2250

ILLINOIS
Director of Insurance
4th Floor, 320 West Washington Street
Springfield, Illinois 62767
(217) 782-4515

INDIANA
Commissioner of Insurance
311 West Washington Street
Indianapolis, Indiana 46204
(317) 232-2386

IOWA
Commissioner of Insurance
State Office Building, G23, Ground Floor
Des Moines, Iowa 50319
(515) 281-5705

KANSAS
Commissioner of Insurance
420 Southwest 9th Street
Topeka, Kansas 66612
(913) 296-3071

KENTUCKY
Insurance Commissioner
229 West Main Street
Frankfort, Kentucky 40602
(502) 564-3630

LOUISIANA
Commissioner of Insurance
P.O. Box 94214
Baton Rouge, Louisiana 70804
(504) 342-5328

MAINE
Superintendent of Insurance
Hollowell Annex
State House, Station #34
Augusta, Maine 04333
(207) 289-3101

MARYLAND
Insurance Commissioner
7th Floor South
501 St. Paul Place
Baltimore, Maryland 21202
(301) 659-6300

MASSACHUSETTS
Commissioner of Insurance
100 Cambridge Street
Boston, Massachusetts 02202
(617) 727-3333

MICHIGAN
Commissioner of Insurance
P.O. Box 30220
Lansing, Michigan 48909
(517) 373-0220

MINNESOTA
Deputy Commissioner of Commerce
5th floor, 500 Metro Square Building
St. Paul, Minnesota 55101
(612) 296-6907

MISSISSIPPI
Commissioner of Insurance
1804 Walter Sillers Building
Jackson, Mississippi 39201
(601) 359-3569

MISSOURI
Director of Insurance
301 West High, Route 630
Jefferson City, Missouri 65102
(314) 751-2451

MONTANA
Commissioner of Insurance
Mitchell Building
Helena, Montana 59601
(406) 444-2040

NEBRASKA
Director of Insurance
301 Centennial Mall South
State Office Building
Lincoln, Nebraska 68509
(402) 471-2201

NEVADA
Commissioner of Insurance
Nye Building
201 South Falls Street
Carson City, Nevada 89710
(702) 885-4270

NEW HAMPSHIRE
Insurance Commissioner
169 Manchester Street
Concord, New Hampshire 03301
(603) 271-2261

NEW JERSEY
Commissioner of Insurance
201 East State Street
Trenton, New Jersey 08625
(609) 292-5363

NEW MEXICO
Superintendent of Insurance
PERA Building, P.O. Drawer 1269
Santa Fe, New Mexico 87504
(505) 827-4535

NEW YORK
Superintendent of Insurance
160 West Broadway
New York, New York 10013
(212) 602-0429 (800) 522-4370

NORTH CAROLINA
Commissioner of Insurance
Dobbs Building
P.O. Box 26387
Raleigh, North Carolina 27611
(919) 733-7343 (800) 662-7777

NORTH DAKOTA
Commissioner of Insurance
Capitol Building, 5th Floor
Bismarck, North Dakota 58505
(701) 224-2444

OHIO
Director of Insurance
2100 Stella Court
Columbus, Ohio 43205
(614) 481-5735

OKLAHOMA
Insurance Commissioner
1901 North Walnut
Oklahoma City, Oklahoma 73105
(405) 521-2828

OREGON
Insurance Commissioner
Insurance Division, Commerce Building
Salem, Oregon 97310
(503) 378-4271

PENNSYLVANIA
Commissioner of Insurance
1326 Strawberry Square
Harrisburg, Pennsylvania 17120
(717) 787-5173

PUERTO RICO
Commissioner of Insurance
P.O. Box 8330
Fernandez Juntos Station
Santurce, Puerto Rico 00910
(809) 724-6565

RHODE ISLAND
Insurance Commissioner
100 North Main Street
Providence, Rhode Island 02903
(401) 277-2223

SOUTH CAROLINA
Insurance Commissioner
1612 Marion Street
Columbia, South Carolina 29202
(803) 737-6160

SOUTH DAKOTA
Director of Insurance
Insurance Building
910 East Sioux
Pierre, South Dakota 57501
(605) 773-3563

TENNESSEE
Commissioner of Commerce and Insurance
1808 West End Building
Nashville, Tennessee 37219
(615) 741-2241

TEXAS
State Board of Insurance
1110 San Jacinto Boulevard
Austin, Texas 78701
(512) 463-6169

UTAH
Commissioner of Insurance
160 East 300 South
Salt Lake City, Utah 84110
(801) 530-6400

VERMONT
Commissioner of Banking and Insurance
State Office Building
Montpelier, Vermont 05602
(802) 828-3301

VIRGINIA
Commissioner of Insurance
700 Jefferson Building
Richmond, Virginia 23209
(804) 786-3741

VIRGIN ISLANDS OF THE UNITED STATES
Commissioner of Insurance
Office of Lieutenant Governor
P.O. Box 450
Charlotte Amalie
St. Thomas, Virgin Islands 00801
(809) 774-2991

WASHINGTON
Insurance Commissioner
Insurance Building AQ21
Olympia, Washington 98504
(206) 753-7301

WEST VIRGINIA
Insurance Commissioner
2100 Washington Street East
Charleston, West Virginia 25305
(304) 348-3386

WISCONSIN
Commissioner of Insurance
P.O. Box 7873
Madison, Wisconsin 53707
(608) 266-3585

WYOMING
Insurance Commissioner
122 West 25th Street, Herschler Building
Cheyenne, Wyoming 82002
(307) 777-7401

U.S. STATE SECURITIES REGULATORS

Anyone dealing with the potential purchase or sale of securities might want to consult with the state regulators listed here. Brokerage firms and financial planners selling securities must pass tests administered by state securities departments. In the event of any malfeasance on the part of those with a license to sell securities, the state securities department will look into the complaint and possibly revoke the license, if such action is called for.

These regulators protect buyers of securities sold in their states in another way: They screen all securities offering documents, such as prospectuses, to ensure that adequate information has been disclosed and that the deal is not fraudulent. The securities office will not judge each deal on its investment potential, but it will reject offerings it deems abusive. This prescreening process is commonly called the blue-sky process, because a judge once asserted that a particular offering had as much value as a patch of blue sky. It is important to ask these state securities regulators, therefore, if a particular security, such as a mutual fund or limited partnership, has passed the blue-sky process in one's state. If it has not, state residents are not allowed to buy it.

Besides watching óver the securities industry in their states and screening new securities offerings, state securities offices can be helpful in explaining the pros and cons of various kinds of securities. They often have helpful literature describing what investors should watch for in making good investments and avoiding bad ones. In general, these offices will be one of the best places to contact about any question that might come up regarding a security sold in one's state.

ALABAMA
Securities Commissioner
2nd Floor, 166 Commerce Street
Montgomery, Alabama 36130
(205) 261-2984

ALASKA
Banking, Securities & Corporations Division
Commerce & Economic Development Department
Post Office Box D
Juneau, Alaska 99811
(907) 465-2521

ARIZONA
Securities Division
Corporation Commission
1200 West Washington
Phoenix, Arizona 85007
(602) 255-4242

ARKANSAS
Securities Commissioner
201 East Markham
Little Rock, Arkansas 72201
(501) 371-1011

CALIFORNIA
Securities Commissioner
Department of Corporations
Suite 205, 1025 P Street
Sacramento, California 95814
(916) 445-8200

COLORADO
Division of Securities
Department of Regulatory Agencies
1560 Broadway, Suite 1450
Denver, Colorado 80202
(303) 866-2607

CONNECTICUT
Securities & Business Investments
Department of Banking
44 Capitol Avenue
Hartford, Connecticut 06106
(203) 566-4560

DELAWARE
Secretary of State
Townsend Building
Dover, Delaware 19901
(302) 736-4111

DISTRICT OF COLUMBIA
Deputy Mayor for Financial Management
Suite 423, 1350 Pennsylvania Avenue, NW
Washington, D.C. 20004
(202) 727-2476

FLORIDA
Securities Division
Department of Banking & Finance
The Capitol
Tallahassee, Florida 32301
(904) 488-9805

GEORGIA
Securities Commissioner
Suite 802W
2 Martin Luther King Jr. Drive
Atlanta, Georgia 30334
(404) 656-2894

HAWAII
Business Registration Division
Commerce & Consumer Affairs Department
1010 Richards Street
Honolulu, Hawaii 96810
(808) 548-6521

IDAHO
Department of Finance
700 West State Street
Boise, Idaho 83720
(208) 334-3313

ILLINOIS
Secretary of State
213 Capitol Building
Springfield, Illinois 62756
(217) 782-2201

INDIANA
Securities Commissioner
Suite 560, 1 North Capitol Street
Indianapolis, Indiana 46204
(317) 232-6681

IOWA
Securities Division
Insurance Department
Lucas State Office Building
Des Moines, Iowa 50319
(515) 281-4441

KANSAS
Securities Commissioner
Suite 212, 503 Kansas Avenue
Topeka, Kansas 66603
(913) 296-3307

KENTUCKY
Financial Institutions Department
Public Protection & Regulation Cabinet
911 Leawood Drive
Frankfort, Kentucky 40601
(502) 564-3390

LOUISIANA
Department of the Treasury
P.O. Box 44154
Baton Rouge, Louisiana 70804
(504) 342-0010

MAINE
Bureau of Banking, Business, Occupational &
  Professional Regulations Department
Suite 36, State House Station
Augusta, Maine 04333
(207) 289-3231

MARYLAND
Division of Securities
Office of the Attorney General
4th Floor, 7 North Calvert Street
Baltimore, Maryland 21202
(301) 576-6360

MASSACHUSETTS
Securities Division
Office of Secretary of Commonwealth
Suite 1719, 1 Ashburton Place
Boston, Massachusetts 02108
(617) 727-7190

MICHIGAN
Securities Division
Department of Commerce
6546 Mercantile Way
Lansing, Michigan 48909
(517) 334-6200

MINNESOTA
Registration & Licensing Division
Department of Commerce
5th Floor, Metro Square Building
St. Paul, Minnesota 55101
(612) 296-2594

MISSISSIPPI
Securities Division
Office of Secretary of State
401 Mississippi Street
Jackson, Mississippi 39201
(601) 359-1350

MISSOURI
Division of Securities
Office of Secretary of State
Truman Building, Box 778
Jefferson City, Missouri 65102
(314) 751-4136

MONTANA
Securities Division
Office of State Auditor
Capitol Station
Helena, Montana 59620
(406) 444-2040

NEBRASKA
Department of Banking & Finance
P.O. Box 95006
301 Centennial Mall South
Lincoln, Nebraska 68509
(402) 471-2171

NEVADA
Securities & Fraud Division
Office of Secretary of State
State Capitol
Carson City, Nevada 89710
(702) 885-5203

NEW HAMPSHIRE
Division of Securities
Department of Insurance
169 Manchester Street
Concord, New Hampshire 03301
(603) 271-2261

NEW JERSEY
Bureau of Securities
Suite 308, 80 Mulberry Street
Newark, New Jersey 07102
(201) 648-2040

NEW MEXICO
Securities Division
Regulation & Licensing Department
Bataan Memorial Building
Santa Fe, New Mexico 87503
(505) 827-7750

NEW YORK
Bureau of Investor Protection & Securities
120 Broadway
New York, New York 10271
(212) 341-2222

NORTH CAROLINA
Division of Securities
Office of Secretary of State
Suite 302, 300 North Salisbury Street
Raleigh, North Carolina 27611
(919) 733-3924

NORTH DAKOTA
Securities Commissioner's Office
9th Floor, State Capitol
Bismarck, North Dakota 58505
(701) 224-2910

OHIO
Division of Securities
Department of Commerce
3rd Floor, 2 Nationwide Plaza
Columbus, Ohio 43215
(614) 466-3440

OKLAHOMA
Securities Commissioner
2915 North Lincoln Boulevard
Oklahoma City, Oklahoma 73105
(405) 521-2451

OREGON
Division of Securities
Department of Commerce
158 12th Street N.E.
Salem, Oregon 97310
(503) 378-4385

PENNSYLVANIA
Securities Commissioner
14th Floor, 333 Market Street
Harrisburg, Pennsylvania 17101
(717) 787-6828

PUERTO RICO
Securities Commissioner
Department of the Treasury
P.O. Box 3508
San Juan, Puerto Rico 00904
(809) 723-1122

RHODE ISLAND
Banking Division
Department of Business Regulation
100 North Main Street
Providence, Rhode Island 02903
(401) 277-2405

SOUTH CAROLINA
Securities Division
816 Keenon Building
Columbia, South Carolina 29201
(803) 734-1089

SOUTH DAKOTA
Division of Securities
Commerce & Regulations Department
State Capitol
Pierre, South Dakota 57501
(605) 773-3177

TENNESSEE
Securities Division
Department of Commerce & Insurance
6th Floor, Tennessee Building
Nashville, Tennessee 37219
(615) 741-2947

TEXAS
Securities Board
P.O. Box 13167
Capitol Station
Austin, Texas 78711
(512) 474-2233

UTAH
Securities Commissioner's Office
Department of Business Regulation
160 East 300 South
Salt Lake City, Utah 84110
(801) 530-6600

VERMONT
Securities Commissioner
Department of Banking & Insurance
120 State Street
Montpelier, Vermont 05602
(802) 828-3301

VIRGINIA
State Corporation Commissioner
13th Floor, Jefferson Building
Richmond, Virginia 23219
(804) 786-3601

VIRGIN ISLANDS OF THE UNITED STATES
Corporations & Trade Names Division
Office of the Lieutenant Governor
P.O. Box 450
St. Thomas, Virgin Islands 00801
(809) 774-2991

WASHINGTON
Securities Division
Department of Licensing
Highways-Licensing Building
Olympia, Washington 98504
(206) 753-6928

WEST VIRGINIA
Securities Division
Office of State Auditor
W-100 State Capitol Complex
Charleston, West Virginia 25305
(304) 348-2257

WISCONSIN
Commissioner of Securities
P.O. Box 1768
111 West Wilson Street
Madison, Wisconsin 53701
(608) 266-3433

WYOMING
Secretary of State
State Capitol
Cheyenne, Wyoming 82002
(307) 777-7378

CANADIAN PROVINCIAL AND TERRITORIAL AGENCIES

The provincial and territorial agencies listed here have many of the same powers as state regulators in the United States. We have listed the two major finance and investment agencies in each province. The Consumer and Corporate Affairs Agencies regulate such areas as consumer protection, mortgages, insurance, credit, and securities. The Finance Departments of each province run the financial affairs of government and collect taxes.

ALBERTA
Consumer & Corporate Affairs Departemnt
1100 Capitol Square
10025 Jasper Avenue
Edmonton, Alberta T5G 3Z5
(403) 427-4095

Treasury Department
434 Terrace Building
9515 107th Street
Edmonton, Alberta T5K 2C3
(403) 427-4106

BRITISH COLUMBIA
Ministry of Consurmer & Corporate Affairs
940 Blanshard Sttreet
Victoria, British Columbia V8W 3E6
(604) 387-3126

Ministry of Finance
Parliament Buildings
Victoria, British Columbia V8V 1 X 4
(604) 387-5801

MANITOBA
Consumer & Corporate Affairs Department
114 Garry Street
Winnipeg, Manitoba R3C 1G1
(204) 956-2040

Department of Finance
Room 103, Legislative Building
Winnipeg, Manitoba R3C OV8
(204) 945-4035

NEW BRUNSWICK
Consumer Affairs Division
Justice Department
P.O. Box 6000
Fredericton, New Brunswick E3B 5H1
(506) 453-2659

Department of Finance
Centennial Building
Fredericton, New Brunswick E3B 5H1
(506) 453-2511

NEWFOUNDLAND
Department of Consumers Affairs and
   Communications
Elizabeth Towers, P.O. Box 4750
St. John's, Newfoundland A1C 5T7
(709) 576-2591

Department of Finance
Confederation Building
St. John's, Newfoundland A1C 5T7
(709) 576-2924

NORTHWEST TERRITORIES and YUKON
   TERRITORY
Department of Finance
P.O. Box 2703
Whitehorse, Yukon Territory Y1A 2C6
(403) 667-5343

NOVA SCOTIA
Department of Consumer Affairs
5151 Terminal Road, P.O. Box 998
Halifax, Nova Scotia B3J 2 X 3
(902) 424-4690

Department of Finance
Provincial Building, Hollis Street
P.O. Box 187
Halifax, Nova Scotia B3J 2N3
(902) 424-5720

ONTARIO
Ministry of Consumer & Commercial Relations
555 Yonge Street
Toronto, Ontario M7A 2H6
(416) 963-1111

Ministry of Treasury and Economics
4th Floor, Frost Building South
Queen's Park, Toronto M7A 1Z2
(416) 965-4746

PRINCE EDWARD ISLAND
Consumer Services Division, Justice
   Department
P.O. Box 2000
Charlottetown, Prince Edward Island
   C1A 7N8
(902) 892-5411

Department of Finance
Shaw Building, 95 Rochford Street
P.O. Box 2000
Charlottetown, Prince Edward Island
  C1A 7NB
(902) 368-4050

QUÉBEC
Ministère des Finances
1025 rue St. Augustin
Québec, P.Q. G1R 4Z6
(418) 643-4426

Ministère de la Protection du Consommateur
6 rue de L'Université
Québec, P.Q. G1R 5G8
(418) 643-1557

SASKATCHEWAN
Department of Consumer and Commercial
  Affairs
1871 Smith Street
Regina, Saskatchewan S4P 3V7
(306) 787-5550

Department of Finance
Treasury Board Division, 10th floor
2350 Albert Street
Regina, Saskatchewan S4P 4A6
(306) 787-6768

FINANCE AND INVESTMENT ORGANIZATIONS

This is a list of 50 of the most important organizations in the finance and investment field. Included are trade associations, which educate the public about their industry and lobby for their political positions in Congress; self-regulatory organizations, which regulate the conduct of the marketplace under the supervision of a federal regulatory agency; and consumer and investor organizations, which educate consumers and investors and help them resolve problems.

American Association of Commodity Traders
10 Park Street
Concord, New Hampshire 03301
(603) 224-2376

Represents traders of commodity futures and options.

American Association of Financial
  Professionals
P.O. Box 1928
Cocoa, Florida 32923
(305) 632-8654

Represents those in the financial planning industry such as CPAs, stockbrokers, tax attorneys, financial planners, and money, managers.

American Association of Individual Investors
612 North Michigan Avenue
Chicago, Illinois 60611
(312) 280-0170

Educates individual investors about opportunities in stocks, bonds, and mutual funds and investment computer software.

American Bankers Association
1120 Connecticut Avenue N.W.
Washington, D.C. 20036
(202) 663-5000

Represents commercial banks in lobbying on bank-related issues and educating the public about banking.

American Council of Life Insurance
1850 K Street, N.W.
Washington, D.C. 20006
(202) 862-4000

Represents life insurance companies in lobbying on life insurance-related issues and educating the public about insurance.

American Financial Services Association
1101 14th Street, N.W.
Washington, D.C. 20005
(202) 289-0400

Represents companies that lend to consumers, mostly finance companies. Lobbies on issues related to consumer lending, and also educates the public about use of credit and budgeting.

American Institute of Certified Public
  Accountants
1211 Avenue of the Americas
New York, New York 10036
(212) 575-6200

Professional society of accountants; establishes auditing and reporting standards and prepares the Uniform CPA Examination for state licensing bodies.

American Insurance Association
85 John Street
New York, New York 10038
(212) 669-0400

Represents property and liability insurance companies in lobbying on insurance-related issues. Educates the public about safety issues and suggests codes to governments on such areas as industrial safety and fire prevention.

American Management Association
135 West 50th Street
New York, New York 10020
(212) 586-8100

Educational organization to improve management skills in government and industry.

American Society of CLU & ChFC
270 Bryn Mawr Avenue
Bryn Mawr, Pennsylvania 19010
(215) 526-2500

Professional society of insurance agents, accountants, attorneys, and trust officers who hold the CLU (Chartered Life Underwriter) or the ChFC (Chartered Financial Consultant) designation, which is awarded after they have attended certain seminars and passed certain examinations.

Appraisers Association of America
60 East 42nd Street
New York, New York 10165
(212) 867-9775

Represents those who give professional appraisals of the value of property, usually for tax or insurance purposes.

Associated Credit Bureaus
16211 Park 10 Place
Houston, Texas 77084
(713) 492-8155

Represents credit bureaus, where consumer credit records are maintained. Consumers can take their complaints about a local credit bureau to the Associated Credit Bureaus for resolution.

Association of Publicly Traded Investment
  Funds
7 St. Paul Street
Baltimore, Maryland 21202
(301) 752-5900

Represents companies that offer closed-end mutual funds to the public, both in public education about the funds and lobbying on issues relating to the funds.

Bond & Share Society
24 Broadway
New York, New York 10004
(212) 943-1880

Society for promoting the hobby of scripophily, that is, the collection and study of antique stock and bond certificates.

Canadian Securities Institute
Suite 360, 33 Yonge Street
Toronto, Ontario M5E 1G4 Canada
(416) 364-9130

Represents Canadian brokerage firms on lobbying matters before the Legislature and promotes public education about the brokerage industry.

College for Financial Planning
9725 East Hampden Avenue
Denver, Colorado 80231
(303) 755-7101

Provides mail-order educational material and administers tests for financial planners. Once someone has passed the College's multipart test, they are a certified financial planner, and are entitled to use the CFP designation.

Credit Union National Association
5710 Mineral Point Road
Madison, Wisconsin 53705
(608) 231-4000

Represents credit unions in lobbying on issues related to credit unions. Promotes credit union membership and the formation of new credit unions, and educates the public about credit unions.

Financial Accounting Foundation
P.O. Box 3821
Stamford, Connecticut 06905
(203) 329-8401

Maintains the Financial Accounting Standards Board, which sets up auditing and accounting procedures for accountants.

Financial Analysts Federation
1633 Broadway
New York, New York 10019
(212) 957-2860

Organization of security analysts from brokerage houses and institutional investors which furthers the education of analysts.

Financial Executives Institute
10 Madison Avenue
Morristown, New Jersey 07960
(201) 898-4600

Organization of executives (such as controllers, treasurers, or vice presidents for finance) who perform finance functions in corporations.

Futures Industry Association
1825 Eye Street, N.W.
Washington, D.C. 20006
(202) 466-5460

Represents brokerage firms that deal in stock index and commodity futures, both in lobbying on futures-related issues and educating the public about the futures industry.

Independent Bankers Association of America
1 Thomas Circle, N.W.
Washington, D.C. 20005
(202) 659-8111

Represents medium and small commercial banks in lobbying on banking issues. Also helps members gain access to the latest banking technologies in areas such as credit card processing, automated teller machines, and computers.

Institute of Certified Financial Planners
10065 East Harvard Avenue
Denver, Colorado 80231
(303) 751-7600

Represents financial planners who have earned the CFP (Certified Financial Planner) designation. Offers continuing education for planners, and refers members of the public who inquire about CFP's in their area.

Institute of Chartered Financial Analysts
P.O. Box 3668
Charlottesville, Virginia 22903
(804) 977-6600

Represents financial analysts who have passed the CFA (Chartered Financial Analyst) examination. Conducts continuing education seminars of financial and investment analysis.

Insurance Information Institute
110 William Street
New York, New York 10038
(212) 669-9200

Represents property and liability insurance companies to educate the public about insurance issues. Maintains a consumer insurance hotline.

Insurance Services Office
160 Water Street
New York, New York 10038
(212) 487-5000

Establishes rate guidelines for property and liability insurance companies.

International Association for Financial Planning
Suite 800, Two Concourse Parkway
Atlanta, Georgia 30328
(404) 395-1605

Represents those in the financial services industry who are involved with financial planning. Promotes education of financial planners and offers assistance to the public in finding planners in their area.

International Consumer Credit Association
243 North Lindbergh Boulevard
St. Louis, Missouri 63141
(314) 991-3030

Represents members of the consumer credit industry. Conducts continuing education programs on consumer credit issues.

International Franchise Association
1350 Connecticut Avenue, N.W.
Washington, D.C. 20005
(202) 628-8000

Represents franchisers and franchisees of many different kinds of businesses by lobbying Congress on issues of concern to the industry. Gives advice to those wanting to evaluate franchise opportunities.

Investment Company Institute
1600 M Street, N.W.
Washington, D.C. 20036
(202) 293-7700

Represents open-end mutual fund companies, both lobbying on mutual fund issues in
Congress and educating the public about the
uses of mutual funds.

Investment Counsel Association of America
20 Exchange Place
New York, New York 10005
(212) 344-0999

Represents firms that invest clients' money in
stocks and bonds for a fee. Provides a list of
money managers for those looking for one.

Investor Responsibility Research Center
1755 Massachusetts Avenue, N.W.
Washington, D.C. 20036
(202) 939-6500

Publishes reports and analyses of social issues and public policies that affect corporations and investors. Focuses on such issues
as investing based on companies' records of
environmental safety, level of involvement in
military programs, and level of support for
oppressive governments.

Mortgage Bankers Association of America
1125 15th Street N.W.
Washington, D.C. 20005
(202) 861-6500

Represents mortgage lenders such as mortgage bankers, commercial banks, savings and
loans, and insurance companies. The MBAA
lobbies on housing finance issues before
Congress and conducts continuing education
seminars for members of the industry.

Municipal Bond Insurance Association
445 Hamilton Avenue
White Plains, New York 10602
(914) 681-1300

Consortium of insurance companies that insure municipal bonds against default of payment of principal and interest.

National Association of Business Economists
28349 Chagrin Boulevard
Cleveland, Ohio 44122
(216) 464-7986

Society of economists employed in corporate
or governmental positions who strive to improve the art of economic analysis and forecasting.

National Association of Investors Corporation
1515 East 11 Mile Road
Royal Oak, Michigan 48067
(313) 543-0612

Represents investment clubs. Helps people
set up such clubs, and monitors performance
of the clubs.

National Association of Personal Financial
  Advisors
3726 Oletangy River Road
Columbus, Ohio 43214
(614) 457-8200

Represents financial planners who work only
for a consulting fee and do not take commissions for selling products.

National Association of Real Estate
  Investment Trusts
1101 17th Street, N.W.
Washington, D.C. 20036
(202) 785-8717

Represents real estate investment trusts before Congress in lobbying on REIT-related issues, and educates the public about REITs.

National Association of Realtors
430 North Michigan Avenue
Chicago, Illinois 60611
(312) 329-8200

Represents Realtors by lobbying Congress on
real estate-related issues and educates the
public about the realty business.

National Association of Securities Dealers
1735 K Street, N.W.
Washington, D.C. 20006
(202) 728-8000

Organization formed under the supervision of
the Securities and Exchange Commission to
self-regulate the securities markets, particularly the over-the-counter market. NASD enforces rules of fair practice in the securities
markets and operates the NASDAQ (National
Association of Securities Dealers Automated
Quotations) system.

National Council of Savings Institutions
1101 15th Street N.W.
Washington, D.C. 20005
(202) 857-3100

Represents savings and loans and savings
banks in educating its members and the public about issues relating to banking and housing finance.

National Association of Small Business Investment Companies
1156 15th Street, N.W.
Washington, D.C. 20005
(202) 833-8230

Represents small business investment companies (SBICs), which are publicly traded or private companies that invest in private small businesses. The Association lobbies Congress on issues related to the industry and educates the public about SBICs.

National Foundation For Consumer Credit
8701 Georgia Avenue
Silver Spring, Maryland 20910
(301) 589-5600

Represents grantors of credit to consumers such as finance companies, retailers, and banks. Sponsors Consumer Credit Counseling Service centers around the country to give free aid to consumers in credit difficulty.

National Futures Association
200 West Madison Street
Chicago, Illinois 60606
(312) 781-1300

Represents and sets standards for brokers in the commodity futures and options business. Resolves disputes between its members and customers with complaints against those members.

National Investor Relations Institute
1629 K Street, N.W.
Washington, D.C. 20036
(202) 861-0630

Represents professionals in the investor relations and corporate communications function inside corporations. Conducts continuing education programs for members.

National Venture Capital Association
1655 North Fort Meyer Drive
Arlington, Virginia 22209
(202) 528-4370

Represents venture capitalists seeking to invest money in growing enterprises. Lobbies in Congress for programs to improve the environment for venture capital investing.

New York Society of Security Analysts
71 Broadway
New York, New York 10006
(212) 344-8450

Affiliate of the Financial Analysts Federation which conducts regular meetings between securities analysts and managements of companies followed by those analysts. This is the largest society in the country, though there are similar societies in most major American cities as well.

No-Load Mutual Fund Association
11 Penn Plaza
New York, New York 10001
(212) 563-4540

Represents no-load mutual funds and provides information to the public on the name, telephone number, and kinds of funds available.

Public Securities Association
40 Broad Street
New York, New York 10004
(212) 809-7000

Represents brokerage firms and banks dealing in municipal and mortgage-backed securities.

Securities Industry Association
120 Broadway
New York, New York 10271
(212) 608-1500

Represents securities broker/dealers, underwriters, and investment bankers in lobbying Congress on issues of concern to the securities industry. Educates the public about the securities industry.

United States League of Savings Institutions
111 East Wacker Drive
Chicago, Illinois 60601
(312) 644-3100

Represents savings and loans in lobbying before Congress on issues affecting the S & L industry. Educates the public about the savings and loan and housing industries.

FINANCE AND INVESTMENT PUBLICATIONS

The following is a list of just about all of the major publications that can help keep you informed about the fast-changing world of finance and investment. The list encompasses the full spectrum of publications, from mass circulation business magazines to investment newsletters that reach only a handful of subscribers. The publications also cover a wide variety of topics, from investment advice about stocks, bonds, money-market instruments, and commodities to mutual funds, taxation, entrepreneurship, and corporate finance. Other subjects covered include international investing, banking, precious metals, collectibles, management trends, economic forecasting, socially conscious investing, estate planning, venture capital, insider trading, real estate, and options. The title of each newsletter will often give you a clue to its subject matter.

Almost all the publications are available for a subscription charge; some also require that you join the organization that puts out the publication. Many will send you a sample either free or for a nominal charge.

Before subscribing to a newsletter, you must assess your needs and level of sophistication. Some letters listed here are designed for the novice investor with a relatively small amount of money to put into stocks or mutual funds. Other publications are aimed at a highly sophisticated audience that is knowledgeable about technical analysis, commodities trading, or some other specialty. In general, the more complex the publication, the higher the subscription fee.

Whichever publications you read, employ an appropriate amount of caution before following specific investment recommendations. Despite many advisors' claims, no one calls every move in the complex financial markets right every time. You should be satisfied if you find a few letters that offer a style you are comfortable with and have a good long-term track record at spotting unfolding investment trends.

A good part of this list was supplied by Jeffrey Dampf of JD Resources, 5 Macopin Avenue, Upper Montclair, New Jersey 07043, to whom we are very grateful.

AAII Journal
612 North Michigan Avenue
Chicago, Illinois 60611 (312) 280-0170

Abacus Futures Forecasting Company
1799 North Highland Avenue, M169
Clearwater, Florida 33515 (813) 442-6057

Addison Report
P.O. Box 402
Franklin, Mass. 02038 (617) 528-8678

ACCU Comm Futures Forecast
Suite 187, 3645 28th Street, Southeast
Grand Rapids, Michigan 49508
(616) 676-9765

Aden Analysis
4425 West Napoleon Avenue
Metairie, Louisiana 70001 (504) 456-0040

AG-Data Index
P.O. Box 49
Mathews, Missouri 63867 (314) 471-0081

AIC Investment Bulletin
7 North Street
Pittsfield, Mass. 01201 (413) 499-1111

Alan Shawn Feinstein Insiders Report
41 Alhambra Circle
Cranston, Rhode Island 02905
(401) 467-5155

Alexander Letter
Brexmarl, P.O. Box 231
Hamilton 5, Bermuda (809) 295-2686

Alexander Paris Report
P.O. Box 471
Barrington, Illinois 60010 (312) 428-6633

America's Fastest Growing Companies
John Herold, Inc.
35 Mason Street
Greenwich, Connecticut 06830
(203) 869-2585

American Banker (newspaper)
One State Street Plaza
New York, New York 10004 (212) 943-8200

American Rare Coin Reporter
Devonshire Financial Corporation at
  Newsletter Management Corporation
10076 Boca Entrada Boulevard
Boca Raton, Florida 33431-0907
(305) 483-2601

American Stock Exchange Weekly Bulletin
86 Trinity Place
New York, New York 10006 (212) 306-1445

Analagous Solar Terrestrial
5816 Webster
Omaha, Nebraska 68132 (402) 551-3203

Anderson Tax Report
Target, Inc., 6612 Owens Drive
Pleasanton, California 94566 (800) 654-4455
(800) 654-4456 (Cal. only)

Armstrong Report
112 Quakerbridge Mall
Lawrenceville, New Jersey 08648
(609) 799-8040

A.S.T.R.O.
5816 Webster
Omaha, Nebraska 68132 (402) 551-3203

Astute Investor
P.O. Box 988
Paoli, Pennsylvania 19301 (215) 296-2411

Astute Investor
Route 3, P.O. Box 310-D
Kingston, Tennessee 37763 (615) 376-2732

Barron's National Business and Financial
  Weekly (newspaper)
200 Liberty Street
New York, New York 10281 (212) 416-2000

Bartlett Letters
P.O. Box 309
Aurora, Illinois 60507 (312) 896-3143

Baxter Letter
1030 East Putnam Avenue
Greenwich, Connecticut 06836
(203) 637-4559

Bench Investment Letter
222 Bridge Plaza South
Fort Lee, New Jersey 07024 (201) 585-2333

Better Investing
National Association of Investors Corp.
1515 East Eleven Mile Road
Royal Oak, Michigan 48067 (313) 543-0612

Big Base Investing
Suite 400, 850 Montgomery Street
San Francisco, California 94133
(415) 421-7503

Big Picture
P.O. Box 9137
Allentown, Pennsylvania 18105

BI Research
P.O. Box 301
South Salem, New York 10590
(914) 763-5816

Blue Book of Canadian Business Service
  Stock Reports
Marpep Publishing Ltd.
133 Richmond Street West
Toronto, Ontario M5H 3M8 Canada
(416) 869-1177

Blue Book of Mutual Fund Reports
Marpep Publishing Ltd.
239 Genesee Street
Utica, New York 13501 (315) 724-4844

Blue Chip Economic Indicators
Blue Chip Economic Worldscan
Blue Chip Energy Forecasts Outlook
Blue Chip Financial Forecasts
Capitol Publications
1300 North 17th Street
Arlington, Virginia 22209 (703) 528-5400
(800) 847-7772

Boardroom Reports
Breakthrough by Boardroom Reports
330 West 42nd Street
New York, New York 10036 (212) 239-9000

Board Watch
Suite 160, 1154 Fort Street Mall
Honolulu, Hawaii 96813 (808) 528-4850

Bonanza Report
BFG Publishers
807 East South Temple
Salt Lake City, Utah 84102 (801) 363-9743

Bond Buyer
One State Street Plaza
New York, New York 10004 (212) 943-8200

Bond Fund Survey
P.O. Box 4180, Grand Central Station
New York, New York 10163 (212) 988-2498

Bondweek
Institutional Investor, Inc.
488 Madison Avenue
New York, New York 10022 (212) 303-3300

Boot Cove Economic Forecast
P.O. Box 200
Lubec, Maine 04652 (207) 733-5593

Bottom Line/Personal
P.O. Box 1027
Millburn, New Jersey 07041 (212) 239-9000

Bowser Report
P.O. Box 6278
Newport News, Virginia 23606
(804) 877-5979

Braun's Incremental System
Braun's Stock Index
Braun's T-Bill Trader
317 Wyatfield Drive
Lewisville, North Carolina 27023
(919) 945-9110

Brennan's IRA Adviser
Brennan Reports On Sophisticated Tax and
  Investment Planning
P.O. Box 882
Valley Forge, Pennsylvania 19482
(215) 783-0647 (800) 523-7289

Bretz's Juncture Recognition
P.O. Box 1209
Pompano Beach, Florida 33061
(305) 564-0643

Broadcast Banking
Broadcast Investor
Broadcast Investor Charts
Paul Kagan Associates
126 Clock Tower Place
Carmel, California 93923 (408) 624-1536

Browning Newsletter
P.O. Box 494
Burlington, Vermont 05402 (802) 658-0322

Bruce Babcock's Computer Trading Tutor
806 Dunbarton Circle
Sacramento, California 95825
(916) 929-5308

Bruce Gould on Commodities
P.O. Box 16
Seattle, Washington 98111

Bullion Report
Investor Metals Services
201-B East 82nd Street
New York, New York 10028 (212) 628-9780
(800) 223-1208

Bullish Consensus
Commodity Spread Trader
Hadady Publications
Suite 309, 61 South Lake Avenue
Pasadena, California 91101 (818) 795-1957

Business Trends Forecaster
Econometrics Newsletter Associates at
  Newsletter Management Corporation
10076 Boca Entrada Boulevard
Boca Raton, Florida 33431-0907
(305) 483-2601

Business Week Magazine
1221 Avenue of the Americas
New York, New York 10020 (212) 512-2511

Cable TV Investor
Cable TV Investor Charts
Motion Picture Investor
Paul Kagan Associates
126 Clock Tower Place
Carmel, California 93923 (408) 624-1536

Cabot Market Letter
P.O. Box 1013
Salem, Massachusetts 01970
(617) 745-5532

Cadence Universe Performance Report,
composed of
Investment Advisors Equity Performance
  Report
Bank & Insurance Company Fund
  Performance Report
Mutual Fund Performance Report
CDA Overview of Market Indices
Computer Directions Advisors
11501 Georgia Avenue
Silver Spring, Maryland 20902-9973
(301) 942-1700

California Technology Stock Letter
Venture Capital Management
155 Montgomery Street
San Francisco, California 94104
(415) 982-0125

Cambridge Commodities Marketletter
Cambridge Commodities Corp.
238 Main Street, Suite 522
Cambridge, Massachusetts 02142
(617) 661-6600

CRB Futures Chart Service
Commodity Research Bureau
100 Church Street
New York, New York 10007
(221) 406-4545

*Canadian Business Service Investment
    Reporter*
Marpep Publishing, Ltd.
133 Richmond Street West
Toronto, Canada M5H 3M8 (416) 869-1177

Canadian Guide To International Investing
CCH Canadian Limited
6 Garamond Court
Don Mills, Ontario M3C 1Z5 (416) 441-2992

Capital Gains
Financial Timing Publications
700 Shelard Plaza North
Minneapolis, Minnesota 55426
(612) 541-9344

Capitalgains
475 Grand Avenue
Palisades Park, New Jersey 07650
(201) 461-4157

Cash Flow Indicator
BFG Publishers
807 East South Temple
Salt Lake City, Utah 84102 (801) 363-9743

Catalyst
Center for Economic Revitalization
28 Main Street
Montpelier, Vermont 05602 (802) 223-3911

Chartcraft:
Bi-Monthly Weekly Bar Charts Book
Industry Groups Point and Figure Chartbook
Long Term Point and Figure Chartbook
*Monthly Point and Figure Chartbook of
    NYSE/ASE*
*Quarterly Non-Option Relative Strength
    Chartbook*
Quarterly Options Point and Figure Chartbook
Quarterly Option Relative Strength Chartbook
*Quarterly Over the Counter Point and Figure
    Chartbook*
Point and Figure Method Book
Weekly Commodity Service
Weekly Options Service
Weekly Service on NYSE/ASE
Technical Indicator Review
Chartcraft, Inc.
1 West Avenue
Larchmont, New York 10538 (914) 834-5181

Charted Course
P.O. Box 88
Westport, Connecticut 06881
(203) 334-5102

Charting The Economy
P.O. Box 829
New Haven, Connecticut 06504
(203) 666-8664

Chartist
P.O. Box 3160
Long Beach, California 90803
(213) 596-2385

Cheap Investor
Suite 10, 36 King Arthur Court
Northlake, Illinois 60164 (312) 562-0021

Clean Yield
P.O. Box 1880
Greensboro Bend, Vermont 05842

CMI:
Hi Performance Trader
Index Futures Trader
Index Option Trader
Market Perspectives
Option Trader
555 Sparkman Drive
Huntsville, Alabama 35805 (205) 837-7920

Coinage Magazine
James Miller Publications
2660 East Main Street
Ventura, California 93003 (805) 643-3664

Coin Dealer Newsletter
P.O. Box 11099
Torrance, California 90510-1099

Coin Market
Krause Publications
700 East State Street
Iola, Wisconsin 54990 (715) 445-2214

Comex Daily Market Report
Comex Quarterly
Comex Weekly Market Report
The Week In Metals
Commodity Exchange, Inc.
9th floor, 4 World Trade Center
New York, New York 10048 (212) 938-2900

Commodities Magazine
Commodities Report
219 Parkade
Cedar Falls, Iowa 50613 (319) 277-1271

Commodity and Currency Reporter
Marpep Publishing Ltd.
133 Richmond Street West
Toronto M5H 3M8, Canada (416) 869-1177

Commodity Closeup
P.O. Box 6
Cedar Falls, Iowa 50613 (319) 277-1271

Commodity Futures Forecast
Commodex
7000 Boulevard East,
Guttenberg, New Jersey 07093
(201) 868-2600

Commodity Journal
American Association of Commodity Traders
10 Park Street
Concord, New Hampshire 03301
(603) 224-2376

Commodity Price Charts
219 Parkade
Cedar Falls, Iowa 50613 (319) 277-1271

Commodity Price Forecast
P.O. Box 138038
Chicago, Illinois 60613

Commodity Research Bureau Outlook
100 Church Street
New York, New York 10007
(212) 406-4545

Commodity Timing
P.O. Box 1781
Kalispell, Montana 59901 (406) 752-2381

Computerized Investing
American Association of Individual Investors
612 North Michigan Avenue
Chicago, Illinois 60611 (312) 280-0170

Concordia Letter
Valley Forge Road
Weston, Connecticut 06883 (203) 226-5300

Confidential Market Report
Vukovich and Associates
1305 South Western
Park Ridge, Illinois 60068 (312) 692-9395

Confidential: Report from Zurich
Devonshire Financial Corporation at
  Newsletter Management Corporation
10076 Boca Entrada Boulevard
Boca Raton, Florida 33431-0907
(305) 483-2601

Consensus
1737 McGee Street
Kansas City, Missouri 64108 (816) 471-3862

Consensus of Insiders
P.O. Box 24349
Fort Lauderdale, Florida 33307
(305) 563-6827

Consultant's Coin Report
P.O. Box 8277
Fountain Valley, California 92728
(714) 662-0237

Contrary Investor
P.O. Box 494
Burlington, Vermont 05402 (802) 658-0322

Corporate Financing Week
Institutional Investor Systems
488 Madison Avenue
New York, New York 10022 (212) 303-3300

Corporate Shareholder
Market Value, Inc.
271 Madison Avenue
New York, New York 10016 (212) 213-0510

Crawford Perspectives
250 East 77th Street
New York, New York 10021 (212) 744-6973

Credit Union News
150 Nassau Street
New York, New York 10038 (212) 267-7707

Creditweek
Standard and Poor's
25 Broadway
New York, New York 10004
(212) 208-8000

Cris Research Reports
Frederick Research Corp.
1441 Prospect Avenue
Plainfield, New Jersey 07060 (201) 753-4514

CSCRPM Journal of Commodity Research
A View From Naples
P.O. Box 2302
Naples, Florida 33939 (813) 263-3114

CTCR (Commodity Traders Consumer Report)
Suite 149, 1731 Howe Avenue
Sacramento, California 95825
(916) 929-5308

Cumulative Stock Profits
P.O. Box 246
Forest Hills, New York 11375 (718) 896-8760

Currency Dealer Newsletter
P.O. Box 11099
Torrance, California 90510-1099

Cylinder Theory Reports
P.O. Box 4526
Albuquerque, New Mexico 87196
(505) 843-7749

Daily Graphs
P.O. Box 24933
Los Angeles, California 90024
(213) 820-2583

Danbell Energy Alert
Danbell Energy Letter
Daniels & Bell
99 Wall Street
New York, New York 10005 (212) 422-1710

Davis-Zweig Futures Hotline
Davis-Zweig Futures, Inc.
900 Third Avenue
New York, New York 10022 (212) 644-0040

Decision Charts
Target, Inc.
6612 Owens Drive
Pleasanton, California 94566 (800) 654-4455
(800) 654-4456 (Cal. only)

Deliberations: The Ian McAvity Market Letter
P.O. Box 182, Adelaide Street Station
Toronto, Ontario M5C 2J1, Canada
(416) 926-0995

Dessauer's Journal of Financial Markets
P.O. Box 1718
Orleans, Massachusetts 02653
(617) 255-1651

Detector Selector Survey
12100-74 Montecito Road
Los Alamitos, California 90720
(213) 596-9584

Dick Davis Digest
P.O. Box 2828, Ocean View Station
Miami Beach, Florida 33140 (305) 531-7777

Dickson's Investment Strategies
Econalyst Research Limited
Suite 3-223, 1750 Kalakaua Avenue
Honolulu, Hawaii 96826 (808) 942-3786

Digest of Investment Advices
516 Fifth Avenue
New York, New York 10036 (212) 564-6090

Dines Letter
Dines Commodity Letter
P.O. Box 22
Belvedere, California 94920 (415) 435-5458

Donoghue's Money Fund Report of Holliston, Mass.
Donoghue's Moneyletter

P.O. Box 540
Holliston, Massachusetts 01746
(617) 429-5930

Dowbeaters
450 Springfield Avenue
Summit, New Jersey 07901 (201) 273-0120

Dow Theory Forecasts
7412 Calumet Avenue
Hammond, Indiana 46324 (219) 931-6480

Dow Theory Letters
P.O. Box 1759
La Jolla, California 92038 (619) 454-0481

Dunn & Hargitt Commodity Service
22 North Second Street, P.O. Box 1100
Lafayette, Indiana 47902 (317) 423-2624

Dun's Business Month
875 Third Avenue
New York, New York 10022 (212) 605-9400

Economic Logic
22855 Essex Way
Southfield, Michigan 48034 (313) 357-1446

Economic News Review and Financial Digest
P.O. Box 94425
Schaumburg, Illinois 60194

Economist, The
10 Rockefeller Plaza
New York, New York 10020 (212) 541-5730
(800) 227-5782

Ehrenkrantz Letter
50 Broadway
New York, New York 10004 (212) 425-5328
(800) 854-0085

Electro-Optics Report
PennWell Publishing Company
119 Russell Street
Littleton, Massachusetts 01460
(617) 486-9501

Eliot Sharp's Financing News
Dealers' Digest, Inc.
150 Broadway
New York, New York 10038 (212) 227-1200

Elliott Wave Theorist
Elliott Wave Commodity Letter
P.O. Box 1618
Gainesville, Georgia 30503 (404) 536-0309

Emerging and Special Situations
Standard and Poor's Corp.
25 Broadway
New York, New York 10004 (212) 208-8000

Emerging Growth Stocks
Dow Theory Forecasts, Inc.
7412 Calumet Avenue
Hammond, Indiana 46324 (219) 931-6480

*Envest, The Business and Investment
   Newsletter of Energy and the Environment*
Glenville Station, P.O. Box 73
Greenwich, Connecticut 06830
(914) 937-6939

Equator Newsletter
4216 Pommard Drive
Kenner, Louisiana 70065 (504) 466-5540

Equity Research Associates
540 Madison Avenue
New York, New York 10022 (212) 940-0218

Estate Planning Review
Commerce Clearing House, Inc.
4025 West Peterson Avenue
Chicago, Illinois 60646 (312) 583-8500

Estate Planning
Prentice Hall
Route 9-W
Englewood Cliffs, New Jersey 07632
(201) 592-2000

Estate Planning Magazine
Warren Gorham and Lamont
210 South Street
Boston, Massachusetts 02111
(617) 423-2020

Estates, Gifts and Trusts Journal
Tax Management, Inc.
Bureau of National Affairs
1231 25th Street, N.W.
Washington, D.C. 20037 (202) 452-4200

FACT Magazine
711 Third Avenue
New York, New York 10017 (212) 687-3965

Factor Report
Route 7, P.O. Box 263
Brainerd, Minnesota 56401 (218) 963-3554

FEDWATCH
Money Market Services
275 Shoreline Drive
Redwood City, California 94065
(415) 595-0610 (800) 227-7304

Financial Analysts Journal
Financial Analysts Federation
1633 Broadway
New York, New York 10019 (212) 957-2860

Financial and Estate Planning
Financial and Estate Planning Ideas & Trends
Commerce Clearing House, Inc.
4025 West Peterson Avenue
Chicago, Illinois 60646 (312) 583-8500

Financial Foresight
The Communicators
8020 East Tuckey
Scottsdale, Arizona 85253 (602) 998-2535

Financial Freedom Report
National Institute of Financial Planning
1831 Fort Union Boulevard
Salt Lake City, Utah 84121 (802) 943-1311

Financial Guidance
P.O. Box 4130
Medford, Oregon 97501 (503) 826-9279

Financial Security Alert
Financial Timing Publications
700 Shelard Plaza North
Minneapolis, Minnesota 55426
(612) 541-9344

Financial Success Report
Target Inc.
6612 Owens Drive
Pleasanton, California 94566 (800) 654-4455
(800) 654-4456 (Cal. only)

Financial Times (newspaper)
14 East 60th Street
New York, New York 10022 (212) 752-4500

Financial World Magazine
1450 Broadway
New York, New York 10018 (212) 869-1616

FinVestor Report, Stocks Around Five Dollars
7322 Pinewood Street
Falls Church, Virginia 22046 (202) 785-0037
(703) 560-2847

First Report
P.O. Box 111050
Carrollton, Texas 75011

Fiscal Fitness
P.O. Box 365
Sandown, New Hampshire 03873
(603) 887-3110

Five Point Investment Strategy
200 West Madison Street, Suite 3850
Chicago, Illinois 60606 (312) 853-2820

Flexible Investor
P.O. Box 265, FDR Station
New York, New York 10022 (212) 832-2405

Focus 100 Series
Equity Research Associates
540 Madison Avenue
New York, New York 10022 (212) 940-0216

Forbes Magazine
60 Fifth Avenue
New York, New York 10011 (212) 620-2200

Ford Investment Management Report
Ford Value Report
Ford Investor Services
11722 Sorrento Valley Road
San Diego, California 92121 (619) 755-1327

Forecaster
Forecaster Publishing Company
19623 Ventura Boulevard
Tarzana, California 91356 (818) 345-4421

Forecasts & Strategies
Phillips Publishing, Inc.
7811 Montrose Road
Potomac, Maryland 20854 (301) 340-2100

Fortune Magazine
Time Incorporated
1271 Avenue of the Americas
New York, New York 10020 (212) 586-1212

Four Corners Advisor
P.O. Box 6
Silverton, Colorado 81433 (303) 387-5684

Franchising/Investments Around the World
P.O. Box 6996
Hollywood, Florida 33021 (305) 966-1530

Fraser Opinion Letter
P.O. Box 494
Burlington, Vermont 05402 (802) 658-0322

Free Market Perspectives
P.O. Box 471
Barrington, Illinois 60010 (312) 428-6633

Futures Forecast
P.O. Box 1682
Racine, Wisconsin 53401 (414) 634-3982

Futures Magazine
219 Parkade
Cedar Falls, Iowa 50613 (319) 277-6341

Futures Market Service
Commodity Research Bureau
75 Montgomery Street
Jersey City, New Jersey 07302
(201) 451-7500

FXC Investors
62-19 Cooper Avenue
Glendale, New York 11385 (718) 417-1330

Gann Angles, The Position Trader's Newsletter
Gannworld, Inc.
Suite 2, 245-A Washington Street
Monterey, California 93940 (408) 649-8822

Garside Forecast
P.O. Box 1812
Santa Ana, California 92702 (714) 544-1670

Gem Market Reporter
Gem Market News
P.O. Box 39890
Phoenix, Arizona 85069 (602) 252-4477

Gemstone Price Reports
Ubige S.P.R.L.
221 Avenue Louis
B-1050, Brussels, Belgium (02) 648-0711

Global Markets
P.O. Box 724
Morrisville, Pennsylvania 19067
(215) 946-8124

Going Public, The IPO Reporter
Two Penn Center Plaza
Philadelphia, Pennsylvania 19102
(215) 988-0010

Gold Newsletter
National Committee for Monetary Reform
4425 West Napoleon Avenue
Metairie, Louisiana 70001 (504) 456-0040

Goldsmith-Nagan Bond and Money Market Letter
1545 New York Avenue N.E.
Washington, D.C. 20002 (202) 628-1600

Gold Standard News
1805 Grand Avenue
Kansas City, Missouri 64108 (816) 842-4653

Gold Stock News
P.O. Box 471
Barrington, Illinois 60010 (312) 428-6633

Good Money
Center for Economic Revitalization
28 Main Street
Montpelier, Vermont 05602 (802) 223-3911

Gordon Market Timer
P.O. Box 938
Englewood Cliffs, New Jersey 07632

Graham-Rea Investment Analysis
10966 Chalon Road
Los Angeles, California 90077
(213) 471-1917

Grandich Letter
Underhill Associates, Inc.
12 Broad Street
Red Bank, New Jersey 07701 (201) 747-4030
(800) 631-2173

Granville Market Letter
P.O. Drawer 23006
Kansas City, Missouri 64141 (816) 474-5353

Graphic Analysis
P.O. Box 96
Gibson, North Carolina 28343
(919) 268-3515

Graphix Commodity Charts
Suite 1432, 30 West Washington Street
Chicago, Illinois 60602 (800) 663-8364

Ground Floor
The Hirsch Organization
6 Deer Trail
Old Tappan, New Jersey 07675
(201) 664-3400

Growth Fund Guide
P.O. Box 6600
Rapid City, South Dakota 57709
(605) 341-1971

Growth Stock Dynamics
Spring Valley Road, Rt. 1, Box 80
Elk Creek, Virginia 24326 (703) 655-4481

Growth Stock Outlook
P.O. Box 15381, 4405 East West Highway
Chevy Chase, Maryland 20815
(301) 654-5205

Growth Stock Report
Unity Publishers Corporation at Newsletter
   Management Corporation
10076 Boca Entrada Boulevard
Boca Raton, Florida 33431-0907
(305) 483-2601

Growth Stock Services
68 Beacon Street
Boston, Massachusetts 02108
(617) 227-9089

Hard Money Digest
3608 Grand Avenue
Oakland, California 94610 (415) 444-2800

Harmonic Research
650 Fifth Avenue, 16th Floor
New York, New York 10019 (212) 246-0300

Harry Browne's Special Reports
207 Jefferson Square, P.O. Box 5586
Austin, Texas 78763 (512) 453-7313
(800) 531-5142

Heim Investment Letter
Suite 308, 720 South West Washington
   Street
Portland, Oregon 97205 (503) 228-9555

Hidden Value, A Review of Overlooked
   Securities
7322 Pinewood Street
Falls Church, Virginia 22046 (202) 785-0037
(703) 560-2847

High Technology Growth Stocks
14 Nason Street
Maynard, Massachusetts 01754
(617) 897-9422

High Tech Investor
HMR Publishing Company
P.O. Box 471
Barrington, Illinois 60010 (312) 428-6633

High Tech Tomorrow, The Insider's Report
High Tech Information, Inc.
330 West 42nd Street
New York, New York 10036 (212) 239-9000

High Technology Investments
Suite 219, Gianturco & Michaels
5925 Kirby Drive
Houston, Texas 77005 (713) 529-1453

Hi-Tech/Defense Advisory
Oil Statistics Co.
One Map Hill Drive, P.O. Box 127
Babson Park, Massachusetts 02157
(617) 237-6620

Holt Investment Advisory
T.J. Holt and Co.
290 Post Road West
Westport, Connecticut 06880 (203) 226-8911

Howard Prenzel Technical Alert Letter
P.O. Box 893
Floral City, Florida 32636 (904) 726-1339

Hulbert Financial Digest
643 South Carolina Avenue, S.E.
Washington, D.C. 20003 (202) 546-2164

Hume MoneyLetter
835 Franklin Court, P.O. Box 105649
Atlanta, Georgia 30348 (404) 426-1920

In Business
P.O. Box 323
Emmaus, Pennsylvania 18049
(215) 967-4135

Inc. Magazine
38 Commercial Wharf
Boston, Massachusetts 02110
(617) 227-4700

Income & Safety, The Consumer's Guide to High Yields
3471 North Federal Highway
Fort Lauderdale, Florida 33306
(305) 563-9000

Independent Thinker
202 Grasmur Turn
Pine Hill, New Jersey 08021 (609) 435-7537

Index Futures Trading Points
P.O. Box 2666
Springfield, Virginia 22152 (301) 953-0935

Index Option Dataguide
1 Richmond Square
Providence, Rhode Island 02906
(401) 331-8950

Indicator Digest
Indicator Research Group
451 Grand Avenue
Palisades Park, New Jersey 07650
(201) 947-8800

Industries in Transition
9 Viaduct Road
Stamford, Connecticut 06906
(203) 325-2208

Industry Forecast
P.O. Box 26
Chappaqua, New York 10514 (914) 238-3665

Insider Indicator
2230 N.E. Brazee Street
Portland, Oregon 97212 (503) 281-8626

Insiders
Institute for Econometric Research
3471 North Federal Highway
Fort Lauderdale, Florida 33306
(305) 563-9000

Insider's Chronicle
Suite 207C
398 West Camino Gardens Boulevard
Boca Raton, Florida 33427 (305) 394-3404

Insiders' Edge
109 Spanish Village
Dallas, Texas 75248 (214) 380-1334

Insiders' Guide to Medical Technology Stocks
P.O. Box 24349
Fort Lauderdale, Florida 33307
(305) 563-6827

Insights
P.O. Box 907
Peck Slip Station
New York, New York 10272 (212) 460-0673

Insight: The Advisory Letter for Concerned Investors
Franklin Research and Development Corp.
711 Atlantic Avenue
Boston, Massachusetts 02111
(617) 423-6655

Institute of Certified Financial Planners Journal
3443 South Galena
Denver, Colorado 80231 (303) 751-7600

Institutional Investor
488 Madison Avenue
New York, New York 10022 (212) 303-3300

Intermarket Magazine
Suite A621, 175 West Jackson Boulevard
Chicago, Illinois 60604 (312) 922-4300

International Advisor
INVESTigate
Market Express
WMP Publishing Co.
Suite 103, 2211 Lee Road
Winter Park, Florida 32789 (305) 628-5300

International Asset Investor
P.O. Box 471
Barrington, Illinois 60010 (312) 428-6633

International Financial Success
Target, Inc.
6612 Owens Drive
Pleasanton, California 94566 (800) 654-4455
(800) 654-4456 (Cal. only)

International Gold Digest
Indicator Research Group
451 Grand Avenue
Palisades Park, New Jersey 07650
(201) 947-8800

International Harry Schultz Letter
FERC Ltd.
P.O. Box 381
1001 Lausanne, Switzerland

International Investor's Viewpoint
P.O. Box 447
Wilsonville, Oregon 97070 (503) 682-2750

International Moneyline Weekly
25 Broad Street
New York, New York 10004 (212) 344-1223

*International Prospector & Developer
   Magazine*
P.O. Box 1240, Station A
621-602 West Hastings Street
Vancouver, British Columbia V6B 1P2 Canada
(604) 684-8032

Intervest CD Rate Report
P.O. Box 794
Beverly Hills, California 90213
(818) 342-0710 (213) 937-8449

InveSearch Investment Briefs
P.O. Box 1445
Severna Park, Maryland 21146
(301) 987-5333

InvesTech Market Letter
522 Crestview Drive
Kalispell, Montana 59901 (406) 755-8527

Investing In Crisis
KCI Communications
1300 North 17th Street
Arlington, Virginia 22209 (703) 276-7100

Investment Alert
18 Lois Street
Norwalk, Connecticut 06851

Investment Dealers' Digest
150 Broadway
New York, New York 10038 (212) 227-1200

Investment Decisions
W.R. Nelson & Company
11 Elm Place
Rye, New York 10580 (914) 967-9100

Investment Educators Commodity Letter
P.O. Box 2354
Des Plaines, Illinois 60017 (312) 699-0225

Investment Highlights
P.O. Box 29190
Richmond, Virginia 23229 (804) 285-9655

Investment Letter
C.H.W. International Investment Services
Suite 1511, Simpson Tower, 401 Bay Street
Toronto, Ontario M5H 2Y4, Canada
(416) 368-7096

Investment Management World
Financial Analysts Federation
1633 Broadway
New York, New York 10019 (212) 957-2860

Investment Planning Guide
Investment Reporter
Marpep Publishing
133 Richmond Street West
Toronto, Ontario M5H 3M8, Canada
(416) 869-1177

Investment Quality Trends
7440 Girard Avenue
La Jolla, California 92037 (619) 459-3818

Investment Strategist
Money Growth Institute
37 Van Reipen Avenue
Jersey City, New Jersey 07306
(201) 792-0801

*Investment Strategy and Market Timing
   Update*
Institute of Wall Street Studies
Suite 200, 1200 North Federal Highway
Boca Raton, Florida 33432 (800) 453-8837

Investment Timing & Selections
P.O. Box 218, R.D. 1
Harvey's Lake
Pennsylvania 18618 (717) 639-1653

Investment Traders
461 Beach 124th Street
Belle Harbor, New York 11694
(718) 474-6568

Investment Values
P.O. Box 517
Mount Kisco, New York 10549
(914) 277-5801

Investor News
Prescott, Ball and Turben
1331 Euclid Avenue
Cleveland, Ohio 44115 (216) 574-7300

Investor Relations Newsletter
Enterprise Publications
20 North Wacker Drive
Chicago, Illinois 60606 (312) 332-3571

Investor Relations Update
National Investor Relations Institute
1730 M Street, N.W.
Washington, D.C. 20036 (202) 861-0630

Investor U.S.A.
Seahorse Financial Advisers
18 Seatuck Lane, P.O. Box 370
Remsenburg, New York 11960
(516) 325-0507

Investor's Clinic
9 Mount Jefferson Terrace
Lake Oswego, Oregon 97034 (503) 635-3501

Investor's Daily (newspaper)
1941 Armacost Avenue
Los Angeles, California 90025
(213) 477-1453

Investor's Digest of Canada
Maclean Hunter Ltd.
777 Bay Street
Toronto, Ontario M5W 1A7 Canada
(416) 596-5670 (800) 387-1300

Investor's Hotline
10616 Beaver Dam Road
Hunt Valley, Maryland 21030 (301) 667-0064

Investor's Notebook
James Blanchard & Co.
4425 West Napoleon Avenue
Metairie, Louisiana 70001 (504) 456-9034

Investors Intelligence
1 West Street
Larchmont, New York 10538 (914) 834-5181

IPO Reporter
150 Broadway
New York, New York 10038 (212) 227-1200

ITA Mutual Fund Advisor
Investment Trend Analysts
828 S.W. Moss
Portland, Oregon 97219 (503) 244-1924

Jenks Southeastern Business Letter
1132 West Peachtree Street
Atlanta, Georgia 30309 (404) 872-9546

Journal of Buyouts and Acquisitions
The Acquisition Mart
Business Publications
7124 Convoy Court
San Diego, California 92111 (619) 268-0782
(800) 523-7543

Journal of Portfolio Management
488 Madison Avenue
New York, New York 10022 (212) 303-3300

Junior Growth Stocks
P.O. Box 15381
Chevy Chase, Maryland 20815
(301) 654-5205

Key-Volume Strategies
P.O. Box 407
White Plains, NY 10602 (914) 997-8551

Kenneth Gerbino Investment Letter
Suite 200, 9595 Wilshire Boulevard
Beverly Hills, California 90212
(213) 550-6304

Kimball Letter
1418 Rummell Road
St. Cloud, Florida 32769 (305) 892-8555

Kinsman's Low-Risk Growth Letter
70 Mitchell Boulevard
San Rafael, California 94903 (415) 479-3200

Kiplinger Washington Letter
1729 H Street, N.W.
Washington, D.C. 20006 (202) 887-6400

Kirkpatrick's Market Strategist
P.O. Box 4376
Portsmouth, New Hampshire 03801
(603) 431-1411

Klein-Wolman Investment Letter
P.O. Box 727
Princeton Junction, New Jersey 08550
(609) 799-3885

Kondratieff Wave Analyst
P.O. Box 977
Crystal Lake, Illinois 60014

Kon Lin Research and Analysis
5 Water Road
Rocky Point, New York 11778
(516) 744-8536

LaLoggia's Special Situation Report
P.O. Box 167
Rochester, New York 14601 (716) 325-7100

Lancz Letter
Alan B. Lancz & Associates
3103 Executive Parkway
Toledo, Ohio 43606 (419) 537-1788

Laser Report
PennWell Publishing Co.
119 Russell Street
Littleton, Massachusetts 01460
(617) 486-9501

Let's Talk Silver and Gold:
The Cumulative Average
Sibbet Publications
Suite 301, 61 South Lake Avenue
Pasadena, California 91101 (213) 681-5319

Long Term Investing
P.O. Box 500
New York, New York 14592 (716) 243-3148

Long Term Values
Daily Graphs, William O'Neil & Co.
P.O. Box 24933
Los Angeles, California 90024
(213) 820-2583

Low-Priced Stock Digest
Idea Publishing Corp.
55 East Afton Avenue
Yardley, Pennsylvania 19067 (215) 493-1810

Low Price Stocks Newsletter
BFG Publishers
807 East South Temple
Salt Lake City, Utah 84102 (801) 363-9743

Low Priced Stock Survey
Dow Theory Forecasts
7412 Calumet Avenue
Hammond, Indiana 46324 (219) 931-6480

Lowe Investment & Financial Letter
Lowe Stock Advisory
P.O. Box 6
Jersey City, New Jersey 07303
(201) 233-5762

Lynch International Investment Survey
Lynch-Bowes, Inc.
1010 Franklin Avenue
Garden City, New York 11530
(516) 746-1122

Lynn Elgert Report
P.O. Box 1283
Grand Island, Nebraska 68802
(308) 381-2121

Magic T Forecast
American Shareholders Investment
 Corporation
3 Thurston's Court
Nantucket, Massachusetts 02554
(617) 228-2995

Main Street Journal
Claremont Economics Institute
250 West First Street
Claremont, California 91711 (714) 625-1441

Major Trends
6971 North Beech Tree Drive
Milwaukee, Wisconsin 53209 (414) 352-8460

Managed Account Reports
LJR Communications
5513 Twin Knolls
Columbia, Maryland 21045 (301) 730-5365

Margo's Market Monitor
P.O. Box 624
Lexington, Massachusetts 02173

Marina's Market Letter
P.O. Box 3608
Vero Beach, Florida 32964 (305) 231-1963
(800) 367-1029

Market Action Letter
KCI Communications
1300 North 17th Street
Arlington, Virginia 22209 (703) 276-7100

Market Alert
James Blanchard Co.
4425 West Napoleon Avenue
Metairie, Louisiana 70001 (504) 456-9034

Market Cash Flow Analysis
Allied Investments Inc.
841 Route 6
Bolton, Connecticut 06040 (203) 649-9034

Market Charts, a Point & Figure Technical
 Library
20 Exchange Place
New York, New York 10005 (212) 509-0944

Market Chronicle (newspaper)
William B. Dana Company
Suite 911, 45 John Street
New York, New York 10038 (212) 233-5200

Market Decisions
P.O. Box 14602
North Palm Beach, Florida 33408
(305) 842-9981

Market Insider Bulletin
P.O. Box 541
Thornhill, Ontario L3T 2CO Canada
(416) 883-4843

Market Insight
Top Farmer Intelligence
AgriData Resources
330 East Kilbourn Avenue
Milwaukee, Wisconsin 53202 (414) 278-7676

Market Insights, Special Situations in the
  Futures Markets
Bruce Babcock, Jr.
Suite 149, 1731 Howe Avenue
Sacramento, California 95825
(916) 929-5308

Market Logic
Institute for Econometric Research
3471 North Federal Highway
Fort Lauderdale, Florida 33306
(305) 563-9000

Market Mania
P.O. Box 1234
Pacifica, California 94044 (415) 355-9666

Market Master
Bastianelli Company
Suite 123, 23161 Lake Center Drive
El Toro, California 92630 (714) 951-8466

Market Perceptions
Serco Investments
Suite 402, 50 Santa Rosa Avenue
Santa Rosa, California 95402 (707) 575-7799

Marketrend
1615 Northern Boulevard
Manhasset, New York 11030 (516) 627-1600

Market Timing Report, Transaction Timing
  Analysis for High Liquidity Investments
P.O. Box 225
Tucson, Arizona 85702 (602) 624-6364

Market Vantage
P.O. Box 517
Mt. Kisco, New York 10549 (914) 277-5801

Marples Business Newsletter, Pacific
  Northwest Investor
Suite 300, 911 Western Avenue
Seattle, Washington 98104 (206) 622-0155

Master Indicator of the Stock Market
P.O. Box 3024
West Palm Beach, Florida 33402
(305) 793-8316

Maxwell Newton's World Market Report
Devonshire Financial Corporation at
  Newsletter Management Corporation
10076 Boca Entrada Boulevard
Boca Raton, Florida 33431-0907
(305) 483-2601

MBH Weekly Commodity Letter
P.O. Box 353
Winnetka, Illinois 60093 (312) 446-9210
outside Illinois (800) 323-5486

McAlvany Intelligence Advisor
P.O. Box 39850
Phoenix, Arizona 85069 (602) 252-4477

McKeever Strategy Letter
P.O. Box 4130
Medford, Oregon 97501 (503) 826-9279

McShane Letter
155 East 55th Street
New York, New York 10022 (212) 688-2387

Media General Financial Weekly (newspaper)
P.O. Box C-32333
Richmond, Virginia 23293-0001
(804) 649-6587

Medical Technology Stock Letter
Venture Capital Management
155 Montgomery Street
San Francisco, California 94104
(415) 982-0125

Medtech Market Letter
Marden Publishing Company
2915 Bissonnet
Houston, Texas 77005 (713) 668-6700

Merrill Lynch Market Letter
P.O. Box 60, Church Street Station
New York, New York 10277 (212) 637-5196

Merrill Lynch Stockfinder Research Service
165 Broadway
New York, New York 10080 (212) 766-5196

Merriman Market Analyst
MMA Gold and Silver Report
P.O. Box 1074
Birmingham, Michigan 48012
(313) 626-3034

Mike Segal's Commodity Advisor
Suite 2305, 150 Broadway
New York, New York 10038 (212) 406-0211
(800) 221-3572

MJF Growth Stock Advisory
P.O. Box 3056
Stamford, Connecticut 06902
(203) 322-3013

Money & Markets
Money Forecasts
P.O. Box 2923
West Palm Beach, Florida 33402
(305) 684-8100

Money Dynamics Letter
1300 Post Oak Boulevard
Houston, Texas 77056 (713) 621-9733

Money Investors Journal
Institute of Wall Street Studies
Suite 200, 1200 North Federal Highway
Boca Raton, Florida 33432 (800) 453-8837

Money Letter For Women
Phillips Publishing, Inc.
7811 Montrose Road
Potomac, Maryland 20854 (301) 340-2100

Money Magazine
Time Incorporated
1271 Avenue of the Americas
New York, New York 10020 (212) 586-1212

Money Maker Magazine
5705 North Lincoln Avenue
Chicago, Illinois 60659 (312) 275-3590

Money Manager Portfolios
H F Pearson & Co.
168 Main Street
Huntington, New York 11743 (516) 427-3107

*Money Market Fund Survey & Bond Fund
   Survey*
P.O. Box 4180, Grand Central Station
New York, New York 10163 (212) 988-2498

*Moneypaper, The, A Financial Publication for
   Women*
Two Madison Avenue
Larchmont, New York 10538 (914) 833-0270

Money Reporter
Marpep Publishing
133 Richmond Street West
Toronto, Ontario M5H 3M8, Canada
(416) 869-1177

Money Trends
Sammut Capital Management
Sherwood House Box 569
Skaneateles, New York 13152
(315) 685-8901

Moody's:
Bank and Finance Manual and News Reports
Bond Record
Bond Survey
Dividend Record
Handbook of Common Stocks
Handbook of OTC Stocks
Industrial Manual and News Reports
Industry Review
International Manual and News Reports
*Municipal and Government Manual and News
   Reports*
OTC Industrial Manual and News Reports
Public Utility Manual and News Reports
Transportation Manual and News Reports
Moody's Investors Service
99 Church Street
New York, New York 10007 (212) 553-0300

Mortgage Commentary
Bank Board Watch
FDIC Watch
Mortgage Marketplace
NCUA Watch
Savings and Loan Reporter
Mortgage Commentary Publications
P.O. Box 30240
Bethesda, Maryland 20814 (301) 654-5580

Multiplier
P.O. Box 3831
Albany, Georgia 31706 (912) 883-7774

Mutual Funds Guide
Commerce Clearing House
4025 West Peterson Avenue
Chicago, Illinois 60646 (312) 583-8500

Mutual Fund Chartist
P.O. Box 6600
Rapid City, South Dakota 57709
(605) 341-1971

Mutual Fund Forecaster
Institute for Econometric Research
3471 North Federal Highway
Fort Lauderdale, Florida 33306
(305) 563-9000

Mutual Fund Investing
Phillips Publishing
7811 Montrose Road
Potomac, Maryland 20854 (301) 340-2100

Mutual Fund Investor
P.O. Box 1301
Portsmouth, New Hampshire 03801
(207) 439-0094

Mutual Fund Letter
205 West Wacker Drive
Chicago, Illinois 60606 (312) 750-9300

Mutual Fund Specialist
P.O. Box 1025
Eau Claire, Wisconsin 54702 (715) 835-9870

Mutual Fund Strategist
P.O. Box 466
Burlington, Vermont 05402 (802) 658-3513

*National Association of Investors Corporation
Investor Advisory Service*
1515 East Eleven Mile Road
Royal Oak, Michigan 48067 (313) 543-0612

National OTC Stock Journal (newspaper)
P.O. Box 24327
Suite 400, 1780 South Bellaire
Denver, Colorado 80222 (303) 758-9131

National Thrift News (newspaper)
212 West 35th Street
New York, New York 10001 (212) 563-4008

National Underwriter (newspaper)
175 West Jackson Boulevard
Chicago, Illinois 60604 (312) 922-2704

Nation's Business
1615 H Street, N.W.
Washington, D.C. 20062 (202) 463-5650

New Issues
Institute for Econometric Research
3471 North Federal Highway
Fort Lauderdale, Florida 33306
(305) 563-9000

New Issues Alert
NIA Corporation at Newsletter Management
 Corporation
10076 Boca Entrada Boulevard
Boca Raton, Florida 33431-0907
(305) 483-2601

New Issues in High Technology
American Investor Information Services
1627 Spruce Street
Philadelphia, Pennsylvania 19103
(215) 732-5350

News for Investors
Investor Responsibility Research Center
1319 F Street, N.W.
Washington, D.C. 20004 (202) 833-3727

Newsletter Digest
2335 Pansy Street
Huntsville, Alabama 35801 (205) 536-0901

*Newsworthy, The Institute of Certified
 Financial Planners*
3443 South Galena
Denver, Colorado 80231 (303) 751-7600

Ney Option Report
Ney Report
Richard Ney & Associates Asset Management
P.O. Box 91109
Pasadena, California 91109 (818) 441-2222

Nicholson Report
7550 Red Road
Coral Gables, Florida 33143 (305) 665-7445

Nielsen's Investment Letter
P.O. Box 7532
Olympia, Washington 98507 (206) 352-7281

No-Load Fund Investor
P.O. Box 283
Hastings-on-Hudson, New York 10706
(914) 478-2381

*NoLoad Fund*X*
Dal Investment Co.
235 Montgomery Street
San Francisco, California 94104
(415) 986-7979

North American Gold Mining Stocks
P.O. Box 871
Woodside, New York 11377 (718) 457-1426

Norwood Index
Norwood Securities
6134 North Milwaukee Avenue
Chicago, Illinois 60646 (312) 763-1540

Nourse Investor Report
P.O. Box 28039
San Diego, California 92128 (619) 578-5089

Ober Income Letter
Securities Investigations, Inc.
Mill Hill Road, P.O. Box 888
Woodstock, New York 12498 (914) 679-2300

Oberweis Management Monthly Review
841 North Lake Street
Aurora, Illinois 60506 (312) 897-7100

Off Shore Banking News
301 Plymouth Drive, N.E.
Dalton, Georgia 30720 (404) 259-6035

Oil/Energy Statistics Bulletin
One Map Hill Drive, Box 127
Babson Park, Massachusetts 02157
(617) 237-6620

Opportunities in Options
Suite 149, 1731 Howe Avenue
Sacramento, California 95825
(916) 929-5308

OTC Handbook
Standard and Poor's Corp.
25 Broadway
New York, New York 10004 (212) 208-8000

Optimum Switch Hitting
Target, Inc.
6612 Owens Drive
Pleasanton, California 94566 (800) 654-4455
(800) 654-4456 (Cal. only)

Option Advisor
P.O. Box 46709
Cincinnati, Ohio 45246 (513) 772-3535

Options Alert
Merrill Lynch
165 Broadway
New York, New York 10006 (212) 637-7455

Options Handbook
Standard and Poor's Corp.
25 Broadway
New York, New York 10004 (212) 208-8000

Ostaro's Market Newsletter
P.O. Box A76
New York, New York 10163 (212) 686-4121

OTC Growth Stock Watch
P.O. Box 305
Brookline, Massachusetts 02146
(617) 327-8420

OTC Insight
P.O. Box 1329
El Cerrito, California 94530 (415) 527-5116

OTC Market Perspective
Campbell & Associates
Suite 4710, 405 North Wabash
Chicago, Illinois 60611 (312) 644-0707

OTC Review
OTC Review Special Situations
Review Publishing Corp.
110 Pennsylvania Avenue
Oreland, Pennsylvania 19075 (215) 887-9000

Ottawa Letter
CCH Canada Limited
6 Garamond Court
Don Mills, Ontario M3C 1Z5, Canada
(416) 441-2992

Outten Quarterly Stock Evaluation
435 Winslow Avenue
Long Beach, California 90814
(213) 498-1965

Partnership Record
P.O. Box 682, 368 Center Street
Southport, Connecticut 06490
(203) 254-0510

Patient Investor
Ariel Capital Management
307 North Michigan Avenue
Chicago, Illinois 60601 (312) 726-0140

Pearson Investment Letter
3801 Sydney Road
Dover, Florida 33527 (813) 659-2560

Penny Fortune Newsletter
P.O. Box 670, 102 South Tejon
Colorado Springs, Colorado 80901
(303) 634-3777

Penny Mining Stock Report
Target, Inc.
6612 Owens Drive
Pleasanton, California 94566 (800) 654-4455
(800) 654-4456 (Cal. only)

Penny Power
3910 N.E. 26th Avenue
Lighthouse Point, Florida 33064
(305) 942-3288

Penny Stock News
8930 J Oakland Center
Columbia, Maryland 21045 (301) 596-0126

Penny Stocks Newsletter
31731 Outer Highway 10
Redlands, California 92373 (714) 794-4316

Penny Stock Performance Digest
Newsletter Management Corp.
10076 Boca Entrada Boulevard
Boca Raton, Florida 33433 (305) 483-2600

Penny Stock Preview
Idea Marketing Corporation
55 East Afton Avenue
Yardley, Pennsylvania 19067 (215) 493-1810

Penny Stock Plays
Dow Theory Forecasts
7412 Calumet Avenue
Hammond, Indiana 46324 (219) 931-6480

Penny Stock Ventures
Money Growth Institute
37 Van Reipen Avenue
Jersey City, New Jersey 07306
(201) 792-0802

Pension and Investment Age
Crain Communications
740 Rush Street
Chicago, Illinois 60611 (312) 649-5200
(800) 331-1750

Pension Investing Strategies
Ridgewood Financial Institute
89 Chestnut Street
Ridgewood, New Jersey 07450
(201) 447-0681

*Pensions and Investments Performance
Evaluation Reports (PIPER)*
Crain Communications
740 Rush Street
Chicago, Illinois 60611 (312) 649-5200

Pension World
6255 Barfield Road
Atlanta, Georgia 30328 (404) 256-9800

*Performance Guide Publications, Mutual
Funds and Timing*
P.O. Box 2604
Palos Verdes, California 90274
(213) 833-2924

Perlow Letter
319 Lovell Avenue
Mill Valley, California 94941 (415) 383-7464

Personal Finance: The Inflation Survival Letter
KCI Communications
Suite 1660, 1300 North 17th Street
Arlington, Virginia 22209 (703) 276-7100
(800) 336-5407

Personal Investing Newsletter
P.O. Box 832
Boston, Massachusetts 02103
(617) 570-5063

Personal Investor Magazine
Plaza Communications, Inc.
4300 Campus Drive
Newport Beach, California 92660
(714) 756-8777

Personal Tax Strategist
PTS Newsletter Associates Ltd. at Newsletter
Management Corporation

10076 Boca Entrada Boulevard
Boca Raton, Florida 33431-0907
(305) 483-2601

Personal Wealth Digest
Unity Publishers Corporation at Newsletter
Management Corporation
10076 Boca Entrada Boulevard
Boca Raton, Florida 33431-0907
(305) 483-2601

Personal Wealth Reporter
Marpep Publishing Ltd.
133 Richmond Street West
Toronto M5H 3M8 Canada (416) 869-1177

Peter Dag Investment Letter
65 Lake Front Drive
Akron, Ohio 44319 (216) 644-2782

Petrodata Letter
Suite 1233, 3130 Villa Norte
La Jolla, California 92037 (619) 458-9926

Petzold On The Market
Petzold On Stocks
4455 Torrance Boulevard
Torrance, California 90503 (213) 431-0180

Philadelphia Adviser
P.O. Box 420491
Atlanta, Georgia 30342 (404) 255-6117

Plain Talk Investor
801 Skokie Boulevard, Suite 218
Northbrook, Illinois 60062 (312) 564-1955

Portfolio Letter
Institutional Investor
488 Madison Avenue
New York, New York 10022 (212) 303-3300

Portfolios Investment Advisory
P.O. Box 997
Lynchburg, Virginia 24505 (804) 845-1335

Powell Alert
Powell Monetary Analyst
Reserve Research Ltd.
181 State Street
Portland, Maine 04101 (207) 879-0611

Practical Stock Picker
68 Edgelawn Avenue
North Andover, Massachusetts 01845
(617) 686-4765

Precision Timing
P.O. Box 11722
Atlanta, Georgia 30305 (404) 355-0447

Predictions
Euler Enterprises
Penthouse 11, 4853 Cordell Avenue
Bethesda, Maryland 20814 (301) 951-3800

Predictor & Tillman Survey
P.O. Box 22008
Santa Barbara, California 93121
(805) 688-9905

Primary Trend
Arnold Investment Counsel
700 North Water Street
Milwaukee, Wisconsin 53202 (414) 271-2726

Prime Investment Alert
Prime Tax Alert
P.O. Box 8308
Portland, Maine 04104 (207) 772-1679

Pring Market Review
P.O. Box 338
Washington Depot, Connecticut 06794
(203) 868-7772

Privileged Information
Boardroom Reports, Inc.
330 West 42nd Street
New York, New York 10036 (212) 239-9000

Professional Investor
P.O. Box 2144
Pompano Beach, Florida 33061-2144
(305) 946-6353

Professional Tape Reader
P.O. Box 2407
Hollywood, Florida 33022 (305) 923-3733

Professional Timing Service
P.O. Box 7483
Missoula, Montana 59807 (406) 543-4131

Profit Report
P.O. Box 7212, Main Post Office
Chicago, Illinois 60680 (312) 486-4666

Prudent Speculator
P.O. Box 1767
Santa Monica, California 90406
(213) 395-5275

PSR Prophet
1001 Bridgeway, P.O. Box 244
Sausalito, California 94965 (415) 381-3777

Public Investor
Government Finance Officers Association
Suite 800, 180 North Michigan Avenue
Chicago, Illinois 60601 (312) 977-9700

Quarterly Performance Report
LJR Communications
5513 Twin Knolls Road
Columbia, Maryland 21045 (301) 730-5365

Quote American
Quote New York
Quote OTC
P.O. Box 213-A
Wichita, Kansas 67201 (316) 262-2111

Rating the Stock Selectors
8949 La Riviera Drive
Sacramento, California 95826
(916) 363-2055

RC Stock News
P.O. Box 2217
Northbrook, Illinois 60065 (312) 498-2645

Real Estate Digest
P.O. Box 26444
Birmingham, Alabama 35226 (800) 633-6050

Real Estate Financial Success
Target, Inc.
6612 Owens Drive
Pleasanton, California 94566 (800) 654-4455
(800) 654-4456 (Cal. only)

Real Estate Intelligence Report
Phillips Publishing
7811 Montrose Road
Potomac, Maryland 20854 (301) 340-2100

Real Estate Investment Digest
REI Newsletter Associates Ltd. at Newsletter
  Management Corporation
10076 Boca Entrada Boulevard
Boca Raton, Florida 33431-0907
(305) 483-2601

Real Estate Investment, Trends &
  Opportunities
Jarvis, Connors and Archibald
404 West Titus Building
Kent, Washington 98031 (206) 852-3910

Realty Stock Review
Audit Investments
230 Park Avenue
New York, New York 10169 (212) 661-1710

Reaper
P.O. 39026
Phoenix, Arizona 85069 (602) 252-4477
(800) 528-0559

Registered Representative
Plaza Communications
4300 Campus Drive
Newport Beach, California 92660
(714) 979-3666

Research Institute of America:
Corporate Capital Transactions Coordinator
Employee Benefits Compliance Coordinator
Employment Coordinator
Employment Alert
Estate Planners Alert
Estate Planning & Taxation Coordinator
Executive Compensation Alert
Executive Compensation & Taxation
  Coordinator
Farmers Federal Tax Alert
Federal Tax Coordinator 2d
Florida Taxation
Internal Revenue Bulletin
International Tax Planners Alert
Oil and Gas Tax Alert
Real Estate Coordinator
RIA Special Studies
Social Security Coordinator
Social Security Alert
Small Business Tax Planner
State Tax Action Coordinator
Tax Action Coordinator
Tax Guide
Tax Preparers Liability Service
Weekly Alert
589 Fifth Avenue
New York, New York 10017 (212) 755-8900
(800) 431-2057

Retirement Financial Success
Target, Inc.
6612 Owens Drive
Pleasanton, California 94566 (800) 654-4455
(800) 654-4456 (Cal. only)

Retirement Fund Advisory
Schabacker Investment Management
8943 Shady Grove Court
Gaithersburg, Maryland 20877
(301) 840-0301

Retirement Letter
Phillips Publishing
7811 Montrose Road
Potomac, Maryland 20854 (301) 340-2100

Retirement Plan Success Letter
Growth Fund Research Building
P.O. Box 6600
Rapid City, South Dakota 57709
(605) 341-1971

Retirement Planning Newsletter
NROCA Press, Department B
P.O. Box 12066
Dallas, Texas 75225

Retirement Security Reporter
Marpep Publishing Ltd.
133 Richmond Street West
Toronto, Canada M5H 3M8 (416) 869-1177

RHM Survey of Warrants, Options & Low-
  Priced Stocks
172 Forest Avenue
Glen Cove, New York 11542 (516) 759-2904

Richland Report
P.O. Box 222
La Jolla, California 92038 (619) 459-2611

RJ Nies Financial Strategies Report
663 Sixth Avenue South
St. Petersburg, Florida 33701
(813) 894-2929

Robbins Report
William Spencer Educational Foundation
3118 Hillcrest Drive
San Antonio, Texas 78201 (512) 733-0051

Rocky Mountain Financial Forecasting
  Newsletter
RMFF Inc.
5601 Sacajawea Way
Loveland, Colorado 80537 (303) 663-4688

Roesch Market Memo
P.O. Box 4242
Shawnee Mission, Kansas 66204
(913) 381-0857

Ronald Sadoff's Major Trends
6971 North Beech Tree Drive
Milwaukee, Wisconsin 53209 (414) 352-8460

Ruff Times
P.O. Box 25
Pleasanton, California 94566 (415) 463-2200

Ryals Investment Report
Suite 202, 2930 Honolulu Avenue
La Crescenta, California 91214
(818) 248-1486

S.A. Advisory
2274 Arbor Lane
Salt Lake City, Utah 84117 (801) 272-4761

Savers Rate News
P.O. Box 145510
Coral Gables, Florida 33114-5510
(305) 441-2062

Savings and Loan Investor
P.O. Box 7163
Long Beach, California 90807-0163
(213) 427-1905

SEC Docket
SEC News Digest
Securities and Exchange Commission
500 North Capitol Street, N.W.
Washington, D.C. 20549 (202) 655-4000

Securities and Federal Corporate Law Report
Clark Boardman Co.
435 Hudson Street
New York, New York 10014 (212) 929-7500

Securities Traders' Monthly
Dealers' Digest, Inc.
150 Broadway
New York, New York 10038 (212) 227-1200

Securities Week
McGraw-Hill Publications
1221 Avenue of the Americas
New York, New York 10020 (212) 997-3144

Sentinel Investment Letter
P.O. Box 189, 52 South Main Street
New Hope, Pennsylvania 18938
(215) 862-5454

Shelburne Securities Forecast
P.O. Box 5566
Arlington, Virginia 22205 (703) 532-4416

Sherwood Moran Investment Timing
7550 Panthera Court
Orlando, Florida 32822-7853 (305) 275-3901

Sideline Business Newsletter
P.O. Box 323, 18 South Seventh Street
Emmaus, Pennsylvania 18049
(215) 967-4135

Silver and Gold Report
P.O. Box 40
Bethel, Connecticut 06801 (203) 748-2036

Silver Baron
Suite 404, 350 South Center Street
Reno, Nevada 89501 (702) 786-0307

Silver Magazine
P.O. Box 1243
Whittier, California 90609 (213) 696-6738

Sindlinger Alert
Sindlinger Digest
Sindlinger Letter
Sindlinger Monday Mailgram
600 North Jackson Street
Media, Pennsylvania 19083 (215) 565-2800

Smart Money
The Hirsch Organization
6 Deer Trail
Old Tappan, New Jersey 07675
(201) 664-3400

South Dakota Gold Newsletter
P.O. Box C
Deadwood, South Dakota 57732
(605) 578-2115

Space Time Forecasting
P.O. Box 2772
Setauket, New York 11733 (516) 941-4084

Special Investment Situations
P.O. Box 4254, 6305 Forest Park Drive
Signal Mountain, Tennessee 37377
(615) 886-1628

Special Situations Newsletter
C.H. Kaplan Research Associates
Suite 1926, 150 Nassau Street
New York, New York 10038 (212) 233-0660

Special Situation Report
P.O. Box 167
Rochester, New York 14601 (716) 325-7100

Special Situation Speculator
P.O. Box 188
Glen Oaks, New York 11004 (212) 347-7532

Special Situations Under $5
Dow Theory Forecasts
7412 Calumet Avenue
Hammond, Indiana 46324 (219) 931-6480

Spectrum by CDA:
Convertibles
US and European Investment Company
Portfolios
US and European Investment Company Stock
Holdings Survey
Institutional Stock Holdings Survey
Institutional Portfolios
Five Percent Ownership based on 13D, 13G
and 14D-1 Filings
Insider Ownership
CDA Technologies
11501 Georgia Avenue
Silver Spring, Maryland 20902
(301) 942-1700

Speculative Ventures
P.O. Box 517
Mount Kisco, New York 10549
(914) 277-5801

Speculator
Money Growth Institute
37 Van Reipen Avenue
Jersey City, New Jersey 07306
(201) 792-0802

Spread Scope Commodity Spread Charts
Spread Scope Spread Letter
Spread Scope Long-Term Weekly Charts
P.O. Box 5841
Mission Hills, California 91345
(818) 365-4579

Standard and Poor's:
Amex Handbook
Analyst's Handbook
Blue List
Bond Guide
Called Bond Record
Commercial Paper Ratings Guide
Corporate Registered Bond Interest Record
Corporation Records
CreditWeek
CUSIP Directories
Daily Stock Price Record (NYSE, AMEX and
OTC)
Directory of Bond Agents
Dividend Record
Earnings Forecaster
Emerging and Special Situations
Growth Stocks Handbook
High Tech Stocks Handbook
Income Stocks Handbook
Index Services
Industry Surveys
Municipal Registered Bond Interest Record
OTC Handbook
Oil and Gas Stocks Handbook

Options Handbook
The Outlook
Register of Corporations, Directors and
Executives
Review of Securities Regulation
Security Dealers of North America
Statistical Service
Stock Guide
Stock Market Encyclopedia of the S&P 500
Stock Reports
Stock Summary
Trendline Stock Chart Services
Unit Investment Trusts
25 Broadway
New York, New York 10004 (212) 208-8786

Stanger Register
Stanger Report
Stanger Review
1129 Broad Street
Shrewsbury, New Jersey 07701
(201) 389-3600

Statistical Sciences Market Letter
4425 Park Alisal
Calabasas, California 91302 (818) 888-6355

Stein Synopsis
P.O. Box 148028
Chicago, Illinois 60614 (312) 880-5090

Stock Market Cycles
2260 Cahuenga Boulevard
Los Angeles, California 90068
(213) 465-5543

Stock Market Growth Stocks
Stocks On Tape Inc.
3 Berglund Avenue
Staten Island, New York 10314
(718) 761-3278

Stock Market Magazine
16 School Street
Yonkers, New York 10701 (914) 423-4566

Stock Market Monitor
P.O. Box 403
Naperville, Illinois 60566 (312) 852-6276

Stock Market Performance Digest
Stock Market Summary Newsletter
Associates Ltd. at Newsletter Management
Corporation
10076 Boca Entrada Boulevard
Boca Raton, Florida 33431-0907
(305) 483-2601

Stock Market Trendex
P.O. Box 1978
San Antonio, Texas 78297 (512) 225-6581

Stock Option Trading Form
P.O. Box 24242
Fort Lauderdale, Florida 33307
(305) 566-4500

Stornelli Investment Review
P.O. Box 248
Auburn, New York 13021 (315) 253-0371

Strategic Trading
P.O. Box 46709
Cincinnati, Ohio 45246 (513) 772-3535

Street Smart Investing
2651 Strang Boulevard
Yorktown Heights, New York 10598
(914) 962-4646

Strongest Funds
P.O. Box 6600
Rapid City, South Dakota 57709
(605) 341-1971

Sunbelt Growth Stocks
P.O. Box 28173
Atlanta, Georgia 30358 (404) 256-4990

Sundex Newsletter
P.O. Box 73, Glenville Station
Greenwich, Connecticut 06830
(914) 937-6939

Supergrowth Technology USA
21st Century Research
8200 Boulevard East
North Bergen, New Jersey 07047
(201) 868-0881

Switch Fund Advisory
Schabacker Investment Management
8943 Shady Grove Court
Gaithersburg, Maryland 20877
(301) 840-0301

Systems and Forecasts
Signalert Corp.
150 Great Neck Road
Great Neck, New York 11021 (516) 829-6444

Tactics and Technics
Herzfeld & Stern, Inc.
30 Broad Street
New York, New York 10004 (212) 480-1800

Taurus
Mega-Trades
Optimum Options
Taurus Corp.
P.O. Box 1607
Winchester, Virginia 22601 (703) 667-4827

Tax Avoidance Digest
Euler Enterprises
Penthouse 11, 4853 Cordell Avenue
Bethesda, Maryland 20814 (301) 951-3800

Tax Hotline
Boardroom Reports, Inc.
330 West 42nd Street
New York, New York 10036 (212) 239-9000

TaxLetter
MoneyLetter
Hume Publishing Company Limited
4141 Yonge Street
Willowdale, Ontario, Canada M2P 2A7
(416) 221-4596

Tax Planning Review
Commerce Clearing House, Inc.
4025 West Peterson Avenue
Chicago, Illinois 60646 (312) 583-8500

Tax Shelter Analyst
Tax Reports Newsletter Associates at
  Newsletter Management Corporation
10076 Boca Entrada Boulevard
Boca Raton, Florida 33431-0907
(305) 483-2601

Tax Shelter Blue Book
Securities Investigations, Inc.
Mill Hill Road, P.O. Box 888
Woodstock, New York 12498 (914) 679-2300

Tax Shelter Insider
Tax Reports Newsletter Associates at
  Newsletter Management Corporation
10076 Boca Entrada Boulevard
Boca Raton, Florida 33431-0907
(305) 483-2601

Tax Shelter Investment Review
Leland Publishing Company
81 Canal Street
Boston, Massachusetts 02114
(617) 227-9314

Tax Shelter Monitor
P.O. Box 512, Grand Central Station
New York, New York 10017 (212) 794-9625

Tax Sheltered Investments Law Report
Clark Boardman Company
435 Hudson Street
New York, New York 10014 (212) 929-7500

*Technical Analysis of Stocks and
  Commodities*
P.O. Box 46518, 9131 California Avenue, S.W.
Seattle, Washington 98146-0518
(206) 938-0570

Technical Forecast
P.O. Box 2298
Edison, New Jersey 08818 (201) 548-7833

Technical Indicator Review
Chartcraft, Inc.
1 West Avenue
Larchmont, New York 10538 (914) 834-5181

Technical Trends
P.O. Box 792
Wilton, Connecticut 06897

Technology Stock Monitor
P.O. Box 471
Barrington, Illinois 60010 (312) 428-6633

Tech Street Journal
Technology Financial Services
4 Courthouse Lane
Chelmsford, Massachusetts 01824
(617) 458-3974

Ted Warren Investolator Stock Market Letter
216-B North Catalina
Redondo Beach, California 90277
(213) 374-7726

Telegen Reporter
Department N, 48 West 38th Street
New York, New York 10018 (212) 944-8500

Telephone Switch Newsletter
P.O. Box 2538
Huntington Beach, California 92647
(714) 840-4747

Terex Report
110-50 71st Road
Forest Hills, New York 11375 (718) 268-3300

Texas Trader's Relative Strength Trendex
P.O. Box 1978
San Antonio, Texas 78297 (512) 225-6581

Timer Digest
P.O. Box 030130
Fort Lauderdale, Florida 33301
(305) 764-8499

Timing
Suite 135, 3320 East Shea Boulevard
Phoenix, Arizona 85028 (602) 996-1800

Tim Hayes' Investigative Report
Devonshire Financial Corporation at
  Newsletter Management Corporation
10076 Boca Entrada Boulevard
Boca Raton, Florida 33431-0907
(305) 483-2601

Tomorrow Newsletter
The Wealth Institute
4425 West Napoleon Avenue
Metairie, Louisiana 70001 (504) 456-0040
(800) 322-6267

Tomorrow's Commodities
Tomorrow's Commodity Options
Tomorrow's Options
Tomorrow's Stocks
Techno-Fundamental Investments
P.O. Box 411
Scottsdale, Arizona 85252 (602) 996-2908

Tony Henfrey's Gold Letter
P.O. Box 9137
Allentown, Pennsylvania 18105

Trading Strategies
P.O. Box 336
Buffalo, New York 14218-0336
(716) 823-6382

Treasurer's Digest
TDCP Associates
1807 Glenview Road
Glenview, Illinois 60025 (312) 998-6688

Trend Capital
P.O. Box 313
Brooklyn, New York 11217 (718) 815-7785

Trends in Mutual Fund Activity
Investment Company Institute
1600 M Street, N.W.
Washington, D.C. 20036 (202) 293-7700

Trusts and Estates Magazine
Communication Channels
6255 Barfield Road
Atlanta, Georgia 30328 (404) 256-9800

Turning Point
P.O. Box 9157
Scottsdale, Arizona 85252 (602) 991-3410

United Business and Investment Report
United Mutual Fund Selector
210 Newbury Street
Boston, Massachusetts 02116
(617) 267-8855

United States Banker
Kalo Communications
One River Road
Cos Cob, Connecticut 06807 (203) 869-8200

Unlisted Market Guide
Unlisted Market Service Corporation
49 Glen Head Road
Glen Head, New York 11545 (516) 759-1253
(800) 642-3840

upTREND Investment Services Limited
P.O. Box 49333
Four Bentall Centre
Vancouver, British Columbia V7X 1L4 Canada
(604) 687-5541

Value Line Investment Survey
Value Line Option & Convertible Survey
Value Line OTC Special Situations Service
711 Third Avenue
New York, New York 10017 (212) 687-3965

Venture, The Magazine For Entrepreneurs
521 Fifth Avenue
New York, New York 10175-0028
(212) 682-7373

Venture Capital Journal
P.O. Box 348, 16 Laurel Avenue
Wellesley Hills, Massachusetts 02181
(617) 431-8100

Vickers Weekly Insider Report
P.O. Box 59
Brookside, New Jersey 07926
(201) 539-1336

Volume Reversal Survey
P.O. Box 1546
Chicago, Illinois 60690-1546 (312) 432-1120
(800) 554-5551

Wall Street Computer Review
150 Broadway
New York, New York 10038 (212) 227-1200

Wall Street Digest
101 Carnegie Center
Princeton, New Jersey 08540 (609) 452-8111

Wall Street Generalist
MarketMetrics, Inc.
Suite 6, 1266 First Street
Sarasota, Florida 33577 (813) 366-5645

Wall Street Inquirer
263 Orange Avenue
Goleta, California 93117 (805) 964-8275

Wall Street Journal, The (newspaper)
200 Liberty Street
New York, New York 10281 (212) 416-2000

Wall Street Letter
Institutional Investor
488 Madison Avenue
New York, New York 10022 (212) 303-3300

Wall Street Micro Investor
WSOL Publishing
Suite 1302, 11 Hanover Square
New York, New York 10005 (212) 884-5408

Wall Street Money Letter
Wall Street Trading Letter
Institute of Wall Street Studies
Suite 200, 1200 North Federal Highway
Boca Raton, Florida 33432 (800) 453-8837

Wall Street Transcript
99 Wall Street
New York, New York 10005 (212) 747-9500

W.D. Gann Technical Review
P.O. Box 0
Pomeroy, Washington 99347 (509) 843-1094

Wealth Formula
Unity Publishers Corporation at Newsletter
  Management Corporation
10076 Boca Entrada Boulevard
Boca Raton, Florida 33431-0907
(305) 483-2601

Wealth Magazine
The Wealth Institute
4425 West Napoleon Avenue
Metairie, Louisiana 70001 (504) 456-0040
(800) 322-6267

Weekly Takeover Target Forecast
Quality Services Co.
5290 Overpass Road
Santa Barbara, California 93111
(805) 964-7841

Weiss Research
P.O. Box 2923
West Palm Beach, Florida 33402
(305) 684-8100

Wellington Alert
Wellington Capital
Wellington Commodity Technician
Wellington Letter
Wellington Special Bulletin
Worry-Free Investing
733 Bishop Street, Honolulu, Hawaii 96813
(808) 524-8063

Wes English's Sound Advice, The Real Estate
& Tax Advisory Letter
P.O. Box 487
Walnut Creek, California 94596
(415) 838-8100 (800) 423-8423

Western Investor Magazine
Western Investor Newsletter
Suite 1115, 400 Southwest Sixth Avenue
Portland, Oregon 97204 (503) 222-0577

Western Monetary Report
P.O. Box 430
Fort Collins, Colorado 80522 (303) 221-2144
(800) 525-4956

Whisper on Wall Street
P.O. Box 8098
Bridgeport, Connecticut 06605
(203) 248-1156

Wiesenberger Investment Companies Service
Current Performance and Dividend Report
Management Results
Warren Gorham and Lamont
210 South Street
Boston, Massachusetts 02111
(617) 423-2020 (800) 922-0066

Williams Trend Indicators
6 Devon Drive
Orangeburg, New York 10962
(914) 359-1129

Wilsearch Investment Letter
620 South 42nd Street
Boulder, Colorado 80303 (303) 494-0404

Wolfe's Version
P.O. Box 99
Blue Springs, Missouri 64015
(816) 229-1666

Women's Investment Newsletter
P.O. Box 670
102 South Tejon
Colorado Springs, Colorado 80901
(303) 634-3777

World Market Perspective
WMP Publishing Co.
Suite 103, 2211 Lee Road
Winter Park, Florida 32789 (305) 628-5300

Worldwide Investment Notes
P.O. Box 16041, 7730 Carondelet Avenue
St. Louis, Missouri 63105 (314) 726-2731

WOW Indexes (Who Owns What In the
Futures Markets)
P.O. Box 2923
West Palm Beach, Florida 33402
(305) 684-8100

Z-900 Report
P.O. Box 794
Beverly Hills, California 90213
(818) 342-0710 (213) 937-8449

Zweig Forecast
900 Third Avenue
New York, New York 10022 (212) 644-0040

COMPUTERIZED DATABASES FOR INVESTORS

The following firms offer investors with computers and modems the opportunity to follow price movements in investment markets with up-to-the-second accuracy. Investors can tap into these data banks to download both current and historical price and volume information as well as news about investment markets. Some of these databases also allow investors to execute trades through their computers.

This list is printed courtesy of *The Individual Investor's Microcomputer Resource Guide,* by Norman Nicholson, American Association of Individual Investors, 612 North Michigan Avenue, Chicago, Illinois 60611 (312) 280-0170.

Bridge Data
Market Data Systems
10050 Manchester Road
St. Louis, Missouri 63122 (314) 821-5660

Bristol Financial Systems
1010 Washington Boulevard
Stamford, Connecticut
(203) 356-9490

Business Research Corporation
12 Farnsworth Street
Boston, Massachusetts 02210 (617) 350-4044

Citicorp Information Services
641 Lexington Avenue
New York, New York 10043 (800) 241-2476

Commodity Quotations
670 White Plains Road
Scarsdale, New York 10583 (914) 725-3477

Compuserve
5000 Arlington Center Boulevard
Columbus, Ohio 43220 (614) 457-8600

Compustat Services
Standard and Poor's Corporation
7400 South Alton Court
Englewood, Colorado 80112 (303) 771-6510

DeskTop Broker
300 Montgomery Street
San Francisco, California 94104
(415) 433-3030

Disclosure, Inc.
5161 River Road
Bethesda, Maryland 20816 (301) 951-1300

Dow Jones News/Retrieval
P.O. Box 300
Princeton, New Jersey 08540 (800) 257-511⟨

FCI-Invest/net
99 Northwest 183rd Street
North Miami, Florida 33169 (305) 652-1710

Ford Investor Services
11722 Sorrento Valley Road
San Diego, California 92121 (619) 755-1327

Hale Systems
1044 Northern Boulevard
Roslyn, New York 11576 (516) 484-4545

Interactive Data Corporation
486 Totten Pond Road
Waltham, Massachusetts 02154
(617) 890-1234

Investment Technologies
Metropark, 510 Thornall Street
Edison, New Jersey 08837 (919) 787-2911

Lotus Information Network Corporation
P.O. Box 3900
Peoria, Illinois 61614
(800) 447-4700, extension 300

Micro Futures
P.O. Box 2255
Naperville, Illinois 60565

Monchik-Weber/McGraw Hill
11 Broadway
New York, New York 10004 (212) 269-5460

National Computer Network
1929 North Harlem Avenue
Chicago, Illinois 60635 (312) 427-5125

Newsnet
945 Haverford Road
Bryn Mawr, Pennsylvania 19010
(215) 527-8030

PC Quote
401 South LaSalle Street
Chicago, Illinois 60605 (312) 786-5400

Quoteline
75 Montgomery Street
Jersey City, New Jersey 07302
(201) 333-6533

Quotron Systems
5454 Beethoven Street
Los Angeles, California 90066
(213) 827-4600

I.P. Sharp Associates
Two First Canadian Place, Exchange Tower
Toronto, Ontario, Canada M5X 1E3
(416) 364-5361

Source Telecomputing
1616 Anderson Road
McLean, Virginia 22102 (703) 734-7500

Telemet America
515 Wythe Street
Alexandria, Virginia 22314 (703) 548-2042

Telerate Systems
1 World Trade Center, 104th floor
New York, New York 10048 (212) 938-5400

Telescan
11011 Richmond Avenue
Houston, Texas 77042 (713) 952-1060

Trade Plus
460 California Avenue
Palo Alto, California 94306 (415) 324-4554

Max Ule & Company
202 East 39th Street
New York, New York 10016 (212) 687-0705

Wall Street On-Line
11 Hanover Square
New York, New York 10005 (212) 514-5780

Warner Computer Systems
One University Place
Hackensack, New Jersey 07601 (201) 489-1580

PERSONAL COMPUTER SOFTWARE FOR INVESTING AND FINANCIAL PLANNING

The following sampling of software packages can help investors to make better investment decisions and to improve record-keeping, as well as to perform personal financial planning. There are, of course, hundreds of software packages on the market to perform these tasks. Those listed here have proven themselves by being on the market for some time. They are all marketed by established companies in the software business.

The first group of programs allows users to screen lists of stocks to isolate the companies that meet certain fundamental investment criteria. The information on companies comes either from a disk that is updated monthly or from a continuously updated online database, which is accessed by telephone line. Usually these disks or online databases are available for an annual fee. There are many kinds of screens investors can perform with this software, depending on what kinds of stocks they want to find. For example, an investor looking for high income could find the highest-yielding stocks in the database. Someone looking for growth stocks could find the companies with fast earnings growth records.

The second group of programs is designed to pick stocks based on technical considerations, such as price movements and volume. These programs usually display data in chart form, allowing investors to isolate stocks with technical indicators thought to point to a good buying or selling opportunity.

The third group of programs enable users to keep track of their investment portfolios. Once stocks, bonds, and other instruments are entered into the computer, the value of the portfolio can be easily updated by tapping into a database. These programs also reveal the tax implications of potential investment moves, such as whether a stock has been held long enough to qualify for long-term capital gains treatment.

The fourth group of software programs is designed to help an individual do financial planning. This means that investments can be tracked, tax strategy formulated, real estate decisions examined, and retirement and estate planning options explored. One particular advantage of these programs is that once data has been entered into the computer for one part of a program, it is stored for use in other parts of the program. For instance, when a stock sale that generates a taxable capital gain is entered in the investment records section, it is also being recorded in the income tax preparation part of the program.

Fundamental Screening Software

Compustock
A.S. Gibson & Sons, Inc.
1412 Vineyard Drive
Bountiful, Utah 84010 (801) 298-4578

Market Microscope
Dow Jones & Company
P.O. Box 300
Princeton, New Jersey 08540 (609) 452-2000

Micro PMS
The Boston Company
One Boston Place
Boston, Massachusetts 02106 (617) 722-7928

Stockpak II
Standard & Poor's Corporation
25 Broadway
New York, New York 10004 (212) 208-8000

Value/Screen Plus
Value Line, Inc.
711 Third Avenue
New York, New York 10017 (212) 687-3965

Technical Analysis Software

Market Analyst
Anidata, Inc.
7200 Westfield Avenue
Pennsauken, New Jersey 08110
(609) 663-0195

Market Analyzer Plus
Dow Jones & Company
P.O. Box 300
Princeton, New Jersey 08540 (609) 452-2000

Technical Investor
Savant Corporation
P.O. Box 440278
Houston, Texas 77244 (713) 556-8363

Telescan
Telescan, Inc.
11011 Richmond Avenue
Houston, Texas 77042 (713) 952-1060

Trendline II
Standard & Poor's Corporation
25 Broadway
New York, New York 10004 (212) 208-8000

Portfolio Management Programs

Ava
Market Maker Investment Software
55 Sutter Street
San Francisco, California 94104
(415) 943-1945

Equalizer
Charles Schwab & Co.
101 Montgomery Street
San Francisco, California 94104
(415) 627-7197

Market Manager Plus
Dow Jones & Company
P.O. Box 300
Princeton, New Jersey 08540 (609) 452-2000

Financial Planning Packages

Dollars & Sense
Monogram
8295 South La Cienega Boulevard
Inglewood, California 90301 (213) 215-0355

Financial Independence
Charles Schwab & Co.
101 Montgomery Street
San Francisco, California 94104
(415) 627-7197

Financier II
Financier Tax Series
Financier, Inc.
P.O. Box 558
Hudson, Massachusetts 01749
(617) 568-0374

Managing Your Money
MECA Software
285 Riverside Avenue
Westport, Connecticut 06880 (203) 222-1000

PC/Taxcut
Best Programs
5134 Leesburg Pike
Alexandria, Virginia 22302 (800) 368-2405

Personal Financial Planner
Lumen Systems
P.O. Box 9893
Englewood, New Jersey 07631
(201) 592-1121

Professional Tax Planner
Aardvark McGraw-Hill
1020 North Broadway
Milwaukee, Wisconsin 53202 (414) 225-7500

2. MAJOR FINANCIAL INSTITUTIONS

This section of the *Finance and Investment Handbook* provides listings of major financial institutions, such as banks, life insurance companies, brokerages, limited partnership sponsors, and securities and commodities exchanges. All provide vital financial services. Personal investors deal directly with most of the institutions, and at least indirectly with all. Introductions to the lists provide background information on the types of institutions covered; for additional information it is best to contact an institution directly.

The first part of this section provides lists of the major institutions of the banking system. The 12 banks and the 25 branches that make up the Federal Reserve System and the 12 banks that comprise the Federal Home Loan Bank System are listed. Then follows a listing of primary dealers in government securities, which interact with the Federal Reserve banks. Next is a compilation of the 100 largest commercial banks in the United States and the commercial banks of Canada, followed by a listing of the 100 largest thrift institutions (savings and loans and savings banks) in the United States and the trust and loans of Canada.

The second major part of this section provides a listing of the top 100 life-insurance companies in the U.S. and Canada. Insurance companies are important not only because of the protection they provide to policyholders, but also because they are major institutional investors.

A listing of the top 100 full-service brokerage firms and a listing of major discount brokers follow. Full-service brokers play a key role in raising capital for corporations and government bodies, and distributing securities and a wide array of financial services to individual and institutional investors. Investors can save on commissions by dealing with discount brokers.

This section continues with a compilation of major sponsors of limited partnerships, broken down by category of investment, such as real estate, oil and gas, and equipment leasing. By allowing individual investors to participate in markets previously accessible mainly to large institutions and the wealthy, these sponsors have greatly broadened the markets in which they compete.

Next is a listing of the 25 leading accounting firms. These firms, which in the past generally restricted their activities to auditing and accounting, have diversified recently into a variety of financial services. The final part of this section presents stock and commodity exchanges around the world. As financial markets have grown and become more interdependent, foreign exchanges have become more important to North Americans looking for investment opportunities.

FEDERAL RESERVE SYSTEM

The following is a list of the names, addresses, and telephone numbers of the 12 banks and 25 branch banks that make up the Federal Reserve System. These banks supervise the activities of commercial banks and savings banks in their regions. Each branch is associated with one of the 12 Federal Reserve banks—on the list of branches, the parent bank is shown in parentheses. Nationally chartered banks must join the Federal Reserve System; state-chartered banks join on a voluntary basis. The Fed banks ensure that the banks they supervise follow Federal Reserve rules and provide member banks with access to emergency funds through the discount window. Each regional bank is owned by the member banks in its region.

The Federal Reserve System was set up by Congress in 1913 to regulate the U.S. monetary and banking system. The System regulates the nation's money supply by buying and selling government securities on the open market, setting reserve requirements for member banks, setting the discount rate at which it lends funds to member banks, supervising printing of the currency at the mint, acting as a clearinghouse for the transfer of funds throughout the banking system, and examining member banks to ensure that they meet Federal Reserve regulations.

Members of the top policy-making body of the Federal Reserve—the Board of Governors—are appointed by the President of the United States with the consent of the Senate. However, in conducting monetary policy, the Fed is designed to operate independently, so that the rate of growth of the money supply is not directly controlled by Congress or the President. To assure independence, members of the Board of Governors of the Federal Reserve are appointed to 14-year terms. Statements by members of the Board of Governors—especially the Chairman—often have much influence in the finance and investment community.

Depositors and borrowers can complain to the Federal Reserve about practices of member banks considered unfair or abusive. The Fed has jurisdiction over consumer credit, for instance, so consumers can bring complaints about problems with bank lending policies, credit cards, or advertising. In addition, consumers wanting to buy U.S. Treasury and government agency securities without the fees that banks and brokers usually charge can buy them directly through any of the Federal Reserve banks or branches on this list. Also, Federal Reserve banks publish a variety of economic reports and studies that can be helpful to an investor.

Board of Governors

Board of Governors of the Federal Reserve System
20th and Constitution Avenue, N.W.
Washington, D.C. 20551
(202) 452-3000

Federal Reserve Banks

ATLANTA
Federal Reserve Bank of Atlanta
104 Marietta Street, N.W.
Atlanta, Georgia 30303
(404) 521-8500

BOSTON
Federal Reserve Bank of Boston
600 Atlantic Avenue
Boston, Massachusetts 02106
(617) 973-3000

CHICAGO
Federal Reserve Bank of Chicago
230 South LaSalle Street
Chicago, Illinois 60690
(312) 322-5322

CLEVELAND
Federal Reserve Bank of Cleveland
1455 East Sixth Street
Cleveland, Ohio 44101
(216) 579-2000

DALLAS
Federal Reserve Bank of Dallas
400 South Akard Street
Dallas, Texas 75222
(214) 651-6111

KANSAS CITY
Federal Reserve Bank of Kansas City
925 Grand Avenue
Kansas City, Missouri 64198
(816) 881-2000

MINNEAPOLIS
Federal Reserve Bank of Minneapolis
250 Marquette Avenue
Minneapolis, Minnesota 55480
(612) 340-2345

NEW YORK
Federal Reserve Bank of New York
33 Liberty Street
New York, New York 10045
(212) 720-5000

PHILADELPHIA
Federal Reserve Bank of Philadelphia
101 Independence Mall
Philadelphia, Pennsylvania 19106
(215) 574-6000

RICHMOND
Federal Reserve Bank of Richmond
701 East Byrd Street
Richmond, Virginia 23219
(804) 643-1250

ST. LOUIS
Federal Reserve Bank of St. Louis
411 Locust Street
St. Louis, Missouri 63102
(314) 444-8444

SAN FRANCISCO
Federal Reserve Bank of San Francisco
101 Market Street
San Francisco, California 94105
(415) 974-2000

Federal Reserve Branch Banks

BALTIMORE (Richmond)
502 South Sharp Street
Baltimore, Maryland 21201
(301) 576-3300

BIRMINGHAM (Atlanta)
1801 Fifth Avenue North
Birmingham, Alabama 35202
(205) 252-3141

BUFFALO (New York)
160 Delaware Avenue
Buffalo, New York 14202
(716) 849-5000

CHARLOTTE (Richmond)
401 South Tryon Street
Charlotte, North Carolina 28230
(704) 336-7100

CINCINNATI (Cleveland)
150 East Fourth Street
Cincinnati, Ohio 45201
(513) 721-4787

DENVER (Kansas City)
1020 16th Street
Denver, Colorado 80202
(303) 572-2300

DETROIT (Chicago)
160 Fort Street West
Detroit, Michigan 48231
(313) 961-6880

EL PASO (Dallas)
301 East Main Street
El Paso, Texas 79999
(915) 544-4730

HELENA (Minneapolis)
400 North Park Avenue
Helena, Montana 59601
(406) 442-3860

HOUSTON (Dallas)
1701 San Jacinto Street
Houston, Texas 77002
(713) 659-4433

JACKSONVILLE (Atlanta)
515 Julia Street
Jacksonville, Florida 32231
(904) 632-4400

LITTLE ROCK (St. Louis)
325 West Capitol Avenue
Little Rock, Arkansas 72203
(501) 372-5451

LOS ANGELES (San Francisco)
409 West Olympic Boulevard
Los Angeles, California 90015
(213) 683-8323

LOUISVILLE (St. Louis)
410 South Fifth Street
Louisville, Kentucky 40201
(502) 568-9200

MEMPHIS (St. Louis)
200 North Main Street
Memphis, Tennessee 38103
(901) 523-7171

MIAMI (Atlanta)
9100 N.W. Thirty-Sixth Street Extension
Miami, Florida 33178
(305) 591-2065

NASHVILLE (Atlanta)
301 Eighth Avenue North
Nashville, Tennessee 37203
(615) 259-4006

NEW ORLEANS (Atlanta)
525 St. Charles Avenue
New Orleans, Louisiana 70161
(504) 586-1505

OKLAHOMA CITY (Kansas City)
226 Dean A. McGee Avenue
Oklahoma City, Oklahoma 73125
(405) 235-1721

OMAHA (Kansas City)
2201 Farnum Street
Omaha, Nebraska 68102
(402) 221-5500

PITTSBURGH (Cleveland)
717 Grant Street
Pittsburgh, Pennsylvania 15230
(412) 261-7800

PORTLAND (San Francisco)
915 S.W. Stark Street
Portland, Oregon 97205
(503) 221-5900

SALT LAKE CITY (San Francisco)
120 South State Street
Salt Lake City, Utah 84111
(801) 322-7900

SAN ANTONIO (Dallas)
126 East Nueva Street
San Antonio, Texas 78204
(512) 224-2141

SEATTLE (San Francisco)
1015 Second Avenue
Seattle, Washington 98104
(206) 442-1376

PRIMARY GOVERNMENT SECURITIES DEALERS

The following is a list of banks and brokerage firms that act as primary government securities dealers, reporting to the Federal Reserve Bank of New York. In this role, they facilitate the Federal Reserve's open market operations by buying and selling U.S. Treasury securities directly through the New York Fed's Securities Department, commonly called The Desk. These dealers are therefore key players in the execution of Federal Reserve policy, as set down by the Federal Open Market Committee, which decides to tighten or loosen the money supply to combat inflation or to stimulate economic growth. When the Fed wants to tighten the money supply, it sells government securities to the primary dealers—the dollars the dealers pay for the securities are thus taken out of circulation, and the money supply contracts. When the Fed, on the other hand, wants to expand the money supply, it buys government securities from the dealers—the proceeds from these sales then go into the economy, and the money supply increases.

When the government issues new Treasury securities, these primary dealers also play a key role, because they are among other large dealers and investors making competitive bids for the securities. Under the competitive bid system, also known as a Dutch auction, bidders offer prices for the securities, and the highest prices are accepted. Most individual investors do not participate in this auction. Rather than risk losing out to a higher bidder, they buy Treasury securities with noncompetitive bids, for which the investor accepts whatever price is determined by the competitive auction.

In order to become a primary dealer, a firm must show the Federal Reserve that the company has an excellent reputation, large capacity for trading in government securities, and adequate staff and facilities. It is considered to be very prestigious to be accepted into the inner circle of primary government securities dealers.

Bank of America N.T. & S.A.
Bank of America Center
San Francisco, California 94104
(415) 622-3456

Bankers Trust Co.
280 Park Avenue
New York, New York 10017
(212) 775-2500

Bear, Stearns & Co., Inc.
55 Water Street
New York, New York 10041
(212) 952-5000

Carroll McEntee & McGinley Inc.
40 Wall Street
New York, New York 10005
(212) 825-6780

Chase Manhattan Government Securities, Inc.
Chase Manhattan Plaza
New York, New York 10081
(212) 552-2222

Chemical Bank
277 Park Avenue
New York, New York 10172
(212) 310-6161

Citibank, N.A.
399 Park Avenue
New York, New York 10043
(212) 559-1000

Continental Illinois National Bank and Trust
of Chicago
231 South LaSalle Street
Chicago, Illinois 60697
(312) 828-2345

Daiwa Securities America Inc.
1 Liberty Plaza
New York, New York 10006
(212) 732-6600

Dean Witter Reynolds, Inc.
5 World Trade Center
New York, New York 10048
(212) 524-2222

Discount Corp. of New York
58 Pine Street
New York, New York 10005
(212) 248-8900

Donaldson, Lufkin & Jenrette Securities Corp.
140 Broadway
New York, New York 10005
(212) 943-0300

Drexel, Burnham Lambert Government
Securities Inc.
60 Broad Street
New York, New York 10004
(212) 480-6000

The First Boston Corp.
Park Avenue Plaza
New York, New York 10017
(212) 909-2000

First Interstate Capital Markets, Inc.
707 Wilshire Boulevard
Los Angeles, California 90017
(213) 614-4111

First National Bank of Chicago
33 North LaSalle Street
Chicago, Illinois 60690
(312) 661-5000

Goldman, Sachs & Co.
85 Broad Street
New York, New York 10004
(212) 902-1000

Greenwich Capital Markets, Inc.
600 Steamboat Road
Greenwich, Connecticut 06830
(203) 629-2570

Harris Trust and Savings Bank
111 West Monroe Street
Chicago, Illinois 60690
(312) 461-2121

E.F. Hutton & Company, Inc.
One Battery Park Plaza
New York, New York 10004
(212) 742-5000

Irving Securities, Inc.
1 Wall Street
New York, New York 10005
(212) 635-1400

Kidder, Peabody & Co. Inc.
10 Hanover Square
New York, New York 10005
(212) 747-2000

Kleinwort Benson Government Securities, Inc
100 Wall Street
New York, New York 10005
(212) 248-5060

Aubrey Lanston & Co., Inc.
20 Broad Street
New York, New York 10005
(212) 943-1200

Manufacturers Hanover Trust Co.
270 Park Avenue
New York, New York 10017
(212) 286-6000

Merrill Lynch Government Securities, Inc.
One Liberty Plaza
New York, New York 10006
(212) 637-7455

Midland-Montagu Government Securities, Inc.
1 Montgomery Street, West Tower
San Francisco, CA 94104
(415) 983-6649

J.P. Morgan Securities, Inc.
23 Wall Street
New York, New York 10015
(212) 483-2323

Morgan Stanley & Co. Inc.
1251 Avenue of the Americas
New York, New York 10020
(212) 974-4000

Nomura Securities International, Inc.
180 Maiden Lane
New York, New York 10038
(212) 208-9300

Paine Webber Inc.
1285 Avenue of the Americas
New York, New York 10020
(212) 713-2000

Wm. E. Pollock Government Securities, Inc.
160 Water Street
New York, New York 10038
(212) 908-5800

Prudential-Bache Securites, Inc.
One Bache Plaza
New York, New York 10292
(212) 791-1000

Refco Partners
One World Trade Center
New York, New York 10048
(212) 466-1610

L.F. Rothschild, Unterberg, Towbin, Inc.
55 Water Street
New York, New York 10041
(212) 412-1000

Salomon Brothers Inc.
One New York Plaza
New York, New York 10004
(212) 747-7000

Security Pacific National Bank
333 South Hope Street
Los Angeles, California 90071
(213) 229-1032

Shearson Lehman Government Securities, Inc.
World Financial Center
New York, New York 10285
(212) 298-2000

Smith Barney Government Securities, Inc.
1345 Avenue of the Americas
New York, New York 10105
(212) 399-6000

Thomson McKinnon Securities, Inc.
One New York Plaza
New York, New York 10004
(212) 482-7000

FEDERAL HOME LOAN BANKS

The following are the names, addresses, and telephone numbers of the 12 banks of the Federal Home Loan Bank System, as well as the System's national headquarters in Washington. The Federal Home Loan Bank System, established by Congress in 1932 after the collapse of the banking system during the Great Depression, raises money by issuing notes and bonds and lends money to savings and loans and other mortgage lenders based on the amount of collateral the borrowing institution can provide. The Federal Home Loan Banks supervise the activities of, and supply credit reserves to, federally charted savings and loans, cooperative banks, and other mortgage lenders in their regions. Each Home Loan Bank is owned by the member banks in its region.

As the chief regulator of the savings and loan industry, the Home Loan Bank System also receives and acts on complaints from depositors and borrowers at member savings and loans. The System regulates savings and loan lending, deposit-taking, and advertising policies, among other areas of endeavor by the industry.

The System is supervised by the three-member Federal Home Loan Bank Board, an independent agency, which also supervises the Federal Savings and Loan Insurance Corporation (FSLIC) and the Federal Home Loan Mortgage Corporation.

National Headquarters
Federal Home Loan Bank System
1776 G Street N.W.
Washington, D.C. 20006
(202) 377-6000

Federal Home Loan Banks

ATLANTA
Federal Home Loan Bank of Atlanta
Coastal States Building
260 Peachtree Street, N.W.
Atlanta, Georgia 30303
(404) 522-2450

BOSTON
Federal Home Loan Bank of Boston
One Financial Center
Boston, Massachusetts 02110
(617) 542-0150

CHICAGO
Federal Home Loan Bank of Chicago
111 East Wacker Drive, Suite 800
Chicago, Illinois 60601
(312) 565-5700

CINCINNATI
Federal Home Loan Bank of Cincinnati
2000 Atrium II
221 East 4th Street
Cincinnati, Ohio 45202
(513) 852-7500

DALLAS
Federal Home Loan Bank of Dallas
500 East John Carpenter Freeway
Dallas/Ft. Worth, Texas 75261
(214) 659-8500

DES MOINES
Federal Home Loan Bank of Des Moines
907 Walnut Street
Des Moines, Iowa 50309
(515) 243-4211

INDIANAPOLIS
Federal Home Loan Bank of Indianapolis
1350 Merchants Plaza, South Tower
115 West Washington Street
Indianapolis, Indiana 46204
(317) 631-0130

NEW YORK
Federal Home Loan Bank of New York
One World Trade Center, Floor 103
New York, New York 10048
(212) 912-4600

PITTSBURGH
Federal Home Loan Bank of Pittsburgh
20 Stanwix Street
One Riverfront Center
Pittsburgh, Pennsylvania 15222
(412) 288-3400

SAN FRANCISCO
Federal Home Loan Bank of San Francisco
600 California Street
San Francisco, California 94120
(415) 393-1000

SEATTLE
Federal Home Loan Bank of Seattle
600 Stewart Street
Seattle, Washington 98101
(206) 624-3980

TOPEKA
Federal Home Loan Bank of Topeka
3 Townsite Plaza
120 East 6th Street
Topeka, Kansas 66603
(913) 233-0508

COMMERCIAL BANKS

The following is an alphabetical list of the names, addresses, and telephone numbers of the headquarters of the 100 largest commercial banks in the United States. The institutions listed here are the largest based on total deposits, the criterion generally used for comparing the size of banks. These deposits are made up of deposits of corporations, individuals, correspondent banks, government agencies, not-for-profit organizations, and many other groups. They are in such forms as checking accounts and certificates of deposit and other time deposits. Another way of ranking banks is by the amount of permanent capital. This capital has been built over the years by offerings of stock to the public and retained earnings. The top 100 institutions would basically be the same using either method of ranking.

Most banks listed here are national banks, because they are chartered by the federal government. Any bank with the initial N (meaning national) or with national in its name is a national bank. Although there are about 14,000 commercial banks in the United States, there is a high amount of concentration of deposits and capital in the largest banks. The two largest, Citibank N.A. and Bank of America N.T. & S.A., have $94 billion and $88 billion in deposits, respectively, and about $7 billion and $4 billion in capital. Only about the top 20 banks have deposits in excess of $10 billion and capital of $1 billion or more. The banks ranking near number 100, in contrast, have about $2 billion in deposits and around $200 million in capital.

In the 1980s there were many bank mergers, as banks sought to compete better in the new, less regulated environment brought about largely by the Depository Institutions Deregulation and Monetary Control Act of 1980. Some large banks operate newly acquired banks as separate subsidiaries. Chase Manhattan's Chase Lincoln First Bank and Mellon Bank's Philadelphia subsidiary, Mellon Bank (East), for example, are larger than many small banks. Since they are run independently, though still under the corporate umbrella, they are listed here separately.

This list of the largest commercial banks (current as of the end of 1985) comes from the *American Banker* newspaper [1 State Street Plaza, New York, New York 10004 (212) 943-6700]. The banks are listed alphabetically, not by size.

Allied Bank of Texas
1000 Louisiana
Houston, Texas 77002
(713) 224-6611

American Bank & Trust Co.
35 North Sixth Street
Reading, Pennsylvania 19603
(215) 320-2000

American Fletcher National Bank & Trust Co.
101 Monument Circle
Indianapolis, Indiana 46277
(317) 639-3000

American National Bank & Trust Co.
33 North LaSalle Street
Chicago, Illinois 60602
(312) 661-5000

American Security Bank, N.A.
730 15th Street, N.W.
Washington, D.C. 20013
(202) 624-4000

AmeriTrust Company, N.A.
900 Euclid Avenue
Cleveland, Ohio 44101
(216) 687-5000

AmSouth Bank, N.A.
1900 Fifth Avenue North
Birmingham, Alabama 35203
(205) 326-5120

Arizona Bank
101 North First Avenue
Phoenix, Arizona 85002
(602) 262-2000

Atlantic National Bank of Florida
200 West Forsyth Street
Jacksonville, Florida 32202
(904) 632-6565

BancOhio National Bank
155 East Broad Street
Columbus, Ohio 43251
(614) 463-7100

Banco Popular de Puerto Rico
Banco Popular Center
Hato Rey
San Juan, Puerto Rico 00936
(809) 842-8000

Bankers Trust Co.
280 Park Avenue
New York, New York 10017
(212) 775-2500

Bank of America National Trust & Savings Assoc.
555 California Street
San Francisco, California 94104
(415) 622-3456

Bank of Hawaii
Financial Plaza of the Pacific
111 South King Street
Honolulu, Hawaii 96813
(808) 537-8111

Bank of New England, N.A.
28 State Street
Boston, Massachusetts 02109
(617) 742-4000

The Bank of New York
48 Wall Street
New York, New York 10015
(212) 530-1784

Bank of Tokyo Trust Co.
100 Broadway
New York, New York 10005
(212) 766-3400

Bank of Virginia
7 North 8th Street
Richmond, Virginia 23219
(804) 747-2000

Barnett Bank of South Florida, N.A.
800 Brickell Avenue
Miami, Florida 33131
(305) 825-5900

Boston Safe Deposit & Trust Co.
1 Boston Place
Boston, Massachusetts 02106
(617) 956-9700

California First Bank
350 California Street
San Francisco, California 94104
(415) 445-0200

Central Fidelity Bank, N.A.
219 East Broad Street
Richmond, Virginia 23219
(804) 782-4000

Chase Lincoln First Bank, N.A.
One Lincoln First Square
Rochester, New York 14643
(716) 258-5000

The Chase Manhattan Bank
One Chase Manhattan Plaza
New York, New York 10081
(212) 552-2222

Chemical Bank
277 Park Avenue
New York, New York 10172
(212) 310-6161

Citibank N.A.
399 Park Avenue
New York, New York 10043
(212) 559-1000

Citibank (New York State)
409 Main Street
Buffalo, New York 14203
(716) 849-2531

Citizens and Southern National Bank
35 Broad Street
Atlanta, Georgia 30303
(404) 581-2121

Comerica Bank
211 West Fort Street
Detroit, Michigan 48275
(313) 222-3300

Connecticut Bank & Trust Co. N.A.
One Constitution Plaza
Hartford, Connecticut 06115
(203) 244-5000

Connecticut Bank & Trust Co. N.A.
One Constitution Plaza
Hartford, Connecticut 06115
(203) 244-5000

Continental Illinois National and Trust Co.
of Chicago
231 South LaSalle Street
Chicago, Illinois 60697
(312) 828-2345

Equitable Bank N.A.
100 South Charles Street
Baltimore, Maryland 21201
(301) 547-4000

European American Bank and Trust Co.
10 Hanover Square
New York, New York 10015
(212) 437-4300

Fidelity Bank, N.A.
135 South Broad Street
Philadelphia, Pennsylvania 19109
(215) 985-6000

First City National Bank
1001 Main Street
Houston, Texas 77002
(713) 658-6011

First Fidelity Bank, N.A.
550 Broad Street
Newark, New Jersey 07192
(201) 565-3200

First Florida Bank, N.A.
1111 Madison Avenue
Tampa, Florida 33602
(813) 224-1111

First Hawaiian Bank
165 South King Street
Honolulu, Hawaii 96813
(808) 525-7000

First Interstate Bank of Arizona, N.A.
First Interstate Bank Plaza
Phoenix, Arizona 85003
(602) 271-6000

First Interstate Bank of California
707 Wilshire Boulevard
Los Angeles, California 90017
(213) 614-4111

First Interstate Bank of Oregon, N.A.
1300 Southwest Fifth Avenue
Portland, Oregon 97201
(503) 225-2111

First Interstate Bank of Washington, N.A.
999 Third Street
Seattle, Washington 98104
(206) 292-3111

The First National Bank of Atlanta
Two Peachtree Street
Atlanta, Georgia 30383
(404) 588-5000

First National Bank of Boston
100 Federal Street
Boston, Massachussetts 02110
(617) 434-2200

First National Bank of Chicago
One First National Plaza
Chicago, Illinois 60670
(312) 732-4000

First National Bank of Maryland
25 South Charles Street
Baltimore, Maryland 21203
(301) 244-4000

First National Bank of Minneapolis
120 South Sixth Street
Minneapolis, Minnesota 55480
(612) 370-4141

First National Bank of St. Paul
332 Minnesota Street
St. Paul, Minnesota 55101
(612) 291-5000

First Pennsylvania Bank, N.A.
Centre Square
16th and Market Streets
Philadelphia, Pennsylvania 19101
(215) 786-5000

First Tennessee Bank, N.A.
165 Madison Avenue
Memphis, Tennessee 38103
(901) 523-4444

First Union National Bank
First Union Plaza
Charlotte, North Carolina 28288
(704) 374-6161

First Wisconsin National Bank
777 East Wisconsin Avenue
Milwaukee, Wisconsin 53202
(414) 765-4321

Fleet National Bank
111 Westminster Street
Providence, Rhode Island 02903
(401) 278-6000

Florida National Bank
The Edward Ball Building
214 Hogan Street
Jacksonville, Florida 32202
(904) 359-5111

Harris Trust & Savings Bank
111 West Monroe Street
Chicago, Illinois 60690
(312) 461-2121

Huntington National Bank
17 South High Street
Columbus, Ohio 43260
(614) 476-8300

Indiana National Bank
One Indiana Square
Indianapolis, Indiana 46266
(317) 266-6000

InterFirst Bank Dallas, N.A.
1401 Elm Street
Dallas, Texas 75283
(214) 744-9600

Irving Trust Co.
One Wall Street
New York, New York 10005
(212) 635-1111

Israel Discount Bank
511 Fifth Avenue
New York, New York 10017
(212) 551-8500

Manufacturers Hanover Trust Co.
270 Park Avenue
New York, New York 10017
(212) 286-6000

Manufacturers National Bank
Manufacturers Bank Tower
Renaissance Center
Detroit, Michigan 48243
(313) 222-4000

Marine Midland Bank, N.A.
140 Broadway
New York, New York 10015
(212) 440-1000

Maryland National Bank
Baltimore and Light Streets
Baltimore, Maryland 21203
(301) 244-5000

MBank Dallas, N.A.
1704 Main Street
Dallas, Texas 75201
(214) 698-6000

MBank Houston, N.A.
910 Travis Street
Houston, Texas 77002
(713) 751-6100

Mellon Bank, N.A.
One Mellon Bank Center
Pittsburgh, Pennsylvania 15258
(412) 234-5000

Mellon Bank (East) N.A.
Broad and Chestnut Streets
Philadelphia, Pennsylvania 19102
(215) 585-2000

Morgan Guaranty Trust Co.
23 Wall Street
New York, New York 10015
(212) 483-2323

National Bank of Detroit
611 Woodward Avenue
Detroit, Michigan 48226
(313) 225-1000

National City Bank
1900 East 9th Street
Cleveland, Ohio 44114
(216) 575-2000

National Westminster Bank USA
175 Water Street
New York, New York 10038
(212) 602-1000

NCNB National Bank of Florida
600 North Florida Avenue
Tampa, Florida 33602
(813) 224-5151

NCNB National Bank of North Carolina
One NCNB Plaza
Charlotte, North Carolina 28255
(704) 374-5000

Northern Trust Co.
50 South La Salle Street
Chicago, Illinois 60675
(312) 630-6000

Norwest Bank Minneapolis, N.A.
Eighth Street and Marquette Avenue
Minneapolis, Minnesota 55479
(612) 372-8123

Philadelphia National Bank
Broad and Chestnut Streets
Philadelphia, Pennsylvania 19101
(215) 629-3100

Pittsburgh National Bank
Fifth Avenue & Wood Street
Pittsburgh, Pennsylvania 15265
(412) 355-2000

Provident National Bank
Broad and Chestnut Streets
Philadelphia, Pennsylvania 19101
(215) 585-5000

Rainier National Bank
1301 Fifth Avenue
Seattle, Washington 98124
(206) 621-4111

RepublicBank Dallas, N.A.
Pacific and Ervay Streets
Dallas, Texas 75201
(214) 922-5000

Republic National Bank of New York
452 Fifth Avenue
New York, New York 10018
(212) 930-6000

Riggs National Bank
1503 Pennsylvania Avenue, N.W.
Washington, D.C. 20013
(202) 835-6000

Seattle-First National Bank
1001 Fourth Avenue
Seattle, Washington 98154
(206) 583-3131

Security Pacific National Bank
333 South Hope Street
Los Angeles, California 90071
(213) 613-6211

Shawmut Bank of Boston, N.A.
One Federal Street
Boston, Massachusetts 02211
(617) 292-2000

South Carolina National Bank
1401 Main Street
Columbia, South Carolina 29226
(803) 771-3954

Southeast Bank, N.A.
1 Southeast Financial Center
Miami, Florida 33131
(305) 375-7500

Sovran Bank, N.A.
111 East Main Street
Richmond, Virginia 23219
(804) 788-2000

State Street Bank & Trust Co.
225 Franklin Street
Boston, Massachussetts 02110
(617) 786-3000

Sumitomo Bank of California
300 California Street
San Francisco, California 94104
(415) 445-8000

Texas Commerce Bank, N.A.
600 Travis Street
Houston, Texas 77252
(713) 236-4865

Trust Company Bank
One Park Place
Atlanta, Georgia 30303
(404) 588-7711

Union Bank
445 South Figueroa Street
Los Angeles, California 90071
(213) 236-5000

United States National Bank of Oregon
U.S. Bancorp Tower
111 Southwest Fifth Avenue
Portland, Oregon 97204
(503) 225-6111

United Virginia Bank
919 East Main Street
Richmond, Virginia 23261
(804) 782-5000

Valley National Bank
241 North Central Avenue
Phoenix, Arizona 85001
(602) 261-2900

Wachovia Bank and Trust Co., N.A.
301 North Main Street
Winston-Salem, North Carolina 27150
(919) 770-5000

Wells Fargo Bank, N.A.
420 Montgomery Street
San Francisco, California 94104
(415) 396-0123

THRIFT INSTITUTIONS

The following is an alphabetical list of the names, addresses, and telephone numbers of the headquarters of the 100 largest savings and loans and savings banks in the United States, based on total deposits at the end of 1985, as tabulated by the *American Banker* newspaper [1 State Street Plaza, New York, New York 10004 (212) 943-6700]. Total deposits, made up mostly of certificates of deposit and money-market accounts, are the best measure of thrift institution size, and they are therefore commonly used in ranking savings and loans and savings banks. Some tabulations compare thrifts by their total assets—mostly mortgage loans. In either case, the list of the top 100 institutions would be similar.

Savings and loans were initially founded predominantly in the western states, particularly California, as a mechanism for pioneer settlers in the 19th century to finance the construction of homes. They were largely regulated by state authorities until 1932, when the Federal Home Loan Bank Board was set up in reaction to the crisis of the banking and home building industries during the Great Depression. Savings and loans are now regulated at both the federal and state levels and most deposits are insured by the Federal Savings and Loan Insurance Corporation (FSLIC).

Savings banks were initially found mainly on the East Coast, where, like savings and loans, they catered to consumers and made home loans. They are chartered and regulated by both state authorities and the Federal Reserve Board, as well as the Federal Home Loan Bank Board in some cases. Most deposits are insured by the Federal Deposit Insurance Corporation (FDIC). Over the years, the few distinctions between savings banks and savings and loans have largely faded away.

Historically, both types of thrifts have been distinguished from commercial banks in that they obtained most of their deposits from consumers and lent that money out in the form of fixed-rate mortgages to homebuyers. To give them an edge in attracting deposits, they were allowed (under Regulation Q) to pay ¼% more interest on passbook savings accounts than commercial banks. Starting in the late 1970s, when the general level of interest rates started to rise dramatically, many thrifts ran into financial trouble, because their income from mortgage loans was fixed at low rates, while they had to pay out higher rates on unregulated certificates of deposit to retain depositors. The pressure from this predicament ultimately led to the Depository Institutions Deregulation and Monetary Control Act of 1980 and the Garn St Germain Act of 1982, which mandated the gradual phase-out of control on interest rates on all deposits and permitted thrifts to offer adjustable-rate mortgages. They were also allowed to enter businesses from which they had previously been banned, such as commercial lending, issuing credit cards, and providing trust services.

By the late 1980s, thrifts played a prominent and highly competitive role in providing financial services. Many institutions went after consumer dollars by paying among the highest interest rates in the country on money-market deposits and certificates of deposit. These savings and loans and savings banks often arranged to take deposits over the phone. They sometimes brought in millions of dollars by allying with a securities brokerage firm to sell certificates of deposit. With the ability to bring in large amounts of money quickly, many thrifts became aggressive lenders as well.

American Savings Bank, FSB
8th Avenue and 42nd Street
New York, New York 10036
(212) 880-7600

American Savings & Loan Assoc.
18401 Van Korman
Irvine, California 92715
(714) 553-6800

American Savings & Loan Assoc.
77 West Second South
Salt Lake City, Utah 84101
(801) 483-5800

American Savings & Loan Assoc. of Florida
17801 N.W. Second Avenue
Miami, Florida 33169
(305) 653-5353

AmeriFirst Federal Savings & Loan Assoc.
One Southeast Third Avenue
Miami, Florida 33131
(305) 577-6100

Anchor Savings Bank, FSB
225 Main Street
Northport, New York 11768
(516) 261-6000

Astoria Federal Savings & Loan Assoc.
37-16 30th Avenue
Long Island City, New York 11103
(718) 545-4400

Atlantic Financial Federal
50 Monument Road
Bala Cynwyd, Pennsylvania 19004
(215) 667-7300

BancWestern Federal Savings Bank
700 17th Street
Denver, Colorado 80202
(303) 370-1212

Benjamin Franklin Federal Savings & Loan Assoc.
501 East Hawthorne Boulevard
Portland, Oregon 97214
(503) 248-1234

Bowery Savings Bank
110 East 42nd Street
New York, New York 10017
(212) 953-8000

Broadview Savings & Loan
6000 Rockside Woods Boulevard
Cleveland, Ohio 44131
(216) 447-1900

California Federal Savings & Loan Assoc.
5670 Wilshire Boulevard
Los Angeles, California 90036
(213) 932-4321

Capitol Federal Savings & Loan Assoc.
700 Kansas Avenue
Topeka, Kansas 66603
(913) 235-1341

Carteret Savings Bank, F.A.
200 South Street
Morristown, New Jersey 07960
(201) 326-1000

CenTrust Savings Bank
101 East Flagler Street
Miami, Florida 33131
(305) 376-5000

Chevy Chase Savings & Loan Inc.
8401 Connecticut Avenue
Chevy Chase, Maryland 20815
(301) 986-7560

Citicorp Savings F.S. & L.A.
180 Grand Avenue
Oakland, California 94604
(415) 891-8600

Citicorp Savings of Illinois, F.S. & L.A.
One South Dearborn Street
Chicago, Illinois 60603
(312) 977-5000

Citicorp Savings of Florida F.S. & L.A.
1790 Biscayne Boulevard
Miami, Florida 33132
(305) 599-5555

Citizens Federal Savings & Loan Assoc.
110 North Main Street
Dayton, Ohio 45402
(513) 223-4234

City Federal Savings & Loan Assoc.
Route 202-206
Bedminster, New Jersey 07921
(201) 658-4100

Coast Savings & Loan Assoc.
855 South Hill Street
Los Angeles, California 90014
(213) 624-2110

Columbia Savings F.S. & L.A.
8840 South Ulster Circle East
Englewood, Colorado 80111
(303) 773-3444

Columbia Savings & Loan Assoc.
8840 Wilshire Boulevard
Beverly Hills, California 90211
(213) 657-6134

Community Federal Savings & Loan Assoc.
1 Community Federal Center
St. Louis, Missouri 63131
(314) 822-5000

Coral Gables Federal Savings & Loan Assoc.
2511 Ponce de Leon Boulevard
Coral Gables, Florida 33134
(305) 447-4711

CrossLand Savings, FSB
211 Montague Street
Brooklyn, New York 11201
(718) 522-0030

Dallas Federal Savings & Loan Assoc.
8333 Douglas Avenue
Dallas, Texas 75225
(214) 750-5000

Dime Savings Bank of New York, FSB
9 DeKalb Avenue
Brooklyn, New York 11201
(718) 643-4200

Dollar Bank, FSB
535 Smithfield Street
Pittsburgh, Pennsylvania 15222
(412) 261-4900

Dollar Dry Dock Savings Bank
2530 Grand Concourse
Bronx, New York 10458
(212) 584-6000

Downey Savings & Loan Assoc.
3200 Bristol Street
Costa Mesa, California 92626
(714) 549-8811

East River Savings Bank
26 Cortlandt Street
New York, New York 10007
(212) 553-9600

Emigrant Savings Bank
5 East 42nd Street
New York, New York 10017
(212) 883-5800

Empire of America, FSB
One Main Place
Buffalo, New York 14202
(716) 845-7000

Empire Savings of America
P.O. Box 689
Baytown, Texas 77520
(713) 422-8355

Farm & Home Savings Assoc.
221 West Cherry
Nevada, Missouri 64772
(417) 667-3333

Far West Savings & Loan Assoc.
4001 MacArthur Boulevard
Newport Beach, California 92660
(714) 833-8383

Fidelity Federal Savings & Loan Assoc.
600 North Brand Boulevard
Glendale, California 91203
(818) 956-7100

First Federal of Michigan
1001 Woodward Avenue
Detroit, Michigan 48226
(313) 965-1400

First Federal Savings & Loan Assoc.
One First Federal Place
Rochester, New York 14614
(716) 454-4010

First Federal Savings & Loan Assoc.
of Mount Oliver
317 Brownsville Road
Pittsburgh, Pennsylvania 15210
(412) 431-3499

First Minnesota Savings Bank, FSB
Minnesota at Fifth Avenue
St. Paul, Minnesota 55101
(612) 298-6400

First Nationwide Savings, F.S. & L.A.
700 Market Street
San Francisco, California 94102
(415) 772-1400

First Texas Savings Assoc.
14951 Dallas Parkway
Dallas, Texas 75240
(214) 960-4500

Florida Federal Savings & Loan Assoc.
360 Central Avenue
St. Petersburg, Florida 33701
(813) 893-1131

Freedom Savings & Loan Assoc.
111 North Dale Mabry Highway
Tampa, Florida 33609
(813) 870-5000

Fulton Federal Savings & Loan Assoc.
21 Edgewood Avenue, Northeast
Atlanta, Georgia 30303
(404) 586-7283

Georgia Federal Bank, FSB
20 Marietta Street NW
Atlanta, Georgia 30303
(404) 588-2600

Gibraltar Savings
9111 Wilshire Boulevard
Beverly Hills, California 90210
(213) 278-8720

Gibraltar Savings Assoc.
13401 North Freeway
Houston, Texas 77060
(713) 872-3100

Glendale Federal Savings and Loan Assoc.
700 North Brand Boulevard
Glendale, California 91203
(818) 500-2000

Goldome, FSB
1 Fountain Plaza
Buffalo, New York 14203
(716) 847-5800

Great American First Savings Bank
600 B Street
San Diego, California 92183
(619) 231-1885

Great Western Savings, F.S. & L.A.
8484 Wilshire Boulevard
Beverly Hills, California 90211
(213) 852-3951

Greater New York Savings Bank
One Penn Plaza
New York, New York 10119
(212) 613-4000

Green Point Savings Bank
807 Manhattan Avenue
Brooklyn, New York 11222
(718) 706-2900

Guarantee Savings F.S. & L.A.
Guarantee Savings Building
1177 Fulton Mall
Fresno, California 93721
(209) 268-8111

Hill Financial Savings Assoc.
400 Main Street
Red Hill, Pennsylvania 18076
(215) 679-3131

Home Federal Savings & Loan Assoc.
of San Diego
707 Broadway
San Diego, California 92101
(619) 699-7000

Home Savings of America, F.S. & L.A.
1001 Commerce Drive
Irwindale, California 91706
(818) 960-6311

Homestead Savings F.S. & L.A.
1777 Murchison Drive
Burlingame, California 94010
(415) 692-1432

Howard Savings Bank
768 Broad Street
Newark, New Jersey 07102
(201) 430-2000

Hudson City Savings Bank
West 80 Century Road
Paramus, New Jersey 07652
(201) 967-1900

Imperial Savings Assoc.
Columbia Centre
8780 Complex Drive
San Diego, California 92123
(619) 292-6464

Lamar Savings Assoc.
800 Brazos Street
Austin, Texas 78701
(512) 474-5966

Lincoln Savings & Loan Assoc.
18200 Von Karman Street
Irvine, California 92715
(714) 553-0200

Lincoln Savings Bank, FSB
200 Park Avenue
New York, New York 10166
(212) 972-9500

Long Island Savings Bank, FSB
50 Jackson Avenue
Syosset, New York 11791
(516) 677-5000

Manhattan Savings Bank
385 Madison Avenue
New York, New York 10017
(212) 688-3000

MeraBank, FSB
20002 North 19th Avenue
Phoenix, Arizona 85027
(602) 581-5638

Midwest Federal Savings & Loan Assoc.
801 Nicollet Mall
Minneapolis, Minnesota 55402
(612) 372-6123

Northeast Savings, F.A.
147 Charter Oak Avenue
Hartford, Connecticut 0610ᶠ
(203) 727-1600

Old Stone Bank, FSB
P.O. Box 1598
Providence, Rhode Island 02903
(401) 278-2000

Pacific First Federal Savings Bank
1145 Broadway
Tacoma, Washington 98402
(206) 383-2511

People's Bank-Bridgeport
Main and State Streets
Bridgeport, Connecticut 06602
(203) 579-7171

Perpetual American Bank, FSB
1749 Old Meadow Road
McLean, Virginia 22102
(703) 893-4930

Philadelphia Saving Fund Society
1212 Market Street
Philadelphia, Pennsylvania 19107
(215) 636-6000

Rochester Community Savings Bank
235 East Main Street
Rochester, New York 14604
(716) 262-5800

San Antonio Savings Assoc.
601 Northwest Loop 410
San Antonio, Texas 78216
(512) 340-7272

San Francisco Federal Savings & Loan Assoc.
88 Kearny Street
San Francisco, California 94108
(415) 955-5800

Santa Barbara Savings & Loan Assoc.
7 West Figueroa Street
Santa Barbara, California 93101
(805) 569-1181

San Jacinto Savings Assoc.
P.O. Box 35700
Houston, Texas 77235
(713) 661-7000

Seamen's Bank for Savings, FSB
30 Wall Street
New York, New York 10005
(212) 797-5000

Sears Savings Bank
701 North Brand Street
Glendale, California 91203
(818) 956-1800

Society for Savings
31 Pratt Street
Hartford, Connecticut 06145
(203) 727-5000

Standard Federal Bank
2401 West Big Beaver Road
Troy, Michigan 48084
(313) 643-9600

St. Paul Federal Bank for Savings
6700 West North Avenue
Chicago, Illinois 60635
(312) 622-5000

Sunbelt Savings Assoc.
422 West Washington Street
Stephenville, Texas 76401
(817) 965-3166

Talman Home Federal Savings & Loan Assoc.
30 West Monroe Street
Chicago, Illinois 60603
(312) 922-9775

Transohio Savings Bank, FSB
1 Pentan Plaza, 1111 Chester Avenue
Cleveland, Ohio 44114
(216) 579-7700

Twin City Federal Savings & Loan Assoc.
801 Marquette Avenue
Minneapolis, Minnesota 55402
(612) 370-7000

United Savings Assoc.
10333 Harwin
Houston, Texas 77036
(713) 981-2300

University Savings Assoc.
1160 Dairy Ashford
Houston, Texas 77079
(713) 596-1000

Valley Federal Savings & Loan Assoc.
6842 Van Nuys Boulevard
Van Nuys, California 91405
(818) 904-3828

Washington Mutual Savings Bank
1101 Second Avenue
Seattle, Washington 98101
(206) 464-4400

Western Savings & Loan Assoc.
3443 North Central Avenue
Phoenix, Arizona 85012
(602) 248-1616

Williamsburgh Savings Bank
One Hanson Place
Brooklyn, New York 11243
(718) 272-4242

World Savings F.S. & L.A.
1901 Harrison Street
Oakland, California 94612
(415) 645-9426

CANADIAN TRUST AND LOANS

The equivalent of the U.S. savings and loan in Canada is called a trust and loan. These trust and loans act as executors, trustees, and administrators of wills and trust agreements; serve as transfer agents, registrars, and bond trustees for corporations; take deposits that are invested in fixed term instruments; offer unit investment trusts; manage profit-sharing and pension plans for companies; and offer mortgage loans, mostly to residential home buyers. The following is an alphabetical list of Canadian trust and loans.

Acadia Trust Co.
798 Prince Street
Truro, Nova Scotia B2N 1H1
(902) 895-5484

Alcan Fiduciaries Ltd.
1188 Sherbrooke Street West
Montréal, Québec H3A 3G2
(514) 848-8000

Atlantic Trust Co. of Canada
1741 Barrington Street
Halifax, Nova Scotia B3J 3C4
(902) 422-1701

Bankers' Trust Co.
630 Dorchester Boulevard West
Montréal, Québec H3B 1S6
(514) 876-2705

Bayshore Trust Co.
825 Eglington Avenue West, 5th Floor
Toronto, Ontario M5N 1E7
(416) 787-1787

Cabot Trust Co.
Suite 605, 1055 Wilson Avenue
Downsview, Ontario M3K 1Y9
(416) 633-4400

Canada Permanent Trust Co.
Canada Permanent Mortgage Corp.
320 Bay Street
Toronto, Ontario M5H 2P6
(416) 361-8131

Canada Trustco Mortgage Co.
Canada Trust Tower
275 Dundas Street
London, Ontario N6A 4S4
(519) 673-6209

Canadian Trust Co.
1 Place Ville Marie
Montréal, Québec H3B 4A8
(514) 397-7044

Central Trust Co.
5151 Terminal Road
Halifax, Nova Scotia B3J 3C8
(902) 425-7390

CIBC Mortgage Co.
Commerce Court Postal Station
Toronto, Ontario M5L 1A2
(416) 784-7391

Citizens Trust Co.
815 West Hastings Street
Vancouver, British Columbia V6C 1B4
(604) 682-7171

Colonial Trust Co.
10208 112 Street
Edmonton, Alberta T5K 1M4
(403) 425-1342

Columbia Trust Co.
625 Howe Street
Vancouver, British Columbia V6C 2T6
(604) 689-8033

Community Trust Co.
2299 Bloor Street West
Toronto, Ontario M6S 1P1
(416) 763-2291

Continental Trust Co.
145 King Street West
Toronto, Ontario M5H 2E2
(416) 860-3911

Co-operative Trust Co. of Canada
333 3rd Avenue North
Saskatoon, Saskatchewan S7K 2M2
(306) 244-1900

Counsel Trust Co.
19 Toronto Street
Toronto, Ontario M5C 2R1
(416) 365-3100

Crédit Foncier
612 St. Jacques Street
Montréal, Québec H3C 1E1
(514) 282-1880

Discovery Trust Co. of Canada
5909 West Boulevard
Vancouver, British Columbia V6M 3X1
(604) 263-2371

Dominion Trust Co.
81 Durham Street South
Sudbury, Ontario P3E 4S6
(705) 674-8311

Eaton Bay Trust Co.
595 Bay Street
Toronto, Ontario M5G 2C6
(416) 591-5222

Effort Trust Co.
242 Main Street East
Hamilton, Ontario L8N 1T5
(416) 528-8956

Evangeline Savings and Mortgage Co.
535 Albert Street
Windsor, Nova Scotia B0N 2T0
(902) 798-8326

Family Trust Corp.
8 Wellington Street West
Markham, Ontario L3P 1A2
(416) 294-1372

Fidelity Trust Co.
10506 Jasper Avenue
Edmonton, Alberta T5J 2W9
(403) 423-3474

Fiduciaries de la Cité et du District de
Montréal Limitée
1253 McGill College
Montréal, Québec H3B 2Z6
(514) 878-3351

Fiducie Canadienne Italienne
6995 Boulevard St-Laurent
Montréal, Québec H2S 3E1
(514) 270-4121

Fiducie du Québec
1 Complexe Desjardins, Tour Sud, C.P. 34
Montréal, Québec H5B 1E4
(514) 286-9441

Fiducie Pret et Revenu (Savings and
Investment Trust)
850 D'Youville
Québec City, Québec G1K 7P3
(418) 692-1221

Financial Trust Co.
2323 Yonge Street
Toronto, Ontario M4P 2C9
(416) 488-1333

First City Trust Co.
14th Floor, 777 Hornby Street
Vancouver, British Columbia V6Z 1S4
(604) 668-5777

Greymac Mortgage Corp.
4 Wellington Street East
Toronto, Ontario M5E 1C5
(416) 862-0111

Guaranty Trust Co. of Canada
366 Bay Street
Toronto, Ontario M5H 2W5
(416) 863-5000

Guardian Trust Co.
618 Rue St. Jacques
Montréal, Québec H3C 1E3
(514) 842-7161

Heritage Savings & Trust Co.
10162 100 Street
Edmonton, Alberta T5J 0P5
(403) 421-7771

HFC Trust Ltd.
150 Kent Street
Charlottetown, Prince Edward Island C1A 8C5
(902) 960-0665

Huronia Trust Co.
2 Mississaga Street East
Orilla, Ontario L3V 6H9
(705) 325-2328

Income Trust Co.
181 Main Street West
Hamilton, Ontario L8P 4S1
(416) 528-9811

Inland Trust & Savings Corp. Ltd.
1054 Portage Avenue
Winnipeg, Manitoba R3G 3M2
(204) 786-6016

Interior Trust Co.
Royal Trust Tower
Toronto Dominion Centre
Toronto, Ontario M5K 1K7
(416) 862-1095

International Trust Co.
Royal Bank Plaza, North Tower
Toronto, Ontario M5J 2J2
(416) 865-0515

Investors Group Trust Co. Ltd.
280 Broadway
Winnipeg, Manitoba R3C 3B6
(204) 943-0361

Mennonite Trust Ltd.
P.O. Box 40
Waldheim, Saskatchewan S0K 4R0
(306) 945-0361

Merchant Trust Co.
1809 Barrington Street
Halifax, Nova Scotia B3J 2T3
(902) 421-1966

Monarch Trust Co.
Suite 1005, 21 St. Clair Avenue East
Toronto, Ontario M4T 1L9
(416) 922-4545

Montréal Trust Co.
1 Place Ville Marie
Montréal, Québec H3B 3L6
(514) 367-7044

Morgan Trust Co. of Canada
Suite 900, 630 Dorchester Boulevard West
Montréal, Québec H3B 1S6
(514) 878-3861

Municipal Trust Co.
70 Collier Street
Barrie, Ontario L4M 4S9
(705) 726-7200

National Victoria & Grey Trust Co.
21 King Street East
Toronto, Ontario M5C 1B3
(416) 361-4222

North Canadian Trust Co.
Suite 104, 386 Broadway
Winnipeg, Manitoba R3C 3R6
(204) 944-8758

North West Trust Co.
7th floor, 10201 Jasper Avenue
Edmonton, Alberta T5J 3R3
(403) 420-6071

Nova Scotia Savings & Loan Co.
1645 Granville Street
Halifax, Nova Scotia B3J 2T3
(902) 421-1556

Pacific & Western Trust Corp.
242 22nd Street East
Saskatoon, Saskatchewan S7K 0E8
(306) 244-1868

Peace Hills Trust Co.
10232 112 Street
Edmonton, Alberta T5K 1M4
(403) 421-1606

Pioneer Trust Co.
P.O. Box 576
Regina, Saskatchewan S4P 3A3
(306) 569-2288

Premier Trust Co.
65 Yonge Street
Toronto, Ontario M5E 1J7
(416) 363-7043

Principal Savings & Trust Co.
10303 Jasper Avenue, 2900 Principal Plaza
Edmonton, Alberta T5J 3N6
(403) 421-2020

Provincial Trust Co.
106 Kent Street
Charlottetown, Prince Edward Island C1A 7L9
(902) 672-8170

Regent Trust Co.
877 Portage Avenue
Winnipeg, Manitoba R3G 0N8
(204) 783-8995

Regional Trust Co.
Suite 1400, 701 West Georgia Street
Pacific Centre
Vancouver, British Columbia V7Y 1B6
(604) 669-1250

Royal Trust Corp. of Canada
Toronto Dominion Centre
Toronto, Ontario M5W 1P9
(416) 867-2000

Saskatchewan Trust Co.
171 2nd Avenue South
Saskatoon, Saskatchewan S7K 1K6
(306) 244-8744

Seaway Trust Co.
Suite 2710, 145 King Street West
Toronto, Ontario M5H 1J8
(416) 364-5330

Security Trust Co.
Suite 205, 5300 Yonge Street
Willowdale, Ontario M2N 5R2
(416) 226-5313

Settlers Savings & Mortgage Co.
877 Portage Street
Winnipeg, Manitoba R3G 0N8
(204) 786-8508

Sherbrooke Trust
75 Wellington Nord
Sherbrooke, Québec J1H 5B5
(819) 563-4011

Societé Nationale de Fiducie
385 Sherbrooke Street East
Montréal, Québec H2X 1E5
(514) 844-2050

Standard Trust Co.
69 Yonge Street
Toronto, Ontario M5E 1K3
(416) 868-6900

Sterling Trust Corp.
Suite 500, 220 Bay Street
Toronto, Ontario M5J 2K8
(416) 364-7495

Trust General du Canada
1100 University Street
Montréal, Québec H3B 2G7
(514) 871-7100

Vanguard Trust of Canada Ltd.
Suite 5420, One First Canadian Place
Toronto, Ontario M5X 1A4
(416) 868-0234

Western Capital Trust Co.
980 One Bentall Centre, 505 Burrard Street
Vancouver, British Columbia V7X 1M4
(604) 689-8766

Yorkshire Trust Co.
1100 Melville Street
Vancouver, British Columbia V6E 4B6
(604) 685-3711

LIFE INSURANCE COMPANIES

The following is an alphabetical list of the headquarters addresses and telephone numbers of the 100 largest life insurance companies in the United States and Canada. The list is provided courtesy of A.M. Best Company of Oldwick, New Jersey 08858 (tel. 201 439-2200), which tracks the life insurance industry.

Life insurance companies are normally ranked in one of three ways: by admitted assets, by life insurance in force, or by total premium income. Although any of these rankings would include most of the same companies, this particular list is based on admitted assets. Such assets include all the assets a life insurance company has accumulated over the years, including investments in real estate, stocks, and bonds, based on the current market value of those assets. Because of the enormous size of these assets, insurance companies have become extremely important institutional investors. The other two methods of ranking these companies, by life insurance in force and by total premium income, show the amount of coverage insurance companies are providing and the dollar amount of their sales. These are also important figures to judge a company by, but they do not provide as direct an indication of a company's importance in the finance and investment markets.

The life insurance industry is characterized by a few giant firms with a high percentage of the industry's total assets and a large number of smaller companies. The top two firms, Prudential Insurance Company of America and Metropolitan Life Insurance Company, had assets in 1985 of $78 billion and $67 billion, respectively. Only the top 14 companies had assets of around $10 billion or more. The 100th largest company had a little more than $1 billion in assets.

The companies on this list represent two distinct types of insurance company. One is owned by stockholders, and its or its parent company's shares are traded on the New York or American stock exchange or over the counter. This type of company is in business to write life insurance policies, invest premiums, and the difference between investment income and insurance claims ultimately reaches shareholders as dividends or increases in shareholder's equity. The other type of company, called a mutual life insurance company (the word mutual usually is in the name), is owned by policyholders, who receive any profits the company may earn. Mutual companies have no outstanding stock traded on an exchange, since the company is owned solely by its policyholders.

As in other areas of the financial services industry, competition has been increasing among life insurers. The advent in the early 1980s of universal life insurance, which ties cash value buildup to money-market rates, put additional pressure on all insurers to make policies competitive. By the later 1980s, the life insurance industry had produced a panoply of products which allow policyholders a wide range of flexibility in paying premiums, building cash value, and buying insurance protection. In addition to traditional whole life and term policies, companies now offer universal life, variable life (where the policyholder chooses between stock, bond, and money-market investments), universal variable life, and a wide range of annuity and Individual Retirement Account products. Many insurers also offer financial planning services.

In addition to their role as insurers of lives, life insurance companies have become an important source of capital for world capital markets. Insurance companies are a major force in the stock market; the municipal, corporate, and government bond markets; in real estate (both as owners and lenders); and as providers of venture capital. Some insurance companies have expanded their offerings by acquiring brokerage and money management firms.

Aid Assoc. for Lutherans
4321 North Ballard Road
Appleton, Wisconsin 54919
(414) 734-5721

Aetna Life Insurance and Annuity Co.
151 Farmington Avenue
Hartford, Connecticut 06156
(203) 273-0123

Aetna Life Insurance Co.
151 Farmington Avenue
Hartford, Connecticut 06156
(203) 273-0123

Allstate Life Insurance Co.
Allstate Plaza
Northbrook, Illinois 60062
(312) 291-5000

American General Life & Accident Insurance
Co.
American General Center
8th and Union Street
Nashville, Tennessee 37250
(615) 749-1000

American National Insurance Co.
One Moody Plaza
Galveston, Texas 77550
(409) 763-4661

American United Life Insurance Co.
One American Square
Indianapolis, Indiana 46204
(317) 263-1877

Anchor National Life Insurance Co.
2201 East Camelback Road
Phoenix, Arizona 85016
(602) 955-0300

Bankers Life & Casualty Co.
4444 West Lawrence Avenue
Chicago, Illinois 60630
(312) 777-7000

Canada Life Assurance Co.
330 University Avenue
Toronto, Ontario CN M5G 1R8 Canada
(416) 597-1456

Capitol Life Insurance Co.
1600 Sherman Street
Denver, Colorado 80203
(303) 861-4065

Charter Security Life Insurance Co.
720 Fifth Avenue
New York, New York 10022
(212) 397-2350

Combined Insurance Co. of America
5050 North Broadway
Chicago, Illinois 60640
(312) 275-8000

Commonwealth Life Insurance Co.
Commonwealth Building
Broadway at Fourth Street
Louisville, Kentucky 40202
(502) 587-7371

Confederation Life Insurance Co.
280 Interstate North
Atlanta, Georgia 30348
(404) 953-5100

Connecticut General Life Insurance Co.
900 Cottage Grove Road
Bloomfield, Connecticut 06002
(203) 726-6000

Connecticut Mutual Life Insurance Co.
140 Garden Street
Hartford, Connecticut 06154
(203) 727-6500

Continental Assurance Co.
CNA Plaza
Chicago, Illinois 60685
(312) 822-5000

Country Life Insurance Co.
1701 Towanda Avenue
Bloomington, Illinois 61702
(309) 557-2111

Crown Life Insurance Co.
120 Bloor Street East
Toronto, Ontario M4W 1B8 Canada
(416) 928-4500

Equitable Life Assurance Society
  of the United States
787 Seventh Avenue
New York, New York 10019
(212) 554-1234

Equitable Life Insurance Co. of Iowa
604 Locust Street
Des Moines, Iowa 50306
(515) 245-6954

Equitable Variable Life Insurance Co.
420 Lexington Avenue
New York, New York 10017
(212) 551-9100

Excelsior Life Insurance Co.
145 King Street West
Toronto, Ontario M5H 3T7 Canada
(416) 864-8000

Executive Life Insurance Co.
9777 Wilshire Boulevard
Beverly Hills, California 90212
(213) 273-4203

Executive Life Insurance Co. of New York
390 North Broadway
Jericho, New York 11753
(516) 931-6400

First Colony Life Insurance Co.
700 Main Street
Lynchburg, Virginia 24504
(804) 845-0911

The Franklin Life Insurance Co.
Franklin Square
Springfield, Illinois 62713
(217) 528-2011

General American Life Insurance Co.
700 Market Street
St. Louis, Missouri 63101
(314) 231-1700

General Reassurance Corp.
Financial Centre
P.O. Box 10351
Stamford, Connecticut 06904
(203) 328-5000

Great American Life Insurance Co.
580 Walnut Street
Cincinnati, Ohio 45202
(513) 369-5000

Great-West Life Assurance Co.
100 Osborne Street North
Winnipeg, Manitoba R3C 3A5 Canada
(204) 946-1190

Guardian Life Insurance Co. of America
201 Park Avenue South
New York, New York 10003
(212) 598-8000

John Hancock Mutual Life Insurance Co.
Hancock Place
Boston, Massachusetts 02117
(617) 421-6000

Hartford Life Insurance Co.
Hartford Plaza
Hartford, Connecticut 06115
(203) 547-5000

Home Life Insurance Co.
253 Broadway
New York, New York 10007
(212) 306-2000

IDS Life Insurance Co.
IDS Tower
Minneapolis, Minnesota 55402
(612) 372-3510

Imperial Life Assurance Co. of Canada
95 St. Clair Avenue West
Toronto, Ontario M4V 1N7 Canada
(416) 926-2600

INA Life Insurance Co.
1600 Arch Street
Philadelphia, Pennsylvania 19103
(215) 241-4000

Independent Order of Foresters
789 Don Mills Road
Don Mills, Ontario M3C 1T9 Canada
(416) 429-3000

Industrial Life Insurance Co.
160 Eglinton Avenue East
Toronto, Ontario M4P 3B5 Canada
(416) 487-4749

Jefferson Standard Life Insurance Co.
101 North Elm Street
Greensboro, North Carolina 27420
(919) 378-2011

Kemper Investors Life Insurance Co.
120 South LaSalle Street
Chicago, Illinois 60603
(312) 781-1121

Keystone Provident Life Insurance Co.
99 High Street
Boston, Massachusetts 02110
(617) 338-3500

Knights of Columbus
One Columbus Plaza
New Haven, Connecticut 06507
(203) 772-2130

Liberty National Life Insurance Co.
2001 Third Avenue South
Birmingham, Alabama 35233
(205) 325-2722

Life Insurance Co. of Virginia
6610 West Broad Street
Richmond, Virginia 23230
(804) 281-6000

Lincoln National Life Insurance Co.
1300 South Clinton Street
Fort Wayne, Indiana 46802
(219) 427-2000

Lincoln National Pension Insurance Co.
1300 South Clinton Street
Fort Wayne, Indiana 46802
(219) 427-2000

London Life Insurance Co.
255 Dufferin Avenue
London, Ontario N6A 4K1 Canada
(519) 432-5281

Lutheran Brotherhood
625 Fourth Avenue South
Minneapolis, Minnesota 55415
(612) 340-7000

Manufacturers Life Insurance Co.
200 Bloor Street East
Toronto, Ontario M4W 1E5 Canada
(416) 928-4100

Manufacturers Life Insurance Co.
111 Westmount Road South
Waterloo, Ontario N2J 4C6 Canada
(519) 888-5111

Maritime Life Assurance Co.
2701 Dutch Village Road
Halifax, Nova Scotia B3J 2X5 Canada
(902) 453-4300

Massachusetts Mutual Life Insurance Co.
1295 State Street
Springfield, Massachusetts 01111
(413) 788-8411

Met Life Security & Insurance Co.
72 Eagle Rock Avenue
East Hanover, New Jersey 07936
(201) 515-1300

Metropolitan Insurance and Accident Co.
1 Madison Avenue
New York, New York 10010
(212) 298-2211

Metropolitan Life Insurance Co.
1 Madison Avenue
New York, New York 10010
(212) 578-2211

Minnesota Mutual Life Insurance Co.
400 North Robert Street
St. Paul, Minnesota 55101
(612) 298-3500

Mutual Benefit Life Insurance Co.
520 Broad Street
Newark, New Jersey 07101
(201) 481-8000

Mutual Life Assurance Co. of Canada
227 King Street South
Waterloo, Ontario N2J 4C5 Canada
(519) 888-2290

Mutual Life Insurance Co. of New York
1740 Broadway
New York, New York 10019
(212) 708-2000

Mutual of America Life Insurance Co.
666 Fifth Avenue
New York, New York 10103
(212) 399-1600

Mutual of Omaha Life Insurance Co.
Mutual of Omaha Plaza
Omaha, Nebraska 68175
(402) 342-7600

National Investors Pension Insurance
2nd and Broadway
Little Rock, Arkansas 72201
(501) 376-3261

National Home Life Insurance Co.
Liberty Park
Frazer, Pennsylvania 19355
(215) 648-5000

National Life Insurance Co.
National Life Drive
Montpelier, Vermont 05604
(802) 229-3333

Nationwide Life Insurance Co.
One Nationwide Plaza
Columbus, Ohio 43216
(614) 249-7111

New England Mutual Life Insurance Co.
501 Boylston Street
Boston, Massachusetts 02117
(617) 266-3700

New York Life Insurance Co.
51 Madison Avenue
New York, New York 10010
(212) 576-7000

New York Life Insurance & Annuity Corp.
51 Madison Avenue
New York, New York 10010
(212) 576-7000

North American Life Assurance Co.
5650 Yonge Street
North York, Ontario M2M 4GH Canada
(416) 229-4515

Northwestern Mutual Life Insurance Co.
720 East Wisconsin Avenue
Milwaukee, Wisconsin 53202
(414) 271-1444

Northwestern National Life Insurance Co.
20 Washington Avenue South
Minneapolis, Minnesota 55440
(612) 372-5432

Pacific Mutual Life Insurance Co.
700 Newport Center Drive
Newport Beach, California 92663
(714) 640-3011

Penn Mutual Life Insurance Co.
Independence Square
Philadelphia, Pennsylvania 19172
(215) 625-5000

Phoenix Mutual Life Insurance Co.
One American Row
Hartford, Connecticut 06115
(203) 275-5000

Provident Life & Accident Insurance Co.
Fountain Square
Chattanooga, Tennessee 37402
(615) 755-1011

Provident Mutual Life Insurance Co.
of Philadelphia
1600 Market Street
Philadelphia, Pennsylvania 19103
(215) 636-5000

Provident National Life Assurance Co.
One Maryland Farms Boulevard
Brentwood, Tennessee 37027
(615) 373-0044

Prudential Insurance Co. of America
745 Broad Street
Newark, New Jersey 07101
(201) 877-6000

Southern Farm Bureau Life Insurance Co.
1401 Livingston Lane
Jackson, Mississippi 39213
(601) 981-7422

Southwestern Life Insurance Co.
Southwestern Life Building
Dallas, Texas 75201
(214) 954-7111

State Farm Life Insurance Co.
112 East Washington Street
Bloomington, Illinois 61701
(309) 766-2311

State Mutual Life Assurance Co. of America
440 Lincoln Street
Worcester, Massachusetts 01605
(617) 852-1000

Sun Life Assurance Co. of Canada
P.O. Box 4150, Station A
Toronto, Ontario M5W 2C9 Canada
(416) 979-9966

Sun Life Insurance Co. of America
Sun Life Building, Charles Center
Baltimore, Maryland 21201
(301) 727-0400

Teachers Insurance & Annuity Assoc.
of America
730 Third Avenue
New York, New York 10017
(212) 490-9000

Transamerica Life Insurance & Annuity Co.
1149 South Broadway
Los Angeles, California 90015
(213) 742-2111

Transamerica Occidental Life Insurance Co.
1150 South Olive Street
Los Angeles, California 90015
(213) 742-2111

Travelers Insurance Co.
One Tower Square
Hartford, Connecticut 06115
(203) 277-0111

The Travelers Life & Annuity Co.
One Tower Square
Hartford, Connecticut 06115
(203) 277-0111

Union Central Life Insurance Co.
Mill and Waycross Roads
Cincinnati, Ohio 45201
(513) 595-2200

Union Labor Life Insurance Co.
111 Massachusetts Avenue, N.W.
Washington, D.C. 20001
(202) 682-0900

Union Mutual Life Insurance Co.
2211 Congress Street
Portland, Maine 04122
(207) 780-2211

United Insurance Co. of America
One East Wacker Drive
Chicago, Illinois 60601
(312) 266-3500

United of Omaha Life Insurance Co.
Mutual of Omaha Plaza
Omaha, Nebraska 68175
(402) 342-7600

Variable Annuity Life Insurance Co.
2929 Allen Parkway
Houston, Texas 77019
(713) 526-5251

Washington National Insurance Co.
1630 Chicago Avenue
Evanston, Illinois 60201
(312) 570-5500

Western & Southern Life Insurance Co.
400 Broadway
Cincinnati, Ohio 45202
(513) 629-1800

BROKERAGE FIRMS

The following is a list of the top 100 full-service and the top 10 discount brokerage firms in the United States and Canada. Traditionally, brokers sold mostly stocks and bonds to their customers, who were primarily persons of substantial means. Today, these firms allow customers to buy and sell stocks, bonds, commodities, options, mutual funds, bank certificates of deposit, limited partnerships, and many other financial products. Brokers also offer asset management accounts, which combine holdings of assets like stocks and bonds with a money-market fund that provides checkwriting and credit card features. Most brokers in addition offer individualized financial planning services. As a result of this wide range of products, brokers today have a much more diverse clientele, ranging from young persons just starting to invest to wealthy retired people who are experienced investors.

On May 1, 1975, known as May Day in the brokerage industry, the era of fixed brokerage commissions ended. This development brought much more competition within the industry and ushered in a new breed of broker—the discounter. These brokers specialize in executing buy and sell orders for stocks, bonds, and options. As a rule, they charge commissions far lower than full-service brokers. Discounters do not give advice about which securities to buy or sell, however, so investors who use them generally are more experienced and knowledgeable. Some discount brokers were acquired in the early 1980s by commercial banks, who under the Glass-Steagall Act of 1933 are not allowed to act as full-service brokers. Banks were allowed to make such acquisitions because discount brokers do not give advice or underwrite securities. Full-service firms offer far more guidance on what investments are appropriate for each client. For this guidance, however, clients must pay significantly higher charges.

Within the full-service brokerage firm category, two varieties exist. The largest firms are known as wire houses, because they have a national network of offices linked by advanced communications equipment. National wire houses also tend to have an important presence overseas. In contrast, regional brokerage firms concentrate on serving customers in a particular area of the country. Such firms typically do not offer as wide an array of financial products, although they usually provide all the basics. Regional firms tend to concentrate on finding investment opportunities not yet discovered by large national firms.

In addition to providing services to individuals, brokers who also engage in investment banking play an important role in raising capital for federal, state, and local governments and for corporations. Such firms underwrite new issues of debt securities for governments and equity and debt issues for corporations and distribute them to both institutional and individual investors. In addition, brokers act as advisers to corporations involved in merger and acquisition activity and other areas of corporate finance. Increasingly, brokerage firms are expanding their operations internationally, to facilitate trading of foreign currencies and foreign debt and equity securities.

This alphabetical list contains the top 100 brokerage firms as measured by amount of capital. Capital is crucial to a brokerage firm because it must constantly be put at risk in underwriting and trading securities. The two largest firms on the list, Merrill Lynch, Pierce, Fenner & Smith Inc. and Salomon Brothers Inc., had about $2.6 billion and $2.3 billion in capital, respectively, in 1986. The next six largest firms, Shearson Lehman Brothers Inc., Dean Witter Financial Services, Prudential Bache Securities Inc., Goldman, Sachs & Co., E.F. Hutton Group, Inc., and First Boston Inc., had capital of more than $1 billion. All other brokerage firms listed here had less than $1 billion of capital. The smallest of the 100 firms on the list had $21.5 million in capital.

Most of these brokerage firms were originally formed as partnerships, but in recent years many incorporated and a number offered shares of stock in their companies to the public. Such public offerings can be the best way for a brokerage firm to raise the additional capital it needs to be competitive.

Following the list of 100 full-service firms is an alphabetical list of the top 10 discount brokers, also ranked by capital. These lists are provided courtesy of the brokerage industry's trade association, the Securities Industry Association [120 Broadway, New York, New York 10005 (212) 608-1500].

Full-Service Brokerage Firms

The Advest Group, Inc.
Six Central Row
Hartford, Connecticut 06103
(203) 525-1421

Alex. Brown & Sons, Inc.
135 East Baltimore Street
Baltimore, Maryland 21202
(301) 727-1700

Allen & Company Inc.
711 Fifth Avenue
New York, New York 10022
(212) 832-8000

Robert W. Baird & Co., Inc.
777 East Wisconsin Avenue
Milwaukee, Wisconsin 53202
(414) 765-3500

Bateman Eichler, Hill Richards Inc.
700 South Flower Street
Los Angeles, California 90017
(213) 625-3545

Bear, Stearns & Co.
55 Water Street
New York, New York 10041
(212) 952-5000

Sanford C. Bernstein & Co., Inc.
767 Fifth Avenue
New York, New York 10153
(212) 486-5800

D.H. Blair & Co., Inc.
44 Wall Street
New York, New York 10005
(212) 968-2000

Arnhold and S. Bleichroeder, Inc.
45 Broadway
New York, New York 10006
(212) 943-9200

Blunt Ellis & Loewi Inc.
225 East Mason Street
Milwaukee, Wisconsin 53202
(414) 347-3400

Boettcher & Co., Inc.
828 Seventeenth Street
Denver, Colorado 80202
(303) 628-8000

J.C. Bradford & Co.
170 Fourth Avenue North
Nashville, Tennessee 37219
(615) 748-9000

Brown Brothers Harriman & Co.
59 Wall Street
New York, New York 10005
(212) 483-1818

Butcher & Singer, Inc.
211 South Broad Street
Philadelphia, Pennsylvania 19107
(215) 985-5000

Clayton Brown & Associates, Inc.
300 West Washington Street
Chicago, Illinois 60606
(312) 641-3300

Cowen & Co.
One Battery Park Plaza
New York, New York 10004
(212) 483-0700

Crowell, Weedon and Co.
One Wilshire Building
Los Angeles, California 90017
(213) 620-1850

Dain Bosworth Inc.
100 Dain Tower
Minneapolis, Minnesota 55402
(612) 371-2711

Daiwa Securities America, Inc.
One Liberty Plaza
New York, New York 10006
(212) 732-6600

Dean Witter Financial Services Inc.
130 Liberty Street
New York, New York 10006
(212) 524-2222

Deutsche Bank Capital Corp.
40 Wall Street
New York, New York 10005
(212) 612-0600

Dillon Read & Co. Inc.
535 Madison Avenue
New York, New York 10022
(212) 906-7000

Dominion Securities Pitfield Ltd.
Commerce Court South
Toronto, Ontario M5L 1A7 Canada
(416) 864-4000

Donaldson, Lufkin and Jenrette Inc.
140 Broadway
New York, New York 10005
(212) 504-3000

Drexel Burnham Lambert Group Inc.
60 Broad Street
New York, New York 10004
(212) 480-6000

Eaton Vance Corp.
24 Federal Street
Boston, Massachusetts 02110
(617) 482-8260

Edward D. Jones & Co.
201 Progress Parkway
St. Louis, Missouri 63043
(314) 851-2000

A.G. Edwards & Sons, Inc.
One North Jefferson
St. Louis, Missouri 63103
(314) 289-3000

Eppler, Guerin & Turner, Inc.
2001 Bryan Tower
Dallas, Texas 75201
(214) 880-9000

First Boston Inc.
Park Avenue Plaza
New York, New York 10055
(212) 909-2000

First Manhattan Co.
437 Madison Avenue
New York, New York 10022
(212) 832-4400

Albert Fried & Co.
40 Exchange Place
New York, New York 10005
(212) 422-7282

Furman Selz Mager Dietz & Birney Inc.
230 Park Avenue
New York, New York 10169
(212) 309-8200

Glickenhaus & Co.
6 East 43rd Street
New York, New York 10017
(212) 953-7800

Goldman Sachs & Co.
85 Broad Street
New York, New York 10004
(212) 902-1000

Gruntal & Co. Inc.
14 Wall Street
New York, New York 10005
(212) 267-8800

Hambrecht & Quist Inc.
235 Montgomery Street
San Francisco, California 94104
(415) 576-3300

Henderson Brothers, Inc.
One Exchange Plaza
New York, New York 10006
(212) 809-1000

Herzog Heine Geduld, Inc.
26 Broadway
New York, New York 10004
(212) 908-4000

E.F. Hutton Group, Inc.
31 West 52nd Street
New York, New York 10019
(212) 969-5300

Integrated Resources Equity Corp.
733 Third Avenue
New York, New York 10017
(212) 551-5000

Interstate Securities Corp.
2700 NCNB Plaza
101 South Tryon Street
Charlotte, North Carolina 28280
(704) 379-9000

Janney Montgomery Scott Inc.
5 Penn Center Plaza
Philadelphia, Pennsylvania 19103
(215) 665-6000

Jeffries & Co., Inc.
445 South Figueroa Street
Los Angeles, California 90071
(213) 624-3333

Keefe, Bruyette & Woods, Inc.
Suite 8566, Two World Trade Center
New York, New York 10048
(212) 349-4321

Kemper Financial Services, Inc.
120 South LaSalle Street
Chicago, Illinois 60603
(312) 781-1121

Kidder Peabody & Co., Inc.
10 Hanover Square
New York, New York 10005
(212) 510-3000

Lazard Freres & Co.
One Rockefeller Plaza
New York, New York 10020
(212) 489-6600

Legg Mason Wood Walker Inc.
7 East Redwood Street
Baltimore, Maryland 21202
(301) 539-3400

Levesque, Beaubien Inc.
360 St. Jacques Street
Montréal, Québec H2Y 1P7 Canada
(514) 879-2222

Mabon, Nugent & Co.
115 Broadway
New York, New York 10006
(212) 732-2820

Bernard L. Madoff
110 Wall Street
New York, New York 10005
(212) 825-3910

McDonald & Co. Securities, Inc.
2100 The Society Building
Cleveland, Ohio 44114
(216) 443-2300

Merrill Lynch, Pierce, Fenner
& Smith Inc.
One Liberty Plaza
New York, New York 10080
(212) 637-7455

MKI Securities Corp.
61 Broadway
New York, New York 10006
(212) 425-2288

Montgomery Securities
600 Montgomery Street
San Francisco, California 94111
(415) 627-2000

Morgan Keegan & Company, Inc.
50 Front Street
Memphis, Tennessee 38103
(901) 524-4100

Morgan Stanley & Co. Inc.
1251 Avenue of the Americas
New York, New York 10020
(212) 703-4000

Moseley Holding Corp.
60 State Street
Boston, Massachusetts 02109
(617) 367-2400

Murphey, Marseilles Smith & Nammack
30 Broad Street
New York, New York 10004
(212) 425-2210

Nesbitt Thomson Bongard Inc.
Sun Life Tower, Sun Life Center
Toronto, Ontario M5H 3W2 Canada
(416) 486-3600

Neuberger & Berman
522 Fifth Avenue
New York, New York 10036
(212) 730-7370

The Nikko Securities Co. International, Inc.
140 Broadway
New York, New York 10005
(212) 747-9800

Nomura Securities International
180 Maiden Lane
New York, New York 10038
(212) 208-9300

John Nuveen and Co. Inc.
333 West Wacker Drive
Chicago, Illinois 60606
(312) 917-7700

The Ohio Co.
155 East Broad Street
Columbus, Ohio 43215
(614) 464-6811

Oppenheimer & Co., Inc.
World Financial Center
New York, New York 10281
(212) 667-7000

Paine Webber Inc.
1285 Avenue of the Americas
New York, New York 10019
(212) 713-2000

Piper Jaffray Inc.
Piper Jaffray Tower
222 South 9th Street
Minneapolis, Minnesota 55440
(612) 342-6000

Prescott, Ball and Turben, Inc.
1331 Euclid Avenue
Cleveland, Ohio 44115
(216) 574-7300

Prudential-Bache Securities Inc.
One Seaport Plaza
199 Water Street
New York, New York 10292
(212) 214-1000

Rauscher Pierce Refsnes, Inc.
2500 North Tower
Plaza of the Americas Building
Dallas, Texas 75201
(214) 978-0111

Raymond James & Associates, Inc.
1400 66th Street, North
St. Petersburg, Florida 33733
(813) 381-3800

The Robinson-Humphrey Co., Inc.
Atlanta Financial Center
3333 Peachtree Road, N.E.
Atlanta, Georgia 30326
(404) 266-6000

L.F. Rothschild, Unterberg, Towbin
55 Water Street
New York, New York 10041
(212) 412-1000

Ryan, Beck & Co.
80 Main Street
West Orange, New Jersey 07052
(201) 325-3000

Salomon Brothers Inc.
One New York Plaza
New York, New York 10004
(212) 747-7000

M.A. Schapiro & Co., Inc.
One Chase Manhattan Plaza
New York, New York 10005
(212) 425-6600

Securities Settlement Corp.
One Whitehall Street
New York, New York 10004
(212) 709-8000

Shearson Lehman Brothers Inc.
World Financial Center
New York, New York 10285
(212) 298-2000

Smith Barney, Harris Upham & Co., Inc.
1345 Avenue of the Americas
New York, New York 10105
(212) 698-6000

Smith New Court Inc.
61 Broadway
New York, New York 10006
(212) 363-3800

Spear Leeds & Kellogg
115 Broadway
New York, New York 10006
(212) 587-8800

Stephens Inc.
114 East Capitol Avenue
Little Rock, Arkansas 72203
(501) 374-4361

Stern Brothers & Co.
1100 Main Street
2200 City Center Square
Kansas City, Missouri 64199
(816) 471-6460

Stifel, Nicolaus & Co., Inc.
500 North Broadway
St. Louis, Missouri 63102
(314) 342-2000

Stone & Youngberg
One California Street
San Francisco, California 94111
(415) 981-1314

Thomson McKinnon Inc.
One New York Plaza
New York, New York 10004
(212) 482-7000

Tucker, Anthony & R.L. Day, Inc.
120 Broadway
New York, New York 10271
(212) 618-7400

UBS Securities, Inc.
299 Park Avenue
New York, New York 10171
(212) 715-3800

Van Kampen Merritt Inc.
1901 North Naper Boulevard
Naperville, Illinois 60566
(312) 369-8880

Wedbush, Noble, Cooke, Inc.
615 South Flower Street
Los Angeles, California 90017
(213) 620-1750

Weiss, Peck & Greer
One New York Plaza
New York, New York 10004
(212) 908-9500

William E. Pollock & Co., Inc.
160 Water Street
New York, New York 10038
(212) 908-5800

Wertheim & Co., Inc.
200 Park Avenue
New York, New York 10166
(212) 578-0200

Wheat, First Securities, Inc.
707 East Main Street
Richmond, Virginia 23211
(804) 649-2311

Wood Gundy Inc.
Toronto Dominion Centre
Toronto, Ontario M5K 1M7 Canada
(416) 869-8100

Yamaichi International (America), Inc.
Two World Trade Center, Suite 9650
New York, New York 10048
(212) 912-6400

The Ziegler Co., Inc.
215 North Main Street
West Bend, Wisconsin 53095
(414) 334-5521

Discount Brokerage Firms

Brown and Company Securities Corp.
20 Winthrop Square
Boston, Massachusetts 02109
(800) 225-6707
(617) 357-4410

Discount Brokerage Corp. of America
67 Wall Street
New York, New York 10005
(800) 328-1268
(212) 806-2888

Fidelity Brokerage Services Inc.
161 Devonshire Street
Boston, Massachusetts 02110
(800) 544-6666
(617) 570-7000

Ovest Financial Services Inc.
90 Broad Street
New York, New York 10004
(800) 255-0700
(212) 668-0600

Pacific Brokerage Services
5757 Wilshire Boulevard
Beverly Hills, California 90211
(800) 421-8395
(213) 939-1100

Quick & Reilly, Inc.
120 Wall Street
New York, New York 10005
(800) 221-5220
(212) 943-8686

Rose & Co. Investment Brokers Inc.
One Financial Place
Chicago, Illinois 60605
(800) 621-3700
(312) 663-8300

Charles Schwab and Co.
101 Montgomery Street
San Francisco, California 94104
(415) 398-1000

Muriel Siebert and Co.
444 Madison Avenue
New York, New York 10022
(800) 872-0711
(212) 644-2400

Spear Securities
626 Wilshire Boulevard
Los Angeles, California 90017
(800) 346-5522
(213) 627-8422

LIMITED PARTNERSHIP SPONSORS

The following is a list of major sponsors of publicly available limited partnerships. All the sponsors act as general partner in managing the assets of the partnership for the benefit of the limited partners. In return for management services, general partners receive management fees and often a percentage of profits generated by partnership investments.

In recent years, there has been a proliferation of different types of limited partnerships. These programs, which formerly were marketed only to wealthy investors, are now sold to investors of more modest means, mostly through brokerage firms and financial planners.

Some partnerships are designed to provide current income—often at least partially sheltered from taxation. Such income is derived from interest on loans the partnership has made, from rents that tenants pay to occupy real estate owned by the partnership, from sales of oil and gas that have been extracted by the partnership, or from other sources.

Other partnerships are designed to produce long-term capital gains for limited These plans pay out little, if any, current income to participants. Capital gains can be achieved through purchases and resale at a higher price of real estate, oil and gas properties, equipment like computers or airplanes, cable television systems, or other investments. The skill of the general partner in buying undervalued properties and increasing their worth over time is key in realizing such capital gains.

Some partnerships strive not only for income or capital gains, but also for tax savings for the limited partners. Tax benefits from depreciation, tax credits, depletion allowances, intangible drilling costs, operating losses or other tax savings under current law, pass directly through to limited partners in direct proportion to their holdings in the partnership. Before 1987, these benefits could be applied without limit to taxable earnings from salaries, investments, or any other source of income. The Tax Reform Act of 1986 severely curtailed the use of limited partnerships as tax shelters by ruling that the applicability of such passive source deductions would, over a five-year transaction period, be limited to income from other passive sources. For purposes of the alternative minimum tax, the new law was even tougher on limited partnerships: Net passive losses were made a tax preference item at 100% of value effective in 1987.

All units of limited partnerships must be purchased through qualified broker/dealers. These dealers have the responsibility of doing a due diligence investigation of the partnership's management, objectives, and track record. Once the deal has cleared this process, brokers are allowed to sell units to customers who meet certain suitability requirements. Usually, a certain level of yearly income and net worth is called for, in addition to the assurance that the investor is sophisticated enough to understand the potential risks of the investment. Investors must be given the partnership's prospectus before they invest. Each unit of a partnership typically costs $1000, and the minimum purchase is from 1 to 5 units. For Individual Retirement Accounts, the minimum is usually 2 units, or $2000. Out of this amount, broker/dealers usually charge a sales commission of at least 5%, and sometimes as much as 10%, of the principal invested. In general, partnership shares are not actively traded, though general partners usually will attempt to buy back partnership interests or place the units with another person if an existing partner wants to liquidate a position. In a few cases, partnership units are listed on the New York or American stock exchanges or traded over the counter.

The listing that follows is divided into the nine main types of limited partnerships. These are Agriculture/Livestock, Cable Television, Commodities and Financial Futures, Equipment Leasing, Film, Master Limited Partnerships, Oil and Gas, Real Estate, and Research and Development. The general partners in each category are the ones with the largest sales to the public in their speciality. They are listed alphabetically, along with their addresses and telephone numbers.

This list and the 1985 sales figures are courtesy of Robert Stanger & Company, a firm which tracks the limited partnership industry. The company publishes an annual *Partnership Sponsor Directory,* available from Stanger at 1129 Broad Street, Shrewsbury, New Jersey 07701 [(201) 389-3600 or (800) 631-2291].

Agriculture/Livestock

Agriculture/Livestock partnerships invest in a wide variety of agricultural properties that pass income and tax benefits through to the limited partners. These programs may involve growing grain or fruits and vegetables or producing lumber. Other partnerships involve raising livestock and selling the cattle for slaughter. The success or failure of the partnership depends on the management of the farm as well as the price the partnership gets for its products. Higher returns in general result when prices are high and rising than when prices are low and falling.

The following partnerships all had at least $5 million in sales during 1985.

First Winthrop Corp.
260 Franklin Street
Boston, Massachusetts 02110
(617) 439-4200

Granada Management Corp.
10900 Richmond
Houston, Texas 77242
(713) 977-7000

IP Forest Resources Co.
77 West 45th Street
New York, New York 10036
(212) 536-7856

Lana Lobell Farms Income, Inc.
Rattlesnake Bridge Road
Bedminster, New Jersey 07921
(201) 534-6161

Marley Orchards Corp.
Cowiche City Street
Cowiche, Washington 98923
(509) 678-4123

Rayonier Forest Resources Co.
1177 Summer Street
Stamford, Connecticut 06904
(203) 348-7000

Cable Television

These partnerships build or buy cable television systems, upgrade their services in an attempt to increase subscriptions, and sell the systems in five to ten years. Limited partners receive capital gains resulting from the sale of the systems as well as any tax benefits that may flow from the partnership's investment in the business. These partnerships typically provide little, if any, current income to partners, since the revenue from operations is generally reinvested in the business.

The following partnerships all had at least $1 million in sales in 1985.

Enstar Communications Corp.
Suite 300, 6100 Lake Forest Drive
Atlanta, Georgia 30328
(404) 252-0061
(800) 241-1005

Integrated Resources
666 Third Avenue
New York, New York 10017
(800) 223-1424

Jones Intercable, Inc.
5275 DTC Parkway
Englewood, Colorado 80111
(800) 572-6520

U.S.A.T.V. Co.
1016 Northwest 82nd Street
Oklahoma City, Oklahoma 73114
(405) 848-0733

Northland Communications Corp.
3500 One Union Square Building
Seattle, Washington 98101
(206) 621-1351

Commodities and Financial Futures

The following partnerships hire money managers who invest in the commodities and financial futures markets for capital gains. These markets are very volatile and are difficult for individuals to play on their own. By pooling resources with many other investors, partnerships allow the small investor to hire professional advisors who follow the markets closely and make timely investment decisions. Each partnership usually will invest in many commodities and financial futures markets simultaneously so that losses in one market can be offset by profits in another. These partnerships are designed to achieve capital gains, not income. With a few profitable trades, the returns to partners can be quite substantial—average annual returns of 20% or more are not uncommon. Limited partners are allowed to take money out of the partnership at specified intervals—usually once or twice a year. The investment advisor will not normally put all the partnership's assets at risk in the markets, so that a cushion remains if the futures positions result in losses. If losses are severe, a partnership may be dissolved, and the remaining capital returned to limited partners.

The partnerships listed here all had sales of at least $1 million in 1985.

Collins Financial Services, Inc.
Suite 1910A, 141 West Jackson Boulevard
Chicago, Illinois 60604
(312) 341-7600
(800) 621-5419

Gruntal Futures Management Corp.
14th Floor, 14 Wall Street
New York, New York 10005
(212) 267-8800

Hayden Commodities Corp.
17 Battery Plaza
New York, New York 10004
(212) 623-9647

Heinold Asset Management, Inc.
250 South Wacker Drive
Chicago, Illinois 60606
(312) 648-8000

Morgan Management Co.
800 West First Street
Los Angeles, California 90012

North American Investment Inc.
800 Connecticut Avenue
East Hartford, Connecticut 06108
(800) 243-4322

Professional Advisor Associates, Inc.
968 Princeton S.E.
Grand Rapids, Michigan 49506
(616) 458-1391

Thomson McKinnon
One New York Plaza
New York, New York 10004
(212) 482-7000

Virginia Futures Management Corp.
Suite 1717A, 141 West Jackson Boulevard
Chicago, Illinois 60604
(312) 922-1717

Equipment Leasing

Equipment Leasing partnerships specialize in buying a wide range of equipment and leasing it to users. For example, one of these partnerships might buy computers and lease them to a company preferring to rent rather than buy. The rental income from the computers is passed through to the limited partners as are all tax benefits, such as depreciation on the equipment. When the lease expires, the partnership either re-leases the computers or sells them and distributes the proceeds to the limited partners. In addition to leasing computer equipment, such partnerships may also lease transportation equipment such as airplanes and railroad cars.

The general partners listed here all had at least $5 million in sales in 1985.

AFG Leasing Associates
Exchange Place
Boston, Massachusetts 02109
(617) 542-1200

Dean Witter Reynolds
130 Liberty Street
New York, New York 10006
(212) 524-5115

Equitec Financial Group
7677 Oakport Street
Oakland, California 94614
(415) 430-9900

Fidelity Leasing Associates General
250 King of Prussia Road
Radnor, Pennsylvania 19087
(215) 964-7008

Finalco Group
1400-66th Street North
St. Petersburg, Florida 33710
(813) 345-3199
(800) 237-4240

Integrated Resources
666 Third Avenue
New York, New York 10017
(800) 223-1424

Leasetec Corp.
Suite 200, 1440 Maria Lane
Walnut Creek, California 94596
(415) 938-3443

Phoenix Leasing, Inc.
2401 Kerner Boulevard
San Rafael, California 94901
(415) 485-4600

PLM Financial Services Inc.
655 Montgomery Street
San Francisco, California 94111
(800) 227-0830
(800) 622-0809

Polaris Aircraft Leasing Corp.
Third Floor, 600 Montgomery Street
San Francisco, California 94111
(415) 362-0333
(800) 227-3530

RJ Leasing, Inc.
1400 16th Street North
St. Petersburg, Florida 33710
(813) 345-3199
(800) 237-4240

Thomson McKinnon
49th floor, 1 New York Plaza
New York, New York 10004
(212) 482-7205

Wellesley Leasing Partnership
600 Atlantic Avenue
Boston, Massachusetts 02210
(617) 722-6020

Film

Film partnerships invest in the producton and distribution of motion pictures. Partners help to finance the production costs of a portfolio of films and receive royalties when the films are released to the public in theaters, on cable television, on videocassette, or otherwise. The success of the partnership, of course, depends on the commercial success of the films that are financed. Limited partners usually receive no income in the start-up phase of the partnership, but receive distributions once a film starts to generate revenues. A certain amount of this income is sheltered by the tax benefits generated by the film production.

The partnerships listed here had at least $1 million in sales in 1985.

Silver Screen Management Inc.
Suite 1100, 595 Madison Avenue
New York, New York 10022
(212) 310-1500

Balcor/American Express Co.
Balcor Plaza, 4849 Golf Road
Skokie, Illinois 60077
(312) 677-2900

Delphi Financial Services Corp.
711 Third Avenue
New York, New York 10017
(212) 986-1921

Master Limited Partnerships

The following is a list of limited partnerships composed of corporate assets, primarily oil and gas reserves, which have been spun off to shareholders and are now traded separately on the New York or American stock exchanges or over the counter. Partnership holders in these companies receive the flow-through of all benefits, including income from the sale of oil and gas and tax benefits. Like real estate investment trusts, master limited partnerships are not taxed at the corporate level. Holders of units must pay taxes on all income received that is not sheltered by tax benefits, however. MLPs usually do not explore for new oil and gas reserves but produce from existing proven reserves. Some MLPs have also been formed to harvest and sell timber.

Apache Corp.
730 2nd Avenue South
Minneapolis, Minnesota 55402
(612) 347-8884
(800) 328-7187

Belden & Blake Oil Production, Inc.
7555 Freedom Avenue
North Canton, Ohio 44720
(216) 499-1660

Diamond Shamrock Exploration Co.
2001 Ross Avenue
Dallas, Texas 75201
(214) 979-5000

Enserch Corp.
Enserch Center, 300 South St. Paul Street
Dallas, Texas 75201
(214) 670-2204

Freeport-McMoran, Inc.
200 Park Avenue
New York, New York 10166
(212) 578-9200

Natural Resource Management
San Jacinto Tower, 2121 San Jacinto Street
Dallas, Texas 75201
(214) 742-9751
(800) 527-1461

Rayonier Forest Resources Corp.
1177 Summer Street
Stamford, Connecticut 06904
(203) 348-7000

Snyder Oil Co.
Suite 1500, 1360 Post Oak Boulevard
Houston, Texas 77056
(713) 963-9188

Sun Exploration & Production Co.
4 North Park, 5656 Blackwell
Dallas, Texas 75231
(214) 890-6000

Transco Exploration Co.
Transco Tower, 2800 Post Oak Boulevard
Houston, Texas 77251
(713) 439-2000

Union Exploration Partnership
1201 West Fifth Street
Los Angeles, California 90017
(213) 977-7600

Oil and Gas

Oil and Gas limited partnerships are involved in the exploration, drilling, and production of oil and gas. The riskiest and potentially most rewarding partnerships do exploratory drilling to find oil and gas reserves. If the driller is successful, revenues from the sale of oil and gas flow through to limited partners, along with tax benefits such as the oil depletion allowance and depreciation on drilling equipment.

More conservative programs either drill where oil and gas reserves are proven or just pump oil and gas from wells that have already been successfully drilled. The success or failure of any oil and gas limited partnership depends not only on finding and pumping petroleum and/or natural gas, however. The price of oil and gas is also a crucial determinant of success. In general, the programs offer higher returns to limited partners when oil and gas prices are high and rising than when prices are low and falling.

The general partners listed here had at least $5 million in sales in 1985.

Angeles/Quinoco Securities, Inc.
10301 West Pico Boulevard
Los Angeles, California 90064
(213) 277-4900
(800) 421-4374

Apache Corp.
730 2nd Avenue South
Minneapolis, Minnesota 55402
(612) 347-8884
(800) 328-7187

Belden & Blake Oil Production, Inc.
7555 Freedom Avenue
North Canton, Ohio 44720
(216) 499-1660

Bogert Oil Co.
Suite 901N, The Oil Center
2601 Northeast Expressway
Oklahoma City, Oklahoma 73112
(405) 848-5808

Clinton Oil Co.
4770 Indianola Avenue
Columbus, Ohio 43214
(614) 888-9588

Coastal Corp.
9 Greenway Plaza
Houston, Texas 77046
(713) 877-6734
(800) 231-3829

Damson Corp.
366 Madison Avenue
New York, New York 10017
(212) 503-8500

Dyco Petroleum Corp.
1100 Shelard Tower
Minneapolis, Minnesota 55426
(612) 545-2828

Egolf Co., The
Suite 1410, 50 Penn Place
Oklahoma City, Oklahoma 73118
(405) 840-3293

Enex Resources Corp.
Suite 212, 2 Kingwood Plaza
Kingwood, Texas 77339
(713) 358-8401
(800) 231-0444

Hawkins Oil and Gas, Inc.
Suite 800, 400 South Boston
Tulsa, Oklahoma 74103
(918) 585-3121

HCW, Inc.
101 Summer Street
Boston, Massachusetts 02110
(617) 542-2880

May Petroleum, Inc.
800 One Lincoln Center
Dallas, Texas 75240
(214) 934-9600
(800) 527-5958

Merrico Resources, Inc.
1000 Energy Center
Ardmore, Oklahoma 73402
(405) 226-6700
(800) 654-4597

Merrill Lynch
1 Liberty Plaza
New York, New York 10005
(212) 637-7455

Natural Resource Management Corp.
2121 San Jacinto Street
Dallas, Texas 75201
(214) 742-9751
(800) 527-1461

Paine Webber
1285 Avenue of the Americas
New York, New York 10020
(212) 730-5826

Parker & Parsley Petroleum Co.
P.O. Box 3178
Midland, Texas 79702
(915) 683-4768
(800) 831-3332

Pioneer Western Energy Corp.
Suite 800, 600 Cleveland Street
Clearwater, Florida 33518
(813) 446-3333
(800) 237-9783

Prudential-Bache Securities
100 Gold Street
New York, New York 10292
(212) 791-1000

Red Eagle Exploration Co.
Suite 1700, 1601 Northwest Expressway
Oklahoma City, Oklahoma 73156
(405) 755-2023

Samson Properties, Inc.
Swanson Plaza, 2 West 2nd Street
Tulsa, Oklahoma 94103
(918) 583-1791
(800) 331-2618

Snyder Exploration Co.
Suite 1500, 1360 Post Oak Boulevard
Houston, Texas 77056
(713) 963-9188

Sterling Drilling and Production Co.
150 Grand Street
White Plains, New York 10601
(914) 684-5830

Stone Petroleum Corp.
P.O. Box 58207
Lafayette, Louisiana 70505
(318) 237-0410

Swift Energy Co.
Suite 200, 652 East North Belt
Houston, Texas 77060
(713) 445-0844

Tenneco Oil Co.
Tenneco Building, 1010 Milam
Houston, Texas 77002
(713) 757-3116

Woods Petroleum Co.
Suite 700, 1 Lakeview Energy Center
3817 Northwest Expressway
Oklahoma City, Oklahoma 73112
(405) 947-7811

Real Estate

Real Estate limited partnerships buy equity interests in, and make loans to owners of, a wide variety of real estate properties, such as office buildings, apartment complexes, shopping centers, and miniwarehouse storage centers. Partnerships that mainly buy such properties plan to sell them in five to ten years and pass through any capital gains to the limited partners. In the meantime, they collect rents and improve the properties, if necessary, passing along income and tax benefits, such as depreciation, to the limited partners.

The other type of real estate partnership makes mortgage loans to real estate owners or those constructing buildings. In some cases, these programs also have some equity participation in the real estate for which they are making loans. In general, mortgage loan partnerships are more conservative investments than equity programs and loan offerings pay higher current income to limited partners.

The general partners listed here had at least $10 million in sales in 1985.

AEI Inc.
101 West Burnsville Parkway
Burnsville, Minnesota 55337
(612) 894-8800
(800) 328-3519

America First Capital Associates
1004 Farnam Street
Omaha, Nebraska 68102
(402) 444-1630

Angeles/Quinoco
10301 West Pico Boulevard
Los Angeles, California 90064
(213) 277-4900
(800) 421-4374

August Financial Partners
3545 Long Beach Boulevard
Long Beach, California 90807
(800) 821-3332
(800) 352-3710

Balcor/American Express
Balcor Plaza, 4849 Golf Road
Skokie, Illinois 60077
(312) 677-2900

Brichard Properties
Suite 608, 220 Montgomery Street
San Francisco, California 94104
(415) 989-2000

Centennial Group, Inc.
282 South Anita Drive
Orange, California 92668
(714) 634-9200

Clifton Investment Properties, Inc.
6400 East El Dorado Circle
Tucson, Arizona 85715
(602) 886-5716

Consolidated Capital Corp.
2000 Powell Street
Emeryville, California 94608
(415) 652-7171
(800) 227-1870

Consolidated Resources Corp. of America
Suite 3, 2245 Perimeter Pike
Atlanta, Georgia 30341
(800) 241-3395

CRI, Inc.
1 Central Plaza, 1130 Rockville Pike
Rockville, Maryland 20852
(301) 468-9200

Dain Bosworth
1820 Dain Tower
Minneapolis, Minnesota 55402
(612) 371-7810

Damson Corp.
366 Madison Avenue
New York, New York 10017
(212) 503-8500

Dean Witter Reynolds
130 Liberty Street
New York, New York 10006
(212) 524-5115

DeAnza Corp.
Suite 627, 9171 Wilshire Boulevard
Beverly Hills, California 90210
(213) 550-1111

Drexel Burnham Lambert Realty, Inc.
405 Lexington Avenue
New York, New York 10017
(212) 986-2800

DSI Properties Inc.
P.O. Box 357
Long Beach, California 90801
(213) 424-2655

EQK Partners, Inc.
3 Bala Plaza East
Bala Cynwyd, Pennsylvania 19034
(212) 747-7000
(212) 730-8500

Equitec Financial Group
7677 Oakport Street
Oakland, California 94614
(415) 430-9900

First Capital Properties Corp.
2 North Riverside Plaza
Chicago, Illinois 60606
(312) 442-0200

Fox Group of Companies
Suite 300, 2755 Campus Drive
San Mateo, California 94403
(415) 574-3333
(800) 227-6557

Franchise Finance Corp. of America
Suite 500, Financial Center
3443 North Central Avenue
Phoenix, Arizona 85012
(602) 264-9639
(800) 528-1179

Freeman Properties Inc.
2517 Lebanon Road
Nashville, Tennessee 37215
(615) 889-8250
(800) 221-3947

Griffin Companies, Inc.
8200 Humboldt Avenue South
Minneapolis, Minnesota 55431
(800) 328-3788

Hall Real Estate Group
Suite 600, 10100 North Central Expressway
Dallas, Texas 75231
(214) 373-4822

HCW Inc.
101 Summer Street
Boston, Massachusetts 02110
(617) 542-2880

E. F. Hutton
1 Battery Park Plaza
New York, New York 10004
(516) 747-8000

Independent American Real Estate, Inc.
Suite 1000, 300 East Carpenter Freeway
Irving, Texas 75062
(214) 252-1234

Integrated Resources
666 Third Avenue
New York, New York 10017
(800) 223-1424

I.R.E. Financial Corp.
1320 South Dixie Highway
Coral Gables, Florida 33146
(800) 665-8100

Jacques-Miller Inc.
211 7th Avenue North
Nashville, Tennessee 37219
(800) 251-2003

JMB Realty Corp.
875 North Michigan Avenue
Chicago, Illinois 60611
(312) 440-5361
(800) 621-1870

Kemper/Cymrot Inc.
630 Hansen Way
Palo Alto, California 94304
(800) 468-4881
(800) 421-0226

Krupp Companies
Harbor Plaza, 470 Atlantic Avenue
Boston, Massachusetts 02210
(617) 423-2233

Landsing Corp.
800 El Camino Real
Menlo Park, California 94025
(415) 321-7100
(800) 227-8228

Liberty Real Estate Corp.
1 Federal Street
Boston, Massachusetts 02110
(617) 722-6060

MB Operating Co.
104 6th Street, S.W.
Canton, Ohio 44702
(216) 456-2454

McClintock, John H. & James H. Pugh Jr.
301-B Park Avenue, North
Winter Park, Florida 32789
(305) 644-9055

McCombs Corp.
2392 Morse Avenue
Irvine, California 92714
(714) 863-1901
(800) 854-3295

The Robert McNeil Corp.
28555 Campus Drive
San Mateo, California 94403
(415) 572-0660
(800) 572-0660

Mellon Real Estate Investment
Management Corporation
551 Madison Avenue
New York, New York 10022
(212) 702-4049

Merrill Lynch Hubbard, Inc.
23rd Floor, 2 Broadway
New York, New York 10004
(212) 908-8409

Murray Realty Investors, Inc.
5520 LBJ Freeway
Dallas, Texas 75240
(214) 851-6672
(800) 527-5909

National Development and Investment Inc.
13555 Bishop's Court
Brookfield, Wisconsin 53008
(800) 558-1312
(800) 242-7732

National Housing Partnership
1133 15th Street N.W.
Washington, D.C. 20005
(202) 857-5700
(202) 857-5891

National Partnerships Investment Corp.
Suite 919, 1880 Century Park East
Los Angeles, California 91903
(213) 277-2422

New England Life Properties, Inc.
535 Boylston Street
Boston, Massachusetts 02116
(617) 267-6600
(800) 343-7104

Nooney Co.
7701 Forsyth Boulevard
St. Louis, Missouri 63105
(314) 863-7700
(800) 325-0893

NTS Properties
10172 Linn Station Road
Louisville, Kentucky 40223
(800) 421-1492

Occidental Land Research
Suite 300, 22632 East Golden Springs Drive
Diamond Bar, California 91765
(714) 861-6211
(800) 831-2078

Oxford Development Corp.
Suite 300, 7316 Wisconsin Avenue
Bethesda, Maryland 20814
(301) 654-3100

Paine Webber Propertie.
1285 Avenue of the Americas
New York, New York 10020
(212) 730-5826

Phoenix Realty Management, Inc.
1 American Row
Hartford, Connecticut 06115
(203) 278-1212

Prudential-Bache
100 Gold Street
New York, New York 10292
(212) 791-1000

Public Storage
990 South Fair Oaks Avenue
Pasadena, California 91102
(800) 421-2856
(800) 331-3388

Rancho Consultants
Suite B-1, 28636 Front Street
Temecula, California 92390
(408) 257-1512
(714) 676-6664

Realty Income Corp.
200 West Grand Avenue
Escondido, California 92025
(800) 854-1967
(800) 542-6030

Robin Linn, Inc. & Linsan Corp.
Suite 102, 21031 Ventura Boulevard
Woodland Hills, California 91364
(818) 992-8999

Security Properties, Inc.
Suite 1500, 2201 6th Avenue
Seattle, Washington 98121
(206) 441-8313
(800) 426-9242

Shearson Lehman Bros., Inc.
World Financial Center
New York, New York 10285
(212) 298-2000

Shelter Resource Corp.
Suite 200, 3880 Michelson Drive
Irvine, California 92715
(714) 786-0506

Shurgard Capital Group
Suite 1001, 999 Third Avenue
Seattle, Washington 98104
(206) 628-3200

Sierra Real Estate Advisors Inc.
Suite 525, 300 Montgomery Street
San Francisco, California 94104
(415) 391-0129
(800) 227-5610

Southmark Corp.
Suite 800, 1601 LBJ Freeway
Dallas, Texas 75234
(214) 241-8787

Teachers Management & Investment Corp.
#6 Upper Newport Plaza
Newport Beach, California 92660
(714) 955-9100

T. Rowe Price Real Estate Fund Management,
Inc.
100 East Pratt Street
Baltimore, Maryland 21202
(800) 638-5660

USAA Financial Services Co.
USAA Building, 9800 Fredericksburg Road
San Antonio, Texas 78288
(512) 690-6916

VMS Realty, Inc.
8700 West Bryn Mawr
Chicago, Illinois 60631
(312) 399-8700

Windsor Corp.
Suite 206, 120 West Grand Avenue
Escondido, California 92025
(800) 821-4715
(800) 821-3736

Research and Development

The following partnerships help finance research into new products or services that small but promising companies cannot finance on their own. In addition, such partnerships use funds to develop and market a product or service so that it will gain acceptance in the marketplace. Most commonly, Research and Development partnerships finance a number of unrelated ventures in the high-technology field. If one of the projects becomes commercially successful, the payoff to limited partners can be great. The risk of loss is also large, however, since many ideas which may be technically feasible do not ultimately become commercially viable. In addition to receiving distributions from the partnership if projects are profitable, limited partners also can receive tax benefits in the form of tax credits and depreciation on equipment. It often takes at least five, and possibly ten, years before a significant discovery is made, tested, and marketed successfully.

The partnerships here all had sales of at least $1 million in 1985.

Daleco Research & Development Inc.
4th Floor, 3388 Via Lido
Newport Beach, California 92663
(800) 432-5326
(800) 432-5336

E.F. Hutton
1 Battery Park Plaza
New York, New York 10004
(212) 747-8000

Merrill Lynch Hubbard
23rd Floor, 2 Broadway
New York, New York 10004
(212) 908-8409

Paine Webber
1285 Avenue of the Americas
New York, New York 10020
(212) 730-5826

Prudential-Bache
100 Gold Street
New York, New York 10292
(212) 791-1000

Technology Funding, Inc.
2000 Alameda De Las Pulgas
San Mateo, California 94403
(415) 345-2200

Windsor Corp., The
Suite 206, 120 West Grand Avenue
Escondido, California 92025
(800) 821-4715
(800) 821-3736

ACCOUNTING FIRMS

The following is a list of the names, addresses, and telephone numbers of the headquarters of the 25 largest U.S. certified public accounting firms, based on revenue generated in 1985. These firms are organized as partnerships of the certified public accountants who work in them. CPAs, who must pass examinations to earn their licenses, mainly do corporate accounting and auditing and prepare tax returns.

The eight largest accounting firms are commonly known as the Big Eight, because they dominate the industry. In alphabetical order, the Big Eight are Arthur Andersen & Co., Coopers & Lybrand, Deloitte Haskins & Sells, Ernst & Whinney, Peat, Marwick, Mitchell & Co., Price Waterhouse & Co., Touche Ross & Co., and Arthur Young and Co. Most major corporations deal with one of these eight firms, whose revenue is far greater than that of other accounting firms. For instance, in 1985, Arthur Andersen & Co., the biggest firm, had annual revenue of a little over $1 billion and Touche Ross & Co., the eighth largest member of the Big Eight, had $448 million in revenue. Only the next four firms had revenue over $100 million, and after that, the revenue per firm dropped dramatically so that the 25th largest firm had just $16 million in revenue. Below this level, the accounting profession splinters into thousands of smaller firms.

There has been a trend toward consolidation in the industry, with medium and smaller-sized accounting firms merging in order to better compete with each other and the giants. In addition, foreign accounting firms have been acquiring interests in American firms. For example, KMG Main Hurdman is affiliated with the giant Amsterdam-based Klynveld Main Goerdeler, one of the major accounting firms of Europe.

Accounting firms have also been branching out beyond their traditional functions of auditing and accounting into other business services, particularly management consulting. A number of these firms now offer specialized advice for clients in such industries as financial services, health care, and telecommunications.

This list is provided courtesy of *Public Accounting Report* [P.O. Box 80280, Atlanta, Georgia 30366 (404) 455-7600], a newsletter that tracks the accounting industry.

Altschuler, Melvoin and Glasser
30 South Wacker Drive
Chicago, Illinois 60606
(312) 207-2800

Arthur Andersen & Co.
69 West Washington Street
Chicago, Illinois 60602
(312) 580-0069

Baird Kurtz & Dobson
318 Park Central East
Springfield, Missouri 65806
(417) 865-8701

Cherry, Bekaert & Holland
One NCNB Plaza
Charlotte, North Carolina 28280
(704) 377-1678

Clifton, Gunderson & Co.
900 Commercial National Bank Building
Peoria, Illinois 61602
(309) 671-4500

Coopers & Lybrand
1251 Avenue of the Americas
New York, New York 10020
(212) 536-2000

Crowe, Chizek
330 East Jefferson Boulevard
South Bend, Indiana 46624
(219) 232-3992

Deloitte Haskins & Sells
1114 Avenue of the Americas
New York, New York 10036
(212) 790-0500

Ernst & Whinney
2000 National City Center
Cleveland, Ohio 44114
(216) 861-5000

Grant Thornton
Prudential Plaza
Chicago, Illinois 60601
(312) 856-0001

KMG Main Hurdman
55 East 52nd Street
New York, New York 10055
(212) 909-5000

Laventhol and Horwath
1845 Walnut Street
Philadelphia, Pennsylvania 10103
(215) 299-1600

Kenneth Leventhal & Co.
2049 Century Park East
Los Angeles, California 90067
(213) 277-0880

Mann Judd Landau
230 Park Avenue
New York, New York 10169
(212) 661-5500

McGladrey Hendrickson & Pullen
640 Capital Square
Des Moines, Iowa 50309
(515) 284-8680

Moss Adams
2830 Bank of California Center
Seattle, Washington 98164
(206) 223-1820

Goe. S. Olive & Co.
320 North Meridian Street
Indianapolis, Indiana 46204
(317) 267-8400

Oppenheim, Appel, Dixon & Co.
101 Park Avenue
New York, New York 10178
(212) 422-1000

Pannell Kerr Forster
262 North Belt East
Houston, Texas 77060
(713) 999-5134

Peat, Marwick, Mitchell & Co.
345 Park Avenue
New York, New York 10022
(212) 758-9700

Plante & Moran
26211 Central Park Boulevard
Southfield, Michigan 48037
(313) 352-2500

Price Waterhouse & Co.
1251 Avenue of the Americas
New York, New York 10020
(212) 489-8900

Seidman & Seidman
15 Columbus Circle
New York, New York 10023
(212) 657-7500

Touche Ross & Co.
1633 Broadway
New York, New York 10019
(212) 489-1600

Arthur Young & Co.
277 Park Avenue
New York, New York 10172
(212) 407-1500

SECURITIES AND COMMODITIES EXCHANGES AROUND THE WORLD

The following is a list of the name and address of major securities and commodities exchanges around the world. Telephone numbers are provided for American and Canadian exchanges. The list is arranged alphabetically by country.

The most active financial markets are those in the industrialized countries of North America, Western Europe, and Japan. In these countries, there is more regulation of securities markets, and companies have to disclose more about their financial status; the regulation and disclosure requirements of U.S. exchanges are by far the strictest. The more active markets are more competitive and therefore are characterized by narrower spreads between bid and asked prices.

The stock markets of the less industrialized countries offer both greater rewards and greater risks to investors. Regulation of these markets tends to be looser and financial disclosure rules less stringent. With less trading activity, the spreads between bid and asked prices tend to be wide. In some cases, investment by nonnationals of the country is banned or strictly limited. Many of these markets provide rich opportunities to participate in some of the world's fastest growing economies, such as South Korea, Hong Kong, and Singapore.

The shares of some prominent companies listed on these and other exchanges are also traded in the United States as American Depositary Receipts (ADRs). For investors who are interested in participating in these foreign markets, but do not have the time or expertise to do so directly, there are a number of mutual funds, both closed-end and open-end, specializing in buying securities in markets around the world.

Argentina

Bolsa de Comercio de Buenos Aires
Sarmiento 299
Buenos Aires 1353

Australia

Stock Exchange of Adelaide
55 Exchange Place
Adelaide, 5001 S.A.

Brisbane Stock Exchange
Network House
344 Queen Street
Brisbane, 4001 Queensland

Stock Exchange of Melbourne
351 Collins Street
Melbourne, 3001 Victoria

Stock Exchange of Perth
68 St. George's Terrace
Perth, 6001 W.A.

Sydney Futures Exchange
13-15 O'Connell Street
Sydney, N.S.W. 2000

Sydney Stock Exchange
Australia Square
Sydney, N.S.W. 2000

Austria

Wiener Boersekammer
A-1011 Wien, 1
Wipplingerstrasse 34

Belgium

Fondsen-En Wisselbeurs Van Antwerpen
Korte Klarenstraat 1
2000 Antwerpen

Bourse de Bruxelles
Palais de la Bourse
1000 Bruxelles

Fondsen-Ed Wisselbeurs Van Gent
Kouter, 29
9000 Gent

Bourse de Fonds Publics de Liège
Boulevard D'Avroy, 3/022
4000 Liège

Brazil

Bolsa de Valores do Rio de Janiero
Praca XV de Novembro 20
Rio de Janiero RJ

Bolsa de Valores de São Paulo
Rua Alvares Penteado No. 151-60 Andar
01012 São Paolo, SP

Canada

Alberta Stock Exchange
300 5th Avenue, S.W.
Calgary, Alberta T2P 3C4
(403) 262-7791

Montréal Exchange
Tour de la Bourse
800 Victoria Square
Montréal, Québec H4Z 1A9
(514) 871-2424

Toronto Futures Exchange
Toronto Stock Exchange
The Exchange Tower
2 First Canadian Place
Toronto, Ontario M5X 1J2
(416) 947-4700

Vancouver Stock Exchange
Stock Exchange Tower
609 Granville Street
Vancouver, British Columbia V7Y 1H1
(604) 689-3334

Winnipeg Commodity Exchange
500 Commodity Exchange Tower
360 Main Street
Winnipeg, Manitoba R3C 3Z4
(204) 949-0495

Winnipeg Stock Exchange
167 Lombard Avenue
Winnipeg, Manitoba R3B 0V3
(204) 942-8431

Chile

Bolsa de Comercio de Santiago
Casilla 123-D
Santiago

China, Republic of (Taiwan)

Taiwan Stock Exchange
8-10th Floor, City Building
85 Yen-Ping South Road
Taipei

Colombia

Bolsa de Bogota
Carrera 8, 13-82 Piso 8
Bogota

Denmark

Københavns Fondsbors
6 Nikolaj Plads
DK-1007 Copenhagen

Ecuador

Bolsa de Valores de Quito
Avenue Rio Amazonas 540 y Jeronimo
Carrion, Piso 8
Apartado Postal 3772
Quito

Egypt

Cairo Stock Exchange
4-A Cherifein Street
Cairo

Finland

Helsingin Arvopaperiporssi
Fabianinkatu 14
00100 Helsinki 10

France

Bourse de Bordeaux
Palais de la Bourse
13-Bordeaux

Bourse de Lille
68 Palais Bourse
Place du Theatre
59-Lille

Bourse de Lyon
Palais du Commerce
Place de la Bourse
69289 Lyon

Bourse de Marseille
Palais de la Bourse
Marseille

Bourse de Nancy
40 rue Henri Poincare
54000 Nancy

Bourse de Nantes
Palais de la Bourse
Place du Commerce
44-Nantes

Bourse de Paris
4,Place de la Bourse
75080 Paris

Paris Commodity Exchange
Bourse de Commerce
2,rue de Viarmes B.P. 53/01
75040 Paris

Great Britain

Belfast Stock Exchange
Northern Bank House
10 High Street
Belfast BT1 2BP

London Commodity Exchange
Cereal House, 58 Mark Lane
London EC3R 7NE

London International Financial Futures
Exchange (LIFFE)
Royal Exchange
London EC3

London Stock Exchange
Old Broad Street
London EC2N 1HP

Midlands & Western Stock Exchange
Margaret Street
Birmingham B3 3J1

Northern Stock Exchange
2/6 Norfolk Street
Manchester M2 1DS

Provincial Stock Exchange
Room 402, 4th floor
London EC2N 1HP

Scottish Stock Exchange
Stock Exchange House
69 St. George's Place
Glasgow G2 1BU
      and
12 Dublin Street
Edinburgh EH1 3PP

Greece

Athens Stock Exchange
10 Sophocleous Street
Athens 121

Hong Kong

Hong Kong Futures Exchange
Hong Kong Stock Exchange
Exchange Square
GPO Box 8888

India

Bombay Stock Exchange
Dalal Street
Fort, Bombay 400001

Calcutta Stock Exchange Association
7, Lyons Range
Calcutta 700001

Delhi Stock Exchange Association
3 & 4/4B Asaf Ali Road
New Delhi 110002

Madras Stock Exchange
Stock Exchange Building
11 Second Line Beach
Madras 600001

Indonesia

Stock Exchange of Indonesia
Perserikatan Perdagangan
Uang dan Efek-Efek
P.O. Box 1224/Dak,
Jakarta-Kota

Ireland

Irish Stock Exchange
28 Anglesea Street
Dublin 2

Israel

Tel-Aviv Stock Exchange
113 Allenby Road
Tel-Aviv 65127

Italy

Borsa Valori di Bologna
Piazza della Costituzione, 8
Palazzo degli Affari
40100 Bologna

Borsa Valori de Firenze
Piazza Mentana, 2
50122 Firenze

Borsa Valori di Genova
Via G. Boccardo, 1
16121 Genova

Borsa Valori di Milano
Piazza degli Affari, 6
20123 Milano

Borsa Valori di Napoli
Via S. Aspreno, 2
80133 Napoli

Borsa Valori di Palermo
Via E. Amari, 11
90139 Palermo

Borsa Valori di Roma
Via de' Burro, 147
00186 Roma

Borsa Valori di Torino
Via S. Francesco da Paola, 28
10123 Torino

Borsa Valori de Trieste
Via Cassa di Risparmio, 2
34100 Trieste

Borsa Valori di Venezia
Via XXII Marzo, 2034
30124 Venezia

Jamaica

Jamaica Stock Exchange
Bank of Jamaica Tower
P.O. Box 621
Nethersole Place, Kingston

Japan

Fukuoka Stock Exchange
2-14-2 Tenjin, Chuohku
Fukuokashi

Hiroshima Stock Exchange
14-18 Ginzancho
Hiroshimashi

Kyoto Stock Exchange
66 Tateuri Nishimachi
Tohdohin Higashihairu
Shijohdohri, Shimokyoku
Kyoto

Nagoya Stock Exchange
3-3-17 Sakae, Naka-ku
Nagoyashi

Niigata Securities Exchange
1245 Hachibancho
Kamiohkawamaedohri
Niigatashi

Osaka Securities Exchange
Kitahama 2-chome
Higashi-Ku
Osaka 541

Sapporo Stock Exchange
5-14-1 Nishi
Minami Ichijoh, Chuoku
Sappororshi

Tokyo Stock Exchange
2-1-1 Nihombashi-Kayaba-cho
Chuo-ku, Tokyo, 103

Kenya

Nairobi Stock Exchange
Stanbank House
Moi Avenue
P.O. Box 43633
Nairobi

Luxembourg

Societé de la Bourse de Luxembourg
11, avenue de la Porte-Neuve
2227 Luxembourg

Malaysia

Kuala Lumpur Stock Exchange
4th Floor Block C, Damansara Centre
Damansara Heights
Kuala Lumpur 23-04

Mexico

Bolsa Mexicana de Valores
Uraguay #68
Mexico 1.D.F.

Bolsa de Valores de Monterrey
Escobedo Sur #733
Monterrey, N.L.

Morocco

Bourse des Valeurs de Casablanca
Chamber of Commerce Building
98 Boulevard Mohamed V
Casablanca

Netherlands

Amsterdam Stock Exchange
Beursplein 5, P.O. Box 19163
1000 GD Amsterdam

European Options Exchange
DAM 21
1012 JS Amsterdam

New Zealand

Auckland Stock Exchange
C.M.L. Centre
Queen Street
Auckland 1

Christchurch Invercargill Stock Exchange
128 Oxford Terrace
P.O. Box 639
Christchurch

Dunedin Stock Exchange
Queens Building
109 Princes Street
P.O. Box 483
Dunedin C.1

Wellington Stock Exchange
Government Life Insurance Building
Brandon Street
P.O. Box 767
Wellington C.1

Nigeria

Nigerian Stock Exchange
NIDB House, 15th floor
63/71, Broad Street
P.O. Box 2457
Lagos

Norway

Aalesunds Børs
Roysegate 14
6001 Aalesund

Bergens Børs
Olav Kyrresgate 11
Postboks 832
5000 Bergen

Fredrikstad Børs
Nygaardsgaten 5
Fredrikstad

Oslo Børs
Tollbugaten 2
Oslo 1

Trondheim Børs
Dronningensgt
Trondheim

Pakistan

Karachi Stock Exchange
Stock Exchange Road
Karachi 2

Lahore Stock Exchange
17 Bank Square
Lahore

Peru

Bolsa de Valores de Lima
Jiron Antonio Miro Quesada 265
Apartado 1538
Lima 100

Philippines

Makati Stock Exchange
Makati Stock Exchange Building
Ayala Avenue
Makati, Metro Manila

Manila Stock Exchange
Manila Stock Exchange Building
Prensa Street, Cor. Muelle de la Industria
Binondo, Manila

Metropolitan Stock Exchange
Padilla Arcade, 2nd floor
Greenhills Commercial Center
San Juan, Metro Manila

Portugal

Bolsa de Valores de Lisboa
Praca do Comercio
Torreao Oriental
Lisboa

Singapore

Stock Exchange of Singapore
702/1403, Hong Leong Building
Raffles Quay
Singapore 0104

Singapore International Monetary Exchange
24 Raffles Place
29-04 Clifford Centre
Singapore 0104

South Africa

Johannesburg Stock Exchange
P.O. Box 1174
Diagonal Street
Johannesburg, 2000

South Korea

Korea Stock Exchange
1-116, Yoido-Dong
Youngdeungpo-Ku
Seoul

Spain

Bolsa de Barcelona
Paseo Isabel II, Consulado 2
Barcelona 3

Bolsa de Bilbao
Jose Maria Olabarri 1
Bilbao 1

Bolsa de Comercio de Madrid
Plaza de la Lealtad 1
Madrid 14

Bolsa Oficial de Comercio de Valencia
Calle Pascual y Genis, 19
Valencia

Sri Lanka

Colombo Brokers' Association
P.O. Box 101
59 Janadipathi Mawatha
Colombo 1

Sweden

Stockholms Fondbörs
Box 1256
S-111 82 Stockholm

Switzerland

Börsenkammer des Kantons Basel-Stadt
Freie Strasse 3
CH-4001 Basel

Berner Börsenverein
Aabergergasse 30
CH-3011 Bern

Chambre de la Bourse de Genève
10, rue Peitot
Case Postale 228
1211 Genève

Bourse de Lausanne
Societé de Banque Suisse
16, Place St-François
CH-1003 Lausanne

Bourse de Neuchâtel
Coq d'Inde 24
2000 Neuchâtel

Effktenbörsenverein Zürich
Bleicherweg 5
Postfach
8021 Zürich

Thailand

Securities Exchange of Thailand
Siam Center, 4th Floor
965 Rama 1 Road
Bangkok, Metropolis 5

United States

American Stock Exchange
AMEX Commodities Corporation
86 Trinity Place
New York, New York 10006
(212) 306-1000

Boston Stock Exchange
One Boston Place
Boston, Massachusetts 02108
(617) 723-9500

Chicago Board of Trade
LaSalle at Jackson
Chicago, Illinois 60604
(312) 435-3500

Chicago Board Options Exchange
LaSalle at Van Buren
Chicago, Illinois 60605
(312) 786-5600

Chicago Mercantile Exchange
International Monetary Market
30 South Wacker Drive
Chicago, Illinois 60606
(312) 930-1000 (800) 843-6372

Chicago Rice & Cotton Exchange
444 West Jackson Boulevard
Chicago, Illinois 60606
(312) 341-3078

Cincinnati Stock Exchange
205 Dixie Terminal Building
Cincinnati, Ohio 45202
(513) 621-1410

Coffee, Sugar & Cocoa Exchange
4 World Trade Center
New York, New York 10048
(212) 938-2800

Commodity Exchange, Inc. (COMEX)
4 World Trade Center
New York, New York 10048
(212) 938-2900

Intermountain Stock Exchange
373 South Main Street
Salt Lake City, Utah 84111
(801) 363-2531

Kansas City Board of Trade
4800 Main Street
Kansas City, Missouri 64112
(816) 753-7500

MidAmerica Commodity Exchange
444 West Jackson Boulevard
Chicago, Illinois 60606
(312) 341-3000

Midwest Stock Exchange
440 South LaSalle Street
Chicago, Illinois 60605
(312) 663-2222

Minneapolis Grain Exchange
150 Grain Exchange Building
Minneapolis, Minnesota 55415
(612) 338-6212

New York Cotton Exchange
4 World Trade Center
New York, New York 10048
(212) 938-2702

New York Futures Exchange
20 Broad Street
New York, New York 10005
(212) 656-4949 (800) 221-7722

New York Mercantile Exchange
4 World Trade Center
New York, New York 10048
(212) 938-2222

New York Stock Exchange
11 Wall Street
New York, New York 10005
(212) 656-3000

Pacific Stock Exchange
301 Pine Street
San Francisco, California 94104
(415) 393-4000

Philadelphia Stock Exchange
Philadelphia Board of Trade
1900 Market Street
Philadelphia, Pennsylvania 19103
(215) 496-5000

Spokane Stock Exchange
225 Peyton Building
Spokane, Washington 99201
(509) 624-4632

West Germany

Berliner Wertpapierbörse
1000 Berlin 12
Hardenbergstrasse 16-18

Rheinisch-Westfälische Börse zu Düsseldorf
4000 Düsseldorf
Ernst-Schneider-Platz 1

Frankfurter Wertpapierbörse
Börsenplatz 6
6000 Frankfurt am Main 1

Hanseatische Wertpapierbörse Hamburg
2000 Hamburg 11
Adolphsplatz, Börse, Zimmer 151

Bayerische Börse in München
8000 München 2
Lenbachplatz 2 a

3. MUTUAL FUNDS

OPEN-END MUTUAL FUNDS

The following is a list of the names, addresses, and telephone numbers of American open-end mutual funds. Most organizations offer more than one fund, and the funds in this list are grouped under the name of the firm to which they belong. In order to obtain information about a fund you may be interested in, look first for the name of its management group. Newspaper listings also usually group mutual funds by family.

The funds on this list are both load and no-load. Load funds are sold through brokers and financial planners for commissions that generally range from about 3% (this is called a low-load fund) to 8½%. In return for this sales charge, customers should expect expert advice on which fund is most appropriate for their investment needs and goals. A broker should also tell the customer when to get out of the fund, as well as when to get in. No-load funds, on the other hand, charge no commissions. Investors buy shares directly from the management companies over the phone, by mail, or in person. The management company representative will offer information on the funds the firm offers, but they may not advise investors on which fund to buy. No one will call when the time comes to switch from one fund to another—that is left totally up to the individual shareholder.

The funds on this list are categorized by the investment objective of the fund manager. The following is a brief characterization of each objective, the abbreviation of which is given in parentheses after each fund's name in the list of funds.

Aggressive Growth (AG) Aggressive-growth funds seek maximum capital gains; current income is not a consideration. Fund managers may use several strategies, such as buying high-technology stocks, emerging growth stocks, or companies that have fallen on hard times or are out of favor. Some aggressive funds make use of options and futures and/or borrow against funds shares to buy stock. Aggressive-growth funds typically provide dramatic gains and losses for shareholders and should therefore be monitored closely.

Balanced (B) Balanced mutual funds generally invest in both stocks and bonds, with the intent of providing capital gains and income. Preservation of principal is a primary objective of balanced fund managers. These funds are for conservative investors who are looking for some growth of capital.

Corporate Bond (CB) Corporate-bond funds seek to pay a high level of income to shareholders by buying corporate bonds. Some conservative bond funds buy only the debt of highly rated corporations. The yield of this kind of fund would be lower than that of a fund buying bonds from lower-rated corporations—frequently called junk bonds.

Although income, not capital gains, is the primary objective of most corporate-bond shareholders, capital gains can be significant if the country's general level of interest rates falls. On the other hand, losses can be substantial if interest rates rise.

Growth (G) Growth funds invest in the common stock of growth companies. The primary aim is to achieve capital gains, and income is of little concern. Growth funds vary widely in the amount of risk they are willing to take, but in general they take less risk than aggressive-growth funds because the stocks they buy are those of more seasoned companies.

Growth and Income (G + I) Growth and income funds seek to provide both capital gains and a steady stream of income by buying the shares of high-yielding conservative stocks. Growth and income fund managers look for companies with solid records of increasing their dividend payments as well as showing earnings gains. These funds are more conservative than pure growth funds.

GNMA Fund (GNMA) These funds buy Government National Mortgage Association (GNMA or Ginnie Mae) certificates, which are securities backed by home mortgages. GNMA funds are designed to provide a high level of current income to shareholders and to minimize risk to capital. These funds are subject to fluctuation because of the ups and downs of interest rates, however. They are also affected by the rates at which homeowners refinance their mortgages. When interest rates fall, more mortgages are refinanced, and therefore shareholders in GNMA funds see their yields fall. When rates rise, on the other hand, fewer mortgages are refinanced, and so the fund maintains its yield, but it does not grow very quickly. GNMA funds are designed for conservative income-oriented investors.

Income (I) Income funds seek to provide a high level of current income by buying government and corporate bonds as well as high-yielding common and preferred stock. Income funds are not designed to provide major capital gains, but their shares do rise in value when interest rates fall. (Conversely, the shares fall in value when interest rates rise.) Income funds are designed for conservative income-oriented investors.

International (INT) International funds invest in stocks of companies around the world as well as in bonds issued by foreign companies and governments. Some funds (also called global funds) buy American and Canadian shares in addition to those of companies in other countries, while others are restricted to buying non-North American shares. International funds provide investors with diversification among countries as well as industries. Such funds are strongly influenced by the rise and fall of foreign-exchange rates—a factor important to consider before buying shares. For Americans, it would generally be beneficial to buy an international fund when the outlook is for the exchange rate of the dollar to fall against other currencies. Conversely, international-fund performance usually suffers when the dollar strengthens. International funds are for those willing to take some risk; understanding of the effect of currency changes on holdings is essential.

Long-Term Municipal Bond (LTMB) These funds aim to provide a high level of tax-exempt income to shareholders by buying the debt obligations of cities, states, and other municipal government agencies.

Depending on the state in which a shareholder resides, interest earned is either totally or partially free of federal, state, and local income taxes. While such funds are designed to provide current income, their value also rises and falls inversely with the country's general level of interest rates. The municipal bonds these funds usually buy tend to mature from 10 to 20 years in the future.

Money Market (MM) Money-market mutual funds buy short-term securities sold in money markets and provide current income to shareholders. Because of the short-term nature of their holdings, these funds reflect changes in short-term interest rates rather quickly. The principal in money-market funds is extremely safe. Some money funds buy commercial instruments like commercial paper, banker's acceptances, and repurchase agreements, while others restrict themselves to buying U.S. Treasury obligations like Treasury bills. The portfolios of some money-market funds are insured by private insurance companies. Most money funds allow checkwriting, often with a minimum check size of $250 or $500. Money market funds are frequently included in asset management accounts offered by brokerage firms and are used as parking places for funds while shareholders decide where the best place to invest long-term might be. Otherwise, money-market funds are for extremely conservative investors, who want virtually no risk of capital loss.

Option Income (OI) Option-income funds provide high current return by writing call options on a portfolio of dividend-paying stocks. The current return derives from dividends on stock as well as premium income earned by writing options. If the value of the stock in the portfolio declines, the net asset value of the fund will also decline, though the income earned will somewhat offset the decline. Option-income funds are designed for investors wanting high current return while being willing to risk declines in the value of their shares.

Precious Metals—Gold (PMG) Such funds invest in the shares of gold and silver mining companies. These shares often pay high dividends, and therefore the funds often have high yields. As with all precious-metal investments, these funds reflect the ups and downs of investor psychology as it relates to the outlook for inflation as well as political upheaval. These funds tend to perform better when inflation is high and rising and there is considerable political turmoil in the world. Some funds invest largely in South African mines, while others restrict themselves to shares in North American mining companies.

Short-Term Minicipal Bond (STMB) These funds buy short-term obligations of cities, states, and other municipal government agencies and pass along tax-exempt income to shareholders. Since the bonds are short-term, they are less risky and usually have a lower yield than longer-term obligations. Some short-term municipal bond funds operate like tax-free money-market funds and allow check writing, usually with a $250 or $500 per check minimum. These funds are generally for conservative investors in income-tax brackets high enough to take full advantage of tax-free income.

State Municipal Bond—Long Term (STMB–LT) These funds buy debt obligations of cities and municipal authorities in one state only. The interest from these bonds is usually tax exempt to residents of the particular state. Thus, shareholders can have a higher after-tax yield than if they bought shares in an out-of-state fund on which they had to pay taxes. These funds typically buy longer-term bonds maturing in 10 to 20 years. As a result, they fluctuate considerably with the ups and downs of the general level of interest rates.

State Municipal Bond—Short Term (STMB–ST) These funds buy the debt obligations of cities and municipal authorities in one state only. The interest from these bonds is usually tax exempt to residents of the particular state. Thus, shareholders can obtain a higher after-tax yield than if they bought the shares in an out-of-state fund on which they had to pay taxes. These funds typically buy short-term debt obligations with maturities from a few days or months to as much as five years. Therefore, they are not as subject to interest rate fluctuations as long-term funds. The funds generally allow shareholders to write checks, typically with a minimum withdrawal of $250 to $500 per check.

U.S. Government Income (USGI) These funds invest only in direct obligations of the U.S. Treasury. The funds therefore buy U.S. Treasury bills, bonds, and notes and federally backed mortgage securities. Shareholders of such funds want a high level of current income as well as maximum safety against default. Some funds have short maturities, while others buy bonds with maturities as long as 20 to 30 years. The longer the portfolio's overall maturity, the more the fund will fluctuate with general interest-rate movements.

This listing of mutual funds was made possible through the generous cooperation of two mutual-fund trade associations, the Investment Company Institute and the No-Load Mutual Fund Association. The Investment Company Institute [1600 M Street, N.W., Washington, D.C. 20036 (202) 293-7700] has both load and no-load members and regularly keeps track of new fund groups and funds. It publishes an annual directory of members.

The No-Load Mutual Fund Association [11 Penn Plaza, Suite 2204, New York, New York 10001 (212) 563-4540] has a large membership of no-load and low-load funds. It also publishes an annual directory of members, which is available for $2 by writing the association at P.O. Box 1010, South Orange, New Jersey 07079.

Abbreviations of Fund Objectives

AG	Aggressive Growth
B	Balanced
CB	Corporate Bond
G	Growth
G+I	Growth and Income
GNMA	Government National Mortgage Association Fund
I	Income
INT	International
LTMB	Long-Term Municipal Bond
MM	Money Market
OI	Option Income
PMG	Precious Metals—Gold
STMB	Short-Term Municipal Bond
SMB–LT	State Municipal Bond—Long Term
SMB–ST	State Municipal Bond—Short Term
USGI	U.S. Government Income

AARP Investments
P.O. Box 2540
Boston, Massachusetts 02208
(800) 253-7777

AARP Capital Growth (G), AARP Ginnie Mae (GNMA), AARP General Bond (B), AARP Growth and Income (G + I), AARP Tax Free Bond (LTMB), AARP Tax Free Shares (STMB)

ABT Funds. *see* Midwest / ABT Funds.

Accrued Equities
295 Northern Boulevard
Great Neck, NY 11021
(516) 466-0808

New Alternatives Fund (G)

Acorn
2 North LaSalle Street
Chicago, IL 60602
(312) 621-0630

Acorn Fund (G)

Aetna
151 Farmington Avenue
Hartford, CT 06156
(203) 273-4808

Aetna Income Shares (CB), Aetna Variable Fund (G)

Afuture Fund. *see* Carlisle-Asher Management Company.

AIM Funds
107 North Adams Street
Rockville, MD 20850
(301) 251-1002, (800) 638-2042

Convertible Yield Fund (I), Dividend/Growth Fund: Dividend Series (G + I), Dividend/Growth Fund: Laser & Advanced Technology Series (G), Greenway Fund (G), High Yield Fund (CB), Summit Fund (AG)

Alex. Brown
135 East Baltimore Street, P.O. Box 515
Baltimore, MD 21203
(301) 727-1700

Flag Investors Fund Telephone Income Shares Series (I)

Alliance/Wood Struthers
1345 Avenue of the Americas
New York, NY 10105
(800) 221-5672, (212) 902-4135

Alliance Bond Fund (USGI), Alliance Bond Fund: High-Grade Portfolio (CB), Alliance Bond Fund: High-Yield Portfolio (CB), Alliance Capital Reserves (MM), Alliance Corporate Cash Reserves (I), Alliance Counterpoint Fund (G), Alliance Global Fund (INT), Alliance Government Reserves (MM), Alliance International Fund (INT), Alliance Mortgage Securities Income Fund (GNMA), Alliance Tax-Exempt Reserves (STMB), Alliance Technology Fund (G), Chemical Fund (G), Decision Funds: Government Income Fund (USGI), Decision Funds: Growth & Income Fund (G + I), Decision Funds: Growth Fund (AG), Decision Funds: Tax-Free Fund (LTMB), Neuwirth Fund (AG), Pine Street Fund (G + I), Quasar Associates (AG), Surveyor Fund (G), deVegh Mutual Fund (G)

Alpha
250 Piedmont Avenue N.E.
Atlanta, GA 30365
(404) 524-4415, (800) 367-6536

Alpha Fund (G)

American Capital
2800 Post Oak Blvd
Houston, TX 77056
(713) 993-0500, (800) 231-3638

American Capital Comstock Fund (G), American Capital Corporate Bond Fund (CB), American Capital Enterprise Fund (AG), American Capital Exchange Fund (G), American Capital Government Securities (USGI), American Capital Growth Fund (G), American Capital Harbor Fund (G + I), American Capital High Yield Investments (CB), American Capital Municipal Bond Fund (LTMB), American Capital Over-The-Counter Securities (AG), American Capital Pace Fund (G), American Capital Reserve Fund (MM), American Capital Tax-Exempt Trust: California Tax-Exempt Trust (SMB-LT), American Capital Tax-Exempt Trust: High Yield Municipal Portfolio (LTMB), American Capital Tax-Exempt Trust: Insured Municipal Portfolio (LTMB), American Capital Tax-Exempt Trust: Money Market Municipal Portfolio (STMB), American Capital Tax-Exempt Trust: New York Municipal Portfolio (SMT-LT), American Capital Venture Fund (AG), American General Equity Accumulation Fund (AG), American General High Yield Accumulation Fund (I), American General Money Market Accumulation Fund (MM), Fund of America (G), Provident Fund for Income (I)

American Express Funds. *see* Shearson Lehman Brothers.

American Fund Advisors
50 Broad Street
New York, NY 10004
(212) 482-8100, (800) 654-0001 (NY only)

National Aviation & Technology Fund (G),
National Telecommunications & Technology
Fund (G), National Value Fund (G)

American General Funds. *see* VALIC.

American Growth
410 17th Street, Suite 800
Denver, CO 80202
(303) 623-6137, (800) 525-2406

American Growth Fund (G)

American Investors
777 W. Putnam Avenue, P.O. Box 2500
Greenwich, CT 06836
(203) 531-5000, (800) 243-5353

American Investors Fund (AG), American
Investors Income Fund (I), American Investors Money Fund (MM)

American National
Two Moody Plaza
Galveston, TX 77550
(409) 763-2767, (800) 231-4639,
(800) 392-9753 (TX only)

American National Bond Fund (CB), American
National Growth Fund (G), American National
Income Fund (G + I), American National Money
Market Fund (MM)

American Pension Investors
P.O. Box 2529
Lynchburg, VA 24501
(800) 544-6060

American Pension Investors Trust (G)

American Pioneer
1121 East Missouri Avenue, Suite 200
Phoenix, AZ 85014
(602) 248-0012

American Pioneer Arizona Tax-Free Securities
(STMB-LT)

American Shares
P.O. Box 3942
St. Petersburg, FL 33731
(813) 823-8712, (800) 237-0738

American Individual Shares Portfolio (G + I),
American Treasury Shares Portfolio (I)

AMEV Funds
P.O. Box 64284
St. Paul, MN 55164
(612) 738-4000, (800) 872-2638

AMEV Capital Fund (G + I), AMEV Fiduciary
Fund (AG), AMEV Growth Fund (G), AMEV
Money Fund (MM), AMEV Special Fund (G),
AMEV Tax-Free Fund: Minnesota Portfolio
(SMB-LT), AMEV U.S. Government Securi-
ties Fund (I).

Amway
7575 East Fulton Road
Ada, MI 49355
(616) 676-6288

Amway Mutual Fund (G + I)

Analytic
2222 Martin Street, Suite 230
Irvine, CA 92715
(714) 833-0294

Analytic Optioned Equity Fund (OI)

Armstrong
311 North Market Street, Suite 205
Dallas, TX 75202
(214) 744-5558

Armstrong Associates (G)

Aster Capital Management
60 East Sir Francis Drake Boulevard,
Suite 306
Larkspur, CA 94939
(415) 461-8770, (800) 446-6662

Meridian Fund (G)

Axe-Houghton
400 Benedict Avenue
Tarrytown, NY 10591
(914) 631-8131

Axe-Houghton Fund B (B), Axe-Houghton Income Fund (I), Axe-Houghton Money Market
Fund (MM), Axe-Houghton Stock Fund (G)

Babson
3 Crown Center, 2440 Pershing Road
Kansas City, MO 64108
(816) 471-5200, (800) 821-5591

Babson Bond Trust (I), Babson Enterprise Fund
(G), Babson Growth Fund (G), Babson Money
Market: Federal Portfolio (MM), Babson Money
Market: Prime Portfolio (MM), Babson Tax
Free Income: Long Term (LTMB), Babson Tax
Free Income: Money Market (STMB), Babson
Tax Free Income: Short Term (STMB), Bab-
son Value Fund (I)

Bailard, Biehl & Kaiser
951 Mariner's Island Boulevard
San Mateo Bay Center, Suite 700
San Mateo, CA 94404
(415) 571-5800

Bailard, Biehl & Kaiser International Fund (AG)

Bankers System
P.O. Box 517, 6815 Saukview Drive
St. Cloud, MN 56302
(612) 251-3060, (800) 328-2342

Bankers Systems GRANIT: Fixed Income Fund
(I), Bankers Systems GRANIT: Government
Securities Fund (USGI), Bankers Systems
GRANIT: Growth Stock Fund (G), Bankers
Systems GRANIT: Money Market Fund (MM),
Bankers Systems GRANIT: Stock Fund (G + I),
Bankers Systems GRANIT: Tax Exempt Fund
(LTMB)

Bank Stock Fund
333 North Tejon Street
Colorado Springs, CO 80901
(303) 473-8100

Bank Stock Fund (G)

Bartlett & Co.
36 East Fourth Street
Cincinnati, OH 45202
(513) 621-0066, (800) 543-0863

Bartlett Management Trust: Corporate Cash
Fund (I), Bartlett Basic Value Fund (G + I),
Fixed Income Fund (I)

Beacon Growth Fund
46 Homestead Park
Needham, MA 02194
(617) 444-2770, (800) 343-4465

Beacon Growth Fund (I)

Beacon Hill Mutual Fund
75 Federal Street
Boston, MA 02110
(617) 482-0795

Beacon Hill Mutual Fund (G)

Benham Capital Management Group
755 Page Mill Road
Palo Alto, CA 94304
(415) 858-2400, (800) 982-6150, (CA only),
(800) 227-8380

Benham California Tax-Free Trust: Intermediate-Term Portfolio (SMB-LT), Benham California Tax-Free Trust: Long-Term Portfolio
(SMB-LT), Benham California Tax-Free Trust:
Money Market Portfolio (SMB-ST), Benham

GNMA Income Fund (GNMA), Benham Na-
tional Tax-Free Trust: Intermediate-Term
Portfolio (LTMB), Benham National Tax-Free
Trust: Long-Term Portfolio (LTMB), Benham
National Tax-Free Trust: Money Market Port-
folio (STMB), Benham National Tax-Free Trust:
Short-Term Portfolio (STMB), Benham Target
Maturities Trust: Series 1990 (USGI), Ben-
ham Target Maturities Trust: Series 1995
(USGI), Benham Target Maturities Trust: Series
2000 (USGI), Benham Target Maturities Trust:
Series 2005 (USGI), Benham Target Maturities
Trust: Series 2010 (USGI), Capital Preserva-
tion Fund II (MM), Capital Preservation Fund
(MM), Capital Preservation Treasury Note Trust
(USGI)

Berger Associates
899 Logan Street, Suite 211
Denver, CO 80203
(303) 837-1020

One Hundred Fund (G), One Hundred and One
Fund (G + I)

BLC Funds
711 High Street
Des Moines, IA 50307
(515) 247-5711

BLC Cash Management Fund (MM), BLC
Growth Fund (G), BLC Income Fund (I). *See also*
Principal Financial Group.

BMI Equity
67 Wall Street
New York, NY 10005
(212) 422-1619

BMI Equity Fund (G)

Boston Company Group
One Boston Place
Boston, MA 02106
(617) 722-7250, (800) 343-6324

Boston Company Fund: Capital Appreciation
Fund (G), Boston Company Fund: Cash Man-
agement Fund (MM), Boston Company Fund:
Government Income Fund (USGI), Boston Com-
pany Fund: Government Money Fund (MM),
Boston Company Fund: Special Growth Fund
(G), Boston Company Tax-Free Municipal Funds:
Massachusetts Tax-Free Money Fund (SMB-ST),
Boston Company Tax-Free Municipal Funds:
Tax-Free Money Fund (STMB)

Boston Mutual
120 Royall Street
Canton, MA 02021
(617) 828-7000

Boston Mutual Fund (G)

Bridges
256 Durnham Plaza, 8401 West Dodge Road
Omaha, NE 68114
(402) 397-4700

Bridges Investment Fund (G + I)

Brown & Co., R.C.
655 Montgomery Street, Suite 1500
San Francisco, CA 94111
(415) 981-4050, (800) 722-6696

R.C. Brown Money Market Fund: General
Portfolio (MM), R.C. Brown Money Market
Fund: Government Portfolio (MM)

Bruce Fund
20 North Wacker Drive, Suite 1425
Chicago, IL 60606
(312) 236-9160

Bruce Fund (AG)

Bull & Bear Group
11 Hanover Square, 11th Floor
New York, NY 10005
(212) 785-0900, (800) 847-4200

Bull & Bear Capital Growth Fund (G), Bull &
Bear Dollar Reserves Fund (MM), Bull & Bear
Equity Income (G + I), Bull & Bear High Yield
Fund (I), Bull & Bear Tax Free Income (LTMB)

Bullock/Equitable
40 Rector Street
New York, NY 10006
(212) 513-4200, (800) 443-4430

Bullock Aggressive Growth Shares (G), Bul-
lock Balanced Shares (B), Bullock Dividend
Shares (G + I), Bullock Growth Shares (G + I),
Bullock High Income Shares (CB), Bullock In-
sured California Tax-Exempt Shares (SMB-LT),
Bullock Monthly Income Shares (CB), Bullock
Tax-Free Shares (LTMB), Bullock U.S. Gov-
ernment Income Shares (USGI), Canadian Fund
(INT), Equitable Money Market Account: Gen-
eral Purpose Portfolio (MM), Equitable Money
Market Account: Government Securities Port-
folio (MM), Equitable Tax-Free Account (STMB)

Calvert Group
1700 Pennsylvania Ave., N.W.
Washington, DC 20006
(301) 951-4820, (800) 368-2748

Calvert Fund Equity Portfolio (G), Calvert Fund
Income Portfolio (CB), Calvert Social Invest-
ment Fund: Managed Growth Portfolio (G + I),
Calvert Social Investment Fund: Money Mar-
ket Portfolio (MM), Calvert Tax-Free Re-
serves: Limited-Term Portfolio (STMB), Cal-
vert Tax-Free Reserves: Long-Term Portfolio
(LTMB), Calvert Tax-Free Reserves: Money
Market Portfolio (STMB), First Variable Rate
Fund for Government Income (MM), Money
Management Plus Government Portfolio (MM),
Money Management Plus: Prime Portfolio
(MM), Money Management Plus: Tax-Free
Portfolio (STMB), Washington Area Growth
Fund (G)

CAM Fund
P.O. Box 1986
Valley Forge, PA 19481
(215) 783-6789, (800) 423-2345,
(800) 362-7400 (PA only)

Consolidated Asset Management Fund (MM)

Capital Cash
200 Park Ave., Suite 4515
New York, NY 10017
(212) 697-6666

Capital Cash Management Trust (MM), Cash
Assets Trust (MM), Churchill Cash Reserves
Trust (MM), Hawaiian Tax-Free Trust (SMB-
LT), Oxford Cash Management Fund (MM),
Prime Cash Fund (MM), Short Term Asset
Reserves (MM), Trinity Liquid Assets Trust
(MM)

Capital Research & Management
333 South Hope Street
Los Angeles, CA 90071
(213) 486-9200, (800) 421-0180,
(213) 486-9651 (collect)

and

Four Embarcadero Center, P.O. Box 7650
San Francisco, CA 94120
(415) 421-9360

AMCAP Fund (G), American Balanced Fund
(B), American Mutual Fund (G + I), Bond Fund
of America (CB), Bond Portfolio for Endow-
ments (CB), Cash Management Trust of
America (MM), Endowments (G + I), Euro-
Pacific Growth Fund (INT), Fundamental
Investors (G + I), Growth Fund of America (G),
Income Fund of America (I), Investment
Company of America (G + I), New Economy
Fund (G), New Perspective Fund (INT), Tax-
Exempt Bond Fund of America (LTMB), Tax-
Exempt Fund of California (SMB-LT), Tax-Ex-
empt Fund of Maryland (SMB-LT), Tax-Ex-
empt Fund of Virginia (SMB-LT), U.S. Gov-
ernment Guaranteed Securities Fund (USGI),
Washington Mutual Investors Fund (G + I)

Cardinal
155 East Broad Street
Columbus, OH 43215
(614) 464-7041, (800) 262-9446,
(800) 848-7734

Cardinal Fund (G), Cardinal Government Securities Trust (MM), Cardinal Tax Exempt Money Trust (STMB)

Carillon Investments
1876 Waycross Road, P.O. Box 5304
Cincinnati, OH 45201
(513) 595-2600

Carillon Fund: The Bond Portfolio (CB), Carillon Fund: The Equity Portfolio (G + I), Carillon Fund: The Money Market Portfolio (MM)

Carlisle-Asher Management Company
Legal Arts Building, Front and Lemon Streets
Media, PA 19063
(215) 565-3131, (800) 523-7594

Afuture Fund (G)

Carnegie
1331 Euclid Avenue
Cleveland, OH 44115
(216) 781-4440, (800) 321-2322

Carnegie Government Securities Trust: Carnegie High Yield Government Series (USGI), Carnegie Government Securities Trust: Money Market Series (MM), Carnegie Tax Free Income Trust (STMB), Carnegie-Cappiello Trust: Growth Series (G), Carnegie-Cappiello Trust: Total Return Series (G + I), Liquid Capital Income Trust (MM)

CCM Partners
44 Montgomery Street, Suite 2265
San Francisco, CA 94104
(415) 398-2727

California GNMA Fund (GNMA), California Money Fund For Investment in Federal Securities (MM), California Tax Free Income Fund (STMB-LT), California Tax Free Money Market Fund (STMB-ST)

Century Shares Trust
One Liberty Square
Boston, MA 02109
(617) 482-3060, (800) 321-1928

Century Shares Trust (G + I)

Charter
1850 Two Lincoln Centre
5420 LBJ Freeway/LB No. 66
Dallas, TX 75240
(214) 980-1800, (800) 392-9681

Associated Planners Stock Fund (G), Charter Fund (G)

Chubb Securities
832 Georgia Avenue
Chattanooga, TN 37402
(615) 756-2887, (800) 251-7202

Chubb America Fund: Gold Stock Portfolio (PMG), Chubb America Fund: Money Market Portfolio (MM), Chubb America Fund: World Growth Stock Portfolio (G)

CIGNA
P.O. Box 7728
Philadelphia, PA 19103
(215) 241-4000, (800) 562-4462
and
1380 Main Street
Springfield, MA 01103
(413) 781-7776, (800) 562-4462

CIGNA Aggressive Growth Fund (AG), CIGNA Cash Fund (MM), CIGNA Growth Fund (G), CIGNA High Yield Fund (CB), CIGNA Income Fund (CB), CIGNA Money Market Fund (MM), CIGNA Municipal Bond Fund (LTMB), CIGNA Tax-Exempt Cash Fund (STMB), CIGNA Value Fund (G + I)

Clipper Fund
9601 Wilshire Boulevard, Suite 828
Beverly Hills, CA 90210
(213) 278-4461

Clipper Fund (G)

Colonial
One Financial Center
Boston, MA 02111
(617) 426-3750, (800) 426-3750

Colonial Advanced Strategies Gold Trust (PMG), Colonial Capital Appreciation Trust (G), Colonial Corporate Cash Trust I (I), Colonial Corporate Cash Trust II (I), Colonial Enhanced Mortgage Trust (GNMA), Colonial Fund (G + I), Colonial Government Securities Plus Trust (USGI), Colonial Growth Shares (G), Colonial High Yield Securities Trust (CB), Colonial Income Fund (CB), Colonial Money Market Trust (MM), Colonial Option Income Trust Portfolio I (OI), Colonial Option Income Trust Portfolio II (OI), Colonial Tax-Exempt Trust: Colonial Tax-Exempt High Yield Fund (LTMB), Colonial Tax-Exempt Trust: Colonial Tax-Exempt Insured Fund (LTMB)

Columbia
1301 S.W. Fifth Avenue, P.O. Box 1350
Portland, OR 97207
(503) 222-3600, (800) 547-1037

Columbia Daily Income Company (MM), Columbia Fixed Income Securities Fund (I), Columbia Growth Fund (G), Columbia Municipal Bond Fund (SMB-LT), Columbia Special Fund (AG)

Commonwealth Group
P.O. Box 8687
1500 Forest Ave., Suite 223
Richmond, VA 23229
(804) 285-8211, (800) 527-9500

Commonwealth Group: Bowser Growth Fund (G), Commonwealth Group: Newport Far East Fund (INT), Commonwealth Group: Nicholson Growth Fund (AG)

Composite
Seafirst Financial Center, 9th Floor
Spokane, WA 99201
(509) 624-4101, (800) 541-0830,
(800) 572-5828 (WA only)

Composite Bond & Stock Fund (B), Composite Cash Management Company (MM), Composite Fund (G + I), Composite Income Fund (I), Composite Tax-Exempt Bond Fund (LTMB), Composite U.S. Government Securities (GNMA)

Concord Fund
60 State Street, Suite 930
Boston, MA 02109
(617) 742-7077

Concord Fund (AG)

Connecticut Mutual
140 Garden Street
Hartford, CT 06154
(203) 727-6500, (800) 243-0018

Connecticut Mutual Financial Services Series Fund I: Total Return Portfolio (G + I), Connecticut Mutual Financial Services Series Fund I: Growth Portfolio (G), Connecticut Mutual Financial Services Series Fund I: Income Portfolio (I), Connecticut Mutual Financial Services Series Fund I: Money Market Portfolio (MM), Connecticut Mutual Investment Account: Connecticut Mutual Growth Account (G), Connecticut Mutual Investment Accounts: Connecticut Mutual Liquid Account (MM), Connecticut Mutual Investment Accounts: Connecticut Mutual Government Securities Account (USGI), Connecticut Mutual Investment Accounts: Connecticut Mutual Income Account (I), Connecticut Mutual Investment Accounts: Connecticut Mutual Total Return Account (G + I)

Continental
6631 East Ironwood Drive
Scottsdale, AZ 85253
(602) 991-1363

Continental Mutual Investment Fund (G + I), Foundation Growth Stock Fund (G)

Continental Equities
180 Maiden Lane
New York, NY 10038
(212) 440-3863, (800) 626-3863

Continental Mutual Funds Trust: Continental Option Income Plus Fund (OI)

Co-Operative Bank
265 Franklin Street
Boston, MA 02110
(617) 439-4416

Co-Operative Bank Investment Fund I (I)

Copley Financial Services
109 Howe Street, P.O. Box 66
Fall River, MA 02724
(617) 674-8459

Copley Tax Managed Trust (I)

Country Capital
1701 Towanda Avenue
Bloomington, IL 61701
(309) 557-2444, (800) 322-3838 (IL only)

Country Capital Growth Fund (G), Country Capital Income Fund (I), Country Capital Money Market Fund (MM), Country Capital Tax-Exempt Bond Fund (LTMB)

Craig-Hallum
701 Fourth Avenue South
Minneapolis, MN 55415
(612) 332-1212

General Securities (G + I)

Criterion Group
333 Clay Street, Suite 4300
Houston, TX 77002
(713) 751-2400, (800) 231-4645,
(800) 392-7802 (TX only)

Commerce Income Shares (I), Criterion Bond Fund: U.S. Government High Yield Trust (USGI), Criterion Technology Fund (AG), Current Interest: Money Market Portfolio (MM), Current Interest: U.S. Government Portfolio (MM), Investment Quality Interest (CB), Lowry Market Timing Fund (AG), Pilot Fund (AG), Sunbelt Growth Fund (G), Tax Free Fund: Current Interest Tax Free Portfolio (STMB), Tax Free Fund: Quality Tax Free Bond Portfolio (LTMB)

Cumberland
614 Landis Avenue, P.O. Box 663
Vineland, NJ 08360
(609) 692-6690, (800) 257-7013,
(800) 232-6692 (NJ only)

Cumberland Growth Fund (G)

Dayton Kahn Heppe Hancock
Architect's Building, Suite 1905
Philadelphia, PA 19103
(215) 988-0277

Gibraltar Fund (G)

Dean Witter
One World Trade Center, 59th Floor
New York, NY 10048
(212) 545-5000, (212) 938-4554,
(800) 222-3326, (800) 221-2685

Active Assets: Government Securities Trust (MM), Active Assets: Money Trust (MM), Active Assets: Tax-Free Trust (STMB), Dean Witter California Tax-Free Income Fund (SMB-LT), Dean Witter Convertible Securities Trust (G + I), Dean Witter Developing Growth Securities Trust (AG), Dean Witter Dividend Growth Securities (G + I), Dean Witter High Yield Securities (CB), Dean Witter Industry-Valued Securities (G), Dean Witter Natural Resource Development Securities (G), Dean Witter New York Tax-Free Income Fund (SMB-LT), Dean Witter Option Income Trust (OI), Dean Witter Tax Advantaged Corporate Trust (I), Dean Witter Tax Exempt Securities (LTMB), Dean Witter U.S. Government Securities Trust (USGI), Dean Witter Variable Annuity Investment Series: Equity Portfolio (G), Dean Witter Variable Annuity Investment Series: High Yield Portfolio (CB), Dean Witter Variable Annuity Investment Series: Money Market Portfolio (MM), Dean Witter World Wide Investment Trust (INT), Dean Witter/Sears Liquid Asset Fund (MM), Dean Witter/Sears Tax-Free Daily Income Fund (STMB), Dean Witter/Sears U.S. Government Money Market Trust (MM), Sears Tax-Exempt Reinvestment Fund (LTMB)

Decision Funds. *see* Alliance/Wood Struthers.

Delaware Group
Ten Penn Center Plaza
Philadelphia, PA 19103
(215) 988-1333, (800) 523-4640,
(800) 523-1918

DMC Tax-Free Income Trust: Pennsylvania (SMB-LT), DMC Tax-Free Income USA: USA Insured Series (LTMB), DMC Tax-Free Income—USA: USA Series (LTMB), Decatur Income Fund (I), Delaware Cash Reserve (MM), Delaware Fund (G + I), Delaware Group Government Fund: GNMA Series (GNMA), Delaware Group Government Fund: U.S. Government Series (USGI), Delaware Tax Free Money Fund (STMB), Delaware Treasury Reserves: Investors Series (USGI), Delaware Treasury Reserves: Money Market Series (MM), Delchester Bond Fund (CB), Delta Trend Fund (AG)

Dodge and Cox
One Post Street, 35th Floor
Crocker Plaza
San Francisco, CA 94104
(415) 981-1710

Dodge & Cox Balanced Fund (B), Dodge & Cox Stock Fund (G + I)

Drexel Burnham Lambert
60 Broad Street
New York, NY 10004
(212) 482-1623, (800) 272-2700

Benefactors Money Market Fund (MM), DBL Cash Fund: Government Securities Portfolio (MM), DBL Cash Fund: Money Market Portfolio (MM), DBL Tax-Free Cash Fund: Limited Term Portfolio (LTMB), DBL Tax-Free Cash Fund: Money Market Portfolio (STMB), Drexel Burnham Fund (G), Drexel Series Trust: Bond-Debenture Series (I), Drexel Series Trust: Emerging Growth Series (AG), Drexel Series Trust: Government Securities Series (USGI), Drexel Series Trust: Growth Series (G), Drexel Series Trust: Money Market Series (MM), Drexel Series Trust: Option Income Series (OI), Fenimore International Fund (INT)

Dreyfus
767 Fifth Avenue
New York, NY 10153
and
666 Old Country Road
Garden City, NY 11530
(718) 895-1396, (718) 895-1206,
(800) 645-6561, (800) 242-8671

Dreyfus A Bonds Plus (CB), Dreyfus California Tax Exempt Bond Fund (SMB-LT), Dreyfus Capital Value Fund (G), Dreyfus Cash Management (MM), Dreyfus Dollar International Fund (MM), Dreyfus Fund (G + I), Dreyfus GNMA Fund (GNMA), Dreyfus Government Cash Management (MM), Dreyfus Growth Opportunity Fund (G), Dreyfus Institutional Money Market Fund: Government Series (MM), Dreyfus Institutional Money Market Fund: Money Market Series (MM), Dreyfus Insured Tax Exempt Bond Fund (LTMB), Dreyfus Intermediate Tax Exempt

Bond Fund (LTMB), Dreyfus Leverage Fund (AG), Dreyfus Liquid Assets (MM), Dreyfus Massachusetts Tax Exempt Bond Fund (SMB-LT), Dreyfus Money Market Instruments: Government Securities Series (MM), Dreyfus Money Market Instruments: Money Market Series (MM), Dreyfus New Leader Fund (G), Dreyfus New York Tax Exempt Bond Fund (SMB-LT), Dreyfus Special Income Fund (I), Dreyfus Strategic Income Fund (I), Dreyfus Strategic Investing Fund (G), Dreyfus Tax Exempt Bond Fund (LTMB), Dreyfus Tax Exempt Cash Management (STMB), Dreyfus Tax Exempt Money Market Fund (STMB), Dreyfus Third Century Fund (G), General Aggressive Growth Fund (AG), General Government Securities Money Market Fund (MM), General Money Market Fund (MM), General Tax Exempt Bond Fund (LTMB), General Tax Exempt Money Market Fund (STMB)

Eaton Vance
24 Federal Street
Boston, MA 02110
(617) 482-8260, (800) 225-6265

Bond Fund For Bank Trust Departments: Government Obligations Portfolio (USGI), Bond Fund For Bank Trust Departments: Near Term Bond Portfolio (CB), Bond Fund For Bank Trust Departments: Tax Free Bond Portfolio (STMB), Bond Fund For Bank Trust Departments: Tax Free Income Portfolio (LTMB), Bond Fund For Bank Trust Departments: Total Return Bond Portfolio (CB), Capital Exchange Fund (G + I), Depositors Fund of Boston (G + I), Diversification Fund (G + I), Eaton & Howard Stock Fund (G + I), Eaton Vance Cash Management Fund (MM), Eaton Vance Government Obligations Trust (USGI), Eaton Vance Growth Fund (G), Eaton Vance High Yield Fund (CB), Eaton Vance Income Fund of Boston (I), Eaton Vance Investors Fund (B), Eaton Vance Municipal Bond Fund (LTMB), Eaton Vance Special Equities Fund (G), Eaton Vance Tax Free Reserves (STMB), Eaton Vance Tax-Managed Trust (G), Equity Fund For Bank Trust Departments: Wright Blue Chip Portfolio (G + I), Equity Fund For Bank Trust Departments: Wright Junior Blue Chip Portfolio (G + I), Equity Fund For Bank Trust Departments: Wright Quality Core Portfolio (G + I), Exchange Fund of Boston (G + I), Fiduciary Exchange Fund (G + I), Leverage Fund of Boston (AG), Money Market Fund For Bank Trust Departments (MM), Nautilus Fund (AG), Second Fiduciary Exchange Fund (G + I), Vance Sanders Exchange Fund (G + I), Vance Sanders Special Fund (G)

EBI Funds. *see* INVESCO Capital Management.

Elfun Funds. *see* General Electric Investment Corporation.

Evergreen Funds
550 Mamaroneck Avenue
Harrison, NY 10528
(914) 698-5711, (800) 635-0003

Evergreen Fund (AG), Evergreen Limited Market Fund (AG), Evergreen Total Return Fund (G + I)

Farm Bureau
5400 University Avenue
West Des Moines, IA 50265
(515) 225-5400, (800) 422-3175, (IA only)
(800) 247-4170

FBL Money Market Fund (MM), Farm Bureau Growth Fund (G + I)

Federated
421 Seventh Avenue
Pittsburgh, PA 15219
(412) 288-1900, (800) 245-3391,
(800) 245-2423

A.T. Ohio Tax-Free Money Fund (SMB-ST), American Leaders Fund (G + I), Automated Cash Management Trust (MM), Automated Government Money Trust (MM), EGT Money Market Trust (MM), Edward D. Jones & Co. Daily Passport Cash Trust (MM), FT International Trust (INT), Federated Bond Fund (CB), Federated Corporate Cash Trust (I), Federated Exchange Fund (G + I), Federated Floating Rate Trust (I), Federated GNMA Trust (GNMA), Federated Growth Trust (AG), Federated High Income Securities (CB), Federated High Quality Stock Fund (G + I), Federated High Yield Trust (I), Federated Income Trust (I), Federated Intermediate Government Trust (USGI), Federated Intermediate Municipal Trust (LTMB), Federated Master Trust (MM), Federated Short-Intermediate Government Trust (USGI), Federated Short-Intermediate Municipal Trust (STMB), Federated Stock Trust (G + I), Federated Stock and Bond Fund (B), Federated Tax-Free Income Fund (LTMB), Federated Tax-Free Trust (STMB), Federated U.S. Government Fund (USGI), Fort Washington Money Market Fund (MM), Fund for U.S. Government Securities (USGI), High Yield Cash Trust (MM), Legg Mason Cash Reserve Trust (MM), Liberty U.S. Government Money Market Trust (MM), Liquid Cash Trust (MM), Lutheran Brotherhood Fund (G + I), Lutheran

Brotherhood Income Fund (I), Lutheran Brotherhood Municipal Bond Fund (LTMB), Lutheran Brotherhood Money Market Fund (MM), Money Market Management (MM), Money Market Trust (MM), Morgan Keegan Daily Cash Trust (MM), New York Tax-Free Trust (SMB-ST), Tax Free Instruments Trust (STMB), Trust for Cash Reserves (MM), Trust for Short-Term U.S. Government Securities (MM), Trust for U.S. Treasury Obligations (MM)

Fidelity
82 Devonshire Street
Boston, MA 02109
(617) 570-7000, (617) 523-1919 (collect, MA only), (800) 544-6666

Congress Street Fund (G + I), Daily Money Fund: Money Market Portfolio (MM), Daily Money Fund: Treasury Portfolio (MM), Daily Tax-Exempt Money Fund (STMB), Equity Portfolio-Growth (AG), Equity Portfolio-Income (I), Fidelity Aggressive Tax Free Fund (LTMB), Fidelity California Tax Free Fund: Municipal Bond Portfolio (SMB-LT), Fidelity California Tax Free Fund: (SMB-ST), Fidelity Cash Reserves (MM), Fidelity Contrafund (G), Fidelity Corporate Bond Fund (CB), Fidelity Daily Income Trust (MM), Fidelity Destiny Fund (G), Fidelity Discoverer Fund (G), Fidelity Equity-Income Fund (G + I), Fidelity Exchange Fund (G), Fidelity Freedom Fund (AG), Fidelity Fund (G + I), Fidelity GNMA Portfolio (GNMA), Fidelity Government Securities Fund (USGI), Fidelity Growth & Income Portfolio (G + I), Fidelity High Income Fund (CB), Fidelity High Yield Municipals (LTMB), Fidelity Institutional Cash Portfolios: U.S. Treasury Portfolio (MM), Fidelity Institutional Cash Portfolios: Money Market Portfolio (MM), Fidelity Institutional Cash Portfolios: U.S. Government Portfolio (MM), Fidelity Institutional Tax-Exempt Cash Portfolios (STMB), Fidelity Limited Term Municipals (LTMB), Fidelity Magellan Fund (AG), Fidelity Massachusetts Tax Free Fund: Money Market Portfolio (SMB-ST), Fidelity Massachusetts Tax Free Fund: Municipal Bond Portfolio (SMB-LT), Fidelity Mercury Fund (AG), Fidelity Michigan Tax Free Fund (SMB-LT), Fidelity Minnesota Tax Free Fund (SMB-LT), Fidelity Money Market Trust: Domestic Money Market Portfolio (MM), Fidelity Money Market Trust: U.S. Government Portfolio (MM), Fidelity Money Market Trust: U.S. Treasury Portfolio (MM), Fidelity Mortgage Securities Fund (GNMA), Fidelity Municipal Bond Fund (LTMB), Fidelity New York Tax Free Fund: In-

sured Tax Free Portfolio (SMB-ST), Fidelity New York Tax Free Fund: Municipal Bond Portfolio (SMB-LT), Fidelity New York Tax Free Fund: Short-Term Municipal Bond Portfolio (SMB-ST), Fidelity OTC Portfolio (AG), Fidelity Ohio Tax Free Fund (SMB-LT), Fidelity Overseas Fund (INT), Fidelity Puritan Fund (G + I), Fidelity Qualified Dividend Fund (I), Fidelity Select Portfolios: Brokerage Portfolio (AG), Fidelity Select Portfolios: Chemicals Portfolio (AG), Fidelity Select Portfolios: Computers Portfolio (AG), Fidelity Select Portfolios: Defense & Aerospace Portfolio (AG), Fidelity Select Portfolios: Electronics Portfolio (AG), Fidelity Select Portfolios: Energy Portfolio (AG), Fidelity Select Portfolios: Financial Services Portfolio (AG), Fidelity Select Portfolios: Food & Agriculture Portfolio (AG), Fidelity Select Portfolios: Health Care Portfolio (AG), Fidelity Select Portfolios: Leisure Portfolio (AG), Fidelity Select Portfolios: MMKT Portfolio (MM), Fidelity Select Portfolios: Precious Metals and Minerals Portfolio (PMB), Fidelity Select Portfolios: Software Portfolio (AG), Fidelity Select Portfolios: Technology Portfolio (AG), Fidelity Select Portfolios: Telecommunications Portfolio (AG), Fidelity Select Portfolios: Utilities Portfolio (G), Fidelity Special Situations Fund (AG), Fidelity Tax-Exempt Money Market Trust (STMB), Fidelity Thrift Trust (CB), Fidelity Trend Fund (G), Fidelity U.S. Government Reserves (MM), Fidelity Variable Annuity (MM), Financial Reserves (MM), Fixed-Income Portfolios, Limited Term Series (CB), North Carolina Cash Management Trust: Money Market Portfolio (MM), Rodney Square Fund: Money Market Portfolio (MM), Rodney Square Fund: U.S. Government Portfolio (MM), Rodney Square Tax Exempt Fund (STMB)

Fiduciary Management
222 East Mason Street
Milwaukee, WI 53202
(414) 271-6666

Fiduciary Capital Growth (G + I)

Financial Programs
6312 South Fiddler's Green Circle,
P.O. Box 2040
Englewood, CO 80111
(303) 779-1233, (800) 532-9145 (CO only)
(800) 525-8085

Financial Bond Shares: Bond Share Portfolio (I), Financial Bond Shares: High Yield Bond Portfolio (I), Financial Daily Income Shares (MM), Financial Dynamics Fund (AG), Financial Group Portfolio: Energy (AG), Financial Group Portfolio: Gold (AG), Financial Group Portfolio: Health Sciences (AG), Financial Group Portfolio: Leisure (AG), Financial Group Portfolio: Pacific Basin (AG), Financial Group Portfolio: Technology (AG), Financial Industrial Fund (G + I), Financial Industrial Income Fund (I), Financial Tax Free Income Shares (LTMB), Financial Tax Free Money Fund (STMB), World of Technology (AG)

Finomic Investment
2600 InterFirst Plaza
1100 Louisiana, Suite 4550
Houston, TX 77002
(713) 659-2611

Finomic Investment Fund (AG)

First Investors
120 Wall Street
New York, NY 10005
(212) 208-6000, (800) 423-4026

First Investors Adjustable Preferred Fund (I), First Investors Bond Appreciation Fund (CB), First Investors Cash Management Fund (MM), First Investors Discovery Fund (AG), First Investors Fund For Growth (AG), First Investors Fund For Income (CB), First Investors Government Fund (USGI), First Investors International Securities Fund (INT), First Investors Natural Resources Fund (G + I), First Investors New York Tax Free Fund (SMB-LT), First Investors Ninety-Ten Fund (OI), First Investors Option Fund (OI), First Investors Special Bond Fund (CB), First Investors Tax Exempt Fund (LTMB), First Investors Tax Exempt Money Market Fund (STMB)

First Mutual
560 Lexington Avenue, 9th Floor
New York, NY 10022
(212) 759-7755

First Mutual Fund (G)

First Pacific Advisors
10301 West Pico Boulevard
Los Angeles, CA 90064
(213) 277-4900, (800) 421-4374

FPA Capital Fund (G), FPA New Income (I), FPA Paramount Fund (G + I), FPA Perennial Fund (G + I)

First Trust
110 North Franklin Street, Room 406
Chicago, IL 60606
(312) 781-9490, (800) 523-0076

First Trust Money Market Fund: The General Purpose Portfolio (MM), First Trust Money Market Fund: The Government Portfolio (MM), First Trust Tax-Free Fund: Money Market Portfolio (STMB)

Flagship
One First National Plaza, Suite 910
Dayton, OH 45402
(513) 461-0332, (800) 227-4648,
(800) 354-7447 (OH only)

Corporate Cash Management Fund (I), Flagship Double Tax Exempt Funds: Michigan Double Tax Exempt Fund (SMB-LT), Flagship Double Tax Exempt Funds: Ohio Double Tax Exempt Fund (SMB-LT)

Flex Funds. see Meeder & Associates.

Florida Mutual Funds Group
7301 West Palmetto Park Road, Suite C-105
Boca Raton, FL 33433
(305) 392-2667, (800) 432-1592

Pinnacle Government Fund (MM)

Forty-Four Management
1 State Street Plaza
New York, NY 10004
(212) 344-4224, (800) 221-7836

44 Wall Street Fund (AG), 44 Wall Street Equity Fund (AG)

Founders Mutual Depositors Corporation
3033 East First Avenue, Suite 810
Denver, CO 80206
(303) 394-4404, (800) 525-2440,
(800) 874-6301 (CO only)

Founders Growth Fund (G), Founders Income Fund (G + I), Founders Money Market Fund (MM), Founders Mutual Fund (G + I), Founders Special Fund (AG)

Franklin Group of Funds
777 Mariners Island Boulevard
San Mateo, CA 94404
(415) 570-3000, (800) 632-2180

AGE High Income Fund (CB), Birr Wilson Money Fund (MM), Franklin California Tax-Free Income Fund (SMB-LT), Franklin California Tax-Free Trust: Franklin California Insured Tax-Free Income Fund (SMB-LT), Franklin California Tax-Free Trust: Franklin California Tax-Exempt Money Fund (SMB-ST), Franklin Corporate Cash Management Fund (I), Franklin Custodian Funds: DynaTech Series (AG), Franklin Custodian Funds: Growth Series (G), Franklin Custodian Funds: Income Series (I),

Franklin Custodian Funds: U.S. Government Securities Series (GNMA), Franklin Custodian Funds: Utilities Series (G + I), Franklin Equity Fund (G), Franklin Federal Money Fund (MM), Franklin Federal Tax Free Income Fund (LTMB), Franklin Gold Fund (PMG), Franklin Institutional Fiduciary Trust: Equity Portfolio (G + I), Franklin Institutional Fiduciary Trust: GNMA Portfolio (GNMA), Franklin Institutional Fiduciary Trust: Money Market Portfolio (MM), Franklin Institutional Fiduciary Trust: Precious Metals Portfolio (PMG), Franklin Institutional Fiduciary Trust: Tax-Exempt Portfolio (LTMB), Franklin Money Fund (MM), Franklin New York Tax-Free Income Fund (SMB-LT), Franklin Option Fund (OI), Franklin Tax-Exempt Money Fund (STMB), Franklin Tax-Free Trust: Franklin Insured Tax-Free Income Fund (LTMB), Franklin Tax-Free Trust: Franklin Massachusetts Insured Tax-Free Income Fund (SMB-LT), Franklin Tax-Free Trust: Franklin Massachusetts Insured Tax-Free Income Fund (SMB-LT), Franklin Tax-Free Trust: Franklin Michigan Insured Tax-Free Income Fund (SMB-LT), Franklin Tax-Free Trust: Franklin Minnesota Insured Tax-Free Income Fund (SMB-LT), Franklin Tax-Free Trust: Franklin Ohio Insured Tax-Free Income Fund (SMB-LT), Franklin Tax-Free Trust: Franklin Puerto Rico Tax-Free Income Fund (SMB-LT)

Furman, Anderson & Co.
19 Rector Street
New York, NY 10006
(212) 509-8532

The Rainbow Fund (G)

Furman Selz
230 Park Avenue, 13th Floor
New York, NY 10169
(212) 309-8400, (800) 221-3780

FundTrust; FundTrust Aggresive Growth Fund (AG), FundTrust: FundTrust Growth & Income Fund (G + I), FundTrust: FundTrust Growth Fund (G), FundTrust: FundTrust Income Fund (I), FundTrust: High Yield Investment Fund (CB), FundTrust: International Equity Fund (INT), FundTrust: Money Fund (MM), Mariner Institutional Fund: Mariner Government Fund (MM), Mariner Institutional Funds: Mariner Cash Management Fund (MM), Mariner Institutional Funds: Mariner U.S. Treasury Fund (MM), Mariner Tax-Free Institutional Funds: Mariner Tax-Free Money Market Fund (STMB)

Gabelli Funds
P.O. Box 1634, Grand Central Station
New York, NY 10163
(212) 490-3670, (800) 422-3554

Gabelli Asset Fund (G)

Gateway
400 TechneCenter Road
Milford, OH 45150
(513) 248-2700, (800) 354-6339

Gateway Growth Plus Fund (G), Gateway Option Income Fund (OI)

GEICO
GEICO Plaza
Washington, DC 20076
(301) 986-2200, (800) 832-6232

GEICO Adjustable Rate Preferred Fund (I), Government Securities Cash Fund (MM)

General Electric Investment Corporation
112 Prospect Street, P.O. Box 7900
Stamford, CT 06904
(203) 357-4104

Elfun Income Fund (I), Elfun Tax Exempt Income Fund (LTMB), Elfun Trusts (G + I), General Electric S&S Program: Growth and Income (G + I), General Electric S&S Program: Long Term (I)

General Funds. see Dreyfus.

General Securities
701 4th Avenue South
Minneapolis, MN 55415
(612) 332-1212

General Securities (G)

Gibraltar Fund. see Dayton Kahn Heppe Hancock.

Gintel Equity Management
Greenwich Office Park, O.P.- 6
Greenwich, CT 06830
(203) 622-6402, (800) 243-5808

Gintel Capital ERISA Fund (G + I), Gintel Fund (G)

GIT Investment Funds
1655 North Fort Myer Drive
Arlington, VA 22209
(703) 528-3600, (800) 336-3063,
(800) 572-2050 (VA only)

GIT Cash Trust: Government Money Market Fund (MM), GIT Cash Trust: Regular Money Market Fund (MM), GIT Equity Trust: GIT Equity Income Fund (I), GIT Equity Trust: GIT Equity Select Growth Fund (G), GIT Equity Trust: GIT Equity Special Growth Fund (AG), GIT Income Trust: GIT Income Trust A-Rated Income Fund: (CB), GIT Income Trust: GIT Income Trust Hedged Mortgage Securities Portfolio (GNMA), GIT Income Trust Maximum Income Fund (CB), GIT Tax-Free Trust: High Yield Fund (LTMB), GIT Tax-Free Trust: Money Market Fund (STMB), Government Investors Trust (MM)

Gradison
580 Building
6th & Walnut Streets
Cincinnati, OH 45202
(513) 579-5700, (800) 582-7062,
(800) 543-1818 (OH only)

Gradison Cash Reserves Trust (MM), Gradison Growth Trust: Emerging Growth Fund (AG), Gradison Growth Trust: Established Growth Fund (G), Gradison U.S. Government Trust (MM)

Granaham-Everitt Investors
303 Wyman Street
Waltham, MA 02154
(617) 890-4415, (617) 350-0330,
(800) 572-0006

Nova Fund (G)

Grantham, Mayo, Van Otterloo
40 Industrial Park Road
Hingham, MA 02043
(617) 749-1416, (800) 235-3322

Ivy Growth Fund (G), Ivy Institutional Fund (G)

Greenspring Fund. see Key Equity Management Corporation.

Growth Industry Shares
135 South LaSalle Street
Chicago, IL 60603
(312) 236-1600, (312) 346-4830

Growth Industry Shares (G)

G.T. Global Funds
601 Montgomery Street, Suite 1400
San Francisco, CA 94111
(415) 392-6181, (800) 824-8361 (CA only),
(800) 824-1580

G.T. Global Growth Funds: G.T. Europe Growth Fund (INT), G.T. Global Growth Funds: G.T. International Growth Fund (INT), G.T. Global Growth Funds: G.T. Japan Growth Fund (INT), G.T. Global Growth Funds: G.T. Pacific Growth Fund (INT)

Guardian Life Insurance
201 Park Avenue South
New York, NY 10003
(212) 598-8000, (800) 221-3253,
(800) 522-7800 (NY only)

Guardian Cash Management Trust (MM), Guardian Park Avenue Fund (G)

Hartford
200 Hopmeadows
Hartford, CT 06104
(203) 683-8163, (800) 862-6667

HVA Advisers Fund (G + I), HVA Aggressive Growth Fund (AG), HVA Fixed Income Fund (CB), HVA Government Securities Fund (MM), HVA Money Market Fund (MM), HVA Stock Fund (G), Hartford Money Market Fund (MM)

Hartwell Management Company
515 Madison Avenue, 31st Floor
New York, NY 10022
(212) 308-3355, (800) 645-6405

Hartwell Growth Fund (AG), Hartwell Leverage Fund (AG)

Heine Management Group
253 Post Road West, P. O. Box 830
Westport, CT 06881
(203) 222-1624, (800) 225-8558

LMH Fund (G + I)

Heine Securities
26 Broadway
New York, NY 10004
(212) 908-4047, (800) 457-0211

Mutual Beacon Fund (G + I), Mutual Qualified Income Fund (G + I), Mutual Shares Corp (G + I)

Heritage Funds
1400 66th Street North
St. Petersburg, FL 33710
(813) 344-8250, (800) 237-0702

Heritage Capital Appreciation Trust (G), Heritage Cash Trust (MM)

Hilliard-Lyons
545 South Third Street
Louisville, KY 40202
(502) 588-8400, (800) 626-2023

Hilliard-Lyons Government Fund (MM)

Home Life
253 Broadway
New York, NY 10007
(212) 306-2000

Home Life Bond Fund (CB), Home Life Equity Fund (G), Home Life Liquid Fund (MM), Home Life Money Management Fund (MM)

Horace Mann
One Horace Mann Plaza
Springfield, IL 62715
(217) 789-2500

Horace Mann Balanced Fund (B), Horace Mann Growth Fund (G), Horace Mann Income Fund (I), Horace Mann Short-Term Investment Fund (I)

Hotckis & Wiley
800 West 6th Street, Suite 540
Los Angeles, CA 90017
(213) 623-4073

Olympic Trust: Total Return Series (B)

Hudson Capital
One Southwest Columbia, Suite 400
Portland, OR 97258
(503) 223-2086

Oregon Municipal Bond Fund (SMB-LT)

E.F. Hutton Group
31 West 52nd Street
New York, NY 10019
(212) 969-5300, (800) 334-2626,
(800) 422-0214 (NY only)

Cash Reserve Management (MM), Hutton AMA Cash Fund (MM), Hutton California Municipal Fund (SMB-LT), Hutton Government Fund (MM), Hutton Investment Series: Bond & Income Series (CB), Hutton Investment Series: Emerging Growth Series (AG), Hutton Investment Series: Government Securities Series (USGI), Hutton Investment Series: Growth Series (G), Hutton Investment Series: Option Income Series (OI), Hutton Investment Series: Short Term Investment Series (MM), Hutton National Municipal Fund (LTMB), Hutton New York Municipal Fund (SMB-LT), Municipal Cash Reserve Management (STMB)

ICU
5710 Mineral Point Road, P. O. Box 431
Madison, WI 53701
(608) 231-4000

CU Members Income Fund (I)

IDEX Fund
600 Cleveland St., Suite 800
P. O. Box 2437
Clearwater, FL 33517
(813) 446-3333, (800) 237-3055

IDEX Fund (G), IDEX II (G)

IDS Mutual Fund Group
1000 Roanoke Building
Minneapolis, MN 55474
(612) 372-3131, (800) 328-8300

IDS Bond Fund (CB), IDS Cash Management Fund (MM), IDS Discovery Fund (AG), IDS Equity Plus Fund (G + I), IDS Extra Income Fund (CB), IDS Federal Income Fund (USGI), IDS Growth Fund (G), IDS High Yield Tax-Exempt Fund (LTMB), IDS International Fund (INT), IDS Life Moneyshare Fund (MM), IDS Life Special Income Fund (I), IDS Managed Retirement Fund (G + I), IDS Mutual (B), IDS New Dimensions Fund (G), IDS Precious Metals Fund (PMG), IDS Progressive Fund (AG), IDS Selective Fund (CB), IDS Stock Fund (G + I), IDS Strategy Fund: Aggressive Equity Portfolio (AG), IDS Strategy Fund: Equity Portfolio (G + I), IDS Strategy Fund: Income Portfolio (CB), IDS Strategy Fund: Money Market Portfolio (MM), IDS Tax Exempt Bond Fund (LTMB), IDS Tax-Free Money Fund (STMB)

Independent CashFlow
One University Plaza, Suite 200
Hackensack, NJ 07601
(201) 487-6677, (800) 336-2468

Independent CashFlow Trust (MM)

Industrial Series Trust Funds. *see* Mackenzie Investment Management.

Integrated Resources
666 Third Avenue
New York, NY 10017
(212) 551-6700, (800) 221-2644

Home Investors Government Guaranteed Income Fund (GNMA), Integrated Capital Appreciation Fund (G), Integrated Corporate Investors Fund (I), Integrated Insured Tax Free Fund (LTMB), Integrated Money Market Securities (MM)

Integrated Resources
One Bridge Plaza
Fort Lee, NJ 07024
(201) 461-0606, (800) 221-2644

Integrated Resources Series Trust: Fixed Income Portfolio (I), Integrated Resources Series Trust: Government Securities Portfolio (USGI), Integrated Resources Series Trust: Growth Portfolio (G), Integrated Resources Series Trust: Money Market Portfolio (MM)

International Investors
122 East 42nd Street
New York, NY 10168
(212) 687-5200, (800) 221-2220

International Investors (PMG), World Trends
Fund (G)

INVESCO Capital Management
1201 Peachtree Street, N.E.
Atlanta, GA 30361
(404) 892-0666, (800) 554-1156

EBI Cash Management (MM), EBI Equity
(G + I), EBI Income (USGI)

Investment Trust of Boston
60 State Street
Boston, MA 02109
(617) 542-0213

Empire Builder Tax Free Fund (LTMB)

IRI Stock Fund
One Appletree Square
Minneapolis, MN 55420
(612) 853-9500, (800) 328-1010

IRI Stock Fund (G)

ISI Corporation
1608 Webster Street, P.O. Box 23330
Oakland, CA 94623
(415) 832-1400, (800) 345-4474

ISI Growth Fund (G), ISI Income Fund (I), ISI
Trust Shares (G + I)

Ivy Funds. see Grantham, Mayo, Van Otterloo.

Janus Group
100 Fillmore Street, Suite 300
Denver, CO 80206
(303) 333-3863, (800) 525-3713

Janus Fund (G), Janus Value Fund (G), Janus
Venture Fund (AG)

John Hancock
John Hancock Place, P. O. Box 111
Boston, MA 02117
(617) 375-1760, (800) 225-5291

John Hancock Bond Trust (CB), John Han-
cock Cash Management Trust (MM), John
Hancock Global Trust (INT), John Hancock
Growth Trust (G), John Hancock Special Equi-
ities Trust (AG), John Hancock Tax-Exempt
Cash Management Trust (STMB), John Han-
cock Tax-Exempt Income Trust (LTMB), John
Hancock U.S. Government Guaranteed Mort-
gages Trust (GNMA), John Hancock U.S.
Government Securities Trust (USGI)

JP Equity Sales
P.O. Box 21008
Greensboro, NC 27420
(919) 378-2448

JP Growth Fund (G), JP Income Fund (I)

Kayne, Anderson Investment Management
1800 Avenue of the Stars
Los Angeles, CA 90067
(213) 556-2721

Rokaand Fund (G + I)

Kemper
120 South LaSalle Street
Chicago, IL 60603
(312) 781-1121, (800) 621-1048

Cash Equivalent Fund: Government Securities
Portfolio (MM), Cash Equivalent Fund: Money
Market Portfolio (MM), Investment Portfo-
lios: Equity Portfolio (G), Investment Portfo-
lios: Government Plus Portfolio (USGI), In-
vestment Portfolios: High Yield Portfolio (I),
Investment Portfolios: Money Market Portfolio
(MM), Investment Portfolios: Option Income
Portfolio (OI), Kemper California Tax-Free
Income Fund (STM-LT), Kemper Government
Money Market Fund (MM), Kemper Growth Fund
(G), Kemper High Yield Fund (CB), Kemper
Income & Capital Preservation Fund (CB), Kem-
per International Fund (INT), Kemper Money
Market Fund (MM), Kemper Municipal Bond
Fund (LTMB), Kemper Option Income Fund (OI),
Kemper Summit Fund (AG), Kemper Total
Return Fund (G + I), Kemper U.S. Government
Securities Fund (USGI), Tax-Exempt Money Mar-
ket Fund (STMB), Technology Fund (G)

Key Equity Management Corporation
Village of Cross Keys, Quadrangle, Suite 322
Baltimore, MD 21210
(301) 435-9000

Greenspring Fund (G)

Keystone Massachusetts Group
99 High Street
Boston, MA 02110
(617) 338-3400, (800) 663-4900

Aggressive Stock Trust (AG), Capital T Money
Fund: Insured Money Market Portfolio (MM),
Capital T Money Fund: Money Market Portfo-
lio (MM), Capital T Tax Free Fund (STMB),
Cash Income Trust (MM), Freedom Fund
Money Market Portfolio (MM), High Yield Bond
Trust (CB), Keystone Custodian Funds: B-1
Series (CB), Keystone Custodian Funds: B-2
Series (CB), Keystone Custodian Funds: B-4
Series (CB), Keystone Custodian Funds: K-1

Series (I), Keystone Custodian Funds: K-2 Series (G), Keystone Custodian Funds: S-1 Series (G + I), Keystone Custodian Funds: S-3 Series (G), Keystone Custodian Funds: S-4 Series (AG), Keystone International Fund (INT), Keystone Liquid Trust (MM), Keystone Precious Metals Holdings (PMG), Keystone Tax Exempt Trust (LTMB), Keystone Tax Free Fund (LTMB), Managed Assets Trust (G + I), Master Reserves Tax Free Trust: Multiple User (STMB), Master Reserves Tax Free Trust: Single Investor Portfolio I (STMB), Master Reserves Tax Free Trust: Single Investor Portfolio II (STMB), Master Reserves Trust: Money Market Portfolio No. 1 (MM), Master Reserves Trust: Money Market Portfolio No. 10 (MM), Master Reserves Trust: Money Market Portfolio No. 11 (MM), Master Reserves Trust: Money Market Portfolio No. 14 (MM), Master Reserves Trust: Money Market Portfolio No. 16 (MM), Master Reserves Trust: Money Market Portfolio No. 17 (MM), Master Reserves Trust: Money Market Portfolio No. 18 (MM), Master Reserves Trust: Money Market Portfolio No. 19 (MM), Master Reserves Trust: Money Market Portfolio No. 3 (MM), Master Reserves Trust: Money Market Portfolio No. 5 (MM), Master Reserves Trust: Money Market Portfolio No. 6 (MM), Master Reserves Trust: Money Market Portfolio No. 8 (MM), Master Reserves Trust: U.S. Government Portfolio No. 1 (MM), Master Reserves Trust: U.S. Government Portfolio No. 10 (MM), Master Reserves Trust: U.S. Government Portfolio No. 11 (MM), Master Reserves Trust: U.S. Government Portfolio No. 16 (MM), Master Reserves Trust: U.S. Government Portfolio No. 3 (MM), Master Reserves Trust: U.S. Government Portfolio No. 5 (MM), Master Reserves Trust: U.S. Government Portfolio No. 6 (MM), Master Reserves Trust: U.S. Government Portfolio No. 8 (MM), Money Market/Options Investments (OI), Salem Funds: The Salem Growth Portfolio (G)

Kidder Peabody Funds. *see* Webster.

Kleinwort Benson International
200 Park Avenue
New York, NY 10166
(212) 687-2515, (800) 237-4218

Transatlantic Fund (INT)

Lazard Frères
One Rockefeller Plaza, 24th Floor
New York, NY 10020
(212) 957-5403

Lazard Cash Management Fund (MM), Lazard Government Fund (MM), Lazard Tax-Free Reserves; Lazard Tax-Free Money Market Fund (STMB)

Legg Mason
7 East Redwood Street, P. O. Box 1476
Baltimore, MD 21203
(301) 539-3400, (800) 822-5544,
(800) 638-1107 (MD only)

Legg Mason Tax-Exempt Trust (STMB), Legg Mason Total Return Trust (G + I), Legg Mason Value Trust (G)

Lehman Group
55 Water Street
New York, NY 10041
(212) 668-8578, (800) 221-5350

Lehman Capital Fund (AG), Lehman Investors Fund (G + I), Lehman Opportunity Fund (G)

Leperq-Istel Trust
345 Park Avenue
New York, NY 10154
(212) 702-0100

Leperq-Istel Fund (G + I)

Lexington Group
Park 80 West—Plaza Two, P. O. Box 1515
Saddle Brook, NJ 07662
(201) 845-7300, (800) 526-0056

Lexington GNMA Income Fund (GNMA), Lexington Goldfund (PMG), Lexington Government Securities Money Market Fund (MM), Lexington Growth Fund (AG), Lexington Money Market Trust (MM), Lexington Research Fund (G), Lexington Tax Free Money Fund (STMB)

Life of Virginia Series
6610 West Broad Street
Richmond, VA 23230
(804) 281-6000, (800) 822-6000

Life of Virginia Series Fund: Bond Portfolio (CB), Life of Virginia Series Fund: Common Stock Portfolio (G), Life of Virginia Series Fund: Money Market Portfolio (MM), Life of Virginia Series Fund: Total Return Portfolio (G + I)

Lincoln Investment Planning
The Benson East, Suite 1000
Jenkintown, PA 19046
(215) 927-7880

Rightime Fund (G)

Lindner Management Corporation
200 South Bemiston, P. O. Box 16900
St. Louis, MO 63105
(314) 727-5305

Lindner Dividend Fund (I), Lindner Fund (G)

Loomis-Sayles/NEL
P.O. Box 449, Back Bay Annex
Boston, MA 02117
(617) 568-6272

Loomis-Sayles Capital Development Fund (G), Loomis-Sayles Mutual Fund (B), NEL Cash Management Trust: Money Market Series (MM), NEL Cash Management Trust: U.S. Government Series (MM), NEL Equity Fund (G + I), NEL Growth Fund (G), NEL Income Fund (I), NEL Retirement Equity Fund (G), NEL Series Fund: Bond Income Series (CB), NEL Series Fund: Capital Growth Series (G), NEL Series Fund: Money Market Series (MM), NEL Tax-Exempt Bond Fund (LTMB), NEL Tax-Exempt Money Market Trust (STMB), New England Life Government Securities Trust (GNMA)

Lord Abbett
63 Wall Street
New York, NY 10005
(212) 425-8720, (800) 223-4224

Affiliated Fund (G + I), Lord Abbett California Tax-Free Income Fund (SMB-LT), Lord Abbett Bond-Debenture Fund (CB), Lord Abbett Cash Reserve Fund (MM), Lord Abbett Developing Growth Fund (AG), Lord Abbett Tax-Free Income Fund: National Series (LTMB), Lord Abbett Tax-Free Income Fund: New York Series (SMB-LT), Lord Abbett U.S. Government Securities Fund (USGI), Lord Abbett Value Appreciation Fund (G)

Lutheran Brotherhood Funds. see Federated.

Mackenzie Investment Management
1665 Palm Beach Lakes Boulevard, Suite 604
West Palm Beach, FL 33401
(305) 471-2929, (800) 222-2274

Industrial Series Trust: Industrial American Fund (G), Industrial Series Trust: Industrial Bond Fund (CB), Industrial Series Trust: Industrial Cash Management Fund (MM), Industrial Series Trust: Industrial Government Securities Plus Fund (USGI), Industrial Series Trust: Industrial Option Income Fund (OI)

ManuLife
200 Bloor Street, East
Toronto, Ontario CAN M4W 1E5
(416) 926-4387

ManuLife Series Fund: Balanced Assets Fund (B), ManuLife Series Fund: Capital Growth Bond Fund (I), ManuLife Series Fund: Emerging Growth Equity Fund (AG), ManuLife Series Fund: Money Market Fund (MM)

Mariner Funds. see Furman Selz.

Massachusetts Financial
200 Berkeley Street
Boston, MA 02116
(617) 423-3500

MFS Government Guaranteed Securities Trust (USGI), MFS Managed California Tax-Free Trust (SMB-LT), MFS Managed High Yield Municipal Bond Trust (LTMB), MFS Managed Multi-State Tax-Exempt Trust: Maryland Series (SMB-LT), MFS Managed Multi-State Tax-Exempt Trust: Massachusetts Series (SMB-LT), MFS Managed Multi-State Tax-Exempt Trust: North Carolina Series (SMB-LT), MFS Managed Multi-State Tax-Exempt Trust: South Carolina Series (SMB-LT), MFS Managed Multi-State Tax-Exempt Trust: Virginia Series (SMB-LT), MFS Managed Multi-State Tax-Exempt Trust: West Virginia Series (SMB-LT), MFS Managed Municipal Bond Trust (LTMB), Massachusetts Capital Development Fund (G), Massachusetts Cash Management Trust: Prime Series (MM), Massachusetts Cash Management Trust: Government Series (MM), Massachusetts Financial Bond Fund (CB), Massachusetts Financial Development Fund (G + I), Massachusetts Financial Emerging Growth Trust (AG), Massachusetts Financial High Income Trust (CB), Massachusetts Financial Special Fund (AG), Massachusetts Financial International Trust Bond Portfolio (INT), Massachusetts Financial Total Return Trust (I), Massachusetts Investors Growth Stock Fund (G), Massachusetts Investors Trust (G + I), Municipal Working Capital Trust (STMB)

MassMutual Liquid Assets
1295 State Street
Springfield, MA 01111
(413) 788-8411, (800) 451-1713

MassMutual Liquid Assets Trust (MM)

Master Reserves Trust. see Keystone Massachusetts Group.

Mathers & Company
125 South Wacker Drive
Chicago, IL 60606
(312) 236-8215

Mathers Fund (AG)

Maxus Fund
30195 Chagrin Boulevard, Suite 205
Pepper Pike, OH 44124
(216) 292-6450

Maxus Fund (G + I)

Medical Research Management
350 Royal Palm Way
Palm Beach, FL 33480
(305) 833-7607, (800) 558-0398

Medical Research Investment Fund (G)

Meeder & Associates
6000 Memorial Drive
Dublin, OH 43017
(614) 766-7000

Flex-Fund (AG), Flex-Fund: The Bond Fund (CB), Flex-Fund: The Capital Gains Fund (G), Flex-Fund: The Corporate Income Fund (I), Flex-Fund: The Money Market Fund (MM), Flex-Fund: The Retirement Growth Fund (G)

Meeschaert & Co.
47 Miller Hill Road
Dover, MA 02030
(617) 244-0432

Meeschaert Capital Accumulation Fund (G)

Merrill Lynch
125 High Street
Boston, MA 02110
(617) 357-1460, (800) 225-1576

CBA Money Fund (MM), CMA Government Securities Fund (MM), CMA Money Fund (MM), CMA Tax-Exempt Fund (STMB), Merrill Lynch Basic Value Fund (G + I), Merrill Lynch California Municipal Series Trust: Merrill Lynch California Tax-Exempt Fund (SMB-LT), Merrill Lynch Capital Fund (G + I), Merrill Lynch Corporate Bond Fund: High Income Portfolio (CB), Merrill Lynch Corporate Bond Fund: High Quality Portfolio (CB), Merrill Lynch Corporate Bond Fund: Intermediate Term Portfolio (CB), Merrill Lynch Corporate Dividend Fund (I), Merrill Lynch Equi-Bond I Fund (I), Merrill Lynch Federal Securities Trust (USGI), Merrill Lynch Fund for Tomorrow (G), Merrill Lynch Government Fund (MM), Merrill Lynch Institutional Fund (MM), Merrill Lynch Institutional Tax-Exempt Fund (STMB), Merrill Lynch International Holdings (INT), Merrill Lynch Municipal Bond Fund: High Yield Portfolio (LTMB), Merrill Lynch Municipal Bond Fund: Insured Portfolio (LTMB), Merrill Lynch Municipal Bond Fund: Limited Maturity Portfolio (STMB), Merrill Lynch Natural Resources Trust (G), Merrill Lynch Pacific Fund (INT), Merrill Lynch Phoenix Fund (AG), Merrill Lynch Ready Assets Trust (MM), Merrill Lynch Retirement Reserves Money Fund (MM), Merrill Lynch Series Fund: Capital Stock Series (G + I), Merrill Lynch Series Fund: Growth Stock Series (G), Merrill Lynch Series Fund: Intermedi-ate Government Bond Series (USGI), Merrill Lynch Series Fund: Long Term Corporate Bond Series (CB), Merrill Lynch Series Fund: Money Market Reserve Series (MM), Merrill Lynch Series Fund: Multiple Strategy Series (G + I), Merrill Lynch Special Value Fund (G), Merrill Lynch U.S.A. Government Reserves (MM), Merrill Lynch Variable Series Funds: Equity Growth Fund (AG), Merrill Lynch Variable Series Funds: High Current Income Fund (CB), Merrill Lynch Variable Series Funds: Prime Bond Fund (CB), Merrill Lynch Variable Series Funds: Quality Equity Fund (G + I), Merrill Lynch Variable Series Funds: Reserve Assets Fund (STMB), Merrill Lynch Variable Series Funds: U.S. Government Money Fund (STMB), SciTech Holdings (INT), Summitt Cash Reserve Fund (MM)

MidAmerica
4333 Edgewood Road N.E.
Cedar Rapids, IA 52499
(319) 398-8511, (800) 553-4287,
(800) 342-4490 (IA only)

MidAmerica High Growth Fund (AG), Mid-America High Yield Fund (CB), MidAmerica Mutual Fund (G), MidAmerica Tax-Exempt Bond Fund (LTMB)

Midwest Life
100 Dain Tower, P. O. Box 690
Minneapolis, MN 55440
(612) 371-7774, (800) 527-5453

Midwest Life Fund: Series A (Money Market Account) (MM), Midwest Life Fund: Series B (Common Stock Account) (G), Midwest Life Fund: Series C (Bond Account) (CB)

Midwest/ABT Funds
Dixie Terminal Building
Cincinnati, OH 45202
(513) 629-2000, (800) 354-0436,
(800) 582-7396 (OH only)

ABT Growth and Income Trust (G + I), ABT Investment Series: ABT Emerging Growth Fund (AG), ABT Investment Series: ABT Security Income Fund (OI), ABT Utility Income Fund (G + I), LG Investment Trust: Fund for Growth (G), LG Investment Trust: Fund for Income (I), LG Investment Trust: U.S. Government Securities Fund (GNMA), Midwest Group Tax Free Trust: Limited Term Portfolio (STMB), Midwest Group Tax Free Trust: Money Market Portfolio (STMB), Midwest Group Tax Free Trust: Ohio Long Term Portfolio (SMB-LT), Midwest Income Trust: Cash Management Fund (MM), Midwest Income Trust: Intermediate Term Government Fund (USGI), Midwest Income Trust: Short Term Government Fund (MM)

The Milwaukee Company
250 East Wisconsin Avenue
Milwaukee, WI 53202
(414) 347-7000, (800) 558-1015

Heartland Value Fund (G)

MIMLIC
400 North Robert Steet
St. Paul, MN 55101
(612) 298-3826, (800) 328-8045

MIMLIC Investors Fund I ((G + I), MIMLIC Investors Fund II (G + I), MIMLIC Money Market Fund (MM), MIMLIC Mortgage Securities Income Fund (GNMA)

Monarch Investment Management Corporation
1 Financial Plaza
Springfield, MA 01102-9002
(413) 781-3000

FVL Growth Fund (G), Variable Stock Fund (G)

Money Management Associates
9922 Fairmount Avenue
Bethesda, MD 20814
(800) 986-7811

Rushmore GNMA Portfolio (GNMA), Rushmore Money Market Portfolio (MM), Rushmore Over-the-Counter Index Plus Portfolio (AG), Rushmore Stock Market Index (G), Rushmore U.S. Government Securities Portfolio (USGI)

Monitor Capital
107D Waters Building
Grand Rapids, MI 49503
(616) 774-0928, (800) 882-1657,
(800) 221-3692 (MI only)

Money Market Fund (MM)

Monitrend Mutual Fund
222 Bridge Plaza South
Fort Lee, NJ 07024
(201) 886-2300

Monitrend Mutual Fund (G)

MONY Variable
1740 Broadway, Mail Drop 21-4
New York, NY 10019
(212) 708-2000

MONY Series Fund: Diversified Portfolio (B), MONY Series Fund: Equity Growth Portfolio (G), MONY Series Fund: Equity Income Portfolio (I), MONY Series Fund: Intermediate Term Bond Portfolio (CB), MONY Series Fund: Long Term Bond Portfolio (CB), MONY Series Fund:

Money Market Portfolio (MM), MONY Variable Account-A (G), MONY Variable Account-B (MM)

Mutual Benefit
520 Broad Street
Newark, NJ 07101
(201) 751-8600

MAP-Government Fund (MM), MBL Growth Fund (G), Mutual Benefit Fund (G)

Mutual Group of Funds. *see* Heine Securities.

Mutual of America
666 Fifth Avenue
New York, NY 10103
(212) 399-1600, (800) 223-0898

Mutual of America Separate Account No. 2: Bond Fund (CB), Mutual of America Separate Account No. 2: Composite Fund (G + I), Mutual of America Separate Account No. 2: Money Market Fund (MM), Mutual of America Separate Account No. 2: Stock Fund (G + I)

Mutual of Omaha
10235 Regency Circle
Omaha, NE 68114
(402) 397-8555, (800) 228-9596,
(800) 642-8112 (NE only)

Mutual of Omaha America Fund (USGI), Mutual of Omaha Cash Reserve Fund (MM), Mutual of Omaha Growth Fund (G), Mutual of Omaha Income Fund (I), Mutual of Omaha Money Market Account (MM), Mutual of Omaha Tax-Free Income Fund (LTMB)

Mutual Selection Management
First National Bank Building, P. O. Box 619
Muscatine, IA 52761
(319) 263-8771

Mutual Selection Fund (G)

NASL Series
129 South Street
Boston, MA 02111
(617) 350-8642

NASL Series Fund: The Bond Portfolio (CB), NASL Series Fund: The Equity Portfolio (G), NASL Series Fund: The Money Market Portfolio (MM)

National Aviation & Technology Fund. *see* American Fund Advisors.

National Securities
605 Third Avenue
New York, NY 10158
(212) 661-3000, (800) 223-7757

California Tax Exempt Bonds (SMB-LT), Fairfield Fund (AG), National Cash Reserves (MM), National Federal Securities Trust (USGI), National Real Estate Stock Fund (AG), National Securities Funds: Balanced Fund (B), National Securities Funds: Bond Fund (CB), National Securities Funds: Growth Fund (G), National Securities Funds; Income Fund (I), National Securities Funds: Preferred Fund (I), National Securities Funds: Stock Fund (G + I), National Securities Funds: Total Return Fund (G + I), National Securities Tax-Exempt Bonds (LTMB)

Nationwide Financial Services
One Nationwide Plaza, Box 1492
Columbus, OH 43216
(614) 249-7855, (800) 848-0920,
(800) 282-1449 (OH only)

Nationwide Investing Foundation: Bond Fund (CB), Nationwide Investing Foundation: Growth Fund (G), Nationwide Investing Foundation: Money Market Fund (MM), Nationwide Investing Foundation: Nationwide Fund (G + I), Nationwide Separate Account Trust: Common Stock Fund (G + I), Nationwide Separate Account Trust: Government Bond Fund (USGI), Nationwide Separate Account Trust: Money Market Fund (MM)

NEL Funds. *see* Loomis-Sayles/NEL.

Neuberger & Berman
342 Madison Avenue
New York, New York 10173
(212) 850-8300, (800) 367-0770,
(800) 922-3700

Energy Fund (G), Guardian Mutual Fund (G + I), Liberty Fund (CB), Manhattan Fund (G), Neuberger & Berman Government Money Fund (MM), Neuberger & Berman Tax-Free Money Fund (STMB), Partners Fund (G)

The New Beginning Mutual Fund Group
1714 First Bank Place West
Minneapolis, MN 55402
(612) 332-3223

"New Beginning" Growth Fund (G), "New Beginning" Income & Growth Fund (I), "New Beginning" Investment Reserve Fund (I), "New Beginning" Yield Fund (I)

New England Life Funds
501 Boylston Street
Boston, MA 02117
(617) 267-6600, (800) 343-7104

NEL Cash Management: Money Market Series (MM), NEL Cash Management: U.S. Government Series (USGI), NEL Equity Fund (G + I), NEL Growth Fund (G), NEL Income Fund (I), NEL Retirement Equity Fund (G), NEL Tax Exempt Bond Fund (LTMB), NEL Tax Exempt Money Market Fund (STMB)

Newton
Two Plaza East, Suite 1150
330 East Kilburn Avenue
Milwaukee, WI 53202
(414) 347-1141, (800) 247-7039,
(800) 242-7229 (WI only)

Newton Growth Fund (G), Newton Income Fund: Newton Income Fund (I), Newton Income Fund: Newton Money Fund (MM)

Nicholas Company
700 North Water Street, Suite 1010
Milwaukee, WI 53202
(414) 272-6133

Nicholas Fund (G), Nicholas II (G), Nicholas Income Fund (I)

Nomura
180 Maiden Lane
New York, NY 10038
(212) 208-9300, (800) 833-0018

Nomura Pacific Basin Fund (INT)

North Star
1100 Dain Tower, P. O. Box 357
Minneapolis, MN 55440
(612) 371-2884

North Star Apollo Fund (G), North Star Bond Fund (CB), North Star Regional Fund (G), North Star Stock Fund (G + I)

Northwestern National (NWNL)
20 Washington Avenue South
Minneapolis, MN 55440
(612) 372-5605

Northwestern Cash Fund (MM), Select Capital Growth Fund (G), Select Cash Management Fund (MM), Select High Yield Fund (CB)

Nuveen
333 West Wacker Drive
Chicago, IL 60606
(312) 917-7700, (800) 621-2431

Nuveen Municipal Bond Fund (LTMB), Nuveen Tax-Exempt Money Market Fund (STMB), Nuveen Tax-Free Reserves (STMB), Tax-Free Accounts (STMB)

NY Muni Fund
One World Trade Center, Suite 8407
New York, New York 10048
(212) 775-0043

California Muni Fund (SMB-LT), California Tax-Free Money Fund (SMB-ST), New York Muni Fund (SMB-LT)

Ohio National Fund
237 William Howard Taft Road
Cincinnati, OH 45219
(513) 861-3600

Ohio National Fund: Bond Portfolio (CB), Ohio National Fund: Equity Portfolio (G), Ohio National Fund: Money Market Portfolio (MM), Ohio National Fund: Omni Portfolio (B)

Oppenheimer/Centennial
3410 South Galena Street, P. O. Box 5061
Denver, CO 80217
(303) 671-3200, (800) 525-9310,
(800) 525-7048
    and
Two Broadway
New York, NY 10004
(212) 668-5000, (800) 221-9839,
(800) 522-3012 (NY only)
    and
200 Liberty Street
New York, NY 10281
(212) 667-7000, (800) 862-7778

Centennial Government Trust (MM), Centennial Money Market Trust (MM), Centennial Tax Exempt Trust (STMB), Daily Cash Accumulation Fund (MM), Hamilton Funds (G + I), Oppenheimer A.I.M. Fund (INT), Oppenheimer Challenger Fund (AG), Oppenheimer Directors Fund (AG), Oppenheimer Equity Income Fund (I), Oppenheimer Fund (AG), Oppenheimer Gold & Special Minerals Fund (PMG), Oppenheimer High Yield Fund (CB), Oppenheimer Money Market Fund (MM), Oppenheimer New York Tax Exempt Fund (SMB-LT), Oppenheimer Premium Income Fund (OI), Oppenheimer Regency Fund (AG), Oppenheimer Retirement Fund: Blue Chip Stocks Fund (G), Oppenheimer Retirement Fund: Quality Money Market Fund (MM), Oppenheimer Retirement Fund: U.S. Government Securities Fund (USGI), Oppenheimer Special Fund (G), Oppenheimer Target Fund (G), Oppenheimer Tax-Free Bond Fund (LTMB), Oppenheimer Time Fund (AG), Oppenheimer U.S. Government Trust (USGI), Quest for Value Fund (AG)

Over-the-Counter
510 Pennsylvania Avenue, Suite 321
P. O. Box 1537
Fort Washington, PA 19034
(215) 643-2510, (800) 523-2578

Over-The-Counter Securities Fund (G)

Pacific American
707 Wilshire Boulevard, Suite 5300
Los Angeles, CA 90017
(213) 614-3231

Pacific American Fund: Money Market Portfolio (MM), Pacific American Fund: Short Term Government Portfolio (MM)

Pacific Horizons Fund
3550 Wilshire Boulevard, Suite 932
Los Angeles, CA 90010
(800) 645-3515

Pacific Horizons Aggressive Fund (AG), Pacific Horizons California Fund (STMB-LT), Pacific Horizons High Yield Fund (I), Pacific Horizons Money Market Portfolio (MM)

Paine Webber
The PaineWebber Building
1285 Avenue of the Americas
New York, NY 10019
(212) 713-2000, (800) 828-6109

PaineWebber ATLAS Fund (INT), Paine-Webber America Fund (G + I), PaineWebber CASHFUND (MM), PaineWebber California Tax Exempt Income Fund (SMB-LT), Paine-Webber Fixed Income Portfolios: GNMA Portfolio (GNMA), PaineWebber Fixed Income Portfolios: High Yield Bond Portfolio (CB), PaineWebber Fixed Income Portfolios: Investment Grade Portfolio (CB), PaineWebber Olympus Fund (G), PaineWebber RMA Money Fund: Money Market Portfolio (MM), PaineWebber RMA Money Fund: U.S. Government Portfolio (MM), PaineWebber RMA Tax-Free Fund (STMB), PaineWebber Tax-Exempt Income Fund (LTMB)

Parker Dillon Carlson & Johnson
Governor Square Office Center
1416 Miamisburg—Centerville Road
Dayton, OH 45459
(513) 439-1010

PDC&J Performance Fund (G), PDC&J Preservation Fund (I)

Parkway
985 Old Eagle School Road
Wayne, PA 19087
(215) 688-8165, (800) 441-7786

Parkway Cash Fund (MM), Parkway Tax-Free Reserve Fund (STMB)

Pax World
224 State Street
Portsmouth, NH 03801
(603) 431-8022

Pax World Fund (B)

Penn Square Management Corporation
2650 Westview Drive
Wyomissing, PA 19610
(215) 670-1031, (800) 523-8440

Penn Square Mutual Fund (G)

Pennsylvania Mutual
1414 Avenue of the Americas
New York, NY 10019
(212) 355-7311, (800) 221-4268

Pennsylvania Mutual Fund (AG), Royce Value Fund (AG)

Phoenix
One American Row
Hartford, CT 06115
(203) 278-8050, (800) 243-4361

P-C Capital Fund (AG), Phoenix Series Fund: Balanced Fund Series (B), Phoenix Series Fund: Convertible Fund Series (I), Phoenix Series Fund: Growth Fund Series (G), Phoenix Series Fund: High Quality Bond Fund Series (CB), Phoenix Series Fund: High Yield Fund Series (CB), Phoenix Series Fund: Money Market Fund Series (MM), Phoenix Series Fund: Stock Fund Series (G)

Piedmont
1010 North Globe Road
Arlington, VA 22201

Piedmont Income Fund (I)

Pilgrim
222 Bridge Plaza South
Fort Lee, NJ 07024
(201) 461-7500, (800) 526-0475

Pilgrim Adjustable Rate Fund (I), Pilgrim GNMA Fund (GNMA), Pilgrim High Yield Trust (I), Pilgrim MagnaCap Fund (G), Pilgrim Preferred Fund (I)

Pioneer
60 State Street
Boston, MA 02109
(617) 742-7825, (800) 225-6292

Pioneer Bond Fund (CB), Pioneer Fund (G + I), Pioneer II (G + I), Pioneer Three (G + I)

PML Securities
1600 Market Street, P. O. Box 7378
Philadelphia, PA 19101
(212) 636-5000

Providentmutual Variable Life Insurance Company: Bond Account (CB), Providentmutual Variable Life Insurance Company: Growth Account (G), Providentmutual Variable Life Insurance Company: Money Market Account (MM)

T. Rowe Price
100 East Pratt Street
Baltimore, MD 21202
(301) 547-2308, (800) 638-5660

T. Rowe Price Equity-Income Fund (G + I), T. Rowe Price GNMA Fund (GNMA), T. Rowe Price Growth & Income Fund (G + I), T. Rowe Price Growth Stock Fund (G), T. Rowe Price High Yield Fund (CB), T. Rowe Price International Fund (INT), T. Rowe Price New America Growth (G), T. Rowe Price New Era Fund (G), T. Rowe Price New Horizons Fund (AG), T. Rowe Price New Income Fund (CB), T. Rowe Price Prime Reserve (MM), T. Rowe Price Short-Term Bond Fund (CB), T. Rowe Price Tax Exempt Money Fund (STMB), T. Rowe Price Tax-Free High Yield Fund (LTMB), T. Rowe Price Tax-Free Income Fund (LTMB), T. Rowe Price Tax-Free Short-Intermediate Fund (LTMB), T. Rowe Price U.S. Treasury Money Fund (MM)

Principal Group
6310 N. Scottsdale Road
Scottsdale, AZ 85253
(602) 998-5557

Principal Arizona Tax Free Fund (SMB-LT), Principal Equity Fund (G), Principal World Fund (INT)

Princor
711 High Street
DesMoines, IA 50309
(515) 247-5711, (800) 247-4123,
(800) 622-5344 (IA only)

Princor Capital Accumulation Fund (G + I), Princor Cash Management Fund (MM), Princor Fund (G + I), Princor Government Securities Income Fund (USGI), Princor Growth Fund (G), Princor Money Market Fund (MM), Princor Tax-Exempt Bond Fund (LTMB)

Prudential-Bache
One Seaport Plaza
New York, NY 10292
(212) 214-1234, (800) 872-7787

Command Government Fund (MM), Command Money Fund (MM), Command Tax-Free Fund (STMB), Prudential-Bache Equity Fund (G), Prudential-Bache Research Fund (G + I), Prudential-Bache Utility Fund (G + I), Prudential-Bache Adjustable Rate Preferred Stock Fund (G + I), Prudential-Bache California Municipal Fund (SMB-LT), Prudential-Bache Global Fund (INT), Prudential-Bache Government Plus Fund (USGI), Prudential-Bache Government Securities Trust: Intermediate Term Series (USGI), Prudential-Bache Government Securities Trust: Money Market Series (MM), Prudential-Bache Growth Opportunity Fund (G), Prudential-Bache High Yield Fund (CB), Prudential-Bache High Yield Municipals (LTMB), Prudential-Bache IncomeVertible Plus Fund (I), Prudential-Bache MoneyMart Assets (MM), Prudential-Bache Municipal Series Fund: Arizona Series (SMB-LT), Prudential-Bache Municipal Series Fund: Georgia Series (SMB-LT), Prudential-Bache Municipal Series Fund: Maryland Series (SMB-LT), Prudential-Bache Municipal Series Fund: Massachusetts Series (SMB-LT), Prudential-Bache Municipal Series Fund: Michigan Series (SMB-LT), Prudential-Bache Municipal Series Fund; Minnesota Series (SMB-LT), Prudential-Bache Municipal Series Fund: New York Money Market Series (SMB-ST), Prudential-Bache Municipal Series Fund: New York Series (SMB-LT), Prudential-Bache Municipal Series Fund: North Carolina Series (SMB-LT), Prudential-Bache Municipal Series Fund: Ohio Series (SMB-LT), Prudential-Bache Municipal Series Fund: Oregon Series (SMB-LT), Prudential - Bache Option Growth Fund (G), Prudential-Bache Quality Income Fund (I), Prudential-Bache Tax Free Money Fund (STMB)

Putnam Funds
One Post Office Square
Boston, MA 02109
(617) 292-1000, (800) 225-2465,
(800) 225-1581

Depositors Investors Trust: Aggressive Growth Fund (AG), Depositors Investors Trust: Capital Growth Fund (G), Depositors Investors Trust: Current Income Fund (I), George Putnam Fund of Boston (B), Putnam California Tax Exempt Income Fund (SMB-LT), Putnam Capital Fund (G), Putnam Convertible Income—Growth Trust (G + I), Putnam Corporate Cash Trust-Adjustable Rate Preferred Portfolio (I), Putnam Corporate Cash Trust-Diversified Strategies Portfolio (I), Putnam Daily Dividend Trust (MM), Putnam Energy-Resources Trust (AG), Putnam Fund for Growth and Income (G + I), Putnam Health Sciences Trust, (AG), Putnam High Income Government Trust (USGI), Putnam High Yield Trust (CB), Putnam Income Fund (I), Putnam Information Sciences Trust (AG), Putnam International Equities Fund (INT), Putnam Investors Fund (G), Putnam New York Tax Exempt Income Fund (SMSB-LT), Putnam Option Income Trust (OI), Putnam Option Income Trust II (OI), Putnam Tax-Free Income Trust: High Yield Portfolio (LTMB), Putnam Tax-Free Income Trust: Insured Long-Term Portfolio (LTMB), Putnam U.S. Government Guaranteed Securities Income Trust (GNMA), Putnam Vista Fund (AG), Putnam Voyager Fund (AG)

Quality Services Company
5290 Overpass Road
Santa Barbara, CA 93111
(805) 964-7841

The Santa Barbara Fund (AG)

Quantum
4000 Town Center, Suite 101
Southfield, MI 48075
(313) 358-2282

Quantum Fund (AG)

Rainbow Fund. see Furman, Anderson & Co.

Rea-Graham
10966 Chacon Road
Los Angeles, CA 90077
(213) 471-1917

Rea-Graham Fund (B)

Reich & Tang Mutual Funds
100 Park Avenue
New York, NY 10017
(212) 370-1240, (800) 221-3079

Connecticut Daily Tax Free Income Fund (SMB-ST), Daily Dollar Reserves (MM), Daily Income Fund (MM), Daily Tax Free Income Fund (STMB), Short-Term Income Fund: Money Market Fund (MM), Short-Term Income Fund: Short-Term Income Government Fund (MM), Soundshore Fund (G), Warburg International Fund (INT)

Retirement Planning Funds. see Venture Advisers.

The Rightime Fund
The Benson East Office Plaza
Jenkintown, PA 19046
(215) 927-7880

The Rightime Fund (G)

Rochester
379 Park Avenue
Rochester, NY 14607
(716) 442-5500

Rochester Growth Fund (G), Rochester Tax Managed Fund (G + I)

Rodney Square Funds. *see* Fidelity.

Rokaand Fund. *see* Kayne, Anderson Investment Management.

Ruane, Cunniff and Co.
1370 Avenue of the Americas, Suite 780
New York, NY 10019
(212) 245-4500

Sequoia Fund (AG)

Rushmore Funds. *see* Money Management Associates.

SAFECO
SAFECO Plaza
Seattle, WA 98185
(206) 545-5530, (800) 426-6730,
(800) 562-6810 (WA only)

SAFECO California Tax-Free Income Fund (SMB-LT), SAFECO Equity Fund (G + I), SAFECO Growth Fund (G), SAFECO Income Fund (G + I), SAFECO Money Market Mutual Fund (MM), SAFECO Municipal Bond Fund (LTMB), SAFECO Tax-Free Money Market Fund (STMB)

Scudder
175 Federal Street
Boston, MA 02110
(617) 482-3990, (800) 225-2470,
(800) 225-5163

Scudder California Tax Free Fund (SMB-LT), Scudder Capital Growth Fund (G), Scudder Cash Investment Trust (MM), Scudder Development Fund (AG), Scudder Government Money Fund (MM), Scudder Government Mortgage Securities Fund (GNMA), Scudder Growth & Income Fund (G + I), Scudder Income Fund (I), Scudder International Fund (INT), Scudder Managed Municipal Bonds (LTMB), Scudder New York Tax Free Fund (SMB-LT), Scudder Target Fund: General 86

(CB), Scudder Target Fund: General 87 (CB), Scudder Target Fund: General 90 (CB), Scudder Target Fund: General 94 (CB), Scudder Target Fund: General 96 (LTMB), Scudder Target Fund: Government 86 (USGI), Scudder Target Fund: Government 87 (USGI), Scudder Target Fund: Government 90 (USGI), Scudder Tax-Free Money Fund (STMB), Scudder Tax-Free Target Fund: Tax Free 87 (LTMB), Scudder Tax-Free Target Fund: Tax Free 90 (LTMB), Scudder Tax-Free Target Fund: Tax Free 93 (LTMB)

Security
700 Harrison Street
Topeka, KS 66636
(913) 295-3127, (800) 432-3536 (KS only),
(800) 255-2461 (800) 255-3557

Security Action Fund (G), Security Cash Fund (MM), Security Equity Fund (G), Security Income Fund: Corporate Bond Series (CB), Security Income Fund: U.S. Government Series (GNMA), Security Investment Fund (G + I), Security Tax-Exempt Fund (LTMB), Security Ultra Fund (AG)

SEI Financial Services
680 East Swedesford Road, No. 7
Wayne, PA 19087
(215) 687-1700, (800) 345-1151

TrustFunds Cash + Plus: Federal Securities Portfolio (MM), TrustFunds Cash + Plus: Money Market Portfolio (MM), TrustFunds Equity Index Funds: Extended Market Index Portfolio (G + I), TrustFunds Equity Index Funds: S&P 500 Index Portfolio (G + I), TrustFunds Liquid Asset Trust: Agency Portfolio (MM), TrustFunds Liquid Asset Trust: Commercial Portfolio (MM), TrustFunds Liquid Asset Trust: Prime Obligation Portfolio (MM), TrustFunds Liquid Asset Trust: Treasury Portfolio (MM), TrustFunds Tax Exempt Trust: Eastern Portfolio (STMB), TrustFunds Tax Exempt Trust: Western Portfolio (STMB)

Selected
230 West Monroe Street
Chicago, IL 60606
(312) 641-7862, (800) 621-7321,
(800) 572-4437 (IL only)

Selected American Shares (G + I), Selected Government Money Market Fund (MM), Selected Money Market Fund (MM), Selected Special Shares (G), Selected Tax-Exempt Bond Fund (LTMB)

Seligman
One Bankers Trust Plaza
New York,NY 10006
(212) 488-0200, (800) 221-7844,-2450,
(800) 522-6869 (NY only)

Liberty Cash Management Fund (MM), Selig-man California Tax-Exempt Fund Series: High-Yield Series (SMB-LT), Seligman California Tax-Exempt Fund Series: Money Market Series (SMB-ST), Seligman California Tax-Exempt Fund Series: Quality Series (SMB-LT), Selig-man Capital Fund (AG), Seligman Cash Man-agement Fund: Government Portfolio (MM), Seligman Cash Management Fund: Prime Portfolio (MM), Seligman Common Stock Fund (G + I), Seligman Communications and Infor-mation Fund (AG), Seligman Frontier Fund (G), Seligman Growth Fund (G), Seligman High Income Fund Series: High-Yield Bond Series (CB), Seligman High Income Fund Series: Se-cured Mortgage Income Series (GNMA), Se-ligman High Income Fund Series: U.S. Gov-ernment Guaranteed Securities Series (USGI), Seligman Income Fund (I), Seligman Tax-Ex-empt Fund Series: Louisiana Tax-Exempt Series (SMB-LT), Seligman Tax-Exempt Fund Series: Maryland Tax-Exempt Series (SMB-LT), Se-ligman Tax-Exempt Fund Series: Massachu-setts Tax-Exempt Series (SMB-LT), Seligman Tax-Exempt Fund Series: Michigan Tax-Ex-empt Series (SMB-LT), Seligman Tax-Exempt Fund Series: Minnesota Tax-Exempt Series (SMB-LT), Seligman Tax-Exempt Fund Series: National Tax-Exempt Series (LTMB), Selig-man Tax-Exempt Fund Series: New York Tax-Exempt Series (SMB-LT), Seligman Tax-Ex-empt Fund Series: Ohio Tax-Exempt Series (SMB-LT)

Sentinel
National Life Drive
Montpelier, VT 05604
(802) 229-3900, (800) 526-3032
and
217 Broadway, Suite 306
New York, NY 10007
(212) 406-0404

Sentinel Cash Management Fund (MM), Sen-tinel Group Funds: Balanced Fund Series (B), Sentinel Group Funds: Bond Fund Series (CB), Sentinel Group Funds: Common Stock Fund Series (G + I), Sentinel Group Funds: Growth Fund Series (G)

Sentry
1800 North Point Drive
Stevens Point, WI 54481

(715) 346-7051, (800) 826-0266,
(800) 472-0280 (WI only)

Sentry Fund (G)

Sequoia Fund. *see* Ruane, Cunniff and Co.

Shearson Lehman Brothers
1600 Los Gamos Road
San Rafael, CA 94911
(415) 492-7730

American Express Variable Annuity Fund Growth: Portfolio (G), American Express Var-iable Annuity Fund: Income Portfolio (I), American Express Variable Annuity Fund: Money Market Portfolio (MM)

Shearson Lehman Brothers
One Boston Place
Boston, MA 02106
(617) 956-9740, (617) 338-0880,
(800) 343-6324

American Telecommunication Trust: Growth Portfolio (G), American Telecommunication Trust: Income Portfolio (G + I)

Shearson Lehman Brothers
1600 Los Gamos Drive
San Rafael, CA 94911
(415) 492-7730
(302) 478-1630, (212) 323-7712,
(800) 221-8120
and
3512 Silverside Road
Wilmington, DE 19810
(302) 478-6945, (800) 441-7450

Arch Fund: Discretionary Portfolio (G), Arch Fund: Non-Discretionary Portfolio (G), Bison Money Market Fund: Discretionary Portfo-lio–Class B (MM), Bison Money Market Fund: Non-Discretionary Portfolio–Class A (MM), Chestnut Street Cash Fund: Portfolio A (MM), Chestnut Street Cash Fund: Portfolio B (MM), Diversified Securities Funds: Capital Appreci-ation Fund (G), First Phoenix Fund: Discre-tionary Portfolio (G), First Phoenix Fund: Non-Discretionary Portfolio (G), International Fund for Institutions (INT), Money Express Reserve Fund (MM), Municipal Fund for California Investors (SMB-ST), Municipal Fund for New York Investors (SMB-ST), Municipal Fund for Temporary Investment: InterMuni Fund (STMB), Municipal Fund for Temporary In-vestment: Muni-Cash (STMB), Municipal Fund for Temporary Investment: Muni-Fund (STMB), Temporary Investment Fund: TempCash Dol-lar (MM), Temporary Investment Fund: TempFund (MM), Trust for Short-Term Federal Securities: FedFund (MM), Trust for Short-Term Federal Securities: T-Fund (MM), Westcore Funds: Discretionary Portfolio–Class A (MM)

Shearson Lehman Brothers
Two World Trade Center
New York, NY 10048
(212) 577-5794, (800) 451-2010

Shearson Aggressive Growth Fund (AG), Shearson California Municipals (SMB-LT), Shearson Fundamental Value Fund (G), Shearson Global Opportunities Fund (INT)

Shearson Lehman Brothers
1300 South University Drive, 6th Floor
University Centre
Fort Worth, TX 76107
(817) 335-3051, (800) 221-3636,
(800) 522-5429 (TX only)

Shearson Appreciation Fund (G), Shearson Daily Dividend (MM), Shearson Daily Tax-Free Dividend (STMB), Shearson FMA Government Fund (MM), Shearson FMA Cash Fund (MM), Shearson FMA Municipal Fund (STMB), Shearson Government and Agencies (MM), Shearson High Yield Fund (CB), Shearson Managed Municipals (LTMB), Shearson Managed Governments (GNMA), Shearson New York Municipals (SMB-LT)

Sherman Dean
6061 N.W. Expressway, Suite 465
San Antonio, TX 78201
(512) 734-1488

Sherman, Dean Fund (AG)

Siebel Capital Management
80 East Sir Francis Drake Boulevard
Larkspur, CA 94939
(415) 461-3850
and
7677 Oakport Street, P. O. Box 2470
Oakland, CA 94614
(415) 430-9900, (800) 445-9020,
(800) 445-9052 (CA only)

Adam Investors (G + I), Equitec Siebel Total Return Fund (G + I), Gamma Partners (G + I), Siebel Capital Partners (G + I)

Sigma
Greenville Center, C-200
3801 Kennett Pike
Wilmington, DE 19807
(302) 652-3091, (800) 441-9490

Sigma Capital Shares (AG), Sigma Government Securities Fund (MM), Sigma Income

Shares (CB), Sigma Investment Shares (G + I), Sigma Money Market Fund (MM), Sigma Special Fund (G), Sigma Tax-Free Bond Fund (LTMB), Sigma Trust Shares (B), Sigma Venture Shares (AG), Sigma World Fund (INT)

SMA Investment Trust
440 Lincoln Street
Worcester, MA 01605
(617) 852-1000

SMA Investment Trust: Growth Fund (G + I), SMA Investment Trust: Income Appreciation Fund (G + I), SMA Investment Trust: Money Market Fund (MM)

Smilen Investment Research & Management
220 East 42nd Street
New York, NY 10017
(212) 953-7700, (800) 431-4111

Sector Investment Fund (G)

Smith Barney
1345 Avenue of Americas
New York, NY 10105
(212) 613-2600, (800) 223-7078,
(800) 221-8806

National Liquid Reserves: NLR Cash Portfolio (MM), National Liquid Reserves: NLR Government Portfolio (MM), Smith Barney Equity Fund (G), Smith Barney Funds: Income & Growth Portfolio (G + I), Smith Barney Funds: Income Return Account Portfolio (I), Smith Barney Funds: U.S. Government Securities Portfolio (GNMA), Tax Free Money Fund (STMB), Vantage Money Market Funds: Vantage Cash Portfolio (MM), Vantage Money Market Funds: Vantage Government Portfolio (MM)

SoGen Securities Corporation
630 Fifth Avenue
New York, NY 10111
(212) 832-0022

SoGen International Fund (INT)

Southern Farm Bureau
1401 Livingston Lane, Suite 300
P. O. Box 691
Jackson, MS 39205
(601) 982-7800, (800) 647-8053,
(800) 872-8514 (MS only)

Southern Farm Bureau Cash Fund (MM)

Sovereign
985 Old Eagle School Road
Wayne, PA 19087
(215) 254-0703

Sovereign Investors (G + I)

Spears, Benzak
10 Rockefeller Plaza, Suite 1120
New York, NY 10020
(212) 903-1200

SBSF Fund (G)

State Bond and Mortgage Company
100-16 North Minnesota Street
New Ulm, MN 56703
(507) 354-2144

State Bond Common Stock Fund (G), State Bond Diversified Fund (I), State Bond Progress Fund (G)

State Farm
One State Farm Plaza
Bloomington, IL 61701
(309) 766-2029

State Farm Balanced Fund (B), State Farm Growth Fund (G), State Farm Interim Fund (I), State Farm Municipal Bond Fund (LTMB)

State Street
One Financial Center, 38th Floor
Boston, MA 02111
(617) 482-3920

State Street Exchange Fund (G + I), State Street Growth Fund (G + I), State Street Investment Corporation (G + I)

Steadman Security Corporation
1730 K Street, N.W.
Washington, DC 20006
(202) 223-1000, (800) 424-8570

Steadman American Industry (G), Steadman Associated (G), Steadman Investment (G), Steadman Oceanographic, Technology & Growth (G)

SteinRoe
300 West Adams Street, 11th Floor
Chicago, IL 60606
(312) 368-7800, (800) 621-0615,
(800) 621-0320

Stein Roe & Farnham Capital Opportunities Fund (G), Stein Roe & Farnham Stock Fund (G), Stein Roe Bond Fund (CB), Stein Roe Cash Reserves (MM), Stein Roe Discovery Fund (AG), Stein Roe Government Reserves (MM), Stein Roe Governments Plus (USGI), Stein Roe High Yield Bonds (CB), Stein Roe High-Yield Municipals (LTMB), Stein Roe Intermediate Municipals (LTMB), Stein Roe Special Fund (AG), Stein Roe Tax-Exempt Bond Fund (LTMB), Stein Roe Tax-

Exempt Money Fund (STMB), Stein Roe Total Return Fund (B), Stein Roe Universe Fund (AG)

Strategic Investment Services
3403 10th Street
Riverside, CA 92501
(714) 686-3388, (800) 972-3863,
(800) 521-5612 (CA only)

YES Fund (USGI)

Stratton
P. O. Box 550, Butler & Skippack Pike
Blue Bell, PA 19422
(215) 542-8025

Stratton Growth Fund (G + I), Stratton Monthly Dividend Shares (I)

Strong Funds
815 East Mason Street
Milwaukee, WI 53202
(414) 765-0620, (800) 368-3863

Strong Investment Fund (G), Strong Money Market Fund (MM), Strong Total Return Fund (G + I)

Sun Growth
One Sun Life Executive Park
Wellesley Hills, MA 02181
(617) 237-6030, (800) 225-3950

Sun Growth Variable Annuity Fund (G)

Templeton
405 Central Avenue, P. O. Box 3942
St. Petersburg, FL 33731
(813) 823-8712, (800) 237-0738,
(800) 282-0106 (FL only)

Templeton Funds: Foreign Fund (INT), Templeton Funds: World Fund (INT), Templeton Global Funds: Templeton Global I (INT), Templeton Global Funds: Templeton Global II (INT), Templeton Income Fund (I)

Tenneco Asset Management
777 Walker Street, Suite 200
P. O. Box 2511
Houston, TX 77001
(713) 757-5656, (800) 262-6686

Fund of the Southwest (G), Plimoney Fund (MM), Plitrend Fund (AG), Southwestern Investors Income Fund (I)

Thomas McKinnon
One New York Plaza
New York, NY 10004
(212) 482-5894, (800) 628-1237,
(800) 482-5894 (NY only)

Cash Accumulation Trust: National Government Fund (MM), Cash Accumulation Trust: National Money Market Fund (MM), Cash Accumulation Trust: National Tax-Exempt Fund (STMB), Thomson McKinnon Investment Trust: Thomson McKinnon Growth Fund (G), Thomson McKinnon Investment Trust: Thomson McKinnon Income Fund (I), Thomson McKinnon Investment Trust: Thomson McKinnon Opportunity Fund (AG), Thomson McKinnon Investment Trust: Thomson McKinnon Short-Term Fund (MM), Thomson McKinnon Investment Trust: Thomson McKinnon U.S. Government Fund (USGI)

Transamerica
Box 2438, Terminal Annex
1150 South Olive
Los Angeles, CA 90051
(213) 742-4141

Transamerica Cash Reserve (MM)

Transatlantic Fund. *see* Kleinwort Benson International.

T. Rowe Price Funds. *see* at Price.

TrustFunds. *see* SEI Financial Services.

Trust Services of America
700 Wilshire Boulevard
Los Angeles, CA 90017
(213) 614-7000, (800) 221-4171

TSA Spectrum Portfolios Trust: TSA-Active Allocation Portfolio (G + I), TSA Spectrum Portfolios Trust: TSA-Active Bond Portfolio (CB), TSA Spectrum Portfolios Trust: TSA-Aggressive Value Equity Portfolio (AG), TSA Spectrum Portfolios Trust: TSA-Core Common Stock Portfolio (G), TSA Spectrum Portfolios Trust: TSA-Emerging Growth Portfolio (AG), TSA Spectrum Portfolios Trust: TSA-Government Securities Portfolio (USGI), TSA Spectrum Portfolios Trust: TSA-Money Market Portfolio (MM)

Tucker Anthony
Three Center Plaza
Boston, MA 02108
(617) 523-3170, (800) 225-6258

Freedom Investment Trust: Freedom Gold & Government Trust (USGI), Tucker Anthony Group of Tax Exempt Funds: Tucker Anthony Tax Exempt Money Fund (STMB), Tucker Anthony Mutual Fund: Cash Management Fund (MM), Tucker Anthony Mutual Fund: Government Securities Fund (MM)

Tudor Management Company
1 New York Plaza
New York, NY 10004
(212) 908-9582, (800) 223-3332

Tudor Fund (G)

Twentieth Century
605 West 47th Street, P. O. Box 200
Kansas City, MO 64141
(816) 531-5575

Twentieth Century Investors: Cash Reserve (MM), Twentieth Century Investors: Giftrust Investors (G), Twentieth Century Investors: Growth Investors (G), Twentieth Century Investors: Select Investors (G + I), Twentieth Century Investors: U.S. Governments (USGI), Twentieth Century Investors: Ultra Investors (AG), Twentieth Century Investors: Vista Investors (AG)

Unified
600 Guaranty Building
Indianapolis, IN 46204
(317) 634-3300, (800) 862-7283

Liquid Green Tax-Free Trust (STMB), Liquid Green Trust (MM), Unified Growth Fund (G), Unified Income Fund (I), Unified Municipal Fund: General Series (LTMB), Unified Municipal Fund: Indiana Series (SMB-LT), Unified Mutual Shares (G + I)

United Funds
2400 Pershing Road, P.O. Box 1343
Kansas City, MO 64141
(816) 283-4000, (800) 821-5664

United Cash Management Fund (MM), United Continental Income Fund (B), United Funds: Accumulative Fund Series (G), United Funds: Bond Fund Series (CB), United Funds: Income Fund Series (I), United Funds: Science & Energy Fund Series (G), United Gold & Government Fund (G + I), United Government Securities Fund (USGI), United High Income Fund (CB), United International Growth Fund (INT), United Municipal Bond Fund (LTMB), United New Concepts Fund (AG), United Retirement Shares (G + I), United Vanguard Fund (AG)

United Services
11330 IH 10 West, Suite 5300
Woodway Park, Building 5000
San Antonio, TX 78249
(512) 696-1234, (800) 531-5777,
(800) 824-4653

United Services Funds (G), United Services Funds: Gold Shares Fund (PMG), United

Services Funds: Good & Bad Times Fund (G), United Services Funds: Growth Fund (G), United Services Funds: U.S. Income Fund (G + I), United Services Funds: U.S. LoCap Fund (AG), United Services Funds: U.S. Prospector Fund (PMG), United Services Funds: U.S. Tax Free Fund (LTMB), United Services Funds: U.S. Treasury Securities Fund (MM)

USAA
USAA Building
San Antonio, TX 78288
(512) 498-7270, (800) 531-8181

USAA Investment Trust: Cornerstone Fund (G), USAA Investment Fund: Gold Fund (PMG), USAA Mutual Fund: Federal Securities Money Market Fund (MM), USAA Mutual Fund: Growth Fund (G), USAA Mutual Fund: Income Fund (I), USAA Mutual Fund: Money Market Fund (MM), USAA Mutual Fund: Sunbelt Era Fund (AG), USAA Tax Exempt Fund: High Yield Fund (LTMB), USAA Tax Exempt Fund: Intermediate-Term Fund (LTMB), USAA Tax Exempt Fund: Short-Term Fund (LTMB), USAA Tax Exempt Fund: Tax Exempt Money Market Fund (STMB)

U.S. Boston Investment
6 New England Executive Park
Burlington, MA 01803
(617) 272-6420

U.S. Boston Investment Company: Boston I (G + I), U.S. Boston Investment Company: Boston International (INT)

VALIC
2929 Allen Parkway, P. O. Box 3206
Houston, TX 77253
(713) 526-5251

American General Series Portfolio Company: Capital Accumulation Fund (AG), American General Series Portfolio Company: Capital Conservation Fund (G + I), American General Series Portfolio Company: Government Securities Fund (USGI), American General Series Portfolio Company: Money Market Fund (MM), American General Series Portfolio Company: Timed Opportunity Fund (G)

Valley Forge Management Corporation
P.O. Box 262
Valley Forge, PA 19481
(215) 688-6839

Valley Forge Fund (G)

Value Line
711 Third Avenue
New York, NY 10017
(212) 687-3965, (800) 223-0818

Value Line Bond Fund (I), Value Line Cash Fund (MM), Value Line Centurion Fund (G), Value Line Convertible Fund (G + I), Value Line Fund (G), Value Line Income Fund (I), Value Line Leveraged Growth Investors (AG), Value Line Special Situations Fund (AG), Value Line Tax Exempt Fund: High Yield Portfolio (LTMB), Value Line Tax Exempt Fund: Money Market Portfolio (STMB)

Van Kampen Merritt
1001 Warrenville Road
Lisle, IL 60532
(312) 719-6000, (800) 225-2222

Van Kampen Merritt U.S. Government Fund (USGI), Van Kampen Merritt Insured Tax Free Income Fund (LTMB), Van Kampen Merritt Tax Free Income Fund (LTMB)

Vanguard Group (The)
Vanguard Financial Center, P. O. Box 2600
Valley Forge, PA 19482
(215) 648-6000, (800) 662-7447,
(800) 362-0530 (PA only)

Explorer Fund (AG), Explorer II (AG), Gemini Fund (G), Naess & Thomas Special Fund (AG), PRIMECAP Fund (G), Trustees' Commingled Fund: International Equity Portfolio (INT), Trustees' Commingled Fund: U.S. Equity Portfolio (G + I), Vanguard Fixed-Income Securities Fund: GNMA Portfolio (GNMA), Vanguard Fixed-Income Securities Fund: High-Yield Bond Portfolio (CB), Vanguard Fixed-Income Securities Fund: Investment Grade Bond Portfolio (CB), Vanguard Fixed-Income Securities Fund: Short Term Bond Portfolio (CB), Vanguard Index Trust (G + I), Vanguard Money Market Trust: Federal Portfolio (MM), Vanguard Money Market Trust: Insured Portfolio (MM), Vanguard Money Market Trust: Prime Portfolio (MM), Vanguard Municipal Bond Fund: High-Yield Portfolio (LTMB), Vanguard Municipal Bond Fund: Insured Long-Term Municipal Bond Portfolio (LTMB), Vanguard Municipal Bond Fund: Intermediate-Term Portfolio (LTMB), Vanguard Municipal Bond Fund: Long-Term Portfolio (LTMB), Vanguard Municipal Bond Fund: Money Market Portfolio (STMB), Vanguard Municipal Bond Fund: Short-Term Portfolio (STMB), Vanguard Qualified Dividend Portfolio I (I), Vanguard Qualified Dividend Portfolio II (I), Vanguard Qualified Dividend Portfolio III (I), Vanguard

STAR Fund (B), Vanguard Specialized Portfolios: Energy Portfolio (AG), Vanguard Specialized Portfolios: Gold & Precious Metals Portfolio (PMG), Vanguard Specialized Portfolios: Health Care Portfolio (AG), Vanguard Specialized Portfolios: Service Economy Portfolio (AG), Vanguard Specialized Portfolios: Technology Portfolio (AG), Vanguard World Fund: International Growth Portfolio (INT), Vanguard World Fund: U.S. Growth Portfolio (G), W. L. Morgan Growth Fund (G), Wellesley Income Fund (I), Wellington Fund (B), Windsor Fund (G + I), Windsor II (G + I)

Venture Advisers
309 Johnson Street, P. O. Box 1688
Santa Fe, NM 87501
(505) 983-4335, (800) 545-2098

New York Venture Fund (AG), Retirement Planning Funds of America: Bond Fund (USGI), Retirement Planning Funds of America: Equity Fund (AG), Retirement Planning Funds of America: Money Market Fund (MM), Venture Income Plus (I), Venture Muni Plus (LTMB)

Wayne Hummer
175 West Jackson Boulevard
Chicago, IL 60604
(312) 431-1700, (800) 621-4477,
(800) 972-5566 (IL only)

Wayne Hummer Growth Fund (G + I), Wayne Hummer Money Fund: Trust Money Market Portfolio (MM)

Wealth Monitors
1001 East 101st Terrace
Kansas City, MO 64131
(816) 941-7990

Wealth Monitors Fund (G)

Webster
20 Exchange Place
New York, NY 10005
(212) 510-5000

Kidder, Peabody Equity Income Fund (G + I), Kidder Peabody Government Income Fund (USGI), Kidder, Peabody Government Money Fund (MM), Kidder, Peabody Premium Account Fund (MM), Kidder, Peabody Special Growth Fund (AG), Kidder, Peabody Tax Exempt Money Fund (STMB), Kidder Peabody Tax Free Income Fund: National Series (LTMB), Webster Cash Reserve Fund (MM)

Weiss Peck & Greer
One New York Plaza, 30th Floor
New York, NY 10004
(212) 908-9582, (800) 223-3332

Tudor Fund (AG), WPG Fund (G + I)

WesterGaard
540 Madison Avenue, Suite 805
New York, NY 10022
(212) 940-0253, (800) 523-8425

WesterGaard Fund (AG)

Working Assets
230 California Street
San Francisco, CA 94111
(415) 989-3200, (800) 223-7010,
(800) 543-8800

Working Assets Money Fund (MM)

YES Fund. *see* Strategic Investment Services.

B. C. Ziegler
215 North Main Street
West Bend, WI 53095
(414) 334-5521, (800) 558-1776

Principal Preservation Tax-Exempt Fund (LTMB), S&P 100 Plus Portfolio (G + I)

CLOSED-END MUTUAL FUNDS

The following is a compilation of the names, ticker symbols, and addresses of American closed-end mutual funds, with the types of investments made by each. The notation *bond* means the fund buys only bonds, and is therefore likely to pay a high yield. The notation *convertible* means that the fund mainly buys convertible bonds, which pay a higher yield than stocks and also have more potential to rise in value than bonds. The notation *dual purpose* means that the fund is split into two, with one part of the fund designed for investors who want income and the other part designed for shareholders intent upon capital gains. The notation *equity* means the fund buys stocks, mostly for capital gains purposes. The notation *gold* means the fund exclusively buys shares of gold-mining companies, which usually have a high yield, but are subject to the ups and downs of gold prices. The notation *specialized equity* means that the fund buys only particular kinds of stocks for the purpose of capital appreciation. Some funds, for instance, only buy stocks of medical companies, while others concentrate on the stocks of a particular foreign country like Japan.

Closed-end mutual funds issue a fixed number of shares, which are then traded either on exchanges or over the counter. Funds traded on the New York Stock Exchange are notated with an NYSE, those traded on the American Stock Exchange, with an ASE, and those traded over the counter, with an OTC. Closed-end funds contrast with open-end mutual funds, which create new shares whenever additional funds are received from customers. But closed-end fund managers buy and sell stocks, bonds, and convertible securities just like open-end mutual fund managers.

Open-end funds sell at the net asset value of their holdings on a particular day (plus a charge, or load, in some cases) and always stand ready to redeem shares at the NAV. In contrast, closed-end funds usually sell above or below the net asset value. The price of the shares is determined by the same forces of supply and demand that affect the value of any publicly traded security. Therefore, those buying shares in a closed-end fund when it is selling below net asset value are, in effect, buying a dollar's worth of securities for less than a dollar, and those buying such a fund when it is trading at a premium to its net asset value receive less than a dollar's worth of securities for each dollar invested.

This list is provided courtesy of Thomas Herzfeld, author of *The Investor's Guide To Closed-End Mutual Funds* and *High-Return, Low-Risk Investment, Combining Market Timing, Stock Selection and Closed-End Mutual Funds* (Mentor Executive Library, 1633 Broadway, New York, New York 10019). Mr. Herzfeld, located at 7800 Red Road, South Miami, Florida 33143 [(305) 665-6500], is an investment advisor specializing in closed-end funds.

Adams Express Company ADX, NYSE
 (Equity)
201 North Charles Street
Baltimore, Maryland 21201 (301) 752-5900

American Capital Convertible Securities, Inc.
 ACS, NYSE (Convertible-Equity)
2777 Allen Parkway, P.O. Box 3121
Houston, Texas 77253 (713) 529-0600

AMEV Securities AMV, NYSE (Bond)
P.O. Box 43284
St. Paul, Minnesota 55164 (612) 738-4000

Anglo American Gold Investment Company,
 Limited AAGIY, OTC (Equity Gold)
44 Main Street
Johannesburg 2001, South Africa

ASA Limited ASA, NYSE (Equity-Gold)
54 Marshall Street
Johannesburg, 2001 South Africa

Baker Fentress & Co. BKFR, OTC (Equity)
Suite 3510, 200 West Madison Street
Chicago, Illinois 60606 (312) 236-9190

Baldwin Securities Corporation BAL, ASE
 (Equity)
595 Madison Avenue
New York, New York 10022 (212) 972-8170

Bancroft Convertible Fund, Inc. BCV, ASE
 (Convertible-Equity)
42 Broadway
New York, New York 10004 (212) 269-9236

Biotech Capital Corporation BITC, OTC
 (Specialized Equity)
600 Madison Avenue
New York, New York 10022 (212) 758-7722

Bunker Hill Income Securities, Inc. BHL,
 NYSE (Bond)
P.O. Box 4602
Pasadena, California 91106 (213) 613-8656

Capital Southwest Corporation CSWC, OTC
 (Equity)
Suite 700, 12900 Preston Road
Dallas, Texas 75230 (214) 233-8242

Castle Convertible Fund, Inc. CVF, ASE
(Convertible-Equity)
75 Maiden Lane
New York, New York 10038 (201) 547-3600

Central Securities Corporation CET, ASE
(Equity)
375 Park Avenue
New York, New York 10022 (212) 688-3011

Circle Income Shares, Inc. CINS, OTC (Bond)
P.O. Box 44027
Indianapolis, Indiana 46244 (317) 639-8180

CL Assets, Inc. CLAS, OTC (Equity)
342 Madison Avenue
New York, New York 10173 (212) 850-8300

Claremont Capital Corporation CCM, ASE
(Equity)
321 16th Street South, P. O. Box 3407
Seattle, Washington 98114 (206) 324-0901

CNA Income Shares, Inc. CNN, NYSE (Bond)
CNA Plaza
Chicago, Illinois 60685 (312) 822-4181

Combined Penny Stock Fund, Inc. PENY,
OTC (Specialized Equity)
2616 West Colorado Avenue
Colorado Springs, CO 80904 (303) 636-1511

Current Income Shares, Inc. CUR, NYSE
(Bond)
P.O. Box 30151, Terminal Annex
Los Angeles, California 90030
(213) 480-6748

Drexel Bond Debenture Trading Fund DBF,
NYSE (Bond)
1500 Walnut Street
Philadelphia, Pennsylvania 19102
(215) 561-8060

Emerging Medical Technology Fund EMT,
ASE (Specialized Equity)
Suite 120, 5 Sentry Parkway West,
P. O. Box 111
Blue Bell, Pennsylvania 19422
(215) 825-0400

Engex, Inc. OTC (Equity)
44 Wall Street
New York, New York 10005 (212) 968-2004

Equity Strategies Fund, Inc. EQST, OTC
(Equity)
Suite 1600, 171 Madison Avenue
New York, New York 10016 (212) 683-7141

Excelsior Income Shares, Inc. EIS, NYSE
(Bond)
Suite 2300, 45 Wall Street
New York, New York 10005 (212) 425-7120

First Australia Fund IAF, ASE
(Specialized Equity)
One Seaport Plaza
New York, New York 10292 (212) 214-1215

First Australia Prime Income Fund FAI, ASE
(Specialized Bond)
One Seaport Plaza
New York, New York 10292 (212) 214-1215

Fort Dearborn Income Securities, Inc. FTD,
NYSE (Bond)
Suite 800, 126 South State Street
Chicago, Illinois 60603 (312) 346-0676

France Fund, Inc. FRN, NYSE
(Specialized Equity)
535 Madison Avenue
New York, NY 10022 (212) 906-7733

Franklin Corporation FKLN, OTC (Equity)
1185 Avenue of the Americas
New York, New York 10036 (212) 719-4844

Gabelli Equity Trust Inc., GAB, NYSE (Equity)
8 Sound Shore Drive
Greenwich, Connecticut 06830
(203) 625-0028

Gemini II Fund GMI, GMI PR, NYSE
(Dual-Purpose)
P.O. Box 1100
Valley Forge, Pennsylvania 19482
(215) 648-6000

General American Investors Company, Inc.
GAM NYSE (Equity)
330 Madison Avenue
New York, New York 10017 (212) 916-8400

Germany Fund, Inc. GER, NYSE
(Specialized Equity)
40 Wall Street
New York, NY 10005 (212) 612-0600

Global Yield Fund, Inc. PGY, NYSE (Bond)
One Seaport Plaza
New York, NY 10292 (212) 214-1215

Greater Washington Investors, Inc. GMII,
OTC (Specialized Equity)
5454 Wisconsin Avenue
Chevy Chase, Maryland 20815
(301) 656-0626

Growth Fund of Florida, Inc. GFLA, OTC
(Equity)
10 West Adams Street
Jacksonville, Florida 32202 (904) 632-8000

Growth Stock Outlook Trust, Inc. GSO, NYSE
(Equity)
4405 East-West Highway
Bethesda, Maryland 20814 (301) 654-5205

Hatteras Income Securities HAT, NYSE
(Bond)
One NCNB Plaza
Charlotte, North Carolina 28255
(704) 333-7808

INA Investment Securities, Inc. IIS, NYSE
(Bond)
P.O. Box 7728
Philadelphia, Pennsylvania 19101
(215) 568-2295

Independent Square Income Securities, Inc.
ISIS, OTC (Bond)
3 Radnor Corporate Center, 100 Matsonford
Road
Radnor, Pennsylvania 19087 (212) 301-0109

Intercapital Income Securities, Inc. ICB,
NYSE (Bond)
One World Trade Center
New York, New York 10048 (212) 938-4500

Italy Fund, Inc. ITA, NYSE
(Specialized Equity)
106th Floor, 2 World Trade Center
New York, New York 10048 (212) 321-7476

Japan Fund, Inc. JPN, NYSE
(Specialized Equity)
345 Park Avenue
New York, New York 10154 (212) 350-8500

John Hancock Income Trust JHS, NYSE
(Bond)
John Hancock Place, P.O. Box 111
Boston, Massachusetts 02117
(617) 421-6320

John Hancock Investors, JHI, NYSE (Bond)
John Hancock Place, P. O. Box 111
Boston, Massachusetts 02117
(617) 421-6320

Korea Fund, Inc. KF, NYSE
(Specialized Equity)
345 Park Avenue
New York, New York 10154 (212) 350-8200

Lehman Corporation LEM, NYSE (Equity)
55 Water Street
New York, New York 10041 (212) 558-2024

Lincoln National Direct Placement Fund, Inc.
LND, NYSE (Bond)
111 West Washington Street
Chicago, Illinois 60602 (312) 630-2445

MassMutual Corporate Investors, Inc. MCI,
NYSE (Bond)
1295 State Street
Springfield, Massachusetts 01111
(413) 788-8411

Mexico Fund, Inc. MXF, NYSE
(Specialized Equity)
633 Third Avenue
New York, New York 10017 (212) 637-4467

Midland Capital Corporation MCAP, OTC
(Equity)
950 Third Avenue
New York, New York 10022 (212) 753-7790

ML Convertible Securities, Inc. MLS, MLS
PR, NYSE (Dual Purpose)
P.O. Box 9011
Princeton, New Jersey 08540-9011
(609) 282-2000

Montgomery Street Income Securities, Inc.
MTS, NYSE (Bond)
Suite 1608, 315 Montgomery Street
San Francisco, California 94104
(415) 982-8020

Mutual of Omaha Interest Shares, Inc. MUO,
NYSE (Bond)
Mutual of Omaha Fund Management
Company
10235 Regency Circle
Omaha, Nebraska 68114 (402) 397-8555

Niagara Share Corporation NGS, NYSE
(Equity)
70 Niagara Street
Buffalo, New York 14202 (716) 856-2600

Pacific American Income Shares, Inc. PAI,
NYSE (Bond)
P.O. Box 983
Pasadena, California 91102 (213) 614-3156

Petroleum & Resources Corporation PEO,
NYSE (Equity)
201 North Charles Street
Baltimore, Maryland 21201 (301) 752-5900

Pilgrim Regional BankShares PBS, NYSE
(Specialized Equity)
1930 Century Plaza West
Los Angeles, California 90067
(213) 551-0833

Pro-Med Capital, Inc. PRMD, OTC
(Specialized Equity)
Suite 225, 1380 NE Miami Gardens Drive
North Miami Beach, Florida 33179
(305) 949-5900

Providence Investors Company OTC
(Specialized Equity)
1902 Fleet National Bank Building
Providence, Rhode Island 02903
(401) 421-1141

Rand Capital Corporation RAND, OTC
(Specialized Equity)
1300 Rand Building
Buffalo, New York 14203 (716) 853-0802

Real Silk Hosiery Mills, Inc. OTC (Equity)
Suite 908, 455 North Pennsylvania Street
Indianapolis, Indiana (317) 632-7359

Revere AE Capital Funds, Inc. PREV, OTC
(Equity)
745 Fifth Avenue
New York, New York 10151 (212) 888-6800

Rockies Fund, Inc. ROCF, OTC (Equity)
4th Floor, 100 Garfield Street
Denver, Colorado 80206 (303) 320-0090

Scandinavia Fund, Inc. SCF, ASE
(Specialized Equity)
136 Nassau Road
Huntington, NY 11743 (516) 385-9580

Source Capital, Inc. SOR, NYSE (Equity)
10301 West Pico Boulevard
Los Angeles, California 90064
(213) 277-4900

Spectra Fund, Inc. OTC (Equity)
75 Maiden Lane
New York, New York 10038 (201) 547-3600

State Mutual Securities SMS, NYSE (Bond)
440 Lincoln Street
Worcester, Massachusetts 01605
(617) 852-1000

Sterling Capital Corporation SPR, ASE
(Equity)
635 Madison Avenue
New York, New York 10022 (212) 980-3360

Transamerica Income Shares, Inc. TAI, NYSE
(Bond)
P.O. Box 2438
Los Angeles, California 90051
(213) 742-4141

Tri-Continental Corporation TY, NYSE
(Equity)
One Bankers Trust Plaza
New York, New York 10006 (212) 432-4000

USLIFE Income Fund, Inc. UIF, NYSE (Bond)
125 Maiden Lane
New York, New York 10038 (212) 709-6000

Vestaur Securities, Inc. VES, NYSE (Bond)
Fifth Floor, Packard Building, 1500 Chestnut
Street
Philadelphia, Pennsylvania 19101
(215) 567-3969

Z-Seven Fund ZSE, Pacific Stock Exchange
(Equity)
Suite 21, 90 Broad Street
New York, New York 10004 (212) 809-1880

Zweig Fund, Inc. ZF, NYSE (Equity)
900 Third Avenue
New York, NY 10022 (212) 486-7110

4. FUTURES AND OPTIONS CONTRACTS

On the following pages, you will find a list of commodity and option contracts traded in the United States and Canada. These contracts are listed by the exchange on which they are traded. Within each exchange, the listings are broken down into the kind of products they are: foreign currency options, futures, futures options, index options, or interest rate options. Each contract is then listed alphabetically within its category.

Contract specifications set by each exchange and approved by either the Commodities Futures Trading Commission or the Securities and Exchange Commission are listed with each contract.

The basic facts about each commodity futures contract include:

Trading Unit   The underlying commodity or group of stocks being traded, and the quantity.

Prices Quoted In   The form in which prices are quoted (such as cents per bushel).

Minimum Price Fluctuation   The smallest move, up or down, the contract can make. This is indicated first in increments that the contract can move in, and then as a dollar figure for the amount of money the move means to the commodity trader.

Dollar Value of a 1 Cent Move   The dollars an investor will make or lose, at least on paper, if a contract moves 1 cent up or down.

Daily Contract Limit   Many exchanges do not allow prices to rise or fall beyond certain limits within a day. Such limits, if any, are shown first in the increment of the contract, and then as a dollar figure.

Settlement   The way contracts are settled when they expire. Some contracts provide for the physical delivery of a commodity. Specific rules must be followed on how and where commodities are delivered from seller to buyer. Other contracts involve no physical delivery. These contracts are settled in cash.

Last Trading Day   The last day trading can occur in a contract.

Contract Months   Although all these contracts trade constantly, most expire only in certain months of the year. This column presents the month in which contracts expire.

Trading Hours   The hours during which a contract is traded, in local time. EST means Eastern Standard Time, CST means Central Standard Time, and PST means Pacific Standard Time.

Ticker Symbol   The symbol by which a contract's current price and trading activity can be checked through an electronic price quote service.

For index, interest rate, and futures options contracts, other information is given:

Exercise Limits Each exchange limits the number of contracts one trader can take a position in, either on the long or short side of a trade.

Strike Prices Strike prices are set both above and below the current market price of the future or index, so puts and calls can be traded in both directions. This column also gives the intervals at which strike prices are set, and when new strike prices are added.

Expiration Day If options are not exercised, they expire. This column details when options expire.

Index by Contract

This index will guide you to a particular contract in the tables that follow. Commodities, financial instruments, and stock indexes are listed alphabetically in the index, along with the contracts available and the exchanges on which the contracts trade. When you find the particular contract that interests you, turn to the relevant exchange in the tables, where exchanges are listed alphabetically. For instance, if you are interested in futures options on cotton, look for the *cotton* entry in the index, which indicates that this contract is traded on the NYCE, or New York Cotton Exchange. Turn to New York Cotton Exchange in the tables, and you will find specifics about the contract. (A key to abbreviations follows the index.)

Airline Index index options (ASE)
Aluminum futures (COMEX)
Bank Certificates of Deposit futures (IMM)
Barley futures (WCE); futures options (CME)
Canadian Dollar foreign currency options (CBOE, PHSE); futures (IMM, MACE); futures options (VSE)
Cocoa futures (CSCE); futures options (CSCE)
Coffee futures (CSCE)
Commodity Research Bureau Price Index futures (NYFE)
Computer Technology Index index options (ASE)
Consumer Price Index-Wages futures (CSCE)
Copper futures (COMEX, MACE); futures options (COMEX)
Corn futures (CBT, MACE); futures options (CBT)
Cotton futures (NYCE); futures options (NYCE)
Crude Oil futures (NYME)
Deutsche Mark foreign currency options (CBOE, PHSE); futures (IMM, MACE); futures options (CME)
Eurodollars futures (IMM); futures options (CME); interest rate options (PHSE)
European Currency Units futures (IMM, NYCE); interest rate options (PHSE)
Feeder Cattle futures (CME)
Flaxseed futures (WCE)
French Franc foreign currency options (CBOE, PHSE); futures (IMM)
Gasoline futures (NYME)
Gold futures (CBT, COMEX, IMM, MACE, ME, WCE); futures options (COMEX, MACE, VSE, WCE); index options (PHSE); options (ASE)
Government National Mortgage Association Mortgages futures (CBT)
Heating Oil futures (NYME)
High Fructose Corn Syrup futures (MGE)
Japanese Yen foreign currency options (CBOE, PHSE); futures (IMM, MACE)

Live Cattle futures (CME, MACE); futures options (CME)

Live Hogs futures (CME, MACE); futures options (CME)

Lumber futures (CME, ME)

Major Market Index futures (CBT); index options (ASE)

Municipal Bond Index futures (CBT)

NASDAQ-100 Index futures (CBT); index options (NASDAQ)

National OTC Index futures (PHSE); index options (PHSE)

NYSE Composite Index futures (NYFE); futures options (NYFE); index options (NYSE)

NYSE Double Index index options (NYSE)

Oats futures (CBT, MACE, WCE)

Oil Index futures (TFE); index options (ASE)

Orange Juice futures (NYCE); futures options (NYCE)

Over The Counter 250 Industrial Stock Price Index futures (CME)

Palladium futures (NYME)

Platinum futures (MACE, NYME)

Pork Bellies futures (CME)

Potatoes futures (NYME)

Propane futures (NYCE)

Rapeseed futures (WCE)

Rough Rice futures (CRCE)

Rye futures (WCE)

Short Staple Cotton futures (CRCE)

Silver futures (CBT, COMEX, MACE, WCE); futures options (CBT, COMEX, TFE, VSE)

Soybeans futures (CBT, MACE); futures options (CBT, MACE)

Soybean Meal futures (CBT, MACE)

Soybean Oil futures (CBT)

Standard and Poor's 100 Index futures (CME); index options (CBOE)

Standard and Poor's 500 Index futures (CME); futures options (CME); index options (CBOE)

Standard and Poor's Over the Counter 250 Index index options (CBOE)

Sugar futures (CSCE); futures options (CSCE)

Swiss Franc foreign currency options (CBOE, PHSE); futures (IMM, MACE); futures options (CME)

Technology Index index options (PSE)

Toronto Stock Exchange 300 futures (TFE)

Treasury Bills futures (IMM, MACE); TFE (Canadian bills) interest rate options (ASE)

Treasury Bonds futures (CBT, MACE); TFE (Canadian bonds) futures options (CBT); TFE (Canadian bonds); futures options (CME); interest rate options (CBOE)

Treasury Index (Five Year) futures (NYCE)

Treasury Notes futures (CBT); futures options (CBT); interest rate options (ASE, CBOE)

U.S. Dollar futures (NYCE, TFE)

Value Line Index futures (KCBT); index options (PHSE)

Wheat futures (CBT, KCBT, MACE, MGE, WCE); futures options (KCBT, MACE, MGE)

Key to Abbreviations of Exchanges

ASE American Stock Exchange

CBT Chicago Board of Trade

CBOE Chicago Board Options Exchange

CME Chicago Mercantile Exchange
CRCE Chicago Rice and Cotton Exchange
CSCE Coffee, Sugar and Cocoa Exchange
COMEX Commodity Exchange, Inc.
IMM International Monetary Market at CME
KCBT Kansas City Board of Trade
MACE MidAmerica Commodity Exchange
ME Montréal Exchange
MGE Minneapolis Grain Exchange
NASDAQ National Association of Securities Dealers Automated Quotations system
NYCE New York Cotton Exchange
NYFE New York Futures Exchange
NYME New York Mercantile Exchange
NYSE New York Stock Exchange
PSE Pacific Stock Exchange
PHSE Philadelphia Stock Exchange
TFE Toronto Futures Exchange
VSE Vancouver Stock Exchange
WCE Winnipeg Commodity Exchange

UNITED STATES SECURITIES
AND COMMODITIES EXCHANGES
American Stock Exchange

Index Options

Contract	Underlying Index	Trading Unit	Prices Quoted In	Minimum Price Fluctuation
● Airline Index	5 major airline stocks	Index × $100	index points	1/16 up to 3, 1/8 over 3
● Computer Technology Index	major computer stocks	Index × $100	index points	1/16 up to 3, 1/8 over 3
● Major Market Index	20 Blue Chip stocks	Index × $100	index points	1/16 up to 3, 1/8 over 3
● Oil Index	15 major oil stocks	Index × $100	index points	1/16 up to 3, 1/8 over 3

Interest Rate Options

Contract	Underlying Security	Trading Unit	Prices Quoted In	Minimum Price Fluctuation
● Treasury Bills	current 13-week T-bill	$1 million T-bills	basis points	1 basis point ($25)
● Treasury Notes	current 10-year T-note	$100,000 T-notes	basis points	1/32 of a point ($31.25)

Amex Commodities Corporation

Options

Contract	Underlying Commodity	Trading Unit	Prices Quoted In	Minimum Price Fluctuation
● Gold Bullion	gold bullion	100 troy ounces	dollars and cents	10 cents ($10)

Strike Prices	Settlement	Contract Months	Trading Hours	Ticker Symbol
5 points apart	in cash	4 nearest months	9:30 A.M.–4:10 P.M. EST	XAI
5 points apart	in cash	Mar, June, Sept, Dec	9:30 A.M.–4:10 P.M. EST	XCI
5 points apart	in cash	4 nearest months	9:30 A.M.–4:10 P.M. EST	XMI
5 points apart	in cash	5 nearest months	9:30 A.M.–4:10 P.M. EST	XOI

Strike Prices	Settlement	Contract Months	Trading Hours
20 basis points apart	in Treasury bills	Mar, June, Sept, Dec	9 A.M.–3 P.M. EST
2 basis points apart	in Treasury notes	Feb, May Aug, Nov	9 A.M.–3 P.M. EST

Strike Prices	Settlement	Last Trading Day	Contract Months	Trading Hours	Ticker Symbol
$10 apart	in cash	3rd Friday of expiration month	Feb, Apr, June, Aug, Oct, Dec	9 A.M.–2:30 P.M. EST	AU

Chicago Board of Trade

Futures

Contract	Trading Unit	Prices Quoted In	Minimum Price Fluctuation
● Corn	5000 bushels	cents and ¼ cents a bushel	¼ of a cent ($12.50)
● Gold	1 kilogram (32.15 troy ounces)	dollars and cents a troy ounce	10 cents a troy ounce ($3.22)
● GNMA-CDR	$100,000 of GNMA 8% coupon	full points and 32nds of a point	$\frac{1}{32}$nd of a point ($31.25)
● Major Market Index	Index of 20 Blue Chip Stocks × $100	full points and $\frac{1}{20}$th of a point	$\frac{1}{20}$th of a point ($5)
● Major Market Index "MAXI"	Index of 20 Blue Chip Stocks × $250	full points and $\frac{1}{20}$th of a point	$\frac{1}{20}$th of a point ($12.50)
● Municipal Bond Index	Bond Buyer Muni Index × $1000	full points and 32nds of a point	$\frac{1}{32}$nd of a point ($31.25)
● NASDAQ-100 Index	100 Large OTC Stocks × $250	full points and $\frac{1}{20}$th of a point	$\frac{1}{20}$th of a point ($12.50)
● Oats	5000 bushels	cents and ¼ cents a bushel	¼ of a cent a bushel ($12.50)
● Silver	1000 troy ounces	dollars and cents a troy ounce	$\frac{1}{10}$ of a cent a troy ounce ($1)
● Soybeans	5000 bushels	cents and ¼ cents a bushel	¼ of a bushel ($12.50)
● Soybean Meal	100 tons (200,000 pounds)	dollars and cents a ton	10 cents a ton ($10)
● Soybean Oil	60,000 pounds	dollars and cents per hundredweight	$\frac{1}{100}$ of a cent per pound ($6)
● Treasury Bonds	$100,000 of Treasury Bond 8% coupon	full points and 32nds of a point	$\frac{1}{32}$nd of a point ($31.25)
● Treasury Notes	$100,000 of Treasury Notes	full points and 32nds of a point	$\frac{1}{32}$nd of a point ($31.25)
● Wheat	5000 bushels	cents and ¼ cents a bushel	¼ of a cent a bushel ($12.50)

Daily Contract Limit	Dollar Value of 1 cent move	Contract Months	Trading Hours	Ticker Symbol
10 cents ($500)	$50	Mar, May, July, Sept, Dec	9:30 A.M.–1:15 P.M. CST	C
$50 a troy ounce ($1607.50)	—	3 nearest months and Feb, Apr, June, Aug, Oct, Dec	8:00 A.M.–1:40 P.M. CST	KI
64/32 per contract ($2000)	—	Mar, June, Sept, Dec	8:00 A.M.–2:00 P.M. CST	M
None	—	3 nearest months and next 3 months in the Mar, June, Sept, Dec cycle	8:15 A.M.–3:15 P.M. CST	MX
None	—	3 nearest months and next 3 months in the Mar, June, Sept, Dec cycle	8:15 A.M.–3:15 P.M. CST	BC
64/32 of a point ($2000)	—	Mar, June, Sept, Dec	8:00 A.M.–2:00 P.M. CST	MB
None	—	3 nearest months and next 3 months in the Mar, June, Sept, Dec cycle	8:15 A.M.–3:15 P.M. CST	ND
10 cents a bushel ($500)	—	Mar, May, July, Sept, Dec	9:30 A.M.–1:15 P.M. CST	O
50 cents a troy ounce ($500)	$10	3 nearest months and Feb, Apr, June, Aug, Oct, Dec	8:05 A.M.–1:25 P.M. CST	AG
30 cents a bushel ($1500)	$50	Jan, Mar, May, July, Aug, Sept, Nov	9:30 A.M.–1:15 P.M. CST	S
$10 a ton ($1000)	$1	Jan, Mar, May, July, Aug, Sept, Oct, Dec	9:30 A.M.–1:15 P.M. CST	SM
1 cent per pound ($600)	—	Jan, Mar, May, July, Aug, Sept, Oct, Dec	9:30 A.M.–1:15 P.M. CST	BO
64/32 of a point ($2000)	—	Mar, June, Sept, Dec	8:00 A.M.–2:00 P.M. CST	US
64/32 of a point ($2000)	—	Mar, June, Sept, Dec	8:00 A.M.–2:00 P.M. CST	TY
20 cents a bushel ($1000)	—	Mar, May, July, Sept, Dec	9:30 A.M.–1:15 P.M. CST	W

Futures Options

Contract	Trading Unit	Prices Quoted In	Minimum Price Fluctuation	Strike Prices
● Corn	1 CBT corn futures contract	⅛ of a cent ($50)	⅛ of a cent ($6.25)	10 cents apart
● Silver	1 CBT silver futures contract	⅒ of a cent ($1)	25 cents a troy ounce ($500)	50 cents apart
● Soybeans	1 CBT soybean futures contract	⅛ of a cent ($50)	⅛ of a point ($6.25)	25 cents apart
● Treasury Bonds	1 CBT T-bond futures contract	1/64th of 1% of $100,000	1/64th of a point ($15.63)	2 points apart
● Treasury Notes	1 CBT T-note futures contract	1/64th of 1% of $100,000	1/64th of a point ($15.63)	2 points apart

Chicago Board Options Exchange

Foreign Currency Options

Contract	Trading Unit	Prices Quoted In	Minimum Price Fluctuation	Strike Prices
● British Pound	25,000 pounds	cents per pound	5 cents ($12.50)	2½ or 5 cents per pound apart
● Canadian Dollar	100,000 dollars	cents per dollar	1 cent ($10)	1 cent per dollar apart
● Deutsche Mark	125,000 marks	cents per mark	1 cent ($12.50)	1 cent per mark apart
● French Franc	250,000 francs	⅒ of a cent per franc	5 cents ($12.50)	⅒ of a cent per franc apart
● Japanese Yen	12.5 million yen	1/100 of a cent per yen	1 cent ($12.50)	1/100 of a cent per yen apart
● Swiss Franc	125,000 francs	cents per franc	1 cent ($12.50)	1 cent per franc apart

Expiration Day	Last Trading Day	Contract Months	Trading Hours	Ticker Symbol
Saturday after last trading day	Friday before futures notice day	Mar, May, July, Sept, Dec	9:30 A.M.– 1:15 P.M. CST	CY (call) PY (put)
Saturday after last trading day	Friday before futures notice day	Feb, Apr, June, Aug, Oct, Dec	8:05 A.M.– 1:25 P.M. CST	AC (call) AP (put)
Saturday after last trading day	Friday before futures notice day	Jan, Mar, May, July, Nov	9:30 A.M.– 1:15 P.M. CST	CZ (call) PZ (put)
Saturday after last trading day	Friday before futures notice day	Mar, June, Sept, Dec	8:00 A.M.– 2:00 P.M. CST	CG (call) PG (put)
Saturday after last trading day	Friday before futures notice day	Mar, June, Sept, Dec	8:00 A.M.– 2:00 P.M. CST	TO (call) TP (put)

Expiration Day	Exercise Limits	Contract Months	Trading Hours	Ticker Symbol
Sat before 3rd Wed of expiration month	25,000 contracts	Mar, June, Sept, Dec, and 2 nearest months	8:00 A.M.– 2:30 P.M. EST	CBP
Sat before 3rd Wed of expiration month	25,000 contracts	Mar, June, Sept, Dec, and 2 nearest months	8:00 A.M.– 2:30 P.M. EST	CCD
Sat before 3rd Wed of expiration month	25,000 contracts	Mar, June, Sept, Dec, and 2 nearest months	8:00 A.M.– 2:30 P.M. EST	CDM
Sat before 3rd Wed of expiration month	25,000 contracts	Mar, June, Sept, Dec, and 2 nearest months	8:00 A.M.– 2:30 P.M. EST	CFF
Sat before 3rd Wed of expiration month	25,000 contracts	Mar, June, Sept, Dec, and 2 nearest months	8:00 A.M.– 2:30 P.M. EST	CJY
Sat before 3rd Wed of expiration month	25,000 contracts	Mar, June, Sept, Dec, and 2 nearest months	8:00 A.M.– 2:30 P.M. EST	CSF

Index Options

Contract	Underlying Index	Trading Unit	Prices Quoted In	Minimum Price Fluctuation
● S&P 100 Index	S&P 100 Stock Index	index × $100	dollars and cents	1/16 up to 3, 1/8 over 3
● S&P 500 Index	S&P 500 Stock Index	index × $100	dollars and cents	1/16 up to 3, 1/8 over 3
● S&P OTC 250 Index	S&P OTC 250 Stock Index	index × $100	dollars and cents	1/16 up to 3, 1/8 over 3

Interest Rate Options

Contract	Underlying Security	Trading Unit	Prices Quoted In	Minimum Price Fluctutation
● U.S. Treasury Bonds	Treasury bonds	$100,000 in bonds	points and 1/32nd of a point	1/32nd of a point ($31.25)
● U.S. Treasury Notes	Treasury notes	$100,000 in notes	points and 1/32nd of a point	1/32nd of a point ($31.25)

Chicago Mercantile Exchange

Futures

Contract	Trading Unit	Prices Quoted In	Minimum Price Fluctuation	Daily Price Limit
● Feeder Cattle	44,000 pounds	dollars per hundred pounds	2.5 cents per hundred pounds ($11)	1.5 cents per pound ($660)
● Live Cattle	40,000 pounds	dollars per hundred pounds	2.5 cents per hundred pounds ($10)	1.5 cents per pound ($600)
● Live Hogs	30,000 pounds	dollars per hundred pounds	2.5 cents per hundred pounds ($7.50)	1.5 cents per pound ($450)

Strike Prices	Settlement	Last Trading Day	Contract Months	Trading Hours	Ticker Symbol
5 points apart	in cash	Sat after 3rd Friday of expiration month	every month	9:30 A.M.– 4:10 P.M. EST	OEX
5 points apart	in cash	Sat after 3rd Friday of expiration month	2 nearest months and three later months in the Mar, June, Sept, Dec cycle	9:30 A.M.– 4:10 P.M. EST	SPX
5 points apart	in cash	Sat after 3rd Friday of expiration month	every month	9:30 A.M.– 4:10 P.M. EST	SCX

Strike Prices	Settlement	Last Trading Day	Contract Months	Trading Hours	Ticker Symbol
2 points apart	in Treasury bonds	Sat after 3rd Fri of expiration month	Mar, June, Sept, Dec	8:00 A.M.– 2:00 P.M. CST	YBQ, YBR
1 point apart	in Treasury notes	Sat after 3rd Fri of expiration month	Mar, June, Sept, Dec	8:00 A.M.– 2:00 P.M. CST	YFD, YFC

Dollar value of 1 cent move	Last Trading Day	Contract Months	Trading Hours	Ticker Symbol
$440	Last Thursday of contract month	Jan, Mar, Apr, May, Aug, Sept, Oct, Nov	9:05 A.M.– 1 P.M. CST	FC
$400	20th day of contract month	Feb, Apr, June, Aug, Oct, Dec	9:05 A.M.– 1 P.M. CST	LC
$300	20th day of contract month	Feb, Apr, June, July, Aug, Oct, Dec	9:10 A.M.– 1 P.M. CST	LH

Contract	Trading Unit	Prices Quoted In	Minimum Price Fluctuation	Daily Price Limit
● Lumber	130,000 board feet	dollars per thousand board feet	10 cents per thousand board feet ($13)	$5 per thousand board feet ($650)
● OTC 250 Industrial Stock Price Index	S&P OTC Industrial Index × $500	index points	½0th of an index point ($25)	none
● Pork Bellies	40,000 pounds	cents per pound	2.5 cents per 100 pounds ($9.50)	2 cents per pound ($760)
● S&P 100 Index	S&P 100 × $200	cents	5 cents (5 points) ($25)	none
● S&P 500 Index	S&P 500 × $500	cents	5 cents ($25)	none

Futures Options

Contract	Trading Unit	Prices Quoted In	Minimum Price Fluctuation	Strike Prices
● British Pound	1 pound futures contract	cents per pound	5 cents ($12.50)	2.5 cents per pound apart
● Deutsche Mark	1 mark futures contract	cents per mark	1 cent ($12.50)	1 cent per mark apart
● Eurodollars	1 Eurodollar futures contract	index points (1.0 points = $25)	.01 point ($25)	50 index points apart
● Live Cattle	1 cattle futures contract	cents per pound	.00025 per pound ($10)	2 cents apart
● Live Hogs	1 hogs futures contract	cents per pound	.00025 per pound ($7.50)	2 cents apart
● S&P 500 Stock Index	1 S&P 500 futures contract	index points (5 points = $25)	5 points ($25)	5 points apart
● Swiss Franc	1 franc futures contract	cents per franc	1 cent ($12.50)	1 cent per franc apart
● Treasury Bills	1 T-bill futures contract	index points (.01 points = $25)	.01 points ($25)	50 index points apart

Dollar value of 1 cent move	Last Trading Day	Contract Months	Trading Hours	Ticker Symbol
$1	15th day of contract month	Jan, Mar, May, July, Sept, Nov	9:00 A.M.– 2:05 P.M. CST	LB
—	3rd Friday of contract month	Mar, June, Sept, Dec	8:30 A.M.– 3:15 P.M. CST	OT
$360	6 days before end of contract month	Feb, Mar, May, July, Aug	9:10 A.M.– 1 P.M. CST	PB
—	3rd Friday of contract month	every month	8:30 A.M.– 3:15 P.M. CST	SX
—	3rd Friday of contract month	Mar, June, Sept, Dec	8:30 A.M.– 3:15 P.M. CST	SP

Expiration Day	Last Trading Day	Contract Months	Trading Hours	Ticker Symbol
on last trading day	2nd Fri before 3rd Wed of month	Mar, June, Sept, Dec	7:20 A.M.– 1:24 P.M. CST	CP (call) PP (put)
on last trading day	2nd Fri before 3rd Wed of month	Mar, June, Sept, Dec	7:20 A.M.– 1:20 P.M. CST	CM (call) PM (put)
on last trading day	same day as Eurodollar futures contract	Mar, June, Sept, Dec	7:20 A.M.– 2:00 P.M. CST	CE (call) PE (put)
on last trading day	last Fri before first day of month	Feb, Apr, June, Aug, Oct, Dec	9:05 A.M.– 1:00 P.M. CST	CK (call) PK (put)
on last trading day	last Fri before first day of month	Feb, Apr, June, July, Aug, Oct, Dec	9:10 A.M.– 1:00 P.M. CST	CH (call) PH (put)
on last trading day	same day as S&P 500 futures contract	Mar, June, Sept, Dec	8:30 A.M.– 3:15 P.M. CST	CS (call) PS (put)
on last trading day	2nd Fri before 3rd Wed of month	Mar, June, Sept, Dec	7:20 A.M.– 1:16 P.M. CST	CF (call) PF (put)
on last trading day	varies	Mar, June, Sept, Dec	7:20 A.M.– 2:00 P.M. CST	CQ (call) PQ (put)

Chicago Rice and Cotton Exchange

Futures

Contract	Trading Unit	Prices Quoted In	Minimum Price Fluctuation
● Rough Rice	2000 hundredweight	cents per hundredweight	.005 per hundredweight ($10)
● Short Staple Cotton	50,000 pounds	cents per pound	1 1/100 of a cent per pound ($5)

Coffee, Sugar & Cocoa Exchange

Futures

Contract	Trading Unit	Prices Quoted In	Minimum Price Fluctuation	Daily Contract Limit
● Cocoa	10 metric tons	dollars per metric ton	$1 per metric ton ($10)	$88 per metric ton
● Coffee	37,500 pounds	cents per pound	1/100 cents per pound ($3.75)	4 cents per pound
● Consumer Price Index–Wages	CPI Index × $1000	index points	1/100 of the index ($10)	3 points ($3000)
● Sugar Number 11	50 long tons	cents per pound	1/100 cents per pound ($11.20)	5/100 of a cent per pound
● Sugar Number 14	50 long tons	cents per pound	1/100 cents per pound ($11.20)	5/100 of a cent per pound

Futures Options

Contract	Trading Unit	Prices Quoted In	Minimum Price Fluctuation	Strike Prices
● Cocoa	1 cocoa futures contract	dollars per metric ton	$1 per ton ($10)	$100 apart
● Sugar	1 sugar futures contract	cents per pound	1/100 cents per pound ($11.20)	1 cent apart

Daily Contract Limit	Last Trading Day	Contract Months	Trading Hours	Ticker Symbol
30 cents per hundredweight ($600)	8th to last day of month	Jan, Mar, May, Sept, Nov	9:00 A.M.– 1:30 P.M. CST	NR
2 cents per pound ($1000)	17th to last day of month	Mar, May, July, Oct, Dec	9:30 A.M.– 2:00 P.M. CST	NO

Last Trading Day	Contract Months	Trading Hours	Ticker Symbol
10th business day before final business day of delivery month	Mar, May, July, Sept, Dec	9:30 A.M.– 3:00 P.M. EST	CC
7th business day before final business day of delivery month	Mar, May, July, Sept, Dec	9:45 A.M.– 2:28 P.M. EST	KC
2nd day before release of index	Jan, Apr, July, Oct	9:30 A.M.– 2:30 P.M. EST	CI
last business day of the month preceding the delivery month	Jan, Mar, May, July, Sept, Oct	10:00 A.M.– 1:43 P.M. EST	SB
8th calendar day of the month preceding the delivery month	Jan, Mar, May, July, Sept, Oct	10:00 A.M.– 1:43 P.M. EST	SE

Expiration Day	Last Trading Day	Contract Months	Trading Hours
on last trading day	first Fri of month before contract month	Mar, May, July, Sept, Dec	9:30 A.M.– 3:00 P.M. EST
on last trading day	2nd Fri of month before contract month	Mar, May, July, Oct	10 A.M.– 1:43 P.M. EST

Commodity Exchange, Inc. (COMEX)

Futures

Contract	Trading Unit	Prices Quoted In	Minimum Price Fluctuation	Daily Contract Limit
● Aluminum	40,000 pounds	cents per pound	$5/100$ of a cent ($20)	5 cents a pound
● Copper	25,000 pounds	cents per pound	$5/100$ of a cent ($12.50)	5 cents a pound
● Gold	100 troy ounces	cents per troy ounce	10 cents per troy ounce ($10)	$25 per troy ounce
● Silver	5000 troy ounces	cents per troy ounce	$1/10$ of a cent per troy ounce ($5)	50 cents per troy ounce

Futures Options

Contract	Trading Unit	Prices Quoted In	Minimum Price Fluctuation	Strike Prices
● Copper	1 copper futures contract	cents per pound	$5/100$ of a cent per pound	1 to 5 cents apart, depending on copper price
● Gold	1 gold futures contract	cents per troy ounce	10 cents per troy ounce	$10 to $40 apart, depending on gold price
● Silver	1 silver futures contract	cents per troy ounce	$1/10$ of a cent per troy ounce	25 cents to $1 apart, depending on silver price

Dollar Value of 1 cent move	Last Trading Day	Contract Months	Trading Hours	Ticker Symbol
$400	3rd last day of month	Jan, Mar, May, July, Sept, Dec, and 2 nearest months	9:30 A.M.– 2:15 P.M. EST	AL
$250	3rd last day of month	Jan, Mar, May, July, Sept, Dec, and 2 nearest months	9:50 A.M.– 2:00 P.M. EST	CU
$1	3rd last day of month	Feb, Apr, June, Aug, Oct, Dec, and 2 nearest months	9:00 A.M.– 2:30 P.M. EST	GC
$50	3rd last day of month	Jan, Mar, May, July, Sept, Dec, and 2 nearest months	9:05 A.M.– 2:25 P.M. EST	SI

Expiration Day	Last Trading Day	Contract Months	Trading Hours	Ticker Symbol
on last trading day	2nd Fri of month before futures delivery	Mar, May, July, Sept, Dec	9:50 A.M.– 2:00 P.M. EST	OP
on last trading day	2nd Fri of month before futures delivery	Feb, Apr, June, Aug, Oct, Dec	9:00 A.M.– 2:30 P.M. EST	OG
on last trading day	2nd Fri of month before futures delivery	Mar, May, July, Sept, Dec	9:05 A.M.– 2:25 P.M. EST	SO

International Monetary Market at the Chicago Mercantile Exchange

Futures

Contract	Trading Unit	Prices Quoted In	Minimum Price Fluctuation
● Bank CDs	3 month, $1 million CDs	100 minus yield	1 point ($25)
● British Pound	25,000 pounds	cents per pound	5 points or $.0005 a pound ($12.50)
● Canadian Dollar	100,000 Canadian dollars	cents per Canadian dollar	1 point or $.0001 per Canadian dollar ($10)
● Deutsche Mark	125,000 marks	cents per mark	1 point or $.0001 per mark ($12.50)
● Eurodollars	3 month, $1 million Eurodollars	cents per Eurodollar	1 point or $.01 per Eurodollar ($25)
● European Currency Units (ECU)	125,000 ECU	dollars per ECU	$.0001 per ECU ($12.50)
● French Franc	250,000 French francs	cents per franc	5 points or $.00005 per franc ($12.50)
● Gold	100 fine troy ounces	dollars per troy ounce	10 points or 10 cents per troy ounce ($10)
● Japanese Yen	12,500,000 yen	cents per yen	1 point or $.0001 per yen ($12.50)
● Swiss Franc	125,000 francs	cents per franc	1 point or $.0001 per franc ($12.50)
● Treasury bills	$1 million	100 minus yield	1 point ($25)

Daily Price Limit	Last Trading Day	Contract Months	Trading Hours	Ticker Symbol
none	2nd to last day of month	Mar, June, Sept, Dec	7:20 A.M.– 2:00 P.M. CST	DC
none	2nd day before 3rd Wed of month	Jan, Mar, Apr, June, July, Sept, Oct, Dec, and spot month	7:20 A.M.– 1:24 P.M. CST	BP
none	2nd day before 3rd Wed of month	Jan, Mar, Apr, June, July, Sept, Oct, Dec, and spot month	7:20 A.M.– 1:26 P.M. CST	CD
none	2nd day before 3rd Wed of month	Jan, Mar, Apr, June, July, Sept, Oct, Dec, and spot month	7:20 A.M.– 1:20 P.M. CST	DM
none	2nd day before 3rd Wed of month	Mar, June, Sept, Dec	7:20 A.M.– 2:00 P.M. CST	ED
none	2nd day before 3rd Wed of month	Mar, June, Sept, Dec	7:20 A.M.– 1:30 P.M. CST	EC
none	2nd day before 3rd Wed of month	Jan, Mar, Apr, June, July, Sept, Oct, Dec, and spot month	7:20 A.M.– 1:28 P.M. CST	FR
none	6th day before contract ends	Jan, Mar, Apr, June, July, Sept, Oct, Dec	7:20 A.M.– 1:30 P.M. CST	GD
none	2nd day before 3rd Wed of month	Jan, Mar, Apr, June, July, Sept, Oct, Dec, and spot month	7:20 A.M.– 1:22 P.M. CST	JY
none	2nd day before 3rd Wed of month	Jan, Mar, Apr, June, July, Sept, Oct, Dec, and spot month	7:20 A.M.– 1:16 P.M. CST	SF
none	2nd day before 3rd Wed of month	Mar, June, Sept, Dec	7:20 A.M.– 2:00 P.M CST	TB

Kansas City Board of Trade

Futures

Contract	Trading Unit	Prices Quoted In	Minimum Price Fluctuation	Daily Contract Limit
• Value Line Maxi Index	index × $500	index points	$25 per tick	none
• Value Line Mini Index	index × $100	index points	$5 per tick	none
• Wheat	5000 bushels	cents and ¼ cents per bushel	¼ cent per bushel ($12.50)	25 cents per bushel ($12.50)

Futures Options

Contract	Trading Unit	Prices Quoted In	Minimum Price Fluctuation	Strike Prices
• Wheat	1 wheat futures contract	cents per bushel	⅛ of a cent per bushel ($6.25)	10 cents per bushel apart

MidAmerica Commodity Exchange
(Affiliate of the Chicago Board of Trade)

Futures

Contract	Trading Unit	Prices Quoted In	Minimum Price Fluctuation
• British Pound	12,500 pounds	Dollars per pound	$.0005 ($6.25)
• Canadian Dollar	50,000 Canadian dollars	U.S. dollars per Canadian dollar	$.0001 ($5)
• Copper	55,000 pounds	cents per pound	$.0005 ($27.50)
• Corn	1000 bushels	dollars and cents per bushel	⅛ of a cent per bushel ($1.25)
• Deutsche Mark	62,500 marks	U.S. dollars per mark	$.0001 ($6.25)
• Gold	33.2 fine troy ounces	dollars per troy ounce	10 cents per fine troy ounce ($3.32)

Dollar Value of 1 cent move	Last Trading Day	Contract Months	Trading Hours	Ticker Symbol
—	3rd Fri of month	Mar, June, Sept, Dec	8:30 A.M.–3:15 P.M. CST	KV
—	3rd Fri of month	Mar, June, Sept, Dec	8:30 A.M.–3:15 P.M. CST	MV
$50	8th day before the end of month	Mar, May, July, Sept, Dec	9:30 A.M.–1:15 P.M. CST	KW

Expiration Day	Last Trading Day	Contract Months	Trading Hours	Ticker Symbol
1st Sat after last trading day	Fri 10 days before last day of month	Mar, May, July, Sept, Dec	9:30 A.M.–1:15 P.M. CST	WC (call) WP (put)

Daily Contract Limit	Last Trading Day	Contract Months	Trading Hours
none	2 days before 3rd Wed	Mar, June, Sept, Dec	7:20 A.M.–1:34 P.M. CST
none	2 days before 3rd Wed	Mar, June, Sept, Dec	7:20 A.M.–1:36 P.M. CST
5 cents per pound ($2750)	3 business days before last business day of the month	Jan, Mar, May, July, Sept, Dec, and 3 nearest months	7:50 A.M.–1:15 P.M. CST
10 cents a bushel ($100)	7 days before end of month	Mar, May, July, Sept, Dec	9:30 A.M.–1:30 P.M. CST
none	2 days before 3rd Wed	Mar, June, Sept, Dec	7:20 A.M.–1:30 P.M. CST
$25 per troy ounce ($830)	2 business days before last business day of the month	Feb, Apr, June, Aug, Oct, Dec	8:00 A.M.–1:40 P.M. CST

Contract	Trading Unit	Prices Quoted In	Minimum Price Fluctuation
● Japanese Yen	6,250,000 yen	U.S. dollars per yen	$.000001 ($6.25)
● Live Cattle	20,000 pounds	cents per pound	$.00025 per pound ($5)
● Live Hogs	15,000 pounds	cents per pound	$.00025 per pound ($3.75)
● Oats	1000 bushels	dollars and cents per bushel	⅛ of a cent per bushel ($1.25)
● Platinum	25 fine troy ounces	cents per troy ounce	10 cents per troy ounce ($2.50)
● Silver	1000 fine troy ounces	cents per troy ounce	⅒ of a cent per troy ounce ($1)
● Soybeans	1000 bushels	dollars and cents per bushel	⅛ of a cent ($1.25)
● Soybean Meal	20 tons	dollars per ton	10 cents per ton ($2)
● Swiss Franc	62,500 francs	U.S. dollars per franc	$.0001 ($6.25)
● Treasury Bills	$500,000 in 90 day T-bills	100 minus T-bill yield	1 basis point ($12.50)
● Treasury Bonds	$50,000 in 15 year T-bonds	in 32nds of a % of par	1/32nd of a percentage point ($15.62)
● Wheat	1000 bushels	dollars and cents per bushel	⅛ of a cent per bushel ($1.25)

Futures Options

Contract	Trading Unit	Prices Quoted In	Minimum Price Fluctuation	Strike Prices
● Gold	1 gold futures contract	dollars per troy ounce	10 cents per troy ounce ($3.32)	$10-$40 per troy ounce apart (depends on price level)
● Soybeans	1 soybean futures contract	cents per bushel	⅛ of a cent per bushel ($1.25)	25 cents per bushel apart
● Wheat	5 wheat futures contracts	cents per bushel	⅛ of a cent per bushel ($1.25)	10 cents per bushel apart

Daily Contract Limit	Last Trading Day	Contract Months	Trading Hours
none	2 days before 3rd Wed	Mar, June, Sept, Dec	7:20 A.M.– 1:32 P.M. CST
$.015 per pound ($300)	20th day of the month	Feb, Apr, June, Aug, Oct, Dec	9:05 A.M.– 1:15 P.M. CST
$.015 per pound ($225)	20th day of the month	Feb, Apr, June, July, Aug, Oct, Dec	9:10 A.M.– 1:15 P.M. CST
10 cents per bushel ($100)	7 days before end of month	Mar, May, July, Sept, Dec	9:30 A.M.– 1:30 P.M. CST
$25 per troy ounce ($625)	4th business day before end of month	Jan, Apr, July, Oct	8:00 A.M.– 1:40 P.M. CST
50 cents per troy ounce ($500)	2 business days before last business day of the month	current month and any subsequent month	8:05 A.M.– 1:40 P.M. CST
30 cents per bushel ($300)	7 days before end of month	Jan, Mar, May, July, Aug, Sept, Nov	9:30 A.M.– 1:30 P.M. CST
$10 per ton ($200)	business day before 12th to last business day of the month	Jan, Mar, May, July, Aug, Sept, Oct, Dec	9:30 A.M.– 1:30 P.M. CST
none	2 days before 3rd Wed	Mar, June, Sept, Dec	7:20 A.M.– 1:26 P.M. CST
none	day before T-bill delivery date on Int. Monetary Mkt.	Mar, June, Sept, Dec	7:20 A.M.– 2:15 P.M. CST
$^{64}/_{32}$ of a percentage point ($1000)	business day before 7th to last business day of contract month	Mar, June, Sept, Dec	8:00 A.M.– 2:15 P.M. CST
20 cents per bushel ($200)	7 days before end of month	Mar, May, July, Sept, Dec	9:30 A.M.– 1:30 P.M. CST

Expiration Day	Last Trading Day	Contract Months	Trading Hours
day after the last day of trading	2nd Fri of month before futures delivery month	Feb, Apr, June, Aug, Oct, Dec	8:00 A.M.– 1:40 P.M. CST
1st Sat after last trading day	last Fri by at least 10 business days before soybean futures notice day	Jan, Mar, May, July, Aug, Sept, Nov	9:30 A.M.– 1:30 P.M. CST
1st Sat after last trading day	last Fri by at least 10 business days before wheat futures notice day	Mar, May, July, Sept, Dec	9:30 A.M.– 1:30 P.M. CST

Minneapolis Grain Exchange

Futures

Contract	Trading Unit	Prices Quoted In	Minimum Price Fluctuation
● High Fructose Corn Syrup	48,000 pounds	dollars and cents per hundredweight	1 cent per trading unit ($4.80)
● Spring Wheat	5000 bushels	cents and ¼ cents per bushel	⅛ of a cent per bushel ($6.25)
● White Wheat	5000 bushels	cents and ¼ cents per bushel	¼ of a cent per bushel ($12.50)

Futures Options

Contract	Trading Unit	Prices Quoted In	Minimum Price Fluctuation	Strike Prices
● Spring Wheat	1 wheat futures contract	⅛ of a cent per bushel	⅛ of a cent per bushel ($6.25)	10 cents per bushel apart

National Association of Securities Dealers Automated Quotations System

Index Option

Contract	Underlying Index	Trading Unit	Prices Quoted In	Minimum Price Fluctuation
● NASDAQ 100 Index	100 of the largest nonfinancial NASDAQ/NMS stocks	index × $100	index points	1/16 of a point

Daily Contract Limit	Last Trading Day	Contract Months	Trading Hours	Ticker Symbol
$1 per hundredweight ($480)	7 days before end of month	Mar, May, July, Sept, Dec	9:00 A.M.– 1:15 P.M. CST	HF
20 cents per bushel ($1000)	7 days before end of month	Mar, May, July, Sept, Dec	9:30 A.M.– 1:15 P.M. CST	MW
20 cents per bushel ($1000)	7 days before end of month	Mar, May, July, Sept, Dec	9:30 A.M.– 1:15 P.M. CST	NW

Expiration Day	Last Trading Day	Contract Months	Trading Hours	Ticker Symbol
1st Sat after last trading day	Fri 10 days before wheat futures notice day	Mar, May, July, Sept, Dec	9:35 A.M.– 1:25 P.M. CST	CW (call) PW (put)

Strike Prices	Last Trading Day	Contract Months	Trading Hours	Ticker Symbol
5 points apart	Fri of the month following 3rd Sat of month	every 3 consecutive months	9:30 A.M.– 4:10 P.M. EST	NDQ

New York Cotton Exchange

Futures

Contract	Trading Unit	Prices Quoted In	Minimum Price Fluctuation	Daily Contract Limit
● Cotton	50,000 pounds	cents and 1/100 of a cent per pound	1/100 of a cent per pound ($5)	2 cents per pound ($1000) (no limit on or after 1st notice day of current delivery month)
● Orange Juice	15,000 pounds	cents and 1/100 of a cent per pound	5/100 of a cent per pound ($7.50)	5 cents per pound ($750)
● Propane	1000 barrels	cents per gallon	1/100 of a cent per gallon ($4.20)	2 cents per gallon ($840)

Futures Options

Contract	Trading Unit	Prices Quoted In	Minimum Price Fluctuation	Strike Prices
● Cotton	1 cotton futures contract	cents and 1/100 of a cent	1/100 of a cent ($5)	1 cent apart
● Orange Juice	1 orange juice futures contract	cents and 1/100 of a cent	5/100 of a cent ($7.50)	250 points apart

FINEX (division of the New York Cotton Exchange)

Futures

Contract	Trading Unit	Prices Quoted In	Minimum Price Fluctuation
● European Currency Units	100,000 ECU	cents and 1/100 of cent per ECU ($1000)	.01 of a cent per ECU ($1000)
● U.S. Dollar	dollar index × $500	index points	.01 of an index point ($5)
● U.S. Treasury Index (Five Year)	5-year U.S. Treasury index × $5000	index points	.005 of an index point ($25)

Dollar Value of 1 cent move	Last Trading Day	Contract Months	Trading Hours	Ticker Symbol
$500	17 days before end of month	Mar, May, July, Oct, Dec	10:30 A.M.– 3:00 P.M. EST	CT
$1.50	9 days before last delivery day	Jan, Mar, May, July, Sept, Nov	10:15 A.M.– 2:45 P.M. EST	JO
$1000	5 days before last delivery day	every month	10:45 A.M.– 3:15 P.M. EST	LP

Expiration Day	Last Trading Day	Contract Months	Trading Hours	Ticker Symbol
on last trading day	1st Fri of month before delivery month	Mar, May, July, Oct, Dec	10:30 A.M.– 3:00 P.M. EST	CT
Sat after last trading day	1st Fri of month before delivery month	Jan, Mar, May, July, Sept, Nov	10:15 A.M.– 2:45 P.M. EST	OJ

Daily Contract Limit	Last Trading Day	Contract Months	Trading Hours	Ticker Symbol
none	3 days before 3rd Thursday of month	Mar, June, Sept, Dec	8:20 A.M.– 2:40 P.M. EST	EU
none	3rd Wed of month	Mar, June, Sept, Dec	8:20 A.M.– 2:40 P.M. EST	DX
none	last Monday of contract month	Mar, June, Sept, Dec	8:25 A.M.– 3:10 P.M. EST	FYTR

New York Futures Exchange

Futures

Contract	Trading Unit	Prices Quoted In	Minimum Price Fluctuation
● CRB Futures Price Index	commodity index × $500	index points	5 basis points ($25)
● NYSE Composite Index	index × $500	index points	5 basis points ($25)

Futures Options

Contract	Prices Quoted In	Minimum Price Fluctuation
● 1 NYSE Composite Index Futures Contract	index points (1 point = $5)	5 points ($25), 1 point if price is less than 5 points

New York Mercantile Exchange

Futures

Contract	Trading Unit	Prices Quoted In	Minimum Price Fluctuation	Daily Contract Limit
● Crude Oil	1000 barrels	dollars and cents per barrel	1 cent per barrel ($10)	$1 per barrel ($1000)
● Gasoline	1,000 barrels	dollars and cents per gallon	.01 cent per gallon ($4.20)	2 cents per gallon ($840)
● Number 2 Heating Oil	1,000 barrels	dollars and cents per gallon	.01 cent per gallon ($4.20)	2 cents per gallon ($840)
● Palladium	100 troy ounces	dollars and cents per troy ounce	5 cents per troy ounce ($5)	$6 per troy ounce ($600)
● Platinum	50 troy ounces	dollars and cents per troy ounce	10 cents per troy ounce ($5)	$25 per troy ounce ($1250)
● Potatoes	50,000 pounds	cents per pound	1 cent per 50 pounds ($10)	40 cents per 50 pounds ($400)

Daily Contract Limit	Last Trading Day	Contract Months	Trading Hours	Ticker Symbol
none	3rd Fri of month	Mar, May, July, Sept, Dec	9:00 A.M.–3:30 P.M. EST	CRB
none	3rd Fri of month	Mar, June, Sept, Dec	9:30 A.M.–4:15 P.M. EST	YX

Strike Prices	Expiration Day	Last Trading Day	Contract Months	Trading Hours
numbers divisible by two	on last trading day	3rd Fri of futures delivery month	Mar, June, Sept, Dec	9:30 A.M.–4:15 P.M. EST

Last Trading Day	Contract Months	Trading Hours	Ticker Symbol
3rd business day before 25th of month before delivery month	every month	9:45 A.M.–3:10 P.M. EST	CL
last business day of month before delivery month	every month	9:50 A.M.–3:05 P.M. EST	HR (leaded gasoline) HU (unleaded gasoline)
last business day of month before delivery month	every month	9:50 A.M.–3:05 P.M. EST	HO
4th business day before end of delivery month	Mar, June, Sept, Dec	8:50 A.M.–2:20 P.M. EST	PA
4th business day before end of delivery month	Jan, Apr, July, Oct	9:00 A.M.–2:30 P.M. EST	PL
10th business day of month	Jan, Feb, Mar, Apr, May, Nov, Dec	9:45 A.M.–2:00 P.M. EST	PC

New York Stock Exchange

Index Options

Contract	Underlying Index	Trading Unit	Prices Quoted In	Minimum Price Fluctuation
• NYSE Double Index	NYSE double index	index × $100	16ths of a point	$\frac{1}{16}$th of a point
• NYSE Options Index	NYSE composite index	index × $100	16ths of a point	$\frac{1}{16}$th of a point

Pacific Stock Exchange

Index Option

Contract	Underlying Index	Trading Unit	Prices Quoted In	Minimum Price Fluctuation
• Technology Index	100 technology stocks	index × $100	$\frac{1}{16}$ up to 3, $\frac{1}{8}$ over 3	$\frac{1}{16}$ of an index point

Philadelphia Stock Exchange

Foreign Currency Options

Contract	Trading Unit	Prices Quoted In	Minimum Price Fluctuation	Strike Prices
• British Pound	12,500 pounds	cents per pound	5 cents ($6.25)	5 cents apart
• Canadian Dollar	50,000 Canadian dollars	cents per Canadian dollar	1 cent apart ($5)	1 cent apart
• Deutsche Mark	62,500 marks	cents per mark	1 cent apart ($6.25)	1 cent apart
• French Franc	125,000 francs	$\frac{1}{10}$ of a cent per franc	5 cents ($6.25)	$\frac{1}{2}$ of a cent apart
• Japanese Yen	6,250,000 yen	$\frac{1}{100}$ of a cent per yen	1 cent ($6.25)	$\frac{1}{100}$ of a cent apart
• Swiss Franc	62,500 francs	cents per franc	1 cent ($6.25)	1 cent apart

Strike Prices	Settlement	Last Trading Day	Contract Months	Trading Hours	Ticker Symbol
5 points apart	in cash	3rd Fri of month	Mar, June, Sept, Dec 4 nearest months	9:30 A.M.– 4:05 P.M. EST	NDX
5 points apart	in cash	3rd Fri of month	Mar, June, Sept, Dec 4 nearest months	9:30 A.M.– 4:05 P.M. EST	NYA

Strike Prices	Settlement	Last Trading Day	Contract Months	Trading Hours	Ticker Symbol
5 points apart	In cash	Sat after 3rd Fri of month	4 nearest months	6:30 A.M.– 1:10 P.M. PST	PSE

Expiration Day	Contract Months	Trading Hours	Ticker Symbol
Sat before 3rd Wed of month	Mar, June, Sept, Dec and 2 nearest months	8:00 A.M.– 2:30 P.M. EST	XBP
Sat before 3rd Wed of month	Mar, June, Sept, Dec and 2 nearest months	8:00 A.M.– 2:30 P.M. EST	XCD
Sat before 3rd Wed of month	Mar, June, Sept, Dec and 2 nearest months	8:00 A.M.– 2:30 P.M. EST	XDM
Sat before 3rd Wed of month	Mar, June, Sept, Dec and 2 nearest months	8:00 A.M.– 2:30 P.M. EST	XFF
Sat before 3rd Wed of month	Mar, June, Sept, Dec and 2 nearest months	8:00 A.M.– 2:30 P.M. EST	XJY
Sat before 3rd Wed of month	Mar, June, Sept, Dec and 2 nearest months	8:00 A.M.– 2:30 P.M. EST	XSF

Futures

Contract	Trading Unit	Prices Quoted In	Minimum Price Fluctuation	Daily Contract Limit
• National OTC Index Futures	index × $500	index points	5 cents per point ($25)	none

Index Options

Contract	Underlying Index	Trading Unit	Prices Quoted In	Minimum Price Fluctuation
• Gold/Silver Index	7 gold and silver mining stocks	index × $100	index points (1 point = $100)	.01 point
• National OTC Index	OTC 100 stocks	index × $100	index points (1 point = $100)	.01 point
• Value Line Composite Index	1700 Value Line stocks	index × $100	index points (1 point = $100)	.01 point

Interest Rate Options

Contract	Underlying Security	Trading Unit	Prices Quoted In	Minimum Price Fluctuation
• Eurodollar Deposits	$1 million in Eurodollars	100 minus Eurodollar yield	percentage points	1 cent per Eurodollar ($25)
• European Currency Units	62,500 ECU	10 European currencies	cents per ECU	1 cent per ECU ($6.25)

Last Trading Day		Contract Months	Trading Hours	Ticker Symbol
3rd Fri of month		Feb, Mar, Apr, June, Sept	9:30 A.M.– 4:15 P.M. EST	OX

Strike Prices	Settlement	Last Trading Day	Contract Months	Trading Hours	Ticker Symbol
5 points apart	in cash	1st day before expiration	Mar, June, Sept, Dec and 2 nearest months	10:00 A.M.– 4:10 P.M. EST	XAU
5 points apart	in cash	1st day before expiration	Mar, June, Sept, Dec and 2 nearest months	10:00 A.M.– 4:10 P.M. EST	XOC
5 points apart	in cash	1st day before expiration	Mar, June, Sept, Dec and 2 nearest months	10:00 A.M.– 4:10 P.M. EST	XVL

Strike Prices	Settlement	Last Trading Day	Contract Months	Trading Hours	Ticker Symbol
25 basis points apart	in cash	Mon before 3rd Wed of month	Mar, June, Sept, Dec	8:30 A.M.– 3:00 P.M. EST	XED
1 cent apart	in ECUs	Fri before 3rd Wed of month	Mar, June, Sept, Dec	8:00 A.M.– 2:30 P.M. EST	ECU

CANADIAN SECURITIES AND COMMODITIES EXCHANGES

Montreal Exchange (Mercantile Division)

Futures

Contract	Trading Unit	Prices Quoted In	Minimum Price Fluctuation
● Gold	100 fine troy ounces	U.S. dollars and cents per troy ounce	10 cents per troy ounce ($10)
● Lumber	140,000 feet board measure (FBM)	U.S. dollars per 1000 FBM	10 cents per 1000 FBM ($14)

Toronto Futures Exchange

Futures

Contract	Trading Unit	Prices Quoted In	Minimum Price Fluctuation
● Oil & Gas Stock Index	Canadian oil & gas stocks	index points	one index points ($10)
● Toronto Stock Exchange 300 Index	300 TSE stocks	index points	one index point ($10)
● Treasury Bills (Canadian)	$1 million of 91-day Canadian T-bills	100 minus T-bill yields	one basis point ($24)
● Treasury Bonds (Canadian)	$100,000 of 15 year Canadian T-bonds	⅟₃₂nds of a point	⅟₃₂nd of a point ($31.25)
● U.S. Dollar	$50,000 U.S. dollars	Canadian dollars per $100 U.S.	1 Canadian cent, 1 point = $5

Daily Contract Limit	Last Trading Day	Contract Months	Trading Hours
$50 a troy ounce	last business day of previous month	current month, next 2 months, and any Feb, Apr, June, Aug, Oct, Dec	9:00 A.M.– 3:30 P.M. EST
$5 per 1000 FBM	business day before the 16th of contract month	Jan, Mar, May, July, Sept, Nov	10:00 A.M.– 2:30 P.M. EST

Daily Contract Limit	Last Trading Day	Contract Months	Trading Hours	Ticker Symbol
250 index points ($2500)	3rd Fri of month	next 3 months	9:20 A.M.– 4:10 P.M. EST	TOX
150 index points ($1500)	3rd Fri of month	next 3 months	9:20 A.M.– 4:10 P.M. EST	TCX
60 basis points ($1440)	T-bill auction before last Fri of delivery month	current month plus Mar, June, Sept, Dec	9:00 A.M.– 3:15 P.M. EST	TBT
2 points ($2000)	6th last day of delivery month	Mar, June, Sept, Dec	9:00 A.M.– 3:15 P.M. EST	GCB
250 points ($12.50)	3rd Wed of month	next 3 months and Mar, June, Sept, Dec	8:30 A.M.– 4:00 P.M. EST	USD

Options

Contract	Trading Unit	Prices Quoted In	Minimum Price Fluctuation	Strike Prices
● Silver	100 ounces	U.S. dollars	one cent	25 cents apart
● Treasury Bonds (Canadian)	$25,000 in T-bonds	.05% of $100 face value	.05% of $100 face value	2.5 points apart

Vancouver Stock Exchange

Commodity Options

Contract	Trading Unit	Prices Quoted In	Minimum Price Fluctuation	Strike Prices
● Canadian Dollar	$50,000 Canadian dollars	U.S. dollars per Canadian dollars	1 cent per Canadian dollar ($5)	2 cents per Canadian dollar apart
● Gold	10 troy ounces	U.S. dollars per ounce	10 cents per ounce ($1)	$20 per ounce apart
● Silver	250 troy ounces	U.S. dollars per ounce	1 cent per ounce ($2.50)	50 cents apart

Expiration Day	Last Trading Day	Contract Months	Trading Hours	Ticker Symbol
Sat after 3rd Fri of month	3rd Fri of month	Mar, June, Sept, Dec	9:05 A.M.– 4:00 P.M. EST	SVR
Sat after 3rd Fri of month	3rd Fri of month	Mar, June, Sept, Dec	9:00 A.M.– 4:00 P.M. EST	OBC

Expiration Day	Last Trading Day	Contract Months	Trading Hours	Ticker Symbol
Mon after 3rd Fri of month	3rd Fri of month	1st 3 months and next 2 months in the Mar, June, Sept, Dec cycle	11:30 A.M.– 4:00 P.M. PST	CAN
Mon after 3rd Fri of month	3rd Fri of month	Feb, May, Aug, Nov	11:30 A.M.– 4:00 P.M. PST	OR
Mon after 3rd Fri of month	3rd Fri of month	Mar, June, Sept, Dec	7:30 A.M.– 4:00 P.M. PST	SI

Winnipeg Commodity Exchange

Futures

Contract	Trading Unit	Prices Quoted In	Minimum Price Fluctuation	Daily Contract Limit
● Barley (Alberta)	20 metric tons	dollars and cents per ton	10 cents per ton	$5 per ton
● Barley (domestic)	20 metric tons	dollars and cents per ton	10 cents per ton	$5 per ton
● Flaxseed	20 metric tons	dollars and cents per ton	10 cents per ton	$10 per ton
● Gold	20 ounces	dollars and cents per ounce	10 cents per 1 ounce	$25 per ounce
● Oats	20 metric tons	dollars and cents per ton	10 cents per ton	$5 per ton
● Rapeseed	20 metric tons	dollars and cents per ton	10 cents per ton	$10 per ton
● Rye	20 metric tons	dollars and cents per ton	10 cents per ton	$5 per ton
● Silver	200 ounces	dollars and cents per ounce	1 cent per ounce	50 cents per ounce
● Wheat	20 metric tons	dollars and cents per ton	10 cents per ton	$5 per ton

Futures Options

Contract	Trading Unit	Prices Quoted In	Minimum Price Fluctuation	Strike Prices
● Gold	1 WCE gold futures contract	dollars and cents	10 cents per ounce	$10-$90 apart, depending on gold price

Last Trading Day	Contract Months	Trading Hours	Ticker Symbol
last business day of contract month	Feb, Apr, June, Sept, Nov	9:30 A.M.– 1:15 P.M. CST	AB
last business day of contract month	Mar, May, July, Oct, Dec	9:30 A.M.– 1:15 P.M. CST	B
last business day of contract month	Mar, May, July, Oct, Dec	9:30 A.M.– 1:15 P.M. CST	F
last business day of contract month	Mar, June, Sept, Dec	10:00 A.M.– 1:25 P.M. CST	G
last business day of contract month	Mar, May, July, Oct, Dec	9:30 A.M.– 1:15 P.M. CST	O
8th day before end of month	Jan, Mar, June, Sept, Nov	9:30 A.M.– 1:15 P.M. CST	RS
last business day of contract month	Mar, May, July, Oct, Dec	9:30 A.M.– 1:15 P.M. CST	R
last business day of contract month	Jan, Apr, July, Oct	10:00 A.M.– 1:25 P.M. CST	SL
last business day of contract month	Mar, May, July, Oct, Dec	9:30 A.M.– 1:15 P.M. CST	W

Expiration Day	Contract Months	Trading Hours	Ticker Symbol
at least 6 days before first delivery day of underlying futures contract	Mar, June, Sept, Dec	10:00 A.M.– 1:25 P.M. CST	GK

5. HISTORICAL DATA

This section of the *Handbook* allows you to follow the major ups and downs of the financial markets and the United States economy during the 20th Century. Although history never repeats itself exactly, it is important to understand historical market cycles if you are to understand where the markets and economy stand today, as well as where they might be going in the future.

The historical section is presented with graphs accompanied by tabular data and explanations of what the information signifies to you as an investor. Graphs are based on end-of-month closing stock index values; municipal bond yields compiled the first week of each month; month-end London morning fix prices of gold; monthly average Treasury bill and bond yields; monthly average discount, prime, and federal funds rates; and monthly or monthly average government economic statistics.

The tabular data show annual highs, lows, and year-end figures on the same monthly bases as the above with these exceptions: stock indexes are based on daily closing figures; the consumer and producer price indexes and money supply (M-1) statistics are annual percentage changes (for instance, November 1985 vs. November 1984); gold prices are daily London morning fixings; and the discount and prime rates are day-end figures.

Note that the month-end data points on which the stock index graphs are based may reflect different highs and lows than the daily closing data. The month-end data plot long-term trends with a minimum of aberrations caused by PROGRAM TRADES and other NOISE, while the daily data are more subject to short-term fluctuations. The graphs showing trends of the discount and prime rates, because they are based on monthly averages, will also differ from the accompanying tables, which are based on day-end rates.

Much of the data have been provided courtesy of Interactive Data Corporation, a financial database service. IDC, with headquarters at 486 Totten Pond Road, Waltham, Massachusetts 02154 (phone: 617-890-1234) provided numbers for the charts as far back as their data banks went. This usually meant 1968, though in some cases indexes were not created until later. If data was received from another source, such as the Federal Reserve Board, the U.S. Bureau of Labor Statistics, Dow Jones and Company, or Standard & Poor's Corporation, both IDC and that source have been credited.

AMEX MARKET VALUE INDEX

Source: American Stock Exchange, Interactive Data Corporation

This graph shows the movement of the American Stock Exchange Market Value Index. Formerly known as the American Stock Exchange Index, the AMVI is a market value-weighted index (i.e., the impact of a component's price change is proportionate to the overall market value of the issue). The index measures the performance of more than 800 issues, representing all major industry groups, including shares, American Depositary Receipts, and warrants. The companies listed on the Amex tend to be medium-sized and smaller growth firms. One unique aspect of this index is that cash dividends paid by the component stocks are assumed to be reinvested and thus are reflected in the index.

Year	High	Low	Close
1968	74.82	48.66	73.69
1969	84.49	57.22	60.01
1970	62.77	36.10	49.21
1971	60.86	49.09	58.49
1972	69.18	58.55	64.52
1973	65.23	42.16	45.16
1974	51.01	29.13	30.16
1975	48.43	31.10	41.74
1976	54.92	42.16	54.92
1977	63.95	54.31	63.95
1978	88.44	59.87	75.28
1979	123.54	76.02	123.54
1980	185.38	107.85	174.49
1981	190.18	138.38	160.31
1982	170.93	118.65	170.30
1983	249.03	169.61	223.01
1984	227.73	189.16	204.26
1985	246.13	202.06	246.13
1986	285.19	240.30	263.27

BOND BUYER INDEX (11 BONDS)

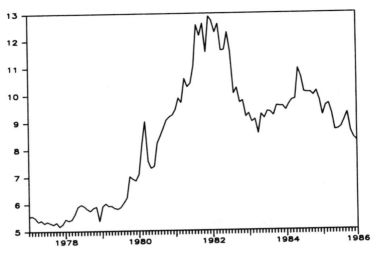

Source: *Bond Buyer*, Interactive Data Corporation

This graph shows the movement of the *Bond Buyer* Index of 11 bonds. The *Bond Buyer* is a daily newspaper covering the municipal bond market. This index is made up of the yields of 11 newly-issued general obligation municipal bonds averaging 20 years to maturity and Aa in rating and selling at par. The issuers of these bonds, whose average rating is second only to Aaa, are among the most creditworthy of all those issuing bonds in the municipal market. The yield offered by these bonds, therefore, is lower than that of less creditworthy municipalities, but it acts as a benchmark against which market participants compare other municipal bond yields.

Year	High	Low	Close
1917	4.55	3.88	4.60
1918	4.65	4.39	4.42
1919	4.53	4.42	4.53
1920	5.25	4.53	5.03
1921	5.16	4.48	4.35
1922	4.37	4.05	4.14
1923	4.38	4.10	4.35
1924	4.35	4.07	4.15
1925	4.23	3.98	4.19
1926	4.19	4.05	4.10
1927	4.10	3.89	3.83
1928	4.15	3.83	4.13
1929	4.47	4.13	4.19
1930	4.25	3.92	4.05
1931	4.23	3.60	4.66
1932	4.66	4.02	3.81

Year	High	Low	Close
1933	4.90	3.81	4.50
1934	4.50	3.38	3.30
1935	3.30	2.79	2.84
1936	2.84	2.35	2.35
1937	2.90	2.35	2.75
1938	2.75	2.42	2.36
1939	2.94	2.26	2.24
1940	2.66	1.82	1.80
1941	2.13	1.57	1.91
1942	2.79	1.72	1.80
1943	1.80	1.35	1.44
1944	1.44	1.30	1.32
1945	1.43	1.06	1.14
1946	1.66	1.04	1.62
1947	2.13	1.53	2.11
1948	2.25	1.98	1.97
1949	2.00	1.84	1.86
1950	1.87	1.54	1.50
1951	2.04	1.43	1.92
1952	2.20	1.84	2.21
1953	2.88	2.21	2.37
1954	2.37	2.10	2.24
1955	2.50	2.22	2.41
1956	3.10	2.29	3.08
1957	3.43	2.81	2.85
1958	3.51	2.70	3.26
1959	3.70	3.17	3.65
1960	3.65	3.12	3.26
1961	3.44	3.16	3.28
1962	3.28	2.92	2.97
1963	3.24	2.95	3.19
1964	3.25	3.06	3.01
1965	3.47	2.99	3.45
1966	4.14	3.43	3.66
1967	4.37	3.32	4.27
1968	4.72	3.96	4.72
1969	6.74	4.68	6.42
1970	7.00	5.02	5.47
1971	6.04	4.75	4.82
1972	5.35	4.78	4.98
1973	5.45	4.87	5.05
1974	6.71	5.04	6.62
1975	7.23	5.94	6.45
1976	6.57	5.36	5.36
1977	5.57	5.18	5.37
1978	6.28	5.32	6.22

Year	High	Low	Close
1979	7.02	5.77	6.85
1980	10.08	6.63	9.27
1981	12.89	9.04	12.89
1982	13.05	8.90	9.18
1983	9.86	8.54	9.57
1984	10.95	9.34	9.78
1985	9.74	8.25	8.26
1986	8.24	6.64	6.70

BOND BUYER INDEX (20 BONDS)

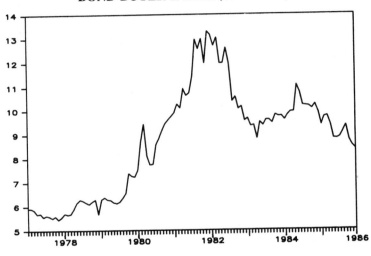

Source: *Bond Buyer*, Interactive Data Corporation

This graph shows the movement of the *Bond Buyer* Index of 20 bonds. The *Bond Buyer* is a daily newspaper covering the municipal bond market. This index is made up of the yields of 20 newly issued general obligation municipal bonds with an average maturity of 20 years, rated from Baa to Aaa (thus including all those of investment grade) and selling at par. The issuers of these bonds are among the most creditworthy of all those issuing bonds in the municipal market.

Year	High	Low	Close
1917	4.56	3.92	4.62
1918	4.72	4.40	4.44
1919	4.55	4.44	4.56
1920	5.27	4.56	5.06
1921	5.26	4.50	4.38
1922	4.41	4.09	4.16

Year	High	Low	Close
1923	4.40	4.11	4.37
1924	4.37	4.11	4.16
1925	4.26	3.99	4.23
1926	4.23	4.10	4.13
1927	4.13	3.93	3.87
1928	4.18	3.87	4.17
1929	4.49	4.17	4.23
1930	4.29	3.97	4.12
1931	4.45	3.74	4.87
1932	5.09	4.57	4.61
1933	5.69	4.48	5.48
1934	5.48	3.89	3.81
1935	3.81	3.23	3.25
1936	3.25	2.69	2.62
1937	3.17	2.62	3.16
1938	3.19	2.83	2.78
1939	3.30	2.66	2.59
1940	3.00	2.18	2.14
1941	2.43	1.90	2.24
1942	2.51	2.13	2.17
1943	2.17	1.69	1.77
1944	1.77	1.59	1.62
1945	1.72	1.35	1.42
1946	1.91	1.29	1.85
1947	2.35	1.78	2.36
1948	2.48	2.20	2.19
1949	2.21	2.08	2.07
1950	2.07	1.70	1.66
1951	2.23	1.58	2.11
1952	2.39	2.03	2.40
1953	3.09	2.40	2.54
1954	2.54	2.26	2.38
1955	2.63	2.37	2.56
1956	3.24	2.42	3.23
1957	3.57	2.96	2.97
1958	3.59	2.85	3.40
1959	3.81	3.26	3.78
1960	3.78	3.27	3.39
1961	3.55	3.26	3.37
1962	3.37	2.98	3.05
1963	3.31	3.01	3.26
1964	3.32	3.12	3.07
1965	3.56	3.04	3.53
1966	4.24	3.51	3.76
1967	4.45	3.40	4.38
1968	4.85	4.07	4.85

Year	High	Low	Close
1969	6.90	4.82	6.61
1970	7.12	5.33	5.74
1971	6.23	4.97	5.03
1972	5.54	4.96	5.08
1973	5.59	4.99	5.18
1974	7.15	5.16	7.08
1975	7.67	6.27	7.13
1976	7.13	5.83	5.83
1977	5.93	5.45	5.66
1978	6.67	5.58	6.61
1979	7.38	6.08	7.23
1980	10.56	7.11	9.76
1981	13.30	9.49	13.30
1982	13.44	9.25	9.56
1983	10.04	8.78	9.76
1984	11.07	9.51	9.91
1985	9.87	8.36	8.36
1986	8.33	6.77	6.83

DOW JONES 30 INDUSTRIALS STOCK AVERAGE

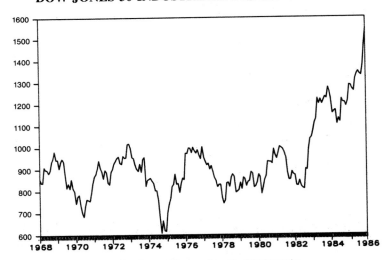

Source: Dow Jones and Company, Interactive Data Corporation

This graph shows the movement of the Dow Jones 30 Industrials Stock Average. This is the oldest and most widely quoted of all stock market indicators. When people ask "What did the market do today?" they usually expect to hear whether this average was up or down for the day. The price-weighted average is comprised of the stocks of 30 blue-chip stocks, primarily manufacturing companies but also service companies like American Express. The components, which change from time to time, represent between 15 percent and 20 percent of the market value of all NYSE stocks. The Dow, as it is known, is calculated by adding the closing prices of the component stocks and using a divisor that adjusts the average for splits and stock dividends equal to 10% or more of the market issue as well as for mergers and changes in the components of the list. The Dow Jones 65 Composite Stock Average is composed of the Dow Jones 30 industrials, the Dow Jones 20 transportations, and the Dow Jones 15 utilities.

The components of the Dow Jones Industrial Average (DJIA) are:

Allied-Signal Company
Aluminum Company of America
American Can Company
American Express Company
American Telephone & Telegraph
Bethlehem Steel
Chevron
DuPont
Eastman Kodak Company
Exxon Corporation
General Electric Company
General Motors Corporation
Goodyear Tire and Rubber Company
Inco Incorporated
International Business Machines Corporation
International Paper Company
McDonalds Corporation
Merck & Company
Minnesota Mining & Manufacturing Company
Navistar International
Owens-Illinois, Inc.
Phillip Morris Company
Proctor & Gamble Corporation
Sears Roebuck and Company
Texaco Incorporated
Union Carbide Corporation
United Technologies Company
USX Corporation
Westinghouse Electric Corporation
F. W. Woolworth & Company

Year	High	Low	Close
1897	55.82	38.49	49.41
1898	60.97	42.00	60.52
1899	77.61	58.27	66.08
1900	71.04	52.96	70.71
1901	78.26	61.52	64.56
1902	68.44	59.57	64.29
1903	67.70	42.15	49.11
1904	73.23	46.41	69.61
1905	96.56	68.76	96.20
1906	103.00	85.18	93.63
1907	96.37	53.00	58.75

Year	High	Low	Close
1908	88.38	58.62	86.15
1909	100.53	79.91	99.05
1910	98.34	73.62	81.36
1911	87.06	72.94	81.68
1912	94.15	80.15	87.87
1913	88.57	72.11	78.78
1914	83.43	53.17	53.17
1915	99.21	54.22	99.15
1916	110.15	84.96	95.00
1917	99.18	65.95	74.38
1918	89.07	73.38	82.20
1919	119.62	79.15	107.23
1920	109.88	66.75	71.95
1921	81.50	63.90	81.10
1922	103.43	78.59	98.73
1923	105.38	85.76	95.52
1924	120.51	88.33	120.51
1925	159.39	115.00	156.66
1926	166.64	135.20	157.20
1927	202.40	152.73	202.40
1928	300.00	191.33	300.00
1929	381.17	198.69	248.48
1930	294.07	157.51	164.58
1931	194.36	73.79	77.90
1932	88.78	41.22	59.93
1933	108.67	50.16	99.90
1934	110.74	85.51	104.04
1935	148.44	96.71	144.13
1936	184.90	143.11	179.90
1937	194.40	113.64	120.85
1938	158.41	98.95	154.76
1939	155.92	121.44	150.24
1940	152.80	111.84	131.13
1941	133.59	106.34	110.96
1942	119.71	92.92	119.40
1943	145.82	119.26	135.89
1944	152.53	134.22	152.32
1945	195.82	151.35	192.91
1946	212.50	163.12	177.20
1947	186.85	163.21	181.16
1948	193.16	165.39	177.30
1949	200.52	161.60	200.13
1950	235.47	196.81	235.41
1951	276.37	238.99	269.23
1952	292.00	256.35	291.90
1953	293.79	255.49	280.90

Year	High	Low	Close
1954	404.39	279.87	404.39
1955	488.40	388.20	488.40
1956	521.05	462.35	499.47
1957	520.77	419.79	435.69
1958	583.65	436.89	583.65
1959	679.36	574.46	679.36
1960	685.47	566.05	615.89
1961	734.91	610.25	731.14
1962	726.01	535.76	652.10
1963	767.21	646.79	762.95
1964	891.71	766.08	874.13
1965	969.26	840.59	969.26
1966	995.15	744.32	785.69
1967	943.08	786.41	905.11
1968	985.21	825.13	943.75
1969	968.85	769.93	800.36
1970	842.00	631.16	838.92
1971	950.82	797.97	890.20
1972	1036.27	889.15	1020.02
1973	1051.70	788.31	850.86
1974	891.66	577.60	616.24
1975	881.81	632.04	852.41
1976	1014.79	858.71	1004.65
1977	999.75	800.85	831.17
1978	907.74	742.12	805.01
1979	897.61	796.67	838.74
1980	1000.17	759.13	963.99
1981	1024.05	824.01	875.00
1982	1070.55	776.92	1046.55
1983	1287.20	1027.04	1258.64
1984	1286.64	1086.57	1211.57
1985	1553.10	1184.96	1546.67
1986	1955.57	1502.29	1895.95

DOW JONES 20 TRANSPORTATION STOCK AVERAGE

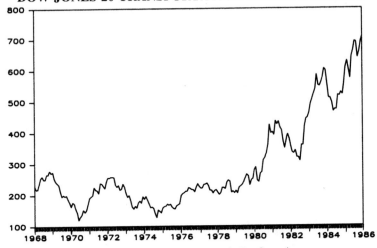

Source: Dow Jones and Company, Interactive Data Corporation

This graph shows the movement of the Dow Jones 20 Transportation Stock Average. This price-weighted average consists of the stocks of 20 large companies in the transportation business, which includes airlines, railroads, and trucking. The Transportation Average is important not only in that it tracks the movement of a major segment of American industry, but also because it is watched by the proponents of Dow Theory, which maintains that a significant trend is not confirmed until both the Dow Jones Industrial Average and the Dow Jones Transportation Average reach new highs or lows; if they don't, the market will fall back to its former trading range, according to this theory. From 1897 to 1969, this average was called the Dow Jones Railroad Average. The Dow Jones 65 Composite Average is composed of the Dow Jones 20 Transportation Stock Average, as well as the Dow Jones 30 industrials and the Dow Jones 15 utilities.

The components of the Dow Jones Transportation Average are:

AMR Corporation
American President Lines
Burlington Northern Railroad
Canadian Pacific Railroad
Carolina Freight Corporation
Consolidated Freight Corporation
CSX Corporation
Delta Air Lines
Federal Express Company
Leaseway Transportation Company
Norfolk Southern Railway
NWA Incorporated
Pan American Corporation
Piedmont Aviation, Inc.
Ryder System Incorporated
Santa Fe Southern Pacific Company
TWA Corporation
UAL Incorporated
Union Pacific Corporation
USAir Group

Year	High	Low	Close
1897	67.23	48.12	62.29
1898	74.99	55.89	74.99
1899	87.04	72.48	77.73
1900	94.99	72.99	94.99
1901	117.86	92.66	114.85
1902	129.36	111.73	118.98
1903	121.28	88.80	98.33
1904	119.46	91.31	117.43
1905	133.51	114.52	133.26
1906	138.36	120.30	129.80
1907	131.95	81.41	88.77
1908	120.05	86.04	120.05
1909	134.46	113.90	130.41
1910	129.90	105.59	114.06
1911	123.86	109.80	116.83
1912	124.35	114.92	116.84
1913	118.10	100.50	103.72
1914	109.43	87.40	88.53
1915	108.28	87.85	108.05
1916	112.28	99.11	105.15
1917	105.76	70.75	79.73
1918	92.91	77.21	84.32
1919	91.13	73.63	75.30
1920	85.37	67.83	75.96
1921	77.56	65.52	74.27
1922	93.99	73.43	86.11
1923	90.63	76.78	80.86
1924	99.50	80.23	98.33
1925	112.93	92.98	112.93
1926	123.33	102.41	120.86
1927	144.82	119.29	140.30
1928	152.70	132.60	151.14
1929	189.11	128.07	144.72
1930	157.94	91.65	96.58
1931	111.58	31.42	33.63
1932	41.30	13.23	25.90
1933	56.53	23.43	40.80
1934	52.97	33.19	36.44
1935	41.84	27.31	40.48
1936	59.89	40.66	53.63
1937	64.46	28.91	29.46
1938	33.98	19.00	33.98
1939	35.90	24.14	31.83
1940	32.67	22.14	28.13
1941	30.88	24.25	25.42
1942	29.28	23.31	27.39

Year	High	Low	Close
1943	38.30	27.59	33.56
1944	48.40	33.45	48.40
1945	64.89	47.03	62.80
1946	68.31	44.69	51.13
1947	53.42	41.16	52.48
1948	64.95	48.13	52.86
1949	54.29	41.03	52.76
1950	77.89	51.24	77.64
1951	90.08	72.39	81.70
1952	112.53	82.03	111.27
1953	112.21	90.56	94.03
1954	146.23	94.84	145.86
1955	167.83	137.84	163.29
1956	181.23	150.44	153.23
1957	157.67	95.67	96.96
1958	157.91	99.89	157.65
1959	173.56	146.65	154.05
1960	160.43	123.37	130.85
1961	152.93	131.06	143.84
1962	149.83	114.86	141.04
1963	179.46	142.03	178.54
1964	224.91	178.81	205.34
1965	249.55	187.29	247.48
1966	271.72	184.34	202.97
1967	274.49	205.16	233.24
1968	279.48	214.58	271.60
1969	279.88	169.03	176.34
1970	183.31	116.69	171.52
1971	248.33	169.70	243.72
1972	275.71	212.24	227.17
1973	228.10	151.97	196.19
1974	202.45	125.93	143.44
1975	174.57	146.47	172.65
1976	237.03	175.69	237.03
1977	246.64	199.60	217.18
1978	261.49	199.31	206.56
1979	271.77	205.78	252.39
1980	425.68	233.69	398.10
1981	447.38	335.48	380.30
1982	464.55	292.12	448.38
1983	612.57	434.24	598.59
1984	612.63	444.03	558.13
1985	723.31	553.03	708.21
1986	866.74	686.97	807.17

DOW JONES 15 UTILITIES STOCK AVERAGE

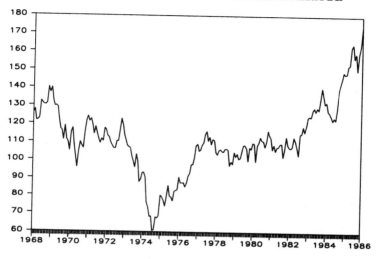

Source: Dow Jones and Company, Interactive Data Corporation

This graph shows the movement of the Dow Jones 15 Utilities Stock Average. This price-weighted average is composed of 15 geographically representative and well-established gas and electric utility companies. Since utilities are heavy borrowers, their stock prices are inversely affected by the ups and downs of interest rates. The Dow Jones 65 Composite Stock Average is composed of the Dow Jones 15 Utilities Stock Average, the Dow Jones 30 industrials, and the Dow Jones 20 transportations.

The components of the Dow Jones Utilities Average are:

American Electric Power Company
Centerior Energy
Columbia Gas System
Commonwealth Edison Company
Consolidated Edison Company
Consolidated Natural Gas Company
Detroit Edison Company
Houston Industries
Niagara Mohawk Power Company
Pacific Gas & Electric Company
Panhandle Eastern Company
Peoples Energy Corporation
Philadelphia Electric Company
Public Service Enterprise Group Incorporated
Southern California Edison Company

Year	High	Low	Close
1929	144.61	64.72	88.27
1930	108.62	55.14	60.80
1931	73.40	30.55	31.41

Year	High	Low	Close
1932	36.11	16.53	27.50
1933	37.73	19.33	23.29
1934	31.03	16.83	17.80
1935	29.78	14.46	29.55
1936	36.08	28.63	34.83
1937	37.54	19.65	20.35
1938	25.19	15.14	23.02
1939	27.10	20.71	25.58
1940	26.45	18.03	19.85
1941	20.65	13.51	14.02
1942	14.94	10.58	14.54
1943	22.30	14.69	21.87
1944	26.37	21.74	26.37
1945	39.15	26.15	38.13
1946	43.74	33.20	37.27
1947	37.55	32.28	33.40
1948	36.04	31.65	33.55
1949	41.31	33.36	41.29
1950	44.26	37.40	40.98
1951	47.22	41.47	47.22
1952	52.64	47.53	52.60
1953	53.88	47.87	52.04
1954	62.47	52.22	62.47
1955	66.68	61.39	64.16
1956	71.17	63.03	68.54
1957	74.61	62.10	68.58
1958	91.00	68.94	91.00
1959	94.70	85.05	87.83
1960	100.07	85.02	100.02
1961	135.90	99.75	129.16
1962	130.85	103.11	129.23
1963	144.37	129.19	138.99
1964	155.71	137.30	155.17
1965	163.32	149.84	152.63
1966	152.39	118.96	136.18
1967	140.43	120.97	127.91
1968	141.30	119.79	137.17
1969	139.95	106.31	110.08
1970	121.84	95.86	121.84
1971	128.39	108.03	117.75
1972	124.14	105.06	119.50
1973	120.72	84.42	89.37
1974	95.09	57.93	68.76
1975	87.07	72.02	83.65
1976	108.38	84.52	108.38
1977	118.67	104.97	111.28

Year	High	Low	Close
1978	110.98	96.35	98.24
1979	109.74	98.24	106.60
1980	117.34	96.04	114.42
1981	117.81	101.28	109.02
1982	122.83	103.22	119.46
1983	140.70	119.51	131.84
1984	149.93	122.25	149.52
1985	174.96	146.54	174.81
1986	219.15	169.47	206.01

DOW JONES 65 COMPOSITE STOCK AVERAGE

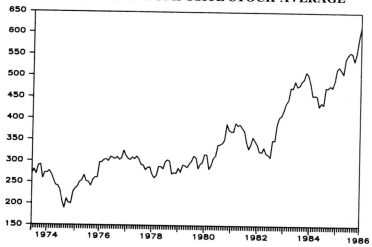

Source: Dow Jones and Company, Interactive Data Corporation

This graph shows the movement of the Dow Jones 65 Composite Stock Average. This average is made up of the 30 stocks in the Dow Jones Industrial Average, the 20 stocks in the Dow Jones Transportation Average, and the 15 stocks in the Dow Jones Utility Average. The average therefore is significant because it combines the three blue chip averages and thus gives a good indication of the overall direction of the largest, most established companies.

Year	High	Low	Close
1939	53.0	40.4	50.6
1940	51.7	37.2	44.0
1941	44.9	35.5	39.4
1942	39.6	31.5	39.6
1943	50.9	39.8	47.1
1944	56.6	47.0	56.6

Year	High	Low	Close
1945	73.5	55.9	73.5
1946	79.4	58.5	65.4
1947	67.1	57.3	65.1
1948	71.9	59.9	64.7
1949	71.9	57.8	71.9
1950	87.2	70.3	87.2
1951	100.0	86.9	97.4
1952	113.6	96.1	113.6
1953	114.0	98.2	108.0
1954	150.2	106.0	150.2
1955	174.2	137.8	174.2
1956	184.1	164.3	174.2
1957	179.9	142.8	149.4
1958	202.4	147.4	202.4
1959	233.5	200.1	219.5
1960	222.6	190.4	206.1
1961	251.4	204.8	249.6
1962	245.8	187.4	228.9
1963	269.1	228.7	269.1
1964	314.2	269.1	307.5
1965	340.9	290.4	340.9
1966	352.4	261.3	290.3
1967	337.3	282.7	314.1
1968	353.1	290.1	352.7
1969	346.2	253.0	268.3
1970	273.2	208.7	273.2
1971	318.4	270.2	310.1
1972	338.5	302.1	338.5
1973	334.1	247.7	272.5
1974	282.5	184.2	199.7
1975	268.2	205.3	261.7
1976	325.5	264.5	325.5
1977	324.9	274.3	287.2
1978	315.3	260.7	272.2
1979	315.1	274.3	298.3
1980	388.9	271.7	373.4
1981	394.6	320.6	347.8
1982	416.3	299.4	409.2
1983	515.1	401.0	502.9
1984	514.0	421.4	489.9
1985	619.4	480.9	616.5
1986	767.9	602.8	736.8

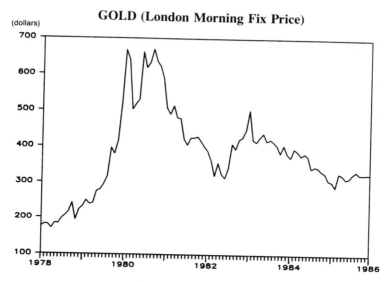

GOLD (London Morning Fix Price)

(dollars)

Source: Interactive Data Corporation

This graph shows the movement of the per troy ounce gold price, according to the month-end morning fixings in London. Twice each business day (at 10:30 A.M. and 3:30 P.M.), five major metals dealers meet in London to fix a benchmark price for gold, after assessing supply and demand at that time. Gold has traditionally been considered a store of value both against the erosion through inflation of a currency's purchasing power and against political instability or turmoil. From the 1930s until the early 70s, gold was fixed at $35 an ounce in the United States. When trading in the metal resumed, gold at first rose to about $200 an ounce, then fell to about $100, then rose again modestly in the mid-1970s. In the late 1970s and early 80s, with inflation driven by rising oil prices, compounded by Middle East tensions, the gold price soared. It then dropped precipitously and after a period of relative stability in the mid-1980s began falling as a reflection of disinflation.

Year	High	Low	Close
1977	168.15	156.65	165.60
1978	243.65	165.60	224.50
1979	524.00	216.50	524.00
1980	843.00	474.00	589.50
1981	599.25	391.75	400.00
1982	488.50	297.00	448.00
1983	511.50	374.75	381.50
1984	406.85	303.25	309.00
1985	339.30	285.00	327.00
1986	442.75	326.00	390.90

NASDAQ NATIONAL MARKET SYSTEM COMPOSITE INDEX

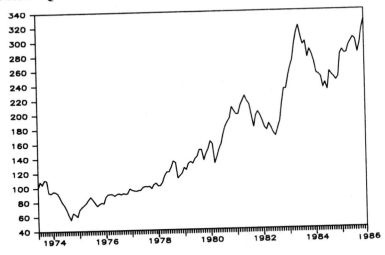

Source: National Association of Securities Dealers, Interactive Data Corporation

This graph shows the movement of the National Association of Securities Dealers
Automated Quotations (NASDAQ) National Market System Composite Index. This
market-value weighted index is composed of all the stocks traded on the National
Market System of the over-the-counter market, which is supervised by the National
Association of Securities Dealers. The companies in this index are smaller growth
companies, many of them in high technology and financial services. The direction
of the index is used by analysts to gauge investor interest in more speculative stocks.
In times of enthusiasm for small stocks, this index will rise dramatically, and it will
fall just as much when investors opt for safety instead of risk.

Year	High	Low	Close
1973	136.84	88.67	92.19
1974	96.53	54.87	59.82
1975	88.00	60.70	77.62
1976	97.88	78.06	97.88
1977	105.05	93.66	105.05
1978	139.25	99.09	117.98
1979	152.29	117.84	151.14
1980	208.15	124.09	202.34
1981	223.47	175.03	195.84
1982	240.70	159.14	232.41
1983	328.91	230.59	278.60
1984	278.90	225.30	247.35
1985	307.76	245.91	324.93
1986	411.16	323.01	348.83

NEW YORK STOCK EXCHANGE COMPOSITE INDEX

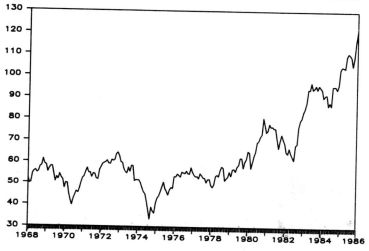

Source: New York Stock Exchange, Interactive Data Corporation

This graph shows the movement of the New York Stock Exchange Composite Index. This market-value weighted index is composed of four subindexes—the NYSE Industrial, Transportation, Utilities, and Finance indexes. As such, the Composite Index provides a broader measure of the performance of the New York Stock Exchange than the more widely quoted Dow Jones Industrial Average. Some newspapers, such as *The New York Times*, provide a graph of the NYSE Composite on a daily basis. Stock index futures and options are traded on the NYSE Composite on the New York Futures Exchange.

Year	High	Low	Close
1968	61.27	48.70	58.90
1969	59.32	49.31	51.53
1970	52.36	37.69	50.23
1971	57.76	49.60	56.43
1972	65.14	56.23	64.48
1973	65.48	49.05	51.82
1974	53.37	32.89	36.13
1975	51.24	37.06	47.64
1976	57.88	48.04	57.88
1977	57.69	49.78	52.50
1978	60.38	48.37	53.62
1979	63.39	53.88	61.95
1980	81.02	55.30	77.86
1981	79.14	64.96	71.41
1982	82.35	58.80	81.03
1983	99.63	79.79	95.18
1984	98.12	85.13	96.38
1985	121.90	94.60	121.58
1986	145.75	117.75	138.58

STANDARD & POOR'S 400 INDUSTRIAL STOCK INDEX

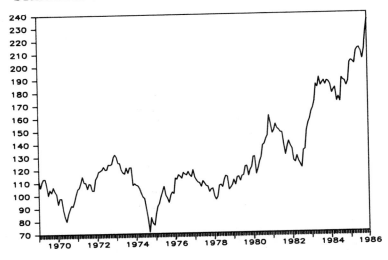

Source: Standard & Poor's Corporation, Interactive Data Corporation

This graph shows the movement of Standard & Poor's 400 Industrial Stock Index, commonly known as the S&P 400. This market-value weighted index is made up of 400 large, established industrial companies, most of which are traded on the New York Stock Exchange. The stocks in the Dow Jones Industrial Average are also included in the S&P 400, but the S&P index provides a much broader picture of the performance of industrial stocks. Standard & Poor's 500 Index is comprised of the S&P 400 plus the S&P 40 Utilities, 20 Transportations, and 40 Financials indexes.

Year	High	Low	Close
1930	20.32	11.33	11.90
1931	14.07	6.02	6.32
1932	7.26	3.52	5.18
1933	10.25	4.24	9.26
1934	10.54	7.63	9.12
1935	12.84	7.90	12.77
1936	17.02	12.67	16.50
1937	18.10	9.73	10.26
1938	13.66	8.39	13.07
1939	13.08	9.92	12.17
1940	12.42	8.70	10.37
1941	10.62	8.47	8.78
1942	9.94	7.54	9.93
1943	12.58	10.00	11.61
1944	13.18	11.43	13.05
1945	17.06	12.97	16.79

Year	High	Low	Close
1946	18.53	13.64	14.75
1947	15.83	13.40	15.18
1948	16.93	13.58	15.12
1949	16.52	13.23	16.49
1950	20.60	16.34	20.57
1951	24.33	20.85	24.24
1952	26.92	23.30	26.89
1953	26.99	22.70	24.87
1954	37.24	24.84	37.24
1955	49.54	35.66	48.44
1956	53.28	45.71	50.08
1957	53.25	41.98	42.86
1958	58.97	43.20	58.97
1959	65.32	57.02	64.50
1960	65.02	55.34	61.49
1961	76.69	60.87	75.72
1962	75.22	54.80	66.00
1963	79.25	65.48	79.25
1964	91.29	79.74	89.62
1965	98.55	86.43	98.47
1966	100.60	77.89	85.24
1967	106.15	85.31	105.11
1968	118.03	95.05	113.02
1969	116.24	97.75	101.49
1970	102.87	75.58	100.90
1971	115.84	99.36	112.72
1972	132.95	112.19	131.87
1973	134.54	103.37	109.14
1974	111.65	69.53	76.47
1975	107.40	77.71	100.88
1976	120.89	101.64	119.46
1977	118.92	99.88	104.71
1978	118.71	95.52	107.21
1979	124.99	107.08	121.02
1980	160.96	111.09	154.45
1981	157.02	125.93	137.12
1982	159.66	114.08	157.62
1983	194.84	154.95	186.24
1984	191.48	167.75	186.36
1985	235.75	182.24	234.56
1986	282.77	224.88	269.93

STANDARD & POOR'S 20 TRANSPORTATION
STOCK INDEX

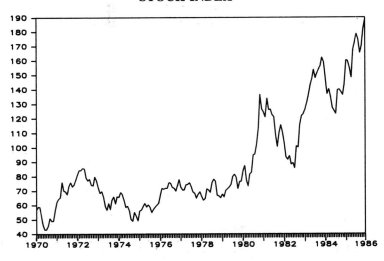

Source: Standard & Poor's Corporation, Interactive Data Corporation

This graph shows the movement of Standard & Poor's 20 Transportation Stock Index. This market-value weighted index is made up of 20 large transportation companies in the airline, trucking, and railroad businesses. It is combined with the S&P 400 Industrials, S&P 40 Utilities, and S&P 40 Financials to make up Standard & Poor's 500 Index.

Year	High	Low	Close
1930	46.34	28.27	30.20
1931	34.75	10.08	10.57
1932	13.02	4.32	8.72
1933	18.97	7.69	13.89
1934	17.77	11.15	12.25
1935	14.81	9.36	14.32
1936	20.95	14.40	18.90
1937	22.07	9.76	9.89
1938	11.23	6.58	11.23
1939	12.04	7.80	10.47
1940	10.78	7.25	9.47
1941	10.22	7.77	8.21
1942	10.12	7.75	9.43
1943	13.34	9.52	11.65
1944	15.85	11.57	15.85
1945	21.33	15.45	20.83
1946	22.74	13.86	15.61
1947	16.46	11.95	14.46

Year	High	Low	Close
1948	17.26	13.34	13.92
1949	14.49	11.24	13.86
1950	19.39	13.34	19.34
1951	21.93	17.59	20.08
1952	25.41	20.16	24.90
1953	25.13	19.79	20.33
1954	30.48	20.42	30.38
1955	35.78	28.54	34.17
1956	37.57	30.45	31.36
1957	32.48	20.82	20.95
1958	34.39	21.57	34.39
1959	38.03	31.98	33.82
1960	34.92	27.17	29.55
1961	35.30	29.64	33.25
1962	34.48	26.81	32.73
1963	40.70	32.88	40.65
1964	49.87	40.54	45.82
1965	51.56	41.06	51.28
1966	56.32	37.91	41.04
1967	51.46	41.35	43.71
1968	56.08	40.82	54.15
1969	56.96	35.26	37.16
1970	38.94	24.65	35.40
1971	48.32	35.03	44.61
1972	48.31	40.40	44.26
1973	45.80	32.50	45.80
1974	47.36	29.38	35.59
1975	40.18	34.02	38.12
1976	78.11	67.57	78.11
1977	78.72	63.29	69.50
1978	82.48	63.14	65.12
1979	84.11	65.33	76.73
1980	136.71	70.72	126.22
1981	135.29	96.13	110.44
1982	126.93	81.77	123.12
1983	164.97	119.45	158.81
1984	161.46	117.21	143.91
1985	192.35	141.56	188.72
1986	217.28	176.16	197.27

STANDARD & POOR'S 40 UTILITIES STOCK INDEX

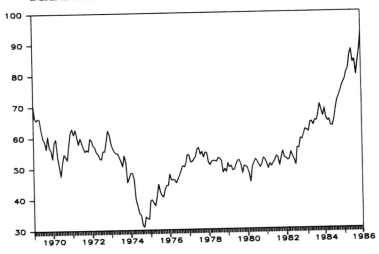

Source: Standard & Poor's Corporation, Interactive Data Corporation

This graph shows the movement of Standard & Poor's 40 Utilities Stock Index. This market-value weighted index is made up of 40 large and geographically representative electric and gas utilities. It is combined with the S&P 400 Industrials, S&P 20 Transportations, and S&P 40 Financials to make up Standard & Poor's 500 Index.

Year	High	Low	Close
1930	67.83	35.33	38.75
1931	49.17	22.38	23.66
1932	26.77	12.49	21.97
1933	27.41	14.73	16.21
1934	21.78	11.35	12.13
1935	20.46	9.52	20.25
1936	24.61	19.36	23.46
1937	25.26	13.47	13.96
1938	17.04	10.90	15.97
1939	17.77	14.23	16.81
1940	17.36	12.65	13.08
1941	13.48	7.77	8.21
1942	8.88	6.65	8.69
1943	12.72	8.79	12.07
1944	13.72	11.98	13.51
1945	20.61	13.63	19.96
1946	23.54	16.95	19.58
1947	19.83	15.89	16.28
1948	18.01	15.56	16.04

Year	High	Low	Close
1949	19.94	15.90	19.93
1950	21.45	18.35	19.42
1951	21.72	19.61	21.72
1952	24.55	21.73	24.55
1953	25.30	22.25	25.10
1954	29.82	25.16	29.82
1955	32.87	29.53	31.70
1956	33.93	31.15	31.76
1957	34.29	28.96	32.14
1958	43.28	32.32	43.28
1959	45.45	41.87	44.74
1960	51.76	43.74	51.76
1961	67.97	51.42	64.83
1962	65.11	50.21	61.09
1963	67.99	61.26	66.42
1964	74.97	66.36	74.52
1965	78.20	72.03	75.51
1966	75.37	59.03	69.35
1967	72.59	62.21	66.08
1968	72.30	61.06	69.69
1969	70.74	54.33	56.09
1970	61.71	47.67	61.71
1971	64.81	54.48	59.83
1972	62.99	52.02	61.05
1973	61.57	43.51	46.91
1974	49.44	29.37	33.54
1975	45.61	35.31	44.45
1976	54.24	44.70	54.24
1977	57.56	51.60	54.73
1978	54.47	48.23	48.47
1979	52.85	47.14	50.24
1980	53.97	43.29	52.45
1981	55.75	48.96	52.98
1982	61.69	50.31	60.45
1983	70.30	60.22	66.17
1984	76.47	62.90	75.89
1985	93.26	74.70	93.17
1986	123.74	90.33	112.29

STANDARD & POOR'S 40 STOCK FINANCIAL INDEX

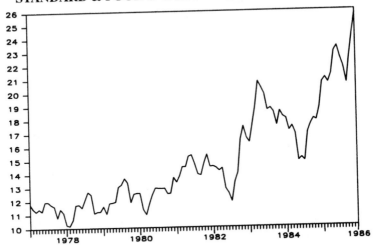

Source: Standard & Poor's Corporation, Interactive Data Corporation

This graph shows the movement of Standard & Poor's Financial Index. This market-value weighted index is composed of 40 large financial institutions such as banks and insurance companies. As such, the stocks in the index tend to move inversely with interest rates. The S&P Financial Index is combined with the S&P 400 Industrials, 20 Transportations, and 40 Utilities to form Standard & Poor's 500, one of the main benchmarks of performance of the stock market.

Year	High	Low	Close
1976	12.79	11.25	12.79
1977	12.67	10.57	11.15
1978	13.18	10.14	11.22
1979	13.90	11.05	12.57
1980	13.76	10.39	13.70
1981	16.56	13.15	14.47
1982	18.05	11.55	16.58
1983	20.99	15.77	18.13
1984	18.88	14.09	18.80
1985	25.87	18.37	25.72
1986	31.13	25.19	26.92

STANDARD & POOR'S 500 STOCK INDEX

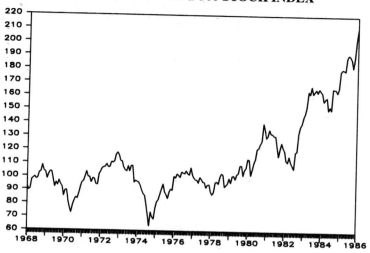

Source: Standard & Poor's Corporation, Interactive Data Corporation

This graph shows the movement of Standard & Poor's 500 Stock Index. This market-value weighted index is composed of the S&P 400 Industrials, the S&P 20 Transportations, the S&P 40 Financials, and the S&P 40 Utilities. Most of the stocks in the S&P 500 are found on the New York Stock Exchange, though there are a few from the American Stock Exchange and the over-the-counter market. The index represents about 80 percent of the market value of all issues traded on the NYSE. The S&P is commonly considered the benchmark against which the performance of individual stocks or stock groups is measured. It is a far broader measure of market activity than the Dow Jones Industrial Average, even though the DJIA is quoted more widely. There are mutual funds, called index funds, which aim to mirror the performance of the S&P 500. Such funds appeal to investors who wish to match the general performance of the stock market. Stock index futures and options are also traded on the S&P 500 and its smaller version, the S&P 100, on the Chicago Mercantile Exchange and the Chicago Board Options Exchange.

Year	High	Low	Close
1930	25.92	14.44	15.34
1931	18.17	7.72	8.12
1932	9.31	4.40	6.89
1933	12.20	5.53	10.10
1934	11.82	8.36	9.50
1935	13.46	8.06	13.43
1936	17.69	13.40	17.18
1937	18.68	10.17	10.55
1938	13.79	8.50	13.21
1939	13.23	10.18	12.49
1940	12.77	8.99	10.58

Year	High	Low	Close
1941	10.86	8.37	8.69
1942	9.77	7.47	9.77
1943	12.64	9.84	11.67
1944	13.29	11.56	13.28
1945	17.68	13.21	17.36
1946	19.25	14.12	15.30
1947	16.20	13.71	15.30
1948	17.06	13.84	15.20
1949	16.79	13.55	16.76
1950	20.43	16.65	20.41
1951	23.85	20.69	23.77
1952	26.59	23.09	26.57
1953	26.66	22.71	24.81
1954	35.98	24.80	35.98
1955	46.41	34.58	45.48
1956	49.74	43.11	46.67
1957	49.13	38.98	39.99
1958	55.21	40.33	55.21
1959	60.71	53.58	59.89
1960	60.39	52.30	58.11
1961	72.64	57.57	71.55
1962	71.13	52.32	63.10
1963	75.02	52.69	75.02
1964	86.28	75.43	84.75
1965	92.63	81.60	92.43
1966	94.06	73.20	80.33
1967	97.59	80.38	96.47
1968	108.37	87.72	103.86
1969	106.16	89.20	92.06
1970	93.46	69.29	92.15
1971	104.77	90.16	102.09
1972	119.12	101.67	118.05
1973	120.24	92.16	97.55
1974	99.80	62.28	68.56
1975	95.61	70.04	90.19
1976	107.83	90.90	107.46
1977	107.00	90.71	95.10
1978	106.99	86.90	96.11
1979	111.27	96.13	107.94
1980	140.52	98.22	135.76
1981	138.12	112.77	122.55
1982	143.02	102.42	140.64
1983	172.65	138.34	164.93
1984	170.41	147.82	167.24
1985	212.02	163.68	211.28
1986	254.00	203.49	242.17

TORONTO 300 COMPOSITE STOCK INDEX

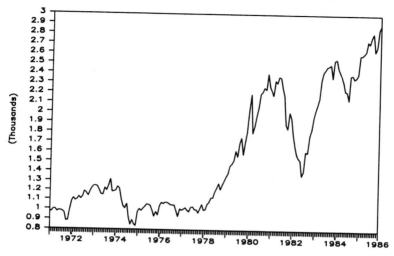

Source: Toronto Stock Exchange, Interactive Data Corporation

This graph shows the movement of the Toronto 300 Composite Stock Index. This is the major index for Canadian stocks, since most of the stock market trading in Canada takes place in Toronto. The index is composed of the Industrial, Transportation, Utilities, and Financial indexes maintained by the Toronto Stock Exchange. Stock index futures are traded on the Composite 300 on the Toronto Futures Exchange.

Year	High	Low	Close
1971	1036.09	879.80	990.54
1972	1226.58	1044.60	1226.58
1973	1319.26	1122.34	1187.78
1974	1276.81	821.10	835.42
1975	1081.96	862.74	942.94
1976	1100.55	931.17	1011.52
1977	1067.35	961.04	1059.59
1978	1332.71	998.19	1309.99
1979	1813.17	1315.82	1813.17
1980	2402.23	1702.51	2268.70
1981	2390.50	1812.48	1954.24
1982	1958.08	1346.35	1958.08
1983	2598.26	1949.81	2552.35
1984	2585.73	2079.69	2400.33
1985	2900.60	2348.55	2900.60
1986	3129.11	2754.06	3066.18

TREASURY BILL (3 MONTH) YIELDS

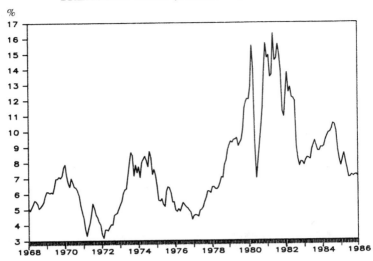

Source: Federal Reserve Bulletin, Interactive Data Corporation

This graph shows the movement of the yields of 3-month Treasury bills. Treasury-bill yields are considered the most important yardsticks of short-term interest rates, and they are therefore watched closely by credit market analysts for signs that rates might be rising or falling. Many floating-rate loans and variable-rate mortgages are tied to the Treasury bill rate. The minimum purchase amount of a Treasury bill is $10,000. Auctions for Treasury bills are held weekly. Individual investors who do not submit a competitive bid are sold bills at the average price of the winning competitive bids. Treasury bills are the primary instrument used by the Federal Reserve in its regulation of the money supply through open market operations. Futures are traded on Treasury bills on the International Monetary Market and the MidAmerica Commodity Exchange. Futures options on T-bills are traded on the Chicago Mercantile Exchange, and the interest rate options on T-bills are traded on the American Stock Exchange.

Year	Average Rate	Year	Average Rate
1965	4.37%	1976	4.35%
1966	4.96%	1977	6.07%
1967	4.96%	1978	9.08%
1968	5.94%	1979	12.04%
1969	7.81%	1980	15.49%
1970	4.87%	1981	10.85%
1971	4.01%	1982	7.94%
1972	5.07%	1983	9.00%
1973	7.45%	1984	8.06%
1974	7.15%	1985	7.10%
1975	5.44%		

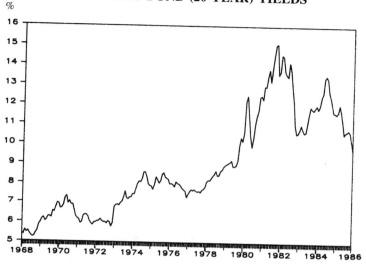

TREASURY BOND (20 YEAR) YIELDS

%

Source: Federal Reserve Bulletin, Interactive Data Corporation

This graph shows the movement of yields of 20-year Treasury bonds. Treasury-bond yields are considered the most important yardsticks of long-term interest rates, and they are therefore watched closely by credit market analysts for signs that rates might be rising or falling. The minimum denomination of a Treasury bond is $1000 and maturities range from 10 to 30 years, with the 20-year T-bond representing a large percentage of the bonds traded. Futures are traded on Treasury bonds on the Chicago Board of Trade and the MidAmerica Commodity Exchange. Futures options on T-bonds are traded on the Chicago Board of Trade, and interest rate options on T-bonds are traded on the Chicago Board Options Exchange.

Year	Average Rate	Year	Average Rate
1965	4.50%	1976	7.30%
1966	4.76%	1977	7.87%
1967	5.59%	1978	8.90%
1968	5.88%	1979	10.18%
1969	6.97%	1980	12.49%
1970	6.28%	1981	13.73%
1971	6.00%	1982	10.62%
1972	5.96%	1983	12.02%
1973	7.29%	1984	11.64%
1974	7.91%	1985	9.75%
1975	8.23%		

VALUE LINE COMPOSITE INDEX

Source: Value Line, Inc., Interactive Data Corporation

This graph shows the movement of the Value Line Composite Index. This equally weighted geometric average is composed of the approximately 1700 stocks traded on the New York Stock Exchange, American Stock Exchange, and over-the-counter that are tracked by the Value Line Investment Survey. This index is particularly broad in scope, since Value Line covers both large industrial companies as well as smaller growth firms. Futures are traded on the Value Line Composite Index on the Kansas City Board of Trade, and index options are traded on the index on the Philadelphia Stock Exchange.

Year	High	Low	Close
1968	188.64	138.92	183.18
1969	183.63	127.40	130.56
1970	135.46	84.23	103.60
1971	125.76	97.36	112.94
1972	125.98	107.11	114.05
1973	116.20	70.50	73.61
1974	83.41	47.03	48.97
1975	80.88	51.12	70.69
1976	93.47	71.62	93.47
1977	96.34	86.53	93.92
1978	119.77	88.67	97.97
1979	125.25	98.88	121.91
1980	149.76	100.60	144.20
1981	159.03	125.66	137.81
1982	161.37	112.32	158.94
1983	208.51	157.70	194.35
1984	200.32	162.46	177.98
1985	214.86	176.61	214.86
1986	246.80	210.84	225.62

WILSHIRE 5000 EQUITY INDEX

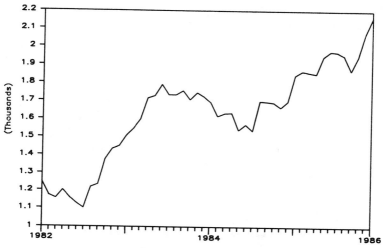

Source: Wilshire Associates, Interactive Data Corporation

This graph shows the movement of the Wilshire 5000 Equity Index. This market-value weighted index of 5000 stocks is the broadest of all the indexes and averages, and represents the value, in billions of dollars, of all New York Stock Exchange, American Stock Exchange, and over-the-counter stocks for which quotes are available. The index is used as a measure of how all stocks are doing as a group, as opposed to a particular segment of the market.

Year	High	Low	Close
1971	955.25	871.15	949.26
1972	1090.31	976.73	1090.31
1973	1059.76	854.60	861.73
1974	863.57	550.04	590.34
1975	840.17	675.54	784.15
1976	954.18	879.52	954.18
1977	919.19	851.60	887.59
1978	1004.15	822.27	922.77
1979	1101.82	935.84	1100.71
1980	1466.64	1026.03	1404.60
1981	1415.04	1208.47	1286.24
1982	1451.59	1099.70	1451.59
1983	1791.70	1508.98	1723.63
1984	1702.11	1536.91	1702.01
1985	2164.69	1845.24	2164.69
1986	2598.03	2109.61	2434.95

CONSUMER PRICE INDEX

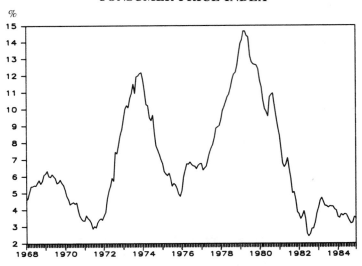

Source: U.S. Bureau of Labor Statistics, Interactive Data Corporation

This graph shows the movement of the Consumer Price Index. The line represents the rolling 12-month average of changes in consumer prices—a method which best shows the ups and downs of the inflation rate. Each month, the U.S. Bureau of Labor Statistics shops a fixed market basket of goods and services available to an average urban wage earner. The market basket of goods is updated every few years. The major groups included in the CPI are food, shelter, fuel oil and coal, gas and electricity, apparel, private transportation, public transportation, medical care, entertainment, services, and commodities. The CPI is important because many pension and employment contracts are tied to changes in it. The inflationary spike of the 1970s did much damage to the world economy and had profound consequences, including the strongly anti-inflationary monetary policies of the middle 1980s. Futures on the Consumer Price Index are traded on the Coffee, Sugar and Cocoa Exchange.

Year	Annual Change in CPI	Year	Annual Change in CPI
1967	2.9%	1977	6.5%
1968	4.2%	1978	7.7%
1969	5.4%	1979	11.3%
1970	5.9%	1980	13.5%
1971	4.3%	1981	10.4%
1972	3.3%	1982	6.1%
1973	6.2%	1983	3.2%
1974	11%	1984	4.3%
1975	9.1%	1985	2.3%
1976	5.8%		

DISCOUNT RATE

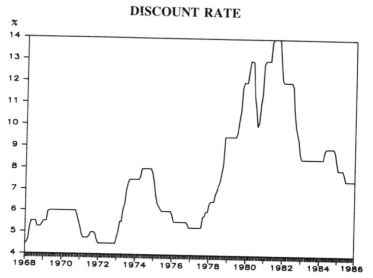

Source: Federal Reserve Board, Interactive Data Corporation

This graph shows the movement of the discount rate, which is the rate the Federal Reserve charges its member banks for loans from the discount window. Credit market analysts watch the Fed's discount rate moves very carefully, since changes in the rate are a major indication of whether the Fed wants to ease or tighten the money supply. When the Fed wants to ease the money supply to stimulate the economy, it cuts the discount rate. When the Fed wants to tighten the money supply to slow the economy and thereby to try to lower the inflation rate, it raises the discount rate. The discount rate acts as a floor on interest rates, since banks set their loan rates, such as the prime rate, a notch above the discount rate.

Year	High	Low	Close
1914	6%	5%	5%
1915	5%	4%	4%
1916	4%	3%	3%
1917	3.50%	3%	3%
1918	3.50%	4%	4%
1919	4.75%	4%	4.75%
1920	7%	4.75%	7%
1921	7%	4.50%	4.50%
1922	4.50%	4%	4%
1923	4.50%	4%	4.50%
1924	4.50%	3%	3%
1925	3.50%	3%	3.50%
1926	4%	3.50%	4%
1927	4%	3.50%	4%
1928	5%	3.50%	5%

Year	High	Low	Close
1929	6%	4.50%	4.50%
1930	4.50%	2%	2%
1931	3.50%	1.50%	3.50%
1932	3.50%	2.50%	2.50%
1933	3.50%	2%	2%
1934	2%	1.50%	1.50%
1935	1.50%	1.50%	1.50%
1936	1.50%	1.50%	1.50%
1937	1.50%	1%	1%
1938	1%	1%	1%
1939	1%	1%	1%
1940	1%	1%	1%
1941	1%	1%	1%
1942	1%	.50%	.50%
1943	1%	.50%	.50%
1944	1%	.50%	.50%
1945	1%	.50%	.50%
1946	1%	.50%	.50%
1947	1%	1%	1%
1948	1.50%	1%	1.50%
1949	1.50%	1.50%	1.50%
1950	1.75%	1.50%	1.75%
1951	1.75%	1.75%	1.75%
1952	1.75%	1.75%	1.75%
1953	2%	1.75%	2%
1954	2%	1.50%	2%
1955	2.50%	1.50%	2.50%
1956	3%	2.50%	3%
1957	3.50%	3%	3%
1958	3%	1.75%	3%
1959	4%	2.50%	4%
1960	4%	3%	3%
1961	3%	3%	3%
1962	3%	3%	3%
1963	3.50%	3%	3.50%
1964	4%	3.50%	4%
1965	4.50%	4%	4.50%
1966	4.50%	4.50%	4.50%
1967	4.50%	4%	4.50%
1968	5.50%	4.50%	5.50%
1969	6%	5.5%	6%
1970	6%	5.5%	5.5%
1971	5%	4.5%	4.5%
1972	4.5%	4.5%	4.5%
1973	7.5%	4.5%	7.5%
1974	8%	7.75%	7.75%

Year	High	Low	Close
1975	7.75%	6%	6%
1976	6%	5.25%	5.25%
1977	6%	5.25%	6%
1978	9.5%	6%	9.5%
1979	12%	9.5%	12%
1980	13%	10%	13%
1981	14%	12%	12%
1982	12%	8.5%	8.5%
1983	8.5%	8.5%	8.5%
1984	9%	8%	8%
1985	8%	7.5%	7.5%
1986	7.5%	5.5%	5.5%

FEDERAL FUNDS RATE

Source: Federal Reserve Board, Interactive Data Corporation

This graph shows the movement of the federal funds rate, which is the rate at which banks with excess reserves lend to banks needing overnight loans to meet reserve requirements. The fed funds rate is the most sensitive of all short-term interest rates, and therefore it is carefully watched by credit market analysts as a precursor of moves in other interest rates. For instance, when the fed funds rate consistently stays below the discount rate, analysts often anticipate that the Federal Reserve will cut the discount rate.

Year	High	Low	Close
1968	6.12%	4.6%	6.02%
1969	9.19%	6.3%	8.97%
1970	8.98%	4.9%	4.9%
1971	5.57%	3.71%	4.14%
1972	5.33%	3.29%	5.33%
1973	10.78%	5.94%	9.95%
1974	12.92%	8.53%	8.53%
1975	7.13%	5.20%	5.20%
1976	5.48%	4.65%	4.65%
1977	6.56%	4.61%	7.75%
1978	10.03%	6.70%	10.03%
1979	13.78%	10.01%	13.78%
1980	18.90%	9.03%	18.90%
1981	19.08%	12.37%	12.37%
1982	14.94%	8.95%	8.95%
1983	9.56%	8.51%	9.47%
1984	11.64%	8.38%	8.38%
1985	8.58%	7.53%	8.27%
1986	16.17%	5.56%	14.35%

INDEX OF LEADING ECONOMIC INDICATORS

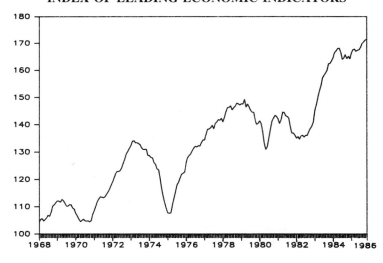

Source: Bureau of Economic Analysis of the U.S. Commerce Department, Interactive Data Corporation

This graph shows the movement of the Index of Leading Economic Indicators. This composite of 12 economic indicators (adjusted for inflation) is designed to forecast whether the economy will gain or lose strength, and is therefore an important tool for economists and others doing business planning. On the whole, it has been an accurate barometer of future economic activity. The 12 components of the Index are: average workweek of production workers; average weekly claims for unemployment insurance; new orders for consumer goods and materials; vendor performance (companies receiving slower deliveries from suppliers); net business formation; contracts for plant and equipment; new building permits; inventory changes; sensitive materials prices; stock prices; money supply as measured by M-2; and business and consumer borrowing. The index is released monthly.

Year	High	Low	December
1968	111.5	104.4	111.5
1969	112.7	109.1	109.1
1970	107.5	104.4	107.3
1971	118.0	108.6	118.0
1972	131.4	119.2	131.4
1973	134.2	128.7	128.7
1974	128.7	109.2	109.2
1975	122.8	107.6	122.8
1976	134.5	126.1	134.5
1977	142.4	134.5	142.4
1978	147.9	141.0	147.2
1979	149.3	140.1	140.5
1980	143.4	130.9	143.0
1981	144.6	136.2	136.2
1982	140.9	134.7	140.9
1983	163.4	145.2	163.4
1984	168.2	163.9	164.1
1985	171.5	166.3	171.5

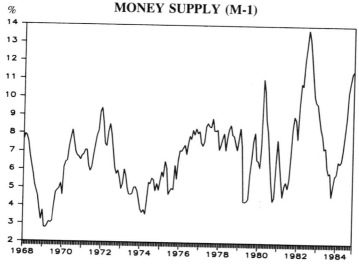

MONEY SUPPLY (M-1)

Source: Federal Reserve Board, Interactive Data Corporation

This graph shows the movement of changes in the money supply in the United States, as measured by M-1. The line represents the rolling 12-month change in the money supply. The percentage change is calculated by comparing, for example, the December 1985 figure with the December 1984 figure. This method best shows the ups and downs of the growth of the amount of money circulating in the economy. The rate of change in the money supply is important because it has an important bearing on how quickly or slowly the economy will be growing in the future. Monetarist economists believe changes in the money supply are the key to economic ups and downs. When the Federal Reserve, which strongly influences the money supply through its conduct of open market operations and by setting bank reserve requirements and the discount rate, wants the economy to expand, it eases the money supply. When the Fed is concerned that inflation may be accelerating, it will slow the economy by tightening the money supply. The components of the M-1 measure of the money supply are: currency in circulation; commercial and mutual savings bank demand deposits; NOW and ATS (automatic transfer from savings) accounts; credit union share drafts; and nonbank travelers checks.

Year	High	Low	December
1968	7.93%	3.21%	3.21%
1969	5.25%	2.77%	5.25%
1970	8.19%	4.61%	6.56%
1971	9.19%	5.93%	9.19%
1972	9.42%	5.52%	5.52%
1973	6.05%	4.36%	4.36%
1974	5.57%	3.55%	4.90%
1975	6.60%	4.68%	6.60%
1976	8.33%	6.90%	8.06%
1977	8.89%	7.37%	8.26%
1978	8.54%	7.13%	7.16%
1979	8.37%	4.30%	6.63%
1980	11.08%	4.34%	6.51%
1981	9.04%	4.59%	8.83%
1982	13.79%	7.79%	8.83%
1983	9.70%	4.64%	5.78%
1984	11.57%	5.89%	11.57%

PRIME RATE

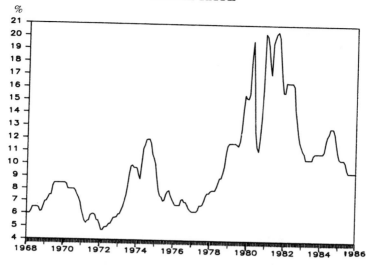

Source: Bureau of Economic Analysis of the U.S. Commerce Department, Interactive Data Corporation

This graph shows the movement of the prime rate, which is the interest rate banks charge their most creditworthy customers. The rate is determined by market forces affecting a bank's cost of funds and the rates borrowers will accept. The prime often moves up or down in concert with the Federal Reserve discount rate. The prime rate tends to become standard across the banking industry when a major bank moves its rate up or down. The rate is a key interest rate, since loans to less-creditworthy customers are often tied to the prime.

Year	High	Low	Close
1968	6.75%	6%	6.75%
1969	8.5%	6.75%	8.5%
1970	8.5%	6.75%	6.75%
1971	6.75%	5.25%	5.25%
1972	6%	5%	6%
1973	10%	6%	10%
1974	12%	8.75%	10.5%
1975	10.5%	7%	7%
1976	7.25%	6.25%	6.25%
1977	7.75%	6.5%	7.75%
1978	11.75%	7.75%	11.75%
1979	15.75%	11.5%	15%
1980	21.50%	10.75%	21.50%
1981	20.5%	15.75%	15.75%
1982	17%	11.5%	11.5%
1983	11.5%	10.5%	11%
1984	13%	10.75%	10.75%
1985	10.75%	9.5%	9.5%
1986	9.5%	6.75%	7.5%

PRODUCER PRICE INDEX

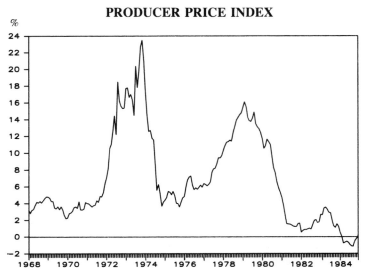

Source: U.S. Bureau of Labor Statistics, Interactive Data Corporation

This graph shows the movement of the Producer Price Index. The line represents the rolling 12–month average of changes in producer prices—a method that best shows the ups and downs of the wholesale inflation rate. Each month, the U.S. Bureau of Labor Statistics measures changes in the prices of all commodities, at all stages of processing, produced for sale in primary markets in the United States. Approximately 3400 commodity prices are collected by the Bureau from sellers. The prices are generally the first significant large-volume commercial transaction for each commodity—either the manufacturer's selling price or the selling price from an organized commodity exchange. The major commodity groups that are represented in the PPI are: farm products; processed food and feed; textiles and apparel; hides, skins, and leather; fuels; chemicals; rubber and plastic products; lumber and wood products; pulp and paper products; metals and metal products; machinery and equipment; furniture and household durables; nonmetallic mineral products; and transportation equipment. The PPI is important not only because it is a good gauge of what is happening in the industrial economy, but also because it gives an indication of the future trend in consumer prices.

Year	Annual Percent Change	Year	Annual Percent Change
1961	−0.2%	1974	18.9%
1962	0%	1975	9.2%
1963	−0.1%	1976	4.6%
1964	0.4%	1977	6.1%
1965	3.4%	1978	7.8%
1966	1.7%	1979	12.6%
1967	1.0%	1980	14.1%
1968	2.8%	1981	9.2%
1969	4.8%	1982	2.0%
1970	2.2%	1983	1.3%

Year	Annual Percent Change	Year	Annual Percent Change
1971	4.0%	1984	2.4%
1972	6.5%	1985	− .6%
1973	13.1%		

UNEMPLOYMENT RATE (CIVILIAN)

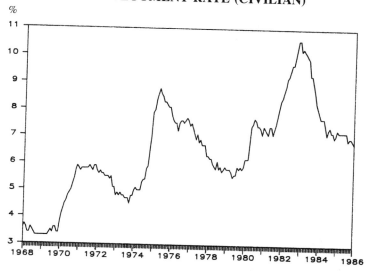

Source: U.S. Bureau of Labor Statistics, Interactive Data Corporation

This graph shows the movement of the unemployment rate. This is the rate of civilians, 16 years of age and older, who were not employed, and who made specific efforts to find a job within the previous four weeks and who were available for work. Persons on layoff from a job or waiting to report to a new job within 30 days are also classified as unemployed. The unemployment rate is a lagging indicator— that is, it rises months after business has already slowed down, and it falls months after business has picked up.

MONTHLY RATE

Year	High	Low	December
1968	3.7%	3.3%	3.3%
1969	3.6%	3.3%	3.4%
1970	5.9%	3.8%	5.9%
1971	5.9%	5.7%	5.9%
1972	5.7%	5.1%	5.1%
1973	4.9%	4.5%	4.8%
1974	7%	5%	7%
1975	8.8%	7.9%	8.1%
1976	7.8%	7.2%	7.6%

Year	High	Low	December
1977	7.5%	6.3%	6.3%
1978	6.3%	5.7%	5.9%
1979	5.9%	5.5%	5.9%
1980	7.7%	6.2%	7.1%
1981	8.4%	7.1%	8.4%
1982	10.6%	8.5%	10.6%
1983	10.3%	8.1%	8.1%
1984	7.9%	7.0%	7.1%
1985	7.3%	6.8%	6.8%

PUBLICLY TRADED COMPANIES

On the following pages, you will find a comprehensive list of the companies whose common stock is traded on the New York Stock Exchange, the American Stock Exchange, and the over-the-counter market—some 4700 companies in all. The OTC stocks listed here are those in the National Market System of NASDAQ (National Association of Securities Dealers Automated Quotation system). Each of the three markets is listed separately. In addition, there is a listing of selected major companies traded on the Toronto Stock Exchange.

Following the overall company lists are two lists of special interest: the first presents companies offering free or reduced-price goods or services to shareholders; the second, foreign companies whose American Depositary Receipts (ADRs) are traded in the United States.

The New York Stock Exchange is the home of almost all the largest, most established public companies, though many smaller companies are traded there as well. The NYSE operates with a specialist system of trading, where buyers and sellers are brought together by a specialist on the floor of the exchange. The specialist steps in to buy or sell shares if there is an imbalance of orders on one side of the market or the other. The requirements the NYSE imposes for being listed on the exchange are the most stringent of all the places where stocks are traded in the United States. Two of the most important requirements are that a corporation must have (1) a minimum aggregate market value of $16 million and (2) an annual net income topping $2.5 million before federal income taxes.

The American Stock Exchange is where mostly medium and smaller-sized companies are traded. In addition, many foreign companies are listed on the AMEX. The American Stock Exchange uses the same specialist trading system employed by the New York Stock Exchange. The AMEX's listing requirements are less stringent than those of the NYSE, though the exchange requires that a company have a reliably profitable business.

The over-the-counter market is populated for the most part with smaller, emerging growth companies without long histories of earnings and dividends. In the 1980s, however, many firms that formerly graduated from the OTC market to the AMEX and NYSE as they increased in size have instead been staying on the OTC market. Unlike on the two exchanges, trading on the OTC market is done under a system of competing marketmakers who communicate by telephone and computer terminal. The market is overseen by the National Association of Securities Dealers, a self-regulatory organization. Price quotes that appear in newspapers come from the NASDAQ electronic system. The requirements for being traded over-the-counter are far less stringent than those of the NYSE and AMEX. For the most part, companies whose shares are being publicly traded for the first time, called initial public offerings, begin to trade on the OTC market. The list of companies in this section does not include every company whose stock is traded over the counter. Instead, it features the great majority of the most actively traded companies on NASDAQ. As a group, they are called the National Market System stocks. There is more price and volume information available on NMS stocks than on other OTC stocks, which tend to be of very small companies.

Each listing includes up to seven elements: the company's name, stock symbol, address, telephone number, line of business, if it has a dividend reinvestment plan, and whether options are traded on the stock.

Company Name   We have used each company's full corporate name, though words such as Incorporated, Company, and Corporation may be abbreviated as Inc., Co., and Corp. The lists are arranged alphabetically, by company name.

Stock Symbol   The stock symbol—usually three or four capital letters—follows each company's name. When asking a broker to look up the price or other information about a stock, it is usually necessary to provide the stock symbol. The symbol is then entered into a computer terminal, which retrieves data about the company. The stock symbol is not the same abbreviation as one sees in newspaper stock tables, however.

Address   The street address or post office box listed refers to the executive office at the headquarters of the company. In the case of foreign companies, the home address of the company usually is listed, though the address of a contact office in the United States may be given.

Telephone Number   The phone number is that of the executive offices at the company's headquarters. If you require further information about the company because you are considering whether to invest in it, you should ask for the investor relations department, which will send annual and quarterly financial reports and other data about the firm.

Line Of Business   This is a brief description of the main business of the company. Some companies specialize in a narrow field—in this case, the description is quite specific to its line of business. Other companies engage in diverse activities, and for them we have listed the largest segments of their business, or when no business is dominant, we have labeled the company a conglomerate. To find out each company's exact product line, you can call or write the firm's investor relations department.

Dividend Reinvestment Plan   If the letters DRP are in brackets on the final line of an entry for a company, this means that shareholders can use a company plan to reinvest cash dividends into more of the company's stock, instead of receiving a cash payment. Usually, there will be little or no commission cost to the shareholder who participates in a plan. Many companies also allow shareholders to make cash payments in addition to reinvesting dividends to buy more shares, usually at no commission charge.

Some companies offer an extra bonus in their dividend reinvestment plan. Companies on the list with a 5% following DRP offer a 5% discount on the purchase price of newly issued stock for the amount of reinvested dividends. Thus, a shareholder who reinvested $100 of dividends would be credited with purchasing $105 worth of stock. Some companies allow the 5% discount on both dividends reinvested as well as additional cash put up by the shareholder.

Most companies allow shareholders to participate in a dividend reinvestment plan while owning as little as one share. If the dividend is not sufficient to purchase a full share, a shareholder's account is credited with the appropriate fractional share.

The information on dividend reinvestment plans was compiled by Duane Frederic, who publishes a monthly list tracking company plans. A sample copy of this list is available for $10 from Mr. Frederic at 8908 East Pilgrim Drive, Chagrin Falls, Ohio 44022, or by calling (216) 543-6327.

Options   Also on the final line of a company entry is a notation of whether options are traded on the company's stock. This is signified with the letter O. Stock options usually are traded on the American Stock Exchange, the Chicago Board Options Exchange, the Pacific Stock Exchange, or the Philadelphia Stock Exchange. Options of larger companies may trade on more than one of these exchanges simultaneously. Stock options can be used by an investor to make a speculative bet on a stock going up or down. Other investors use options to increase their income or hedge the value of their stock holdings.

The information in these lists was supplied mainly by the New York Stock Exchange, the American Stock Exchange, the National Association of Securities Dealers, and the Toronto Stock Exchange. We would like to thank these organizations for their enormous help.

In today's fast-moving world of finance and investment, a company may merge with another, add or drop a line of business, change its address or telephone number, move from one exchange to another, or even go out of business. Despite such changes, this list will remain an indispensable resource for investors and others in the finance and investment community.

NEW YORK STOCK EXCHANGE

AAR Corp. AIR
2100 Touhy Avenue
Elk Grove Village, IL 60007 (312) 439-3939
aerospace components   [DRP]

Abbott Laboratories ABT
Abbott Park
North Chicago, IL 60064 (312) 937-6100
medical supplies   [DRP O]

ACCO World Corp. ACO
2215 Sanders Road Suite 250
Northbrook, IL 60062 (312) 480-9700
office supplies

Acme Electric Corp. ACE
20 Water Street
Cuba, NY 14760 (716) 968-2400
power conversion equipment, transformers

Acme-Cleveland Corp. AMT
Pepper Pike Place Suite 300, Chagrin Blvd
Cleveland, OH 30195 (216) 292-2100
machine tools   [DRP]

Adams Express Co. ADX
201 North Charles Street
Baltimore, MD 21201 (301) 752-5900
closed-end mutual fund   [DRP]

Adams-Millis Corp. ALL
225 North Elm
High Point, NC 27261 (919) 889-7071
hosiery, yarn

Adobe Resources Corp. ADB
645 Madison Avenue
New York, NY 10022 (212) 754-0050
oil and gas exploration and development

Advanced Micro Devices, Inc. AMD
901 Thompson Place
Sunnyvale, CA 94086 (408) 732-2400
semiconductors   [O]

Advanced Systems Inc. ASY
2340 South Arlington Heights Road
Arlington Heights, IL 60005 (312) 981-4260
video training courses

Advest Group (The) ADV
6 Central Row
Hartford, CT 06103 (203) 525-1421
brokerage firm   [DRP]

Aetna Life And Casualty Co. AET
151 Farmington Avenue
Hartford, CT 06115 (203) 273-0123
insurance   [DRP 5%]

AFG Industries AFG
18200 von Karmen Suite 700
Irvine, CA 92715 (714) 553-9026
glass products

A.G. Edwards Inc. AGE
1 North Jefferson
St. Louis, MO 63103 (314) 289-3000
brokerage firm   [O]

AGS Computers Inc. AGS
1139 Spruce Drive
Mountainside, NJ 07092 (201) 687-9200
software and engineering services

Ahmanson H.F. & Co. AHM
3731 Wilshire Boulevard
Los Angeles, CA 90010 (213) 487-4277
savings and loan   [O]

Aileen Inc. AEE
331 East 38th Street
New York, NY 10016 (212) 679-7010
apparel, sportswear

Air Products and Chemicals Inc. APD
P. O. Box 538
Allentown, PA 18105 (215) 481-4911
industrial gases/equipment, chemicals [DRP O]

Airborne Freight Corp. ABF
3101 Western Avenue
Seattle, WA 98111 (206) 285-4600
freight forwarding

Ala Moana Hawaii Properties ALA
615 Battery Street Suite 600
San Francisco, CA 94111 (415) 627-9205
real estate

Alaska Air Group Inc. ALK
19300 Pacific Highway South
Seattle, WA 98188 (206) 433-3200
regional airline   [O]

Alberto Culver Co. ACV
2525 Armitage Ave
Melrose Park, IL 60164 (312) 450-3000
personal care products

Albertsons Inc. ABS
250 Parkcenter Boulevard
Boise, ID 83707 (208) 344-7441
food stores

Alcan-Aluminum, Ltd AL
1188 Sherbrooke Street West
Montreal Quebec CDA HC3 3H2 (514) 848-8000
aluminum refining   [DRP 5% O]

Alco Standard Corp. ASN
P O Box 834
Valley Forge, PA 19482 (215) 296-8000
conglomerate, industrial products,coal [DRP O]

Alexander & Alexander Services,Inc. AAL
1211 Avenue of the Americas
New York, NY 10036 (212) 840-8500
insurance brokers   [O]

Alexanders Inc. AL
500 7th Avenue
New York, NY 10018 (212) 560-2121
retailing

Alleghany Corp. Y
Park Avenue Plaza
New York, NY 10055 (212) 752-1356
financial services, steel tubing, screws

Allegheny International, Inc. AG
2 Oliver Plaza
Pittsburgh, PA 15230 (412) 562-4000
appliances and industrial equipment   [DRP]

Allegheny Power System Inc. AYP
320 Park Avenue
New York, NY 10022 (212) 752-2121
electric utility   [DRP]

Allen Group Inc. ALN
534 Broad Hollow Road
Melville, NY 11746 (516) 293-5500
auto parts,testing equipment   [DRP]

Allied Products Corp. ADP
10 South Riverside Plaza
Chicago, IL 60606 (312) 454-1020
agricultural products, fasteners

Allied-Signal Inc. ALD
Columbia Road & Park Avenue
Morristown, NJ 07960 (201) 455-2000
aerospace, chemicals, electronics   [DRP O]

Allied Stores Corp. ALS
1114 Avenue Of The Americas
New York, NY 10036 (212) 764-2000
department stores   [DRP O]

Allied Supermarkets ASU
8711 Meadowdale
Detroit, MI 48228 (313)943-3300
food supermarket chain

Allis-Chalmers Corp. AH
1205 South 70th Street
West Allis, WI 53214 (414) 475-2000
agricultural and industrial equipment   [O]

ALLTEL Corp. AT
100 Executive Parkway
Hudson, OH 44236 (216) 650-7000
telephone equipment and services   [DRP O]

Aluminum Co. of America AA
1501 Alcoa Building, 425 6th Avenue
Pittsburgh, PA 15219 (412)553-4545
aluminum production   [DRP]

Amax Inc. AMX
Amax Center
Greenwich, CT 06836 (203) 629-6000
minerals mining, oil and gas   [DRP 5% O]

AMCA International Ltd. AIL
Dartmouth National Bank Bldg
Hanover, NH 03755 (603) 643-5454
engineering and heavy construction

Amerada Hess Corp. AHC
1185 Avenue Of The Americas
New York, NY 10036 (212) 997-8500
oil and gas refining and marketing   [DRP O]

American Agronomics Corp. AGR
4600 West Cypress Street Suite 300
Tampa, FL 33607 (813) 872-9909
orange groves

American Bakeries Co. ABA
100 Park Avenue-17th Floor
New York, NY 10017 (212) 687-7225
baked foods

American Brands Inc. AMB
245 Park Avenue
New York, NY 10167 (212) 880-4200
tobacco, consumer products   [DRP O]

American Building Maintenance Ind. ABM
333 Fall Street
San Francisco, CA 94102 (415) 864-5150
building maintenance

American Business Products Inc. ABP
2690 Cumberland Parkway
Atlanta, GA 30339 (404) 434-1000
business forms   [DRP]

American Can Co. AC
American Lane
Greenwich, CT 06836 (203) 552-2000
containers, financial services   [DRP O]

American Capital Bond Fund, Inc. ACB
P O Box 3528
Houston, TX 77253 (713) 993-0500
closed-end bond fund   [DRP]

American Capital Convertible Sec. Inc. ACS
P O Box 3121
Houston, TX 77001 (713) 993-0500
closed end convertible fund   [DRP]

American Capital Management & Research ACA
P O Box 1411
Houston, TX 77251-1411 993-0500
investment advisory and distribution

American Century Corp. ACT
140 E Houston Street
San Antonio, TX 78205 (512) 226-2222
savings and loan, real estate

American Cyanamid Co. ACY
859 Berdan Ave One Cyanamid Plaza
Wayne, NJ 07470 (201) 831-2000
chemicals, drugs   [DRP O]

American District Telegraph Co. ADT
1 World Trade Center, Suite 9200
New York, NY 10048 (212) 558-1100
electronic protection services   [DRP]

American Electric Power Co., Inc. AEP
1 Riverside Plaza
Columbus, OH 43215 (614) 223-1000
electric utility   [DRP O]

American Express Co. AXP
American Express Plaza
New York, NY 10004 (212) 323-2000
financial services, travel   [DRP O]

American Family Corp. AFL
1932 Wynnton Road
Columbus, GA 31905 (404) 323-3431
insurance   [DRP]

American General Corp. AGC
2929 Allen Parkway
Houston, TX 77019 (713) 522-1111
insurance, financial services   [DRP O]

American Heritage Investment Corp AHL
11 E Forsyth
Jacksonville, FL 32202 (904) 354-1776
insurance   [DRP]

American Hoist and Derrick Co AHO
345 St Peter Street
St Paul, MN 55102 (612) 293-4567
cranes and construction equipment

American Home Products Corp AHP
685 Third Avenue
New York, NY 10017 (212) 878-5000
drugs, food and medical products   [DRP O]

American Information Technologies Corp AIT
225 West Randolph Street
Chicago, IL 60606 (312) 750-5000
telecommunications services   [DRP O]

American International Group Inc, AIG
70 Pine Street
New York, NY 10270 (212) 770-7000
insurance   [O]

American Medical International Inc. AMI
433 North Camden Drive
Beverly Hills, CA 90210 (213) 278-6200
hospitals, health services   [DRP]

American Motors Corp. AMO
27777 Franklin Road
Southfield, MI 48034 (313) 827-1000
auto manufacturer

American Standard Inc. AST
40 West 40th Street
New York, NY 10018 (212) 840-5100
plumbing and industrial products   [DRP]

American President Co. Ltd APS
1800 Harrison Street
Oakland, CA 94612 (415) 272-8000
shipping   [O]

American Savings & Loan Assoc. of Fla. AAA
17801 NW 2nd Avenue PO Box 4620
Miami, FL 33169 (305) 653-5353
savings and loan

American Ship Building Co. ABG
2502 Rocky Point Road
Tampa, FL 33607 (813) 228-8457
ship building

American Stores Co. ASC
709 East South Temple
Salt Lake City, UT 84127 (801) 539-0112
food and drug stores

American Telephone and Telegraph Co. T
550 Madison Avenue
New York, NY 10022 (212) 644-1000
telecommunications, computers   [DRP O]

American Water Works Co. Inc. AWK
3908 Kennett Pike
Wilmington, DE 19807 (302) 656-1681
water utility

Americana Hotels And Realty Corp AHR
532 South Michigan Avenue
Chicago, IL 60605 (312) 435-8900
hotels and real estate

Americus Trust for AT&T Common Shares TUA
15 West 39th Street
New York, NY 10018 (212) 575-8670
unit trust for AT&T holding companies

Ameron Inc. AMN
4700 Ramona Boulevard P O Box 3000
Monterey Park, CA 91754 (213) 268-4111
pipe, construction, steel products

Ames Department Stores ADD
248 Main Street
Rocky Hill, CT 06067 (203) 563-8234
department stores   [DRP]

Ametek Inc. AME
410 Park Avenue
New York, NY 10022 (212) 935-8640
instruments and industrial equipment

AMEV Securities Inc. AMV
Box 1386
St Paul, MN 55164 (612) 544-1531
closed-end investment company

Amfac, Inc. AMA
700 Bishop Street PO Box 3230
Honolulu, HI 96801 (415) 772-2000
hotels, retailing, food   [DRP]

Amfesco Industries Inc. QAFS
2 Amfesco Drive
Plainview, NY 11803 (516) 694-7272
casual footwear/slippers

Amoco Corp. AN
200 East Randolph Drive
Chicago, IL 60680 (312) 856-6111
oil and gas production and marketing [DRP O]

AMP Inc. AMP
470 Friendship Road
Harrisburg, PA 17109 (717) 564-0100
electronic connecting devices   [DRP O]

Ampco-Pittsburgh Corp. AP
700 Porter Building
Pittsburgh, PA 15219 (412) 456-4400
air and liquid handling equipment, metals

AMR Corp. AMR
P O Box 619616
DFW Airport, TX 75261 (817) 355-1234
airline flights and services   [O]

AMREP Corp. AXR
16 West 61st Street
New York, NY 10023 (212) 541-7300
real estate, magazine distributor

Amsouth Bancorporation ASO
1400 First National-Southern
Birmingham, AL 35288 (205) 583-4419
banking   [DRP 5%]

Amsted Industries Inc. AD
3700 Prudential Plaza
Chicago, IL 60601 (312) 645-1700
construction and railroad equipment

Anacomp,Inc. AAC
11550 N Meridian Street Suite 600
Carmel, IN 46032 (317) 844-9666
computer and micrographic services

Analog Devices, Inc. ADI
Route 1 Industrial Park
Norwood, MA 02062 (617) 329-4700
electronic measuring equipment

Anchor Hocking Corp. ARH
109 North Broad St
Lancaster, OH 43132 (614) 687-2111
glass products   [DRP]

Anderson Clayton Co. AYL
Suite 3800, 1100 Louisiana
Houston, TX 77001 (713) 651-0641
food products, insurance

Anderson, Greenwood & Co. AGV
5425 South Rice Avenue
Houston, TX 77081 (713) 668-0631
valve manufacturer   [DRP O]

Angelica Corp. AGL
700 Rosedale Avenue
St Louis, MO 63112 (314) 991-4150
uniform renting and manufacturing

Anheuser Busch Co. BUD
721 Pestalozzi Street
St Louis, MO 63118 (314) 577-2000
breweries and baking   [DRP O]

Anixter Brothers Inc. ANX
4711 Gold Road
Skokie, IL 60076 (312) 677-2600
cable distributor

Anthem Electronics Inc. ATM
174 Component Drive
San Jose, CA 95131 (408) 295-4200
semiconductor distributor

Anthony Industries, Inc. ANT
4900 Triggs Street
City Of Commerce, CA 90022 (213) 268-4877
sporting goods and apparel

Apache Corp. APA
730 Second Avenue
Minneapolis, MN 55402 (612) 347-8700
oil/gas exploration and production   [DRP O]

Apache Petroleum Co. APP
Forshay Tower
Minneapolis, MN 55402 (612) 347-8700
oil and gas partnerships

APL Corp. APL
PO Drawer K, 6917 Collins Avenue
Miami Beach, Florida 33141 (305) 866-7771
tissue paper, plastic products

Applied Magnetics Corp. APM
75 Robin Hill Road
Goleta, CA 93117 (805) 964-4881
computer equipment and components

Archer Daniels Midland Co. ADM
4666 Faries Parkway
Decatur, IL 52525 (217) 424-5200
grain processing, food products   [O]

Arkansas Best Corp. ABZ
1000 South 21st Street
Fort Smith, AR 92901 (501) 785-6000
trucking

Arkla, Inc. ALG
PO Box 21734, 525 Milam Street
Shreveport, LA 71151 (318) 226-2700
natural gas, various manufacturing   [DRP O]

Arlen Corp. ARE
1501 Broadway
New York, NY 10036 (212) 719-9911
steel products

Armada Corp. ABW
630 Buhl Building
Detroit, Michigan 48226 (313) 963-3100
specialty alloys

Armco, Inc. AS
703 Curtis Street
Middletown, OH 45043 (513) 425-6541
steel producer   [O]

Armstrong Rubber Co. ARM
500 Sargent Drive
New Haven, CT 06536 (203) 784-2200
tires and rubber products

Armstrong World Industries, Inc. ACK
P O Box 3001 West Liberty Street
Lancaster, PA 17604 (717) 397-0611
flooring products   [DRP]

Arrow Electronics Inc. ARW
767 Fifth Avenue
New York, NY 10153 (212) 935-6100
electronics distributor

Artra Group Inc. ATA
500 Central Avenue
Northfield, IL 60093 (312) 628-2554
plastics, metals, machinery

Arvin Industries Inc. ARV
1531 13th Street
Columbus, IN 47201 (812) 379-3000
auto parts   [DRP]

ARX, Inc. ARX
South Service Road
Plainview, NY 11803 (516) 694-6700
military and industrial products

ASA Ltd.Inc. ASA
P O Box 39
Chatham, NJ 07928 (201) 635-0122
closed-end gold mutual fund   [DRP O]

ASARCO Inc. AR
180 Maiden Lane
New York, NY 10038 (212) 510-2000
metals mining   [DRP O]

Ashland Oil Inc. ASH
Ashland Drive
Russell, KY 41169 (606) 329-3333
oil refining, chemicals, coal   [DRP 5% O]

Associated Dry Goods Corp. DG
417 5th Avenue
New York, NY 10016 (212) 679-8700
department stores   [DRP]

Athlone Industries Inc. ATH
200 Webro Road
Parsippany, NJ 07054 (201) 887-9100
specialty metals, fasteners

Atlantic City Electric Co. ATE
1199 Black Horse Pike
Pleasantville, NJ 08232 (609) 645-4100
electric utility   [DRP]

Atlantic Richfield Co. ARC
515 South Flower Street
Los Angeles, CA 90075 (213) 486-3511
oil/gas exploration and marketing   [DRP O]

Atlas Corp. AZ
353 Nassau Street
Princeton, NJ 08540 (609) 921-2000
hose manufacturer, uranium mining

Augat, Inc. AUG
89 Forbes Blvd PO Box 425
Mansfield, MA 02048 (617) 543-4300
electromechancial components

Automatic Data Processing Inc. AUD
One ADP Boulevard
Roseland, NJ 07068 (201) 994-5000
data processing   [O]

Avalon Corp. AVL
645 Madison Avenue
New York, NY 10022 (212) 751-8700
real estate, oil and gas exploration

AVEMCO Corp. AVE
411 Aviation Way
Frederick, MD 21701 (301) 694-5700
insurance, finance, aviation

Avery International Corp. AVY
150 North Orange Grove Boulevard
Pasadena, CA 91103 (818) 304-2000
self-adhesive labels and paper products

Avnet Inc. AVT
767 Fifth Avenue
New York, NY 10153 (212) 644-1050
electronics distributor   [DRP O]

Avon Products, Inc. AVP
9 West 57th Street
New York, NY 10019 (212) 546-6015
cosmetics, health care   [DRP O]

AVX Corp. AVX
60 Cutter Mill Road
Great Neck, NY 11021 (516) 829-8500
ceramic capacitors

Aydin Corp. AYD
700 Dresher Road PO Box 349
Horsham, PA 19044 (215) 657-7510
microwave, data communications equipment

AZP Group Inc. AZP
411 North Central Avenue
Phoenix, AZ 85036 (602) 250-1000
electric utility   [DRP]

Bairnco Corp BZ
200 Park Avenue
New York, NY 10017 (212) 490-8722
lighting and electrical products

Baker International Corp. BKO
P O Box 2274 Terminal Annex
Los Angeles, CA 90054 (714) 634-2333
oil field services, heavy machinery   [DRP O]

Baldor Electric Co. BEZ
5711 South 7th Street
Fort Smith, AR 72902 (501) 646-4711
electric motors

Baldwin United Corp. QBDW
1801 Gilbert Avenue
Cincinnati, OH 45202 (513) 852-7821
financial services

Ball Corp. BLL
345 South High Street
Muncie, IN 47305 (317) 747-6100
metal/glass containers, aerospace   [DRP 5%]

Bally Manufacturing Corp. BLY
2640 West Belmont Avenue
Chicago, IL 60618 (312) 399-1300
casino, health clubs, theme parks   [O]

Bally's Park Place Inc. BPP
Park Place and the Boardwalk
Atlantic City, NJ 08401 (609) 340-2000
hotels, motels, resorts

Baltimore Gas & Electric BGE
Gas & Electric Building, Charles Center
Baltimore, MD 21203 (301) 234-5811
electric and gas utility   [DRP]

Banc One Corp. ONE
100 East Broad Street
Columbus, OH 43271 (614) 463-5631
banking   [DRP]

Banco Central SA BCM
50 Broadway
New York, NY 10004 (212) 785-0700
banking

BancTEXAS Group Inc. BTX
1525 Elm Street
Dallas, TX 75201 (214) 969-6111
banking

Bandag Inc. BDG
Bandag Center
Muscatine, IA 52861 (319) 262-1400
tire retreader

Bank of Boston Corp. BKB
100 Federal Street
Boston, MA 02110 (617) 434-2200
banking   [DRP 5%]

Bank of New York Inc. BK
48 Wall Street
New York, NY 10005 (212) 530-1784
banking   [DRP 5% O]

Bank of Virginia Co. BKV
P O Box 25970
Richmond, VA 23260 (804) 771-7372
banking   [DRP 5%]

BankAmerica Corp. BAC
Bank Of America Center
San Francisco, CA 94104 (415) 622-3456
banking   [DRP O]

BankAmerica Realty Investors BRE
Bank of America Center, Suite 4275
San Francisco, CA 94104 (415) 622-3960
real estate investment trust

Bankers Trust NY Corp. BT
280 Park Avenue
New York, NY 10019 (212) 850-1120
banking and financial services   [DRP 3% O]

Banner Industries Inc. BNR
24500 Chagrin Blvd
Cleveland, OH 44122 (216) 464-3650
aerospace parts,tire retreading

Bard C R Inc. BCR
731 Central Avenue
Murray Hill, NJ 07974 (201) 277-8000
medical supplies   [DRP O]

Barnes Group Inc. B
123 Main Street
Bristol, CT 06010 (203) 583-7070
auto parts distributor   [DRP]

Barnett Banks Of Florida BBF
1 Laura Street
Jacksonville, FL 32202 (904) 791-7720
banking   [DRP]

Barry Wright Corp. BAR
1 Newton Executive Park
Newton Lower Falls, MA 02162 (617) 965-5800
computer shock protection equipment   [DRP]

BASIX Corp. BAS
110 East 59th Street
New York, NY 10022 (212) 758-1990
oil and gas equipment

Bausch & Lomb Inc. BOL
1 Lincoln First Square
Rochester, NY 14601 (716) 338-6000
contact lenses, optical instruments   [DRP O]

Baxter Travenol Laboratories Inc. BAX
1 Baxter Parkway
Deerfield, IL 60015 (312) 948-2000
medical supplies   [DRP O]

Bay Financial Corp. BAY
2 Faneuil Hall Marketplace
Boston, MA 02109 (617) 742-7550
real estate investment trust

Baystate Gas Co. BGC
120 Royall Street
Canton, MA 02021 (617) 828-8650
gas utility   [DRP]

Bear Stearns Companies Inc. BSC
55 Water Street
New York, NY 10041 (212) 952-5000
brokerage firm

Bearings Inc. BER
3600 Euclid Ave
Cleveland, OH 44115 (216) 881-2828
bearings and power transmissions

Becor Western Inc. BCW
1100 Milwaukee Avenue
South Milwaukee, WI 53172 (414) 768-4400
mining machinery, aerospace systems   [O]

Becton Dickinson Co. BDX
Mack Centre Drive
Paramus, NJ 07652 (201) 967-3700
medical supplies   [DRP O]

Beker Industries QBKI
124 West Putnam Avenue
Greenwich, CT 06830 (203) 622-5700
phosphate fertilizers

Belding Hemingway Co. Inc. BHY
1430 Broadway
New York, NY 10018 (212) 944-6040
fabrics, threads, buttons

Bell And Howell Co. BHW
5215 Old Orchard Road
Skokie, IL 60077 (312) 470-7100
educational aids, information systems   [DRP]

Bell Atlantic Corp. BEL
1600 Market Street
Philadelphia, PA 19103 (215) 466-9900
telecommunications   [DRP O]

Bell Canada Enterprises Inc. BCE
Box 6190 Station A
Montreal, QB, CDA H3C 3A7 (514) 394-7000
telecommunications   [DRP 5% O]

Bell Industries BI
11812 San Vicente Boulevard
Los Angeles, CA 90067 (213) 826-6778
electronics distributor, recreation

BellSouth Corp. BLS
1155 Peachtree Street NE
Atlanta, GA 30367-6000 (404) 249-2000
telecommunications   [DRP 54% O]

Belo A H Corp. BLC
Young & Houston Streets
Dallas, TX 75265 (214) 745-8730
publishing, broadcasting and CATV

Bemis Co. Inc. BMS
800 Northstar Center
Minneapolis, MN 55402 (612) 340-6000
consumer/industrial packaging material [DRP]

Beneficial Corp. BNL
Beneficial Building
Wilmington, DE 19899 (302) 798-0800
personal credit, financial services   [DRP]

Benequity Holdings BH
3700 Wilshire Boulevard
Los Angeles, CA 90010 (213) 387-6537
real estate

Benguet Corp. BE
1110 Vermont Avenue Suite 600
Washington, DC 20085
gold and copper mining

Berkey Inc. BKY
1 Water Street
White Plains, NY 10601 (914) 997-9700
photo equipment and supplies

Best Products Co. BES
Parham Road at Interstate 95
Richmond, VA 23227 (804) 261-2000
catalog showroom retailing

Bethlehem Steel Corp. BS
701 East Third Street
Bethlehem, PA 18016 (215) 694-2424
steel mills, steel products   [DRP O]

Beverly Enterprises BEV
873 South Fair Oaks Avenue
Pasadena, CA 90105 (818) 577-6111
nursing homes   [DRP O]

B.F. Saul Real Estate Investment Trust BFS
8401 Connecticut Avenue
Chevy Chase, MD 20015 (301) 986-6000
real estate investment trust

Big Three Industries Inc. BIG
3535 West 12th Street
Houston, TX 77008 (713) 868-0333
oil and gas services, industrial gases

Biocraft Laboratories Inc. BCL
92 Route 46
Elmwood Park, NJ 07407 (201) 796-3434
generic drugs

Black & Decker Corp. BDK
701 East Joppa Road
Towson, MD 21204 (301) 583-3900
power tools and household appliances [DRP O]

Black Hills Power And Light Co. BHP
625 9th Street
Rapid City, SD 57709 (605) 348-1700
electric utility, coal mining   [DRP 5%]

Blair John Co. BJ
717 5th Avenue
New York, NY 10022 (212) 603-5000
TV and radio, marketing services

Block (H&R) Inc. HRB
4410 Main Street
Kansas City, MO 64111 (816) 753-6900
tax return preparation, databases   [DRP]

BMC Industries Inc. BMC
1150 Amer. Nat. Bank Building
St Paul, MN 55101 (612) 228-6310
electronic equipment, optics

Boeing Co. BA
7755 East Marginal Way South
Seattle, WA 98108 (206) 655-2121
aircraft manufacturer   [O]

Boise Cascade Corp. BCC
1 Jefferson Square
Boise, ID 83728 (208) 384-6161
paper and wood products   [DRP O]

Bolt Beranek And Newman Inc. BBN
10 Moulton Street
Cambridge, MA 02238 (617) 491-1850
research, consulting services

Borden Inc. BN
277 Park Avenue
New York, NY 10017 (212) 573-4000
dairy and food products, chemicals   [DRP O]

Borg-Warner Corp. BOR
200 South Michigan Avenue
Chicago, IL 60604 (312) 322-8500
capital goods, plastics, financial   [DRP O]

Borman's Inc. BRF
P O Box 466, 18718 Borman Avenue
Detroit, MI 48232 (313) 270-1000
supermarkets

Boston Edison Co. BSE
800 Boylston Street
Boston, MA 02199 (617) 424-2000
electric utility   [DRP 5%]

Bowater Inc. BOW
1500 East Putnam Ave
Old Greenwich, CT 06870 (203) 656-7200
newsprint, coated paper   [DRP 5%]

Briggs & Stratton Corp. BGG
12301 West Wirth Street
Wauwatosa, WI 53222 (414) 259-5333
power equipment engines, locks   [DRP]

Bristol-Myers Co. BMY
345 Park Avenue
New York, NY 10022 (212) 546-4000
drugs, cosmetics, personal care   [DRP O]

British Land of America BLA
90 Broad Street - 12th floor
New York, NY 10004 (212) 509-4840
real estate investment trust

British Petroleum Co Ltd BP
620 5th Avenue 4th Floor
New York, NY 10020 (212) 887-9300
oil and gas production

British Telecommunications PLC BTY
150 East 52nd Street
New York, NY 10017 (212) 319-6518
telecommunications services in UK

Brock Hotel Corp. BHC
4441 West Airport Freeway
Irving, TX 75062 (214) 258-8500
lodging, restaurants

Brockway, Inc. BRK
Mc Cullough Avenue
Brockway, PA 15824 (814) 268-3015
glass/metal/plastic containers   [DRP]

Brooklyn Union Gas Co. BU
195 Montague Street
Brooklyn, NY 11201 (718) 643-2000
gas utility   [DRP]

Brown & Sharpe Manufacturing Co. BNS
P O Box 456, Frenchtown Road
North Kingston, RI 02852 (401) 886-2000
machine tools, hydraulics   [DRP]

Brown Group Inc. BG
8400 Maryland Avenue
St Louis, MO 63105 (314) 854-4000
footwear   [DRP]

Browning Ferris Industries Inc. BFI
14701 St. Mary's
Houston, TX 77079 (713) 870-8100
waste management   [DRP O]

Brunswick Corp. BC
1 Brunswick Plaza
Skokie, IL 60076 (312) 470-4700
recreation products   [DRP O]

Brush Wellman Inc. BW
17876 St Clair Avenue
Cleveland, OH 44110 (216) 443-1000
beryllium products   [DRP]

Bundy Corp. BNY
333 West Fort Street - 20th fl
Detroit, MI 48226 (313) 964-4244
steel tubing and engineered plastics

Bunker Hill Income Securities Inc. BHL
P O Box 4602, 1000 East Walnut Street
Pasadena, CA 91106 (213) 613-8656
closed-end bond mutual fund   [DRP]

Burlington Coat Factory Warehouse Corp BCF
Route 130
Burlington, NJ 08016 (609) 386-3374
apparel stores

Burlington Industries Inc. BUR
3330 West Friendly Avenue
Greensboro, NC 27420 (919) 379-2000
textiles,apparel   [DRP]

Burlington Northern Inc. BNI
999 Third Avenue
Seattle, WA (206) 467-3838
railroads, oil, gas, forest products   [DRP O]

Burndy Corp. BDC
Richards Avenue
Norwalk, CT 06850 (203) 838-4444
electrical connectors   [DRP]

Butler International Inc. BTL
110 Summit Avenue PO Box 460
Montvale, NJ 07645 (201) 573-8000
aircraft manufacturing and service

Buttes Gas & Oil Co. QBGO
1221 Broadway P O Box 2071
Oakland, CA 94612 (415) 839-1600
oil and gas production

C3 Inc. CEE
11425 Isaac Newton Square South
Reston, VA 22090 (703) 471-6000
computer systems,software

Cabot Corp. CBT
125 High Street
Boston, MA 02110 (617) 423-6000
carbon black, oil, gas   [DRP]

Caesars World Inc. CAW
1801 Century Park East
Los Angeles, CA 90067 (213) 552-2711
entertaining, gaming, resort facilities   [O]

CalFed Inc. CAL
5670 Wilshire Boulevard
Los Angeles, CA 90036 (213) 932-4200
banking and insurance   [O]

California REIT CT
601 Montgomery Street
San Francisco, CA 94111 (415) 433-1805
real estate investment trust

Callahan Mining Corp. CMN
6245 North 24th Street
Phoenix, AZ 85016 (602) 954-6115
silver mining, flexible hose

CalMat Co. CZM
3200 San Fernando Road
Los Angeles, CA 90065 (213) 258-2777
cement, concrete, stone products

Cameron Iron Works Inc. CIW
13013 Northwest Freeway
Houston, TX 7704 (713) 939-2211
oil tools, forgings, and valves

Campbell Red Lake Mines Ltd CRK
Suite 2700,1 First Canadian Place
Toronto, ON, CDA M5X 1H1 (416) 364-3453
gold mining   [O]

Campbell Resources Inc. CCH
55 Yonge Street
Toronto, ON, CDA M58 1J4 (416) 366-5201
copper mining

Campbell Soup Co. CPB
Campbell Place
Camden, NJ 08101 (609) 342-4800
food/canned and frozen   [DRP O]

Canadian Pacific Ltd. CP
123 Front Street West
Toronto, ON, CDA M5J 2M8 (403) 231-6100
integrated transportation systems   [DRP O]

Cannon Group Inc. CAN
640 San Vicente Boulevard
Los Angeles, CA 90048 (213)651-4700
film production and distribution

Capital Cities Communications-ABC Inc. CCB
24 East 51st Street
New York, NY 10022 (212) 421-9595
radio/TV broadcasting, publishing   [O]

Capital Holding Corp. CPH
Commonwealth Building
Louisville, KY 40232 (502) 560-2000
life, accident, health insurance   [DRP]

Carling O'Keefe Ltd CKB
79 St Clair Avenue East
Toronto, ON, CDA (416) 922-4848
brewers, wine, oil and gas   [O]

Carlisle Corp. CSL
1700 Dubois Tower, 511 Walnut Street
Cincinnati, OH 45202 (513) 241-2500
rubber, plastics, tires, wire

Carolina Freight Corp. CAO
1201 E Church Street PO Box 697
Cherryville, NC 28021 (704) 435-6811
trucking   [DRP]

Carolina Power & Light Co. CPL
P O Box 1551
Raleigh, NC 27602 (919) 836-6111
electric utility   [DRP 3%]

Carpenter Technology Corp. CRS
101 West Bern Street
Reading, PA 19603 (215) 371-2000
steel mills   [DRP]

Carrols Corps. CRL
968 James Street
Syracuse, NY 13203 (315) 424-0513
restaurant franchises, candy shops

Carson Pirie Scott & Co. CRN
1 South Street
Chicago, IL 60603 (312) 245-8000
department stores, floor coverings

Carter Hawley Hale Stores Inc. CHH
550 South Flower Street
Los Angeles, CA 90071 (213) 620-0150
retail/department stores   [DRP 5% O]

Carter-Wallace Inc. CAR
767 Fifth Ave
New York, NY 10022 (212) 758-4500
health care/personal care/pet products

Cascade Natural Gas Corp. CGC
222 Fairview Avenue North
Seattle, WA 98124 (206) 624-3900
gas utility   [DRP]

Castle & Cooke, Inc. CKE
50 California Street
San Francisco, CA 94111 (415) 986-3000
food products, real estate

Caterpillar Tractor Co. CAT
100 North East Adams Street
Peoria, IL 60602 (309) 675-1000
farm/construction/mining machinery [DRP O]

CBI Industries Inc. CBH
800 Jorie Boulevard
Oak Brook, IL 60521 (312) 654-7000
steel plate structures, tanks   [DRP]

CBS Inc. CBS
51 West 52nd Street
New York, NY 10019 (212) 975-6075
broadcasting, publishing   [DRP O]

CCX Inc. CCX
1 Old Country Road
Carle Place, NY 11514 (516)294-3380
wire and cable, alloy steels

Ceco Industries Inc. CCP
1400 Kensington Road
Oak Brook, IL 60521 (312) 789-1400
building products and concrete   [DRP]

Celanese Corp. CZ
1211 Avenue of the Americas
New York, NY 10036 (212) 719-8000
fibers, chemicals, plastics, paints   [DRP O]

Cenergy Corp. CRG
10210 North Central Expressway, Suite 500
Dallas, TX 75231 (214) 692-3800
oil and gas exploration, pipeline

Centel Corp. CNT
O'Hare Plaza 5725 East River Road
Chicago, IL 60631 (312) 399-2500
telephone,communications systems   [DRP]

Centerior Energy CX
3000 Madison Avenue
Toledo, OH 43652 (419) 259-5000
electric utility

Centex Corp. CTX
4600 Republic National Bank Tower
Dallas, TX 75201 (214) 748-7901
residential construction,oil and gas

Central & South West Corp. CSR
2121 San Jacinto Street,Suite 2500
Dallas, TX 72666-0164 (214) 754-1000
electric utility,gas and oil pipelines   [DRP]

Central Hudson Gas & Electric Corp CNH
South Road
Poughkeepsie, NY 12601 (914) 452-2000
electric and gas utility   [DRP]

Central Illinois Public Service Co CIP
607 East Adams Street
Springfield, IL 62701 (217) 523-3600
electric and gas utility   [DRP]

Central Louisiana Electric Co. CNL
415 Main Street
Pineville, LA 71360 (318) 445-8264
electric utility   [DRP 5%]

Central Maine Power Co. CTP
Edison Drive
Augusta, ME 04332 (207) 623-3521
electric utility   [DRP 5%]

Central Vermont Public Service Corp CV
77 Grove Street
Rutland, VT 05701 (802) 773-2711
electric utility   [DRP 5%]

Centronics Data Computer Corp. CEN
P O Box CS0905
Hudson, NH 03051 (603) 883-0111
computer printers

Century Telephone Enterprises, Inc. CTL
520 Riverside Drive
Monroe, IA 71201 (318) 387-5541
communications service   [DRP 5%]

Cenvill Investors, Inc. CVI
Century Village Adm. Building
West Palm Beach, FL 33409 (305) 686-2577
real estate investment trust

Certain-teed Corp. CRT
P O Box 860
Valley Forge PA 19482 (215) 687-5000
building materials,insulation

Champion International Corp. CHA
1 Champion Plaza
Stamford, CT 06921 (203) 358-7000
paper and containers, forest products   [O]

Champion Spark Plug Co. CHM
900 Upton Avenue P O Box 910
Toledo, OH 43601 (419) 535-2567
auto parts, accessories   [DRP]

Charter Co. QCHR
21 West Church Street
Jacksonville, FL 32231 (904) 358-4111
oil refining/marketing/production, gas [DRP]

Chase Manhattan Corp. CMB
1 Chase Manhattan Plaza
New York, NY 10005 (212) 552-2222
banking   [DRP 5% 0]

Chelsea Industries Inc. CHD
1360 Soldiers Field Road
Boston, MA 02135 (617) 787-9010
plastic products, electronic components

Chemed Corp. CHE
1200 Dubois Tower
Cincinnati, OH 45202 (513) 762-6900
specialty chemicals, health products   [DRP]

Chemical New York Corp. CHL
277 Park Avenue
New York, NY 10017 (212) 310-6161
banking   [DRP 5% 0]

Chesapeake Corp. CSK
19th & Main Streets
West Point, VA 23181 (804) 843-5000
paper products, containers   [DRP]

Chesebrough-Pond's Inc. CBM
33 Benedict Place
Greenwich, CT 06830 (203) 661-2000
health and beauty products, food   [DRP 5% 0]

Chevron Corp. CHV
225 Bush Street
San Francisco, CA 94120 (415) 894-7700
oil production/refining/marketing   [DRP O]

Chicago Milwaukee Corp. CHG
401 North Michigan Avenue
Chicago, IL 60606 (312) 822-0400
manufacturer/distributor of food equipment

Chicago Pneumatic Tool Co. CGG
6 East 44th Street
New York, NY 10017 (212) 850-6800
pneumatic and electrical machinery/tools

Chock Full O'Nuts Corp. CHF
370 Lexington Avenue
New York, NY 10017 (212) 532-0300
coffee, real estate

Christiana Companies,The CST
225 Broadway 7th Floor
San Diego, CA 92101 (714) 232-7399
real estate development

Chromalloy American Corp. CRO
Chromalloy Plaza,120 South Central Ave
St Louis, MO 6310 (314) 726-9200
metal fabrication, transportation, apparel

Chrysler Corp. C
12000 Chrysler Drive
Highland Park, MI 48288 (313) 956-5252
auto manufacturer   [DRP O]

Chubb Corp. CB
15 Mountain View Road
Warren, NJ 07061 (212) 612-4050
fire, marine, casualty insurance   [DRP]

Church's Fried Chicken Inc. CHU
P O Box BH001
San Antonio, TX 78284 (512) 735-9392
restaurants   [O]

Chyron Corp. CHY
865 Spagnoli Road
Melville, NY 11747 (516) 249-3018
electronic TV titling, graphics equipment

CIGNA Corp. CI
1 Logan Square
Philadelphia, PA 19103 (215) 557-5000
life, auto, fire, casualty insurance   [DRP O]

CILCORP Inc. CER
300 Liberty Street
Peoria, IL 61602 (309) 672-5271
electric utility   [DRP]

Cincinnati Bell Inc. CSN
201 East 4th Street
Cincinnati, OH 45202 (513) 397-9900
telephone service   [DRP]

Cincinnati Gas & Electric Co. CIN
139 East 4th Street
Cincinnati, OH 45202 (513) 381-2000
electric and gas utility   [DRP]

Cincinnati Milacron Inc. CMZ
4701 Marburg Ave
Cincinnati, OH 45209 (513) 841-8100
machine tools and accessories   [DRP O]

Circle K Corp. CKP
4500 South 40th Street
Phoenix, AZ 85040 (602) 437-0600
convenience food stores

Circuit City Stores Inc. CC
2040 Thalbro Street
Richmond, VA 23230 (804) 257-4292
retailer of video equipment, appliances

Circus Circus Enterprises Inc. CIR
2880 Las Vegas Boulevard South
Las Vegas, NV 89109 (702) 734-0410
casino-hotels

Citicorp CCI
399 Park Avenue
New York, NY 10043 (212) 559-1000
banking, financial services   [DRP O]

Clabir Corp. CLG
475 West Putnam Avenue
Greenwich, CT 06830 (203) 625-0300
military ordnance,food

Claire's Stores Inc. CLE
6095 N.W. 167th Street
Miami, FL 33015 (305) 558-2577
apparel stores

Clark Equipment Co. CKL
Circle Drive
Buchanan, MI 49107 (616) 697-8000
fork lifts, construction machinery   [DRP]

Clayton Homes Inc. CMH
7131 Clinton Highway
Knoxville, TN 37912 (615) 938-2529
manufactured homes producer

CLC of America Inc. CLC
1655 Des Peres Road
St Louis, MO 63131 (314) 966-3757
highway/marine transportation

Cleveland Cliffs Inc. CLF
1460 Union Commerce Building
Cleveland, OH 44115 (216) 241-2356
iron ore, oil and gas drilling

Clevepak Corp. CLV
2500 Westchester Avenue
Purchase, NY 10577 (914) 682-0400
paperboard, packaging products

Clorox Co. CLX
P O Box 24305
Oakland, CA 94605 (415) 271-7000
soaps and cleansers   [DRP O]

Club Med Inc. CMI
309 Grand Cayman Islands
Georgetown, British West Indies
operator of vacation resorts

CNA Financial Corp. CAF
CNA Plaza
Chicago, IL 60685 (312) 822-5000
fire, marine, casualty, title insurance

CNA Income Shares Inc. CNN
CNA Plaza
Chicago, IL 60685 (312) 822-4181
closed end bond mutual fund   [DRP]

CNW Corp. CNW
1 Northwestern Center
Chicago, IL 60606 (312) 559-7000
railroads [O]

Coachmen Industries Inc. COA
601 East Beardsley Avenue
Elkhart, IN 46515 (219) 262-0123
recreational vehicles

Coastal Corp. CGP
9 Greenway Plaza
Houston, TX 77046 (713) 877-1400
refining and marketing of oil, gas, coal [O]

Coca Cola Co. KO
P O Box 1734
Atlanta, GA 30301 (404) 898-2121
soft drinks, juices, entertainment [DRP O]

Coleco Industries Inc. CLO
945 Asylum Avenue
West Hartford, CT 06105 (203) 725-6000
toys and video games [O]

Coleman Co., Inc. CLN
250 North St Francis Avenue
Wichita, KS 67202 (316) 261-3211
outdoor products, heating equipment

Colgate Palmolive Co. CL
300 Park Avenue
New York, NY 10022 (212) 310-2000
household/personal/health items [DRP O]

Collins & Aikman Corp. CK
210 Madison Avenue
New York, NY 10016 (212) 578-1200
specialized textile products [DRP]

Collins Food International Inc. CF
12731 East Jefferson Boulevard
Los Angeles, CA 90066 (213) 827-2300
restaurants

Colt Industries Inc. COT
430 Park Avenue
New York, NY 10022 (212) 940-0400
diverse industrial products [DRP O]

Columbia Gas System, Inc. CG
20 Montchanin Road
Wilmington, DE 19807 (302) 429-5000
gas utility [DRP]

Columbia Savings and Loan Association CSV
8840 Wilshire Boulevard
Beverly Hills, CA 90211 (213) 657-6134
savings and loan

Combined International Corp. PMA
222 North Dearborn Street
Chicago, IL 60601 (312) 269-4000
insurance [DRP]

Combustion Engineering, Inc. CSP
900 Long Ridge Road
Stamford, CT 06902 (203) 329-8771
energy generation, engineering [DRP O]

Comdisco Inc. CDO
6400 Shafer Court
Rosemont, IL 60018 (312) 698-3000
remarket/lease IBM computer equipment [O]

Commercial Metals Co. CMC
3000 Diamond Park Drive
Dallas, TX 75247 (214) 631-4120
metals fabrication

Commodore International Ltd. CBU
950 Rittenhouse Road
Norristown, PA 19403 (215) 666-7950
computer systems, electronic products [O]

Commonwealth Edison Co. CWE
1 First National Plaza, 37th Floor
Chicago, IL 60690 (312) 294-4321
electric utility [DRP 5% O]

Commonwealth Energy System CES
P O Box 190
Cambridge, MA 02139 (617) 864-3100
electric and gas utility [DRP]

Communications Satellite Corp. CQ
950 L'Enfant Plaza South S W
Washington, DC 20024 (202) 863-6000
satellite telecommunications [DRP O]

Community Psychiatric Centers CMY
510 Washington Street
San Francisco, CA 94111 (415) 397-6151
acute psychiatric hospitals [O]

COMPAQ Computer Corp. CPQ
20555 FM 149
Houston, TX 77070 (713) 370-0670
computers

Compugraphic Corp. CPU
200 Ballarduale Street
Wilmington, MA 01887 (617) 658-5600
photo and typesetting equipment

Computer Sciences Corp. CSC
650 North Sepulveda Boulevard
El Segundo, CA 90245 (213) 615-0311
computer services [O]

Computervision Corp. CVN
201 Burlington Road
Bedford, MA 01730 (617) 275-1800
industrial automation computers   [O]

ConAgra Inc. CAG
Conagra Center, 1 Central Park Plaza
Omaha, NE 68102 (402) 978-4000
bakery, flour, feeds, poultry   [DRP]

Connecticut Energy Corp. CNE
880 Broad Street
Bridgeport, CT 06601 (203) 727-3000
gas utility   [DRP]

Connecticut Natural Gas Corp. CTG
233 Pearl Street
Hartford, CT 06103 (203) 727-3000
gas utility   [DRP]

Conrac Corp. CAX
3 Landmark Square
Stamford, CT 06901 (203) 348-2100
communications equipment,instruments [DRP]

Consolidated Edison Co. ED
4 Irving Place
New York, NY 10003 (212) 460-3458
electric and gas utility   [DRP O]

Consolidated Freightways Inc. CNF
3240 Hillview Avenue,P O Box 10340
Palo Alto, CA 94303 (415) 494-2900
trucking

Consolidated Natural Gas Co. CNG
4 Gateway Center
Pittsburgh, PA 15222 (412) 227-1000
gas utility, oil and gas production   [DRP]

Consumers Power Co. CMS
212 Michigan Avenue West
Jackson, MI 49201 (517) 788-0550
electric and gas utility

Continental Corp. CIC
180 Maiden Lane
New York, NY 10038 (212) 440-3980
property-casualty, life insurance   [DRP]

Continental Illinois Corp. (NEW) CIL
231 South La Salle Street
Chicago, IL 60697 (312) 828-2345
banking

Continental Illinois Holding Corp CIH
231 South La Salle Street
Chicago, IL 60697 (312) 828-2345
banking

Continental Information Systems Corp CNY
1000 James Street
Syracuse, NY 13203 (315) 425-1900
computer leasing

Continental Telecom Inc. CTC
245 Perimeter Center Parkway
Atlanta, GA 30345 (404) 391-8000
communications service and equipment [DRP O]

Control Data Corp. CDA
8100-34th Avenue South
Minneapolis, MN 55440 (612) 853-8100
computer hardware and services   [DRP O]

Cook United Inc. QCCF
16501 Rockside Road
Maple Heights, OH 44137 (216) 475-1000
discount department, wholesaler

Cooper Industries Inc. CBE
P O Box 4446
Houston, TX 77210 (713) 739-5400
electrical/electronic products   [DRP O]

Cooper Tire & Rubber Co. CTB
Lima & Western Avenues
Findlay, OH 45840 (419) 423-1321
tires

Coopervision Inc. EYE
3145 Porter Drive
Palo Alto, CA 94304 (415) 856-5000
eye care products   [O]

Copperweld Corp. COS
2 Oliver Plaza
Pittsburgh, PA 15222 (412) 263-3200
alloy steel,specialty tubing   [DRP]

Cordura Corp. CDU
2029 Century Park East,Suite 3210
Los Angeles, CA 90067 (213) 553-4646
insurance estimating data, services

Core Industries, Inc. CRI
500 North Woodward Avenue
Bloomfield Hills, MI 48013 (313) 642-3400
electronics,farm equipment,fluid controls

Corning Glass Works GLW
Houghton Park
Corning, NY 14830 (607) 974-9000
glass products, medical equipment   [DRP O]

Corroon & Black Corp. CBL
Wall Street Plaza
New York, NY 10005 (212) 363-4100
insurance brokers   [DRP]

Countrywide Credit Industries Inc. CCR
155 North Lake Avenue
Pasadena, CA 91109 (818) 304-8400
mortgage loan servicing

CP National Corp. CPN
1355 Willow Way
Concord, CA 94520 (415) 680-2606
electric,gas telephone utility   [DRP 5%]

CPC International Inc. CPC
International Plaza
Englewood Cliffs, NJ 07632 (201) 894-4000
grocery products,corn   [DRP]

Craig Corp. CRA
921 West Artesia Boulevard
Compton, CA 90220 (213) 537-1233
consumer electronics

Crane Co. CR
300 Park Avenue
New York, NY 10022 (212) 980-3600
fluid control equipment

Cray Research, Inc. CYR
608 2nd Avenue South
Minneapolis, MN 55402 (612) 333-5889
supercomputers   [O]

CRI Insured Mortgage Investments CRM
1 Central Plaza,11300 Rockville Pike
Rockville, MA 20852 (301) 468-9200
real estate investment partnerships

Crompton and Knowles Corp CNK
345 Park Avenue
New York, NY 10018 (212) 754-1660
industrial chemicals and machinery   [DRP]

Crown Cork & Seal Co., Inc. CCK
9300 Ashton Road
Philadelphia, PA 19136 (215) 698-5100
metal cans, filling & packaging machinery

Crown Zellerbach Corp. ZB
1 Bush Street
San Francisco, CA 94104 (415) 951-5000
paper and packaging   [DRP O]

CRS/Sirrine Inc. DA
1177 West Loop South
Houston, TX 77027 (713) 658-9511
architecture and engineering services

Crystal Brands Inc. CBR
1411 Broadway
New York, NY 10018 (212) 760-3200
sportswear, accessories

CSX Corp. CSX
1500 Federal Reserve Building
Richmond, VA 23219 (804) 782-1400
railroads, coal   [DRP O]

CTS Corp. CTS
905 North West Boulevard
Elkhart, IN 46514 (219) 293-7511
electronic components, metal products

Culbro Corp. CUC
605 3rd Avenue
New York, NY 10016 (212) 561-8700
tobacco products,snack foods

Cullinet Software, Inc. CUL
400 Blue Hill Drive
Westwood, MA 02090 (617) 329-7700
software   [O]

Cummins Engine Co. CUM
P O Box 3005
Columbus, IN 47202-3005 (812) 377-5000
diesel engines   [DRP]

Current Income Shares Inc. CUR
P O Box 30151 Terminal Annex
Los Angeles, CA 90030 (213) 480-6748
closed end bond mutual fund   [DRP]

Curtiss-Wright Corp. CW
1 Passaic Street
Woodridge, NJ 07075 (201) 777-3820
aerospace, process equipment

Cyclops Corp. CYL
650 Washington Road
Pittsburgh, PA 15228 (412) 343-4000
specialty steel,toll carbon   [DRP]

Dallas Corp. DLS
6750 LBJ Freeway
Dallas, TX 75240 (214) 233-6611
construction products and equipment

Damon Corp. DMN
115 4th Avenue
Needham Heights, MA 02194 (617) 449-0800
medical/institutional supplies

Dana Corp. DCN
4500 Dorr Street
Toledo, OH 43601 (419) 535-4500
auto parts, accessories   [DRP]

Danaher Corp. DHR
1645 Palm Beach Lakes Boulevard, Suite 700
West Palm Beach, FL 33401 (305) 471-2700
real estate investment trust

Daniel Industries Inc. DAN
P O Box 19097,1 River Way
Houston, TX 77056 (713) 960-1300
measuring and fluid control devices

Data Design Laboratories DDL
7925 Center Ave
Cucamonga, CA 91730 (714) 987-2511
engineering services

Data General Corp. DGN
4400 Computer Drive
Westboro, MA 01580 (617) 366-8911
minicomputers   [O]

Datapoint Corp. DPT
9725 Datapoint Drive
San Antonio, TX 78284 (512) 699-4427
data processing systems   [O]

Dayco Corp. DAY
333 West First Street
Dayton, OH 45402 (513) 226-7000
rubber and plastic products   [DRP]

Dayton Power & Light Co. DPL
Courthouse Plaza Southwest
Dayton, OH 45401 (513) 224-6000
electric and gas utility   [DRP]

Dayton-Hudson Corp. DH
777 Nicollet Mall
Minneapolis, MN 55402 (612) 370-6948
department/discount/specialty stores [DRP O]

DCNY Corp DCY
58 Pine Street
New York, NY 10005 (212) 248-8900
investment broker and banker

Dean Foods Co. DF
3600 North River Road
Franklin Park, IL 60131 (312) 625-6200
dairy and other food products   [DRP]

Deere & Co. DE
John Deere Road
Moline, IL 61265 (309) 752-8000
farm/construction/mining machinery [DRP O]

Delmarva Power & Light Co. DEW
800 King Street
Wilmington, DE 19899 (302) 429-3011
electric utility   [DRP]

Delta Air Lines, Inc. DAL
Atlanta Airport
Atlanta, GA 30320 (404) 765-2600
airline   [DRP O]

Deltona Corp. DLT
3250 S W 3rd Avenue
Miami, FL 33129 (305) 854-1111
real estate development

Deluxe Check Printers, Inc. DLX
1080 West Country Road
St. Paul, MN 55112 (612) 483-7355
imprinted bank checks, forms

Dennison Manufacturing Co. DSN
300 Howard Street
Framingham, MA 01701 (617) 890-6350
paper products,stationery   [DRP]

DeSoto Inc. DSO
1700 South Mt Prospect Road
Des Plaines, IL 60018 (312) 391-9000
paints, coatings, detergents

Detroit Edison Co. DTE
2000 2nd Avenue
Detroit, MI 48226 (313) 237-8000
electric utility   [DRP]

Dexter Corp., The DEX
1 Elm Street
Windsor Locks, CT 06096 (203) 627-9051
specialty chemicals   [DRP]

Di Giorgio Corp. DIG
P O Box 3574
San Francisco, CA 94119 (415) 362-8972
meat processor, food/drug distributor [DRP]

Diamond Shamrock Corp. DIA
717 North Harwood Street, Shamrock Towers
Dallas, TX 75201 (214) 922-2000
oil and gas, chemicals,coal   [O]

Diamond Shamrock Offshore Partners Ltd. DSP
717 North Harwood Street
Dallas, TX 75201 (214) 979-5000
oil investment partnership

Diana Corp. DNA
111 East Wisconsin Avenue
Milwaukee, WI 53202 (414) 289-9797
industrial park investments

Diebold Inc. DBD
818 Mulberry Road S E
Canton, OH 44711 (216) 489-4000
record storage, bank security,ATMs   [O]

Digital Equipment Corp. DEC
111 Powdermill Road
Maynard, MA 01754 (617) 897-5111
minicomputers   [O]

Disney, Walt Productions DIS
500 South Buena Vista Street
Burbank, CA 91504 (213) 840-1000
amusement parks, films, TV   [DRP O]

Diversified Energies, Inc. DEI
201 South 7th Street
Minneapolis, MN 55402 (612) 372-5032
gas and oil pipelines and exploration   [DRP]

Diversified Industries Inc. DMC
1034 South Brentwood Boulevard
Richmond Heights, MO 63117 (314) 862-8200
metals trading, railroad equipment

Dome Mines Ltd. DM
P O Box 270, First Canadian Place
Toronto, ON, CDA M5X 1B1 (416) 364-3453
gold mining   [O]

Dominion Resources Inc. D
1 James River Plaza
Richmond, VA 23261 (804) 771-3000
electric utility   [DRP O]

Donaldson Co., Inc. DCI
14400 West 94th Street
Minneapolis, MN 55440 (612) 887-3131
engine air cleaners, mufflers   [DRP]

Donnelley, R R, & Sons Co. DNY
2223 Martin Luther King Drive
Chicago, IL 60616 (312) 326-8000
printing   [DRP]

Dorsey Corp. DSY
400 West 45th Street
Chattanooga, TN 37410 (615) 267-2973
plastic containers, highway trailers

Dover Corp. DOV
277 Park Avenue
New York, NY 10017 (212) 826-7160
elevators, petroleum equipment

Dow Chemical Co. DOW
2030 Dow Center
Midland, MI 48640 (517) 636-1000
chemicals, plastics, pharmaceuticals [DRP O]

Dow Jones & Co. Inc. DJ
22 Cortland Street
New York, NY 10007 (212) 285-5000
business and financial news services   [DRP]

Downey Savings & Loan Association DSL
3200 Bristol Street
Costa Mesa, CA 92626 (714) 549-8811
savings and loan

Dravo Corp. DRV
1 Oliver Plaza
Pittsburgh, PA 15222 (412) 566-3000
engineering construction   [DRP]

Dresser Industries Inc. DI
1505 Elm Street
Dallas, TX 75201 (214) 740-6000
oil and gas services   [DRP O]

Drexel Bond-Debenture Trading Fund DBF
1500 Walnut Street
Philadelphia, PA 19101 (215) 561-8060
closed-end bond mutual fund   [DRP]

Dreyfus Corp., The DRY
767 5th Avenue
New York, NY 10022 (212) 715-6000
mutual fund management and investment [DRP]

Duke Power Co. DUK
422 South Church Street P O Box 33189
Charlotte, NC 28202 (704) 373-4579
electric utility   [DRP O]

Duke Realty Investments Inc. DRE
8445 Keystone Crossing
Indianapolis, IN 46240 (317) 257-8688
real estate investment trust

Dun & Bradstreet Corp. DNB
299 Park Avenue
New York, NY 10017 (212) 593-6800
business info publishing/marketing/TV   [O]

Dupont de Nemours, E.I., & Co. DD
1007 Market Street
Wilmington, DE 19898 (302) 774-1000
chemicals, oil and gas production   [DRP O]

Duquesne Light Co. DQU
1 Oxford Centre, 301 Grant Street
Pittsburgh, PA 15279 (412) 456-6000
electric utility   [DRP 3%]

Dynamics Corp. of America DYA
475 Steamboat Road
Greenwich, CT 06830 (203) 869-3211
appliances, metal fabrication

E-Systems ESY
6250 LBJ Freeway P O Box 6030
Dallas, TX 75266 (214) 661-1000
electronic and aerospace equipment [DRP O]

Eagle-Picher Industries Inc. EPI
580 Walnut Street P O Box 779
Cincinnati, OH 45201 (513) 721-7010
auto parts, industrial machinery   [DRP]

Easco Corp. ES
201 North Charles Street
Baltimore, MD 21201 (301)837-9550
hand tools, aluminum components   [DRP]

Eastern Gas & Fuel Associates EFU
1 Beacon Street
Boston, MA 02108 (617) 742-9200
coal, river barging,gas utility   [DRP O]

Eastern Utilities Associates EUA
P O Box 2333
Boston, MA 02107 (617) 357-9590
electric utility   [DRP 5%]

Eastman Kodak Co. EK
343 State Street
Rochester, NY 14650 (716) 724-4000
photographic equipment,chemicals [DRP O]

Eaton Corp. ETN
100 Erie View Plaza
Cleveland, OH 44114 (216) 523-5000
electronics, electrical components [DRP 5%]

Echlin Inc. ECH
Echlin Road & US 1
Branford, CT 06405 (203) 481-5751
auto parts, accessories

Edison Brothers Stores, Inc. EBS
400 Washington Avenue
St Louis, MO 63102 (314) 331-6000
women's shoe stores

EDO Corp. EDO
14004 111th Street
College Point, NY 11356 (212) 445-6000
marine and military electronic equipment

Educational Computer Corp. ECC
5882 South Tampa Avenue
Orlando, FL 32809 (305) 859-7410
computer controlled simulators

EG&G Inc. EGG
45 William Street,Wellesley Office Park
Wellesley, MA 02181 (617) 237-5100
electronic,nucleonic systems   [DRP O]

El Torito Restaurants Inc. ET
Grace Plaza
New York, NY 10036 (714) 863-6400
restaurants

Elcor Corp. ELK
2100 Wilco Building
Midland, TX 79701 (915) 685-0200
roofing and industrial products

Electronic Associates, Inc. EA
185 Monmount Parkway
West Long Branch, NJ 07764 (201) 229-1100
simulator computer systems

Electrospace Systems Inc. ELE
1601 North Plano Road
Richardson, TX 75083-1359 (214) 231-9303
communication,navigation equipment

Elgin National Industries Inc. ENW
120 South Riverside Plaza
Chicago, IL 60606 (312) 454-1900
coal/mineral plant construction, watches

Elscint Ltd. ELT
Advanced Technology Center,P O Box 5258
Haifa, Israel
scientific,medical instruments

Emerson Electric Co. EMR
8000 West Florissant P O Box 4100
St Louis, MO 63136 (314) 553-2000
electrical and electronic products   [DRP O]

Emerson Radio Corp. EME
1 Emerson Lane
North Bergen, NJ 07047 (201) 854-4800
consumer and medical electronics

Emery Air Freight Corp. EAF
P O Box 322
Wilton, CT 06897 (203) 762-8601
air freight   [DRP O]

Emhart Corp. EMH
P O Box 2730
Hartford, CT 06101 (203) 678-3000
hardware, electronics, fasteners   [DRP]

Empire District Electric Co. EDE
602 Joplin Street
Joplin, MO 64801 (417) 623-4700
electric utility   [DRP 5%]

Energen Corp. EGN
2101 6th Avenue North
Birmingham, AL 35203 (205) 326-8100
gas utility   [DRP]

Energy Exchange Corp. QEEX
6555 South Lewis
Tulsa, OK 74136 (918) 437-3000
oil and gas exploration and production

Engelhard Corp. EC
Menlo Park CN-40
Edison, NJ 08818 (201) 632-6000
specialty catalysts, precious metals   [DRP O]

Ennis Business Forms Inc. EBF
107 North Sherman Street
Ennis, TX 75119 (214) 875-3818
business forms, paper products

Enron Corp. ENE
P.O. Box 1188
Houston, TX 77001 (713) 654-6161
oil and gas pipelines   [DRP O]

ENSERCH Corp. ENS
300 South St. Paul Street
Dallas, TX 75201 (214) 651-8700
oil and gas, gas utility/pipeline   [DRP O]

Enserch Exploration Partners Ltd. EP
1817 Wood Street
Dallas, TX 75201 (214) 748-1110
oil investment partnerships

Ensource Inc. EEE
5575 DTC Parkway
Englewood, CO 80111 (303) 740-7038
oil and gas production

Enterra Corp. EN
Radnor Corporate Center, P O Box 26
Radnor, PA 19087 (215) 293-9500
oil and gas services, fire protection

Entex Energy Development Ltd. EED
1200 Milam P O Box 2628
Houston, TX 77001 (713) 654-5600
oil and gas production   [DRP]

Entex Inc. ETX
P O Box 2628
Houston, TX 77001 (713) 654-5100
gas utility   [DRP]

EQK Realty Investors I EKR
3 Bala Plaza East Suite 500
Bala Cynwyd, PA 19004 (215) 667-2300
real estate investment trust

Equifax Inc. EFX
P O Box 4081
Atlanta, GA 30302 (404) 885-8000
risk management, financial services   [DRP]

Equimark Corp. EQK
Equibank Building, 2 Oliver Plaza
Pittsburgh, PA 15222 (412) 288-5000
banking

Equitable Resources Inc. EQT
420 Boulevard of the Allies
Pittsburgh, PA 15219 (412) 471-7600
gas utility   [DRP]

Equitec Financial Group Inc. EFG
7677 Oakport Street P O Box 2470
Oakland, CA 94614 (415) 430-9900
financial services, real estate

Erbamont N V ERB
1266 Main Street
Stamford, CT 06902 (203) 967-4882
drugs

Esselte Business Systems Inc. ESB
71 Clinton Road
Garden City, NY 11530 (516) 741-1477
office supply/graphics products

Essex Chemical Corp. ESX
1401 Broad Street
Clifton, NJ 07015 (201) 773-6300
chemicals, sealants, coatings

Esterline Corp. ESL
CBT Plaza, 1120 Post Road
Darien, CT 06820 (203) 655-7651
scientific and automotive equipment

Ethyl Corp. EY
330 South 4th Street P O Box 2189
Richmond, VA 23219 (804) 788-5000
chemicals, plastics, insurance   [DRP]

Ex-Cell-O Corp. XLO
2855 Coolidge Highway
Troy, MI 48084 (313) 649-1000
auto/aerospace/defense components   [DRP]

Excelsior Income Shares EIS
20 Exchange Place
New York, NY 10005 (212) 425-7120
closed end bond mutual fund   [DRP]

Exxon Corp. XON
1251 Avenue of the Americas
New York, NY 10020 (212) 333-1000
oil/gas production and marketing   [DRP O]

Fabri-Centers of America FCA
23550 Commerce Park Road
Beachwood, OH 44122 (216) 464-2500
retail fabric stores

Facet Enterprises Inc. FCT
7030 South Yale, Suite 800
Tulsa, OK 74136 (918) 492-1800
filters and auto components

Fairchild Industries, Incorporated FEN
300 West Service Road, P O Box 10803
Chantilly, VA 22021 (703) 478-5800
aerospace   [DRP]

Fairfield Communities, Inc. FCI
1207 Rebsamen Road
Little Rock, AR 72202 (501) 664-6000
real estate development,time sharing

Family Dollar Stores FDO
P O Box 25800, 10401 Old Monroe Road
Charlotte, NC 28212 (704) 847-6961
discount stores

Fansteel Inc. FNL
1 Tantalum Place
North Chicago, IL 60064 (312) 689-4900
specialty metals refining

Far West Financial Corp. FWF
4001 MacArthur Boulevard
Newport Beach, CA 92660 (714) 833-8585
savings and loan

Farah Manufacturing Co. Inc. FRA
P O Box 9519
El Paso, TX 79985 (915) 593-4444
jeans and slacks for men and boys

Fay's Drug Co. FAY
7245 Henry Clay Boulevard
Liverpool, NY 13088 (315) 451-8000
discount drug stores   [DRP]

Fedders Corp. FJQ
158 Highway 206, P O Box 265
Peapack, NJ 07977 (201) 234-2100
air conditioning equipment

Federal Co. FFF
1755-D Lynnfield Road, Suite 149
Memphis, TN 38117 (901) 761-3610
consumer foods, animal by-products   [DRP]

Federal Express Corp. FDX
2990 Airways Boulevard,P O Box 727
Memphis, TN 38194 (901) 369-3600
freight and package forwarding   [O]

Federal National Mortgage Assoc. FNM
3900 Wisconsin Avenue, NW
Washington, DC 20016 (202) 537-7000
mortgage-backed securities   [DRP O]

Federal Paper Board Co., Inc. FBO
75 Chestnut Ridge Road
Montvale, NJ 07645 (201) 391-1776
paperboard, pulp, folding cartons   [DRP]

Federal Realty Investment Trust FRT
5454 Wisconsin Avenue
Chevy Chase, MD 20815 (301) 652-3360
real estate investment trust   [DRP 5%]

Federal Signal Corp. FSS
1415 22nd Street Room 1100
Oak Brook, IL 60521 (312) 920-2700
electric outdoor signs and signals   [DRP]

Federal-Mogul Corp. FMO
26555 Northwestern Highway
Southfield, MI 48034 (313) 354-7700
auto/machinery/aerospace components [DRP]

Federated Department Stores, Inc. FDS
227 West Seventh Street
Cincinnati, OH 45202 (513) 579-7000
department stores, supermarkets   [DRP O]

Ferro Corp. FOE
1 Erieview Plaza
Cleveland, OH 44144 (216) 641-8580
specialty coatings and chemicals   [DRP]

Fieldcrest-Cannon Mills Inc. FLD
326 East Stadium Drive
Eden, NC 27288 (919) 627-3000
home furnishing textile products, yarns

Financial Corp. of America FIN
18401 von Karman Boulevard
Irvine, CA 92715 (714) 553-6900
savings and loan   [O]

Financial Corp. Santa Barbara FSB
3908 State Street P O Box 1109
Santa Barbara CA 93102 (805) 682-5000
savings and loan

Fireman's Fund Corp. FFC
777 San Marin Drive
Novato, CA 94998 (415) 899-2000
property and casualty insurance

Firestone Tire & Rubber Co. FIR
1200 Firestone Parkway
Akron, OH 44317 (216) 379-7000
tires, wheel products, rubber   [DRP O]

First Bank System Inc. FBS
1400 1st National Bank Building
Minneapolis, MN 55402 (612) 370-5100
banking, financial services   [DRP 5%]

First Boston Inc. FBC
Park Avenue Plaza
New York, NY 10055 (212) 909-2000
investment bankers and brokers   [O]

First Capital Holdings FCH
1900 Avenue of the Stars
Los Angeles, CA 90667 (213) 551-1000
mutual funds, insurance

First Chicago Corp. FNB
1 First National Plaza
Chicago, IL 60670 (312) 732-4000
banking   [DRP 5% O]

First City Bancorp of Texas FBT
1001 Main Street
Houston, TX 77002 (713) 658-6044
banking   [DRP]

First City Industries Inc. FCY
8383 Wilshire Boulevard Suite 800
Beverly Hills, CA 90211 (213) 852-0499
real estate

First Federal Savings Bank of Arizona FED
3003 North Central Avenue
Phoenix, AZ 85012 (602) 248-4221
banking

First Fidelity Bancorporation FFB
550 Broad Street
Newark, NJ 07192 (201) 565-3200
banking   [DRP 5%]

First Interstate Bancorp I
707 Wilshire Boulevard
Los Angeles, CA 90054 (213) 614-3001
banking   [DRP]

First Mississippi Corp. FRM
656 North Street P O Box 1249
Jackson, MS 38205 (601) 948-7550
sulphur, fertilizer, oil/gas exploration   [O]

First Pennsylvania Corp. FPA
36th and Market Street
Philadelphia, PA 19101 (215) 786-5000
banking

First Union R.E. Eq. Mtge. Investments FUR
55 Public Square
Cleveland, OH 44113 (216) 781-4030
real estate investment trust   [DRP]

First Virginia Banks Inc. FVB
6400 Arlington Boulevard
Falls Church, VA 22042 (703) 241-4000
banking   [DRP 5%]

First Wachovia Corp. FWWI
P O Box 3099
Winston-Salem, NC 27102 (919) 770-5000
banking   [DRP 5%]

First Wisconsin Corp. FWB
777 East Wisconsin Avenue
Milwaukee, WI 53201 (414) 765-4985
banking   [DRP]

Fischbach Corp. FIS
485 Lexington Avenue
New York, NY 10017 (212) 986-4100
electrical and mechanical contracting

Fisher Foods Inc. FHR
5300 Richmond Road
Bedford Heights, OH 44146 (216)292-7000
food products, supermarkets

Fleet Financial Group, Inc. FLT
55 Kennedy Plaza
Providence, RI 02903 (401) 278-5800
banking, financial services   [DRP]

Fleetwood Enterprises, Inc. FLE
P O Box 7638 3125 Myers Street
Riverside, CA 92523 (714) 351-3500
mobile homes, travel trailers   [O]

Fleming Companies Inc. FLM
North Broadway Plaza Box 26647
Oklahoma City, OK 73126 (405) 840-7200
wholesale food distributor   [DRP 5%]

Flightsafety International, Inc. FSI
Marine Air Terminal, LaGuardia Airport
Flushing, NY 11371 (718) 565-4100
pilot and marine training

Floating Point Systems, Inc. FLP
3601 SW Murray Boulevard
Beavertown, OR 97005 (503) 641-3151
hi-speed array processor computers

Florida East Coast Industries Inc. FLA
1 Malaga Street
St Augustine, FL 32084 (904) 829-3421
railroads, real estate

Florida Progress Corp. FPC
3201 34th Street South
St Petersburg, FL 33711 (813) 895-1700
electric utility   [DRP 5%]

Florida Steel Corp. FLS
P O Box 23328
Tampa, FL 33622 (813) 251-8811
steel mills

Flow General, Inc. FGN
7655 Old Springhouse Road
McLean, VA 22102 (703) 893-5915
biomedical products, research services

Flowers Industries, Inc. FLO
US Highway 19 South
Thomasville, GA 31792 (912) 226-9110
baked goods, snack foods, frozen foods

Fluor Corp. FLR
333 Michelson Drive
Irvine, CA 92730 (714) 975-2000
general contracting,coal, metals   [DRP O]

FMC Corp. FMC
200 East Randolph Drive
Chicago, IL 60601 (312) 861-6000
chemicals and machinery   [DRP]

Foote Cone Belding Communications Inc. FCB
401 North Michigan Avenue
Chicago, IL 60611 (312) 467-9200
advertising agency   [DRP]

Ford Motor Co. F
The American Road
Dearborn, MI 48120 (313) 322-3000
auto/truck/farm/defense equipment [DRP O]

Fort Dearborn Securities Inc. FTD
126 South State Street Room 800
Chicago, IL 60603 (312) 346-0676
closed end bond mutual fund   [DRP]

Fort Howard Paper Co. FHP
P O Box 130
Green Bay, WI 54305 (414) 435-8821
household paper goods, food containers [DRP]

Foster Wheeler Corp. FWC
111 South Orange Avenue
Livingston, NJ 07039 (201) 533-1100
energy and process equipment/plants [DRP O]

Fox Photo Inc. FPI
8750 Tesoro Drive
San Antonio, TX 78286 (512) 828-9111
photo equipment, processing   [DRP 5%]

Foxboro Co., The FOX
38 Neponset Avenue
Foxboro, MA 02035 (617) 543-8750
industrial control instrument systems   [DRP]

FPL Group Inc. FPL
P O Box 529100
Miami, FL 33152 (305) 552-3552
electric utility   [DRP]

Freeport McMoran Energy Partners Ltd. FMP
3421 North Causeway Boulevard
Metairie, LA 70002 (504) 835-4700
oil investment partnerships

Freeport McMoran Inc. FTX
200 Park Avenue 55th Floor
New York, NY 10017 (212) 578-9200
sulphur, oil and gas, copper   [O]

Freeport McMoran O & G Royalty Trust FMR
200 Park Avenue
New York, NY 10017 (212) 578-9200
oil and gas royalty trust

Freeport-McMoran Gold Co. FAU
1615 Poydras Street
New Orleans LA 70161 (504) 582-4000
mining, processing gold ore

Frigitronics, Inc. FRG
770 River Road
Shelton, CT 06484 (203) 929-6321
eyeglasses, medical supplies

Fruehauf Corp. FTR
P O Box 238
Detroit, MI 48232 (313) 267-1000
transportation equipment

Fuqua Industries Inc. FQA
3800 First National Bank Tower
Atlanta, GA 30303 (404) 658-9000
sporting goods, lawn equipment, seating

GAF Corp. GAF
1361 Alps Road
Wayne, NJ 07470 (201) 628-3000
specialty chemicals, roofing, insulation   [O]

Galveston-Houston GHX
P O Box 2207
Houston, TX 77001 (713) 966-2500
oilfield hardware and services

Gannett Co. Inc. GCI
1000 Wilson Boulevard
Arlington, VA 20044 (703) 276-5900
newspapers, TV and radio stations   [DRP O]

Gap, Inc. (The) GPS
900 Cherry Avenue P O Box 60
San Bruno, CA 94066 (415) 952-4400
apparel and accessory stores

GATX Corp. GMT
120 South Riverside Plaza
Chicago, IL 60680 (312) 621-6200
railcar leasing,shipping   [DRP]

GCA Corp. GCA
Burlington Road
Bedford, MA 01730 (617) 275-5400
semiconductor instruments and equipment [O]

Gearhart Industries Inc. GOI
1100 Everman Road P O Box 1936
Fort Worth, TX 76101 (817) 293-1300
well evaluation services for oil and gas

GEICO Corp. GEC
GEICO Plaza
Chevy Chase, MD 20076 (301) 986-2500
property and casualty insurance

Gelco Corp. GEL
1 Gelco Drive
Eden Prairie, MN 55344 (612) 828-1000
auto and truck rental/leasing/managing

Gemini II Inc. Capital Shares GMI
1300 Morris Drive P O Box 2600
Valley Forge, PA 19482 (215) 648-6000
closed end dual purpose mutual fund

GenCorp Inc. GY
1 General Street
Akron, OH 44309 (216) 798-3000
tires, aerospace, defense products   [DRP O]

General American Investors Co. Inc. GAM
330 Madison Avenue
New York, NY 10017 (212) 916-8400
closed-end stock mutual fund   [DRP]

General Bancshares Corp. GBS
720 Olive Street
St Louis, MO 63166 (314) 241-3600
banking

General Cinema Corp. GCN
P O Box 1000 27 Boylston Street
Chestnut Hill, MA 02187 (617) 232-8200
soft drink bottling, movie theatres   [DRP]

General Datacomm Industries, Inc. GDC
1 Kennedy Avenue
Middlebury, CT 06762-1299 (203) 574-1118
electronic data transmission systems

General Development Corp. GDV
1111 South Bayshore Drive
Miami, FL 33131 (305) 350-1200
develops planned communities

General Dynamics Corp. GD
Pierre LaClede Center
St Louis, MO 63105 (314) 889-8200
aerospace industries,submarines   [O]

General Electric Co. GE
3135 Eastern Turnpike
Fairfield, CT 06431 (203) 373-2431
consumer/industrial/defense products [DRP O]

General Homes Corp. GHO
7322 Southwest Freeway
Houston, TX 77074 (713) 270-4177
construction of single family homes

General Host Corp. GH
22 Gate House Road
Stamford, CT 06902 (203) 357-9900
convenience stores, food processing

General Housewares Corp. GHW
6 Suburban Avenue,P O Box 10265
Stamford, CT 06904-2265 (203) 325-4141
cookware and giftware

General Instrument Corp. GRL
767 5th Avenue
New York, NY 10153 (212) 207-6200
electronic components and systems   [O]

General Mills, Inc. GIS
P O Box 1113
Minneapolis, MN 55440 (612) 540-2311
foods, restaurants, apparel, toys   [DRP O]

General Motors Corp. GM
3044 West Grand Boulevard
Detroit, MI 48202 (313) 556-5000
autos, trucks, defense, space   [DRP O]

General Nutrition, Inc. GNC
921 Penn Avenue
Pittsburgh, PA 15222 (412) 288-4600
health food production and retailing   [DRP]

General Public Utilities Corp. GPU
100 Interpace Parkway
Parsippany, NJ 07054 (201) 263-6500
electric utility

General Re Corp. GRN
Financial Centre P O Box 10351
Stamford, CT 06904 (203) 328-5000
property-casualty and life reinsurance

General Refractories Inc. GRX
225 City Avenue
Bala Cynwyd, PA 19004 (215) 667-7900
energy conservation products

General Signal Corp. GSX
High Ridge Park
Stamford, CT 06904 (203) 357-8800
electrical control equipment   [DRP]

Genesco Inc. GCO
111 7th Avenue South
Nashville, TN 37202 (615) 367-7000
produces/sells footwear and men's wear

Genrad Inc. GEN
300 Baker Avenue
Concord, MA 01742 (617) 369-4400
electronic test equipment   [O]

Genstar Corp. GST
4 Embarcadero Center
San Francisco, CA 94111 (415) 986-7200
building materials,land development [DRP O]

Genuine Parts Co. GPC
2999 Circle 75 Parkway
Atlanta, GA 30339 (404) 953-1700
distribution of auto and industrial parts   [O]

GEO International Corp. GX
1 Landmark Square
Stamford, CT 06901 (203) 964-1955
oilfield services and equipment   [DRP]

Georgia-Pacific Corp. GP
133 Peachtree NW
Atlanta, GA 30303 (404) 521-4000
building products, packaging, paper [DRP O]

Gerber Products Co. GEB
445 State Street
Fremont, MI 49412 (616) 928-2000
baby foods, apparel, toys, furniture   [DRP]

Gerber Scientific Inc. GRB
83 Gerber Road West
South Windsor, CT 06074 (203) 644-2581
automatic electronic drafting systems   [O]

Getty Petroleum Corp. GTY
175 Sunnyside Boulevard
Plainview, NY 11803 (516) 486-0905
distribution of gasoline, gas stations

GF Corp. GFB
229 East Dennick Avenue
Youngstown, OH 44505 (216) 759--8888
metal office furniture

Giant Group Ltd. GPO
9500 Wilshire Boulevard
Beverly Hills, CA 90212 (213) 273-5678
cement

Gibraltar Financial Corp. GFC
9111 Wilshire Boulevard
Beverly Hills, CA 9021 (213) 278-8720
savings and loan

Gifford-Hill & Co. GFH
P O Box 47127
Dallas, TX 75247 (214) 258-7000
cement, concrete, metal pre-fabs   [DRP]

Gillette Co. GS
Prudential Plaza
Boston, MA 02199 (617) 421-7000
personal care products, pens   [DRP O]

Gleason Corp. GLE
1000 University Avenue
Rochester, NY 14692 (716) 473-1000
bevel gear machinery, tooling

Glendale Federal Savings & Loan Assoc GLN
700 North Grand Boulevard
Glendale, CA 91203 (818) 500-2424
savings and loan

Global Marine Inc. GLM
777 North Eldridge
Houston, TX 77079 (713) 596-5100
offshore drilling, oil and gas exploration

Golden Nugget, Inc. GNG
129 Fremont Street
Las Vegas, NV 89101 (702) 385-7111
hotel-casino complexes   [O]

Golden West Financial Corp. GDW
1970 Broadway Suite 1000
Oakland, CA 94612 (415) 645-9420
savings and loan   [O]

Goodrich, BF, Co. GR
500 South Main Street
Akron, OH 44318 (216) 374-2000
chemical and plastic products, tires   [DRP]

Goodyear Tire and Rubber GT
1144 East Market Street
Akron, OH 44316 (216) 796-2121
rubber/plastic/chemical products [DRP 5% O]

Gordon Jewelry Corp. GOR
820 Fannin Street
Houston, TX 77003 (713) 222-8080
retail jewelry store chain   [DRP]

Gould Inc. GLD
10 Gould Center
Rolling Meadows, IL 60008 (312) 640-4000
electronic systems   [DRP O]

Grace, W R Co. GRA
Grace Plaza,1114 Avenue of the Americas
New York, NY 10036 (212) 819-5500
chemicals, energy, consumer products [DRP O]

Grainger, W W Inc. GWW
5500 West Howard Street
Skokie, IL 60077 (312) 982-9000
manufacture/retailing of electric motors

Great American First Savings Bank GTA
600 B Street
San Diego, CA 92183 (619) 231-1885
savings and loan

Great Atlantic & Pacific Tea Co., Inc. GAP
2 Paragon Drive
Montvale, NJ 07645 (201) 573-9700
supermarkets, coffee processing, bakeries

Great Northern Iron Ore Properties GNI
W-1481 1st National Bank Building
St Paul, MN 55101 (612) 224-2385
leasing iron ore properties to mine firms

Great Northern Nekoosa Corp. GNN
75 Prospect Street
P O Box 9309
Stamford, CT 06901 (203) 359-4000

Great Western Financial Corp. GWF
8484 Wilshire Boulevard
Beverly Hills, CA 90211 (213) 852-3411
savings and loan   [DRP O]

Green Mountain Power Corp. GMP
25 Green Mountain Drive
Burlington, VT 05402 (802) 864-5731
electric utility   [DRP 5%]

Green Tree Acceptance Inc. GNT
1100 Amhoist Tower,345 St Peter Street
St Paul, MN 55102 (612) 293-3400
purchases housing contracts

Greyhound Corp. G
Greyhound Tower
Phoenix, AZ 85077 (602) 248-4000
intercity bus transport, food, leasing   [O]

Grolier Inc. GLR
Sherman Turnpike
Danbury, CT 06816 (203) 797-3500
book publishing, electronic publishing

Grow Group Inc. GRO
200 Park Avenue
New York, NY 10166 (212) 599-4400
specialty coatings, chemical products   [DRP]

Growth Stock Outlook Trust GSO
4405 East West Highway
Bethesda, MD 20814 (301) 654-5205
closed-end stock mutual fund

Grubb & Ellis Co. GBE
1 Montgomery Street 31st Floor
San Francisco, CA 94014 (415) 956-1990
real estate broker

Grumman Corp. GQ
1111 Stewart Avenue
Bethpage, NY 11714 (516) 575-0574
government aircraft, trucks, radar   [DRP O]

Gruntal Financial Corp. GRU
14 Wall Street
New York, NY 10005 (212) 267-8800
regional securities broker

GTE Corp. GTE
1 Stamford Forum
Stamford, CT 06904 (203) 965-2000
telecommunication systems, equipment
                                          [DRP O]

Guilford Mills Inc. GFD
4925 West Market Street
Greenboro, NC 27407 (919) 292-7550
textiles for apparel/upholstery/autos

Gulf & Western Industries Inc. GW
1 Gulf & Western Plaza
New York, NY 10023 (212) 333-7000
entertainment, publishing, financial   [DRP O]

Gulf Resources & Chemical Corp. GRE
1100 Milam Building 47th Floor
Houston, TX 77002 (713) 658-0471
mineral mining, chemicals, oil and gas

Gulf States Utilities Co. GSU
P O Box 1671
Beaumont, TX 77704 (713) 838-6631
electric companies, gas utilities   [DRP]

Hall, Frank B & Co., Inc. FBH
549 Pleasantville Road
Briarcliff Manor, NY 10610 (914) 769-9200
insurance brokers   [O]

Halliburton Co. HAL
3211 Southland Center
Dallas, TX 75201 (214) 748-7261
oil field services/engineering   [O]

Hallwood Group Inc. HWG
1900 E. Ninth Street
Cleveland, OH 44114 (216) 696-1111
real estate investment trust

Hammermill Paper Co. HML
East Lake Road
Erie, PA 16501 (814) 456-8811
wholesale paper and forest products   [DRP]

Handleman Co. HDL
500 Kirts Boulevard
Troy, MI 48084 (313) 362-4400
sells and distributes music and books   [DRP]

Handy and Harman HNH
850 3rd Avenue
New York, NY 10022 (212) 752-3400
metals, auto parts, electronic items   [DRP]

Hannaford Brothers Co. HRD
P.O. Box 1000
Portland, ME 04104 (207) 883-2911
food distributor, food/drug stores   [DRP]

Hanson Trust HAN
410 Park Avenue
New York, NY 10022 (212) 759-8477
diversified manufacturing

Harcourt Brace Jovanovich Inc. HBJ
6277 Sea Harbor Drive
Orlando, FL 32821 (305) 345-2000
book, journal, and magazine publishing

Harland, John H Co. JH
2939 Miller Road
Decatur, GA 30035 (404) 981-9460
check printing

Harnischfeger Corp. HPH
4400 West National Avenue
Milwaukee, WI 53246 (414) 671-4400
cranes and material handling equipment

Harper & Row Publishers Inc. HPR
10 East 53rd Street
New York, NY 10032 (212) 593-7000
book publishing

Harris Corp. HRS
1025 West Nassau Boulevard
Melbourne, FL 32919 (305) 727-9100
electronic communications equipment [DRP O]

Harsco Corp. HSC
P O Box 8888
Camp Hill, PA 17011 (717) 763-7064
metals fabrication   [DRP]

Hartmarx Corp. HMX
101 North Wacker Drive
Chicago, IL 60606 (312) 372-6300
clothing manufacturer/retailer   [DRP]

Hatteras Income Securities Inc. HAT
1 NCNB Plaza P O Box 120
Charlotte, NC 28255 (704) 333-7808
closed-end bond mutual fund   [DRP]

Hawaiian Electric Industries Inc. HE
P O Box 2750
Honolulu, HA 96813 (808) 548-7771
electric utility   [DRP 5%]

Hayes-Albion Corp. HAY
2701 North Dettman Road
Jackson, MI 49201 (517) 782-9421
auto parts and light metals

Hazeltine Corp. HZ
Commack, NY 11725 (516) 462-5100
military electronic systems and equipment

Hazleton Labs Corp. HLC
9200 Leesburg Turnpike
Vienna, VA 22100 (703) 893-5400
independent contract bio-research labs

Health Care Property Investors Inc. HCP
3200 Park Center Drive
Costa Mesa, CA 92626 (714) 751-0989
real estate investment trusts

HealthAmerica Corp. HMO
3310 West End Avenue
Nashville, TN 38203 (615) 385-7300
health maintenance organizations

HealthCare USA Inc. HSA
1626 East 4th Street
Santa Ana, CA 92701 (714) 633-5420
hospitals

Heck's Inc. HEX
McJunken Road
Nitro, WV 25143 (304) 755-8351
discount department stores

Hecla Mining Co. HL
Hecla Building
Wallace, ID 83873 (208) 752-1251
mining of silver, lead, and zinc   [O]

Heileman, G Brewing Co. Inc. GHB
100 Harborview Plaza
La Crosse, WI 54601 (608) 785-1000
malt beverages, snack foods, jet parts [DRP]

Heilig Meyers Co. HMY
3228 West Cary Street
Richmond, VA 21221 (804) 359-9171
retail furniture stores

Heinz, H J Co. HNZ
P O Box 57
Pittsburgh, PA 15230 (412) 456-5700
food products   [DRP O]

Helene Curtis Industries, Inc. HC
325 North Wells Street
Chicago, IL 60610 (312) 661-0222
beauty and hair care products

Helmerich and Payne Inc. HP
1579 East 21st Street
Tulsa, OK 74115 (918) 742-5531
oil field services/exploration

Hercules Inc. HPC
900 Market Place
Wilmington, DE 19899 (302) 575-5000
chemicals and plastics products   [DRP O]

Heritage Communications Inc. HCI
2195 Ingersoll Avenue
Des Moines, Iowa 50312 (515) 245-7585
constructs and operates cable TV systems

Herman's Sporting Goods Inc. HER
2 Germack Drive
Carteret, NJ 07008 (201) 541-1550
sporting goods/apparel stores

Hershey Foods Corp. HSY
100 Mansion Road East
Hershey, PA 17033 (717) 534-4000
candy, pasta, restaurants   [DRP]

Hesston Corp. HES
P O Box 788 420 West Lincoln Boulevard
Hesston, KS 67062 (316) 327-4000
farm/construction/mining machinery

Hewlett-Packard Co. Inc. HWP
3000 Hanover Street
Palo Alto, CA 94304 (415) 857-1501
measurement and computation products   [O]

Hexcel Corp. HXL
650 California Street
San Francisco, CA 94108 (415) 956-3333
honeycomb cores for aerospace   [DRP 5%]

Hi-Shear Industries, Inc. HSI
3333 New Hyde Park Road
North Hills, NY 10042 (516) 627-8600
aerospace fastener devices

High Voltage Engineering Corp. HVE
South Bedford Street
Burlington, MA 01803 (617) 272-1313
electrical systems for electric utilities

Hillenbrand Industries Inc. HB
Highway 46
Batesville, IN 430064 (812) 934-7000
burial caskets, medical equipment, luggage

Hilton Hotels Corp. HLT
9990 Santa Monica Boulevard
Beverly Hills, CA 90210 (213) 278-4321
hotels and casinos   [O]

Hitachi, Ltd HIT
6, Kanda-Surugadai 4 Chome
Chiyoda-Ku, Tokyo 101, Japan
electrical and industrial equipment

Holiday Corp. HIA
1023 Cherry Road
Memphis, TN 38117 (901) 362-4001
hotels, hotel-casinos, restaurants   [DRP O]

Holly Sugar Corp. HLY
P O Box 1052
Colorado Springs, CO 80901 (303) 471-0123
manufactures sugar from sugarbeets

Home Depot Inc. HD
6300 Powers Ferry Road
Atlanta, GA 30339 (404) 952-5504
retail building material stores   [O]

Home Federal Savings and Loan Assoc. HFD
707 Broadway
San Diego, CA 92101 (619) 238-7581
savings and loan

Homestake Mining Co. HM
650 California Street
San Francisco, CA 94108 (415) 981-8150
gold/uranium/lead/zinc/silver mining [DRP O]

Homestead Financial Corp. HFL
1777 Murchison Drive
Burlingame, CA 94010 (415)692-1432
savings and loan

Honda Motor Co. Ltd HMC
1270 Avenue of the Americas
New York, NY 10020 (212) 765-3804
motorcycles, autos, light trucks   [O]

Honeywell Inc. HON
Honeywell Plaza
Minneapolis, MN 55408 (612) 870-5200
controls, data processing systems   [DRP O]

Horizon Bancorp HZB
334 Madison Avenue
Morristown, NJ 07960 (201) 539-7700
banking   [DRP 5%]

Horizon Corp. HZN
16838 East Palisades Boulevard
Fountain Hill, AZ 85751 (602) 837-1685
develops and sells planned communities

Hospital Corp. of America HCA
P O Box 550
Nashville, TN 37202 (615) 327-9551
owns and operates hospitals   [DRP 5% O]

Hotel Investors Trust HOT
5530 Wisconsin Avenue
Chevy Chase, MD 20815 (301) 654-9200
real estate investment trust   [DRP]

Houghton Mifflin Co. HTN
2 Park Avenue
Boston, MA 02107 (617) 725-5000
text and trade books   [DRP]

House of Fabrics HF
13400 Riverside Drive
Sherman Oaks, CA 91423 (818) 995-7000
retailer of notions and fabrics

Household International Inc. HI
2700 Sanders Road
Prospect Heights, IL 60070 (312) 564-5000
consumer finance, car rentals, tools [DRP O]

Houston Industries Inc. HOU
611 Walker Street
Houston, TX 77002 (713) 228-2474
electric utility   [DRP]

Houston Oil Royalty Trust RTH
P O Box 809
Houston, TX 77001 (713) 658-6011
royalties of oil and gas properties

Howell Corp. HWL
1010 Lamar
Houston, TX 77002 (713) 658-4000
coal, oil, and gas refining

HRE Properties HRE
530 5th Avenue - 21st floor
New York, NY 10036 (212) 642-4800
real estate investment trust   [DRP 5%]

Huffy Corp. HUF
7701 Byers Road
Miamisburg, OH 45342 (513) 866-6251
bicycles and outdoor power equipment [DRP]

Hughes Supply Inc. HUG
521 West Central Boulevard
Orlando, FL 32802 (305) 841-4710
retailer of electrical and plumbing items

Hughes Tool Co. HT
5425 Polk Avenue
Houston, TX 77023 (713) 924-2222
oil and gas equipment and services   [DRP O]

Humana Inc., HUM
PO Box 1438 500 West Main Street
Louisville, KY 40201-1438 (502) 580-1000
acute care community hospitals   [DRP O]

Hunt Manufacturing Co. HUN
1405 Locust Street
Philadelphia, PA 19102 (215) 732-7700
art and office supplies

Hutton, E.F. Group Inc. EFH
1 Battery Park Plaza
New York, NY 10004 (212)742-5000
brokerage firm, life insurance

Hydraulic Co. THC
835 Main Street
Bridgeport, CT 06609 (203) 367-6621
water utility   [DRP 5%]

IC Industries Inc. ICX
1 Illinois Center 111 East Wacker
Chicago, IL 60601 (312) 565-3000
packaged foods, rail shipping   [DRP O]

ICM Property Investors Inc. ICM
600 3rd Avenue
New York, NY 10016 (212) 986-5640
real estate investment trust   [DRP]

ICN Pharmaceuticals INC ICN
222 North Vincent Avenue
Covina, CA 91722 (213) 967-0771
pharmaceuticals

Idaho Power Co. IDA
P O Box 70 1220 Idaho Street
Boise, ID 83707 (208) 383-2200
electric utility   [DRP]

Ideal Basic Industries Inc. IDL
P O Box 8789
Denver, CO 80201 (303) 623-5661
portland cement and potash

Illinois Power Co. IPC
500 South 27th Street
Decatur, IL 62521 (217) 424-6600
electric and gas utility   [DRP 5%]

Illinois Tool Works ITW
8501 West Higgins Road
Chicago, IL 60631 (312) 693-3040
fasteners, tools, plastic containers

Imperial Chemical Industries PLC ICI
Imperial Chemical House, Millbank
London England SW1P 3JF
chemicals

Imperial Corp. of America ICA
P O Box 631
San Diego, CA 92112 (714) 292-6300
savings and loan

INA Investment Securities Inc. IIS
1617 JFK Boulevard
Philadelphia, PA 19101 (215) 568-2295
closed-end bond mutual fund   [DRP]

INCO Ltd. N
1 New York Plaza
New York, NY 10004 (212) 612-5500
nickel, copper, precious metals   [DRP O]

Indiana Energy Inc. IGC
1630 North Meridian Street
Indianapolis, IN 46202 (317) 926-3351
gas utility   [DRP]

Inexco Oil Co. INX
700 Louisiana Street Suite 2100
Houston, TX 77002-2702 (713) 346-3500
oil and gas production

Ingersoll-Rand Co. IR
200 Chestnut Ridge Road
Woodcliff Lake, NJ 07675 (201) 573-0123
non-electrical machinery and equipment [DRP]

Ingredient Technology Corp. ITC
10 Pelham Parkway
Pelham Manor, NY 10803 (914) 738-6420
flavors, sweeteners, fragrances, spices

Inland Steel Co. IAD
30 West Monroe Street
Chicago, IL 60603 (312) 346-0300
steel, limestone, coal, iron ore   [DRP]

Insilco Corp. INR
1000 Research Parkway
Meriden, CT 06460 (203) 634-2000
multi-industry   [DRP]

Inspiration Resources Corp IRC
250 Park Avenue
New York, NY 10177 (212) 503-3100
metals, petroleum, agricultural chemicals

Integrated Resources Inc. IRE
666 3rd Avenue
New York, NY 10017 (212) 551-6000
financial services, insurance brokerage

Intelogic Trace IT
8415 Datapoint Drive
San Antonio, TX 78229 (512) 699-5700
services dispersed data processing systems

Inter-Regional Financial Group, Inc. IFG
100 Dain Tower
Minneapolis, MN 55402 (612) 371-7750
investment banking, securities brokerage

Intercapital Income Securities Inc. ICB
1 World Trade Center
New York, NY 10048 (212) 938-4500
closed-end bond mutual fund   [DRP]

INTERCO Inc. ISS
P O Box 8777 10 Broadway
St Louis, MO 63102 (314) 231-1100
apparel, footwear, home furnishings

InterFirst Corp. IFC
P O Box 83000
Dallas, TX 75283-1014 (214) 977-2866
banking   [DRP]

Interlake Inc. IK
Commerce Plaza 2015 Spring Road
Oak Brook, IL 60521 (312) 986-6600
metals, materials handling   [DRP 5%]

Intermedics ITM
4000 Technology Drive
Angleton, TX 77515 (409) 848-4000
pacemakers and heart valves

International Aluminum Corp. IAL
767 Monterey Pass Road
Monterey Park, CA 91754 (213) 264-1670
aluminum products

International Business Machines IBM
Old Orchard Road
Armonk, NY 10504 (914) 765-1900
computers, information systems   [DRP O]

International Controls Corp. INC
549 North Federal Highway,P O Box 3010
Boca Raton, FL 33431 (305) 997-7400
electronics, aerospace

International Flavors & Fragrances Inc. IFF
521 West 57th Street
New York, NY 10019 (212) 765-5500
industrial flavor and fragrance products   [O]

International Minerals & Chemical Corp IGL
2315 Sanders Road
Northbrook, IL 60062 (312) 564-8600
fertilizer materials   [O]

International Multifoods Corp. IMC
Multifoods Tower Box 2942
Minneapolis, MN 55402 (612) 340-3300
consumer and animal foods, restaurants [DRP]

International Paper Co. IP
77 West 45th Street
New York, NY 10036 (212) 536-6000
pulp, paper, lumber, plywood   [DRP O]

International Rectifier Corp. IRF
9220 Sunset Boulevard
Los Angeles, CA 90069 (213) 278-3100
semiconductors, drugs, alloys

Interpublic Group of Companies Inc. IPG
1271 Avenue of the Americas
New York, NY 10020 (212) 399-8000
advertising agencies   [DRP]

Interstate Bakeries Corp. IBC
P O Box 1627 12 East Armour Boulevard
Kansas City, MO 64141 (816) 561-6600
produces and distributes baked goods

Interstate Power Co. IPW
1000 Main Street
Dubuque, IA 52001 (319) 582-5421
electric utility   [DRP]

Interstate Securities Inc. IS
2700 NCNB Plaza
Charlotte, NC 28280 (704) 379-9000
securities brokerage

Iowa Electric Light and Power Co. IEL
Security Building P O Box 351
Cedar Rapids, IA 52801 (319) 398-4411
electric utility   [DRP]

Iowa Resources Inc. IOR
P O Box 657 666 Grand Avenue
Des Moines, IA 50303 (515) 281-2900
electric and gas utility   [DRP 5%]

Iowa-Illinois Gas & Electric Co. IWG
216 East 2nd Street
Davenport, IA 52808 (319) 326-7111
gas and electric utility   [DRP 5%]

IP Timberlands Ltd IPT
77 West 45th Street
New York, NY 10036 (212) 536-6000
investment partnerships - timber

IPALCO Enterprises Inc. IPL
P O Box 15953
Indianapolis, IN 46206 (317) 261-8261
electric utility   [DRP]

IPCO Corp. IHS
1025 Westchester Avenue
White Plains, NY 10604 (914) 682-4500
manufactures/distributes medical supplies

IRT Property Co. IRT
200 Galleria Parkway,Suite 1400
Atlanta, GA 30339 (404) 955-4406
real estate investment trust

Irving Bank Corp. V
1 Wall Street
New York, NY 10005 (212) 487-2121
banking   [DRP 5%]

Italy Fund Inc. ITA
2 World Trade Center -- 106th floor
New York, NY 10048 (212) 321-7476
closed-end italian stock mutual fund   [DRP]

ITT Corp. ITT
320 Park Avenue
New York, NY 10022 (212) 752-6000
telecommunications, defense, insurance [DRP O]

IU International Corp. IU
1105 North Market Street
Wilmington, DE 19801 (302) 571-5000
trucking, waste management, distribution [DRP]

James River Corp. of Virginia JR
P O Box 2218 Tredegar Street
Richmond, VA 23217 (804) 644-5411
paper products

Jamesway Corp. JMY
49 Hartz Way
Secaucus, NJ 07094 (201) 330-6000
discount department stores

Japan Fund Inc. JPN
345 Park Avenue
New York, NY 10154 (212) 350-8500
closed-end japanese stock fund   [DRP]

Jefferson-Pilot Corp. JP
P O Box 21008
Greensboro, NC 27420 (919) 378-2011
life, accident, health insurance   [DRP]

Jewelcor Inc. JC
72 North Franklin Street
Wilkes Barre, PA 18773 (717) 824-8761
jewelry

John Hancock Income Securities Trust JHS
John Hancock Place P O Box 111
Boston, MA 02117 (617)421-6320
closed-end bond mutual fund   [DRP]

John Hancock Investors Trust JHI
John Hancock Place P O Box 111
Boston, MA 02117 (617) 421-6320
closed-end bond mutual fund   [DRP]

Johnson & Johnson Co. JNJ
501 George Street
New Brunswick, NJ 08933 (201) 524-0400
health care products   [O]

Johnson Controls Inc. JCI
575 North Green Bay Avenue P O Box 591
Milwaukee, WI 53201 (414) 228-1200
building automation systems, batteries [DRP]

Jorgensen, Earle M Co. JOR
10700 Alameda Street
Lynwood, CA 90262 (213) 567-1122
distribution of metals   [DRP]

Jostens Inc. JOS
5501 Norman Center Drive
Minneapolis, MN 55437 (612) 830-3300
custom mementos for schools, business [DRP]

Joy Manufacturing Co. JOY
301 Grant Street
Pittsburgh, PA 15219 (412) 562-4500
capital equipment for oil/gas/mining [DRP O]

JWT Group Inc. JWT
466 Lexington Avenue
New York, NY 10017 (212) 210-7000
advertising agencies

K mart Corp. KM
3100 West Big Beaver
Troy, MI 48084 (313) 643-1000
discount and variety stores   [O]

Kaiser Aluminum & Chemical Corp. KLU
300 Lakeside Drive
Oakland, CA 94643 (415) 271-3300
aluminum products, oil, gas, chemicals

Kaiser Cement Corp. KCC
Kaiser Building 300 Lakeside Drive
Oakland, CA 94612 (415) 271-2000
cement, concrete, aggregates

Kaneb Services Inc. KAB
14141 Southwest Freeway
Sugarland, TX 77210 (713) 490-5000
oil/gas/coal exploration/production   [DRP O]

Kansas City Power & Light Co. KLT
P O Box 1437
Kansas City, MO 64141 (816) 556-2200
electric utility   [DRP]

Kansas City Southern Industries Inc. KSU
114 West 11th Street
Kansas City, MO 64105 (816) 556-0365
railroads, financial services

Kansas Gas & Electric Co. KGE
201 North Market Street
Wichita, KS 67202 (316) 261-6611
electric utility   [DRP 5%]

Kansas Power & Light Co. KAN
P O Box 889
Topeka, KS 66612 (913) 296-6300
electric and gas utility   [DRP]

Katy Industries Inc. KT
853 Dundee Avenue
Elgin, IL 60120 (312) 379-1121
multi-industry

Kaufman & Broad Inc. KB
11601 Wilshire Boulevard
Los Angeles, CA 90025 (213) 312-5000
residential construction, life insurance

KDI Corp. KDI
5721 Dragon Way
Cincinnati, OH 45227 (513) 272-1421
electrical/electronic components

Kellogg Co. K
235 Porter Street
Battle Creek, MI 49016 (616) 966-2000
convenience foods, cereal   [DRP O]

Kellwood Co. KWD
600 Kellwood Parkway
St Louis, MO 63017 (314) 576-3100
apparel, home fashions, recreational items

Kenai Corp. KEN
477 Madison Avenue
New York, NY 10022 (212) 688-6600
oil field services, refining, marketing

Kennametal Inc. KMT
1 Lloyd Avenue
Latrobe, PA 15650 (412) 539-5000
tungsten-based carbide tools   [DRP 5%]

Kenner Parker Toys Inc. KPT
50 Dunham Road
Beverly, MA 01915 (617) 927-7600
toys and games

Kentucky Utilities Co. KU
1 Quality Street
Lexington, KY 40507 (606) 255-1461
electric utility   [DRP]

Kerr Glass Manufacturing Corp. KGM
501 South Shatto Place
Los Angeles, CA 90020 (213) 487-3250
glass containers

Kerr McGee Corp. KMG
Kerr McGee Building P O Box 25861
Oklahoma City, OK 73125 (405) 270-1313
oil and gas exploration/production   [DRP O]

KeyCorp KEY
60 State Street
Albany, NY 12207 (518) 447-3500
banking   [DRP]

Keystone Consolidated Industries Inc. KES
4835 LBJ Freeway Suite 345
Dallas, TX 75244 (214) 458-0028
steel and wire products

Keystone International Inc. KII
9700 West Gulf Bank Road
Houston, TX 77040 (713) 466-1176
flow control products and systems   [DRP]

Kidde Inc. KDE
Park 80 West Plaza 2 Box 5555
Saddle Brook, NJ 07662 (201) 368-9000
multi-industry   [DRP]

Kimberly-Clark Corp. KMB
P O Box 619100
Dallas, TX 75261 (214) 830-1200
paper products, lumber, pulp, newsprint [DRP]

KLM Royal Dutch Airlines KLM
437 Madison Avenue
New York, NY 10022 (212)759-2400
international airline

Knight-Ridder Newspapers Inc. KRN
1 Herald Plaza Suite 624
Miami, FL 33101 (305) 376-3800
newspapers, business information

Knogo Corp. KNO
100 Tec Street
Hicksville, NY 11801 (516) 822-4200
electronic detector systems

Koger Properties Inc. KOG
3986 Boulevard Center Drive
Jacksonville, FL 32207 (904) 396-4811
owns and operates office buildings [DRP 5%]

Kollmorgen Corp. KOL
60 Washington Street
Hartford, CT 06106 (203) 547-0600
electrical and electronic equipment   [DRP]

Koppers Co. Inc. KOP
Koppers Building
Pittsburgh, PA 15219 (412) 227-2000
chemicals, road materials, metal items [DRP]

Korea Fund Inc. KF
c/o Scudder Stevens & Clark 345 Park Ave
New York, NY 10154 (212) 350-8200
closed-end korean stock fund   [DRP]

Kraft Inc. KRA
2211 Sanders Road
Northbrook, IL 60062 (312) 498-8000
food/dairy marketing and manufacturing [DRP]

Kroger Co. KR
1014 Vine Street
Cincinnati, OH 45201 (513) 762-4000
supermarkets, foods, drug stores   [DRP]

Kubota Ltd KUB
405 Lexington Avenue 59th Floor
New York, NY 10174 (212) 490-8050
agricultural machinery, pipe

Kuhlman Corp. KUH
2565 West Maple Road
Troy, MI 48084 (313) 649-9300
transformers, auto parts, springs   [DRP]

Kyocera Corp. KYO
Yamashina-Ku,
Kyoto 607, Japan
ceramics for industrial and electronic use

Kysor Industrial Corp. KZ
1 Madison Avenue
Cadillac, MI 49601 (616) 775-4645
truck parts, machine tools, hardware

L&N Housing Corp. LHC
2001 Bryan Tower
Dallas, TX 75201 (214) 746-7178
real estate investment trusts

La Quinta Motor Inns Inc. LQM
10010 San Pedro
San Antonio, TX 78216 (512) 349-1221
motor inns and restaurants

Lac Minerals Ltd LAC
Suite 2105 North Tower, Royal Bank Plaza
Toronto, ON, CDA M5 J 2J4 (416)865-0722
gold, oil and gas exploration, development

Laclede Gas Co. LG
720 Olive Street
St Louis, MO 63101 (314) 342-0500
gas utility   [DRP]

Lafarge Corp. LAF
12700 Park Central Place,Suite 1900
Dallas, TX 75251 (214) 991-6800
cement, concrete products   [DRP]

LaMaur Inc. LMR
5601 East River Road
Minneapolis, MN 55432 (612) 571-1234
hair care, personal grooming products

Lamson & Sessions Co. LMS
1600 Bond Court 1300 East 9th Street
Cleveland, OH 44114 (216) 781-5000
industrial fasteners

Lawter International Inc. LAW
990 Skokie Boulevard
Northbrook, IL 60062 (312) 498-4700
chemicals for inks and paints

Lea-Ronal Inc. LRI
272 Buffalo Avenue
Freeport, NY 11520 (516) 868-8800
electro-plating and metal finishing

Lear Petroleum Corp. LPT
4925 Greenville Avenue
Dallas, TX 75206 (214) 363-6085
oil and gas exploration and production

Lear Siegler Inc. LSI
P O Box 2158
Santa Monica, CA 90406 (213) 391-7211
multi-industry   [DRP O]

Leaseway Transportation Corp. LTC
2700 Park East Drive
Cleveland, OH 44122 (216) 464-3300
transportation   [DRP]

Lee Enterprises Inc. LEE
130 East 2nd Street
Davenport, IA 52801 (319) 383-2202
newspaper publishing

Legg Mason Inc. LM
7 East Redwood Street
Baltimore, MD 21203 (301) 539-3400
brokerage services

Leggett and Platt Inc. LEG
18th Road
Carthage, MO 64836 (417) 358-8131
furniture springs

Lehigh Valley Industries LEH
200 East 42nd Street
New York, NY 10017 (212) 867-0300
textiles, castings, shoes

Lehman Corp. LEM
55 Water Street
New York, NY 10041 (212) 558-2024
closed-end stock mutual fund   [DRP]

Lennar Corp. LEN
700 Northwest 107th Avenue
Miami, FL 33172 (305) 559-4000
residential construction

Leucadia National Corp. LUK
315 Park Avenue South
New York, NY 10010 (212) 460-1900
consumer financing, insurance, real estate

Liberty Corp. LC
P O Box 789 Wade Hampton Boulevard
Greenville, SC 29602 (803) 268-8111
insurance, broadcasting

Lilly, Eli and Co. LLY
307 East McCarty Street
Indianapolis, IN 46285 (317) 261-2000
medicines, medical tools, cosmetics [DRP O]

Limited Inc., The LTD
1 Limited Parkway
Columbus, OH 43230 (614) 475-4000
women's apparel stores   [DRP O]

Lincoln National Corp. LNC
1300 South Clinton Street
Fort Wayne, IN 46801 (219) 427-2000
life/health/casualty insurance   [DRP]

Lincoln Nat'l Direct Placement Fund LND
1300 South Clinton Street
Fort Wayne, IN 46801 (312) 630-2445
closed-end bond mutual fund   [DRP]

Litton Industries Inc. LIT
360 North Crescent Drive
Beverly Hills, CA 90213 (213) 859-5000
electronic, defense, automation systems [O]

LL&E Royalty Trust LRT
1st City National Bank of Houston
Houston, TX 77002 (713) 658-7145
oil and gas exploration

LLC Corp. LLC
8300 Dunwoody Place
Dunwoody, Georgia 30338 (404) 587-5200
restaurants, cabinet hardware

Lockheed Corp. LK
2555 North Hollywood Way
Burbank, CA 91503 (818) 847-6121
aerospace, aeronautic, marine systems   [O]

Loctite Corp. LOC
705 North Mountain Road
Newington, CT 06111 (203) 278-1280
adhesives, sealants   [DRP]

Loews Corp. Inc. LTR
666 5th Avenue
New York, NY 10103 (212) 841-1000
insurance, cigarettes, watches, hotels   [O]

Logicon Inc. LGN
3701 Skypark Drive
Torrance, CA 90505 (213) 373-0220
electronic systems, aerospace

Lomas & Nettleton Financial Corp LNF
2001 Bryan Tower
Dallas, TX 75222 (214) 746-7111
mortgage and construction loan service

Lomas Mortgage Corp. LMC
2001 Bryan Tower
Dallas, TX 75201 (214) 746-7111
invests in single-family mortgages

Lomas Nettleton Mortgage Investors LOM
2001 Bryan Tower P O Box 225644
Dallas, TX 75265 (214) 746-7111
real estate investment trust

Lone Star Industries Inc. LCE
1 Greenwich Plaza
Greenwich, CT 06830 (203) 661-3100
cement, concrete, sand, crushed stone [DRP]

Long Island Lighting Co. LIL
175 East Old Country Road
Hicksville, NY 11501 (516) 933-4590
electric and gas utility

Longs Drug Stores Corp. LDG
141 North Civic Drive
Walnut Creek, CA 94596 (415) 937-1170
drugstore chain

Loral Corp. LOR
600 3rd Avenue
New York, NY 10016 (212) 697-1105
military electronics, plastics   [O]

Louisiana General Services Inc. LGS
1233 West Bank Expressway
Harvey, LA 70058 (504) 367-7000
gas utility and pipeline   [DRP]

Louisiana Land and Exploration Co LLX
P O Box 60350
New Orleans, LA 70160 (504) 566-6500
oil and gas exploration and production   [O]

Louisiana-Pacific Corp. LPX
1300 SW 5th Avenue
Portland, OR 97201 (503) 221-0800
lumber, plywood, pulp   [DRP O]

Louisville Gas & Electric Co. LOU
P O Box 32010
Louisville, KY 40232 (502) 566-4011
electric and gas utility   [DRP]

Lowe's Companies LOW
Highway 268 Box 1111
North Wilkesboro, NC 28656 (919) 651-4000
retailer of building products   [DRP]

LTV Corp. LTV
P O Box 5003
Dallas, TX 75265 (214) 979-7711
steel products, aerospace   [O]

Lubrizol Corp., The LZ
P O Box 3057
Wickliffe, OH 44092 (216) 943-4200
chemical additives for petroleum industry

Luby's Cafeterias, Inc. LUB
P O Box 33069 211 NE Loop 410
San Antonio, TX 78233 (512) 654-9000
cafeterias

Lucky Stores Inc. LKS
6300 Clark Avenue
Dublin, CA 94566 (415) 833-6000
retailer of food and non-food items   [DRP]

Lukens Inc. LUC
Modena Road
Coatesville, PA 19320 (215) 383-2000
plate steel   [DRP]

M/A-Com Inc. MAI
South Avenue
Burlington, MA 01803 (617) 272-9600
microwave and digital communications   [O]

MacMillan Bloedel Ltd. MMB
1075 West Georgia Street
Vancouver, BC CDA V6E 3R9 (604) 661-8000
lumber, newsprint, pulp

Macmillan Inc. MLL
866 3rd Avenue
New York, NY 10022 (212) 702-2000
educational publishing and services   [DRP]

Macy, R H Co. Inc. MZ
151 West 34th Street
New York, NY 10001 (212) 560-3600
retail department stores   [O]

Magic Chef Inc. MGC
740 King Edward Avenue
Cleveland, TN 37311 (615) 472-3371
major home appliances, air/heat equipment

M A Hanna Co. HNM
100 Erieview Plaza
Cleveland, OH 44114 (216) 589-4000
iron mining

Manhattan Industries Inc. MHT
1271 Avenue of the Americas
New York, NY 10019 (212) 265-3700
apparel manufacturing and retailing   [DRP]

Manhattan National Corp. MLC
111 West 57th Street
New York, NY 10019 (212) 484-9300
life, accident, health insurance   [DRP 5%]

Manor Care Inc. MNR
10750 Columbia Pike
Silver Spring, MD 20901 (301) 593-5600
nursing homes for elderly, inns

Manpower Inc. (MN)
1 Parker Place
Jamesville, WI 53546 (608) 755-7000
writing instruments, ink, temp services

Manufacturers Hanover Corp. MHC
270 Park Avenue
New York, NY 10017 (212) 286-4966
banking   [DRP O]

Manville Corp. QMAN
Greenwood Plaza P O Box 5108
Denver, CO 80217 (303) 978-2000
forest products, mining

MAPCO Incorporated MDA
1880 South Baltimore Avenue
Tulsa, OK 74110 (918) 584-4471
produces/markets coal/oil/gas liquid [DRP O]

Marantz Co. Inc. MTZ
20525 Nordhoff Street
Chatsworth, CA 91311 (818) 998-9333
consumer audio-electronic products

Marcade Group Inc. MAR
21 Caven Point Avenue
Jersey City, NJ 07305 (201) 433-0100
discount and variety stores

Marine Midland Banks Inc. MM
2400 Marine Midland Center
Buffalo, NY 14200 (716) 843-2424
banking   [DRP]

Marion Laboratories Inc. MKC
10263 Bunker Ridge Road
Kansas City, MO 64137 (816) 966-5000
pharmaceuticals   [DRP O]

Mark Controls Corp. MK
1900 Dempster Street
Evanston, IL 60204 (312) 866-8840
building control and flow control systems

Marriott Corp. MHS
Marriott Drive
Washington, DC 20058 (301) 897-9000
hotels, resorts, food services, cruises   [O]

Marsh & McClennan Corp. MMC
1221 Avenue of the Americas
New York, NY 10020 (212) 997-2000
insurance brokerage and agency services [DRP]

Martin Marietta Corp. ML
6801 Rockledge Drive
Bethesda, MD 20034 (301) 897-6000
aerospace, defense, communications [DRP O]

Masco Corp. MAS
21001 van Born Road
Taylor, MI 48180 (313) 274-7400
plumbing and ventilation products

Massey-Ferguson Ltd. MSE
595 Bay Street
Toronto ON, CDA M5C 2C3 (416) 593-3811
farm machinery

MassMutual Corporate Investors Inc. MCI
1295 State Street
Springfield, MA 01111 (413) 788-8411
closed-end bond mutual fund   [DRP]

MassMutual Income Investors Inc. MIV
1295 State Street
Springfield, MA 01101 (413) 788-8411
closed-end bond mutual fund   [DRP]

Matsushita Electric Industrial Co Ltd MC
1 Panasonic Way
Secaucus, NJ 07094 (201) 348-7705
consumer electrical products

Mattel Inc. MAT
5151 Rosecrans Avenue
Hawthorne, CA 90250 (213) 978-5150
toys

MAXXAM Group Inc. MXM
350 Park Avenue
New York, NY 10022 (212) 576-0500
real estate, lumber

May Department Stores Co. MA
611 Olive Street
St Louis, MO 63101 (314) 342-6300
department, discount, shoe stores

Maytag Co. MYG
403 West 4th Street North
Newton, IA 50208 (515) 792-7000
major home appliances, repair parts   [DRP]

MCA Inc. MCA
100 Universal City Plaza
Universal City, CA 91608 (213) 985-4321
film entertainment, records   [DRP O]

McDermott International Corp. MDR
1010 Common Street
New Orleans, LA 70112 (504) 587-4411
construction in energy industries   [DRP O]

McDonald & Co. Investments Inc. MDD
2100 Central National Bank Building
Cleveland, OH 44114 (216) 623-2000
banking and investment brokerage

McDonald's Corp. MCD
McDonald's Plaza
Oak Brook, IL 60521 (312) 887-3200
fast-food restaurant chain   [O]

McDonnell Douglas Corp. MD
P O Box 516
St Louis, MO 63166 (314) 232-6357
aerospace industries   [O]

McGraw-Hill Inc. MHP
1221 Avenue of the Americas
New York, NY 10020 (212) 997-1221
books, magazines, info services, TV [DRP O]

McIntyre Mines Ltd. MP
3 Calgary Place 355 4th Avenue SW
Calgary, AL, CDA T2P 9J3 (403) 267-4511
coal mining

McKesson Corp. MCK
Crocker Plaza 1 Post Street 37th Floor
San Francisco, CA 94104 (415) 983-8300
distributor of drugs, food, wine   [DRP]

McLean Industries Inc. MII
660 Madison Avenue
New York, NY 10021 (212) 593-3325
shipping, real estate development

McNeil Corp. MME
666 West Market Street
Akron, OH 44303 (216) 434-6000
production support systems and equipment

MCorp MBK
P O Box 5415
Dallas, TX 75222 (214) 698-5000
banking   [DRP 5%]

MDC Holdings INC MDC
3600 South Yosemite Street Suite 900
Denver, CO 80237 (303) 773-1100
developer of houses and real estate

MDU Resources Group Inc. MDU
400 North 4th Street
Bismark, ND 58501 (701) 222-7900
electric/gas utility, gas pipeline   [DRP 5%]

Mead Corp. MEA
World Headquarters Courthouse Plaza NE
Dayton, OH 45463 (513) 222-6323
paper, wood products, publishing   [DRP]

Measurex Corp. MX
1 Result Way
Cupertino, CA 95014 (408) 255-1500
paper industry process control systems

Medtronic Incorporated MDT
3055 Old Highway Eight P O Box 1453
Minneapolis, MN 55440 (612) 574-4000
implantable medical devices, monitoring   [O]

Mellon Bank Corp. MEL
1 Mellon Bank Center Room 750
Pittsburgh, PA 15258 (412) 234-4100
banking   [DRP 5%]

Melville Corp. MES
3000 Westchester Avenue
Harrison, NY 10528 (914) 253-8000
stores: footwear, apparel, health, toys

Mercantile Stores Co. Inc. MST
100 West 10th Street
Wilmington, DE 19899 (302) 575-1816
department stores, beauty salons

Merck and Co. Inc. MRK
Lincoln Avenue
Rahway, NJ 07067 (201) 574-4000
human and animal health products   [DRP O]

Meredith Corp. MDP
1716 Locust Street
Des Moines, IA 50303 (515) 284-3000
magazine and book publishing, broadcasting

Merrill Lynch & Co. Inc. MER
1 Liberty Plaza 26th Floor
New York, NY 10006 (212) 637-7455
investment services and brokerage   [DRP O]

Mesa Ltd. Partnership MLPWI
1 Mesa Square P O Box 2009
Amarillo, TX 79189 (806) 378-1000
oil and gas exploration and production

Mesa Offshore Trust MOS
1 Mesa Square P O Box 2009
Amarillo, TX 79189 (806) 378-1000
royalties of oil and gas production

Mesa Petroleum Co. MSA
320 South Polk Street P O Box 2009
Amarillo, TX 79105 (806) 378-1000
oil and gas exploration and production   [O]

Mesa Royalty Trust MTR
c/o Texas Commerce Bank P O Box 2558
Houston, TX 77002 (713) 236-4631
royalty interests in oil and gas

Mesabi Trust MSB
P O Box 318 Church Street Station
New York, NY 10015 (212) 618-2352
leasehold royalties, land fees, interest

Mestek Inc. MCC
209 Moon Clinton Rd
Coraopolis, PA 15108 (412) 269-5800
steel mill machinery and equipment

Metropolitan Financial Corp. MFC
215 North Fifth Street
Fargo, ND 58108 (701) 293-2600
financial services   [DRP]

Mexico Fund Inc. MXF
165 Broadway
New York, NY 10005 (212) 637-4467
closed-end mexico stock fund   [DRP]

MGM/UA Communications MGM
450 North Roxbury Drive
Beverly Hills, CA 90210 (213) 281-4000
movie producer

Michigan Energy Resources Co. MCG
899 South Telegraph Road, P O Box 729
Monroe, MI 48161 (313) 242-5210
gas utility   [DRP 5%]

Mickelberry Corp. MBC
405 Park Avenue
New York, NY 10022 (212) 832-0303
printing, advertising agencies

MidCon Corp. MCN
701 East 22nd Street
Lombard, IL 60148 (312) 691-2500
oil/gas services/pipelines, coal   [DRP 5% O]

Middle South Utilities MSU
P O Box 610005
New Orleans, LA 70161 (504) 529-5262
electric utility   [O]

Midland-Ross Corp. MLR
20600 Chagrin Boulevard
Cleveland, OH 44112 (216) 491-8400
thermal systems, mechanical controls [DRP]

Midwest Energy Co. MWE
401 Douglas Street P O Box 778
Sioux City, IA 51102 (712) 277-7400
electric and gas utility   [DRP]

Milton Roy Co. MRC
1 Plaza Place NE
St Petersburg, FL 33733 (813) 823-4444
pumps and pollution control devices   [DRP]

Minnesota Mining & Manufacturing Co MMM
3M Center Building 220-600-05
St. Paul MN 55144 (612)733-1110
tapes, abrasives   [DRP O]

Minnesota Power & Light Co. MPL
30 West Superior Street
Duluth, MN 55802 (218) 722-2641
electric utility   [DRP]

Mission Insurance Group Inc. MEQ
2601 Wilshire Boulevard
Los Angeles, CA 90057 (213) 381-6811
fire, marine, casualty, title insurance

Mitel Corp. MLT
350 Legget Drive
Kanata, ON CDA H2K 1B3 (613) 592-2122
telecommunications equipment   [O]

ML Convertible Securities Inc. MLS
P.O. Box 9011
Princeton, NJ 08540 (609)282-2000
closed-end dual purpose mutual fund

Mobil Corp. MOB
150 East 42nd Street
New York, NY 10017 (212) 883-4242
oil refining and marketing   [DRP O]

Mobile Home Industries Inc. QMH
1309 Thomasville Road
Tallahassee, FL 32304 (904) 224-5111
manufacture/sale of mobile homes/parks

Modular Computer System Inc. MSY
1650 McNab Road
Fort Lauderdale, FL 33309 (305) 974-1380
computer system measures and controls

Mohasco Corp. MOH
57 Lyon Street
Amsterdam, NY 12020 (518) 841-2111
furniture and carpeting   [DRP]

Mohawk Data Sciences Corp. MDS
7 Century Drive
Parsippany, NJ 13602 (201) 540-9080
electronic data processing equipment

Monarch Capital Corp. MON
1 Financial Plaza
Springfield, MA 01102 (413) 781-3000
life and disability insurance

Monarch Machine Tool Co. MMO
North Oak Ave
Sidney, OH 45365 (513) 492-4111
lathes for metal-working industry

Monsanto Co. MTC
800 North Lindbergh Boulevard
St Louis, MO 63166 (314) 694-1000
chemicals and chemical products   [DRP O]

Montana Power Co., The MTP
40 East Broadway
Butte, MT 59701 (406) 723-5421
electric and gas utility   [DRP 5%]

Montgomery Street Income Securities Inc. MTS
315 Montgomery Street Suite 1608
San Francisco, CA 94104 (415) 982-8020
closed-end bond mutual fund   [DRP]

MONY Real Estate Investors MYM
1740 Broadway
New York, NY 10019 (212) 586-6716
real estate investment trust   [DRP]

Moore Corp. Ltd MCL
1 First Canadian Place P O Box 78
Toronto, ON, CDA M5X 1G5 (416) 364-2600
business forms   [DRP 5% O]

Moore McCormack Resources Inc. MMR
1 Landmark Square
Stamford, CT 06901 (203) 358-2200
cement, concrete, iron ore, energy   [DRP]

Morgan Keegan Inc. MOR
2800 One Commerce Square
Memphis, TN 38103 (901) 524-4100
regional brokerage services

Morgan, JP Co. Inc. JPM
23 Wall Street
New York, NY 10015 (212) 483-2323
banking and financial services   [DRP 5% O]

Morgan Stanley Group Inc. MS
1251 Avenue of the Americas
New York, NY 10020 (212)974-4000
investment banking, brokerage

Morrison Knudsen Corp. MRN
1 Morrison Knudsen Plaza
Boise, ID 83729 (208) 386-8000
marine engineering, construction   [DRP]

Morse Shoe Inc. MRS
555 Turnpike Street
Canton, MA 02021 (617) 828-9300
shoe stores

Mortgage & Realty Trust MRT
7320 Old York Road
Melrose Park, PA 19126 (215) 782-2055
real estate investment trust   [DRP 5%]

Morton Thiokol Inc. MTI
110 North Wacker Drive
Chicago, IL 60606 (312) 621-5200
chemicals, aerospace motors, salt

Motorola Inc. MOT
Motorola Center 1303 East Algonquin Road
Schaumburg, IL 60196 (312) 397-5000
electronic equipment and systems   [DRP O]

Munford Inc. MFD
68 Brookwood Drive NE
Atlanta, GA 30309 (404) 352-6641
convenience food stores, import stores

Munsingwear Inc. MUN
718 Glenwood Avenue
Minneapolis, MN 55405 (612) 340-4700
men's undergarments

Murphy Oil Corp. MUR
200 Peach Street
El Dorado, AR 71730 (501) 862-6411
oil and gas services,exploration   [O]

Murray Ohio Manufacturing Co.
P O Box 268
Brentwood, TN 37027 (615) 373-6500
bicycles and power motors   [DRP]

Mutual of Omaha Income Shares MUO
10235 Regency Circle
Omaha, NE 68114 (402) 397-8555
closed-end bond mutual fund   [DRP]

Myers, L E Co. Group MYR
1010 Jurie Boulevard
Oakbrook, IL 60521 (312) 325-4666
construction of electric utility plants

NAFCO Financial Group Inc. NAF
5801 Pelican Bay Boulevard
Naples, FL 33340 (813) 597-1611
savings and loan

Nalco Chemical Co. NLC
2901 Butterfield Road
Oak Brook, IL 60521 (312) 887-7500
specialized industrial chemicals

Nashua Corp. NSH
44 Franklin Street
Nashua, NH 03060 (603) 880-2323
office copy products, adhesives

National Convenience Stores Inc. NCS
100 Waugh Drive
Houston, TX 77007 (713) 863-2200
self-service food stores

National Distillers & Chemical Corp. DR
99 Park Avenue
New York, NY 10016 (212) 949-5000
chemicals, brass, liquor [DRP O]

National Education Corp. NEC
4361 Birch Street
Newport Beach, CA 92660 (714) 955-9400
home study courses

National Enterprises NEI
Earle Avenue at Wallace Street
Lafayette, IN 47904 (317) 448-2000
real estate

National Fuel Gas Co. NFG
30 Rockefeller Plaza
New York, NY 10012 (212) 541-7533
gas utility [DRP]

National Home Corp. NHX
Earl Avenue & Wallace Street
Lafayette, IN 47905 (317) 448-2000
pre-fabricated and mobile homes

National Intergroup Inc. NII
20 Stanwix Street
Pittsburgh, PA 15222 (412) 394-4100
steel, aluminum, coal, financial services

National Medical Enterprises Inc. NME
11620 Wilshire Boulevard
Los Angeles, CA 90025 (213) 479-5526
general hospitals [DRP O]

National Mine Service Co. NMS
4900/600 Grant Street
Pittsburgh, PA 15219 (412) 281-0688
mining equipment and supplies

National Presto Industries Inc. NPK
3925 North Hastings Way
Eau Claire, WI 54701 (715) 839-2121
electrical appliances

National Semiconductor Corp. NSM
2900 Semiconductor Drive
Santa Clara, CA 95051 (408) 737-5000
electronic components, digital systems [O]

National Service Industries Inc. NSI
1180 Peachtree Street NW
Atlanta, GA 30312 (404) 892-2400
conglomerate [DRP]

National Standard Co. NSD
8th & Howard Streets
Niles, MI 49100 (616) 683-8100
wire products and machinery

Navistar Inc. NAV
401 West Michigan Avenue 24th Floor
Chicago, Illinois 60601 (312) 836-2000
truck manufacturer

NBD Bancorp Inc. NBD
611 Woodward Avenue
Detroit, MI 48226 (313) 225-1000
banking [DRP]

NBI Inc. NBI
3450 Mitchell Lane P O Box 9001
Boulder, CO 89301 (303) 444-5710
software, word processing systems [O]

NCH Corp. NCH
P O Box 2170 2727 Chemsearch Boulevard
Irving, TX 75062 (214) 438-0251
cleaning and other chemicals

NCNB Corp. NCB
1 NCNB Plaza
Charlotte, NC 28255 (704) 374-5000
banking [DRP 5%]

NCR Corp. NCR
1700 South Patterson Boulevard
Dayton, OH 45479 (513) 445-5000
business info processing systems [DRP O]

NERCO Inc. NER
111 Southwest Columbia
Portland, OR 97201 (503) 796-6600
coal and precious metals, gas

Nevada Power Co. NVP
P O Box 230
Las Vegas, NV 89101 (702) 367-5000
electric utility [DRP]

Nevada Savings and Loan Association NEV
201 Las Vegas Boulevard South
Las Vegas, NV 89101 (702) 385-2222
savings and loan

New England Electric System NES
25 Research Drive
Westborough, MA 01582 (617) 366-9011
electric utility [DRP 5%]

New Jersey Resources Corp. NJR
601 Bangs Avenue
Asbury Park, NJ 07719 (201) 938-1480
gas supplier [DRP]

New York State Electric & Gas Corp NGE
Ithaca-Dryden Road
Ithaca, NY 14850 (607) 729-2551
electric and gas utility   [DRP]

Newell Co. NWL
Newell Center,29 East Stephenson Street
Freeport, IL 61032 (815-235-4171)
home furnishings manaufacturer

Newhall Investment Properties NIP
23823 Valencia Boulevard
Valencia, CA 91355 (805) 255-4000
real estate investment trust

Newhall Land and Farming Dep. Recpts. NHL
23823 Valencia Boulevard
Valencia, CA 91355 (805) 255-4000
land development

Newhall Resources NR
23823 Valencia Boulevard
Valencia, CA 91355 (808) 253-4200
oil and gas limited partnership

Newmont Mining Corp. NEM
200 Park Avenue 36th Floor
New York, NY 10166 (212) 953-6900
coal, copper, lead, zinc, fertilizer   [DRP O]

Newpark Resources Inc. NP
2900 Ridgelake Drive
Metaire, LA 70002 (504) 838-8222
oil field services

Niagara Mohawk Power Corp. NMK
300 Erie Boulevard West
Syracuse, NY 13202 (315) 474-1511
electric and gas utility   [DRP]

Niagara Share Corp. NGS
70 Niagara Street
Buffalo, NY 14202 (716) 856-2600
closed-end investment company   [DRP]

Nicolet Instrument Corp. NIC
5225 Verona Road
Madison, WI 53711 (608) 271-3333
electronic measurement instruments   [DRP]

NICOR Inc. GAS
P O Box 200
Naperville, IL 60566 (312) 242-4470
gas utility, oil/ gas production   [DRP 5%]

N L Industries Inc. NL
1230 Avenue of the Americas
New York, NY 10020 (212) 621-9400
oil products, services, equipment   [DRP O]

Noble Affiliates Inc. NBL
P O Box 1967 330 Neustadt Plaza
Ardmore, OK 73402 (405) 226-1900
oil and gas exploration and production   [O]

Nord Resources Corp. NRD
8111 Timberlodge Trail
Dayton, OH 45459 (513) 433-6307
explores and develops minerals and ores

Norfolk Southern Corp. NSC
8 North Jefferson Street
Norfolk, VA 23510 (804) 629-2600
railroad   [DRP O]

Norlin Corp. NRL
44 South Broadway
White Plains, NY 10605 (212) 966-5900
musical instruments,financial printing

Norstar Bancorp Inc. NOR
1450 Western Avenue
Albany, NY 12203 (518) 447-4043
banking   [DRP 5%]

Nortek Inc. NTK
50 Kennedy Plaza
Providence, RI 02903 (401) 751-1600
multi-industry

North American Coal Corp. NC
12800 Shaker Boulevard
Cleveland, OH 44120 (216) 752-1000
mines and markets coal and lignite

North American Philips Corp. NPH
100 East 42nd Street
New York, NY 10017 (212) 697-3600
electrical and electronic products

North European Oil Royalty Trust NET
43 West Front Street Suite 16
Red Bank, NJ 07701 (201) 741-4008
oil and gas producer

Northeast Utilities NU
P O Box 270
Hartford, CT 06101 (203) 666-6911
electric utility   [DRP]

Northern Indiana Public Service Co. NI
5265 Hohman Avenue
Hammond, IN 46325 (219) 853-5200
electric and gas utility

Northern States Power Co. NSP
414 Nicollet Mall
Minneapolis, MN 55401 (612) 330-5500
electric and gas utility   [DRP]

Northern Telecom Ltd. NT
P O Box 458 Mississauga, ON
CDA L5A 3A2 (416) 275-0960
telecommunications equipment

Northgate Exploration Ltd. NGX
Suite 3140 1 First Canadian Place
Toronto, ON, CDA M5X 1C7 (416) 363-6683
base metal products

Northrop Corp. NOC
1800 Century Park East Century City
Los Angeles, CA 90067 (213) 553-6262
aerospace products and services   [DRP O]

Northwestern Steel & Wire Co. NSW
Avenue B & Wallace Street
Sterling, IL 61081 (815) 625-2500
steel and steel products

Norton Co. NRT
1 New Bond Street
Worcester, MA 01606 (617) 853-1000
abrasives, oil/gas services/products   [DRP]

Norwest Corp. NOB
1200 Peavey Building
Minneapolis, MN 55479 (612) 372-8123
diversified financial services   [DRP 5%]

Novo Industri A/S NVO
575 Madison Avenue
New York, NY 10022
industrial enzymes, insulin   [O]

Nucor Corp. NUE
4425 Randolph Road
Charlotte, NC (704) 366-7000
steel products   [DRP]

NUI Corp. NUI
1011 Route 22
Bridgewater, NJ 08807 (201) 685-3900
gas utility, drilling, softwear   [DRP 5%]

Nutri/System Inc. NTR
2655 Philmont Avenue
Huntington Valley, PA 19006 (215) 947-9700
weight loss centers, prepackaged foods

N V F Co. NVF
P O Drawer K
Miami Beach, FL 33140 (305) 866-7771
steel, paper, plastics, coal

NWA Inc. NWA
Minneapolis/St Paul Airport
St Paul, MN 55001 (612) 726-2111
airline   [O]

NYNEX Corp. NYN
333 Madison Avenue
New York, NY 10017 (212) 370-7400
telecommunications services   [DRP O]

Oakite Products Inc. OKT
50 Valley Road
Berkeley Heights, NJ 07922 (201) 464-6900
cleaning and conditioning chemicals   [DRP]

Occidental Petroleum Corp. OXY
10889 Wilshire Boulevard
Los Angeles, CA 90024 (213) 879-1700
oil/coal/gas exploration/production   [DRP O]

Ocean Drilling and Exploration Co. ODR
1600 Canal Street
New Orleans, LA 70112 (504) 561-2811
oil and gas contract drilling   [O]

Ogden Corp. OG
277 Park Avenue
New York, NY 10017 (212) 754-4000
conglomerate

Ohio Edison Co. OEC
76 South Main Street
Akron, OH 44308 (216) 384-5100
electric utility   [DRP]

Ohio Mattress Co., The OMT
1300 East 9th Street
Cleveland, OH 44114 (216) 522-1310
bedding and textile products

Oklahoma Gas & Electric Co. OGE
P O Box 321 321 North Harvey Avenue
Oklahoma City, OK 73101 (405) 272-3217
electric utility   [DRP]

Olin Corp. OLN
120 Long Ridge Road
Stamford, CT 06904 (203) 356-2000
chemicals, glass, paper, guns

Omnicare Inc. OCR
1300 Fountain Square South
Cincinnati, OH 45202 (513) 762-6666
hospital services, equipment, supplies

Oneida Ltd. OCQ
Oneida, NY 13421 (315) 361-3000
tableware/cookware, industrial wire
                                       [DRP 5%]

ONEOK Inc. OKE
P O Box 871
Tulsa, OK 74102 (918) 588-7000
oil and gas exploration/production [DRP 5%]

Orange and Rockland Utilities Inc. ORU
1 Blue Hill Plaza
Pearl River, NY 10965 (914) 352-6000
electric and gas utility   [DRP]

Orange-co Inc. OJ
P O Box 127
Lake Hamilton, FL 33851 (813) 439-1585
juices, restaurants

Orion Capital Corp. OC
30 Rockefeller Plaza
New York, NY 10020 (212) 541-4646
life, accident, health insurance

Orion Pictures Corp. OPC
711 5th Avenue 6th Floor
New York, NY 10022 (212) 758-5100
film-making, publishing

Outboard Marine Corp. OM
100 Sea Horse Drive
Waukegan, IL 60085 (312) 689-6200
outboard motors, lawn/turf equipment [DRP]

Overnite Transportation Co. OVT
1000 Semmes Avenue
Richmond, VA 23224 (804) 231-8236
trucking

Overseas Shipholding Group Inc. OSG
511 5th Avenue
New York, NY 10017 (212) 869-1222
bulk ocean transport

Owens-Corning Fiberglas OCF
Fiberglas Tower
Toledo, OH 43659 (419) 248-8000
glass fiber insulation and textiles   [DRP O]

Owens-Illinois Inc. OI
1 Seagate
Toledo, OH 43666 (419) 247-5000
glass products, packaging products [DRP O]

Oxford Industries Inc. OXM
222 Piedmont Avenue NE
Atlanta, GA 30312 (404) 659-2424
men's and women's apparel

Pacific American Income Shares Inc. PAI
P O Box 983
Pasadena, CA 92102 (213) 614-3156
closed-end bond mutual fund   [DRP]

Pacific Gas & Electric Co. PCG
77 Beale Street
San Francisco, CA 94106 (415) 781-4211
electric and gas utility   [DRP]

Pacific Lighting Corp. PLT
P O Box 54790 Terminal Annex
Los Angeles, CA 90054 (213) 689-3481
gas utility   [DRP]

Pacific Resources Inc. PRI
733 Bishop Street
Honolulu, HI 96813 (808) 547-3111
oil refining and marketing

Pacific Scientific Co. PSX
1350 South State College Boulevard
Anaheim, CA 9820 (714) 535-8141
electronic instruments and controls

Pacific Telesis Group PAC
140 New Montgomery Street
San Francisco, CA 94105 (415) 882-8000
telecommunications services   [DRP O]

Pacific Tin Consolidated Corp. PTC
289 Park Avenue
New York, NY 10017 (212) 557-2020
minerals, metal products, petroleum

PacifiCorp PPW
920 SW 6th Avenue
Portland, OR 97204 (503) 243-1122
electric utility   [DRP]

Paine-Webber Group Inc. PWJ
1285 Avenue of the Americas
New York, NY 10019 (212) 713-2000
investment services, brokerage   [DRP O]

Pan Am Corp. PN
Pan Am Building
New York, NY 10156 (212) 880-1234
airline

Pan American Banks, Inc. PAB
150 Southeast 3rd Avenue
Miami, FL 33131 (305) 577-5974
banking

Pandick Inc. PI
345 Hudson Street
New York, NY 10014 (212) 741-5555
printing: prospectuses and annual reports

Panhandle Eastern Corp. PEL
PO Box 1642
Houston, TX 77001 (713) 664-3401
gas pipelines   [DRP 5% O]

Pansophic Systems Inc. PNS
709 Enterprise
Oak Brook, IL 60521 (312) 986-6000
standardized systems software products

Pantry Pride Inc. PPR
6500 North Andrews Avenue
Fort Lauderdale, FL 33309 (305) 771-8300
supermarkets, drug stores, food, cosmetics

Paradyne Corp. PDN
8550 Ulmerton Road
Largo, FL 33354 (813) 530-2000
data communication products, systems   [O]

Park Electrochemical Corp. PKE
5 Dakota Drive
Lake Success, NY 11042 (516) 354-4100
printed circuit materials

Parker Drilling Co. PKD
Parker Building 3rd & Main Streets
Tulsa, OK 74103 (918) 585-8221
contract oil drilling service

Parker-Hannifin Corp. PH
17325 Euclid Avenue
Cleveland, OH 44112 (216) 531-3000
fluid power systems and components

Patrick Petroleum Co. PPC
P O Box 747
Jackson, MI 49204 (517) 787-6633
oil and gas exploration and production

Pay 'n Pak Stores Inc. PNP
1209 South Central
Kent, WA 98031 (206) 854-5450
retail plumbing and electrical materials

Payless Cashways Inc. PCI
1 Pershing Square
2301 Main Street
Kansas City, MO 64108 (816) 471-5500

Pengo Industries Inc. PGO
1400 Everman Road
Fort Worth, TX 76140 (817) 293-7110
oil field equipment, services

Penn Central Corp. PC
500 West Putnam Avenue
Greenwich, CT 06836 (203) 629-5000
electronics, oil, and telecommunications   [O]

Penn Power & Light Co. PPL
2 North 9th Street
Allentown, PA 18101 (215) 770-5151
electric utility   [DRP]

Penney, J C Co. Inc. JCP
1301 Avenue of the Americas
New York, NY 10019 (212) 957-4321
merchandise retailer   [DRP O]

Pennwalt Corp. PSM
Penwalt Building 3 Parkway
Philadelphia, PA 19102 (215) 587-7000
chemicals, health products, equipment [DRP]

Pennzoil Co. PZL
P O Box 2967 1 Pennzoil Place
Houston, TX 77001 (713) 546-4000
oil and gas, mineral mining   [DRP O]

Peoples Energy Corp. PGL
122 South Michigan Avenue
Chicago, IL 60603 (312) 431-4000
gas utility   [DRP]

Pep Boys-Manny Moe & Jack PBY
3111 West Allegheny Avenue
Philadelphia, PA 19132 (215) 229-9000
auto parts retail chain

PepsiCo Inc. PEP
World Headquarters
Purchase, NY 10057 (914) 253-2000
beverages, snack foods, restaurants [DRP O]

Perkin-Elmer Corp., The PKN
Main Avenue
Norwalk, CT 06851 (203) 762-1000
analytic equipment, optics, avionics [DRP O]

Permian Basin Royalty Trust PBT
P O Box 1317
Fort Worth, TX 76102 (817) 390-6905
royalty oil interests

Perry Drug Stores Inc. PDS
5400 Perry Drive
Pontiac, MI 48056 (313) 334-1300
drug stores, drug/auto/home center stores

Petrie Stores Corp. PST
70 Enterprise Avenue
Secaucus, NJ 07094 (201) 866-3600
women's specialty store chain

Petroleum & Resources Corp. PEO
201 North Charles Street
Baltimore, MD 21201 (301) 752-5900
closed-end investment company   [DRP]

Petroleum Investments Ltd. PIL
50 Penn Place Suite 1410
Oklahoma City, OK 73118 (405) 840-3293
oil and gas limited partnerships

Pfizer Inc. PFE
235 East 42nd Street
New York, NY 10017 (212) 573-2323
health/agriculture/chemical products [DRP O]

Phelps Dodge Corp. PD
300 Park Avenue
New York, NY 10022 (212) 940-6400
copper mining, silver, gold, molybdenum [O]

PHH Group, Inc. PHH
11333 McCormick Road
Hunt Valley, MD 21031 (301) 667-4000
personnel/vehicle fleet/leasing services

Philadelphia Suburban Corp. PSC
762 Lancaster Avenue
Bryn Mawr, PA 19010 (215) 527-8000
water utility   [DRP]

Philadelphia Electric Co. PE
2301 Market Street
Philadelphia, PA 19101 (215) 841-4000
electric utility

Philip Morris Companies Inc. MO
100 Park Avenue
New York, NY 10017 (212) 880-5000
cigarettes, brewing, food   [DRP O]

Philips Industries Inc. PHL
4801 Springfield Street P O Box 943
Dayton, OH 45401 (513) 253-7171
construction, building products

Phillips Petroleum Co. P
244 Adams Building
Bartlesville, OK 74004 (918) 661-6600
oil production/refining/marketing   [DRP O]

Phillips-Van Heusen Corp. PVH
1290 Avenue of the Americas
New York, NY 10019 (212) 541-5200
men's apparel, apparel stores

Piedmont Aviation Inc. PIE
P O Box 2720
Winston-Salem, NC 27156 (919) 768-5171
air transport of passengers, cargo, mail   [O]

Piedmont Natural Gas Co. Inc. PNY
P O Box 33068
Charlotte, NC 28233 (704) 364-3120
gas utility   [DRP 5%]

Pier 1 Inc. PIR
2520 West Freeway
Fort Worth, TX 76102 (817) 335-7031
import specialty stores

Pilgrim Regional Bank Shares Inc. PBS
222 Bridge Plaza South
Fort Lee, NJ 07024 (201) 461-7500
mutual fund sponsor   [DRP]

Pillsbury Co. PSY
Pillsbury Center
Minneapolis, MN 55402 (612) 330-8870
consumer foods, restaurants   [DRP O]

Pioneer Corp. PNA
P O Box 511
Amarillo, TX 79163 (806) 373-6054
oil and gas exploration and production   [O]

Pioneer Electronic Corp. PIO
4-1 Meguro 1-Chome Meguro-Ku
Tokyo 153 Japan
high-fidelity stereo products

Pitney-Bowes Inc. PBI
Walter H Wheeler Jr Drive
Stamford, CT 06926 (203) 356-5000
business equipment and supplies   [DRP O]

Pittston Co. PCO
1 Pickwick Plaza
Greenwich, CT 06830 (203) 622-0900
coal, freight forwarding, security   [DRP O]

Plains Petroleum Co. PLP
143 Union Boulevard Suite 1000
Lakewood, CO 80228 (303) 969-9325
oil and gas exploration and production

Planning Research Corp. PLN
1500 Planning Research Drive
McLean, VA 22102 (703) 556-1000
computer systems info and engineering

Plantronics Inc. PLX
1762 Technology Drive Suite 225
San Jose, CA 95110 (408) 998-8388
telecommunications,headsets

Playboy Enterprises Inc. PLA
919 North Michigan Avenue Suite 1300
Chicago, IL 6061 (312) 751-8000
magazines, clubs, entertainment

Plessey Co. Ltd. PLY
277 Park Avenue 30th Floor
New York, NY 10017 (212) 752-4441
electrical and electronic components

Pogo Producing Co. PPP
P O Box 2504 707 McKinney Street
Houston, TX 77001 (713) 651-4300
oil and gas exploration and development

Polaroid Corp. PRD
119 Windsor Street
Cambridge, MA 02139 ((617) 577-2000
photographic equipment and film   [DRP O]

Ponderosa Inc. PON
P O Box 578
Dayton, OH 45401 (513) 890-6400
self-service steak houses, meat processing

Pope and Talbot Inc. POP
1500 West 1st Avenue
Portland, OR 97201 (503) 228-9161
wood, pulp, and paper products

Portec Inc. POR
300 Windsor Drive
Oak Brook, IL 60521 (312) 920-4600
railway track equipment

Portland General Electric Co. PGN
121 Southwest Salmon Street
Portland, OR 97204 (503) 226-8333
electric utility   [DRP]

Potlatch Corp. PCH
P O Box 3591
San Francisco, CA 94119 (415) 981-5980
pulp, paperboard, lumber, paper   [DRP]

Potomac Electric Power Co. POM
1900 Pennsylvania Avenue N W
Washington, DC 20006 (202) 872-2797
electric utility   [DRP]

PPG Industries Inc. PPG
1 PPG Place
Pittsburgh, PA 15272 (412) 434-3131
glass, paint, resins, fiber glas   [DRP O]

Premier Industrial Corp. PRE
4415 Euclid Avenue
Cleveland, OH 44103 (216) 391-8300
electronic and industrial products   [DRP]

Primark Corp. PMK
535 Griswold Street Suite 22
Detroit, MI 48226 (313) 961-6161
gas utility, aircraft and TV leasing   [DRP]

Prime Computer Inc. PRM
Prime Park
Natick, MA 01760 (617) 655-8000
mini-computers and systems   [O]

Prime Motor Inns Inc. PDQ
700 Route 46 East
Fairfield, NJ 07006 (201) 882-1010
motels and construction   [O]

Procter and Gamble Co. PG
2 Procter & Gamble Plaza TN-7
Cincinnati, OH 45202 (513) 562-1100
household/food/grooming products   [DRP O]

Products Research & Chemical Corp PRC
5430 San Fernando Road
Glendale, CA 91203 (213) 240-2060
sealants, coatings, specialty chemicals

Proler International Corp. PS
P O Box 286
Houston, TX 77001 (713) 675-2281
upgrades ferrous scrap metal

Prudential Realty Trust Capital Shares PRT
Prudential Plaza
Newark, NJ 07101 (201) 877-4302
real estate investment trust

PSA Inc. PSA
3225 North Harbor Drive
San Diego, CA 92101 (714) 574-2100
airline, fuel sales, jet engine servicing

Public Service Co of New Hampshire PNH
P O Box 330
Manchester, NH 03105 (603) 669-4000
electric utility

Public Service Co. of Colorado PSR
550 15th Street
Denver, CO 80202 (303) 571-7511
electric and gas utility   [DRP]

Public Service Co. of New Mexico PNM
Alvarado Square
Albuquerque, NM 87158 (505) 848-2700
electric utility   [DRP 3%]

Public Service Enterprise Grp. Inc. PEG
800 Park Place
Newark, NJ 07101 (201) 430-7000
electric and gas utility   [DRP]

Public Service of Indiana Inc. PIN
1000 East Main Street
Plainfield, IN 46188 (317) 839-9611
electric utility

Publicker Industries Inc. PUL
777 West Putnam Avenue P O Box 1978
Greenwich, CT 06830 (203) 531-4500
industrial alcohols, chemicals, liquor

Pueblo International Inc. PII
375 Park Avenue
New York, NY 10022 (212) 935-1710
supermarkets

Puerto Rican Cement Co. Inc. PRN
P O Box 4487
San Juan, Puerto Rico 00936
cement

Puget Sound Power & Light Co. PSD
Puget Power Building
Bellevue, WA 98009 (206) 454-6363
electric utility   [DRP]

Pullman-Peabody Co., The PMN
182 Nassau Street
Princeton, NJ 08540 (609) 683-1770
industrial equipment

Pulte Home Corp. PHM
6400 Farmington Road
West Bloomfield, MI 48033 (313) 661-1500
home design and construction   [O]

Purolator Courier Corp. PCC
131 Morristown Road
Basking Ridge, NJ 07920 (201) 953-6400
package delivery, vehicle filters and caps

Pyro Energy Corp. BTU
653 South Hebron Avenue
Evansville, IN 47715 (812) 473-8600
coal mining, oil and gas production

Quaker Oats Co. OAT
Merchandise Mart Plaza
Chicago, IL 60654 (312) 222-7111
grocery products, toys   [DRP O]

Quaker State Oil Refining Corp. KSF
P O Box 989
Oil City, PA 16031 (814) 676-7676
auto products, lubricants, fuels   [DRP]

Quanex Corp. NX
1900 West Loop South Suite 1500
Houston, TX 77027 (713) 961-4600
seamless and welded steel tubing, bars

Questar Corp. STR
P O Box 11368
Salt Lake City, UT 84111 (801) 534-5555
gas utility, oil and gas exploration   [DRP]

Quick & Reilly Group Inc. BQR
120 Wall Street
New York, NY 10005 (212) 943-8686
discount brokerage firm

Radice Corp. RI
600 Corporate Drive
Fort Lauderdale, FL 33334 (305) 493-5003
develops and sells houses and condominiums

Ralston Purina Co. RAL
Checkerboard Square
St Louis, MO 63119 (314) 982-1000
groceries, pet foods, feed, restaurants   [O]

Ramada Inns Inc. RAM
3838 East Van Buren Street
Phoenix, AZ 85008 (602) 273-4000
hotels, casino-hotels

Ranco Inc. RNI
555 Metro Place North P O Box 248
Dublin, OH 43017 (614) 764-3733
thermo/pressure controls   [DRP]

Ranger Oil Ltd. RGO
425 1st Street SW
Calgary, AL, CDA T2P 3L8 (403) 263-1500
oil and gas exploration and production   [O]

Raychem Corp. RYC
300 Constitution Drive
Menlo Park, CA 94025 (415) 329-3333
plastic and elastomeric products   [O]

Raymark Corp. RAY
100 Oakview Drive
Trumbull, CT 06611 (203) 371-0101
asbestos, rivets, other friction products

Rayonier Timberlands LOG
1177 Summer Street
Stamford, CT 06904 (203)348-7000
timber limited partnerships

Raytheon Co. RTN
141 Spring Street
Lexington, MA 02173 (617) 862-6600
electric and electronic products   [DRP O]

R B Industries Inc. RBI
2323 Southeast Main Street
Irvine, CA 92714 (714) 979-4000
retail furniture showrooms

Reading & Bates Corp. RB
2200 Mid-Continent Tower
Tulsa, OK 74103 (918) 583-8521
oil/gas construction/production   [DRP O]

Realty Refund Trust RRF
National City Center 13th Floor
Cleveland, OH 44115 (216) 771-7660
real estate investment trust

Recognition Equipment Inc. REC
P O Box 222307
Dallas, TX 75222 (214) 579-6000
optical character recognition systems

Redman Industries Inc. RE
2550 Walnut Hill Lane
Dallas, TX 75229 (214) 353-3600
manufactured housing, building components

Reece Corp. RCE
200 Prospect Street
Waltham, MA 02154 (617) 894-9220
industrial sewing machines

Regal International Inc. RGL
256 North Belt East
Houston, TX 77060 (713) 445-7700
rubber products for oil and gas industry

Reichhold Chemicals Inc. RCI
RCI Building 525 North Broadway
White Plains, NY 10602 (914) 682-5700
specialty chemicals and synthetic resins

Republic Gypsum Co. RGC
3625 Miller Park Drive
Garland, TX 75042 (214) 272-0441
wallboard, mobile and modular homes

Republic New York Corp. RNB
452 5th Avenue
New York, NY 10018 (212) 930-6000
banking

Republicbank Corp. RPT
P O Box 222102
Dallas, TX 75222 (214) 922-6023
banking

Research Cottrell Inc. RC
P O Box 1500
Somerville, NJ 08876 (201) 685-4000
environmental control systems

Revco DS Inc. RDS
1925 Enterprise Highway
Twinsburg, OH 44087 (216) 425-9811
discount drugstores, health aids   [DRP O]

Revere Copper & Brass Inc. QRVB
605 3rd Avenue
New York, NY 10016 (212) 578-1500
fabrication of aluminum, copper, brass

Revlon Group REV
36 East 63rd Street
New York, NY 10021 (212) 593-4300
supermarkets, food, cosmetics

Rexham Corp. RXH
90 Park Avenue
New York, NY 10016 (212) 883-0915
packaging materials   [DRP]

Rexnord Inc. REX
350 North Sunny Slope Road
Brookfield, WI 53005 (414) 797-6900
mechanical and electronic components [DRP]

Reynolds Metals Co. RLM
Reynolds Metals Building
Richmond, VA 23261 (804) 281-2000
aluminum products   [DRP] [O]

RJR Nabisco RJR
4th & Main Streets
Winston-Salem, NC 27192 (919) 773-2000
tobacco, food, spirits, restaurants   [DRP O]

Rite Aid Corp. RAD
PO Box 3165
Harrisburg, PA 17105 (717) 761-2633
discount drug store chain   [O]

River Oaks Industries Inc. ROI
Sand Mountain Industrial Park
Boaz, AL 35857 (205) 593-9240
mobile homes, toys

RLC Corp. RLC
1 Rollins Plaza P O Box 1971
Wilmington, DE 19899 (302) 429-2929
trucking/leasing, pollution control   [DRP]

Robertson, HH Co. RHH
2 Gateway Center
Pittsburgh, PA 15222 (412) 281-3200
metal building products, construction [DRP]

Robins, AH Co. Inc. QRAH
1407 Cummings Drive
Richmond, VA 23220 (804) 257-2141
pharmaceuticals

Rochester Gas & Electric Corp. RGS
89 East Avenue
Rochester, NY 14604 (716) 546-2700
electric and gas utility   [DRP]

Rochester Telephone Corp. RTC
100 Midtown Plaza
Rochester, NY 14604 (716) 325-9851
telephone service   [DRP]

Rockefeller Center Properties Inc. RCP
1230 Avenue of the Americas
New York, NY 10020 (212) 489-3000
real estate investment trust

Rockwell International Corp. ROK
600 Grant Street
Pittsburgh, PA 15219 (412) 565-2000
military electronics, aerospace   [DRP]

Rohm and Haas Co. ROH
Independence Mall West
Philadelphia, PA 19105 (215) 592-3000
chemicals, plastics

Rohr Industries Inc. RHR
Foot of H Street
Chula Vista, CA 92012 (619) 691-4111
aircraft, jet engine, aerospace components

Rollins Communications Inc. ROC
2170 Piedmont Road NE
Atlanta, GA 30324 (404) 888-2000
cable broadcasting, outdoor advertising

Rollins Environmental Services Inc. REN
2200 Concord Pike
Wilmington, DE 19803 (302) 492-2700
industrial waste disposal   [DRP]

Rollins Inc. ROL
P O Box 647
Atlanta, GA 30301 (404) 888-2216
pest control, fire security   [DRP]

Ronson Corp. RON
1 Ronson Road
Bridgewater, NJ 08807 (201) 526-5900
household appliances and lighters

Roper Corp. ROP
1905 West Court Street
Kankakee, IL 60901 (815) 937-6000
power mowers, kitchen appliances   [DRP]

Rorer Group Inc. ROR
500 Virginia Drive
Fort Washington, PA 19034 (215) 628-6541
health products, medical instruments   [O]

Rothschild, Unterberg, Towbin Inc. R
55 Water Street
New York, NY 10041 (212) 412-1000
investment banking and brokerage

Rowan Companies Inc. RDC
1900 Post Oak Tower Bldg 5051 Westheimer
Houston, TX 77027 (713) 621-7800
contract drilling, air charter service   [O]

Royal Dutch Petroleum Co. RD
1 Rockefeller Plaza
New York, NY 10020 (212) 262-7400
oil production   [O]

Royal International Optical Corp RIO
2760 Irving Boulevard
Dallas, TX 75207 (214) 638-1397
optical stores

RPC Energy Services Inc. RES
2170 Piedmont Road NE
Atlanta, GA 30324 (404) 888-2000
oil and gas industry services, equipment

RTE Corp. RTE
235 North Executive Drive
Brookfield, WI 53005 (414) 786-2559
electric power industry equipment

Rubbermaid Corp. RBD
1147 Akron Road
Wooster, OH 44691 (216) 264-6464
plastic and rubber products

Russ Berrie & Co. Inc. RUS
111 Bauer Drive
Oakland, NJ 07436 (201) 891-7500
gift items

Russ Togs Inc. RTS
27-11 49th Avenue
Long Island City, NY 11101 (718) 937-1000
apparel for women and girls

Ryan Homes Inc. RYN
100 Ryan Court
Pittsburgh, PA 15205 (412) 276-8000
residential construction

Ryder System Inc. RDR
PO Box 520816
Miami, FL 33152 (305) 593-3671
truck leasing/services/stops   [DRP]

Ryland Group Inc. RYL
10221 Wincopin Circle
Columbia, MD 21044 (301) 730-7222
single-family home construction

Rymer Co. RYR
1701 Gulf Road 3 Continental Towers
Rolling Meadows, IL 60008 (312) 952-2920
meat processing, parking meters

Sabine Corp. SAB
1200 Mercantile Bank Building
Dallas, TX 75201 (214) 979-6900
oil and gas exploration and production

Sabine Royalty Trust SBR
1200 Mercantile Bank Building
Dallas, TX 75201 (214) 979-6900
royalties of oil and gas properties

Safeguard Business Systems Inc. SGB
470 Maryland Drive
Fort Washington, PA 19034 (215) 641-5000
business systems and forms

Safeguard Scientific Inc. SFE
630 Park Avenue
King of Prussia, PA 19406 (215) 265-4000
power transmission, metal finishing

Safety Kleen Corp. SK
777 Big Timber Road
Elgin, IL 60120-1499 (312) 697-8460
parts cleaning services

Safeway Stores Inc. SA
4th & Jackson Streets
Oakland, CA 94660 (415) 891-3000
food/liquor stores, food processing   [DRP]

Saga Corp. SGA
1 Saga Lane
Menlo Park, CA 94025 (415) 854-5150
restaurants, food services

Saint Joseph Light & Power Co. SAJ
520 Francis Street
St Joseph, MO 64502 (816) 233-8888
electric utility   [DRP]

Salant Corp. QSLT
330 5th Avenue
New York, NY 10001 (212) 502-1900
slacks, jeans, outerwear

Salomon Inc. PBS
1221 Avenue of the Americas
New York, NY 10020 (212) 764-3700
investment services, commodity trading   [O]

San Diego Gas & Electric Co. SDO
P O Box 1831
San Diego, CA 92112 (619) 696-2000
electric/gas utility, gas pipelines   [DRP]

San Juan Basin Royalty Trust SJT
Fort Worth National Bank, 500 Throckmorton
Fort Worth, TX 76102 (817) 338-8607
oil & gas production

San Juan Racing Association Inc. SJR
2000 L Street Suite 609
Washington, DC 20006 (809) 724-9220
racetrack, real estate

Sanders Associates Inc. SAA
Daniel Webster Highway
South Nashua, NH 03061 (603) 885-4321
aircraft defense, graphics electronics   [O]

Santa Anita Realty Enterprises Inc. SAR
1 Wilshire Building Suite 2303
Los Angeles, CA 90017 (213) 485-9220
racetrack, commercial real estate   [DRP 5%]

Santa Fe Southern Pacific Corp SFX
224 South Michigan Avenue
Chicago, IL 60604 (312) 427-4900
railroad   [DRP O]

Sara Lee Corp. SLE
3 First National Plaza
Chicago, IL 60603 (312) 726-2600
food processor, consumer products   [DRP O]

Sargent Welch Scientific Co. SWS
7300 North Linder Avenue
Skokie, IL 60077 (312) 677-0600
school research laboratory equipment

Savannah Electric and Power Co. SAV
P O Box 968
Savannah, GA 31402 (912) 232-7171
electric utility   [DRP]

Savin Corp. SVB
9 West Broad Street P O Box 10270
Stamford, CT 06904 (203) 967-5000
copying machines

SCANA Corp. SCG
P O Box 764
Columbus, SC 29202 (803) 748-3000
electric and gas utility   [DRP]

Schering-Plough Corp. SGP
Galloping Hill Road
Kenilworth, NJ 07033 (201) 822-7000
drugs, personal care products   [DRP O]

Schlumberger NV SLB
277 Park Avenue
New York, NY 10172 (212) 350-9400
oil drilling services, semiconductors   [O]

Scientific Atlanta Inc. SFA
Box 105600
Atlanta, GA 30348 (404) 449-2000
communications equipment   [O]

Scott Paper Co. SPP
Scott Plaza
Philadelphia, PA 19113 (215) 521-5000
paper products   [DRP O]

Scotty's Inc. SHB
Recker Highway
Winter Haven, FL 33880 (813) 299-1111
building materials retailer

Sea Containers Ltd. SCR
1 World Trade Center Suite 2831
New York, NY 10048 (212) 938-1507
sea cargo container chassis, crane leasing

Sea Land Corp. SLN
10 Parsonage Road
Edison, NJ 08817 (201) 632-2000
containerized freight shipping   [O]

SeaCo Inc. SCN
1 World Trade Center Suite 2831
New York, NY 10048 (212) 938-1500
leisure and property development

Seagram Co. Ltd. VO
1430 Peel Street
Montreal 2, QU, CDA H3A1S9 (514) 849-5271
wine and distilled spirits, chemicals   [O]

Seagull Energy Corp. SGO
1st National Bank Building
Houston, TX 77002 (713) 951-4700
natural gas pipeline

Sealed Air Corp. SEE
Park 80 Plaza East
Saddle Brook, NJ 07662 (201) 791-7600
packaging products

Sealed Power Corp. SPW
2001 Sanford Street
Muskegon, MI 49443 (616) 724-5011
engine parts, piston rings   [DRP]

Sears Roebuck & Co. S
Sears Tower 41st Floor
Chicago, IL 60684 (312) 875-1466
retailing, financial services   [DRP O]

Security Pacific Corp. SPC
333 South Hope Street
Los Angeles, CA 90071 (213) 613-6696
banking   [DRP 5% O]

Service Corp. International SRV
P O Box 13548
Houston, TX 77019 (713) 522-5141
funeral services, cemetery

Shaklee Corp. SHC
444 Market Street
San Francisco, CA 94111 (415) 954-3000
vitamins, food supplies   [DRP O]

Shaw Industries Inc. SHX
616 East Walnut Avenue
Dalton, GA 30720 (404) 278-3812
carpet manufacturer

Shell Transport & Trading Co. SC
1 Wall Street 6th Floor
New York, NY 10005 (212) 262-2244
oil and gas exploration and production

Sherwin Williams Co. SHW
101 Prospect Avenue NW
Cleveland, OH 4415 (216) 566-2000
paint and varnish manufacturer   [DRP]

Shoe-Town Inc. SHU
994 Riverview Drive
Totowa, NJ 07512 (201) 785-1900
shoe retailer

Showboat Inc. SBO
2800 East Fremont Street
Las Vegas, NV 89104 (702) 385-9123
hotel and casino

Sierra Pacific Resources SRP
P O Box 30150
Reno, NV 89520 (702) 689-3600
electric, gas, water utility   [DRP]

Singer Co., The SMF
8 Stamford Forum
Stamford, CT 06904 (203) 356-4200
aerospace and marine systems   [O]

Skyline Corp. SKY₁
2520 By-pass Road
Elkhart, IN 46514 (219) 294-6521
mobile homes, recreational vehicles   [O]

SL Industries Inc. SL
3 Greentree Center Suite 201
Marlton, NJ 08053 (609) 596-7800
specialty industrial products

Slattery Group Inc. SGI
15 South Third Street
Easton, PA 18042 (215) 258-6231
construction, cement

Smith International Inc. SII
P O Box 1860
Newport Beach, CA 92660 (714) 752-9000
oil drilling equipment, services   [DRP O]

Smithkline Beckman Corp. SKB
1500 Spring Garden Street
Philadelphia, PA 19130 (215) 751-4000
drugs, medical instruments   [DRP O]

Smucker, JM Co. SJM
Strawberry Lane North
Orrville, OH 44667 (216) 682-0015
preserves, jams and jellies   [DRP]

Snap-on Tools Corp. SNA
2801 80th Street
Kenosha, WI 53140 (414) 654-8681
hand tools

Snyder Oil Partners SOI
1-10 West 7th Street - Suite 415
Fort Worth, TX 76102 (817) 338-4043
oil and gas property management

Sonat Inc. SNT
PO Box 2563
Birmingham, AL 35202 (205) 325-3800
gas pipeline, oil and gas drilling   [DRP O]

Sony Corp. SNE
9 West 57th Street
New York, NY 10019 (212) 371-5800
consumer and industrial electronics

Soo Line Corp. SOO
800 Soo Line Building Box 530
Minneapolis, MN 55440 (612) 332-1261
railroad   [DRP]

Source Capital Inc. SOR
10301 West Pico Boulevard
Los Angeles, CA 90064 (213) 277-4900
closed-end mutual fund   [DRP]

South Jersey Industries Inc. SJI
1 South Jersey Plaza Route 4
Folsom, NJ 08037 (609) 561-9000
gas, fuel, oil, sand

Southdown Inc. SDW
2 Allen Center Suite 2200
Houston, TX 77002 (713) 658-8921
oil and gas exploration and production

Southeast Banking Corp. STB
100 South Biscayne Boulevard
Miami, FL 33131 (305) 577-4000
banking   [DRP 5%]

Southeastern Public Service Co. SPV
6917 Collins Avenue
Miami, FL 33141 (305) 866-7771
electric utility

Southern California Edison Co. SCE
2244 Walnut Grove Avenue
Rosemead, CA 91700 (213) 572-1212
electric utility   [DRP]

Southern Co. SO
64 Perimeter Center East
Atlanta, GA 30346 (404) 393-0650
electric utility   [DRP O]

Southern Indiana Gas & Electric Co. SIG
20-24 NW 4th Street
Evansville, IN 47741 (812) 424-6411
gas and electric utility   [DRP]

Southern New England Telephone Co. SNG
227 Church Street
New Haven, CT 06506 (203) 771-3226
telephone service   [DRP]

Southern Union Co. SUG
1800 First International Building
Dallas, TX 75270 (214) 748-8511
oil and gas pipeline   [DRP]

Southland Corp. SLC
P O Box 719
Dallas, TX 75221 (214) 828-7011
convenience stores, gasoline refiner   [DRP O]

Southland Royalty Co. SRO
1600 1st National Building
Fort Worth, TX 76102 (817) 390-9200
oil and gas exploration

Southmark Corp. SM
1601 LBJ Park West - Suite 800
Dallas, TX 75234 (214) 241-8787
real estate, financial services

Southwest Airlines Inc. LUV
P O Box 37611 Love Field
Dallas, TX 75235 (214) 353-6100
regional airline   [O]

Southwest Forest Industries Inc. SWF
6225 North 25th Street
Phoenix, AZ 85016 (602) 956-6000
paper and building materials

Southwest Gas Corp. SWX
5241 Spring Mountain Road, P O Box 15015
Las Vegas, NV 89114 (702) 876-7250
natural gas utility   [DRP]

Southwestern Bell Corp. SBC
1010 Pine Street
St Louis, MO 63101 (312) 241-4540
telecommunications service   [DRP O]

Southwestern Energy Co. SWN
1001 Sain Street
Fayetteville, AR 72702 (501) 521-1141
gas utility, oil and gas exploration   [DRP]

Southwestern Public Service Co. SPS
P O Box 1261
Amarillo, TX 79170 (806) 378-2121
electric utility   [DRP]

Sparton Corp. SPA
2400 East Canson
Jackson, MI 49202 (517) 787-8600
sonobuoys, conveyors, auto parts

Spectra-Physics Inc. SPY
3333 North First Street
San Jose, CA 95134 (408) 946-6080
lasers

Springs Industries, Inc. SMI
205 North White Street
Fort Mill, SC 29715 (803) 547-2901
fabrics, home furnishings

SPS Technologies Inc. ST
P O Box 1000
Newton, PA 18940 (215) 860-3000
industrial fasteners, materials handling

Square D Co. SQD
Executive Plaza, 1415 South Rosell Street
Palatine, IL 60067 (312) 397-2600
electrical equipment   [DRP]

Squibb Corp. SQB
P.O. Box 4000
Princeton, NJ 08540 (609) 921-4000
drugs, cosmetics   [DRP O]

Staley Continental Inc. STA
2200 East Eldorado Street
Decatur, IL 62525 (312) 981-1696
corn processing, food service   [DRP]

Standard Brands Paint Co. SBP
4300 West 190th Street
Torrance, CA 90509 (213) 542-5901
paint and home decorating centers

Standard Motor Products Inc. SMP
37-18 Northern Boulevard
Long Island City, NY 11101 (718) 392-0200
auto parts

Standard Oil Co. SOH
1445 Midland Building
Cleveland, OH 44115 (216) 575-4141
oil and copper refining/marketing   [DRP O]

Standard Products Co., The SPD
2130 West 110th Street
Cleveland, OH 44102 (216) 281-8300
auto parts   [DRP]

Standard-Pacific Corp. SPF
1565 West MacArthur Boulevard
Costa Mesa, CA 92626 (714) 546-1161
homebuilder

Standex International Corp. SXI
Manor Parkway
Salem, NH 03079 (603) 893-9701
diversified manufacturing   [DRP]

Stanhome Inc. STH
333 Western Avenue
Westfield, MA 01085 (413) 562-3631
soaps and personal care products

Stanley Works SWK
195 Lake Street
New Britain, CT 06052 (203) 225-5111
hardware products, tools   [DRP]

Starret, L S Co. SCX
121 Crescent Street
Athol, MA 01331 (617) 249-3551
mechanics' measuring tools

State Mutual Securities Inc. SMS
440 Lincoln Street
Worcester, MA 01605 (617) 852-3805
closed-end mutual fund   [DRP]

Steego Corp. STG
319 Clematis Street
West Palm Beach, FL 33401 (305) 655-9700
auto and farm parts

Sterling Bancorp STL
540 Madison Avenue
New York, NY 10022 (212) 826-8000
banking

Sterling Drug Inc. STY
90 Park Avenue
New York, NY 10016 (212) 907-2000
drugs, household cleansers   [DRP O]

Stevens, JP Co. STN
1185 Avenue of the Americas
New York, NY 10036 (212) 930-2000
textile manufacturer   [DRP]

Stewart-Warner Corp. STX
1826 Diversey Parkway
Chicago, IL 60614 (312) 883-6000
electrical products and systems   [DRP]

Stone and Webster Inc. SW
P O Box 1244
New York, NY 10116 (212) 290-7401
engineering/construction contractors   [DRP]

Stone Container Corp. STO
360 North Michigan Avenue
Chicago, IL 60601 (312) 346-6600
paperboard packaging products

Stop & Shop Co. Inc. SHP
P O Box 369
Boston, MA 02101 (617) 770-8000
food supermarkets   [DRP]

Storage Equities Inc. SEQ
990 South Fair Oaks Avenue
Pasadena, CA 91105-2626 (213) 682-3601
real estate investment trust   [DRP 5%]

Storage Technology Co. QSTK
2270 South 88th Street
Louisville, CO 80027 (303) 673-5151
computer data storage equipment, printers

Strategic Mortgage Investments Inc. STM
700 North Central Avenue
Glendale, CA 91203 (818) 247-6057
mortgage loan partnerships

Stride Rite Corp. SRR
5 Cambridge Center
Cambridge, MA 02142 (617) 491-8800
children's shoe retailer, manufacturer   [DRP]

Student Loan Marketing Association SLM
1050 Thomas Jefferson Street NW
Washington, DC 20007 (202) 333-8000
student loan financing

Suave Shoe Corp. SWV
14100 NW 60th Avenue
Miami Lakes, FL 33014 (305) 822-7880
shoe manufacturer and importer, apparel

Sun Chemical Corp. SNL
200 Park Avenue
New York, NY 10017 (212) 986-5500
printing inks, specialty chemicals

Sun Co. Inc. SUN
100 Matsonford Road
Radnor, PA 19087 (215) 293-6000
oil and gas production, marketing   [DRP O]

Sun Electric Corp. SE
1 Sun Parkway
Crystal Lake, IL 60014 (815)459-7700
automotive test equipment

Sun Energy Partners Ltd. Partnerships SLP
5656 Blackwell East
Dallas, TX 75231 (214) 890-6000
oil and gas exploration,production

Sundstrand Corp. SNS
4751 Harrison Avenue
Rockford, IL 61101 (815) 226-6000
aerospace parts, power transmissions [DRP]

Sunshine Mining Co. SSC
500 Plaza of the Americas South
Dallas, TX 57201 (214) 748-9872
silver mining

SunTrust Banks Inc. STI
1 Park Place NE
Atlanta, GA 30303 (404) 588-7711
banking   [DRP]

Super Valu Stores Inc. SVU
P O Box 990
Minneapolis, MN 55440 (612) 828-4000
grocery wholesaler and retailer

Supermarkets General Corp. SGL
301 Blair Drive
Woodbridge, NJ 07095 (201) 499-3000
food supermarket chain

Swank Inc. SNK
PO Box 869
Attleboro, MA 02703 (617) 222-3400
leather goods, jewelry

Syms Corp. SYM
300 Chubb Street
Lyndhurst, NJ 07071 (201) 935-7500
discount apparel stores

Syntex Corp. SYN
3401 Hillview Avenue
Palo Alto, CA 94304 (415) 855-5050
drugs, agribusiness   [O]

Sysco Corp. SYY
1177 West Loop South
Houston, TX 77017 (713) 877-1122
food distribution and service

Tacoma Boatbuilding Co. QTBO
1840 Marine View Drive
Tacoma, WA 98422 (206) 572-3600
medium size aluminum and steel vessels

Taft Broadcasting Co. TFB
1906 Highland Avenue
Cincinnati, OH 45219 (513) 721-1414
broadcasting, films   [DRP]

Talley Industries Inc. TAL
2702 North 4th Street
Phoenix, AZ 85008 (602) 957-7711
clocks, watches, apparel

Tambrands Inc. TMB
10 Delaware Drive
Lake Success, NY 10042 (516) 437-8800
feminine hygiene products   [DRP]

Tandy Corp. TAN
1800 One Tandy Center
Fort Worth, TX 76102 (817) 390-3700
consumer electronics, computer retailer   [O]

Tandycrafts Inc. TAC
2727 West 70th Street
Fort Worth, TX 76107 (817) 870-0361
leather crafts, picture frames

TDK Corp. TDK
12 Harbor Park Drive
Port Washington, NY 11050 (516) 625-0100
ferrite, ceramics, magnetic tape

TECO Energy Inc. TE
P O Box 111
Tampa, FL 33601 (813) 228-4111
electric utility

Tektronix Inc. TEK
P O Box 500
Beavertown, OR 97077 (503) 627-7111
oscilloscopes, electronic equipment   [O]

Telecom Corp. TEL
1341 West Mockingbird Lane
Dallas, TX 75247 (214) 638-0638
heating and air conditioning equipment

Teledyne Inc. TDY
1901 Avenue of the Stars
Los Angeles, CA 90027 (213) 277-3311
conglomerate   [O]

Telerate Inc. TLR
1 World Trade Center
New York, NY 10048 (212) 938-5200
computerized financial information network

Telex Corp. TC
6422 West 41st Street
Tulsa, OK 74101 (918) 628-2268
computer peripherals, audio equipment   [O]

Temple-Inland Inc. TIN
303 South Temple Drive
Diboll, TX 79541 (409) 829-5511
paper, containers, building products   [DRP]

Tenneco Inc. TGT
P O Box 2511
Houston, TX 77001 (713) 757-2131
oil and gas exploration, farm equipment [DRP]

Teradyne Inc. TER
183 Essex Street
Boston, MA 02111 (617) 482-2700
electronic test equipment   [O]

Tesoro Petroleum Corp. TSO
8700 Tesoro Drive
San Antonio, TX 78286 (512) 828-8484
oil and gas exploration and production   [O]

Texaco Inc. TX
2000 Westchester Avenue
White Plains, NY 10650 (914) 253-4000
oil refining and retailing   [DRP O]

Texas American Bancshares Inc. TXA
500 Throckmorton Street
Fort Worth, TX 76102 (817) 338-8671
banking   [DRP]

Texas Commerce Bancshares TCB
600 Travis Street
Houston, TX 77002 (713) 236-4865
banking   [DRP 5%]

Texas Eastern Corp. TET
P O Box 2521
Houston, TX 77001 (713) 759-3131
gas pipeline   [DRP]

Texas Industries Inc. TXI
8100 Carpenter Freeway
Dallas, TX 75247 (214) 637-3100
cement, concrete products, and aggregates

Texas Instruments Inc. TXN
13500 North Central Expressway
Dallas, TX 75265 (214) 995-2011
electronic components, digital products   [O]

Texas International Co. TEI
6525 North Meridian
Oklahoma City, OK 73116 (405) 728-5100
oil and gas exploration

Texas Pacific Land Trust TPL
61 Broadway
New York, NY 10006 (212) 269-2266
oil land holdings

Texas Utilities Co. TXU
2001 Bryan Tower
Dallas, TX 75201 (214) 653-4600
electric utility   [DRP 5%]

Texfi Industries Inc. TXF
400 English Road
Rocky Mount, NC (919) 443-5001
fabrics for the apparel industry

Textron Inc. TXT
40 Westminster Street
Providence, RI 12903 (401) 421-2800
aerospace, financial services, tools   [DRP O]

TGI Fridays Inc. TGI
14665 Midway Road
Dallas, TX 75234 (214) 450-5400
restaurant chain

Thackeray Corp. THK
9200 South Dadeland Boulevard
Miami, FL 33156 (305) 662-5673
ribbons, wire, cable, real estate

The Williams Companies WMB
1 Williams Center
Tulsa, OK 74172 (918) 588-2000
gas pipelines, fertilizer, oil, gas　　　　[O]

Thermo Electron Corp. TMO
101 First Avenue
Waltham, MA 02254 (617) 890-8700
industrial equipment

Thomas & Betts Corp. TNB
920 Route 202
Raritan, NJ 08869 (201) 685-1600
electrical and electronic connectors　　[DRP]

Thomas Industries Inc. TII
207 East Broadway
Louisville, KY 40202 (502) 582-3771
electric light fixtures, tools, hardware

Thompson Medical Co. Inc. TM
919 3rd Avenue
New York, NY 10022 (212) 688-4422
appetite suppressants

Thrifty Corp. TFD
5051 Rodeo Road
Los Angeles, CA 90016 (213) 293-5111
drug and discount store chain　　　　[O]

Tidewater Inc. TDW
1440 Canal Street Suite 2100
New Orleans, LA 70112 (504) 568-1010
offshore oil service vessels　　　　　[O]

Tiger International TGR
1888 Century Park East
Los Angeles, CA 90067 (213) 552-6300
air freight, trucking

Time Inc. TL
1271 Avenue of the Americas
New York, NY 10020 (212) 586-1212
magazines, books, cable television　[DRP O]

Timeplex Inc. TIX
1 Communication Plaza
Rochelle Park, NJ 07662 (201) 368-1113
data communications equipment

Times Mirror Co., The TMC
Times Mirror Square
Los Angeles, CA 90053 (213) 972-3700
newspaper and book publishing, tv

Timken Co. TKR
1835 Deuber Ave SW
Canton, OH 44706 (216) 438-3000
bearings, rock bits, alloy steel　　　[DRP]

Titan Corp. TTN
9191 Towne Centre Drive La Jolla Gateway
San Diego, CA 92122 (619) 298-9367
memory systems for computers

TNP Enterprises Inc. TNP
501 West Sixth Street
Fort Worth, TX 76102 (817) 731-0099
electric and gas utility　　　　　　[DRP]

Todd Shipyards Corp. TOD
1 State Street Plaza
New York, NY 10004 (212) 668-4700
construction and overhaul of ships

Tokheim Corp. TOK
1603 Wabash Avenue
Fort Wayne, IN 46801 (219) 423-2552
equipment for gas stations

Tonka Corp. TKA
6000 Clearwater Drive
Minnetonka, MN 55343 (612) 936-3300
toys

Tootsie Roll Industries Inc. TR
7401 South Cicero Avenue
Chicago, IL 60629 (312) 838-3400
candies

Torchmark Corp. TMK
2001 3rd Avenue
Birmingham, AL 35233 (205) 325-4200
insurance and financial services　　[DRP]

Toro Corp. TTC
1 Appletree Square 8009 34th South Avenue
Minneapolis, MN 55240 (612) 888-8801
yard maintenance equipment　　　　[DRP]

Tosco Corp. TOS
2401 Colorado Boulevard
Santa Monica, CA 90406 (213) 207-6000
oil and gas exploration and development

Towle Manufacturing Co. TOW
144 Addison Street
Boston, MA 02128 (617) 569-7600
silverware, giftware, crystal

Toys "R" Us Inc. TOY
395 West Passaic Street
Rochelle Park, NJ 07662 (201) 845-5033
toy supermarkets　　　　　　　　　[O]

Tracor Inc. TRR
6500 Tracor Lane
Austin, TX 78721 (512) 926-2800
electronic equipment　　　　　　[DRP 5%]

Trammell Crow Real Estate Investors TCR
3500 LTV Center
Dallas, TX 75201 (214) 979-5100
real estate investment trust

Trans World Airlines Inc. TWA
605 3rd Avenue
New York, NY 10158 (212) 692-3000
airline

Transamerica Corp. TA
600 Montgomery Street
San Francisco, CA 94111 (415) 983-4000
insurance, travel, manufacturing   [DRP O]

Transamerica Income Shares TAI
P O Box 2438
Los Angeles, CA 90051 (415) 983-4000
closed end bond mutual fund   [DRP]

Transamerica Realty Investors TAR
600 Montgomery Street
San Francisco, CA 94115 (415) 983-5430
real estate investment

TransCanada PipeLines Ltd. TRP
Commerce Court West Suite 5400
Toronto, ON, CDA M5L 1C2 (416) 869-2111
gas pipeline   [O]

Transco Energy Co. E
P O Box 1396
Houston, TX 77001 (713) 439-2000
oil and gas pipelines   [DRP O]

Transco Exploration Partners LTD EXP
2800 Post Oak Boulevard
Houston, TX 77056 (713) 439-2000
oil and gas exploration

Transcon Inc. TCL
P O Box 92220
Los Angeles, CA 90009 (213) 640-1800
trucking

TRANSOHIO Financial Corp. TFC
1 Penton Plaza
Cleveland, OH 44114 (216) 579-7700
savings and loan

Transworld Corp. TW
605 3rd Avenue
New York, NY 10158 (212) 972-4700
food/hotel/real estate services   [O]

Travelers Corp. TIC
1 Tower Square
Hartford, CT 06183 (203) 277-0111
insurance, financial services   [DRP O]

TRE Corp. TRE
9460 Wilshire Boulevard
Los Angeles, CA 90212 (213) 470-7120
aerospace material, hardware

Tri-Continental Corp. TY
1 Bankers Trust Plaza
New York, NY 10006 (212) 488-0200
closed-end mutual fund   [DRP O]

Triangle Industries Inc. TRI
P O Box 2500
New Brunswick, NJ 0890 (201) 745-55003
vending and coin-operated machines   [DRP]

Triangle Pacific Corp. TPC
P O Box 660100
Dallas, TX 75266 (214) 931-3000
home cabinets, wood flooring

Tribune Co. TRB
435 North Michigan Avenue
Chicago, IL 60611 (312) 222-9100
newspaper publishing, broadcasting

Tricentrol PLC TCT
Capal House New Broad Street
London EC2M 1JS England
oil and gas production

Trico Industries Inc. TRO
15707 South Main Street
Gardenia, CA 90248 (213) 532-9400
oil production equipment

Trinity Industries TRN
4001 Irving Building
Dallas, TX 75207 (214) 631-4420
railcars, structural and marine products

Triton Energy Corp. OIL
4925 Greenville Avenue
Dallas, TX 75206 (214) 691-5200
oil and gas exploration and development

TRW Inc. TRW
23555 Euclid Avenue
Cleveland, OH 44117 (216) 291-7500
high-technology conglomerate   [DRP O]

Tucson Electric Power Co. TEP
220 West 6th Street P O Box 711
Tucson, AZ 85701 (602) 622-6661
electric utility   [DRP]

Tultex Corp. TTX
22 East Church Street
Martinsville, VA 24115 (703) 632-2961
sportswear and yarn

Twin Disc Inc. TDI
1328 Racine Street
Racine, WI 53403 (414) 634-1981
power transmission equipment   [DRP]

Tyco Laboratories Inc. TYC
Tyco Park
Exeter, NH 03833 (603) 778-7331
fire protection systems

Tyler Corp. TYL
Southland Center
Dallas, TX 75201 (214) 747-7800
electronic components, pipe, coatings

UAL Inc. UAL
P O Box 66919
Chicago, IL 60606 (312) 952-4000
airline, hotels, car rental   [O]

UCCEL Corp. UCE
UCC Tower Exchange Park
Dallas, TX 75235 (214) 353-7100
computer services and software

UDC Universal Development LP UDC
4800 Three First National Plaza
Chicago, IL 60602 (312) 726-1885
home building, land development

UGI Corp. UGI
Box 858
Valley Forge, PA 19482 (215) 337-1000
gas utility, oil field services   [DRP 5%]

UNC Resources Inc. UNC
7700 Leesburgh Pike
Falls Church, VA 22043 (703) 821-7900
uranium mining, nuclear power equipment

Unifirst Corp. UNF
15 Olympia Avenue
Woburn, MA 01888 (617) 933-5800
garment rental services

Unilever NV UN
10 East 53rd Street
New York, NY 10022 (212) 888-1260
food, chemicals, paper

Unilever PLC UL
10 East 53rd Street
New York, NY 10022 (212) 888-1260
foods, chemicals, paper

Union Camp Corp. UCC
1600 Valley Road
Wayne, NJ 07470 (201) 628-2000
paper, packaging, wood products   [DRP]

Union Carbide Corp. UK
39 Old Ridgebury Road
Danbury, CT 06817 (203) 794-2000
chemicals, plastics, gases, metals   [DRP O]

Union Corp. UCO
Jones Street
Verona, PA 15147 (412)362-1700
diversified manufacturing and services

Union Electric Co. UEP
P O Box 149
St Louis, MO 63166 (314) 621-3222
electric and gas utility   [DRP]

Union Exploration Partners Ltd. UXP
900 Exec. Plaza West 4635 SW Freeway
Houston, TX 77207 (713) 623-8000
oil and gas exploration and production

Union Pacific Corp. UNP
345 Park Avenue
New York, NY 10022 (212) 418-7800
railroads, oil, gas mining, real estate   [DRP]

Unisys UIS
Burroughs Plaza
Detroit, MI 48232 (313) 972-7000
computers   [O]

United Brands Co. UB
1271 Avenue of the Americas
New York, NY 10020 (203) 573-2000
food processing/distribution, plastics

United Cable Television Corp. UCT
4700 South Syracuse Parkway
Denver, CO 80239 (303) 779-5999
cable television systems

United Illuminating Co. UIL
80 Temple Street
New Haven, CT 06506 (203) 787-7200
electric utility   [DRP]

United Industrial Corp. UIC
18 East 48th Street
New York, NY 10017 (212) 752-8787
defense, health, and combustion products

United Inns Inc. UI
5100 Poplar Avenue
Memphis, TN 38137 (901) 767-2880
hotels, furniture

United Jersey Banks UJB
P O Box 2066
Princeton, NJ 08540 (609) 987-3200
banking   [DRP]

United Merchants and Manufacturers UMM
1407 Broadway
New York, NY 10018 (212) 930-3900
textiles, apparel, yarns, adhesives

United Park City Mines Co. UPK
309 Kearns Building
Salt Lake City, UT 84101 (801) 532-4031
mine leasing

United States Leasing International Inc. USL
633 Battery Street
San Francisco, CA 94111 (415) 627-9000
equipment leasing and financing   [DRP]

United States Shoe Corp. USR
1658 Herald Avenue
Cincinnati, OH 45207 (513) 527-7000
footwear   [DRP]

United Stockyards Corp. COW
717 Fifth Avenue
New York, NY 10017 (212) 826-6040
operates stockyards

United Technologies Corp. UTX
United Technologies Building
Hartford, CT 06101 (203) 728-7000
aerospace, air conditioning, elevators   [O]

United Telecommunications Inc. UT
P O Box 11315
Kansas City, MO 64112 (913) 676-3000
telephone service   [DRP]

United Water Resources Inc. UWR
200 Old Hook Road
Harrington Park, NJ 07640 (201) 784-9434
water utility   [DRP 5%]

Unitrode Corp. UTR
5 Forbes Road
Lexington, MA 02173 (617) 861-6540
semiconductor devices

Univar Corp. UVX
1600 Norton Building
Seattle, WA 98104 (206) 447-5911
industrial chemicals, graphics products

Universal Foods Corp. UFC
433 East Michigan Street
Milwaukee, WI 53202 (414) 271-6755
foods and beverages   [DRP 5%]

Universal Leaf Tobacco Co. Inc. UVV
Hamilton Street at Broad
Richmond, VA 23260 (804) 359-9311
tobacco processing, title insurance   [DRP]

Unocal Corp. UCL
461 South Boylston StreetC
Los Angeles, CA 90017 (213)977-6718
oil exploration and production   [DRP O]

Upjohn Co. UPJ
7000 Portage Road
Kalamazoo, MI 49002 (616) 323-4000
pharmaceuticals, health care, seeds [DRP O]

URS Corp. URS
155 Bovet Road
San Mateo, CA 94402 (415) 574-5000
engineering and architectural services

USAir Group Inc. U
1911 Jefferson Davis Highway
Arlington, VA 22202 (703) 892-7226
regional airline   [O]

USF&G Corp. FG
100 Light Street
Baltimore, MD 21002 (301) 547-3000
auto/life insurance, workmen's comp [DRP 5%]

USG Corp. USG
101 South Wacker Drive
Chicago, IL 60606 (312) 321-4000
gypsum-based and other building products [DRP]

US Home Corp. UH
1800 West Loop South
Houston, TX 77027 (713) 877-2300
residential construction

USLIFE Corp. USH
125 Maiden Lane
New York, NY 10038 (212) 709-6000
insurance and financial services   [DRP]

USLIFE Income Fund Inc. UIF
125 Maiden Lane
New York, NY 10038 (212) 709-6000
closed-end mutual fund   [DRP]

US Tobacco Co. UBO
100 West Putnam Avenue
Greenwich, CT 06830 (203) 661-1100
tobacco products, wines, farmland   [DRP]

US West Inc. USW
70800 East Orchard Road Room 290
Englewood, CO 80111 (303) 793-6500
telecommunications service   [DRP O]

USX Corp. X
660 Grant Street Room 6026
Pittsburgh, PA 15230 (412) 433-1121   [O]
steel, oil and gas   [DRP]

Utah Power & Light Co. UTP
P O Box 899
Salt Lake City, UT 84110 (801) 535-2000
electric utility   [DRP]

Utilicorp United Inc. UCU
10700 East 305 Highway
Kansas City, MO 64138 (816) 737-9393
gas and electric utility   [DRP]

Valero Energy Corp. VLO
530 McCullough Avenue P O Box 500
San Antonio, TX 78292 (512) 246-2000
gas pipelines, gas transportation   [O]

Valley Industries Inc. VI
105 South 9th Street
St Louis, MO 63102 (314) 231-2160
steel products

Van Dorn Co. VDC
2700 East 79th Street
Cleveland, OH 44104 (216) 361-5234
containers, plastic molding machinery [DRP]

Varco International Inc. VRC
800 North Eckhoff Street
Orange, CA 92668 (714) 978-1900
oil and gas drilling tools and equipment

Varian Associates Inc. VAR
611 Hansen Way
Palo Alto, CA 94394 (415) 493-4000
microwave tubes, semiconductor items [DRP O]

Varo Inc. VRO
2203 West Walnut Street
Garland, TX 75040 (214) 272-1571
electronics and aerospace products

Veeco Instruments Inc. VEE
515 Broad Hollow Road
Melville, NY 11746 (516) 694-4200
standard power supplies   [O]

Vendo Co. VEN
7209 North Ingram Avenue
Pinedale, CA 93650 (209) 439-1770
soft drink vending machines

Vestaur Securities Inc. VES
Packard Building 5th Floor
Philadelphia, PA 19101 (215) 567-3969
closed-end investment company   [DRP]

Vestron Inc. VV
1011 High Ridge Road
Stamford, CT 06905 (203) 968-0000
marketing of pre-recorded videocassettes

V F Corp. VFC
1047 North Park Road
Wyomissing, PA 19610 (215) 378-1151
intimate and leisure apparel   [DRP]

Viacom International Inc. VIA
1211 Avenue of the Americas
New York, NY 10022 (212) 575-5175
creates/acquires/distributes TV programs [O]

Vishay Intertechnology Inc. VSH
63 Lincoln Highway
Malvern, PA 19355 (215) 644-1300
electronic resistors

Vornado Inc. VNO
174 Passaic Street
Garfield, NJ 07026 (201) 773-4000
real estate leasing

Vulcan Materials Co. VMC
1 Metroplex Drive
Birmingham, AL 35209 (205) 877-3000
concrete products, chemicals, metals   [DRP]

Wackenhut Corp. WAK
1500 San Remo Avenue
Coral Gables, FL 33146 (305) 666-5656
security and investigative services

Wainoco Oil Corp. WOL
1200 Smith Street Suite 1500
Houston, TX 77002 (713) 658-9900
oil and gas exploration and production

Wal-Mart Stores Inc. WMT
P O Box 116
Bentonville, AR 72212 (501) 273-4000
discount stores   [O]

Walgreen Co. WAG
200 Wilmot Road
Deerfield, IL 60015 (312) 940-2500
drug stores   [DRP O]

Walker, Hiram Resources Ltd HWR
1 First Canadian Place Suite 600
Toronto, ON, CDA M5X 1A9 (416) 864-3300
liquor distiller and gas utility   [DRP 5% O]

Wallace Computer Services Inc. WCS
4600 West Roosevelt Road
Hillside, IL 60162 (312) 626-2000
business forms and catalogs

Walter, Jim Corp. JWC
1500 North Dale Mabry Highway
Tampa, FL 33607 (813) 871-4811
homes, building materials, minerals [DRP O]

Warnaco Inc. WRC
350 Lafayette Street
Bridgeport, CT 06602 (203) 579-8272
knit sportswear

Warner Communications Inc. WCI
75 Rockefeller Plaza 25th Floor
New York, NY 10019 (212) 484-8000
film, television, records, magazines   [O]

Warner-Lambert Co. WLA
201 Tabor Road
Morris Plains, NJ 07950 (201) 540-2000
medical products, drugs, gums, mints [DRP O]

Washington Gas Light Co. WGL
1100 H Street NW
Washington, DC 20080 (202)750-4440
gas utility   [DRP]

Washington National Corp. WNT
1630 Chicago Avenue
Evanston, IL 60201 (312) 570-5500
insurance   [DRP 5%]

Washington Water Power Co. WWP
P O Box 3727
Spokane, WA 99220 (509) 489-0500
electric and gas utility   [DRP]

Waste Management Inc. WMX
3003 Butterfield Road
Oak Brook, IL 60521 (312) 654-8800
solid/chemical waste management   [DRP O]

Watkins-Johnson Co. WJ
333 Hillview Avenue
Palo Alto, CA 94304 (415) 493-4141
electronic systems and devices

Wayne Gossard Corp. WKT
701 Market Street Suite 922
Chattanooga, TN 37401 (615) 756-8146
hosiery, knitwear, apparel

Wean United Inc. WID
948 Fort Duquesne Boulevard
Pittsburgh, PA 15222 (412) 456-5300
sheet and strip steel machinery

Webb, Del E Corp. WBB
3800 North Central Avenue
Phoenix, AZ 85012 (602) 264-8011
hotels, casinos, real estate development

Wedtech Corp. WDT
595 Gerard Avenue
Bronx, NY 10451 (212) 993-0500
specialty coatings and defense products

Weingarten Realty Inc. WRI
2600 Citadel Plaza Drive
Houston, TX 77008 (713) 868-6361
real estate investment trust

Weis Markets Inc. WMK
1000 South 2nd Street
Sunbury, PA 1780 (717) 286-4571
supermarkets   [DRP]

Wells Fargo and Co. WFC
420 Montgomery Street
San Francisco, CA 94163 (415) 396-0123
banking   [DRP]

Wells Fargo Mortgage & Equity Trust WFM
475 Sansome Street
San Francisco, CA 94111 (415) 396-2887
real estate investment trust   [DRP]

Wendy's International Inc. WEN
4288 West Dublin Granville Road
Dublin, OH 43017 (614) 764-3100
fast-food restaurants   [DRP O]

West Co. Inc. WST
West Bridge Street
Phoenixville, PA 19460 (215) 935-4500
pharmaceutical packaging

West Point-Pepperell Inc. WPM
West 10th Street
West Point, GA 31833 (205) 756-7111
household/ apparel/industrial fabrics   [DRP]

Westcoast Transmission WTC
1333 West Georgia Street
Vancouver BC CDA V6E 3K9 (604) 664-5500
gas pipeline   [DRP 5% O]

Western Air Lines Inc. WAL
6060 Avion Drive
Los Angeles, CA 90045 (213) 646-2345
regional airline

Western Co. North America WSN
6000 Western Place P O Box 186
Fort Worth, TX 76101 (817) 731-5100
oil drilling services

Western Pacific Industries Inc. WPI
345 Park Avenue 17th Floor
New York, NY 10022 (212) 751-6464
counting devices, fasteners

Western Savings and Loan Association WSL
3443 North Central Avenue
Phoenix, AZ 85012 (602) 248-4600
savings and loan

Western Union Corp. WU
1 Lake Street
Upper Saddle River, NJ 07450 (201) 825-5000
communications systems,services   [DRP O]

Westinghouse Electric Corp. WX
Westinghouse Building Gateway Center
Pittsburgh, PA 15222 (412) 642-3546
defense and utility electric equipment   [O]

Westvaco Corp. W
299 Park Avenue
New York, NY 10017 (212) 688-5000
pulp, paper, paper products, lumber   [DRP]

Weyerhaeuser Co. WY
33663 32nd Drive South
Auburn, WA (206) 924-2345
pulp, paper, packaging, logs, chips   [DRP O]

Wheeling-Pittsburgh Steel Corp. QWHX
4 Gateway Center P O Box 118
Pittsburgh, PA 15230 (412) 288-3600
steel and steel products, iron ore, coal

Whirlpool Corp. WHR
2000 U S 33 North
Benton Harbor, MI 49022 (616) 926-5000
major home appliances   [DRP]

Whitehall Corp. WHT
2659 Nova Drive
Dallas, TX 75229 (214) 247-8747
seismic survey and defense electronics

Whittaker Corp. WKR
10880 Wilshire Boulevard
Los Angeles, CA 90024 (213) 475-9411
medical, aerospace, chemicals, metal [DRP O]

WICOR Inc. WIC
777 East Wisconsin Avenue
Milwaukee, WI 53202 (414) 291-7000
gas utility   [DRP]

Wilfred American Educational Corp. WAE
1657 Broadway
New York, NY 10019 (212) 562-6690
career school systems

Willcox & Gibbs Inc. WG
1440 Broadway
New York, NY 10018 (212) 869-1800
apparel and textile supplies and equipment

Williams Electronics Inc. WMS
3401 North California Avenue
Chicago, IL 60618 (312) 267-2240
coin-operated amusement games

Wilshire Oil Co. of Texas WOC
921 Bergen Avenue Suite 27
Jersey City, NJ 07306 (201) 420-2800
oil and gas exploration and production

Winn-Dixie Stores Inc. WIN
5050 Edgewood Court
Jacksonville, FL 32205 (904) 783-5000
supermarkets   [DRP]

Winnebago Industries Inc. WGO
P O Box 152
Forest City, IA 50436 (515) 582-3535
motor homes and recreational vehicles   [O]

Winners Corp. WNR
101 Winners Circle Maryland Farms
Brentwood, TN 37027 (615) 377-4400
fast food restaurants

Winter, Jack Inc. JWI
8100 North Teutonia Avenue
Milwaukee, WI 53209 (414) 354-4100
manufacturer/retailer of apparel

Wisconsin Electric Power Co. WPC
231 West Michigan Street
Milwaukee, WI 53201 (414) 277-2345
electric utility   [DRP]

Wisconsin Power & Light Co. WPL
222 West Washington Avenue
Madison, WI 53703 (608) 252-3311
electric and gas utility   [DRP]

Wisconsin Public Service Corp. WPS
700 North Adams Street
Green Bay, WI 54305 (414) 433-1598
electric and gas utility

Witco Corp. WIT
520 Madison Avenue
New York, NY 10022 (212) 605-3800
oil, chemical, and detergent products

Wolverine World Wide Inc. WWW
9341 Courtland Drive NE
Rockford, MI 49351 (616) 874-8448
footwear

Woolworth, F W Co. Z
233 Broadway
New York, NY 10279 (212) 553-2000
variety/apparel/shoe store chains   [DRP O]

World Airways Inc. WOA
Oakland Internat'l Airport
Oakland, CA 94614 (415) 577-2000
airline

Wrigley, Wm Jr Co. WWY
410 North Michigan Avenue
Chicago, IL 60611 (312) 644-2121
chewing gum   [DRP]

Wurlitzer Co. WUR
403 East Gurler Road
De Kalb, IL 60115 (815) 756-2771
pianos and electronic organs

Wyle Laboratories WYL
128 Maryland Street
El Segundo, CA 90245 (213) 678-4251
distribution of electronic components   [DRP]

Wynn's International Inc. WN
2600 East Nutwood Avenue
Fullerton, CA 92631 (714) 992-2000
engine additives and treatment solutions

Xerox Corp. XRX
P O Box 1600
Stamford, CT 06904 (203) 329-8700
copying/office automation equipment [DRP O]

XTRA Corp. XTR
2625 Concord Pike
Wilmington, DE 19803 (302) 478-0705
leases intermodal transportation equipment

Zale Corp. ZAL
901 West Walnut Hill Lane
Irving, TX 75038-1003 (214) 257-4000
jewelry stores

Zapata Corp. ZOS
Zapata Tower P O Box 4240
Houston, TX 77210 (713) 226-6000
oil/gas production and services, fish   [O]

Zayre Corp. ZY
770 Cochituate Road
Framingham, MA 01701 (617) 620-5000
discount department and apparel stores

Zenith Electronics Corp. ZE
1000 Milwaukee Avenue
Glenview, IL 60025 (312) 391-7000
consumer electronics   [O]

Zenith Laboratories ZEN
140 LeGrand Avenue
Northvale, NJ 07647 (201) 767-1700
pharmaceuticals

Zero Corp. ZRO
777 Front Street
Burbank, CA 91503 (213) 846-4191
electronic equipment, enclosures   [DRP]

Zurn Industries Inc. ZRN
1 Zurn Place
Erie, PA 16512 (814) 452-2111
environmental quality control systems [DRP]

AMERICAN STOCK EXCHANGE

ACI Holdings ACF
3636 Birch Street
Newport Beach, CA 92660 (714) 752-7000
airline

Acme Precision Products, Inc. ACL
3750 East Outer Drive
Detroit, MI 48234 (313) 891-3400
precision cutting tools

Acme United Corp. ACU
425 Post Road
Fairfield, CT 06430 (203) 255-2744
medical shears and scissors

Action Industries, Inc. ACX
Allegheny Industrial Park
Cheswick, PA 15024 (412) 782-4800
merchandising programs for retailers

Acton Corp. ATN
One Acton Place
Acton, MA 01720 (617) 263-7711
owner/operator of cable tv systems

Adams Resources & Energy, Inc. AE
P.O. Box 844
Houston, TX 77001 (713) 797-9966
markets and transports petro products

Adams-Russell Co., Inc. AAR
1380 Main Street
Waltham, MA 02154 (617) 894-8540
defense electronics, cable tv

ADI Electronics, Inc. ADE
101 Trade Zone Drive P.O. Box 1221
Ronkonkoma, NY 11779 (516) 737-1800
electronics components

Aeronca, Inc. ARN
7415 Pineville Matthews
Charlotte, NC 28226 (704) 541-1700
aerospace electronics and components

Affiliated Publications, Inc. AFP
135 William T. Morrissey Boulevard
Boston, MA 02107 (617) 929-2889
newspaper publishing, broadcasting

Air Express International Corp. AEX
120 Tokeneke Road
Darien, CT 06820 (203) 655-7900
freight forwarding

Air Cal., Inc. ACF
3636 Birch Street
Newport Beach, CA 92660 (714) 752-7000
airline

A.L. Laboratories, Inc. BMD
452 Hudson Terrace
Englewood Cliffs, NJ 07632 (312) 625-6411
pharmaceuticals, animal health products

ALAMCO, Inc. AXO
200 West Main Street P.O.Drawer 1740
Clarksburg, WV 26301 (304) 623-6671
oil and gas exploration and production

Alba-Waldensian, Inc. AWS
201 St. Germain Avenue, SW P.O. Box 100
Valdese, NC 28690 (704) 874-2191
hosiery, fabrics

Aloha Airlines, Inc. ALO
Honolulu Int'l. Airport P.O. Box 30028
Honolulu, HI 96820 (808) 836-4101
airline

Alpha Industries, Inc. AHA
20 Sylvan Road
Woburn, MA 01801 (617) 935-5150
microwave computer devices

Alpine Group ALGA
1290 Avenue of the Americas
New York, NY 10104 (212) 489-0110
precision machine parts, buttons

Altex Industries AOC
1660 Wynkoop Street Suite 800
Denver, CO 80202 (303) 534-2667
oil and gas

ALZA Corp. AZA
950 Page Mill Road P O Box 10950
Palo Alto, CA 94303 (415) 494-5000
pharmaceutical research

AM International, Inc. AM/AM Pf
333 W. Wacker Drive Suite 900
Chicago, IL 60602 (312) 558-1966
graphic and data business equipment

AmBrit, Inc. ABI
5400 118th Avenue North
Clearwater, FL 33520 (813) 576-8424
manufactures/distributes ice cream bars

AMC Entertainment, Inc. AEN
106 West 14th Street Suite 1700
Kansas City, MO 64105 (816) 474-6150
operates movie theaters

Amdahl Corp. AMH
1250 East Arques Avenue P O Box 470
Sunnyvale, CA 94086 (408) 746-6000
high-performance computer systems   [O]

Amedco Inc. AMY
625 South Second Street
Springfield, IL 62704 (217) 753-5700
hospital and funeral equipment

American Biltrite Inc. ABL
57 River Street
Wellesley Hills, MA 02181 (617) 237-6655
floor coverings, electrical tape products

American Capital Corp. ACC
5555 Biscayne Boulevard
Miami, FL 33137 (305) 754-5555
savings and loan

American Controlled Industries, Inc. ACI
Six East Fourth Street
Cincinnati, OH 45202 (513) 621-2280
heat transfer products, real estate

American Fructose Corp. AFC.A
41 Harbor Plaza Drive
Stamford, CT 06904 (203) 356-9000
corn syrups and sugar products

American Healthcare Management, Inc. AHI
14160 Dallas Parkway Suite 900
Dallas, TX 75240 (214) 385-7000
health care facilities

American Israeli Paper Mills Ltd. AIP
c/o Becker, Ross & Stone 41 East 42nd St.
New York, NY 10017 (212) 697-2310
paper manufacturing from imported pulp

American Maize-Products Co. AZEA
41 Harbor Plaza Drive P.O. Box 10128
Stamford, CT 06904 (203) 356-9000
corn sweeteners and corn starches

American Medical Buildings, Inc. A
735 North Water Street
Milwaukee, WI 53202 (414) 276-2277
construction of medical buildings, clinics

American Oil and Gas Corp. AOG
333 Clay Street
Houston, TX 77002 (713) 650-0510
oilfield crews and rigs

American Petrofina, Inc. API.A
P.O. Box 2159
Dallas, TX 75221 (214) 750-2400
oil refining and marketing   [DRP]

American Plan Corp. APN
1001 Industrial Blvd. Amdall Complex
Plano, TX 75074 (214) 423-8250
property/casualty insurance

American Precision Industries Inc. APR
2777 Walden Avenue
Buffalo, NY 14225 (716) 684-9700
industrial processing equipment

American Realty Trust ARB
3900 North Fairfax Avenue
Arlington, VA 22202 (703) 522-5100
real estate investment trust

American Royalty Trust ARI
1301 Fannin Street
Houston, TX 77002 (713) 658-7145
royalties of oil and gas properties

American Science & Engineering, Inc. ASE
Fort Washington
Cambridge, MA 02130 (617) 868-1600
energy, space, medical systems

Americus Trust for Exxon Shares XNU
15 West 39th Street
New York, NY 10018 (212) 575-8670
unit trust for Exxon capital appreciation

Ampal-American Israel Corp. AIS.A
10 Rockefeller Plaza
New York, NY 10020 (212) 586-3232
loans/investments in Israel

Andal Corp. ADL
60 Madison Avenue
New York, NY 10010 (212) 683-9191
specialty steel, tubing

Anderson Jacobson Inc. AJ
521 Charcot Avenue
San Jose, CA 95131 (408) 263-8520
remote data terminals, modems

Andrea Radio Corp. AND
11-40 45th Road
Long Island City, NY 11101 (718) 729-8500
audio-electronic equipment

Angeles Corp. ANG
10301 West Pico Boulevard
Los Angeles, CA 90064 (213) 277-4900
oil/gas/real estate partnerships

Angeles Finance Partners ANF
10301 West Pico Boulevard
Los Angeles, CA 90064 (213) 277-4900
short-term secured loans

Anglo Energy Ltd. AEL.A
233 Broadway 17th Floor
New York, NY 10279 (212) 619-4242
contract drilling and services

AOI Coal Co. AOI
1100 Western United Life Building
Midland, TX 79701
coal mining/processing/marketing

Argo Petroleum Corp. ARG
1661 Lincoln Boulevard Suite 400
Santa Monica, CA 90404 (213) 452-8676
oil and gas exploration and development

Arley Merchandise Corp. ARY
42 Adams Street
Taunton, MA 02780 (617) 822-7133
curtains, drapes, bedcovers

Armatron International, Inc. ART
Two Main Street
Melrose, MA 02176 (617) 321-2300
industrial pumps, electrical products

Armel, Inc. AML
5545 N.W. 35th Avenue
Ft. Lauderdale, FL 33309 (305) 486-6161
athletic/leisure footwear retailer

Arrow Automotive Industries, Inc. AI
5 Speen St. P.O. Box 856
Framingham, MA 01701 (617) 872-3711
rebuilds auto replacement parts

Arundel Corp. ARL
110 West Road
Baltimore, MD 21204 (301) 296-6400
heavy construction, building materials

Astrex, Inc. ASI
150 Fifth Avenue
New York, NY 10011 (212) 989-5000
electronics showrooms/distribution

Astrotech International Corp. AIX
Two Chatham Center Suite 240
Pittsburgh, PA 15219 (412) 391-1896
superalloys for jet engines

AT&T Stock Fund - Equity Income Fund
One Liberty Plaza 165 Broadway
New York, NY 10080 (212) 637-7455
closed-end stock mutual fund

Atlas Cons. Mining & Dev. Corp. ACM.B
177 Summer Street Suite 104
Stamford, CT 06901
copper and gold in the Philippines

Audiotronics Corp. ADO
7428 Bellaire Avenue
North Hollywood, CA 91605 (818) 765-2645
audio and visual components/equipment

Ausimont Compo N.V. AUS
128 Roberts Road
Waltham, MA 02254
chemicals, carpeting, footwear materials

Avondale Mills AVD
Avondale Avenue
Sylacauga, AL 35150 (205) 245-5221
cotton and synthetic materials

Badger Meter, Inc. BMI
4545 West Brown Deer Road
Milwaukee, WI 53223 (414) 355-0400
fluid meters, accessories

Baker, Michael Corp. BKR
4301 Dutch Ridge Road Box 280
Beaver, PA 15009 (412) 495-7711
engineering consulting services

Baldwin Securities BAL
595 Madison Avenue Suite 716
New York, NY 10173 (212) 223-1210
closed-end investment company

Bancroft Convertible Fund, Inc. BCV
42 Broadway
New York, NY 10004 (212) 269-9236
closed-end investment company   [DRP]

Bank Bldg. & Equip. Corp. of America BB
1130 Hampton Avenue
St. Louis, MO 63139 (314) 647-3800
designs/builds/remodels/equips banks [DRP]

Barco of California BRC
350 West Rosecrans Avenue
Gardena, CA 90248 (213) 770-1012
medical uniforms

Barnes Engineering Co. BIR
30 Commerce Road
Stamford, CT 06904 (203) 348-5381
infrared electro-optical systems

Barnwell Industries, Inc. BRN
2828 Paa Street
Honolulu, HI 96819 (808) 836-0136
oil and gas

Barry, R G Corp. RGB
13405 Yarmouth Road N.W.
Pickerington, OH 43147 (213) 770-1012
slippers, comfort footwear

Baruch-Foster Corp. BFO
4925 Greenville Ave.,1160 One Energy Sq.
Dallas, TX 75206 (214) 368-5886
oil and gas development

BDM International, Inc. BDM
7915 Jones Branch Drive
McLean, VA 22102 (703) 821-5000
technical services for government

Beard Oil Co. BOC
2000 Classen Center Bldg. Suite 200 South
Oklahoma City, OK 73106 (405) 528-2323
oil and gas exploration and development

Belden & Blake Energy Co. BBE
7555 Freedom Avenue, N.W.
North Canton, OH 44720 (216) 499-1660
oil and gas exploration and development

Beltran Corp. BTN
One Acton Place
Acton, MA 01720 (617) 264-4900
restaurant/institution food distribution

Bergen Brunswig Corp. BBC.A
1900 Avenue of the Stars Suite 1185
Los Angeles, CA 90067 (213) 879-4991
drugs, health products, video software

Bethlehem Corp. BET
25th & Lennox Streets P.O. Box 348
Easton, PA 18042 (215) 258-7111
energy and environmental products

BIC Corp. BIC
Wiley Street
Milford, CT 06460 (203) 878-9341
low-cost disposable pens, lighters, razors

Big V Supermarkets, Inc. BIV
176 North Main Street
Florida, NY 10921 (914) 651-4411
supermarkets

Binks Manufacturing Co. BIN
9201 West Belmont Avenue
Franklin Park, IL 60131 (312) 671-3000
coatings application equipment

Bio-Rad Laboratories, Inc. BIO.B
2200 Wright Avenue
Richmond, CA 94804 (415) 234-4130
medical test kits, analytic instruments

Blessings Corp. BCO
645 Martinsville Road
Liberty Corner, NJ 07948 (201) 647-7980
diaper rental, disposable medical supplies

Blocker Energy Corp. BLK
800 Bering Drive
Houston, TX 77057 (713) 578-3677
contract drilling, oil and gas exploration

Blount Inc BLT.A
4520 Executive Park Drive P O Box 949
Montgomery, AL 36116 (205) 272-8020
construction/engineering, steels   [DRP]

Bolar Pharmaceutical Co., Inc. BLR
130 Lincoln St.
Copiague, NY 11726 (516) 842-8383
generic prescription drugs

Bowl America Inc. BWL.A
6446 Edsall Road
Alexandria, VA 22312 (703) 941-6300
bowling centers

Bowmar Instrument Corp. BOM
531 Main Street
Acton, MA 01720 (617) 263-8365
electromechanical components

Bowne & Co., Inc. BNE
345 Hudson Street
New York, NY 10014 (212) 924-5500
financial printer

Brown-Forman, Inc. BFDB
850 Dixie Highway P.O. Box 1080
Louisville, KY 40201 (502) 585-1100
wine, spirits, china, whiskey barrels   [DRP]

BRT Realty Trust BRT
60 Cutter Mill Road Suite 303
Great Neck, NY 11021 (516) 466-3100
real estate investment trust

BSD Bancorp, Inc. BSD
225 Broadway Suite 260
San Diego, CA 92101 (619) 237-5367
banking

BSN Corp. BSN
11414 Mathis Drive
Dallas, TX 75234 (214) 869-0486
sports equipment

Buckhorn Inc. BKN
3592 Corporate Drive P.O. Box 689
Columbus, OH 43216 (614) 895-1895
material handling, rubber/plastic products

Buell Industries, Inc. BUE
130 Huntington Avenue
Waterbury, CT 06708 (203) 574-1800
fasteners for auto industry

Bush Industries BSH
312 Fair Oak Street
Little Valley, NY 14755 (716) 938-9101
electronics furniture

Cablevision System Corp. CVC
One Media Crossways
Woodbury, NY 11797 (516) 364-8400
operates cable systems

Caesars New Jersey, Inc. CJN
Caesars Boardwalk Regency Hotel/Casino
Atlantic City, NJ 08401 (609) 340-5300
casino-hotel

Caesars World, Inc. CAW
1801 Century Park East Suite 2600
Los Angeles, CA 90067 (213) 552-2711
casino-hotels, honeymoon resorts

Cagle's Inc. CGL.A
1155 Hammond Drive, N.E.
Atlanta, GA 30328 (404) 394-8223
poultry producer, food distributor

Calprop Corp. CPP
5456 McConnell Avenue
Los Angeles, CA 90066 (213) 306-4314
builder of home rental properties

Camco, Inc. CAM
P.O. Box 14484
Houston, TX 77021 (713) 747-4000
oilfield services/products, electronics

Campanelli Industries, Inc. CAP
One Campanelli Drive
Braintree, MA 02184 (617) 843-8280
home-builder

Canandaigua Wine Co., Inc. CDG
116 Buffalo Street
Canandaigua, NY 14424 (716) 394-3630
domestic wine producer

Cardiff Equities Corp. CEQ
3333 North Torrey Pines Court
La Jolla, CA 92037 (619) 450-1901
bathroom vanities, food products

Cardillo Travel Systems, Inc. TVL
5710 Hannum Avenue
Culver City, CA 90230 (213) 649-6160
travel planning for commercial clients

Cardis Corp. CDS
9401 Wilshire Boulevard Suite 500
Beverly Hills, CA 90212 (213) 275-3866
distributes auto parts and supplies

Care Corp. KRE.B/A
200 Trust Building
Grand Rapids, MI 49503 (616) 459-1071
health care, recreation, housing

Care Enterprises CRE.B/A
23046 Avenida de la Carlota #700
Laguna Hills, CA 92653 (714) 837-8800
nursing and rehabilitation services

Casablanca Industries, Inc. CAB
450 North Baldwin Park Boulevard
City of Industry, CA 91746 (818) 369-6441
ceiling fans, wholesale sundry merchandise

Castle, A.M. & Co. CAS
3400 N. Wolf Road
Franklin Park, IL 60131 (312) 625-6411
metal products distributor

Castle Convertible Fund, Inc. CVF
c/o Fred Alger Management 75 Maiden Lane
New York, NY 10004 (212) 806-8800
closed-end investment company

Castle Industries Inc. CSE
Saltillo Road
Conway, AR 72032 (501) 327-1381
mobile home manufacturer

CDI Corp. CDI
Ten Penn Center Plaza
Philadelphia, PA 19103 (215) 569-2200
engineering and technical services

Centennial Group, Inc. CEG
5131 Owl Creek Road P.O. Box 5848
Snowmass Village, CO 81615 (303) 923-3031
real estate and development

Central Securities Corp. CET
375 Park Avenue
New York, NY 10022 (212) 688-3011
closed-end investment company

Century Business Credit Corp. CTY
444 Fifth Avenue
New York, NY 10018 (212) 221-4400
factoring and financing

Cetec Corp. CEC
9900 Baldwin Place
El Monte, CA 91731 (818) 442-8840
electronics

Champion Home Builders Co. CHB
5573 East North Street
Dryden, MI 48428 (313) 796-2211
manufactured housing, motor homes

Champion Products, Inc. CH
3141 Monroe Street P. O. Box 850
Rochester, NY 14618 (716) 385-3200
imprinted attire for school, business   [DRP]

Charter Medical Corp. CMD.A/B
577 Mulberry Street 11th Floor
Macon, GA 31298 (912) 742-1161
psychiatric and acute-care hospitals

Chicago Rivet & Machine Co. CVR
55731 Frontenac Road
Naperville, IL 60540 (312) 357-8500
rivets, fasteners, wire

Citadel Holding Corp. CDL
600 N. Brand Boulevard
Glendale, CA 91203 (213) 956-7100
savings and loan

Citizens First Bancorp, Inc. CFB
208 Harrison Road
Glen Rock, NJ 07452 (201) 445-3400
banking

City Gas Co. of Florida CGF
955 East 25th Street
Hialeah, FL 33013 (305) 691-8710
gas utility

Claremont Capital Corp. CCM
321 16th Avenue South P.O. Box 3407
Seattle, WA 98114 (206) 324-0901
closed-end investment company

Clark Consolidated Industries, Inc CLK
20575 Center Ridge Road Suite 300
Rocky River, OH 44116 (216) 333-8200
paper tubes, pulleys, electrical supplies

Clarostat Manufacturing Co., Inc. CLR
Washington Street
Dover, NH 03820 (603) 742-1120
controls, resistors, switches

Clopay Corp. CPY
101 E. 4th Street Clopay Building
Cincinnati, OH 45202 (513) 381-4800
specialty plastic films and home products

CMI Corp. CMX
I-40 and Morgan Road P.O. Box 1985
Oklahoma City, OK 73101 (405) 787-6020
automated road-building equipment

CMX Corp. CXC
3303 Scott Boulevard
Santa Clara, CA 95050 (408) 988-2000
computer-controlled tape-editing systems

Cognitronics Corp. CGN
c/o Am. Computer Corp. 4915 Mercury St.
San Diego, CA 92111 (203) 327-5397
optical scan/voice response components

Cohu, Inc. COH
807 LaJolla Rancho Road
La Jolla, CA 92037 (619) 277-6700
electronic devices, tv equipment

ComFed Savings Bank CFK
45 Central Street
Lowell, MA 01852 (617) 454-5663
banking

CompuDyne Corp. CDC
100 South Wacker Drive
Chicago, IL 60606 (312) 346-7878
communications and control equipment

Computer Consoles, Inc. CCS
97 Humboldt Street
Rochester, NY 14609 (716) 482-5000
data management systems

Computer Factory Inc. CFA
805 Third Avenue
New York, NY 10022 (212) 980-1700
sells and services personal computers

Conchemco, Inc. CKC
c/o Wescon Products Co.
P.O. Box 7710
Wichita, KS 67277 (316) 946-4280
machining and mechanical controls

Concord Fabrics Inc. CIS
1359 Broadway
New York, NY 10018 (212) 760-0300
woven and knitted fabrics

Connelly Containers, Inc. CON
Righters Ferry Rd. and Schuylkill Rv.
Bala Cynwyd, PA 19004 (215) 839-6400
containers, food processing

Conner Corp. CNR
US 70 Bypass East P.O. Box 520
Newport, NC 28570 (919) 223-5121
mobile homes

Conquest Exploration Co. CQX
P.O. Box 4512
Houston, TX 77210 (713) 440-2000
oil and gas exploration and development

Consolidated Oil & Gas, Inc. CGS
1860 Lincoln St., Lincoln Tower Building
Denver, CO 80295 (303) 861-5252
oil and gas products, land development

Consolidated Stores Corp. CNS
2020 Corvair Avenue
Columbus, OH 43207 (614) 224-1297
retailer of close-out merchandise

Continental Airlines Corp. QCAI
2929 Allen Parkway P.O. Box 4607
Houston, TX 77210 (713) 630-5285
airline

Continental Materials Corp. CUO
325 N. Wells Street
Chicago, IL 60610 (312) 661-7200
minerals, building materials

Convest Energy Partners, Ltd. CEP
2401 Fountain View Drive Suite 700
Houston, TX 77057 (713) 780-1952
oil and gas exploration and development

Copley Properties, Inc. COP
535 Boylston Street
Boston, MA 02116 (617) 578-4900
real estate investment

Cosmopolitan Care Corp. CCA
308 Madison Avenue
New York, NY 10017 (212) 986-0500
temporary health and clerical personnel

Countrywide Mortgage Investments, Inc. CWM
155 North Lake Avenue
Pasadena, CA 91109 (818) 304-8400
investments in single-family mortgages   [DRP]

Crest-Foam Corp. CFO
100 Carol Place
Moonachie, NJ 07074 (201) 641-9030
polyurethane foam

Cross, A.T. Co. ATXA
One Albion Road
Lincoln, RI 02865 (401) 333-1200
high-priced writing instruments/accessories

Crowley, Milner & Co. COM
2301 West Lafayette Blvd.
Detroit, MI 48216 (313) 962-2400
department stores

Crown Central Petroleum Corp. CNP.A/B
One North Charles P.O. Box 1168
Baltimore, MD 21203 (301) 539-7400
oil producing and refining

Crown Crafts, Inc. CRW
Edmond St., P.O. Box 371
Calhoun, GA 30701 (404) 629-7941
home furnishings products

Crutcher Resources Corp. CTR
50 Briar Hollow Lane P.O. Box 3227
Houston, TX 77001 (713) 871-9000
oil services; pipeline equipment

Crystal Oil Co. COR
229 Milam Street P.O. Box 21101
Shreveport, LA 71120 (318) 222-7791
oil and gas

CSS Industries, Inc. CSS
1401 Walnut Street
Philadelphia, PA 19102 (215) 569-9900
department/specialty/furniture stores

Cubic Corp. CUB
9333 Balboa Avenue
San Diego, CA 92123 (714) 277-6780
military electronic systems

Curtice-Burns, Inc. CBI
One Lincoln First Square P.O. Box 681
Rochester, NY 14602 (716) 325-1020
canned, frozen, snack foods   [DRP]

Custom Energy Services, Inc. CUS
Route 513
Califon, NJ 07830 (201) 832-5171
specialty piping components

Damon Creations, Inc. DNI
16 East 34th Street
New York, NY 10016 (212) 683-2465
men's furnishings and sportswear

Damson Oil Corp. DAM
366 Madison Avenue
New York, NY 10017 (212) 503-8500
oil and gas development/investments

Dataproducts Corp. DPC
6200 Canoga Avenue
Woodland Hills, CA 91365 (213) 887-8000
data communication products   [O]

Dataram Corp. DTM
Princeton Road
Cranbury, NJ 08512 (609) 799-0071
minicomputer-related products

De Rose Industries, Inc. DRI
8504 Adamo Drive
Tampa, FL 33619 (813) 623-2685
mobile homes

Decorator Industries, Inc. DII
2755 W. 8th Avenue
Hialeah, FL 33010 (305) 885-4661
manufactures and distributes draperies

De Laurentiis Entertainment Group, Inc. DEG
8670 Wilshire Boulevard
Beverly Hills, CA 90211 (213) 854-7000
movie production

Del Laboratories, Inc. DLI
565 Broad Hollow Road
Farmingdale, NY 11735 (516) 293-7070
drugs and cosmetics

Del-Val Financial Corp. DVL
24 River Road
Bogota, NJ 07603 (201) 487-1300
mortgage loans   [DRP]

Delmed, Inc. DMD
437 Turnpike St.
Canton, MA 02021 (617) 821-0500
disposable medical products

Designatronics, Inc. DSG
55 South Denton Ave.
New Hyde Park, NY 11040 (516) 328-3300
electro-mechanical components

Designcraft Industries, Inc. DJI
23 W. 47th Street
New York, NY 10036 (212) 719-3960
gold rings, earrings, pendants

Development Corp. of America DCA
2514 Hollywood Boulevard
Hollywood, FL 33020 (305) 920-6600
builder and developer

Devon Resource Investors DIN
1500 Mid-America Tower
Oklahoma City, OK 73102 (405) 235-3611
oil and gas development and production

Diagnostic/Retrieval Systems, Inc. DRS.A/B
16 Thornton Road
Oakland, NJ 07436 (201) 337-3800
anti-submarine warfare computer systems

Digicon Inc. DGC
3701 Kirby Drive
Houston, TX 77098 (713) 526-5611
oil industry data services

Dillard Department Stores Inc. DDSA
900 West Capitol Avenue P O Box 486
Little Rock, AR 72203 (501) 376-5200
department stores   [DRP]

Diodes, Inc. DIO
9957 Canoga Avenue
Chatsworth, CA 91311 (818) 998-4445
semi-conductor devices

Direct Action Marketing, Inc. DMK
3601 Hempstead Turnpike
Levittown, NY 11756 (516) 579-6200
retail marketing by direct mail

Drillers, Inc. DRL
450 Gears Road Suite 625
Houston, TX 77067 (713) 874-0202
onshore contract drilling

Driver-Harris Co. DRH
308 Middlesex Street
Harrison, NJ 07029 (201) 483-4800
electricity- and heat-resisting alloys

Ducommun Inc. DCO
611 West Sixth Street Suite 2500
Los Angeles, CA 90017 (213) 612-4200
electronics distribution, aerospace items

Duplex Products Inc. DPX
1947 Bethany Road
Sycamore, IL 60178 (815) 895-2101
continuous business forms

Duro-Test Corp. DUR
2321 Kennedy Boulevard
North Bergen, NJ 07047 (201) 867-7000
light bulbs

DWG Corp. DWG
6917 Collins Avenue
Miami Beach, FL 33141 (305) 866-7771
diversified technological services

Dyneer Corp. DYR
The Riverside Building
Westport, CT 06880 (203) 226-1071
mechanical power and electronic equipment

EAC Industries, Inc. EAC
135 South LaSalle Street Suite 1400
Chicago, IL 60603 (312) 346-2015
hardware, aircraft and defense products

Eagle Clothes, Inc. EGL
350 Fifth Avenue Suite 6501
New York, NY 10118 (212) 947-6635
manufacture and retail of menswear

Eastern Co. EML
112 Bridge Street
Naugatuck, CT 06770 (203) 729-2255
mine roof supports, metals fabrication [DRP]

East Group Properties
120 North Congress St. P.O. Box 22728
Jackson, MS 39225 (601) 948-4091
real estate investment trust

Echo Bay Mines, Ltd. ECO
3300 Manulife Place, 10180 101st Street
Edmonton, AL, CDA T5J354 (403) 429-5811
gold mining

EECO Inc. EEC
1601 East Chestnut Avenue
Santa Ana, CA 92701 (714) 835-6000
electronic equipment, digital modules

Electro Audio Dynamics, Inc. EAD
98 Cutter Mill Road
Great Neck, NY 11021 (516) 466-5100
antennas, precision motors, circuitry

Electronics Corp. of America ECA
265 Winter Street
Waltham, MA 02154 (617) 466-8000
electronic controls and systems

ElectroSound Group, Inc. ESG
800 Veterans Memorial Highway
Hauppauge, NY 11788 (516) 724-3700
record pressing, audio equipment

Elsinore Corp. ELS
300 South 4th Street Suite 501
Las Vegas, NV 89101 (702) 382-2385
resort hotels and casinos

Emerging Medical Technology Fund, Inc. EMT
5 Sentry Parkway West P.O. Box 1111
Blue Bell, PA 19422 (215) 825-0400
closed-end investment company

Empire of Carolina, Inc. EMP
Daniel Street
Tarboro, NC 27886 (919) 823-4111
children's plastic toys

Energy Development Partners Ltd. EDP
P.O. Box 387111
Denver, CO 80237
oil and gas exploration and production

Energy Oil, Inc. EOI
1960 Industrial Circle
Longmont, CO 80501 (303) 776-4354
oil and gas exploration and development

EnerServ Products, Inc. ESV
6914 Industrial Blvd.
El Paso, TX 79915 (915) 779-4812
oil-field tubular goods

Engineered Systems & Development Corp. ESD
600 Meridian Avenue
San Jose, CA 95126 (408) 289-0111
automation systems and equipment

ERC International Inc. ERC
2070 Chain Bridge Road Suite 400
Vienna, VA 22180 (312) 346-2015
provides engineering technical services

Ero Industries, Inc. ERO
5940 West Touhy Avenue
Chicago, IL 60648 (312) 647-0700
outdoor sporting goods

ESI Industries, Inc. ESI
6440 North Central Expwy.
Dallas, TX 75206 (214) 361-6663
specialized truck bodies

Espey Mfg. & Electronics Corp. ESP
Ballston & Congress Aves. P.O. Box 422
Saratoga Springs, NY 12866 (518) 584-4100
electronic power supply systems

Esprit Systems, Inc. ETI
100 Marcus Drive
Melville, NY 11747 (516) 293-5600
markets video display terminals

Esquire Radio & Electronics, Inc. EE
4100 First Avenue
Brooklyn, NY 11232 (718) 499-0020
private brand radios, hi-fi

Everest & Jennings International EJ.A/B
2310 So. Sepulveda Blvd.
Los Angeles, CA 90064 (213) 479-4141
wheelchairs, medical equipment

Excel Industries, Inc. EXC
1120 North Main Street
Elkhart, IN 46514 (219) 264-2131
windows for vehicles

Fab Industries, Inc. FIT
200 Madison Avenue
New York, NY 10016 (212) 279-9000
fabrics and laces

Fairmont Financial, Inc. FFI
4111 West Alameda Avenue
Burbank, CA 91505 (213) 843-0755
workers' compensation insurance

Fairmount Chemical Co., Inc. FMT
117 Blanchard Street
Newark, NJ 07105 (201) 344-5790
agricultural and graphics chemicals

Fidata Corp. FID
67 Broad Street
New York, NY 10004 (212) 530-2400
financial computer clearance service

First Australia Fund, Inc. IAF
One Seaport Plaza
New York, NY 10292
closed-end investment company

First Capital Holdings Corp. FCH
1900 Avenue of the Stars
Los Angeles, CA 90067 (213) 551-1000
mutual fund investor advisory services

First Conn. Small Business Inv. Co. FCO
177 State Street
Bridgeport, CT 06604 (203) 366-4726
loans to small businesses

First Wyoming BanCorp. FWO
18th St. & Carey Avenue
Cheyenne, WY 82001 (307) 632-0504
banking

Firstcorp, Inc. FCR
300 South Salisbury St.
Raleigh, NC 27601 (919) 828-8241
savings and loan

Fischer & Porter Co. FP
200 Witmer Road
Horsham, PA 19044 (215) 674-6000
industrial process control equipment

Fitchburg Gas & Electric Light Co. FGE
120 Royall Street
Canton, MA 02021 (617) 828-8660
electric and gas utility

Flanigan's Enterprises, Inc. QBDL
16565 N.W. 15th Avenue
Miami, FL 33169 (305) 624-9681
liquor stores, cocktail lounges

Florida Rock Industries, Inc. FRK
155 East 21st Street
Jacksonville, FL 32206 (904) 355-1781
ready-mixed concrete products, aggregates

Fluke, John Mfg. Co., Inc. FKM
Post Office Box C9090
Everett, WA 98206 (206) 356-5310
test and measurement instruments/systems

Foodarama Supermarkets, Inc. FSM
303 W. Main Street P.O. Box 592
Freehold, NJ 07728 (201) 462-4700
supermarkets

Foote Mineral Co. FTE
Route 100
Exton, PA 19341 (215) 363-6500
mining and processing of raw materials

Foothill Group, Inc. FGI
2049 Century Park East Suite 600
Los Angeles, CA 90067 (213) 556-1222
commercial finance

Forest City Enterprises, Inc. FCE.A/B
10800 Brookpark Road
Cleveland, OH 44130 (216) 267-1200
real estate, building materials

Forest Laboratories, Inc. FRX
150 East 58th Street 20th Floor
New York, NY 10155 (212) 421-7850
ethical and non-prescription drugs

Fotomat Corp. FOT
205 Ninth Street North
St. Petersburg, FL 33701 (813) 823-2027
film processing, kiosks

FPA Corp. FPO
2501 Palm-Aire Drive North
Pompano Beach, FL 33060 (305) 971-6000
community development, leisure services

Frantz Manufacturing Co. FRZ
301 West Third Street
Sterling, IL 61081 (815) 625-0163
overhead garage doors, hardware

Frederick's of Hollywood FHD
6608 Hollywood Boulevard
Hollywood, CA 90028 (213) 466-5151
apparel stores, mail order

Frequency Electronics, Inc. FEI
55 Charles Lindbergh Boulevard
Mitchel Field, NY 11553 (516) 794-4500
electronic control products

Friedman Industries, Inc. FRD
Homestead Road
Houston, TX 77028 (713) 672-9433
processes steel coils into plates/sheets

Fries Entertainment, Inc. FE
9200 Sunset Boulevard Suite 700
Los Angeles, CA 90069 (213) 859-9957
produces made-for-tv-movies

Frisch's Restaurants, Inc. FRS
2800 Gilbert Avenue
Cincinnati, OH 45206 (513) 961-2660
operates coffee shops, motels

Fur Vault, Inc. FRV
350 Seventh Avenue
New York, NY 10001
wholesaler/retailer of fur apparel

Galaxy Carpet Mills, Inc. GXY
850 Arthur Avenue
Elk Grove Village, IL 60007 (312) 593-0555
manufacturer/distributor of tufted carpets

Galaxy Oil Co. GOX
918 Lamar Drawer GALY
Wichita Falls, TX 76307 (817) 766-0193
oil and gas development and sales

Garan, Inc. GAN
350 Fifth Avenue
New York, NY 10118 (212) 563-2000
knitted/woven apparel

Gates Learjet Corp GLJ
P O Box 11186
Tucson, AZ 85734 (602) 746-5100
business jet aircraft, avionics equipment

Gelman Sciences, Inc. GSC
600 South Wagner Road Box 1448
Ann Arbor, MI 48106 (313) 665-0651
lab health devices, filters

Gemco National, Inc. GNL
1350 Ave. of the Americas
New York, NY 10019 (212) 489-0610
metal/glass architectural fabrication

General Defense Corp. GDF
230 Schilling Circle Schilling Plz.S
Hunt Valley, MD 21031 (301) 666-5900
tank ordnance

General Employment Enterprises, Inc. JOB
150 South Wacker Drive
Chicago, IL 60606 (312) 977-9300
personnel placement service

General Microwave Corp. GMW
5500 New Horizons Blvd.
Amityville, NY 11701 (516) 694-3600
electron measuring and control equipment

Genisco Technology Corp. GES
18435 Susana Road
Rancho Dominguez, CA 90221 (213) 537-4750
diversified electronics manufacturer

Genovese Drug Stores, Inc. GDX
80 Marcus Drive
Melville, NY 11747 (516) 420-1900
drug and general merchandise chain

Geothermal Resources International, Inc. GEO
1825 South Grant Street Suite 900
San Mateo, CA 94402 (415) 349-3232
equipment leasing and service

Giant Food, Inc. GFSA
6300 Sheriff Road
Landover, MD 20785 (301) 341-4100
supermarkets, drug stores, foods   [DRP]

Glatfelter, P.H. Co. GLT
228 South Main Street
Spring Grove, PA 17362 (717) 225-4711
printing/writing/technical papers

Glenmore Distilleries Co. GDS
Citizens Plaza
Louisville, KY 40202 (502) 589-0130
domestic, imported liquors

Global Natural Resources, Inc. GNR
5300 Memorial Drive
Houston, TX 77007 (713) 880-5464
oil and gas exploration and production

GNC Energy Corp. GLE
2320 South Tower, Plaza of the Americas
Dallas, TX 75201 (214) 748-0244
health food stores

Golden West Homes, Inc. GWH
1308 East Wakeham Avenue
Santa Ana, CA 92705 (714) 835-4200
mobile home manufacturer

Goldfield Corp. GV
65 East NASA Boulevard Suite 101
Melbourne, FL 32901 (305) 724-1700
electrical construction, silver mining

Gorman-Rupp Co. GRC
P.O. Box 1217
Mansfield, OH 44901 (419) 755-1011
pump products manufacturer

Gould Investors Trust GTR
60 Cutter Mill Road
Great Neck, NY 11021 (516) 466-3100
real estate investment trust

Graham Corp. GHM
20 Florence Avenue
Batavia, NY 14020 (716) 343-2216
vacuum and heat transfer equipment

Graham-McCormick Oil & Gas Partners GOP
P.O. Box 8058
Melanie, LA 70011 (504) 834-9332
oil and gas exploration and production

Grand Auto, Inc. GAI
7200 Edgewater Drive
Oakland, CA 94621 (415) 568-6500
retail auto stores

Grant Industries Inc. GTX
High Street
West Nyack, NY 10994 (914) 358-4400
mechanical slides

Graphic Technology, Inc. GRT
14824 W. 117th Street
Olathe, KS 66062 (913) 829-8000
bar-coded labels for inventory control

Great Lakes Chemical Corp. GLK
Highway 52 Northwest P. O. Box 2200
West Lafayette, IN 47906 (317) 463-2511
bromine and bromine derivatives

Greenman Brothers, Inc. GMN
105 Price Parkway
Farmingdale, NY 11735 (516) 293-5300
wholesale/retail distribution of toys

Greiner Engineering, Inc. GII
300 E. Carpenter Freeway Suite 1210
Irving, TX 75062 (214) 258-6208
community development services

GRI Corp. GRR
65 E. South Water Street The GRI Bldg.
Chicago, IL 60601 (312) 977-3700
consumer products by mail

GTI Corp. GTI
10060 Willow Creek Road
San Diego, CA 92131 (619) 578-3111
electronic sealer components

Guardsman Chemicals, Inc. GRV
P.O. Box 1521
Grand Rapids, MI 49501 (616) 957-2600
paints and varnishes

Gull, Inc. GLL
395 Oser Avenue
Smithtown, NY 11787 (516) 231-3737
aircraft instrument systems

HAL, Inc. HA
Honolulu Int'l Airport P.O. Box 30008
Honolulu, HI 96820 (808) 537-5100
air transport system

Halifax Engineering, Inc. HX
5250 Cherokee Avenue
Alexandria, VA 22312 (703) 750-2202
professional/technical support services

Hampton Industries, Inc. HAI
P.O. Box 614
Kinston, NC 28501 (919) 527-8011
men's and boys' clothing

Handyman Corp. HMN
6666 Convoy Court
San Diego, CA 92111 (619) 560-6666
retail home improvement centers

Harley-Davidson, Inc. HDI
3700 West Juneau Avenue
Milwaukee, WI 53208 (414) 342-4680
motorcycle manufacturer

Harvey Group Inc. HRA
245 Great Neck Road
Great Neck, NY 11022 (516) 466-5790
distributes electronics, brokers food   [O]

Hasbro, Inc. HAS
1027 Newport Avenue
Pawtucket, RI 02862 (401) 727-5000
toys, board and card games

Hastings Manufacturing Co. HMF
325 North Hanover Street
Hastings, MI 49058 (616) 945-2491
manufactures auto replacement parts

Health Care REIT, Inc. HCN
1865 North McCullough St. P.O. Drawer C
Lima, OH 45802 (419) 227-3760
real estate investment trust   [DRP 4%]

Health-Chem Corp. HCH
1107 Broadway
New York, NY 10010 (212) 691-7550
industrial and health care products

Health-Mor, Inc. HMI
151 East 22nd Street
Lombard, IL 60148 (312) 953-9700
vacuum cleaners, metal tubing

Healthcare International HII
9737 Great Hills Trail
Austin, TX 78759 (512) 346-4300
psychiatric, general health services

HEICO Corp. HEI
3000 Taft Street   P.O. Box 7209
Hollywood, FL 33021 (305) 987-6101
medical lab equipment, jet engine parts

Hein-Werner Corp. HNW
1200 National Avenue
Waukesha, WI 53187 (414) 542-6611
hydraulic jacks and pumps

Heldor Industries, Inc. HDR
1 Corey Road
Morristown, NJ 07960 (201) 898-9445
in-ground swimming pools

Helm Resources, Inc. H
Two Hammarskjold Plaza
New York, NY 10017 (212) 355-7788
oil services, agricultural equipment

Heritage Entertainment HHH
9229 Sunset Boulevard
Los Angeles, CA 90069 (213) 278-1566
distributes tv programs, films

Hershey Oil Corp. HSO
101 West Walnut Street
Pasadena, CA 91103 (818) 405-8888
oil and gas exploration and development

Hinderliter Industries Inc. HND
P.O. Box 35505
Tulsa, OK 74135 (918) 494-0992
energy industry equipment, auto parts

Hipotronics, Inc. HIP
Route 22 P.O. Box A
Brewster, NY 10509 (914) 279-8091
high volt testing/power supply equipment

HMG Property Investors, Inc. HMG
2701 South Bayshore Drive
Coconut Grove, FL 33133 (305) 854-6803
real estate investment trust

Hofmann Industries, Inc. HOF
3145 Shillington Road
Sinking Spring, PA 19608 (215) 678-8051
steel tubing, gray iron castings

Holly Corp. HOC
2600 Diamond Shamrock Tw.
Dallas, TX 75201 (214) 979-0210
petroleum refining and marketing

Home Group, Inc. HME
59 Maiden Lane
New York, NY 10038 (212) 530-6157
insurance

Home Shopping Network, Inc. HSN
1529 U.S. Highway 19 South
Clearwater, FL 33546 (813) 530-9455
sells merchandise on tv

Hormel, George A. & Co. HRL
501 16th Avenue, N.E. P.O. Box 800
Austin, MN 55912 (507) 437-5611
meat processor, especially pork products

Horn & Hardart Co. HOR
1163 Ave. of the Americas
New York, NY 10036 (212) 398-9000
fast food restaurants, mail order items

Hotel Investors Trust, Inc. HPS
21031 Ventura Boulevard Suite 315
Woodland Hills, CA 91364 (818) 883-9520
real estate investment trust   [DRP]

Hovnanian Enterprises, Inc. HOV
10 Route 35 P. O. Box 500
Red Bank, NJ 07701 (201) 747-7800
multifamily-home builder

Howell Industries, Inc. HOW
17515 West Nine Mile Road
Southfield, MI 48075 (313) 424-8220
auto steel parts, seat guides

Hubbell, Harvey Inc. HUBB
584 Derby Milford Road
Orange, CT 06477 (203) 789-1100
heavy electrical equipment   [DRP]

HUBCO, Inc. HCO
3100 Bergenline Ave.
Union City, NJ 07087 (201) 348-2300
banking   [DRP]

Hudson Foods HFI
P.O. Box 777
Rogers, AR 72757 (501) 636-1100
produces/markets poultry products

Hudson General Corp. HGC
111 Great Neck Road
Great Neck, NY 11021 (516) 487-8610
aviation services, land development

I.C.H. Corp. ICH
4211 Norbourne Boulevard P. O. Box 7597
Louisville, KY 40207 (502) 897-1861
insurance

ICEE - USA ICY
1330 N. Knollwood Center
Anaheim, CA 92801 (714) 761-5441
markets semi-frozen beverages

ICO, Inc. ICO
6000 Western Place Suite 120
Ft. Worth, TX 76107 (814) 735-1331
tubular services to the oil industry

Imperial Industries, Inc. III
13939 N.W. 60th Avenue
Miami Lakes, FL 33014 (305) 557-2525
building materials distributor, paints

Inflight Services, Inc. INF
485 Madison Avenue
New York, NY 10022 (212) 751-1800
films aboard aircraft

Instron Corp. ISN
100 Royall Street
Canton, MA 02021 (617) 828-2500
material testing equipment

Instrument Systems Corp. ISY
100 Jericho Quadrangle
Jericho, NY 11753 (516) 938-5544
products for home, industry, defense

Intermark Inc. IMI
1020 Prospect Street P. O. Box 1149
La Jolla, CA 92038 (619) 459-3841
operating/holding company   [DRP]

International Banknote Co., Inc. IBK
230 Park Avenue
New York, NY 10169 (212) 697-6600
currencies/securities printing/equipment

International Hydron Corp. HYD
210 Crossways Park Drive
Woodbury, NY 11797 (516) 364-1700
manufactures soft contact lenses

International Income Property, Inc. IIP
100 Park Avenue
New York, NY 10017 (212) 759-9534
real estate investment trust   [DRP]

International Power Machines Corp. PWR
3328 Executive Boulevard
Mesquite, TX 75149 (212) 288-6471
uninterruptible power systems

International Proteins Corp. PRO
123 Fairfield Road
Fairfield, NJ 07006 (201) 227-2710
manufacturer/distributor of fishmeal

International Seaway Trading Corp. INS
1382 West 9th Street
Cleveland, OH 44113 (216) 696-7800
imported footwear

Internat'l Thoroughbred Breeders Inc. ITB
202 Abbington Drive
East Windsor, NJ 08520 (609) 443-6111
breeding, thoroughbred/harness race tracks

Interwest Corp. IWC
1525 Elm Street LTV Building
Dallas, TX 75201 (214) 720-0118
closed-end investment company

Ionics, Inc. ION
65 Grove Street
Watertown, MA 02172 (617) 926-2500
electro-chemical processing equipment

IPM Technology, Inc. IPM
6851 West Imperial Hwy.
Los Angeles, CA 90045 (213) 646-2994
airport ancillary services

Iroquois Brands Ltd. IBL
41 West Putnam Avenue
Greenwich, CT 06830 (203) 622-9000
nutritional and gourmet products, brews

IRE Financial Corporation IREF
1320 South Dixie Highway
Coral Gables, FL 33146 (605) 665-8100
diversified financial services

IRT Corp. IX
3030 Callan Road
San Diego, CA 92121 (619) 450-4343
scientific engineering/technical services

ISS International Service System, Inc. ISI
360 Lexington Avenue
New York, NY 10017 (212) 382-9800
building maintenance

Jaclyn, Inc. JLN
635 59th Street
West New York, NJ 07093 (201) 868-9400
popular-priced handbags

Jacobs Engineering Group Inc. JEC
251 South Lake Avenue
Pasadena, CA 91101 (213) 681-3781
full-service engineering organization

Jet America Airlines, Inc. JA
3521 East Spring Street
Long Beach, CA 90806 (213) 492-6000
limited domestic air service

Jetronic Industries, Inc. JET
Main & Cotton Streets
Philadelphia, PA 19127 (215) 482-7660
electronic equipment manufacturer

Johnson Products Co., Inc. JPC
8522 South Lafayette Ave.
Chicago, IL 60620 (312) 483-4100
hair products, cosmetics geared to blacks

Johnstown American Companies JAC
5775-A Peachtree Dunwoody
Atlanta, GA 30342 (404) 252-8780
property management, real estate services

Johnstown Industries, Inc. JII
111 Crossways Park West P.O. Box 1000
Woodbury, NY 11797 (516) 921-1500
auto/truck parts, textiles

Jumping-Jacks Shoes, Inc. JJS
100 Fifth Street
Monett, MO 65708 (417) 235-3122
manufacturer/distributor children's shoes

Kapok Corp. KPK
923 McMullen Booth Road
Clearwater, FL 33519 (813) 726-4734
restaurants, tin plate, pipe

Kappa Networks, Inc.
1443 Pinewood Street
Rahway, NJ 07065 (201) 541-1600

Kay Corp. KAY
320 King Street
Alexandria, VA 22314 (703) 683-3800
international trading, jewelry stores

Kay Jewelers, Inc. KJI
320 King Street
Alexandria, VA 22314 (703) 683-3800
jewelry stores

Kearney-National, Inc. KNY
Two Continental Towers 1701 Golf Road
Rolling Meadows, IL 60008 (312) 593-6046
electric utility equipment

Kenwin Shops, Inc. KWN
505 Eighth Avenue
New York, NY 10018 (212) 695-1850
ladies' and children's apparel

Ketchum & Co., Inc. KCH
33 Riverside Avenue
Westport, CT 06880 (203) 227-8084
drug distributor and manufacturer

Key Pharmaceuticals, Inc. KPH
18425 NW Second Avenue
Miami, FL 33169 (305) 578-5800
prescription and non-prescription drugs

Keystone Camera Products Corp. KYC
468 Getty Avenue
Clifton, NJ 07015 (201) 546-2800
35 mm cameras and photographic equipment

Killearn Properties, Inc. KPI
P.O. Box 12789
Tallahassee, FL 32317 (904) 893-2111
developer of communities

Kinark Corp. KIN
7060 South Yale Avenue P.O. Box 1499
Tulsa, OK 74136 (918) 494-0964
chemical packaging

Kirby Exploration Co., Inc. KEX
P.O. Box 1745
Houston, TX 77001 (713) 629-9370
transport services, insurance, oil and gas

Kit Manufacturing Co. KIT
530 East Wardlow Road P.O. Box 848
Long Beach, CA 90801 (213) 595-7451
mobile homes, recreational vehicles

Kleer-Vu Industries, Inc. KVU
711 Polk Street Suite 500
Houston, TX 77002 (713) 654-1344
plastic transparent items

Knoll International, Inc. KNL
153 East 53rd Street Suite 5901
New York, NY 10022 (212) 826-2400
office furniture manufacturer

Koger Co. KGR
3986 Boulevard Center Dr.
Jacksonville, FL 32207 (904) 396-4817
owns/operates office buildings   [DRP 5%]

La Pointe Industries, Inc. LPI
155 West Main Street
Rockville, CT 06066 (203) 872-8571
electronic equipment manufacturer

LaBarge, Inc. LB
707 North Second Street
St. Louis, MO 63178 (314) 231-5960
tubular furniture, electronics

Landmark Bancshares Corp. LBC
10 South Brentwood Blvd.
Clayton, MO 63105 (314) 889-9500
banking   [DRP]

Landmark Land Co., Inc. LML
100 Clock Tower Place Suite 200
Carmel, CA 93923 (408) 625-4060
land developing, building materials

Landmark Savings Association LSA
335 Fifth Avenue
Pittsburgh, P.A. 15222 (412) 471-9800
mortgage and consumer loans

Laurentian Capital Corp. LQ
P O Box 3600
Winter Park, FL 32790 (305) 647-3111
life, accident, and health insurance

Lazare Kaplan International, Inc. LKI
529 Fifth Avenue
New York, NY 10017 (212) 972-9700
cutter and merchant of diamonds

Lear Petroleum Partners Ltd. LPT
4925 Greenville Avenue
Dallas, TX 75206 (214) 363-6085
oil and gas exploration and production

Lee Pharmaceuticals LPH
1444 Santa Anita Avenue P. O. Box 3836
South El Monte, CA 91733 (213) 442-3141
nail care, orthodontic products

Lehigh Press, Inc. LP
7001 North Park Drive
Pennsauken, NJ 08109 (609) 665-5200
commercial printing

Leisure & Technology, Inc. LVX
12233 West Olympic Blvd.
Los Angeles, CA 90064 (213) 826-1000
retirement recreational communities

Levitt Corp. LVT
7777 Glades RoadSuite 410
Boca Raton, FL 33434 (305) 482-5100
single family homes

Liberty Financial Group, Inc. LFG
202 North Broad Street
Philadelphia, PA 19102 (215) 864-7630
savings and loan

Lifestyle Restaurants, Inc. LIF
401 Park Avenue South
New York, NY 10016 (212) 696-7700
restaurant chain

Lincoln N.C. Realty Fund, Inc. LRF.E
101 Lincoln Center Drive
Foster City, CA 94404 (415) 571-2250
real estate investment trust

Lionel Corporation LIO
441 Lexington Avenue Suite 703
New York, NY 10017 (212) 818-6300
toy supermarkets, electrical components

Littlefield, Adams & Co. LFA
81 Adams Drive
Totowa, NJ 07512 (201) 256-8600
imprinted leisurewear

Lodge & Shipley Co. LSP
3055 Colerain Avenue
Cincinnati, OH 45225 (513) 541-4774
machine tools, packaging machinery

Lori Corp. LRC
500 Central Avenue Box 8902
Northfield, IL 60093 (312) 441-7300
distributor of costume jewelry

Lorimar-Telepictures Inc. LRM
3970 Overland Avenue
Culver City, CA 90230 (213) 202-2000
tv programming/production/distribution

LSB Industries, Inc. LSB
Post Office Box 754
Oklahoma City, OK 73101 (405) 235-4546
bearings, machine tools, air conditioning

Lundy Electronics & Systems, Inc. LDY
One Robert Lane
Glen Head, NY 11545 (516) 671-9000
data entry systems, military electronics

Luria, L, & Son, Inc. LUR
5770 Miami Lakes Drive
Miami Lakes, FL 33014 (305) 557-9000
catalog showroom retailer

Lydall, Inc. LDL
One Colonial Road
Manchester, CT 06040 (203) 646-1233
diversified industrial products

Lynch Communication Systems, Inc. LYC
204 Edison Way
Reno, NV 89520 (702) 786-4020
hardware for telephone systems

Lynch Corp. LGL
369 Passaic Avenue
Fairfield, NJ 07006 (201) 882-0900
glass machinery, test equipment, quartz

MacGregor Sporting Goods, Inc. MGS
25 East Union Avenue
East Rutherford, NJ 07073 (201) 935-6300
manufactures/imports athletic equipment

MacNeal-Schwendler Corp. MNS
815 Colorado Boulevard
Los Angeles, CA 90041 (213) 258-9111
software for computer-aided engineering

Macrodyne Industries, Inc. MCT
4465 Wilshire Blvd. Suite 303
Los Angeles, CA 90010 (213) 930-1043
aircraft parts, jet engine parts

Magnet Bank MAG
1 Piedmont Road
Charleston, WV 25328 (304) 347-9600
savings bank

Maine Public Service Co. MAP
209 State Street Drawer 1209
Presque Isle, ME 04769 (207) 768-5811
electric utility

Mangood Corp. MAB
676 N. St. Clair
Chicago, IL 60611 (312) 943-3900
instruments for weighing and batching

Marathon Office Supply, Inc. MAO
10323 Santa Monica Blvd. Suite D
Los Angeles, CA 90025 (213) 557-2708
distributes office products, furniture

Mark IV Industries, Inc. IV
388 Evans Street
Williamsville, NY 14221 (716) 632-7050
plastic products, control equipment

Martin Processing, Inc. MPI
Post Office Box 690
Rocky Mount, VA 24151 (703) 483-0261
film and textile yarn

Masland, C.H. & Sons MLD
P.O. Box 40
Carlisle, PA 17013 (717) 249-1866
carpeting for homes and autos

Matec Corp. MXC
75 South Street
Hopkinton, MA 01748 (617) 435-9039
electronic components/systems manufacturer

Material Sciences Corp. MSC
2300 East Pratt Boulevard
Elk Grove Village, IL 60007 (312) 439-8270
steel coil protective coatings

Materials Research Corp. MTL
Route 303
Orangeburg, NY 10962 (914) 359-4200
film coating, etching, high purity metals

Matrix Corp. MAX
1 Ramland Avenue
Orangeburg, NY 10962 (914) 365-0190
imaging instrumentation

May Energy Partners, Ltd. MEP
800 One Lincoln Ctr. 5400 LBJ Frwy.
Dallas, TX 75240 (214) 934-6263
oil and gas exploration and development

Mayflower Corp. MFL
9998 North Michigan Road
Carmel, IN 46032 (317) 875-1000
hauling/storage, school busing, cassettes

McDowell Enterprises, Inc. ME
P.O. Box 149
Nashville, TN 37202 (615) 366-4141
asphalt paving, construction

MCO Holdings, Inc. MCO
10880 Wilshire Boulevard
Los Angeles, CA 90024 (213) 879-5252
oil and gas, pipeline, land development

MCO Resources, Inc. MCR
5718 Westheimer
Houston, TX 77057 (713) 953-7777
oil, gas, geothermal exploration/development

McFaddin Ventures, Inc. MV
1900 Yorktown Suite 100
Houston, TX 77056 (713) 871-0212
operates entertainment clubs

McRae Industries, Inc. MRI
P.O. Box 726
Mount Gilead, NC 27306 (919) 439-6147
combat boots, apparel

Media General, Inc. MEGA
333 East Grace Street
Richmond, VA 23219 (804) 649-6000
newspaper publishing, newsprint   [DRP]

MEDIQ, Inc. MED
One MEDIQ Plaza
Pennsauken, NJ 08110 (609) 665-9300
medical services/equipment leasing

MEM Co., Inc. MEM
Union Street Extension
Northvale, NJ 07647 (201) 767-0100
men's toiletries, packaging materials

Mercury Savings and Loan Association MSL
7812 Edinger Avenue
Huntington Beach, CA 92647 (714) 842-9333
savings and loan

Met-Pro Corp. MPR
160 Cassell Road
Harleysville, PA 19438 (215) 723-6715
pollution control, fluid handling

Metex Corp. MTX
970 New Durham Road P.O. Box 358
Edison, NJ 08818 (201) 287-0800
antenna systems; high temperature seals

Metrocare, Inc. MEE
5398 Park Street North
St. Petersburg, FL 33709 (813) 546-2461
health care services, land development

Michigan General Corp. MGL
1555 Valwood Parkway Suite 150
Carrollton, TX 75006 (214) 247-3800
homebuilding products, clothing stores

Mid-America Industries Inc MAM
900 Rogers Avenue
Fort Smith, AR 72901 (501) 785-1461
auto replacement parts distributor

Midland Co. MLA
P.O. Box 1256
Cincinnati, OH 45201 (513) 721-3777
insurance, mobile homes, barge

Mission West Properties MSW
110 15th Street P.O. Box 2530
Del Mar, CA 92014 (619) 481-5181
real estate business trust

Mitchell Energy & Development Corp. MND
2001 Timberlock Road P.O. Box 4000
The Woodlands, TX 77380 (713) 363-5657
oil and gas, real estate development   [O]

Money Management Corp. MGT
1000 East 80th Place P.O. Box 8030
Merrillville, IN 46410 (219) 738-6283
banking   [DRP]

Moog, Inc. MOG.A/B
East Aurora, NY 14052 (716) 652-2000
aerospace servovalves, industrial controls

Moore Medical Corp. MMD
P.O. Box 3070
New Britain, CT 06050 (203) 225-2225
drugs, medical/beauty products distributor

Mortgage Growth Investors MTG
One Post Office Square
Boston, MA 02109 (617) 423-4747
real estate investment trust

Mortgage Investments Plus, Inc. MIP
5955 DeSoto Avenue Suite 140
Woodland Hills, CA 91367 (818) 715-0311
real estate investment trust   [DRP]

MorTronics, Inc. MR
1300 South Main St. Suite 1000
North Canton, OH 44720 (216) 494-6722
coin-operated video games, restaurants

Mott's Super Markets, Inc. MSM
59-65 Leggett Street
East Hartford, CT 06108 (203) 289-3301
supermarkets

Mountain Medical Equipment, Inc. MTN
10488 West Centennial Rd.
Littleton, CO 80127 (303) 973-1200
oxygen concentrators

Movie Star, Inc. MVS.A
392 Fifth Avenue
New York, NY 10018 (212) 563-3000
lingerie and loungewear

Movielab, Inc. MOV
619 West 54 Street
New York, NY 10019 (212) 586-0360
film and tv processing lab

MSA Realty Corp. SSS
115 West Washington St.
Indianapolis, IN 46204 (317) 263-7030
real estate investment trust

MSI Data Corp. MSI
340 Fischer Avenue
Costa Mesa, CA 92626 (714) 549-6000
portable data collection systems

MSR Exploration Ltd. MSR
CBM Building Box 176
Cut Bank, MT 59427 (406) 873-2235
oil and gas exploration and development

Murphy Industries, Inc. MIH
2801 Rockcreek Parkway
North Kansas City, MO 64116 (816) 474-0300
electric wiring assemblies

Myers Industries, Inc. MYE
1293 South Main Street
Akron, OH 44301 (216) 253-5592
tire service equipment and supplies

Nantucket Industries, Inc. NAN
105 Madison Avenue
New York, NY 10016 (212) 889-5656
hosiery and underwear

National Gas & Oil Co. NLG
1500 Granville Road P.O. Drawer A-F
Newark, OH 43055 (614) 344-2102
gas utility

National Patent Development Corp. NPD
375 Park Avenue
New York, NY 10022 (212) 826-8500
emerging technology commercial products   [O]

New Mexico and Arizona Land Co. NZ
2810 North Third Street Suite 203
Phoenix, AZ 85004 (602) 266-5455
uranium, land rental

New Plan Realty Trust NPR
469 Fifth Avenue
New York, NY 10017 (212) 684-6200
real estate investment trust   [DRP 5%]

New Process Co. NOZ
220 Hickory Street
Warren, PA 16366 (814) 723-3600
mail order apparel and home furnishings

New World Pictures, Ltd. NWP
1888 Century Park East 5th floor
Los Angeles, CA 90067 (213) 551-1444
motion picture producer and distributor

New York Times Co. NYT.A
229 West 43rd Street
New York, NY 10036 (212) 556-1234
newspapers, magazines, tv, cable tv   [DRP]

Newbery Corp. NBE
1430 West Broadway
Tempe, AZ 85282 (602) 966-6243
electrical contracting

Newcor, Inc. NEW
3270 West Big Beaver Rd. Suite 430
Troy, MI 48084 (313) 643-7730
specialized industrial machinery

Newmark & Lewis, Inc. NLI
595 South Broadway
Hicksville, NY 11802 (516) 681-6900
retail electrical/appliance stores

Newport Electric Corp. NPT
12 Turner Road P.O. Box 4128
Middletown, RI 02840 (401) 847-4480
electric utility   [DRP]

Nichols Institute LAB
26441 Via de Anza
S.J. Capistrano, CA 92675 (714) 661-8000
clinical testing services

Nichols, S.E. Inc. NCL
500 8th Avenue
New York, NY 10018 (212) 695-5120
discount department stores

Noel Industries, Inc. NOL
350 Fifth Avenue
New York, NY 10001 (212) 563-2700
apparel manufacturer

Nolex Corp. NLX
2049 Century Park East Suite 450
Los Angeles, CA 90067 (213) 553-9400
distributes printing and industrial papers

NRM Energy Co. NRM
2121 San Jacinto Street
Dallas, TX 75201 (214) 742-9751
oil and gas exploration and production

Nu Horizons Electronics Corp. NUH
238 Route 109
Farmingdale, NY 11735 (516) 694-2500
distributor of semi-conductor parts

Nuclear Data, Inc. NDI
Hamilton Lakes 500 Park Boulevard
Itasca, IL 60143 (312) 773-0200
printed circuit boards

O'Okiep Copper Co. Limited OKP
200 Park Avenue 12th Floor
New York, NY 10166
copper mines in South Africa

O'Sullivan Corp. OSL
P. O. Box 3510
Winchester, VA 22601 (703) 667-6666
heels and soles: plastic parts

Oakwood Homes Corp. OMH
2225 South Holden Road P.O. Box 7386
Greensboro, NC 27407 (919) 292-7061
manufactured homes

Odetics, Inc. O.A/B
1515 S. Manchester Avenue
Anaheim, CA 92802 (714) 774-5000
electronic recording equipment

OEA, Inc. OEA
34501 East Quincy Ave. P. O. Box 10488
Denver, CO 80210 (303) 693-1248
aerospace escape systems

Ohio Art Co. OAR
720 East High Street P.O. Box 111
Bryant, OH 43506 (419) 636-3141
manufactures toys, musical items

Olla Industries, Inc. OLA
518 Gregory Avenue
Weehawken, NJ 07087 (201) 865-4253
ladies' handbags

Olsten Corp. OLS
One Merrick Avenue
Westbury, NY 11590 (516) 832-8200
temporary personnel services

Oppenheimer Industries, Inc. OPP
P.O. Box 19657
Kansas City, MO 64108 (816) 471-1750
cattle agency, ranch broker

Oriole Homes Corp. OHC.A/B
1151 N.W. 24th Street
Pompano Beach, FL 33064 (305) 972-7660
homes and condominium apartments

Ormand Industries, Inc. OMD
P.O. Box 7025
City of Industry, CA 91744 (818) 968-9301
manufactures containers, well services

Oxford First Corp. OFC
6701 North Broad Street
Philadelphia, PA 19126 (215) 276-5000
financial services

Ozark Holdings, Inc. OZA
Lambert-St. Louis Int'l. Airport
St. Louis, MO 63145 (314) 895-6600
airline

Pacific Gas Transmission Co. PGT
77 Beale Street
San Francisco, CA 94106 (415) 781-0474
imports, transmits, and sells gas

Paine Webber Residential Realty Inc. PWM
1285 Avenue of the Americas
New York, NY 10019 (212) 713-2000
real estate investment trust

Pall Corp. PLL
30 Sea Cliff Avenue
Glen Cove, NY 11542 (516) 671-4000
fluid filters and equipment   [DRP]

Pantasote Inc. PNT
P.O. Box 1800
Greenwich, CT 06836 (203) 661-0400
plastic and rubber products

Park Chemical Co. PAK
8074 Military Avenue
Detroit, MI 48204 (313) 895-7215
auto and industrial chemical items

Patient Technology, Inc. PTI
80 Davids Drive
Hauppauge, NY 11788 (516) 434-0905
electrical medical monitor devices

Pauley Petroleum, Inc. PP
10000 Santa Monica Blvd.
Los Angeles, CA 90067 (213) 879-5000
oil and gas exploration and refining

Pay-Fone Systems, Inc. PYF
11255 West Olympic Blvd.
West Los Angeles, CA 90064 (213) 473-2935
payroll service systems

PEC Israel Economic Corp. IEC
511 Fifth Avenue
New York, NY 10017 (212) 687-2400
finance and organize companies in Israel

Peerless Tube Co. PLS
58-76 Locust Avenue
Bloomfield, NJ 07003 (201) 743-5100
metal plastic aerosol containers   [DRP]

Penn Engineering & Mfg. Corp. PNN
P. O. Box 1000
Danboro, PA 18916 (215) 766-8853
self-clinching fasteners

Penn Traffic Co. PNF
319-347 Washington Street
Johnstown, PA 15901 (814) 536-4411
supermarkets, dairy, shopping centers [DRP]

Pennsylvania Engineering Corp. PEC
32nd Street & AVRR
Pittsburgh, PA 15201 (412) 288-6800
steel mill equipment

Pennsylvania Real Estate Investment Trust PEI
12 South Twelfth Street
Philadelphia, PA 19107 (215) 927-1700
real estate investment trust

Penobscot Shoe Co. PSO
North Main Street P.O. Box 545
Old Town, ME 04468 (207) 827-4431
casual sport footwear

Penril Corp. PNL
5520 Randolph Road
Rockville, MD 20852 (301) 881-8151
data communication equipment   [DRP]

Pentron Industries, Inc. PEN
1655 North Main Street Suite 240
Walnut Creek, CA 94596 (415) 939-6526
housewares, coils, plastics

Perini Corp. PCR
73 Mount Wayte Avenue
Framingham, MA 01701 (617) 875-6171
construction, real estate, coal

Perini Investment Properties, Inc. PNV
490 Union Avenue
Framingham, MA 01701 (617) 875-6975
commercial general contractor/developer

Petro-Lewis Corp. PTL
717 Seventeenth Street P.O. Box 2250
Denver, CO 80201 (303) 620-1000
oil and gas exploration and development

Pico Products, Inc. PPI
103 Commerce Boulevard
Liverpool, NY 13088 (315) 451-7700
electrical devices for cable tv industry

Pioneer Systems, Inc. PAE
Pioneer Industrial Park
Manchester, CT 06040 (203) 644-1581
parachutes

Pitt-Des Moines Inc. PDM
Neville Island
Pittsburgh, PA 15225 (412) 331-3000
steel fabricating, contracting

Pittsburgh & West Virginia Railroad PW
600 Grant Street
Pittsburgh, PA 15219 (212) 687-4956
leased rail line

Pittway Corp. PRY
333 Skokie Boulevard
Northbrook, IL 60062 (312) 498-1260
aerosol products, burglar and smoke alarms

Pizza Inn, Inc. PZA
2930 Stemmons Freeway
Dallas, TX 75247 (214) 638-7250
pizza restaurant chain

PLM Financial Services, Inc. PLM.B
655 Montgomery Street 12th floor
San Francisco, CA 94111 (415) 989-1860
transport equipment leasing/managing

PlyGem Industries, Inc. PGI
919 Third Avenue 6th Floor
New York, NY 10022 (212) 832-1550
specialty wood products, filtration products

Plymouth Rubber Co., Inc. PLR.A/B
104 Revere Street
Canton, MA 02021 (617) 828-0220
plastic and rubber specialties

Pneumatic Scale Corp. PNU
65 Newport Avenue
Quincy, MA 02171 (617) 328-6100
packaging and bottling machinery

Pope, Evans and Robbins, Inc. PER
49 West 37th Street
New York, NY 10018 (212) 921-4260
knitwear importer, fabric retailer

Porta Systems Corp. PSI
575 Underhill Blvd.
Syosset, NY 11791 (516) 364-9300
manufactures telecommunications equipment

Postal Instant Press PIP
8201 Beverly Boulevard
Los Angeles, CA 90048 (213) 653-8750
centers which print while you wait

Pratt & Lambert, Inc. PM
75 Tonowanda Street P.O. Box 22
Buffalo, NY 14240 (716) 873-6000
architectural finishes, special coatings

Pratt-Read Corp. PRA
Main Street
Ivoryton, CT 06442 (203) 767-8282
wood/metal products, piano/organ parts

Premier Resources, Ltd. PRL
600 17th Street Suite 1300 No.
Denver, CO 80202 (303) 298-1600
oil and gas exploration, contract drilling

Presidential Realty Corp. PDL.A/B
180 South Broadway
White Plains, NY 10605 (914) 948-1300
real estate investment trust

Presidio Oil Co. PRS
1700 Broadway Suite 1411
Denver, CO 80290 (303) 861-1411
interest in oil and gas wells

Price Communications PR
45 Rockefeller Plaza
New York, NY 10020 (212) 757-5600
tv/radio, newspaper, outdoor advertising

Property Capital Trust PCL
200 Clarendon Street 47th Floor
Boston, MA 02116 (617) 536-8600
real estate investment trust

Providence Energy Corp. PVY
100 Weybosset Street
Providence, RI 02901 (401) 272-5040
gas utility   [DRP]

Punta Gorda Isles, Inc. PGA
1 Matecumbe Key Road
Punta Gorda, FL 33955 (813) 639-4151
land development, home building, inn

Ragan, Brad Inc. BRD
112 Greenwood Road
Spruce Pine, NC 28777 (704) 765-9611
tire retreading, retail stores

RAI Research Corp. RAC
225 Marcus Boulevard
Hauppauge, NY 11788 (516) 273-0911
battery membranes

Ransburg Corp. RBG
P. O. Box 88511
Indianapolis, IN 46208 (317) 298-5000
industrial equipment and systems   [DRP]

Raven Industries, Inc. RAV
3550 South Highway 100 P.O. Box 1007
Minneapolis, MN 55416 (605) 336-2750
sportswear, tanks, balloons

RB & W Corp. RBW
5970 Heisley Road
Mentor, OH 44060 (216) 357-1200
industrial fasteners

Realty South Investors RSI
1850 Parkway Place
Marietta, GA 30067 (404) 426-0331
real estate investment trust   [DRP]

RE Capital Corp. RCC
518 Gregory Avenue
Weehawken, NJ 07087
reinsurance, ladies handbags

Regal-Beloit Corp. RBC
Rockton Road P.O. Box 38
South Beloit, IL 61080 (815) 389-1920
cutting tools, gauges, gear drives

Residential Mortgage Investments, Inc. RMI
2624 West Freeway
Fort Worth, TX 76102 (817) 390-2000
real estate investment trust

Resorts International, Inc. RTA
915 Northeast 125th Street
North Miami, FL 33161 (305) 891-2500
casino-hotels

Restaurant Associates Industries, Inc. RA.B
1540 Broadway
New York, NY 10036 (212) 997-1400
operates restaurants and hotels

Rex-Noreco, Inc. RNX
616 Palisade Ave.
Englewood Cliffs, NJ 07632 (201) 567-8300
railroad car-leasing and management

Riblet Products Corp. RIB
1003 Industrial Parkway P.O. Box 1124
Elkhart, IN 46516 (219) 522-0995
mobile home components

RMS Electronics, Inc. RMS
50 Antin Place
Bronx, NY 10462 (212) 892-6700
electronic communications equipment

Robert Halmi Inc. RHI
6 East 45th Street
New York, NY 10017 (212) 867-1460
film production for tv and theatre

Rockaway Corp. RKY
Waterview Plaza Suite 400
Parsippany, NJ 07054 (201) 335-1126
package and mail service, produce shipping

Rogers Corp. ROG
Rogers, CT 06263 (203) 774-9605
polymer products, electronic interconnectors

Rooney Pace Group Inc. RP
11 Broadway
New York, NY 10004 (212) 908-7700
investment banking and brokerage

Royal Palm Beach Colony, Inc. RPB
8080 Northeast 5th Avenue
Miami, FL 33138 (305) 757-2711
real estate

Ruddick Corp. RDK
2000 First Union Plaza
Charlotte, NC 28282 (704) 372-5404
supermarkets, threads, business forms

Rykoff-Sexton, Inc. RYK
761 Terminal Street
Los Angeles, CA 90021 (213) 622-4131
processed food, janitorial/paper products

S M D Industries, Inc. SDI
65 South Street
Hopkinton, MA 01748 (617) 237-6477
picture frames, paper products

Sage Energy Co. SAG
700 N. St. Mary's Suite 1990
San Antonio, TX 78205 (512) 271-7200
oil/gas exploration/development/driling

St. Joe Gold Corporation SJG
7733 Forsyth Boulevard
Clayton, MO 63105 (314) 726-9500
gold/silver mining

Salem Corp. SBS
P.O. Box 2222
Pittsburgh, PA 15230 (412) 923-2200
heavy equipment for coal/metal industries

Samson Energy Company Ltd. Partnership SAM
2 West Second Street Samson Plaza
Tulsa, OK 74103 (918) 583-1791
oil and gas exploration and development

Sandy Corp. SDY
1500 West Big Beaver Road
Troy, MI 48084 (313) 649-0800
markets corporate training programs

Sanmark - Stardust Inc. SMK
145 Madison Avenue
New York, NY 10016 (212) 684-3400
manufacturer of women's apparel

Saunders Systems Inc SAU.A/B
201 Office Park Drive
Birmingham, AL 35223 (205) 879-2131
leasing of trucks, tractors, trailers

Saxon Oil Development Partners SAX
Diamond Shamrock Tower 717 N. Harwood
Dallas, TX 75210 (214) 745-1300
oil and gas exploration and development

Sbarro, Inc. SBA
One Huntington Quadrangle
Melville, NY 11747 (516) 454-6710
Italian fast-food restaurants

Scandinavia Fund, Inc. SCF
136 Nassau Road
Huntington, NY 11743 (516) 385-9580
closed-end mutual fund

Scheib, Earl Inc. ESH
8737 Wilshire Boulevard
Beverly Hills, CA 90211 (213) 652-4880
auto paint shop chain

School Pictures, Inc. PIX
P.O. Box Drawer 570
Jackson, MS 39205 (601) 354-2361
processes school pictures

Schwab Safe Co., Inc. SS
3000 Main Street P.O. Box 5088
Lafayette, IN 47902 (317) 447-9470
manufactures safes

Science Management Corp. SMG
P.O. Box 0600
Basking Ridge, NJ 07920 (201) 647-7000
management consulting services

Scientific Leasing Inc. SG
790 Farmington Avenue
Farmington, CT 06032 (203) 677-8700
leases medical equipment to hospitals

Scope Industries SCP
233 Wilshire Boulevard Suite 790
Santa Monica, CA 90401 (213) 458-1574
waste material recycling, beauty schools

Seaboard Corp. SEB
200 Boylston Street
Newton, MA 02167 (617) 332-8492
flour milling, grain storage

Seaport Corp. SEO
1155 7th Street
Oakland, CA 94607 (415) 834-3130
auto replacement parts

Security Capital Corp. SCC
1290 Ave. of the Americas
New York, NY 10014 (212) 408-2900
finances, invests in, operates real estate

Seis Pros, Inc. SEI
16850 Park Row
Houston, TX 77084 (713) 494-0028
seismic data for the oil industry

Selas Corp. of America SLS
Limekiln Pike & Dreshertown Rd.
Dresher, PA 19025 (215) 646-6600
heat processing equipment

Seligman & Associates, Inc. SLG
24901 Northwestern Highway
Southfield, MI 48037 (313) 355-2400
builds homes, manages property

Semtech Corp. SMH
652 Mitchell Road
Newbury Park, CA 91320 (805) 498-2111
manufactures silicon rectifiers

SERVISCO SVO
470 Mundet Place
Hillside, NJ 07205 (201) 964-7500
garment rental and maintenance service

Servo Corp. of America SCA
111 New South Road
Hicksville, NY 11802 (516) 938-9700
manufactures railroad safety equipment

Servotronics, Inc. SVT
3901 Union Road
Buffalo, NY 14225 (716) 633-5990
manufactures cutlery and servocontrols

Seton Co. SEL
849 Broadway
Newark, NJ 07104 (201) 485-4800
leather products   [DRP]

SFM Corp. SFM
900 North Avenue
Plainfield, NJ 07062 (201) 561-4500
machinery and electric motors

Shaer Shoe Corp. SHS
Canal & Dow Streets
Manchester, NH 03101 (603) 625-8566
women's fashion footwear

Shopwell, Inc. SH
400 Walnut Avenue
Bronx, NY 10454 (212) 579-3400
supermarkets

Sierra Health Services, Inc. SIE
888 South Rancho Drive
Las Vegas, NV 89106 (702) 877-8603
owns and operates an HMO

Sierra Spring Water Co. WTR
1801 "R" Street
Sacramento, CA 95814 (916) 446-5341
produces and markets bottled spring water

Sierracin Corp. SER
12780 San Fernando Road
Sylmar, CA 91342 (818) 362-6802
aerospace components

SIFCO Industries, Inc. SIF
970 East 64th Street
Cleveland, OH 44103 (216) 881-8600
precision forgings, machined parts   [DRP]

Sikes Corp. SK.A
One Sikes Boulevard
Lakeland, FL 33801 (813) 687-7171
ceramic tile products

Silvercrest Industries, Inc. SLV
P.O. Box 759
Corona, CA 91720 (714) 734-6610
manufactures mobile homes

SJW Corp. SJW
374 W. Santa Clara Street
San Jose, CA 95196 (408) 279-7900
water service   [DRP]

Smith, A.O. Corp. SMC.A/B/PrC
11270 West Park Place
Milwaukee, WI 53224 (414) 359-4000
auto and truck equipment, farm equipment

Solitron Devices, Inc. SOD
1177 Blue Heron Boulevard
Riviera Beach, FL 33404 (305) 848-4311
microwave semiconductors

Sorg Printing Co., Inc. SRG
111 Eighth Avenue
New York, NY 10011 (212) 741-6600
financial and corporate printing

Southwest Bancorp SWB
1737 West Vista Way
Vista, CA 92083 (619) 726-5870
banking

Southwest Realty, Ltd. SWL
7424 Greenville Avenue
Dallas, TX 75231 (214) 369-1995
real estate limited partnership

Spectrum Group, Inc. BUG
P.O Box 6246
Jacksonville, FL 32236 (904) 359-3005
pest control, household products

Speed-O-Print Business Machines Corp. SBM
1801 W. Larchmont Avenue
Chicago, IL 60613 (312) 477-2000
office copy-making machines

Aaron Spelling Productions SP
1041 North Formosa Avenue
Los Angeles, CA 90046 (213) 850-2413
tv and movie production

Spencer Companies, Inc. SPN
450 Summer Street
Boston, MA 02210 (617) 542-8120
shoe manufacturer/retailer, apparel

Spendthrift Farm, Inc. SFI
Iron Works Pike
Lexington, KY 40588 (606) 299-5271
thoroughbred breeding/boarding/training

Standard Havens Inc. SHV
8800 East 63rd Street
Kansas City, MO 64133 (816) 737-0400
hot asphalt production equipment

Standard Shares, Inc. SWD
230 Park Avenue
New York, NY 10169 (212) 697-4767
financial holding company

Stanwood Corp. SNW
4819 Park Road P. O. Box 11813
Charlotte, NC 28220 (704) 527-5270
sportswear, underwear, sleepwear

Starrett Housing Corp. SHO
909 Third Avenue
New York, NY 10022 (212) 751-3100
develops/constructs multi-unit housing

Statex Petroleum, Inc. SEP
300 E. Carpenter Freeway Suite 1100
Irving, TX 75062 (214) 257-1771
oil and gas exploration and production

Stepan Co. SCL
Edens & Winnetka
Northfield, IL 60093 (312) 446-7500
basic/intermediate chemicals

Sterling Capital Corp. SPR
635 Madison Avenue
New York, NY 10022 (212) 980-3360
investment company

Sterling Electronics Corp. SEC
4201 Southwest Freeway
Houston, TX 77027 (713) 623-6600
manufactures electronic equipment

Sterling Extruder Corp. SLX
901 Durham Avenue
South Plainfield, NJ 07080 (201) 561-3700
plastic extrusion machinery and equipment

Sterling Software, Inc. SSW
370 Campbell Center
Dallas, TX 75206 (214) 987-6464
markets computer software products

Struthers Wells Corp. SUW
1003 Pennsylvania Avenue
Warren, PA 16365 (814) 726-1000
heat transfer equipment

Summit Energy, Inc. SUM
1925 Mercantile Dallas Bldg.
Dallas, TX 75201 (214) 748-0221
oil and gas exploration and development

Sunbelt Nursery Group, Inc. SBN
500 Terminal Road
Fort Worth, TX 76106 (817) 624-7253
retailer of lawn and garden products

Sun City Industries, Inc. SNI
1200 NW 78th Avenue
Miami, FL 33126 (305) 593-2355
produces and markets shell eggs

Sun Savings and Loan Association SSL
6390 Greenwich Drive Suite 100
San Diego, CA 92122 (619) 457-4786
savings and loan

Sunshine-Jr. Stores, Inc. SJS
17th St. & June Avenue P.O. Box 2498
Panama City, FL 32402 (904) 769-1661
wholesale food and machine distribution

Super Food Services, Inc. SFS
3185 Elbee Road
Dayton, OH 45439 (513) 294-1731
food wholesaler

Superior Care, Inc. SI
287 Northern Blvd.
Great Neck, NY 11021 (516) 487-4181
home health care services

Superior Industries International SUP
7800 Woodley Avenue
Van Nuys, CA 91406 (213) 781-4973
highly stylized car wheels, accessories

Superior Surgical Mfg. Co., Inc. SGC
Seminole Boulevard at 100 Terrace
Seminole, FL 33542 (813) 397-9611
hospital and industrial uniforms

Susquehanna Corp. SQN
P.O. Box 5170
Denver, CO 80217 (303) 779-0777
building materials

Swift Energy Co. SFY
652 E. North Belt Suite 200
Houston, TX 77060 (713) 445-0844
oil and gas exploration and development

Swift Independent Corp. SFT
115 West Jackson Blvd.
Chicago, IL 60604 (312) 431-3500
meat packer of beef and pork

Synalloy Corp. SYO
Post Office Box 5627
Spartanburg, SC 29304 (803) 585-3605
metal and chemical processor

Systems Engineering & Mfg. Corp. SEM
44 Campanelli Parkway
Stoughton, MA 02072 (617) 344-1700
electroplating systems

T-Bar Inc. TBR
141 Danbury Road P. O. Box T
Wilton, CT 06897 (203) 834-8227
data switching and control equipment

Tab Products Co. TBP
1400 Page Mill Road
Palo Alto, CA 94304 (415) 852-2400
office/computer access equipment

Tandy Brands, Inc. TAB
550 Bailey Suite 400
Fort Worth, TX 76107 (817) 334-8200
leather goods/accessories

Tasty Baking Co. TBC
2801 Hunting Park Avenue
Philadelphia, PA 19129 (215) 221-8500
small cakes, pies, graphic equipment

Team, Inc. TMI
1020 Holcombe Boulevard Suite 802
Houston, TX 77030 (713) 795-0014
energy conservation services

TEC Inc TCK
2727 North Fairview Avenue
Tucson, AZ 85705 (602) 792-2230
electronic computer components

Tech-Sym Corp. TSY
10500 West Office Drive
Houston, TX 77042 (713) 785-7790
military electronics systems, hardware

Tech/Ops, Inc. TO
One Beacon Street
Boston, MA 02108 (617) 523-2030
technology-based products and services

TechAmerica Group, Inc. TCH
Elkan Estates Industrial Park
Elwood, KS 66024 (913) 365-9076
animal health care products

Technical Tape, Inc. TTI
One LeFevre Lane
New Rochelle, NY 10801 (914) 235-1000
industrial and consumer tapes, bedding

Technitrol, Inc. TNL
1952 E. Allegheny Avenue
Philadelphia, PA 19134 (215) 426-9105
computer components

Technodyne Inc. TND
98 Cutter Mill Road
Great Neck, NY 11021 (516) 466-5100
electro-mechanical products

Tejon Ranch Co. TRC
P. O. Box 1000
Lebec, CA 93243 (805) 327-8481
seed, cattle, oil, land

TeleConcepts Corp. TCC
36 Holly Drive
Newington, CT 06111 (203) 666-5666
decorative telephones

Teleflex, Inc. TFX
155 South Limerick Rd.
Limerick, PA 19468 (215) 948-5100
car/boat/plane precision equipment

Telephone & Data Systems, Inc. TDS
79 West Monroe Street Suite 905
Chicago, IL 60603 (312) 630-1900
telephone service   [DRP]

TeleSciences, Inc. TSC
124 Gaither Drive
Mt. Laurel, NJ 08054 (609) 866-1000
computer phone support systems

Telesphere International, Inc. TSP
2211 York Road Suite 115
Oak Brook, IL 60521 (312) 655-2169
long-distance telephone service

Tenney Engineering, Inc. TNY
1090 Springfield Road
Union, NJ 07083 (201) 686-7870
environmental test equipment

Tensor Corp. TEN
333 Stanley Avenue
Brooklyn, NY 11207 (718) 649-2000
distributes silk flowers/plants

Texas Air Corp. TEX
4040 Capital Bank Plaza
Houston, TX 77002 (713) 658-9588
airline

Texas American Energy Corp. TAE
300 West Wall Avenue Suite 400
Midland, TX 79701 (915) 683-4811
oil and gas production and refining

Thor Energy Resources Inc THR
719 West Front Street
Tyler, TX 75702 (214) 531-6000
engineering services

Three D Departments, Inc. TDD.B
801 Silver Lane
East Hartford, CT 06118 (203) 569-6720
domestics departments in discount stores

TIE/Communications, Inc. TIE
Five Research Park
Shelton, CT 06484 (203) 929-7373
key telephone systems

TII Industries, Inc. TI
1375 Akron Street
Copiague, NY 11726 (516) 789-5000
overvoltage protectors

Tofutti Inc. TOF
1638 63rd Street
Brooklyn, NY 11204 (718) 232-1031
non-dairy frozen products

Torotel, Inc. TTL
P. O. Box 608
Raymore, MO 64083 (816) 331-8400
magnetic components

Total Petroleum N.A. Ltd. TPN
One Denver Place 999 18th Street
Denver, CO 80202 (303) 291-2000
integrated oil and gas

Trans-Lux Corp. TLX
110 Richards Avenue
Norwalk, CT 06854 (203) 853-4321
display/print-out equipment, teleprinters

TransTechnology Corp. TT
15233 Ventura Boulevard
Sherman Oaks, CA 91403 (818) 990-5920
aerospace-defense products, textiles

Tranzonic Companies TNZ
30195 Chagrin Boulevard
Pepper Pike, OH 41124 (216) 831-5757
vending/food services, wholesaler

Tri-State Motor Transit Co. of Delaware TSM
Post Office Box 113
Joplin, MO 64801 (417) 624-3131
explosives, radioactive material

Triangle Corp. TRG
P.O. Box 1881
Stamford, CT 06904 (203) 327-9050
mechanics' hand tools

Triangle Home Products, Inc. THP
945 East 93rd Street
Chicago, IL 60619 (312) 374-4400
lighting fixtures, metal products

Tridex Corp. TDX
580 Spring Street
Windsor Locks, CT 06096 (203) 623-2481
electronic components and relays

Turner Broadcasting System, Inc. TBS
1050 Techwood Drive N.W.
Atlanta, GA 30318 (404) 827-1717
cable news, tv broadcasting, sports

Turner Corp. TUR
633 Third Avenue
New York, NY 10017 (212) 878-0400
diversified builder, real estate

Turner Equity Investors, Inc. TEQ
10014 North Dale Mabry Highway
Tampa, FL 33618 (813) 963-0786
real estate investment trust

Ultimate Corp. ULT
717 Ridgedale Avenue
East Hanover, NJ 07936 (201) 388-8800
integrated computer systems

U.N.A. Corp. UNA
600 Atlantic Ave., Fed. Reserve Plaza
Boston, MA 02210 (617) 973-9600
importer/distributor of specialty steel

Unicorp American Corp. UAC
1133 Ave. of the Americas Suite 2516
New York, NY 10036 (212) 398-6300
real estate investments

United Aircraft Products, Inc. UAP
P.O. Box 1335
Dayton, OH 45401 (513) 898-1811
aerospace industry components

United Cos. Financial Corp. UCF
4041 Essen Lane P.O. Box 1591
Baton Rouge, LA 70809 (504) 924-6007
consumer loans and insurance

United Foods, Inc. UFD.A/B
100 Dawson Avenue
Bells, TN 38006 (901) 663-2335
frozen vegetables and fruits

United Medical Corp. UM
56 South Haddon Avenue
Haddonfield, NJ 08033 (609) 354-2200
health services and products

Unitel Video, Inc. UNV
510 West 57th Street
New York, NY 10019 (212) 265-3600
videotape recording, post-production

UNITIL Corp. UTL
436 South River Road R.F.D. #9
Bedford, NH 03102 (603) 625-4114
electric utility   [DRP 5%]

Universal Communication Systems, Inc. UCS
1401 Municipal Road, N.W.
Roanoke, VA 24019 (703) 362-3701
telephone interconnect system

Universal Resources Corp. UVR
5400 Valley View Trail P.O. Box 802426
Dallas, TX 75380 (214) 661-3876
oil and gas exploration and production

Universal-Rundle Corp. URI
P.O. Box 29
New Castle, PA 16103 (412) 658-6631
bath fixtures/fittings/cabinets

University Patents, Inc. UPT
1465 Postroad East P.O. Box 901
Westport, CT 06880 (203) 255-6044
patent service

USR Industries Inc UIN
1717 Woodstead Court
The Woodlands, TX 77380 (713) 367-2821
luminescent chemicals, oil and gas, metal

Valley Resources, Inc. VR
1595 Mendon Road
Cumberland, RI 02864 (401) 333-1595
gas utility   [DRP 5%]

Valspar Corp. VAL
1101 Third Street South
Minneapolis, MN 55415 (612) 332-7371
paints and coatings

Verit Industries, Inc. VER
11131 Dora Street
Sun Valley, CA 91352 (213) 875-0480
meat processing, speaker systems

Vermont American Corp. VAC.A
100 East Liberty Street
Louisville, KY 40202 (502) 587-6851
cutting tools, power tool accessories

Vermont Research Corp. VRE
Precision Park
N. Springfield, VT 05150 (802) 886-2256
magnetic computer memories

Verna Corp. VNA
One 1800 Bering Drive
Houston, TX 77057 (713) 266-3333
oil and gas contract drilling

Vernitron Corp. VRN
2001 Marcus Avenue
Lake Success, NY 11042 (516) 775-8200
motors, controls, electrical measurers

Vertipile, Inc. VRT
Scott Drive
Leominster, MA 01453 (617) 534-6191
upholstery fabrics supplier

Viatech, Inc. VTK
One Aerial Way
Syosset, NY 11791 (516) 822-4940
engineering and consulting services

Vicon Industries, Inc. VII
525 Broad Hollow Road
Melville, NY 11747 (516) 293-2200
closed-circuit tv security equipment

Vintage Enterprises, Inc. VIN
3825 Northeast Expressway
Atlanta, GA 30340 (404) 458-3144
manufacturer/retailer mobile homes

Virco Manufacturing Corp. VIR
15134 S. Vermont Avenue
Gardena, CA 90247 (213) 532-3570
chairs, tables, contract seating

Visual Graphics Corp. VGC
5701 Northwest 94th Ave.
Tamarac, FL 33321 (305) 722-3000
photographic typesetting equipment

VMS Hotel Investment Trust VHT
8700 West Bryn Mawr Avenue
Chicago, IL 60631 (312) 399-8700
real estate investment trust

VMS Short Term Income Trust VST
8700 West Bryn Mawr Avenue
Chicago, IL 60631 (312) 399-8700
real estate investment trust

Voplex Corp. VOT
1100 Pittsford-Victor Road
Pittsford, NY 14534 (716) 248-5350
plastic auto parts

Vulcan Corp. VUL
6 East 4th Street
Cincinnati, OH 45202 (513) 621-2850
shoe lasts/heels, bowling pins

Vyquest Inc. VY
925 Clifton Avenue
Clifton, NJ 07013 (201) 473-6550
manufactured homes, recreational vehicles

Wang Laboratories, Inc. WAN.B/C
One Industrial Avenue
Lowell, MA 01851 (617) 459-5000
computer and word processing systems   [O]

Washington Homes, Inc. WHI
P. O. Box 1006
Waldorf, MD 20601 (301) 843-8900
single family homes

Washington Post Co. WPO.B
1150 15th St. N.W.
Washington, DC 20071 (202) 223-6000
newspapers, magazines, tv, newsprint

Washington Real Estate Investment Trust WRE
4936 Fairmont Avenue
Bethesda, MD 20814 (301) 652-4300
real estate investment trust   [DRP]

Watsco, Inc. WSO.A/B
1800 West 4th Avenue
Hialeah, FL 33010 (305) 885-1911
refrigeration/air conditioning controls

Weatherford International Inc. WII
P.O. Box 27608
Houston, TX 77227 (713) 439-9400
oil field services/equipment/rental

Webb, Del E Investment Prop. Inc. DWP.A
3800 North Central Avenue P O Box 29040
Phoenix, AZ 85038 (602) 264-8011
hotels-casinos, real estate

Webcor Electronics, Inc. WER
107 Charles Lindbergh Boulevard
Garden City, NY 11530 (516) 794-6200
telephones, watches, calculators

Wedco Technology, Inc. WED
P.O. Box 397
Bloomsbury, NJ 08804 (201) 479-4181
grinding services, machinery manufacture

Wedgestone Realty Investors Trust WDG
181 Wells Avenue
Newton, MA 02159 (617) 965-8330
real estate investment trust

Weiman Co., Inc. WC
4801 W. Peterson
Chicago, IL 60646 (312) 286-1121
photo service, home furnishings

Welded Tube Co. of America WTA
1818 Market Street 36th Floor
Philadelphia, PA 19103 (215) 557-9777
welded steel tubing

Weldotron Corp. WLD
1532 So. Washington Ave.
Piscataway, NJ 08854 (201) 752-6700
industrial food packaging systems

Wellco Enterprises, Inc. WLC
P. O. Box 188
Waynesville, NC 28786 (704) 456-3545
manufacturer of footwear, shoe machinery

Wells American Corporation WAC
3243 Sunset Boulevard
West Columbia, SC 29169 (803) 796-7801
desktop microcomputers

Wells-Gardner Electronics Corp. WGA
2701 North Kildare Avenue
Chicago, IL 60639 (312) 252-8220
video monitors, tv receivers

Wesco Financial Corp. WSC
315 E. Colorado Boulevard
Pasadena, CA 91109 (818) 449-2345
savings and loan

Wespercorp WP
14321 New Myford Road
Tustin, CA 92680 (714) 730-6250
computer components and systems

Westbridge Capital Corp. WBC
777 Main Street Suite 900
Fort Worth, TX 76102 (817) 838-3300
life, accident, and health insurance

Western Digital Corp. WDC
2445 McCabe Way
Irvine, CA 92714 (714) 863-0102
digital component systems

Western Health Plans, Inc. WHP
3702 Ruffin Road
San Diego, CA 92123 (619) 571-3102
health maintenance services

Western Investment Real Estate Trust WIR
4330 California Street
San Francisco, CA 94118 (415) 221-3111
real estate investment trust

Wherehouse Entertainment, Inc. WEI
14100 So. Kingsley Drive
Gardena, CA 90249 (213) 538-2314
record and tape store chain

Wichita Industries, Inc. WRO
1801 California Street Suite 4500
Denver, CO 80202 (303) 293-8167
oil and gas exploration and production

Wickes Companies, Inc. WIX
3340 Ocean Park Boulevard
Santa Monica, CA 90405 (213) 452-0161
lumber, building products, home furnishing

Wiener Enterprises WPB
5725 Powell Street P.O. Box 23607
Harahan, LA 70183 (504) 733-7055
retail apparel and shoe stores

Wilson Brothers WLB
6917 Collins Avenue
Miami Beach, FL 33141 (305) 866-7771
men's shirts, sportswear

Winn Enterprises WNN.B
231 East 23rd Street
Los Angeles, CA 90011 (714) 992-6130
processes and distributes dairy products

Winthrop Insured Mortgage Investors WMI
260 Franklin Street
Boston, MA 02119 (617) 439-4200
investments in insured mortgage loans

Wolf, Howard B. Inc HBW
3809 Parry Avenue
Dallas, TX 75226 (214) 823-9941
women's fashion apparel

Woodstream Corp. WOD
69 North Locust Street
Lititz, PA 17543 (717) 626-2125
sporting goods, pest traps

Work Wear Corp. WKW
1768 East 25th Street
Cleveland, OH 44114 (216) 771-4040
work clothes manufacture and rental

Worldwide Energy Corp. WWE
1700 Lincoln Center Suite 4400
Denver, CO 80203 (303) 861-8615
oil and gas production, gas transmission

Worthen Banking Corp. WOR
Worthen Bank Building 200 West Capitol
Little Rock, AR 72203 (501) 378-1811
banking   [DRP 5%]

Wrather Corp. WCO
270 North Canon Drive
Beverly Hills, CA 90210 (213) 278-8521
owns tv syndication rights, hotel

WTC International N.V. WAF
23740 Hawthorne Boulevard
Torrance, CA 90505 (213) 373-0411
freight forwarding

Yankee Cos., Inc. YNK
49 Margin Street The Oaks
Cohasset, MA 02025 (617) 383-1500
diversified energy and financial services

Zimmer Corp. ZIM
5801 Congress Avenue P.O. Box 3058
Boca Raton, FL 33431 (305) 997-0700
manufactured homes

NASDAQ NATIONAL MARKET SYSTEM

A & M Food Services, Inc. AMFD
1924 South Utica Avenue
Tulsa, OK 74104 (918) 749-4423
restaurants

ABS Industries, Inc. ABSI
Interstate Square, Suite 300
Willoughby, OH 44094 (216) 946-2274
finished metal

ACMAT Corp. ACMT
141 Prestige Park Road
East Hartford, CT 06108 (203) 289-6493
interior contractors

ADAC Labs. ADAC
4747 Hellyer Avenue
San Jose, CA 95138 (408) 365-2000
medical supplies

ADC Telecommunications, Inc. ADCT
5501 Green Valley Drive
Bloomington, MN 55437 (612) 835-6800
communications

ADIA Services, Inc. ADIA
64 Willow Place
Menlo Park, CA 94025 (415) 324-0696
temporary personnel

AEC, Inc. AECE
850 Pratt Blvd.
Elk Grove Village, IL 60007 (312) 593-5000
water cooling equipment

AEL Industries, Inc. AELN
306 Richardson Road
Montgomeryville, PA 18936 (215) 822-2929
electronic defense equipment

ALC Communication Corp. ALCC
30300 Telegraph Road
Birmingham, MI 48010 (313) 647-6920
communication

ARGOSystems, Inc. ARGI
310 North Mary Avenue
Sunnyvale, CA 94086 (408) 737-2000
electronics

ASK Computer Systems, Inc. ASKI
730 Distel Drive
Los Altos, CA 94022 (415) 969-4442
computer systems

AST Research, Inc. ASTA
2121 Alton Avenue
Irvine, CA 92714 (714) 863-1333
computer equipment

A. T. & E. Corp. ATEC
One Maritime Plaza
San Francisco, CA 94111 (415) 433-0430
electronic equipment

ATE Enterprises Inc. ATEE
617 Vine Street
Cincinnati, OH 45202 (513) 381-7424
land development

Aaron Rents, Inc. ARON
1100 Aaron Bldg.
Atlanta, GA 30363 (404) 231-0011
furniture rental

Abrams Industries, Inc. ABRI
5775-A Glenridge Drive, N.E.
Atlanta, GA 30328 (404) 256-9785
contracting and engineering

Aca Joe ACAJ
25 Taylor Street
San Francisco, CA 94102 (415) 777-4222
apparel retailer

Academy Insurance Group, Inc. ACIG
One Valley Forge Plaza
Valley Forge, PA 19487 (215) 337-1400
insurance

Acapulco Restaurants ALAR
2690 East Foothill Blvd.
Pasadena, CA 91107 (213) 449-5467
restaurants

Acceleration Corp. ACLE
475 Metro Place North
Dublin, OH 43017 (614) 764-7000
insurance

AccuRay Corp. ACRA
650 Ackerman Road
Columbus, OH 43202 (614) 261-2495
electronic instruments   [DRP]

Aceto Corp. ACET
126-02 Northern Blvd.
Flushing, NY 11368 (718) 898-2300
chemicals

Activision, Inc. AVSN
2350 Bayshore Frontage Road
Mountain View, CA 94043 (415) 960-0410
toys and games

Actmedia, Inc. ACTM
777 Boston Post Road
Darien, CT 06820 (203) 655-2211
in-store marketing services

Adage, Inc. ADGE
One Fortune Drive
Billerica, MA 01821 (617) 667-7070
electronic equipment

Addison-Wesley Publishing Co., Inc. ADSN
Jacob Way
Reading, MA 01867 (617) 944-3700
publishing   [DRP]

Advance Circuits, Inc. ADVC
560 16th Avenue South
Hopkins, MN 55343 (612) 935-5695
electronic equipment

Advanced Computer Techniques Corp. ACTP
16 East 32nd Street
New York, NY 10016 (212) 696-3600
software, data processing

Advanced Genetic Sciences, Inc. AGSI
6701 San Pablo Avenue
Oakland, CA 94608 (415) 547-2395
biotechnology

Advanced Semiconductor Materials Int'l. ASMI
Jan Steenlaan 9
Bilthoven, The Netherlands
electronic products

Advanced Telecommunications Corp. ATEL
148 International Blvd.
Atlanta, GA 30303 (404) 688-2475
communication

Aequiton Medical, Inc. AQTN
14130 Twenty-Third Avenue
Minneapolis, MN 55441 (612) 559-2012
health services and supplies

Aero Systems, Inc. AESM
5415 N.W. 36th Street
Miami, FL 33152 (305) 871-1300
aircraft manufacturer, service

Affiliated Bank Corp. of Wyoming ABWY
P.O. Box 2799
Casper, WY 82602 (307) 266-1100
banking

Affiliated Bankshares of Colorado, Inc. AFBK
1101 Arapahoe Avenue
Boulder, CO 80302 (303) 449-2030
banking   [DRP]

Agency Rent-A-Car, Inc. AGNC
30000 Aurora Road
Solon, OH 44139 (216) 349-1000
auto rental

Agnico-Eagle Mines Ltd. AEAG
Suite 1612, 401 Bay Street
Toronto, Ont. M5H 2Y4 (416) 947-1212
metal mining

Air Cargo Equipment Corp. ARCE
4171 North Mesa
El Paso, TX 79902 (915) 544-7722
transportation equipment

Air Midwest, Inc. AMWI
2203 Air Cargo Road
Wichita, KS 67277 (316) 942-8137
regional airline

Air Wis Services, Inc. ARWS
Outagamie County Airport
Appleton, WI 54915 (414) 739-5123
regional airline

Alaska Bancorporation ASKA
507 "E" Street
Anchorage, AK 99501 (907) 277-6244
banking

Alaska Mutual Bancorporation AMAB
1500 West Benson Blvd.
Anchorage, AK 99509 (907) 274-3561
banking

Alaska National Bank of the North ANBN
Pouch 6608
Anchorage, AK 99502 (907) 278-4581
banking

AlaTenn Resources, Inc. ATNG
P.O. Box 918
Florence, AL 35631 (205) 383-3631
gas utility

Alco Health Services Corp. AAHS
P.O. Box 834
Valley Forge, PA 19482 (215) 296-4480
health services, supplies

Alexander & Baldwin, Inc. ALEX
822 Bishop Street
Honolulu, HI 96813 (808) 525-6622
shipping, sugar, real estate

Alex. Brown Inc. ABSB
135 East Baltimore Street
Baltimore, MD 21202 (301) 727-1700
securities brokerage

Alfin Fragrances, Inc. ALFN
720 Fifth Avenue
New York, NY 10019 (212) 333-7700
cosmetics and personal care

Algorex Corp. ALGO
70 Corporate Drive
Hauppauge, NY 11788 (516) 434-9400
electronics

Alico, Inc. ALCO
P.O. Box 338
La Belle, FL 33935 (813) 675-2966
agricultural production

Allegheny & Western Energy Corp. ALGH
1600 Kanawha Valley Bldg.
Charleston, WV 25329 (304) 343-4327
oil and gas

Allegheny Beverage Corp. ABEV
Macke Circle
Cheverly, MD 20781 (301) 341-6188
soft drinks

Allen Organ Co. AORG
150 Locust Street
Macungie, PA 18062 (215) 966-2200
musical instruments

Allied Bancshares, Inc. ALBN
1000 Louisiana
Houston, TX 77002 (713) 224-6611
banking　　　　　　　　　　　　　　　　[DRP]

Allied Capital Corp. ALLC
1625 Eye Street, N.W.
Washington, DC 20006 (202) 331-1112
investment company

Allied Research Associates, Inc. ARAI
P.O. Box 1000
Severna Park, MD 21146 (301) 727-1164
sporting goods

Ally & Gargano, Inc. AGAI
805 Third Avenue
New York, NY 10022 (212) 688-5300
advertising

Alpha Microsystems ALMI
3501 Sunflower Street
Santa Ana, CA 92704 (714) 957-8500
computers

Alternacare Corp. ALTN
11500 Olympic Blvd.
Los Angeles, CA 90064 (213) 312-4500
health services

Altos Computer Systems ALTO
2641 Orchard Pkwy.
San Jose, CA 95134 (408) 946-6700
computers

Altron Inc. ALRN
One Jewel Drive
Wilmington, MA 01887 (617) 658-5800
electronics

Amcast Industrial Corp. ACST
P.O. Box 98
Dayton, OH 45401 (513) 298-5251
steel mill

Amcole Energy Corp. AMLE
6421 Camp Bowie Blvd.
Fort Worth, TX 76116 (817) 731-3721
oil and gas

Amer. First Fed. Guaranteed Mortgage Fund
AMER
1004 Farnam Street
Omaha, NE 68102 (402) 444-1630
financial brokers

America West Airlines, Inc. AWAL
222 South Mill Avenue
Tempe, AZ 85281 (602) 894-0800
regional airline

American Adventure, Inc. GOAA
12910 Kingsgate Way NE
Kirkland, WA 98083 (206) 821-7766
hotels, motels, resorts

American Bank of Connecticut AMSA
Two West Main Street
Waterbury, CT 06723 (203) 757-9401
banking

Amer. Bankers Ins. Group, Inc. ABIG
11222 Quail Roost Drive
Miami, FL 33157 (305) 253-2244
insurance

Amer. Barrick Resources Corp. ABXF
Suite 3001, South Tower
Toronto, Ont. M5J 2J1 (416) 865-0005
metal mining

American Businessphones, Inc. ABPI
9 Mason
Irvine, CA 92718 (714) 472-2200
communications equipment

American Carriers, Inc. ACIX
9393 West 110th Street
Overland Park, KS 66210 (913) 451-2811
freight forwarding

Amer. City Business Journals, Inc. AMBJ
3535 Broadway
Kansas City, MO 64111 (816) 753-4300
publishing

American Continental Corp. AMCC
P.O. Box 29099
Phoenix, AZ 85038 (602) 957-7170
building construction

American Ecology Corp. ECOL
30423 Canwood Street
Agoura Hills, CA 91301 (818) 991-7361
waste disposal

American Exploration Co. AXCO
4500 RepublicBank Center
Houston, TX 77002 (713) 237-0800
oil and gas

Amer. Fed. S&L Assn. of Colorado AFSL
5475 Tech Center Drive
Colorado Springs, CO 80919 (303) 599-7400
savings and loan

American Filtrona Corp. AFIL
P.O. Box 34668
Richmond, VA 23234 (804) 275-2631
tobacco filters   [DRP]

American First Corp. AFCO
Suite 1340, American First Tower
Oklahoma City, OK 73102 (405) 270-5300
insurance

American Fletcher Corp. AFLT
111 Monument Circle
Indianapolis, IN 46277 (317) 639-3000
banking   [DRP]

American Furniture Co., Inc. AFUR
P.O. Box 5071
Martinsville, VA 24112 (703) 632-2061
furniture

American Greetings Corp. AGRE
10500 American Road
Cleveland, OH 44144 (216) 252-7300
greeting cards   [DRP O]

American Income Life Ins. Co. AINC
1200 Wooded Acres Drive
Waco, TX 76797 (817) 772-3050
insurance

Amer. Indemnity Financial Corp. AIFC
One American Indemnity Plaza
Galveston, TX 77550 (409) 766-4600
insurance

Amer. Insured Mortgage Investors AIMA
666 Third Avenue
New York, NY 10017 (212) 551-6000
mortgage limited partnership

American Integrity Corp. AIIC
Two Penn Center Plaza
Philadelphia, PA 19102 (215) 561-1400
insurance

Amer. Investors Life Ins. Co., Inc. AILI
P.O. Box 2039
Topeka, KS 66601 (913) 232-6945
insurance

American Land Cruisers, Inc. ALCR
7740 N.W. 34th Street
Miami, FL 33122 (305) 591-7511
auto sales

American List Corp. ALST
98 Cutter Mill Road
Great Neck, NY 11021 (516) 466-0602
business services

American Locker Group, Inc. ALGI
15 West Second Street
Jamestown, NY 14702 (716) 664-9600
furniture, lockers

American Magnetics Corp. AMMG
13535 Ventura Blvd.
Sherman Oaks, CA 91423 (213) 783-8900
computers and business equipment

Amer. Management Systems, Inc. AMSY
1777 North Kent Street
Arlington, VA 22209 (703) 841-6000
business services, data processing

Amer. Medical Services Inc. AMSR
1051 East Ogden Avenue
Milwaukee, WI 53202 (414) 271-1300
health services

American Midland Corp. AMCO
270 Sylvan Avenue
Englewood Cliffs, NJ 07632 (201) 871-3800
hotels, motels, resorts

American National Holding Co. ANHC
136 East Michigan Avenue
Kalamazoo, MI 49007 (616) 383-6700
banking

Amer. National Insurance Co. ANAT
One Moody Plaza
Galveston, TX 77550 (409) 763-4661
insurance

Amer. Physicians Service Group, Inc. AMPH
1301 Capital of Texas Hwy.
Austin, TX 78746 (512) 328-0888
business services

American Pioneer Savings Bank APIO
135 West Central Blvd.
Orlando, FL 32801 (305) 423-7300
savings and loan

American Restaurants Corp. AMRS
5528 Everglades Street
Ventura, CA 93003 (805) 656-3602
restaurants

American Savings Bank AMSB
820 South A Street
Tacoma, WA 98402 (206) 272-8305
banking

Amer. Savings Bank F.S.B. ABNY
380 Madison Avenue
New York, NY 10020 (212) 880-7600
banking

American Security Corp. ASEC
730 Fifteenth Street, N.W.
Washington, DC 20013 (202) 624-4000
banking   [DRP 5%]

American Software, Inc. AMSW
443 East Paces Ferry Road N.E.
Atlanta, GA 30305 (404) 261-4381
software, data processing

American Surgery Centers Corp. SRGY
6991 East Camelback Road
Scottsdale, AZ 85251 (602) 994-9609
health services

American Technical Ceramics Corp. ATCC
One Norden Lane
Huntington Station, NY 11746 (516) 271-9600
ceramics

American TV & Commun. Corp. ATCMA
160 Inverness Drive West
Englewood, CO 80112 (303) 799-1200
cable tv systems

American Western Corp. AWST
1208 West Elkhorn
Sioux Falls, SD 57117 (605) 334-0334
plastic products

AmeriTrust Corp. AMTR
P.O. Box 5937
Cleveland, OH 44101 (216) 687-5413
banking   [DRP]

Ameriwest Financial Corp. AMWS
6400 Uptown Blvd., N.E.
Albuquerque, NM 87110 (505) 883-3100
savings and loan

Amgen AMGN
1900 Oak Terrace Lane
Thousand Oaks, CA 91320 (805) 499-5725
biotechnology, drugs

Amistar Corp. AMTA
2675 Skypark Drive
Torrance, CA 90505 (213) 539-7200
electronics

Amoskeag Bank Shares, Inc. AMKG
875 Elm Street
Manchester, NH 03105 (603) 624-3200
banking

Amoskeag Co. AMOS
Prudential Center
Boston, MA 02199 (617) 262-4000
food products

Ampad Corp. AMPD
104 Lower Westfield Road
Holyoke, MA 01040 (413) 536-3511
paper products

Anadite, Inc. ADIT
5301 West Roosevelt Road
Chicago, IL 60650 (312) 656-8558
finished metal and forgings

Analogic Corp. ALOG
8 Centennial Drive
Peabody, MA 01961 (617) 246-0300
electronics

Analysts International Corp. ANLY
7615 Metro Blvd.
Minneapolis, MN 55435 (612) 835-2330
software, data processing

Anaren Microwave, Inc. ANEN
6635 Kirkville Road
East Syracuse, NY 13057 (315) 432-8909
electronic equipment

Andersen Group, Inc. ANDR
1280 Blue Hills Avenue
Bloomfield, CT 06002 (203) 242-0761
health equipment

Andover Controls Corp. ANDO
York and Haverhill Streets
Andover, MA 01801 (617) 470-0555
automation systems

Andrew Corp. ANDW
10500 West 153rd Street
Orland Park, IL 60462 (312) 349-3300
communications

Andros Analyzers Inc. ANDY
2332 Fourth Street
Berkeley, CA 94710 (415) 849-1377
scientific instruments

Animed, Inc. VETS
25 Lumber Road
Roslyn, NY 11576 (516) 484-2700
veterinary services

Anitec Image Techology Corp. ANTC
40 Charles Street
Binghamton, NY 13902 (201) 573-6908
photo equipment

Apogee Enterprises, Inc. APOG
7900 Xerxes Avenue South
Minneapolis, MN 55431 (612) 835-1874
building materials-glass

Apollo Computer Inc. APCI
330 Billerica Road
Chelmsford, MA 01824 (617) 256-6600
computers

Apple Bank for Savings APPL
205 East 42nd Street
New York, NY 10017 (212) 573-8000
savings bank

Apple Computer, Inc. AAPL
20525 Mariani Avenue
Cupertino, CA 95014 (408) 996-1010
computers   [O]

Applied Biosystems, Inc. ABIO
850 Lincoln Centre Drive
Foster City, CA 94404 (415) 570-6667
scientific instruments

Applied Communications, Inc. ACIS
330 South 108th Avenue
Omaha, NE 68154 (402) 390-7600
electronics

Applied Data Communications, Inc. ADCC
14272 Chambers Road
Tustin, CA 92680 (714) 731-9000
communications equipment

Applied Materials, Inc. AMAT
3050 Bowers Avenue
Santa Clara, CA 95051 (408) 727-5555
electronic equipment

Applied Solar Energy Corp. SOLR
15251 East Don Julian Road
City of Industry, CA 91746 (213) 968-6581
solar plumbing and heating

Arabian Shield Development Co. ARSD
10830 North Central Expressway
Dallas, TX 75231 (214) 692-7872
oil and gas

Archive Corp. ACHV
1650 Sunflower Avenue
Costa Mesa, CA 92626 (714) 641-0279
computer tape drives

Arizona Bancwest Corp. AZBW
101 North First Avenue
Phoenix, AZ 85003 (602) 262-2000
banking   [DRP]

Ark Restaurants Corp. ARKR
215 West 29th Street
New York, NY 10001 (212) 760-0520
restaurants

Arnold Industries, Inc. AIND
625 South Fifth Avenue
Lebanon, PA 17042 (717) 274-2521
trucking

Arrow Bank Corp. AROW
250 Glen Street
Glens Falls, NY 12801 (518) 793-4121
banking

Artel Communications Corp. AXXX
P.O. Box 100
Worcester, MA 01602 (617) 752-5690
fiber optics

Ashton-Tate TATE
20101 Hamilton Avenue
Torrance, CA 90502 (213) 329-8000
computer software

Associated Banc-Corp. ASBC
222 Cherry Street
Green Bay, WI 54307 (414) 433-3166
banking

Associated Communications Corp. ACCM
Gateway Towers
Pittsburgh, PA 15222 (412) 281-1907
communication

Associated Companies, Inc. ASCI
8935 North Meridian Street
Indianapolis, IN 46260 (317) 848-7025
insurance

Associated Hosts, Inc. AHST
8447 Wilshire Blvd.
Beverly Hills, CA 90211 (213) 653-6010
restaurants

Astro-Med, Inc. ALOT
600 East Greenwich Avenue
West Warwick, RI 02893 (401) 828-4000
precision instruments

Astrocom Corp. ACOM
120 West Plato Blvd.
St. Paul, MN 55107 (612) 227-8651
computers

Astronics Corp. ATRO
80 South Davis Street
Orchard Park, NY 14127 (716) 662-6640
packaging

Astrosystems, Inc. ASTR
Six Nevada Drive
Lake Success, NY 11042 (516) 328-1600
electronics, aerospace

Atcor, Inc. ATCO
16100 South Lathrop Avenue
Harvey, IL 60426 (312) 995-6000
metals fabrication

Athens Fed. Savings Bank AFSB
124 East Hancock Avenue
Athens, GA 30613 (404) 546-5440
banking

Athey Products Corp. ATPC
Route 1-A North
Raleigh, NC 27602 (919) 556-5171
transporation equipment

Atico Financial Corp. ATFC
150 S.E. Third Avenue
Miami, FL 33131 (305) 577-7781
agricultural products

Atkinson (Guy F.) Co., ATKN
10 West Orange Ave.
San Francisco, CA 94080 (415) 876-1000
building construction

Atlanta Gas Light Co. AGLT
235 Peachtree Street, N.E.
Atlanta, GA 30302 (404) 572-0123
utility   [DRP]

Atlantic American Corp. AAME
4370 Peachtree Road, N.E.
Atlanta, GA 30319 (404) 231-1010
insurance

Atlantic Fed. S&L Assn. of Ft. Lauderdale ASAL
1750 East Sunrise Blvd.
Fort Lauderdale, FL 33304 (305) 764-1110
savings and loan

Atlantic Financial Federal ATLF
50 Monument Road
Bala Cynwyd, PA 19004 (215) 668-9440
savings and loan

Atlantic Permanent Fed. S&L Assn. APER
740 Boush Street
Norfolk, VA 23510 (804) 446-0500
savings and loan

Atlantic Research Corp. ATRC
5390 Cherokee Avenue
Alexandria, VA 22312 (703) 642-4000
aerospace components

Atlantic Southeast Airlines, Inc. ASAI
1688 Phoenix Pkwy.
College Park, GA 30349 (404) 996-4562
regional airline

Atwood Oceanics, Inc. ATWD
15835 Park Ten Place Drive
Houston, TX 77218 (713) 492-2929
offshore oil and gas drilling

Audio/Video Affiliates, Inc. AVDO
2875 Needmore Road
Dayton, OH 45414 (513) 276-3931
electronics retailer

Austron, Inc. ATRN
P.O. Box 14766
Austin, TX 78761 (512) 251-2341
measuring instruments

Auto-Trol Technology Corp. ATTC
12500 North Washington
Denver, CO 80233 (303) 452-4919
automated design

Autoclave Engineers, Inc. ACLV
2930 West 22nd Street
Erie, PA 16512 (814) 838-2071
special industrial machines

Autodesk, Inc. ACAD
2320 Marinship Way
Sausalito, CA (415) 332-2344
computer-aided design

Automated Medical Labs. Inc. AUML
2201 West 76th Street
Hialeah, FL 33016 (305) 558-4000
health services

Automated Systems, Inc. ASII
1505 Commerce Avenue
Brookfield, WI 53005 (414) 784-6400
software, data processing

Automatix Inc. AITX
1000 Technology Park Drive
Billerica, MA 01821 (617) 667-7900
special industrial machines

Autotrol Corp. AUTR
5730 North Glen Park Road
Glendale, WI 53209 (414) 228-9100
waste management

Auxton Computer Enterprises, Inc. AUXT
851 Trafalgar Court
Maitland, FL 32751 (305) 660-8400
software, data processing

Avacare, Inc. AVAC
9200 Carpenter Freeway
Dallas, TX 75247 (214) 638-7686
health products

Avant-Garde Computing, Inc. AVGA
8000 Commerce Pkwy.
Mt. Laurel, NJ 08054 (609) 778-7000
computer software

Avantek, Inc. AVAK
4401 Great America Pkwy.
Santa Clara, CA 95054 (408) 727-0700
electronic equipment

Avatar Holdings, Inc. AVTR
201 Alhambra Circle
Coral Gables, FL 33134 (305) 442-7000
real estate

Aviation Group, Inc. (The) LIFT
P.O. Box 28187
Raleigh, NC 27611 (919) 872-0868
air freight

Aztec Manufacturing Co. AZTC
400 North Tarrant Street
Crowley, TX 76036 (817) 297-4361
heavy machinery

BBDO International, Inc. BBDO
383 Madison Avenue
New York, NY 10017 (212) 415-6143
advertising

BGS Systems, Inc. BGSS
One University Office Park
Waltham, MA 02254 (617) 891-0000
software, data processing

BIW Cable Systems, Inc. BIWC
65 Bay Street
Boston, MA 02125 (617) 265-2102
cable manufacturer

BPI Systems, Inc. BPII
3001 Bee Cave Road
Austin, TX 78746 (512) 328-5400
software, data processing

BR Communications BRHF
P.O. Box 61989
Sunnyvale, CA 94088 (408) 734-1600
communications equipment

BRAE Corp. BRAE
Four Embarcadero Center
San Francisco, CA 94111 (415) 951-1500
railroad-car leasing

BRIntec Corp. BRIX
1600 West Main Street
Willimantic, CT 06226 (203) 456-8000
electronics

BT Financial Corp. BTFC
532-534 Main Street
Johnstown, PA 15907 (814) 536-7801
non-bank finance

BTR Realty, Inc. BTRI
817 Maiden Choice Lane
Baltimore, MD 21228 (301) 247-4991
real estate

Baird Corp. BATM
125 Middlesex Turnpike
Bedford, MA 01730 (617) 276-6000
precision electronic instruments

Baker, Fentress & Co. BKFR
Suite 3510, 200 West Madison Street
Chicago, IL 60606 (312) 236-9190
closed-end mutual fund

Baldwin & Lyons, Inc. BWIN
3100 North Meridian Street
Indianapolis, IN 46208 (317) 925-3501
Insurance

Baltek Corp. BTEK
10 Fairway Court
Northvale, NJ 07647 (201) 767-1400
wood products

Baltimore Bancorp BBCM
P.O.Box 896
Baltimore, MD 21203 (301) 244-3360
banking

BancOklahoma Corp. BOKC
Bank of Oklahoma Tower
Tulsa, OK 74192 (918) 588-6348
banking   [DRP]

BancTec, Inc. BTEC
4435 Spring Valley Road
Dallas, TX 75244 (214) 450-7700
business data processing

Banco Popular de Puerto Rico BPOP
Banco Popular Center
Hato Rey, PR 00918 (809) 751-9800
banking

Bancorp Hawaii, Inc. BNHI
P.O. Box 2900
Honolulu, HI 96846 (808) 537-8111
banking   [DRP 5%]

Bangor Hydro-Electric Co. BANG
33 State Street
Bangor, ME 04401 (207) 945-5621
utility

Bank of Delaware Corp. BDEL
P.O. Box 788
Wilmington, DE 19899 (302) 429-2200
banking

Bank of Granite GRAN
123 North Main Street
Granite Falls, NC 28630 (704) 396-3141
banking

Bank of New England Corp. BKNE
28 State Street
Boston, MA 02109 (617) 742-4000
banking   [DRP 3%]

Bank South Corp. BKSO
55 Marietta Street
Atlanta, GA 30303 (404) 529-4075
banking   [DRP]

BankEast Corp. BENH
One Wall Street
Manchester, NH 03105 (603) 624-6013
banking

Bankers First Corp. BNKF
985 Broad Street
Augusta, GA 30913 (404) 823-3200
banking

Banknorth Group, Inc. BKNG
8 North Main Street
St. Albans, VT 05478 (802) 524-5951
banking

Banks of Iowa, Inc. BIOW
520 Walnut
Des Moines, IA 50306 (515) 245-6320
banking

Banks of Mid-America, Inc. BOMA
100 Broadway
Oklahoma City, OK 73102 (405) 231-6000
banking   [DRP]

BankVermont Corp. BKVT
148 College Street
Burlington, VT 05402 (802) 658-1810
banking

Ban Ponce Corp., BDEP
268 Munoz Rivera Ave.
San Juan, PR 00918 (809) 754-9400
banking

George Banta Co., Inc. BNTA
Curtis Reed Plaza
Menasha, WI 54952 (414) 722-7771
printing

Barden Corp. (The) BARD
200 Park Avenue
Danbury, CT 06810 (203) 744-2211
machinery

Baron Data Systems BDSY
1700 Marina Blvd.
San Leandro, CA 94577 (415) 352-8101
business data processing

Barris Industries, Inc. BRRS
9100 Wilshire Blvd.
Beverly Hills, CA 90212 (213) 278-9550
television production

Barton Valve Co., Inc. BART
2401 North Hwy. 177
Shawnee, OK 74801 (405) 273-7660
oil drilling equipment

Base Ten Systems, Inc. BASE
Number One Electronics Drive
Trenton, NJ 08619 (609) 586-7010
electronic equipment

Basic American Medical, Inc. BAMI
P.O. Box 27249
Indianapolis, IN 46227 (317) 783-5461
health services, supplies

Basic Res. Int'l. (Bahamas) Ltd. BBAH
650 Fifth Avenue
New York, NY 10019 (212) 541-8920
oil and gas

Bassett Furniture Industries., Inc. BSET
P.O. Box 626
Bassett, VA 24055 (703) 629-7511
furniture

Battle Mountain Gold Co. BMGC
Pennzoil Place
Houston, TX 77251 (713) 546-4715
metal mining

Bay Pacific Health Corp. BPHC
1111 Bayhill Drive
San Bruno, CA 94066 (415) 952-5000
health services

Baybanks, Inc. BBNK
175 Federal Street
Boston, MA 02110 (617) 482-1040
banking   [DRP]

Bayly Corp. BAYL
1400 Ford Bldg.
Detroit, MI 48226 (313) 222-0870
apparel

Bayou Resources, Inc. BYOU
1200 Milam
Houston, TX 77002 (713) 658-9937
oil and gas

Beeba's Creations, Inc. BEBA
4388 Jutland Drive
San Diego, CA 92117 (619) 270-5750
apparel stores

Begley Co. BGLY
P.O. Box 1000
Richmond, KY 40475 (606) 623-2550
retailing

Bel Fuse Inc. BELF
198 Van Vorst Street
Jersey City, NJ 07302 (201) 432-0463
electronic equipment

Bell (W.) & Co., Inc. BLLW
12401 Twinbrook Pkwy.
Rockville, MD 20852 (301) 468-5662
catalog showroom retailing

Ben & Jerry's Homemade, Inc. BJIC
Route 100
Waterbury, VT 05676 (802) 244-5641
dairy products

Bench Craft, Inc. SOFA
State Hwy. 15
Blue Mountain, MS 38610 (601) 685-4711
furniture

Benihana National Corp. BNHN
P.O. Box 020210
Miami, FL 33102 (305) 593-0770
restaurants

Bercor, Inc. BECR
14450 Industry Circle
La Mirada, CA 90638 (714) 670-7644
wholesale distributor

Berkley (W. R.) Corp. BKLY
165 Mason Street
Greenwich, CT 06836 (203) 629-2880
insurance

Berkline Corp. (The) BERK
One Berkline Drive
Morristown, TN 37814 (615) 586-1461
furniture

Berkshire Gas Co. (The) BGAS
115 Cheshire Road
Pittsfield, MA 01201 (413) 442-1511
utility   [DRP]

Berkshire Hathaway Inc. BKHT
1440 Kiewit Plaza
Omaha, NE 68131 (402) 346-1400
insurance, investments

Best Buy Co., Inc. BBUY
4400 West 78th Street
Bloomington, MN 55435 (612) 831-4552
retailing

Betz Laboratories, Inc. BETZ
4636 Somerton Road
Trevose, PA 19047 (215) 355-3300
specialty chemicals

Big B, Inc. BIGB
2600 Morgan Road, S.E.
Birmingham, AL 35023 (205) 785-0335
drugstores

Big Bear, Inc. BGBR
770 West Goodale Road
Columbus, OH 43212 (614) 464-6500
retail food stores

Bindley Western Industries, Inc. BIND
4212 West 71st Street
Indianapolis, IN 46268 (317) 298-9900
drugs

Binghamton Savings Bank (The) BING
58-68 Exchange Street
Binghamton, NY 13902 (607) 773-2525
banking

Bio-Response, Inc. BIOR
1978 West Winton Avenue
Hayward, CA 94545 (415) 786-9744
health services, supplies

Biogen N.V. BGEN
C/O Biogen Inc.
Cambridge, MA 02142 (617) 864-8900
biotechnology

Biomet, Inc. BMET
Airport Industrial Park
Warsaw, IN 45680 (219) 267-6639
medical supplies

Biosearch Medical Products Inc. BMPI
35 Industrial Pkwy.
Somerville, NJ 08876 (201) 722-5000
medical supplies

Biotech Research Laboratories, Inc. BTRL
1600 East Gude Drive
Rockville, MD 20850 (301) 251-0800
biotechnology

Bird Inc. BIRD
Washington Street
East Walpole, MA 02032 (617) 668-2500
building materials

Birdfinder Corp. BFTV
2251 Cattlemen Road
Sarasota, FL 33582 (813) 377-5231
broadcasting and cable tv

Birdview Satellite Communications, Inc. BVSC
P.O. Box 25788
Overland Park, KS 66225 (913) 451-2636
communications equipment

Birtcher Corp. (The) BIRT
4501 North Arden Drive
El Monte, CA 91731 (213) 575-8144
medical electronics

Bishop Graphics, Inc. BGPH
5388 Sterling Center Drive
Westlake Village, CA 91359 (213) 991-2600
graphic equipment

Black Industries, Inc. BLAK
2816 North Roxboro Street
Durham, NC 27704 (919) 477-0485
construction

Blasius Industries, Inc. BLAS
1099 Wall Street West
Lyndhurst, NJ 07071 (201) 438-2801
rubber products

Block Drug Co., Inc. BLOC
257 Cornelison Avenue
Jersey City, NJ 07302 (201) 434-3000
drugs

Blue Ridge Real Est. Co. Big Boulder Corp. BLRG
Route 940 and Mosey Wood Road
Blakeslee, PA 18610 (717) 443-8433
lodging

Boatmen's Bancshares, Inc. BOAT
100 North Broadway
St. Louis, MO 63102 (314) 425-7525
banking   [DRP]

Bob Evans Farms, Inc. BOBE
3776 South High Street
Columbus, OH 43207 (614) 491-2225
restaurants   [DRP]

Bohemia Inc. BOHM
2280 Oakmont Way
Eugene, OR 97401 (503) 342-6262
wood products

Bolt Technology Corp. BOLT
Four Duke Place
Norwalk, CT 06854 (203) 853-0700
oil field services

Boole & Babbage, Inc. BOOL
510 Oakmead Pkwy.
Sunnyvale, CA 94086 (408) 735-9550
software and data processing

Boonton Electronics Corp. BOON
791 Route 10
Randolph, NJ 07869 (201) 584-1077
scientific instruments

Booth, Inc. BOTH
2025 Royal Lane
Dallas, TX 75229 (214) 484-3222
machinery

Boothe Financial Corp. BCMP
100 Bush Street
San Francisco, CA 94104 (415) 989-6580
computer leasing

Boston Bancorp. SBOS
460 West Broadway
South Boston, MA 02127 (617) 268-2500
banking

Boston Digital Corp. BOST
Granite Park
Milford, MA 01757 (617) 473-4561
computer equipment

Boston Five Cents Savings Bank FSB BFCS
10 School Street
Boston, MA 02108 (617) 742-6000
banking

Bradley Real Estate Trust BRLY
250 Boylston Street
Boston, MA 02116 (617) 421-0750
real estate

Brady (W. H.) Co. BRCO
727 West Glendale Avenue
Milwaukee, WI 53201 (414) 332-8100
chemical products

Branch Corp. BNCH
223 West Nash Street
Wilson, NC 27893 (919) 399-4291
banking   [DRP]

Brenco, Inc. BREN
P.O. Box 389
Petersburg, VA 23804 (804) 732-0202
railroad equipment

Bridge Communications, Inc. BLAN
1345 Shorebird Way
Mountain View, CA 94043 (415) 969-4400
electronic communication

Bridgford Foods Corp. BRID
1308 North Patt Street
Anaheim, CA 92801 (714) 526-5533
frozen foods

Britton Lee, Inc. BLII
14600 Winchester Blvd.
Los Gatos, CA 95030 (408) 378-7000
business data processing

Bruno's, Inc. BRNO
P.O. Box 2486
Birmingham, AL 35201 (205) 785-9400
food stores

Buffton Corp. BUFF
1415 Interfirst Tower
Fort Worth, TX 76102 (817) 332-4761
pipe, cable

Builders Transport, Inc. TRUK
U.S. Hwy. 1
Camden, SC 29020 (803) 432-1400
trucking and shipping

Bull & Bear Group, Inc. BNBG
11 Hanover Square
New York, NY 10005 (212) 785-0900
investment services

Burnham Service Corp. BSCO
5000 Burnham Blvd.
Columbus, GA 31907 (404) 563-1120
trucking

Burnup & Sims, Inc. BSIM
One North University Drive
Fort Lauderdale, FL 33324 (305) 587-4512
cable systems installation

Burr-Brown Corp. BBRC
6730 South Tucson Blvd.
Tucson, AZ 85706 (602) 746-1111
precision instruments

Burritt InterFinancial Bancorporation BANQ
267 Main Street
New Britain, CT 06050 (203) 225-7601
savings and loan

Business Men's Assurance Co. of America BMAC
BMA Tower
Kansas City, MO 64108 (816) 753-8000
insurance   [DRP]

Businessland, Inc. BUSL
3600 Stevens Creek Blvd.
San Jose, CA 95117 (408) 554-9300
computer retailing

John O. Butler Co. BUTC
4635 West Foster Avenue
Chicago, IL 60630 (312) 777-4000
cosmetics and personal care

Butler Manufacturing Co. BTLR
BMA Tower, Penn Valley Park
Kansas City, MO 64141 (816) 968-3000
building products   [DRP]

Butler National Corp. BUTL
8246 Nieman Road
Lenexa, KS 66214 (913) 888-8585
electronic machinery

C B & T Bancshares, Inc. CBTB
1148 Broadway
Columbus, GA 31902 (404) 571-2197
banking   [DRP]

C-Cor Electronics, Inc. CCBL
60 Decibel Road
State College, PA 16801 (814) 238-2461
electronics

CACI, Inc. CACI
1815 N. Fort Myer Drive
Arlington, VA 22209 (703) 841-7800
computer analysis and services

CCB Financial Corp. CCBF
111 Corcoran Street
Durham, NC 27702 (919) 683-7777
banking   [DRP]

CCNB Corp. CCNC
331 Bridge Street
New Cumberland, PA 17070 (717) 774-7000
banking

CCX Network Inc. CCXN
301 Industrial Blvd.
Conway, AR 72032 (501) 329-6836
business services

CF&I Steel Corp. CFIP
P.O. Box 316
Pueblo, CO 81002 (303) 561-6500
metals fabrication

CFS Financial Corp., Inc. CFSC
4020 University Drive
Fairfax, VA 22030 (703) 691-4400
savings and loan

CML Group, Inc. CMLI
524 Main Street
Acton, MA 01720 (617) 264-4155
apparel stores

C.O.M.B. Co. CMCO
14605 28th Avenue North
Plymouth, MN 55441 (612) 559-8000
retailing

COMNET Corp. CNET
5185 MacArthur Blvd., N.W.
Washington, DC 20016 (202) 537-2500
computer services

CORCOM, Inc. CORC
1600 Winchester Road
Libertyville, IL 60048 (312) 680-7400
electronic filters

C.P. Rehab Corp. CRHB
240 Madison Avenue
New York, NY 10016 (212) 685-3570
health services

CPI Corp. CPIC
1706 Washington Avenue
St. Louis, MO 63103 (314) 231-1575
portrait studios, residence cleaning

CPT Corp. CPTC
8100 Mitchell Road
Eden Prairie, MN 55344 (612) 937-8000
computers

CSP, Inc. CSPI
40 Linnell Circle
Billerica, MA 01821 (617) 272-6020
electronic equipment, data processing

CVB Financial Corp. CVBF
12808 Central Avenue
Chino, CA 91710 (714) 627-7316
investments

Cable TV Industries CATV
10801 National Blvd.
Los Angeles, CA 90064 (213) 204-4440
electronic equipment

Cache, Inc. CACH
2090 North Miami Avenue
Miami, FL 33127 (305) 576-2130
apparel stores

Cadbury Schweppes p.l.c. CADBY
1-4 Connaught Place
London, England W2 2EX
food products

Cadmus Communications Corp. CDMS
2901 Byrdhill Road
Richmond, VA 23261 (804) 264-2885
printing

California Amplifier, Inc. CAMP
460 Calle San Pablo
Camarillo, CA 93010 (805) 987-9000
electronics

California Biotechnology, Inc. CBIO
2450 Bayshore Frontage Road
Mountain View, CA 94043 (415) 966-1550
biotechnology

California First Bank CFBK
350 California Street
San Francisco, CA 94104 (415) 445-0200
banking   [DRP 5%]

California Jockey Club CJOC
P.O. Box 5050
San Mateo, CA 94402 (415) 574-7223
amusement

California Microwave, Inc. CMIC
990 Almanor Avenue
Sunnyvale, CA 94086 (408) 732-4000
electronic communications equipment

California Silver Ltd. CALS
6th Floor, 535 Howe Street
Vancouver, B.C. V6C 2C2 (604) 669-7888
metal mining

California Water Service Co. CWTR
1720 North First Street
San Jose, CA 95112 (408) 298-1414
utility   [DRP]

Callon Petroleum Co. CLNP
200 North Canal Street
Natchez, MS 39120 (601) 442-1601
oil and gas

Calny, Inc. CLNY
1650 Borel Place, Ste 101
San Mateo, CA 94402 (415)574-2455
restaurants

Calumet Industries, Inc. CALI
3 Illinois Center, Suite 424
Chicago, IL 60601 (312) 565-4120
oil refining

Canal-Randolph Ltd. Partnership CANL
717 Fifth Avenue
New York, NY 10022 (212) 826-6040
investment co.

Canrad, Inc. CNRD
100 Chestnut Street
Newark, NJ 07104 (201) 589-4300
electronic machinery

Capital Southwest Corp. CSWC
12900 Preston Road
Dallas, TX 75230 (214) 233-8242
investment company

Capitol Bancorporation CAPB
One Bulfinch Place
Boston, MA 02114 (617) 723-5300
banking

Capitol Fed. S&L Assn. of Denver CFSD
3300 South Parker Road
Aurora, CO 80014 (303) 671-1000
savings and loan

Capitol Transamerica Corp. CATA
4610 University Avenue
Madison, WI 53705 (608) 231-4450
insurance

Captain Crab, Inc. CRAB
Bayshore Executive Plaza
Miami, FL 33161 (305) 895-9505
restaurants

Cardinal Distribution, Inc. CDIC
555 Metro Place North
Columbus, OH 43017 (614) 766-6662
wholesale food and drug distributor

Cardis Corp. CRDS
9401 Wilshire Blvd.
Beverly Hills, CA 90212 (213)272-0242
auto parts distributor

CareerCom Corp. CRCM
Suite 540, Irwin Bldg.
King of Prussia, PA 19406 (215) 337-7176
educational services

Caremark, Inc. CMRK
4340 Von Karman
Newport Beach, CA 92660 (714) 851-2311
health services

Carl Karcher Enterprises, Inc. CARL
1200 North Harbor Blvd.
Anaheim, CA 92801 (714) 774-5796
restaurants

Carlsberg Corp. CRLS
2800 28th Street
Santa Monica, CA 90405 (213) 450-6800
real estate

Carolin Mines Ltd. CRLN
5th Fl., 535 Howe Steet
Vancouver, B.C. V6C 2C2 (604) 685-4368
metal mining

Carriage Industries, Inc. CARG
P.O. Box 542
Calhoun, GA 30701 (404) 629-9234
rugs and carpets

Carteret S&L Association, F.A. CFCC
200 South Street
Morristown, NJ 07960 (201) 326-1000
savings and loan

Cascade Corp. CASC
Park Center
Portland, OR 97201 (503) 227-0024
construction and mining machinery

Casey's General Stores, Inc. CASY
1299 N.E. Broadway Avenue
Des Moines, IA 50313 (515) 263-3700
retail food stores

Catalyst Energy Development Corp. CEDC
180 Maiden Lane
New York, NY 10038 (212) 968-1700
energy services

Cencor, Inc. CNCR
P.O. Box 26610
Kansas City, MO 64196 (816)474-4750
financial services

Centerre Bancorporation CTBC
One Centerre Plaza
St. Louis, MO 63101 (314) 554-6515
banking   [DRP]

Centocor, Inc. CNTO
244 Great Valley Pkwy.
Malvern, PA 19355 (215) 296-4488
health services, supplies

Centrafarm Group N.V. CFNV
Nieuwe Donk 9
The Netherlands
drugs

Central Bancorporation, Inc. (The) CBAN
Fifth & Main Streets
Cincinnati, OH 45202 (513) 651-8915
banking   [DRP]

Central Bancshares of the South, Inc. CBSS
701 South 20th Street
Birmingham, AL 35296 (205) 933-3000
banking   [DRP]

Central Fidelity Banks, Inc. CFBS
Broad at Third Street
Richmond, VA 23219 (804) 782-4000
banking   [DRP]

Central Jersey Bancorp CJER
Route Nine
Freehold Township, NJ 07728 (201) 462-0011
banking   [DRP]

Central Pennsylvania Savings Assn. CPSA
100 West Independence Street
Shamokin, PA 17872 (717) 644-0861
savings bank

Central Reserve Life Corp. CRLC
343 West Bagley Road
Berea, OH 44017 (216) 826-4100
insurance

Central Sprinkler Corp. CNSP
451 North Cannon Avenue
Lansdale, PA 19446 (215) 362-0700
sprinkler systems

Central Wisconsin Bancshares, Inc. CWCB
P. O. Box 2138
Wausau, WI 54401 (715)845-3133
banking

Centuri, Inc. CENT
300 Plaza Drive
Binghamton, NY 13903 (607) 729-6316
recreation equipment

Century Papers, Inc. CPAP
P.O. Box 1908
Houston, TX 77251 (713) 877-1100
paper and containers

Ceradyne, Inc. CRDN
16781-A Milliken Avenue
Irvine, CA 92714 (714) 549-0421
aerospace products

Cerberonics, Inc. CRBR
5600 Columbia Pike
Bailey's Crossroads, VA 22041 (703) 379-4500
defense engineering services

Cermetek Microelectronics Inc. CRMK
1308 Borregas Avenue
Sunnyvale, CA 94088 (408) 734-8150
electronics

Certified Collateral Corp. CARX
640 North LaSalle Street
Chicago, IL 60610 (312) 787-2640
financial services

Cetus Corp. CTUS
1400 Fifty-Third Street
Emeryville, CA 94608 (415) 420-3300
drugs, electronic instruments   [O]

Champion Parts Rebuilders, Inc. CREB
2525-22nd Street
Oak Brook, IL 60521 (312) 986-6100
auto parts

Chancellor Corp. CHCR
Federal Reserve Plaza
Boston, MA 02210 (617) 723-3500
equipment leasing

Chaparral Resources, Inc. CHAR
621 17th Street
Denver, CO 80293 (303) 293-2340
oil and gas

Chapman Energy, Inc. CHPN
6350 LBJ Freeway
Dallas, TX 75240 (214)350-2469
oil and gas

Chargit, Inc. CHGT
1501 Broadway
New York, NY 10036 (212) 944-9669
ticket sales

Charlotte Charles, Inc. CAKE
2501 North Elston Avenue
Chicago, IL 60647 (312) 772-8310
food products

Charming Shoppes, Inc. CHRS
450 Winks Lane
Bensalem, PA 19020 (215) 245-9100
apparel stores

Charter Fed. S&L Association CHFD
110 Piedmont Avenue
Bristol, VA 24201 (703) 669-5101
savings and loan

Charvoz-Carsen Corporation CHZC
5 Daniel Road East
Fairfield, NJ 07006 (201) 227-6500
scientific equipment distribution

Chatham Manufacturing Co. CHAT
P.O. Box 620
Elkin, NC 28621 (919) 835-2211
weaving mills

Chattem, Inc. CHTT
1715 West 38th Street
Chattanooga, TN 37409 (615) 821-4571
cosmetics and personal care

Check Technology Corp. CTCQ
1284 Corporate Center Drive
Saint Paul, MN 55121 (612) 454-9300
check printing

Checkpoint Systems, Inc. CHEK
550 Grove Road
Thorofare, NJ 08086 (609) 848-1800
electronic theft detection equipment

Chemex Pharmaceuticals, Inc. CHMX
1401 17th Street
Denver, CO 80202 (303) 292-3603
drugs

Chemical Fabrics Corp. CMFB
701 Daniel Webster Hwy.
Merrimack, NH 03054 (603)424-9000
textiles, apparel

ChemLawn Corp. CHEM
8275 North High Street
Columbus, OH 43085 (614) 888-3572
lawn care

Cherokee Group (The) CHKE
12544 Saticoy Street
North Hollywood, CA 91605 (213) 875-1002
apparel and shoe stores

Cherry Electrical Products Corp. CHER
3600 Sunset Avenue
Waukegan, IL 60087 (312) 662-9200
electrical equipment

Chesapeake Utilities Corp. CHPK
P.O. Box 615
Dover, DE 19903 (302) 734-7443
utility

Chi-Chi's, Inc. CHIC
P.O. Box 32338
Louisville, KY 40232 (502) 244-1800
restaurants   [O]

Chicago Pacific Corp. CPAC
200 South Michigan Avenue
Chicago, IL 60604 (312) 435-7300
conglomerate

Chief Automotive Systems Inc. CHFS
1924 East 4th Street
Grand Island, NE 68802 (308) 384-9747
auto parts

Chili's, Inc. CHLI
6820 LBJ Freeway, #200
Dallas, TX 75240 (214) 980-9917
restaurants

Chiron Corp. CHIR
4560 Horton Street
Emeryville, CA 94608 (415) 655-8730
health services, supplies

Chittenden Corp. CNDN
Two Burlington Square
Burlington, VT 05401 (802) 658-4000
banking

Chronar Corp. CRNR
330 Bakers Basin Road
Trenton, NJ 08638 (609)587-8000
energy equipment

Church & Dwight Co., Inc. CRCH
CN 5297, 469 North Harrison Street
Princeton, NJ 08540 (609) 683-5900
specialty chemicals

Cincinnati Financial Corp. CINF
11295 Princeton Road
Cincinnati, OH 45246 (513) 771-2000
insurance and investment services   [DRP]

Cincinnati Microwave, Inc. CNMW
One Microwave Plaza
Cincinnati, OH 45249 (513) 489-5400
radar detectors

Cintas Corp. CTAS
11255 Reed Hartman Hwy.
Cincinnati, OH 45241 (513) 489-4000
uniform sale and rental

Cipher Data Products, Inc. CIFR
P.O. Box 85170
San Diego, CA 92138 (619) 693-7200
computer equipment   [O]

Ciprico, Inc. CPCI
2955 Xenium Lane
Plymouth, MN 55441 (612) 559-2034
computer equipment

Circadian, Inc. CKDN
3960 North First Street
San Jose, CA 95134 (408) 943-9222
health services, supplies

Circon Corp. CCON
749 Ward Drive
Santa Barbara, CA 93111 (805) 967-0404
electronic equipment

Citizens and Southern Corp. (The) CITS
1801 Main Street
Columbia, SC 29222 (803) 765-8423
banking

Citizens and Southern Corp. CSOU
P.O. Box 4899
Atlanta, GA 30302 (404) 581-2121
banking   [DRP]

Citizens Banking Corp. CBCF
One Citizens Banking Center
Flint, MI 48502 (313) 766-7500
banking

Citizens Cable Communications, Inc. CITI
720 Taylor Street
Fort Wayne, IN 46804 (219) 456-9000
communication

Citizens Fidelity Corp. CFDY
Citizens Plaza
Louisville, KY 40202 (502) 581-2100
banking   [DRP]

Citizens Financial Group, Inc. CITN
870 Westminister Street
Providence, RI 02903 (401) 456-7000
banking

Citizens Growth Properties CITG
200 Peoples Bank Bldg.
Jackson, MS 39201 (601) 948-4091
real estate

Citizens Savings Financial Corp. CSFC
999 Brickell Avenue
Miami, FL 33131 (305) 577-0400
savings and loan

Citizens Utilities Co. CITU
High Ridge Park
Stamford, CT 06905 (203) 329-8800
utility   [DRP]

City National Corp. CTYN
400 North Roxbury Drive
Beverly Hills, CA 90210 (213) 550-5400
banking

CityFed Financial Corp. CTYF
293 South County Road
Palm Beach, FL 33480 (305) 655-5919
savings and loan   [DRP 5%]

Citytrust Bancorp, Inc. CITR
945 Main Street
Bridgeport, CT 06601 (203) 384-5400
banking   [DRP]

Clark (J.L.) Manufacturing Co. CLRK
2300 Sixth Street
Rockford, IL 61125 (815) 962-8861
packaging products, metal cans

Classic Corp. WBED
8214 Wellmoor Court
Jessup, MD 20794 (301) 953-1133
furniture

Clear Channel Communications, Inc. CLCH
500 Two RepublicBank Plaza
San Antonio, TX 78205 (512) 225-4231
radio stations

CleveTrust Realty Investors CTRI
1020 Ohio Savings Plaza
Cleveland, OH 44114 (216) 621-3366
real estate

Clothestime, Inc. (The) CTME
5325 East Hunter Avenue
Anaheim, CA 92807 (714) 779-5881
apparel stores

Co-operative Bancorp COBK
97 Lowell Road
Concord, MA 01742 (617) 369-2400
banking

Coast Federal S&L Association CFSF
1777 Main Street
Sarasota, FL 33578 (813) 366-7000
savings and loan

Coast R.V. Inc. CRVI
1723 Junction Avenue
San Jose, CA 95112 (408) 297-0471
recreational vehicles

Coastal International, Ltd. CSTI
Sterling House
Hamilton 5, Bermuda (809) 295-8639
oil and gas

Coastal Savings Bank CSBK
426 Forest Avenue
Portland, ME 04104 (204) 774-5000
banking

Coated Sales, Inc. RAGS
P. O. Box 999
Laurence Harbor, NJ 08879 (201) 583-9600
coated textiles

Cobanco, Inc. CBCO
55 River Street
Santa Cruz, CA 95060 (408) 458-6315
financial services

Cobb Resources Corp. COBB
313 Washington S.E.
Albuquerque, NM 87108 (505) 265-2622
oil and gas

Cobe Laboratories, Inc. COBE
1201 Oak Street
Lakewood, CO 80215 (303) 232-6800
medical instruments

Coca-Cola Bottling Co. Consolidated COKE
P.O. Box 31487
Charlotte, NC 28231 (704) 334-6851
soft drinks   [DRP]

Codenoll Technology Corp. CODN
1086 North Broadway
Yonkers, NY 10701 (914) 965-6300
electronic machinery

Coeur D'Alene Mines Corp. COUR
416 River Street
Wallace, ID 83873 (208) 556-1121
metal mining

Cogenic Energy Systems, Inc. CESI
127 East 64th Street
New York, NY 10021 (212) 772-7500
energy-saving machinery

Coherent, Inc. COHR
3210 Porter Drive
Palo Alto, CA 94304 (415) 493-2111
scientific and medical instruments

Collaborative Research Inc. CRIC
128 Spring Street
Lexington, MA 02173 (617) 861-9700
drugs

Collagen Corp. CGEN
2500 Faber Place
Palo Alto, CA 94303 (415) 856-0200
medical supplies

Collective Federal S&L Association COFD
158 Philadelphia Avenue
Egg Harbor City, NJ 08215 (609) 965-1234
savings and loan

Collins Industries, Inc. COLL
P.O. Box 58
Hutchinson, KS 67501 (316) 663-4441
vehicles

Colonial American Bankshares Corp. CABK
10 Franklin Road S.E.
Roanoke, VA 24011 (703) 982-3249
banking

Colonial Bancgroup, Inc. (The) CLBG
671 South Perry Street
Montgomery, AL 36102 (205) 834-5500
banking

Colonial Gas Co. CGES
40 Market Street
Lowell, MA 01853 (617) 458-3171
utility   [DRP]

Colonial Group, Inc. (The) COGR
75 Federal Street
Boston, MA 02110 (617) 426-3750
investment services

Colonial Life & Accident Ins. Co. CACC
P.O. Box 1365
Columbia, SC 29202 (803) 798-7000
insurance

Color Tile, Inc. TILE
515 Houston Street
Fort Worth, TX 76102 (817) 870-9634
tile products

Colorado National Bankshares Inc. COLC
950 Seventeenth Street
Denver, CO 80202 (303) 629-1968
banking   [DRP 5%]

Columbia Federal Savings Bank CFSB
30 South Mission Street
Wenatchee, WA 98801 (509) 662-3641
banking

Columbus Mills, Inc. COLM
P.O. Box 1560
Columbus, GA 31993 (404) 324-0111
rugs and carpets

Comair, Inc. COMR
P.O. Box 75021
Greater Cincinnati, OH 45275 (606) 525-2550
regional airline

Comarco, Inc. CMRO
160 S. Springs Road
Anaheim, CA 92808 (714) 921-0672
engineering and computer services

Comcast Corp. CMCS
One Belmont Avenue
Bala Cynwyd, PA 19004 (215) 667-4200
cable tv systems

Comcoa, Inc. CCOA
411 North Webb Road
Wichita, KS 67206 (316) 683-4411
restaurants, rental services

Comdata Network, Inc. CASH
2209 Crestmoor Road
Nashville, TN 37215 (615) 385-0400
money-transfer systems

Comdial Corp. CMDL
2340 Commonwealth Drive
Charlottesville, VA 22906 (804) 978-2506
communications

Comerica, Inc. CMCA
211 West Fort Street
Detroit, MI 48275 (313) 370-5430
banking

Command Airways, Inc. COMD
Dutchess County Airport
Wappingers Falls, NY 12590 (914) 462-6100
regional airline

Commerce Bancorp, Inc. COBA
336 Route 70
Marlton, NJ 08053 (609) 983-6300
banking

Commerce Bancshares, Inc. CBSH
720 Main Street
Kansas City, MO 64199 (816) 234-2000
banking

Commerce Clearing House, Inc. CCLR
4025 W. Peterson Avenue
Chicago, IL 60646 (312) 583-8500
publishing

Commerce Union Corp. COMU
One Commerce Place
Nashville, TN 37219 (615) 749-3333
banking

Commercial Bancorporation of Colorado CBOC
3300 East First Avenue
Denver, CO 80206 (303) 321-1234
banking

Commercial Bancshares, Inc. CBNJ
15 Exchange Place
Jersey City, NJ 07302 (212) 434-5100
banking   [DRP]

Commercial Federal Corp. CFCN
2120 South 72nd Street
Omaha, NE 68124 (402) 554-9200
savings and loan

Commercial National Corp. CNCL
P.O. Box 21119
Shreveport, LA 71152 (318) 226-4614
banking

Commercial Shearing, Inc. CSHR
1775 Logan Avenue
Youngstown, OH 44501 (216) 746-8011
metals fabrication

Commonwealth Bancshares Corp. CBKS
101 West Third Street
Williamsport, PA 17703 (717) 327-5011
banking

Commonwealth National Financial Corp. CNHC
10 South Market Square
Harrisburg, PA 17108 (717) 564-9500
banking

Commonwealth S&L Association F.A. COMW
P.O. Box 9548
Ft. Lauderdale, FL 33310 (305) 979-0500
savings and loan

Commonwealth Savings Association CFGI
2223 West Loop South
Houston, TX 77027 (713) 439-7200
savings and loan

Commonwealth Telephone Enterprises, Inc. CWTE
46 Public Square
Wilkes-Barre, PA 18703 (717) 825-1100
communications   [DRP]

Communications Corp. of America CCPA
500 Twin Towers South
Dallas, TX 75247 (214) 638-5444
communications

Communications Industries Inc. COMM
3811 Turtle Creek Blvd.
Dallas, TX 75219 (214) 651-4250
communications equipment

Communications Systems Inc. CSII
213 South Main Street
Hector, MN 55342 (612) 848-6231
communications equipment

Community Shares Ltd. CSLT
P. O. Box 230
Fond Du Lac, WI 54935 (414) 923-7700
savings and loan

Comp-U-Card International, Inc. CUCD
707 Summer Street
Stamford, CT 06901 (203) 324-9261
computerized discount shopping

Comp-U-Check, Inc. CMUC
16250 Northland Drive
Southfield, MI 48075 (313) 569-1448
check verification

Component Technology Corp. CTEC
3409 West 14th Street
Erie, PA 16505 (814) 838-1971
business equipment

Comprehensive Care Corp. CMPH
18551 Von Karmen Avenue
Irvine, CA 92714 (714) 851-2273
health services

Compression Labs, Inc. CLIX
2305 Bering Drive
San Jose, CA 95131 (408) 946-3060
business equipment

CompuSave Corp. CPSV
16842 Von Karman
Irvine, CA 92714 (714) 863-9250
electronic catalogs

Compuscan, Inc. CSCN
81 Two Bridge Road
Fairfield, NJ 07006 (201) 575-0500
scanning equipment

Computer & Communications Technology
Corp. CCTC
460 Ward Drive
Santa Barbara, CA 93111 (805) 964-0771
computers

Computer Associates International, Inc. CASI
The Computer Associates Bldg.
Jericho, NY 11753 (516) 333-6700
software, data processing

Computer Automation, Inc. CAUT
2181 Dupont Drive
Irvine, CA 92713 (714) 833-8830
computers

Computer Data Systems, Inc. CPTD
One Curie Court
Rockville, MD 20850 (301) 921-7000
software, data processing

Computer Entry Systems Corp. CESC
2141 Industrial Pkwy.
Silver Spring, MD 20904 (301) 622-3500
electronic equipment

Computer Horizons Corp. CHRZ
747 Third Avenue
New York, NY 10017 (212) 371-9600
software, data processing

Computer Identics Corp. CIDN
5 Shawmut Road
Canton, MA 02021 (617) 821-0830
electronic equipment

Computer Language Research, Inc. CLRI
2395 Midway Road
Carrollton, TX 75006 (214) 250-7000
software, data processing

Computer Memories Inc. CMIN
P.O. Box 2740
Chatsworth, CA 91311 (818) 709-6445
computer equipment

Computer Products, Inc. CPRD
2900 S.W. 14th Street
Pompano Beach, FL 33069 (305) 974-5500
computer equipment

Computer Resources, Inc. CRII
4520 West 160th Street
Cleveland, OH 44135 (216) 362-1020
computer equipment

Computer Task Group, Inc. CTSK
800 Delaware Avenue
Buffalo, NY 14209 (716) 882-8000
software, data processing

ComputerCraft, Inc. CRFT
1616 South Voss Road
Houston, TX 77057 (713) 977-8419
computer retailing

Computone Systems Inc. CTON
One Dunwoody Park, Suite 200
Atlanta, GA 30338 (404) 393-3010
computer software and equipment

Computrac, Inc. CTTX
222 Municipal Drive
Richardson, TX 75080 (214) 234-4241
computer software

Comshare, Inc. CSRE
3001 South State Street
Ann Arbor, MI 48104 (313) 994-4800
software and data processing

Comstock Group, Inc. CSTK
38 Old Ridgebury Road
Danbury, CT 06810 (203) 792-9800
construction services

Comtrex Systems Corp. COMX
109 Gaither Drive
Mt. Laurel, NJ 08054 (609) 778-0090
electronics

Concept Development, Inc. CDII
10854 John Galt Blvd.
Omaha, NE 68137 (402) 896-0997
hotels, restaurants

Concept, Inc. CCPT
12707 U.S. Hwy. 19 South
Clearwater, FL 33546 (813) 536-2791
medical supplies

Concord Computing Corp. CEFT
7 Alfred Circle
Bedford, MA 01730 (617) 275-1730
computers

Congress Street Properties, Inc. CSTP
200 Peoples Bank Bldg.
Jackson, MS 39201 (601) 948-4091
real estate

Conifer Group, Inc. (The) CNFG
370 Main Street
Worcester, MA 01608 (617) 752-5661
banking   [DRP]

Connecticut Water Service, Inc. CTWS
93 West Main Street
Clinton, CT 06413 (203) 669-8636
utility   [DRP 5%]

Consolidated Capital Income Opportunity
Trust CCOT
2000 Powell Street
Emeryville, CA 94608 (415) 652-7171
real estate

Consolidated Capital Income Trust CCIT
2000 Powell Street
Emeryville, CA 94608 (415) 652-7171
real estate   [DRP]

Consolidated Capital Realty Investors CCPL
2000 Powell Street
Emeryville, CA 94608 (415) 652-7171
real estate   [DRP]

Consolsolidated Capital Special Trust CCST
2000 Powell Street
Emeryville, CA 94608 (415) 652-7171
real estate   [DRP]

Consolidated Fibres, Inc. CFIB
50 California Street
San Francisco, CA 94111 (415) 788-5300
recyclable waste paper

Consolidated Papers, Inc. CPER
P. O. Box 50
Wisconsin Rapids, WI 54494 (715) 422-3111
paper products

Consolidated Products, Inc. COPI
500 Century Bldg.
Indianapolis, IN 46204 (317) 633-4100
restaurants

Consolidated-Tomoka Land Co. CTLC
P.O. Box 2400
Daytona, FL 32015 (813) 385-0141
agricultural products

Constellation Bancorp CSTL
68 Broad Street
Elizabeth, NJ 07207 (201) 354-4080
banking   [DRP]

Consul Restaurant Corp. CNSL
4815 West 77th Street
Minneapolis, MN 55435 (612) 893-0230
restaurants

Consumers Financial Corp. CFIN
1110 Fernwood Avenue
Camp Hill, PA 17011 (717) 761-4230
insurance

Consumers Water Co. CONW
Four Canal Plaza
Portland, ME 04112 (207) 773-6438
utility   [DRP]

Continental Bancorp, Inc. CBRP
1500 Market Street
Philadelphia, PA 19102 (215) 564-7000
banking   [DRP]

Continental Federal S&L Association CONF
P.O. Box 838
Oklahoma City, OK 73101 (405) 236-3641
savings and loan

Continental General Insurance Co. CGIC
8901 Indian Hills Drive
Omaha, NE 68114 (402) 397-3200
insurance

Continental Health Affiliates, Inc. CTHL
900 Sylvan Avenue
Englewood Cliff, NJ 07632 (201) 569-8833
health services

Continental Healthcare Systems, Inc. CHSI
8900 Indian Creek Pkwy.
Overland Park, KS 66210 (913) 451-6161
health services

Continuum Co., Inc. (The) CTUC
3429 Executive Center Drive
Austin, TX 78731 (512) 345-5700
software, data processing

Control Laser Corp. CLSR
11222 Astronaut Blvd.
Orlando, FL 32821 (305) 851-2540
scientific instruments

Control Resource Industries, Inc. CRIX
670 Mariner Drive
Michigan City, IN 46360 (219) 872-5591
air-filtration systems

Convenient Food Mart, Inc. CFMI
9701 West Higgins Road
Rosemont, IL 60018 (312) 751-1500
food stores

Convergent Technologies, Inc. CVGT
30 East Pulmeria
San Jose, CA 95134 (408) 945-8877
computers

Converse, Inc. CVRS
55 Fordham Road
Wilmington, MA 01887 (617) 657-5500
footwear

Cooper Development Co. BUGS
75 Willow Road
Menlo Park, CA 94025 (415) 853-6000
health services, supplies

Cooper LaserSonics, Inc. ZAPS
3145 Porter Drive
Palo Alto, CA 94304 (415) 856-5000
health services, supplies

Adolph Coors Co. ACCO
Golden,CO 80401 (303) 279-6565
brewer   [O]

Copytele, Inc. COPY
900 Walt Whitman Road
Huntington Station, NY 11746 (516) 549-5900
communcations

Cordis Corp. CORD
P.O. Box 525700
Miami, FL 33102 (305) 551-2000
medical supplies

CoreStates Financial Corp. CSFN
N. E. Corner Broad & Chestnut Sts.
Philadelphia, PA 19101 (215) 629-3100
banking   [DRP]

Corp. for Entertainment & Learning, Inc. CELC
515 Madison Avenue
New York, NY 10022 (212) 421-4030
movies

Corvus Systems, Inc. CRVS
2100 Corvus Drive
San Jose, CA 95124 (408) 559-7000
computers

Cosmo Communications Corp. CSMO
16501 N.W. 16th Court
Miami, FL 33169 (305) 621-4227
consumer electronics

Cotton States Life and Health Insurance Co. CSLH
244 Perimeter Center Pkwy.
Atlanta, GA 30346 (404) 391-8600
insurance

Courier Corp. CRRC
165 Jackson Street
Lowell, MA 01852 (617) 458-6351
printing

Courier Dispatch Group, Inc. CDGI
P.O. Box 4924
Atlanta, GA 30348 (404) 955-8646
freight forwarding

Cousins Properties Inc. COUS
800 North Omni International
Atlanta, GA 30335 (404) 577-5400
real estate

Covington Technologies COVT
2451 East Orangethorpe Avenue
Fullerton, CA 92631 (714) 879-0111
real estate

Cracker Barrel Old Country Store, Inc. CBRL
P.O. Box 787
Lebanon, TN 37088 (615) 444-5533
restaurants

Craddock-Terry Shoe Corp. CDCK
3100 Albert Lankford Drive
Lynchburg, VA 24506 (804) 845-3411
footwear   [DRP]

Cramer, Inc. CRMR
625 Adams Street
Kansas City, KS 66105 (913) 621-6700
furniture

Crazy Eddie, Inc. CRZY
2845 Coney Island Avenue
Brooklyn, NY 11235 (718) 934-0100
consumer electronics stores

Crestek, Inc. CRST
Scotch Road
Trenton, NJ 08628 (609) 883-4000
oil and gas

Cronus Industries, Inc. CRNS
12700 Pk. Central Drive
Dallas, TX 75251 (214) 386-2900
metals fabrication

Cross & Trecker Corp. CTCO
505 North Woodward Avenue
Bloomfield Hills, MI 48013 (313) 644-4343
machine tools   [DRP]

CrossLand Savings, FSB CRLD
211 Montague Street
Brooklyn, NY 11201 (718) 780-0400
banking

Crown Auto, Inc. CRNI
7550 Corporate Way
Eden Prairie, MN 55344 (612) 831-5232
auto parts retailing

Crown Books Corporation CRWN
3300 75th Avenue
Landover, MD 20785 (301) 731-1200
book retailing

Crump Companies, Inc. (The) CRMP
P.O. Box 171377
Memphis, TN 38117 (901) 761-1550
insurance

Cullum Companies, Inc. CULL
14303 Inwood Road
Dallas, TX 75234 (214) 661-9700
food stores

Cullen/Frost Bankers, Inc. CFBI
100 West Houston Street
San Antonio, TX 78205 (512) 220-4011
banking

Culp, Inc. CULP
2020 Logan Street
High Point, NC 27263 (919) 889-5161
furniture

Custom Creamery Systems, Inc. OJAY
645 Madison Avenue
New York, NY 10022 (212) 308-6920
wholesale durable goods

Cycare Systems, Inc. CYCR
P.O. Box 1278
Dubuque, IA 52001 (319) 556-3131
software, data processing

Cypress Savings Association CYPS
One North University Drive
Plantation, FL 33324 (305) 474-2303
savings and loan

Cyprus Minerals Co. CYPM
7200 South Alton Way
Englewood, CO 80112 (303) 740-5000
hard coal mining

D' Lites of America, Inc. DLIT
6075 The Corners Pkwy.
Norcross, GA 30092 (404) 448-0654
restaurants

DBA Systems, Inc. DBAS
1103 West Hibiscus Blvd.
Melbourne, FL 32901 (305) 725-3711
aerospace systems analysis

DCNY Corp. DCNY
58 Pine Street
New York, NY 10005 (212) 248-8900
investment brokers and bankers

DDI Pharmaceuticals, Inc. DDIX
518 Logue Avenue
Mountain View, CA 94043 (415) 964-7676
drugs

DEP Corp. DEPC
2101 East Via Arado
Rancho Dominguez, CA 90220 (213) 604-0777
cosmetics and personal care

DH Technology, Inc. DHTK
575 Maude Court
Sunnyvale, CA 94086 (408) 738-2082
computer equipment

DICKEY-John Corp. DKJC
15½ Country Club Road
Auburn, IL 62615 (217) 438-3371
electronic equipment

DNA Plant Technology Corp. DNAP
2611 Branch Pike
Cinnaminson, NJ 08077 (609) 829-0110
biotechnology, food production

DSC Communications Corp. DIGI
707 East Arapaho Road
Richardson, TX 75083 (214) 238-4000
electronic communications equipment   [O]

D.O.C. Optics Corp. DOCO
19800 West Eight Mile Road
Southfield, MI 48075 (313) 354-7100
optical products retailing

Dahlberg, Inc. DAHL
7731 Country Club Drive
Minneapolis, MN 55427 (612) 545-3721
hearing aids

Dairy Mart Convenience Stores, Inc. DMCV
240 South Road
Enfield, CT 06082 (203) 745-1661
food stores

Daisy Systems Corp. DAZY
700 Middlefield Road
Mountain View, CA 94039 (415) 960-0123
computerized engineering systems

Damon Biotech, Inc. DBIO
119 Fourth Avenue
Needham Heights, MA 02194 (617) 449-6002
biotechnology, medical supplies

Danners, Inc. DNNR
P.O. Box 1146
Indianapolis, IN 46206 (317) 291-8011
retailing

Dart Group Corp. DRUG
3300 75th Avenue
Landover, MD 20785 (301) 731-1200
drug stores

Data Architects, Inc. DRCH
245 Winter Street
Waltham, MA 02154 (617) 890-7730
computer software

Data Card Corp. DATC
P.O. Box 9355
Minneapolis, MN 55440 (612) 933-1223
credit card processing equipment

Data I/O Corp. DAIO
10525 Willows Roads N.E.
Redmond, WA 98073 (206) 881-6444
software, data processing

Data Switch Corp. DASW
One Enterprise Drive
Shelton, CT 06484 (203) 926-1801
computer control systems

Datamarine International, Inc. DMAR
53 Portside Drive
Pocasset, MA 02559 (617) 563-7151
specialized computer equipment

Datapower, Inc. DPWR
3328 West First Street
Santa Ana, CA 92703 (714) 775-2000
computer equipment

Datascope Corp. DSCP
580 Winters Avenue
Paramus, NJ 07652 (201) 265-8800
medical instruments

Datasouth Computer Corp. DSCC
4216 Stuart Andrew Blvd.
Charlotte, NC 28210 (704) 523-8500
computer equipment

Datron Systems, Inc. DTSI
200 West Los Angeles Avenue
Simi Valley, CA 93065 (805) 584-1717
electronic equipment

Datum, Inc. DATM
1363 South State College
Anaheim, CA 92806 (714) 533-6333
scientific instruments

Dauphin Deposit Corp. DAPN
P.O. Box 2961
Harrisburg, PA 17105 (717) 255-2121
banking

Davis Water & Waste Industries, Inc. DWWS
P. O. Box 1419
Thomasville, GA 31792 (912) 226-5733
pollution control equipment

Dawson Geophysical Co. DWSN
208 South Marienfeld
Midland, TX 79701 (915) 682-7356
oil and gas services

Daxor Corp. DAXR
645 Madison Avenue
New York, NY 10022 (212) 935-1430
human sperm bank

Days Inns Corp. DAYS
2751 Buford Hwy., N.E.
Atlanta, GA 30324 (404) 325-4000
lodging

Deb Shops, Inc. DEBS
9401 Blue Grass Road
Philadelphia, PA 19114 (215) 676-6000
apparel stores

Decision Data Computer Corp. DDCC
400 Horsham Road
Horsham, PA 19044 (215) 674-3300
computer equipment

Decom Systems, Inc. DSII
340 Rancheros Drive
San Marcos, CA 92069 (619) 744-1002
electronic equipment, aerospace parts

Decor Corp. DCOR
1519 South Alum Creek Drive
Columbus, OH 43209 (614) 258-2871
luxury and recreation products

De Kalb AgResearch, Inc. DKLB
3100 Sycamore Road
De Kalb, IL 60115 (815) 758-3461
hybrid seeds, farm products

Delchamps, Inc. DLCH
305 Delchamps
Mobile, AL 36633 (205) 433-0431
food stores

Delta Data Systems Corp. DDSC
2595 Metropolitan Drive
Trevose, PA 19047 (215) 322-5400
computer equipment

Delta Natural Gas Co., Inc. DGAS
Route 1, Box 30-A
Winchester, KY 40391 (606) 744-6171
utility

Deltak Corp. DLTK
P. O. Box 9496
Minneapolis, MN 55440 (612) 544-3371
electrical equipment

Delta U.S. Corp. DLTA
InterFirst Plaza Tower, P. O. Box 2012
Tyler, TX 75702 (214) 595-7700
oil and gas services

Dento-Med Industries, Inc. DTMD
1680 N.E. 205 Terrace
N. Miami Beach, FL 33179 (305) 652-9766
dental instruments

Deposit Guaranty Corp. DEPS
210 East Capitol Street
Jackson, MS 39201 (601) 354-8564
banking   [DRP]

Designhouse International, Inc. DHIN
6348 Dawson Blvd.
Norcross, GA 30093 (404) 449-6636
furniture stores

Detector Electronics Corp. DETX
6901 West 110th Street
Minneapolis, MN 55438 (612) 941-5665
fire detection systems

Detrex Chemical Industries, Inc. DTRX
4000 Town Center
Southfield, MI 48075 (313) 358-5800
specialty chemicals

Detroit & Northern Savings, F.A. DNSF
400 Quincy Street
Hancock, MI 49930 (906) 482-2700
savings and loan

DeVry, Inc. DVRY
2201 West Howard Street
Evanston, IL 60202 (312) 328-8100
educational services

Dewey Electronics Corp. (The) DEWY
27 Muller Road
Oakland, NJ 07436 (201) 337-4700
electronic machinery and light equipment

Diagnostic Products Corp. DPCZ
5700 West 96th Street
Los Angeles, CA 90045 (213) 776-0180
medical supplies

Diamond Crystal Salt Co. DSLT
916 South Riverside Avenue
St. Clair, MI 48079 (313) 329-2211
salt, condiments

Diasonics, Inc. DNIC
1708 McCarthy Blvd.
Milpitas, CA 95035 (408) 946-9001
health services, supplies

Dibrell Bros., Inc. DBRL
512 Bridge Street
Danville, VA 24541 (804) 792-7511
tobacco products

Diceon Electronics, Inc. DICN
2500 Michelson Drive
Irvine, CA 92714 (714) 833-0870
electronic circuit boards

Dicomed Corp. DCOM
12000 Portland Avenue South
Minneapolis, MN 55440 (612) 885-3000
computer output microfilm

Digilog, Inc. DILO
1370 Welsh Road
Montgomeryville, PA 18936 (215) 628-4530
electronic equipment

Digital Communications Associates, Inc. DCAI
1000 Alderman Drive
Alpharetta, GA 30201 (404) 442-4000
computer communications networks

Dinner Bell Foods, Inc. DINB
P.O. Box 388
Defiance, OH 43512 (419) 782-9015
meat products

Dionex Corp. DNEX
1228 Titan Way
Sunnyvale, CA 94086 (408) 737-0700
chromatography systems

Dionics, Inc. DION
65 Rushmore Street
Westbury, NY 11590 (516) 997-7474
electronics

Distributed Logic Corp. DLOG
1555 South Sinclair Street
Anaheim, CA 92806 (714) 937-5700
electronic equipment

Diversified Human Resources Group, Inc. HIRE
15400 Knoll Trail Drive, #212
Dallas, TX 75248 (214) 980-0071
business services

Divi Hotels, N.V. DIVH
520 West State Street
Ithaca, NY 14850 (607) 277-3484
lodging

Dixon Ticonderoga Co. DIXY
P.O. Box 3504
Vero Beach, FL 32960 (305) 231-3190
writing products, real estate

Dollar General Coporation DOLR
427 Beech Street
Scottsville, KY 42164 (502) 237-5444
general merchandise retailing

Dominion Bankshares Corp. DMBK
213 South Jefferson Street
Roanoke, VA 24040 (703) 563-7000
banking   [DRP 5%]

Donovan Companies, Inc. DONO
1080 Montreal Avenue
St. Paul, MN 55116 (612) 690-1761
utility

Dorchester Hugoton, Ltd. DHUL
9708 Skillman Street
Dallas, TX 75243 (214) 739-2002
oil and gas

Douglas & Lomason Co. DOUG
24600 Hallwood Court
Farmington Hills, MI 48018 (313) 478-7800
auto parts

Doyle Dane Bernbach Group, Inc DOYL
437 Madison Avenue
New York, NY 10022 (212) 415-2000
advertising

Dranetz Technologies, Inc. DRAN
1000 New Durham Road
Edison, NJ 08818 (201) 287-3680
electrical test instruments

Dresher, Inc. DRES
7200 South Mason
Chicago, IL 60638 (312) 594-8900
furniture

Dress Barn (The) DBRN
88 Hamilton Avenue
Stamford, CT 06902 (203) 327-4242
apparel stores

Drew Industries Inc. DRWI
200 Mamaroneck Avenue
White Plains, NY 10601 (914) 428-9098
finished metal

Drexler Techology Corp. DRXR
2557 Charleston Road
Mountain View, CA 94043 (415) 969-7277
plastic card-making electronic equipment

Dreyer's Grand Ice Cream, Inc. DRYR
5929 College Avenue
Oakland, CA 94618 (415) 652-8187
dairy products

Dual Lite Inc. DUAL
63 South Main Street
Newtown, CT 06470 (203) 426-8011
lighting equipment

Dumagami Mines Ltd. DMGI
401 Bay Street, Suite 1612
Toronto, Ont. M5H 2Y4 (416) 947-1212
metal mining

Dunkin' Donuts Inc. DUNK
P.O. Box 317
Randolph, MA 02368 (617) 961-4000
restaurants   [DRP]

Duquesne Systems, Inc. DUQN
Two Allegheny Center
Pittsburgh, PA 15212 (412) 323-2600
software, data processing

Durakon Industries, Inc. DRKN
2101 N. Lapeer Road
Lapeer, MI 48446 (313) 664-0850
auto parts, accessories

Durham Corp. DUCO
P.O. Box 27807
Raleigh, NC 27611 (919) 782-6110
insurance

Duriron Co., Inc. (The) DURI
425 North Findlay Street
Dayton, OH 45404 (513) 226-4000
processing equipment   [DRP]

Durr-Fillauer Medical, Inc. DUFM
P.O. Box 951
Montgomery, AL 36192 (205) 271-3512
medical supplies

Dycom Industries, Inc. DYCO
450 Australia Avenue South
West Palm Beach, FL 33401 (305) 659-6301
financial services

Dynamics Research Corp. DRCO
60 Concord Street
Wilmington, MA 01887 (617) 658-6100
computer services, encoders

Dynascan Corp. DYNA
6460 West Cortland Street
Chicago, IL 60635 (312) 889-8870
communications equipment

Dynatech Corp. DYTC
3 New England Executive Park
Burlington, MA 01803 (617) 272-3304
medical laboratory products

E'Town Corp. EWAT
One Elizabethtown Plaza
Elizabeth, NJ 07202 (201) 354-4444
utility   [DRP]

E-H International, Inc. EHIL
696 East Trimble Road
San Jose, CA 95131 (408) 946-9100
electronic testing equipment

E-Z-EM, Inc. EZEM
7 Portland Avenue
Westbury, NY 11590 (516) 333-8230
health services, supplies

ECI Telecom Ltd. ECIL
88, Yigal Allon Street
Tel-Aviv, Israel 67891 (972) 333-3241
computers, communications equipment

E.I.L. Instruments, Inc. EILI
10 Loveton Circle
Sparks, MD 21152 (301) 771-4800
electronic equipment distribution

EIP Microwave, Inc. EIPM
4500 Campus Drive
Newport Beach, CA 92660 (714) 540-6655
microwave test equipment

EMC Insurance Group, Inc. EMCI
717 Mulberry Street
Des Moines, IA 50309 (515) 280-2587
insurance

EMF Corp. EMFC
15110 N.E. 95th Street
Redmond, WA 98052 (206) 883-0045
paper-sorting machinery

EPSCO, Inc. EPSC
411 Providence Hwy.
Westwood, MA 02090 (617) 329-1500
electronic equipment

Eagle Telephonics, Inc. EGLA
375 Oser Avenue
Hauppauge, NY 11788 (516) 273-6700
communications equipment

Early California Industries, Inc. ERLY
10960 Wilshire Blvd.
Los Angeles, CA 90024 (213) 879-1480
food products

Eastmet Corp. EMET
P.O. Box 1975
Baltimore, MD 21203 (301) 522-6200
iron and steel

Eastover Corp. EAST
P.O. Box 22728
Jackson, MS 39225 (601) 948-4091
investment services

Eaton Financial Corp. EATO
27 Hollis Street
Framingham, MA 01701 (617) 620-0099
computer leasing

Eaton Vance Corp. EAVN
24 Federal Street
Boston, MA 02110 (617) 482-8260
investments

Economics Laboratory, Inc. ECON
Osborn Bldg., 370 Wabasha
St. Paul, MN 55102 (612) 293-2233
specialty chemicals   [DRP]

Edgcomb Steel of New England, Inc. ESNE
385 West Hollis Street
Nashua, NH 03061 (603) 883-7731
metals fabrication

Edison Sault Electric Co. EDSE
725 East Portage Avenue
Sault Ste. Marie, MI 49783 (906) 632-2221
utility

El Chico Corp. ELCH
12200 Stemmons Freeway
Dallas, TX 75234 (214) 241-5500
restaurants

El Paso Electric Co. ELPA
P.O. Box 982
El Paso, TX 79960 (915) 543-5958
utility   [DRP]

Elan Corp., PLC ELAN
1300 Gould Drive
Gainesville, GA 30501 (404) 534-8239
drugs

Elbit Computers Ltd. ELBT
Advanced Technology Center
Haifa 31053, Israel
computers, data processing

Elco Industries, Inc. ELCN
1111 Samuelson Road
Rockford, IL 61125 (815) 397-5151
fasteners, stampings

Elder-Beerman Stores Corp. (The) ELDR
3155 Elbee Road
Dayton, OH 45439 (513) 296-2700
general merchandise stores

Eldon Industries, Inc. ELDN
9920 Lacienega Blvd.
Inglewood, CA 90301 (213) 642-7716
office equipment

Eldorado Bancorp ELDB
24012 Calle da la Plata
Laguna Hills, CA 92653 (714) 830-8800
banking

Eldorado Motor Corp. EDMC
P.O. Box 266
Minneapolis, KS 67467 (913) 392-2171
transportation equipment

Electro Rent Corp. ELRC
3340 Ocean Park Blvd.
Santa Monica, CA 90405 (213) 452-3200
leases electronic equipment

Electro Scientific Industries, Inc. ESIO
13500 N.W. Science Park Drive
Portland, OR 97229 (503) 641-4141
laser scientific instruments

Electro-Biology, Inc. EBII
Calle Box EBI
Guaynabo, Puerto Rico 00657 (809) 790-6855
bone fracture medical devices

Electro-Catheter Corp. ECTH
2100 Felver Court
Rahway, NJ 07065 (201) 382-5600
medical supplies

Electro-Nucleonics, Inc. ENUC
350 Passaic Avenue
Fairfield, NJ 07006 (201) 227-6700
medical supplies, centrifuges

Electro-Sensors, Inc. ELSE
7251 Washington Avenue South
Minneapolis, MN 55435 (612) 941-8171
medical supplies

Electromagnetic Sciences, Inc. ELMG
125 Technical Park/Atlanta
Norcross, GA 30092 (404) 448-5770
microwave components

Electronic Tele-Communications Inc. ETCI
1915 MacArthur Road
Waukesha, WI 53188 (414) 542-5600
electronic communications equipment

Electronics, Missiles & Communications, Inc.
ECIN
P.O. Box 68
White Haven, PA 18661 (717) 443-9575
electronic tv equipment

Elron Electronic Industries, Ltd. ELRN
1211 Avenue of the Americas
New York, NY 10036 (212) 819-1644
electronic weapons systems

Emett and Chandler Companies, Inc. EMCC
1800 Avenue of the Stars
Los Angeles, CA 90067 (213) 553-4600
insurance brokers

Empi, Inc. EMPI
261 South Commerce Circle
Minneapolis, MN 55432 (612) 571-2855
medical supplies

EMS Systems, Ltd. EMSIF
4546 Beltway Drive
Dallas, TX 75244 (214) 991-9585
oil and gas, electronics

Emulex Corp. EMLX
3545 Harbor Blvd.
Costa Mesa, CA 92626 (714) 662-5600
computer disk and tape controllers

Encore Computer Corp. ENCC
One Federal Street
Boston, MA 02110 (617) 426-4600
computers

Endata, Inc. DATA
501 Great Circle Road
Nashville, TN 37228 (615) 244-0244
business data processing

Endo-Lase Inc. ENDL
10 Columbus Circle
New York, NY 10019 (212) 757-7800
medical lasers

Endotronics ENDO
8500 Evergreen Boulevard
Coon Rapids, MN 55433 (612) 786-0302
electronics

Energas Co. EGAS
301 Taylor Street
Amarillo, TX 79101 (806) 378-3370
utility

Energy Conversion Devices, Inc. ENER
1675 West Maple Road
Troy, MI 48084 (313) 280-1900
energy-saving electronic controls

Energy Factors, Inc. EFAC
1495 Pacific Hwy.
San Diego, CA 92101 (619) 239-9900
cogeneration systems

EnergyNorth, Inc. ENNI
1260 Elm Street
Manchester, NH 03105 (603) 625-4000
gas utility

Engineered Support Systems, Inc. EASI
1270 N. Price Road
St. Louis, MO 63132 (314) 993-5880
military systems

Engineering Measurements Co. EMCO
600 Diagonal Highway
Longmont, CO 80501 (303) 651-0550
flow measuring devices

Engraph, Inc. ENGH
Suite 900
Atlanta, GA 30345 (404) 329-0332
paper products   [DRP]

Entertainment Publications, Inc. EPUB
1400 North Woodward Avenue
Birmingham, MI 48011 (313) 642-8300
publishing

Entré Computer Centers, Inc. ETRE
1951 Kidwell Drive
Vienna, VA 22180 (703) 556-0800
computer retailing

Envirodyne Industies, Inc. ENVR
222 West Adams Street
Chicago, IL 60606 (312) 822-0030
plastic products

Environmental Processing, Inc. EPIC
1321 North Plano Road
Richardson, TX 75081 (214) 669-0830
electronics

Environmental Tectonics Corp. ENVT
County Line Industrial Park
Southampton, PA 18966 (215) 355-9100
waste measuring equipment

Enviromental Treatment & Certification Corp. ETCC
284 Raritan Center Pkwy.
Edison, NJ 08818 (201) 225-6700
waste management testing

Enzo Biochem, Inc. ENZO
325 Hudson Street
New York, NY 10013 (212) 741-3838
biotechnology, drugs

Epsilon Data Management, Inc. EPSI
50 Cambridge Street
Burlington, MA 01803 (617) 273-0250
computer-based marketing consultants

Equatorial Communications Co. EQUA
189 North Bernardo Avenue
Mountain View, CA 94043 (415) 969-9500
communications equipment, earth stations

Equion Corp. (The) EQUI
Tapp Road
Harrodsburg, KY 40330 (606) 734-7178
machinery

Equitable Bancorporation EBNC
100 South Charles Center
Baltimore, MD 21201 (301) 547-4395
banking

Equitable of Iowa Companies EQIC
P.O. Box 1635
Des Moines, IA 50306 (515) 245-6911
insurance

Equity Oil Co. EQTY
10 West 3rd South, Suite 806
Salt Lake City, UT 84110 (801) 521-3515
oil and gas

Erb Lumber Co. ERBL
375 South Eton Road
Birmingham, MI 48012 (313) 644-5300
building materials

Ericsson Telephone Co. (L.M.) ERIC
Dept-DJF
Stockholm, Sweden
communications equipment

Erie Lackawanna, Inc. ERIE
1302 Midland Bldg.
Cleveland, OH 44115 (216) 621-4617
investment company

Essex Corp. ESEX
333 North Fairfax Street
Alexandria, VA 22314 (703) 548-4500
business services

Evans & Sutherland Computer Corp. ESCC
580 Arapeen Drive
Salt Lake City, UT 84108 (801) 582-5847
computer graphic systems

Evans, Inc. EVAN
36 South State Street
Chicago, IL 60603 (312) 855-2000
apparel stores

Evergood Products Corp. EVGD
175 Lauman Lane
Hicksville, NY 11801 (516) 822-1230
retail food stores

Exchange International Corp. EXCG
120 South LaSalle Street
Chicago, IL 60603 (312) 781-8000
banking

Exovir, Inc. XOVR
111 Great Neck Road
Great Neck, NY 11021 (516) 466-2110
health services, supplies

Expeditors International of Washington, Inc.
EXPD
2013 Third Street
Seattle, WA 98121 (206) 343-5111
freight and shipping

Exposaic Industries, Inc. EXPO
180 West Independence Blvd.
Mount Airy, NC 27030 (919) 786-2141
building materials, cement

F & M National Corp. FMNT
38 Rouss Avenue
Winchester, VA 22601 (703) 665-4200
banking

FDP Corp. FDPC
2140 South Dixie Hwy.
Miami, FL 33133 (305) 858-8200
software, data processing

FMI Financial Corp. FMIF
31 Ocean Reef Drive
Key Largo, FL 33037 (305) 532-7361
insurance

Fabric Wholesalers, Inc. FBRC
2035 N.E. 181st Avenue
Portland, OR 97230 (503) 666-4511
textile retailing

Fair Lanes, Inc. FAIR
1112 North Rolling Road
Baltimore, MD 21228 (301) 788-6300
bowling centers, restaurants

Famous Restaurants, Inc. FAMS
4455 East Camelback Road
Phoenix, AZ 85018 (602) 840-8001
restaurants

Faraday Labs., Inc. FDLB
100 Hoffman Place
Hillside, NJ 07205 (201) 375-3304
chemical products

Farm & Home Savings Association FAHS
221 West Cherry
Nevada, MO 64772 (417) 667-3333
savings and loan

Farm Fresh, Inc. FFSH
3487 Inventors Road
Norfolk, VA 23501 (804) 853-7461
food stores

Farm House Foods Corp. FHFC
111 East Wisconsin Avenue
Milwaukee, WI 53202 (414) 271-5050
wholesale food distributor, drugstores

Farmer Bros. Co. FARM
20333 South Normandie Avenue
Torrance, CA 90502 (213) 320-1212
grocery wholesalers

Farmers Group, Inc. FGRP
4680 Wilshire Blvd.
Los Angeles, CA 90010 (213) 932-3200
insurance

Farr Co. FARC
2301 Rosecrans Avenue
El Segundo, CA 90245 (213) 772-5221
filtration equipment

Federal Screw Works FSCR
3401 Martin Avenue
Detroit, MI 48210 (313) 841-8400
auto parts

Federated Group, Inc. (The) FEGP
5655 East Union Pacific Avenue
City of Commerce, CA 90022 (213) 728-5100
home-entertainment products

Federated Guaranty Corp. FDGC
P.O. Box 11000
Montgomery, AL 36198 (205) 288-3900
insurance

Ferrofluidics Corp. FERO
40 Simon Street
Nashua, NH 03061 (603) 883-9800
computer equipment

Fibronics International, Inc. FBRX
325 Stevens Street
Hyannis, MA 02601 (617) 778-0700
communications, fiber optics

Fidelcor, Inc. FICR
1200 East Lancaster Avenue
Rosemont, PA 19010 (215) 527-1410
banking

Fidelity Federal S&L Association FFED
6958 Torresdale Avenue
Philadelphia, Pa 19135 (215) 624-9000
savings and loan

Fifth Third Bancorp FITB
38 Fountain Square Plaza
Cincinnati, OH 45263 (513) 579-5300
banking   [DRP]

Figgie Intern'l Holdings, Inc. FIGI
1000 Virginia Center Parkway
Richmond, VA 23295 (804) 264-5600
diversified manufacturing

Filtertek, Inc. FILT
P.O. Box 135
Hebron, IL 60034 (815) 648-2416
filters

Finalco Group, Inc. FLCO
8200 Greensboro Drive
McLean, VA 22102 (703) 790-0970
data processing equipment

Financial News Network, Inc. FNNI
2525 Ocean Park Blvd.
Santa Monica, CA 90405 (213) 450-2412
broadcasting

Financial Security S&L Association FSSL
100 East Linton Blvd.
Del Ray Beach, FL 33444 (305) 276-8900
savings and loan

Financial Trust Corp. FITC
1 West High Street
Carlisle, PA 17013 (717) 243-3212
financial services

Fingermatrix, Inc. FINX
30 Virginia Road
North White Plains, NY 10603 (914) 428-5441
anti-theft machinery

Finnigan Corp. FNNG
355 River Oaks Pkwy.
San Jose, CA 95134 (408) 946-4848
scientific instruments

First Alabama Bancshares, Inc. FABC
P.O. Box 1448
Montgomery, AL 36102 (205) 832-8490
banking   [DRP]

First Albany Companies, Inc. FACT
41 State Street
Albany, NY 12207 (518) 447-8500
securities brokerage

First Amarillo Bancorporation, Inc. FAMA
P.O. Box 1331
Amarillo, TX 79180 (806) 378-1870
banking

First of America Bank Corp. FABK
108 East Michigan Avenue
Kalamazoo, MI 49007 (616) 383-9000
banking   [DRP 5%]

First American Bank and Trust FIAM
401 Northlake Blvd.
North Palm Beach, FL 33408 (305) 863-9800
banking   [DRP 5%]

First American Corp. FATN
First American Center
Nashville, TN 37237 (615) 748-2000
banking

First American Federal S&L Association FAMF
1900 Memorial Pkwy.
Huntsville, AL 35801 (205) 539-5761
savings and loan

First American Financial Corp. (The) FAMR
114 East Fifth Street
Santa Ana, CA 92701 (714) 558-3211
insurance

First Bancorporation of Ohio FBOH
106 South Main Street
Akron, OH 44308 (216) 384-8000
banking   [DRP]

First Capital Corp. FCAP
248 East Capitol Street
Jackson, MS 39205 (601) 354-5111
banking

First Colonial Bankshares Corp. FCOL
5850 West Belmont Avenue
Chicago, IL 60634 (312) 283-3700
banking

First Columbia Financial Corp. FCLF
5850 DTC Pkwy. Bldg. #14
Englewood, CO 80111 (303) 773-3444
financial services, real estate

First Commerce Corp. FCOM
210 Baronne Street
New Orleans, LA 70112 (504) 561-1371
banking   [DRP]

First Commercial Bancorp FCOB
550 J Street
Sacramento, CA 95814 (916) 447-7700
banking

First Commercial Corp. FCLR
P.O. Box 1471
Little Rock, AR 72203 (501) 371-7000
banking

First Connecticut Bancorp, Inc. FCBC
101 Pearl Street
Hartford, CT 06103 (203) 241-2400
banking

First Continental REIT FCRE
1360 Post Oak Blvd.
Houston, TX 77056 (713) 622-2084
real estate

First Eastern Corp. FEBC
11 West Market Street
Wilkes-Barre, PA 18768 (717) 826-4600
banking

First Empire State Corp. FEMP
One M&T Plaza
Buffalo, NY 14240 (716) 842-5445
banking   [DRP]

First Executive Corp. FEXC
P.O. Box 6090
Inglewood, CA 90312 (213) 273-4202
insurance

First Farwest Corp. FFWS
400 South West Sixth Avenue
Portland, OR 97204 (503) 222-0339
insurance

First Federal Bank, FSB FFBN
223 Main Street
Nashua, NH 03060 (603) 889-2123
banking

First Federal of Michigan FFOM
1001 Woodward Avenue
Detroit, MI 48226 (313) 965-1400
savings and loan

First Federal Savings, F.A. FFSA
1201 Boston Post Road
Westbrook, CT 06443 (203) 399-7901
savings and loan

First Federal Savings Bank of California FFSB
401 Wilshire Blvd.
Santa Monica, CA 90401 (213) 458-3011
banking

First Federal Savings Bank of Montana FFSM
202 Main Street
Kalispell, MT 59901 (406) 755-7101
banking

First Federal S&L Association of Brooksville FFBV
201 North Howell Avenue
Brooksville, FL 33512 (904) 796-6751
savings and loan

First Federal S&L Association of Charleston FFCH
34 Broad Street
Charleston, SC 29401 (803) 724-0800
savings and loan

First Federal S&L Association of Fort Myers FFMY
2201 Second Street
Fort Myers, FL 33901 (813) 334-4106
savings and loan

First Federal S&L Association of Kalamazoo FFKZ
346 West Michigan Avenue
Kalamazoo, MI 49007 (616) 342-7200
savings and loan

First Federal S&L Association of Roanoke
FFSL
36 West Church Avenue
Roanoke, VA 24011 (703) 345-1535
·savings and loan

First Federal S&L Association of SC FTSC
301 College Street
Greenville, SC 29601 (803) 271-7222
savings and loan

First Financial Bancorp FFBC
108 South Main Street
Monroe, OH 45050 (513) 867-4700
banking

First Financial Corp. FFHC
1305 Main Street
Stevens Point, WI 54481 (715) 341-0400
savings and loan

First Financial Management Corp. FFMC
3 Corporate Square
Atlanta, GA 30329 (404) 321-0120
financial data processing

First Florida Banks, Inc. FFBK
First Florida Tower
Tampa, FL 33601 (813) 224-1455
banking

First Hawaiian, Inc. FHWN
165 South King Street
Honolulu, HI 96813 (808) 525-7000
banking

First Illinois Corp. FTIL
800 Davis Street
Evanston, IL 60204 (312) 866-6000
banking

First Indiana Federal Savings Bank FISB
One North Pennsylvania Street
Indianapolis, IN 46204 (317) 269-1200
savings and loan

First Interstate Corp. of Alaska FIBK
716 West Fourth Avenue
Anchorage, AK 99501 (907) 276-7200
banking

First Interstate Corp. of Wisconsin FIWI
636 Wisconsin Avenue
Sheboygan, WI 53081 (414) 459-2000
banking

First Interstate of Iowa, Inc. FIIA
900 United Central Bank Bldg.
Des Moines, IA 50309 (515) 245-7134
banking

First Jersey National Corp. FJNC
Two Montgomery Street
Jersey City, NJ 07302 (201) 547-7000
banking   [DRP 5%]

First Kentucky National Corp. FKYN
101 South Fifth Street
Louisville, KY 40202 (502) 581-4498
banking   [DRP]

First Maryland Bancorp FMDB
25 South Charles Street
Baltimore, MD 21201 (301) 244-4000
banking

First Michigan Bank Corp. FMBC
101 East Main Street
Zeeland, MI 49464 (616) 396-9245
banking

First Midwest Bancorp, Inc. FMBI
1230 East Diehl Road
Naperville, IL 60566 (815) 727-4545
banking

First Midwest Corp. FMWC
1010 Plymouth Bldg.
Minneapolis, MN 55402 (612) 339-9391
financial services

First Mutual Savings Association of Florida FMSA
70 North Baylen street
Pensacola, FL 32501 (904) 434-1361
savings and loan

First NH Banks, Inc. FINH
1000 Elm Street
Manchester, NH 03101 (603) 668-5020
banking   [DRP]

First National Bancorp (of Gainesville) FBAC
111 Green Street, N.E.
Gainesville, GA 30503 (404) 535-5500
banking

First National Cincinnati Corp. FNAC
425 Walnut Street
Cincinnati, OH 45201 (513) 632-4000
banking   [DRP]

First National Corp. FNBC
401 West A Street
San Diego, CA 92101 (619) 233-5588
banking

First National Corp. FTNC
2011 Riverside Drive
Columbus, OH 43221 (614) 486-7114
restaurants

First Northern S&L Association FNGB
P.O. Box 100
Green Bay, WI 54305 (414) 437-7101
savings and loan

First Ohio Bancshares Inc. FIRO
606 Madison Avenue
Toledo, OH 43604 (419) 259-6960
banking

First Oklahoma Bancorporation, Inc. FOKL
P.O. Box 25189
Oklahoma City, OK 73125 (405) 272-4942
banking

First Railroad & Banking Co. of GA FRRG
699 Broad Street
Augusta, GA 30913 (404) 823-2753
banking

First Savings Bank of Florida, FSB FSBF
101 Federal Place
Tarpon Springs, FL 33589 (813) 934-5721
banking

First Security Corp. FSCO
79 South Main
Salt Lake City, UT 84130 (801) 350-5325
banking   [DRP 5%]

First Security Corp. of Kentucky FSKY
One First Security Plaza
Lexington, KY 40507 (606) 231-1000
banking

1st Source Corp. SRCE
100 North Michigan Street
South Bend, IN 46601 (219) 236-2000
banking

First Southern Federal S&L Association FSFA
First Southern Federal Tower
Mobile, AL 36606 (205) 473-0500
savings and loan

First Tennessee National Corp. FTEN
165 Madison Avenue
Memphis, TN 38103 (901) 523-4161
banking   [DRP]

First Union Corp. FUNC
First Union Plaza
Charlotte, NC 28288 (704) 374-6565
banking   [DRP 5%]

First United Bancshares, Inc. UNTD
Main and Washington Streets
El Dorado, AR 71730 (501) 863-3181
banking

First United Financial Services, Inc. FUFS
111 East Busse Avenue
Mount Prospect, IL 60056 (312) 398-4000
financial services

First Valley Corp. FIVC
One Bethlehem Plaza
Bethlehem, PA 18018 (215) 865-8411
banking

First Vermont Financial Corp. FIVT
215 Main Street
Brattleboro, VT 05301 (802) 254-8711
banking

First Western Financial Corp. FWES
P.O. Box 18430
Las Vegas, NV 89114 (702) 871-2000
savings and loan

Firstier, Inc. FRST
Farnam at Seventeenth
Omaha, NE 68102 (402) 348-6000
banking, travel agency

Flagler Bank Corp. (The) FLGL
Flagler Center
West Palm Beach, FL 33401 (305) 659-2265
banking

Flakey Jake's, Inc. FJAK
15375 S.E. 30th Place
Bellevue, WA 98007 (206) 644-9467
restaurants

Flexsteel Industries, Inc. FLXS
P.O. Box 877
Dubuque, IA 52001 (319) 556-7730
furniture

Florafax International, Inc. FIIF
4175 South Memorial Drive
Tulsa, OK 74145 (918) 622-8415
flower marketing

Florida Commercial Banks, Inc. FLBK
950 S.W. 57th Avenue
Miami, FL 33144 (305) 266-2600
banking

Florida Federal S&L Association FLFE
360 Central Avenue
St. Petersburg, FL 33701 (813) 893-1131
savings and loan

Florida National Banks of Florida, Inc. FNBF
214 Hogan Street, P.O. Box 689
Jacksonville, FL 32201 (904) 359-5111
banking   [DRP 5%]

Florida Public Utilities Co. FPUT
401 South Dixie Hwy.
West Palm Beach, FL 33402 (305) 832-2461
utility

Flow Systems, Inc. FLOW
21440 68th Avenue South
Kent, WA 98032 (206) 938-3569
waterjet cutting systems

Fluorocarbon Co. (The) FCBN
27611 La Paz Road
Laguna Niguel, CA 92677 (714) 831-5350
rubber and plastic products

Fonar Corp. FONR
110 Marcus Drive
Melville, NY 11747 (516) 694-2929
medical equipment

Food Lion, Inc. FDLN
P.O. Box 1330
Salisbury, NC 28145 (704) 633-8250
food stores

Foremost Corp. of America FCOA
P.O. Box 2450
Grand Rapids, MI 49501 (616) 942-3233
insurance

Forest Oil Corp. FOIL
78 Main Street
Bradford, PA 16701 (814) 368-7171
oil and gas

Forschner Group, Inc. (The) FSNR
151 Long Hill Crossroads
Shelton, CT 06484 (203) 929-6391
housewares

Fortune Financial Group, Inc. FORF
2120 U.S. 19 South
Clearwater, FL 33546 (813) 538-1000
savings and loan

Fortune Systems Corp. FSYS
300 Harbor Blvd.
Belmont, CA 94002 (415) 593-9000
computers

Forum Group, Inc. FOUR
8900 Keystone Crossing
Indianapolis, IN 46240 (317) 846-0700
health services

Foster (L.B.) Co. FSTR
415 Holiday Drive
Pittsburgh, PA 15220 (412) 928-3400
railroad, construction equipment

Franklin Corp. FKLN
1185 Avenue of the Americas
New York, NY 10036 (212) 719-4844
financial services

Franklin Electric Co., Inc. FELE
400 East Spring Street
Bluffton, IN 46714 (219) 824-2900
electrical equipment

Franklin Resources, Inc. FRRI
777 Mariners Island Boulevard
San Mateo, CA 94404 (415) 570-3000
investment services, mutual funds

Freedom Federal Savings Bank FRFE
600 Hunter Drive
Oak Brook, IL 60521 (312) 789-1075
banking

Freedom S&L Association FRDM
P.O. Box 24024
Tampa, FL 33630 (813) 870-5000
savings and loan

Fremont General Corp. FRMT
525 South Virgil Avenue
Los Angeles, CA 90020 (213) 483-0991
insurance, health services

Frost & Sullivan, Inc. FRSL
106 Fulton Street
New York, NY 10038 (212) 233-1080
industry reports

Frozen Food Express Industries, Inc. FEXP
318 Cadiz Street
Dallas, TX 75207 (214) 428-7661
trucking

Fuddruckers, Inc. FUDD
Suite 700, Lincoln Center
San Antonio, TX 78230 (512) 366-4481
restaurants

Fuller (H. B.) Co. FULL
2400 Kasota Avenue
St. Paul, MN 55108 (612) 481-1588
specialty chemicals   [DRP]

Fulton Financial Corp. FULT
One Penn Square
Lancaster, PA 17604 (717) 291-2411
financial services

FundsNet, Inc. FNET
385 Nordhoff Place
Englewood, NJ 07631 (201) 569-7764
financial computer transactions

Funtime, Inc. FNTM
1060 Aurora Road
Aurora, OH 44202 (216) 562-7131
amusement

G&K Services, Inc. GKSR
400 South County Road 18
Minneapolis, MN 55426 (612) 546-7440
textiles

GNI, Inc. GNUC
202 Medical Center Blvd.
Webster, TX 77598 (713) 332-3581
electronic machinery

GTECH Corp. GTCH
101 Dyer Street
Providence, RI 02903 (401) 273-7700
lottery computer systems

GTS Corp. GTSC
16801 Greenspoint Park Drive
Houston, TX 77060 (713) 874-9300
oil and gas services

GWC Corp. GWCC
3219 Philadelphia Pike
Claymont, DE 19703 (302) 798-3883
utility

Galactic Resources Ltd. GALC
Ste. #935, 355 Burrard Street
Vancouver, B.C. V6C 2G8   (604) 687-7169
metal mining

Galileo Electro-Optics Corp. GAEO
Galileo Park
Sturbridge, MA 01518 (617) 347-9191
precision instruments and photography

Arthur J. Gallagher & Co. AJGC
10 Gould Center
Rolling Meadows, IL 60008 (312) 640-8500
insurance sales

Lewis Galoob Toys, Inc. GATO
500 Forbes Blvd.
South San Francisco, CA 94080 (415) 952-1678
toys

Gamma Biologicals, Inc. GAMA
3700 Mangum Road
Houston, TX 77092 (713) 681-8481
medical supplies

Gandalf Technologies Inc. GAND
9 Slack Road
Nepean, Ont. K2B 0B7 (613) 225-0565
communications equipment

Gateway Bank GTWY
50 Main Street
South Norwalk, CT 06856 (203) 853-2265
banking

Genentech, Inc. GENE
460 Point San Bruno Blvd.
South San Francisco, CA 94080 (415) 952-1000
biotechnology, drugs   [O]

General Binding Corp. GBND
One GBC Plaza
Northbrook, IL 60062 (312) 272-3700
office machines and supplies

General Ceramics, Inc. GCER
Greenwood Avenue
Haskell, NJ 07420 (201) 839-1600
specialty containers

Gen. Magnaplate Corp. GMCC
1331 U.S. Route One
Linden, NJ 07036 (201) 862-6200
coatings

General Physics Corp. GPHY
10650 Hickory Ridge Road
Columbia, MD 21044 (301) 964-6000
trains electric co. personnel

General Shale Products Corp. GSHL
P.O. Box 3547, CRS
Johnson City, TN 37601 (615) 282-4661
building materials   [DRP]

Genetic Engineering, Inc. GEEN
P.O. Box 33554
Denver, CO 80233 (303) 457-1311
biotechnology, agricultural products

Genetic Labs., Inc. GENL
1385 Centennial Drive
St. Paul, MN 55113 (612) 636-4112
biotechnology

Geneve Capital Group, Inc. GCGI
485 Madison Avenue
New York, NY 10022 (212) 355-4141
insurance

Genex Corp. GNEX
16020 Industrial Drive
Gaithersburg, MD 20877 (301) 258-0552
biotechology, drugs

Genova, Inc. GNVA
7034 East Court Street
Davison, MI 48423 (313) 744-4500
building materials, plumbing and heating

Georgia Bonded Fibers, Inc. GBFH
P.O. Box 751
Buena Vista, VA 24416 (703) 261-2181
leather products

Georgia Federal Bank, FSB GFED
P.O. Box 1723
Atlanta, GA 30301 (404) 588-2600
banking

Geriatric & Medical Centers, Inc. GEMC
63rd and Walnut Streets
Philadelphia, PA 19139 (215) 476-2250
health services

Germania F.A. GMFD
543 East Broadway
Alton, IL 62002 (618) 465-5543
savings and loan

Gibson (The C. R.) Co. GIBS
32 Knight Street
Norwalk, CT 06856 (203) 847-4543
stationery

Gibson Greetings, Inc. GIBG
2100 Section Road
Cincinnati, OH 45237 (513) 841-6600
printing, greeting cards

Giga-Tronics Inc. GIGA
2495 Estand Way
Pleasant Hill, CA 94523 (415) 680-8160
electronic equipment

Gilbert Associates, Inc. GILB
P.O. Box 1498
Reading, PA 19603 (215) 775-2600
engineering and consulting services

Godfrey Co. GDFY
1200 West Sunset Drive
Waukesha, WI 53187 (414) 542-9311
food wholesaler and retailer   [DRP]

Golden Corral Realty Corp. GCRA
5151 Glenwood Avenue
Raleigh, NC 27612 (919) 781-5310
real estate

Golden Enterprises, Inc. GLDC
2101 Magnolia Avenue
Birmingham, AL 35205 (205) 326-6101
food products

Good Guys (The), Inc. GGUY
601 Van Ness Avenue
San Francisco, CA 94102 (415) 885-2121
retailing

GoodMark Foods, Inc. GDMK
4909 Windy Hill Drive
Raleigh, NC 27609 (919) 872-2880
food products

Goody Products, Inc. GOOD
969 Newark Turnpike
Kearny, NJ 07032 (201) 997-3000
personal-care products

Gotaas-Larsen Shipping Corp. GOTL
The Perry Bldg.
Hamilton 5-24, Bermuda (809) 295-3457
shipping

Goulds Pumps, Inc. GULD
240 Fall Street
Seneca Falls, NY 13148 (315) 568-2811
water pumps   [DRP]

Graco, Inc. GRAC
4050 Olson Memorial Hwy.
Golden Valley, MN 55422 (612) 623-6000
lubricating, pumping equipment

Gradco Systems, Inc. GRCO
3421 West Segerstrom Avenue
Santa Ana, CA 92704 (714) 549-9175
business equipment

GranTree Corp. GTRE
2501 S.W. First Avenue
Portland, OR 97208 (503) 223-1161
furniture

Graphic Industries, Inc. GRPH
2155 Monroe Drive, N.E.
Atlanta, GA 30324 (404) 874-3327
printing

Graphic Media, Inc. GMED
373 Route 46 West
Fairfield, NJ 07006 (201) 227-5000
printing

Graphic Scanning Corp. GSCC
329 Alfred Avenue
Teaneck, NJ 07666 (201) 837-5100
communications

Gray and Co. Public Communications Int.
Inc. GRCM
The Power House
Washington, DC 20007 (202) 333-7400
public relations

Great American Corp. GTAM
One American Place
Baton Rouge, LA 70825 (504) 346-6000
banking

Great American Partners GAPR
701 "B" Street, Suite 1100
San Diego, CA 92112 (619) 239-2006
oil and gas

Great Lakes Federal S&L Association GLFS
401 East Liberty Street
Ann Arbor, MI 48107 (313) 769-8300
savings and loan

Great Southern Federal Savings Bank GSFB
132 East Broughton Street
Savannah, GA 31401 (912) 944-6200
savings and loan

Great Western Savings Bank GWSB
P.O. Box C-91080
Bellevue, WA 98004 (206) 451-2000
savings and loan

Greater Washington Investors, Inc. GWII
5454 Wisconsin Avenue
Chevy Chase, MD 20815 (301) 656-0626
investment services

Grey Advertising Inc. GREY
777 Third Avenue
New York, NY 10017 (212) 546-2000
advertising

Griffin Technology Inc. GRIF
6132 Victor-Manchester Road
Victor, NY 14564 (716) 924-7121
business data processing

Grist Mill Co. GRST
21405 Hamburg Avenue
Lakeville, MN 55044 (612) 469-4981
food products

Growth Fund of Florida, Inc. (The) GFLA
10 West Adams Street
Jacksonville, FL 32202 (904) 632-8000
investment co.

Grubb & Ellis Realty Income Trust GRIT
One Montgomery Street
San Francisco, CA 94104 (415) 956-1990
real estate

Guarantee Financial Corp. of California GFCC
1177 Fulton Mall
Fresno, CA 93721 (209) 268-8111
savings and loan

Guaranty National Corp. GNIC
P.O. Box 3329
Englewood, CO 80155 (303) 790-8200
insurance

Guardian Packaging Corp. GPCK
6590 Central Avenue
Newark, CA 94560 (415) 797-3710
specialty packaging materials

Guest Supply, Inc. GEST
720 U.S. Hwy. One
North Brunswick, NJ 08902 (201) 246-3011
personal care items for hotel guests

Guilford Industries, Inc. GILD
P.O. Box 179
Guilford, ME 04443 (207) 876-3331
textiles

Gulf Applied Technologies, Inc. GATS
41 East 42nd Street
New York, NY 10017 (212) 661-7780
engineering services

Gulf Broadcast Co. GBCO
13101 Preston Road
Dallas, TX 75240 (214) 233-2972
tv and radio stations, real estate

H & H Oil Tool Co., Inc. HHOT
201 South Hallock Drive
Santa Paula, CA 93060 (805) 647-5595
oil and gas drilling equipment

HBO & Co. HBOC
400 Perimeter Center Terrace
Atlanta, GA 30346 (404) 668-9680
hospital computer information systems

HCC Industries HCCI
16311 Ventura Blvd.
Encino, CA 91436 (213) 995-4131
hermetic seals and transducers

HCW, Inc. HCWO
101 Summer Street
Boston, MA 02110 (617) 542-2880
oil and gas

HEI Corp. HEIC
7676 Woodway
Houston, TX 77063 (713) 780-7802
health services

HEI, Inc. HEII
1495 Steiger Lake Lane
Victoria, MN 55386 (612) 443-2500
electrical equipment

HETRA Computer and Communications
Industries Inc HETC
1151 South Eddie Allen Road
Melbourne, FL 32901 (305) 723-7731
computers and data processing

HMO America, Inc. HMOA
540 North LaSalle Street
Chicago, IL 60610 (312) 751-7500
health services

Haber, Inc. HABE
470 Main Road
Towaco, NJ 07082 (201) 263-0990
chemicals

Hadco Corp. HDCO
10 Manor Pkwy.
Salem, NH 03079 (603) 898-8000
electronics

Hadson Petroleum Corp. HADS
101 Park Avenue
Oklahoma City, OK 73102 (405) 236-5207
oil and gas

Hamilton Oil Corp. HAML
1600 Broadway
Denver, CO 80202 (303) 861-2456
oil and gas

Hammond Co. (The) THCO
4910 Campus Drive
Newport Beach, CA 92663 (714) 752-6671
insurance, mortgage banking

Hanover Companies Inc. HHHC
118 Mill Road
Park Ridge, NJ 07656 (201) 930-0300
real estate

Hanover Insurance Co. (The) HINS
440 Lincoln Street
Worcester, MA 01605 (617) 852-1000
insurance

Harlyn Products, Inc. HRLN
1515 South Main Street
Los Angeles, CA 90015 (213) 746-0745
jewelry

Harper Group (The) HARG
260 Townsend Street
San Francisco, CA 94107 (415) 978-0600
freight forwarding

Hartford National Corp. HNAT
777 Main Street
Hartford, CT 06115 (203) 728-2000
banking   [DRP 5%]

Hartford Steam Boiler Insp. & Insurance Co.
HBOL
One State Street
Hartford, CT 06102 (203) 722-1866
insurance   [DRP]

Harvard Industries, Inc. HAVA
4321 Semple Avenue
St. Louis, MO 63120 (314) 382-5590
furniture

Hathaway Corp. HATH
5250 East Evans Avenue
Denver, CO 80222 (303) 756-8301
electronics

Hauserman, Inc. HASR
5711 Grant Avenue
Cleveland, OH 44105 (216) 883-1400
office furniture, plumbing and heating

Haverty Furniture Companies, Inc. HAVT
866 West Peachtree Street
Atlanta, GA 30308 (404) 881-1911
furniture stores

Hawkeye Bancorporation HWKB
600 First Bldg., 6th Floor
Des Moines, IA 50307 (515) 284-1930
banking   [DRP]

Health Information Systems Inc. HISI
4522 Fort Hamilton Pkwy.
Brooklyn, NY 11219 (212) 435-6300
hospital computerized information systems

Healthco International, Inc. HLCO
25 Stuart Street
Boston, MA 02116 (617) 423-6045
health services equipment

Healthcare Services Group, Inc. HCSG
405 Masons Mill Road
Huntingdon Valley, PA 19006 (215) 657-7020
medical supplies

Healthcare Services of America, Inc. HSAI
2000 Southbridge Pkwy.
Birmingham, AL 35209 (205) 879-8970
health services

Healthdyne, Inc. HDYN
2253 N.W. Pkwy.
Marietta, GA 30067 (404) 955-9555
medical supplies and services

Hechinger Co. HECH
3500 Pennsy Drive
Landover, MD 20785 (301) 341-1000
building materials retailing

Heist (C.H.) Corp. CHHC
810 North Belcher Road
Clearwater, FL 33575 (813) 461-5656
special construction

Helen of Troy Corp. HELE
6827 Market Street
El Paso, TX 79915 (915) 779-6363
cosmetics and personal care

Helix Technology Corp. HELX
266 Second Avenue
Waltham, MA 02254 (617) 890-9292
electrical equipment

HemoTec, Inc. HEMO
7103 South Revere Pkwy.
Englewood, CO 80112 (303) 770-1539
medical supplies

Henley Group HENG
375 Park Avenue
New York, NY 10152 (212) 832-2200
diversified manufacturing

Henredon Furniture Industries, Inc. HDON
P.O. Box 70
Morganton, NC 28655 (704) 437-5261
furniture

Heritage Federal S&L Association HFLA
230 North Beach Street
Daytona Beach, FL 32014 (904) 253-9227
savings and loan

Herley Microwave Systems, Inc. HRLY
10 Industry Drive
Lancaster, PA 17603 (717) 397-2777
electronics

Hibernia Corp. HIBC
313 Carondelet Street
New Orleans, LA 70130 (504) 586-5552
banking   [DRP 5%]

Dow B. Hickam, Inc. DBHI
P.O. Box 2006
Sugar Land, TX 77478 (713) 240-1000
drugs

High Plains Oil Corp. HPOC
1475 Lawrence Street
Denver, CO 80202 (303) 572-1122
oil and gas

Highland Superstores, Inc. HIGH
21405 Trolley Drive
Taylor, MI 48180 (313) 291-7800
electrical equipment retailing

Highlands-National, Inc. HLNI
200 Peoples Bank Bldg.
Jackson, MS 39201 (601) 948-4091
investment services

Hogan Systems, Inc. HOGN
5080 Spectrum Drive
Dallas, TX 75248 (214) 386-0020
banking software

Holmes (D.H.) Co., Ltd. HLME
819 Canal Street
New Orleans, LA 70112 (504) 561-6611
discount drug stores

Home Federal Savings Bank of Georgia HFGA
Washington & Green Streets
Gainesville, GA 30503 (404) 535-0950
savings and loan

Home Beneficial Corp. HBEN
3901 West Broad Street
Richmond, VA 23230 (804) 358-8431
insurance

Home Federal Bank of Florida, F.S.B. HFBF
P.O. Box 12288
St. Petersburg, FL 33733 (813) 823-1111
banking

Home Federal S&L Association of Arizona
HMAZ
32 North Stone Avenue
Tucson, AZ 85701 (602) 623-7771
savings and loan

Home Federal S&L Association of Atlanta
HOMA
79 West Paces Ferry Road, N.W.
Atlanta, GA 30355 (404) 266-2255
savings and loan

Home Federal S&L Association of the Rockies
HROK
P.O. Box 2182
Fort Collins, CO 80522 (303) 482-3216
savings and loan

Home Owners Federal S&L Association HFSL
21 Milk Street
Boston, MA 02109 (617) 482-0630
savings and loan

HomeClub, Inc. HCLB
140 Orangefair Mall
Fullerton, CA 92632 (714) 441-0171
building materials retailing

Homecrafters Warehouse, Inc. HCWH
P.O. Box 10084
Birmingham, AL 35202 (205) 972-8500
building materials retailing

Hon Industries Inc. HONI
414 East Third Street
Muscatine, IA 52761 (319) 264-7400
office furniture

Hooper Holmes, Inc. HOOP
170 Mt. Airy Road
Basking Ridge, NJ 07920 (201) 766-5000
health services, supplies

Horizon Air Industries, Inc. HZIR
1221 South 188th Street
Seattle, WA 98148 (206) 241-6757
regional airline

Horizon Industries, Inc. HRZN
P.O. Box 12069
Calhoun, GA 30701 (404) 629-7721
rugs and carpets

Horizons Research Inc. HRES
18531 South Miles Road
Cleveland, OH 44128 (216) 475-0555
photographic technology

Howard Bancorp HOBC
111 Main Street
Burlington, VT 05401 (802) 658-1010
banking

Howard Savings Bank (The) HWRD
200 South Orange Avenue
Livingston, NJ 07039 (201) 430-2000
banking

Hunt (J.B.) Transport Services, Inc. JBHT
Hwy. 71 North
Lowell, AR 72745 (501) 659-8800
trucking

Huntingdon International Holdings PLC HRCL
Huntingdon, Cambridgeshire
England, PE 18 6ES
health services, supplies

Huntington Bancshares Inc. HBAN
41 South High Street
Columbus, OH 43260 (614) 469-7000
banking   [DRP 5%]

Hurco Companies, Inc. HURC
6602 Guion Road
Indianapolis, IN 46268 (317) 293-5309
machine tools

Hyde Athletic Industries, Inc. HYDE
Centennial Drive/P.O. Box 6046
Peabody, MA 01961 (617) 532-6703
footwear, apparel

Hyponex Corp. HYPX
2013 South Anthony Blvd.
Fort Wayne, IN 46803 (219) 422-6511
lawn and garden products

Hytek Microsystems, Inc. HTEK
980 University Avenue
Los Gatos, CA 95030 (408) 358-1991
electronics

IBI Security Service, Inc. IBIS
29-19 39th Avenue
Long Island City, NY 11101 (718) 729-5599
security services

ICOT Corp. ICOT
3801 Zanker Road
San Jose, CA 95150 (408) 423-3300
data communications

IDC Services, Inc. IDCS
303 East Ohio Street
Chicago, IL 60611 (312) 943-7500
market research

IEC Electronics Corp. IECE
105 Norton Street
Newark, NY 14513 (315) 331-7742
electronics

I.I.S. Intelligent Information Systems Ltd. IISL
Technion City
Haifa 31015, Israel
computers

ILC Technology, Inc. ILCT
399 Java Drive
Sunnyvale, CA 94089 (408) 745-7900
electrical equipment

I.M.S. International, Inc. IMSI
800 Third Avenue
New York, NY 10022 (212) 371-2310
market research services

IPL Systems, Inc. IPLS
360 Second Avenue
Waltham, MA 02154 (617) 890-6620
computers

ISC Systems Corp. ISCS
Box TAF-C8
Spokane, WA 99220 (509) 536-5050
financial data terminal systems

IVB Financial Corp. IVBF
1700 Market Street
Philadelphia, PA 19103 (215) 496-4000
banking

Idle Wild Foods, Inc. IDLE
P. O. Box 118
Worcester, MA 01613 (617) 757-7761
meat and poultry

Imatron Inc. IMAT
389 Oyster Point Blvd.
South San Francisco, CA 94080
(415) 583-9964
health service and supplies

Immunex Corp. IMNX
51 University Street
Seattle, WA 98101 (206) 587-0430
drugs

Immuno Nuclear Corp. INUC
1951 North Western Avenue
Stillwater, MN 55082 (612) 439-9710
health services and supplies

ImmunoGenetics, Inc. IGEN
2285 East Landis Avenue
Vineland, NJ 08360 (609) 691-2411
biotechnology, drugs

Inacomp Computer Centers, Inc. INAC
1824 West Maple Road
Troy, MI 48084 (313) 649-5580
computer retailing

Independence Bancorp, Inc. INBC
Corporate Center, North Fifth
Perkasie, PA 18944 (215) 453-3000
banking

Independence Holding Co. INHO
96 Cummings Point Road
Stamford, CT 06902 (203) 358-8000
real estate

Independent Bankshares, Inc. IBSI
500 Chestnut Street
Abilene, TX 79604 (915) 677-2661
banking

Indian Head Banks, Inc. IHBI
One Indian Head Plaza
Nashua, NH 03060 (603) 880-5000
banking

Indiana Financial Investors, Inc. IFII
151 North Delaware Street
Indianapolis, IN 46204 (317) 266-5250
investment co.

Indiana National Corp. INAT
One Indiana Square
Indianapolis, IN 46266 (317) 266-6000
banking   [DRP]

Indianapolis Water Co. IWTR
1220 Waterway Blvd.
Indianapolis, IN 46202 (317) 639-1501
utility   [DRP 3%]

Industrial Acoustics Co., Inc. IACI
1160 Commerce Avenue
Bronx, NY 10462 (212) 931-8000
noise control building products

Industrial Electronic Hardware Corp. IEHC
109 Prince Street
New York, NY 10012 (212) 677-1881
electronic machinery

Inertia Dynamics Corp. TRIM
7125 West Galveston
Chandler, AZ 85224 (602) 961-1002
lawn and garden products

Information International, Inc. IINT
5933 Slauson Avenue
Culver City, CA 90230 (213) 390-8611
computer equipment

Information Resources Inc. IRIC
150 North Clinton Street
Chicago, IL 60606 (312) 726-1221
market analysis services

Information Science Inc. INSI
95 Chestnut Ridge Road
Montvale, NJ 07645 (201) 391-1600
computer software

Information Solutions, Inc. ISOL
6486 South Quebec Street
Englewood, CO 80111 (303) 694-9180
office machines

InfoTech Management, Inc. INFC
24-20 Jackson Avenue
Long Island City, NY 11101 (718) 729-5000
special construction

Infotron Systems Corp. INFN
Cherry Hill Industrial Center
Cherry Hill, NJ 08003 (609) 424-9400
data communications systems

Infrared Industries, Inc. INFR
P.O. Box 14200
Orlando, FL 32857 (305) 282-7700
precision instruments and photography

Inland Vacuum Industries, Inc. IVAC
35 Howard Avenue
Churchville, NY 14428 (716) 293-3330
refining

Inmed Corp. NMED
3030-B Holcomb Bridge Road
Norcross, GA 30071 (404) 446-3004
medical supplies

Innovex, Inc. INVX
1313 Fifth Street South
Hopkins, MN 55343 (612) 938-4155
machinery

Insituform East, Inc. INEI
3421 Pennsy Drive
Landover, MD 20785 (301) 386-4100
sewer and pipe repair

Insituform Group Ltd. IGLS
Borough House, Trinity Square
Guernsey, Channel Islands
sewer and pipe repair

Insituform of North America, Inc. INSU
P.O. Box 181071
Memphis, TN 38118 (901) 363-2105
sewer and pipe repair

Instinet Corp. INET
757 Third Avenue
New York, NY 10017 (212) 310-9500
computerized security trading

Intech Inc. INTE
282 Brokaw Road
Santa Clara, CA 95050 (408) 727-0500
electronics

InteCom, Inc. INCM
601 InteCom Drive
Allen, TX 75002 (214) 727-9141
telecommunications products

Integrated Circuits Inc. ICTM
10301 Willows Road
Redmond, WA 98052 (206) 882-3100
electronic equipment

Integrated Device Technology, Inc. IDTI
3236 Scott Blvd.
Santa Clara, CA 95051 (408) 727-6116
electronics

Integrated Genetics, Inc. INGN
31 New York Avenue
Framingham, MA 01701 (617) 875-1336
biotechnology, medical products

Integrated Software Systems Corp. ISCX
10505 Sorrento Valley Road
San Diego, CA 92121 (619) 452-0170
software, data processing

Integrity Financial Group Inc. (The) INTY
Mack Centre II
Paramus, NJ 07652 (201) 262-9300
insurance

Intel Corp. INTC
3065 Bowers Avenue
Santa Clara, CA 95051 (408) 987-8080
semiconductors   [O]

IntelliCorp, Inc. INAI
1975 El Camino Real West
Mountain View, CA 94040 (415) 965-5500
biotechnology software

Intelligent Systems Corp. INTS
4355 Shackelford Road
Norcross, GA 30093 (404) 441-0611
computers and accessories

Inter-Tel, Inc. INTL
6505 West Williams Field Road
Chandler, AZ 85224 (602) 961-9000
commmunications equipment

Interactive Radiation, Inc. INRD
181 Legrand Avenue
Northvale, NJ 07647 (201) 767-1910
radiation detection systems

Interand Corp. IRND
3200 West Peterson Avenue
Chicago, IL 60659 (312) 478-1700
electronic machinery

Interface Flooring Systems, Inc. IFSI
Orchard Hill Road
LaGrange, GA 30241 (404) 882-1891
carpet, tiles

Interface Systems, Inc. INTF
5855 Interface Drive
Ann Arbor, MI 48103 (313) 769-5900
computer equipment

Intergraph Corp. INGR
One Madison Industrial Park
Huntsville, AL 35807 (205) 772-2000
computer graphic systems   [O]

Intermagnetics General Corp. INMA
Charles Industrial Park
Guilderland, NY 12084 (518) 456-5456
electrical equipment, magnets

Intermec Corp. INTR
4405 Russell Road
Lynnwood, WA 98046 (206) 743-7036
printing and reading products

Intermet Corp. INMT
2849 Paces Ferry Road
Atlanta, GA 30339 (404) 436-1102
metal fabrication

Intermetrics, Inc. IMET
733 Concord Avenue
Cambridge, MA 02138 (617) 661-1840
computer software

International Bank IBKW
1701 Pennsylvania Avenue
Washington, DC 20006 (202) 452-6500
financial services, fund management   [DRP]

International Capital Equipment Ltd. ICEY
1840 Palmer Avenue
Larchmont, NY 10538 (914) 834-5011
equipment leasing

International Clinical Labs., Inc. ICLB
5 Park Plaza
Nashville, TN 37203 (615) 327-1025
medical services and supplies

International Container Systems, Inc. ICSI
5401 West Kennedy Blvd.
Tampa, FL 33609 (813) 872-9940
containers

International Game Technology IGAM
520 South Rock Blvd.
Reno, NV 89502 (702) 323-5060
toys and games, entertainment

International Holding Capital Corp. ISLH
1111 Bishop Street
Honolulu, HI 96813 (808) 547-5110
financial services

International King's Table, Inc. IKNG
1500 Valley River Drive
Eugene, OR 97401 (503) 686-8030
restaurants

International Lease Finance Corp. ILFC
8484 Wilshire Blvd.
Beverly Hills, CA 90211 (213) 658-7871
aircraft leasing

International Mobile Machines Corp. IMMC
100 North 20th Street
Philadelphia, PA 19103 (215) 569-3880
communications equipment

International Remote Imaging Systems, Inc.
IRIS
9825 DeSoto Avenue
Chatsworth, CA 91311 (818) 709-1244
scientific instruments

International Research and Development
Corp. IRDV
500 North Main Street
Mattawan, MI 49071 (616) 668-3336
safety evaluation

International Shipholding Corp. INSH
650 Poydras Street
New Orleans, LA 70130 (504) 529-5461
shipping

International Totalizator Systems, Inc. ITSI
11095 Flintkote Avenue
San Diego, CA 92121 (619) 457-4680
computer systems

Interphase Corp. INPH
2925 Merrell Road
Dallas, TX 75229 (214) 350-9000
electronics

Interprovincial Pipe Line Ltd. IPIP
1 First Canadian Place
Toronto, Ont. M5X 1A9 (416) 362-1343
pipelines   [DRP]

Intertrans Corp. ITRN
8505 Freeport Parkway
Irving, TX 75603 (214) 258-4888
freight and shipping

IntraWest Financial Corp. INTW
Terminal Annex Box 5605
Denver, CO 80217 (303) 293-2000
banking

Invacare Corp. IVCR
P.O. Box 4028
Elyria, OH 44036 (216) 329-6000
health services, supplies

Investors GNMA Securities Trust, Inc. INVG
55 Water Street
New York, NY 10041 (212) 558-1500
investments

Investors S&L Association ISLA
5008 Monument Avenue
Richmond, VA 23230 (804) 254-1300
savings and loan

Iomega Corp. IOMG
4646 South 1500 West
Ogden, UT 84403 (801) 392-7581
computer disk drives

Iowa Southern Utilities Co. IUTL
300 Sheridan Avenue
Centerville, IA 52544 (515) 437-4400
utility

Isomedix Inc. ISMX
11 Apollo Drive
Whippany, NJ 07981 (201) 887-4700
medical supplies

Itel Corp. ITEL
55 Francisco Street
San Francisco, CA 94133 (415) 984-4000
equipment leasing

JB's Restaurants, Inc. JBBB
1010 West 2610 South
Salt Lake City, UT 84119 (801) 972-1405
restaurants

JLG Industries, Inc. JLGI
JLG Drive
McConnellsburg, PA 17233 (717) 485-5161
farm and construction machinery

JMB Realty Trust JMBR
875 North Michigan Avenue
Chicago, IL 60611 (312) 440-5300
real estate

J.P. Industries, Inc. JPII
325 East Eisenhower Pkwy.
Ann Arbor, MI 48104 (313) 663-6749
auto parts

Jackpot Enterprises, Inc. JACK
2900 South Highland Drive
Las Vegas, NV 89109 (702) 369-3424
amusement

Jackson National Life Insurance Co. JNAL
5901 Executive Drive
Lansing, MI 48910 (517) 394-3400
insurance

Jacobson Stores, Inc. JCBS
1200 North West Avenue
Jackson, MI 49202 (517) 787-3600
apparel stores

Jacor Communications, Inc. JCOR
602 Main Street
Cincinnati, OH 45202 (513) 579-8240
communication

Jaguar plc JAGR
600 Willow Tree Road
Leonia, NJ 07605 (201) 592-5200
automobiles

Jamaica Water Properties, Inc. JWAT
410 Lakeville Road
Lake Success, NY 11042 (516) 488-4600
water utility

Jefferies Group, Inc. JEFG
445 South Figueroa Street
Los Angeles, CA 90071 (213) 624-3333
investment services

Jefferson Bankshares, Inc. JBNK
123 East Main Street
Charlottesville, VA 22901 (804) 972-1100
banking

Jefferson Smurfit Corp. JJSC
401 Alton Street
Alton, IL 62002 (618) 463-6000
paper and containers

Jeffrey Martin, Inc. JFRY
410 Clermont Terrace
Union, NJ 07083 (201) 687-4000
health services, supplies

Jerrico, Inc. JERR
101 Jerrico Drive
Lexington, KY 40511 (606) 268-5211
restaurants

John Adams Life Corp. JALC
11777 San Vicente Blvd.
Los Angeles, CA 90049 (213) 826-3656
insurance

Johnson Electronics, Inc. JHSN
4301 Metric Drive
Winter Park, FL 32793 (305) 677-4030
electronics

Jones & Vining Inc. JNSV
166 Forbes Road
Braintree, MA 02184 (617) 848-7310
shoes and leather

Jones Intercable, Inc. JOIN
5275 DTC Pkwy.
Englewood, CO 80111 (303) 740-9700
communication, cable tv

Josephson International, Inc. JSON
40 West 57th Street
New York, NY 10019 (212) 556-5600
talent agency, financial services

Judy's Inc. JUDY
7710 Haskell Avenue
Van Nuys, CA 91406 (213) 873-6200
apparel stores

Juno Lighting, Inc. JUNO
2001 South Mt. Prospect Road
Des Plaines, IL 60018 (312) 827-9880
electrical lighting equipment

Justin Industries, Inc. JSTN
2821 West 7th Street
Fort Worth, TX 76107 (817) 336-5125
building materials, shoes and leather   [DRP]

Keithley Instruments, Inc. KEII
28775 Aurora Road
Solon, OH 44139 (216) 248-0400
scientific instruments

KLA Instruments Corp. KLAC
2051 Mission College Blvd.
Santa Clara, CA 95054 (408) 988-6100
electronic test systems

Kelly Services, Inc. KELY
999 West Big Beaver Road
Troy, MI 48084 (313) 362-4444
temporary personnel

KMW Systems Corp. KMWS
8307 Hwy. 71 West
Austin, TX 78735 (512) 288-1453
electronic equipment

Kemper Corp. KEMC
Kemper Center
Long Grove, IL 60049 (312) 540-2000
insurance

K-Tron International, Inc. KTII
7975 North Hayden Road
Scottsdale, AZ 85258 (602) 998-0900
measuring equipment

KenCope Energy Companies KCOP
12500 San Pedro
San Antonio, TX 78216 (512) 494-1179
oil and gas services and exploration

K-V Pharmaceutical Co. KVPH
2503 South Hanley Road
St Louis, MO 63144 (314) 645-6600
drugs

Kennington Ltd., Inc. KENN
3209 Humboldt Street
Los Angeles, CA 90031 (213) 225-1655
apparel

Kaman Corp. KAMN
1332 Blue Hills Avenue
Bloomfield, CT 06002 (203) 243-6324
aerospace contractor   [DRP]

Kentucky Central Life Insurance Co. KENC
Kincaid Towers
Lexington, KY 40508 (606) 253-5111
insurance

Kamenstein, (M) Inc. MKCO
190 East Post Road
White Plains, NY 10601 (914) 948-2290
furniture

Kevex Corp. KEVX
1101 Chess Drive
Foster City, CA 94404 (415) 573-5866
measuring instruments

Kappa Networks, Inc. KAPA
1443 Pinewood Street
Rahway, NJ 07065 (201) 541-1600
electronics

Kevlin Microwave Corp. KVLM
26 Conn Street
Woburn, MA 01801 (617) 935-4800
microwave equipment

Kasler Corp. KASL
27400 East Fifth Street
San Bernardino, CA 92402 (714) 884-4811
special contractors

Kewaunee Scientific Equipment Corp. KEQU
1213 Wilmette Avenue
Wilmette, IL 60091 (312) 251-7100
scientific instruments

Kaydon Corp. KDON
2860 McCracken Street
Muskegon, MI 49443 (616) 755-3741
bearings and filters

Key Tronic Corp. KTCC
N. 4424 Sullivan
Spokane, WA 99216 (509) 928-8000
computer accessories

Kaypro Corp. KPRO
533 Stevens Avenue
Solana Beach, CA 92075 (619) 481-4300
computers

Keystone Financial, Inc. KSTN
P.O. Box 708
Altoona, PA 16603 (814) 946-6689
banking

Keane, Inc. KEAN
210 Commercial Street
Boston, MA 02109 (617) 742-5210
business data processing

Keystone Heritage Group, Inc. KHGI
P.O.Box 448
Lebanon, PA 17042 (717) 274-6800
investments

Kimball International, Inc. KBAL
1600 Royal Street
Jasper, IN 47546 (812) 482-1600
furniture, musical instruments

Kimbark Oil and Gas Co. KIMB
1580 Lincoln Street
Denver, CO 80203 (303) 839-5504
oil and gas

Kincaid Furniture Co., Inc. KNCD
P.O. Box 605
Hudson, NC 28638 (704) 728-3261
furniture

Kinder-Care Learning Centers, Inc. KNDR
2400 Presidents Drive
Montgomery, AL 36116 (205) 277-5090
day care centers

King World Productions, Inc. KING
480 Morris Avenue
Summit, NJ 07901 (201) 522-0100
broadcasting and cable tv programs

Kloss Video Corp. KLOS
640 Memorial Drive
Cambridge, MA 02139 (617) 577-1000
video equipment

Knape & Vogt Manufacturing Co. KNAP
2700 Oak Industrial Drive
Grand Rapids, MI 49505 (616) 459-3311
specialty hardware

Kreisler Manufacturing Corp. KRSL
5960 Central Avenue
St. Petersburg, FL 33707 (813) 347-1144
transportation equipment

Kroy, Inc. KROY
7720 East Evans Drive
Scottsdale, AZ 85260 (602) 951-3000
business lettering systems

Krueger (W.A.) Co. KRUE
7301 East Helm Drive
Scottsdale, AZ 85260 (602) 948-5650
printing

Kulicke and Soffa Industries, Inc. KLIC
507 Prudential Road
Horsham, PA 19044 (215) 674-2800
electronics, scientific instruments

Kustom Electronics, Inc. KUST
8320 Nieman Road
Shawnee Mission, KS 66214 (913) 492-1400
electronics

LCS Industries, Inc. LCSI
120 Brighton Road
Clifton, NJ 07012 (201) 778-5588
marketing services

LD Brinkman Corp. LDBC
444 Sidney Baker South
Kerrville, TX 78028 (512) 257-2000
rugs and carpets

LESCO, Inc. LSCO
20005 Lake Road
Rocky River, OH 44116 (216) 333-9250
lawn-care products

LIN Broadcasting Corp. LINB
1370 Avenue of the Americas
New York, NY 10019 (212) 765-1902
broadcasting, communication   [O]

LSB Bancshares, Inc. LXBK
One LSB Plaza
Lexington, NC 27292 (704) 246-6500
investment co.

LSI Lighting Systems Inc. LYTS
4201 Malsbary Road
Cincinnati, OH 45242 (513) 793-3200
electrical lighting equipment

LSI Logic Corp. LLSI
1551 McCarthy Blvd.
Milpitas, CA 95035 (408) 263-9494
custom semiconductors   [O]

LTX Corp. LTXX
LTX Park at University Avenue
Westwood, MA 02090 (617) 329-7550
semiconductor test equipment

La Petite Academy, Inc. LPAI
12th and Baltimore City Center
Kansas City, MO 64196 (816) 474-4750
day care centers

La-Z-Boy Chair Co. LAZB
1284 North Telegraph Road
Monroe, MI 48161 (313) 242-1444
furniture   [DRP]

Lacana Mining Corp. LCNA
Sun Life Centre, 150 King St.
Toronto, Ont. M5H 1J9 (416) 591-6640
metal mining

Laclede Steel Co. LCLD
Equitable Bldg., 10 Broadway
St. Louis, MO 63102 (314) 425-1400
iron and steel

Ladd Furniture, Inc. LADF
One Plaza Center
High Point, NC 27261 (919) 889-0333
furniture

Laidlaw Industries, Inc. LWSI
15 Spinning Wheel Road
Hinsdale, IL 60521 (312) 887-8181
waste management

Laidlaw Transportation Ltd. LDMF
490-110 King Street West
Hamilton, Ont. L8P 4S6 (416) 521-1800
waste management, trucking

Lam Research Corp. LRCX
47531 Warm Springs Blvd.
Fremont, CA 94539 (415) 659-0200
electronics

Lancaster Colony Corp. LANC
37 West Broad Street
Columbus, OH 43215 (614) 224-7141
housewares   [DRP]

Lance, Inc. LNCE
8600 South Blvd.
Charlotte, NC 28232 (704) 554-1421
food products   [DRP]

Lancer Corp. LACR
235 West Turbo
San Antonio, TX 78216 (512) 344-3071
beverage-dispensing equipment

Land Of Lincoln S&L LOLS
6655 West Cermak Road
Berwyn, IL 60402 (312) 749-1900
savings and loan

Landmark Savings Association LMRK
335 Fifth Avenue
Pittsburgh, PA 15222 (412) 471-9800
savings and loan

Lane Co. Inc. (The) LANE
Franklin Avenue
Altavista, VA 24517 (804) 369-5641
furniture

Langley Corp. LCOR
310 Euclid Avenue
San Diego, CA 92112 (619) 264-3181
electronic equipment

Larsen Co. (The) LARS
P.O. Box 19027
Green Bay, WI 54303 (414) 435-5301
food products

Lawson Products, Inc. LAWS
1666 East Touhy Avenue
Des Plaines, IL 60018 (312) 827-9666
fastener distribution

Leader Development Corp. LDCO
1050 Kingsmill Pkwy.
Columbus, OH 43229 (614) 846-7410
oil and gas

Lee Data Corp. LEDA
7075 Flying Cloud Drive
Eden Prairie, MN 55344 (612) 828-0300
computer terminals

Leiner (P.) Nutritional Products Corp. PLIN
1845 West 205th Street
Torrance, CA 90501 (213) 328-9610
food products

Leisure Concepts Inc. LCIC
116 Central Park South
New York, NY 10019 (212) 765-1489
character licensing

Palmer G. Lewis Co., Inc. LWIS
525 C Street N.W.
Auburn, WA 98001 (206) 941-2600
building materials

Lexicon Corp. LEXI
1541 North West 65th Avenue
Ft. Lauderdale, FL 33313 (305) 792-4400
computers

Lexidata Corp. LEXD
755 Middlesex Turnpike
Billerica, MA 01865 (617) 663-8550
graphic display computers

Liberty Homes, Inc. LIBH
P.O. Box 35
Goshen, IN 46526 (219) 533-0431
homebuilding

Liberty National Bancorp, Inc. LNBC
416 West Jefferson
Louisville, KY 40232 (502) 566-2000
banking   [DRP]

Lieberman Enterprises Inc. LMAN
9549 Penn Avenue South
Minneapolis, MN 55431 (612) 887-5300
entertainment

Liebert Corp. LIEB
1050 Dearborn Drive
Columbus, OH 43329 (614) 888-0246
computer control systems

Life Investors Inc. LINV
4333 Edgewood Road, North East
Cedar Rapids, IA 52499 (319) 398-8511
insurance

Lifetime Communities, Inc. LFTM
3740 Beach Blvd.
Jacksonville, FL 32207 (904) 399-3750
real estate

Lilly Industrial Coatings Inc. LICI
P.O. Box 946
Indianapolis, IN 46206 (317) 634-8512
industrial coatings

Lily Tulip, Inc. LILY
P.O. Box 1808
Augusta, GA 30903 (404) 823-5459
paper containers, boxes   [O]

Lincoln Telecommunications Co. LTEC
1440 M Street
Lincoln, NE 68508 (402) 474-2211
communication   [DRP]

Lindberg Corp. LIND
8600 West Bryn Mawr Avenue
Chicago, IL 60631 (312) 693-2021
metals fabrication

Linear Corp. LINE
2055 Corte del Nogal
Carlsbad, CA 92008 (619) 438-7000
electronic security

Liqui-Box Corp. LIQB
6950 Worthington-Galena Road
Worthington, OH 43085 (614) 888-9280
plastic products and packaging

Liquid Air Corp. LANA
One Embarcadero Center
San Francisco, CA 94111 (415) 765-4500
industrial gases, welding products

Arthur D. Little Inc. LTLE
Acorn Park
Cambridge, MA 02140 (617) 864-5770
business consulting

Liz Claiborne, Inc. LIZC
1441 Broadway
New York, NY 10018 (212) 354-4900
apparel   [O]

Loan America Financial Corp. LAFC
9549 Koger Blvd.
St. Petersburg, FL 33702 (305) 577-0600
financial services

Local Federal S&L Association LOCL
3601 North West 63rd Street
Oklahoma City, OK 73126 (405) 841-2100
savings and loan

Lodgistix, Inc. LDGX
7701 East Kellogg
Wichita, KS 67207 (316) 685-2216
software, data processing

London House, Inc. LOND
1550 N.W. Hwy.
Park Ridge, IL 60068 (312) 298-7311
institutional services

Lone Star Steel Co. LSST
2200 W. Mockingbird Lane
Dallas, TX 75235 (214) 352-3981
steel products

Longview Fibre Co. LFBR
P.O. Box 639
Longview, WA 98632 (206) 425-1550
paper and wood products

Lotus Development Corp. LOTS
161 First Street
Cambridge, MA 02142 (617) 492-7171
software   [O]

Louis Vuitton S.A. LVTN
30 rue la Boetie
75008 Paris, France (331) 563-0900
luggage, handbags

Louisiana Bancshares, Inc. LABS
P.O. Box 3399
Baton Rouge, LA 70821 (504) 389-4206
banking

Lynden Inc. LYND
18000 Pacific Hwy. South
Seattle, WA 98188 (206) 241-8778
trucking

LyphoMed, Inc. LMED
2020 Ruby Street
Melrose, IL 60160 (312) 345-6170
health services, supplies

M/A/R/C Inc. MARC
4230 LBJ Freeway
Dallas, TX 75244 (214) 661-5900
market research

MBI Business Centers, Inc. MBOX
1201 Seven Locks Road
Rockville, MD 20854 (301) 279-0551
computer retailing

MCI Communications Corp. MCIC
1133 19th Street, N.W.
Washington, DC 20036 (202) 872-1600
telecommunications   [O]

Malrite Communications Group, Inc. MALR
1200 Statler Office Tower
Cleveland, OH 44115 (216) 781-3010
broadcasting and cable tv

MICOM Systems, Inc. MICS
4100 Los Angeles Avenue
Simi Valley, CA 93062 (805) 583-8600
data communications equipment

Management Science America, Inc. MSAI
3445 Peachtree Road, N.E.
Atlanta, GA 30326 (404) 239-2000
software, data processing

MIW Investors Of Washington MINV
1825 Eye Street, N.W.
Washington, DC 20006 (202) 429-1999
real estate investment trust

Manitowoc Co., Inc. (The) MANT
500 South Sixteenth Street
Manitowoc, WI 54220 (414) 684-6621
construction machinery

MMI Medical, Inc. MMIM
1902 Royalty Drive
Pomona, CA 91767 (714) 620-0391
health services, supplies

Manufactured Homes, Inc. MANH
P.O. Box 24549
Winston-Salem, NC 27114 (919) 768-9890
manufactured home sales

MPSI Systems, Inc. MPSG
8282 South Memorial Drive
Tulsa, OK 74133 (918) 250-9611
software

Manufacturers National Corp. MNTL
One Hundred Renaissance Center
Detroit, MI 48243 (313) 222-4000
banking

Mack Trucks, Inc. MACK
2100 Mack Blvd.
Allentown, PA 18105 (215) 439-3426
truck manufacturer

Marcus Corp. (The) MRCS
212 West Wisconsin Avenue
Milwaukee, WI 53203 (414) 272-6020
hotels, restaurants

Madison Gas and Electric Co. MDSN
133 South Blair Street
Madison, WI 53701 (608) 252-7964
utility   [DRP]

Margaux Controls, Inc. MRGX
2940 North First Street
San Jose, CA 95134 (408) 942-0909
electronic equipment

Magma Power Co. MGMA
631 South Witmer Street
Los Angeles, CA 90017 (213) 483-2285
utility

Marine Corp. (The) MCRP
111 East Wisconsin Avenue
Milwaukee, WI 53201 (414) 765-2418
banking   [DRP 5%]

Magna Group, Inc. MAGI
19 Public Square
Belleville, IL 62220 (618) 234-0020
banking

Marine Transport Lines, Inc. MTLI
150 Meadowland Pkwy.
Secaucus, NJ 07094 (201) 330-0200
shipping

Magna International Inc. MAGA
36 Apple Creek Blvd.
Markham, Ont. L3R 4Y4 (416) 477-7766
transportation equipment

Mark Twain Bancshares, Inc. MTWN
8820 Ladue Road
St. Louis, MO 63124 (314) 727-1000
banking   [DRP]

Magnetics International, Inc. MAGN
5400 Dunham Road
Maple Heights, OH 44137 (216) 662-8484
magnets

Market Facts, Inc. MFAC
676 North Saint Clair Street
Chicago, IL 60611 (312) 280-9100
market research

Major Realty Corp. MAJR
5750 Major Blvd.
Orlando, FL 32819 (305) 351-1111
real estate

Marquest Medical Products, Inc. MMPI
11039 East Lansing Circle
Englewood, CO 80112 (303) 790-4835
medical supplies

Mars Stores, Inc. MXXX
P.O. Box 678
North Dighton, MA 02764 (617) 822-1500
discount and variety stores

Marsh Supermarkets, Inc. MARS
501 Depot Street
Yorktown, IN 47396 (317) 759-6211
food stores   [DRP]

Marshall & Isley Corp. MRIS
770 North Water Street
Milwaukee, WI 53202 (414) 765-7801
banking   [DRP]

Maryland National Corp. MDNT
10 Light Street
Baltimore, MD 21203 (301) 244-6737
banking   [DRP 5%]

Masco Industries, Inc. MASX
21001 Van Born Road
Taylor, MI 48180 (313) 274-7405
plumbing and heating equipment

Massachusetts Computer Corp. MSCP
One Technology Park
Westford, MA 01886 (617) 692-6200
computers and data processing

Masstor Systems Corp. MSCO
5200 Great America Pkwy.
Santa Clara, CA 95050 (408) 988-1008
computer data storage equipment

Matrix Science Corp. MTRX
435 Maple Avenue
Torrance, CA 90503 (213) 328-0271
aircraft electrical connectors

Maverick Restaurant Corp. MAVR
302 North Rock Road
Wichita, KS 67206 (316) 685-8281
restaurants

Maxicare Health Plans, Inc. MAXI
5200 West Century Blvd.
Los Angeles, CA 90045 (213) 568-9000
health services

Maxtor Corp. MXTR
150 River Oaks Pkwy.
San Jose, CA 95134 (408) 942-1700
computer equipment

Maxwell Laboratories, Inc. MXWL
8835 Balboa Avenue
San Diego, CA 92123 (619) 279-5100
electrical power systems

May Petroleum, Inc. MAYP
800 One Lincoln Centre
Dallas, TX 75240 (214) 934-9600
oil and gas

Mayfair Super Markets, Inc. MYFR
681 Newark Avenue
Elizabeth, NJ 07208 (201) 352-6400
food stores

Maynard Oil Co. MOIL
8080 North Central Expressway
Dallas, TX 75206 (214) 891-8880
oil and gas

Mays, (J. W.) Inc. MAYS
510 Fulton Street
Brooklyn, NY 11201 (212) 624-7400
retailing

McCormick & Co., Inc. MCCRK
11350 McCormick Road
Hunt Valley, MD 21031 (301) 667-7301
spices, food products   [DRP]

McFarland Energy, Inc. MCFE
10425 South Painter Avenue
Santa Fe Springs, CA 90670 (213) 944-0181
oil and gas

McGill Manufacturing Co. Inc. MGLL
909 North Lafayette Street
Valparaiso, IN 46383 (219) 465-2200
electrical products

McGrath RentCorp MGRC
10760 Bigge Street
San Leandro, CA 94577 (415) 568-8866
equipment rental and sales

Mechtron International Corp. MCHT
2140 West Washington Street
Orlando, FL 32805 (305) 843-9880
machinery

Med-Chem Products, Inc. MDCH
236 West Cummings Park
Woburn, MA 01801 (617) 938-9328
medical supplies, drugs

Medalist Industries, Inc. MDIN
10218 North Port Washington
Mequon, WI 53092 (414) 241-8500
sporting goods   [DRP]

Medar, Inc. MDXR
38700 Grand River Avenue
Farmington Hills, MI 48018 (313) 477-3900
electronics

Medco Containment Services, Inc. MCCS
491 Edward H. Ross Drive
Elmwood Park, NJ 07407 (201) 791-8200
drugs

Medex, Inc. MDEX
3637 Lacon Road
Hilliard, OH 43026 (614) 876-2413
medical supplies

Medical Care International, Inc. MEDC
1300 Post Oak Road
Houston, TX 77056 (713) 961-5333
health services, surgery centers

Medical Graphics Corp. MGCC
501 West County Road E
Saint Paul, MN 55112 (612) 484-4874
scientific instruments

Medical Sterilization, Inc. MSTI
225 Underhill Blvd.
Syosset, NY 11791 (516) 496-8822
health services

Medicare-Glaser Corp. MGCO
2320 Schuetz Road
St. Louis, MO 63146 (314) 569-1100
drug retailing

Medicine Shoppe International, Inc. MSII
10121 Paget Drive
St. Louis, MO 63132 (314) 993-6000
drug retailing and wholesaling

Mediplex Group, Inc. (The) MPLX
15 Walnut Street
Wellesley, MA 02181 (617) 235-6650
health services, supplies

Megadata Corp. MDTA
35 Orville Drive
Bohemia, NY 11716 (516) 589-6800
computers

Mellon Participating Mortgage Trust MPMT
551 Madison Avenue
New York, NY 10022 (212) 702-4040
real estate

Mentor Corp. MNTR
600 Pine Avenue
Goleta, CA 93117 (805) 967-3451
biomedical engineering and research

Mentor Graphics Corp. MENT
8500 S.W. Creekside Place
Beaverton, OR 97005 (503) 626-7000
computer aided engineering software

Mercantile Bancorporation, Inc. MTRC
P.O. Box 524
St. Louis, MO 63166 (314) 425-2525
banking   [DRP]

Mercantile Bankshares Corp. MRBK
2 Hopkins Plaza
Baltimore, MD 21203 (301) 237-5900
banking   [DRP 5%]

Merchant Bank of California (The) MCAL
9100 Wilshire Blvd.
Beverly Hills, CA 90212 (213) 274-9820
banking

Merchants Bancorp, Inc. MRBA
702 Hamilton Mall
Allentown, PA 18101 (215) 821-7215
banking

Merchants Bancshares, Inc. MBVT
123 Church Street
Burlington, VT 05401 (802) 658-3400
banking

Merchants Bank of Boston MCBKB
125 Tremont Street
Boston, MA 02108 (617) 484-2800
banking

Merchants Bank of New York (The) MBNY
434 Broadway
New York, NY 10013 (212) 669-6600
banking

Merchants National Corp. MCHN
One Merchants Plaza
Indianapolis, IN 46255 (317) 267-6100
banking

Meridian Bancorp, Inc. MRDN
35 North Sixth Street
Reading, PA 19603 (215) 320-2000
banking   [DRP 5%]

Meritor Savings Bank MTOR
1212 Market Street
Philadelphia, PA 19107 (215) 636-6000
banking

Merrimac Industries, Inc. MMAC
41 Fairfield Place
West Caldwell, NJ 07007 (201) 575-1300
electronic equipment

Merry Land & Investment Co., Inc. MERY
624 Ellis Street
Augusta, GA 30901 (404) 722-6756
real estate

Merry-Go-Round Enterprises, Inc. MGRE
1220 East Joppa Road
Towson, MD 21204 (301) 828-1000
apparel stores

Mesaba Aviation, Inc. MESA
6201 34th Avenue South
Minneapolis, MN 55450 (218) 326-6657
regional airline

Met-Coil Systems Corp. METS
5480 Sixth Street, S.W.
Cedar Rapids, IA 52404 (319) 364-9181
machinery

Methode Electronics, Inc. METH
7444 Wilson Avenue
Harwood Heights, IL 60656 (312) 867-9600
electronic equipment

Metro Airlines, Inc. MAIR
8505 Freeport Parkway
Irving, TX 75063 (214) 594-3400
regional airline

Metro-Tel Corp. MTRO
15 Burke Lane
Syosset, NY 11791 (516) 364-3377
telephone-testing equipment

MetroBanc, Federal Savings Bank MTBC
201 Monroe Avenue, N.W.
Grand Rapids, MI 49503 (616) 459-3161
savings and loan

Metromail Corp. MTML
901 West Bond Street
Lincoln, NE 68521 (402) 475-4591
direct mail, telephone marketing

Metropolitan Federal S&L Association MFTN
230 Fourth Avenue North
Nashville, TN 37219 (615) 259-2800
savings and loan

Metropolitan S&L Association MSLA
5944 Luther Lane
Dallas, TX 75225 (214) 369-2700
savings and loan

Michaels Stores, Inc. MIKE
9212 Royal Lane
Irving, TX 75063 (214) 258-8668
retail department stores

Michigan National Corp. MNCO
P.O. Box 589
Bloomfield Hills, MI 48303 (313) 642-9001
banking

Micro D, Inc. MCRD
2801 South Yale Street
Santa Ana, CA 92704 (714) 540-4781
computer software distribution

Micro Mask, Inc. MCRO
695 Vaqueros Avenue
Sunnyvale, CA 94086 (408) 245-7342
electronic equipment

Microdyne Corp. MCDY
491 Oak Road
Ocala, FL 32672 (904) 687-4633
communications equipment

Micron Technology, Inc. DRAM
2805 East Columbia Road
Boise, ID 83706 (208) 383-4000
computer components

Micropolis Corp. MLIS
21123 Nordhoff Street
Chatsworth, CA 91311 (818) 709-3300
computer disk drives

MicroPro International Corp. MPRO
33 San Pablo Avenue
San Rafael, CA 94903 (415) 499-1200
software

Micros Systems, Inc. MCRS
12000 Baltimore Avenue
Beltsville, MD 20705 (301) 490-2000
electronic equipment

Microsemi Corp. MSCC
2830 South Fairview Street
Santa Ana, CA 92704 (714) 979-8220
semiconductor devices

Microsoft Corporation
16011 N.E. 36th Street
Redmond, WA 98073 (206) 828-8080
computer software

Microwave Filter Co., Inc. MFCO
6743 Kinne Street
East Syracuse, NY 13057 (315) 437-3953
electronic equipment

Mid Pacific Air Corp. MPAI
P.O. Box 30843
Honolulu, HI 96820 (808) 833-0026
regional airline

Mid-America Bancorp MABC
500 West Broadway
Louisville, KY 40202 (502) 562-5439
banking

Mid-American National Bank and Trust Co.
MIAM
222 South Main Street
Bowling Green, OH 43402 (419) 352-5271
banking

Mid-State Federal S&L Association MSSL
Paddock Park Business Center
Ocala, FL 32674 (904) 732-9977
savings and loan

Middlesex Water Co. MSEX
P.O. Box 1500
Iselin, NJ 08830 (201) 634-1500
water utility   [DRP]

Midlantic Banks, Inc. MIDL
Metro Park Plaza
Edison, NJ 08818 (201) 321-8100
banking   [DRP]

Midway Airlines, Inc. MDWY
5700 South Cicero Avenue
Chicago, IL 60638 (312) 838-0001
regional airline

Midwest Commerce Corp. MCBC
121 West Franklin Street
Elkhart, IN 46516 (219) 294-6621
banking

Midwest Financial Group, Inc. MFGC
301 South West Adams Street
Peoria, IL 61631 (309) 655-5200
financial services

Herman Miller, Inc. MLHR
8500 Byron Road
Zeeland, MI 49464 (616) 772-3300
office furniture

Millicom Inc. MILL
733 Third Avenue
New York, NY 10017 (212) 687-0055
communication

Millipore Corp. MILI
80 Ashby Road
Bedford, MA 01730 (617) 275-9200
filters, mechanical devices   [DRP]

Miltope Group, Inc. MILT
733 Third Avenue
New York, NY 10017 (212) 661-6343
computers

Miniscribe Corp. MINY
1861 Lefthand Circle
Longmont, CO 80501 (303) 651-6000
computer disk drives

Minnetonka, Inc. MINL
Jonathan Industrial Center
Chaska, MN 55318 (612) 448-4181
soap, cosmetics and personal care

Minstar, Inc. MNST
1215 Marshall Street, N.E.
Minneapolis, MN 55413 (612) 379-1800
conglomerate

Mischer Corp. (The) MSHR
2727 North Loop West, #200
Houston, TX 77008 (713) 869-7800
building construction

Mitsui & Co., Ltd. MITS
2-1, Ohtemachi 1-Chome
Chiyoda-ku, Tokyo, Japan
Conglomerate

Mobile Communications Corp. of America MCCA
1500 Capital Towers
Jackson, MS 39201 (601) 969-1200
communication

Mobile Gas Service Corp. MBLE
2828 Dauphin Street
Mobile, AL 36652 (205) 476-2720
utility   [DRP]

Modern Controls, Inc. MOCO
6820 Shingle Creek Pkwy.
Minneapolis, MN 55430 (612) 560-2900
precision instruments and photography

Modine Manufacturing Co. MODI
1500 DeKoven Avenue
Racine, WI 53401 (414) 636-1200
auto parts, accessories

Modulaire Industries, MODX
425 Second St., S.E.
Cedar Rapids, IA 52401 (319) 365-5211
modular offices

Molecular Genetics, Inc. MOGN
10320 Bren Road East
Minnetonka, MN 55343 (612) 935-7335
biotechnology, drugs

Molex Inc. MOLX
2222 Wellington Court
Lisle, IL 60532 (312) 969-4550
electronic equipment

Monarch Avalon, Inc. MAHI
4517 Harford Road
Baltimore, MD 21214 (301) 254-9200
printing, toys and games

Monfort of Colorado, Inc. MNFT
1930 AA Street
Greeley, CO 80632 (303) 353-2311
beef products

Moniterm Corp. MTRM
5740 Green Circle Drive
Minnetonka, MN 55343 (612) 935-4151
business data processing

Monitor Technologies Inc. MLAB
10180 Scripps Ranch Blvd.
San Diego, CA 92131 (619) 578-5060
measuring equipment

Monoclonal Antibodies, Inc. MABS
2319 Charleston Road
Mountain View, CA 94043 (415) 960-1320
biotechnology, drugs

Monolithic Memories, Inc. MMIC
2175 Mission College Blvd.
Santa Clara, CA 95054 (408) 970-9700
semiconductors

Monumental Corp. MONU
1111 North Charles Street
Baltimore, MD 21201 (301) 685-2900
insurance   [DRP 5%]

Moore Financial Group Inc. MFGI
101 South Capitol Blvd.
Boise, ID 83733 (208) 383-7000
banking   [DRP]

Moore Products Co. MORP
Sumneytown Pike
Spring House, PA 19477 (215) 646-7400
industrial instruments and gauges

Mor-Flo Industries, Inc. MORF
18450 South Miles Road
Cleveland, OH 44128 (216) 663-7300
gas and electric water heaters

Morgan Products, LTD MGAN
601 Oregon Street
Oshkosh, WI 54903 (414) 235-7170
wood products

Morlan International, Inc. MORL
Philmont Avenue & Byberry Road
Philadelphia, PA 19116 (215) 947-7770
real estate

Morris County Savings Bank (The) MCSB
21 South Street
Morristown, NJ 07960 (201) 539-0500
banking

Morrison Inc. MORR
4721 Morrison Drive
Mobile, AL 36625 (205) 344-3000
restaurants

Moseley Holding Corp. MOSE
60 State Street
Boston, MA 02109 (617) 367-2400
investment services

Mosinee Paper Corp. MOSI
1244 Kronenwetter Drive
Mosinee, WI 54455 (715) 693-4470
paper products

Motor Club of America MOTR
484 Central Avenue
Newark, NJ 07107 (201) 733-1234
auto club, insurance

Mr. Gasket Co. MRGC
8700 Brookpark Road
Brooklyn, OH 44129 (216) 398-8300
auto parts

Mt. Baker Bank, A Savings Bank MBSB
1621 Cornwall Avenue
Bellingham, WA 98227 (206) 676-2300
banking

Paul Mueller Co. MUEL
1600 West Phelps Street
Springfield, MO 65802 (417) 831-3000
heavy machinery

Multibank Financial Corp. MLTF
1400 Hancock Street
Quincy, MA 02169 (617) 471-3800
banking   [DRP 3%]

Multimedia, Inc. MMED
P.O. Box 1688
Greenville, SC 29602 (803) 298-4373
publishing, tv, radio and cable broadcasting

Mutual Federal S&L Assoc. MUTU
201 West Main Street
Elkin, NC 28261 (919) 835-1522
savings and loan

Mutual Savings Life Insuance Co. MUTS
P.O. Box 2222
Decatur, AL 35601 (205) 552-7011
insurance

Mylan Laboratories, Inc. MYLN
1030 Century Bldg.
Pittsburgh, PA 15222 (412) 232-0100
generic drugs   [O]

NAC Re Corporation NREC
25 Valley Drive
Greenwich, CT 06830 (203) 622-1127
insurance

NBSC Corp. NSCB
207 North Main Street
Sumter, SC 29150 (803) 775-1211
banking

NCA Corp. NCAC
3250 Jay Street
Santa Clara, CA 95054 (408) 986-1800
software, data processing

NEC Corp. NIPN
33-1, Shiba 5-chome
Minato-ku, Tokyo 108 Japan
electronic equipment, communications

NIKE, Inc. NIKE
3900 South West Murray
Beaverton, OR 97005 (503) 641-6453
footwear and apparel

NMS Pharmaceuticals, Inc. NMSI
1533 Monrovia Avenue
Newport Beach, CA 92663 (714) 645-2111
drugs

Nanometrics Inc. NANO
690 East Arques Avenue
Sunnyvale, CA 94086 (408) 735-1044
electronics

Napa Valley Bancorp NVBC
One Financial Plaza
Napa, CA 94558 (707) 255-8300
banking

Napco International Inc. NPCO
1600 Second Street South
Hopkins, MN 55343 (612) 931-2400
auto parts, accessories

Napco Security Systems, Inc. NSSC
6 Di Tomas Court
Copiague, NY 11726 (516) 842-9400
security systems

Nash-Finch Co. NAFC
3381 Gorham Avenue
St. Louis Park, MN 55426 (612) 929-0371
food wholesaling   [DRP]

Nashville City Bank & Trust Co. NCBT
315 Union Street
Nashville, TN 37201 (615) 251-9200
banking

Nathan's Famous, Inc. NATH
1515 Broadway
New York, NY 10036 (212) 869-0600
restaurants

National Bancorp of Alaska, Inc. NBAK
301 West Northern Lights Blvd.
Anchorage, AK 99510 (907) 276-1132
banking

National Bankshares Corp. of Texas NBCT
430 Soledad Street
San Antonio, TX 78205 (512) 225-2511
banking

National Capital Real Estate Trust NCET
50 California Street
San Francisco, CA 94111 (415) 989-2661
real estate   [DRP]

National City Bancorporation NCBM
75 South Fifth Street
Minneapolis, MN 55402 (612) 340-3183
banking

National City Corp. NCTY
1900 East Ninth Street
Cleveland, OH 44114 (216) 575-2000
banking   [DRP]

National Commerce Bancorporation NCBC
One Commerce Square
Memphis, TN 38150 (901) 523-3242
banking

National Community Bank of New Jersey NCBR
24 Park Avenue
Rutherford, NJ 07070 (201) 845-1000
banking   [DRP]

National Computer Systems, Inc. NLCS
11000 Prairie Lakes Drive
Eden Prairie, MN 55344 (612) 830-7600
computer products

National Controls, Inc. NCIS
P.O. Box 1501
Santa Rosa, CA 95402 (707) 527-5555
electronic equipment

National Data Corp. NDTA
One National Data Plaza
Atlanta, GA 30329 (404) 329-8500
telephone computer services, billing   [DRP]

National Guardian Corp. (The) NATG
191 Mason Street
Greenwich, CT 06830 (203) 629-3391
security services

National HMO Corp. NHMO
930 S. Harbor City Blvd.
Melbourne, FL 32901 (305) 729-8362
health services

National Hardgoods Distributors, Inc. NHRD
365 Washington Street
Stoughton, MA 02072 (617) 341-1810
hardware stores

National Health Corp. NHCC
814 South Church Street
Murfreesboro, TN 37130 (615) 896-5921
health services

National Lumber & Supply, Inc. NTLB
17102 Newhope Street
Fountain Valley, CA 92708 (714) 751-3970
building materials retailing

National Micronetics, Inc. NMIC
5600 Kearney Mesa Road
San Diego, CA 92111 (619) 279-7500
computer memory components

National Penn Bancshares, Inc. NPBC
Philadelphia and Reading
Boyertown, PA 19512 (215) 367-6001
banking

National Pizza Co. PIZA
P.O. Box 62643
Pittsburg, KS 66762 (316) 231-3390
restaurants

National Properties Corp. NAPE
4500 Merle Hay Road
Des Moines, IA 50310 (515) 278-1132
real estate

National Security Insurance Co. NSIC
661 East Davis Street
Elba, AL 36323 (205) 897-2273
insurance

National Technical Systems NTSC
24007 Ventura Blvd.
Calabasas, CA 91302 (818) 873-7303
educational services

National Western Life Insurance Co. NWLI
850 East Anderson Lane
Austin, TX 78776 (512) 836-1010
insurance

Nationwide Power Corp. NPWR
1300 S.W. 12th Avenue
Pompano Beach, FL 33069 (305) 782-3110
power equipment

Nature's Bounty, Inc. NBTY
90 Orville Drive
Bohemia, NY 11716 (516) 567-9500
food supplements and vitamins

Nature's Sunshine Products, Inc. AMTC
P.O. Box 1000
Spanish Fork, UT 84660 (801) 798-9861
vitamins

Naugles, Inc. NAUG
2932 East Nutwood Avenue
Fullerton, CA 92634 (714) 524-0181
restaurants

Thomas Nelson, Inc. TNEL
Nelson Place at Elm Hill Pike
Nashville, TN 37214 (615) 889-9000
bible publishing

Nelson Research & Development Co. NELR
1001 Health Sciences Road West
Irvine, CA 92715 (714) 856-3100
drugs

Network Security Corp. NTWK
16901 North Dallas Pkwy.
Dallas, TX 75248 (214) 931-1910
fire and security alarms

Network Systems Corp. NSCO
7600 Boone Avenue North
Minneapolis, MN 55428 (612) 425-2202
high-speed computer networks   [0]

Networks Electronic Corp. NWRK
9750 De Soto Avenue
Chatsworth, CA 91311 (818) 341-0440
bearings, ordnance

Neutrogena Corp. NGNA
5755 West 96th Street
Los Angeles, CA 90045 (213) 642-1150
cosmetics and personal care

Nevada National Bancorporation NENB
200 South Virginia Street
Reno, NV 89501 (702) 785-6590
banking

New Brunswick Scientific Co., Inc. NBSC
44 Talmadge Road
Edison, NJ 08818 (201) 287-1200
scientific instruments

New England Business Service, Inc. NEBS
500 Main Street
Groton, MA 01450 (617) 448-6111
office supplies

New Hampshire Savings Bank Corp. NHSB
27 North State Street
Concord, NH 03301 (603) 224-7711
banking

New Jersey National Corp. NJNB
One West State Street
Trenton, NJ 08603 (609) 771-5700
banking   [DRP 5%]

NewCentury Bank Corp. NUCY
108 West School Street
Frankenmuth, MI 48734 (517) 652-3283
banking

Neworld Bank For Savings NWOR
55 Summer Street
Boston, MA 02110 (617) 482-2600
banking

Newport Corp. NEWP
18235 Mount Baldy Circle
Fountain Valley, CA 92708 (714) 963-9811
laser and electro-optical systems

Newport Electronics, Inc. NEWE
630 East Young Street
Santa Ana, CA 92705 (714) 540-4914
scientific instruments

Newport Pharmaceuticals International, Inc.
NWPH
P.O. Box 1990
Newport Beach, CA 92663 (714) 642-7511
drugs

Ni-Cal Development Ltd. NICL
2550 Via Tejon
Palos Verdes, CA 90274 (213) 378-4297
metal mining

Nobel Insurance Ltd. NOBL
3010 LBJ Freeway
Dallas, TX 75234 (214) 484-5626
insurance

Noble Drilling Corp. NDCO
1924 South Utica
Tulsa, OK 74104 (918) 749-9901
oil and gas drilling

Nodaway Valley Co. NVCO
220 North First Street
Clarinda, IA 51632 (712) 542-5125
financial services

Noland Co. NOLD
2700 Warwick Blvd.
Newport News, VA 23607 (804) 244-8441
building materials distibutor

Nordson Corp. NDSN
555 Jackson Street
Amherst, OH 44001 (216) 988-9411
industrial and packaging machinery

Nordstrom, Inc. NOBE
1501 Fifth Avenue
Seattle, WA 98101 (206) 628-2111
apparel stores

Norsk Data A.S. NORK
Postboks 4 Lindeberg Gard
Oslo-10, Norway
business data processing

Norstan, Inc. NRRD
15755 - 32nd Avenue North
Plymouth, MN 55447 (612) 553-3200
precision gears, telephone service

North American National Corp. NAMC
1251 Dublin Road
Columbus, OH 43216 (614) 253-7453
insurance

North Atlantic Industries, Inc. NATL
60 Plant Avenue
Hauppauge, NY 11788 (516) 582-6500
electronic equipment

North Carolina Natural Gas Corp. NCNG
150 Rowan Street
Fayetteville, NC 28302 (919) 483-0315
utility

North Fork Bancorporation, Inc. NFBC
245 Love Lane
Mattituck, NY 11952 (516) 298-8366
banking   [DRP]

North Hills Electronics, Inc. NOHL
Alexander Place
Glen Cove, NY 11542 (516) 671-5700
electronics

North-West Telecommunications, Inc. NOWT
901 Kilbourn Avenue
Tomah, WI 54660 (608) 372-4151
communication

Northeast Bancorp, Inc. NBIC
Church and Elm Streets
New Haven, CT 06502 (203) 773-5815
banking   [DRP]

Northeast Savings, F.A. NESA
500 State Street
Schenectady, NY 12301 (518) 370-8400
banking

Northern Air Freight, Inc. NAFI
16400 Southcenter Pkwy.
Seattle, WA 98188 (206) 575-3360
air freight

Northern Trust Corp. NTRS
50 South LaSalle Street
Chicago, IL 60675 (312) 630-6000
banking

Northview Corp. NOVC
10021 Willow Creek Road
San Diego, CA 92131 (619) 578-8710
lodging

Northwest Natural Gas Co. NWNG
220 N.W. Second Avenue
Portland, OR 97209 (503) 226-4211
utility   [DRP]

Northwest Teleproductions, Inc. NWTL
4455 West 77th Street
Minneapolis, MN 55435 (612) 835-4455
movies

Northwestern National Life Insurance Co.
NWNL
20 Washington Avenue South
Minneapolis, MN 55440 (612) 372-5432
insurance

Northwestern Public Service Co. NWPS
N.W. National Bank Bldg.
Huron, SD 57350 (605) 352-8411
utility   [DRP 5%]

Norwesco, Inc. NWES
7850 Metro Pkwy.
Minneapolis, MN 55420 (612) 854-1120
injection molded plastic products

Novametrix Medical Systems Inc. NMTX
One Barnes Industrial Park
Wallingford, CT 06492 (203) 265-7701
scientific instruments

Novar Electronics Corp. NOVR
24 Brown Street
Barberton, OH 44203 (216) 745-0074
anticrime electronics

Novell, Inc. NOVL
748 North, 1340 West
Orem, UT 84057 (801) 226-8202
business services

Novo Corp. NOVO
1075 Central Park Avenue
Scarsdale, NY 10583 (914) 472-2252
home improvement products, film

Noxell Corp. NOXL
11050 York Road
Hunt Valley, MD 21030 (301) 628-7300
cosmetics and personal care

Nu-Med, Inc. NUMS
16633 Ventura Blvd.
Encino, CA 91436 (818) 990-2000
health services

Nuclear Metals, Inc. NUCM
2229 Main Street
Concord, MA 01742 (617) 369-5410
metals fabrication

Nuclear Pharmacy Inc. NURX
1730 Montano Road N.W.
Albuquerque, NM 87107 (505) 345-1641
drug distributor

Nuclear Support Services, Inc. NSSI
P.O. Box 3120
Hershey, PA 17033 (717) 838-8125
electrical equipment, business services

Numerax, Inc. NMRX
230 Passaic Street
Maywood, NJ 07607 (201) 368-0170
transportation services

Numerex Corp. NUMR
7101 Northland Circle
Minneapolis, MN 55428 (612) 533-4716
machinery

Numerica Financial Corp. NUME
1000 Elm Street
Manchester, NH 03101 (603) 624-2424
banking

NuVision, Inc. NUVI
2284 South Ballenger Hwy.
Flint, MI 48503 (313) 767-0900
optical retailing

OCG Technology, Inc. OCGT
42 Executive Blvd.
Farmingdale, NY 11735 (516) 454-0981
machinery

ORFA Corp. of America ORFA
800 Kings Hwy.
Cherry Hill, NJ 08034 (609) 482-2300
utility

ORS Automation, Inc. ORSI
440 Wall Street
Princeton, NJ 08540 (609) 924-1667
computers

Oak Hill Sportswear Corp. OHSC
1411 Broadway
New York, NY 10018 (212) 354-0444
apparel

Oceaneering International, Inc. OCER
16001 Park Ten Place
Houston, TX 77084 (713) 578-8868
offshore drilling

Ocilla Industries, Inc. OCIL
3000 Marcus Ave.
Lake Success, NY 11042 (516) 354-6333
mobile homes

Offshore Logistics, Inc. OLOG
900 East University Avenue
Lafayette, LA 70505 (318) 233-1221
offshore oilfield services

Ogilvy Group, Inc. (The) OGIL
2 East 48th Street
New York, NY 10017 (212) 907-3595
advertising   [DRP]

Oglebay Norton Co. OGLE
1100 Superior Avenue
Cleveland, OH 44114 (216) 861-3300
freight, water transportation

Ohio Bancorp OHBC
801 Dollar Bank Bldg.
Youngstown, OH 44503 (216) 744-2093
banking

Ohio Casualty Corp. OCAS
136 North Third Street
Hamilton, OH 45025 (513) 867-3000
insurance   [DRP]

Oil-Dri Corp. of America OILC
520 North Michigan Avenue
Chicago, IL 60611 (312) 321-1515
absorbent minerals mining

Oilgear Co. (The) OLGR
2300 South 51st Street
Milwaukee, WI 53219 (414) 327-1700
oil drilling equipment

Old Fashion Foods, Inc. OFFI
5521 Collins Blvd., S.W.
Austell, GA 30001 (404) 948-1177
vending machine retailing

Old Kent Financial Corp. OKEN
One Vandenberg Center
Grand Rapids, MI 49503 (616) 774-5000
banking

Old National Bancorp OLDB
420 Main Street
Evansville, IN 47708 (812) 464-1200
banking

Old Republic International Corp. OLDR
307 North Michigan Avenue
Chicago, IL 60601 (312) 346-8100
insurance   [DRP]

Old Spaghetti Warehouse, Inc. OSWI
1815 North Market Street
Dallas, TX 75202 (214) 651-1450
restaurants

Old Stone Corp. OSTN
150 South Main Street
Providence, RI 02903 (401) 278-2000
banking   [DRP]

Olson Industries, Inc. OLSN
13400 Riverside Drive
Sherman Oaks, CA 91413 (818) 995-1238
agricultural products, meat

Omni Equities, Inc. OEQU
701 West Cypress Creek Road
Fort Lauderdale, FL 33309 (305) 492-8155
solar water-heating equipment

On-Line Software International Inc. OSII
Fort Lee Executive Park
Fort Lee, NJ 07024 (201) 592-0009
software

One Bancorp (The) TONE
One Maine Savings Plaza
Portland, ME 04101 (207) 871-1111
banking

One Liberty Properties, Inc. TIRE
515 Madison Avenue
New York, NY 10022 (212) 935-0931
investments

Optical Coating Laboratory, Inc. OCLI
2789 Northpoint Pkwy.
Santa Rosa, CA 95407 (707) 545-6440
coated lenses and filters

Optical Radiation Corp. ORCO
1300 Optical Drive
Azusa, CA 91702 (818) 969-3344
electro-optical systems

Opto Mechanik, Inc. OPTO
1216 East Prospect Avenue
Melbourne, FL 32902 (305) 724-2017
precision instruments and photography

Optrotech Ltd. OPTK
P.O. Box 69
Nes-Ziona 70450 Israel
electro-optical systems

Orbanco Financial Services. Corp. ORBN
1001 S.W. Fifth Avenue
Portland, OR 97204 (503) 222-7960
banking

Orbit Instrument Corp. ORBT
80 Cabot Court
Hauppauge, NY 11788 (516) 435-8300
electronic equipment

Oregon Metallurgical Corp. OREM
530 West 34th Avenue
Albany, OR 97321 (503) 926-4281
produces aircraft alloys

Orion Research Inc. ORIR
840 Memorial Drive
Cambridge, MA 02139 (617) 864-5400
scientific instruments

Oshkosh B'Gosh, Inc., GOSH
112 Otter St.
Oshkosh, WI 54901 (414) 231-8800
apparel

Oshkosh Truck Corp., OTRK
2307 Oregon St.
Oshkosh, WI 54903 (414) 235-9150
truck manufacturer

Oshman's Sporting Goods, Inc. OSHM
2302 Maxwell Lane
Houston, TX 77023 (713) 928-3171
sporting goods retailing

Osmonics, Inc. OSMO
5951 Clearwater Drive
Minnetonka, MN 55343 (612) 933-2277
filters

Otter Tail Power Co. OTTR
215 South Cascade Street
Fergus Falls, MN 56537 (218) 736-5411
utility   [DRP]

Overland Express, Inc. OVER
1631 West Thompson Road
Indianapolis, IN 46207 (317) 787-4300
trucking

Owens & Minor, Inc. OBOD
P.O. Box 27626
Richmond, VA 23261 (804) 747-9794
drug and hospital supplies wholesaler

Oxoco Inc. OXCO
1360 Post Oak Blvd.
Houston, TX 77056 (713) 961-1770
oil and gas production and services

PACCAR Inc. PCAR
777-106th Avenue, N.E.
Bellevue, WA 98004 (206) 455-7400
truck and rail car manufacturer

PACE Membership Warehouse, Inc. PMWI
3350 Peoria Street
Aurora, CO 80010 (303) 364-0700
merchandise wholesaling and retailing

PAR Technology Corp. PARR
220 Seneca Turnpike
New Hartford, NY 13413 (315) 738-0600
computer terminal systems

PDA Engineering PDAS
1560 Brookhollow Drive
Santa Ana, CA 92705 (714) 556-2800
software, data processing

PENWEST, LTD. PENW
300 One Bellevue Center
Bellevue, WA 98004 (206) 462-6000
food products

PNC Financial Corp. PNCF
Foster Plaza, Holiday Drive
Pittsburgh, PA 15222 (412) 355-2666
banking   [DRP 5%]

PT Components, Inc. PTCS
7545 Rockville Road
Indianapolis, IN 46224 (316) 273-5813
auto parts, accessories

Pacific First Financial Corp. PFFS
1102 Pacific Avenue
Tacoma, WA 98402 (206) 383-2511
savings and loan

Pacific Gamble Robinson Co. PGAM
10829 N. E. 68th Street
Kirkland, WA 98033 (206) 828-6200
grocery wholesaling   [DRP]

Pacific Telecom, Inc. PTCM
805 Broadway
Vancouver, WA 98668 (206) 696-0983
communication

Pacific Western Bancshares PAWB
333 West Santa Clara Street
San Jose, CA 95113 (408) 244-1700
banking

Packaging Systems Corp. PAKS
275 North Middletown Road
Pearl River, NY 10965 (914) 735-9200
packaging products

Paco Pharmaceutical Services, Inc. PPSI
1200 Paco Way
Lakewood, NJ 08701 (201) 367-9000
drug packaging products

Pacwest Bancorp PWST
1211 Southwest Fifth Avenue
Portland, OR 97204 (503) 790-7501
banking

Page America Group, Inc. PAGE
60 Broad Street
New York, NY 10004 (212) 286-8901
communication

Palmetto Fed. Savings Bank PALM
107 Chesterfield Street South
Aiken, SC 29801 (803) 648-0171
savings and loan

Panatech Research and Development Corp.
PNTC
655 Deep Valley Drive
Rolling Hills Estates, CA 90274 (213) 541-0221
medical supplies

Pancho's Mexican Buffet, Inc. PAMX
3500 Noble Avenue
Fort Worth, TX 76111 (817) 831-0081
restaurants

Par Pharmaceutical, Inc. PARP
12 Industrial Avenue
Upper Saddle River, NJ 07458 (201) 825-8848
drugs

Parisian, Inc. PASN
1101 North 26th Street
Birmingham, AL 35234 (205) 251-1300
apparel stores

Park Communications, Inc. PARC
P.O. Box 550
Ithaca, NY 14851 (607) 272-9020
broadcasting, newspapers

Park-Ohio Industries, Inc. PKOH
20600 Chagrin Blvd.
Cleveland, OH 44122 (216) 991-9700
oil and gas production, pipelines

Parkway Co. (The) PKWY
120 North Congress Street
Jackson, MS 39225 (601) 948-4091
financial services

Parlex Corp. PRLX
145 Milk Street
Methuen, MA 01844 (617) 685-4341
electronics

Pasadena Technology Corp. PACE
4546 Beltway Drive
Dallas, TX 75244 (214) 991-9585
oil and gas, electronics

Pasquale Food Co., Inc. PASQ
19 West Oxmoor Road
Birmingham, AL 35209 (205) 942-3371
hotels, restaurants

Pasta & Cheese, Inc. PANC
21-51 Borden Avenue
Long Island City, NY 11101 (718) 729-8489
food products

Patient Medical Systems Corp. PATS
790 Madison Avenue
New York, NY 10021 (212) 737-5771
health services

Patlex Corp. PTLX
533 South Avenue West
Westfield, NJ 07090 (201) 654-6620
patent enforcement

Patrick Industries, Inc. PATK
1800 South 14th Street
Elkhart, IN 46515 (219) 294-7511
building materials

Patriot Bancorporation PATB
63 Franklin Street
Boston, MA 02110 (617) 451-9100
banking

Paul Harris Stores, Inc. PHRS
6003 Guion Road
Indianapolis, IN 46268 (317) 293-3900
apparel stores

Pawling Savings Bank PSBK
Route 22
Pawling, NY 12564 (914) 855-1333
banking

Pawnee Industries, Inc. PWNE
101 S. Ridge Road
Wichita, KS 67209 (316) 722-7212
rubber products

Frank Paxton Co. PAXT
9229 Ward Pkwy.
Kansas City, MO 64114 (816) 361-7110
wood products

Paychex, Inc. PAYX
P.O. Box 25397
Rochester, NY 14625 (716) 385-6666
payroll services

Payco American Corp. PAYC
180 North Executive Drive
Brookfield, WI 53005 (414) 784-9035
collection agency

Peak Health Care, Inc. PHCI
North Creek 1, Suite 200
Colorado Springs, CO 80919 (303) 548-8600
health services

Peerless Manufacturing Co. PMFG
2811 Walnut Hill Lane
Dallas, TX 75220 (214) 357-6181
machinery

Pegasus Gold, Inc. PGUL
West 801 Riverside Avenue
Spokane, WA 99201 (509) 624-4653
metal mining

Penn Virginia Corp. PVIR
2500 Fidelity Bldg.
Philadelphia, PA 19109 (215) 545-6600
soft coal mining

Pennbancorp PNBA
Pennbank Center
Titusville, PA 16354 (814) 827-2751
banking

Pennsylvania Enterprises, Inc. PENT
39 Public Square
Wilkes-Barre, PA 18711 (717) 829-8600
utility   [DRP]

Pennsylvania National Financial Corp. PNFC
1002 North Seventh Street
Harrisburg, PA 17102 (717) 622-4200
financial services

Pentair, Inc. PNTA
1700 West Hwy. 36
St. Paul, MN 55113 (612) 636-7920
paper products   [DRP]

People Express, Inc. PEXP
Newark International Airport
Newark, NJ 07114 (201) 961-2935
airline

Peoples Ban Corp. PEOP
1414 Fourth Avenue
Seattle, WA 98111 (206) 344-2330
banking

Peoples Bancorporation PBNC
130 South Franklin Street
Rocky Mount, NC 27801 (919) 977-4800
banking

Perceptronics, Inc. PERC
6271 Variel Avenue
Woodland Hills, CA 91367 (818) 884-7470
electronics

Perle Systems Ltd. PERL
360 Tapscott Road
Scarborough, Ont. M1B 3C4 (416) 299-4999
software, data processing

Perpetual American Bank, F.S.B. PASB
2034 Eisenhower Avenue
Alexandria, VA 22314 (703) 838-6000
banking

Personal Computer Products, Inc. PCPI
11590 West Bernardo Court
San Diego, CA 92127 (619) 485-8411
computers

Petrol Industries, Inc. PTRL
1200 North Market Street
Shreveport, LA 71107 (313) 424-6396
oil and gas

Petroleum Equipment Tools Co. PTCO
P.O. Box 4301
Houston, TX 77210 (713) 658-1141
oil and gas drilling equipment

Petrolite Corp. PLIT
100 North Broadway
St. Louis, MO 63102 (314) 241-8370
specialty chemicals

Petrominerals Corp. PTRO
12362 Beach Blvd.
Stanton, CA 90680 (714) 895-6370
oil and gas

Pharmacia AB PHAB
800 Centennial Ave.
Piscataway, NJ 08854 (201) 457-8000
drugs

PharmaControl Corp. PHAR
661 Palisade Avenue
Englewood Cliffs, NJ 07632 (201) 567-9004
drug testing equipment

Pharmakinetics Laboratories, Inc. PKLB
104 East 25th Street
Baltimore, MD 21218 (301) 366-2001
health services, supplies

Philips Gloeilampenfabrieke NV PGLO
Bldg. VH-1
5600 MD Eindhoven, The Netherlands
electrical equipment

Phoenix American Inc. PHXA
P.O. Box 2008
San Rafael, CA 94912 (415) 485-4500
equipment leasing limited partnerships

Phoenix Medical Technology, Inc. PHNX
P.O. Box 346
Andrews, SC 29510 (803) 221-5100
medical supplies

Phone-A-Gram System, Inc. PHOG
1201 Corporate Blvd.
Reno, NV 89502 (702) 348-1000
health services, supplies

Photo Control Corp. PHOC
4800 Quebec Avenue North
Minneapolis, MN 55428 (612) 537-3601
photographic equipment

Photronics Corp. PHOT
P.O. Box 11368
Hauppauge, NY 11788 (516) 231-9500
precision instruments and photography

Physicians Insurance Co. of Ohio PICO
P.O. Box 281
Pickerington, OH 43147 (614) 864-7100
insurance

Pic 'N' Save Corp. PICN
P.O. Box 58667
Los Angeles, CA 90058 (213) 537-9220
discount and variety stores

Piccadilly Cafeterias, Inc. PICC
P.O. Box 2467
Baton Rouge, LA 70821 (504) 293-9440
restaurants

Piedmont BankGroup Inc. PBGI
P.O. Box 4751
Martinsville, VA 24115 (703) 632-2971
banking

Piedmont Management Co. Inc. PMAN
99 John Street
New York, NY 10038 (212) 732-5210
insurance, investment services

Pioneer Federal S&L Association PION
112 Main Street
Hopewell, VA 23860 (804) 458-9893
savings & loan

Pioneer Group, Inc. (The) PIOG
60 State Street
Boston, MA 02109 (617) 742-7825
investment services, mutual funds

Pioneer Hi-Bred International Inc. PHYB
6800 Pioneer Pkwy.
Johnston, IA 50131 (515) 270-3100
agricultural products, seeds   [DRP]

Pioneer Savings Bank PSBF
5770 Roosevelt Blvd.
Clearwater, FL 33520 (813) 530-7600
banking

Pioneer-Standard Electronics, Inc. PIOS
4800 East 131st Street
Garfield Heights, OH 44105 (216) 587-3600
electronics

Piper Jaffray, Inc. PIPR
Piper Jaffray Tower
Minneapolis, MN 55440 (612) 342-6000
brokerage

Planters Corp. (The) PNBT
131 North Church Street
Rocky Mount, NC 27801 (919) 977-8211
banking   [DRP]

Plaza Commerce Bancorp PLZA
55 Almaden Blvd.
San Jose, CA 95113 (408) 294-8940
banking

Plenum Publishing Corp. PLEN
233 Spring Street
New York, NY 10013 (212) 620-8000
publishing, books

Po Folks, Inc. POFO
2201 Murfreesboro Road
Nashville, TN 37217 (615) 366-0900
restaurants

Policy Management Systems Corp. PMSC
One PMS Center
Blythewood, SC 29016 (803) 735-4000
software for insurance companies

Ponce Federal Bank, F.S.B. PFBS
P.O. Box 7304
Ponce, PR 00732 (809) 844-8100
banking

Popular Bancshares Corp. PBAN
100 East Flagler Street
Miami, FL 33131 (305) 579-3000
banking

Porex Technologies Corp. PORX
491 Edward H. Ross Drive
Elmwood Park, NJ 07407 (201) 794-1000
medical plastic components

Possis Corp. POSS
750 Pennsylvania Avenue South
Minneapolis, MN 55426 (612) 545-1471
machinery

Poughkeepsie Savings Bank, F.S.B. (The) PKPS
21 Market Street
Poughkeepsie, NY 12602 (914) 454-1100
banking

Powell Industries, Inc. POWL
8550 Mosley Drive
Houston, TX 77075 (713) 944-6900
electrical distribution equipment

Power Conversion, Inc. PWRC
495 Blvd.
Elmwood Park, NJ 07407 (201) 796-4800
electronic power equipment

Powertec, Inc. PWTC
20550 Nordhoff Street
Chatsworth, CA 91311 (213) 882-0004
power supplies for electronic equipment

Pratt Hotel Corp. PRAT
4099 McEwen
Dallas, TX 75244 (214) 386-9777
lodging

Pre-Paid Legal Services, Inc. LEGL
P.O. Box 145
Ada, OK 74820 (405) 436-1234
insurance, legal services

Precision Castparts Corp. PCST
4600 S.E. Harney Drive
Portland, OR 97206 (503) 653-8210
precision castings

Preferred Financial Corp. PFCO
2130 South Dahlia Street
Denver, CO 80222 (303) 759-2400
financial services, insurance

Preferred Health Care Ltd. PHCC
800 Cross River Road
Katonah, NY 10536 (914) 763-8134
health services

Preferred Risk Life Insurance Co. PFDR
1111 Ashworth Road
West Des Moines, IA 50265 (515) 225-5000
insurance

Preferred Savings Bank PSLA
600 North Hamilton Street
High Point, NC 27262 (919) 889-3132
savings & loan

Presidential Life Corp. PLFE
69 Lydecker Street
Nyack, NY 10960 (914) 358-2300
insurance

Preston Corp. PTRK
151 Easton Blvd.
Preston, MD 21655 (301) 673-7151
trucking

Preway Inc. PREW
1430 Second Street North
Wisconsin Rapids, WI 54494 (715) 423-1100
home heating and plumbing appliances

Priam Corp. PRIA
20 West Montague Expressway
San Jose, CA 95134 (408) 946-4600
computer disk drives

Price Co. (The) PCLB
2657 Ariane Drive
San Diego, CA 92117 (619) 581-4600
wholesale membership merchandise outlets

Prime Medical Services PMSI
240 Madison Avenue
New York, NY 10016 (212) 685-3570
health services

Princeville Development Corp. PVDC
1860 Lincoln Street
Denver, CO 80295 (303) 861-5252
real estate

Printronix, Inc. PTNX
17500 Cartwright Road
Irvine, CA 92713 (714) 863-1900
computer printers

Prodigy Systems, Inc. PDGY
21 Meridian Road
Edison, NJ 08820 (201) 321-1717
computers

Production Operators Corp. PROP
11302 Tanner Road
Houston, TX 77041 (713) 466-0980
oil and gas services

Professional Investors Insurance Group, Inc.
PROF
9933 East 16th Street
Tulsa, OK 74128 (918) 665-8280
insurance

Profit Systems, Inc. PFTS
80 West Sunrise Hwy.
Valley Stream, NY 11581 (516) 791-1551
air freight

Programming and Systems, Inc. PSYS
269 West 40th Street
New York, NY 10018 (212) 944-9200
educational services

Progress Federal Savings Bank PBNK
One Montgomery Plaza
Norristown, PA 19401 (215) 272-3500
banking

Progressive Corp. (The) PROG
6300 Wilson Mills Road
Mayfield Village, OH 44143 (216) 461-5000
insurance

ProGroup, Inc. PRGR
99 Tremont Street
Chattanooga, TN 37405 (615) 267-5631
sporting goods

Property Investors of Colorado PRCL
5325 South Valentia Way
Englewood, CO 80111 (303) 779-8100
real estate

Property Trust of America PTRA
4487 North Mesa
El Paso, TX 79902 (915) 532-3901
real estate

Protective Life Corp. PROT
2801 Hwy. 280 South
Birmingham, AL 35223 (205) 879-9230
insurance

Protocol Computers, Inc. PCII
6150 Canoga Avenue
Woodland Hills, CA 91367 (818) 716-5500
computer equipment

Provident American Corp. PRAM
2500 DeKalb Pike
Norristown, PA 19404 (215) 279-2500
insurance

Provident Institution for Savings in Boston
PROV
30 Winter Street
Boston, MA 02108 (617) 423-9600
banking

Provident Life and Accident Insurance Co.
PACC
Fountain Square
Chattanooga, TN 37402 (615) 755-1011
insurance

Prudential Bancorporation PBSB
1100 Third Avenue
Seattle, WA 98101 (206) 382-7500
banking

Prudential Financial Services Corp. PFSL
127 East 33rd South
Salt Lake City, UT 84115 (801) 467-0501
financial services

Pubco Corp. PUBO
7209 St. Clair Avenue
Cleveland, OH 44103 (216) 391-6303
publishing

Public Service Co. of NC, Inc. PSNC
400 Cox Road
Gastonia, NC 28053 (704) 864-6731
utility

Puget Sound Bancorp PSNB
1119 Pacific Avenue
Tacoma, WA 98402 (206) 593-3600
banking

Pulaski Furniture Corp. PLFC
P.O. Box 1371
Pulaski, VA 24301 (703) 980-7330
furniture

Puritan-Bennett Corp. PBEN
P.O. Box 25905
Overland Park, KS 66225 (913) 661-0444
medical supplies

Q E D Exploration, Inc. QEDX
1616 Glenarm Place, Suite 1560
Denver, CO 80202 (303) 572-7832
oil and gas

QMS, Inc. QMSI
One Magnum Pass
Mobile, AL 36618 (205) 633-4300
computer printers

QT & T, Inc. QTNT
448 Suffolk Avenue
Brentwood, NY 11717 (516) 273-2800
electronic equipment

Quadrex Corp. QUAD
1700 Dell Avenue
Campbell, CA 95008 (408) 370-4247
nuclear power engineering services

Quaker Chemical Corp. QCHM
Elm and Lee Streets
Conshohocken, PA 19428 (215) 828-4250
specialty chemicals

Quality Systems, Inc. QSII
17822 East 17th Street
Tustin, CA 92680 (714) 731-7171
software, data processing

Quantronix Corp. QUAN
225 Engineers Road
Smithtown, NY 11788 (516) 273-6900
scientific instruments

Quantum Corp. QNTM
1804 McCarthy Blvd.
Milpitas, CA 95035 (408) 262-1100
computer disk drives

Quarex Industries, Inc. QRXI
4705 Metropolitan Avenue
Ridgewood, NY 11385 (718) 821-0011
food products

QuesTech, Inc. QTEC
6858 Old Dominion Drive
McLean, VA 22101 (703) 556-8666
business services

Quest Medical, Inc. QMED
3312 Wiley Post Road
Carrollton, TX 75006 (214) 387-2740
medical supplies

Quintel Corp. QNTL
2078 East University Drive
Tempe, AZ 85281 (602) 894-1981
scientific instruments

Quixote Corp. QUIX
One East Wacker Drive
Chicago, IL 60601 (312) 467-6755
highway safety products

Quotron Systems, Inc. QUOT
5454 Beethoven Street
Los Angeles, CA 90066 (213) 827-4600
financial information services   [O]

R.J. Financial Corp. RJFN
1400 66th Street North
St. Petersburg, FL 33710 (813) 344-8200
investment services

RLI Corp. RLIC
9025 North Lindbergh Drive
Peoria, IL 61615 (309) 692-1000
insurance

RPM, Inc. RPOW
P.O. Box 777
Medina, OH 44258 (216) 225-3192
specialty chemicals, building products [DRP]

Radiation Systems, Inc. RADS
1501 Moran Road
Sterling, VA 22170 (703) 450-5680
communication antennas, aerospace

Radiation Technology, Inc. RTCH
108 Lake Denmark Road
Rockaway, NJ 07866 (201) 625-8400
health services, supplies

Radionics, Inc. RADX
1800 Abbott Street
Salinas, CA 93901 (408) 757-8877
signal communication systems

Ragen Corp. RAGN
9 Porete Avenue
North Arlington, NJ 07032 (201) 997-1000
electric and electronic components

Rainier Bancorporation RBAN
1301 Fifth Avenue
Seattle, WA 98124 (206) 621-4111
banking   [DRP 5%]

Ramapo Financial Corp. RMPO
64 Mountain View Blvd.
Wayne, NJ 07470 (201) 696-6100
banking

Ramtek Corp. RMTK
2211 Lawson Lane
Santa Clara, CA 95050 (408) 988-2211
computer graphic displays

Rangaire Corp. RANG
501 South Wilhite Street
Cleburne, TX 76031 (817) 477-2161
home appliances

Rauch Industries, Inc. RCHI
6048 South York Road
Gastonia, NC 28053 (704) 867-5333
luxury and recreation products

Rax Restaurants, Inc. RAXR
1266 Dublin Road
Columbus, OH 43215 (614) 486-3669
restaurants

Raymond Corp. (The) RAYM
Canal Street
Greene, NY 13778 (607) 656-2311
mining and materials handling machinery

Raymond Engineering Inc. REIN
217 Smith Street
Middletown, CT 06457 (203) 632-1000
electronic systems, aerospace

Reading Co. RDGC
Reading Center
Philadelphia, PA 19107 (215) 922-3303
real estate

REIT of California REIT
1201 San Vicente Blvd.
Los Angeles, CA 90049 (213) 476-9986
real estate

Recoton Corp. RCOT
46-23 Crane Street
Long Island City, NY 11101 (718) 392-6442
consumer electronics accessories

Rectisel Corp. RECT
21 Gray Oaks Avenue
Yonkers, NY 10710 (914) 965-4400
electronics

RediCare, Inc. REDI
18662 MacArthur Blvd.
Irvine, CA 92715 (714) 476-8743
health services

Redken Laboratories, Inc. RDKN
6625 Variel Avenue
Canoga Park, CA 91303 (818) 992-2700
cosmetics and personal care

Reebok International Ltd. RBOK
500 Bodwell Street Extension
Avon, MA 02322 (617) 580-1600
apparel, footwear

Reeves Communications Corp. RVCC
605 Third Avenue
New York, NY 10158 (212) 573-6700
broadcast programming

Refac Technology Development Corp. REFC
122 East 42nd Street
New York, NY 10168 (212) 687-4741
investments

Regency Electronics, Inc. RGCY
7707 Records Street
Indianapolis, IN 46226 (317) 543-4845
communications, navigation equipment

Regency Equities Corp. RGEQ
131 S. Rodeo Drive
Beverly Hills, CA 90212 (213) 276-6224
financial services

Regina Company, Inc. (The) REGI
313 Regina Avenue
Rahway, NJ 07065 (201) 381-1000
appliances

Regis Corp. RGIS
5000 Normandale Road
Edina, MN 55436 (612) 929-6776
hair salons

Reid-Ashman, Inc. REAS
590 Laurelwood Road
Santa Clara, CA 95050 (408) 727-6706
electronics

Reid-Provident Laboratories, Inc. REID
640 Tenth Street, N.W.
Atlanta, GA 30318 (404) 898-1000
drugs, chemicals

Reliability Inc. REAL
16400 Park Row
Houston, TX 77218 (713) 492-0550
semiconductor testing equipment

Renal Systems, Inc. RENL
14905 28th Avenue North
Minneapolis, MN 55441 (612) 553-3300
health services, supplies

Rent-A-Center, Inc. RENT
9920 East Harry Street
Wichita, KS 67207 (316) 686-7411
household goods rental

Repco Inc. RPCO
2421 North Orange Blossom
Orlando, FL 32804 (305) 843-8484
communications

Republic Automotive Parts, Inc. RAUT
22777 Kelly Road
East Detroit, MI 48021 (313) 779-7700
auto parts

Republic Health Corp. REPH
14951 Dallas Pkwy.
Dallas, TX 75240 (214) 851-3100
health services

Republic Pictures Corp. RPIC
12636 Beatrice Street
Los Angeles, CA 90066 (213) 306-4040
movies

Research, Inc. RESR
P.O. Box 24064
Minneapolis, MN 55424 (612) 941-3300
construction and heating equipment

Reserve Oil and Minerals Corp. ROIL
20 First Plaza
Albuquerque, NM 87102 (505) 247-2384
metal mining

Resource Exploration, Inc. REXI
2876 South Arlington Road
Akron, OH 44312 (216) 644-6626
oil and gas

Resources Pension Shares 1 RPSA
666 Third Avenue
New York, NY 10017 (212) 551-6000
real estate

Resources Pension Shares 2 RPSB
666 Third Avenue
New York, NY 10017 (212) 551-6000
real estate

Resources Pension Shares 3 RPSC
666 Third Avenue
New York, NY 10017 (212) 551-6000
real estate

Restaurant Management Services, Inc. RESM
4848 Mercer University Drive
Macon, GA 31210 (912) 474-5633
restaurants

Reuter, Inc. REUT
410 - 11th Avenue South
Hopkins, MN 55343 (612) 935-6921
precision instruments

Reuters Holdings PLC RTRS
Reuters Limited, 1700 Broadway
New York, NY 10017 (212) 603-3520
financial information services

Revere AE Capital Fund PREV
745 Fifth Avenue
New York, NY 10151 (212) 888-6800
investments

Rexon Inc. REXN
5800 Uplander Way
Culver City, CA 90230 (213) 641-7110
computers

Reynolds and Reynolds Co. (The) REYN
P.O. Box 2608
Dayton, OH 45401 (513) 443-2000
computer systems, business forms

Rhodes, Inc. RHDS
4370 Peachtree Road, N.E.
Atlanta, GA 30319 (404) 264-4600
furniture stores

Ribi Immunochem Research, Inc. RIBI
P.O. Box 1409
Hamilton, MT 59840 (406) 363-6214
drugs

Richardson Electronics, Ltd. RELL
3030 North River Road
Franklin Park, IL 60131 (312) 456-0600
electronics

Richton International Corp. RIHL
1345 Avenue of the Americas
New York, NY 10105 (212) 765-6480
jewelry

Riggs National Corp. RIGS
1503 Pennsylvania Avenue, N.W.
Washington, DC 20005 (202) 835-6000
banking

Ritzy's, Inc. (G.D.) RITZ
1535 Bethel Road
Columbus, OH 43220 (614) 459-3250
restaurants

Rival Manufacturing Co. RIVL
36th Street and Bennington
Kansas City, MO 64129 (816) 861-1000
housewares

River Forest Bancorp RFBC
7727 Lake Street
River Forest, IL 60305 (312) 771-2500
banking

Roadway Services, Inc. ROAD
1077 Gorge Blvd.
Akron, OH 44309 (216) 384-8184
trucking   [DRP]

Roanoke Electric Steel Corp. RESC
102 Miller Street, N.W.
Roanoke, VA 24017 (703) 342-1831
steel mills

Robbins & Myers, Inc. ROBN
1400 Kettering Tower
Dayton, OH 45423 (513) 222-2610
household machinery, ceiling fans

Robert C. Brown & Co., Inc. RCBI
655 Montgomery Street
San Francisco, CA 94111 (415) 981-4050
financial services

Robeson Industries Corp. RBSN
49 Windsor Avenue
Mineola, NY 11501 (516) 741-0420
appliances

Robinson Nugent, Inc. RNIC
800 East Eighth Street
New Albany, IN 47150 (812) 945-0211
electromechanical products

Robotic Vision Systems, Inc. ROBV
425 Rabro Drive East
Hauppauge, NY 11788 (516) 273-9700
special industrial machines

Rockwood Holding Co. RKWD
118 West Main Street
Somerset, PA 15501 (814) 443-1471
insurance

Rocky Mount Undergarment Co., Inc. RMUC
1536 Boone Street
Rocky Mount, NC 27801 (919) 446-5188
apparel

Rocky Mountain Natural Gas Co., Inc. RGAS
1600 Sherman Street
Denver, CO 80203 (303) 861-4072
utility

Rogers Cablesystems of Amer., Inc. RCCA
Twelfth and Market Streets
Wilmington, DE 19899 (302) 658-8128
cable television

Ropak Corp. ROPK
660 S. State College Blvd.
Fullerton, CA 92631 (714) 871-0171
rubber products

Rose's Stores, Inc. RSTO
P. H. Rose Bldg.
Henderson, NC 27536 (919) 492-8111
discount and variety stores

Rospatch Corp. RPCH
3101 Walkent Drive, N.W.
Grand Rapids, MI 49504 (616) 784-1000
fabric labels, packaging material

Ross Stores, Inc. ROST
P.O. Box 728
Newark, CA 94560 (415) 790-4400
discount and drug stores

RoTech Medical Corp. ROTC
724 Franklin Lane
Orlando, FL 32801 (305) 841-2115
health services

Royal Resources RRCO
1660 Wynkoop Street
Denver, CO 80202 (303) 573-1660
oil and gas

Royale Airlines, Inc. RYAL
Shreveport Regional Airport
Shreveport, LA 71109 (318) 635-8168
regional airline

Rule Industries, Inc. RULE
Cape Ann Industrial Park
Gloucester, MA 01930 (617) 281-0440
machinery

Rusty Pelican Restaurants, Inc RSTY
2862 McGaw Avenue
Irvine, CA 92714 (714) 660-9011
restaurants

Ryan's Family Steak Houses, Inc. RYAN
2711 Wade Hampton Blvd.
Greenville, SC 29615 (803) 244-7265
restaurants

SAB Harmon Industries, Inc. SHRM
P.O. Box 600
Grain Valley, MO 64029 (816) 249-9501
railroad electronic equipment

S.A.Y. Industries, Inc. SAYI
163 Pioneer Drive
Leominster, MA 01453 (617) 537-4001
paper and containers

SCI Systems, Inc. SCIS
5000 Technology Drive
Huntsville, AL 35807 (205) 882-4800
computer electronic systems

SEI Corp. SEIC
680 East Swedesford Road
Wayne, PA 19087 (215) 293-2932
data services for banks

SFE Technologies SFEM
1501 First Street
San Fernando, CA 91340 (818) 361-1176
capacitors and filters

SHL Systemhouse Inc. SHKI
99 Bank Street
Ottawa, Ont. K1P 6B9 (613) 236-9734
business data processing

SIS Corp. SISB
30400 Detroit Road
Westlake, OH 44145 (216) 835-2775
restaurants

S-K-I Ltd. SKII
c/o Killington Ltd.
Killington, VT 05751 (802) 422-3333
lodging

S.P.I.-Suspension and Parts Inds. Ltd. SPIL
345 Park Avenue
New York, NY 10154 (212) 486-9500
transportation equipment

SRI Corp. SRIC
Wantage Avenue
Branchville, NJ 07890 (201) 948-3000
insurance   [DRP]

STV Engineers, Inc. STVI
11 Robinson Street
Pottstown, PA 19464 (215) 326-4600
engineering and architectural services

Saatchi & Saatchi Co., PLC SACH
625 Madison Avenue
New York, NY 10022 (212) 350-1169
advertising

SafeCard Services, Inc. SFCD
2995 North Dixie Hwy.
Fort Lauderdale, FL 33334 (305) 565-2131
credit card protection services

Safeco Corp. SAFC
Safeco Plaza T-14
Seattle, WA 98185 (206) 545-5000
insurance

Safeguard Health Enterprises, Inc. SFGD
505 North Euclid Street
Anaheim, CA 92803 (714) 778-1284
insurance

St. Joseph Bancorporation, Inc. STJO
202 South Michigan Street
South Bend, IN 46601 (219) 237-5200
banking

St. Jude Medical, Inc. STJM
One Lillehei Plaza
St. Paul, MN 55117 (612) 483-2000
medical supplies

St. Paul Companies, Inc. (The) STPL
385 Washington Street
St. Paul, MN 55102 (612) 221-7911
insurance

Salem Carpet Mills, Inc. SLCR
NCNB Plaza, Suite 1100
Winston-Salem, NC 27101 (919) 727-1200
carpeting

Salick Health Care, Inc. SHCI
407 North Maple Drive
Beverly Hills, CA 90210 (213) 276-0732
health services, supplies

San/Bar Corp. SBAR
9999 Muirlands Pkwy.
Irvine, CA 92718 (714) 855-9911
telecommunications products

Sandwich Chef, Inc. SHEF
2310 Airport Interchange
Memphis, TN 38116 (901) 345-1020
restaurants

Saratoga Standardbreds, Inc. STGA
Route 116 and Keeler Lane
North Salem, NY 10560 (914) 669-8003
horse training

Satellite Music Network, Inc. SMNI
12655 North Central Expressway
Dallas, TX 75243 (214) 991-9200
broadcasting

Satellite Syndicated Systems, Inc. SSSN
P.O. Box 702160
Tulsa, OK 74170 (918) 481-0881
communication

Savannah Foods & Industries, Inc. SVAN
P.O. Box 339
Savannah, GA 31402 (912) 234-1261
sugar refining, corn products   [DRP]

Saver's Bancorp, Inc. SVRS
85 Main Street
Littleton, NH 03561 (603) 444-5321
banking

Savings Bank of Puget Sound, FSB SBPS
815 Second Avenue
Seattle, WA 98104 (206) 447-5700
banking

Saxon Oil Co. SAXO
717 North Harwood
Dallas, TX 75201 (214) 745-1300
oil and gas

Scan-Optics, Inc. SOCR
22 Prestige Park Circle
East Hartford, CT 06108 (203) 289-6001
optical data entry systems

Scan-Tron Corp. SCNN
2021 East Del Amo Blvd.
Rancho Dominquez, CA 90220 (213) 638-0520
optical mark reading equipment

Scherer (R. P.) Corp. SCHC
2075 West Big Beaver Road
Troy, MI 48084 (313) 649-0900
drugs

Scholastic, Inc. SCHL
730 Broadway
New York, NY 10003 (212) 505-3000
publishing

Schulman (*A), Inc. SHLM
3550 West Market Street
Akron, OH 44313 (216) 666-3751
engineered plastic compounds

Science Dynamics Corp. SIDY
1919 Springdale Road
Cherry Hill, NJ 08003 (609) 424-0068
electronics

Scientific Communications, Inc. SCFC
2908 National Drive
Garland, TX 75041 (214) 840-4900
communications equipment

Scientific Computers, Inc. SCIE
10101 Bren Road East
Minnetonka, MN 55343 (612) 933-4200
software, data processing

Scientific Micro Systems, Inc. SMSI
339 North Bernardo Avenue
Mountain View, CA 94039 (415) 964-5700
computers

Scientific Software-Intercomp, Inc. SSFT
1801 California Street
Denver, CO 80202 (303) 292-1111
software, data processing

Scientific System Services, Inc. SSSV
2000 Commerce Drive
Melbourne, FL 32901 (305) 725-1300
computer systems installation

SciMed Life Systems, Inc. SMLS
13000 County Road 6
Minneapolis, MN 55441 (612) 559-9504
medical supplies

Scitex Corp. Ltd. SCIX
Hamada Street
Herzlia B 46 103, Israel
computer imaging systems

Scott Cable Communications, Inc. JSCC
700 West Airport Freeway
Irving, TX 75062 (214) 438-9450
broadcasting and cable tv

Scripps-Howard Broadcasting Co. SCRP
1100 Central Trust Tower
Cincinnati, OH 45202 (513) 977-3000
broadcasting

Sea Galley Stores, Inc. SEAG
7036-220th S.W.
Mountlake Terrace, WA 98043 (206) 775-0411
restaurants

Seacoast Banking Corp. of Florida SBCF
815 Colorado Avenue
Stuart, FL 33494 (305) 287-4000
banking

Seagate Technology SGAT
920 Disc Drive
Scotts Valley, CA 95066 (408) 438-6550
computer disk drives

Seal Inc. SINC
550 Spring Street
Naugatuck, CT 06770 (203) 729-5201
photographic laminating equipment

Seaman Furniture Co. SEAM
393 Old Country Road
Carle Place, NY 11514 (516) 333-8365
furniture retailing

Seaway Food Town, Inc. SEWY
1020 Ford Street
Maumee, OH 43537 (419) 893-9401
food stores

Second National Building & Loan, Inc. SNBL
Rowe Blvd. & Melvin Avenue
Annapolis, MD 21404 (301) 268-9400
savings and loan

Security American Financial Enterprises, Inc.
SAFE
6681 Country Club Drive
Minneapolis, MN 55427 (612) 544-2121
insurance

Security Bancorp, Inc. SECB
16333 Trenton Road
Southgate, MI 48195 (313) 281-5000
banking   [DRP]

Security Tag Systems, Inc. STAG
P.O. Box 23000
St. Petersburg, FL 33742 (813) 576-6399
anti-theft devices

Seeq Technology, Inc. SEEQ
1849 Fortune Drive
San Jose, CA 95131 (408) 262-5041
computer memory devices

Seibels Bruce Group, Inc. (The) SBIG
1501 Lady Street
Columbia, SC 29201 (803) 748-2000
insurance   [DRP 5%]

Selecterm, Inc. SLTM
153 Andover Street
Danvers, MA 01923 (617) 246-1300
computer leasing

Semicon, Inc. SEME
15 New England Executive Park
Burlington, MA 01803 (617) 229-6290
electronic equipment

Sensormatic Electronics Corp. SNSR
1150 Broken Sound Pkwy., N.W.
Boca Raton, FL 33431 (305) 994-9700
anti-theft devices

Servamatic Systems, Inc. SSSI
2610 Crow Canyon Road
San Ramon, CA 94583 (415) 838-1511
solar heating systems

Service Fracturing Co. SERF
P.O. Box 1741
Pampa, TX 79066 (806) 665-7221
oil and gas services

Service Merchandise Co., Inc. SMCH
P.O. Box 24600
Nashville, TN 37202 (615) 251-6666
catalog showroom retailer

Servicemaster Industries Inc. SMAS
2300 Warrenville Road
Downers Grove, IL 60515 (312) 964-1300
health care and industrial cleaning service

Servico Inc SRVI
1601 Belvedere Road
West Palm Beach, FL 33406 (305) 689-9970
lodging

Seven Oaks International, Inc. QPON
4564 Warden Road
Memphis, TN 38122 (901) 683-7055
coupon processing

Shared Medical Systems Corp. SMED
51 Valley Stream Pkwy.
Malvern, PA 19355 (215) 296-6300
hospital computer information services

Shawmut Corp. SHAS
One Federal Street
Boston, MA 02211 (617) 292-2000
banking   [DRP]

Shelby Williams Industries, Inc. SWIX
1348 Merchandise Mart
Chicago, IL 60654 (312) 527-3593
furniture

Sheldahl, Inc. SHEL
P.O. Box 170
Northfield, MN 55057 (507) 663-8000
printed circuits

Shoney's, Inc. SHON
1727 Elm Hill Pike
Nashville, TN 37210 (615) 361-5201
restaurants

Shoney's South, Inc. SHNS
2158 Union Avenue
Memphis, TN 38104 (901) 725-6400
restaurants

Shopsmith, Inc. SHOP
6640 Poe Avenue
Dayton, OH 45414 (513) 898-6070
woodworking tools

Sierra Real Estate Equity Trust '83 SETB
One Maritime Plaza
San Francisco, CA 94111 (415) 982-4141
real estate

Sierra Real Estate Equity Trust '84 SETC
One Maritime Plaza
San Francisco, CA 94111 (415) 982-4141
real estate

Sigma Research, Inc. SIGR
3200 George Washington Way
Richland, WA 99352 (509) 375-0663
research services

Sigma-Aldrich Corp. SIAL
3050 Spruce Street
St. Louis, MO 63103 (314) 771-5765
specialty chemicals

Sigmaform Corp. SGMA
2401 Walsh Avenue
Santa Clara, CA 95051 (408) 727-6510
tubing and molded shapes

Silicon General, Inc. SILN
940 Detroit Avenue
Concord, CA 94518 (415) 686-6660
electronic equipment

Silicon Systems, Inc. SLCN
14351 Myford Road
Tustin, CA 92680 (714) 731-7110
semiconductors

Silicon Valley Group, Inc. SVGI
541 East Trimble Road
San Jose, CA 95131 (408) 945-9300
semiconductor equipment

Siliconix Inc. SILI
2201 Laurelwood Road
Santa Clara, CA 95054 (408) 988-8000
electronic components

Siltec Corp. SLTC
190 Independence Drive
Menlo Park, CA 94025 (415) 365-8600
silicon wafers, ceramic packaging

Silvar-Lisco SVRL
1080 Marsh Road
Menlo Park, CA 94025 (415) 324-0700
engineering software

Silver State Mining Corp. SSMC
1600 Hudson's Bay Centre
Denver, CO 80202 (303) 629-1515
metal mining

Simmons Airlines, Inc. SIMM
11 East Goethe Street
Chicago, IL 60610 (312) 280-8222
regional airline

Simpson Industries, Inc. SMPS
32100 Telegraph Road
Birmingham, MI 48010 (313) 540-6200
auto parts   [DRP

Sippican, Inc. SOSI
Seven Barnabas Road
Marion, MA 02738 (617) 748-1160
oceanagraphic instruments

Sizzler Restaurants International, Inc. SIZZ
P.O. Box 92092
Los Angeles, CA 90009 (213) 827-2300
restaurants

Skipper's, Inc. SKIP
14450 N.E. 29th Place
Bellevue, WA 98007 (206) 454-3456
restaurants

Sky Express Inc. SKYX
145 Avenue, Bldg. #11
Valley Stream, NY 11581 (718) 528-9080
freight forwarding

Sloan Technology Corp. SLON
602 East Montecito Street
Santa Barbara, CA 93103 (805) 963-4431
vacuum-deposited thin film

Smith Laboratories, Inc. SMLB
2215 Sanders Road
Northbrook, IL 60062 (312) 564-5700
drugs

Smithfield Foods, Inc. SFDS
1777 North Kent Street
Arlington, VA 22209 (703) 276-7200
meat products

Snelling and Snelling, Inc. SNEL
Snelling Plaza
Sarasota, FL 33581 (813) 922-9616
employment services

Society Corp. SOCI
127 Public Square
Cleveland, OH 44114 (216) 622-9000
banking   [DRP]

Society For Savings SOCS
P.O. Box 2200
Hartford, CT 06145 (203) 727-5000
banking

Softech, Inc. SOFT
460 Totten Pond Road
Waltham, MA 02154 (617) 890-6900
software

Software AG Systems, Inc. SAGA
11800 Sunrise Valley Drive
Reston, VA 22091 (703) 860-5050
software

Software Publishing Corp. SPCO
1901 Landings Drive
Mountain View, CA 94043 (415) 962-8910
software

Somerset Bancorp, Inc. SOMB
P. O. Box 711
Somerville, NJ 08876 (201) 685-8852
banking

Sonesta International Hotels Corp. SNST
200 Clarendon Street
Boston, MA 02116 (617) 421-5400
lodging

Sonoco Products Co. SONO
North Second Street
Hartsville, SC 29550 (803) 383-3700
paper and packaging products   [DRP]

Sooner Federal S&L Association SFOK
5100 East Skelly Drive
Tulsa, OK 74101 (918) 665-6600
savings and loan

Sound Warehouse, Inc. SWHI
10911 Petal Street
Dallas, TX 75238 (214) 343-4700
record, videotape retailer

Southbrook International Television Co., PLC
SITV
55 South Audley Street
London, England W1Y 5FA
movies, television

South Carolina National Corp. SCNC
1426 Main Street
Columbia, SC 29226 (803) 765-4390
banking   [DRP]

Southeastern Michigan Gas Enterprises, Inc.
SMGS
405 Water Street
Port Huron, MI 48061 (313) 987-7900
utility   [DRP]

Southern Bancorporation, Inc. STBN
P.O. Box 1329
Greenville, SC 29602 (803) 255-8000
banking   [DRP 5%]

Southern California Water Co. SWTR
3625 West Sixth Street
Los Angeles, CA 90020 (213) 251-3610
water utility   [DRP]

Southern Hospitality Corp. SHOS
P.O. Box 48
Nashville, TN 37215 (615) 327-3311
restaurants

Southern National Corp. SNAT
500 North Chestnut Street
Lumberton, NC 28358 (919) 739-2801
banking

Southland Financial Corp. SFIN
5215 North O'Connor Blvd.
Dallas, TX 75039 (214) 556-0500
insurance, real estate

SouthTrust Corp. SOTR
112 North 20th Street
Birmingham, AL 35290 (205) 254-5680
banking   [DRP]

Southwest National Corp. SWPA
111 South Main Street
Greensburg, PA 15601 (412) 834-2310
banking

Southwest Water Co. SWWC
16340 East Maplegrove Street
La Puente, CA 91744 (818) 918-1231
water utility

Southwestern Electric Service Co. SWEL
1310 Mercantile Bank Bldg.
Dallas, TX 75201 (214) 741-3125
utility

Sovereign Corp. SOVR
30 West Sola Street
Santa Barbara, CA 93101 (805) 963-7871
insurance

Sovran Financial Corp. SOVN
One Commercial Place
Norfolk, VA 23510 (804) 441-4000
banking   [DRP 5%]

Span-America Medical Systems, Inc. SPAN
Commerce Center, Route #15
Greenville, SC 29615 (803) 288-8877
health services, supplies

Spearhead Industries, Inc. SPRH
9971 Valley View Road
Eden Prairie, MN 55344 (612) 941-9171
chemicals

Specialty Composites Corp. SPCM
650 Dawson Drive
Newark, DE 19713 (302) 738-6800
rubber products

Spectradyne, Inc. SPDY
1501 North Plano Road
Richardson, TX 75081 (214) 234-2721
hotel movie systems

SpecTran Corp. SPTR
50 Hall Road
Sturbridge, MA 01566 (617) 347-2261
optical fibers

Spectrum Control, Inc. SPEC
2185 West Eighth Street
Erie, PA 16505 (814) 455-0966
pollution control devices

Spire Corp. SPIR
Patriots Park
Bedford, MA 01730 (617) 275-6000
electronics

Square Industries, Inc. SQAI
921 Bergen Avenue
Jersey City, NJ 07306 (201) 798-0090
auto repair

Staar Surgical Co. STAA
1911 Walker Avenue
Monrovia, CA 91016 (818) 303-7902
health services, supplies

Staff Builders, Inc. STAF
122 East 42nd Street
New York, NY 10168 (212) 867-2345
temporary personnel

Stanadyne, Inc. STNA
100 Deerfield Road
Windsor, CT 06095 (203) 525-0821
engine components, plumbing products

Standard Commercial Tobacco Co., Inc.
(The) STOB
2201 Miller Road
Wilson, NC 27893 (919) 291-5507
tobacco

Standard Microsystems Corp. SMSC
35 Marcus Blvd.
Hauppauge, NY 11788 (516) 273-3100
semiconductors

Standard Register Co. (The) SREG
626 Albany Street
Dayton, OH 45401 (513) 223-6181
business forms

Stanford Telecommunications, Inc. STII
2421 Mission College Blvd.
Santa Clara, CA 95054 (408) 748-1010
satellite earth stations

Stanhome Inc. STHM
333 Western Avenue
Westfield, MA 01085 (413) 562-3631
soaps and personal care products

Stanline, Inc. STAN
12851 Alondra Blvd.
Norwalk, CA 90650 (213) 921-0966
building products

Stansbury Mining Corp. STBY
1831 North Fort Canyon Road
Alpine, UT 84003 (801) 756-5464
mining

State Street Boston Corp. STBK
225 Franklin Street
Boston, MA 02101 (617) 786-3000
banking   [DRP]

State-O-Maine, Inc. SOME
One Astor Plaza
New York, NY 10036 (212) 244-1111
wholesaling

Statesman Group, Inc. (The) STTG
1400 Des Moines Bldg.
Des Moines, IA 50309 (215) 284-7500
insurance

Status Game Corp. STGM
56 Budney Road
Newington, CT 06111 (203) 666-1960
toys and games

Steiger Tractor, Inc. STGR
3101-1st Avenue North
Fargo, ND 58102 (701) 293-4650
farm machinery

Stereo Village, Inc. STVL
1833 Lawrenceville Hwy.
Decatur, GA 30033 (404) 325-0049
consumer electronics stores

Sterner Lighting Systems Inc. SLTG
351 Lewis Avenue West
Winsted, MN 55395 (612) 473-1252
lighting equipment

Stewart & Stevenson Services, Inc. SSSS
2707 North Loop West
Houston, TX 77008 (713) 868-7700
engines and turbines

Stewart Information Services Corp. SISC
2200 West Loop South
Houston, TX 77027 (713) 871-1100
insurance   [DRP]

Stewart Sandwiches, Inc. STEW
5732 Curlew Drive
Norfolk, VA 23502 (804) 466-9200
prepackaged sandwiches

Stifel Financial Corp. STFL
500 North Broadway
St. Louis, MO 63102 (314) 342-2000
investment services

Stocker & Yale, Inc. STKR
P.O. Box 494
Beverly, MA 01915 (617) 927-3940
measuring equipment

Stockholder Systems, Inc. SSIA
4411 East Jones Bridge Road
Norcross, GA 30092 (404) 441-3387
computer software

Stokely U.S.A, Inc. STKY
626 East Wisconsin Avenue
Oconomowoc, WI 53066 (414) 567-1731
food products

Stratus Computer, Inc. STRA
55 Fairbanks Blvd.
Marlboro, MA 01752 (617) 460-2000
computers

Strawbridge & Clothier STRW
801 Market Street
Philadelphia, PA 19105 (215) 629-6779
retail stores

Stryker Corp. STRY
420 East Alcott Street
Kalamazoo, MI 49001 (616) 381-3811
medical supplies

Stuart Department Stores, Inc. STUS
45 South Street
Hopkinton, MA 01748 (617) 435-9711
retail stores

Stuart Hall Co., Inc. STUH
P.O. Box 1381
Kansas City, MO 64141 (816) 221-8480
stationery and office supplies

Sturm, Ruger & Co., Inc. STRM
Lacey Place
Southport, CT 06490 (203) 259-7843
sporting goods

Subaru of America, Inc. SBRU
7040 Central Hwy.
Pennsauken, NJ 08109 (609) 488-8500
auto retailer

Suburban Airlines, Inc. SALI
Reading Municipal Airport
Reading, PA 19603 (215) 375-8551
regional airline

Suburban Bancorp SUBC
6610 Rockledge Drive
Bethesda, MD 20817 (301) 493-2890
banking

Sudbury Holdings, Inc. SUDS
3733 Park East Drive
Cleveland, OH 44122 (216) 464-7026
auto parts

Suffield Savings Bank SSBK
66 North Main Street
Suffield, CT 06078 (203) 668-1261
banking

Sumitomo Bank Of California SUMI
365 California Street
San Francisco, CA 94104 (415) 445-8000
banking

Summa Medical Corp. SUMA
4272 Balloon Park Road, N.E.
Albuquerque, NM 87109 (505) 345-8891
drugs

Summcorp SMCR
One Summit Square
Fort Wayne, IN 46801 (219) 461-7713
investment co.

Summit Bancorporation (The) SUBN
367 Springfield Avenue
Summit, NJ 07901 (201) 522-8400
banking   [DRP]

Summit Health Ltd. SUMH
1800 Avenue of the Stars
Los Angeles, CA 90067 (213) 201-4000
health services

Sun Coast Plastics, Inc. SUNI
2202 Industrial Blvd.
Sarasota, FL 33580 (813) 355-7166
plastic products

Sunair Electronics, Inc. SNRU
3101 S.W. Third Avenue
Fort Lauderdale, FL 33315 (305) 525-1505
electronic equipment

Sunrise Medical, Inc. SNMD
970 West 190th Street
Torrance, CA 90502 (213) 516-8568
home health care products

Sunstar Foods, Inc. SUNF
P.O. Box 27501
Minneapolis, MN 55427 (612) 546-2506
food products

Sunstates Corp. SUST
1325 San Marco Blvd.
Jacksonville, FL 32207 (904) 396-1600
real estate

Sunwest Financial Services, Inc. SFSI
303 Roma Avenue N.W.
Albuquerque, NM 87103 (505) 765-2403
banking   [DRP 5%]

Sunworld International Airways, Inc. SUNA
2333 Renaissance Drive
Las Vegas, NV 89119 (702) 798-0088
regional airline

Super Rite Foods, Inc. SRFI
3900 Industrial Road
Harrisburg, PA 17110 (717) 232-6821
food, tobacco wholesaler

Super Sky International, Inc. SSKY
10301 North Enterprise Drive
Mequon, WI 53092 (414) 242-2000
glass skylight systems

Superior Electric Co. (The) SUPE
383 Middle Street
Bristol, CT 06010 (203) 582-9561
electrical equipment

Supertex, Inc. SUPX
1350 Bordeaux Drive
Sunnyvale, CA 94088 (408) 744-0100
electronics

Supreme Equipment & Systems Corp. SEQP
170 - 53rd Street
Brooklyn, NY 11232 (718) 439-3800
business equipment

Surgical Care Affiliates, Inc. SCAF
4515 Harding Road
Nashville, TN 37205 (615) 385-3541
health services

Survival Technology, Inc. SURV
8101 Glenbrook Road
Bethesda, MD 20814 (301) 656-5600
medical supplies

Susquehanna Bancshares, Inc. SUSQ
9 East Main Street
Lititz, PA 17543 (717) 626-4721
banking

Sym-Tek Systems, Inc. SYMK
3912 Calle Fortunada
San Diego, CA 92123 (714) 569-6800
computers

Symbion, Inc. SYMB
825 North 300 West
Salt Lake City, UT 84103 (801) 531-7022
medical supplies

Symbol Technologies, Inc. SMBL
1101 Lakeland Avenue
Bohemia, NY 11716 (516) 563-2400
laser scanners

Symbolics, Inc. SMBX
Eleven Cambridge Center
Cambridge, MA 02142 (617) 577-7500
software and data processing   [O]

Syntech International Inc. SYNE
10864 Audelia Road
Dallas, TX 75238 (214) 340-0379
computers for gaming

Syntrex Inc. STRX
246 Industrial Way West
Eatontown, NJ 07724 (201) 542-1500
office automation equipment

Syscon Corp. SCON
1000 Thomas Jefferson St.,N.W.
Washington, DC 20007 (202) 342-4000
computer, engineering services

System Industries, Inc. SYSM
1855 Barber Lane
Milpitas, CA 95035 (408) 942-1212
computer disk storage systems

System Integrators, Inc. SINT
4111 North Freeway Blvd.
Sacramento, CA 95834 (916) 929-9481
publication composition systems

Systematics, Inc. SYST
4001 Rodney Parham Road
Little Rock, AR 72212 (501) 223-5100
software

Systems & Computer Technology Corp. SCTC
Great Valley Corporate Center
Malvern, PA 19355 (215) 647-5930
software and data processing

Systems Associates, Inc. SAIN
P.O. Box 36305
Charlotte, NC 28236 (704) 333-1276
hospital computer systems

T C B Y Enterprises, Inc. TCBY
11300 Rodney Parham Road
Little Rock, AR 72212 (501) 225-0349
restaurants

TBC Corp. TBCC
4770 Hickory Hill Road
Memphis, TN 38115 (901) 363-8030
auto parts

TCA Cable TV, Inc. TCAT
3027 S.E. Loop 323
Tyler, TX 75701 (214) 595-3701
cable tv

T.R.V. Minerals Corp. TRVM
Penthouse Suite 2390
Vancouver, B.C. V6E 2E9 (604) 689-5300
oil and gas

TS Industries, Inc. TNDS
11801 E. Smith Avenue
Santa Fe Springs, CA 90670 (213) 942-7000
paper products

TSI Inc. TSII
500 Cardigan Road
Shoreview, MN 55112 (612) 483-0900
electronic instruments

TSO Financial Corp. TSOF
Five TSO Financial Center
Horsham, PA 19044 (215) 657-4000
personal credit

TSR, Inc. TSRI
400 Oser Avenue
Hauppauge, NY 11788 (516) 231-0333
software, toys and games

Taco Viva, Inc. TVIV
7100 West Camino Real
Boca Raton, FL 33433 (305) 394-4446
restaurants

Tandem Computers Inc. TNDM
19333 Vallco Pkwy.
Cupertino, CA 95014 (408) 725-6488
computers   [O]

Tandon Corp. TCOR
20320 Pairie Street
Chatsworth, CA 91311 (818) 993-6644
computer disk drives

Technalysis Corp. TECN
6700 France Avenue South
Minneapolis, MN 55435 (612) 925-5900
software, data processing

Technical Communications Corp. TCCO
100 Domino Drive
Concord, MA 01742 (617) 862-6035
electrical equipment

Technical Equities Corp. TEQT
1922 The Alameda
San Jose, CA 95126 (408) 246-7502
rubber products

Technology Inc. TNLG
1115 Talbott Tower
Dayton, OH 45402 (513) 224-9066
aerospace components

Technology for Communications Intern'l TCII
1625 Stierlin Drive
Mountain View, CA 94043 (415) 962-5200
communications equipment

Tecumseh Products Co. TECU
100 East Patterson Street
Tecumseh, MI 49286 (517) 423-8411
refrigeration products

Telco Systems, Inc. TELC
1040 Marsh Road
Menlo Park, CA 94025 (415) 324-4300
communications equipment

Tele-Communications, Inc. TCOM
54 Denver Technological Center
Englewood, CO 80111 (303) 771-8200
cable tv systems   [O]

Telecom Plus International, Inc. TELE
48-40 34th Street
Long Island City, NY 11101 (718) 392-7700
communications equipment

Telecrafter Corp. TLCR
12596 West Bayaud Avenue
Lakewood, CO 80228 (303) 987-2900
cable tv

Telecredit, Inc. TCRD
1901 Avenue of the Stars
Los Angeles, CA 90067 (213) 277-4061
check verification systems

Telemation, Inc. TLMT
143 South Main
Salt Lake City, UT 84111 (801) 364-4477
movies

Televideo Systems, Inc. TELV
P.O. Box 6602
San Jose, CA 95150 (408) 971-0255
computer terminals

Tellabs, Inc. TLAB
4951 Indiana Avenue
Lisle, IL 60532 (312) 969-8800
telecommunications equipment

Telxon Corp. TLXN
3330 West Market Street
Akron, OH 44313 (216) 867-3700
hand-held computers

Temco Home Health Care Products, Inc. TEMC
125 South Street
Passaic, NJ 07055 (201) 472-3173
health services, supplies

Templeton Energy, Inc. TMPL
509 Market Street
Shreveport, LA 71101 (800) 772-9417
oil and gas

Temtex Industries, Inc. TMTX
Park West, 1601 LBJ Freeway
Dallas, TX 75234 (214) 484-1845
metals fabrication

Tender Loving Care Health Care, Inc. TLCI
One Hollow Lane
Lake Success, NY 11042 (516) 365-3100
health services

Tennant Co. TANT
701 North Lilac Drive
Minneapolis, MN 55440 (612) 540-1200
floor cleaning machines

Tera Corp. TRRA
2150 Shattuck Avenue
Berkeley, CA 94704 (415) 845-5200
computer software

Termiflex Corp. TFLX
316 Daniel Webster Hwy.
Merrimack, NH 03054 (603) 424-3700
electronics

Terminal Data Corp. TERM
21221 Oxnard Street
Woodland Hills, CA 91367 (818) 887-4900
document microfilming

Texon Energy Corp. TXON
1212 Main Street
Houston, TX 77002 (713) 658-9586
oil and gas

Thermal Profiles, Inc. THPR
59 Mall Drive
Commack, NY 11725 (516) 349-9188
building products

Thermedics Inc. THMD
470 Wildwood Street
Woburn, MA 01888 (617) 938-3786
health services

Thetford Corp. THFR
7101 Jackson Road
Ann Arbor, MI 48106 (313) 769-6000
plumbing products

Third National Corp. TDAT
Third National Bank Bldg.
Nashville, TN 37244 (615) 748-4891
banking

Thor Industries, Inc. THOR
419 West Pike Street
Jackson Center, OH 45334 (513) 596-6849
sport vehicles

Thoratec Laboratories Corp. TTEC
2448 Six Street
Berkeley, CA 94710 (415) 549-9600
health services

Thorn Apple Valley, Inc. TAVI
18700 West Ten Mile Road
Southfield, MI 48075 (313) 552-0700
food products

Thousand Trails, Inc. TRLS
15325 SE 30th Place
Bellevue, WA 98007 (206) 644-1100
lodging, real estate

3Com Corp. COMS
1365 Shorebird Way
Mountain View, CA 94043 (415) 961-9602
computers

Tierco Group, Inc. (The) TIER
1140 N.W. 63rd Street
Oklahoma City, OK 73116 (405) 843-9906
real estate

Timberland Industries, Inc. TIMB
3805 108th Avenue N.E.
Bellevue, WA 98004 (206) 828-3565
wood products

Time Energy Systems, Inc. TIME
2900 Wilcrest Drive
Houston, TX 77042 (713) 780-8532
energy saving consulting

Times Fiber Communications, Inc. TFCI
P.O. Box 384
Wallingford, CT 06492 (203) 265-8500
cable for communication industry

Tipperary Corp. TIPR
511 West Ohio
Midland, TX 79701 (915) 684-7151
oil refining and marketing

Toledo Trustcorp, Inc. TTCO
Three Seagate
Toledo, OH 43603 (419) 259-8209
banking   [DRP]

Tom Brown, Inc. TMBR
P.O. Box 2608
Midland, TX 79701 (915) 682-9715
oil and gas

Tony Lama Co., Inc. TLAM
1137 Tony Lama Street
El Paso, TX 79915 (915) 778-8311
leather products

Toreador Royalty Corp. TRGL
1140 Hartford Bldg.
Dallas, TX 75201 (214) 747-9497
oil and gas

Total System Services, Inc. TSYS
1000 Fifth Avenue
Columbus, GA 31902 (404) 571-2204
software, data processing

Toys Plus, Inc. TOYS
1600 Heritage Landing
St. Charles, MO 63301 (314) 928-1990
toy retailing

Trak Auto Corp. TRKA
3300 75th Avenue
Landover, MD 20785 (301) 731-1200
auto parts

Trans Louisiana Gas Co., Inc. TRLA
201 Rue Iberville
Lafayette, LA 70508 (318) 234-4782
utility   [DRP 5%]

Trans-Industries, Inc. TRIN
2637 North Adams Road
Auburn Heights, MI 48057 (313) 852-1990
manufacturing

Transducer Systems, Inc. TSIC
1510 Delp Drive
Kulpsville, PA 19443 (215) 256-4611
measuring equipment

Transnet Corp. TRNT
1945 Route 22
Union, NJ 07083 (201) 688-7800
computer services

Transtector Systems, Inc. TTOR
Coeur D'Alene Airport
Post Falls, ID 83854 (208) 772-8515
electrical equipment

Transworld Bancorp TWBC
5430 Van Nuys Blvd.
Sherman Oaks, CA 91401 (818) 783-7501
banking

Travelers REIT TRAT
99 High Street
Boston, MA 02110 (617) 338-3460
real estate   [DRP]

Travelers Realty Income Investors TRII
99 High Street
Boston, MA 02110 (617) 338-3460
real estate

Triad Systems Corp. TRSC
1252 Orleans Drive
Sunnyvale, CA 94086 (408) 734-9720
computer systems

Triangle Microwave, Inc. TRMW
31 Farinella Drive
East Hanover, NJ 07936 (201) 884-1423
microwave equipment

Trilogy Ltd. TRIL
10500 Ridgeview Court
Cupertino, CA 95014 (408) 973-9333
semiconductors

Trion, Inc. TRON
101 McNeill Road
Sanford, NC 27331 (919) 775-2201
air conditioning

Triton Group Ltd. TRRO
1900 Avenue of the Stars
Los Angeles, CA 90067 (213) 553-3900
graphic products

Trus Joist Corp. TJCO
9777 West Chinden Blvd.
Boise, ID 83704 (208) 375-4450
wood products

Trustco Bank Corp NY TRST
320 State Street
Schenectady, NY 12305 (518) 377-3311
banking

Tucker Drilling Co., Inc. TUCK
P.O. Box 1876
San Angelo, TX 76902 (915) 655-6773
oil and gas services

II Morrow, Inc. MORW
2777 19th Street, S.E.
Salem, OR 97302 (503) 581-8101
navigation equipment

Tylan Corp. TYLN
23301 South Wilmington Avenue
Carson, CA 90745 (213) 518-6310
semiconductor equipment

Tyson Foods, Inc. TYSN
P.O. Drawer E
Springdale, AR 72764 (501) 756-4000
foods, poultry

U.S. Bancorp USBC
P.O. Box 8837
Portland, OR 97208 (503) 225-5702
banking

U.S. Capital Corp. USCC
1400 Main Street
Columbia, SC 29201 (803) 779-2170
real estate

U.S. Design Corp. USDC
5100 Philadelphia Way
Lanham, MD 20706 (301) 577-2880
design services

U.S. Energy Corp. USEG
Glen L. Larson Bldg.
Riverton, WY 82501 (307) 856-9271
metal mining

U.S. Health Inc. USHI
300 East Joppa Road
Towson, MD 21204 (301) 296-8800
health services

U.S. Precious Metals, Inc. USPM
535 Howe Street, 6th Floor
Vancouver, B.C. V6C 2C2 (604) 669-6115
metal mining

U.S. Shelter Corp. USSS
1 Shelter Place
Greenville, SC 29602 (803) 239-1000
real estate

U.S. Truck Lines, Inc. UTRK
785 Huntington Bldg.
Cleveland, OH 44115 (216) 241-5326
trucking

U.S. Trust Corp. USTC
45 Wall Street
New York, NY 10005 (212) 806-4500
banking

U.S.A. Cafes USCF
8080 North Central Expressway
Dallas, TX 75206 (214) 891-8400
restaurants

U.S.BANCORP, Inc. USBP
Main and Franklin Streets
Johnstown, PA 15901 (814) 533-5300
banking

U.S.LICO Corp. USVC
1701 Pennsylvania Avenue N.W.
Washington, DC 20006 (202) 342-0535
insurance   [DRP]

U.S.P. REIT USPT
4333 Edgewood Road, N.E.
Cedar Rapids, IA 52499 (319) 398-8511
real estate

U.S.PCI, Inc. UPCI
2000 Classen Center Bldg.
Oklahoma City, OK 73106 (405) 528-8371
waste management

U.S.T Corp. USTB
40 Court Street
Boston, MA 02108 (617) 726-7000
banking

UTL Corp. UTLC
4500 West Mockingbird Lane
Dallas, TX 75209 (214) 350-7601
electronic equipment

Ultra Bancorporation ULTB
1125 Route 22 West
Bridgewater, NJ 08807 (201) 685-8300
banking

Ultrasystems Inc. ULTR
16845 Von Karman Avenue
Irvine, CA 92714 (714) 863-7000
space defense construction

Ungermann-Bass, Inc. UNGR
2560 Mission College Blvd.
Santa Clara, CA 95052 (408) 496-0111
computer network systems

Unibancorp, Inc. UBCP
Sears Tower
Chicago, IL 60606 (312) 876-4200
banking

Unifi, Inc. UNFI
P.O. Box 19109
Greensboro, NC 27419 (919) 294-4410
knitting mills

Uniforce Temporary Personnel, Inc. UNFR
1335 Jericho Turnpike
New Hyde Park, NY 11040 (516) 437-3300
temporary personnel

Unimed, Inc. UMED
35 Columbia Road
Somerville, NJ 08876 (201) 526-6894
drugs

Union Bancorp Inc. UBAN
200 Ottawa Avenue, N.W.
Grand Rapids, MI 49503 (616) 451-7393
banking

Union Federal S&L Association UFSL
523 West Sixth Street
Los Angeles, CA 90014 (213) 688-8400
savings and loan

Union National Corp. UNBC
P. O. Box 837
Pittsburgh, PA 15278 (412) 644-8184
banking   [DRP]

Union Planters Corp. UPCM
P.O. Box 387
Memphis, TN 38147 (901) 523-6000
banking

Union Special Corp. USMA
400 North Franklin Street
Chicago, IL 60610 (312) 266-4000
industrial sewing machines

Union Trust Bancorp UTBC
Baltimore and St. Paul Streets
Baltimore, MD 21203 (301) 332-5445
banking

Union Warren Savings Bank UWSB
133 Federal Street
Boston, MA 02110 (617) 482-4590
banking

United Artists Communications, Inc. UACI
172 Golden Gate Avenue
San Francisco, CA 94102 (415) 928-3200
movies

United Bancorp of Arizona UBAZ
3300 North Central Avenue
Phoenix, AZ 85012 (602) 248-2399
banking

United Bancorporation Alaska, Inc. UBAK
440 E. 36th Street
Anchorage, AK 99503 (907) 276-1911
banking

United Bank, A Savings Bank UNSB
1102 Commerce Street
Tacoma, WA 98401 (206) 572-5220
banking

United Bank, S.S.B. UBSF
711 Van Ness Avenue
San Francisco, CA 94102 (415) 928-0700
banking

United Bankers, Inc. UBKR
P.O. Box 8436
Waco, TX 76714 (817) 776-7600
banking

United Banks of Colorado, Inc. UBKS
One United Bank Center
Denver, CO 80274 (303) 861-4700
banking

United Carolina Bancshares Corp. UCAR
306 South Madison Street
Whiteville, NC 28472 (919) 642-5131
banking   [DRP]

United Cities Gas Co. UCIT
5300 Maryland Way
Brentwood, TN 37027 (615) 373-0104
utility   [DRP 5%]

United Dominion Realty Trust, Inc. UDRT
5 East Franklin Street
Richmond, VA 23241 (804) 780-2691
real estate

United Education & Software UESS
15720 Ventura Blvd.
Encino, CA 91436 (818) 907-6649
education and software

United Financial Group, Inc. UFGI
10333 Harwin
Houston, TX 77036 (713) 981-2300
savings and loan

United First Federal S&L Association UNFF
P.O. Box 1478
Sarasota, FL 33578 (813) 366-1500
savings and loan

United Healthcare Corp. UNIH
300 Opus Center
Minnetonka, MN 55343 (612) 936-1300
health services

United Home Life Insurance Co. UHLI
1000 North Madison Avenue
Greenwood, IN 46142 (317) 888-4421
insurance

United Missouri Bancshares, Inc. UMSB
P. O. Box 1771
Kansas City, MO 64141 (816) 556-7000
banking

United New Mexico Financial Corp. BNKS
P.O. Box 1081
Albuquerque, NM 87103 (505) 765-5086
banking

United Oklahoma Bankshares, Inc. UOBI
1217 South Agnew
Oklahoma City, OK 73108 (405) 239-5800
banking

United Presidential Corp. UPCO
217 Southway Blvd. East
Kokomo, IN 46902 (317) 453-0602
insurance

U.S. Antimony Corp. USAC
P.O. Box 643
Thompson Falls, MT 59873 (406) 827-3523
metal mining

U.S. Health Care Systems, Inc. USHC
P.O. Box 1109
Blue Bell, PA 19422 (215) 628-4800
health services   [O]

U.S. Surgical Corp. USSC
150 Glover Avenue
Norwalk, CT 06856 (203) 866-5050
medical supplies

United Stationers Inc. USTR
2200 East Golf Road
Des Plaines, IL 60016 (312) 699-5000
wholesale office products

United Telecontrol Electronics, Inc. UTEL
3500 Sunset Avenue
Asbury Park, NJ 07712 (201) 922-1000
electronics

United Television, Inc. UTVI
8501 Wilshire Blvd.
Beverly Hills, CA 90211 (213) 854-0426
television stations

United Tote, Inc. TOTE
10115 Cabin Creek Road
Shepherd, MT 59079 (406) 373-5507
apparel, recreation products

United Vermont Bancorporation UVTB
80 West Street
Rutland, VT 05701 (802) 775-2525
banking

United Virginia Bankshares, Inc. UVBK
919 East Main Street
Richmond, VA 23261 (804) 782-5000
banking   [DRP 5%]

United-Guardian, Inc. UNIR
230 Marcus Blvd.
Smithtown, NY 11787 (516) 273-0900
drugs

Universal Furniture Ltd. UFUR
37 Queen's Road
Central, Hong Kong
Furniture

Universal Health Services, Inc UHSI
367 South Gulph Road
King of Prussia, PA 19406 (215) 768-3300
health services

Universal Holding Corp. UHCO
100 Jericho Quadrangle
Jericho, NY 11753 (516) 935-9440
insurance

Universal Security Instruments, Inc. USEC
10324 South Dolfield Road
Owings Mills, MD 21117 (301) 363-3000
security products

University Federal Savings Bank UFSB
6400 Roosevelt Way N.E.
Seattle, WA 98115 (206) 526-1000
savings and loan

University National Bank & Trust Co. UNNB
361 Lytton Avenue
Palo Alto, CA 94301 (415) 327-0210
banking

Up-Right, Inc. UPRI
1013 Pardee Street
Berkeley, CA 94710 (415) 843-0770
work platforms

Upper Peninsula Power Co. UPEN
616 Shelden Avenue
Houghton, MI 49931 (906) 482-0220
utilities   [DRP]

V Band Systems, Inc. VBAN
5 Odell Plaza
Yonkers, NY 10701 (914) 964-0900
electronics

VLI Corp. VLIS
2031 Main Street
Irvine, CA 92714 (714) 863-9511
drugs, medical supplies

VLSI Technology, Inc. VLSI
1109 McKay Drive
San Jose, CA 95131 (408) 942-1810
semiconductors

VMS Mortgage Investors L.P. VMLP
8700 West Bryn Mawr Avenue
Chicago, IL 60631 (312) 399-8700
real estate

VMX, Inc. VMXI
1241 Columbia Drive
Richardson, TX 75081 (214) 699-1461
voice mail systems

VSE Corp. VSEC
2550 Huntington Avenue
Alexandria, VA 22303 (703) 960-4600
engineering services

Valid Logic Systems Inc. VLID
2820 Orchard Pkwy.
San Jose, CA 95134 (408) 945-9400
computer engineering workstations

Vallen Corp. VALN
13333 N.W. Freeway
Houston, TX 77040 (713) 462-8700
industrial health and safety products

Valley Bancorporation VYBN
P.O. Box 1061
Appleton, WI 54912 (414) 738-3830
banking   [DRP]

Valley Federal S&L Association VFED
6842 Van Nuys Blvd.
Van Nuys, CA 91405 (818) 904-3000
savings and loan

Valley Forge Corp. VALF
1850 Craigshire Drive
St. Louis, MO 63146 (314) 576-1700
electrical equipment

Valley National Bancorp VNBP
935 Allwood Road
Clifton, NJ 07012 (201) 777-1800
banking   [DRP]

Valley National Corp. VNCP
241 North Central Avenue
Phoenix, AZ 85001 (602) 261-2099
banking

Valley Utah Bancorporation VUBN
50 West Broadway
Salt Lake City, UT 84118 (801) 481-5386
banking

Valmont Industries, Inc. VALM
West Hwy. 275
Valley, NE 68064 (402) 359-2201
steel tubing

Valtek Inc. VALT
Mountain Springs Pkwy.
Springville, UT 84663 (801) 489-8611
automatic control valves

Value Line, Inc. VALU
711 Third Avenue
New York, NY 10017 (212) 687-3965
investment advisory services

Van Dusen Air Inc. VAND
2626 East 82nd Street
Minneapolis, MN 55420 (612) 854-8776
aircraft parts wholesaling

Van Schaack & Co. VANS
950 Seventeenth Street
Denver, CO 80202 (303) 572-5000
real estate

Vanzetti Systems, Inc. VANZ
111 Island Street
Stoughton, MA 02072 (617) 828-4650
electronic equipment

Vari-Care, Inc. VCRE
814 Medical Arts Bldg.
Rochester, NY 14607 (716) 325-6940
health services

Varlen Corp. VRLN
One Crossroads of Commerce
Rolling Meadows, IL 60008 (312) 398-2550
tubular metal products

Velo-Bind, Inc. VBND
650 Almanor Avenue
Sunnyvale, CA 94068 (408) 732-4200
binding supplies, office equipment

Ventrex Laboratories, Inc. VTRX
217 Read Street
Portland, ME 04103 (207) 773-7231
medical supplies

Vermont Financial Services Corp. VFSC
100 Main Street
Brattleboro, VT 05301 (802) 257-7151
banking

Versa Technologies, Inc. VRSA
1300 South Green Bay Road
Racine, WI 53405 (414) 554-7575
rubber and plastic products

Vicon Fiber Optics Corp. VFOX
90 Secor Lane
Pelham Manor, NY 10803 (914) 738-5006
fiber optics

Vicorp Restaurants, Inc. VRES
400 West 48th Avenue
Denver, CO 80216 (303) 296-2121
restaurants

Victoria Bankshares, Inc. VICT
One Twenty Main Place
Victoria, TX 77902 (512) 573-5151
banking   [DRP]

Victoria Station Inc. VSTA
Wood Island
Larkspur, CA 94939 (800) 227-2155
restaurants

Video Display Corp. VIDE
P.O. Box 542
Stone Mountain, GA 30083 (404) 938-2080
video equipment

Vie De France Corp. VDEF
8201 Greensboro Drive
McLean, VA 22102 (703) 442-9205
french breads, food products

Viking Freight System, Inc. VIKG
3405 Victor Street
Santa Clara, CA 95050 (408) 988-6111
trucking

Vipont Laboratories, Inc. VLAB
220 East Olive Street
Fort Collins, CO 80524 (303) 482-3126
dental supplies

Viratek, Inc. VIRA
3300 Hyland Avenue
Costa Mesa, CA 92626 (714) 545-0100
drugs

Virginia Beach Federal S&L Association VABF
210 25th Street
Virginia Beach, VA 23451 (804) 428-9331
savings and loan

Virginia First Savings, F.S.B. VFSB
P.O. Box 2009
Petersburg, VA 23804 (804) 733-0333
banking

Visual Electronics Corp. VISC
285 Emmet Street
Newark, NJ 07114 (201) 242-6600
electronics

Visual Technology Inc. VSAL
1703 Middlesex Street
Lowell, MA 01851 (617) 459-4903
computer equipment

Vitramon, Inc. VITR
Route 25
Monroe, CT 06468 (203) 268-6261
electronic capacitors

Vodavi Technology Corp. VTEK
8300 East Raintree Drive
Scottsdale, AZ 85260 (602) 998-2200
telephone systems

Voit Corp. VOIT
45 Gould Street
Rochester, NY 14610 (716) 442-4663
sporting goods

Volt Information Sciences, Inc. VOLT
101 Park Avenue
New York, NY 10178 (212) 309-0200
services to telephone companies

Volvo (A B) VOLV
S-405 08
Göteborg, Sweden
auto manufacturer

Vortec Corp. VRTX
525 Vine Street
Cincinnati, OH 45242 (513) 651-1000
air-compressing equipment

WD-40 Co. WDFC
1061 Cudahy Place
San Diego, CA 92110 (619) 275-1400
oil lubricants

WICAT Systems, Inc. WCAT
1875 South State Street
Orem, UT 84057 (801) 224-6400
educational computers

WNS, Inc. WNSI
7915 FM 1960 West
Houston, TX 77070 (713) 890-5900
home-decorating products

Walbro Corp. WALB
6242 Garfield Avenue
Cass City, MI 48726 (517) 872-2131
carburetors for electrical equipment

Walker Telecommunications Corp. WTEL
200 Oser Avenue
Hauppauge, NY 11788 (516) 435-1100
communications consulting

Wall to Wall Sound & Video, Inc. WTWS
200 South Route 130
Cinnaminson, NJ 08077 (609) 786-8300
consumer electronics stores

Warehouse Club, Inc. WCLB
7235 North Linden Avenue
Skokie, IL 60077 (312) 679-6800
membership warehouse retailing

Washington Energy Co. WECO
815 Mercer Street
Seattle, WA 98111 (206) 622-6767
utility   [DRP 5%]

Washington Federal S&L Association Of
Seattle WFSL
1423 Fourth Avenue
Seattle, WA 98101 (206) 624-7930
savings and loan

Washington Mutual Savings Bank WAMU
1101 Second Avenue
Seattle, WA 98101 (206) 464-4400
banking

Washington Scientific Industries Inc. WSCI
2605 West Wayzata Blvd.
Long Lake, MN 55356 (612) 473-1271
precision equipment

Waters Instruments Inc. WTRS
2411 Seventh St., N.W.
Rochester, MN 55901 (507) 288-7777
medical equipment

Wausau Paper Mills Co. WSAU
One Clark's Island
Wausau, WI 54401 (715) 845-5266
paper products

Waverly Press Inc. WAVR
428 E. Preston Street
Baltimore, MD 21202 (301) 528-4000
publishing

Wavetek Corp. WVTK
9191 Towne Centre Drive
San Diego, CA 92122 (619) 450-9971
electronic test instruments

Waxman Industries, Inc. WAXM
24460 Aurora Road
Bedford Heights, OH 44146 (216) 439-1830
electric and plumbing products

Webb Co. (The) WBBC
1999 Shepard Road
St Paul, MN 55116 (612) 690-7200
publishing

Weigh-Tronix, Inc. WGHT
1000 Armstrong Drive
Fairmont, MN 56031 (507) 238-4461
electronic instruments

Weisfield's, Inc. WEIS
800 South Michigan Street
Seattle, WA 98108 (206) 767-5011
jewelry retailing

Welbilt Corp. WELB
3333 New Hyde Park
New Hyde Park, NY 11042 (516) 365-5040
plumbing and heating

Wespac Investors Trust WESP
4701 Van Karman
Newport Beach, CA 92660 (714) 851-5032
real estate

Wespac Investors Trust II WPTR
4701 Von Karman
Newport Beach, CA 92660 (714) 851-5032
real estate

Westamerica Bancorporation WSAM
1108 Fifth Avenue
San Rafael, CA 94901 (415) 456-8000
banking   [DRP]

Westchester Financial Services Corp. WFSB
North Avenue and Huguenot
New Rochelle, NY 10802 (914) 636-6400
banking

Western Capital Investment Corp. WECA
1675 Broadway, Suite 1700
Denver, CO 80202 (303) 623-5577
savings and loan

Western Commercial WCCC
111 East Shaw Avenue
Fresno, CA 93710 (209) 228-0771
banking

Western Federal Savings Bank WFPR
P.O. Box WFS
Mayaguez, PR 00709 (809) 834-8000
banking

Western Federal S&L Association WFSA
13160 Mindanao Way
Marina del Rey, CA 90292 (213) 306-6500
savings and loan

Western Micro Technology Inc. WSTM
10040 Bubb Road
Cupertino, CA 95014 (408) 725-1660
semiconductor distributor

Western Microwave, Inc. WMIC
1271 Reamwood Avenue
Sunnyvale, CA 94089 (408) 734-1631
microwave equipment

Western States Life Insurance Co. WSTS
700 South Seventh Street
Fargo, ND 58108 (701) 237-5700
insurance

Western Steer Mom 'n' Pop's, Inc. WSMP
Box 399
Claremont, NC 28610 (704) 459-7626
restaurants

Westmoreland Coal Co. WMOR
2500 Fidelity Bldg
Philadelphia, PA 19109 (215) 545-2500
soft coal mining

Westwood One, Inc. WONE
9540 Washington Blvd.
Culver City, CA 90232 (213) 204-5000
broadcasting programs

Westworld Community Healthcare Inc. WCHI
23072 Lake Center Drive
Lake Forest, CA 92630 (714) 768-2981
health services

Wetterau Inc. WETT
8920 Pershall Road
Hazelwood, MO 63042 (314) 524-5000
grocery wholesaling   [DRP]

Weyenberg Shoe Manufacturing Co. WEYS
234 East Reservoir Avenue
Milwaukee, WI 53201 (414) 374-8900
footwear

Wholesale Club, Inc. (The) WHLS
7260 Shadeland Station
Indianapolis, IN 46256 (317) 842-0351
membership merchandise warehouses

Widcom, Inc. WIDE
1500 East Hamilton Avenue
Campbell, CA 95008 (408) 377-9981
data-transmission equipment

Wiland Services, Inc. WSVS
1426 Pearl Street
Boulder, CO 80302 (303) 449-5347
business data processing

Wiley & Sons, Inc. (John) WILL
605 Third Avenue
New York, NY 10158 (212) 850-6000
publishing

Willamette Industries, Inc. WMTT
3800 First Interstate Tower
Portland, OR 97201 (503) 227-5581
paper products

William E. Wright Co. WRIT
South Street
West Warren, MA 01092 (413) 436-7732
sewing materials

Williams (A. L.) Corp. ALWC
3120 Breckinridge Blvd.
Duluth, GA 30199 (404) 381-1674
insurance

Williams Industries, Inc. WMSI
2849 Meadow View Road
Falls Church, VA 22042 (703) 560-1505
building and heavy construction

W. W. Williams Co. (The) WWWM
835 West Goodale Blvd.
Columbus, OH 43212 (614) 228-5000
construction machinery distributor

Williams-Sonoma, Inc. WSGC
5750 Hollis Street
Emeryille, CA 94608 (415) 652-1555
mail order cookware

Wilmington Trust Co. WILM
Rodney Square North
Wilmington, DE 19890 (302) 651-1000
banking

Wilson Foods Corp. WILF
4545 Lincoln Blvd.
Oklahoma City, OK 73105 (405) 525-4545
meat packer

Wilton Enterprises, Inc. WLTN
2240 West 75th Street
Woodridge, IL 60517 (312) 963-7100
consumer kitchenware

Windmere Corp. WDMR
4920 N.W. 165th Street
Hialeah, FL 33014 (305) 621-2611
personal care products

Wings West Airlines, Inc. WING
P.O. Box 8115
Santa Monica, CA 93403 (213) 453-0431
regional airline

Wisconsin Southern Gas Co., Inc. WISC
120 E. Sheridan Springs Road
Lake Geneva, WI 53147 (414) 248-8861
utility   [DRP]

Wiser Oil Co. (The) WISE
P.O. Box 192
Sisterville, WV 26175 (304) 652-3861
oil and gas

Wolohan Lumber Co. WLHN
1740 Midland Road
Saginaw, MI 48603 (517) 793-4532
building materials retailing

Wolverine Technologies, Inc. WOLA
1650 Howard Street
Lincoln Park, MI 48146 (313) 386-0800
aluminum siding

Wood Bros. Homes, Inc. WBRO
55 Madison Avenue, Suite 800
Denver, CO 80206 (303) 355-8000
homebuilder

Woodhead Industries, Inc. WDHD
3411 Woodhead Drive
Northbrook, IL 60062 (312) 272-7990
electrical equipment

Worthington Industries, Inc. WTHG
1205 Dearborn Drive
Columbus, OH 43085 (614) 438-3210
steel mills   [DRP]

Writer Corp. (The) WRTC
27 Inverness Drive East
Englewood, CO 80112 (303) 790-2870
homebuilder

Wyman - Gordon Co. WYMN
P.O. Box 789
Worcester, MA 01613 (617) 756-5111
metals fabrication

Wyse Technology WYSE
3571 North First Street
San Jose, CA 95134 (408) 433-1000
electronic equipment

XL/Datacomp, Inc. XLDC
907 North Elm Street
Hinsdale, IL 60521 (312) 323-1200
computers

Xebec XEBC
2221 Old Oakland Road
San Jose, CA 95131 (408) 263-4100
disk drive controllers

Xicor, Inc. XICO
851 Buckeye Court
Milpitas, CA 95035 (408) 946-6920
semiconductor devices

Xidex Corp. XIDXW
2141 Landings Drive
Mountain View, CA 94043 (415) 965-7350
photographic supplies, floppy disks

Yellow Freight System, Inc. of Delaware YELL
10990 Roe Avenue
Overland Park, KS 66207 (913) 345-3000
trucking

York Financial Corp. YFED
101 South George Street
York, PA 17405 (717) 846-8777
savings and loan

Zehntel, Inc. ZNTL
1600 South Main Street
Walnut Creek, CA 94596 (415) 946-0400
automated factory equipment

Zenith National Insurance Corp. ZNAT
15760 Ventura Blvd.
Encino, CA 91436 (818) 990-9300
insurance

Zentec Corp. ZENT
2400 Walsh Avenue
Santa Clara, CA 95050 (408) 727-7662
computer control systems

Zeus Components ZEUS
100 Midland Avenue
Port Chester, NY 10573 (914) 937-7400
semiconductor distributing

Ziegler Co., Inc. (The) ZEGL
215 North Main Street
West Bend, WI 53095 (414) 334-5521
financial services, fund management

Zions Utah Bancorporation ZION
1190 Kennecott Bldg.
Salt Lake City, UT 84133 (801) 524-4787
banking   [DRP]

Zitel Corp. ZITL
399 West Trimble Road
San Jose, CA 95131 (408) 946-9600
semiconductor equipment

Ziyad, Inc. ZIAD
100 Ford Road
Denville, NJ 07834 (201) 627-7600
paper feeding equipment for computers

Zondervan Corp. (The) ZOND
1415 Lake Drive, S.E.
Grand Rapids, MI 49506 (616) 459-6900
publishing

Zycad Corp. ZCAD
3499 Lexington Avenue North
Arden Hills, MN 55112 (612) 631-3175
computers

ZyMOS Corp. ZMOS
477 North Mathilda Avenue
Sunnyvale, CA 94086 (408) 730-8800
semiconductor equipment

Zygo Corp. ZIGO
Laurel Brook Road
Middlefield, CT 06455 (203) 347-8506
precision instruments

TORONTO STOCK EXCHANGE

Alberta Energy Co. Ltd. AEC
1200, 10707-100 Avenue
Edmonton, AB T5J 3M 1 (403) 266-8111
petroleum and natural gas   [O]

Alberta Natural Gas Co. Ltd. ANG
425 First Street SW 24th Floor
Calgary, AB T2P 3L8 (403) 260-9911
natural gas pipeline

Alcan Aluminum Ltd. AL
1188 Sherbrooke Street West
Montreal, PQ H3A 362 (514) 848-8000
aluminum   [DRP O]

AMCA International Ltd. AIL
200 Ronson Drive
Rexdale, ON M9W 529 (416) 243-9343
structural steel fabrication

American Barrick Resources Corp. ABX
24 Hazelton Avenue
Toronto, ON M5R 2E2 (416) 923-9400
exploration and development

Asamera Inc. ASM
144 4th Avenue SW Suite 2100
Calgary, AB T2P 3N4 (403) 269-5521
oil and gas exploration and development   [O]

Bank of British Columbia BBC
Two Bentall Centre 555 Burnard Street
Vancouver, BC V7X 1K1 (604) 668-4499
banking   [O]

Bank of Montreal BMO
129 St. James West
Montreal, PQ H2Y 1L6 (514) 877-6835
banking   [DRP O]

Bank of Nova Scotia BNS
44 King Street West
Toronto, ON M5H 1H1 (416) 866-6179
banking   [DRP O]

Bell Canada Enterprises B
P.O. Box 3500
Tour de la Bourse
Montreal, PQ H42 1L3 (514) 394-7000
telephone company   [DRP O]

Bonanza Resources Ltd. BNZ
1400 Central Park Plaza 340 12th Avenue SW
Calgary, AB T2K 1L5 (403) 263-6250
oil and gas exploration and development

Bow Valley Industries Ltd. BVI
321 6th Ave. SW
Calgary, AB T2P 3R2 (403) 261-6100
oil and gas exploration and development   [O]

Breakwater Resources Ltd. BWR
1440 625 Howe Street
Vancouver, BC V6C 2T6 (604) 669-1918
gold exploration and development

British Columbia Forest Products Ltd. BCF
1050 West Pender Street
Vancouver, BC V6E 2X3 (604) 665-3865
forest products

British Columbia Resources Invest. Corp. BCI
1176 West Georgia Street
Vancouver, BC V6E 4B9 (604) 687-2600
investment holding company

CAE Industries Ltd. CAE
Suite 3060 P.O. Box 30 Royal Bank Plaza
Toronto, ON M5J 2JM (416) 865-0070
holdings and management   [O]

Campbell Red Lake Mines Ltd. CRK
P.O. Box 270, 1 First Canadian Place
Toronto, ON M5X 1H1 (416) 364-3453
gold production   [O]

Canada Development Corp. CDC
200 444 Yonge Street
Toronto, ON M5B 2H4 (416) 598-7200
investment company   [DRP O]

Canada Trustco Mortgage Co. CT
Drawer 5703 Terminal A
London, ON N6A 4S4 (519) 663-1596
mortgage and loan

Canadian Imperial Bank of Commerce CM
Commerce Court
Toronto, ON M5L 1A2 (416) 862-3044
banking   [O]

Canadian Pacific Enterprises ENT
Windsor Station
Montreal, PQ H3C 3E4 (403) 231-6100
transportation

Canadian Pacific Ltd. CP
P.O. Box 6042, Station "A"
Montreal, PQ H3C 3E4 (514) 395-6592
transportation   [DRP O]

Canadian Tire Corp. Ltd. CTR.A
P.O. Box 770, Station ''K''
Toronto, ON M4P 2V8 (416) 480-3000
auto supplies   [O]

Carma Ltd. CVP.A
Deerfoot Business Centre Suite 300
67 15-8 Street NE
Calgary, AB T2E 7H7 (403) 275-5555
land development

Cineplex Odeon Corp. CPX
214 King Street West Suite 600
Toronto, ON M5H 3S6 (416) 596-2200
theatres and film distribution

Cominco Ltd. CLT
200 Granville Street
Vancouver, BC V6C 2R2 (604) 682-0611
mining and smelting   [O]

Computer Innovations Distribution Inc. CIC
3415 American Drive
Mississauga, ON L4V 1T4 (416) 673-3222
design and manufacture of computers

Consumers Distributing Co. Ltd. CDG.B
62 Belfield Road
Rexdale, ON M9W 162 (416) 864-9700
gas distribution and production

Crownx Inc. CRX
120 Bloor Street East
Toronto, ON M4W 1B8 (416) 928-7722
health care services

Czar Resources Ltd. CZR
700-425 1st Street SW
Calgary, AB T2P 3L8 (403) 265-0270
oil and gas

Daon Development Corp. DAO
1050 West Pender Street
Vancouver, BC V6T 2W7 (604) 688-2171
diversified real estate

Dome Canada Ltd. DCD
Scotia Centre, 700 2nd Street SW 37th floor
Calgary, AB T2P 2H8 (403) 231-1795
oil and gas exploration

Dome Mines Ltd. DM
P.O. Box 270 1 First Canadian Place
Toronto, ON M5X 1H1 (416) 364-3453
gold production   [O]

Dorset Resources Ltd. DOT.A
400, 602-12th Avenue SW
Calgary, AB T2R 1J3 (403) 264-4394
oil and gas exploration and development

Drummond Petroleum Ltd. DRU
2100 Fifth Avenue Place 425-1st Street SW
Calgary, AB T2P 3L8 (403) 269-8850
oil and gas exploration and development

Echo Bay Mines Ltd. ECO
3300 Manulife Place
Edmonton, AB T5J 354 (403) 429-5811
mineral exploration and development   [O]

Falconbridge Ltd. FL
Commerce Court West 40th floor
Toronto, ON M5L 1B4 (416) 863-7000
nickel copper

Franco-Nevada Mining Corp. FN
1201 2300 Yonge Street
Toronto, ON M4P 1E4 (416) 485-1010
exploration and development

Futurtek Communications Inc. FTK
1941 O'Farrell Street
San Mateo, CA 94403 (415) 345-8422
high-tech telecommunications

Genstar Corp. GST
1177 West Hastings Street Suite 2600
Vancouver, BC V6E 343 (604) 689-1611
diverse industrial operations   [O]

Granges Exploration Ltd. GEX
900, 625 Howe Street
Vancouver, BC V6C 2T6 (604) 687-2831
mining exploration and development

Gulf Canada Ltd. GOC
130 Adelaide Street West
Toronto, ON M5H 3R6 (416) 869-8600
integrated oil   [O]

Gulfstream Resources Canada Ltd. GUR
P.O. Box 80 First Canadian Place
Toronto, ON M5K 1B1
oil and gas production

Husky Oil Ltd. HYO
707 8th Avenue SW
Calgary, AB T2P 1H5 (403) 298-6111
integrated oil   [O]

Imasco Ltd. IMS
4 Westmount Square P.O. Box 6800
Montreal, PQ H32 2S8 (514) 937-9111
tobacco production   [O]

Imperial Oil Ltd. IMO.A
111 St. Clair Avenue West
Toronto, ON M5W 1K3 (416) 968-4345
integrated oil   [O]

Inco Ltd. N
1 First Canadian Place P.O. Box 44
Toronto, ON M5X 1C4 (416) 361-7527
mining and smelting N

Inter-City Gas Corp. ICG
444 St. Mary Avenue
Winnipeg, MB R3C 3T7 (204) 944-9920
gas distribution   [DRP O]

International Thomson Organisation Ltd. ITO
20 Queen Street West Suite 2206 P.O. Box 45
Toronto, ON M5H 3R3 (416) 977-8700
holding company

Joutel Resources Ltd. JTL
916, 111 Richmond Street West
Toronto, ON M5H 264 (416) 364-3182
copper production

Lac Minerals Ltd. LAC
Royal Bank Plaza
North Tower Suite 2105 P.O. Box 156
Toronto, ON M5J 2J4 (416) 865-0722
mining exploration and development   [O]

Laidlaw Transportation Ltd. LDM.B
65 Guise Street East
Hamilton, ON L8P 4S6 (416) 521-1800
trucking service

Lochiel Exploration Ltd. LHX.A
890 Calgary House 550 6th Avenue SW
Calgary, AB T2P 0S2 (403) 265-8405
oil exploration

MacLean Hunter Ltd. MHP.X
MacLean Hunter Building 777 Bay Street
Toronto, ON M5W 1A7 (416) 596-5157
printing and publishing

MacMillan Bloedel Ltd. MB
1075 West Georgia Street
Vancouver, BC V6E 3R9 (604) 661-8000
newsprint

Magna International MG.A/B
36 Apple Creek Boulevard
Markham, ON L3R 4Y4 (416) 477-7766
metal fabricating

Manitoba Properties Inc. MPI.PR.A
c/o Buchwald Asper Henteleff 25th floor
Commodity Exchange Tower 360 Main Street
Winnipeg, MB R3C 4H6 (204) 956-0560
office properties

Mark's Work Wearhouse Ltd. MWW
300, Southland Tower 10655 Southport Road SW
Calgary, AB T2W 4Y1 (403) 271-9400
retail clothing store

Massey-Ferguson Ltd. MF
595 Bay Street
Toronto, ON M56 2C3 (416) 593-3811
farm machinery

Mitel Corp. MLT
350 Legget Drive P.O. Box 3089
Kanata, ON K2K 1X3 (613) 592-2122
electronic telephone equipment   [O]

Moore Corp. Ltd. MCL
1 First Canadian Place P.O. Box 78
Toronto, ON M5X 165 (416) 364-2600
business forms   [DRP O]

National Bank of Canada NA
600 rue de la Gauchetiere Ouest
Montreal, PQ H3B 4L2 (514) 394-4000
banking   [DRP O]

Noranda Inc. NOR
Commerce Court West P.O. Box 45
Toronto, ON M5L 1B6 (416) 867-7111
mining and smelting   [O]

Norcen Energy Resources Ltd. NCN
Norcen Tower 715 5th Avenue SW
Calgary, AB T2P 2X7 (403) 231-0111
oil and gas exploration   [O]

Northern Telecom Ltd. NTL
P.O. Box 458 Station "A"
Mississauga, ON L5A 3A2 (416) 275-0960
telecommunications equipment   [DRP O]

Nova, An Alberta Corp. NVA.A
P.O. Box 2535 Postal Station M
Calgary, AB T2P 2N6 (403) 290-6000
natural gas pipeline   [O]

Nu-West Group Ltd. NUW.A
301 14th Street NW
Calgary, AB T2P 2R6 (403) 280-7607
land development builder

Oakwood Petroleums Ltd. OAK.A
1800-311 6th Avenue SW
Calgary, AB T2P 3H2 (403) 265-2740
oil and gas

Pacific Trans-Ocean Resources Ltd. PTX
1868 10303 Jasper Avenue
Edmonton, AB T5J 3N6 (403) 426-3339
mining and mineral exploration

Pagurian Corp. Ltd. PGC.A
401 Bay Street Box 32
Toronto, ON M5H 221 (416) 363-9381
investment holding company

Pennant Resources Ltd. PNR
906, 101 Richmond Street West
Toronto, ON M5H 1T1 (416) 364-9126
oil and gas exploration and development

Penn West Petroleum Ltd. PWT
1250 Elveden House,717-7th Avenue SW
Calgary, AB T2P 023 (403) 237-0120
oil and gas exploration and development

Placer Development Ltd. PDL
1600-1055 Dunsmuir Street
Vancouver, BC V7X 1P1 (604) 682-7082
holding and investment company   [O]

Power Corp. of Canada POW
759 Victoria Square
Montreal, PQ H24 2K4 (514) 286-7424
holding and management company   [O]

Ranger Oil RGO
425 1st Street SW 27th floor
Calgary, AB T2P 3L8 (403) 263-1500
oil and gas   [O]

Reed Stenhouse Companies Ltd. RSS.S
TD Centre P.O. Box 250
Toronto, ON M5K 156 (416) 868-5500
insurance brokerage

Rogers Cablesystems Inc RCI.B
Commercial Union Tower TD Centre
P.O. Box 249
Toronto, ON M5K 1J5 (416) 864-2373
cable television

Royal Bank of Canada RY
The Royal Bank of Canada Building Box 6001
Montreal, PQ H3C 3A9 (514) 874-2110
banking   [DRP O]

Royal Trustco Ltd. RYL.A
P.O. Box 7500 Station "A"
Toronto, ON M5W 1P9 (416) 867-2000
trust company

Royex Gold Mining Corp. RGM
400 111 Richmond Street
Toronto, ON M5H 264 (416) 366-5201
mining exploration and development

Seagram Co. Ltd. VO
1430 Peel Street
Montreal, PQ H3A 1S9 (514) 849-5271
distillery   [O]

Sears Canada Inc. SCC
222 Jarvis Street
Toronto, ON MSB 2B8 (416) 941-4422
retail mail order

Shell Canada Ltd. SHC
P.O. Box 100 Station "M"
Calgary, AB T2P 2H5 (403) 232-3111
integrated oil   [O]

Sherritt Gordon Mines SE
P.O. Box 28, Commerce Court West
Toronto, ON M5L 1B1 (416) 363-9241
minerals mining

Southam Inc. STM
150 Bloor Street West Suite 900
Toronto, ON M5S 248 (416) 927-1877
newspapers and publishing

Stelco Inc. STE.A
Toronto Dominion Centre P.O. Box 205
Toronto, ON M5K 1J4 (416) 362-2161
steel mills   [O]

Teck Corp. TEK.B
1 First Canadian Place Suite 7000
P.O. Box 170
Toronto, ON M5X 169 (416) 862-7102
gold, oil, and gas

Texaco Canada Inc. TXC.R
960 Wynford Drive Don Mills
North York, ON M3C 1K5 (416) 441-7450
integrated oil

Toronto-Dominion Bank TD
Toronto-Dominion Centre P.O. Box 1
Toronto, ON M5K 1AZ (416) 982-8091
banking   [O]

Total Petroleum (North America) Ltd. TPN
639 Fifth Ave. SW
Calgary, AB T2P 0M9 (403) 267-3000
oil exploration and development   [O]

TransAlta Utilities Corp. TAU.A
110-12th Avenue SW Box 1900
Calgary, AB T2P 2MI (403) 267-7110
electric power   [DRP O]

TransCanada Pipelines Ltd. TRP
Commerce Court West P.O. Box 54
Toronto, ON M5L 1CZ (416) 869-2559
gas pipeline   [DRP O]

Treasure Valley Explorations Ltd. TVX
2111, 65 Queen Street West
Toronto, ON M5H 2M5 (416) 366-8160
mining exploration and development

Trimac Ltd. TMA
535 7th Avenue
Calgary, AB T2P 2P9 (403) 298-5100
transportation company

Turbo Resources Ltd. TBR
901-8 Avenue SW
Calgary, AB T2P 3E9 (403) 262-4636
diversified hyrdrocarbons

Ulster Petroleums Ltd. ULP
500 700 4th Avenue SW
Calgary, AB T2P 3J4 (403) 269-6911
oil and gas

Union Enterprises Ltd. UEL
50 Keil Drive North P.O. Box 2001
Chatham, ON N7M 5M1 (519) 436-4504
natural gas production and distribution

Walker, Hiram Resources Ltd. HWR
1 First Canadian Place Suite 600 P.O. Box 33
Toronto, ON M5X 1A9 (416) 864-3343
distillery and natural gas   [DRP O]

Woodward's Ltd. WDS.A
101 West Hastings Street
Vancouver, BC V6B 1H4 (604) 666-4140
department stores   [O]

AMERICAN DEPOSITARY RECEIPTS (ADRs)

Investors wishing to buy shares in some companies headquartered outside the United States can avoid dealing directly with foreign exchanges by purchasing American Depositary Receipts in U.S. markets. ADRs are traded on the New York Stock Exchange, the American Stock Exchange, and the over-the-counter market.

ADRs are receipts for foreign-based corporations' shares, which are held in American bank vaults. A buyer of an ADR in America is entitled to the same dividends and capital gains accruing to a shareholder purchasing shares on an exchange in the home country of the company. ADRs are denominated in dollars, so quoted prices reflect the latest currency exchange rates. ADR prices are listed in *The Wall Street Journal* and other newspapers, as well as in electronic databases.

The companies with ADRs generally are well-established, financially stable corporations with worldwide operations. In many cases, Americans would be familiar with their products and services because they are offered in the United States. A total of about 700 ADRs are traded. Most of the trading activity, however, is limited to some 100 issues. It is these actively traded issues that are presented here in alphabetical order, courtesy of Wilshire Associates [1299 Ocean Avenue, Santa Monica, California 90401 (213) 451-3051]. The entry for each company includes (1) the firm's name, (2) its stock symbol, (3) the exchange where it trades (NYSE for New York Stock Exchange, ASE for American Stock Exchange, and OTC for Over-The-Counter market), (4) its main line of business, and (5) the country where it is headquartered.

Advanced Semiconductor Materials [ASMIF] OTC, electronics, The Netherlands

American Israeli Paper [AIP] ASE, paper manufacturing, Israel

Anglo American Corp. [ANGL] OTC, gold mining, South Africa

Anglo American Gold Investors [AAGI] OTC, gold mining, South Africa

ASA Ltd. [ASA] NYSE, gold mining closed-end mutual fund, South Africa

ASEA AB [ASEA] OTC, electrical equipment, Sweden

Banco Central S.A. [BCM] NYSE, banking, Spain

BAT Industries Ltd. [BTI] ASE, tobacco and retailing, United Kingdom

Bayer A.G. [BAYRY] OTC, chemicals, West Germany

Beecham Group Ltd. [BHAM] OTC, food and health services, OTC, United Kingdom

Blyvoorjitzicht Gold Mining [BLYVY] OTC, gold mining, South Africa

Bowater Ind. PLC [BWTRY], OTC, paper and containers, United Kingdom

British Petroleum Ltd. [BP] NYSE, oil refining and marketing , United Kingdom

British Telecommunications PLC [BTT] NYSE, communications, United Kingdom

Broken Hill Proprietary Co. [BRKXY] OTC, metals mining, Australia

Buffelsfontein Gold Mines [BFEL] OTC, gold mining, South Africa

Burmah Oil, Ltd. [BURMY] OTC, oil refining and marketing, United Kingdom

Cadbury Schweppes PLC [CADBY] OTC, food products, beverages, United Kingdom

Canon Inc. [CANN] OTC, business equipment and photography, Japan

Central Pacific Minerals, N.L. [CPMN] OTC, metals mining, Australia

Club Méditerranée [CMI] NYSE, resorts, France

Compania de Alumbrad [ELSA] OTC, utility, El Salvador

Computer Service Corp. [CSKK] OTC, business machines, Japan

Courtaulds Ltd. [COU] ASE, apparel and chemicals, United Kingdom

Daiei Inc. [DAIE] OTC, retailing, Japan

De Beers Consolidated Mines [DBRSY] OTC, diamonds and metal mining, South Africa

Deltec International [DLTC] NYSE, finance, United Kingdom

Dresdner Bank A.G. [DRSD] OTC, banking, West Germany

Driefontein Consolidated Mines [DRFNY] OTC, gold mining, South Africa

Dunlop Holdings [DLP] ASE, rubber and tires, United Kingdom

ECI Telecom, Ltd. [ECILF] OTC, computers, Israel

Elan PLC [ELAN] OTC, conglomerate, Ireland

Elbit Computers, Ltd. [ELBTF] OTC, business data processing, Israel

Elscint Ltd. [ELT] NYSE, medical equipment, Israel

Ericsson, L.M. [ERIC] OTC, communications equipment, Sweden

Expo Oil, N.L. [EXPO] OTC, energy, Australia

Fanuc [FJFJ] OTC, industrial equipment, Japan

Ferrovandium Corp., N.L. [OTC] metals mining, Australia

Fisons Ltd. [FISN] OTC, farm products and chemicals, United Kingdom

Free State Geduld [FREEY] OTC, gold mining, South Africa

Fuji Photo Film Ltd. [FUJIY] OTC, photographic equipment, Japan

Fujitsu Ltd. [FULD] OTC, electronic equipment, Japan

Gambro A.B. [GAMBY] OTC, health services, Sweden

Gevaert Photo Products [GEVA] OTC, photographic equipment, Belgium

Glaxo Holdings PLC [GLXOY] OTC, drugs, United Kingdom

Gold Fields of South Africa OTC, gold mining, South Africa

Gotaas-Larsen Shipping Corp. [GOTLP] OTC, shipping, Sweden

Great Eastern Mines Ltd. [GOLD] OTC, mining, Australia

Harmony Gold Mining Ltd. [HGM] ASE, gold mining, South Africa

Hartogen Energy Ltd. [HTEN] OTC, energy, Australia

Heineken N.V. [HENK] OTC, brewing, The Netherlands

Highveld Steel and Vanadium [HSVL] OTC, steel, South Africa

Hitachi Ltd. [HIT] NYSE, electronic equipment, Japan

Honda Motor Ltd. [HMC] NYSE, auto and motorcycle manufacturer, Japan

Huntington International Holding [HRCLY] OTC, drugs, United Kingdom

IDB Bankholding Co. [IDBY] OTC, banking, Israel

IEM, S.A. [IEMS] OTC, capital goods, Mexico

Imperial Chemical Industries [ICI] NYSE, chemicals, United Kingdom

Imperial Group PLC [IMT] ASE, tobacco and food, United Kingdom

Instrumentarium Corp. [INMRY] OTC, health services and drugs, Finland

Ito Yokado Ltd. [IYCOY] OTC, retailing, Japan

Jaguar [JAGRY] OTC, auto manufacturer, United Kingdom

Japan Air Lines [JAPN] OTC, airline, Japan

Kirin Brewery Ltd. [KNBW] OTC, breweries and wineries, Japan

KLM Royal Dutch Air Lines [KLM] NYSE, airline, The Netherlands

Kloof Gold Mining [KLOFY] OTC, gold mining, South Africa

Kubota Ltd. [KUB] NYSE, farm, construction, and building machinery, Japan

Kyocera Ltd. [KYO] NYSE, electronics and ceramics, Japan

Lydenburg Platinum [LYDP] OTC, metals mining, South Africa

Makita Electric Works, Ltd. [MKTAY] OTC, electrical equipment, Japan

Marubeni Corp. [MRBN] OTC, conglomerate, Japan

Matsushita Electric Industrial [MC] NYSE, electronic equipment, Japan

Meridian Oil, N.L. [MEDL] OTC, oil drilling and refining, The Netherlands

Minerals and Resources Corp. [MNRC] OTC, metals mining, United Kingdom

Mitsubishi Electric [MECJ] OTC, electronics, Japan

Mitsui & Company Ltd. [MITSY] OTC, conglomerate, Japan

NEC Corp. [NIPN] OTC, electronic equipment, Japan

Nimslo International Ltd. [NIMS] OTC, photography, Japan

Nippon Electric Ltd. [NIPN] OTC, electric products, Japan

Nissan Motors [NSAN] OTC, auto manufacturer, Japan

Norsk-Data, A.S. [NORK] OTC, business data processing, Norway

Novo Industri A/S [NVO] NYSE, drugs, Denmark

Oce-Van Der Grinten [OCEN] OTC, copying machines and office supplies, The Netherlands

O Okiep Copper Ltd. [OKP] ASE, metals mining, South Africa

Palabora Mining Ltd. [PALA] OTC, metals mining, South Africa

Pelsart Resources N.L. [PELR] OTC, energy, The Netherlands

Pharmacia, A.B. [PHAB] OTC, drugs, Sweden

Philips, N.V. [PGLO] OTC, electrical equipment, The Netherlands

Pioneer Electric Corp. [PIO] NYSE, consumer electronics, Japan

Plessey Ltd. [PLY] NYSE, communications, United Kingdom

President Brand Gold Mining [PRES] OTC, gold mining, South Africa

President Steyn Gold Mining [PSTYY] OTC, gold mining, South Africa

Randfontein Estates [RNDE] OTC, gold mining, South Africa

Rank Organization [RANKY] OTC, media, United Kingdom

Reuters Holding PLC [RTRS] OTC, news and financial information agency, United Kingdom

Rodime PLC [RODM] OTC, electronics, United Kingdom

Royal Dutch Petroleum Co. [RD] NYSE, oil refining and marketing, The Netherlands

Saatchi and Saatchi Co. PLC [SACH] OTC, advertising and financial services, United Kingdom

Santos Ltd. [STOS] OTC, oil and gas production, Australia

Sanyo Electric Ltd. [SANY] OTC, electronics, Japan

Scitex [SCIXF] OTC, software and data processing, Israel

Sharp Corp. [SHAP] OTC, business data processing and consumer electronics, Japan

Shell Transport & Trading Co. PLC [SC] NYSE, oil ˙refining and marketing, United Kingdom

Siemens A.G. [SIEM] OTC, electrical equipment, West Germany

Sony Corp. [SNE] NYSE, consumer and industrial electronics, Japan

Southern Pacific Petroleum, N.L. [SPPT] OTC, oil refining and food, Australia

St. Helena Gold Mines [SGOLY] OTC, gold mining, South Africa

Svenska Cellulosa A.K. [SCAP] OTC, drugs, Sweden

Swan Resources Ltd. [SWAN] OTC, mining, Australia

TDK Electronics, Ltd. [TDK] NYSE, electronic equipment, Japan

Telephonos de Mexico [TFON] OTC, telephone utility, Mexico

Teva Pharmaceutical [TEVI] *OTC, drugs,* Israel

Tokio Marine & Fire [TKIOY] OTC, fire, marine, casualty, and title insurance, Japan

Toshiba [TOKY] OTC, electrical equipment, Japan

Toyota Motor Co. [TOYX] OTC, auto manufacturer, Japan

Tricentrol PLC [TCT] NYSE, oil and gas production, United Kingdom

Trio Kenwood Corp. [KENW] OTC, electronics, Japan

Tubos de Acero [TAM] ASE, steel, Mexico

Unilever Ltd. PLC [UL] NYSE, food, United Kingdom

Unilever N.V. [UN] NYSE, soaps and cleansers, The Netherlands

Universal Money Centers [UMUK] OTC, finance, United Kingdom

Vaal Reefs Exploration & Mining [VAALY] OTC, gold mining, South Africa

Volvo A.B. [VOLV] OTC, auto manufacturer, Sweden

Vuitton Luis S.A. [LVTNY] OTC, apparel, France

Wacoal Corp. [WACL] OTC, apparel, Japan

Welkom Gold Mining Ltd. [WLKM] OTC, gold mining, South Africa

Western Deep Levels [WDEPY] OTC, gold mining, South Africa

Western Holdings [WHLD] OTC, gold mining, South Africa

FREE AND DISCOUNTED GOODS AND SERVICES FOR SHAREHOLDERS

The following is a list of American corporations that give free or discounted merchandise or services to their shareholders. In order to make a claim, shareholders usually must write or call the company, since most companies do not know the names of all shareholders (shares often are held in street name by a brokerage firm). These freebies usually are not taxed as income to shareholders.

This list is provided courtesy of Eamonn Fingleton and Roland Turner, who have written a book, *Shareholder Freebies* [Buttonwood Press, 41 Park Avenue, New York, New York 10016 (212) 689-4643]. The book describes more programs and offers more detail than can be presented here. Mr. Fingleton and Mr. Turner also offer updated lists through electronic databases and via electronic mail.

American Brands   Product pack including cigarettes, office products, locks, and food.

American Family Corporation   Two-week trip to see the company's Japanese operation for the stockholders who guess the company's earnings per share most accurately.

American Recreation Centers   Shareholders with at least 300 shares are allowed free use of the company's bowling centers.

Amfac   Discounts on accommodations in Amfac hotels for shareholders who attend the annual meeting. The meeting is held in Hawaii every other year.

Berkshire Hathaway   Contribution by the company to a charity of the shareholder's choice.

Bristol-Myers   Product pack including over-the-counter drugs, shampoo, and toiletries.

Chesebrough-Pond's   Product pack including cosmetics, key rings, tennis accessories, and Q-tips for shareholders with an initial purchase of at least 100 shares held in the individual's own name.

Circuit City Stores   Discounts of 10% on consumer electronics worth up to $1000 sold in the company's stores.

CSX Corporation   15% discount for weekend retreats at The Greenbrier, a West Virginia mountain resort.

Delta Queen Steamship Company   Discounts of up to 25% on cruise vacations on the Mississippi and Ohio rivers.

General Mills Discounts on meals at Red Lobster restaurants, Care Bear books, and Izod clothing. Christmas gift pack includes food items from Betty Crocker division and Parker Brothers games.

H.J. Heinz Company Stockholders with at least 15 shares are offered a product pack with a small warming tray and discount coupons for Heinz food products. Product samples frequently given out at annual meeting.

IU International 15% discount on products of its subsidiary Mauna Loa Macadamia Nut Corporation.

Kimberly-Clark Product pack, with the company's paper products such as Kleenex, Kotex, and Huggies, offered at Christmastime.

Marriott Corporation Discounts of up to 50% on stays at the company's hotels. Discounts of 10% on cruises with the company's Sun Line subsidiary. Annual meeting attendees receive coupons for meals in Marriott-owned restaurants.

Minnesota Mining and Manufacturing Offers product pack including Scotch tape, Micropore medical tapes, and Scotch-Brite scouring pads.

Penril Corporation Discounts of up to 50% on company's audio products such as Thorens turntables and Epicure speakers.

Pepsico Gift packs of soft drinks and food products handed out at annual meeting.

Pfizer Discounts of up to 75% on discontinued cosmetic and toiletry products made available through a catalog sent at Christmastime.

Quaker Oats Cents-off coupons mailed to shareholders with quarterly dividend checks. Quaker products given to annual meeting attendees.

Ramada Inns Discounts of 10% on rooms in Ramada Hotels. Some larger discounts, such as 25% on weekend stays and 50% on Las Vegas Ramada stays.

RJR Nabisco Discount coupons for Del Monte and Hawaiian Punch food products sent with quarterly reports.

Satellite Data Discounts of up to 40% on satellite dishes and other equipment for receiving satellite television signals.

Scott Paper Boxes of tissues, paper towels, and other paper products sent at a discount to shareholders who request them around Christmastime.

Squibb Corporation Discounts of 40% or more on Charles of the Ritz fragrances and cosmetics.

Sterling Drug Product pack of over-the-counter medicines such as aspirin and household products such as Lysol disinfectants and pine action cleaners.

Tandy Corporation Discounts of 10% on purchases in Radio Shack stores at Christmastime.

Appendix

SELECTED FURTHER READING

Overall Bibliography

Daniells, Lorna M. *Business Information Sources.* rev. ed. Berkeley: University of California Press, 1985.

Economics

Friedman, Milton. *Capitalism and Freedom.* Chicago: University of Chicago Press, 1981.

A leading exponent of the monetarist ("Chicago") school of economics sets forth his views in this basic work, first published in 1962.

Heilbroner, Robert L. and Lester C. Thurow. *The Economic Problem.* 7th ed. Englewood Cliffs: Prentice-Hall, 1984.

An established introductory text by two noted economists; covers the background, economic tools, market systems, and major challenges in both macroeconomics and microeconomics.

Keynes, John Maynard. *The General Theory of Employment, Interest and Money.* London: Macmillan, 1936.

The definitive work of the British economist and government advisor, whose influential theories advocating government intervention (fiscal policy) as a solution to economic problems have become known as Keynesian economics.

McConnell, Campbell R. *Economics: Principles, Problems, and Policies.* 9th ed. New York: McGraw-Hill, 1984.

A highly regarded introduction to the fundamental problems and principles of economics and the policy alternatives available to countries, both from a national and international perspective.

Samuelson, Paul A. and W. Nordhaus: *Economics.* 12th ed. New York: McGraw-Hill, 1985.

This famous and widely used introductory economics text has been thoroughly revised and updated. It takes students from fundamental to sophisticated levels of understanding of income and production factors including international trade and finance and current economic problems.

Smith, Adam. *An Inquiry into the Nature and Causes of the Wealth of Nations.* New York: Random House (Modern Library), 1937.

The definitive work, first published in 1776, of the most famous of the classical economists, who held that economies function best when under a laissez-faire system in which market forces are free to operate without government interference.

International Economics, Finance, and Investment

George, Abraham M. and Ian H. Giddy, eds. *International Finance Handbook*. 2 vol. New York: John Wiley & Sons, 1983.

A massive reference written by 56 authorities for the nonspecialist practitioner in international financing, banking, and investment.

Lindert, Peter H. and Charles P. Kindleberger. *International Economics*. 7th ed. Homewood, Illinois: Dow Jones-Irwin, 1982.

A classic text covering aspects of international economics and finance on theoretical and practical levels, plus an examination of larger problems concerning international mobility of people and factors of production.

Pring, Martin J. *International Investing Made Easy*. New York: McGraw-Hill, 1980.

A wide-ranging discussion for the investor new to foreign securities, clearly written by a well-known authority.

Root, Franklin R. *International Trade and Investment*. 5th ed. Cincinnati: South-Western, 1984.

Covers theory, policy, and the marketplace of international trade, including international payments, development financing, and international investments and multinational enterprises.

Roussakis, Emmanuel N., ed. *International Banking: Principles and Practices*. New York: Praeger, 1983.

Twenty-three experts discuss international banking, focusing on lending policies and procedures and on risk and credit analysis.

Walker, Townsend. *A Guide for Using the Foreign Exchange Market*. New York: John Wiley and Sons, 1981.

This beginner's explanatory guide, with case studies and exercises, emphasizes techniques, analysis, and calculations used in foreign exchange.

Money and Banking

Cochran, John A. *Money, Banking and the Economy*. 5th ed. New York: Macmillan, 1983.

An introductory text covering money; the money and capital markets; commercial banks and their competitors; commercial banking practices; central banking; monetary and income theory; and public policy.

DeRosa, Paul and Gary H. Stern. *In the Name of Money: A Professional's Guide to the Federal Reserve, Interest Rates & Money*. New York: McGraw-Hill, 1981.

A practical (rather than theoretical) discussion of Federal Reserve policy and operations and their effects on interest rates, money supply, and the financial markets. Not for the beginner.

Kaufman, George G. *The U.S. Financial System: Money, Markets and Institutions*. 2d ed. Englewood Cliffs: Prentice-Hall, 1983.

Assuming a basic knowledge of economics, this text covers in terms of theory and practice the evolution and operations of the national and international financial markets as well as instruments, institutions, and regulation. The Federal Reserve System and other aspects of the economic macrostructure are also examined.

Ritter, Lawrence S. and William L. Silber. *Principles of Money, Banking and Financial Markets.* 4th ed. New York: Basic Books, 1983.

A comprehensive introductory text that covers money and banking fundamentals; banks and other intermediaries; central banking; monetary theory; financial markets and interest rates; and international finance.

Bond and Money Markets

Darst, David M. *The Handbook of the Bond and Money Markets.* New York: McGraw-Hill, 1981.

For professionals and nonprofessionals, this volume analyzes long- and short-term fixed-income securities, the marketplace, and investment strategies. Comprehensively covers such related subjects as Federal Reserve operations and the makeup and meaning of economic and debt statistics.

Donoghue, William E. with Thomas Tilling. *William E. Donoghue's Complete Money Market Guide.* New York: Harper & Row, 1981.

A readable guide to the money market and investing through money market funds, by a prominent specialist in the field.

Fabozzi, Frank J. and Irving M. Pollock, eds. *The Handbook of Fixed Income Securities.* Homewood, Illinois: Dow Jones-Irwin, 1983.

Includes 47 chapters, each by an expert, covering general investment information; securities and instruments; bond investment management; interest rates and rate forecasting. More extensive than the volume by David M. Darst, but similarly designed for the layperson and professional.

Holt, Robert L. *The Complete Book of Bonds.* rev. ed. San Diego: Harcourt Brace Jovanovich, 1985.

An in-depth examination of bonds and the markets in which they are traded; for both the beginner and the professional.

Stigum, Marcia. *The Money Market.* rev. ed. Homewood, Illinois: Dow Jones-Irwin, 1983.

A comprehensive guide, by a working professional, to the U.S. money market. It covers (1) the various instruments traded, how yields are calculated, and the role of the Federal Reserve; (2) the major participants, including Eurobanks; and (3) particular markets, such as those for commercial paper, Treasury bills, and CDs. Includes financial futures.

Corporate Finance

Altman, Edward I., ed. *Financial Handbook.* 5th ed. New York: John Wiley and Sons, 1981.

With 38 chapters written by 45 authorities, this exhaustive reference divides the world of finance into four sections: U.S. Financial Markets and Institutions; International Financial Markets and Institutions; Securities and Portfolio Management; and Corporate Financial Management. The last category includes 15 chapters on such subjects as planning and control techniques, financial forecasting, capital budgeting, and mergers and acquisitions.

Brigham, Eugene F. *Financial Management: Theory and Practice.* 4th ed. Hinsdale, Illinois: Dryden Press, 1985.

A well-written discussion of basic concepts in financial management and their use in maximizing the value of a firm. Using real-life examples, the text covers financial forecasting, working capital management, capital budgeting, and other relevant subjects, including international financial management and mergers and acquisitions.

Van Horne, James C. *Fundamentals of Financial Management.* 6th ed. Englewood Cliffs: Prentice-Hall, 1986.

An excellent introductory text with sections on principles of financial returns, tools of financial analysis and planning, working capital management, investing in capital assets, capital structure and dividend policies, long-term financing and markets, and special areas including cash-management models and option pricing.

Weston, J. Fred and Eugene F. Brigham. *Essentials of Managerial Finance.* 7th ed. Hinsdale, Illinois: Dryden Press. 1985.

A fine introductory text emphasizing decision rather than theory, with sections on fundamental concepts; financial analysis, planning and control; working capital management; investment decisions; cost of capital and valuation; long-term financing decisions; and integrated topics in managerial finance.

Securities Markets, Securities Analysis, and Portfolio Management

Amling, Frederick. *Investments, An Introduction to Analysis and Management.* 5th ed. Englewood Cliffs: Prentice-Hall, 1984.

A text for the beginning investor or aspiring investment professional. Using practical cases to demonstrate principles, the book deals with various aspects of fundamental analysis, modern portfolio theory, and technical analysis.

Arbel, Avner. *How to Beat the Market with High-Performance Generic Stocks.* New York: William Morrow, 1985.

In an original contribution to the literature of investing, Professor Arbel sets forth an investment strategy based on generic stocks, which lack name recognition but represent potential appreciation because their values have been ignored by the brokerage community.

Cohen, Jerome B., Edward D. Zinbarg, and Arthur Zeikel. *Investment Analysis and Portfolio Management.* 4th ed. Homewood, Illinois: Dow Jones-Irwin, 1982.

An introductory text, notable because it is comprehensive and discusses modern portfolio theory and security valuation techniques in a nonmathematical, readable fashion. It also covers the current investment scene and industry and company analysis.

Dreman, David. *The New Contrarian Investment Strategy: The Psychology of Stock Market Success.* New York: Random House, 1983.

An updated version of an established title, this book discusses a contrarian's approach to successful investing in a 1980s environment marked by widely fluctuating interest rates and market prices.

Engel, Louis and Brendan Boyd. *How to Buy Stocks.* 7th ed. Boston: Atlantic-Little Brown, 1983.

A highly readable, clear, and informative introduction to investing in the stock market, this book has been a deserved fixture in the literature on investing for over three decades.

Fischer, Donald E. and Ronald J. Jordan. *Security Analysis and Portfolio Management.* 3d ed. Englewood Cliffs: Prentice-Hall, 1983.

By using the fast-food industry and McDonald's Corporation as an example to illustrate the practical applications of security analysis and portfolio management theory, the authors of this introductory text manage to keep an essentially mathematical subject relatively nonmathematical and understandable.

Graham, Benjamin, David L. Dodd, and Sidney Cottle. *Security Analysis: Principles and Techniques.* 4th ed. New York: McGraw-Hill, 1962.

This classic work, originally published in 1934, remains the bible for students of the fundamentalist approach to securities analysis. It consists of six parts: survey and approach; analysis of financial statements; fixed-income securities; the valuation of common stocks; senior securities with speculative features; and other aspects of security analysis.

Loll, Leo M. and Julian G. Buckley. *The Over-The-Counter Securities Markets.* 4th ed. Englewood Cliffs: Prentice-Hall, 1981.

A training manual for would-be stockbrokers preparing for the NASD examination and a generally valuable book for any investor wishing to learn more about the over-the-counter markets, securities underwriting, stock and bond trading, regulation, and the securities business in general.

Pring, Martin J. *Technical Analysis Explained: The Successful Investor's Guide to Spotting Investment Trends and Turning Points.* 2d ed. New York: McGraw-Hill, 1985.

An excellent and comprehensive introduction to technical analysis, made especially useful by its many illustrative charts.

Rolo, Charles J. *Gaining on the Market: Your Complete Guide to Investment Strategy.* Boston: Atlantic-Little Brown, 1982.

A superb guide to investing in stocks. It discusses stock picking and market timing as well as forces influencing stock prices and includes practical advice on dealing with brokers and using information sources.

Teweles, Richard J. and Edward S. Bradley. *The Stock Market.* 4th ed. New York: John Wiley and Sons, 1982.

This is a revision of a work originally authored by George L. Leffler in 1951. It examines the stock market in five sections dealing with fundamental information, the exchanges, securities houses, regulations, investing practices, and special instruments.

Train, John. *The Money Masters.* New York: Harper & Row, 1980.

Interesting stories, by an investment counselor, about the investment strategies of nine distinguished portfolio managers, such as T. Rowe Price, Benjamin Graham, and John Templeton, with commentary on their methods and personalities.

Commodity and Financial Futures Markets

Huff, Charles and Barbara Marinacci. *Commodity Speculation for Beginners: A Guide to the Futures Market.* New York: Macmillan, 1980.

Using an informal, chatty narrative style, this book takes the beginner to a considerable depth of understanding of commodities trading and its marketplace, including personal trading programs.

Kaufman, Perry J. *Handbook of Futures Markets: Commodity, Financial, Stock Index, Options.* New York: John Wiley and Sons, 1984.

An extensive manual and reference guide comprising 49 chapters written by over 50 experts. Twenty-five chapters deal with individual commodities, including financial futures. Others deal with markets, forecasting, hedging, risk and money management, and other technical aspects.

Powers, Mark J. *Getting Started in Commodity Futures Trading.* 4th ed. Cedar Falls, Iowa: Investor Publications, 1983.

A combination of theory and practical information for the beginner; includes history, exchanges, choosing a broker, trading programs, hedging, and forecasting. Deals with financial futures.

Rothstein, Nancy H. and James M. Little, eds. *The Handbook of Financial Futures: A Guide for Investors and Professional Financial Managers.* New York: McGraw-Hill, 1984.

A comprehensive reference focusing on concepts and methods for using and analyzing financial futures for hedging and trading purposes, including regulatory, accounting, and tax implications. For the professional as well as the novice.

Schwager, Jack D. *A Complete Guide to the Futures Markets: Fundamental Analysis, Technical Analysis, Trading, Spreads, and Options.* New York: John Wiley and Sons, 1984.

Assumes a basic familiarity with futures trading, but otherwise provides a nontechnical discussion of various analytical techniques, including regression analysis and chart analysis. Has sample charts and a section on trading guidelines.

Options Markets

Ansbacher, Max G. *The New Options Market.* rev. ed. New York: Walker & Co., 1979.

An easy-to-read, yet comprehensive rundown, by a professional trader, of options and option strategies. For the speculator as well as the conservative investor.

————. *The New Stock-Index Market, Strategies for Profit in Stock Index Futures and Options.* New York: Walker & Co., 1983.

This veteran trader and clearheaded writer discusses the relatively new and growing area of index futures and options; for beginner as well as seasoned investors and speculators.

Gastineau, Gary L. *The Stock Options Manual.* 2d ed. New York: McGraw-Hill, 1979.

Assuming a basic knowledge of options and how they are used, Gastineau discusses option valuation methods and their applications in portfolio analysis and management. The book also covers option investment and trading strategies and tax implications.

McMillan, Lawrence G. *Options as a Strategic Investment.* Englewood Cliffs: Prentice-Hall, 1980.

An advanced discussion of option strategies, focusing on which ones work where and why. Includes chapters on arbitrage, mathematical applications, and tax ramifications.

Tso, Lin. *Complete Investor's Guide to Listed Options: Calls & Puts.* Englewood Cliffs: Prentice-Hall, 1981.

A leading expert discusses the fundamentals of puts and calls and the uses, risks, and rewards of listed options for investors of all types.

CURRENCIES OF THE WORLD

The following is a list of the currencies of independent countries of the world. The list will be helpful to anyone doing business or touring in these countries as well as to those tracking finance and investment abroad.

The countries are listed alphabetically. The basic unit of currency is given for each plus the principal subunits. For example, the U.S. dollar (basic unit) is divided into 100 cents (subunits).

Because exchange rates are not fixed, the relative value of the currencies changes continually. For up-to-date exchange rates, check the financial pages of a major newspaper; *The New York Times, The Wall Street Journal,* and the *Financial Times,* for example, print extensive listings. A bank or other financial institution may also be able to provide current exchange rates.

Afghanistan 1 afgani = 100 puls
Albania 1 new lek = 100 qintar
Algeria 1 dinar = 100 centimes
Andorra 1 Spanish peseta = 100 centimos; 1 French franc = 100 centimes
Angola 1 kwanza = 100 centavos
Antigua and Barbuda 1 East Caribbean dollar = 100 cents
Argentina 1 austral = 100 centavos
Australia 1 dollar = 100 cents
Austria 1 schilling = 100 groschen
Bahamas 1 dollar = 100 cents
Bahrain 1 dinar = 1000 fils
Bangladesh 1 taka = 100 paise
Barbados 1 dollar = 100 cents
Belgium 1 franc = 100 centimes
Belize 1 dollar = 100 cents
Benin 1 CFA franc = 100 centimes
Bhutan 1 ngultrum = 100 chetrum
Bolivia 1 peso = 100 centavos
Botswana 1 pula = 100 cents
Brazil 1 cruzado = 100 new centavos
Brunei 1 dollar = 100 cents
Bulgaria 1 lev = 100 stotinki
Burkina Faso 1 CFA franc = 100 centimes
Burma 1 kyat = 100 pyas
Burundi 1 franc = 100 centimes
Cameroon 1 CFA franc = 100 centimes
Canada 1 dollar = 100 cents

Cape Verde 1 escudo = 100 centavos
Central African Republic 1 CFA franc = 100 centimes
Chad 1 CFA franc = 100 centimes
Chile 1 peso = 100 centavos
China 1 yuan = 10,000 jen min piao
Colombia 1 peso = 100 centavos
Comoros 1 CFA franc = 100 centimes
Congo 1 CFA franc = 100 centimes
Costa Rica 1 colón = 100 centimos
Cuba 1 peso = 100 centavos
Cyprus 1 pound = 1,000 mils; 1 Turkish lira = 100 centesimi
Czechoslovakia 1 koruna = 100 hellers
Denmark 1 krone = 100 øre
Djibouti 1 franc = 100 centimes
Dominica 1 East Caribbean dollar = 100 cents
Dominican Republic 1 peso = 100 centavos
East Germany 1 ostmark = 100 pfennig
Ecuador 1 sucre = 100 centavos
Egypt 1 pound = 100 piasters
El Salvador 1 colón = 100 centavos
Equatorial Guinea = 1 CFA franc = 100 centimes
Ethiopia 1 birr = 100 cents
Fiji 1 dollar = 100 cents
Finland 1 markka = 100 pennis
France 1 franc = 100 centimes

Gabon 1 CFA franc = 100 centimes
Gambia, The 1 dalasi = 100 bututs
Ghana 1 new cedi = 100 pesewas
Greece 1 drachma = 100 lepta
Grenada 1 East Caribbean dollar = 100 cents
Guatemala 1 quetzal = 100 centavos
Guinea 1 syli = 100 centimes
Guinea-Bissau 1 peso = 100 centavos
Guyana 1 dollar = 100 cents
Haiti 1 gourde = 100 centimes
Honduras 1 lempira = 100 centavos
Hong Kong 1 dollar = 100 cents
Hungary 1 forint = 100 fillers
Iceland 1 new króna = 100 aurar
India 1 rupee = 100 paise
Indonesia 1 rupiah = 100 sen
Iran 1 rial = 100 dinars
Iraq 1 dinar = 1000 fils
Ireland 1 pound (punt) = 100 pennies
Israel 1 shekel = 100 new agorot
Italy 1 lira = 100 centesimi
Ivory Coast 1 CFA franc = 100 centimes
Jamaica 1 dollar = 100 cents
Japan 1 yen = 100 sen
Jordan 1 dinar = 1000 fils
Kampuchea 1 riel = 100 sen
Kenya 1 shilling = 100 cents
Kiribati 1 Australian dollar = 100 cents
Kuwait 1 dinar = 1000 fils
Laos 1 kip = 100 at
Lebanon 1 pound = 100 piasters
Lesotho 1 maloti = 100 cents
Liberia 1 dollar = 100 cents
Libya 1 dinar = 1000 fils
Liechtenstein 1 Swiss franc = 100 centimes
Luxembourg 1 franc = 100 centimes
Macau 1 pataca = 100 avos
Madagascar 1 franc = 100 centimes
Malawi 1 kwacha = 100 tambala
Malaysia 1 ringgit = 100 sen
Maldives 1 rufiyaa = 100 cents
Mali 1 franc = 100 centimes
Malta 1 lire = 100 centesimi
Mauritania 1 ouguiya = 5 khoums
Mauritius 1 rupee = 100 cents
Mexico 1 peso = 100 centavos
Monaco 1 French franc = 100 centimes
Mongolia 1 tugrik = 100 mongos
Morocco 1 dirham = 100 Moroccan francs
Mozambique 1 metical = 100 centavos

Nauru 1 Australian dollar = 100 cents
Nepal 1 rupee = 100 pice
Netherlands, The 1 guilder = 100 cents
New Zealand 1 dollar = 100 cents
Nicaragua 1 cordoba = 100 centavos
Niger 1 CFA franc = 100 centimes
Nigeria 1 naira = 100 kobo
North Korea 1 won = 100 chon
Norway 1 krone = 100 øre
Oman 1 rial = 100 dinars
Pakistan 1 rupee = 100 paisa
Panama 1 balboa = 100 centesimos
Papua New Guinea 1 kina = 100 cents
Paraguay 1 guarani = 100 centimos
Peru 1 sol = 100 centavos
Phillipines 1 peso = 100 centavos
Poland 1 zloty = 100 groszy
Portugal 1 escudo = 100 centavos
Qatar 1 riyal = 100 dirhams
Romania 1 leu = 100 bani
Rwanda 1 franc = 100 centimes
St. Christopher and Nevis 1 East Caribbean dollar = 100 cents
St. Lucia 1 East Caribbean dollar = 100 cents
St. Vincent and the Grenadines 1 East Caribbean dollar = 100 cents
San Marino 1 Italian lira = 100 centesimi
São Tomé and Príncipe 1 dobra = 100 centavos
Saudi Arabia 1 riyal = 20 gurshes
Senegal 1 CFA franc = 100 centimes
Seychelles 1 rupee = 100 cents
Sierra Leone 1 leone = 100 cents
Singapore 1 dollar = 100 cents
Solomon Islands 1 dollar = 100 cents
Somalia 1 shilling = 100 cents
South Africa 1 rand = 100 cents
South Korea 1 won = 100 chon
Spain 1 peseta = 100 centimos
Sri Lanka 1 rupee = 100 paise
Sudan 1 pound = 100 piasters = 1000 milliemes
Suriname 1 guilder = 100 cents
Swaziland 1 emalangeni = 100 cents
Sweden 1 krona = 100 öre
Switzerland 1 franc = 100 centimes
Syria 1 pound = 100 piasters
Taiwan 1 new dollar = 100 cents
Tanzania 1 shilling = 100 cents
Thailand 1 baht = 100 satang

Togo 1 CFA franc = 100 centimes
Tonga 1 pa'anga = 100 cents
Trinidad and Tobago 1 dollar = 100 cents
Tunisia 1 dinar = 1000 milliemes
Turkey 1 lira = 100 centesimi
Tuvalu 1 Australian dollar = 100 cents
Uganda 1 shilling = 100 cents
Union of Soviet Socialist Republics 1 ruble = 100 kopecks
United Arab Emirates 1 dirham = 100 francs
United Kingdom 1 pound = 100 pennies (pence)
United States 1 dollar = 100 cents
Uraguay 1 new peso = 100 centesimos

Vatican City 1 lira = 100 centesimi
Venezuela 1 bolivar = 100 centimos
Vietnam 1 dong = 100 cents
Western Samoa 1 talà = 100 cents
West Germany 1 deutsche mark = 100 pfennig
Yemen Arab Republic 1 rial = 100 dinars
Yemen, People's Democratic Republic of 1 dinar = 1000 fils
Yugoslavia 1 dinar = 100 paras
Zaire 1 zaire = 100 makutu
Zambia 1 kwacha = 100 newee
Zimbabwe 1 dollar = 100 cents

ABBREVIATIONS AND ACRONYMS

A

A Includes Extra (or Extras) (in stock listings of newspapers)

AAII American Association of Individual Investors

AB Aktiebolag (Swedish stock company)

ABA American Bankers Association

ABA American Bar Association

ABLA American Business Law Association

ABWA American Business Women's Association

ACE AMEX Commodities Exchange

ACRS Accelerated Cost Recovery System

A-D Advance-Decline Line

ADB Adjusted Debit Balance

ADR Automatic Dividend Reinvestment

ADR Asset Depreciation Range System

ADRS Asset Depreciation Range System

AE Account Executive

AFL-CIO American Federation of Labor-Congress of Industrial Organizations

AG Aktiengesellschaft (West German stock company)

AICPA American Institute of Certified Public Accountants

AID Agency for International Development

AIM American Institute for Management

AMA American Management Association

AMA Asset Management Account

AMEX American Stock Exchange

AON All or None

APB Accounting Principles Board

APR Annual Percentage Rate

Arb Arbitrageur

ARF American Retail Federation

ARM Adjustable Rate Mortgage

ARPS Adjustable Rate Preferred Stock

ASAP As Soon as Possible

ASE American Stock Exchange

ATM Automatic Teller Machine

B

B Annual Rate Plus Stock Dividend (in stock listings of newspapers)

BAC Business Advisory Council

BAN Bond Anticipation Note

BBB Better Business Bureau

BD Bank Draft

BD Bills Discontinued

B/D Broker-Dealer

BE Bill of Exchange

BF Brought Forward

BL Bill of Lading

BLS Bureau of Labor Statistics

BO Branch Office

BO Buyer's Option

BOM Beginning of the Month

BOP Balance of Payments

BOT Balance of Trade

BOT Bought

BOT Board of Trustees

BPW Business and Professional Women's Foundation

BR Bills Receivable

BS Balance Sheet

BS Bill of Sale

BS Bureau of Standards

BW Bid Wanted

C

C Liquidating Dividend (in stock listings of newspapers)

CA Capital Account

CA Chartered Accountant

CA Commercial Agent

CA Credit Account

CA Current Account

CACM Central American Common Market

CAD Cash against Documents

CAF Cost Assurance and Freight

C&F Cost and Freight

CAPM Capital Asset Pricing Model

CATS Certificate of Accrual on Treasury Securities

CATV Community Antenna Television

CBA Cost Benefit Analysis

CBD Cash Before Delivery

CBOE Chicago Board Options Exchange

CBT Chicago Board of Trade

CC Chamber of Commerce

CCH Commerce Clearing House

CD Certificate of Deposit

CD Commercial Dock

CEA Council of Economic Advisors

CEO Chief Executive Officer

CF Certificates (in bond listings of newspapers)

CF Carried Forward

CFC Chartered Financial Counselor

CFC Consolidated Freight Classification

CFI Cost, Freight, and Insurance

CFO Chief Financial Officer

CFP Certified Financial Planner

CFTC Commodities Futures Trading Commission

CH Clearing House

CH Custom House

Cía Compañía (Spanish company)

Cie Compagnie (French company)

CIF Corporate Income Fund

CIF Cost, Insurance, and Freight

CLD Called (in stock listings of newspapers)

CLU Chartered Life Underwriter

CME Chicago Mercantile Exchange

CMO Collateralized Mortgage Obligation

CMV Current Market Value

CN Consignment Note

CN Credit Note

CNS Continuous Net Settlement

CO Cash Order

CO Certificate of Origin

Co. Company

COB Close of Business (with date)

COD Cash on Delivery

COD Collect on Delivery

CODA Cash or Deferred Arrangement

COLA Cost-of-Living Adjustment

COMEX Commodity Exchange (New York)

COMSAT Communications Satellite Corporation

CPA Certified Public Accountant

CPD Commissioner of Public Debt

CPFF Cost Plus Fixed Fee

CPI Consumer Price Index

CPM Cost per Thousand

CPPC Cost plus a Percentage of Cost

CR Carrier's Risk

CR Class Rate

CR Company's Risk

CR Current Rate

CRCE Chicago Rice and Cotton Exchange

CSCE Coffee, Sugar and Cocoa Exchange

CSE Cincinnati Stock Exchange

CSVLI Cash Surrender Value of Life Insurance

CUNA Credit Union National Association

CUSIP Committee on Uniform Securities Identification Procedures

CV Convertible Security

CWO Cash with Order

D

DA Deposit Account

DA Documents against Acceptance

DAC Delivery against Cost

D&B Dun and Bradstreet

DC Deep Discount Issue (in bond listings of newspapers)

DCFM Discounted Cash Flow Method

DDB Double-Declining-Balance Depreciation Method

DF Damage Free

DIDC Depository Institutions Deregulatory Committee

DISC Domestic International Sales Corporation

DJIA Dow Jones Industrial Average

DJTA Dow Jones Transportation Average

DJUA Dow Jones Utility Average

DK Don't Know

DN Debit Note

DNR Do Not Reduce

D/O Delivery Order

DP Documents against Payment

DPI Disposable Personal Income

DS Days After Sight

DTC Depository Trust Company

DUNS Data Universal Numbering System (Dun's Number)

DVP Delivery Versus Payment

E

E Declared or Paid in the Preceding 12 Months (in stock listings of newspapers)

E&OE Errors and Omissions Excepted

EBIT Earnings Before Interest and Taxes

ECM European Common Market

ECT Estimated Completion Time

EDD Estimated Delivery Date

EEC European Economic Community

EEOC Equal Employment Opportunity Commission

EMP End-of-Month Payment

EOA Effective On or About

EOM End of Month

EPR Earnings Price Ratio

EPS Earnings Per Share

ERISA Employee Retirement Income Security Act of 1974

ERTA Economic Recovery Tax Act of 1981

ESOP Employee Stock Ownership Plan

ETA Estimated Time of Arrival

ETD Estimated Time of Departure

ETLT Equal To or Less Than

EUA European Unit of Account

EXIMBANK Export-Import Bank

F

F Dealt in Flat (in bond listings in newspapers)

FA   Free Alongside

FACT   Factor Analysis Chart Technique

FAS   Free Alongside

FASB   Financial Accounting Standards Board

FAT   Fixed Asset Transfer

FAX   Facsimile

FB   Freight Bill

FCA   Fellow of the Institute of Chartered Accountants

FCC   Federal Communications Commission

FCUA   Federal Credit Union Administration

FDIC   Federal Deposit Insurance Corporation

Fed   Federal Reserve System

FET   Federal Excise Tax

F&F   Furniture and Fixtures

FFCS   Federal Farm Credit System

FGIC   Financial Guaranty Insurance Corporation

FHA   Farmers Home Administration

FHA   Federal Housing Administration

FHLBB   Federal Home Loan Bank Board

FHLMC   Federal Home Loan Mortgage Corporation (Freddie Mac)

FICA   Federal Insurance Contributions Act

FICB   Federal Intermediate Credit Bank

FIFO   First In, First Out

FIGS   Future Income and Growth Securities

FIT   Federal Income Tax

FITW   Federal Income Tax Withholding

FLB   Federal Land Bank

FMC   Federal Maritime Commission

FNMA   Federal National Mortgage Association (Fannie Mae)

FOB   Free on Board

FOC   Free of Charge

FOCUS   Financial and Operations Combined Uniform Single Report

FOI   Freedom of Information Act

FOK   Fill or Kill

FOMC   Federal Open Market Committee

FOR   Free on Rail (or Road)

FOT   Free on Truck

FP   Floating Policy

FP   Fully Paid

FRA   Federal Reserve Act

FRB   Federal Reserve Bank

FRB   Federal Reserve Board

FRD   Federal Reserve District

FREIT   Finite Life REIT

FRS   Federal Reserve System

FS   Final Settlement

FSC   Foreign Sales Corporation

FSLIC   Federal Savings and Loan Insurance Corporation

FTC   Federal Trade Commission

FTI   Federal Tax Included

FVO   For Valuation Only

FX   Foreign Exchange

FY   Fiscal Year

FYA   For Your Attention

FYI   For Your Information

G

G   Dividends and Earnings In Canadian Dollars (in stock listings of newspapers)

GAAP   Generally Accepted Accounting Principles

GAAS   Generally Accepted Auditing Standards

GAI   Guaranteed Annual Income

GAINS   Growth and Income Securities

GAO   General Accounting Office

GATT   General Agreement on Tariffs and Trade

GDR German Democratic Republic (East Germany)

GE Federal Republic of Germany (West Germany)

GINNIE MAE Government National Mortgage Association

GM General Manager

GmbH Gesellschaft mit beschränkter Haftung (West German limited liability company)

GNMA Government National Mortgage Association

GNP Gross National Product

GO General Obligation Bond

GPM Graduated Payment Mortgage

GTC Good Till Canceled

GTM Good This Month

GTW Good This Week

H

H Declared or Paid After Stock Dividend or Split-Up (in stock listings of newspapers)

H/F Held For

HFR Hold For Release

HQ Headquarters

HR U.S. House of Representatives

HR U.S. House of Representatives Bill (with number)

HUD Department of Housing and Urban Development

I

I Paid This Year, Dividend Omitted, Deferred, or No Action Taken at Last Dividend Meeting (in stock listings of newspapers)

IBES Institutional Broker's Estimate System

IBRD International Bank for Reconstruction and Development (World Bank)

ICC Interstate Commerce Commission

ICFTU International Confederation of Free Trade Unions

ICMA Institute of Cost and Management Accountants

IDB Industrial Development Bond

IET Interest Equalization Tax

IFC International Finance Corporation

ILA International Longshoremen's Association

ILGWU International Ladies' Garment Workers' Union

ILO International Labor Organization

IMF International Monetary Fund

IMM International Monetary Market of the Chicago Mercantile Exchange

Inc. Incorporated

INSTINET Institutional Networks Corporation

IOC Immediate-Or-Cancel Order

IOU I Owe You

IPO Initial Public Offering

IR Investor Relations

IRA Individual Retirement Account

IRB Industrial Revenue Bond

IRC Internal Revenue Code

IRR Internal Rate of Return

IRS Internal Revenue Service

ISBN International Standard Book Number

ISSN International Standard Serial Number

ITC Investment Tax Credit

ITS Intermarket Trading System

J

JA Joint Account

Jeep Graduated Payment Mortgage

K

K Declared or Paid This Year on a Cumulative Issue with Dividends in Arrears (in stock listings of newspapers)

K Kilo- (prefix meaning multiplied by one thousand)

KCBT   Kansas City Board of Trade

KD   Knocked Down (disassembled)

KK   Kabushiki-Kaisha (Japanese stock company)

KW   Kilowatt

KWH   Kilowatt-hour

KYC   Know Your Customer Rule

L

L   Listed (securities)

LBO   Leveraged Buyout

L/C   Letter Of Credit

LCL   Less-Than-Carload Lot

LCM   Least Common Multiple (mathematics)

LDC   Less Developed Country

L/I   Letter of Intent

LIBOR   London Interbank Offered Rate

LIFO   Last In, First Out

LMRA   Labor-Management Relations Act

LP   Limited Partnership

Ltd   Limited (British Corporation)

LYONS   Liquid Yield Option Notes

M

M   Matured Bonds (in bond listings in newspapers)

M   Mill- (prefix meaning divided by one thousand)

M   Mega- (prefix meaning multiplied by one million)

M   One Thousand (Roman Numeral)

MACE   MidAmerica Commodity Exchange

Max   Maximum

MBA   Master of Business Administration

MBIA   Municipal Bond Insurance Association

MBO   Management By Objective

MBS   Mortgage-backed Security

MC   Marginal Credit

MC   Member of Congress

M-CATS   Municipal Certificates of Accrual on Tax-exempt Securities

MD   Months After Date

ME   Montreal Exchange

MFN   Most Favored Nation (tariff regulations)

MGE   Minneapolis Grain Exchange

MGM   Milligram

MHR   Member of the U.S. House of Representatives

MIG-1   Moody's Investment Grade

MIMC   Member of the Institute of Management Consultants

Min   Minimum

MIS   Management Information System

Misc   Miscellaneous

MIT   Market if Touched

MIT   Municipal Investment Trust

M&L   Matched And Lost

MLR   Minimum Lending Rate

MM   Millimeter (metric unit)

MMDA   Money Market Deposit Account

MO   Money Order

MSB   Mutual Savings Bank

MSE   Midwest Stock Exchange

MSRB   Municipal Securities Rulemaking Board

MTU   Metric Units

N

N   New Issue (in stock listings of newspapers)

NA   National Association (National Bank)

NAIC   National Association of Investment Clubs

NAM   National Association of Manufacturers

NAPA National Association of Purchasing Agents

NASA National Aeronautics and Space Administration

NASD National Association of Securities Dealers

NASDAQ National Association of Securities Dealers Automated Quotations system

NAV Net Asset Value

NBS National Bureau of Standards

NC No Charge

NCUA National Credit Union Administration

NCV No Commercial Value

ND Next Day Delivery (in stock listings of newspapers)

NEMS National Exchange Market System

NH Not Held

NIP Normal Investment Practice

NIT Negative Income Tax

NL No Load

NLRA National Labor Relations Act

NLRB National Labor Relations Board

NMAB National Market Advisory Board

NMB National Mediation Board

NMS National Market System

NNP Net National Product

NOW National Organization for Women

NOW Negotiable Order Of Withdrawal

NP No Protest (banking)

NP Notary Public

N/P Notes Payable

NPV Net Present Value

NPV´ No Par Value

NQB National Quotation Bureau

NQB No Qualified Bidders

NR Not Rated

NSBA National Small Business Association

NSCC National Securities Clearing Corporation

NSF Not Sufficient Funds

NSTS National Securities Trading System

NTU Normal Trading Unit

NV Naamloze Vennootschap (Dutch corporation)

NYCE New York Cotton Exchange

NYCSCE New York Coffee, Sugar and Cocoa Exchange

NYCTN,CA New York Cotton Exchange, Citrus Associates

NYFE New York Futures Exchange

NYME New York Mercantile Exchange

NYSE New York Stock Exchange

O

O Old (in options listing of newspapers)

OAPEC Organization of Arab Petroleum Exporting Countries

OB Or Better

OBV On-Balance Volume

OCC Options Clearing Corporation

OD Overdraft, overdrawn

OECD Organization for Economic Cooperation and Development

OMB Office of Management and Budget

OPD Delayed Opening

OPEC Organization of Petroleum Exporting Countries

OPM Options Pricing Model

OPM Other People's Money

O/T Overtime

OTC Over The Counter

OW Offer Wanted

P

P Paid this Year (in stock listings of newspapers)

P Put (in options listings of newspapers)

PA Power of Attorney

PA Public Accountant

PA Purchasing Agent

PAC Put and Call (options market)

P&L Profit and Loss Statement

PAYE Pay as You Earn

PBGC Pension Benefit Guaranty Corporation

PC Participation Certificate

PE Price Earnings Ratio (in stock listings of newspapers)

PER Price Earnings Ratio

PF Preferred Stock (stock tables)

PFD Preferred Stock

PHLX Philadelphia Stock Exchange

PL Price List

PLC (British) Public Limited Company

PN Project Note

PN Promissory Note

POA Power of Attorney

POD Pay on Delivery

POE Port of Embarkation

POE Port of Entry

POR Pay on Return

PPS Prior Preferred Stock

PR Preferred Stock (ticker tape)

PR Public Relations

PRIME Prescribed Right to Income and Maximum Equity

Prop Proprietor

PSA Public Securities Association

PSE Pacific Stock Exchange

PUC Public Utilities Commission

PUHCA Public Utility Holding Company Act of 1935

PVR Profit/Volume Ratio

Q

QB Qualified Buyers

QC Quality Control

QI Quarterly Index

QT Questioned Trade

QTIP Qualified Terminable Interest Property Trust

R

R Declared or Paid in the Preceding 12 Months plus Stock Dividend (in stock listings of newspapers)

R Option Not Traded (in option listings in newspapers)

RAM Reverse Annuity Mortgage

RAN Revenue Anticipation Note

R&D Research and Development

RCIA Retail Credit Institute of America

RCMM Registered Competitive Market Maker

REIT Real Estate Investment Trust

REMIC Real Estate Mortgage Investment Conduit

Repo Repurchase Agreement

ROC Return on Capital

ROE Return on Equity

ROI Return on Investment (Return on Invested Capital)

ROP Registered Options Principal

ROS Return on Sales

RP Repurchase Agreement

RRP Reverse Repurchase Agreement

RT Royalty Trust

RTW Right to Work

S

S No Option Offered (in option listings of newspapers)

S Signed (before signature on typed copy of a document, original of which was signed)

S Split or Stock Dividend (in stock listings of newspapers)

SA Sociedad Anónima (Spanish corporation)

SA Société Anonyme (French corporation)

SAA Special Arbitrage Account

SAB Special Assessment Bond

S&L Savings and Loan

S&L Sale and Leaseback

S&P Standard and Poor's

SB Savings Bond

SB Short Bill

SBA Small Business Administration

SBIC Small Business Investment Corporation

SBLI Savings Bank Life Insurance

SCORE Special Claim on Residual Equity

SD Standard Deduction

SDB Special District Bond

SDBL Sight Draft, Bill of Lading Attached

SDRs Special Drawing Rights

SE Shareholders' Equity

SEAQ Stock Exchange Automated Quotations

SEC Securities and Exchange Commission

SEP Simplified Employee Pension Plan

SF Sinking Fund

SG&A Selling, General and Administrative Expenses

SIA Securities Industry Association

SIAC Securities Industry Automation Corporation

SIC Standard Industrial Classification

SIPC Securities Investor Protection Corporation

SL Sold

SLMA Student Loan Marketing Association (Sallie Mae)

SLO Stop-Limit Order, Stop-Loss Order

SMA Society of Management Accountants

SMA Special Miscellaneous Account

SML Security Market Line

SN Stock Number

Snafu Situation Normal, All Fouled Up

SOP Standard Operating Procedure

SOYD Sum of the Years' Digits Method

SpA Società per Azioni (Italian corporation)

SPDA Single Premium Deferred Annuity

SPQR Small Profits, Quick Returns

SPRI Société de Personnes à Responsabilité Limitée (Belgian corporation)

Sr Senior

SRO Self-Regulatory Organization

SRP Salary Reduction Plan

SRT Spousal Remainder Trust

SS Social Security

SSA Social Security Administration

STAGS Sterling Transferable Accruing Government Securities

STB Special Tax Bond

STRIPS Seperate Trading of Registered Interest and Principal of Securities

SU Set Up (freight)

T

T- Treasury (as in T-bill, T-bond, T-note)

TA Trade Acceptance

TA Transfer Agent

TAB   Tax Anticipation Bill

TAN   Tax Anticipation Note

TC   Tax Court of the United States

TD   Time Deposit

TEFRA   Tax Equity and Fiscal Responsibility Act of 1982

TFE   Toronto Futures Exchange

TIGER   Treasury Investors Growth Receipt

TIP   To Insure Promptness

TL   Trade-Last

TM   Trademark

TSE   Toronto Stock Exchange

TT   Testamentary Trust

TVA   Tennessee Valley Authority

U

UAW   United Automobile Workers

UCC   Uniform Commercial Code

UGMA   Uniform Gifts To Minors Act

UIT   Unit Investment Trust

UL   Underwriters' Laboratories

ULC   Underwriter's Laboratories of Canada

ULI   Underwriter's Laboratories, Inc

UMW   United Mine Workers

UN   United Nations

UPC   Uniform Practice Code

US   United States (of America)

USA   United States of America

USBS   United States Bureau of Standards

USC   United States Code

USCC   United States Chamber of Commerce

USIT   Unit Share Investment Trust

USJCC   United States Junior Chamber of Commerce (JAYCEES)

USS   United States Senate

USS   United States Ship

UW   Underwriter

V

VA   Veterans Administration

VAT   Value Added Tax

VD   Volume Deleted

Veep   Vice President

VI   In bankruptcy or receivership; being reorganized under the Bankruptcy Act; securities assumed by such companies (in bond and stock listings of newspapers)

VIP   Very Important Person

VL   Value Line Investment Survey

VOL   Volume

VP   Vice President

VRM   Variable Rate Mortgage

VSE   Vancouver Stock Exchange

VTC   Voting Trust Certificate

W

WB   Waybill

WCA   Workmen's Compensation Act

WCE   Winnipeg Commodity Exchange

WD   When Distributed (in stock listings of newspapers)

WHOOPS   Washington Public Power Supply System

WI   When Issued (in stock listings of newspapers)

WR   Warehouse Receipt

WSJ   Wall Street Journal

WT   Warrant (in stock listings of newspapers)

W/Tax   Withholding Tax

WW   With Warrants (in bond and stock listings of newspapers)

X

X   Ex-Interest (in bond listings of newspapers)

XD   Ex-Dividend (in stock listings of newspapers)

X-Dis   Ex-Distribution (in stock listings of newspapers)

XR Ex-Rights (in stock listings of newspapers)

XW Ex-Warrants (in bond and stock listings of newspapers)

Y

Y Ex-Dividend and Sales in Full (in stock listings of newspapers)

YLD Yield (in stock listings of newspapers)

YTB Yield to Broker

YTC Yield to Call

YTM Yield to Maturity

Z

Z Zero

ZBA Zero Bracket Amount

ZBB Zero-Based Budgeting

ZR Zero Coupon Issue (Security) (in bond listings of newspapers)

INDEX

This index is coordinated with the Dictionary of Finance and Investment on pages 157 to 541. Entries found there usually are not duplicated in the Index. It is advisable for the user of the *Handbook* to do a double lookup: once in this Index and once in the Dictionary.